SARAH SIDDONS

by Gainsborough

A
BIOGRAPHICAL
DICTIONARY

OF

ACTORS, ACTRESSES, MUSICIANS, DANCERS,
MANAGERS & OTHER STAGE PERSONNEL
IN LONDON, 1660–1800

Volume 14: S. Siddons *to* Thynne

by

PHILIP H. HIGHFILL, JR., KALMAN A. BURNIM
and
EDWARD A. LANGHANS

SOUTHERN ILLINOIS UNIVERSITY PRESS
CARBONDALE AND EDWARDSVILLE

Copyright © 1991 by the Board of Trustees, Southern Illinois University

All rights reserved

Printed in the United States of America

Designed by Andor Braun and George Lenox

Publication of this work was made possible in part through a
grant from the National Endowment for the Humanities.

Library of Congress Cataloging-in-Publication Data
(Revised for Vol. 14)

Highfill, Philip H.
  A biographical dictionary of actors, actresses,
musicians, dancers, managers & other stage personnel in
London, 1660–1800.

  Includes biographical references.
  1. Performing arts—England—London—Biography—Dictionaries. 2. Actors—
England—London—Biography—Dictionaries. 3. Theatrical managers—England—
London—Biography—Dictionaries. 4. London (England)—Biography—Dictionaries.
I. Burnim, Kalman A., joint author. II. Langhans, Edward A., joint author. III. Title.
PN2597.H5   790.2′092′2 [B]   71–157068
ISBN 0–8093–1526–2

Volume 14

S. Siddons *to* Thynne

Siddons, Mrs William, Sarah, née Kemble *1755–1831, actress, singer.*

Sarah Kemble was born at the Shoulder of Mutton Inn in Brecon, Wales, on 5 July 1755, the first of 12 children of the provincial manager Roger Kemble. Her mother Sarah Ward was an actress and the daughter of John and Sarah Ward, managers of a respected company of itinerant players. Sarah's brother John Philip Kemble became the premier actor and manager of his period. Her brothers Charles and Stephen and her sisters Frances (Mrs Francis Twiss), Elizabeth (Mrs Charles Whitlock), and Julia Ann (Mrs William Hatton) all performed in London and are noticed in this *Dictionary.* Her sister Jane (Mrs Henry Mason) was not on the London stage in the eighteenth century but she acted in the provinces in the 1790s. The surname Kemble, often interchangeable with Campbell, was common in Herefordshire and Wiltshire, where earlier members of the family, having remained loyalists, lost lands. The best-known ancestor was Father John Kemble (1599?–1679), who was executed for complicity in the Titus Oates plot. Information on the family background is given in the notice of Roger Kemble in volume 8 of this *Dictionary.*

Sarah's certificate of baptism, copied from the registry of St Mary's in Brecon and dated 14 July 1755, incorrectly listed her father's Christian name as George. Sarah's father Roger Kemble had been trained as a barrister, but in 1752, at the age of 30, he turned actor and was soon engaged in John Ward's company at Birmingham. At Cirencester on 6 June 1753 he married Sarah Ward, his manager's seventeen-year-old daughter. Her mother, also an actress, was the daughter of Mr and Mrs Stephen Butcher, provincial players. It was to her mother's line that Sarah Kemble owed her beauty and her aristocratic bearing. Though originally John Ward had objected to his daughter's marrying an actor, eventually Roger Kemble was accepted and with his wife toured in Ward's company for about eight years. It was at Brecon, while the company was touring Wales in 1755, that their first child was born. Sarah was baptized a Protestant, the persuasion of her mother, as were all the subsequent Kemble daughters. The sons were raised as Catholics, like their father.

Sarah's education was received on the move, at day schools in Worcester, Wolverhampton, and other towns throughout England's western and northern circuits where the Kembles resided for short periods, as they played in inns, barns, and ill-equipped playhouses. In the spring of 1766 when John Ward retired to Leominster, Roger Kemble took over the management of the company. His family grew and his business prospered well enough, though Thomas Holcroft, a onetime member of the troupe, said it was "more respectable than many other companies of strolling players; but it was not in so flourishing a condition as to place the manager beyond the reach of immediate smiles or frowns of fortune."

While at Mrs Harris's school for young ladies, called Thornlea House, in Worcester, young Sarah received some rebuffs because she was the child of a stroller, but she displayed talent and resourcefulness in school theatricals. Though Roger Kemble wished for none of his children to go upon the stage, each surviving one did, and all except Frances married performers. The well-known playbill of a performance of *Charles the First* at the King's Head, Worcester, on 12 February 1767 records five Kembles in the cast: Roger as Colonel Fairfax, Mrs Kemble as Lucy Fairfax, John Philip as the Duke of York, Frances as the Duke of Gloucester, and Sarah as Princess Elizabeth. But the children had been coming onto provincial stages before that time. The company had been at Coventry from August to December 1766, and the Coventry *Mercury* of 22 December 1766 records Sarah's first known role, Ariel in *The Tempest,* a part she did not recollect when telling her life-story to Thomas Campbell, her official biographer.

After remaining in Coventry during part of January, Kemble's brood went to Worcester, where they settled from mid-January to July 1767. Performing Princess Elizabeth in *Charles the First,* at Worcester on 12 February 1767, Miss Kemble also sang during the musical program which legitimized the evening (the play was performed "gratis" between the parts of the concert). Also in *Charles the First,* playing the Duke of Richmond, was William Siddons, her future husband. At Worcester that season Sarah also performed Rosetta in *Love in a Village.* (That night admission was granted

Henry E. Huntington Library and Art Gallery

SARAH SIDDONS, as the TRAGIC MUSE

by Reynolds

WILLIAM SIDDONS
By Opie

to those purchasing packets of Mr Latham's tooth powder at 2*s*, 1*s*, or 6*d*.) On 16 April she appeared again as Ariel.

In July 1767 the company was at Droitwich, then at Bromsgrove from July to September and at Bath from October 1767 to May 1768. They played Coventry in September and October 1768 and then were again in Worcester from November to February 1769. The following month they were at Wolverhampton. Sarah performed at Warwick in January 1770 and at Coventry in February.

In 1770 Sarah was taken off the stage and sent to serve the widowed Lady Mary Greatheed at Guy's Cliffe in Warwick, first as maid and then as companion, at £10 per year. She remained in that situation almost two years. In her later years, Sarah often returned to Guy's Cliffe. Lady Greatheed said that even when seventeen-year-old Sarah was her servant the

mistress "felt an irresistible inclination" (as Roger Manvell puts it in his *Sarah Siddons*, 1970) "to rise from the chair when Sarah came in to attend her." Sarah had been sent into service, originally, in part to cool her affections for William Siddons, who was some 11 years her senior. At the same time Roger Kemble dismissed Siddons from the company. At Guy's Cliffe Sarah spent her free time sculpturing and reciting passages from Milton, Shakespeare, and Rowe in the servants' hall.

Sarah's affection for William Siddons remained constant; eventually her parents bowed to the inevitable, and she and Siddons were married in Holy Trinity Church, Coventry, on 26 November 1773. A fortnight or so after their marriage the bride appeared in the roles of Charlotte Rusport in *The West Indian* and Leonora in *The Padlock* at her father's theatre in Worcester on 13 December 1773. That same month she acted those parts with her father's troupe at Wolverhampton. They were at Leicester in February 1774.

Shortly thereafter Sarah and William left the family company to strike out on their own, joining Chamberlain and Crump's barnstormers. They played in various country towns, but their situation was precarious until in the summer of 1774 the company came to Cheltenham. There Sarah's acting of Belvidera in *Venice Preserv'd* won the tears and eventually the friendship of Henrietta Boyle, the rich and fashionable stepdaughter of Lord Bruce. Bruce was so impressed by her talent that he offered expensive clothes for Sarah's wardrobe, and Miss Boyle, according to Sarah's own account to Campbell, "even condescended to make part of my Dresses with her own dear hand." Upon Lord Bruce's return to London he recommended Sarah to David Garrick at Drury Lane.

During her engagement at Cheltenham Sarah was far advanced in pregnancy; she gave birth to her first child, Henry Siddons, on 4 October 1774 at Wolverhampton. At some point Garrick had sent his friend and leading comedian Tom King to Cheltenham to see her act Calista in *The Fair Penitent*. King was greatly impressed, but Garrick delayed. In 1775 the Siddonses were working in Joseph Younger's company, playing at Leicester in February, Worcester in March, and Cheltenham again for the summer. Garrick's interest was renewed, and on 31 July 1775 he wrote to his friend the Rev Henry Bate: "If you pass by Cheltenham on Your Way to Worcester, I wish you would see an actress there, a Mrs *Siddons*, She has a desire I hear to try her Fortune with Us; if she seems in Your Eyes worthy of being transplanted, pray desire to know upon what conditions She would make ye Tryal, & I will write to her the post after I receive Your Letter." Bate took the assignment, saw her as Rosalind in *As You Like It*, and wrote back to Garrick on 12 August:

I own she made so strong an impression upon me that I think she cannot fail to be a valuable acquisition to Drury Lane. Her figure must be remarkably fine, when she is happily delivered of a big belly. . . . Her face (if I could judge from where I saw it) is one of the most strikingly beautiful for stage effect that ever I beheld. . . . She will most certainly be of great use to you at all parts on account of the great number of characters she plays, all of which I venture to assert she fills with propriety tho' I have yet seen her in but one—She is as you have been informed a very good breeches figure, and plays Widow Brady I am informed admirably: I should not wonder from her ease, figure, and manner if she made the proudest of either house tremble in genteel comedy. . . .

Bate jibed at Garrick, "nay beware yourself *Great Little Man,* for she plays Hamlet to the satisfaction of the Worcestershire Critics." (Presumably Bate was not simply pulling Garrick's leg, and she had already attempted Hamlet at a date unknown to us. Two years later, on 19 March 1777, she acted the role at Birmingham. She was billed as making her "2d appearance" in that character.)

On 15 August 1775 Garrick wrote back to Bate asking him to secure Mrs Siddons, assure her of every reasonable and friendly encouragement, and tell her husband that he must be satisfied "with the state of life in which it has pleased Heaven to call her." Garrick asked about her pregnancy and date of delivery. He directed Bate to get some kind of memorandum signed by her and her husband. Garrick hoped he could direct her fire against his battery of difficult actresses. He requested a list of parts she had played and what she liked best herself. "If she has merit . . . and will be wholly governed by me," he proclaimed, "I will make her theatrical fortune." Bate replied on 19 August that the child was expected in early December (it was actually born in early

November) and suggested that until she was able to appear at Drury Lane Garrick should support her and her family somewhere in the country. Accompanying Bate's letter was a list of 23 characters in which Sarah had appeared, with some underlined as her favorite roles; the latter group included Alicia in *Jane Shore,* Portia in *The Merchant of Venice,* Belvidera in *Venice Preserv'd,* Widow Brady in *The Irish Widow,* Rosalind in *As You Like It,* and Clarinda in *The Suspicious Husband.* Among the others were Jane Shore, Monimia in *The Orphan,* Juliet in *Romeo and Juliet,* Cordelia in *King Lear,* and Euphrasia in *The Grecian Daughter.*

A letter from William Siddons at Gloucester to Bate on 4 September 1775 stated his intention for Sarah to remain in Gloucester until her baby should be delivered. On 7 October Garrick wrote a pleasant letter to Siddons, inquiring after Sarah's health and advising them to stay at Gloucester until Sarah should be able to journey to London. He offered any financial assistance they might need. Again, on 19 October he wrote that "Whenever you please to draw upon Me for the fifteen pounds I shall pay it immediately." On 9 November Siddons wrote to advise Garrick that on the evening of 4 November his wife had been taken ill unexpectedly while performing and early the following morning had produced a fine girl—Sarah Martha Siddons. It was probably at the Barton Street Theatre in Gloucester that her sudden onset of labor occurred. Sarah Martha was baptized at St Michael's in that city on 30 November 1775. Siddons received £20 through a Mr Dinwoody; the Drury Lane account book shows the advance recorded, paid to a Mr Becket by Garrick's order on 16 November 1775. The previous day Garrick had written to urge the Siddonses to come to London as soon as Sarah could safely travel; otherwise her debut might have to be put off until the next season. Garrick wrote that he had no objection to her appearing as Rosalind, except that Mrs King had recently made her debut in that role.

Sarah and William arrived in London in mid-December with their two young children. Garrick decided to bring Sarah on as Portia in *The Merchant of Venice,* and, announced as "a Young Lady (being her first appearance)," she made her debut in that role on 29 December 1775, with Tom King as Shylock. The prompter Hopkins wrote in his Diary: "Mrs. Siddons—first app upon this stage, a good figure rather handsome—wants spirit and ease in her Voice a little course [*sic*] very well received."

But her debut was a disaster. Still in a weakened condition and no doubt intimidated by the capital city (which evidently she had never before visited), she suffered stage fright and a collapse of talent. She lost her voice, moved badly and uncertainly; and even her costume, an ugly dress from the theatre wardrobe, conspired against her. The press uniformly damned her—except for Bate's *Morning Post*. The *Middlesex Journal* of 30 December 1775, echoing other reviews, lamented:

There is not room to expect anything beyond mediocrity. Her figure and face . . . have nothing striking, her voice . . . is far from being favourable . . . she possesses a monotone not to be got rid of; there is a vulgarity in her tones, ill calculated to sustain that line in a theatre she has at first been held forth in.

Sarah's failure was unmistakable, and her fortunes did not improve significantly as the season progressed. She did somewhat better when she repeated Portia on 2 January but was embarrassed again on 13 January 1776 when she came on in Colman's abridgment of *Epicoene*, in which she, in the title role, had to play a boy disguised as a woman, in a part obviously written for a man. The incongruity persisted in performances on 15 and 17 January, but finally, on 23 January, Sarah was replaced by Lamash.

On 1 February she was the original Julia in Bate's opera *The Blackamoor Wash'd White*, which caused, according to Hopkins, "much hissing and Crying out no more no more!" The *Morning Chronicle*, however, thought "All played well except Mrs. Siddons who, having no comedy in her nature, rendered that ridiculous which the author evidently intended to be pleasant." Sarah played the ingenue Emily in the premiere of Mrs Cowley's *The Runaway* on 15 February 1776, and after five performances she was replaced in the part by Mrs King. The author of the anonymous "Critique on the Comedy of the Runaway" (manuscript in the Folger Shakespeare Library) wrote: "If a certain appearance of stupidity, and want of animation be a sure token of love in a female Quixote Mrs Siddons acquitted herself very

well in Miss Emily Morley. She is nonetheless on the whole very tolerable." On 15 April she was the original Maria in *Love's Metamorphoses*, a farce by Vaughan. On 23 May she appeared as Mrs Strickland in *The Suspicious Husband*, with Garrick as Ranger and Miss Young as Jacintha; she acted well enough to have her performance praised in the *Post* as being not inferior to that of the principals.

During his last round of characters before his retirement from the stage, Garrick acted Richard III on 27 May 1776 and entrusted Sarah with Lady Anne. Garrick gave a performance that according to Hopkins was "never finer," demonstrating that "those Amazing powers he has always possess'd are now as brilliant as ever." Sarah was greatly intimidated, and, as she recollected to John Taylor, "there was such an expression in his acting, that it entirely overcame her," to the degree that the critics found her lamentable. She played the role again on 3 and 5 May. That season Garrick also cast her as Venus in his revival of *The Jubilee* on 27 December 1775, earning her the "insidious appellation of *Garrick's Venus*," as Mrs Siddons herself put it in her *Reminiscences* (edited by William Van Lennep [1942], from her manuscript autobiographical notes provided to Thomas Campbell now in the Harvard Theatre Collection). She concluded that in so obviously displaying his deference to her, Garrick was using her cruelly as a foil with which to battle the several troublesome leading ladies of the company.

As Roger Manvell has observed, nervous timidity inhibited everything Sarah tried during those "painful six months" at Drury Lane. She revealed little, either of her great talent or the passion lying within her. After subscribing 10s. 6d. to the Drury Lane Fund, she went to play the summer season at Birmingham under Yates, carrying hopes of a reengagement at Drury Lane for the next season. Soon she received a letter from the prompter Hopkins advising that her services were no longer needed. The rejection threw her into a depression that nearly destroyed her, she wrote, but

for the sake of my poor babies . . . I exerted myself to shake off this dispondency, and my endeavours were blessed with success, in spite of the degradation I had suffer'd from being banished Drury Lane as a worthless candidate for fame and fortune.

SARAH SIDDONS
by Romney

From October to December 1776 she was at Liverpool, and then at Manchester from December to March 1777. She joined Wilkinson's company at York, where, still in bad health, she made her debut on 15 April 1777 as Euphrasia in *The Grecian Daughter*, with Wilkinson as Evander. She then played Rosalind, the title role in *Matilda*, Lady Townly in *The Provok'd Wife*, and Lady Alton in *The English Merchant*, winning great praise from audiences and critics. She was equally successful as Indiana in *The Conscious Lovers*, the Irish Widow in *Woman Is a Riddle* (in which her husband acted Colonel Manly on 29 April), Arpasia in *Tamerlane*, and Horatia in *The Roman Father*. For her benefit on 17 May 1777 she appeared in the title role of *Semiramis*.

Wilkinson in his *Wandering Patentee* remembered that "so great a favourite . . . Mrs. Siddons was in that short period" everyone there was astonished that she could have been rejected by London audiences and by Garrick. "In her Arpasia, I recollect her fall and figure after the dying scene was . . . most elegant; nor do I recognize such a mode of disposing the body in so picturesque and striking a man-

ner as Mrs. Siddons does on such prostrate occasions."

After a few weeks in May at Manchester, Sarah returned to Liverpool to play for Joseph Younger. On 21 June 1777 her brother John Philip Kemble was added to the Liverpool paylist at a modest £1 per week. He had but recently turned actor, having left school at Douai to tour with Chamberlain and Crump's ragtag troupe. Sarah and John went with Younger's company to Worcester and Manchester that winter; at Manchester on 29 January 1778 she acted Desdemona to his Othello, with Younger as Iago. On 19 March 1778 she played Hamlet, and Kemble acted Laertes.

In the spring of 1778 the Siddonses and John Kemble spent an idyllic interval in a country retreat on Russel Moor with the Inchbalds, during which period Kemble and Mrs Inchbald enjoyed each other's company while Joseph Inchbald was engrossed in his painting. That bucolic interlude ended in April when the Siddonses left to play at Liverpool and Manchester again. In her diaries, edited by James Boaden, Mrs Inchbald gave a portrait of Mrs Siddons as "indefatigable in her domestic concerns, for her husband and child [ren]; . . . she neither felt degraded nor unhappy, but cheerfully lightened her task by *singing* away the time."

Upon John Henderson's recommendation Mrs Siddons was engaged at £3 per week at the Orchard Street Theatre in Bath, beginning with the autumn season of 1778. Sarah and her family arrived at Bath in September, and on 24 October 1778 she made her debut before Bath audiences as Lady Townly in *The Provok'd Husband*. Three nights later, on 27 October, she offered Mrs Candour in *The School for Scandal*, but she caused little stir in either comedy. When, however, on 3 November she acted Elvina in More's tragedy *Percy*, the Bath *Chronicle* acclaimed her "in the judgment of the town, as the most capital actress that has performed here these many years." That season at Bath and also at Bristol (where she began to appear on 15 March as the Countess in *The Countess of Salisbury*) she played a remarkable variety of characters: Mrs Lovemore in *The Way to Keep Him*, Lady Jane in *Know Your Own Mind*, Belvidera in *Venice Preserv'd*, Lady Brumpton in *The Funeral*, the Queen in *Hamlet*, Portia in *The Merchant of Venice*, Euphrasia in *The Grecian*

Daughter, Millwood in *The London Merchant*, Rosamond in *Henry II*, the Queen in *The Spanish Fryar*, Juliet in *Romeo and Juliet*, Imoinda in *Oroonoko*, Bellario in *Philaster*, the Princess in *The Law of Lombardy*, Imogen in *Cymbeline*, Miss Aubrey in *The Fashionable Lover*, Queen Elizabeth in *Richard III*, Emmeline in *Edgar and Emmeline*, Sigismunda in *Tancred and Sigismunda*, Lady Randolph in *Douglas*, Emmeline in the *Fatal Falsehood*, and the title role in *Jane Shore*. Twice that season she recited Sheridan's monody on Garrick, who had died on 20 January 1779; she found the monody very moving, writing to a friend, "I never yet was able to read that lovely poem without weeping."

When one adds to her repertoire the roles she had played in Liverpool—among them Clarinda in *The Suspicious Husband*, Statira in *Alexander the Great*, Cleopatra in *All for Love*, Miranda in *The Busy Body*, Miss Richland in *The Good-Natured Man*, and Mrs Claremont in *The Tender Husband*—the industry of the 24-year-old actress is astonishing, especially since she was pregnant during the latter half of the season and gave birth to her third child, Maria, in early July 1779.

Her powers of pathos reduced her Bath auditors to tears, and John Taylor that autumn wrote to Garrick in retirement at Hampton shortly before his death that she was "as much a mistress of her business as ever female I saw." Her success changed the habits of Bath society, who had been accustomed to attending the Thursday night Cotillion Balls in the Assembly rooms. The theatre was usually vacant on those evenings, but as Sarah's attraction grew, the attendance at the balls thinned, and the fashionable began to flock to Orchard Street on Thursdays and any other night on which she acted.

The next season at Bath she began by playing Lady Macbeth on 27 September 1779; and, during that and the following two seasons at Bath and Bristol, she performed more than 100 characters, adding to her repertoire such roles as Isabella in *Measure for Measure*, Queen Katherine in *Henry VIII*, Calista in *The Fair Penitent*, Constance in *King John*, Zara in *The Mourning Bride*, and, in comedy, Miss Hardcastle in *She Stoops to Conquer*, Mrs Oakly in *The Jealous Wife*, and Nell in *The Devil to Pay*. She labored incessantly, performing almost every night, studying new roles into the early hours

of the morning, caring for a husband and three young children. William helped by sharing in child care and taking pains to drill her in lines and coach her (according to the actress Mrs Summers, he "was sometimes very cross with her when she did not act to please him") and occasionally playing small roles himself.

They settled in Axford's Buildings, on the east side of the London road, about a half mile from the theatre. When in Bristol they lodged at Mr Staines's in Bridge Street. While playing a brief engagement at Stroud in July 1780, Sarah lodged with a Mrs Romien, who kept a ladies' school near the top of Nelson Street, where, according to Hannam-Clark (*Drama in Gloucestershire*), "a boarder spoke of her quiet and respectable habits." At Bath Sarah was cultivated by the fashionable and important, including the Duchess of Devonshire, the Rev Thomas Sedgewick Whalley, Sophia Weston, Mrs Thrale, Hannah More, Anna Seward, the Sheridans, and the Linleys. She also was highly flattered by the literary charlatan and sometime actor Samuel Jackson Pratt (Courtney Melmoth). In Bath she met for the first time Thomas Lawrence, a precocious child who would as an adult cause her family much unhappiness.

The Duchess of Devonshire and the former Bath actor John Henderson may have been responsible for inducing the Drury Lane management, now headed by R. B. Sheridan (with his father Tom as acting coach), to bring Sarah back to London. Both Sheridans saw her act at Bath, and the enormous popular and artistic success she garnered there could hardly be ignored much longer. So Mrs Siddons decided to leave the comfort and security of Bath to accept an offer of ten guineas per week and venture once more into the capital.

At her final Bath benefit on 21 May 1782 she acted Hermione in *The Distrest Mother* and Nell in *The Devil to Pay*. An interlude entertainment called a *Holiday Fête* was also offered. As William Siddons informed the public in a footnote to the bills, it was "not only calculated to please, but to fill up the time, while Mrs Siddons dresses, which otherwise would hang very heavy on the audience." At the conclusion of the mainpiece Sarah delivered a farewell address of her own composition in verse, offering her "THREE REASONS" for quitting the Bath theatre. At the timely moment in her address she brought onto the stage her three children, Henry, Sarah ("Sally"), and Maria. (A fourth child, Frances Emilia, baptized on 26 April 1781, had died in infancy, and at the time of this benefit Sarah was eight months pregnant.) Sarah declared:

> These are the moles that bear me from your side;
> Where I was rooted—where I could have died.
> Stand forth, ye elves, and plead your Mother's cause;
> Ye little magnets, whose soft influence draws
> Me from a point where every gentle breeze
> Wafted my bark to happiness and ease—
> Sends me adventurous on a larger main,
> In hopes that you may profit by my gain.

The full address was printed (a newspaper clipping is in an annotated collection of Bath playbills in the Folger Shakespeare Library). The Bath benefit brought her £145 18s.; tickets were purveyed by Mr Siddons at Mr Telling's on Horse Street Parade (probably a convenient place to sell tickets and not the Siddons residence). Sarah repeated the farewell address at her final benefit at Bristol on 17 June 1782, when she took £106 13s. Some of her colleagues thought she was somewhat overdoing the sentiment by exhibiting the children on stage; it was said that two local actresses were planning to bring on their "Reasons" for *not* leaving the Bristol stage.

Between the Bath and Bristol benefits Sarah produced her fifth child, Elizabeth Ann, born on 2 June 1782. On 19 June she gave her last performance of the Bath season as Mrs Belville in *The School for Wives*. She played at Bristol in July, and in August, after an appearance in Cheltenham, she joined her husband and children for some sea air and relaxation at Weymouth, before setting off for London.

Late in September 1782 the Siddons family settled in lodgings at No 149, the Strand. After some deliberation over the appropriate role in which to make her debut, she took the strong advice of Tom Sheridan and decided upon the pathetic Isabella in *Isabella; or, The Fatal Marriage*. In that role she reappeared on the stage of Drury Lane Theatre on 10 October 1782, with a cast that included "Gentleman" Smith as Biron, Packer as Count Baldwin, Farren as Carlos, and Robert Palmer as Belford, eight years after her initial failure there. The tumultuous applause for her began before

the final curtain. The house was drenched in tears, and Boaden wrote that "literally the greater part of the spectators were too ill to use their hands in her applause." It was one of those famous nights in theatrical history, perhaps comparable to those engendered by Garrick and Kean, certainly equal to the debut of her brother John as Hamlet on the same stage a year later. It must have been a heady evening for Sarah's eight-year-old son Henry, who played Isabella's child, one of the roles he had been accustomed to appearing in at Bath.

The merit in Mrs Siddons's portrayal of Isabella was "infinite," reported the *Morning Chronicle* next day, "and when Isabella expired her death was rendered glorious by the theatre's resounding with thundering applause for more than a minute." When Sylas Neville saw her act the role on 21 October, one of the 24 nights that season on which she appeared as Isabella, he wrote in his diary: "She enters into her part with infinite judgment, energy & propriety. Her action is good, her voice pleasing. She excels in the pathetic." But Neville felt that she was "by no means equal to a Yates or Barry." Horace Walpole saw her in the role on 28 October 1782 and was more reserved in his response:

She is a good figure, handsome enough, though neither nose nor chin according to the Greek's standard, beyond which both advance a good deal. Her hair is either red, or she has no objection to it being thought so, and had used red powder. Her voice is clear and good; but I thought she did not vary its modulations enough, nor ever approach enough to the familiar—but this may come when more habituated to the awe of the audience of the capital. Her action is proper, but with little variety; when without motion, her arms are not genteel. . . .

As the season progressed Mrs Siddons gained more confidence, recapturing her estimable powers of concentration. Accolades came from all over town. It is said that people breakfasted near the theatre in order to be among the first to queue up for seats. The Drury Lane management ceremoniously gave her Garrick's dressing room on the stage level.

Her next character was Euphrasia in *The Grecian Daughter* on 30 October 1782, a role in which she drew "sobs and shrieks" for a total of 11 performances that season. As Jane Shore on 8 November her realistic portrayal of the starving heroine made men sob and women go

SARAH SIDDONS

by Beechey

off into hysterics; according to Campbell, "fainting fits were long and frequent in the house." That role was succeeded on 16 November by Mrs Montague in *The Fatal Interview,* a bad prose tragedy by Thomas Hull which proved unpopular and was taken off after three performances. But as Calista in *The Fair Penitent* on 29 November she was magnificent:

"Such acting as Mrs Siddons's," wrote Campbell, "had never been brought to Rowe's poetry at least during the last century." In the third act, according to Tom Davies's *Dramatic Miscellanies,* she was "so far affected, with assuming the mingled passions of pride, fear, anger, and conscious guilt," that despite the rouge on her cheeks some "paleness" showed in her countenance. Before a distinguished and over-flowing audience at her first benefit on 14 December 1782, she acted Belvidera in *Venice Preserv'd,* and she excelled her earlier triumphs of the season.

The account books show her total profit for a benefit clear of charges to have been £335 5s., but this amount was augmented by sub-scriptions and gifts from her many admirers, including 100 guineas from a hundred barris-ters, until it surpassed £800, according to the *Public Advertiser* of 25 December 1782. In an advertisement on 17 December Sarah ex-pressed her gratitude for her splendid benefit, and reported that she had been told that "the emoluments arising from it, exceeded any-thing ever recorded on a similar account, in the annals of the English Stage." Her perform-ance of Belvidera inspired Brereton, who acted Jaffeir, to such a level of excellence that the audience was doubly astonished. The critic in the *Morning Post* of 16 December claimed that she left "no opening for criticism, because there did not appear a *single error* in her per-formance."

Mrs Siddons, in her 13 performances of Bel-videra that season, eclipsed the reputation of Mrs Ann Crawford (formerly Mrs Barry) in that role, but there remained some die-hard supporters of Mrs Crawford. In *A Review of Mrs. Crawford, and Mrs. Siddons in the Character of Belvidera: in a letter to a gentleman at Bath* (1792), a "Mr. W." of Edinburgh compared the two actresses scene by scene. He found that Mrs Crawford was generally sweeter, more suc-cessful at pathos, and more passionate, and wore a loose chemise in the mad scene; whereas Mrs Siddons used her face more than her voice, was sometimes inaudible, and wore a full dress in the mad scene. Crawford adherents, how-ever, were much in the minority. Audiences for years thereafter remained spellbound by the genius shown in Sarah's powerful portrayal of Belvidera. Tom Davies described her appear-ance and her art about this time:

The person of Mrs. Siddons is greatly in her favour; just rising above the middle stature, she looks, walks, and moves like a woman of superior rank. Her countenance is expressive, her eyes so full of information, that the passion is told from her look before she speaks. Her voice, though not so har-monious as Mrs. Cibber's is strong and pleasing; nor is a word lost for want of due articulation. . . .

She excels all persons in paying attention to the business of the scene; her eye never wanders from the person she speaks to, or should look at when she is silent.

Her last new role that season was Zara in *The Mourning Bride,* for her second benefit on 18 March 1783. It was rumored that this ben-efit brought her another £650, but the account books show gross receipts of £329 16s. 6d., with a house charge of £108 17s. 4d. imposed on this occasion. (She had played Zara at Liv-erpool for the first time on 21 October 1776.)

In her first full season at Drury Lane she performed some 80 times. In January 1783 the King and Queen came to see her act Euphrasia on the second, Belvidera on the ninth, Calista on the twentieth, Jane Shore on the twenty-third, and Isabella on the twenty-eighth, a flurry of playgoing for the monarch theretofore unprecedented. Sarah was also instrumental in introducing London audiences to her sister Frances Kemble (later Mrs Twiss) on 6 January 1783 as Alicia to her Jane Shore. Frances re-ceived mixed reviews. On 22 February of that year another sister, Elizabeth (later Mrs Charles Whitlock), made her first appearance on the Drury Lane stage as Portia in *The Mer-chant of Venice.* Both sisters remained at that theatre for several seasons and accompanied Sarah on summer tours.

On 31 March 1783 the *Morning Herald* re-ported that her salary for the current year had been raised to £12 per week, a figure which her original articles had scheduled her to re-ceive in the third year of her engagement: "And to crown all, we hear that within a few days past they [the managers] have entirely given up her first articles, desire her to fix her own terms in the future, which are said to be mu-tually settled for the next season at the rate of *twenty pounds* per week."

When the Drury Lane season closed in early June, she set out for Ireland, playing at Liver-pool that month on the way. After a terrible crossing from Holyhead, her party, including her husband, her sister Frances, Francis Aickin, and Mr and Mrs Brereton, arrived at Dublin in the early morning hours of 16 June. In Dublin she met her brother John Philip Kemble, who had been the mainstay (along with Dorothy Jordan) of Daly's Company at the Smock Alley Theatre since the autumn of

1781. Mrs Siddons had engaged with the notorious Daly for 12 nights; after the charges calculated at £60 per night were deducted she was to have half the receipts. Brother John was receiving £10 per week.

On 21 June 1783 she made her debut at Smock Alley as Isabella. The box office was besieged by three o'clock that Saturday afternoon, and desperate persons of fashion were offering a guinea for a seat in the pit and a guinea and a half for one in the gallery. The *Dublin Evening Post* found her figure "elegant and interesting in the extreme" and especially noted that her eyes pointed up "the full force and meaning" of the several passions the role required. That critic also compared her to Ann Crawford, who was a local favorite. In his view, Mrs Siddons "in the gentler parts was superior to anything we may have seen, nor was she much surpassed by Mrs. Crawford in the impassioned." But while Mrs Siddons excelled, Mrs Crawford, "like Garrick, by her versatility, must keep the unrivalled possession of the dramatic throne."

Sarah played Belvidera before a brilliant and crowded audience headed by the Lord Lieutenant on 23 June, and this time there were no reservations about her superiority. The *Freeman's Journal* and the *Dublin Evening Post* carried the same review: "It is impossible for language to paint, or for words to convey an adequate idea of the unrivalled excellence of Mrs Siddons. . . . Siddons, thou child of Nature! to thee belongs the praise." Her other characters that summer included Euphrasia, Jane Shore, Zara, and Calista. Her costume for Calista was lauded as "one of the richest and most elegant ever seen in Dublin." At the conclusion of her 12 nights she played six charity benefits. Though she was acclaimed "the most . . . affecting actress . . . ," she had detractors. The *Dublin Daily Post* on 10 June 1783 called her acting "truly great" but observed that it sometimes had "the appearance of being preconceived." While Mrs Crawford had less grandeur, she had more nature, the critic thought. Though Sarah enjoyed Dublin society's affection, she also felt a certain hostility that never allowed her to be truly comfortable in Ireland. Before leaving the country she acted a few nights at Cork.

She reappeared at Drury Lane on 8 October 1783, acting the title role in *Isabella* before the King and Queen. After playing several other familiar characters she essayed her first Shakespearean role in London, Isabella in *Measure for Measure,* on 3 November 1783 (a part she had played at Bath on 11 December 1779), and turned the moral, intellectual, and passionless character into a brilliant success. That October she had visited Samuel Johnson, who wrote to Mrs Thrale on the twenty-seventh:

Mrs Siddons . . . behaved with great modesty and propriety, and left nothing behind her to be censured or despised. Neither praise nor money, two powerful corruptions of mankind, seem to have depraved her. I shall be glad to see her again. Her brother Kemble calls on me, and pleases me very well. Mrs Siddons and I talked of plays; and she told me of exhibiting this winter the characters of Constance, Catherine, and Isabella in Shakespeare.

Sarah's brother John had made his impressive debut at Drury Lane as Hamlet on 30 September 1783. He repeated that role four times and then acted the title role in *Edward the Black Prince,* followed by Richard III and Sir Giles Overreach. Excitement heightened when John and Sarah appeared together as Mr and Mrs Beverley in *The Gamester* on 22 November 1783. Kemble's Beverley was "all we could wish," proclaimed the *Public Advertiser* of 9 December, and in the last scene brother and sister drew from the house "as many tears as ever were shed in a theatre on one evening." For a command performance on 10 December 1783, John acted King John and Sarah made her first London appearance as Constance (she had acted the role at Bath on 18 April 1782). He received mixed reviews, most critics finding him too solemn and monotonous; but Sarah created one of her grand portrayals of "a lofty and proud spirit." Her early biographer claimed that in no other role was she so "noble in mind and commanding in person and demeanour."

For her benefit on 22 December 1783 (receipts were £303 8s. 6d. free of house charges) she acted Lady Randolph in *Douglas,* a role she had first played at Manchester on 5 February 1777. Again she was compared to Mrs Crawford, this time by the *Public Advertiser* of 24 December 1783: "The Siddons, younger and more rich in natural Gifts, certainly offers much to the Mind, and yet much more to the Eye. The Crawford, by some means or other, offers more to the Heart."

Ashmolean Museum, Oxford

SARAH SIDDONS
by Romney

Mrs Crawford, after an absence of five years from the London stage, had returned to challenge Sarah's popularity by playing Lady Randolph at Covent Garden on 13 November 1783, a month before Sarah's appearance, but she had to yield to the new tragedy queen. One reviewer did give her "pre-eminence over the Lady Randolph of Mrs Siddons," but otherwise there seemed little question of Mrs Siddons's superiority. As Boaden wrote, when compared to Mrs Crawford, who was 49, Sarah, at 28, "had many advantages . . . — youth, beauty, a finer figure, more power of eye, a voice in its whole compass sound and unbreaking."

Sarah's next new character was the title role in *The Countess of Salisbury* on 6 March 1784 (first acted by her at Bath on 25 November 1778); the *Public Advertiser* of 8 March deplored the revival of Hartson's play. "So thoroughly wretched, so utterly destitute of all Requisites . . . that it excites with Wonder not a little Indignation that the unexampled Genius of such an actress should be wasted on Dullness if possible yet more unexampled." An illness required her to postpone her second

benefit, scheduled for 18 March 1784. She was sufficiently recovered to act Isabella on 25 March, for Smith's benefit. Her own benefit finally occurred on 24 April, when she acted Sigismunda and her brother played Tancred in a revival of Thomsons' *Tancred and Sigismunda* which drew torrents of tears. (She had acted that role for the first time at Manchester on 10 January 1778.) Tickets could be had of her at No 7, Leicester Fields, and receipts were £324 1s. less house charges of £106 10s. 1d.

After the Drury Lane season ended, Sarah immediately left for the north, again to begin a heavy schedule of acting in the provinces. Her summer labors were to bring her substantial additional income, but she would injure her health in the process. She seemed driven through much of her life to make money while she could in order to care for a large and growing family and a husband who seems not to have been able to secure any kind of permanent employment. Her industry contributed to her reputation for stinginess.

Sarah went directly to Edinburgh, where she engaged with Jackson under very advantageous terms. She appeared on 22 May 1784 as Belvidera, and from that evening throughout the remainder of her engagement, according to Dibdin's *Annals of the Edinburgh Stage,* "the scenes that took place in front of the theatre baffle descriptions. . . . Enormous crowds attended hours before the performance, for the chance of getting in, and when, to oblige the crowds, they were admitted at 3 o'clock, they began to assemble at 12." It is said that as many as 2557 applications were made in one day for 630 places, and that persons merely passing by the theatre were swept in by the mob, which also attracted enterprising pickpockets all the way from London. In 12 nights playing her tragic repertoire she realized £967 7s. 7d., including a subscription of £200 from a group of gentlemen and presents of gold plate and tickets worth £120. She also received a present of a silver tea vase inscribed "As a Mark of Esteem [for] Unrivalled Talents . . ."

While she was in Edinburgh the General Assembly was obliged to yield to the Siddons fever and avoided conducting its business during the time of her performances in order to accommodate a considerable number of the members. And John Wesley found his congregants being stolen from his preachings. Thomas Moore reported Walter Scott's testimony to the power of her acting. Scott recollected the heiress Catherine Gordon of Gight (who later married Captain John Byron and gave birth to the poet) hysterically disrupting an Edinburgh performance, "harrowing the house by the desperate and wild way in which she shrieked out Mrs Siddons's exclamation in the character of Isabella. 'Oh my Biron! . . .' The remarkable circumstance was, that the lady had not then seen Captain Byron."

After Scotland came Ireland. Mrs Siddons was engaged by Daly, at Smock Alley in Dublin, at £50 a night for 20 nights. After settling in a house at No 28, Dawson Street, near St Stephen's Green and opposite the Lord Mayor's residence, she began her short season with Belvidera. Her performances drew rave reviews—the *Freeman's Journal* of 7 August 1784 acclaimed her "the greatest star in the theatrical hemisphere." She added the title role in *Cleone* to her repertoire at Smock Alley, and the *Hibernian Journal* of 14 August asked, "What words can express the astonishing powers which the Siddons displayed in every scene?" But her visit was marred by two distressing incidents. The first occurred on 10 July when the performance of *Douglas* was disturbed by the audience's hostility toward the presence of the Lord Lieutenant of Ireland, the Duke of Rutland.

Of more serious consequence for Mrs Siddons was a story circulated that she had refused to play for the benefit of West Digges, who earlier that summer had suffered a paralytic stroke at rehearsal. She was severely criticized in the press: the *Hibernian Journal* complained that "this enriched actress gave no sign of doing a benefit for any private or public charity, nor will she lend to Heaven, where the interest is so long delayed." It was maliciously charged that she had changed her mind and would play, but only if Digges paid £50. Indeed she did act Belvidera on 23 August 1784 for Digges's benefit and Mrs Siddons explained that she and her husband by "indefatigable labour and cruel annoyances" had gathered a company of actors who would play the benefit with her. In her *Memoirs* she lamented, "I acted Belvidera without having previously seen the face of one of the actors. Poor Mr Digges was most materially benefited by this most ludicrous performance; and I put my disgust into my pocket, since money passed into his." After the benefit the *Freeman's Journal* complimented her generosity to a fellow player.

Much of the hostility directed at Mrs Siddons had originated in an earlier incident that summer concerning her refusal to play for Brereton's benefit at Smock Alley unless she received some payment, on the grounds that Brereton was hardly indigent and was a well-paid actor at Drury Lane in the winter season. She did agree to accept £20 instead of her customary £30 for such service. She became ill, however, and there was one delay after another of Brereton's benefit, until, according to Brereton, it became impossible for her to play at all. About that time Thomas published at Dublin *The Siddoniad* (1784), a gushy poem praising her as an actress, woman, wife, and mother; appended was an invocation of the muses to protect her in her "severe illness."

Sarah was scheduled to act at Cork and Belfast, but could meet only the Cork engagement. The *Belfast Newsletter* of 13–17 August 1784 reported, "Mrs Siddons has withdrawn her engagement at the Theatre, as her late indisposition renders it impractical for her to make good both her engagements at Cork and this place, and be in London as early as the time appointed for her appearance there." The same newspaper (10–14 September 1784) claimed that by "a modest calculation," Mrs Siddons had cleared 3000 guineas for her summer excursion—1500 guineas from Edinburgh, the same amount from Dublin, and £500 from Cork to cover expenses.

Her reputation for stinginess at the expense of her fellow players followed her to London, and when she made her first appearance of the season at Drury Lane on 5 October 1784, as Mrs Beverley in *The Gamester,* she was hissed. She had tried to forestall such a reception by having her husband publish an explanation of the Dublin business in several London newspapers on 30 September 1784. On 3 October William Siddons published Brereton's letter in which he acknowledged that Mrs Siddons "did agree to perform at my benefit for a less sum than for any other performer, but her illness prevented it; and that she would have played for me after that had not the night been appointed after she had played three times in the same week—and that the week after her illness." (We erroneously stated in our notice of William Brereton that she acted Jane Shore for him on 19 August 1784.)

But neither letter succeeded, and her appearance as Mrs Beverley was held up for some 40 minutes while attempts to restore order were made and Mrs Siddons herself tried to address the hostile audience. Driven off the stage, she fainted in John Kemble's arms. When recovered she could not be dissuaded from going out once more, and now with the audience suddenly quiet she explained that the "stories which have been circulated against me are calumnies" and she saw no reason for "having deserved your censure." The audience appreciated her courage and directness. The *Town and Country Magazine* of that month perceived "that the lady supported herself with a great degree of firmness at this very aweful trial—a trial, which, in great measure, determined her future fame—perhaps her residence in this metropolis." Betsy Sheridan in her *Journal* complained that the Breretons had used Mrs Siddons "shockingly." Mrs Brereton (who was playing Charlotte that night) was "mean enough to sneak off the stage and leave her to stand the insults of a malicious party tho' she knew the whole disturbance was on her account and that her husband [playing Lewson] had at least been obliged to contradict the reports that concern'd him." Brereton said nothing, though in late October a letter from him reached the *Morning Chronicle* in which he delcared: "I did not pay Mrs Siddons for playing my benefit." John Kemble sent the press a vindication of his sister, signing himself "Laertes." (The irony of the situation would be compounded when, after Brereton's death three years later, his widow Priscilla would marry Kemble.) Mrs Siddons was so shaken by the humiliating events that she gave serious thought to abandoning the stage. On 15 October 1784 her husband wrote to their friend Sir Charles Hotham that Mrs Siddons had "stood the rude shock with greater firmness than could have been expected" and had decided that, though for her children's sake "she shall be obliged to continue in her profession, it will never have those pleasing charms it had before."

She had already resumed acting, appearing as Lady Randolph on 9 October 1784, four

nights after the *The Gamester* incident. She acted regularly that season in her accustomed repertoire. On 3 November 1784 she played Margaret of Anjou in *The Earl of Warwick,* and on 17 November the title role in *Zara,* a somewhat frigid character in which she failed to challenge the late Susanna Maria Cibber's still memorable portrayal. The most successful new production of the season was Cumberland's *The Carmelite,* which opened on 2 December and ran 13 performances; as Matilda she was, according to the play's author, "inimitable." Her other original role was Camiola in *The Maid of Honour,* a disappointing adaptation by John Kemble of Massinger's drama that lasted only three nights.

The high point of the 1784–85 season occurred on 2 February 1785 when Mrs Siddons assumed, for her first time in London, the character of Lady Macbeth and set so extraordinary a standard in the role that it has seldom been approached since. Theatrical history deems Sarah Siddons and Lady Macbeth to be synonymous. "We speak of Lady Macbeth," wrote Charles Lamb, "while in reality we are thinking of Mrs. S." If she had failed to equal Mrs Cibber as Zara, she did eclipse Mrs Pritchard's great reputation and achievement as Lady Macbeth. The latter's performance was well within living memory and had been made legendary by its coupling with Garrick's Macbeth.

One of Sarah's departures from tradition was to put the candle down in the sleepwalking scene in order to leave her hands free for the pantomime of washing. Earlier somnambulists, including Mrs Pritchard, had always carried the candle throughout the scene. Some critics carped because Mrs Siddons wore a white dress in that scene—"She is supposed to be asleep, not mad"—but the *Public Advertiser* of 7 February 1785 defended her: "Yet there is an obvious reason why a person walking in their sleep should wear a white dress of the loose kind wore by Mrs Siddons. . . . It [is] the nearest resemblance which theatrical effect will admit to the common sort of night dresses." The first night of her Lady Macbeth was for her benefit, which brought in £346 16*s.,* free of house charges.

In the *Morning Post* of 3 February 1785 John Taylor wrote that "Throughout the first and second acts Mrs Siddons never exhibited such chaste, such accomplished acting." He noted the absence of some of her usual faults:

There being little or no declamation, our ears were not wounded with the repetition of the *lark's shrill note,* nor the blundering distribution of a vitiated emphasis; the total absence of the pathetic prevented that perpetual shaking of the head and tossing of the chin, which we have before remarked as her principal defects in that line of acting, and the violent exertion of her arms, which shocks the critical spectator in Belvidera and Calista was suited to the masculine ferocity of the heroine in this drama.

Though she was admirable immediately before and after the murder of Duncan, in the banquet scene she did not shine with so much luster because she adopted "too much the *familiar* manner," thought Taylor, and, unlike most other critics, he found her defective in the candle scene: "The faces she made were

Theatre Museum, London

SARAH SIDDONS, as Euphrasia

engraving by Caldwell, after Hamilton

horrid and even ugly, without being strictly just or expressive" and her enunciation was "too confined."

Taylor's reviews aside, however, over the years her portrayal of Lady Macbeth was accounted nearly perfect. The *Public Advertiser* of 24 February believed that her sleepwalking scene was "the greatest act that has in our memory adorned the stage"—but the critic lamented the monstrous marring of one scene by the weird sisters: "Mrs Wrighten laughing and talking the whole time, [and Miss] George who cannot help joining in a laugh." On 31 March 1785 John Kemble joined Sarah and played Macbeth for his first time in London. (Sarah's earlier Macbeth had been William Smith.) In the following year Thomas Beach exhibited at the Royal Academy his painting of Kemble and Mrs Siddons in the scene after the murder (reproduced in this *Dictionary* 8:364).

Her triumph as Lady Macbeth was followed a month later, on 8 March 1785, by an impressive portrayal of Desdemona, with John Kemble as a moving Othello (they had played these roles together at Manchester on 29 January 1777). Her biographer Campbell—who first saw her play the role at Edinburgh when he was a young man and thought her then a great actress—was astonished by the persuasiveness "with which she won over the Moor to Cassio's interest. In that scene it is my belief that no other actress ever softened and sweetened tragedy so originally." Mrs. Thrale, who came slowly to an appreciation of Mrs Siddons's art, found "Her coaxing Scene in Othello . . . prodigiously fine indeed." One critic wrote that "in this wonderful transition from Lady Macbeth to the bride of Othello. Mrs Siddons had shown her genius to be a star of the first magnitude."

Next she appeared in the title role of Mason's dull *Elfrida,* "By Command of Their Majesties," on 14 April 1785, followed by Rosalind in *As You Like It* for her benefit on 20 April (when tickets were available from her in Gower Street, Bedford Square, and receipts were £327 8s. 6d., less house charges of £105 15s. 10d.) Rosalind was a role not particularly suited to Sarah, and she did not enhance the performance by the strange manner in which she suited the role; apparently suffering hesitation about wearing boy's clothes, she costumed herself with something like a gardener's apron in front and a petticoat behind, and wore hussar's boots. Colman called her Rosalind "a frisking Grog," and the *Morning Post* complained of her "frittering refinement" and an odd sinking of the voice. Her attempts at archness were met with irony by the *Public Advertiser:* "The mournful tone, the pathetic countenance, and the long-drawn expression pervaded the sprightly scenes of Rosalind as effectually as if the play had been *Isabella*." Anna Seward described Sarah's Rosalind in a letter to Sophia Weston on 20 July 1786: ". . . the playful scintillation of colloquial wit, which most strongly mark that character, suits not the dignity of the Siddonian form and countenance. Her dress was injudicious . . . an ambiguous vestment, that seemed neither male nor female."

Despite her lack of success as Rosalind, the role in which she made her final appearance of the season on 18 May 1785, it had been a stunning season for Mrs Siddons, who after only three years on the London stage was awarded in *The New Rosciad* (1785) the chair of Roscius. She was earning some 23 guineas per week at Drury Lane and her benefit takings were substantial. Reynolds had already painted his famous picture of her as the "Tragic Muse"—in the attitude she had first and instinctively assumed when the artist requested, "Ascend your undisputed throne, and graciously bestow upon me some good idea of the tragic muse." Sarah had attracted to her performances royalty, politicians, and literary figures including Burke, Fox, Windham, and Gibbon. She enjoyed the friendship of Lord and Lady Harcourt, at whose estate at Nuneham, near Oxford, she and her family became regular visitors. Among her other close friends were the Rev and Mrs Sedgewick Whalley (he was a well-known Bath dilettante and godfather to Sarah's daughter, Cecilia), and soon she would be more assiduously cultivated by Hester Thrale Piozzi. Before too long she would have the honor of attending their majesties at Windsor. But she suffered a grueling experience despite the honor, for she was kept standing for a long time and fed nothing. Peter Pindar (John Wolcot) criticized the Royal Family for their lack of hospitality in his *Ode Upon Ode* (1787):

Poor MRS. SIDDONS, she *was order'd out—*
To *wait upon their M—j——ies, to spout—*
To *read old Shakespear's* As you like it *to 'em;*
And *how to mind their Stops, and Commas, shew*
　　'em.
She *read, and spouted—almost lost her Breath—*
And *standing all the time, was tir'd to Death;*
Whilst *both their M—j——ies, in Royal Style,*
At *perfect ease were sitting all the while.*
Not *offer'd to her was one Drop of Beer,*
Nor *Wine, nor Chocolate, her Heart to cheer.*
Ready *to drop to earth, she must have sunk,*
But *for a Child, that at the Hardship shrunk—*
A *little* PRINCE, *who mark'd her Situation;*
Thus, *pitying, pour'd a tender Exclamation:*
. . . [She] *would, I'm sure, be happy in a* Chair.
What *follow'd—Why?,* The R—y—l *Pair*
　　arose,
Surly *enough—one fairly may suppose;*
And *to a Room adjoining made retreat,*
To *let her, for one Minute,* steal *a seat.*

In addition, it was claimed, she received no compensation for her command appearance.

In the autumn of 1784 Mrs Siddons had moved her family (four surviving children and her husband) to No 14, Gower Street in Bloomsbury. (They acquired the lease until 1814 but sold it in 1790 when they moved to No 49, Great Marlborough Street, Soho.) There were some hints of domestic problems that would later cause their estrangement, but Sarah and William Siddons were in happy financial circumstances by the summer of 1785, though the driven Sarah seldom took the time to enjoy her good fortune.

As was her custom, within a very brief time after finishing the London season she began her provincial summer tour, opening a six-night engagement in Manchester on 23 May 1785 as Isabella. Subsequently she attracted huge audiences in Liverpool, Belfast, Edinburgh, and Glasgow.

At Drury Lane in 1785–86 among her new roles were the Duchess in *Braganza*, Hermione in *The Distrest Mother*, and Mrs Lovemore in *The Way to Keep Him*. On 11 February 1786 she and her brother John appeared together as Belvidera and Jaffeir in *Venice Preserv'd* for the first time in London. She was magnificent as usual, and Kemble, though really unsuited for the tumultuous Jaffeir, provided more than adequate support. In later years Sarah wrote that she did not like to play Belvidera to John's Jaffeir because he was "too cold, too formal," and she much preferred playing in that piece when her brother Charles Kemble had the part. The *Public Advertiser* of 14 February 1786, nevertheless, found Kemble's Jaffeir to have been "a perfect performance." Mrs Siddons's delivery of "'O Jaffeir—Remember twelve—Aye, but that husband trusted her'— and, above all, the narrative of the night with Renault—were given with the most miraculous organs of varied emphasis, modulation, delicacy, and propriety." On 25 February 1786 she went across the road to Covent Garden Theatre to act Belvidera for the benefit of the widow of the estimable actor John Henderson, who had suffered premature death from a heart attack on 25 November 1785, at 30. The poetical address delivered by Mrs Siddons before the play was written by Arthur Murphy. The *Public Advertiser* of 27 February called it "so very dull."

Back at Drury Lane she was the original Malvina in Delap's unsuccessful tragedy *The Captives* on 9 March 1786. Elvina to Kemble's Percy in *Percy* followed on 25 March. For Kemble's benefit on 6 April he acted Bassanio and Sarah acted Portia in *The Merchant of Venice*. The *Morning Chronicle* of 8 April was delighted with her delivery of the "quality of mercy" speech "as it certainly should be spoken—but as in truth we never heard it spoken—as a reply to 'On what compulsion must I?' From every other Portia it has always appeared as a *recitation*, prepared for the occasion." For her own benefit on 15 May 1786 she succeeded as Ophelia to Kemble's Hamlet. The *Public Advertiser* of 17 May proclaimed that Kemble in the apparent assumption of madness and in the melancholy of the character "is not equalled by any of his predecessors," and until Mrs Siddons acted Ophelia "there never was, in sensible discrimination, as there ought to be, the real madness of Ophelia from the feigned distraction of Hamlet. Till then, the dignity, the love, even the pathos of the part [were] but poorly, if at all administered." That night she also acted the Lady in *Comus,* the afterpiece. Her last performance of the season was as Rosalind in *As You Like It* on 7 June 1786. William Windham noted in his *Diary* next day that she was much better as Rosalind than the first time he had seen her, but he believed that her playing of comedy was not equal to her playing of tragedy. "The highest praise that can be given

to her comedy is," he wrote, "that it is the perfection of art; but her tragedy is the perfection of nature."

In the summer of 1786 she was again at Liverpool in June and July, playing 16 nights and splitting the net receipts half-and-half with the management. After an engagement at Manchester she joined Wilkinson's company at York, where she was eagerly awaited and enjoyed an extraordinary reception, beginning 29 July. Wilkinson called that time in Yorkshire "the Siddonian Year," which he feared would be "unequalled in the Yorkshire Theatrical Annals." Mobs followed her everywhere. At her benefit on 3 August 1786 when she acted Belvidera, the receipts were £192 9s. 6d., the greatest ever taken in the three kingdoms, outside London. In four nights in mid-August at Hull, where she was seen as Euphrasia, Zara, Belvidera, and Isabella, the total receipts were £448 14s. 6d. After another three nights in York (on the third night appearing as Margaret of Anjou for her brother Stephen Kemble's benefit), she went on to Leeds and took £437 18s. in four nights and then appeared in September at Wakefield and Chester (in conjunction with the Third Chester Musical Festival).

She returned to Drury Lane on 3 October 1786 to open her season as Belvidera. The *Daily Universal Register* of the next day provided the details of her costume: ". . . a French grey satin gown, trimmed with tiffany, and trimmed with the same as the gown, a girdle of the same colour, a dark sage coloured cane hat ornamented with feathers and edged with gold, with a band of gauze and large bows, the ends fastened to the waist." On 22 November she played the title role in *Cleone* to John Kemble's Sifroy. When she acted Hermione in *The Distrest Mother* on 6 December she was criticized for losing her vocal control: "When [Mrs Siddons] begins a dialogue of scorn, at the top of her voice (as she did last night in the fifth act) the climax must inevitably be sacrificed." For her benefit on 29 January 1787 she appeared for the first time in London as Imogen in *Cymbeline* (a role she had first acted at Bath on 15 April 1779), with Kemble as Posthumus. Boaden called Kemble "the best Posthumus of my time." Sarah's Imogen was wonderfully delicate and dignified, yet strong and energetic. Though Sarah realized about

In the collection of the Stirlings of Keir

SARAH SIDDONS, as Euphrasia

by Sherwin

£650 to £700 at the benefit, the vehicle did not prove popular with the public.

Her other new roles that season included Hortensia in *The Count of Narbonne* (with Kemble as Raymond) on 8 March, Lady Restless in *All in the Wrong* (she had acted the role at Manchester on 17 February 1777), for the benefit of Kemble, who played Beverley, and the title role in the premiere of *Julia,* a tragedy written expressly for her by Robert Jephson but in which Kemble as the romantic Italian lover Montevole carried off all the acting honors. At Sarah's second benefit on 7 May 1787, at which she cleared £232, Londoners saw her for the first time as Alicia in *Jane Shore* (a role she had first acted at York on 26 April 1777).

After concluding the 1786–87 season on 29 May with Rosalind, Sarah was determined to pass a quiet summer at Nuneham, where Lord and Lady Harcourt made her welcome. Probably she felt less pressure to take on summer work, for she could write on 1 October 1786 to the Whalleys that "I have at last . . . attained the *ten thousand pounds* which I set my

heart upon, and am now perfectly at ease with respect to fortune. I thank God, who has enabled me to procure myself so comfortable an income." On 15 August 1787 she visited the Queen at the Royal Lodge in Windsor, on which occasion she read from *The Provok'd Husband*. Fanny Burney, then in attendance to the Queen, was Sarah's hostess and wrote her impressions in her *Diary:*

I found her the heroine of Tragedy—sublime, elevated and solemn. In face and person, truly noble and commanding; in manner, quiet and stiff; in voice, deep and dragging; and in conversation, formal, sententious, calm, and dry. I expected her to have been all that is interesting; the delicacy and sweetness with which she seizes every opportunity to strike and to captivate upon the stage had persuaded me that her mind was formed with that peculiar susceptibility which, in different modes, must give equal powers to attract and to delight in common life. But I was very much mistaken. . . .

In the 1787–88 season her new roles included Cordelia to Kemble's Lear on 21 January 1788 for her benefit, Chelonice in the premier of Mrs Cowley's *The Fate of Sparta,* Catherine to Kemble's Petruchio in *Catherine and Petruchio* for his benefit on 13 March, and Dianora in *The Regent* on 29 March. The last was an insipid verse drama by Bertie Greatheed, head of the family with which she had lived at Guy's Cliffe when a girl. Mrs Siddons was taken ill after the second performance on 1 April—suffering a miscarriage, according to Mrs Thrale. Two weeks later Sarah lost her youngest daughter Elizabeth Ann Siddons, almost six, who died on 16 April 1788 and was buried at Marylebone Church. Sarah returned to the stage on 26 April for a third performance of *The Regent;* Anna Seward described it as "a strange composition," but Sarah's performance managed to keep it on for a total of nine nights. Her last new role that season was Cleopatra in *All for Love,* with Kemble as Marc Antony, for her benefit on 5 May 1788.

In the summer of 1788 she resumed her touring habits, appearing at Newcastle, Edinburgh, Glasgow, and Norwich. At Norwich she acted nine nights in September, causing what was described as "perhaps the greatest theatrical event in the city's history." Total receipts were reported to have been £852 for the nine nights, half of which constituted Sarah's share. While in Norwich she stayed at the house of Mrs Curtis in St Gregory's Street.

During that summer, Thomas King, dismayed by the distraught manner in which Sheridan conducted Drury Lane's affairs, resigned as acting manager. Sheridan finally persuaded John Kemble to assume the task, and on 23 September 1788 Kemble officially undertook the management. He was to rely heavily on his sister as a very important artistic partner in the years he would manage at Drury Lane through 1795–96 (and then at Covent Garden from 1803). Their first important production was the revival of *Henry VIII* on 25 November 1788, with Sarah as Queen Katherine and John as Cromwell, with new costumes, scenery, decorations, and a splendid procession. She was a figure of grandeur and enormous majestic energy. It was in that role, wrote Leigh Hunt, that her dignity "was seen in all its perfection; never was so lofty grief so equally kept up, never a good conscience so nobly prepared, never a dying hour so royal and considerate to the last." Another great success came to her as Volumnia to Kemble's Coriolanus on 7 February 1789. That production was largely responsible for the identification of Kemble with "Roman roles," and Coriolanus was regarded as one of his finest throughout his career. He wrote in his journal on opening night: "This play was very splendidly ornamented—Mrs Siddons was prodigiously admired, and it was said that I never acted better." The actor Young described Volumnia coming down the stage during Coriolanus's triumphal entry:

She came along, marching and beating time to the music; rolling (if that not be too strong a term to describe her motion) from side to side, swelling with the triumph of her son. Such was the intoxication of joy which flashed from her eye and lit up her whole face that the effect was irresistible. She seemed to me to reap all the glory of that procession to herself. I could not take my eye from her.

For her free benefit on 16 February 1789 (receipts £340) Sarah acted the Princess in a revival of Jephson's *The Law of Lombardy* and the Fine Lady in *Lethe*, neither of which can be counted among her better efforts. She was the original Mary Queen of Scots in St John's tragedy of that name which opened on 21 March 1789; it was a bad play but enjoyed a good cast, including Kemble as Norfolk, Fawcett as Paulet, and Mrs Ward as Queen Elizabeth. Yvonne ffrench assigns Elizabeth to Mrs Fawcett, but the playbills state Mrs Ward. On 21 April Sarah went over to the King's Theatre to participate in a gala sponsored by Brooks's Club in celebration of George III's recovery of his sanity; Robert Merry's ode was delivered by Sarah dressed "a la Britannia, with a spear," at the conclusion of which "a Transparent Painting dropped upon her, and she was no more seen." For her second benefit and her last appearance of the season, on 11 May 1789 she acted Juliet, for her first time in London, to Kemble's Romeo. Mrs Thrale believed that "the pouting Scene with the old Nurse was the cleverest thing I ever saw—so pretty, so Babyish, so charming."

Suffering declining health and tired of squabbles with Sheridan over the delays in paying her salary, Sarah removed herself from Drury Lane for the 1789–90 season, thereby depriving her brother John of her substantial support. In the summer of 1789 she made an extensive tour through England, playing at York, Leeds, Wakefield, Sheffield, Weymouth (where in August she acted Lady Townly in *The Provok'd Husband* before the King and Queen), and Exeter. In the north of England she was, as Tate Wilkinson put it, "that radiant Siddonian queen, that never-failing magnet." At York, Leeds, and Wakefield, Wilkinson realized over £1300 in 13 nights, though much of it he had to pay to Sarah.

She acted at Plymouth in September and October and at Truro in the latter month. At Liverpool, where John Kemble and Francis Aickin had taken over the theatre's lease the previous January, Sarah tried to bolster up the venture by playing in November and December. She also passed time at Bath in November but did not act, and in the spring of 1790 she enjoyed a long visit with Mr and Mrs Piozzi at Streatham. While there she continued to suffer from an ailment which, as she would later discover, was not, as she then believed, "Nerves and Nerves only." On 17 May 1790 Hester Piozzi noted in her diary that "the Physicians have Mistaken her case under a silly notion of Scorbutic Humours—dosed that poor Dear with Mercurial Medicines, till they have torne the fine Vessells to pieces, & shattered all the nerves that her profession had not ruined before. . . ." (About a year later Hester learned the real nature of Sarah's illness: "And poor Mrs Siddons's disorder that we have all been at such a stand about," Mrs Piozzi wrote in her diary, "turns upon close examination to be neither more nor less than the P——given by her husband. What a World it is!")

During those months of much-needed idleness and relaxation, the Siddonses moved from Gower Street into the house at No 49, Great Marlborough Street, which they had bought from General Boyer. The house was later renumbered to 54 (see *Notes and Queries,* 6 July 1907, p. 12). In the summer Sarah and William visited their daughters Sally and Maria at their boarding school in Calais; then they traveled to Lisle and toured the Netherlands. They returned in early August.

Announced as making her first appearance in two years (actually about a year and a half), Mrs Siddons returned to Drury Lane on 7 December 1790 to act Isabella. On 14 December she played Euphrasia and then appeared only four more times: as Jane Shore on 21 March, Desdemona on 28 March, Mrs Beverley on 4 April (for her benefit), and Zara in *The Mourning Bride* on 14 May 1791. A German visitor, F. W. von Hassell, described Mrs Siddons acting Jane Shore as she made a timid approach to the house of a friend whose lover she had won away: "She staggers up to the door, timidly lifts the knocker, releases it as if she had committed a mortal sin, seizes it a second time and—knocks. It is impossible to describe how she knocked, but I shall never forget her in this situation, never forget the tone of her voice in answer to the servant, never the timidity, the anguish of her expression and movements."

The receipts that night (21 March 1791) totaled £337 7s. 6d., the largest amount, according to *The London Stage,* taken at Drury Lane Theatre, on a night not designated a benefit, between 1776 and 4 June 1791, the date of the last performance there before that Drury Lane Theatre was closed for demolition.

Sarah did not act in the summer of 1791; her continuing bad health sent her back to the Rectory cottage at Nuneham, which she had begun to rent regularly from the Harcourts. Mrs Piozzi visited her at Nuneham that August and found the cottage "a fairy Habitation" and Sarah busy modeling in clay. But during

Mrs Piozzi's visit Sarah miscarried, and Mrs Piozzi suffered a general discomfort: "the Eating & Drinking at Mrs Siddons's was insupportably ill dress'd, dirty, and scanty." Mrs Piozzi's maid was worse fed and lodged. So, with "the Pleasure faded away," Mrs Piozzi cut short her visit. In September Sarah passed some time with the Greatheeds at Guy's Cliffe. She then went to Harrowgate, seeking relief for her continuing ailment, "to try the effect of the water for a complaint," she wrote to a friend in Glasgow, "which tho' not dangerous has been an unspeakable torment to me." The Siddonses were back in London by 14 January 1792, the date the Pantheon burned to the ground. They watched the fire from their window, on an icy night, and (if the speculation of Aylward in *The House of Angelo* is correct) as a consequence they both were in later years martyrs to rheumatism.

While the Drury Lane company were waiting for their new theatre, they played at the King's Theatre in 1791–92. Sarah made her first appearance there on 21 January 1792, as Isabella. The *London Chronicle* of 23 January reported that when her entrance was anticipated, and almost before she was in view of the audience, "the applause commenced on all sides, and continued for some minutes." The *Morning Chronicle* of the same day wrote of:

The same bold, nervous articulation, with the same violent bursts of passion—bursts that confound criticism, though they harrow up the soul. . . . There is a dignified deportment even in her shocks of surprise—her starts of horror—her agonies of death. She never descends to superfluous motion.

She acted Queen Elizabeth in *Richard III* for her first time in London on 7 February 1792 (she first acted the role at Liverpool on 10 September 1777), with John Kemble as Richard. The *European Magazine* that month praised Mrs Siddons for bringing to the role "that degree of excellence which she displays in all her tragic performances" and declared that she would prove that though the part was small it was not unworthy of the first actress of the stage. For her free benefit on 26 March 1792 she acted Queen Katherine in *Henry VIII* and at the end of the play recited Collins's *Ode on the Passions.* The receipts were an impressive £493 16s.; she also received £30 per night for acting 24 nights. She appeared as Mrs Oakly

SARAH SIDDONS
by Stuart

in *The Jealous Wife* for her first time in London on 28 April (the first time she had acted the role was at Manchester on 21 March 1777). In that character she made her final appearance of the season on 5 May 1792.

Sarah went north in the summer of 1792, playing at Birmingham in June and part of July, and at Edinburgh in July and August. In Edinburgh she tried to boost the fortunes of her brother Stephen Kemble, who as manager there was embroiled in frustrating litigation with John Jackson and Mrs Esten. Sarah also acted at Newcastle in August. She now found out that the cause of her illness was a venereal infection from her husband, and Mrs Piozzi wrote to Sophie Pennington: "Poor Siddons pities my very soul to see her; an indignant melancholy sits on her fine face, and care corrodes her very vitals, I do think . . . she is all resentment."

Again Sarah began her London season late, appearing as Jane Shore at the King's Theatre on 21 December 1792. She acted fewer than 20 times from then to June 1793, and her only new role was Ariadne in the premiere of Mur-

phy's *The Rival Sisters* on 18 March 1792 (not 12 March as stated in *The Dictionary of National Biography*). For her benefit that night she took in £451, less house charges of £154. Some of her performances were given at the little Haymarket Theatre, where the Drury Lane company played when the King's Theatre was occupied with operas and oratorios.

By the autumn of 1793 Sarah seemed on the road to recovery, and rather than remaining in London she toured to the north. While she was visiting her sister Mrs Twiss near Norwich, William Beechey painted two full-length portraits of her. In December and January she was in Dublin. She opened a six-night engagement at Liverpool on 21 October 1793 and played Rosalind on 25 October. After Liverpool she acted at Shrewsbury, Chester, and Manchester, and opened in Dublin on 2 December 1793. Remarking that Mrs Siddons looked "incomparably better," Mrs Piozzi wrote to Mrs Pennington in September 1793 about Sarah "setting off for Ireland in this stormy season, but it will answer to her husband and family, *she* has fame and fortune enough." She returned to London in mid-January, considerably "enriched," and three months pregnant. Some reconciliation with William Siddons must have occurred, however tentative.

The spacious and handsome new Drury Lane theatre was opened to the public on 12 March 1794 with a concert. On 21 April 1794 Kemble brought his company on in the inaugural production, of *Macbeth*. Sarah acted Lady Macbeth, John appeared in the title role, and their brother Charles began his Drury Lane engagement by acting Malcolm. The event was a great success, due largely to the lavish new costumes and scenery and an elaborate stage banquet. Sarah was nervous at the prospect of playing in such a large theatre. Later she would call it "a wilderness of a place" and be grateful that she had made her reputation in a smaller theatre. She was also by then big with child. Mrs Piozzi wrote in her diary that for that reason she feared she would not be well received, "for People have a Notion She is covetous, and this unnecessary Exertion to gain Money will confirm it." In the few months remaining in the season Sarah acted some 19 times, most frequently as Lady Macbeth, Hermione, Queen Katherine, Mrs Beverley, and Matilda (in *Douglas*) were her other characters.

Cecilia, her seventh and last child, was born on 25 July 1794. Sarah recuperated at Nuneham Rectory after what she described in a letter to Mrs Piozzi on 27 August 1794 as a "very Safe, tho a long, and *Laborious* time." She had returned to London to act Mrs Beverley for Mrs Stephen Kemble's benefit at the Haymarket Theatre on 20 August 1794, and for over a week after she had to keep to her room "with a pain and weakness" in her back.

At Drury Lane in 1794–95 Mrs Siddons added to her London repertoire Countess Orsina in *Emilia Galotti* (Berington's alteration from Lessing) on 28 October 1794, Horatia in *The Roman Father* on 15 November (she had first acted the role at York on 10 May 1777), and on 21 March 1795 Elgiva in the premiere of Frances D'Arblay's (Fanny Burney) tragedy *Edwy and Elgiva,* a play so bad that its death scene provoked laughter that not even Mrs Siddons could prevent. It was given only one performance. She also acted Palmyra in *Mahomet the Imposter* and Emmeline (disguised as a man) in *Edgar and Emmeline* on 27 April 1795. Her benefit that night drew £569 8s. 6d., less £204 in house charges.

By March 1795 she had acquired a country cottage on Putney Heath, but, given her playing schedule in London and her summer touring, she must have found little time to enjoy it. Soon after her last performance at Drury Lane that season on 2 May 1795 she was off to Scotland to act with her brother Stephen's company. The press announced that William Siddons was prevented by an "Indisposition" from accompanying her. At Edinburgh and Glasgow in May and June she made £800 for herself and brought £1600 into Stephen's treasury. Subsequently she appeared at Berwick, Newcastle, and Birmingham. She was back in London by 29 August 1795, when she acted Lady Randolph to John Kemble's Douglas for Mrs Kemble's benefit at the Haymarket Theatre.

At Drury Lane in 1795–96, a season in which she suffered recurrent illnesses, she acted Roxana in *Alexander the Great,* Almeyda in the premiere of Sophia Lee's *Almeyda* on 20 April 1796, and Julia in *Such Things Are* on 2 May, for her benefit. On 29 April 1796 she played, for the first time in London, Gertrude in *Hamlet* (her first presentation had been at Liverpool on 23 July 1777). Sarah had shown good taste and sense in turning down the role of Rowena in Kemble's production on 2 April 1796 of *Vortigern,* the ridiculous Ireland forgery of Shakespeare that had brought down peals of satirical laughter.

That summer Sarah returned to play in the north: Manchester, Liverpool, Leeds, and York. The effect of her acting upon one young woman is preserved in a letter (Enthoven collection, Theatre Museum) from the daughter of Sir Thomas Franklin to her father, written after seeing Mrs Siddons at the Summer Assizes at York:

I am almost crazy with Dear Divine Angelic Mrs. Siddons, last night is beyond every thing that ever was, or ever will be the play Isabella (Fatal Marriage I mean) you see I am cracked; her screams, two falls flat upon her face are too dreadful—as well as the madness with which she ends the play. She cried in reality much and the Child (Miss Cummins) was terrified & wept most bitterly nothing will cure me but seeing her every night which I intend to do. to-night I go with pretty Mrs. Hunter (the play The Distressed Mother) tomorrow I am in hopes is Belvidere. Saturday the Grecian Daughter & Mrs S. also acts in the farce. Mama told you about our seeing her in Court, when her countenance during the Trial was almost like seeing her upon the Stage, her smile is bewitching & in short if I don't hear her speak in Private Room (which Betsey & I are determined to do) I shall be miserable—Uncle W. says he had no idea she was so great beyond all imagination he says she terrifies him out of his senses . . .

Sarah returned to London in the autumn of 1796 to find Drury Lane under the managership of Richard Wroughton, because her brother John Kemble would tolerate Sheridan's malfeasance no longer. Despite the fact that he was owed £1367 in back salary, Kemble did stay on to act at £24 per week. Sarah was paid £20 a night. When she acted Isabella on 24 September 1796 the critic in the *Oracle* of 27 September noticed that in the huge space of the new theatre Mrs Siddons could not be heard in all parts of the house: "To be so she would strain her voice unnaturally. She does not choose to make the sacrifice, and preserved her excellence with the near, whatever she may lose to the remote." She was seen as Eleonora in a revival of *Edward and Eleonora* on 22 October. She was the original Vitellia in Jephson's *The Conspiracy* on 15 November 1796; her brothers John and Charles acted Sextus and Publius, respectively. On 28 November she played for her first time in London Millwood to Charles's Barnwell in *The London Merchant.* (Her first appearance in that role had been at Liverpool on 11 October 1776.)

On 20 January 1797 she acted Athenais to John Kemble's Varanes in a revival of *Theodosius.* Her appearance on 3 February 1797 as Arpasia in *Tamerlane* (not acted at Drury Lane since 4 November 1780) was marked by an unusual circumstance. "Mrs. Siddons's manner of receiving the death of Monesis," reported the *True Briton* of 4 February, "and the struggle that ended in her own, was one of the best efforts of art we ever beheld. This effort, however, was too much for her powers; for after her fall, her groans were so audible that the curtain was properly dropped" in the middle of Act V. The curtain was raised again and the act concluded, but the audience would not allow the farce to begin until Whitfield came out to assure them that "she was perfectly recovered."

She appeared for her first time as Dido in *The Queen of Carthage* on 28 April 1797. For her benefit on 1 May she chose to appear as Agnes in Lillo's *The Fatal Curiosity.* In Colman's farce afterpiece, *The Deuce Is in Him,* she acted Emily. The gross receipts of £618 2s. (less £211 1s. for house charges to her) reflect the increased seating capacity of the new house. Sarah concluded the evening by delivering a somewhat tactless address, evidently written by Mrs Piozzi, complimenting Elizabeth Farren on her recent marriage to Lord Derby and her retirement from the stage. As a favor to the actor Alexander Pope Sarah went over to Covent Garden Theatre to act Mrs Beverley to his Beverley in *The Gamester* for his benefit on 4 May 1797.

The following season at Drury Lane her new roles were Julia in *The Rivals* on 24 November 1797 (first played by her at Bath on 6 January 1780) and Mrs Haller in *The Stranger* on 24 March 1798. The latter play, an adaptation by Benjamin Thompson of Kotzebue's *Menschenhass und Reue,* with John Kemble in the title role, was something of a sensation and ran 26 nights that season. Campbell proclaimed her

performance of Mrs Haller "the most delicate and judicious that can be imagined." In this Gothic romantic play Mrs Haller, having lived in sin with her seducer, returns to her husband and children. "She shewed," wrote Campbell

what the poet clearly intended us to feel, namely, that the reconcilement was not a conclusion anticipated as a matter of reason or principle by either party, but a burst of nature, overwhelming all abstracted feelings of pride and considerations of stern propriety. She therefore sustained the part with tearless self-command till the end of the very last scene, denoting that she had neither hope nor wish, beyond a promise from her husband that he would not hate her. . . . Mrs Siddons accordingly conducted herself with a reserve and calmness that threw pride into humility; and thus, by contrast, made the effect of her agitation, in the last scene, undescribable.

In 1788–99 Sarah's salary was £20 per night, and in 1799–1800 it was raised to £31 10s. per night. And her benefit proceeds remained substantial. But articles seemed hardly to matter to Sheridan, who was always in arrears with salaries. Several times Sarah threatened to leave Drury Lane, but each time was wooed back by the persuasive Sheridan. In November 1799 Sheridan still owed her over £2100, not including her benefit proceeds from the previous season. Nevertheless she continued to act, as her husband's negotiations with the manager went on and the debt piled higher each night she acted. Sarah described Sheridan's pocket as "that drowning gulf," from which "no plea of right or justice can save its victims."

Her new roles at Drury Lane over the next several seasons included Miranda in *Aurelio and Miranda* on 29 December 1798, the Countess of Montval in *The Castle of Montval* on 23 April 1799 (a Gothic tragedy by her friend Whalley which she managed through extraordinary care to save from failure), an unspecified part in the anonymous *Trials of a Heart* (a piece never printed and acted only once, for King's benefit on 24 April 1799), the original Elvira in Sheridan's wildly successful *Pizarro* on 11 December 1799 and 35 other times that season, Adelaide in Pye's *Adelaide* on 25 January 1800, Jane in Joanna Baillie's *De Montfort* on 29 April 1800, Helena in Godwin's *Antonio; or, The Soldier's Return* on 13 December 1800, and Agnes

Courtesy of the Garrick Club

HENRY and SARAH SIDDONS in *Isabella*
by Hamilton

in Sotheby's *Julian and Agnes* on 25 April 1801 (her last original role). On 25 March 1802 she added to her repertoire Hermione in *The Winter's Tale,* the last time she would play a new role, and nearly the last time she would act any role, for while she was standing as the statue on the pedestal her billowy costume floated out and was ignited by the lamps. Only the quick action of an alert scene shifter saved her from severe burns or worse. Sarah reported in her *Reminiscences* that she "well rewarded the good man."

According to a notation by John Kemble on a playbill of *De Montfort,* he had adapted Miss Baillie's piece for the stage. Sarah played Jane well enough, but Thomas Dutton in the *Dramatic Censor* found that she was "apt to fall at times in *rant* and exaggerated declamation." After acting the part on 3 May 1800 she had so fatigued herself "with her exertions" that she was unable to speak the epilogue. But as Dutton wrote, "An apology was accordingly made for its omission, and very favourably received by a drowsy audience, who were happy to find the Tragedy had reached its conclusion." Kemble and his sister sustained *De Montfort* for eight performances. When Sarah chose the play for her benefit on 5 May 1800, she was "honoured with a fashionable, but not a numerous house." Total receipts, in fact, were only £296 8s. and once the house charges of £207 14s. were deducted Sarah suffered one of her worst benefits ever. Ticket sales dropped off considerably for the next three performances.

In summer, however, she could still be found attracting large numbers of people and amounts of money in the provinces. She made regular excursions to Margate, Coventry, Manchester, Liverpool, Birmingham, Exeter, and Plymouth in 1797; to Cheltenham, Gloucester, Worcester, Hereford, Birmingham, and Brighton in 1798; to Bath, Bristol, Newcastle, Edinburgh, Glasgow, Lancaster, Pontefract, York, Leeds, Wakefield, Doncaster, Sheffield, and Hull in 1799; to Margate, Birmingham, Cheltenham, and Brighton in 1800; and back to many of those places in 1801, adding Preston, Durham, and Southampton. She was driven to this labor: either enticed by the large sums of money she could take in on summer tours or actually needing the money to compensate for Sheridan's constant failures to pay her. At Liverpool on 26 June 1797, *King Lear* was acted for her benefit—as the advertisements proclaimed—of "the divine Sarah," it being the last night of her engagement. The *Monthly Mirror* of August 1798 reported her to have been very successful at Hereford, playing Calista, Jane Shore, Isabella, Mrs Beverley, and Lady Randolph. It was said that she made £500 at Bath in 1799.

The turn of the century brought sorrow and sickness to Sarah. The death of daughter Maria in 1798 and the subsequent machinations of Thomas Lawrence in connection with her daughter Sally (who would die in 1803) wore heavily upon her. In 1800 she suffered an operation—Mrs Piozzi wrote to Penelope Pennington, "she is now thin as a lath, and light as air, but safe, as everybody thinks. Her behaviour—angelic creature—was in this tryal, as in all her tryals, exemplary; firm, but unostentatious." In 1801 she was attacked by erysipelas on her lips, which caused her burning pain. It was an affliction from which she was never fully cured. That summer while at Bath and Bristol her acting remained wonderful but she was completely depressed. Mrs Piozzi wrote to Mr and Mrs Chappelow:

We are all mad about dear charming Siddons, who attracts crowds to our theatre three times a week . . . She commissioned me to tell you . . . that *nothing* does her any good . . . or produces any but a momentary Relief . . . that anxiety of mind increases it almost to Distraction, but that she has Martyr'd herself with unavailing Remedies, and will try no more. Since Maria's Death it has returned upon her Terribly, and she is as lean as yourself; but very beautiful and light and grace in her Figure. . . .

Sarah was taking laudanum, "externally and internally for this horrid Torment—poor Soul!" Mrs Piozzi asked for secrecy, though she herself was not discreet in describing Sarah's condition to persons who were not her intimate friends:

So now *swear* to me you *will not tell;* but say Mrs Siddons is here and acting divinely, which is the strictest Truth: and that she looks better than ever, which is the strictest Truth likewise: Confession of Illness is to her a Ruin. . . . Say not that anything ails her for Heaven's sake.

By the end of the 1801–2 season at Drury Lane Sarah and her brother John decided they no longer could tolerate Sheridan's financial bunglings and smiling promises. Kemble resigned, began negotiations to buy into the Covent Garden Theatre, and went abroad until March 1803. Leaving her family behind at Bath in May 1802, Sarah went again to Ireland, where she was to remain for a year. Accompanying her was young Martha (Patty) Wilkinson, daughter of the York manager Tate Wilkinson; she had come to live in the Siddons household in 1799, originally as a companion for Sally Siddons; but she became more devoted to Mrs Siddons, accompanied Sarah on all her travels, and never left her until her death.

Soon after her arrival in Dublin, Sarah subscribed five guineas to the Masonic Female Charity School of Ireland, no doubt a genuine gesture, but also perhaps calculated to defuse any renewal in Dublin of the charges that she was miserly. (In fact rumors were already circulating that she would earn £150 per night in Ireland and that her visit would total £10,000, which would be added to some £53,000 she had amassed in her English funds.) Nevertheless, a confusion developed publicly over whether or not she had refused to act for the Dublin Lying-in Hospital. She had the manager Frederick Jones publish her letter in the press, in which she regretted the sad necessity "of vindicating my character." The air was cleared when the trustees of the hospital came to her rescue and stated that she never refused to play for the institution and indeed had never been requested to do so.

A journal kept by an anonymous playgoer (manuscript in the National Library of Ireland) documents Sarah's portrayals at Dublin. At a performance by Mrs Siddons of Zara in *The Morning Post* that playgoer was particularly struck

with the ease & peculiar grandeur of her attitudes; her first appearance is in this piece in the procession of an haughty conqueror, she paid not the smallest attention to the peals of applause from the audience, but advancing to the front crossed her arms in one of her fine attitudes of haughty contempt incident to the character & proceeded—her face is an exact counterpart of her brother Kemble, & possesses . . . even stronger power of expression—in viewing Mrs Siddons performance you see nothing which can in the slightest degree convey the idea of an actress, every motion, every look is the natural result of the passion.

But it seems that Mrs Siddons was no longer the lean figure described by Mrs Piozzi the previous year. "She is rather too fat," wrote the anonymous journalist, "& her voice from long continued exertion has acquired too masculine a tone." When he went to the theatre on 14 June the press of the crowd had increased: ". . . I thought I would secure a peaceable entrance by a Box Ticket, & pass from there into the pit—I found however near 100 people squeezing at the Box door also before it was opened & all these paying price for pit seats." When Sarah acted Lady Macbeth at her benefit on 21 June 1802 it was supposed that she would "from the number of golden offerings" receive above 600 guineas. As Elvira in *Pizarro* on 22 June "the amazing truth of her attitude & expressions of her fine conception in situations where the poet can claim little merit," struck more forcibly "upon the Spectator at every opportunity of witnessing them." Her chilling performance of Lady Macbeth on 12 July sent involuntary shudders throughout the audience.

Perhaps the most extraordinary event of the Dublin season was Sarah's appearance as Hamlet on 27 July 1802:

. . . the House groaned under the weight of spectators & on the 1st appearance of Hamlet, the applauses were excessive—In this 1st Scene she seemed oppressed with the novelty of her appearance (Notwithstanding she wore a kind of black scarf which was very nearly the equivalent of a petticoat) her voice was weak, & I expected a very indifferent performance of the character, but she soon recovered herself & the audience was rapt in admiration of her excellence; her superiority even to her brother was first discernible where the secret of the Ghosts appearance is disclosed to Hamlet. . . . The Fencing scene in the last Act was capital; Galindo who is a master of the art, was put into the character of Laertes purposely for an Exhibition & Mrs. S. had practiced under him so successfully that she astonished the cognoscenti of the audience—Notwithstanding the very fine acting of the character, the effect was considerably injured by the awkwardness of the dress & the feminine gait, which was sometimes ludicrous—if Mrs. S— could correct these, she would be an unrivalled Hamlet.

SARAH SIDDONS, as Lady Macbeth
by Harlow

In March 1803 Sarah, by the desire of the Lord Lieutenant, gave four readings from *Paradise Lost* at the Rotunda "to the whole fashionable world," for the benefit of the hospital. The last night, 16 March, had the added attractions of a card assembly, ball, and promenade:

. . . all the beauty & fashion of Dublin, in all the pomp of feathers, diamonds, etc. ⅔ of the company could not possibly hear a syllable of the reading, but the sight of so splendid an assemblage only was worth the admission ticket—It struck me that there was something of a profanation in reading Milton to a multitude of gay people, two out of three much more deeply intent upon the dancing which was to follow & all assembled more under an idea of amusement than to time their souls to the inspired strain of Milton.

Sarah played at Limerick and Cork in August and September 1803, followed by two months at Belfast in September and October. After the Dublin season ended in March 1803 she returned to Cork. Sarah about this time received notification of the death of her father, the family patriarch Roger Kemble, at London on 6 December 1802. Bad weather prevented her return to England until early April. At Shrewsbury, on her way to London, she received first a letter from William Siddons written an hour before their daughter Sally's death, and then additional news, by word of mouth, that she had died on 24 March 1803 of emphysema brought on by asthma.

By 16 April 1803 Sarah was back in London. She worked no more that summer, retiring to Birch Farm at Cheltenham, to take the waters. In addition to all her other problems, Sarah, who had been the very image of piety and uprightness, untainted by scandal, was now suffering separation from a lover.

Since leaving Dublin Sarah had been writing letters to Mr and Mrs Galindo, with whom she had begun an enthusiastic friendship while in that city. (Galindo, as noted above, had acted Laertes to her Hamlet on 27 July 1802. Mrs Galindo had played Andromache to Mrs Siddon's Hermione in *The Distrest Mother* on 14 June 1802, and the Dublin diarist had been disgusted by her inferiority.) Sarah probably had met P. Galindo (only his first initial is known) when he was a member of the Bath and Bristol Company in 1798–99. Since 1793 he had been operating a fencing academy in Shannon Court, off Corn Street, in Bristol. At that time he was, it seems, married or a widower, for a Miss Galindo was playing children's roles at Bristol in 1798. (She could, of course, have been his young sister.) And he had not yet married Catherine Gough (1765–1829), who had made her debut at Covent Garden Theatre in October 1795. She and Mrs Siddons may have crossed paths in the late 1790s during their summer excursions. During her engagement at Dublin in 1799–1800 Miss Gough became acquainted with Galindo, who by then was also in that city. They married sometime between 24 June and 4 November 1801; after the latter date Miss Gough was advertised in the bills as Mrs Galindo.

Sarah's visit to Dublin in 1802 began a bizarre episode in her life. It was, of course, a time when the forty-seven-year-old Sarah, overworked and overwrought, now separated from her family, nearly estranged from her husband and in need of emotional sustenance, was most vulnerable. According to the story told in *Mrs Galindo's Letter to Mrs. Siddons,* not published until 1809 and written with much bombast and pathos, Mrs Siddons had infatuated Galindo and indulged in a physical affair with him, all the time pretending friendship to Mrs Galindo. The threesome often traveled together, and Sarah was named godmother to a daughter born to the Galindos in July 1803. That year Sarah persuaded Harris the Covent Garden manager to engage Galindo, but John Kemble, embarrassed by his sister's improprieties, became so furious that Harris was forced to withdraw the offer. Galindo, nevertheless, left Dublin in order to be near Sarah in London, leaving Mrs Galindo to fend for herself and family, and to deliver yet another child by him. Mrs Galindo eventually joined her husband in London, where they remained until about 1808, when the fencing master borrowed £1000 from Sarah to enter into a partnership with William Macready for the lease of the Manchester Theatre. When the venture failed and Galindo could not repay Mrs Siddons, he also cooled toward her. In her pamphlet Mrs Galindo charged Sarah with taking revenge by demanding instant repayment of the loan, thereby threatening to ruin him, his wife, and their three children. It seems that Sarah never recovered her money. After 1809 Galindo's movements elude us. Catherine Galindo died in Dublin in 1829 (see her notice, under Gough, in volume 6 of this *Dictionary*).

The summer's stay at Cheltenham in 1803 was an idyllic respite for Sarah, who had suffered the agony of the deaths of two loved ones and the anxiety of her then secret affair with Galindo. She wrote to the Galindos in May of living outdoors as much as possible, reading by the haystack, rambling the fields, or musing in the orchard—"with no observer near to say I am mad, foolish, or melancholy." She could now sleep comfortably once more, "the bitterness and anguish of selfish grief begins to subside."

In April 1803 John Kemble had concluded his negotiations with the Harrises for a one-sixth share in Covent Garden. It was agreed that Kemble should manage the operation as well as act. When Covent Garden opened in September 1803 under his management, it was host to a pride of Kembles. Brother Charles made his first appearance on 12 September and sister Sarah hers on 27 September as Isabella. Also gathered into the clan were Sarah's son Henry Siddons and his wife Harriet (née Murray). Sarah continued to act at Covent Garden until her retirement in 1812, except that during the Master Betty craze in 1804–5 she refused to appear. She played with the Covent Garden company at the King's Theatre and the Haymarket after Covent Garden burned in September 1808.

Though Sarah still commanded high wages and drew large crowds and benefits (her salary in 1805–6, for example, was £1685 4*s.*, according to a pay ledger now in the Harvard Theatre Collection), audiences were beginning to sense a waning of her powers and observe the widening of her girth. No new roles were assumed by her. She continued in sure-fire favorites like Lady Macbeth, Isabella, Belvidera, Elvira, and even Desdemona, a role she had, it would seem, quite literally outgrown. She was also plagued in those later years at Covent Garden by the further deterioration of her health and her marriage.

By February 1804 Galindo was in London. Sarah and William were again living together, now in Hampstead where Sarah had taken a cottage. She hoped for a cure from her ongoing rheumatism by subjecting herself to new electrical treatments that often brought more pain than the crippling arthritis. Eventually the problem spread from her hips to her toes, making it impossible for her to use her left side and keeping her in bed for weeks at a time. But the treatments did provide some relief, and she recovered sufficiently to open the 1804–5 season.

Wicked rumors began to circulate about Sarah's relations, not with Galindo, but with Thomas Lawrence, who had come back into her life when he painted her picture. According to Farrington's diary on 2 March 1804, "Mrs Siddons sat to Lawrence for a *whole length last night by Lamplight,* till 2 o'clock this morning." The true extent of any intimacy Sarah may have shared with Lawrence is not established, but Lawrence had quite a reputation for womanizing, and enough gossip circulated to cause William Siddons to advertise in the press in December his offer of £1000 to anyone who would identify the slanderer. There were no takers. But by October 1804 the Siddonses had already separated, as a matter of mutual agreement and convenience. William, also in declining health and suffering rheumatism, went to live at Bath, where he socialized, dabbled in writing addresses for the Bath theatre, and wrote letters to Mrs Piozzi providing news of Bath events.

Sarah had moved out of the large house in Marlborough Street to Hampstead and then in the autumn of 1804, with her daughter Cecilia and Patty Wilkinson, into Mr Nixon's lodgings in Prince's Street, Hanover Square. In April 1805, she settled into a new cottage at Westbourne Farm, on what is the present Harrow Road. (Westbourne Farm was demolished over 150 years ago. According to Dr Herbert Friend, who died in 1942 after long association with the parish, the cottage was sited in the rectangle formed by the Harrow Road, Woodchester Street, Cirencester Street, and a stone passage that links the latter two and stood about opposite the present St Martha's Hall.) In their separation Sarah and her husband remained friends. On occasion she went to visit William at Bath and he came to see her at Westbourne Farm. On one visit to her William was prompted to write an ode "On Mrs. Siddons's Cottage at Westbourne," which is printed by Yvonne ffrench.

William Siddons died at Bath on 11 March 1808 and was buried at Bath Abbey. Sarah interrupted her acting for a fortnight. Once a handsome man, he had been an actor of some service but, obviously, he remained overshadowed by his wife. He had been born at Walsall on 5 September 1744. Most of his early performing was done at Norwich, York, and other northern cities in the 1760s and 1770s. He acted supporting roles at Bristol and Bath from 1779 to 1782, and at Birmingham in 1792. He never acted in London. In 1799 he became for a short time a shareholder in Sadler's Wells but seems to have played no active role in the affairs of that theatre. It was Sarah's money that had bought him the partial proprietorship. In her *Diary*, Fanny Burney wrote of her surprise when she heard "that she had bought the proprietorship at Sadler's Wells" and expressed her amusement at so extraordinary a combination as Mrs Siddons and Sadler's Wells. William had managed Sarah's business affairs; and after their separation she contemplated having Galindo provide that service, but did not do so.

Siddons seems to have been a petulant and nagging man and no match for his more attractive and more socially acceptable spouse. Yet in his relationship with his wife he came to be regarded by Mrs Piozzi as more sinned against than sinning (despite his having given Mrs Siddons the pox). In November 1805 Mrs Piozzi wrote that Mr Siddons had been a very agreeable companion while visiting, and she knew not why Mrs Siddons had turned him out "in his Old Age Poor Fellow."

In his will dated 28 December 1804, some three years before his death, William Siddons described himself as of Great Marlborough Street, St James's, Westminster, and he left the house there to his eldest son Henry Siddons. To his son George John Siddons, he bequeathed the house in Gower Street, Bedford Square. To Cecilia Siddons, his only surviving daughter, he left £2000 on interest payable to her at 21 or on the day of her marriage. All other effects and residue of his estate he bequeathed to his wife Sarah and named her sole executrix. In a codicil on 24 February 1806 he added to Cecilia's legacy another £2000 and his share in the new Theatre Royal, Bath. In another codicil on 18 November 1806 he left to Henry his gold-cased and jeweled watch and his books (mostly classical Greek and Roman works in translation). The will was proved at London by Sarah Siddons on 2 April 1808.

Almost five months after William Siddons's death Mrs Piozzi remarked in her journal: "Mrs Siddons is said to be engaged to marry Lord Erskine when her year of widowhood is expired—*I* say she always did continue to shine brightly in her *last Act*, however fatigued before." Several years earlier Mrs Piozzi had noticed that "Neither Mr Erskine or Mrs Siddons have their imagination under a very tight rein." Nothing permanent came of whatever relationship Sarah may have had with Thomas Erskine (who was a famous barrister and in 1806 was made Lord Chancellor), and she never remarried.

During the early years of the nineteenth century Mrs Siddons continued to make summer excursions throughout the three kingdoms, except in 1804, 1808, and 1811, when she did not act in the summer. In the winter season 1807–8 she took time off from her

Courtesy of Martha Arnott

SARAH SIDDONS
by Opie

engagement at Covent Garden to play at Richmond, Surrey, in October, at Bath and Bristol in January and February, and then at Hull in February and Edinburgh in March 1808. By that time there were rumors that she was to retire. Her engagement at Bath that year had been announced as her last professional visit, and indeed it was, though she continued to act for several more seasons in London and elsewhere.

Tragedy continued to stalk the Tragic Muse. Less than a year before William Siddon's death in March 1808, Sarah's mother, Sarah Kemble, had died in London, on April 24 1807 at the age of 71. On 20 September 1808 the fire that gutted Covent Garden killed 22 persons and took with it all the theatre's properties, scenery, costumes, Handel's organ, many manuscripts by him and by Arne, and the wines of the Beef Steak Club. Kemble was close to ruin. Sarah lost costumes and jewelry, and a lace veil once belonging to Marie Antoinette said to be worth £1500. In an incredibly short time a new Covent Garden Theatre was built and opened on 18 September 1809, with Sarah and

John acting *Macbeth,* to inaugurate a season marred for her and her brother especially by the O. P. riots.

The Covent Garden fire and the O. P. riots had taken their toll of Mrs Siddon's spirits as well as of Kemble's. The riots she described in a letter to her daughter-in-law Harriet Siddons as a "barbarous outrage to decency and reason, which is a National disgrace." Her enthusiasm for the stage had waned. She was in her mid-fifties and growing stouter. Her brother John admitted to Joseph Farington that her voice was failing when, as Lady Constance in *King John,* she had not the power to express a passage properly. Her admirer Lawrence told Farington that she ought to retire. Henry Crabb Robinson saw her act in the spring of 1811 and regretted that "Her advancing old age is really a cause of pain to me," but nevertheless she remained "the only actor I ever saw with a conviction that there never was nor ever will be her equal." On 4 April 1811 she acted Margaret of Anjou in *The Earl of Warwick* "most nobly"; Robinson wrote in his diary:

The character is one of those to which she can still render justice. She looked ill and I thought her articulation indistinct and her voice more than usually drawing and funereal during the first act; but as she advanced in the piece, her genius triumphed over her natural impediments. She was all that could be wished. The scene in which she wrought upon the mind of Warwick was perfect, and in the last act her triumphant joy at the entrance of Warwick whom she had stabbed was incomparable. She laughed convulsively and staggered off the stage as if drunk with delight; And in every limb of her body shewed the tumult of passion with an accuracy and at the same time a force equally impressive upon the criticial [*sic*] and feeling spectator.

A few weeks later, however, her voice "appeared to have lost its brilliancy (like a beautiful face through a veil)," and when Robinson saw her as Euphrasia on 2 May 1811 she played the expressions of joy, scorn, contempt, and heroic firmness in her "very best style," but "in the expression of plaintive sorrow and in pathos her voice had lost its power and she labours." As Queen Katherine on 19 May she was "perfection":

I think never saw Mrs Siddon's pantomime in higher excellence—In the dying scene her truth of imitation was so exact as almost to go beyond the bounds of beautiful imitation—viz. by shifting her pillow with the restlessness of a person in pain. And the suspended breath in moving which usually denotes suffering.

As the Fine Lady in *Comus* on 5 June she was heard for the first time by Robinson "without pleasure." She was costumed "most unbecomingly with a low gypsy hat and feathers hanging down the side." Robinson was dismayed to see her looking "old and I had almost said ugly—her fine features were lost in the distance [he was seated far from the stage] and her disadvantage of years and bulk made as prominent as possible."

During her final season at Covent Garden, 1811–12, she acted 57 times, offering a round of her famous roles. Her farewell benefit came on the final night of the season, 29 June 1812 (and not on 22 June, as misprinted in Manvell's book). A house packed with emotion watched her act Lady Macbeth, and after the sleep-walking scene the applause continued for some time, causing Kemble to conclude, correctly, that the audience wished the play to stop at that point, so the curtain was dropped. After some time (as Farington described the emotional event played out in a theatre grown insufferably hot):

. . . the Curtain was drawn up and Mrs Siddons appeared sitting at a table in Her own character. She was dressed in White Satin and had a long veil. She arose but it was some time before she could speak the clapping and other sounds of approbation rendering it impossible for Her to be heard. She curtsied and bowed, and at last there was silence. At 10 o'clock precisely she began to speak her farewell address which took up Eight minutes during which time there was profound silence. Having finished, the loudest claps followed, and she withdrew bowing, and led off by an attendant. . . . Her appearance was that of a person distressed and sunk in spirits, but I did not perceive that she shed tears . . .

Her brother John did weep, however, and when he asked the audience if the play should continue they did not allow it. Sarah's farewell address, 37 lines of uninspired verse, had been written for her by her nephew Horace Twiss. A notation by Kemble on a British Library manuscript (Add 31975) indicates that total receipts for the night were over £820.

Mrs Siddons returned to Westbourne Farm

(though in 1812 she had taken temporary lodgings in Pall Mall). She occupied herself with giving fashionable parties, sculpturing, and traveling. She had studios for her sculpturing at Westbourne and later in Upper Baker Street. It is said that she first took up sculpting when she went into a shop in Birmingham to see a bust of herself on display and decided she could do better. Her friend Mrs Anne Seymour Damer gave her lessons and they spent many hours together modeling in Mrs Damer's studio at Strawberry Hill, where Sarah was a frequent visitor. In 1813 with her daughter Cecilia and Patty Wilkinson she visited Paris for two months.

Bath society wanted a farewell performance in that city but she decided against it. She did, however, present private readings at Windsor Castle and readings from Milton and Shakespeare at the Argyll Rooms in the first half of 1813. Her six "performances" at the latter place, at half-a-guinea per seat, brought a profit of £1300. Mrs Siddons gave the proceeds on one of the nights to the widow of the actor Andrew Cherry. That year Mrs Siddons resisted an organized effort to persuade her to return full-time to the stage, but she did appear at Drury Lane on 25 May 1813 to act Mrs Beverley for the benefit of the Theatrical Fund, and a few weeks later she played the same role at the same theatre for the same charity on 22 June 1813. On 11 June 1813 she appeared as Lady Macbeth for her brother Charles's benefit at Covent Garden. In July 1815 another attempt to lure her to Drury Lane was made by a committee headed by Lord Byron, but she remained adamant. That autumn, however, she traveled up to Edinburgh after the death of her son Henry Siddons, the Edinburgh manager, and acted for the benefit of his widow and children, appearing on 18 November 1815 as Lady Macbeth and on nine other nights as Lady Randolph, Queen Katherine, Constance, or Mrs Beverley.

Mrs Siddons's subsequent occasional performances, all at Covent Garden, were: as Queen Katherine on 31 May 1816 for the benefit of Mr and Mrs Charles Kemble; Lady Macbeth on 8 and 22 June 1816 by the express desire of Princess Charlotte; Queen Katherine on 29 June 1816 for the Theatrical Fund; Lady Macbeth on 5 June 1817 for Charles Kemble's benefit; and, her final appearance, Lady Randolph on 9 June 1819 for the benefit of the Charles Kembles. In those performances she was received with some enthusiasm, but William Hazlitt saw her Lady Macbeth in 1817 and thought her portrayal "inferior to what it used to be." She spoke too slowly and had lost some of her sweeping majesty. He concluded:

An actress who appears only once a-year cannot play so well as if she was in the habit of acting once a-week. We, therefore, wish Mrs Siddons would either return to the stage, or retire from it altogether. By her present uncertain wavering between public and private life, she may diminish her reputation, while she can add nothing to it.

In 1817 Mrs Siddons left Westbourne Farm to take a house at No 27, Upper Baker Street, Marylebone, at the top of the row on the right side leading to Regent's Park. (Westbourne Farm was later occupied by Mme Vestris and Charles Mathews when it was known as Desborough Lodge; see *Notes and Queries,* 8 April, 20 May, 17 June, 22 July, and 16 September 1893.) Mrs Siddons resided in Upper Baker Street until her death. Until the house was demolished in 1904, it was marked by a memorial tablet placed by the Society of Artists. In her London house Sarah gave parties, received guests to whom she read from Shakespeare, and watched her coterie of old friends pass away. Mrs Piozzi died in 1821, Dr Whalley in 1828, and Lawrence in 1830. Her brother John had died in 1823 (she had visited him at Lausanne in 1821).

She aged, as her old friend Joseph Jekyll wrote, like "a majestic ruin." She made occasional public appearances, "a solemn female figure in black," as Fanny Kemble recollected her. "Weariness, vacuity, and utter deadness of spirit," Fanny wrote of her aunt. "She has stood on a pinnacle till all things have come to look flat and dreary; mere shapeless, colourless, level monotony to her. . . ." In 1822 Sarah published her only written work, an abridged edition of *Paradise Lost* for children: *The Story of our first Parents, Selected from Paradise Lost: For the Use of Young Persons.* Despite her moroseness, she remained honestly religious throughout her life, possessing a strong spirit, courage, and a fixed moral attitude about right and wrong.

On 31 May 1831 she caught a cold on a drive out, and erysipelas attacked both legs.

She suffered severe vomiting and high fever. On the evening of 7 June she lapsed into a coma, and at about eight the next morning, 8 June 1831, she died at her house in Upper Baker Street, at the age of 76. On 15 June an impressive cortege, which included representatives from Covent Garden and Drury Lane and was viewed by large crowds in the streets and buildings, escorted her body to the Paddington churchyard of St Mary's, where some 5000 persons saw her laid to rest. The inscription on her tomb, lines chosen by herself, reads:

Sacred to the Memory of
SARAH SIDDONS
who departed this life June 8th, 1831,
in her 76th year.
Blessed are the dead who die in the Lord.

Largely through the efforts of W. C. Macready, a large statue of her by the sculptor Thomas Campbell was raised in Westminster Abbey (north transept, east aisle) in 1849. A small sculpture of her by L. Chavalliand, after Reynolds's famous painting of her as the Tragic Muse, stands on Paddington Green; it was unveiled on 14 June 1897 by Sir Henry Irving. Mrs Siddons's bust of herself is in the Dyce Collection at the Victoria and Albert Museum.

Sarah Siddons had seven children by her husband William Siddons, born over a period of 19 years between 1775 and 1794. She had the misfortune to see five of them buried. On 11 March 1799 Mrs Piozzi noted in her journal that Mrs Siddons had returned triumphant to play at Bath after 19 years absence and was "more beautiful, more brilliant, & more just deserving that universal Applause . . . ," but:

I think she is not happy in her children tho'. The eldest son [Henry] will be a strolling player. The second [George] has bad eyes—almost to blindness. The pretty daughter [Maria] died; & Sally seems almost entirely ruined by an Asthma which they call Constitutional, & scarce try to remove. The little Baby, my God child, called Cecilia, is sick and spoild, and fretful & fragile,—her Mother has put her to Miss Lee for education [at the Belvidera School in Bath], but they are fearful she will not live.

The eldest son, Henry Siddons, born at Wolverhampton on 4 October 1774, made his debut at Drury Lane at the age of eight playing the Child to his Mother's Isabella on 10 Octo-

SARAH SIDDONS, as Rosalind

artist unknown

ber 1782. Later he married the actress Harriet Murray and managed at Edinburgh before his death there of tuberculosis on 12 April 1815, at the age of 40. Information on his career and family is given in his notice on these pages.

The second child and first daughter, Sarah Martha (called Sally), was born at Gloucester on 5 November 1755 and was baptized at St Michael's, Gloucester, on 30 November 1775. The third child, Maria, was baptized at Bath Abbey on 24 February 1799 (the date of 1 July 1799 given by Ms ffrench for Maria's birth thus is incorrect). The two girls became the objects of Thomas Lawrence's vacillating affections. He first fell in love with Sally and jilted her for Maria, then turned back to Sally. Maria was

heartbroken, but it was tuberculosis that killed her. She died at Clifton Hot Wells on 7 October 1798 at the age of 19, after great suffering that is said to have turned her appearance into that of an old woman. On her deathbed Maria warned Sally about Lawrence and extracted a promise that Sally would never marry him. Sally died unmarried in London on 24 March 1803, of emphysema, at the age of 27.

A fourth child, Frances Emilia, was baptized at Bath Abbey on 26 April 1781 but soon died. Another daughter, Elizabeth Ann, was born at Bath on 2 June 1782; she also died young, at London on 16 April 1788, and was buried at Marylebone Church.

The Siddons's second son and sixth child, George John, was born at London on 27 February 1785. He went into the Bengal Civil Service in India in 1803 and became Collector of Calcutta Customs; he married Mary Fonbelle and had seven children: (a) Frances, who married Professor Horace Wilson and had six daughters; (b) George Siddons of the Bengal Cavalry, who had one child, Mary (married to J. Hawtry and alive in January 1887); (c) Harriot Emma, who married her cousin Henry Siddons (son of Henry Siddons) and left one child, Sarah Siddons, who married William Grant of Rothiemercus and left no issue; (d) Sarah, who married William Young of the Bengal Civil Service and was alive in 1887 with two sons and two daughters; (e) Henry Siddons, of the Madras Cavalry, who had one child, Henry G. F. Siddons, a Major in the Royal Artillery at Liverpool in January 1887 (see *Notes and Queries* for 1 January 1887, pp. 4–5); (f) William Siddons of the Bengal Native Infantry, who left four children, all alive in 1887: Mary Scott Siddons (who married but kept the family name), Harriet Siddons (unmarried), William Siddons of the Bengal Uncovenanted Service (married with two daughters), and Henry Siddons (unmarried); (g) Mary, who married Robert Thornhill of the Bengal Civil Service; he was killed at Cawnpore, and was survived by two sons and a daughter. George John Siddons died on 5 November 1848 and was buried at St Mary's, Paddington, on 10 November.

Sarah and William Siddons's seventh and final child was Cecilia, born in London on 25 July 1794. She was sickly and remained with her mother for many years; after Sarah's death Cecilia in 1833 married George Coombe, Writer to the Signet in Edinburgh; she died without issue in 1868, having outlived most of the Siddonses of her generation.

Sarah Siddons was survived by her sisters Jane Mason (d. 1834), Elizabeth Whitlock (d. 1836), and Ann Julia Hatton (d. 1838) and by her brother Charles Kemble (d. 1854). Her brother John Philip Kemble had died in 1823 and her brother Stephen and sister Frances Twiss in 1822.

Sarah's sister Ann Julia, the seventh child of their parents Roger and Sarah Kemble, precocious like all the Kembles but eccentric like no other, became the family black sheep. Though she openly criticized her celebrated sister she also traded on her fame. She published in 1783 a collection of her *Poems on Miscellaneous Subjects: By Ann Curtis, sister of Mrs Siddons*. Afflicted as a young child with lameness and a squint, she was unfit for the stage, though in 1783 she was employed by the quack doctor James Graham to give lectures at his establishment located at Schomberg House, Pall Mall. In October of that year she tried to intimidate Sarah and her brother John by advertising in the papers for donations, which, she claimed, were necessary for her to solicit because her sister and brother had refused her applications for relief. According to James Winston, Sarah settled an allowance of £100 a year upon Ann provided she should remain at least 100 miles away from London, but there is no evidence to that effect. Sarah did indeed allow Ann £20 a year, and her brother John gave her £40 a year, an allowance he raised to £60 in his will. Her first marriage to C. Curtis, a provincial actor, ended in disaster when he proved a bigamist. In 1792 she married William Hatton, not an actor, at Marylebone. After Sarah's death Ann railed against her stinginess and hard-heartedness— "I did not see Mrs Siddons for more than fifty years," she wrote to J. P. Collier in August 1832. Collier and Thomas Campbell refused her offer of help in writing Mrs Siddons's biography. In 1834 she was still trying to peddle her life of Mrs Siddons, offering it to R. Bentley in London to support her proposed publication of her latest poetic effort "The Raconteur." Neither was accepted.

Sarah Siddons had made a lengthy will on 18 May 1815, giving her address as Westbourne Green, Paddington, and naming John Philip Kemble and her nephew Horace Twiss of the Temple as executors. The first bequest was to her companion Martha Wilkinson— "her bed and all the furniture of her bedchamber at Westbourne Green, and I confirm the provision of £5500 five per cent bank annuities which I have already made for her by transfer of such annuities in trust" to Samuel Pepys Cocknell and William Mayrick. To her daughter Cecilia Siddons, Sarah left all her furniture, portraits, drawings, books, plates, carriages, and horses. For her "poor sister" Ann Hatton she continued during her life the annuity of £20 which she had been receiving for many years. Small bequests included the portraits of her brother Charles Kemble painted by Clark to his widow Maria Theresa; her inkstand, made of a mulberry tree said to have been planted by Shakespeare at Stratford, to John Philip Kemble; a mourning ring to Charlotte Fitzhugh of upper Grosvenor Street; and £20 for mourning to her sister Frances Twiss. The residue of her estate she left in trust to be divided in three equal parts among her daughter Cecilia Siddons, her son George Siddons (after his decease to his widow Mary), and Harriet Siddons, widow of her son Henry, for maintenance of herself and children. In a codicil signed on 8 April 1824, her brother John having died, she gave the inkstand of mulberry wood and the gloves worn by Garrick to her son George and her daughter Cecilia. The will was proved at London on 8 July 1831 by William Mayrick, now the executor. An additional administration, shown in a marginal notation, was granted to George Siddons, one of the residuary legatees, Horace Twiss having renounced (and apparently Mayrick having died), and Cecilia, now the wife of George Coombe, also having renounced.

The household furniture, china, glass, and plated articles from Mrs Siddons's house at No 27, Upper Baker Street, were sold on the premises by Nixon on 27 and 28 July 1831. The sales catalogue lists 287 lots. At the same time there was "sold the Lease of the House, 40 years of which are unexpired, at a Ground-rent of £7 7s." The house at No 49 (later 54) Great Marlborough Street, with a storey added by 1907, was badly damaged in World War II and was razed in 1953. A small mural tablet was placed by Ellen Terry on 17 October 1922 at No 33, Paragon, Bath, where Mrs Siddons had sometimes lived. The burial ground at St Mary's Church on the northern end of Paddington Green has been cleared of most of the tombstones, but Mrs Siddons's grave remains well tended. Buried beside her is Patty Wilkinson, who died in 1847, and in the next grave over rests Sarah's son George John Siddons, who died on 5 November 1848 at No 10, Harewood Square, and was buried on 10 November. During World War II a bomb blast (some say small children throwing stones) damaged the statue of Mrs Siddons on the Green, causing it to lose part of its nose, some fingers, and a great toe. A committee headed by her descendants Lady Butler and the actor Rupert Siddons and Dame Sybil Thorndike persuaded the Paddington Borough Council to restore the statue and clear out the surrounding area of brush. The sculptor Alfred Banks did the repairs and the inscription was recut.

As with most star actors, a mythology of relics surrounds Sarah Siddons. The Garrick gloves that she bequeathed to her son and daughter were said to have belonged originally to Shakespeare. On 17 October 1931 in *Notes and Queries* Albert Matthews of Boston, Massachusetts, cited a letter dated from Philadelphia on 3 April 1874 written by Fanny Kemble to the effect that she had received the Garrick gloves from Cecilia Coombe's will. Fanny gave them to Dr Howard Furness (1833–1912), editor of Shakespeare; these relics are now in the Furness Collection, University of Pennsylvania. Gloves alleged to have been the Bard's were given to Garrick by John Meacham, mayor of Stratford-upon-Avon in 1769. About 1800 the gloves came into the hands of Thomas Keats of Chelsea College. They were given by his daughter to her cousin Charlotte Benson, whose daughter, Mrs Cockerell of Oxford, presented them to the Shakespeare Memorial Theatre in 1908. The slippers that Mrs Siddons wore in her final performance of Lady Macbeth were presented by the actress to Mrs Davenport, wife of Dr James Davenport, vicar of Stratford. They passed to Miss Sally Booth, then to Mrs J. H. Clyndes, and from the latter to the Shakespeare Memorial Theatre in 1889. Mrs Siddons's make-up table, designed for her by Sheraton, is owned by the Theatre Museum, London. An exhibition of other Siddons relics was held at the Saville Theatre in July 1955.

Numerous articles and books have been written about Sarah Siddons. James Boaden issued his *Memoirs of Mrs Siddons* in 1827. Thomas Campbell, her chosen biographer, published his *Life of Mrs Siddons* in 1836 with the assistance of an autobiographical memoir provided by her. The original manuscript of the memoir is in the Harvard Theatre Collection and was published in 1942 as *The Reminiscences of Sarah Kemble Siddons*, edited by William Van Lennep. Modern books include Mrs Clement Parsons's *The Incomparable Siddons* (1909), Yvonne ffrench's *Mrs Siddons, Tragic Actress* (1936, revised 1954), and Roger Manvell's *Sarah Siddons, Portrait of an Actress* (1970), to all of which this entry is much indebted. *The Letters of Sarah and William Siddons to Hester Lynch Piozzi in the John Rylands Library*, edited by Kalman A. Burnim, appeared in the *Bulletin of the John Rylands Library*, 52 (Autumn 1969). About 200 letters, probably the largest single collection of letters by Sarah Siddons, are in the Harvard Theatre Collection. A detailed account of her acting is provided in Bertram Joseph's *The Tragic Actor* (1959). Her acting of Lady Macbeth is treated in Joseph Donohue's *Dramatic Character in the English Romantic Age* (1970) and by the same author in *Theatre Notebook* 21, in Dennis Bartholomeuz's *Macbeth and the Players* (1969), and in A. C. Sprague's *Shakespearean Players and Performances* (1953). During her lifetime many pamphlets, periodical pieces, and poems were published in her praise, and she is mentioned in many memoirs, diaries, and letters of the period. A useful bibliography is in Manvell's biography of her.

Except for the episode with Galindo and some gossip about her and Lawrence, Mrs Siddons's private character seems to have been worthy of the respect that was accorded to her by the public and friends alike. (In 1804 Joseph Farington heard "reports of Mrs Siddons being gone off with a young artist, who had courted two of her daughters in succession, both of whom had died," but he called the story a "foul calumny" and an attempt to injure both Sarah's and Lawrence's reputations.) She was determined to make money to assure her family's security, and she worked hard to that end. Though sharp in money matters, she

Tate Gallery

SARAH SIDDONS
by Lawrence

thought austere. She was motivated, it seems, by two overwhelming factors: a motherly affectionate heart and an intense devotion to her profession.

Although never the intellectual or social lioness, as Garrick had been the lion, Mrs Siddons could be at ease in the parlor. Her company was sought by the Johnsonians and the Blue Stockings. But most of her professional life she harnessed herself resolutely to the demands of stage life, out of her concern for her family. After retirement she often commented that she had spent most of the early evenings of her life preparing to go on stage. She was never easy away from the theatre, it seems. Samuel Rogers in his *Recollections* claimed that after she left the stage, "Mrs Siddons, for want of excitement, was never happy." She did express jealousy over the great ceremony attendant on John Kemble's retirement from the stage, and was reported to have said, "Well, perhaps in the next world women will be more valued than they are in this."

She was a genius in her art, as beautiful as she was talented. That great beauty of countenance waned but little in her later years, despite the fact that her increased girth sometimes caused her to become stuck in chairs. On stage she had to be helped out of her chair, and in order not to call attention to this necessity all other females on the stage would be similarly assisted.

Although William Hazlitt had been pained by the performances that Sarah had given in the last days of her career, she had been for him in her greatest days the epitome of the Muse of Tragedy. He wrote in the *Examiner* on 16 June 1816:

She raised the tragedy to the skies. . . . It was something above nature. We can conceive of nothing grander. She embodied to our imagination the fables of mythology, of the heroic and dignified mortals of elder time. She was not less than a goddess, or than a prophetess inspired by the gods. Power was seated on her brow, passion emanated from her breast as from a shrine. She was Tragedy, personified. She was the stateliest ornament of the public mind. . . . To have seen Mrs Siddons was an event in everybody's life. . . .

In the *London Magazine* for January 1820 Hazlitt despaired that no actress would ever be able to fill the void left by her retirement:

seems not to have deserved the reputation of being stingy. Like her brother John, she tended toward formality, especially with strangers. She was apt, it was said, to speak in formal rhythmic phrases. Fanny Burney came to admire Mrs Siddons, though she never warmed to her. Fanny found her "a woman of excellent character" who behaved with great propriety—"very calm, modest, quiet, and unaffected." There was "a steadiness in her manner and deportment by no means engaging," wrote Fanny in her *Diary,* and Mrs Thrale (Mrs Piozzi) was heard to say, "Why, this is a leaden goddess we are all worshipping! however, we shall soon gild it." Her biographer Thomas Campbell described her as "a great simple being, who was not shrewd in her knowledge of the world, and was not herself well understood in some of the particulars by the majority of the world." She commanded respect but was

Who shall in our time. . . . fill the stage, like her, with the dignity of their persons, and the emanations of their minds? Or shall sit majestic on the throne of tragedy—a Goddess, a prophetess, and a Muse—from which the lightning of her eyes flashed o'er the mind, startling its inmost thoughts—and the thunder of her voice circled through the labouring breast, rousing deep and scarce-known feelings from their slumber? . . . Who shall walk in sleepless ecstasy of soul, and haunt the mind's eye forever after with the dread pageantry of suffering and of guilt? Who shall make tragedy once more stand with its feet upon the earth, and with its head raised above the skies, weeping tears and blood?

No claim for completeness is made for the list of portraits that follows. Many, but not all, of the pictures are described in detail. Often more information about a picture may be found in the catalogue of the gallery or museum owning it or in studies of the artist. We express our gratitude and appreciation to Peter Siddons for his invaluable assistance and advice. The following list of portraits of Sarah Siddons has been researched and compiled by Kalman A. Burnim and Peter Siddons.

The iconography is organized as follows:

I. Original paintings and drawings of Sarah Siddons in private character, known now to exist or to have existed; listed alphabetically by *artist*. Engraved versions of these are sub-listed alphabetically by engraver.

II. Engraved portraits in private character for which no original paintings or drawings are known or identified, although an artist may have provided a design, listed alphabetically by *engraver.*

III. Original and engraved portraits in stage roles, listed alphabetically by name of the *character* portrayed. Within the character listing, the items are given alphabetically by artist or engraver. Engraved versions of original portraits are sub-listed.

IV. Caricatures and satires: drawings and prints.

V. Portraits in other media: sculptures, medallions, porcelains, other artifacts.

For convenient reference, we have placed in parentheses the numbers of the descriptions, when applicable, of engravings listed in the *Catalogue of Engraved Dramatic Portraits in the Harvard Theatre Collection.*

I. ORIGINAL PAINTINGS AND DRAWINGS IN PRIVATE CHARACTER.

1. By Elias Bancroft, after Gainsborough. Oil, exhibited at Hereford Old House in 1931, when owned by Mrs L. M. Bancroft.

2. By James Barry. Pencil on white paper, 7½″ × 5⅞″. Head, possibly of Mrs Siddons but unlikely. Bought in March 1952 from De Beer by L. G. Duke as "A portrait study of a Lady," and identified as Mrs Siddons by Duke. It—or a similar drawing (6″ × 5½″)—was sold at Sotheby's on 16 July 1970 as the property of L. G. Duke and was bought by Flaxman for £10. Now in the Ulster Museum, purchased through Colnaghi at Sotheby's on 28 January 1971.

3. After John Bateman. Noted in the Huntington Library art file. Present location unknown. An engraving by T. Burke, after Bateman, was published by Birchall in 1783 and does not show the tiara, feathers, or veil. A later engraving by Burke was published by Laurie & Whittle, 1795. (1)

4. By Thomas Beach, 1782, exhibited at the Society of Artists, 1783 (No 28). In the City Art Gallery, Auckland, New Zealand, acquired 1928. Engraving by W. Ridley, published as a plate to *General Magazine and Impartial Review,* 1791. (2) An engraving in reverse by an unknown engraver was published in the *Hibernian Magazine,* December 1793. (3)

5. By Thomas Beach. Lady in the character of Melancholy in Milton's "Il Penseroso," said to be Mrs Siddons. Exhibited at The Society of Artists, 1783 (No 24). Full-length, flowing robes, hands clasped below waist, Gothic building in background. Engraving by W. Dickinson, published by B. Richards, 1782, with ten lines of Milton's text below. Listed as No 259 by Elise S. Beach, *Thomas Beach* (1934).

6. By Thomas Beach. Sometimes called another version of the picture of her as Melancholy (see above, No 5) because the catalogue of the Society of Artists exhibition for 1783 lists this item No 25 as "ditto, ditto" after No 24. But possibly a picture of Mrs Siddons as Calista; see below, No 199.

7. By William Beechey. Full-length, 81½″ × 43½″, standing against background of dark forest; in white gown; arms crossed, a book in left hand, her head turned to right, giving

three-quarter-view of her face. In the Art Institute of Chicago since 1924, the gift of William A. Goodman.

8. By William Beechey, signed and dated 1793. Exhibited at the Royal Academy, 1794 (No 127). "Mrs Siddons with the Emblems of Tragedy," 96½" × 60½". Full-length, holding dagger in her right hand and mask in her left. On right a plate inscribed "Sacred to the Memory of Will Shakespeare," with a mourning Cupid seated upon it. In the artist's sale at Christie's in June 1836 (No 67). Sold by Lord Brooke (now the Earl of Warwick), as removed from Warwick Castle, at Christie's on 22 March 1968 (lot 75). Bought by Leggatt Brothers for Daniel MacDonald who presented it to the National Portrait Gallery in 1970. It has been exhibited frequently, most recently at Kenwood House in February and March 1986. A copy by W. Horn Rosenberg was sold at the Irving sale at Christie's on 14 December 1905 (lot 187). A bust detail, engraved by Sansom, after Beechey, was published as a plate to *Lady's New Pocket Magazine*, 1795. (4)

9. By William Beechey. Small-scale full-length, 26" × 18", standing; to left in a woodland setting; holding a dagger. Owned by Mrs Arthur Bull at Brynderwen, Usk, in 1962. The portrait is from the collection of the late Sir Otto Beit, formerly at Tewin Water, Hertfordshire. Possibly an oil study for Beechey's larger picture exhibited at the Royal Academy in 1794; see No 8, above.

10. By W. Beechey. Oil sketch. Head only, facing right, hair around head. A photograph of the portrait is in the Harvard Theatre Collection, permission of Messrs Keppel & Co. Present location unknown.

11. By Henry Bone, after Thomas Lawrence, inscribed: "Mrs Siddons after Lawrence for HRH the Prince of Wales 1798." Drawing on graph paper. In the National Portrait Gallery (Bone drawings, I: 91). After No 81, below. A version of Bone is in the Royal Collection, inscribed "after a picture in oil by Thomas Lawrence, R.A./1798."

12. By Henry Bone, exhibited at the Royal Academy, 1798 (No 797). Miniature in enamel, in frame with several other portraits. Possibly the same as a miniature after Downman that was in a private collection, Kent, in 1970.

13. By Henry Briggs. In the archives of the National Portrait Gallery is an unsent postcard of poor quality, with NPG date stamp 7 September 1920, on which is a portrait of Mrs Siddons by Briggs.

14. By Henry Briggs, c. 1830. At age 75, pictured with Fanny Kemble, at age 21. In the Boston Athenaeum. Reproduced by J. C. Furnas, *Fanny Kemble*, 1982.

15. By John Brown. Watercolor drawing, oval, 3½" × 2¾", head and shoulders to left, inscribed as Mrs Siddons by J. Brown. In the National Gallery of Scotland (No 2001). Engraving by P. Thompson, published by A. Hogg. (5)

16. By George Chinnery, signed and dated 1803. Miniature oval, 4½" × 3½", on pendant, once called "Mrs Siddons and Child." Shows woman in lace cap, embraced by child from behind. The identification of the sitter is unlikely since Chinnery was in India when he painted this miniature. Strickland suggests that the portrait may be of Lady Clare. It belonged to Jeffery Whitehead in 1889 (in the Burlington Fine Arts Club Exhibition) and 1891 (in the Guelph Exhibition, New Gallery, London). Sold from the Edward Peter Jones collection at Sotheby's on 3 July 1961 (lot 37); and sold there again on 27 April 1964 (lot 38), illustrated in the catalogue. Also reproduced in *The Illustrated London News*, 5 August 1961.

17. By George Clint. Called Mrs Siddons, but unlikely. Seated, three-quarter-length; curly hair, lace kerchief tied under chin; high-necked dress with lace collar; left arm resting on arm of chair. Photograph in the Harvard Theatre Collection places the portrait in the collection of Shirley Woodthorpe, Parkstone Poole, Dorset.

18. By Richard Collins. Whitley in *Artists and Their Friends* (II, 34–35) cites a letter from Mrs Siddons on 23 February [1785?] in which she states that she "will as soon as possible sit to Mr Collins." The picture remains untraced, and it is not known whether or not the sitting occurred.

19. By Peter Contencin. Possibly Mrs Siddons. Colored lithograph portrait, signed and dated December 1800.

20. Attributed to Peter Contencin. Possibly Mrs Siddons. Black and red chalk on paper, 10½" × 8". In a private collection, London.

21. Attributed to Peter Contencin. Possibly Sarah Siddons. Black, blue and red chalk on

Courtesy of Sotheby Parke Bernet Inc

SARAH SIDDONS
by Lawrence

paper, 9¼" × 7¼". In a private collection, London.

22. By Richard Cosway? Called Mrs Siddons seated in a grotto. Canvas, 17" × 23¾". Sold at Sotheby's on 18 March 1964 (lot 40) and illustrated in the catalogue. In the collection of T. Laughton, Scarborough. The sitter is doubtful, and the artist possibly is Wright of Derby.

23. By Richard Cosway. As Tragedy. Pencil, gray wash, and watercolors, 9" × 7". Once with Martyn Gregory, London; at Phillips on 28 March 1983 (lot 119); now in a private collection, London. Possibly the portrait described in the *Morning Herald* of 12 March 1785 as a "delicate small whole-length" of Mrs Siddons, nearly finished.

24. By Richard Cosway. Miniature, owned by Jeffery Whitehead when shown in the Guelph Exhibition at the New Gallery, London, in 1891 (No 1033).

25. By Richard Cosway. Miniature, owned by Jeffery Whitehead when at the Burlington Fine Arts Club in 1889 (case XVII, No 33).

26. By Richard Cosway. Miniature belong-ing to Mrs Bonnor when Williamson published *Richard Cosway* in 1898. Perhaps the same miniature by Cosway, owned by G. Bonnor, that was at the Burlington Fine Arts Club in 1889 (case I, No 14).

27. By Richard Cosway. Miniature owned by W. M. Ponsonby when Williamson published *Richard Cosway* in 1898.

28. By Richard Cosway. Miniature owned by the Rev Hill Wickham when exhibited at South Kensington in 1865 (No 1304).

29. By Richard Cosway. Miniature owned by E. Joseph when exhibited at the Burlington Fine Arts Club in 1889 (case XL, No 29).

30. By Richard Cosway. Miniature pictured in the *Illustrated London News,* 7 June 1890.

31. By Richard Cosway. Small half-length in oval frame. In the E. M. Hodgkins collection in 1905.

32. By Richard Cosway. Called Mrs Siddons. Half-length, in square frame; Elizabethan dress; full head of curly hair. Location unknown. Photograph in the Witt Library.

33. By Richard Cosway. Head and shoulders in small oval, 9" × 6". Offered in the Jaffé sale, at Weberle's, Cologne, 27–30 March 1905 (lot 190); and in the Davidson sale, at Perl's, Berlin, 27–28 December 1924 (lot 49). Not the picture engraved by J. Brown and published by R. Bentley, 1862 (see below, No 34).

34. By Richard Cosway. At the age of 27. Location unknown, but evidently not the picture offered several times in Germany (see above, No. 33). Engraving by J. Brown, published by R. Bentley, 1862. (10)

35. By Richard Cosway. Large miniature, oval, 7" high, seated, with head resting on right arm, looking upwards, high piled hair falling in a plaited tress over her left shoulder. Offered at Sotheby's on 31 July 1961 (lot 72) and illustrated in the catalogue.

36. By Richard Cosway. Oval miniature, 1¾" high, of a woman, in the Walters Art Gallery, Baltimore, had been said to be of Mrs Siddons, but is now tentatively identified as Mrs Henrietta Sheridan.

37. By Richard Crosse. Exhibited at the Royal Academy, 1783 (No 334). In the Victoria and Albert Museum. Illustrated in the *Connoisseur,* November 1929, and as frontispiece to Basil Long's *British Miniaturists* (1929). Another miniature by Crosse at Soth-

eby's on 31 July 1961 (lot 72) was incorrectly called Sarah Siddons, but it is a portrait of Maria Waldegrave, Duchess of Gloucester, and was correctly identified when it re-appeared at Sotheby's on 28 April 1981 (lot 141, illustrated in the catalogue).

38. By George Dawe. Colored chalk on brown paper, 12¼" × 9¼". In the British Museum (No 1931-5-9-244).

39. By Samuel De Wilde, August 1815. Chalk drawing, 8" × 7¾", in the Garrick Club (No 631), presented in 1937 by Ludovic G. Foster. Formerly in the possession of the descendants of De Wilde and said to have been drawn by him while he was sitting in the stalls of the theatre.

40. By Samuel De Wilde. Colored chalk and pencil, 6¼" × 4½". With a lyre. Owned by Ian Mayes when exhibited at the Northampton Central Art Gallery, 1971 (No 57).

41. By Samuel De Wilde, 1813. Pencil and watercolor drawing on paper, 19½ cm × 14½ cm. Half-length to front, head turned and looking to left, veil over hair, arms folded. In the Harvard Theatre Collection (MS Thr 158.10).

42. By Samuel De Wilde, inscribed and dated 1802. Various head studies, including of Sarah Siddons. Drawings on whole sheet, 9" × 12¾", pen-and-ink, and colored chalks. At Sotheby's on 20 April 1972 (lot 1). Now in the Yale Center for British Art.

43. By John Donaldson, c. 1788. Miniature. In the collection of J. P. Morgan in 1907, and owned by W. H. Tapp when it was illustrated in the *Apollo,* December 1942.

44. By John Downman, signed and dated 1787. Exhibited at the Royal Academy, 1788 (No 463). Chalk drawing, 8" × 6¾", oval. In the National Portrait Gallery (No 2651), given by Mrs D. E. Knollys, 1934. (Previously owned by Sir A. Vere Foster?) A copy by Downman, signed and dated 1787 (7½" × 6"), was sold in the Duff sale (as the property of Mrs Mango) at Christie's on 25 July 1924 (lot 16) and was bought by Thistlethwaite for 260 guineas; it was offered as the property of the late Mrs E. S. Borthwick-Norton at Christie's on 15 November 1988 (lot 65), but was withdrawn before the sale; that drawing was again offered by Mrs Borthwick-Norton's executors at Christie's on 10 July 1990 (lot 84) and was bought for £2420. The National Por-

trait Gallery version is inscribed by the artist on a piece of paper attached to the mount: "Mrs Siddons 1787. Original. The Great Tragic Actress/I drew this for the Duke of Richmond but he preferred the Duplicate. Off the stage I thought her face more inclined to the Comic." Another version inscribed 1779 probably is a copy of the Tomkins engraving. For a copy by Henry Bone, see above No 12.

a. Engraving by P. W. Tomkins. Published by R. Cribb, 1797. (11)

b. Engraving by Leon Salles.

c. Engraving by E. Stodart. (13)

d. By unknown engraver. (12)

e. By unknown engraver. (14)

45. By Thomas Gainsborough, 1785. In the National Gallery (No 683). With Gainsborough in 1786 and then owned by Sarah Siddons to her death in 1831. By descent from Mrs Henry Siddons eventually to Major Arthur Mair (husband of the sitter's grandchild Elizabeth Harriet Mair) who sold it to the National Gallery in 1862. Many copies after Gainsborough exist, including: one in the Theatre Royal, Bristol; another (31" × 26") at the Folger Shakespeare Library (in the Augustine Daly sales catalogue in 1912); one was with Frank T. Sabin in 1937; an oval miniature (5" high) in a private collection, London; and a bad copy (26" × 19½") was in the collection of F. Boldini, Lugano. A miniature (2⅞" diameter), inset in the lid of a circular wooden box, was sold at Christie's on 19 February 1963 (lot 1) and bought for 19 guineas by Sternberg.

a. Engraving by T. L. Atkinson. Published by H. Graves & Co, 24 February 1869. (15)

b. Engraving by R. Graves. (16)

c. Engraving by T. Johnson (17)

d. Engraving by Malcolm Osborne. Published in *Art Journal* by Virtue & Co.

e. Engraving by R. B. Parkes. Published by J. Noseda, 1876.

f. Engraving by P. A. Rajon. Published as a plate to *Gazette des beaux arts,* 1873. (18)

g. Engraving by C. Roberts. (19)

h. By Annan & Swan. Process print published as frontispiece to Doran's *Annals of the English Stage* (1888), III. (22)

i. By unknown engraver. Published by Johnson, Fry & Co. (20)

j. Various other engravings by unknown artists.

46. By Thomas Gainsborough. Chalk draw-

ing, 18″ × 13½″, a study for the portrait now in the National Gallery. At Christie's in the Roupell sale in July 1887 (lot 1331), in the Pfungst sale on 15 June 1917 (lot 30), in the A. T. Reid sale on 27 March 1942 (lot 37); then owned by W. Katz, London. At Christie's on 23 December 1954; bought for £52 10s. by Hensing. Now in the Cleveland Museum of Art, acquired 1977.

47. By Thomas Gainsborough. Half-length, 29½″ × 24″), large feather in hat. Sometimes called Mrs Robinson by Reynolds. Offered by Sedelmeyer in 1901. A variant (30″ × 25″), much damaged, was in the E. F. Gange collection, Hereford, when it was photographed for the Witt Library. An engraving by J. B. Armytage was published in the *Hibernian Magazine,* May 1783. (24) The sitter seems not to be Mrs Siddons.

48. By School of Gainsborough. Called Sarah Siddons, but probably not. In the Castellane sale at Terris's, Nice, 5–9 March 1934 (lot 48). Present location unknown. Photograph in the Witt Library. A portrait by "a follower of Gainsborough," of a lady said to be Mrs Siddons—small, half-length, wearing a purple satin gown, in a painted oval (13⅞″ × 11″)—was at Christie's on 18 March 1988 (lot 171) and sold for £605.

49. Attributed to Thomas Gainsborough. Owned by Lord Llangattock at the Hendrie, Monmouth. Reproduced in the *Connoisseur* (1907), 17: 158. Called Mrs Siddons, but unlikely.

50. By Thomas Gainsborough. Included in the *Mathews Collection Catalogue* (No 167), but not now in the Garrick Club. Present location unknown.

51. After Gainsborough? Called Sarah Siddons? Pastel oval, 23½″ × 19½″. At the Lawrence Fine Art Salesroom, Crewkerne, Somerset, on 25 November 1982 (lot 141); bought for £55.

52. Attributed to William Hamilton. Called Mrs Siddons, but unlikely. Oil, 52″ × 45″, oval, full-length standing, left arm resting on pedestal. In the possession of T. Arthur Highton of Adelaide, Australia. Photograph in the Witt Library.

53. By William Hamilton, signed and dated 1793. Black and red chalk drawing, 20½″ × 13½″, with touches of watercolor. Full-length, glove in right hand, shawl over

left arm; turban hat. Owned by J. Whitehead, 1868, and then by the Duchess of Rutland. Bought at Sotheby's on 13 March 1969 (lot 97) for £300 by Sherrick. Sold in the Dr Theodore Besterman sale at Christie's on 14 December 1971 (lot 54, illustrated in the catalogue); bought by W. Katz for 260 guineas. Advertised by Katz, of London, in *Burlington Magazine,* December 1975. Present location unknown. A variant (18½″ × 11″), signed and dated 1793, shows the balcony rail in the left background raked down to the right, with figure in reverse. It was offered—called "Portrait of a Lady"—in the Ednam sale at Christie's on 17 July 1925 (lot 18) and was bought by Martin for 19 guineas.

54. By William Hamilton. Watercolor drawing, 20″ × 12½″, on two joined sheets, signed and dated 1786. Small full-length, standing; studying a part with a book in her right hand. In the Dyce collection (24 DG36), Victoria and Albert Museum.

55. By William Hamilton. Miniature watercolor, 3½″ × 2¾″, half-length, oval. Low-cut dress, with string of pearls, and small feathered headdress. Owned by Jeffery Whitehead in 1879 when it was exhibited at the Royal Academy, and was still in his possession in May 1908 when it was illustrated in the *Connoisseur.*

56. By William Hamilton. With John Kemble and Charles Kemble. Owned by Bernard Weller when in the Shakespeare Exhibition, Whitechapel Art Gallery, 1910.

57. By George Henry Harlow. Pencil touched with color, wash, 8½″ × 7″. Half-length, face turned left, body front, white strap under chin, holding book in right hand. Inscribed on the reverse of the frame, "Sarah Siddons at about 65 years of age." Formerly in the Siddons Budgen collection and then at Brodie Castle. Now in a private collection, London. Anonymous engraving, after Harlow (25); the *British Museum Catalogue of Engraved British Portraits* credits the engraving to Mrs D. Turner (28). In the Harvard Theatre Collection it is credited, as a rare plate, to Mrs Davison.

58. By George Henry Harlow. Brown wash, profile to left, head bowed down. A note on the back states that the drawing came from the collections of Lord Warwick and L. G. Duke. Now in a private collection, London.

"How to harrow up the soul"

by "Annabal Scratch"

59. By George Henry Harlow. Exhibited at the Royal Academy, 1818 (No 262). Called "The Virtue of Faith" or "Christ Healing the Woman with an Issue of Blood," the picture was thought by its contemporaries to contain portraits of Mrs Siddons and Charles Kemble. The large picture was bought by Mr Tomkisson, who appears to have cut the picture into pieces and framed the individual heads. (It has been said that the large picture was destroyed by fire, but there seems to be no evidence to that effect.) A large sketch, 51¼″ × 44″, signed and dated 1811 was at Sotheby's on 30 May 1956 (lot 97) and was bought for £18 by Walsh. The sketch was again at Sotheby's on 23 July 1958 (lot 82) and was bought for £35 by Sherrick.

60. By John Henning. Pencil drawing, 7¼″ × 5″, exhibited at the Society of Artists, 1808

(No 36). One of twelve studies from life of important figures by Henning. The album of the 12 drawings was at Christie's on 4 March 1975 (lot 2); bought for 90 guineas by Pierre Jeannerat; again at Sotheby's on 15 March 1984 (lot 25, illustrated in the catalogue), the property of the Jeannerat estate, and sold for £2400. The drawing is a study sketch for the medallion portrait in wax by Henning; see below, No 369.

61. By Prince Hoare. Black and red chalk, 10¼″ × 8¾″, inscribed on the reverse. Offered at Sotheby's on 1 August 1974 (lot 247); bought for £35 by D. F. L. Cooke. The portrait is very similar to one by Lawrence in a private collection, London; see below, No 89.

62. By Horace Hone, 1784. Miniature watercolor on ivory, oval, 3½″ × 3″, signed and dated. White dress, flowing curls, bust figure slightly to right. Owned by Sir William Drake in 1889, then by Mrs Hornsby Drake, and then by Sir Clair Thompson who bequeathed it in 1946 to the Royal Shakespeare Memorial Theatre.

63. By Horace Hone. Miniature, painted in Dublin, signed and dated 1784. Half-length oval, 3½″ high. Shows Mrs Siddons facing left, her hair piled high and large curl falling to her shoulders. In 1934 the miniature was in the collection of Catherine Evans Gordon; it was sold at Sotheby's on 19 June 1967 (lot 41, illustrated in the catalogue), bought by Willet for £650. The miniature is now in the National Gallery of Ireland (No. 7318). Daphne Foskett in her *Dictionary of British Miniature Painters* (1972) says that there are two versions of this miniature, both dated 1784. A similar version, dated 1785, was sold at Sotheby's on 4 December 1985 (lot 201) and was bought by Portland for £2200. An enamel miniature was exhibited at the Royal Academy in 1822 (No 554), and perhaps is one of the above.

a. Engraving by Bartolozzi. Published in Dublin, 1785. (26)

b. Engraving by G. F. Phillips. Published by A. Buego, 1825. (24)

c. By unknown engraver. Published in *Magazine of Art,* 1887. (28)

64. By Horace Hone. Miniature, called Mrs Siddons, but does not resemble her. Exhibited at the Burlington Fine Arts Club, 1889, when it was lent by Jeffery Whitehead.

65. By Horace Hone. Miniature enamel, signed and dated 1790. Owned by J. Lumsden Propert when exhibited at Burlington Fine Arts Club in 1889, at Guelph Exhibition, New Gallery, London, in 1891, and in the Fair Women Exhibition at the Grafton Gallery in 1894.

66. By Horace Hone. Miniature rectangle, 3⅝" high. Three-quarter to left, wearing white muslin dress with fur tippet, in ormolu frame. Offered at Christie's on 2 May 1961 (lot 97).

67. By Horace Hone. Miniature signed and dated 1775, 2¾" high. Half-length, full-face, in low-cut dress; seated playing a mandolin. Said to be Mrs Siddons, but unlikely. At Sotheby's on 22 October 1956 (lot 34, with a miniature "of an Actor").

68. By John Hoppner. Said to be of Mrs Siddons, but probably of Mrs Harriet Siddons, her daughter-in-law. Formerly with Knoedler, London, and H. Young, New York (1928), and now in the Detroit Institute of Art. Some Hoppner experts deny its attribution to that artist; possibly the picture is by Beechey.

69. By John Hoppner? Called Mrs Siddons. In the Jacquemart-André Museum, Paris. Photograph in the Witt Library.

70. By John Hoppner. Called Mrs Siddons. Half-length, wearing hat, with flowing curls to back of head. Sold at Petit Palais, Paris, 22 April 1929 (lot), and offered in the Renner Sale at Wertheim's in Berlin on 30 April 1930 as from the collection of B. Svenonius, Stockholm. Photograph in the Witt Library.

71. By John Hoppner. Pen-and-ink drawing on paper, 8" × 6", three-quarter-length, standing to left, wearing an enormous hat with festoons and dangles. Called Mrs Siddons but possibly not. Exhibited at the Victoria Art Gallery, Bath, 1918. Owned by Francis Wellesley, Westfield Common, Woking, when sold at Sotheby's on 2 July 1920 (lot 454); with Frank Bailey in 1985 and Peter Richardson (dealer) also 1985. Now in a private collection, London.

72. By John Hoppner. A portrait of "very fine quality painted on a millboard" was sold at Christie's in 1901, according to William McKay and W. Roberts, *John Hoppner, RA* (1914). Perhaps this is the picture of Mrs Siddons by Hoppner referred to in Sandby's *History of the Royal Academy,* I: 308.

73. By John Hoppner? Half-length to left, looking at viewer, white dress and brown shawl, white high-crowned hat trimmed with blue ribbons. Present location unknown. Reproduced in *The Masterpieces of Hoppner* (1912), and credited to that artist by William McKay and W. Roberts, *John Hoppner, RA* (1914). According to McKay and Roberts the original was bought by Shepherd at Christie's on 16 July 1909 (lot 136). Shepherd sold it to Sedelmeyer who lent it to the exhibition *Les Modes à travers Trois Siecles* (No 78) at Bagatelle, 1911. C. M. Mount, however, claims the portrait is by Gilbert Stuart. See below, No 145.

74. By Huena. Listed (No 38) in a *Catalogue of . . . Pictures . . . Property of a Gentleman Retiring,* sold by Mr Edwards, Tom's Coffee House, Cornhill, on 12 February 1804.

75. By Ozias Humphry. Called Mrs Siddons (formerly called Elizabeth Farren). Oval miniature, 2⅝" high, in gold frame; white muslin dress and white bandau in flowing hair. In the National Gallery of Ireland (No 3869). A similar or a copy was at Christie's on 2 May 1961 (lot 197).

76. By Joseph Inchbald, 1777 (?). F. M. Parsons in *Nineteenth Century,* September 1917 (p. 618), suggests that Inchbald did Mrs Siddons's portrait when the Inchbalds, John Kemble, and Sarah all lived together in country lodgings on Russell Moor in the spring of 1777. Supposedly Inchbald also did portraits of his wife Elizabeth and of Kemble. Parsons writes that Inchbald, "who laboured hard to become a Cosway . . . painted in the apartment of Mrs Siddons." No portrait of Mrs Siddons by Inchbald has been traced.

77. By G. F. Joseph, exhibited at the Royal Academy, 1797 (No 203). A large portrait of Mrs Siddons as the Tragic Muse. Present location unknown. A study by Joseph for the painting is owned by Yvonne ffrench. A painting on chicken skin by Joseph of Mrs Siddons was owned by Mrs James Arkhill when it was shown in the exhibition observing the centenary of Sarah Siddons's death, at Old House, Hereford, in 1931.

78. Attributed to Angelica Kauffmann. See Mrs Siddons as Euphrasia, by Sherwin, see below, No 236.

79. By William Lane. Drawing in crayons. Present location unknown. On 12 March 1785 the *Morning Herald* reported "a drawing in cra-

yons and an ingenious model in wax executed by Mr. Lane are likewise intended for the ensuing exhibition of the Academy." The model—in enamel for a gem—was exhibited at the Royal Academy, 1785 (No 266). The drawing was catalogued by the Royal Academy that year in error as "Mr. Siddons."

80. By Thomas Lawrence. Exhibited at the Royal Academy 1804. Full-length, 100" × 58¼". Standing, facing front, in the act of recitation, left hand turning page of a large volume. Presumably as she used to appear when summoned to read before their Majesties. Mrs Fitzhugh, of Bannisters, near Southampton, who originally commissioned the picture, presented it to the National Gallery in 1843. Now in the Tate Gallery (No 188). Lawrence reported on 4 August 1804 to Mrs Fitzhugh that he was also preparing two small copies. Kenneth Garlick in his catalogue raisonné of Lawrence's works (1964) suggests that one of these perhaps was "the study for a portrait of Mrs Siddons full-length panel" (13" × 8"), that was sold as the property of a gentleman at Sotheby's on 25 April 1945 (lot 144) and was bought by Lord Stanley of Alderney; that picture was sold again as the property of a nobleman at Christie's on 28 November 1958 (lot 100). A copy of the head and bust (30" × 25") was offered at Sotheby's on 4 December 1957 (lot 138), and was bought for £10 by Kurke. One of the above may have been the pastel drawing attributed to J. R. Smith, after Lawrence—in the dress Mrs Siddons wore when reading before royalty—that was presented to the Garrick Club in 1978 by Sir Ralph Cusack.

a. Engraving by W. Say. Published by E. Orme, 1810.

b. Engraving by S. H. Gimber. Published by Harper & Bros 1834 (29).

c. Engraving by T. Lupton. Published by E. Wilson as a plate to Campbell's *Life of Mrs Siddons,* 1834 (30).

81. By Thomas Lawrence, c. 1797? 30" × 25", seated, facing viewer, scarf bound wimple-fashion around neck and head, white dress, green coat slipped over left shoulder, gold chain wound three times around neck. Bequeathed by Cecilia Coombe (née Siddons) to the National Gallery, 1868, and for some years the painting was in the Tate Gallery (No 785), until 1968 when it was placed on loan in the

National Portrait Gallery (No L143). The portrait traditionally has been called Mrs Siddons as Mrs Haller in *The Stranger,* but Kenneth Garlick has pointed out in *Sir Thomas Lawrence* that if this is the second Lawrence portrait of her mentioned by Farrington on 2 January 1797, it could not be a representation of her as Mrs Haller, since Kotzebue's play did not appear in London until March 1798. Not until Thompson's engraving of it in 1820 was the picture connected with Mrs Haller. There are at least six other versions of this painting, only one of which is noted in Garlick.

II. An unfinished variant (30" × 25") once owned by Fanny Kemble, descended through the family and was owned by Alice, Lady Butler, of London in 1964.

III. A version described as "after" Lawrence (28¾" × 24¾") has been in the London Museum at least since 1970.

IV. A version (29½" × 24½") from the "studio" of Lawrence was bought from the Lawrence sale at Christie's on 12 June 1831 (lot 102) by Wansey, father-in-law of Dr Edward Hamilton. Sold by Dr Edward Hamilton in 1902 to R. W. M. Walker, and descending from him to his grandson, who sold it at Christie's on 29 January 1982 (lot 88) for £1620. Present owner unknown.

V. A version (29½" × 24½"), "after" Lawrence, was offered at Sotheby's on 14 July 1982, in the sale of the estate of W. H. D. Ridley-Smith at Bridge House. Loxwood, West Sussex; buyer unknown.

VI. A smaller version (24" × 20") was advertised by Sabin Galleries in *Apollo,* June 1967, for sale at the Antique Dealers' Fair, Grosvenor House. It differs somewhat from the National Portrait Gallery picture.

VII. A copy by Mannix in Ireland was offered to a private collection in Ireland in 1985.

There are at least 13 engravings of the original, most of which are catalogued in the Harvard Theatre Collection as Mrs Siddons as Mrs Haller:

a. Engraving by J. Chapman. (115)

b. Engraving by S. A. Edwards. (116)

c. Engraving by D. Edwin. Published as a plate to the *Mirror of Taste,* 1811. (117)

d. Engraving by F. Flameng. Published as a plate to *The Portfolio,* 1877. (118)

e. Engraving by J. Heath. Published by Heath, 1799. (119)

Benefit ticket for SARAH SIDDONS

by Boyne

f. Engraving by T. Hollis. Published by E. Moxon, 1839. (120)

g. Engraving by N. Kenealy. Published by C. E. Clifford, 1891. (121)

h. Engraving by Del Orme and Butler. Published in Doran's *Annals of the English Stage,* 1888.

i. Engraving by J. Thomson. Published by Simpkin & Marshall, and Chapple, 1820. (122)

j. Engraving by C. Turner. Published as frontispiece to her *Memoirs* by Boaden, 1826. (123)

k. By unknown engraver. (124)

l. By unknown engraver. (lithograph). (125)

m. By unknown engraver. Published as a plate to the *Hibernian Magazine,* July 1805.

82. After Thomas Lawrence. 29½" × 24½", half-length. Wearing a white dress and bonnet. Sold at Christie's on 4 October 1967 (lot 91). Perhaps a variant of Lawrence's portrait of her, c. 1797, the so-called Mrs Haller picture, see above, No 81.

83. After Lawrence, by Henry Bone. See above, No 11.

84. By Thomas Lawrence. Probably exhibited at the Royal Academy, 1797, 30" × 25". Seated, facing front, white dress and head scarf, blue sash belt below bodice, black scarf over left arm. Painted for Miss Harriet Lee of Bristol. Until recently owned by the heirs of W. H. Lee-Ewart at Mont-au-Prêtre, Jersey. Offered at Christie's on 21 June 1974 (lot 140) as the property of W. J. Ewart; bought by Leylan for 7500 guineas. Present location unknown. Engraving by C. Turner, published as frontispiece to Boaden's *Memoirs of Mrs. Siddons,* 1826; the engraving is listed incorrectly in the Hall catalogue of engraved portraits in the Harvard Theatre Collection (No 123) as a copy of Lawrence's picture, somewhat similar, that is in the National Portrait Gallery, sometimes called Mrs Siddons as Mrs Haller. See above, No 81. A variant of the above, but without the scarf over the arm, was sold by Mrs Macilwain and sisters at Robinson & Fisher on 25 July 1929 and was bought by Mitchell. In 1929 it was bought from Arthur de Casseres, London, by the Ehrich Galleries, New York; a photograph appeared in the *International Studio,* November 1929.

85. By Thomas Lawrence. 50" × 40", three-quarter-length figure seated in profile to right, her left arm raised in a gesture, her right arm resting on a paisley shawl that covers part of an embankment. Formerly in the collections of James Cowen, Paisley and Ross Hall, Renfrewshire, New Brunswick, and of James Henry Smith, New York, 1910. Offered in the Whitney sale at Parke Bernet, New York, 29–30 April 1942 (lot 266). Present location unknown. When it was engraved by an anonymous artist, undated, it was described as "from a painting in the Blakeslee Collection." (33) A Blakeslee sale occurred in New York on 11 April 1902, when the painting sold for £3541.

86. By Thomas Lawrence. 35" × 27", in white dress with blue sash. Sold at Christie's on 16 March 1907 for 160 guineas.

87. By Thomas Lawrence. Oil, 49" × 39". In white dress and red scarf, seated holding a book. In the "Theatrical Loan Exhibition" at Dudley House, London, February–March 1933 (No 583) when it was owned by Mrs

Cecil Stevens. Sold at Christie's on 22 June 1956 (lot 168) as the property of Capt G. C. Stevens and from the collection of the late G. N. Stevens; bought by Green for £16.

88. Attributed to Thomas Lawrence. Portrait study, red and black chalk, 13¾" × 10". Sold at Sotheby's on 24 July 1963 (lot 309, with a portrait of a lady), and bought by Sir N. Buchan-Hepburn for £22; sold again at Sotheby's on 8 January 1964 (lot 51), bought for £16 by G. Castle.

89. By Thomas Lawrence. Black and red chalk drawing, 11" × 9". Once in the collection of Mrs Siddons Budgen. Now in a private collection in London. Very similar to a drawing by Prince Hoare, see above, No 61.

90. By, or after, Thomas Lawrence. As a young lady. In the Theatre Royal, Bristol.

91. By Thomas Lawrence, 1786. Pastel drawing, 12" × 10", oval. Bequeathed to the National Gallery by Miss Julia Gordon, 1896. Now in the Tate Gallery (No 2222). The portrait bears a striking resemblance to Hone's drawing at the National Gallery of Ireland (see above, No 63).

92. By Thomas Lawrence. Miniature, black chalk and pen-and-ink drawing, 2½" × 1⅛". In the Victoria and Albert Museum, bequeathed by H. H. Harrod. An inscription on the back of the original mount stated that the drawing was formerly in the collection of Sir Charles Robinson (1824–1913), the first superintendent of art collections at the South Kensington Museum.

93. By Thomas Lawrence. Pastel drawing in oval, 11½" × 9½", in white dress, with powdered hair. At Christie's on 9 December 1955 (lot 205), bought by McLaren (?) for £35 14s.

94. By Thomas Lawrence. Drawing signed and dated Thursday, 1797, and inscribed "This drawing is Miss Siddons'." Half-figure, face in profile, with white dress, and white cap; she wears a long gold necklace, from which a cameo is suspended. Present location unknown. An identical copy signed and dated May 1798 (9" × 8") was owned by J. P. Morgan in 1907 (see the *Connoisseur*, February 1907) and is now in the Pierpont Morgan Library. Another version, dated 1797, in black crayon on paper (8½" × 6½"), with a touch of red on lips and cheeks, belongs to John Cavanagh, Mottisfont Abbey; that drawing

may be a copy after the engraving. Another version or a copy, pencil drawing (9" × 8"), is in the Art Gallery of New South Wales, Sydney, bought in Sydney from G. V. F. Mann in 1938. A lithograph by R. J. Lane was published by J. Dickinson, 1830.

95. By (or after) Thomas Lawrence. Crayon drawing. Half-left, in riding habit, large hat with black ribbon. In the Garrick Club, presented by Sophie Andrae, 1978. An anonymous engraving was published in the *Westminster Magazine* by J. Walker, 31 January 1783, ". . . From a Crayon Painting in her own Possession." (35) An engraving by F. Jukes was also published in 1783. (34)

96. By Thomas Lawrence. Pencil drawing, 8¾" × 7". Head in profile, wearing hat with ribbon under chin. In the Garrick Club (No 137). Provenance unknown, in the collection by 1888 (presented by H. R. Willett, 1835?). Engraving by W. Nicholls, published by J. Hassell, December 1810. (31)

97. By Thomas Lawrence. Black and red chalk drawing, 8" × 6½", head only, front, knitted brows. As the Tragic Muse. Owned by F. H. M. Fitzroy Newdegate, Arbury, Nuneaton, when reproduced in Yvonne ffrench, *Mrs. Siddons* (1954). Exhibited at the Royal Academy in 1961 (No 50) by the same owner.

98. By Thomas Lawrence. Pencil and red chalk on paper, oval, 7¾" × 5¾"; head only, to front. Purchased at Colnaghi & Co in January 1967 by Peter Wick, Assistant Director of the Fogg Art Museum, Harvard University, and given by Peter and Kathleen Wick to the Harvard Theatre Collection in honor of Helen D. Willard, the curator of that collection from 1960 to 1972.

99. By Thomas Lawrence. Exhibited at Worcester in 1882 (No 447) when owned by J. Homfray, according to Algernon Graves, *Century of Loan Exhibitions 1813–1912. Second Agenda* (1915).

100. By Thomas Lawrence. Shown in the International Exhibition in 1862 (No 218) when owned by R. Tait, according to Algernon Graves, *Century of Loan Exhibitions 1813–1912. Second Agenda* (1915).

101. By Thomas Lawrence. Sketch of head of Mrs Siddons, with lace bonnet. In the Yale University Library (Denham Album, No 13).

102. By Thomas Lawrence. Head of Mrs Siddons. Purchased at the Lawrence sale on 18

June 1831. Sold in the Matthew Hutchinson sale at Christie's on 22 February 1861 (lot 137).

103. By Thomas Lawrence. Said to be Mrs Siddons, but unlikely. Head and shoulders, facing front, long hair flowing over shoulders. In the Watney sale at Christie's on 13 June 1924; in the Cognac Musée, Paris, in 1930. Photograph in Witt Library.

104. By Thomas Lawrence. "Satan Summoning up his Legions," oil, 170″ × 108″ exhibited in 1797 at the Royal Academy (No 170), where it hangs, having been bought in the Lawrence sale at Christie's on 18 June 1831 (lot 151) by Samuel Woodburn and presented by him in 1837 to the Royal Academy. The nude figure of Satan was posed for by the pugilist John Jackson, but the face is that of J. P. Kemble. Originally there was a writhing demon with a profile of Sarah Siddons in a pit at Satan's feet, but Lawrence later obscured the face with clouds. A study for the painting in pencil and black and white chalk on two sheets of brown paper joined together (41″ × 26½″) was at Sotheby's on 19 July 1979 (lot 106) as the property of the late W. A. Brandt; sold for £14,000.

105. By Thomas Lawrence. Pencil on paper, 7½″ × 4¹³⁄₁₆″, head and shoulders, almost full-face, one arm resting on back of chair. In the Lysons sale, Gloucester, on 21 April 1887 (lot 322), bought by Mrs W. E. Price; in the Mrs Alan Davidson sale at London on 2 March 1976 (lot 142); both times as "Emma Hamilton." It was bought at the latter sale for £240 by Leger Galleries and was sold by Leger to the Goldyne family. Acquired in 1977 by the Fine Arts Museum of San Francisco, Achenbach Foundation for Graphic Arts, the gift of the Goldyne family in memory of Dr Alfred J. Goldyne. An engraving was etched by the artist; the impression in the British Museum is inscribed, "This plate was etched as an experiment which failed, T. L."

106. By Thomas Lawrence. Pencil sketch. Owned by Miss Faulder when it was shown in the exhibition observing the centenary of Sarah Siddons's death, at Old House, Hereford, in 1931.

107. After Thomas Lawrence. Head of Mrs Siddons. Oil, oval, 20″ × 16″. Sold at Christie's on 17 June 1912 (lot 64).

108. After Thomas Lawrence. Pen and watercolor drawing, perhaps by J. P. Harding? In the H. R. Beard collection, Theatre Museum, London (No S.2.33).

109. After Thomas Lawrence. Head and shoulders sketch, 23″ × 19½″. Sold for £352 in the Mellon sale at Sotheby's on 18 November 1981 (lot 287). A copy of the National Portrait Gallery (L143) picture; see above, No 81.

110. After Thomas Lawrence. Oil, 32½″ × 27½″. In the City Art Gallery, Hereford.

111. By Mrs Lightfoot. Miniature oval, 3½″ high, on plaster. Silhouette of a lady said to be Mrs Siddons. Head and shoulders in profile, hair dress with ribbons and two plumes. At Sotheby's on 1 May 1972 (lot 11, illustrated in the catalogue); bought by Mrs De Peyer for £130.

112. By C. Linsell. Portrait of Mrs Siddons, inscribed "Penseroso," pencil drawing, 9¼″ × 7⅛″. Sold at Sotheby's on 25 January 1967 (lot 334), bought by C. C. Embree for £4.

113. By David Martin. Study in black chalk, heightened with white, on blue paper, 13¾″ × 10⅝″. In the National Gallery of Scotland, Edinburgh (No D. 293A), Laing Bequest, 1910.

114. By John Masquerier. Pastel drawing, 12″ × 9¾″, oval. Half-length, in white dress. At one time owned by H. A. Tipping, F. S. A., sold as the property of Ian Menzies at Christie's on 14 June 1977 (lot 216) for £140. Present location unknown.

115. By Jeremiah Meyer. Miniature oval, 3½″ high. At Sotheby's on 5 April 1944 (lot 96) as the property of Mrs Siddons Budgeon; at Sotheby's, as the property of a gentleman (Nyberg Collection) on 2 February 1970 (lot 84), bought by Mudd for £130; and again at Sotheby's on 29 March 1976 (lot 37) but not sold; in the sale of the Grosvenor Paine collection at Christie's on 28 October 1980 (lot 67) but withdrawn. On the back of this miniature is a silhouette of Mrs Siddons by John Miers. The engraving of Meyer's miniature by Bartolozzi states that it is after "Benjamin" Meyer.

116. By John Miers. Two miniatures by John Miers were exhibited in the British Theatrical Loan Exhibition at Dudley House, London, 1933, lent by Mrs Nevill Jackson: one on ivory (No 347E and the other on plaster (No 347F). The silhouette on ivory is on the back of a miniature by Jeremiah Meyer (see above,

Royal Shakespeare Theatre, Stratford-upon-Avon

SARAH SIDDONS

by J. Smith

No 115). That miniature is the one that was noted in a Sotheby sales catalogue of 1 May 1972 (*re* lot 11) as in the Pollak collection, and it is illustrated in Peggy Hickman's *Two Centuries of Silhouettes,* 1971 (p. 84). The second silhouette was reproduced (as by "an unknown artist") in Roger Manvell's *Sarah Siddons,* 1970, pl. 47, at that time in the collection of A. N. McKenchnie of Bath.

117. By W. T. Newton. Sarah with her brothers John and Charles. Watercolor drawing. Shown in the Guelph Exhibition at the New Gallery, London, 1891 (No 1895), owned by Mrs H. Llewellyn Bird.

118. By John Opie, c. 1785–90. Canvas, 15″ × 11½″, bust, full-face, leaning forward, a gauze scarf over left shoulder. Once in the possession of William Cox, Pall Mall, from

Christie's, and sold for 15*s.* at the sale of Mrs Cox's pictures at Christie's on 18 February 1884. In the Henry Irving sale at Christie's on 16 December 1905 (lot 134) and bought for five guineas by Parsons. The picture was sold at Christie's on 19 November 1965 (lot 81) and was bought for 110 guineas by Kyrle Fletcher. It is now in the possession of Mrs Martha Arnott, widow of the late Professor James Arnott, Glasgow.

119. By John Opie. Half-length, body front, looking right, with right hand holding scarf in front, short hair. In the Normanton collection, 1900. Photograph in the Witt Library. Engraving by unknown artist, process print in the Harvard Theatre Collection. (36) The identification of the sitter is doubtful.

120. By John Opie. 50″ × 38″. Sold at Christie's on 23 July 1909, bought by Beale for eight guineas. Listed in Earland's *Opie,* 1911.

121. By John Opie? Called Mrs Siddons. But the attributions of artist and sitter are very unlikely. Bought at the Wendell sale, American Art Galleries, on 21 October 1919, by H. C. Folger, and now in the Folger Shakespeare Library.

122. By John Opie. Listed without details by Earland, *Opie,* 1911, as owned at that time by Lionel Phillips. Possibly one of the above by Opie.

123. By William Quiller Orchardson. Called "Mrs Siddons in the Studio of Sir Joshua Reynolds," 39″ × 53″, exhibited at the Royal Academy, 1903 (No 201). The picture depicts Mrs Siddons rehearsing the role of Lady Macbeth. A school friend of the artist's daughter, "a Jewess aged about twelve," posed for Mrs Siddons and Sir David Murray posed for Reynolds. Other persons in the picture are Burke, Kemble, Sheridan, Macklin, Mrs "Jordaans," and "Le Flaneur." See O. H. Grey, *The Life of Sir W. Q. Orchardson, R.A.,* where the picture is illustrated. The painting sold for 400 guineas from the collection of Stephen Holland at Christie's in 1908 (see the *Connoisseur,* 1908, 21: 279). It reappeared at Sotheby's on 12 March 1969 (lot 7), as earlier from the collection of T. R. Cowie, and was bought by Mrs Ferguson for £420.

124. By Alexander Pope. Pastel drawing, 10¾″ × 8½″, full-length, facing half-right. Named and dated 1783, on a label at back of

a modern frame. Owned by Her Majesty Queen Elizabeth II, Windsor Castle. The picture bears little resemblance to Mrs Siddons. See also Pope's picture of her as Isabella, below, No 253.

125. By Henry Raeburn. Oil study, 50½" × 40½". Three-quarter-length, face to left. Black hair, right hand hangs loose, left hand rests on table. In *Illustrated Catalogue of the Joseph Widener Collection,* privately printed, Pennsylvania, 1923.

126. By Henry Raeburn. Perhaps Mrs Siddons. Bust, side view, face to viewer, white cape and ruff, dark jacket. Probably the portrait called Mrs Siddons that was sold from the stock of the late S. T. Smith, art dealer, at Robinson & Fisher on 16 November 1905 (lot 109) and bought for 130 guineas. It was with Shepherd in 1910 and was listed by James Grieg in *Henry Raeburn* in 1911. The picture was offered at Christie's on 24 November 1933 (lot 138), sold by Stephen Mitchell, bought by Frost and Reid. It appeared at Sotheby Park Bernet, New York, 22–23 April 1983 (lot 46, illustrated), and was exhibited at the Leger Galleries, 12 October to 25 November 1983 (No 21). But the sitter is almost certainly not Mrs Siddons.

127. By B. Wesley Rand. Mrs Siddons reading before Garrick. Printed as a plate to Boaden's *Mrs Sarah Siddons,* the edition published by the Grolier Society, London [n.d.], frontispiece to volume 2.

128. By Joshua Reynolds. Exhibited at the Royal Academy, 1784 (No 190). As the Tragic Muse, 93" × 56", full-length, classical figure seated on throne, reminiscent of Michelangelo's Isaiah on the ceiling of the Sistine Chapel. In her *Reminiscences,* Mrs Siddons described the first sitting: ". . . he took me by the hand, saying, 'Ascend your undisputed throne, and graciously bestow upon me some grand Idea of the Tragic Muse.' I walked up the steps and seated myself instantly in the attitude in which She now appears. This idea satisfyed him so well that he without one moments hesitation, determined not to alter it." The painting for some time remained with the artist, until eventually it was bought by C. A. de Calonne for 800 guineas. It was sold in de Calonne's sale at Skinner and Dyke on 28 March 1795 (lot 97) to William Smith, of Norwich, for £336. Smith sold it privately to G. Watson

Taylor for £900. In the Taylor sale at Christie's on 13 June 1823 (lot 64) it was bought for £1837 10s. by the Earl Grosvenor, who was created Marquis of Westminster in 1831. It was sold by the second Duke of Westminster at Christie's on 4 July 1919 (lot 25), and was bought by Sir Joseph Duveen, who sold it to Henry Huntington in 1921. The picture now hangs in the Huntington Art Gallery, San Marino, California. An inferior version by Reynolds (94½" × 58"), painted five years later, in 1789, was bought from the artist by Desenfans in 1790 for £735. It came to the Dulwich College Picture Gallery through the Bourgeois Bequest in 1811.

At least five other versions exist, though they are probably copies, not by Reynolds himself. A letter to the *Sunday Times* on 23 August 1938 located an excellent replica at Langley Park, Stowe, the seat of Mr Harvey, M.P., said to have been given by Reynolds to Mr Harvey's grandfather. A full-length copy by Mary, Countess of Temple, is in the collection of Lord Normanton. A painting of only the upper part of the figure was in the possession of Mrs Cecilia Coombe (née Siddons) of Edinburgh, and a similar half-figure is reported in the Sternberg collection, New York (photograph in the Witt Library). Another, oil (40" × 50"), three-quarter-length, is by Charles McLagen, after Reynolds; painted after 1883, it was owned by Robert Tait when it was in the National Portrait Exhibition at South Kensington in 1868 (No 95); Henry Tait lent it to the *Fair Women* exhibition at the Grafton Gallery, London, in 1894 (No 122). It is now in the Coventry Art Gallery, a gift of the Bennett Trust in September 1938.

There are numerous engraved versions:

a. By C. Brand. Printed by A. Kneissel. (147)

b. By J. Bromley. Published by Moon, Boys & Graves, 2 July 1832, and another changed to Hodgson, Boys & Graves, 1834. (143)

c. By A. Cardon. Published by Bill as a plate to *La Belle Assemblée,* 1812. (148). Another copy was published by Jones as a plate to *British Drama,* 1825. (149)

d. By H. Dawe. Published by J. Bulcock, 1827. (139). A smaller version of the Dawe engraving was also issued. (140)

e. By S. Freeman. Published by Jones & Co, 1827. (150)

f. By F. Haward. Published by the engraver, 1787, the first engraving of the picture. (138)

g. By W. Holl. Published as a plate to *Knight's Portrait Gallery,* 1835. (151)

h. By Richard Josey, 1892.

i. By J. B. Longacre (n. d.).

j. By Page. Published by Dean & Munday, 1816. (152)

k. By S. W. Reynolds. Published by the engraver. (141)

l. By E. Smith. Published by Virtue as a plate to *Cabinet Gallery.* (142)

m. By J. Webb. Published by Humphrey, 1798. (144)

n. By Annan & Swan, for Doran's *Annals of the English Stage,* 1888.

o. By anonymous engravers, including Harvard 153 & 154.

129. By George Romney, 1783. Oil sketch, 29½″ × 25″. Half-length, chin resting on her right hand; white dress, wreath in hair. Owned by Daniel Braithwaite; thence by descent to his son-in-law, Dr Batty (who lived next door to Mrs Siddons), and then to the Martineau family, in whose house it hung for nearly 100 years. Sold for 2500 guineas from the collection of a gentleman (C. S. Montefiore) at Christie's on 26 May 1906; owned by Mrs Nelke in 1933. Sold at Christie's on 24 June 1977 (lot 82) as the property of the late Countess Anton Apponyi of Lausanne. Advertised by Leger Galleries in *Burlington Magazine,* March 1978. Now in a private collection, London. An engraving said to be by Bartolozzi was issued, without date. A version of the portrait by Romney (24½″ × 23¼″), called an oval but actually a rectangle when out of the frame, was offered at Sotheby's on 16 November 1983 (lot 50) as the property of a charitable trust; earlier it had been owned by Lord Glentanar. Its earlier provenance included the Romney sale at Christie's on 27 April 1807 (lot 28), bought for £4 6s. by Tresham; the Rev C. Este sale at Christie's on 13 December 1828, unsold; Christie's on 10 January 1829 (lot 85), unsold; and Christie's on 12 December 1829 (lot 42), when attributed to "Stewart," and bought by Piercy. The 1983 sale catalogue called it a portrait of Lady Hamilton as "Contemplation," but it is manifestly a finished version of the 1783 portrait of Mrs Siddons. This second version is now in the same private collection with the sketch. A third painting is

also referred to in Romney's ledger (in the Fitzwilliam Museum Library). That ledger also shows that both finished versions were cut down from full-length to three-quarters, which explains why contemporary newspapers referred to a full-length. See also below, No 130.

130. By George Romney. Gray watercolor over black chalk. Preparatory drawing for Romney's 1783 portrait (see above, No 129). In the Fitzwilliam Museum (called to our attention by Jennifer Watson).

131. By George Romney. "Siddonian Recollections," canvas, 26½″ × 23¼″. Three heads, with terror-stricken faces, on diagonal from bottom left corner to upper right corner. Sometimes associated with Lady Macbeth, also known as Mrs Siddons as Medea. Sold at Christie's, 28 March 1924 (lot 12), 27 April 1925 (lot 86), bought by Deacon for 15 guineas, and 22 March 1929 (lot 130), bought by Leger for 23 guineas. In 1945 it was owned by A. V. Newton of New York; in 1962 it was purchased from V. D. Spark of New York by its present owners, Mr and Mrs Thomas J. McCormick, Norton, Massachusetts.

132. By George Romney. Pen-and-ink sketch on sheet with five other sketches. Head in profile left. Once with Colnaghi. Photograph in the Witt Library.

133. By George Romney. Oil sketch, 17½″ × 14½″, head only, three-quarter-length. At Sotheby's on 19 December 1934 (lot 89), bought by Glen for £44.

134. By George Romney. Owned by W. Percival Boxall when shown in the "Works of Art and Industry" exhibition at the New Assembly Rooms, the Royal Pavilion, Brighton, in 1867 (No 24). Perhaps one of the above.

135. By George Romney. "The Infant Shakespeare attended by Nature and the Passions." The figure kneeling over the infant is said to be Mrs Siddons as "Sorrow." Oil sketch on panel, 18½″ × 24″. In the Royal Shakespeare Theatre Picture Gallery, Stratford-upon-Avon, presented by H. Graves. The finished version (80″ × 55″) was in the Boydell Gallery and was in the Boydell sale in 1805 (lot 41); it was purchased by Bryan for 62 guineas. It was at the Grafton Gallery in 1900, owned by T. Chamberlyne. Present location unknown. An engraving by Benjamin Smith was published in volume 1 of Boydell's *Shake-*

National Galleries of Scotland

SARAH SIDDONS
by Martin

speare and was issued separately on 29 September 1799.

136. By Thomas Rowlandson. Watercolor drawing, 7½" × 4¾", half-length, seated, arms folded on her lap. In the collection of Archibald G. B. Russell, the Lancaster Herald, when it was reproduced in the *Connoisseur,* July 1924. Offered in the Russell sale at Sotheby's on 9 May 1929 (lot 28), but not sold.

137. By John Russell. Exhibited at the Royal Academy, 1787 (No 156). Three-quarter-length, to right. Scarf around neck and head. Broad sash around neck and waist. Owned by R. Leicester, Esq. The picture at one time belonged to a Mr Noseda, a dealer in the Strand who sold it to J. Whitehead, but by 1893 the latter had sold it. It was reproduced in the *Connoisseur* (1906), vol 15, with the statement, "Now at last it has come to light again, and we are able to present to our readers a coloured representation of the charming portrait which has hitherto been known only through the engraving made of it by Heath." But the Heath engraving is clearly a different portrait. See below, No 138.

138. By John Russell. Bust to front, head left, veil over left shoulder, pearl cross hanging from choker around neck; and holding the veil across her chest. Present location unknown but see above, No 137. Engraving by Heath, oval (3¹³⁄₁₆" × 3"), in the Harvard Theatre Collection but not in the Hall *Catalogue.*

139. Attributed to John Russell. Pastel drawing, 45" × 35". At Sotheby's on 5 October 1950 (lot 927), from the property of Farnham Hall, Ware, Hertfordshire, the residence of the late Lady Brocket.

140. By Samuel Shelley. Miniature oval, 3⅜" high, initialed and dated 1783. In brown dress, with white edge; a child (her daughter?) at her shoulder. Sold at Christie's on 27 July 1976 (lot 96) for £180; illustrated in the catalogue. The miniature had been exhibited at the Burlington Fine Arts Club in 1889 (case X, No 6), when owned by Jeffery Whitehead.

141. By Charles Sheriff. According to Daphne Foskett, *British Portrait Miniaturists,* Sheriff painted miniatures of Sarah Siddons and her brother John Philip Kemble. In her biography Mrs Parsons states that Sheriff painted Sarah alone and with Kemble. Perhaps the Sherriff portrait is the miniature of Mrs Siddons on a snuffbox prepared for Whalley. About December 1785 Mrs Siddons wrote to the Whalleys: "I am very much disappointed in Sherriffe's picture of me, and am afraid to employ him about your snuff-box. . . . I shall sit for it as soon as possible" (letter cited by Mrs Kennard in *Mrs Siddons,* p 153). The snuffbox (with the miniature) was shown in the exhibition on the centenary of Mrs Siddons's death held at the Old House, Hereford, in 1931, when it was owned by Mrs Ellwood, who had received it from Thomas Sidgewick Whalley, her great uncle. See also below, the Sheriff picture of *Tancred and Sigismunda,* No 328.

142. By J. K. Sherwin. A small head of Mrs Siddons by Sherwin was listed in *The Plan of the Descriptive Catalogue of the European Museum,* in King Street, St James Square, in 1801 and 1804. Possibly the original for Sherwin's engraving of Mrs Siddons as Euphrasia; see below, No 236.

143. By John Smart. Miniature, head of Mrs Siddons. Sold as the property of Mrs Dyer, the great-granddaughter of the artist, at Christie's on 26 November 1937 (lot 34).

144. By Gilbert Stuart, c. 1785. Mrs Siddons at about age 30. Canvas, 29½" × 24½", half-length, seated. At one time in the possession of Horace Twiss, Mrs Siddons's nephew. Presented by John Thaddeus Delane (the husband of Horace Twiss's daughter) to the National Portrait Gallery (No 50) in July 1858. Now on loan to No 10, Downing Street. For some time this portrait was attributed to William Beechey (see W. Roberts, *Sir William Beechey*). A copy by W. Horn Rosenberg was sold in the Irving sale at Christie's on 14 December 1905 (lot 187).

145. By Gilbert Stuart. C. M. Mount in *Gilbert Stuart* argues that a picture of Mrs Siddons long called a Hoppner is actually by Stuart. It was reproduced in *The Masterpieces of Hoppner* (1912). Present location unknown. See above, No 73.

146. By Mary, Countess of Temple. Mrs Siddons as the Tragic Muse. A copy of the Reynolds original (see above, No 128). In the collection of the Earl of Normanton at Somerly, Hampshire, in 1958.

147. By Richard Westall, signed and dated 1795. Watercolor over pencil, heightened with body color and gum arabic, 24" × 19". At Sotheby's on 6 November 1969 (lot 86), bought for £55; again at Sotheby's on 15 March 1984 (lot 105), bought for £550, illustrated in the catalogue.

148. By William Wood. Miniature. Owned by J. Lumsden Propert when it was in the *Fair Women Exhibition* at the Grafton Gallery, 1894 (No 330A).

149. By unknown artist. Noted in the Huntington Library art files as having been in the Davidson sale at Perl, Berlin, 1924.

150. By unknown artist. "Portrait of an Actress," called Mrs Siddons. Watercolor, 19¾" × 13⅞", nineteenth century. In the Yale Center for British Art (No B1976.1.3).

151. By unknown artist. Noted in the Huntington Library art files as in the collection of James T. Reed, California.

152. By unknown artist. Noted in the Huntington Library art files as in the collection of E. M. Hodgkins.

153. By unknown artist. Canvas, 21¾" × 15¾". Head, three-quarters to right. In the Theatre Museum, London (D. 76). Reproduced in Roger Manvell's *Sarah Siddons,* pl. 17.

154. By unknown artist. Oval, half-length, looking to right; gauze veil over right shoulder, long hair. Photograph in Witt Library.

155. By unknown artist. Full-length, seated on bench, chin resting on right hand, elbow on back of bench. Location unknown. Photograph in Witt Library.

156. By unknown artist. Half-length, slightly to right, eyes slightly raised. Location unknown. Photograph in the Witt Library.

157. By unknown artist. Miniature oval, 3½" high, enamel on porcelain. Sold at Christie's on 15 April 1958 (lot 32), bought for 10 guineas by Mills.

158. By unknown artist. Miniature in the collection of the Countess Waldegrave, Chewton House, Mendip. Photograph in Witt Library.

159. By unknown artist. Miniature drawing on paper. Called Sarah Siddons. In the Holbourne of Menstrie Museum, Bath. The curator suggests that the sitter may be Jean, Duchess of Gordon, and the artist John Brown.

160. By unknown artist. Watercolor drawing of a woman in a turban. Possibly Mrs Siddons (but doubtful) and possibly by De Wilde. In the Maugham Bequest, the National Theatre, London.

161. By unknown artist. Silhouette, feathered headdress, in oval frame. In the possession of A. N. McKechnie of Bath. Reproduced in Roger Manvell's *Sarah Siddons,* pl. 47.

162. By unknown artist. Called Sarah Siddons (?). Watercolor and gray wash drawing, 9.5 cm × 7.3 cm; head, profile to right; lace bound around head. In the Folger Shakespeare Library (Art Box S. 658).

163. By unknown artist, after Gainsborough, 1785. Oil on canvas. In the Auckland City Art Gallery, acquired in 1941.

164. By unknown artist. Mrs Siddons reading at Clifton, February 1808. Seated at table, profile to right. Location unknown; a photograph of the portrait is in a private collection.

165. By unknown artist. Miniature, the back of which contains hair, with initials "S. S." in gold. Owned by Mrs Siddons Budgen when in the exhibition observing the centenary of Mrs Siddons's death, at the Old House, Hereford, in 1931.

166. By unknown artist. Miniature. Owned by Mrs Charles Kemble when in the exhibition

observing the centenary of the death of Mrs Siddons, at the Old House, Hereford, in 1931.

167. By unknown artist. Miniature. Owned by Arthur Lucas when in the Guelph Exhibition, the New Gallery, London, 1891 (No 1194A).

168. By unknown artist. Miniature. Owned by Moss Cockle when in the *Fair Women* exhibition at the Grafton Gallery, London, 1894 (No 76).

169. By unknown artist. Mrs Siddons at church, pencil drawing inscribed "From recollection a short time previous to her death," and dated 1821 (she died 1831). Property of the American Shakespeare Theatre, Stratford, Connecticut, sold by auction at Sotheby Parke Bernet, New York, on 15 January 1976 (lot 55). Present location unknown. See also below, No 170.

170. By unknown artist. With David Garrick. Watercolor portraits, each about 9″ × 6″, framed as one. Property of the American Shakespeare Theatre, Stratford, Connecticut, sold by auction at Sotheby Park Bernet, New York City, on 15 January 1976. These two pictures and the one above sold for a total of $140 (lot 55). Present location unknown.

171. By unknown artist. Portrait group called Mrs Siddons and her family. Watercolor, 11″ × 7¾″. Sold from the collection of Desmond Coke at Christie's on 15 July 1969; bought by Gloyne for 18 guineas.

II. ENGRAVED PORTRAITS IN PRIVATE CHARACTER FOR WHICH NO ORIGINAL PAINTINGS OR DRAWINGS ARE KNOWN.

172. Engraving by R. Blyth, after W. Hamilton. Bust to right, wearing hat. Oval. Published by the engraver, 1780.

173. Engraving after L. Chavalliaud. Copy of the statue on Paddington Green. (7)

174. Engraving: "Drawn & Engraved by J. Condé." Oval. Published as a plate to *Thespian Magazine*, April 1793. (8)

175. Engraving by Cook. Published as a plate to *Universal Magazine*, 1783. (9)

176. Engraving by T. Cook. As the Tragic Muse. Standing, right arm extended downward to left, headdress with feathers. Published as a plate to *Bell's British Theatre*, May 1783. (155)

177. Engraving by R. Ibbot. Oval medallion, bust, profile to right. Published by R. Ibbot, Bath, March 1783. Three other copies, without backgrounds (two of these reversed), by unknown engravers were also issued; one was published by Whitworth & Yates, Birmingham, October 1784. (42) All are in the British Museum.

178. Engraving by Mackenzie. Published by Vernor & Hood, October 1802. (40)

179. With Dr Johnson. Drawn and etched by Adrien Marcel. She is standing, holding a muff. Dr Johnson seated. The portrait of Mrs Siddons is after Gainsborough. Published as a plate to Boaden's *Mrs Siddons,* edition by the Grolier Society, London [n.d.]. (41)

180. Engraving by R. Page. Published as a plate to *British Lady's Magazine*, January 1817. (38)

181. Engraving by R. W. Page. Published as a plate to *Lady's Magazine*, January 1813. (39)

182. Engraving by W. Ridley, after S. Siddons. From a medallion. Published as a plate to the *Monthly Mirror*, August 1796. (37)

183. Engraving by Thornton. Called "Mrs S——." Clipped book illustration (n.d.) in the Harvard Theatre Collection (but not listed in the Hall *Catalogue*).

184. By unknown engraver. Published in Walker's *Hibernian Magazine*, December 1793.

185. By unknown engraver. Head, facing and looking to right, hair hanging. (44)

186. By unknown engraver, after T. Campbell. Copy of the statue in Westminster Abbey. (6)

187. By unknown engraver. Woodcut signed "P. M.", Mrs Siddons selling benefit tickets at her house in Gower Street. A copy is in the Harvard Theatre Collection, but it is not listed in the Hall *Catalogue*.

188. By unknown engraver, after Richard Westall. 9⅝″ × 7⅝″, half-length, seated to left, head in profile to left, looking upwards; long hair. A copy is in the Harvard Theatre Collection, but not in the Hall *Catalogue*.

189. By unknown engraver. 8¼″ × 6³⁄₁₆″, Mrs Siddons standing in profile over a monument to John Philip Kemble. A long inscription about Kemble by "SW." In the Harvard Theatre Collection, but not in the Hall *Catalogue*.

III. ORIGINAL AND ENGRAVED PORTRAITS IN STAGE ROLES.

190. As Andromache? Watercolor drawing

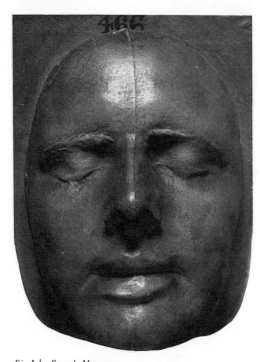

Sir John Soane's Museum

Life mask of SARAH SIDDONS

by William Wellings. 7¼″ × 5½″, dated 1790. In the Victoria and Albert Museum (E.3421–1932), given by Mr A. P. Charles. Engraving by unknown artist. (46) A lithograph copy was also issued. (47)

191. As Andromache. By unknown artist. Pencil and watercolor, 33.3 cm × 23.8 cm; whole-length, standing to front, left hand extended to right; wearing crown with plumes above. In the Folger Shakespeare Library, Art Box C842.6 (1).

192. As Belvidera, with J. P. Kemble as Jaffeir, in *Venice Preserv'd.* Engraving by J. Alais, after Adam Buck. Published by J. Roach, February 1802.

193. As Belvidera. By Daniel Gardner, 1784, but not exhibited at the Royal Academy, according to Whitley, *Artists and their Friends in England.* Present location unknown. Probably the picture engraved by an unknown engraver published by R. Randall, 1785. (40) See also below, No 337, by Gardner (?), in character.

194. As Belvidera. Watercolor by John Nixon, signed and dated 1783. Full-length, standing, head in profile to left, arms extended. At Christie's on 5 November 1974 (lot 94), the property of the French Hospital of La Providence, and again at Christie's on 24 March 1981 (lot 23). Now in a private collection, London.

195. As Belvidera, in the mad scene. Watercolor drawing by Thomas Stothard, 5¼″ × 3½″. In a private collection, London. Engraving by J. Heath, published as a plate to Lowndes's *New English Theatre,* September 1783. (48)

196. As Mrs Beverley, with J. P. Kemble as Beverley, in *The Gamester.* Engraving by J. Alais, after an unknown artist. Published by Roach, October 1804.

197. As Mrs Beverley with J. P. Kemble as Beverley. Engraving by T. Cook, after W. Miller. Published by T. Davies, 1783.

198. As Mrs Beverley, with J. P. Kemble as Beverley, and two others. Engraving by J. Heath, after Thomas Stothard. Published as a plate to *New English Theatre,* December 1783.

199. As Calista in *The Fair Penitent.* By Thomas Beach. The *Morning Chronicle* in May 1783 (cited in the *Connoisseur,* July 1918) described a full-length by Beach's "pencil" of Mrs Siddons as Calista exhibited at the Society of Artists as "one of the most capital likenesses of the lady." This portrait was No 25 in that exhibition, sometimes called in the character of Melancholy, and one of three exhibited that year by Beach. Listed as No 260 by Elise S. Beach, *Thomas Beach* (1934). See above, Nos 5 and 6.

200. As Calista. Engraving by J. Heath after Thomas Stothard. Published as a plate to Lowndes's *New English Theatre,* July 1783. (52)

201. As Calista. Engraving by J. Ogborn, after Sylvester Harding. Published by T. Macklin, 1783. (50). A copy in reverse by an unknown engraver was published as a plate to the *Yorkshire Magazine.* (51)

202. As Calista. Engraving by G. F. Phillips, after C. Turner. Listed in the Harvard *Catalogue of Engraved Dramatic Portraits* as by an unknown engraver. Mrs Siddons in her thirtieth year. (43)

203. As Calista. By unknown engraver. Profile, hands upraised. (53)

204. As Calista. By unknown engraver.

Quotation: "Now think thou curst Calista, now behold." Published as a plate to *Hibernian Magazine*. Inscribed "Mrs. Achmet," but it is a portrait of Mrs Siddons which appeared in an earlier number of the magazine with correct title. (54)

205. As Calista. By unknown engraver. The *Belfast Newsletter*, 17–20 August 1784, contains an advertisement for *Gentleman's and London Magazine* for July 1784; the table of contents lists a "copper-plate, elegantly engraved" of "an animated likeness of the celebrated Mrs Siddons in the Character of Calista."

206. As Cassandra. By Angelica Kauffman. Sold in 1913 for £57 15s. by R. P. Attenborough, according to Lady Manners and Williamson, *Angelica Kauffmann*, 1924.

207. As Cleone, with Julia Granger as the Child, in *Cleone*. By William Hamilton. Oil in circular frame, 19¼" in diameter. In the National Theatre. Reproduced in this *Dictionary 6: 303*. An engraving by A. Smith was published in *Bell's British Theatre*, 1792.

208. As Cleone. Engraving by Thornthwaite, after William Hamilton. Published as a plate to *Bell's British Theatre*, March 1792. (55)

209. As Cleopatra. By Anthony Stewart, c. 1810. Watercolor. Full-length, standing to front, looking to right, wearing tiara. In the collection of T. Balston when it was exhibited at the Burlington Fine Arts Club, 1929–30. The identification of the sitter is doubtful.

210. As Constance (?) in *The Twin Rivals*. By R. Corbauld. A collection of 46 drawings (including many of actors) by R. Corbauld was offered at Christie's on 14 March 1952 (lot 217), the property of Mrs Fitzroy Newdegate, removed from Arbury, Nuneaton. One of the drawings was identified as Mrs Siddons in "Twin Rivals." Mrs Siddons is not known to have appeared in Farquhar's play. The lot was bought for £33 12s. by Eisemann.

211. As Constance in *King John*. By A. E. Chalon, inscribed "Siddons/I hang a calf skin on your requient limbs" and dated 1811. Pen and pencil sketch. Exhibited at Dudley House, London, in February and March 1933 (No 326), lent by Robert Farquharson. Sold with a collection of 29 sketches at Sotheby's on 30 November 1973 (lot 380).

212. As Constance. By John Flaxman. Five pencil drawings showing seven poses, three with Prince Arthur. In the British Museum.

Shown in the "Shakespeare and the Theatre Exhibition" at the Guildhall, 1964 (Nos 50–51).

213. As Constance. Engraving by C. Warren, after John Thurston. Published by G. Kearsley, December 1804. (57)

214. As Constance. Engraving by J. G. Wooding. On a sheet with an engraving of Mrs Billington as Clara. Published as a plate to *New Lady's Magazine*, November 1786. (56)

215. As Constance. Anonymous etching after a drawing by Thomas. To front, looking left, arms upraised holding ribbons fastened to hair and beneath chin. Wearing crown. In the Harvard Theatre Collection, but not listed in Hall catalogue.

216. As Constance. By unknown engraver. Half-length to front. Crown, with shawl wrapped over and around head. In the Brecknock Museum, Brecon, Wales.

217. As Constance. By unknown engraver. Full-length, standing, left arm extended down, right arm at breast; veil over head, long dress. Engraving in the Brecknock Museum, Brecon, Wales.

218. As Constance. By unknown engraver. In crown and veil, right arm upraised. (58)

219. As Constance, with three other figures. By unknown artist. Oil painting in the Folger Shakespeare Library. Possibly representing a cast from 1793, including Aickin as King Philip, Phillimore as Austria, and Kemble as King John.

220. As Cordelia, with J. P. Kemble as Lear, in *King Lear*. Engraving by Reading, after Adam Buck. Published by Roach, May 1801.

221. As Desdemona in *Othello*. By Johann H. Ramberg. India ink, wash and pen drawing. In the British Museum (Burney *VIII*, 167). Engraved by C. Sherwin as a plate to *Bell's Shakespeare*, November 1785. (59)

222. As Elvira in *Pizarro*. Engraving by R. Dighton. Published by the artist, 1799. (60)

223. As Elvira. Engraving by Hixon. Kneeling, shawl covering head. Published by A. Macpherson, February 1805. (61)

224. As Epicoene in *The Silent Woman*. By unknown engraver. Listed in Francis Harvey's index to illustrations in Genest's *History of the English State*, published in 1876 (VIII 484).

225. As Euphrasia in *The Grecian Daughter*. Engraving by J. Barlow. Half-length, looking upward to right, flourishing a dagger, oval.

Published in October 1784 [2?] and as a plate to *Town and Country Magazine,* 1785. Listed in the Harvard *Catalogue of Engraved Dramatic Portraits* as by an unknown engraver. (72)

226. As Euphrasia. Oval, half-length, facing right, with dagger in right hand at breast. Engraving by Francesco Bartolozzi, after G. B. Cipriani. Published by J. Matthews, February 1784. Not listed in the Harvard *Catologue of Engraved Dramatic Portraits.*

227. As Euphrasia. By Peter Contencin, signed and dated 1819. Colored chalk drawing, 16¼″ × 11¾″. Sold at Christie's on 31 July 1979 (lot 55, with three other drawings) for £55.

228. As Euphrasia. By Samuel De Wilde, 1792. Pen and wash drawing, 13″ × 9″. In the Victoria Art Gallery, Bath, purchased in 1940. Engraving by J. Condé, published as a plate to *Bell's British Theatre,* 1792. (62) An engraving by W. Leney was published as a plate to the same work, 1792. (63)

229. As Euphrasia. Silhouette drawing by August Edouart, after William Hamilton (the Royal Academy painting, 1780, see below, No 231). Full-length, standing to left, left hand upraised. In the National Portrait Gallery.

230. As Euphrasia. Gray wash and pencil drawing, 18″ × 13½″, by William Hamilton. Standing full-length, looking right, right arm raised holding dagger, left arm extended to side. In the "Exhibition of Early British Drawings, Watercolours, and Pastels" at William Drummond Convent Garden Galleries, 28 January to February 1982 (No 44). Sold for £400 to the Rijksmuseum, Amsterdam.

231. As Euphrasia. By William Hamilton, signed and dated 1780, exhibited at the Royal Academy, 1780 (No 339). Large canvas, 92 ¼″ × 61″. Sold by Noel at Christie's on 10 April 1813 (lot 48) and bought for £21 by Hill. On loan for many years to the Town Hall, Stratford-upon-Avon, from the Marquess of Zetland; it was sold by the Earl of Gainsborough at Sotheby's on 23 March 1977 (lot 77) and was bought for £4800 by the Stratford Corporation. It still hangs in the Town Hall. According to Geoffrey Ashton, "Paintings in the Mander & Mitchenson Collection," *Apollo* 114 (1981), there are at least three reduced paintings by Hamilton in pairs with his painting of Mrs Siddons as Isabella. The largest pair, measuring 91.4 cm × 66 cm, is in a private collection in London. Perhaps these are the two (33″ × 22½″) sold from the property of the Rt Hon Lord Aberdare, No 83, Eaton Square, at Christie's on 3 June 1932 (lot 95), and bought for £12 11s. 6d. by Strauss. A second pair, measuring 83.8 cm × 57.2 cm, is divided between the Garrick Club (No 638, Isabella) and a New York private collector. The smallest pair, measuring 66 cm × 47 cm, was sold at Christie's in the Robinson sale on 13 April 1927 (lot 107), and was bought for 24 guineas by Christie. It was owned by H. Clifford Smith in 1933, when it was exhibited at Dudley House, London (No 351). The picture appeared at Sotheby's on 10 December 1958 (lot 156, when it noted as once having been in the collection of Viscount Bearsted), and was bought by Moores for £20; and again at Sotheby's on 16 February 1966, bought by Mrs Hayes for £20. An engraving by J. Caldwell was published by Hamilton & Caldwell on 1 March 1788 and again on 1 March 1789. (64) Probably one of the above paintings was the portrait by Hamilton of Mrs Siddons as Euphrasia that was listed in the *Catalogue of the European Museum* at King Street, St James's Square, between 1801 and 1804. And one of these drawings by Hamilton of Mrs Siddons as Euphrasia was owned by Caesar Schlesinger when it was in the "Shakespeare Exhibition" at the Whitechapel Art Gallery (No 71) in 1910.

232. As Euphrasia. By William Hamilton. Oval, about half-length. In the Victoria and Albert Museum. Different from Hamilton's Royal Academy portrait (see above, No 231) but similar to the pastel by Lawrence, engraved by Trotter.

233. As Euphrasia. By Thomas Lawrence, c. 1782. Pastel, profile left, right hand on hilt of dagger at waist. In the Matthew Hutchinson sale at Christie's on 22 February 1861 (lot 74), sold for one guinea. Present location unknown. An engraving by T. Trotter was published by the painter at Bath, 1783. (65) The engraving was dedicated by Lawrence to Count de Bruhl.

234. As Euphrasia. By Macklin. E. Barrington Nash in "Some Portraits of Sarah Siddons," *Magazine of Art,* 1887, refers to Euphrasia as having inspired the pencils of several artists, including Macklin.

235. As Euphrasia. Engraving by W. Sharp,

after Thomas Stothard. Right arm across front, dagger in hand. Published as a plate to Lowndes's *New English Theatre,* April 1783. (69)

236. As Euphrasia. By J. K. Sherwin. Profile left, hair hanging, with scarf and tiara, 10″ × 8″. Oil in the Dyce collection (D77), Victoria and Albert Museum. Another version (9½″ × 7⅞″) is in the collection of the Stirlings of Keir, and it is attributed, evidently incorrectly, to Angelica Kauffmann. Engraving by the artist, published December 1782. (67) A copy, with the tiara omitted, was engraved by W. Holl and published by H. Symonds, November 1880. (68) A pencil copy (9¾″ × 8″), oval, of the engraving after Sherwin was at Christie's on 12 November 1968 (lot 185). See also above, No 142, the small head by Sherwin.

237. As Euphrasia. By Henry Walton, 30″ × 27″. Sold at Sotheby's on 22 July 1970 (lot 248), from the collection of Sir William Atherton and earlier from the collection of Thomas Willis; bought for £35 by Chancellor.

238. As Euphrasia. Engraving by C. Watson, after Robert Edge Pine. With two others: Dionysius on floor and Euphrasia's father standing, in chains. She standing, with dagger upraised in right hand. Published by Pine in February 1784 and then by J. Boydell, May 1784. (66)

239. As Euphrasia. By unknown artist. Watercolor, 33.3 cm × 24.8 cm, full-length to front, standing, looking left, dagger in raised right hand; tiara, white gauze cap, white dress with gold fringes. In the Folger Shakespeare Library, Art Box C842.6 (4).

240. As Euphrasia. By unknown engraver, after H. Repton. In the British Museum.

241. As Euphrasia. By unknown engraver. Standing in a cave. Published by Robinson as a plate to *Lady's Magazine,* 1783. (71)

242. As Euphrasia. By unknown engraver. Standing, dagger in upraised hand. Printed by C. Cooke, March 1808. (70)

243. As Mrs. Haller in *The Stranger?* By Thomas Lawrence. See above, No 81.

244. As Hermione in *The Winter's Tale.* Engraving by J. Alais, after Adam Buck. Published by J. Roach, 1802. (73)

245. As Hermione. Painting by George Hounsom. Standing, elbow resting on pedestal. Location unknown. Engraving by P. Roberts published on 1 November 1802 by Hounsom; the engraving is in the Harvard Theatre Collection but is not listed in the Hall *Catalogue.*

246. As Isabella in *Isabella.* By W. Birch, exhibited at the Royal Academy, 1783 (No 325). Miniature oval enamel, 1½″ high in gold frame. Half-length, profile to left, wearing white dress; trailing veil and powdered hair. Property of the late John Edward Green when sold at Messrs Skinner, Dyke, & Co on 28 May 1805. Sold as the property of L. H. Gilbert of Lisbon at Christie's on 3 December 1963 (lot 146); bought for 55 guineas by Woollett. A Victorian copy (dated 1784 verso) was sold at Phillips's on 1 October 1986 (lot 268) for £520.

247. As Isabella. By S. De Wilde, 14″ × 10½″. Sold at Christie's on 2 April 1971 (lot 100) and bought for 400 guineas by Nash, with a portrait of Mrs Pope as Zara. Engraving by W. Leney, published as a plate to *Bell's British Theatre,* 1792. (74)

248. As Isabella, with her son Henry Siddons as the Child. Engraving by C. Grignion, after Dodd. Published by S. Bladon, 29, March 1783. (75)

249. As Isabella, with her son Henry Siddons as the Child. By William Hamilton, 1784. Oil, 32½″ × 22½″. Full-length, nearly in profile, stooping and holding the Child's left hand in both of hers. Bought at Christie's on 3 June 1932 (lot 95) by Strauss for £6. Presented in 1940 by F. J. Nettlefold to the Garrick Club (No 638). For other versions painted with Hamilton's portrait of Mrs Siddons as Euphrasia, see above, No 231. A pastel (24″ × 17½″) was sold as the property of the Rt Hon Lord Burgh at Christie's on 9 July 1926 (lot 20) and is said to have been in the collection of General Sir James Willoughby Gordon. An engraving by J. Caldwall was published by Hamilton and Caldwall, 1785. (76). A copy, head only, engraved by Cook was published as a plate to Oxberry's *New English Drama,* 1831. (77) It is possible that the Garrick Club picture is not the original; see below, No 250.

250. As Isabella. By William Hamilton, 1783. 30″ × 25″. Top half of figure only from the Garrick Club version above, No 249. Sold at Christie's on 11 June 1948 (lot 115) from the collection of the Rt Hon Viscount Harcourt and bought by Dent for five guineas.

Then at Christie's on 29 June 1956 (lot 91), bought by Doyle for £21; sold by the Countess of Southesk at Christie's on 7 November 1980 (lot 33), bought by C. Berg for £320. The picture was sold at Bonham's on 9 February 1981 (lot 144) and was bought by a private collector, London. A portrait head of Henry Siddons in this scene is in the Scottish National Portrait Gallery (No 1487). It is possible that both half-figures were cut from a version of the larger full-length picture by Hamilton which was the original.

251. As Isabella. By William Hamilton? Ink drawing, 9⅛" × 10⅞". Crouching on ground with child kneeling at her side; soldiers standing in background. In the British Museum (1931–5–9–243).

252. As Isabella. Engraving by J. Heath, after Thomas Stothard. Full-length, to front, standing, looking at man standing at left. Published as a plate to Harrison's *British Magazine*, 1782. (79) Also engraved by Edwin Roffe (n. d.).

253. As Isabella. By Alexander Pope. Small full-length done by the actor Alexander Pope in August 1783 when Mrs Siddons went to Cork, making her first appearance there, as Isabella, on the eleventh. Exhibited at the Royal Academy, 1785 (No 112). In a letter to Whalley from Cork on 29 August 1783 Mrs Siddons wrote, "I have sat to a young man in this place, who has made a small full-length of me in Isabella, upon the first entrance of Biron" (cited by Mrs Kennard, *Mrs Siddons,* [1893] p. 89). Probably that was the portrait engraved by Scheener, after Pope, and published by the engraver, 1784. (78) Possibly this portrait is the one by Pope at Windsor Castle; see above, No 124.

254. As Isabella. Engraving by W. Sharp, after Thomas Stothard. Full-length, standing and bending forward, holding son by the hand. Published as a plate to Lowndes's *New English Theatre,* May 1783. (80)

255. As Isabella. By Thomas Stothard. A. C. Coxhead in *Thomas Stothard* (1909) states: "There is also a small cut of this [Isabella], in which she lies senseless upon the ground and the child over her." Untraced.

256. As Isabella. By unknown engraver, after Thomas Stothard. Nearly three-quarter-length, right hand in front, left arm extended; backed by an artist's palette. (81) A copy, half-

length, in oval, engraved by Murray, was published by Harrison & Co, July 1795. (82)

257. As Isabella. By unknown engraver. Published by Roach, April 1800. (84)

258. As Isabella. By unknown engraver. Full-length, left hand extended, fan in right hand, feathers in hair. Published as a plate to the *Hibernian Magazine,* August 1784. (83)

259. As Isabella in *Measure for Measure.* By Johann H. Ramberg. Gray ink, wash and watercolor drawing, 8.9 cm × 6 cm, oval in rectangle, inscribed "H. Ramberg/del. 1785/ Mrs Siddons,/justice O royal Duke . . ." Whole-length, to right, arm extended, beseeching. In the Folger Shakespeare Library (Art Box R. 167). Engraving by Hall, published as a plate to *Bell's British Theatre,* March 1785. (86) Another engraving by E. Scriven was published by Cawthorn as a plate to an edition of the play, 1808. (85)

260. As Isabella in *Measure for Measure.* Kneeling. By unknown engraver. Published as a plate to *Lady's Magazine,* 1786. (87)

261. As Ismena in *Timanthes.* By James Roberts. Original painting for *Bell's British Theatre,* sold at Leigh and Sotheby's on 25 May 1805 (lot 278), when it was attributed to Graham. Engraving by P. Audinet, after Roberts, published as a plate to that publication, December 1795. (88)

262. As Jane Shore in *Jane Shore.* Engraving by J. Alais. Published by Roach, December 1806. (96)

263. As Jane Shore. By William Hamilton. Oil, 60" × 66". Illustrated by C. R. Grundy, *A Catalogue of the Pictures and Drawings in the Collection of Frederick John Nettleford* (privately published, 1935). The central figure is Mrs Siddons (?), right arm upraised; man on horse in background.

264. As Jane Shore. By William Hamilton, dated 1791. Watercolor drawing, oval, 9½" × 6¼". In the Dyce collection, Victoria and Albert Museum. Engraved versions include:

a. By Leney. Published as a plate to *Bell's British Theatre,* 1791. (92)

b. By Houston. Published by Jones as a plate to *British Theatre,* 1792. (90)

c. By Chapman. Printed by Cooke, 1807 and published as a plate to *British Drama,* 1817. (89)

d. By unknown engraver. Published as a plate to Ireland's *Mirror.* (91)

265. As Jane Shore. Engraving by J. Heath, after Thomas Stothard. Published as a plate to Lowndes's *New English Theatre,* May 1783. (94)

266. As Jane Shore. By R. K. Porter. Original sketches of her, 1799. In the H. R. Beard collection, Theatre Museum, London.

267. As Jane Shore. Engraving by T. Ryder, after Miss Langham. Standing, right hand on door knocker. Oval, published by S. Watts, February 1790. (93)

268. As Jane Shore. By Henry Thompson. Seated on ground, leaning against arch or doorway. Location unknown. Engraving by H. Moses, published by Longman & Co. (n. d.) in the Theatre Museum, London. Another engraving by C. Heath was published by Longman & Co, March 1816.

269. As Jane Shore. Silhouette. Engraving by P. W. Tomkins, after Lady Templeton. Published by Tomkins, June 1792. (95)

270. As Jane Shore. By unknown engraver. Standing, right hand on door knocker. (97)

271. As Julia in *Julia.* Watercolor drawing by John Nixon, initialed and dated 1787. Full-length, standing, in high plumed hat, left arm across waist. At Christie's on 5 November 1974 (lot 94), the property of the French Hospital of La Providence; again at Christie's on 24 March 1981 (lot 23). Now in a private collection, London.

272. As Lady Macbeth in *Macbeth.* Engraving by J. Alais. Sleepwalking. Quotation: "Out! damned spot." (108)

273. As Lady Macbeth, with J. P. Kemble as Macbeth. By Thomas Beach, exhibited at the Royal Academy, 1786 (No 199). Oil, 70 ½" × 60". Said to have been painted for Lord Le Despencer. Sold with his effects from Mereworth Castle at Christie's on 9 May 1865 (lot 138). Also sold at Puttick and Simpson's on 13 July 1921 (lot 159), bought by Mason for 120 guineas. Listed as No 261 by Elise S. Beach, *Thomas Beach* (1934). Presented in 1940 by F. J. Nettlefold to the Garrick Club (No 637), where it now hangs. Reproduced in this *Dictionary,* 8: 364.

274. As Lady Macbeth. By Thomas Beach, exhibited at the Royal Academy, 1786. Full-length, said to be life-size, standing, wearing black draperies. Listed as No 258 by Elise S. Beach, *Thomas Beach* (1934). According to J. Steegman, *Portraits in Welsh Homes,* (1957), this portrait was formerly at Brogyntyn (formerly Porkington), in the possession of Lord Harlech. Lady Harlech, widow of Lord Harlech, advises us that there is no record of their ever having owned the picture.

275. As Lady Macbeth. By Thomas Beach. Property of Lord Falmouth, at Mereworth Castle, Maidstone, listed as No 257 by Elise S. Beach, *Thomas Beach* (1934). Said to have been with Messrs Foster in 1923. Description unknown.

276. As Lady Macbeth. By Henry Bone? In sleepwalking scene; carrying lamp in upraised left hand, veil over head; nurse and doctor in background. Pencil, brown wash and watercolor, 19⅞" × 13¾". Incorrectly attributed to G. H. Harlow when it was in the Gross sale at Anderson, New York, in January 1927. Owned by Louis Kirstein; and then the American Shakespeare Theatre, Stratford, Connecticut, from whom the Yale Center for British Art acquired it in 1976. Attributed to Bone by Geoffrey Ashton in *Shakespeare and British Art* (Yale Center for British Art, 1981). But is unlikely that this generalized figure is a portrait of Mrs Siddons.

277. As Lady Macbeth. Engraving by T. Chessman, after Richard Westall. Half-length to front, looking up to right, profile. Dagger held down in right hand. Not listed in the Hall *Catalogue,* but in the Harvard Theatre Collection.

278. As Lady Macbeth. Engraving by J. M. Delattre, after Johann H. Ramberg. Sleepwalking. Published as a plate to *Bell's Shakespeare,* August 1784. (102) Another impression, reworked, was published by Cawthorn, 1806; and an anonymous woodcut copy was also issued. (103)

279. As Lady Macbeth. By Samuel De Wilde. Sold by the executor of the late Lady Desborough at Christie's on 16 October 1953 (lot 149, which also included a portrait of a boy in a green coat); bought by Singer for £3 3s. Said previously to have been in the Cowper collection from Panshanger.

280. As Lady Macbeth. By M. S. Walter Fox. Full-length standing to front, right arm raised holding dagger, veil across front and left arm. Reproduction titled "The Sybarite." A copy in a private collection has pencil notations, "Designed in England" and "Otto Troitzach."

281. As Lady Macbeth. By Henry Fuseli.

Oil, 40″ × 50″. Scene depicts Lady Macbeth seizing the daggers, with Macbeth to the left, emerging from Duncan's bedchamber. Said to be Mrs Siddons when sold as the property of Mrs John Stanley-Clarke at Sotheby's on 10 March 1965 (lot 107); bought for the Tate Gallery (T733) for £3800. The painting has also been described as representing David Garrick and Mrs Pritchard, but it probably is not a representation of any actual actors. For a list of exhibitions and provenance, see *Henry Fuseli,* edited by Gert Schiff, the catalogue of the Fuseli exhibition at the Tate Gallery in 1975.

282. As Lady Macbeth, in the sleepwalking scene. By George Henry Harlow. Oil, 24½″ × 14¾″. Full-length, hands clasped before her; in white gown with white drapery over her head. In the Garrick Club (No 43). At least three versions in drawings by Harlow exist. A pencil and chalk (8½″ × 7¼″), half-length, probably Harlow's study for the Garrick Club oil, was formerly in the collection of Mrs Siddons Budgen and then at Brodie Castle; it is now in a private collection, London. Another version, chalk and pencil (9″ × 7¼″), once the property of John Baskett, who sold it in 1968 to the Henry E. Huntington Library (No 68.34), is illustrated in R. R. Wark's *British Portrait Drawings 1600–1900.* Yet another version was in the collection of the Marquis of Landsdowne, and is now owned by his son the Earl of Shelburne, at Bowood House, Calne, Hampshire.

a. Engraving by R. Cooper. Published as a plate to *Terry's Theatrical Gallery,* 1822. (98).

b. Lithograph by R. J. Lane, December 1813.

c. Engraving, half-length only, by J. Rogers. Published as a plate to Oxberry's *Dramatic Biography,* 1825. (99).

d. Engraving, head only, by Mrs D. Turner. Vignette in the British Museum.

e. Anonymous line engraving, head only (n. d.).

283. As Lady Macbeth. By G. H. Harlow, 94½″ × 58″. Full-length, left arm across breast, holding paper, right arm by side. Owned by the Arkwright family (related by marriage to the Kembles), of Sutton Scarsdale, Chesterfield, Derbyshire; then by descent to Major General Robert H. B. Arkwright of Pen-y-Bryn Hall, Montgomery. Bought at the

Hawkesworth sale at Christie's on 14 April 1950 (lot 155) by Syrett for £27 6s. The painting is now in the collection of Bob Jones University, South Carolina, acquired from Leger Galleries, 1969. A smaller version (23¼″ × 14¼″) by Harlow is in the Garrick Club (No 31). An engraving by C. Rolls was published by Longman & Co as a plate to *Literary Souvenir,* November 1830. (100)

284. As Lady Macbeth. By Benjamin Robert Haydon. Charcoal on paper, 16″ × 19″. On 10 March 1821 Haydon spent the evening with Mrs Siddons and she read from *Macbeth.* Exhibited as from the collection of the American Shakespeare Theatre, at Knoedler & Co, 3–28 March 1964 (No 32).

285. As Lady Macbeth. Drawings by Miss Langham. In a letter to the Whalleys (1784?) Sarah Siddons writes that Miss Langham "has drawn me in Macbeth asleep and awake; but I think she has been unsuccessful in this effort" (cited by Mrs Kennard in *Mrs Siddons,* 1893). The drawings are unlocated.

286. As Lady Macbeth. By William Loftis, 1792. Pencil, pen-and-ink and watercolor, 15.6 cm × 11.1 cm. Full-length, standing to front, face in profile to left. Hands extended at sides; red and green costume and hat, tartan band around waist. In the Folger Shakespeare Library, Art Box C. 16 (36).

287. As Lady Macbeth. Drawn and etched by Adrien Marcel. Published as a plate to Boaden's *Mrs Siddons,* edition by the Grolier Society, London (n.d.)

288. As Lady Macbeth. Watercolor drawing by John Nixon, initialed and dated 1785. Full-length, in the sleepwalking scene, standing, holding candle in both hands. At Christie's on 5 November 1974 (lot 94) as the property of the French Hospital of La Providence; again at Christie's on 24 March 1981 (lot 23). Now in a private collection, London.

289. As Lady Macbeth. By John Nixon, initialed and dated 1785. Half-length profile to right, large hat with feathers, left arm raised. At Christie's on 5 November 1974 (lot 94) as the property of the French Hospital of La Providence; again at Christie's on 24 March 1981 (lot 23). Now in a private collection, London.

290. As Lady Macbeth. Drawn and engraved by Georgina North. Standing, a dagger

in each hand, Macbeth crouched, his left hand covering his face. Printed by Graf & Soret. (101)

291. As Lady Macbeth. By George Romney. Pen, pencil, and ink and wash drawing, 14½" × 11". Sold for £620 at Sotheby's on 22 March 1979 (lot 128) from the collection of Sir Robert Witt. Illustrated in the sales catalogue.

292. As Lady Macbeth. Scene by Robert Smirke, 28" × 23". Bought from E. Parsons by Henry C. Folger on 1 September 1927. Now in the Folger Shakespeare Library. The identification of Mrs Siddons as the figure of Lady Macbeth is doubtful.

293. As Lady Macbeth. Engraving by J. Thornthwaite. Sleepwalking. Published as a plate to *Bell's Shakespeare,* August 1784. (107)

294. As Lady Macbeth. By Richard Westall, 90½" × 54½". Whole-length, standing, holding a scroll to her breast in her left hand, her clenched right hand stretched down before her. Commissioned by Boydell; sold at Christie's on 20 May 1805. Presented in 1899 by Sir Squire Bancroft to the Garrick Club (No 434). An engraving by James Parker was published in Boydell's *Shakespeare,* 1800. A watercolor study for this portrait by Westall was owned in 1968 by John Boyt, Boston, Massachusetts.

a. Engraving by J. Parker. Published by Boydell, June 1800. (104)

b. Engraving by Dick; archway in background. (105)

c. By unknown engraver. Copyrighted 1888 by Gebbie & Co. (106)

295. As Lady Macbeth. By Richard Westall. Color wash drawing. Full-length, standing to right, wringing hands (sleepwalking), two figures in background. In the Folger Shakespeare Library.

296. As Lady Macbeth. By unknown artist. Watercolor, 31.45 cm × 22.55 cm, full-length, standing to left, looking front, right forefinger raised, lamp in left hand; blue dress and long veil. In the Folger Shakespeare Library, Art Box C842.6(2).

297. As Lady Randolph in *Douglas.* By William Hamilton. Mrs Parsons, *Incomparable Siddons,* states that Hamilton painted her as Lady Randolph. Edwards, *Anecdotes of Painters . . .* (1808) also claims that Hamilton painted a

full-length picture of Sarah as Lady Randolph with her son, and that the picture was bought by Samuel Whitbread.

298. As Lady Randolph, with two others. By John Kay, 1784. Hugh Paton in *A Descriptive Catalogue of Original Portraits, &c. Drawn and Etched by the Late John Kay* (Edinburgh 1816) identified the other performers as Mr Charteris as Old Norval and Mrs Mills as Anna. Mander and Mitchenson in *A Pictorial History of the British Stage* call them Sutherland and Mrs Woods.

299. As Lady Randolph. Engraving by J. Roberts, after I. R. Cruikshank. Published as a plate to *British Stage,* August 1819.

300. As Lady Restless in *All in the Wrong.* Engraving by F. Engleheart, after Henry Singleton. Standing with Sir John, his arm around her waist. Published by Longman & Co, 1806. (110)

301. As Margaret in *The Earl of Warwick.* By unknown engraver. (111)

302. As Matilda in *The Carmelite.* By Charles R. Ryley, 1785. The last scene of the fifth act as performed at Drury Lane on 2 December 1784; others in the painting include Aickin as De Courci, Smith as St Valori, Packer as Byfford, and J. P. Kemble as Montgomeri. "The Original Picture, from which no engraving has been made," sold in the James Winston collection at Puttick & Simpson's on 15 December 1849 (lot 1025), and bought for £7 7s. 6d. by Makepeace. Present location unknown.

303. As Matilda. Engraving by J. Thornthwaite, after William Hamilton. Published as a plate to *Bell's British Theatre,* 1791. (112)

304. As Medea in *Medea.* Engraving by J. Thornthwaite. Published as a plate to *Bell's British Theatre,* February 1792. (113)

305. As Miranda in *The Tempest,* with J. P. Kemble as Ferdinand, an unknown actor as Prospero, and an unknown pretty boy as Ariel. Called "Vision." By John Downman. Tinted drawing, 16" × 21¼". In a private collection. Photograph in the Witt Library.

306. As Olivia, with others, in *Twelfth Night.* By Johann H. Ramberg, signed and dated 1789. Oil, 62" × 86". Noted in the catalogue of the exhibition of the Shakespearean pictures in the collection of the American Shakespeare Festival Theatre, at

Knoedler & Co, 3–28 March 1964 (No 55), that "it is believed Olivia is Mrs Siddons."

307. As Portia, with others, in the trial scene in *The Merchant of Venice*. By B. Wesley Rand. Plate to James Boaden's *Mrs Siddons,* edition published by the Grolier Society, London (n.d.), (frontispiece to Volume I).

308. As Portia, with J. P. Kemble as Shylock. By unknown artist, 25" × 18¾", oil on metal. In the possession of John Boyt, Boston, Massachusetts, in 1968. A photograph is in the Harvard Theatre Collection.

309. As Queen Elizabeth, with Miss Brunton as Lady Rutland, in *The Earl of Essex.* Engraving by J. Alais. Published by Roach, May 1807. (127)

310. As Princess Katherine in *Henry V.* Engraving by J. Thornwaite, after E. F. Burney. Published as a plate to *Bell's British Theatre,* 1785. (126)

311. As Queen Katherine in *Henry VIII,* supported by an attendant. By Adam Buck. Drawing in pencil and pen-and-ink, with gray and green wash. Whole-length, standing to right, head to left, left arm extended, swooning. In the Folger Shakespeare Library (Art Box S.658). Engraving by J. Alais. (133)

312. As Queen Katherine. By A. E. Chalon, inscribed "Siddons. Off the state" and dated 1816. Pen-and-ink drawing, 4¼" × 3". In the Victoria and Albert Museum (No E.941–1924).

313. As Queen Katherine? By William Hamilton. Half-length 29" × 24½", black dress, veil over head and draped over shoulders; right arm bent and resting against fingers. The identification of the sitter is doubtful. Offered from the collection of Mrs Quinn at Christie's on 25 November 1977 (lot 74); again offered by Mrs Quinn at Sotheby's on 14 March 1984 (lot 60) and sold for £1500.

314. As Queen Katherine. By G. H. Harlow. In the artist's sketchbook are seven drawings showing Mrs Siddons in the 1806 revival of *Henry VIII.* In the Folger Shakespeare Library, acquired by Henry C. Folger in 1922. One drawing (6¼" × 6½") depicts her in the Vision Scene; almost knee-length, seated, leaning against arm of chair, turned slightly right, head to left, eyes closed. Geoffrey Ashton suggests that this drawing may have been developed in an oil painting; lot 61 at Chris-

tie's on 28 November 1903 was catalogued as a portrait of Mrs Siddons seated, by Harlow.

315. As Queen Katherine in the Trial Scene. By George Henry Harlow. The painting does not represent an actual performance, though the central figure is Sarah Siddons, with Stephen Kemble as Henry *VIII,* Charles Kemble as Cromwell, and J. P. Kemble as Cardinal Wolsey. Harlow also painted many friends into the painting. For details on versions and engravings, see our portrait list for Stephen Kemble in this *Dictionary,* volume 8: 402 (No 15). To the versions noted there may be added a version, oil on panel (63" × 86") exhibited at the Royal Academy, "Royal Opera House Retrospectives 1732–1982," from December 1982 to February 1983, belonging to the Walter Morrison collection, Sudeley Castle, Gloucestershire; an oil on panel (22 1" × 31") in the collection of John Cavanagh at Mottisfont Abbey; and a black and red chalk drawing (15¾" × 19½") in the British Museum (1912–4–16–43).

The single figure of Mrs Siddons in the painting was variously engraved, including:

a. By W. T. Fry. Half-length. Published by T. Boys, February 1822. (128)

b. By J. Rogers. Half-length. Published as a plate to Oxberry's *New English Drama,* 1824. (127)

c. By unknown engraver. Three-quarter-length. Published by Rogerson & Taxford, 1852. (130)

d. By unknown engraver. Half-length. (131)

316. As Queen Katherine. By John Hayter. There are four drawings of a portrait of Mrs Siddons by Hayter. One, dated 1826 in black, red, and white chalk on brown paper (6" × 4½"), with another figure in the background, is in the British Museum (1913–5–28–39 No 10). The second, signed and dated 1827, in black and red chalk on a card (8½" × 5⅜") is in the Harvard Theatre Collection. The third, dated 1828, black and red chalk touched with white on blue paper (5" × 4½"), is titled "Remembrance of Mrs Siddons reading to Mme Pasta." At one time it belonged to Anne A. Proctor (from her mother), who gave it to R. J. Lane in 1856. The drawing is now in a private collection, London. The fourth version, in pencil (9" × 6⅛") is with the same

collector. A lithograph by W. Sharp, after J. Hayter, was published by J. Dickinson, 1829. (132)

317. As Queen Katherine. By John Hunter. Pencil and red chalk drawing on card, 18.45 cm × 12.7 cm), inscribed *"Mrs Siddons— Queen Catherine/Vide Shakespeare/John Hunter fecit 1827."* In the Harvard Theatre Collection. Head profile to right, looking up, wearing crown, with drapes down back, band under chin.

318. As Queen Katherine. "The Divorcing of Catherine of Arragon," with Stephen Kemble as the King. Engraving by J. Jones, after Thomas Stothard, published by Harris, May 1801.

319. As Queen Katherine, with J. P. Kemble as Cromwell. Miniature by William Wellings, exhibited at the Royal Academy, 1794. Cited by Arthur Mayne, *British Profile Miniaturists* (1970), p 45.

320. As Queen Katherine. By Richard Westall. Titled "The Benevolent Cardinal," watercolor, 11¼" × 15". Offered at Sotheby's on 14 December 1972 (lot 176), illustrated in the catalogue.

321. As Queen Katherine. By unknown artist. Oil on canvas, 32" × 22". In the Folger Shakespeare Library, purchased in the Libbie sale (from the Old National Theatre, Boston, 1905).

322. As Queen Katherine. By unknown artist. Wash drawing in the Huntington Library.

323. As Queen Katherine. By unknown engraver. Tiara and veil, beads with cross pendant. (134)

324. As Rosalind in *As You Like It*. Caricature engraving by J. Barlow. Listed in Francis Harvey's index to illustrations in Genest's *History of the English Stage*, published in 1876.

325. As Rosalind. By unknown artist. Oil. Full-length, seated with legs crossed; slight landscape background. Owned by Miss Edith Craig when lent to the Theatrical Loan Exhibition at Dudley House, London, 1933 (No 83).

326. As Rosalind. By unknown engraver. (135) A copy was also issued. (136)

327. As Sigismunda in *Tancred and Sigismunda*. Chalk drawing by Thomas Lawrence, 1790s. Lying on a couch, arms crossed on breast. Present location unknown. Engraving

by R. J. Lane, printed on a sheet with other sketches of family members and published by J. Dickinson, May 1830. (137)

328. As Sigismunda, with J. P. Kemble as Tancred. By Charles Sherriff. On 12 March 1785 the *Morning Herald* announced that Sherriff was "giving the finishing touches to an elegant miniature" of Mrs Siddons and Mr Kemble in the characters of Sigismunda and Tancred. Exhibited at the Royal Academy, 1785 (No 310). Present location unknown. Engraving by C. Watson, published December 1785. (142)

329. As Zara in *The Mourning Bride*. By J. Collyer, after Thomas Stothard. Published as a plate to Lowndes's' *New English Theatre,* May 1783. (158)

330. As Zara. By William Hamilton. Bust, oval, 29½" × 24½". Wearing a plumed hat. Owned by Sir Foord-Bowes, Barnard Trollope, and Adelaide Greatheed (1861, and thence by descent). Sold as the property of Mrs O. M. Heber-Percy at Christie's on 21 November 1975 (lot 51) for £190. A second version, three-quarter-length (50" × 40"), was owned by E. J. Sartoris when exhibited at the Royal Academy, 1876 (No 62). Sold at Sotheby's on 5 February 1947 (lot 78) as the property of Mrs Siddons Budgen, formerly in the collection of Mrs Cecilia Coombe, Sarah's daughter (and by family descent). Bought by Mallet for £180. Waterhouse in his *Dictionary of British 18th Century Painters,* states that this second version was "formerly in the Los Angeles County Museum."

331. As Zara. Pastel by Thomas Lawrence, c. 1782. Shown in the "Shakespeare Tercentenary Exhibition" at Stratford-upon-Avon, 1864 (No 3), lent by Hogarth. Owned by Mrs George Macdonald, Wickham, Hants, in 1964. Isabel J. Morant, Mrs Macdonald's mother, received it from Sir Henry Hawley, 1889. Earlier the picture had sold for £3 15s. in the Matthew Hutchinson sale at Christie's on 22 February 1861 (lot 54). Engraving by J. R. Smith, published by Lawrence at Bath, 18 June 1783. The engraving was dedicated to Lady James. (156)

332. As Zara? Drawing by Thomas Lawrence. Looking upward. Present location unknown. Engraving by F. C. Lewis. (157). Published in P. G. Patmore's *Catalogue of Gems*

(1837) where the sitter is said to be Lady Hamilton. (157)

333. As Zara. By unknown artist. Watercolor, 11¼″ × 8¼″. Facing front, head profile left, arms to right in chains. In a batch of seven miscellaneous costume studies (four women, three men) in the Folger Shakespeare Library, Art Box C842.6(3). Bought by H. C. Folger from John Anderson, Jr, on 14 December 1929.

334. As Zenobia in *Zenobia*. Engraving by Fittler, after Craig. Published as a plate to Cawthorn's *British Library*, 9 March 1796.

335. In character. By Samuel De Wilde. Called portraits of Mrs Siddons in characters, a pair, 13½″ × 10½″. Sold at Christie's on 29 June 1951 (lot 141); bought for £47 5s. by Bernard.

336. In character. By John Flaxman. Drawing in pen-and-ink owned by Yvonne ffrench. Reproduced in Roger Manvell's *Sarah Siddons* (1970).

337. In character, with another actress, 79″ × 54″. By Gardner? In the Hart sale at Christie's on 28 November 1927 (lot 85); bought by Westmore for 210 guineas. Attribution of artist and identification of sitter are doubtful.

338. In character in an unidentified play, with an actor. Attributed to Georgiana Keate. Watercolor, 13¼″ × 10¾″, inscribed on the back "Bath." In the Westminster Public Library. The actor is said to be John Edwin the elder, but is more likely the younger. The elder Edwin was at Bath with Mrs Siddons on occasions only from 1780 to 1782, when the artist was between seven and nine years old.

339. In character? By unknown engraver. Three-quarter-length, left profile, arms crossed on breast. Published by W. Turner, 1 July 1783. (159)

340. The British Museum holds a sketchbook by the amateur artist Mary Sackville-Hamilton containing numerous sketches of the costumes and attitudes of Mrs Siddons in a variety of characters at Dublin in 1802–3 and 1805. But there are no faces shown. Many were reproduced in *Theatre Notebook*, 9.

341. Called a scene from *Henry VI*, "Gloucester's Murderer Denounced," painted by William Hamilton. Large oil on canvas, 106½″ × 82″. This picture is said to show Mrs Siddons, but the painting is more in the tradition of the Boydell paintings, and the prominent female figure seems not to be Mrs Siddons. In the collection of the Bob Jones University, South Carolina (No 458). Mrs Siddons never appeared in *Henry VI*, which also was never produced in London during the artist's lifetime. A clipping in the Harvard Theatre Collection calls this picture a scene from *Macbeth*.

IV. CARICATURES AND SATIRES, DRAWINGS, AND PRINTS.

342. Satirical print: Melpomene, standing on stage, reaching for a bag of gold, coins dropping from her cup. Pen-and-ink drawing by James Gillray, 1784. In a private collection, London. Engraving published by J. Ridgway, December 1784. (114) *British Museum Catalogue of Political and Personal Satires*, No 6712.

343. Satirical print: "Theatrical Mendicants relieved." The Duke of Northumberland gives J. P. Kemble £10,000 for rebuilding Covent Garden Theatre. Also depicted: a plump Mrs Siddons and Charles Kemble. By James Gillray. Published by Humphrey, 15 January 1809. *British Museum Catalogue of Political and Personal Satires*, No 11413.

344. By Thomas Rowlandson. A watercolor caricature, 12″ × 19″, showing Mrs Siddons rehearsing in the Green Room with her father Roger Kemble and John Henderson. At Christie's on 10 February 1950 (lot 43), bought for £84 by Colnaghi. With the National Trust, Ellen Terry Museum, Smallhythe; another copy in the Victoria and Albert Museum. *British Museum Catalogue of Political and Personal Satires*, No 7591.

345. Satirical print: "Melpomene in the Dumps. or Child's Play Defended by Theatrical Monarchs." J. P. Kemble attempts to placate Mrs Siddons, who had refused to appear on stage with Master Betty, the child prodigy. By Thomas Rowlandson. Published by Ackermann, December 1804. *British Museum Catalogue of Political and Personal Satires*, No 10318.

346. Caricature: "How to harrow up the Soul—Oh-h-h!." Standing, right hand upraised, left hand over heart. Engraving by "Annabal Scratch." Published as a plate to *Attic Miscellany*, Theatrical Portraiture, No. 6, August 1790. (45)

347. Satirical print: "The Castle Spectre and her Ernest Admirers." Full-length, standing to

left, arms extended; a diaphonous ghost is being viewed through a spy glass by an army officer kneeling at left. By unknown engraver. Published by W. Holland, 14 March 1793.

348. Satirical print: "Lady Randolph and Douglas." Mrs Siddons holds Master Betty on her lap. Published by W. Holland, 21 December 1804.

349. Satirical print: "The Centaur-ian Manager." Kemble as a centaur serves as a mount for Mrs Siddons. A satire on equestrian performers at Covent Garden. Engraving by "The Caricaturist General." Published in *The Satirist*, 1 October 1811. *Catalogue of Political and Personal Satires in the British Museum*, No 11773.

350. Caricature "In Tragedy." Full-length, right arm up to right, left arm bent with hand across breast. By unknown engraver. In the Harvard Theatre Collection, but not in the Hall *Catalogue*. In the *British Museum Catalogue of Engraved British Portraits* (no 79).

351. Satirical print: "The Rival Queens of Covent Garden and Drury Lane Theatres, at a Gymnastic Rehearsal!" A pugilistic encounter between Mrs Siddons and Mrs Yates (or Mrs Crawford), referring, it seems, to their rivalry in the role of Euphrasia in the season 1782–83. By unknown engraver. Published about October–November 1782. *Catalogue of Political and Personal Satires in the British Museum*, No 6126.

352. Satirical print: "The Ladies Church Yard." By unknown engraver. Published on 22 September 1783 by B. Pownall. Mock gravestones surround that of the Prince of Wales. One stone reads: *"Here lies Mrs S—D—NS Her fate weep not Whom her survive For in our mem'ry She's alive."* *Catalogue of Political and Personal Satires in the British Museum*, No 6263.

353. Satirical print: "The Orators Journey." By unknown engraver. Published on 7 February 1785 by S. W. Fores. Fox and Burke ride a galloping horse beside a milestone marked *"1 Mile to Perdition."* Between them sits Mrs Siddons, whom Burke holds round the waist. *Catalogue of Political and Personal Satires in the British Museum*, No 6776.

354. Satirical print: "The Caricatures Stock in Trade." Engraving by W. M.[ansell]. Published on 26 March 1786 by W. Humphrey. Thirteen heads arranged in four rows. One head is of Mrs Siddons, wearing a low crown inscribed *"Queen Rant,"* looking wildly over her shoulder. *Catalogue of Political and Personal Satires in the British Museum*, No 6931.

355. Satirical print: "Blowing up the Pic Nic's;—or—Harlequin Quixotte Attacking the Puppets." Drawn and engraved by James Gillray. Published on 2 April 1802 by H. Humphrey. Sheridan leads the forces of the professionals against the amateurs of the Pic Nic Society, who are performing on a small elegant stage. With Sheridan's forces is Mrs Siddons clutching a dagger (as Lady Macbeth?). *Catalogue of Political and Personal Satires in the British Museum*, No 9916.

356. Satirical print: "The Genius of Theatricals—Bringing John Bull to his Senses!!!" Engraving by Williams. Published on 28 January 1806 by S. W. Fores. John Bull sits on the ground goggling at a tiny Roscius. Mrs Siddons wearing a Greek costume bends benignly toward him. An anticipation of the end of the craze over Master Betty. *Catalogue of Political and Personal Satires in the British Museum*, No 10635.

357. Satirical print: "The Rehearsal or the Baron and the Elephant." Engraving by G. Cruikshank. Published on 1 January 1812 by M. Jones. A satire on a pantomime of 1812–13 that caused a sensation by including the performance of an elephant on the Covent Garden stage. In the scene Mrs Siddons walks off the stage with a majestic swagger, carrying a huge money bag on each hip. *Catalogue of Political and Personal Satires in the British Museum*, No 11935.

358. Satirical print: "Theatrical Jealousy—or—the Rival Queens of Covent Garden." Engraving by Williams. Published in June 1816 by J. Sidebotham. Mrs Siddons with sour and irate expression walks toward Miss O'Neill; they are dressed in similar fashion. After her retirement in 1812, Mrs Siddons returned to the stage on occasion, as on 6 and 12 June 1816 when she acted Lady Macbeth at the request of Princess Charlotte. Her performances were deplored in the *Examiner* on 16 June, and she was compared unfavorably with the new much-admired tragic actress Eliza O'Neill. *Catalogue of Political and Personal Satires in the British Museum*, No 12829.

359. Satirical print: "The Moment of Imagination." By unknown engraver. Published by W. George on 13 January 1785. Depicts Ed-

ward Topham seated, in profile. On the wall hangs an oval bust of Mrs Siddons, in profile to left. *Catalogue of Political and Personal Satires in the British Museum,* No 6840.

360. Satirical print: "Young Roscius and his Pappa in Company with John Bull." Engraving by I. Cruikshank. Published by S. W. Fores, 4 January 1805. John Bull seated at a table, with Betty and his son. Pinned to the wall are portraits of Sarah Siddons (profile to right) and J. P. Kemble. *Catalogue of Political and Personal Satires in the British Museum,* No 10458.

361. Satirical print: "Public Characters." Engraving attributed to Thomas Rowlandson. Published c. 1800. Numerous heads of well-known people, including Sarah Siddons. *Catalogue of Political and Personal Satires in the British Museum,* No 9570.

V. PORTRAITS IN OTHER MEDIA.

362. Bust, by Thomas Banks, exhibited at the Royal Academy in 1796, called a "Bust of Melpomene." Identified in the *True Briton* on 26 April 1796 as of Mrs Siddons.

363. Bust, by George Bullock, exhibited at the Royal Academy 1808 (No 916): described as a "Colossal" bust of Mrs Siddons as Melpomene.

364. Statue, marble relief, by T. Campbell. Exhibited at the Royal Academy, 1856 (No 1295). Given by J. T. Gibson-Craig in 1881 to the National Portrait Gallery (No 642). An anonymous engraved picture of the statue is in the Harvard Theatre Collection, but is not listed in the Hall *Catalogue.*

365. Statue, by Thomas Campbell, 1845. In Westminster Abbey. Sometimes attributed to Chantrey. An anonymous engraving of the statue is in the Harvard Theatre Collection (6).

366. Statue in Carrara marble, by L. Chavalliaud. Whole-length, seated on throne. Erected on Paddington Green by public subscription, unveiled by Sir Henry Irving on 14 June 1897. An anonymous engraving of the statue is in the Harvard Theatre Collection (7).

367. Bust, as Melpomene, by Mrs Damer, of Strawberry Hill. Horace Walpole saw it on 27 September 1794, but no description survives. The plaster original (?) was exhibited at the Royal Academy, 1795 (No 733). Present location unknown.

368. Wax portrait, as Lady Macbeth, by John Flaxman, 1784, for Wedgwood. Flaxman kept the original wax and sent Wedgwood a plaster mold. Wedgwood made oval pieces, white jasper, dark blue dip (also in green jasper), and white relief. Another version was issued by Wedgwood in 1955.

369. Medallion portrait in wax, by the elder John Henning, 1807. Noted in a list sent by Henning to Wedgwood. In the National Portrait Gallery of Scotland. See also above, No 60, sketch by Henning.

370. Statuette in marble, full-length, as Cassandra. By John Hickey. Exhibited at the Royal Academy, 1786, then owned by the Earl Fitzwilliam. Sold at Christie's on 15 July 1986 (lot 92) for £4500. Present owner unknown. A model in small for the marble statue was exhibited at the Royal Academy, 1785 (No 637). A copy in marble was sold at Christie's on 15 March 1798 (lot 44) when it was described as "after the original by Mr. Hickey in the collection of Earl Fitzwilliam."

371. Model in wax, in enamel for a gem. By William Lane. Exhibited at the Royal Academy, 1785 (No 266)—"an ingenious model" according to the *Morning Herald* of 12 March 1785. Also see above, No 79, the drawing by Lane.

372. Bust, by B. Papera, supplied to Wedgwood, 1802.

373. Bust, by J. C. F. Rossi, exhibited at the Royal Academy, 1792.

374. Plaster bust, 26" high, of herself, by Sarah Siddons. In the Victoria and Albert Museum (Dyce No 3329).

375. Bronze statue, 25" high on plinth 5 ½" high. Sarah Siddons as Queen Katherine? By Sarah Siddons? In an exhibition of paintings, drawings, and sculptures in the collection of the American Shakespeare Festival Theatre and Academy, Stratford, Connecticut, given at Knoedler & Co, London, 3 to 28 March 1964 (No 94).

376. Bust, by Joachim Smith, 1812. Exhibited at the Royal Academy and afterwards in the Green Room of Drury Lane Theatre, where it remains. The sculptor claimed that this was the only bust of Mrs Siddons modeled from the life. A replica was at Guy's Cliff, Warwick. A plaster cast of it was presented by Miss Watts in 1907 to the Shakespeare Memorial Theatre, Stratford-upon-Avon. Perhaps the latter was

the "fine plaster bust" of Mrs Siddons that was in the John Philip Kemble sale at Robins on 14 and 15 December 1820 (lot 61).

377. Wax bust, 19.8 cm high, as Lady Macbeth. By unknown sculptor. In the National Gallery of Ireland (No 8231).

378. Colored wax relief. By unknown artist. Owned by Miss Georgina Pennant when exhibited at Dudley House, London, February-March 1933.

379. Staffordshire figurines of Mrs Siddons as Lady Macbeth are in the Thomas Balston collection at Stapleford Park, Melton Mowbray, Leicestershire. Statuettes of her in other characters are to be found in various museums and in the hands of private collectors. See this *Dictionary*, 6: 103, item 271 in the Garrick iconography.

380. Plaster bust, as Queen Katherine. W. J. Lawrence records in notes at the National Library of Ireland a bust of Mrs Siddons "in nice plaster, as Queen Katherine, was to be seen in the Liverpool Museum in Dame Street," about the beginning of the nineteenth century.

381. A waxwork of Mrs Siddons, with those of other actors, was exhibited as Mr Clark's waxworks in Fleet Street from about 1788 to 1812 and at Madame Tussaud's from about 1819. See *Theatre Notebook*, 30 (1976).

382. Plaster life mask. In the Sir John Soane Museum (M.466). Believed to have been taken at about the time of her retirement.

383. Miniature set in diamond ring, by unknown artist. According to Mrs Parsons, *Incomparable Siddons* (p. 95), the ring belonged to Lord Inchiquin.

384. Miniature on a stone intaglio brooch. Engraving by Benedetto Pistrucci, c. 1815. Lent by the Baroness Burdett-Coutts to the *Fair Women* exhibition at the Grafton Galleries, summer 1894 (No 426).

385. Portraits of Sarah Siddons and David Garrick are set on a dark blue scent-bottle case owned by the Hon Mrs Ionides when exhibited at Dudley House, London, in February-March 1933 (No 105). Another scent-bottle case with Sarah's portrait on it was in the same exhibition, owned by Egan Mew (No 23A).

386. Engraved portraits of Sarah Siddons are on commemorative wine glasses. See Churchill, *Glass Notes* 16: December 1956,

and Sotheby's sales catalogues for 26 May 1981 (lot 50) and 1 November 1982 (lot 31).

387. Mrs Siddons is said to portray the figure of the Queen (as Lady Macbeth) on a Wedgwood chess set designed by John Flaxman. One hundred and thirty sets were sold between 1785 and 1795. See Ian Mackintosh and Geoffrey Ashton, *The Georgian Playhouse* (Nos 112 A and B), catalogue of the exhibition at the Hayward Gallery, 1975.

Sidney, Laurence [*fl. 1774–1807?*], actor.

The provincial actors Laurence Sidney (or Sydney) and his wife were with Whitley's troupe at Derby in September 1774. Sidney was again there, playing at the new theatre, from 15 September 1775. In 1776 he acted Macsarcasm in *Love à la Mode* at Whitley's booth at Stourbridge Fair in Cambridge. On 21 July 1777 at China Hall, Rotherhithe, Sidney played the Duke in *Othello,* one of his rare appearances in the London area. With the Derby, Nottingham, and Leicester Company of Comedians Sidney, performed again at Derby from 18 to 25 September 1778.

There is almost a ten-year blank in Sidney's record after that. He acted at the Theatre Royal in Liverpool during the summer of 1786, sharing a benefit on 11 August. On 26 March 1787 at the Red Lion Inn, Stoke Newington, for his benefit he acted Sir Oliver Surface in *The School for Scandal,* Old Philpot in *The Citizen,* and concluded the evening with an *Occasional Address of Thanks.* In 1787–88 Sidney was once more in Derby. Perhaps he was the Sidney in Butler's company (from Richmond, Yorkshire) playing in Whitby in 1793–94. The *Thespian Magazine* placed him at Derby again in 1794. He returned in the spring of 1799 and then acted in Nottingham in the summer. At Chesterfield on 17 January 1800 Sidney played the Old Blind Man in *Pizarro* and Snarl in *The Village Lawyer.* At Chesterfield also were his wife and daughter. Miss Sidney seems not to have acted in the London area in the eighteenth century.

When Sidney appeared at the Haymarket Theatre in London on 16 September 1800, the playbill hailed him as from Richmond (Yorkshire?). The *Monthly Mirror* in November 1801 reported from Halifax, Yorkshire, that "Our old friend Sidney still retains his situation amongst us." The Manchester correspondent for the same journal wrote in 1802 that "Our old friend Sidney has given us many fresh proofs of his abilities, in a routine of characters, particularly Brummagem, Cockle-top, Solomon (Stranger), Sir Abel Handy, &c." Perhaps Laurence Sidney was the Mr "Sydney" who was granted a license by the Lord Chamberlain to present an entertainment at the Haymarket in London on 13 April 1807.

Sidney, Mrs [Laurence] [fl. 1770–1802], actress, singer.

Though they seem not always to have performed together, we believe the Mr and Mrs Sidney who were active in the provinces and, occasionally, in London were Laurence Sidney and his wife. Mrs Sidney acted at the Capel Street Theatre in Dublin in 1770–71. We have found no record of Mr Sidney's being there, though he may have been. In September 1774 both were in Whitley's company at Derby. Mrs Sidney was in Pero's troupe at Derby in 1783–84, though Mr Sidney is not known to have been there that season.

On 16 November 1784 at the Haymarket Theatre in London Mrs "Sydney" played Mrs Belville in The School for Wives and Mrs Di Strangeways in The Romance of an Hour. She was Widow Brady "(with Epilogue Song)" in The Irish Widow at that house on 13 December. Though Laurence Sidney seems not to have acted in London that winter, we take the actress to have been his wife. The couple were at the Theatre Royal in Liverpool in 1786; Mrs Sidney had a benefit on 13 December, when The Beggar's Opera and High Life below Stairs were presented. Mrs "Sydney" was acting at Manchester from 5 March 1787. Later that month Mr Sidney performed at Stoke Newington in London. From 24 September 1787 to May 1788 Mrs "Sydney" acted at the new theatre in Hanley, while in 1787–88 Laurence Sidney was performing at Derby, about 30 miles away; the two towns were on the same circuit, and one company served both.

At the Haymarket in London Mrs Sidney acted Zara in The Mourning Bride on 22 February 1796, the Queen in The Battle of Eddington on 28 March, Queen Elizabeth in The Earl of Essex on 27 April, and Mrs Di Strangeways

in The Romance of an Hour on 10 May. The Monthly Mirror placed Mr and Mrs Sidney in Nottingham in the summer of 1799, and a bill for the Chesterfield theatre on 17 January 1800 shows Mr, Mrs, and Miss Sidney acting. Mrs Sidney played the Priestess of the Sun in Pizarro and Mrs Scout in The Village Lawyer. Mr and Mrs Sidney acted at Manchester in 1802, according to the Monthly Mirror.

Sidow. See SEEDO.

Sidus, Georgina. See GEORGE, GEORGINA.

"Siface," stage name of Giovanni Francesco Grossi 1653–1697, singer.

Giovanni Francesco Grossi was born on 12 February 1653 in Uzzanese Chiesina, Tuscany. A castrato, he supposedly studied under Tommaso Redi of Siena (though Redi was his contemporary); Grossi made his stage debut in Rome at the Teatro Tordinona in 1672, after which he sang in the Papal chapel until 1677 and then went into the service of the Duke of Modena. In 1678 in Venice (the New Grove says 1671 in Rome) he sang the role of Siface (Syphax) in Scipione Africano, after which success he was called "Siface" by opera lovers. Though in the employ of the Duke of Modena, Siface seems regularly to have journeyed to Venice and Rome, his fame growing steadily, to the point that he was treated royally. He insulted the French ambassador to Rome by refusing to perform for him without payment. The Modenese representative, Ercole Panciroli, quoted Siface as saying he "wanted doubloons for his singing, and not merely ices, which was all one ever got from the French." (The translation is in Heriot's The Castrati in Opera.)

Siface sang in Naples with great success in 1683–84 and 1685–86 and in Florence in 1686, after which he was sent to London, by way of Paris, to sing for Mary of Modena, sister of the Duke his master and wife of James II of England. Siface paused in Paris, where he pleased the Dauphine but was ignored by Louis XIV.

Arriving in London on 16 January 1687, Siface sang at the King's Catholic Chapel and was heard privately but gave no public recitals.

Evelyn heard him on two occasions, the first being on 30 January at Whitehall: "I heard the famous Cifeccio (Eunuch) sing, in the new popish chapell this afternoon, which was indeede very rare, & with greate skill: He came over from Rome, esteemed one of the best Voices in Italy, much crowding, little devotion." On 19 April Evelyn heard Siface at the home of Samuel Pepys:

I heard the famous Singer the Eunuch Cifacca, esteemed the best in Europe & indeede his holding out & delicatenesse in extending & loosing a note with that incomparable softnesse was admirable: For the rest, I found him a meere wanton, effeminate child; very Coy, & prowdly conceited to my apprehension: He touch'd the Harpsichord to his Voice rarely well, & this was before a select number of some particular persons whom Mr. Pepys (Secretary of the Admiralty & a greate lover of Musick) invited to his house, where the meeting was, & this ["favour" deleted] obtained by peculiar favour & much difficulty of the Singer, who much disdained to shew his talent to any but Princes. . . ."

By the middle of June the singer was anxious to leave England. On the sixteenth the Queen wrote from Windsor to her brother:

This letter will be given you by Siface, who is returning to your service, as the air of this country is so little conformable with his genius and health that he could not stay any longer. It is with my full leave that he is going, and I am more than satisfied with him; I believe him to be the finest *musico* in the world. Take good care of him, and remember that if after some time you should be willing to send him back to me, I should be obliged to you.

Siface returned to Modena, then to Rome, and to Naples for the 1687–88 opera season. He sang in Florence in 1688, in Parma in 1690, and in Reggio in 1696. Siface was murdered near Ferrara on 29 May 1697 by assassins hired by the brothers of Countess Elena Forni, née Marsilii, the widow of a Modenese nobleman. Siface was buried at San Paolo in Ferrara.

Tosi in his *Observations* had high praise for Siface:

His Manner of Singing was remarkably plain, consisting particularly in the *Messa di Voce*, the putting forth his Voice, and the Expression.
There is an *Italian* Saying, that an hundred Perfections are required in an excellent Singer, and he that hath a fine Voice has ninety-nine of them.

It is also certain, that as much as is allotted to Volubility and Tricks, so much is the Beauty of the Voice sacrificed; for the one cannot be done without Prejudice to the other.

Tosi called Siface's voice mellifluous.

Sigel, The Messrs [*fl. 1774–1776*], acrobats.

A clipping in the Finsbury Public Library, hand-dated April 1775, tells of two acrobats at Sadler's wells named Sigel (or Sigels):

The two new performers of the name of Sigel, are, without exaggeration, the most excellent in the line of their profession ever seen in England; by the amazing ease with which they execute their postures, leaps, and attitudes, they remove from the mind of the spectator that kind of fear generally prevalent on such occasions. . . . Their performance excited universal astonishment, accompanied with the most perfect satisfaction.

The Sigels were named in the Sadler's Wells bill of 23 September 1774 as lately arrived from Paris. They were cited again on 1 May 1775 and on 25 April 1776.

Sigioni. *See* SAGGIONE and GALLIA.

Signior. *See* SEIGNIER.

Sikes, George Stephen   1767–1800, instrumentalist.

George Stephen Sikes was born in 1767 and was 21 when he was admitted to the Royal Society of Musicians on 1 June 1788. He was described in his recommendation for membership as single, employed at the Royalty Theatre, the Ancient Academy, Ranelagh Gardens, and by the Portuguese ambassador. He was proficient on the violin, viola, violoncello, harpsichord, and organ and had a number of students. The cello seems to have been his favorite instrument, for he played it at the Handel Memorial Concerts at Westminster Abbey and the Pantheon in May and June 1784 (when he was only 17) and at the Society's St Paul's concerts in 1789, 1790, and 1792. On 15 May 1789 he was one of the instrumentalists in a performance of the *Messiah* at Freemason's Hall for the benefit of the Lying-In Hospital. Doane in his *Musical Directory* of 1794 cited Sikes as from Worcester, and it was at Gloucester on 11 December 1794 that Sikes married Sidney Mealy. They had a child, Elizabeth Parry Sikes, in 1799.

By 5 January 1800 Sikes had become one of the Governors of the Royal Society of Musicians, but he did not enjoy that office for long. On 5 October of that year the Governors granted Mrs Sikes £8 for her husband's funeral expenses and £3 7s. 6d. for the support of herself and her daughter. Young Elizabeth Sikes was last mentioned in the Society's Minute Books on 7 February 1813. Mrs Sikes died in 1829.

Related to George Stephen Sikes was Stephen Sikes of Gloucester, who was listed by Doane as being a violinist and organist, a subscriber to the New Musical Fund, and a participant in the Oxford Meeting of 1793. He seems not to have performed in London.

"Silenus." *See* **LEVERIDGE, RICHARD.**

Sillert, Mr [fl. 1798], *scene painter.*
Covent Garden Theatre paid Mr Sillert (or Siller) £7 12s. 3d. on 10 February 1798 for scene painting. A week later he was paid £2 17s. 9d.

Silvester. *See also* **SYLVESTER.**

Silvester, Mr [fl. 1776–1800], *actor, singer, playwright?*
Mr Silvester's benefit tickets were accepted at Drury Lane Theatre on 18 May 1776 and 2 June 1777. On 29 April 1778 he shared a benefit at the Haymarket Theatre with Roe and played a principal but unspecified role in *All the World's a Stage.* Tickets were available from Silvester at Mrs Hobbe's in Stanhope Street, Clare Market. He continued at the Haymarket through 2 September, playing a Servant in *The Female Chevalier* and a Porter in *The Apprentice.* He was at Brighton under Buckle's management in the summer of 1787. Perhaps he was the Silvester who wrote the comedy *Ranger in Wedlock,* which was performed at the Haymarket in 1788, according to Nicoll (*The London Stage* does not list the play). At the Haymarket on 29 September 1790 Silvester played Old Cockney in *The Romp* and Sir Charles Marlow in *She Stoops to Conquer;* he was back on 24 October 1791 to appear as Priuli in *Venice Preserv'd,* and on 26

November 1792 he acted Manuel in *The Mourning Bride.* In 1798–99 and 1799–1800 he was in the company at Covent Garden Theatre, playing an officer in *Ramah Droog* and singing in the chorus of *Joanna.* He doubtless had other, similar, supernumerary chores.

Silvester, Mr [fl. 1794], *scene painter.*
Mr Silvester was paid £2 on 1 October 1794 for working for two weeks as a scene painter at Covent Garden Theatre.

Silvester, Edward [fl. 1783–1793], *property man.*
Edward Silvester was a property man at the King's Theatre in 1783–84 and 1784–85, according to the Lord Chamberlain's accounts. A letter among the Sheridan papers at the British Library, dated 6 January 1786, speaks of "Mr Silvester's unfortunate situation"—financial difficulties, apparently—but we cannot be sure the Silvester in question was Edward. Edward Silvester was still at the King's Theatre in 1787, but on 22 April 1793 a Silvester, property man at the Haymarket Theatre, was paid £2 for work performed up to 20 April, and on 5 June 1793 he was again cited in the Drury Lane accounts as a property man at the Haymarket. A Mr Sylvester was a machinist at the Haymarket in 1800 and 1801, but we have considered him a different person.

Silvester, Harriett. *See* **LITCHFIELD, MRS JOHN.**

Silvester, Henry [fl. 1705], *singer.*
The *Calendar of Treasury Books* for January–March 1705 show that clothing worth £9 was delivered to Henry Silvester, one of the former children of the Chapel Royal, whose voice had changed.

Silvester, John [fl. 1794], *singer.*
Doane's *Musical Directory* of 1794 listed John Silvester, of Goswell Street, as a bass who sang for the Portland Chapel Society and in the oratorios at Drury Lane Theatre.

Simcock, Matthew 1771–1860, *violinist, violist.*
According to the records of the Royal Society of Musicians, Matthew Simcock (or Simp-

cock) was born on 7 December 1771 in the parish of Holy Rood in Southampton, the son of a barber and peruke maker, Matthew Simcock the elder, and his wife Martha. The boy was not christened until 7 May 1772. On 4 December 1796 in London the younger Simcock was recommended for membership in the Royal Society of Musicians. He was then described as a bachelor, a violinist and violist, leader of the band at the Theatre Royal, Brighthelmstone, and a member of the band at Covent Garden Theatre in London. Simcock was unanimously elected in March 1797.

He played violin in the Society's St Paul's concerts in 1797 and subsequent years, his last notice being in 1804. At Covent Garden, the account books show, he was being paid 5s. 10d. nightly in 1799–1800; by 1821–22 he was working at Drury Lane for £1 16s. weekly. He remained active in the Society, serving as a Governor until 1804 and on the Court of Assistants in 1833, 1834, and 1835. He died on 26 April 1860.

Simcoll. *See* SYMCOLL.

Simes, Mr ₍*fl.* 1792₎, *manager.*
The Pie Powder Court Book at the London Guildhall lists the showman Simes as having produced a pantomime at Bartholomew Fair in 1792.

Siminon. *See* VALLOUIS.

Simkinson. *See* SIMPKINSON.

Simmonds. *See* SIMMONS, SIMONDS, SIMONS, SYMONDS.

Simmons. *See also* SIMONDS, SIMONS, SYMONDS.

Simmons, Mr ₍*fl.* 1770–1771₎, *actor.*
Mr "Simons" acted Glenalvon in *Douglas* at the Haymarket Theatre on 19 March 1770. On 4 March 1771 "Simonds" played Blandford in *Oroonoko,* and "Simmonds" was Dick in *The King and the Miller of Mansfield* at the Haymarket; both references were surely to the same man. Mrs Simmons (fl. 1771–1787?) also acted that evening, and one supposes she was our subject's wife. Simmons played the Chap-

lain in *The Orphan* at the Haymarket on 20 April 1771; Mrs Simmons was also in the cast. Our spelling of the name is the one most often found for the couple.

Simmons, Mr ₍*fl.* 1786–1816₎, *box office keeper.*
The Mr Simmons who was named in benefit bills at Covent Garden Theatre from 2 June 1786 to 25 May 1792 and was cited in the theatre's accounts as a house servant earning 12s. weekly from 1800 to 1803 was probably a box office keeper. That was certainly his position at the Royal Circus, according to a playbill dated 26 May 1806. T. J. Dibdin in his *Reminiscences* called him a receiver of tickets and orders at the Surrey Theatre in 1816, probably during the summer; that year Simmons was also employed at the Lyceum during the spring or fall. Dibdin said Simmons was the father of a "talented little actor of that name, who so many years delighted the town at Covent-Garden." The little actor was Samuel Simmons; the *Index to The London Stage* conflates the references to the father and son.

Simmons, Mrs ₍*fl.* 1742₎, *actress.*
Mrs Simmons played Lady Ruff in *The Indian Merchant* on 25 August 1742 at Bartholomew Fair.

Simmons, Mrs ₍*fl.* 1771–1787?₎, *actress.*
Mrs Simmons acted Peggy in *The King and the Miller of Mansfield* at the Haymarket Theatre on 4 March 1771; in the cast also was Mr "Simmonds," and our guess is that they were husband and wife. Their name was spelled so many different ways in the bills and accounts that we cannot be certain which was correct and have chosen Simmons, the spelling most frequently found. Mrs "Simmonds" acted Mrs Fulmer in *The West Indian* at the Haymarket on 15 April 1771 and on the twentieth (as Mrs Simmons) played Florella in *The Orphan.*

On 2 February 1775 Mrs Simmons was back at the Haymarket, playing Lucinda in *Love in a Village,* and the following 23 March she appeared as Nerissa in *The Merchant of Venice.* She was at China Hall, Rotherhithe, on 25 June 1777, acting (as Mrs "Symmonds") Dorcas in *The Mock Doctor.* Mrs "Symons" was on the

payroll of the Theatre Royal in Liverpool at
15*s*. weekly in October and December 1777
and again from June to mid-October 1778.
Perhaps our subject was the Mrs "Simmonds"
acting at Bristol in July 1787.

Simmons, Miss [*fl. 1781–1790?*], actress.

Miss Simmons played the Masked Lady in
Love and a Bottle at the Haymarket Theatre on
26 March 1781. Perhaps she was the Miss
"Simmonds" who acted Sally in *She Stoops to
Conquer* and Miss La Blond in *The Romp* at the
Haymarket on 29 September 1790.

Simmons, Samuel *c. 1773–1819, actor, dancer, singer.*

Samuel Simmons was born about 1777, according to *The Dictionary of National Biography*,
but other evidence, as will be seen, suggests a
birthdate about 1773. His father was a house
servant at Covent Garden Theatre as early as

Courtesy of the Garrick Club

SAMUEL SIMMONS
by Turneau

1786 and appears to have been a box office
keeper. Master Samuel's first notice in playbills
in *The London Stage* came on 4 November
1783, when he played the Boy in *The Poor
Soldier* at Covent Garden. On 17 September
1784 Master "Symmonds" was the Duke of
York in *Richard III* at the Haymarket Theatre.
The *Authentic Memoirs of the Green Room* state
that "the late Mr. Bannister recommended him
at the Haymarket theatre, to perform the parts
of children." (The *DNB* dates that performance
21 September and places it at Covent Garden;
Master Simmons *did* act in *Richard III* at Covent Garden on 11 October.) At the Haymarket
on 13 July 1785 the lad played the Giant of
the Causeway in *Harlequin Teague*.

He was again at Covent Garden in 1785–
86, playing the Duke of York, the title role in
Tom Thumb, and the Page in *The Orphan*. (The
Index to The London Stage incorrectly assigns to
Samuel Simmons benefit notices that belong
clearly to his father.) On 4 September 1786 at
the Haymarket Samuel was again in *Harlequin
Teague*. Between 1786–87 and 1791–92 Mas-
ter Simmons added to his repertoire Zozeb in
Aladin, the Boy in *The Toy*, the Page in *The
Gamesters*, Prince Edward in *Richard III*, the
Lover's Servant in *Harlequin Chaplet*, the
Waiter in *Wild Oats*, and the Footboy in *Blue-
Beard*. He also acted in *The Road to Ruin* and
A Peep behind the Curtain. The *DNB* states that
Master Simmons disappeared from the bills
from 1785 to 1796, which is clearly not the
case; it reports that at some point he acted the
Boy in *The Contrivances*, which is certainly
likely.

Master Simmons (called in the *Thespian
Magazine* in 1792 "Mr Simmonds") acted at
the Theatre Royal in Richmond in July 1792.
He was Dick in *The Belle's Stratagem*, danced in
a piece called *The Rustic Villagers*, played Jacob
in *The Road to Ruin*, and acted Peter in *A Day
in Turkey*. At Covent Garden in 1793–94 Simmons—now no longer called Master and probably just turned 21—was paid £1 weekly for
his chores.

Through the 1799–1800 season at Covent
Garden Simmons was seen in such new roles
as Donalbain in *Macbeth*, the Taylor and Zany
in *Harlequin and Faustus*, Fifer in *The Battle of
Hexham*, a Taylor in *Catherine and Petruchio*, a
Groom in *The Rage*, Postillion in *The Road to
Ruin*, Manly's Servant in *The Provok'd Husband*,

SAMUEL SIMMONS, as Beau Mordecai
by De Wilde

a Jew in *Lord Mayor's Day,* Fop's Servant in
Harlequin's Treasure, Sweep in *The Way to Get
Un-Married,* and the Apothecary in *Romeo and
Juliet.*

Also a Waiter in *Hartford Bridge,* a Thin Man
in *Barataria,* Simple in *The Merry Wives of
Windsor,* Filch in *The Beggar's Opera,* Jeffery in
Animal Magnetism, Buckram in *Love for Love,*
Abel in *The Honest Thieves,* Verges in *Much Ado
about Nothing,* Tipstaff in *Abroad and at Home,*
Cymon in *The Irishman in London,* Oliver in
Wives as They Were and Maids as They Are,
Clinch in *The Ghost,* Rundy in *The Farmer,*
Daniel in *The Conscious Lovers,* the Gentleman
Usher in *King Lear,* Jack in *False Impressions,*
Francis in *Henry IV,* a Scotch Pedlar in *Oscar
and Malvina,* Ezekiel Spotless in *Retaliation,*
Linco in *Cymon,* Kiddy Wigsby in *The Witches
Revels,* Diggory in *She Stoops to Conquer,* Benin
in *The Highland Reel,* Roger in *The Mayor of
Garratt,* Phisgig in *The Magic Oak,* Midships
in *The Death of Captain Cook,* Stopgap in *Man-
agement,* an Old Peasant in *The Mouth of the
Nile,* a Barber in *The Turnpike Gate,* a Ballad
Singer in *The Volcano,* Cloddy in *The Mysteries
of the Castle,* Verdun in *Lovers' Vows* (he "gave
promise of considerable comic talents," wrote
Thomas Dutton), Sir Christopher Hatton in
The Critic, Parchment in *Liberal Opinions,* Dick
in *Five Thousand a Year,* and Quiz in *Love in a
Camp.* Simmons also sang in choruses on occasion, and some of his roles—such as Sammy
Scrip in *Harlequin's Return*—featured his singing. Our subject was the Simmons who acted
at Liverpool in June 1797. The *Monthly Mirror,*
which reported that activity, also placed Simmons at Liverpool in 1799 and 1801.

At Covent Garden in 1799–1800 "little"
Simmons, as William Hazlitt so often described him later, was earning £2 10*s.*
weekly—a small salary for one who was kept
so busy, albeit in small roles. By 1801–2 he
was up to £3 10*s.*, and he kept climbing to £9
weekly by 1814–15. His summers in Liverpool were increasingly successful, too. The
Monthly Mirror said that his benefit on 9 September 1801 brought in ". . . £20 more than
any former period. Such was the desire to serve
this little deserving comedian, that the greatest part of the audience was content to stand
during the performance. The manager had a
very plentiful harvest. . . ." Simmons's benefit
at Liverpool in 1802 brought in £206. The
Authentic Memoirs of the Green Room said that
Simmons also acted at some point at Windsor.

From 1800 to his death in 1819 Samuel
Simmons added to his Covent Garden reper-
toire such roles as a Witch in *Macbeth,* Jerry in
Seaside Story, Dr Infallible in *Folly,* Manikin in
The Cabinet, Squire Supplejack in *Family Quar-
rels,* Pistol in *Henry V,* the Old Woman in *Rule
a Wife and Have a Wife,* Feeble in *2 Henry IV,*
Shallow in *The Merry Wives of Windsor,* Stubby
in *We Fly by Night,* Lord Sands in *Henry VIII,*
Fulmer in *The West Indian,* Dr Pinch in *The
Comedy of Errors,* Moses in *The School for Scan-
dal,* Probe in *A Trip to Scarborough,* Peter in
Romeo and Juliet, Stephano in *The Tempest,* Flute
in *A Midsummer Night's Dream,* Argus in *The
Barber of Seville,* and Saddletree in *The Heart of
Midlothian.*

The *Authentic Memoirs* noted that Simmons
specialized in three sorts of comic characters:
simpleton types, such as Matthew in *Every
Man in His Humour;* "forward coxcombry still
accompanied with silliness," as in Mordecai in

Harvard Theatre Collection

SAMUEL SIMMONS, as Baron Munchausen
by De Wilde

Love à la Mode and the oratorical Plebeian in *Coriolanus;* and "ridiculous fretfulness," as in Fainwould in *Raising the Wind* or Jonathan Oldskirt in *Who Wants a Guinea?* The *Monthly Mirror* in April 1801 wrote of Simmons as Justice Greedy in *Sir Giles Overreach:* he was "highly entertaining, but he rather *buffoons* the part too much, and we would advise him, as he seems to have original powers, to avoid any imitation of Mr. Quick."

But Hazlitt called Samuel Simmons

one of the most correct, pointed, *naive,* and whimsical comic actors, we have for a long time had, or are likely to have again. He was not a buffoon, but a real actor. He did not play *himself,* nor play tricks, but played the part the author had assigned him. This was the great merit of the good old style of acting. He fitted into it like a brilliant into the setting of a ring, or as the ring fits the finger. We

shall look for him often in Filch, in which his appearance was a continual *double entendre,* with one eye leering at his neighbour's pockets, and the other turned to the gallows:—also in the spangled Beau Mordecai, in Moses, in which he had all the precision, the pragmaticalness, and impenetrable secresy of the Jew money-lender; and in my Lord Sands, where he had all the stage to himself, and seemed to fill it by the singular insignificance of his person, and the infinite airs he gave himself. We shall look for him in these and many other parts, but in vain, or for any one equal to him.

The last role Simmons acted was Moses in *The School for Scandal* on 8 September 1819. On 11 September he collapsed in Hanover Square in a fit of apoplexy. Oxberry in his *Dramatic Biography* stated that Simmons's wife Margaret was with her husband that day when he died, attended by Dr Hyam. The couple had been married for 16 years. Yet on 27 September 1819 administration of the estate of Samuel Simmons, *bachelor,* comedian, was granted to his sister and next of kin, Sarah Compignea, late of York Buildings. The estate was worth only £200. Could Oxberry have confused Samuel Simmons with his father?

Portraits of Samuel Simmons include:

1. By Samuel De Wilde. Half-length, looking to front. Location untraced. Engraving by S. Freeman, published by Vernor & Hood as a plate to the *Monthly Mirror,* 1808.

2. By John Nixon. Picture showing Simmons and a Mr Hamilton as part of the Margravin's party in the meadows near Richmond. Pen, and gray ink, and watercolor (6¼" × 8¾"). Sold as the property of the French Hospital of La Providence at Christie's on 5 November 1974 (lot 80); bought by Waldron for 90 guineas.

3. By John Turneau. Black chalk and watercolor drawing, 6" × 4¾", head and shoulders, in profile to right; fair hair, white neckcloth, and dark coat. In the Garrick Club (No 545).

4. By John Turmeau. Pencil and watercolor drawing, 5¾" × 4⅝", head and shoulders in profile to left. The head is in watercolor, the rest is in pencil. Brown hair, neckcloth, and high collar. In the Garrick Club (No 561b).

5. As Abel in *Honest Thieves.* Watercolor by Samuel De Wilde, September 1805. In the Harvard Theatre Collection. An engraving by R. Smith was published as a plate to Cawthorn's *Minor British Theatre,* 1806; a copy

Courtesy of the Garrick Club

SAMUEL SIMMONS, as Master Matthew
by De Wilde

engraved by J. Kennerley was published as a plate to *The British Stage,* April 1831.

6. As Baron Munchausen in *Harlequin Munchausen.* Watercolor by Samuel De Wilde, June 1819. In the Harvard Theatre Collection. An engraving by R. Cooper was published as a plate to *Terry's Theatrical Gallery,* 1822.

7. As Baron Munchausen. Pencil drawing by Samuel De Wilde. In the Garrick Club (inscribed "as Major Galbraith in the Legend of Montrose"—not listed in printed catalogue).

8. As Beau Mordecai in *Love a la Mode.* Painting by Samuel De Wilde. Full-length, 14″ × 11″, standing, facing viewer, open snuff box in left hand, from which he has taken a pinch of snuff; books on shelves behind. In the Garrick Club (No 467), presented in 1854 by William A. Commerell.

9. As Beau Mordecai. Pencil and watercolor drawing by Samuel De Wilde. Full-length, 14″ × 9″, standing, facing viewer, taking a pinch of snuff. Similar to No 8, above. In the Garrick Club (No 67).

10. As Beau Mordecai. By Samuel De Wilde. Standing, taking a pinch of snuff. An engraving by E. Scriven was published as a plate to the *Theatrical Inquisitor,* 1815. This portrait is different from the two above by De Wilde.

11. As Jonathan Oldskirt in *Who Wants a Guinea?* Pencil and watercolor drawing by Samuel De Wilde. Full-length, 14¾″ × 9¾″, standing, feet apart, wig askew, hat in his left hand and stick in his right. In the Garrick Club (No 47), presented in 1842 by Major-General Wood.

12. As Little Dickey in *Home and Abroad.* Watercolor over pencil drawing by Samuel De Wilde. Full-length, 14¼″ × 9″, standing, legs apart, left hand on sword at waist, right hand at waist. Offered at Sotheby's on 17 November 1988 (lot 72), but not sold (illustrated in the sale catalogue). Similar in size and technique to De Wilde's drawing in the Victoria and Albert Museum of George D. Harley as Kent in *King Lear.*

13. As Master Matthew in *Every Man in His Humour.* By Samuel De Wilde. Oil, 9″ × 7¼″, half-length, facing viewer, pointing to a paper in his left hand. In the Garrick Club (No 232). A pencil and black chalk version (7¾″ × 10″) by De Wilde, dated 1802, is in the collection of the Earl of Leicester at Holkham Hall.

14. As Master Matthew. By Samuel De Wilde, 1807. Pencil and watercolor on paper, 14″ × 8¾″, full-length, front to viewer, stick in his right hand, his left hand on hip. In the Garrick Club (No 69b).

15. As Mother Goose, with Grimaldi as Clown, John Bologna as Harlequin, Luigi Bologna as Pantaloon, and Miss Searle as Colombine, in *Harlequin and Mother Goose.* By T. M. Grimshaw, c. 1806. Pencil and watercolor drawing. In the London Museum. Reproduced in this *Dictionary* 2: 190.

16. As Mother Goose. By unknown engraver (George Cruikshank?), after Samuel De Wilde. 11½″ × 7⅞″. Published by De Wilde, 1807. A copy (6½″ × 4½″) was published by De Wilde in the same year.

17. As Mother Goose. By unknown engraver. Published by John Fairburn.

18. As Simkin in *The Deserter.* By Samuel De Wilde, August 1805. Pencil and watercolor drawing, 14½″ × 9″. Owned by Her Maj-

esty Queen Elizabeth II. An engraving by Maddocks was published as a plate to Cawthorn's *Minor Theatre,* 1806.

Simms. *See also* SIMS.

Simms, Mr [*fl.* 1746–1748], *actor.*
Mr Simms played Peto in *1 Henry IV* at Goodman's Fields Theatre on 29 October 1746 (according to the *Daily Advertiser;* Hogan in *Shakespeare in the Theatre* lists Simons in that role). At Southwark Fair on 7 September 1748 Simms played Sycorax in *The Tempest.* Possibly he was the Simms who acted in Dublin from 1725–26 to 1730–31, but there is not enough evidence to make an identification.

Simon. *See also* SIMPSON.

Simon, Mrs [*fl.* 1749], *actress.*
Mrs Simon played Pert in *The Adventures of Sir Lubberly Lackbrains and His Man Blunderbuss* at Cushing's booth at Bartholomew Fair on 23 August 1749.

Simonds. *See also* SIMMONS, SIMONS, SYMONDS.

Simonds, Henry *d. 1740, violoncellist, organist.*
On 25 October 1711 Henry Simonds (or Simmonds, Symonds) was granted livery as a member of the royal musical establishment. Lord Chamberlain's warrants over the following years named him as a member of the "Instrumental Musick." His salary was £40 annually. In July 1718 he was paid £2 beyond his regular salary for attending the installation of Prince Frederick and the Duke of York, and from August to October he was with the royal family at Hampton Court. About 15 February 1720 Simonds was paid £60 as a violoncellist for the Academy of Music, and by 1724 he was organist of St Martin, Ludgate. On 4 March 1724 he and other musicians were suspended for neglecting their duties at court, but the suspension was rescinded on 10 April. In July 1726 Simonds attended the installation of the Duke of Richmond and Sir Robert Walpole at Windsor. Simonds became one of the original subscribers to the Royal Society of Musicians on 28 August 1739, but within a few months

he was dead. On 12 March 1740 he was replaced in the King's Musick, according to several Lord Chamberlain's warrants. He had died on 6 January, according to *The Royal Society of Musicians* (1985).

Simonds's will, made on 6 March 1739, identified him as a member of the royal musical establishment. He had been living at the house of Robert Doyley in the parish of St George the Martyr. Simonds left his estate to his two grandchildren, Ann and Thomas "Symonds" when they should come of age. Until that time the estate was to be in the hands of Thomas Ricketts of the Strand, woolen draper, and Joseph Mahoon of York Buildings, harpsichord maker. The will was proved on 14 March 1740.

Simonet, Leonora *b. c. 1773, dancer, singer.*
Leonora (or Eleanor) Simonet, born about 1733, was one of the three daughters of the dancers Louis and Adelaide Simonet, performers on the London stage in the last two decades of the eighteenth century. She seems to have been the middle daughter, the eldest having been Rosine Simonet (later Mrs William Wilde) and the youngest Theresa Simonet. Leonora, brought by her parents from Paris in 1775 or 1776, may first have danced at the King's Theatre in 1781–82, where by 1782–83 she was appearing regularly with her sister Rosine. For about ten years their careers were closely intertwined, so it is difficult to specify with assurance particular roles in which Leonora danced. Moreover, her sister Theresa also began to perform occasionally in the 1780s.

Leonora's "first appearance" was advertised for 10 December 1782, when she danced a pas de deux with Master Laborie at the King's Theatre. In October 1783 she danced with Rosine Simonet in *Le Noce du Chateau* and *The Phantom of a Day* at the Royal Circus, and the Misses Simonet and Laborie, with others, appeared at that house in a *Dance of the Coopers* in October 1784. Between 1784 and 1789 Leonora was a dancer at the King's Theatre.

On 21 May 1785 Leonora ascended in a balloon from the Barbican with Jean-Pierre Blanchard. She was the second female balloonist in Great Britain and at the time could not have been more than about 13 years old, for the first female balloonist in Britain was her elder sister Rosine, who less than three weeks earlier ascended with Blanchard on 3 May 1785. Rosine (though called only Miss Simonet and identified as the daughter of a dancer) was described as "but fourteen years and a half old when she accompanied M. Blanchard."

Leonora was also engaged at Covent Garden in 1789–90 and at the Pantheon from 1790 to 1792. She had summer engagements at the Haymarket from 1785 to 1789 and in 1792. Among her parts were Henry in *The Deserter* (ballet version) at the Haymarket in 1785 and appearances at the King's in such historical and pantomime ballets as *Acis and Galatea, Les Deux Solitaires, Les Offrandes à l'Amour,* and *L'Embarquement pour Cythère.* At Covent Garden in 1789–90 she appeared in *The Deserter* on 13 November 1789 and then danced in *Harlequin's Chaplet, The Guardian Outwitted,* and specialty dances.

On 14 April 1792 at the Haymarket she and her sister were introduced as singers in the seraglio scene of *La discordia conjugale;* their duet, accompanied on the harp by young Meyer, was considered by the *Morning Herald* to have been "very pleasing." After her final performance at the Pantheon in June 1792, Leonora Simonet seems to have left the London stage. We believe it was her sister Rosine who became the wife of the actor William Wilde.

Simonet, Louis   [fl. 1765?–1817?], dancer, ballet master, violinist, choreographer.

Louis Simonet was a member of a family of dancers who performed on the Continent in the 1760s. Perhaps he was the Simonet who was a member of Noverre's company at Stuttgart by November 1765, when he was noted in the account books there to receive a bonus of 400 gulders. He was, no doubt, young and learning, for in November 1767 Noverre claimed 1500 florins from the Privy Council at Stuttgart "for teaching the dancer Simonet." That Simonet was evidently the person who went with Noverre to Vienna in 1767 and directed that master's "Theatrical Dance School" at the Vienna Opera until 1774.

In 1774, a Simonet, presumably our subject Louis, was performing at Bristol, where he was also to be found the next year. By the end of the 1774–75 season, Simonet was in London, and he performed some service for Drury Lane Theatre in connection with the Fund Night, a benefit that occurred on 25 May 1775. On that date the treasurer recorded as part of the expenses for the Fund Night, "Salary to Mr Simonet, Sg Como, Sga Crespi, & Mrs Hartle £1 10s." All were dancers, though their names do not appear in the bills that night. A Simonet, perhaps Louis, was a figure dancer at the Paris Opéra in 1776.

By the autumn of 1776 Louis Simonet and his family were settled in London. His wife, also a dancer, was Adelaide De Camp, sister of the flutist George Louis De Camp and the dancer Sophia De Camp. Louis and Adelaide Simonet were accompanied by three young children—Rosine, Leonora, and Theresa— and perhaps also by a young adult named Rosine Simonet, who probably was Louis's sister. One Rosine Simonet at some time in the 1770s married the scene designer and reputed dancer Thomas Frederick Luppino; she had several children by the end of that decade, during which time and afterward the child dancer Rosine Simonet was performing in London.

Louis Simonet and his wife made their debuts at the King's Theatre on 2 November 1776, when they were announced as making their first appearance in England. If that announcement was true, then the Simonet at Bristol in 1774 and 1775 was someone else. That night the dances were composed by Simonet and Vallois. Simonet and his wife performed in a "Grand Serious Ballet" at the end of Act I of the opera *Astarto* and in a new ballet *Les Amusemens champêtres* at the conclusion of the opera. During that season Simonet, usually with his wife, also appeared in such ballets as *L'Épouse Persane* and *La Clochette* and in various specialty dances. When they had their benefit on 1 May 1777, tickets were available from Simonet at Leary's, near the White Bear, Piccadilly. The following year his address was No 5, Dover Street, Piccadilly, where the family still lived in 1782. By March 1784 they resided at No 33, Pall Mall.

Simonet continued to dance at the King's Theatre until June 1788. By 1781 he was also serving as ballet master to the opera, a position he held until 1791, three years after his retirement as a performer.

After 1791 Simonet seems not to have been reappointed at the King's Theatre. In the Public Record Office is a petition (undated but obviously from about 1791) to the Lord Chamberlain, signed by Louis Simonet, in which the dancer complains that his principal source of income—"plus de Cent livres Sterling de salaire"—has been delayed, causing him considerable embarrassment.

On 3 January 1792 the *Morning Herald* announced that the father to the Misses Simonet was available for dancing lessons. He continued his connection with the King's Theatre, however, for in 1794 Doane's *Musical Directory* described him as a dancing master and a violinist at the Opera and gave his address as No 28, Poland Street. He performed some service at Covent Garden Theatre in the autumn of 1797; the account books record on 25 November 1797: "Paid Simonet for 4 rehearsals £8 8s."

As late as 1817 a Simonet was employed as first violinist at the King's Theatre but that person may have been F. Simonet, who was on the Drury Lane payroll at £2 2s. per week in 1807–8 and 1808–9, probably as a musician. (In her *Pre-Romantic Ballet*, M. H. Winter mentions a François Simonet as being in London but seems to have confused him with Louis.)

Louis Simonet's wife Adelaide performed in London through 1790–91, after which season we lose track of her. She and their three daughters, who came upon the London stage as children in the 1770s and 1780s, are noticed separately.

Harvard Theatre Collection

ADELAIDE SIMONET, as the Princess
engraving by Thornthwaite, after Roberts

Simonet, Mme Louis, Adelaide, née De Camp ₍*fl. 1776–1791*₎, *dancer.*

Adelaide De Camp was the daughter of Jean De Camp, of Luneville in Lorraine. Nothing is known of her life before she accompanied her brother, the flutist George Louis De Camp, and his family and her sister Sophia De Camp, to England in the middle of the 1770s. By that time, however, she was the wife of the dancer Louis Simonet, a member of a French family of performers.

On 2 November 1776 Mme Simonet and her husband, announced as making their first appearances in England, danced at the King's Theatre in "A Grand Serious Ballet" and in *Les Amusemens champêtres,* ballets designed by Louis Simonet. She made other appearances that season in *L'Épouse Persane* and *La Clochette* and in a variety of specialty dances.

Mme Simonet's career was closely connected with that of her husband, who danced at the King's Theatre until 1788 and served as ballet master there until 1791. She was engaged as a featured dancer in the operas as the King's through June 1784. She appeared in her husband's new ballet *The Country Gallant* on 25 November 1780, dancing in men's clothes. That season an accident kept her off the stage for a while, and when she returned to dance the Countess in Vestris's *Ninette à la cour* on 22 February 1781, it was announced that "as she is not perfectly recovered from the consequences of her late Accident, she hopes for the indulgence of the Public, from whom she has already received so many flattering proofs of Approbation." She played Medée in *Medée et Jason* when that ballet had its first London performance on 29 March 1781. Though the elder Vestris claimed the ballet as his own in

London, the work had been created by Noverre at Stuttgart in 1763. The *London Magazine* for April 1781 reported that Vestris's "forcible manner of characterizing the passions in the part of Jason distinguished him as an actor superior to all his contemporaries" and that Mme Simonet was "equal to him as an actress." Her performance of Fatima in *L'Épouses Persane* on 15 February 1783 was similarly praised by the *Public Advertiser* of 18 February: "Mme Simonet displayed all that power of acting for which she has been so justly celebrated. . . ."

After her engagement at the King's Theatre concluded in June 1784, Mme Simonet danced at the Royal Circus, appearing there in a new dance *Nobody; or, Two Faces are better than one* in the spring of 1786, in *The Industrious Mechanick* in October 1786, and as a principal dancer there in the summer of 1787. In 1790–91 she was engaged at the Pantheon with her daughters Leonora and Rosine, making her first appearance there on 17 February 1791 in D'Auberval's new ballet *Amphion et Thalie*, performed 19 times that season. Her last performance of record was in that ballet on 28 June 1791.

Her husband, who remained active in the London theatres perhaps as late as 1817, and her three daughters—Rosine, Leonora, and Theresa—are noticed separately.

Mme Adelaide Simonet was the aunt of Maria Theresa De Camp (later Mrs Charles Kemble), Vincent De Camp, Adelaide De Camp, and Sophia De Camp (later Mrs Frederick Brown), all of whom were children of her brother George Louis De Camp and all of whom were on the London stage in the eighteenth century.

Mme Simonet was pictured as the Princess in *Ninette à la cour* in an engraving by Thornthwaite, after J. Roberts, which was published as a plate to *Bell's British Theatre*, 1781. An engraving published by Boydell in 1781 shows her as Medea and Gaetano Vestris as Jason.

Simonet, Rosine, later Mrs William Wilde? *b. c. 1770, dancer, singer.*

Rosine, Leonora, and Theresa Simonet, three daughters of the French dancers Louis and Adelaide Simonet, danced as children on the London stage from the late 1770s until about 1797. All three seem to have been born before their parents came to England from

ROSINE SIMONET, as Skirmish

engraving by Pergolesi, after Garnery

Paris in 1775 or 1776. The careers of the three girls, especially of Rosine and Leonora, are closely intertwined, so it is likely that details of their respective appearances and engagements given in their notices may be credited to the wrong one.

We assume that Rosine Simonet was the eldest sister, born about 1770. She, at any rate, seems to have been the first upon the stage. The name of Miss Simonet, no doubt Rosine, first appeared in the bills on 11 November 1777, when she danced at Covent Garden Theatre with Master Holland and Master D'Egville in a new dance piece called *The Garden of Love*. Later that season, on 22 May 1778, again at Covent Garden, she performed with Master Holland in *The Prince of Wales's New Court Minuet*.

In the fall of 1778 Miss Simonet, presumably Rosine, danced at Drury Lane Theatre, probably in Sheridan's new musical entertainment *The Camp*, though her name did not appear in the bills. The Drury Lane account books indicate that on 30 December 1778 Mr Simonet was paid £3 3s. for "Miss Simonet's

Dancg. 6 nights to 29th Octr inclusive." On 10 November 1778 she danced at Covent Garden with Master D'Egville in *La Soirée à la Mode*. On 10 April 1779 Drury Lane paid Miss Simonet 10*s*. 6*d*. for dancing one night. Her other performances that season, however, were at the King's Theatre, where her parents were engaged. Her first notice in the King's playbills was for dancing in a fairy ballet in the comic opera *Zemira e Azore* on 23 February 1779. That season she also danced Cupid in *Les Forges de Vulcain* (in which her mother danced as Venus) on 25 March 1779.

At the King's Theatre in 1779–80, Rosine danced in a new Indian ballet on 27 November 1779 and that season was seen in *Il desertore, La bergère coquette* (with her mother), *The Rural Sports,* and a new pastoral ballet. Again she appeared at Drury Lane, though she was not named in the bills, for on 11 January 1780 that theatre paid her £2 5*s*. for "3 days Dancing." Announced as from the opera house, she danced with Master D'Egville in *The Prince of Wales's New Court Minuet* at Covent Garden on 18 May 1780. Throughout 1780–81 she also was engaged at Drury Lane, named in the bills there for the first time on 18 October 1780 in *The Force of Love*. On 28 October 1780 she was paid £3 for four nights and on 4 November 1780 she received £1 10s. for two nights.

Rosine was regularly engaged at the King's Theatre throughout the 1780s, until it burned in June 1789. She was probably the Miss Simonet who danced at the Haymarket Theatre in the spring and summer of 1785.

According to Hodgson's *History of Aeronautics in Great Britain,* when Jean-Pierre Blanchard ascended in a balloon from the Barbican on 3 May 1785, he was accompanied by a Miss Simonet, who was identified by Horace Walpole as the daughter of a dancer. She was "but fourteen years and a half old" at that time, according to Monck Mason's *Aeronautica* (1838). That adventurous lass seems to have been Rosine, and she was the "first female that ascended in Great Britain." Less than three weeks later, on 21 May 1785, Miss Simonet's younger sister ascended with Blanchard. That second flying Simonet was, we believe, Leonora, who could not have been more than 13 years old.

Perhaps by 1781–82, Rosine's sister Leonora had also begun to dance at the King's Theatre.

Certainly in the next season, 1782–83, Leonora was appearing regularly with her sister, and their careers then ran parallel, it seems, for about ten years. The third sister, Theresa Simonet, began dancing by April 1781. Rosine and Leonora also performed together occasionally at the Royal Circus, where their appearances included dancing in *Le noce du chateau* and *The Phantom of a Day* in October 1783 and in *The Dance of the Coopers,* with Laborie and others, in October 1784. They also were at the Royalty Theatre in 1788.

With her sister Leonora, Rosine was also engaged at the Haymarket in the summer of 1789, at Covent Garden in 1789–90, and at the Pantheon between 1790 and 1792. At the Haymarket Theatre on 14 April 1792, the Misses Simonet (Rosine and Leonora?) were introduced as vocal performers, when they sang a duet in the seraglio scene of *La discordia conjugale,* accompanied by young Meyer on the harp, and they were, according to the *Morning Herald* (16 April), "very pleasing."

Sometime soon after that April appearance, and before mid-July of that year, it seems that one of the Simonet sisters married the actor William Wilde. We have guessed that it was Rosine, but we offer no assurances. In any event, a Mrs Wilde was performing at Richmond, Surrey, in July 1792, while Mr Wilde was an actor in that company. She danced in *The Rustic Villagers* on 13 July, in *A Day in Turkey* on 23 July, and no doubt in other pieces that summer. (A dancer named "Mlle Rosine" was in the King's company in 1794–95; possibly that person was our subject, but we believe she was not.)

In the summer of 1796 Mrs Wilde and her husband performed at Birmingham. Announced as Mrs Wilde, late Miss Simonet, Rosine began an engagement at Drury Lane on 26 December 1796, as Colombine in the pantomime *Robinson Crusoe*. On 12 January 1797 she danced with Gentili in the masquerade in *Much Ado about Nothing* and during the season appeared in such pieces as *The Labyrinth, The Last of the Family, Les Délassemens militaires, Peggy's Love,* and *Cupid and Psyche*.

Mrs Wilde began the season 1797–98 at Covent Garden Theatre, appearing with a group of dancers borrowed from the King's Theatre, in *Les Délassemens militaires* and *Peggy's Love* on 21 October 1797. That bill was repeated on 24 October. On 4 November she danced in *Cupid and Psyche,* and on 7 November in that piece and *Les Délassemens militaires.* Thereafter, her name disappeared from the London bills.

A portait of Rosine Simonet as Skirmish in *The Deserter* was engraved by M. A. Pergolesi, after P. Garnery, and was published in 1781.

Simonet, Theresa *b. 1775, dancer, singer.*

Announced as a child of six, Theresa Simonet danced a minuet and gavotte with her father Louis Simonet at the King's Theatre on 26 April 1781. The performance was for the benefit of her mother Adelaide Simonet. Theresa, who followed her elder sisters Rosine and Leonora upon the stage, made only occasional appearances over the next seven or eight years. On 30 April 1782 she came onto the King's Theatre stage, announced as seven years old and appearing for that night only, again to dance with her father for her mother's benefit. A year later, on 1 May 1783, the bills announced: "an entirely new ballet, composed by Simonet, *Le Déjeuner Espagnol,* in Part I of which *Sento ch'in Seno* by Giordani, sung by Miss Theresa Simonet, only 8 years old, and who will dance a *Minuet* with her Father, and in Part II . . . a *Chaconne,* composed by Simonet, by Miss Theresa Simonet." Also dancing that night was young Maria Theresa De Camp, daughter of the flutist George Louis De Camp and cousin to Theresa Simonet (Theresa's mother was the flutist's sister. Maria Theresa De Camp became the wife of Charles Kemble in 1806.)

The two cousins appeared together at the King's on 11 March 1784, when Theresa (who, the bill announced, never appeared but at her mother's benefit) danced a pas seul to a French air by Marlborough. At the end of the opera Miss Simonet and Miss De Camp ("neither of whom has yet completed her ninth year") performed a minuet and a gavotte. Possibly Theresa was the Mlle Simonet who played Cupid in the opera *Orfeo* at the King's on 12 May 1785.

Theresa may have been one of the Misses Simonet who appeared at the King's and the Haymarket in 1788–89, but we believe that these and subsequent performances by the Misses Simonet at London were given by Rosine and Leonora.

A Miss Simonet, perhaps Theresa, became a familiar performer at Handy's Circus in Bristol during the 1790s, as a dancer and maybe also as an equestrienne. The Bristol papers advertised her to be with Handy and Franklin's Riding School, "behind the Full Moon," Stoke's Croft, from 22 March to the end of May 1790; the company returned to perform between 30 August and 25 October 1790, and Miss Simonet had a benefit on 11 October. She was with Handy's Circus in Limekiln Lane, Bristol, in March and April 1793, January through March 1794, and in March 1797, when she had a benefit on 18 March and offered two new dances on 25 March. That Miss Simonet was also a performer at the Royal Circus, London, in April 1798.

Simonetti, Lodovico [*fl. 1784–1786*], *singer.*

The libretto of *Andromeda e Perseo,* published in Rome in 1784, named Lodoviso Simonetti as one of the singers. He came to London in 1786 to sing at the King's Theatre: an unspecified part in *Perseo* on 21 March, Tito in *Guilio Sabino* on 30 March, Lucius Virginius in *Virginia* on 4 May, and Sir Thomas in *L'Inglese in Italia* on 20 May.

Simoni, Giuseppe [*fl. 1786–1793*], *singer.*

Giuseppe Simoni sang at La Scala in Milan between 1786 and 1793. According to Haydn's *First London Notebook,* Simoni was a tenor singing in London in 1792. He had been engaged by Salomon and had sung earlier at the Théâtre de Monsieur in Paris. A portrait of him as Floreski in (presumably) Dejaure's *Lodoiska* was engraved by Johann Neidle, after Johann Ziterer, and published in Vienna.

Simonin. *See* VALLOUIS.

Simons. *See also* SIMMONS, SIMONDS, SYMONDS.

Simons, Mr *b. 1728?, dancer.*

Master Simons danced a Peasant in *The Savoyard Travelers* at Drury Lane Theatre on 9 November 1749. He was a Shepherd in *Acis and Galatea* on 27 November but was dropped from the cast two days later. The bills called

Civica Raccolta Stampe A. Bertarelli, Castello Sforzesco, Milan

GIUSEPPE SIMONI, as Floreski

engraving by Neidle, after Ziterer

him Simons rather than Master Simons on 27 and 29 November, so perhaps he had just reached his majority.

Simpcock. *See* SIMCOCK.

Simpkinson, Mr [*fl. 1778–1781*], *actor, singer.*

Mr Simpkinson (or Simkinson) sang in the *Macbeth* chorus at the Haymarket Theatre on 7 September 1778 and appeared fairly regularly during the following seasons at Covent Garden Theatre in the winters and the Haymarket in the summers. His first mention in the Covent Garden bills came on 17 April 1779, when he and others sang some catches and glees. His assignments were usually modest. He was Jupiter in *Midas* in the summer of 1779 at the Haymarket and in the fall at Covent Garden; in the spring of 1780 at Covent Garden he was a Gypsy in *The Norwood Gypsies,* and he repeated that part the following fall; he sang "We be three poor mariners" in *The Fête,* with Davies and Doyle, in the spring of 1781; and

he was the Ghost of Gaffer Thumb in *Tom Thumb* at the Haymarket on 22 and 24 August 1781. He was omitted from the *Macbeth* chorus on 12 November 1781 and may have left the London stage.

Simpson. *See* SIMSON.

Simpson, Mr [*fl. 1756*], *slack-wire dancer.*

The *Daily Advertiser* for 18 March 1756 reported that "Simpson, the slack wire performer, ran a sword into his leg at a performance at The Theatre, James St., near the Haymarket; he has recovered and will continue."

Simpson, Mr *d. 1758, actor, house servant.*

The Simpson who played Harry in *The Mock Doctor* at the Haymarket Theatre on 20 March 1733 was perhaps the Simpson who was Monsieur in *Love Makes a Man* at Lincoln's Inn Fields Theatre on 29 August 1735. He is probably also to be identified as the "Simson" who acted Dick in *The Confederacy* at Lincoln's Inn Fields on 14 March 1743 for the benefit of himself, Rogers, and Chetwood. Tickets could then be had of him "at Mr. Gill's a shoemaker, Basinghall Street."

After performing Aimwell in *The Stratagem* once and Horatio in *Hamlet* three times at the Haymarket Theatre from May to October 1744, Simpson was steadily at Drury Lane in the winter seasons, 1744–45 through 1756–57, though without attaining much celebrity. An 1807 obituary notice of his daughter Mary in the *Gentleman's Magazine* averred that he was a native of Aberdeen and that he "was Mr. G[arrick]'s assistant and particular friend." He and his wife Elizabeth, who also acted, were parents of at least six children, among whom were Mary, who performed later as Mrs Charles Fleetwood and then as Mrs White; John Joseph, who, after acting as a child and youth, became an army officer; and the actress Elizabeth, who married the manager Samuel Jerrold.

The Mr Simpson of this notice assumed his Drury Lane service in 1744–45 as the Bailiff in *The Committee* and followed that with Angus in *Macbeth,* Tyrrell in *Richard III,* Dr Bolus in *The Double Gallant,* Falconbridge in *King John,* a Senator in *Othello*, Burgundy in *King Lear*, Ernesto in *The Orphan*, Balthazar in *The Merchant of Venice*, the King of Fiddlers in *Chrononhotonthologos*, Dick in *The King and the Miller of Mansfield;* in 1745–46, Rosencrantz in *Hamlet*, Ben Budge in *The Beggar's Opera*, Gratiano in *Othello*, Father Thomas in *Measure for Measure*, Ernesto in *The Orphan*, John in *Sir Courtly Nice*, an Officer in *Twelfth Night*, Henroost in *The Humours of the Army*, and Gayless in *The Lying Valet;* in 1746–47, Lord Pride in *The Intriguing Chambermaid*, Phormio in *The Comical Lovers*, Myris in *All for Love*, Smirk in *The Man of Mode*, and the First Murderer in *Macbeth;* in 1747–48, Scale in *The Recruiting Officer*, Westmoreland in *Henry V,* and Buckram in *Love for Love;* in 1748–49, Welldo in *A New Way to Pay Old Debts*, the Second Watch in *The London Cuckolds*, and the Apothecary in *Romeo and Juliet;* and in 1749–50, Hubert in *King John*, the Lawyer in *Love's Last Shift*, Scrapeall in *The Squire of Alsatia*, the Dauphin in *Edward the Black Prince*, the Town Clerk in *Much Ado about Nothing*, Friendly in *The School Boy*, and Cabinet in *The Funeral.*

In 1750–51, Simpson added the Uncle in *The London Merchant*, Humphry in *The Conscious Lovers*, Jaques de Bois in *As You Like It*, Selim in *The Mourning Bride*, a Gentleman in *The Pilgrim*, Ratcliff in *Jane Shore*, Spinoza in *Venice Preserv'd*, and the Younger Brother in *Comus;* in 1751–52, Antonio in *Much Ado about Nothing*, Loveland in *Don Quixote in England*, the Physician in *King Lear*, Hali in *Tamerlane*, Bramble in *Eastward Hoe*, Gates in *Lady Jane Gray*, Surrey in *Henry VIII*, Phoenix in *The Distrest Mother*, Duke Frederick in *As You Like It*, and Freeman in *A Bold Stroke for a Wife;* in 1752–53, Ross in *Macbeth;* in 1753–54, Tom in *The Rehearsal* and Fenton in *The Merry Wives of Windsor;* in 1754–55, Titus Lartius in *Coriolanus* and an Officer in *Tancred and Sigismunda;* in 1755–56, a Steward in *All's Well that Ends Well;* and in 1756–57, some part unspecified in *The Author.*

On 5 May 1756 the prompter Cross noted in his journal: "Benefit for Mr Mrs Simson Their Son & Daughter." The family lived then and for several years in lodgings in Wild Passage, Wild Street, Lincoln's Inn Fields. Among the many insignificant, or at most secondary, parts which Simpson owned, the important role of Falconbridge stands out starkly.

Thomas Davies in his *Dramatic Miscellanies* gives the explanation for his being given the part: David Garrick, reviving *King John* after many years, on 20 February 1745, with himself in the title role, "was at a loss, for some time, to fix upon a Robert Falconbridge to set off his own figure; at last he picked out poor Simson, a Scotchman, a modest and honest man, but as feeble in person as he was in acting."

John Lee in *The Bath Comedians*, poked fun at the heroes Simpson was sometimes allowed to act in the provinces:

> *Now tremble, Sir, for very Fear-o,*
> *For here comes strutting S–p–n's Hero:*
> *In* Romeo, Jaffier, *and* Varanes,
> *He does his best to entertain us*

According to Lee he lacked "power" and was unfit for comedy. James Dibdin, in *The Annals of the Edinburgh Stage*, wrote that, on 11 June 1752, "Mr Simson, from Drury Lane, played Hamlet" at the Edinburgh house. Norma Armstrong found that he there added to his roles Blandford in *Oroonoko* on 4 July 1748 and Castalio in *The Orphan* on 2 July 1752.

According to British Library Additional MS 18586, the Simpson who had played Falconbridge at Drury Lane ("very meagre!") died in March 1758.

Simpson, Mr [*fl.* 1792–1809], *dancer, actor.*

Mr Simpson, a dancer and pantomime actor, seems first to have come into public notice in London on 2 October 1793, when the pantomime *Harlequin's Chaplet* was revived at Covent Garden Theatre. But payments to him totaling £7 15s. were recorded in the Drury Lane accounts on 14 and 28 January and 6 March 1792 for dancing in *Cymon* 31 nights at 5s. per night. Simpson never returned after that season to Drury Lane but was on the Covent Garden roster well into the nineteenth century. Among his known roles there were an Indian in *The Shipwreck*, Harlequin in *Harlequin's Treasure*, Harlequin in *Harlequin and Oberon*, Draco in *Oscar and Malvina*, Harlequin in *Harlequin's Medley*, Kildare in *The Round Tower*, Tasner in *The Magic Oak*, and a Servant in *The Votary of Wealth.*

At the theatre at Richmond, Surrey, in the summer of 1793 Simpson was a featured dancer. In the course of the pantomimes he leapt through "A Hoop of Daggers (Eight Feet High)." He was listed in the opera de ballet at the King's Theatre on 7 July 1796, when a benefit was given for the choreographer Charles-Louis Didelot. When Mme Rose took her benefit at the King's on 6 April 1797, he sustained the role Alcée in the ballet *Sapho et Phaon.* Simpson was employed at the Royal Circus, St George's Fields, in the summer of 1798, and for his benefit he introduced, in *Mirth's Medley; or, Harlequin at Home,* "A leap through a Hogshead of Water; a Flight across the Stage, from Balcony to Balcony; an Escape through a Cask of Fire," as well as his accustomed leap through the daggers. He also presented "the Dying and Skeleton Scenes," an offering not explained. He danced at Sadler's Wells during the summer-fall seasons of 1799 and 1800.

Scattered surviving bills show Simpson figuring in performances at the Royal Circus in spring, summer and fall from 1802 though 1805: on 16 August 1802, as King Ferdinand in "The splendid spectacle" *Gonsalvo de Cordova; or, The Conqest of Granada;* giving unspecified dances on 20 and 27 September 1802; as Harlequin Frolic in *The Rival Statues; or, Harlequin Humorist* on 11 April 1803; as Ascanio in *Louisa of Lombardy* on 25 April, following; as Harlequin in the *Grand Caledonian Pantomime* on 15 November 1803; as Harlequin in a "Comic Pantomime," unnamed, on 29 November following; as Harlequin in *Harlequin Woodcutter* on 5 November 1804; and as a Principal Character in *A Mogul Tale* on 3 June and Petrino in *Abellino; or, The Bravo's Bride,* at some date unknown in 1805. Simpson's name was in Sadler's Wells playbills as a dancer in 1806, 1808, and 1809. His address in 1798 and 1800 was given on benefit bills as No 14, Sweetings Alley, the Royal Exchange.

Simpson was depicted as Kildare, with John Follett as Maon, in *The Round Tower* in an engraving by W. C. Alvey that was published in 1797. That picture is reproduced in this *Dictionary,* 5: 318.

Simpson, Mrs *d.* 1769? *See* SIMPSON, ELIZABETH.

Simpson, Miss. *See also* JERROLD, MRS SAMUEL THE FIRST.

Simpson, Miss ₁*fl.* 1776–1786₁, *actress, singer, dancer.*

The Miss Simpson who was with Tate Wilkinson on the York circuit in 1776 was identified by Wilkinson in *The Wandering Patentee* as "daughter of Mr. Simpson, late of Drury Lane Theatre." Wilkinson remembered that "She had some promise, played Sylvia with a degree of approbation, [but] a year or two after she left me." She was, therefore, the daughter of the actress Elizabeth Simpson and her actorhusband (first name unrecorded) and the (evidently somewhat younger) sister of the performers John Joseph Simpson; of Mary Simpson, who became, first, the wife of the younger Charles Fleetwood and then Mrs White; and of Elizabeth, who married Samuel Jerrold. There were two other girls in the family, about whom nothing is known.

Our present Miss Simpson's London debut was, in fact, in the role of Sylvia in *Cymon* at Drury Lane on 17 January 1778, billed simply as a "Young Lady." The *Morning Chronicle* identified her on 19 January and informed its readers that she had acted at York and at Plymouth (where she had perhaps been during the two years after leaving York).

At Drury Lane for nine seasons, through 1785–86, Miss Simpson played chambermaids, serving wenches, and country maidens, and often, as time went on, some secondary ingenues, as a reward for her constancy. She then retreated to the provinces or to marriage. She seems to have been with the Richmond, Surrey, company in the summer of 1781, for the playbill of 1 September advertised her benefit. Her London roles, in the order they were added, were: in the spring of 1778, Phebe in *Belphegor;* in 1778–79, a part unspecified in *The Wonders of Derbyshire; or, Harlequin of the Peak,* a new pantomime by R. B. Sheridan, and Gillian in *The Quaker;* in 1779–80, Wilhelmina in *The Waterman* and a Country Girl in *The Elopement;* in 1780–81, Lady Charlotte in *High Life below Stairs,* a Shepherdess in *Cymon,* Nell in *The Camp,* Iras in *All for Love,* Bianca in *Catherine and Petruchio,* and Lucy Weldon in *Oroonoko;* in 1781–82, Gymp in *Bon Ton,* a Niece in *The Critic,* a Maid in Richard Tickell's new comic opera *The Carnival of Venice,* Dame Pliant in *The Alchemist,* Clara in *The Capricious Lovers,* Leonora in *Don Juan,* Mincing in *The Way of the World,* and the original Miss Melcomb in Frederick Pilon's comic opera *The Fair American;* in 1782–83, Sally in *False Delicacy,* Gipsy in *The Stratagem,* and some minor part in Tom King's new pantomime *The Triumph of Mirth;* in 1783–84, a Bacchant in *Comus,* Corinna in *The Citizen,* and a Chambermaid in *A Trip to Scotland;* in 1784–85, a Beggar in *The Ladies' Frolic;* and in 1785–86, a role unspecified in *Hurly-Burly.*

Simpson, C. H.   *b. 1771, pleasure-garden master of ceremonies.*

On 19 August 1833, C. H. Simpson took for himself what he assured his prospective patrons was the first benefit ever granted by Vauxhall Gardens. He then had printed and distributed a large benefit bill in which he advertised himself as "Master of the Ceremonies of the Royal Gardens, Vauxhall, upwards of Thirty-Six Years." This remarkable document bears a portrait of Simpson at the Gardens greeting visitors, attired as a typical dandy of the time of George IV.

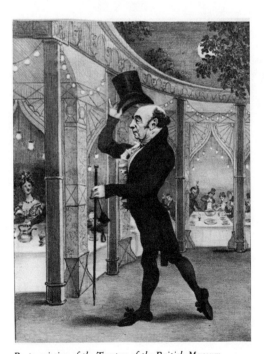

By permission of the Trustees of the British Museum

C. H. SIMPSON
by Gear

On the bill, in a rambling address to his patrons, Simpson gave some information about his life: he was then, he said, "in the Sixty-third Year of my Age." When he was 11 years old "the gallant Captain Sir James Wallace, who was a friend of my father, took me on board his ship the Warrior, 74 gun[s], as an acting Midshipman. . . ." He was honorably discharged at 13. "I very respectfully beg leave to make known, that I am one of the very few Survivors . . . of that bloody and furious battle that lasted from daylight in the Morning until dark, fought by Admiral Rodney in the West Indies, on the 12th of April, 1782, when the British Standard completely annihilated . . . the French Fleet. . . ."

When the Gardens closed for the season on 9 September 1833, Simpson announced his retirement and issued another bill, with an enlarged cut of his figure, in an affected posture of greeting—top hat raised from balding head, one foot extended delicately behind him, executing a courtesy of which he was evidently proud. For as he informs us, "I . . . very dutifully beg to make known that the immense Portrait of myself, in its proper Costume, so much admired at my Benefit, will be, for the last time, exhibited in variegated Lamps; and also, that my own figure, in Fire Works, will appear very beautiful, and bow as representing Life." And a clipping accompanying an announcement of still another of his "retirement" benefits, on 21 July 1834 (a copy of which, like copies of the first two bills, is now in the Minet Library of the Lambeth Library) makes much of his bow, the "celebrated fascinating attitude, when with the ease and dignity of the courtier he elevates his hat and inclines his head to a graceful angle with his body."

When, exactly, Simpson finally retired we do not know. The Minet Library bills show that he resumed his professional duties at Vauxhall in 1835.

Portraits of C. H. Simpson include:

1. Engraving by G. Cruikshank. Walking on stilts, raising hat, stick in right hand.

2. Engraving by G. Cruikshank. Full-length, walking in Vauxhall Gardens.

3. Engraving by R. Cruikshank. Full-length, standing, shaking hands with an officer, his colossal likeness in variegated lamps in background. Drawn in the Gardens on the night of his benefit, 19 August 1833.

C. H. SIMPSON
by G. Cruikshank

4. Lithograph engraving by J. W. Gear. Full-length, walking in the cafe at Vauxhall Gardens, raising his hat, stick in left hand. Published by J. W. Gear. Copies were engraved by G. E. Madeley on a music sheet, "What Think you of Simpson the Beau?," published by Collard & Collard; by "C. J. C." as a plate to the *Magazine of Curiosity and Wonder,* 7 January 1836; by an unknown artist, at the head of his address to the public on the occasion of his benefit on 19 August 1833.

Simpson, Edward   *d. 1664?, trumpeter.*

Edward Simpson was a trumpeter in the King's Music at £40 annually as of 22 September 1661. On 16 May 1664 he was replaced by John Crowther, Simpson (or Sympson) having died, probably very shortly before that date. It is certain that our subject was the Edward Simpson of St Martin-in-the-Fields whose estate was administered by his widow Isabella on 11 June 1664, for in the Lord Chamberlain's accounts on 1 April 1667 "Isabell" Simpson is cited as petitioning against the serjeant trumpeter and other trumpeters in the King's Musick, probably for money they owed her husband at his death.

Simpson, Elizabeth. *See also* INCHBALD, MRS JOSEPH *and* JERROLD, MRS SAMUEL THE FIRST.

Simpson, Mrs Elizabeth   ₁*fl. 1744–1774*₁,   *actress*

The actress of this account married Simpson, an actor (whose first name is unknown), and was the mother, by him, of a brood of at least six children. Among them were at least four performers: a daughter, acting as Miss Simpson, whose first name is not known; John Joseph; Elizabeth (who married Samuel Jerrold); and Mary (who married, successively, the younger Charles Fleetwood and a Mr White). (Mrs Elizabeth Simpson's first name was given in her signature to a letter in the *General Advertiser* of 18 November. Details of the family were supplied in the will drawn by her son John Joseph on 28 November 1765. Of all the baffling Simpsons [Simsons] she is perhaps the most difficult to disentangle from the others.)

Elizabeth was probably the Mrs Simpson who played Lady Bountiful in *The Stratagem*

(her husband was the Aimwell) and Dorcas in *The Mock Doctor* in a benefit performance at the Haymarket on 16 May 1744. She began to appear again, infrequently, at Drury Lane Theatre in 1748–49, acting a few roles of maids and eccentrics and appearing in pantomimes during most seasons, as Simpson or Simson, until the end of 1773–74. From 1752 through at least 1764 a Mrs Simpson displayed the Drury Lane actress's line of characters at Jacob's Wells Theatre, Bristol, every summer and was probably our subject. The Drury Lane actress's husband died in March 1758, and on the following 10 May a performance was given at Drury Lane as a "Benefit for Mrs Simson and 3 Children," according to the prompter Cross's diary.

Though a Mrs Simpson (or Simson) in a similar line of characters continued active virtually uninterruptedly through 1773–74, as stated, there are some troubling difficulties in trying to pin down an identity. First, Joseph Reed, in his usually reliable "Notitia Dramatica" manuscript in the British Library, states that Mrs Simpson "of Drury Lane Theatre" died about Christmas, 1769 ("She was niece to Old [John] Hippesley"). Second, administration of John Joseph Simpson's property was granted on 11 May 1770 "to his Mother Eliz. Simson, he having died in Madras, East Indies." Finally, the complete company list dated 9 February 1765, purportedly in Garrick's hand, lists contiguously *both* a "Mrs Simpson" at 4s. 2d. per diem (£1 5s. per week) *and* a "Mrs Simson" at 3s. 4d. (£1).

Very likely at Drury Lane for some period of time there were both Elizabeth and another Mrs Simpson (Simson). If the death-date of 1769 is veritable it cannot belong to Elizabeth Simpson, because of the will. Thus we do not have to distribute roles after that date, for they all belong to Elizabeth. But which ones before "Christmas 1769" are owned by the "other" Mrs Sim[p]son—if there was one—it is impossible to decide. Only one other paylist of the period can be cited—that of two years later, 24 January 1767—and that one listed only "Mrs Simpson" at £1 5s.

Simpson, George   *c. 1752–1795, actor, singer, dancer.*

George Simpson belonged to a large and prominent family of Roman Catholic farmers at Standingfield, near Bury St Edmunds, Suffolk. The names of most of his siblings have perished. One was the Elizabeth Simpson who later earned a degree of fame as Mrs Inchbald, both as an actress and as a writer of plays and novels. George is now an indistinct figure compared to her. But he did have a provincial theatrical career, and he played for a while in London.

In James Boaden's biography of his sister, Elizabeth Inchbald, George Simpson is mentioned several times. His early departure for a provincial stage career is said to have inspired Elizabeth's own attempt to win her way in the theatre. The family were fond of watching theatricals at Bury, and George, fired by the sight of those professionals, had left home to try their life. He played in a company at Norfolk in the spring of 1770, along with Joseph Inchbald, his sister's future husband. In January 1771 he married a provincial actress, Miss George. They were probably the people referred to by a notation in the *Committee Books* of the Norwich Theatre on 24 August 1772: "Ordd That Mr & Mrs Simpson be discharged."

According to W. S. Clark, in *The Irish Stage in the County Towns,* Simpson was at the Capel Street Theatre, Dublin, on 14 December 1773 and remained there during the 1773–74 season. Presumably his wife was with him, as she was when he turned up at the Theatre Royal, Shakespeare Square, in Edinburgh, under the management of West Digges in 1775. Only one of George Simpson's roles there is known: Malcolm in *Macbeth.* The Simpsons were at Edinburgh again in 1776 and back at Norwich in 1778 and 1779 (on 28 May 1779 it was "Agreed That Mr & Mrs Simpson's Salary be advanced to £2.12.6 p week").

Tate Wilkinson says in *The Wandering Patentee* only that the Simpsons were with him on the York circuit in 1781. But an excerpt which Sybil Rosenfeld has given us from Wilkinson's manuscript account book adds that on 26 December 1781 Simpson forfeited his week's salary for refusing to play a small part in *Duplicity.* The account book shows, further, that Simpson was with the York company in 1782 and 1783 and that in 1783 he had come from Edinburgh in late May.

Those sketchy facts are supplemented by the lengthy list of characters played by him at Edinburgh, as assembled by Norma Armstrong. The list shows that he was at the Theatre Royal, Shakespeare Square, from early January through early August in 1782, and from early January to mid-May in 1783, but was there only from January until late March in 1784. During those three seasons he played about 75 supporting roles, most of them inconsiderable, like Alonzo in *The Mourning Bride,* Bates in *The Gamester,* Charon in *Lethe,* the Cook in *The Devil to Pay,* Dick in *The Belle's Stratagem,* and Duke Frederick in *As You Like It* but with an occasional plum like Charles Dudley in *The West Indian.*

The two years of George Simpson's career following the Edinburgh experience are lost to us. But it seems highly likely, in view of his usual lines of roles, that he was the Simpson who turned up, with his wife, at the Windsor Castle Inn, Hammersmith, for five performances, on 28 and 30 June and 5, 7, and 10 July 1786 to play Sparkish in *The Country Girl,* the Taylor in *Catherine and Petruchio,* Sir Felix Friendly in *The Agreeable Surprise,* Patrick in *The Poor Soldier,* and Prompt in *The Heiress.* In December that year Simpson moved over to the Haymarket to join a hastily assembled company which, by special permission, gave three performances scattered over the following four months. On 18 December Simpson was Lord Randolph in *Douglas.* (In the afterpiece that night an *R.* Simpson was also playing.) On 8 January 1787 George Simpson played Dr Apozem in *The Devil upon Two Sticks,* and on 12 March Stockwell in *The West Indian.*

Doubtless the Mr and Mrs Simpson who were at the Red Lion Inn, Stoke Newington, that month were also Mr and Mrs George Simpson. Simpson was recorded as Sir Peter Teazle in *The School for Scandal* on 26 March, on the following night Dick in *The Miller of Mansfield* and Acasto in *The Orphan,* on 28 March Aladin in *Barbarossa,* on 29 March Tony Lumpkin in *She Stoops to Conquer* and Sir John Trotley in *Bon Ton,* and on 30 March Coupée in *The Virgin Unmask'd* and Don Diego in *The Padlock.*

On 30 April 1787 Simpson was again concerned in a special Haymarket performance, acting Doctor Cantwell in *The Hypocrite* and Freeman in *The Musical Lady.* In July George Simpson (now identified by first name in the bills) turned up in the ever-changing group of performers persuaded by John Palmer to share the uncertain fortunes of his new Royalty Theatre on Wellclose Square, London. We can record only three roles for Simpson from the few surviving bills of the Royalty: on 3 July 1787 he was a Valet in *Hobson's Choice,* a Chinese Servant in *Harlequin Mungo* at some time in November 1787, and (as a dancer) in some unspecified part in Reeve's panto-drama *The Deserter of Naples* on 25 February 1788. Inasmuch as the bill claimed that performance was the thirty-ninth repetition of the piece, it is likely that Simpson had been at the Royalty all season, until that point. But on 9 April 1788 Simpson was again at the Haymarket, playing, for the benefit of the actresses Mrs Greville and Mrs Hunter, Lord Trinket in *The Jealous Husband* and Kecksey in *The Irish Widow.* We believe that the actor who played Jacob Gawkey in *The Chapter of Accidents* and afterward spoke the monologue *Jacob Gawkey's Ramble through Bath* at the Haymarket on 2 June 1794 was also George Simpson. His wife played Bridget in the afterpiece, and it was their benefit night. (The latter identification is strengthened by the fact that three of the performers were said to be from the theatres at Edinburgh, Dublin, and Norwich, places with which the George Simpsons were, as we have seen, closely associated.)

(*The London Stage 1660–1800* has given all of the London performances cited above—excepting only those at the Royalty, which it has not listed at all—to the British provincial and American actor John Simpson. But the Simpson we have been following through the 1780s was accompanied by a wife who acted. *John Simpson did not marry Juliana Frisby Westray until June 1792, until which date she had acted as Mrs Westray. Westray had died in 1789. There is no evidence that John Simpson ever acted in London, and it is practically certain that Juliana Frisby Westray Simpson never acted there as Mrs Simpson.*)

The 1794 performance by George Simpson was his last known London appearance. The British Library's Additional MS 18586 declares that Simpson, "Mrs Inchbald's brother," was "Killed in [a] duel [in] Hamburg Jan 1795." He was 42 years old, added the *Thespian Dictionary* (1805). The *Norwich Mercury* of 9 December 1797 reported that his widow married a Mr Thomas "of the Southampton Cavalry Corps" in 1797. She died in 1802 and was buried in Portsmouth Cathedral on 14 February 1802, according to the burial register.

Simpson, Mrs George, née George, later Mrs Thomas *d. 1802, actress, singer.*

The provincial actress Miss George married the actor George Simpson, a brother of the actress-playwright Elizabeth Inchbald, in January 1771, according to James Boaden in his memoir of Mrs Inchbald. In the summer of 1772 George Simpson and his wife were at the Norwich playhouse. They were at the Capel Street Theatre, Dublin, in 1773 and at Smock Alley, Dublin, in and after February 1774. The couple were in Edinburgh in 1775 and 1776. There Mrs Simpson acted the following parts: Belinda in *All in the Wrong,* Celia in *As You Like It,* Charlotte Rusport in *The West Indian,* Cherry in *The Beaux' Stratagem,* Clarinda in *The Suspicious Husband,* Colombine in *Harlequin in England,* Jenny in *The Deserter,* Lavinia in *The Fair Penitent,* Leonora in *The Padlock,* Lucinda in *Love in a Village,* Maria in *The Citizen,* Miss Biddy in *Miss in Her Teens,* Miss Bridgemore in *The Fashionable Lover,* Miss Hardcastle in *She Stoops to Conquer,* Peggy in *The Gentle Shepherd,* the title role in *Polly Honeycomb,* a "Singing Witch" in *Macbeth,* and Valeria in *The Roman Father.*

The Simpsons returned to Norwich again in 1778 and 1779 where in the former year they earned jointly £2 5s. a week and in the latter advanced to £2 12s. 6d. Hannah More found Mrs Simpson's presentation of Fanny in *The Clandestine Marriage* most pleasing when she acted it with the Norwich company in June 1777. The couple joined Tate Wilkinson on the York circuit in 1781–82 according to *The Wandering Patentee:* "The pretty Mrs. Simpson (by [West] Digges always called the *Diamond in Cotton*) was engaged for the winter, 1781: She made her first appearance on Friday, October the 26th, at Hull, in Sigismunda, and was received with great good greeting." Her husband was also at Hull, but Wilkinson thought more of the wife.

Simpson, and presumably his wife, alternated during 1782, 1783, and 1784, between a season in Edinburgh beginning early in January and ending anywhere from March to August, and trouping with Wilkinson in the summers. (They therefore could not have been the Simpsons whom Arnold Hare lists in the company at Orchard Street, Bath, in 1782–83 and 1783–84, though our subject played there often later in her career. We believe George to have been the Simpson who was at Windsor Castle Inn, Hammersmith, in the summer of 1786 and at the Haymarket briefly in the winter of 1786–87, but there survives no record of his wife's acting at those places. Seemingly they were the Simpsons who performed at the Red Lion Inn, Lordship Road, Stoke Newington, from 12 through 31 March 1787, she playing Maria in *The School for Scandal,* Serina in *The Orphan,* an Attendant in *Barbarossa,* Miss Neville in *She Stoops to Conquer,* Lady Minikin in *Bon Ton,* Dorinda in *The Beaux' Stratagem,* and Bridget in *The Chapter of Accidents.*

A Mrs Simpson was in the Bath and Bristol company in the seasons 1787–88 through 1790–91 and was advertised "from Bath" at Margate in July 1792. She was certainly our subject, inasmuch as Tate Wilkinson, remarking our Mrs Simpson's presence in his company opening at Hull in November 1792, wrote:

That lady was from the Bath stage, where she was a great favourite, and so established in that comfortable and elegant situation, that I rather am inclined to think she was very wrong to quit it. . . . Her person [was] . . . little but delicate in the extreme; She is a very pleasing elegant actress, both in tragedy and comedy, but not powerful or great . . . ; but she is always sure to gain the good word of gentlemen and ladies, and all the parts of a good-natured theatre.

Kathleen Barker cites Mrs Simpson's performances of "heroines" at Bristol in those same years. Mrs Simpson was still at York in October of 1793 when her mother Mrs George died. We believe that the Simpsons who on 2 June 1794 hired the Haymarket for a benefit night and induced actors from Edinburgh, Dublin, and York to play for them were surely the George Simpsons. She played one of her old parts, Bridget in *The Chapter of Accidents.*

George Simpson was killed in a duel in Hamburg in January 1795. Mrs Simpson continued to act in the provinces. In 1797 she married a Mr Thomas "of the Southampton Cavalry Corps" according to the *Norwich Mercury* on 9 December 1797. She was performing as Mrs Thomas at the Portsmouth theatre when she died in February 1802, of a "paralytic stroke," according to the *Thespian Dictionary* (1802). She was buried on 14 February in Portsmouth Cathedral.

Simpson, James *1749–1800, violist, violinist.*

James Simpson, performer on the viola and violin, belonged to a family of musicians, instrument-makers, and music publishers. Charles Humphries and William Smith, in *Music Publishing in the British Isles,* list people who must have been Simpson's immediate forebears.

John Simpson, probably James's grandfather, was a musical instrument maker, engraver, and publisher at the sign of the Viol and Flute in Swithen's (or Swithin's, later Sweeting's) Alley opposite the Royal Exchange from 1734 to about 1749, when, presumably, he died. His widow Ann Simpson carried on the business in her own name until her marriage with John Cox, probably in 1751, and then jointly with Cox. A son of John and Ann Simpson, James Simpson (who must have been the father of James the violist), ran the shop in Sweeting's Alley from about December 1764 until 1767, when he took his elder son John into partnership. Presumably James the violist, who we know was born in 1749, was too young at the time for a partnership. But, also presumably, he was the "James junior" whom Humphries and Smith cite as a music seller in Sweeting's Alley c. 1799. He published and sold there, at about that date, *Unless with my Amanda blest. A Favorite Song. Composed by S. Porter. The words by the celebrated James Thompson* [*sic*].

When James Simpson was recommended to the Royal Society of Musicians on 7 July 1776 he had "studied and practiced music for more than 7 years," was married, and had two children. His admission papers are missing from his file, so his age is not stated, but other documents present show him to have been born in 1749, and thus 27 at the time of his induction. According to Mollie Sands, in *The Eighteenth-Century Pleasure Gardens at Marylebone,* Simpson played concertos at the gardens as early as 1776.

Simpson's performance career, like that of

many musicians, was both varied and obscure. William C. Smith in *The Italian Opera in London* lists him as playing for the opera at both the Pantheon and the Haymarket in 1791. Charles Burney lists him among the "tenors" (violas) in the Handel Memorial Concerts at Westminster Abbey and the Pantheon in May and June 1784. The Minute Books of the Royal Society of Musicians show that he was directed by the Governors to play at the annual benefit concerts at St Paul's Cathedral in 1789, 1793, 1795, and 1796. Doane's *Musical Directory* of 1794 added to his credits performances at Ranelagh Gardens, called him an executant on the violin as well as the viola, and gave his address as Rosemary Lane.

The bills show that he also found employment with the Ashleys in Covent Garden spring oratorios in 1792, 1794, 1795, 1796, and 1797. But that he was underemployed is certain. The Minute Books of the Society contain a petition for financial relief dated 5 December 1795 in which he states that he "is a married man, 46 yrs. of age and by being deprived of his only winters engagement the Italian opera, . . . he is reduced to extreme distress. The only support he has had for sometime past has arisen from the Sale of a few necessaries which are exhausted. . . ." He was granted 15 guineas for temporary relief. On 3 July 1796, his possessions about to be seized for nonpayment of rent, he was allowed four guineas per month. On 3 February 1799, having suffered an accident, he was granted four guineas for medicines. On 2 February 1800 Mary Simpson informed the Governors that her husband James had died. She was granted £8 for his funeral and a widow's pension of £2 12s. 6d. per month provided that she produce their marriage certificate.

Mary Simpson survived her husband James for many years, drawing her pension and being given several special donations. A notation of 3 September 1837 in the Minute Books of the Society states that she had recently died and £8 had been paid for her funeral. Perhaps James and Mary Simpson's son was the James Clement Simpson, "Box Street: Professor of Music," who with his wife Mary Ann appeared at St Paul, Covent Garden, on 8 August 1834 to christen their son Gustavus Alphonso, born on 24 July.

Simpson, ₁John?₁ ₁*fl. 1707?–1708*₁, *bill carrier.*

The Mr Simpson cited in the Coke papers at Harvard as a bill carrier at the Queen's Theatre on 8 March 1708 at 4s. daily may have been John Simpson (or Sympson) who testified on 22 August 1707 in a case brought by Lord Tunbridge against the opera manager Owen Swiney. Tunbridge had taken umbrage at Swiney, and on 15 August when Swiney was entering the Queen's Theatre, he was accosted by two gentlemen who drew their swords without provocation. Swiney, according to Simpson, did not draw his sword but went inside the theatre and avoided a scuffle.

Simpson, Mrs John, Juliana, née Frisby, earlier Mrs Anthony Westray *d. 1836, actress.*

According to the *Miscellanea Genealogica et Heraldica,* Juliana Frisby was married to Anthony Westray on 18 September 1777. The anonymous "lady" who was said to be making her first appearance on any stage, in the title role Jane Shore at the Haymarket Theatre on 9 September 1788, was identified by the *European Magazine* for September as Mrs Westray. The critic for the magazine felt that, inasmuch as he was unable to hear her when she spoke, he was unable either to praise or condemn her. If she had hoped by that late-summer appearance to be hired by one of the patent theatres preparing to open their winter seasons she was disappointed. She was in fact one of those suppliants who came on only once in London and then departed permanently to the provinces.

Mrs Westray's husband Anthony had died on 1 May 1789, says the *Miscellanea.* He was buried at Lambeth, so the Westrays had probably been living in London. It is perhaps reasonable to suppose that Juliana had taken to the stage because of her husband's illness. He does not seem to have acted, but the couple had produced three daughters, all actresses later on.

After her London rebuff Juliana Westray was at Brighton in the fall of 1789 and from about 15 February until June 1790 at Manchester. She was said to be from Manchester when she came to the York circuit in 1790. But Porter, in his *History of the Theatres of Brighton,* says that Mrs Westray was present when on 13 July

1790 Joseph Fox opened Brighton's Duke Street Theatre, along with Hodgkinson and others whose paths Juliana was later to cross in America. According to the *Miscellanea,* she married the actor John Simpson at Devizes on 2 June 1792. The *Hibernian Journal* recorded a Crow Street, Dublin, debut for the couple on 3 December 1792, when they were said to be from Bath. The *Thespian Magazine* for October 1793 reported them as having been in late summer at the Windsor Theatre advertised as "from the Dublin theatre."

Very likely Mrs Simpson accompanied her husband to Bath and Bristol in 1794–95 and 1795–96. In the fall of 1796 the Boston, Massachusetts, manager C. S. Powell recruited both the Simpsons and her daughters by Westray—Juliana, Eleanora, and Elizabeth Ann (the first girl was later well known as Mrs William Burke Wood and the second as Mrs John Darley; the third went under the name of her first husband Thomas C. Villiers and later acted as Mrs William Twaits). The family of five acted successfully in Boston from the opening night, 26 December 1796, through the next summer season. (Only a scattering of the roles of any of them has been preserved, though it is known that Mrs Simpson played Mrs Rackett in *The Belle's Stratagem,* with her husband playing Hardy, on that opening night.) Seilhamer found a bill placing the family at Newport, Rhode Island, on 22 November 1797, with Simpson as Toby Allspice, his wife as Lady Sorrel, Juliana as Clementina, and Eliza as Fanny in *The Way to Get Married.*

The Simpsons and Westrays again moved as a family, this time to New York, in the fall of 1797 for the last season of the old John Street Theatre. The only role which G. C. D. Odell preserved in the *Annals* for Mrs John Simpson that year was the third Witch in *Macbeth.* She returned to Park Street in 1798–99 and was engaged in New York, with one daughter still to care for, when her husband John died of yellow fever at age 42 on 13 October 1801. She played in Providence, Rhode Island, in the summer of 1803, was with Hallam's company in Albany also in 1803, was again at Providence in the summer of 1805, and went back to Park Street for the winter seasons of 1805–6 through 1807–8. She is traceable to the Placide-Green company at Charleston in 1808–9 and Richmond in 1809; to the Fed-

eral Street Theatre, Boston, in 1810; to Alexandria, Virginia, in 1815, to Baltimore in 1822, and to Philadelphia in 1823. Some of her known parts were: Queen Eleanor in *King John,* Lady Capulet in *Romeo and Juliet,* Mrs Maggs in *The London Hermit,* Mrs Scatter in *Cheap Living,* the Marchioness in *The Italian Monk,* Dame Harrowby in *The Poor Gentleman,* The Countess in *Modern Magic,* Dame Freeland in *Too Many Cooks,* Mrs Glastonbury in *Who Wants a Guinea?,* Mrs O'Dennis in *Julia,* Mrs Reference in *The Will for the Deed,* the Hostess in 1 *Henry IV,* the Old Lady in *Mr. H.,* Lady Litigious in *Arbitration,* Mrs Moreen in *Town and Country,* and Lady Esther in *The Secret.*

According to the *Miscellanea Genealogica,* she was buried at St Stephen's in Philadelphia on 8 February 1836.

The London Stage identifies the Mr and Mrs Simpson who performed at the Red Lion Inn, Stoke Newington, in 1787 as John and Juliana Simpson, an error repeated in the *Index to the London Stage 1660–1800.* But Juliana, as we have seen, was Mrs Westray in 1787, did not begin to perform until 1788, and was not married to Simpson until 1792. It may be that Juliana was John's second wife. But there is no evidence for that, and no proof that he ever acted in London.

Simpson, John Joseph   *d. c. 1770, actor, dancer.*

John Joseph Simpson was one of six children of the actress Elizabeth Simpson and her husband, also an actor, whose first name is not known. John's siblings included the Miss Simpson who acted in Plymouth and York in 1776 and in London in 1778; Mary, afterwards acting successively as Mrs Charles Fleetwood and Mrs White; and Elizabeth, also a performer, who married Samuel Jerrold.

John Joseph accompanied his parents to Edinburgh in 1752 but was recorded in only one role there, the Page in *The Orphan,* on 2 July. It may have been his debut. He came on at Drury Lane Theatre as a Page in *Love Makes a Man* on 8 November 1752, his parents and at least one sister being members of the company that season. He played similar juvenile walk-ons his first few seasons, being awarded more mature and more important roles as his age and experience grew. His other parts during the eight winter seasons he remained at

Drury Lane included, in the order he assumed them: in 1752–53, some character unspecified in *The Genii*, the Duke of York in *Richard III*, and Oberon in *The Oracle* (on 7 May 1753, when he shared a benefit with his mother and father). In 1753–54, he added Prince Arthur in *King John* and Robin in *The Merry Wives of Windsor*; in 1754–55, Tom in *Tom Thumb* and Fribble in *Miss in Her Teens*; in 1755–56, Donalbain in *Macbeth* and Prince Edward in *Richard III*. On 5 May 1756 he danced a louvre and minuet with one of his sisters. The prompter Cross wrote in his diary: "Benefit for Mr Mrs Simson [*sic*] Their Son & Daughter." In 1756–57, he acted the Second Spirit in *Comus*, Aminadab in *A Bold Stroke for a Wife*, and the original Bolgolam in Garrick's lamentable farce for juvenile actors, *Lilliput*; and in 1758–59, some part in *Mercury Harlequin*. He added nothing new in 1757–58 or 1759–60.

On 10 May 1758, the family's father having died in March, a benefit had been given for Mrs Simpson and three of her children, and again Master Simpson and his sister had danced.

At the end of the season 1759–60, Master Simpson disappeared from sight. He evidently joined the army in his teens, for by the time he made his will on 28 November 1765 he was styled "John Joseph Simpson of Craven St., Gentleman, lieutenant in the 95th Regt. [of] ffoot." Very likely the will was made in anticipation of his being sent out to India. Administration of his property was granted "his mother Eliz[abeth] Simson," on 11 May 1770, "he having died in Madras, East Indies." To his mother and five sisters, to Samuel Marsh, and to Mr Simpson of Gray's Inn he left a guinea apiece for mourning rings and "to Miss Elizabeth Sale, a mourning ring to be made under the particular direction of my mother." The rest of his estate, not itemized, was to go to his mother, then after her death to Marsh, an executor for his sisters Elizabeth and Mary.

Simpson, Mary, later Mrs Charles Fleetwood and then Mrs ₍Edward?₎ White *d. 1807, actress, dancer.*

Mary Simpson (sometimes Simson) was one of the eldest of at least six children of the London and provincial actor Simpson (first name unknown) and of his wife Elizabeth, who also acted. Mary's documented siblings were

the Miss Simpson who played at Drury Lane from the spring of 1778 through 1785–86; the actor and soldier John Joseph Simpson (d. c. 1770); and Elizabeth Simpson, who became the first Mrs Samuel Jerrold. Nothing is known of the other children.

An obituary notice in the *Gentleman's Magazine* for February 1807 asserted that Mary had been "one of the infant pupils of the celebrated Garrick." That probably means that she was the Miss Simpson who was first noticed in the Drury Lane playbills on 7 May 1753, as Cynthia in the afterpiece *The Oracle*, with her brother John Joseph as Oberon, the piece "To conclude with a *Minuet* by the two principal characters of the Farce." The occasion was a "Benefit for Simson Mrs Simson and Master Simson," according to the diary of Cross the prompter. Mary was doubtless too young for consideration as a recipient. But it was probably not her first appearance, even in that character, for on the previous 24 March *The Oracle* had also been given, with "The characters by Children." In 1753 the family lived "in Wild-Passage, Wild Street, near Lincoln's Inn Fields."

Mary's parents were both in the Drury Lane company and, indeed, her father was called an "assistant" and special favorite of Garrick in the obituary cited above. Thus she had sufficient tutelage and encouragement. She was brought along slowly, dancing with her brother (when her parents or others required juvenile novelty at a benefit) and playing children's parts of slightly increasing length until she arrived at puberty.

The known roles of Mary Simpson at Drury Lane (after Cynthia) in the order added were: in 1753–54, the little Milliner in *The Suspicious Husband*; in 1754–55, Miss Biddy in *Miss in Her Teens* (once); and in 1756–57, a Page in *The Orphan* and Lady Flimnap in Garrick's trifle called *Lilliput* (her brother was Bolgolam). In March 1758 Mary's father died and on 10 May following a benefit performance was given at Drury Lane "for Mrs Simpson and 3 Children" according to the prompter's diary. Mary and her brother danced a minuet and louvre and spoke an epilogue together. In the season of 1758–59 she added Gipsy in *The Stratagem* and the title role in *Tom Thumb* and in 1759–60 some part unspecified in *Every Woman in Her Humour* and Prince Edward in *Richard III*. She was apparently allowed to step out of juvenile retirement to play Charlotte in *The Mock Doctor* on 31 May 1763 for the benefit of "the Distress'd Actors who formerly belong'd to the theatre."

Mary was off the stage between 1763 and 1766. On 10 December 1766 she made her adult debut, billed only as "A Young Gentlewoman" when she played Violante in *The Wonder! A Woman Keeps a Secret,* opposite the Don Felix of Cautherley, Garrick's protégé and perhaps his son. (The part was not that night played by Garrick himself as the *Gentleman's Magazine* long afterward said it was. Nor could she have been just fourteen years old, as it also claimed.) In the few short months after her adult debut as Violante in December 1766 Mary added Bridget in *Every Man in His Humour,* Miss Godfrey in *The Lyar,* Lucinda in *The Conscious Lovers,* Serina in *The Orphan,* Phoebe in *As You Like It,* and one "heavy" role, Parisatis in *The Rival Queens.* We have no record of her roles in the provinces.

Mary Simpson acted at Drury Lane Theatre under her maiden name only until the end of the 1767–68 season and then departed. At some later date she married Charles Fleetwood, an actor and a son of the Charles Fleetwood who had been a patentee of Drury Lane. There is some question as to whether she was his first wife or his second. He seems to have left the acting profession, and perhaps so did she for a time, as there is no record of a Mrs Fleetwood of her generation. He is said to have gone to India in 1769, and the *Morning Chronicle* on 7 July 1773 reported that he was again performing, in Madras. By some accounts he died in India, but his death may be confused with that of Mary's brother John Joseph Simpson, a captain in the army, who certainly died at Madras in 1769 or 1770.

At any rate, Mary Simpson Fleetwood married, apparently about 1791, an actor named White who performed in the provinces and perhaps briefly in London. We are unable to determine whether or not they were the couple named White acting with Thornton's company at Newbury, Berkshire, in 1792, or (Mrs White only) at St Albans in November 1792, or at Stowmarket, Suffolk, in April 1793. The name White is ubiquitous in the provincial bills. Our actress and her second husband may have been the Edward Whites who were at

Norwich at various times from 1794 to 1800, and/or the White (he alone, apparently) at Edinburgh from February to July 1802. The Edward Whites had a son who acted as Master White at Norwich in April 1799, when he was five years old. Edward White died in December 1808 in Edinburgh, according to a checklist supplied to us by Alick Williams of Norwich.

Mrs White had died on 22 January 1807. She was described in the obituary cited above as having been married to White for 16 years and as being a member of the Belfast company.

Simpson, R. [*fl. 1786*], *actor.*

A performer billed as R. Simpson played the Cook in the afterpiece *The Lying Valet* in a specially licensed performance at the Haymarket Theatre on 18 December 1786. He may have been the Simpson—without an initial—who played Lord Randolph in *Douglas* that night, but he probably was not. The *Index to the London Stage* has awarded roles at the Haymarket on 8 January and 12 March 1787 to R. Simpson. We believe the actor on those dates was George Simpson. There appears no reason to assign a series of small parts at Drury Lane Theatre ten years later to R. Simpson, as the *Index* has done. The playbills read only "Simpson."

Simpson, Redmond *c. 1730–1787, oboist, kettledrummer.*

Redmond Simpson was born about 1730 (if we judge from his age—57—at his death in 1787). Nothing is known of his parentage or his musical education. But many notices of his professional activities remain to demonstrate that he was, as his brief obituary in the *Gentleman's Magazine* for February 1787 said, "for many years the first performer on the hautboy in this kingdom." He was also said to have been early in life a member of the band of a regiment of foot guards.

Simpson entered the royal musical establishment probably about 1749, according to an ambiguous document in the Lord Chamberlain's accounts. The first record we have of his performance is the one that Deutsch cites in his *Handel,* playing in the *Messiah* at the Foundling Hospital in May 1754. When the royal music was confirmed by the Lord

Chamberlain in 1759 he was listed as a kettle-drummer.

From that year Simpson was also a member of the band at Covent Garden Theatre. For the following quarter of a century he was featured there on dozens of occasions as a soloist. At various times he contributed his services to benefits, like that for "Ferdinand Tenducci, musician, arrested for debt and . . . in the King's Bench [prison] for eight months," on 28 January 1761 at the Great Room in Dean Street, Soho. Simpson played solos in oratorios at the Haymarket Theatre on 13 November 1764, on 19 February 1765, and on 10 February and 10 March 1769.

In 1761 Simpson had been one of the entourage accompanying Princess Charlotte from the Continent before her marriage to George III, and from shortly thereafter he was a member of the Queen's Chamber Band. He was so described in *Mortimer's London Directory* (1763), which placed his residence in "Brewer-street, Golden-square." In 1767–68 his salary at Covent Garden was 10s. 6d. per week. That season he was engaged in a feud with Charles Dibdin, reasons for which are now obscure. On 24 April 1770 his address was stated to be in Russell Street when he was admitted to the livery and made free of the Worshipfull Company of Musicians. When he gave a deposition in the 1770 theatrical squabble between Colman and Powell on the one side and Rutherford and Harris on the other, over the management of Covent Garden, he had been "8 years in the theatre, 7 of which he [had] been director of music."

A document among the Lord Chamberlain's records shows Simpson to have been a member of the opera band at the King's Theatre in 1783–84. He was assistant to Joah Bates in organizing the great Handel Memorial Concerts at Westminster Abbey and the Pantheon in May and June of 1784.

Simpson had joined the Royal Society of Musicians on 1 January 1758. He was prominent enough in the Society's affairs to be a Governor in 1785 and chairman of that body in February of that year.

Simpson died on 23 January 1787 and was buried on 2 February in the North Cloister of Westminster Abbey. He had married Elizabeth Dubourg, daughter of Matthew Dubourg the celebrated violinist, on 22 September 1753,

but apparently they had become estranged. His will was signed on 4 July 1786 at his residence in King Street, Westminster and proved on 27 January 1787. It made James Galloway of Cumberland House and Ellis Needham of Pimlico executors of an estate that included "the sum of two thousand pounds reduced three per cent Bank Annuities," the income of which was to benefit Simpson's wife "now living in Union Street, Westminster." May Elizabeth Douglas, wife of Archibald Douglas, Esq, of Mecklenburg Street, Dublin, was residuary legatee. She was, however, to receive the dividends from an investment of the sum of £700. Mrs Maria Kirkman, widow of Simpson's "late friend" Alderman John Kirkman of London, was to receive the income from another sum of £700, and Mrs May Bourke, "wife of John Bourke of Token House Yard Lothbury in the City of London," the income from a third £700. Other bequests were: £200 to Mrs Mary Galloway, wife of James Galloway; £100 in stocks to Simpson's niece Helen, wife of Captain Rush of Galway, £200 to another niece, Elizabeth Hickey; £100 to the physician of George III, Sir Richard Jebb, Simpson's "worthy ffriend"; and £100 each to James Madden, to William Sharp, "surgeon of the Old Jewry," to Nathan Drake, "colourman in Long Acre," and to the executors.

To "Doctor Samuel Arnold Organist and Composer to his Majesty" Simpson left "all the Manuscript and printed Musick in the closet of my first floor one pair of stairs" to be sold to satisfy the creditors of his late friend Edward Toms, Sergeant Trumpeter, whose executor Simpson had been. Evidently that music had belonged to Toms, for Simpson left all of his own music and his instruments, "to my worthy ffriend William Page Esquire of Tillichery in the East Indies."

Redmond Simpson had a large collection of portraits, including Handel's by Hudson, which, with others, he gave to the Royal Society of Musicians.

Simpson, Strangeways [*fl. c. 1708–1720*], *violinist.*

Mr Simpson petitioned to play violin in the operas at the Queen's Theatre about 1708 for £1 nightly, but, like other musicians who asked for outrageous fees, he had to settle for far less: 8*s*. nightly or £30 annually. He was named in a number of documents among the Coke papers at Harvard; sometimes he was listed as a second violinist, sometimes as a first, and by about 1713 his salary was up to 10*s*. nightly. The Simpson referred to in the documents was evidently Strangeways Simpson, who on 23 June 1712 signed a receipt. In the Portland papers at Nottingham, Simpson is listed in February 1720 as a second violinist in the Academy of Music opera orchestra at £40.

Simpson, Thomas [*fl.* 1687?–1704], actor, manager.

Thomas Simpson is listed in *The London Stage* as a member of the United Company at the Drury Lane and Dorset Garden theatres in 1687–88, though he may not have joined the troupe until 23 May 1688, when he was officially sworn in. No roles are known for Simpson until after the company split in 1695. He remained with the manager Christopher Rich at Drury Lane (and, for spectacle shows, Dorset Garden), his first known part being Macquaire in *Bonduca* in September 1695. He was Hottman in *Oroonoko* in November, the King in *Agnes de Castro* and the King in Settle's *Philaster* in December, Curio in *Neglected Virtue* in mid-February 1696, Mufti in Pix's *Ibrahim* in late May, and Trusty in *The Cornish Comedy* in June.

Before the end of the century he was also seen as Bull in *The Relapse*, Montano in *The Triumphs of Virtue*, Seleucus in *The Humorous Lieutenant*, Annius Minutianus in *Caligula*, Don Leon in *The Campaigners*, and the Duke of Norfolk in *Richard III*. In the early 1700s he acted the Governor of Segovia in *The Pilgrim*, Armando in *The Perjured Husband*, the Governor in *Love Makes a Man*, Du Law in *The Unhappy Penitent*, Lord Bellamy in *Sir Harry Wildair*, Neoptolemus in *The Virgin Prophetess*, Meroan in *The Generous Conqueror*, Mendez in *All for the Better*, and Uberto in *The Patriot*. A curious warrant issued by the Lord Chamberlain on 23 February 1702 swore Tobias Thomas Simpson and other players as members of Rich's troupe. That would appear to be a confusing of two actors—Tobias Thomas and Thomas Simpson; in any case, the warrant was canceled.

No new parts are known for Simpson after December 1702, but on 24 August 1703 he was co-manager with Pinkethman and Bullock of a booth at Bartholomew Fair, where they presented *Jephtha's Rash Vow*. Morley in *Memoirs of Bartholomew Fair* has the same partners presenting the same work at the same fair in 1704.

Simpson, Thomas [*fl.* 1699–1706], acrobat.

Thomas Brown wrote to George Moult on 12 September 1699, commenting on how much like the late summer fairs the entertainments at the regular playhouses had become. He supposed that soon "we shall be entertain'd here with all sorts of sights and shows, as, jumping thro' a hoop; (for why should not that be as proper as Mr Sympson's vaulting upon the wooden-horses?) dancing upon the high ropes, leaping over eight men's heads[?] . . ." and so on. Thomas Frost in *Circus Life* in 1875 cited a bill of 1702 for Husbands's booth at one of the fairs and gave Simpson's Christian name as Thomas. *The London Stage* lists Simpson as at Bartholomew Fair on 27 August 1706. There was vaulting "By Simpson, that most celebrated Master, the famous Vaulter, who Performs with Mr Penkethman at the Request of the Quality, being lately arriv'd from Italy."

Sims. *See also* SIMMS *and* SYMMS.

Sims, [George?] *c*. 1748–1823, actor, theatrical agent.

For his own benefit at the Haymarket Theatre on 15 October 1792 a Mr Sims acted William in *The Country Girl* in a specially licensed performance by a pickup company. Tickets were "to be had of Sims, the Theatrical Register, Wrekin Tavern, Broad Court, Long Acre." That was the single performance of Sims in London.

The biographical sketch of Sarah Sims, singer and actress, in *Authentic Memoirs of the Green Room* (1806), called her the daughter "of a respectable hair-dresser and perfumer, who some years since kept the Crown and Thistle in Russel-Court, a kind of Theatrical House of Call, much frequented by Performers, Country-Managers, and persons of a theatrical turn in general." The account further states that "The moment she secured the means of competence, with a proud spirit of laudable aspiring, she prevailed upon her father to relinquish his [public] house in Russel-court." Evidently Sims relinquished it to his son, for E. L. Blanchard, in an article quoted by Cuthbert Bede in *Notes and Queries* for May 1872, asserted that "'The Harp,' in Little Russel Street, was long notorious as the resort of poor and disengaged actors. Here Sims the elder flourished for many years. He was succeeded by his son, a tablet to whose memory may still be seen in the parlour of the aforesaid hostelry." No doubt the Crown and Thistle changed its name along with its management. (The son, William, who died on 9 February 1841 at age 54, was facetiously called "Sir William" and referred to as "Lord Mayor." It is possible that he had been the Master Sims who had performed at Birmingham in the summers of 1798 and 1799, when he would have been 11 or 12 years old.)

Perhaps Sarah Sims rescued her father from trade in order that he might pursue art. For he seems to have acted in the provinces. A notice taken from a Bristol newspaper by Kathleen Barker cites the marriage on 12 August 1800 of George Sims, son of Sims of Lilliput Alley, Bath, to Mrs Clifford, "widow of the late Mr. Clifford, of our theatre, and daughter of Mr. Robins, the drawing-master." Mrs Clifford, like her first husband, had had both a London and a provincial acting career. She was on the stage from the age of 17, first as Miss Robins, then as Mrs Clifford. It seems probable that her second husband George Sims was the London actor and publican Sims and that he was also the Sims recorded acting in Sheffield in 1799 and Liverpool in 1801. He was almost certainly the Sims whom Dr Barker cites playing minor farce characters in the Bath-Bristol company in the seasons of 1805–6, 1806–7, 1807–8, and 1808–9, for Sarah Sims appeared in that company during the latter two seasons. Mrs Sims also acted with the company every season from 1805–6 through 1808–9.

A manuscript document of unknown provenance and uncertain authority, in the Folger Library, mentions Mr Sims "theatrical agent [who] died Sep: 19, 1823, aged 75."

Sims, Mrs George. *See* CLIFFORD, MRS, NÉE ROBINS.

By permission of the Trustees of the British Museum

SARAH SIMS, as Fanny

engraving by Alais, after Foster

Sims, Sarah, later Mrs William Penson
[*fl.* 1796–1816], *actress, singer, dancer.*

Sarah Sims was, in the words of the *Authentic Memoirs of the Green Room* (1806), daughter "of a respectable hair-dresser and perfumer, who some years since kept the Crown and Thistle, in Russell-Court, a kind of Theatrical House of Call, much frequented by Performers, Country-Managers, and persons of a theatrical turn in general."

That Sims, whose first name was probably George, was a provincial performer as well, perhaps, as a sort of theatrical agent. "At the early age of four years, [Sarah] discovered a taste and talent for music, which encouraged her father to have her instructed." The account continues, furnishing a dubious tale of a rich patroness who died just at the point where she should have sent Miss Sims to France to further her musical instruction. Sarah had at least one sibling, William, who seems also to have acted, in the provinces, and who succeeded his father as tavern-keeper.

Sarah first began to appear in public at Sadler's Wells, in melodramas like *The Magicians*, in which she played Harriet on 26 September 1796, and such musical spectaculars as *Sadak and Kalasrade,* in which, in 1797, she acted Codan. When she performed at Covent Garden for the first time on 20 October 1797 the *Monthly Mirror* reported:

The *Maid of the Mill* was cut down to a farce, to introduce the the young lady in the character of *Fanny,* with *new songs* adapted to the compass of her voice, which is of a very peculiar nature.

It is a complete *tenor,* something resembling that of *Mrs. Kennedy,* and produces similar effects. Few women are possessed of this singular faculty, and therefore it is to be prized when we meet with it.

The power mostly lies in the *low* notes, which, of Miss Sims, are round, deep, and capacious. To us they sounded not unlike the under *tones* of [Madame] Storace. Should the musicians think it worth their while to *compose for her,* she will make rapid improvement as a singer—that is, if her ear be good—of which we are rather in doubt at present.

The account in *Authentic Memoirs* perhaps overstates the case in saying that, from the moment of her "regular debut" as Fanny, "She was received with unbounded applause and permanently engrafted on the establishment." But she did continue to sing and act as Miss Sims at Covent Garden and also at Sadler's Wells far into the next century, and Dutton's *Dramatic Censor* of 1800 commended her: "Miss Sims improves rapidly. Her personation of Young Edward [in *Every One Has His Fault*] was highly interesting, and replete with feeling. With time there is no doubt but her name will rank in the list of the *principal* performers of the Theatre. It were only to be wished that her musical talents were better cultivated." Surviving manuscript company lists at the British Library and Folger Library show that she was paid £3 per week in 1799–1800, £4 in 1800–1801, and £5 in 1801–2.

In the summer season of 1798 she had made her first appearance at Birmingham. The *Monthly Mirror* of December 1802 reported that she had taken £213 in a benefit at Liverpool. She was at Bristol in 1807–8. The 1806 edition of *Authentic Memoirs* had suggested that success on the London boards had paved an easy way for provincial engagements and testified vaguely that she had sung at Vauxhall, "performed [by 1806] two summers at Birmingham," and "then visited Liverpool, during the recess of the Winter houses. . . ."

Evidently her maiden name was of professional value to her, for she kept it in the playbills for some seasons after her marriage, at St Nicholas, Liverpool, on 26 August 1804 to William Penson, a provincial musician. She was using his name, however, when she acted at Edinburgh in 1807. She returned there for the following nine winter-spring seasons, through 1816. Her husband was leader of the band at the Edinburgh Theatre Royal from 1810 to 1816. (He may also have acted there, though it is likely that the considerable list of roles from 1814 through 1816 credited to him in Norma Armstrong's manuscript calendar belong to the provincial actor-manager John Penson—whose relationship to William is not known.)

By the end of her 20-year career Sarah Sims Penson commanded a repertoire of at least 160 roles, in "lines" which stretched from pantomime and comic opera through farce and comedy of manners—roles such as Leonora in *Two Strings to Your Bow,* Fanny in *The Maid of the Mill,* Nerissa in *The Merchant of Venice,* Miss Leeson in *The School for Wives,* Zekiel Homespun in *The Heir at Law,* and Cowslip in *The Agreeable Surprise.* She was the first representative of several characters: Connor in J. C. Cross's pantomime *The Round Tower,* Edwin in his pantomime *Joan of Arc,* Agra in James Cobb's comic opera *Ramah Droog,* Mary in his musical farce *Paul and Virginia,* Nancy in T. J. Dibdin's musical interlude *The Naval Pillar,* Taffline in his musical farce *St David's Day,* Ozora in his interlude *The Hermione,* and Peggy in Thomas Knight's comic opera *The Turnpike Gate.*

Analysis of her roles during her earlier years reveals the extent to which her success depended on a good voice and a petite figure. She seems not only to have appeared "to considerable advantage, as a breeches figure," as the *Authentic Memoirs* testified, but to have been unusually small, as her assumption of pageboy roles and other children's parts in her maturity shows (Prince Edward in *Richard III,* Paul in *Paul and Virginia,* William in *Rosina,* and so on). "Arch and waggish parts" were her forte, because of her "remarkably gay and sprightly disposition."

Nor did her essential talents seem to diminish as the years rolled on. The extensive record of her parts in the Edinburgh theatre, where she was popular for more than a decade, shows that though she moved into more mature rules, like Mrs Candour in *The School for Scandal*, she retained most of her former "sprightly" parts and added others.

There are four songs "as sung by" Miss Sims at Vauxhall listed in the *Catalogue of Printed Music in the British Museum*.

A portrait of Sarah Sims as Fanny in *The Maid of the Mill* was engraved by Alais, after Foster, and published by Roach as a plate to *Authentic Memoirs of the Green Room*, 1806.

Simson. *See also* SIMPSON.

Simson, Mrs ₍*fl.* 1765₎, *actress. See* SIMPSON, MRS ELIZABETH.

Simson, Master ₍*fl.* 1780₎, *actor.*
At the Crown Inn, Lower Street, Islington, on 27 March 1780 a Master Simson was one of the Countrymen in *The Camp*. At the same place, on 19 April following, he played Buckle in *The Suspicious Husband*.

Sinclair, Mr ₍*fl.* 1779–1792₎, *actor.*
Mr Sinclair played Frederick in *The Students* at the Haymarket Theatre on 11 January 1779. He shared a benefit with Mitchell on 10 May, giving his address as Church Lane, near St Martin's Church in the Strand. A Sinclair was at the Haymarket on 12 December 1791, playing Mause in *The Gentle Shepherd,* and he acted Brabantio in *Othello* on 6 February 1792. We are unable to determine if he was the "poor Sinclair" who was duped by Mrs John Booth, according to J. E. Burghall's *A Statement of Facts* in 1797.

A Mrs Sinclair, who may have been a relative, acted in Belfast in 1794 and 1795.

Sincock, Mr ₍*fl.* 1778–1791₎, *actor.*
Mr Sincock played Bertran in *The Spanish Fryar* at the Haymarket Theatre on 26 January 1778 and returned on 26 September 1791 to appear as Sir William Worthy in *The Gentle Shepherd.* On the latter date Mrs Sincock acted Dorothy in *The Double Amour,* and though nothing more is known of Mr Sincock, she came back to the Haymarket on 27 April 1796 to act the Countess of Nottingham in *The Earl of Essex.* On 23 January 1797 she was Lady Dunder in *Ways and Means,* and Master Sincock

was in *The Battle of Eddington.* Then she acted Lady Pride in *Barnaby* on 26 January and Lady Strangeways in *The Romance of an Hour* on 10 May, on which date a Master Sincock sang "A Sea Song" and "The Muffin Man." Mrs Sincock's name then disappeared from the bills, but at the Haymarket Theatre on 3 August 1797 Master Sincock sang a song by Webbe.

Sincock, Mrs ₍*fl.* 1791–1797₎, *actress. See* SINCOCK, MR.

Sincock, Master ₍*fl.* 1797₎, *singer. See* SINCOCK, MR.

Singer, Mr ₍*fl.* 1782₎, *actor.*
Mr Singer played an unspecified character in *The Taylors* at the Haymarket Theatre on 25 November 1782.

"Singes, Le Chevalier de" ₍*fl.* 1767–1768₎, *trained animal.*
"Le Chevalier de Singes" was Signor Spinacuti's trained monkey, who appeared at Sadler's Wells in 1767 walking and dancing on the tightrope with a pole and on the wire with and without a pole, vaulting on the slack rope, and turning the Catherine wheel. He was pictured in a print of 1768 doing a number of his feats. Arundell in *The Story of Sadler's Wells* wonders if the monkey was a man in a monkey suit, but the print seems to make it clear that Le Chevalier de Singes was a real monkey, and a very talented one. That print is reproduced with our notice of Spinacuta.

"Singing Sandy." *See* GORDON, ALEXANDER.

Singleton, Mr ₍*fl.* 1747–1748₎, *boxkeeper.*
Mr Singleton received 10*s.* from Covent Garden Theatre on 31 January 1747 for five days' work. He was named in the accounts as one of the boxkeepers in 1747–48 and shared a benefit with other house servants on 5 May 1748. Perhaps he was the father of the house servant (Thomas?) Singleton of 20 years later.

Singleton, John *d.* 1686, *instrumentalist, singer?*
John Singleton appears to have been appointed a violinist in the King's Musick at the

Restoration and placed at the head of a small group of musicians within the main musical establishment. Pepys recorded in his diary on 19 November 1660 that Jonson's *Epicoene* was presented at court and "the King did put a great affront upon Singleton's musique, he bidding them stop and bade the French musique play, which, my Lord says, do much outdo all ours." On 24 January 1661 Singleton was named to receive a New Year's gift as one of the King's "private consort." In addition to being a violinist, Singleton seems also to have been proficient on the lute and sackbut.

On 18 April 1662 he was named to attend the King on a journey to Portsmouth, and the following year he waited upon his majesty at Windsor. On 20 December 1664 Singleton was ordered to perform at the Theatre Royal in Bridges Street whenever the manager, Thomas Killigrew, should need him; named also were eight other royal musicians, and it is probable that members of the King's Musick frequently performed at the public theatres. For his court services Singleton received £45 10s. 10d. annually, plus livery. Whenever he attended the royal family outside London, as he did in 1670 at Dover and 1674 at Hampton Court, he received "riding charges." Singleton played violin in the court masque *Calisto* on 15 February 1675.

His work at the theatre was interrupted in May 1677, when Charles Killigrew dismissed Singleton and four other royal musicians for reasons unknown; the musicians petitioned against Killigrew, but the outcome of of of their plea is also unknown. Singleton's association with the theatre may have been closer than the records indicate, for in *MacFlecknoe* Dryden made reference to him:

That, pale with envy, Singleton forswore
The lute and sword which he in triumph bore,
And vowed he ne'er would act Villerius more.

Was Singleton a singer? Villarius was a principal character in Sir William Davenant's "opera" *The Siege of Rhodes*.

There were several John Singletons in London in the Restoration period, so one cannot be certain that the following facts concerned our musician. The Westminster Abbey registers, which contain many entries concerning royal musicians, show that on 19 February 1680 a John Singleton married Elizabeth Fisher—probably the widow of Lawrence Fisher, who had been one of the Abbey's singers. Singleton's former wife, the editor of the registers notes, was Mary Singleton, who was buried at St Bride, Fleet Street, on 16 April 1670. By her, John had had a son John and daughters Rebecca (later Mrs Joshua Hopkins) and Elizabeth (later Mrs John Rollestone).

In *Music in Purcell's London* Harley notes that Singleton was living in Villiers Street, according to the Strand Book for the Highways in 1684 and 1686 and the Poor Rate Book of 1689, but those references must have been to another John Singleton, for our man died in 1686. In his edition of Shadwell's works Montague Summers claimed that Singleton was buried at St Paul, Covent Garden, on 7 April 1686, though the musician's will of 21 January 1685 described him as of the parish of St Martin-in-the-Fields.

At the time he drew up his will Singleton was owed an unspecified amount by the King, and out of it he wished to make the following bequests: 20s. for a ring for Mary Staggins (the musician Isaac Staggins's wife); 20s. for a ring for her son, the musician Nicholas Staggins; £10 for his cousin Grace Farthuier; 20s. each for rings for the court musicians William Clayton, Thomas Farmer, and Henry Brockwell; 20s. for a ring for John Merefield; £5 for Singleton's son-in-law John Hicks; £5 for his brother-in-law John Smith; £5 to Elizabeth Mason; £100 to Mary Meggs ("Orange Moll" of Drury Lane Theatre?); and everything else to his grandson Alexander Hicks. Hicks and Mary Meggs were to be executors, but only Mrs Meggs proved the will, on 23 November 1686. No mention was made in the will of Singleton's wife.

That will, with its mention of several court musicians, surely pertains to our John Singleton, yet another will, dated 15 December 1684 and proved on 17 April 1686, seems also to have been made by our man. In this one he described himself as of Waltham Holy Cross, Essex, and left everything to his wife Elizabeth, including "moneys due upon my places from his Majesty." A sentence pertaining to that will, clearly identifying Singleton as from Waltham Holy Cross, also names Mary Meggs and Alexander Hicks, along with Elizabeth

Singleton. The estate seems finally to have been settled on Elizabeth.

Singleton, John   [fl. 1744–1767], actor, violinist.

John Singleton acted Marplot in *The Busy Body* on 29 November 1744 at Goodman's Fields Theatre. He then appeared as Brazen in *The Recruiting Officer* on 30 November and Clodio in *Love Makes a Man* on 18 December. He was seen in those characters through the end of April 1745. At the Haymarket Theatre on 30 March 1748 he acted Flash in *Miss in Her Teens;* at the New Wells, Leman Street (not Clerkenwell, as *The London Stage* has it) he acted Brazen again; and at Bartholomew Fair on 24 August he played Solomon Slender in *The Consequences of Industry and Idleness.* He returned to the New Wells, Leman Street, on 27 February 1749 as Abel in *The Committee* and on 23 August was Ramble in *The Adventures of Sir Lubberly Lackbrains and His Man Blunderbuss.*

Singleton then left England for America with Hallam's troupe. His American debut was in Williamsburg on 5 September 1752, when he played Gratiano in *The Merchant of Venice.* His first New York appearance was on 17 September 1753 at the Nassau Street Theatre, as Tom in *The Conscious Lovers.* He acted in Philadelphia in the late spring of 1754. He is known to have acted Lothario in *The Fair Penitent* at Charleston, and in Virginia he advertised for violin students. As a member of Hallam's troupe, he acted such parts as Mercutio in *Romeo and Juliet,* Edgar in *King Lear,* Stanley in *Richard III,* and Archer in *The Stratagem.* He also served as the company poet, writing prologues and altering texts for production.

Singleton journeyed to the West Indies, where he married and settled, giving up his stage career. In 1767 he published *A General Description of the West Indian Islands, as Relates to British, Dutch, and Danish Governments, from Barbados to Saint Croix. Attempted in Blank Verse.* It was reprinted in London in 1776, but we do not know whether or not Singleton was then still alive.

"Singleton, Mary." See BROOKE, MRS JOHN.

Singleton, [Thomas?] [fl. 1766–1780], house servant, actor.

Mr Singleton was cited in Egerton MS 2272 in the British Library as the second gallery office keeper at Covent Garden Theatre in 1766. Perhaps he was the son of the Mr Singleton who served that playhouse in the 1740s. On 14 September 1767 Singleton was named on the Covent Garden paylist as a billsticker at 2s. daily, and on 20 May 1769 his benefit tickets were accepted at the theatre, as they were annually through 1774. Singleton began appearing onstage as early as 1770. On 10 February he was paid £1 10s. for being "in the Lyon" for 12 nights in *Harlequin's Jubilee.* That ignominious duty continued to the end of the season. On 26 April 1774 he was paid for unspecified appearances in *The Sorcerer, Henry VIII, Macbeth, The Fair,* and *The Sylphs.* Our guess is that Singleton then left London, for we find no further references to him in London theatrical documents, though a Singleton was in Younger's company in the summer and fall of 1775, and Thomas Singleton, his wife, and his daughter worked at the Theatre Royal, Liverpool, in the late 1770s.

Singleton's duties at Liverpool, which chiefly concerned properties, brought him 6s. weekly in 1777 but 15s. weekly in 1778. One note in the Liverpool accounts has "Singleton & wife" down for £1 10s. per week. Thomas Singleton's name was attached to an inventory of theatre properties in September 1780. His wife and daughter were with him at Birmingham in the summer of 1775 and were at Liverpool later. Both were apparently actresses, Mrs Singleton earning 10s. 6d. weekly at Liverpool in 1778; Miss Singleton was cited for the same wage in 1777 and 1778.

Singleton, Mrs [Thomas?] [fl. 1773–1778], actress.

The Covent Garden Theatre accounts on 21 May 1773 contain the following note: "Paid Mrs Singleton for walking 13 nights in *Henry VIII,* the 8th to 15th February £3 5s. and for walking 28 nights in the *Sorcerer* to the 13th inst. £3 10s." She was very likely the wife of Thomas Singleton, who was a house servant at Covent Garden and worked at the Theatre Royal, Liverpool, with his wife and daughter in the late 1770s. The family was at Birmingham in the summer of 1775 and at Liverpool by 1777. Mrs Singleton's weekly wage in 1778 was 10s. 6d.

Siprutini, Emanuel [fl. 1758–1775?], violoncellist, composer.

Emanuel Siprutini performed on the violoncello at the Great Room in Dean Street, Soho, on 5 April 1758 and took a benefit there on 26 February 1761. He played a cello concerto at Drury Lane Theatre on 26 February 1762, a solo at the Haymarket on 16 March, and another on 22 April. Siprutini and John Crosdill played a duet for two cellos in 1764, according to the entry on Crosdill in *The Dictionary of National Biography.* The last notice we have of Siprutini is 11 March 1765, when he played a concerto for cello at the Haymarket Theatre. He busied himself with composing, however, as the *Catalogue of Printed Music in the British Museum* shows. There are a number of works, mostly for violoncello, dating from about 1764 to about 1775.

Sirbun. *See* SHERBURN.

Sirmen, Signora Ludovico, Maddalena Laura, née Lombardini *b. 1735, violinist, violoncellist?, harpsichordist, singer, composer.*

Maddalena Laura Lombardini, the *New Grove* tells us, was born in 1735 in Venice and received her early training at the Mendicanti there. She became a student of Tartini in Padua, and even after returning to Venice in 1760 she continued studying with him through letters. Her correspondence lessons have given us a most important statement on the great Tartini's principals, and the most helpful letter, dated 5 March 1760, was translated into French, German, and English. Maddalena was on a concert tour of Italy at some time between then and 1768; she met and married the violinist, composer, and *maestro di cappella* of Santa Maria Maggiore in Bergamo, Ludovico Sirmen (or Sireman, Syrmen). The couple went to Paris in 1768 and were highly praised for a double violin concerto of their own composition which they played to great applause. It was evident to critics, however, that she was the better performer.

Signora Sirmen came to London—alone, apparently—to perform at the King's Theatre.

Civica Raccolta Stampe A. Bertarelli, Castello Sforzesco, Milan

MADDALENA SIRMEN

engraving by Costa, after "F. C."

According to *The London Stage,* she was in the pit orchestra playing violoncello (*recte* violin?) for the 1770–71 opera season. On 10 January 1771 she played a violin concerto between the acts, and so, too, at subsequent performances that spring. On 15 February at Covent Garden Theatre she also provided an entr'acte solo. After appearing frequently at both theatres she also made recital engagements, one being according to the *Public Advertiser,* at Almack's on 15 May, when she played the harpsichord. She continued her successful stay to the end of May 1771. During that visit she was living in Half Moon Street, Piccadilly. The *New Grove* has her returning to England in 1774, but the fifth edition of Grove brings her back (correctly) in 1772. She played a concerto on the violin at Covent Garden on 6 March 1772, after a performance of the *Messiah.* When she repeated it on 11 March the *Theatrical Review* reported: "Her tone and style of playing is very pleasing, and her execution truly chaste, without any of those unnecessary and extravagant liberties, which . . . solo players on the violin too frequently give in to." At the end of *The Resurrec-*

tion on 20 March she played "a new Concerto . . . composed by Cirri." Her "last time of performing in England" on that second visit was at a *"Concerto Spirituale"* at Covent Garden on 10 April.

Remarkably, after making her mark as a first-rate violinist, Signora Sirmen decided to become an opera singer. *The London Stage* shows her for her benefit at the King's Theatre on 1 June 1773 singing, for the first time, the title role in *La buona figliuola*. It also lists her on the roster at Marylebone Gardens in the summer of 1773, but the bills do not mention her. Dr Burney was disappointed with her decision to try singing:

In 'Sofonisba' and 'The Cid' Madame Syrmen, the scholar of Tartini who was justly admired for her polished and expressive manner of playing the violin, appeared as a singer in the second woman, but having been a first woman so long upon her instrument, she degraded herself by assuming a character in which, though not destitute of voice and taste, she laid no claim to superiority.

Yet Signora Sirmen (or Lombardini-Sirmen) continued her "unsuccessful" singing career for a number of years. She was in Dresden singing secondary parts in 1782, for example. But in May 1785 at the Concert Spirituel in Paris she tried to resume her career as a violinist. By then her style was considered old-fashioned and the pieces she played were no longer popular. She seems then to have retired.

Signora Sirmen composed a number of works featuring the violin. A list can be found in the *New Grove*.

A portrait of Signora Sirmen engraved by Agostino Costa, after "F. C.", is in the Civiche Raccolta delle Stampe Achille Bertarelli, Milan.

Skaggs or "Skegginello." *See* SKEGGS.

Skeggs, Matthew   *d. 1773, musician.*

Edward Edwards in his *Anecdotes* (1808), commenting on a painting of Matthew Skeggs playing on a broomstick, wrote:

[He] for some time kept a public-house [the Hoop and Bunch of Grapes in St Albans Street], and was one of those who, with others, formed a club, calling themselves Choice Spirits; and, to support their claim to this title, they practised some silly buffooneries; but this college of witlings has been

MATTHEW SKEGGS

engraving by Houston, after King

long forgotten. About the same time in which this society existed, there was a burlesque entertainment exhibited at the little theatre in the Haymarket, called 'Mother Midnight's Oratorio,' in which Skeggs bore a part as a musical performer, by playing upon a broom-stick, his voice, which was tolerably good, supplying the tones of an instrument.

Skeggs, like most of such would-be wits, wanted prudence, and, in the latter part of his life, was obliged to retire to Shefford in Bedfordshire, where he resided in 1772.

The portrait was by the painter Thomas King. It was engraved in mezzotint by R. Houston about 1752 and was captioned "Skeggs, in the Character of Seignor Bumbasto."

A similar mezzotint, dating from 1752, was captioned "*A Tragi-comical DIALOGUE Between My Lord SKAGGS and his BROOMSTICK. By H. Howard. G. Pigganinni Fecit London Printed for John Ryall, at Hogarth's Head, in Fleet*

Street." Hugh Howard wrote the dreadful verses that accompanied the print:

Each Buck & jolly Fellow has heard of Skegginello,
    The famous Skegginello that grunts so pretty
Upon his Broomsticado, such Music he has
    made, O
    Twill spoil the fiddling trade, O
        And thats a Pity.
But have you heard of or seen, O, His Phyz,
        so pretty
    In Picture Shops so grinn, O
    With comic Nose and Chin, O,
    Who'd think a man cou'd shine so,
        At Eh, Eh, Eh, Eh.

On 12 May 1752 Horace Walpole wrote to G. Montagu:

I was t'other night to see what is now grown the fashion, Mother Midnight's Oratory. It appeared the lowest buffoonery in the world, even to me, who am used to my uncle Horace. . . . Two or three men intend to persuade you that they play on a broomstick, which is drolly brought in, carefully shrouded in a case, so as to be mistaken for a bassoon or bass-viol; but they succeed in nothing but the action.

Skegg's name was not mentioned, but the references to him suggest that he may have been the "Signor Bombasto" or "Bombastini" or "Mynheer Von Poop-Poop Broomstickado" or all three; they were pseudonyms used in 1751–52 and 1757–1760 by the producer of zany entertainments at the Haymarket, Christopher Smart. All three are entered in the second volume of this *Dictionary*.

The first mention of Skeggs in London bills came on 6 May 1757, when he "*sang*" a solo on a broomstick at Covent Garden Theatre, advertised as making his first appearance on that stage. He also presented "A Mock Italian and English *Cantata*." On 28 December 1758 at the Haymarket *Galigantus* was performed, with an additional scene by Skeggs and Massey. The pair also participated in *Britannia's Triumph* at the Haymarket on 30 April 1760; the evening was another Christopher Smart concoction. *Musgrave's Obituary* records the death of Matthew Skeggs on 9 April 1773.

The portrait of Skeggs (12 1/2" × 10") mentioned above, engraved by R. Houston, after T. King, was published by M. Jackson and M. Skeggs (n.d.); it was copied on a smaller plate, bust only, in circle (2 1/2" di-

ameter), with a pig on the broomstick, and published by J. Ryall (n. d.). An engraving by Hogarth shows Skeggs playing on his broomstick in a burlesque band assembled for a performance at Ranelagh Gardens of Bonnell Thornton's spoof of Handel's "Ode of St Cecelia's Day." An article by Bellamy Gardner in the *Connoisseur* 106: 186–189 (1940) suggests that the first performance of the burlesque band should be assigned to 1759, but Thornton's *Burlesque Ode on St Cecelia's Day, adapted to the Ancient British Music* was published in 1749.

Skellern. See SKILLERN.

Skerrett, Mr [fl. 1794–1802], *actor.*
Mr Skerrett played Charles in *The School for Scandal* at Hammersmith on 24 March 1794. He was probably the Skerrett cited in the *Monthly Mirror* of December 1802 as having brought in £114 at his benefit in Liverpool.

Skevidge, Mr [fl. 1716], *pitkeeper.*
The King's Theatre accounts show that as of 15 December 1716 Mr Skevidge was a pitkeeper at that house.

Skiddy, Mr [fl. 1731], *musician?*
A benefit concert was held on 9 August 1731 for Mr Skiddy, presumably a musician, at the Great Room in St Alban's Street.

Skidmore. See SCUDAMORE.

Skillern, Thomas 1776–1849, *instrumentalist.*
Thomas Skillern, the son of Joseph and Melina Skillern, was baptized on 24 June 1776 at St Nicholas, Gloucester. When Doane's *Musical Directory* came out in 1794, Skillern was listed as a violinist who had participated in the Handel performances at Westminster Abbey and had played at Ranelagh Gardens. He lived in St Martin's Lane, where also lived the elder Thomas Skillern, apparently his uncle, a music publisher and seller. From 1796 to 1799 Skillern played in the oratorios at Covent Garden Theatre.

He was admitted to the Royal Society of Musicians on 1 December 1799, at which time he was described as 23 years old, single, and proficient on the violin, viola, and double bass. He was still performing at Ranelagh as well as at Covent Garden and had "private business"—presumably students. In 1800 and subsequent years he played in the Society's St Paul's Concerts, usually performing on the double bass. From about 1802 to 1806 he published and sold music at a shop at No 25, Greek Street, Soho; about 1806 the firm became Skillern and Challoner. After 1810 Skillern ran the business by himself at the shop in Greek Street until 1816, then at No 138, Oxford Street until 1819, and finally at No 247, Regent Street until 1826. He continued playing at the theatres; as of 1821–22 he was in the band at Drury Lane at a weekly salary of £1 15s.

According to the Minute Books of the Royal Society of Musicians, Thomas Skillern died in 1849.

Skinner, Mr ₍fl. 1774–1775₎, actor?

A Mr Skinner is on a Drury Lane manuscript company list dating probably 1774–75 in the Forster Collection in the Victoria and Albert Museum.

Skinner, Mr ₍fl. 1794₎, bassoonist.

A Mr Skinner, "Bassoon . . . Windsor," is listed in Doane's *Musical Directory* (1794) as having been concerned in one or more of the Handel commemorations at Westminster Abbey.

Skinner, Charlotte ₍fl. 1747–1750₎, actress.

In the spring of 1747 Samuel Foote and a small company gave a series of 35 performances, illegal under the terms of the Licensing Act, at the Haymarket Theatre. They operated under the pretense that Foote was selling refreshments and that his *"Diversions"* were gratis. The *Monthly Mirror* for July 1804 gave a sketch of the actor Thomas Jefferson which spoke of the well-known Charlotte Skinner, "formerly engaged in Foote's Tea" who "advertised a play at the Little Theatre [in the Haymarket] to be performed by amateurs. . . ." The performance referred to was the one on 10 November 1750 in which Charlotte Skinner played Calista in *The Fair Penitent*, "Tickets to be had at Miss Skinner's Lodgings, No. 4, in Angel Court, Windmill St., Haymarket."

None of Miss Skinner's amateur actors are named in the bill, and the program was said to be for her benefit.

The bill anxiously advised: "As no money can be taken, only those given tickets by Miss Skinner can be admitted. As this Advertisement was sent too late to be altered in the *Daily Advertiser,* it is hoped that the Advertisement inserted in that Paper for this Entertainment will not be regarded, as to any Money being taken for places."

The *Monthly Mirror* sketch of Jefferson (who is supposed to have made his debut that evening of 10 November in the part of Horatio) provides an instructive sidelight on this one among many successful attempts at evading the Licensing Act:

As soon as [Jefferson] had perfected himself in the character, he again waited on the lady [Charlotte Skinner]; but the High constable had, in the mean time, prohibited the performance, and nothing but an application to [Samuel] Foote could enable them to exhibit the intended entertainments. Anxious to obtain his consent, our hero immediately repaired to him at Mr. Delaval's, in Dover-Street. Both these gentlemen agreed, in case permission could not be procured from Henry Fielding, the [Bow Street] magistrate, (who, on being applied to, declined to interfere) that the house should be opened gratis; and they promised, in person, to collect an optional contribution from every person who might be present; they did so, and at the end of Act III, sent [Miss Skinner] one hundred guineas; no collection had then been made from the gallery, which also produced a handsome sum.

Miss Skinner never appeared in a London bill again.

Skinner, J. ₍fl. 1734–1735₎, boxkeeper.

A Mr J. Skinner was a boxkeeper for the French company that gave a series of plays in the French language at the new Haymarket in 1734–35. He shared a benefit with other boxkeepers—Mason, Cossins, and Evans—on 25 April 1735.

Skinner, Mrs Robert. *See* BRISTOW, MRS.

Skipwith, Thomas c. 1652–1710, manager.

Sir Thomas Skipwith was the partner of Christopher Rich in the management of the company of players at Drury Lane and Dorset Garden theatres in the 1690s and the early years of the eighteenth century. Of his personal life we know little, though his lineage seems clear. The *Complete Baronetage* tells us that his father was Thomas Skipwith, son of Edward Skipwith of Gosberton and Grantham, Lincolnshire, and his wife Elizabeth, the daughter of Sir John Hatcher of Careby, Lincolnshire. The elder Thomas married, about 1650, Elizabeth, daughter of Ralph Latham of Upminster, Essex. The younger Thomas Skipwith was born about 1652. His mother died before 30 April 1673, when his father remarried. Thomas the elder was knighted on 29 May 1673, made Serjeant-at-Law on 21 April 1675, created baronet as of Metheringham, Lincolnshire, on 27 July 1678, and died on 2 June 1694 at his home in Lincoln's Inn Fields. He was buried at Upminster, beside his first wife. The second marriage of the elder Thomas Skipwith was alleged by Christopher Rich of Gray's Inn, a relative, one guesses, of the Christopher Rich who became the younger Thomas Skipwith's theatrical partner.

The younger Thomas Skipwith was admitted to Gray's Inn on 5 August 1670. At some point he married Margaret, the widow of William Brownlow of Snarford, Lincolnshire, and daughter of George Brydges, sixth Baron Chandos of Sudely. The following entries in the registers of St Giles in the Fields tell of their children. On 3 September 1685 Thomas, the son of Thomas Skipwith, Esquire, and his wife Margaret, was christened. The child had been born on 23 August. On 14 November 1686 George Bridges son of Thomas and Margaret was christened; he had been born on 7 November.

The elder Skipwith's will, which named the younger Thomas as heir, was found in his chambers of Serjeant's Inn, Fleet Street, by Christopher Rich (previously Sir Thomas's clerk), Samuel Stephens (his present clerk), and Thomas Skipwith the younger. Rich testified to the authenticity of the will on 30 March 1694. Sir Thomas the younger proved his father's will on 7 June. It had been made in August 1688.

The earliest theatrical notices of Thomas Skipwith date from 31 March 1682, when Dame Mary Davenant, widow of the theatre manager-playwright Sir William Davenant,

sold her half share in the Duke's Company to Skipwith. By that time it had become apparent that London could not support two acting companies, and a union was made in 1682 that lasted until 1695. During the early 1680s Skipwith seems to have remained on the fringes of theatre life, merely purchasing interest in theatrical property or lending money to people involved in theatrical affairs. On 30 August 1687 the slippery Alexander Davenant paid his brother Charles £2400 for Charles's interest in the United Company. What Charles did not know was that Alexander had negotiated with Skipwith and Christopher Rich for the money, and of the £2400, only £400 was Alexander's own; the rest, presumably, was Skipwith's. On 12 September Skipwith made over his five-sixths interest to Alexander for seven years; Alexander was to farm out the shares to his advantage and pay Skipwith £312 rent per year in weekly payments of £6. Skipwith was to receive rights to theatre tickets every week. What is so curious about this arrangement is that the interest concerned the Dorset Garden Theatre (the old Duke's Company house) and other Duke's Company property that now belonged to the United Company, but the company acted mostly at Drury Lane, the old King's Company house.

Years later, in December 1693, Skipwith and Rich admitted that Skipwith's real share of the £2400 purchase money was £1500, not £2000. By that time others, including the actor Thomas Betterton, had become concerned at the way Alexander Davenant (who had fled to the Canary Islands) had farmed out their shares. Christopher Rich thereupon arrogated the whole power of the government of the company to himself, though he pretended to share it with Charles Davenant.

Rich proved to be a tyrannical manager, and by December 1694 Betterton and a number of the more seasoned players sent a long list of grievances to the Lord Chamberlain; the answers came from Rich and Skipwith, and we cannot tell how much Skipwith actually had to say in the matter. In 1693 and 1694, said the patentees, Skipwith had made only one percent profit on his investment. In another part of the answer made up by Rich and Skipwith, the patentees stated that the patent cost them £3600 and that in 1693–94 they cleared less than £30.

On 25 March 1695 Betterton and his group were granted a license to open a theatre of their own, and Skipwith and Rich continued holding both of the old patents and operating at Drury Lane and Dorset Garden. In 1694–95 there were ten shares in the United Company; Skipwith held 1.75 shares, Rich the same, and Sir John Brownlow 2; the rest of the shares were divided among 13 people, none of whom held more than three-quarters of a share.

Just what did Skipwith do at the theatre? Rich seems clearly to have been the dominant patentee, and the little evidence we have suggests that Skipwith may have done little more than arrange contracts with the actors. The contracts signed by the actors John Verbruggen on 10 April 1695, William Bullock on 15 April 1695, and Thomas Dogget on 3 April 1696, were with Skipwith, rather than Skipwith and Rich jointly. Colley Cibber, then a young actor in the troupe, told in his *Apology* (1740) of Sir Thomas entertaining actors at his house. There Colley met Cardell Goodman, who had acted in earlier years. Cibber said that, as Skipwith "was an agreeable Companion himself, [he] liked Goodman for the same quality." From December 1696 to 1698 Sir Thomas was M.P. for Malmesbury.

In Mrs Manley's *Rivella* of 1714 (but containing incidents dating about 1696–97) she wrote of meeting Sir Thomas in the hopes of getting her works produced. He had

then Interest enough to introduce upon one Stage whatever Pieces he pleas'd; This Knight had a very good Face, but his Body was grown fat: He was naturally short, and his Legs being what they call somewhat bandy, he was advis'd to wear his Cloaths very long, to help conceal that Defect, insomuch that his Dress made him look shorter than he was: He was following a handsom Lady in the *Mall*, after a World of Courtship, and begging her in vain to let him know where she liv'd; seeing she was prepared to leave the *Park* he renew'd his Efforts, offering to go down upon his knees to her, to have her grant this Request; the Lady turn'd gravely upon him, and told him she thought, *he had been upon his knees all this Time:* The Knight conscious of his duck Legs and long Coat, retired in the greatest Confusion, notwithstanding his natural and acquired Assurance. Sir *Peter* [Mrs Manley's fictional name for Sir Thomas] was supposed to be towards Fifty when he became acquainted with *Rivella* [Mrs Manley], and his Constitution broken by those Excesses, of which in his Youth he had been guilty;

He was married young to a Lady of Worth and Honour, who brought him a very large Joynture.

His wife, according to Mrs Manley's fictionalized account, was a good and doting person, but Sir Thomas "was detestably vain, and lov'd to be thought in the Favour of the Fair, which was indeed his only Fault, for he had a great deal of Wit and good Nature; but sure no Youth of Twenty had so vast a *Foible* for being admired." He and Rivella became intimately acquainted, but "because he found she was a Woman of Fire, more than perhaps he could answer," he put her off, saying he was more interested in another woman. So Rivella became his confidante. His mistress was "Mrs. *Settee*"—that is, Mrs Pym, who had become infatuated with him at the Temple Revels ten years before. She had put him off for three years, however, only writing him love letters and not revealing her name. She cost him £300 yearly and £2000 worth of jewels in trade for allowing him to see her once a week and give her supper on Fridays. Everyone knew of the arrangement and joked about his Fridays. It was expensive for him to prevent his wife and Mrs Pym's husband from discovering the affair. He claimed that though they slept naked together, they had never had intercourse for fear of complications.

He was very attentive to Rivella, showing her Mrs Settee's letters; though he and Rivella were only friends, Mrs Settee became jealous. When he stopped seeing Rivella, Mrs Settee gave herself to him completely. But

either the Weakness of his Constitution, or the Greatness of his Passion, was prejudicial to his Health: He grew proud of the Disorder, and went into a publick course of Physick, as if it were a worse Matter; finding it extreamly for his Credit, that the Town should believe so well of him. . . .

Rivella was thought to be the cause of his disease for a time, but the source was clearly Mrs Settee.

How much of what Mrs Manley put into *Rivella* can be taken as truth we may never know. But since the whole town could identify the originals of her fictional names, some of the story may well have been based on fact.

Meanwhile, at the theatre, Sir Thomas signed contracts with actors; he with Rich received petitions, such as that of John Lacy's widow's appeal for the pension due her; and he encouraged Vanbrugh to give *Aesop* to the Drury Lane company (but he failed to get *The Provok'd Wife,* which went to Lincoln's Inn Fields). In legal documents he was regularly paired with Rich, as in 1700–1701, when Charles Killigrew and other investors tried unsuccessfully to oust Rich and Skipwith from their positions as dominant shareholders. But Judith Milhous found among some Chancery papers a case in 1705–6 in which Skipwith was asked about company finances in the 1690s, and he claimed to have no knowledge of the company books for that period, and that he did not, in any case, understand bookkeeping.

He certainly did not profit much from his shares. As Cibber told the story in his *Apology,* Skipwith visited his friend Colonel Brett of Sandywell, Gloucestershire, and offered Brett his share of the Drury Lane patent, saying he had made nothing on it the previous ten years. A conveyance was legally signed on 6 October 1707. Brett paid a nominal 10*s.* for the patent. About 1709, when Rich was trying to squeeze Brett out of the company, Skipwith aided him by claiming in Chancery on 1 February 1709 that the deed of conveyance was intended to be in trust, not an outright gift. Though Brett denied that, he made no attempt to hang onto his claim, and within weeks he gave up his theatrical venture. Skipwith and a number of other investors petitioned the Queen about summer 1709 to lift the silencing of Rich and the Drury Lane company. They did not succeed.

William Collier on 13 September 1709 wrote to the Lord Chamberlain in anticipation of being able to open Drury Lane's 1709–10 season. "I will consent too for Sir Thomas Skipwith and myself, for the matters are now carried so high that I think it impracticable to sue for favour by any other method than the rules of Westminster Hall." The implication was that Skipwith still held an interest in the patent and, with Collier and other shareholders, was involved in trying to get Drury Lane open again. Exactly what happened to his shares of the patent we do not know. Collier was proprietor of Drury Lane in 1709–10, with Aaron Hill serving as manager.

Sir Thomas Skipwith, Bart., died at Bath on 15 June 1710 and was buried at Upminster.

His will was proved on 8 July. His widow Margaret died on 1 January 1732 at the age of 94 and was buried at Westminster Abbey on 8 January.

Sky, Mr [*fl.* 1775], *doorkeeper.*

In the Forster collection at the Victoria and Albert Museum is a manuscript list of stage personnel showing that a Mr Sky was an outer doorkeeper at Drury Lane Theatre as of 5 October 1775.

Skyo, Mr [*fl.* 1792], *actor.*

Mr Skyo played Dennis O'Connor in a performance of *The Apprentice* at the Haymarket Theatre on 26 November 1792.

Skypwith. *See* SKIPWITH.

Skyrme, John [*fl.* 1677–*c.* 1702], *drummer.*

The Lord Chamberlain's accounts first cited John Skyrme on 8 May 1677, when he was appointed a drummer in ordinary in the King's Musick but waiting for the first "avoydance." That did not come until 27 December 1683, upon the death of Edward Wharton. Skyrme then came into wages of 12*s.* daily plus livery. He marched in the coronation parade for James II on 23 April 1685 and continued active in the musical establishment at court until at least 1702. He was earning £24 annually at that point.

Slack, Elizabeth, later Mrs Henry Brown [*fl.* 1764–1777], *singer, actress.*

Advertised as "A Young Gentlewoman," Miss E. Slack made her stage debut on 28 November 1764 singing Phoebe in *The Capricious Lovers* at Drury Lane Theatre. She was Selinda in *Pharnaces* on 15 February 1765 and, for her shared benefit on 26 April, she played Perdita in *The Winter's Tale* and Margery Pinchwife in an alteration of *The Country Wife.* Tickets were available from her at Mr Bates's in Charles Street, Covent Garden. A paylist dated 9 February 1765 shows Miss Slack among the singers at a weekly salary of £4.

In August 1765 Miss Slack performed at the New Richmond Theatre under Love's management. The *Universal Museum* that month noted that tho' she by no means can arrive at a comparison for musical excellence with many other ladies on the stage, nevertheless [she] goes through the songs of *Rosetta* [in *Love in a Village*] with considerable degree both of delicacy and spirit; and enters into the speaking part of the character with an elegance and propriety so superior to any thing we ever saw in town, that we shall for the future consider the original actress of that amiable run-away, as a *vox et praeterea nihil,* even when we are most ready to commend her as a singer, on account of her uncommon abilities.

(Miss Brent had been the original Rosetta.) Miss Slack's benefit tickets for the 31 August 1765 performance on *Love in a Village* were available from her at Mrs Clay's on Richmond Green.

On 6 December 1765, according to *Faulkner's Dublin Journal,* Miss Slack made her Dublin debut at the Smock Alley Theatre, advertised as from Drury Lane in London. Miss Slack continued performing in Dublin until 1767, making appearances at Cork in September and October of 1766. *Lloyd's Evening Post* in November 1768 reported that

a cause came to be tried in the Court of Common Pleas at Westminster, in which Mr William Bates, Music Master, was Plaintiff and Spranger Berry, Esq the celebrated tragedian, defendent, upon a demand made by the plaintiff for a large sum of money due to him from the Defendant, for the performance of Miss Slack, the Plaintiff's apprentice, at the Theatre in Cork. . . . After a short hearing a verdict was given in favour of the Plaintiff.

By 1770, Miss Slack had married the actor Henry Brown, who had made his stage debut at Drury Lane in 1753. He died sometime before 27 February 1770, according to *Faulkner's Dublin Journal.* As Mrs Brown, our subject continued performing in Ireland, chiefly in Dublin, through 1777. One of her characters, as we learn from a contemporary print, was Mrs Hardcastle in *She Stoops to Conquer.*

Miss Slack is pictured by an unknown engraver as Mrs Hardcastle, with John O'Keefe as Tony Lumpkin and George Parker as Mr Hardcastle, in a scene from *She Stoops to Conquer.* Since O'Keefe never acted in London, the engraving no doubt represents a performance in Dublin about 1770. The picture is reproduced in this *Dictionary* 11: 206.

Slade, Mr   [*fl.* 1794], *singer.*

Doane's *Musical Directory* of 1794 listed Mr Slade, of No 20, Union Street, Whitechapel, as a tenor who sang for the Choral Fund and the Handelian Society.

Slade, Elizabeth   *d.* 1717?, *actress.*

Elizabeth Slade's first known role was Camilla in *An Evening's Love* at the Bridges Street Theatre on 12 June 1668. She then acted Lucy in *Love and a Wood* in March 1671, Belisa in *Marriage à la Mode* about April 1672 (at the King's Company temporary home in the old Lincoln's Inn Fields Theatre), and Melinda in *Love in the Dark* on 10 May 1675 at the new Drury Lane playhouse. She was silenced, for some reason, by the Lord Chamberlain on 25 November 1675, but a warrant dated 25 November 1675 shows her as receiving allowances from the King's Company. At the British Library is a separately printed epilogue to *Like Father, Like Son,* dated by Narcissus Luttrell 5 April 1682. Thomas Jevon spoke the lines and said, among other things,

Here Mistris Betty, Hah! she's grown a very
      Woman,
Thou'st got me Child, better me than no man.

(Betty Cox may have left the stage by that time, and, in any case, would have been too old for the remark; Betty Hall had left the stage in 1668. The reference may have been to Betty Slade, though we know of no performances by her after 1675.)

She was clearly not a major player, yet in February 1745 the *Gentleman's Magazine* reminisced

Of Hart, of Mohun, and all the female train,
Coxe, Marshall, Dryden's Reeve,
Bet. Slade, and Charles's reign.

Perhaps our subject was the Elizabeth Slade who was buried at St Paul, Covent Garden, on 23 July 1717.

Slade, Thomas   [*fl.* 1667–1683?], *tailor.*

The London Stage lists Thomas Slade as a member of the Duke's Company at the Lincoln's Inn Fields Theatre in 1667–68. He was cited in the Lord Chamberlain's accounts on 10 February 1668 as the company tailor.

Henry Williams sued Slade for a debt on 13 September 1671, and Thomas Pearcy, a linen draper, went to court against him on 20 August 1672, also for a debt. These may have been company debts. Possibly the following entry in the registers of St Paul, Covent Garden, refers to our subject and his wife: Katherine Slade, the wife of Thomas, was buried on 15 December 1683.

Slape, William Henry   1786–1868,
dancer, singer, pianist, bassoonist.

William Henry "Slapp," according to *The Royal Society of Musicians* (1985), was born on 21 April 1786. His family name was evidently Slape, but he did not get around to correcting the Society records for many years. Master Slape was an Indian in *Ramah Droog* on 12 November 1798 at Covent Garden Theatre, danced in *Albert and Adelaide* on 11 December, sang in *Raymond and Agnes* beginning 13 April 1799 and in *Joanna* beginning 16 January 1800, and, with others, sang "Sigh no more, Ladies" on 17 May. He was first proposed for membership in the Royal Society of Musicians on 3 July 1808, having been a student of Mazzinghi; he was described as a pianist and a teacher of piano and singing. William Henry was rejected in November but proposed again the following month and, finally, elected on 5 March 1809. He was to play the bassoon in the St Paul's concert in May 1811, but he asked to be allowed to send a deputy. The same thing happened in 1812. On 5 November 1820, according to the Minute Books of the Society, he informed the organization that he had changed his name from Slapp to Slape, under which name he was cited thereafter in the books. Slape died on 26 April 1868.

Slater, Mr   [fl. 1724–1727], *house servant.*

Mr Slater's job is not known, but the accounts of Lincoln's Inn Fields Theatre in September 1724 show him to have been receiving a weekly salary of £1 1s., apparently as a house servant. He was last mentioned on 18 April 1727.

Slater, Mr   [fl. 1750], *actor.*

Mr Slater played Squire Gawky in *The Imprisonment of Harlequin* and Whisk *The Constant Couple* at Southwark Fair on 7 September 1750 and repeated the latter role on 12 and 13 September.

Slater, Mr   [fl. 1758–1762], *office keeper.*

Mr Slater was named in benefit bills at Covent Garden Theatre from 12 May 1758 through 21 May 1762. A paylist dated 22 September 1760 described him as the first gallery office keeper and gave his daily salary as 2s.

Slater, Mr   [fl. 1784], *singer.*

Mr Slater, a countertenor, sang in the Handel Memorial Concerts at Westminster Abbey and the Pantheon in May and June 1784.

Slater, Mr   [fl. 1784], *singer.*

Mr Slater Junior sang bass in the Handel Memorial Concerts at Westminster Abbey and the Pantheon in May and June 1784.

Slater, Mr   [fl. 1789–1801], *doorkeeper.*

Mr Slater was earning 9s. weekly at Drury Lane Theatre in 1789–90. The accounts described him in 1801 as a doorkeeper, still at the same salary.

Slater, Mrs   [fl. 1761], *house servant?*

Mrs Slater was added to the Covent Garden Theatre paylist on 10 October 1761 at 10s. weekly. She was probably a house servant.

Slater, Mrs   [fl. 1789], *actress.*

At Bartholomew Fair in 1789, according to Sybil Rosenfeld in *The Theatre of the London Fairs*, Mrs Slater played in *The Recruiting Serjeant* and was Colombine in *The Enchanted Urn*.

Slater, Miss   [fl. 1774?-1775?], *dancer.*

In the Forster Collection at the Victoria and Albert Museum is a manuscript letter indicating that Miss Slater was a dancer at Drury Lane Theatre, probably in the 1774–75 season.

Slater, Edmund   c. 1644–1670, *singer.*

On 14 September 1669 Edmund Slater of Windsor, a clerk and a bachelor about 25 years old, married Mrs Catherine Paradine of the parish of St Andrew, Holborn, a widow about 28 years old. Slater (or Slauter, Slaughter) was sworn a Gentleman of the Chapel Royal on 13 October, but without a salary. Upon the death of Andrew Carter on 18 October 1669, according to the *Old Cheque Book of the Chapel Royal*, Slater, a bass singer, received a salaried post. But Slater did not live to enjoy his new position; he died on 10 September 1670.

Slatter, Master   [*fl.* 1794], *singer.*

The new *Catalogue of Printed Music in the British Library* lists two songs composed by Hayes and sung by Master Slatter: *On an Orange Flow'r put into a Lady's Bosom* and *when Delia on the plain appears,* both published in 1794.

Slaughter. *See also* OSBORN, MARGARET, *and* SLATER, EDMUND.

"Slaughter"   [*fl.* 1762], *actor.*

Some actor masquerading under the name "Slaughter" played the Butcher in *The Orators* on 25 October 1762.

Slaughter, Mr   [*fl.* 1767]. *See* SLAUGHTER, MRS [*fl.* 1765–1772].

Slaughter, Mrs   [*fl.* 1765–1772], *wardrobe mistress.*

Mrs Slaughter was listed as working in the wardrobe at Drury Lane Theater at 5*s.* daily or £1 10*s.* weekly as of 9 February 1765. *The London Stage* turns her into a man in a similar list dated 24 January 1767, but that is certainly an error. The accounts on 4 June 1767, 15 October and 5 December 1771, and on 28 January, 10 June, and 16 December 1772 show payments to her (once for "paint dishes"). She was not *the* wardrobe mistress, for Mrs Johnston and Mr and Mrs Heath also worked in the wardrobe. The *Index to the London Stage* calls Mrs Slaughter a tavern keeper, but we have found no evidence that she was.

Sledge, Miss   [*fl.* 1757–1766], *actress, singer.*

Miss Sledge made her stage debut, advertised as a young gentlewoman, playing Lucy in *Wit without Money* on 28 January 1757 at Covent Garden Theatre. She was Valeria in *The Rover* on 10 May, when her benefit tickets were accepted. Miss Sledge continued at Covent Garden through 1763–64, left there, perhaps to perform in the provinces, and returned for a few appearances in the fall of 1766. Among her new assignments were Prudence in *The Amorous Widow,* Gipsey in *The Stratagem,* Melinda in *The Recruiting Officer,* a chorus singer in *Comus,* Molly and Sukey in *The Beggar's Opera,* a Beggar Woman in *The Jovial Crew,* Jenny in *The Tender Husband,* Mrs Fainall in *The Way of the World,* a Black-moor Lady in *The English Tars in America,* Bertha in *The Royal Merchant,* and Mademoiselle in *The Funeral.* From 1763 on, Miss Sledge's career deteriorated. The last notice of her was in the accounts on 17 October 1766, when she was paid £1 10*s.* for walking ten nights in *The Coronation.*

Sleep, John   [*fl.* Restoration?], *booth operator.*

In *The Theatre of the London Fairs* Sybil Rosenfeld reported on a playbill at Harvard for The Whelp and Bacon Musick Booth at Bartholomew Fair, undated but probably for the Restoration period. The booth was run by John Sleep from the Rose Tavern in Turnmill Street.

Sleep, Richard   [*fl.* 1739–1755], *musician.*

On 28 August 1739 Richard Sleep, a City Wait and possibly the father of Charles Burney's wife Esther, became one of the original subscribers to the Royal Society of Musicians. He was active at least to 1755, according to *The Royal Society of Musicians* (1985).

Sleigh, Mr   [*fl.c.* 1798], *singer.*

Yard Arm and Yard Arm, a song published about 1798, was sung at the Royal Circus by Mr Sleigh. Mrs Sleigh composed a ballad called *Come buy my sweet Flowers,* published about 1800.

Slezack, Mr   [*fl.* 1794–1807], *violinist, music copyist.*

Doane's *Musical Directory* of 1794 listed Mr Slezack, of King Street, Golden Square, as a violinist who played at the Oxford Meeting in 1793, for the Academy of Ancient Music in London, and in the Handel performances at Westminster Abbey. The Drury Lane account books reveal that Slezack (or Slezak) worked at the theatre as a music copyist, at least in 1795, and that he was a member of the band from 23 June 1794 through 16 September 1807 at £1 15s. weekly. He also played in the oratorios at Covent Garden Theatre in 1798, 1799, and 1800.

Slicks, Mr. *See* HICKS, MR *d. 1796.*

Slim, Mr [*fl. 1754*], *actor.*
An actor named, or (probably) called, Slim played Shadow in *The Humourists* at Drury Lane on 2 July 1754 for Theophilus Cibber's benefit. The play was a selection of scenes from Shakespeare, with Cibber as Pistol.

Slinck, Mr [*fl. 1702*], *actor.*
Mr Slinck, otherwise unknown, was one of five actors brought before the King's Bench on 16 February 1702 and charged with using "abominable" language in performances of *Love for Love* and *The Sham Doctor* (*The Anatomist*). The players were found guilty and fined £5 each.

Slingsby, Lady. *See* LEE, MRS JOHN, MARY.

Slingsby, Samuel. *See* SLINGSBY, SIMON.

Slingsby, Simon *d. 1811, dancer, choreographer, manager.*
The earliest notice we have found of the dancer Simon Slingsby dates to the late spring of 1759, when he performed at the Crow Street Theatre in Dublin. On 19 May he shared a benefit with three others. He was there again in 1761–62 and 1763–64, after which he came to London to make his first appearance at Drury Lane Theater on 29 September 1764 in a tambourin dance with Miss Baker. He danced in *The Medley* on 20 November, and, for his solo benefit on 27 April 1765, Slingsby and Miss Baker offered their tambourin and a new pantomime dance called *The Metamorphosis*. A girl of nine, one of Slingsby's students, danced a hornpipe. Slingsby was paid £3 weekly for his season's work.

In 1765–66 Slingsby danced at the Opéra in Paris. George Colman was in Paris in the summer of 1766. Garrick wrote Colman on 31

July: "if you are well enough to see the Dancer *Slingsby,* hint to him from Yrself that he did wrong to send his Brother to make an Engagement with us & then fly off—we have a good Case in Equity—he is engag'd to ye Opera—however—the Managers of ye Opera dislike the trick he has play'd us." Slingsby's brother had negotiated with Drury Lane for Simon to dance there in 1765–66, but the dancer went to Paris instead. (The brother in question may have been Captain John Slingsby, who committed suicide in 1790. The *Gentleman's Magazine* of 15 October 1790, in reporting his death, described Captain Slingsby as "brother to a once celebrated dancer of that name.")

In 1766–67 Simon Slingsby danced at the King's Theatre, making his initial appearance on 25 November 1766 in an untitled ballet. He was not mentioned in the bills again until his solo benefit on 30 April 1767, when he danced a tambourin with Signora Radicati. The solo benefit would indicate that he worked throughout the season, perhaps as a ballet master if not as a dancer, after which Slingsby may have returned to the Continent. His next notice in London was on 5 May 1768, when he shared a benefit at the King's Theatre with Morigi. That night he danced a new hornpipe and, with Signora Radicati, a new allemande. He remained at the King's for the 1768–69 and 1769–70 seasons, again being cited in the bills but rarely.

After a season's absence Slingsby returned to the King's Theatre in 1771–72, and during that season and the next he was frequently mentioned in advertisements. On 4 February 1772, for his first appearance "on this stage these two years," he danced *"Provenzal"* with Signora Radicati. Then he was named for such dances as a *Pastoral Dance*, a *New Dutch Dance*, *"Un Pas de trois en Berger Gallante,"* and many dances with undescriptive titles (*"New Grand Serious Ballet,"* and so forth) through 19 June 1773. In 1773–74 his name appeared in the bills only once.

On 5 November 1774 he returned to the stage of Drury Lane to dance in *The Maid of the Oaks.* The prompter Hopkins noted that "Mr Slingsby & Sga Hidou danc'd for the first time & were Amazingly well Rec'd." The pair also offered entr'acte turns during the season. Slingsby made over £202 at his benefit on 30

March 1775, though he had difficulty getting an actress to play Andromache in *The Distrest Mother.* Hopkins noted that

. . . Mrs Yates would not play for Mr Slingsby altho' her name has been advertis'd from the beginning—Mrs Hartly of Covent Garden was ask'd to do the part, She refus'd it as it was to be done there for a Benefit the week after at Last Mr Reddish said Mrs Canning Should do it, & Such a performance I think was never Seen in Drury Lane Theatre very bad indeed many hisses.

The accounts early in the season indicate that Slingsby had borrowed £150 or more from the management, but no reason was given. Since he was the Slingsby who shared with Jefferson the management of the Richmond Theatre from 1774 to 1778 (probably in the summers), perhaps the loan had to do with that venture. The Richmond parish registers reveal that Simon and Elizabeth Slingsby had a son who was baptized Smith Saville Slingsby on 3 July 1776.

Slingsby spent his winter seasons at Drury Lane through 1777–78. The accounts show him to have been paid over £11 weekly, the third highest male salary in the company. For that sum he appeared as a dancer in such works as *The Hunting of Savages*, a *Grand Garland Dance*, an allemande, and a *"Grand Provencalle."* For so handsome a salary he must also have been serving as a ballet master or choreographer or both, though the bills name only *"The Provencalle"* as his work.

Slingsby returned to the King's Theatre in 1778–79 and continued until his retirement at the end of the 1784–85 season. He was advertised as a principal dancer and paid £500 during his last season; it is probable that he earned more earlier, for the 1782–83 season was announced as his last, even though he continued appearing for two more seasons. He began his new association with the King's on 24 November 1778 as Lubin in the pantomime ballet *Annette et Lubin.* Thereafter he was seen in such pieces as a *Pas de Deux Anacréontique*, *Le Couronnement de Zémire*, *Hippomène et Atalante*, *Les Forges de Vulcain* (in which he danced the title character), a *Pastoral Ballet* (which he and Zuchelli composed), *La Bergère Coquete*, *Il Filosofo*, *La Fête Pastorale*, *The Fortunate Escape*, *The Rural Sports*, *Ninette à la cour*, *Medée et Jason*,

Les Amans Réunis (he danced the Chief of the Island), *Les Petits Riens*, *Apollon et les Muses*, *The Four Nations*, *Le Tuteur Trompé*, *Pas de Lapons*, *Epouses Persanes* (he was Osman), *La Recrue par Force*, *La Bégueule*, *The Pastimes of Terpsychore*, a *Caledonian Reel* from the ballet *Auld Robin Gray*, *Friendship Leads to Love*, *Le Réveil du Bonheur*, *The Deserter* (he danced Skirmish), and *Macbeth.* His last appearance was at his benefit on 21 April 1785.

From the spring of 1781 on (and perhaps earlier) Slingsby lived at No 34, Upper Seymour Street, Portman Square. (He may have lived in the Richmond parish only until 1778, when his association with the Richmond Theatre ended.) In their edition of David Garrick's *Letters,* Little and Kahrl call our subject Samuel Slingsby, but a deed of trust among the Lord Chamberlain's papers concerning the King's Theatre refers to the dancer several times as Simon Slingsby. The name Samuel comes from the *Gentleman's Magazine* of April 1811, which reported that "Samuel" Slingsby, dancer, had died recently at West Cowes (on the Isle of Wight).

Sloper, George [*fl. 1778–1805*], *machinist, carpenter, dancer?*

Egerton MS 2280 at the British Library names George Sloper as a sceneman at Covent Garden Theatre on 27 January 1778; his benefit tickets were accepted at the theatre on 31 May 1783. A Mr Sloper, described in *The London Stage* as a dancer, was down for Peacock in *Harlequin's Chaplet* from 21 December 1789 through 10 December 1790; but the Sloper in question was George, and the Peacock was not a dancing character but a machine. On 13 June 1794 *Harlequin and Faustus* was presented, and the bill stated that Sloper was "The Peacock." That performance was a benefit for Sloper and two others and brought in over £357. The accounts from 1793 through 1804–5 named Sloper as the theatre's master carpenter at £100 annually, and the bills regularly cited him as sharing the responsibility for the machinery in spectacle productions.

John Williams in *A Pin Basket to the Children of Thespis* in 1797 gave Sloper considerable attention: "Mr. SLOPER is a worthy and ingenious man, and Carpenter to Covent-Garden Theatre. He performed the part of the *Peacock*, in the Pantomime of *Jewels New Set* [*The Chaplet*], for many nights, with uncommon applause from a very discerning audience!" He continued in verse, hinting darkly about Sloper's parentage and then commenting on his peacock:

> *He was got by* Sylvanus *from Pan's shaggy sister;*
> *He's coz-german to* Faunus, *and he too has kist*
> *her:*
> *While his nut-brown Mama heard the vows of her*
> *lover,*
> *Young Dryads with boughs wove the twain a green*
> *cover.*
>
> ....
>
> *What an actor is SLOPER—how vast is his taste!*
> *He's no vulgar grimace—his demeanor is chaste!*
> *When he spreads his gay rump, how the Galleries*
> *roar!*
> *When he screws up his tail, how the belles cry,*
> *Encore!*

On 4 June 1798 at Sloper's shared benefit *Unanimity* was presented, "In which [was] introduced the celebrated piece of machinery, The Peacock, by Sloper."

A note in the registers of St Paul, Covent Garden, may concern our subject: On 5 July 1795 George, the son of George Sloper from St Martin-in-the-Fields, was buried.

Small, Robert *b. 1773, pianist, singer, double-bass player.*

Robert Small was born on 1 August 1773 at Harolds Cross, near Dublin, according to the testimony of his mother, Susanna Small of Lisburn, in 1801. (*The Royal Society of Musicians* [1985] gives 12 August 1773.) He became a member of the Irish Musical Fund but was expelled on 5 July 1789 for not paying his subscription. Perhaps that was because he had left Ireland. Dr Burney wrote to Fanny Burney on 25 May 1799:

Sunday dined w.ᵗʰ my fr.ᵈ Dicky Cox—then to a great Concert in Ormond Street—& after that ended at L.ʸ Rothes's—& last night was at a great assembly at L.ʸ Macartney's—where besides seeing all the 1.ˢᵗ people in London. I heard M.ʳ Small sing—he is a young man who has studied 5 years in Italy—has an agreeable chamber voice, & sings in a very good taste. S.ʳ W.ᵐ Hamilton, & L.ᵈ [Maca]rtney, who saw him at Naples espouse & recommend him much [mo]re for his honour than

Courtesy of Geoffrey Ashton

ROBERT SMALL
by G. Dance

a legion of others, L.ʸ Clarges patronizes him very much to her own & his credit. . . .

Small sang in *The Creation* at Covent Garden Theatre on 2 April 1800, and on 1 March 1801 he was recommended for membership in the Royal Society of Musicians. In 1801 Small was still single and earning his living as a teacher and a performer on the pianoforte. He was admitted to the Society on 7 June and participated in the St Paul's concerts in 1802, 1803 (on the double bass), and 1804.

A portrait of Robert Small (9 1/2" × 7½") was drawn in pencil by George Dance, signed and dated 5 September 1800 and inscribed "at Brighton." It was sold as the property of the Rev George Dance (the artist's grandson) at Christie's on 1 July 1898 (lot 129). It was again at Christie's on 16 July 1974 and on 18 November 1975. The drawing is now owned by Geoffrey Ashton, London.

Smalley, Miss [*fl. 1798–1801*], *actress.*

Miss Smalley played an unspecified character in *The Eleventh of June* on 5, 7, and 13 June

1798 at Drury Lane. On 6 November 1800 she was again named in the bills, as Fernando in *Pizarro,* and sometime in 1800–1801 she acted the Child in *Isabella.*

Smallshaw, Fredrick [*fl.* 1790?–1794], *singer, organist.*

The Master Smallshaw who sang in *Arthur* at the Royalty Theatre on 5 April 1790 may have been the tenor and organist Fredrick Smallshaw of a few years later or Fredrick's son. Doane's *Musical Directory* of 1794 listed Fredrick Smallshaw as organist at the Silver Street Chapel and a participant in the oratorios at Covent Garden Theatre and Westminster Abbey and in performances by the Concert of Ancient Music.

Smallwood, Henry [*fl.* 1776–1784], *constable.*

Henry Smallwood, identified in the *Morning Chronicle* of 22 May 1777 as the Constable at Covent Garden Theatre, was mentioned in that theatre's benefit bills from 22 May 1776 through 29 May 1784.

Smallwood, John *d.* 1748?, *pugilist.*

Among the Burney papers at the British Library is a clipping advertising a boxing match at the Great Booth in Tottenham Court on 24 March 1743. Undefeated John Smallwood, "brother to the famous Thomas Smallwood," challenged William Chetham, who accepted. The outcome of the battle is not known. Perhaps the John Smallwood who was buried at St Paul, Covent Garden, on 4 December 1748 was the boxer.

Smart, Mr [*fl.* 1769], *singer.*

A "Smart, Jr." sang at Finch's Grotto Gardens, George Street, St George's Fields, Southwark, in August 1769, according to the Rendle manuscript notes at the Folger Library. He was probably related to the violinist Smart who performed there in 1771, and who may have been George Smart.

Smart, Mr *d.* 1792?, *musician.*

A member of the Royal Society of Musicians named Smart (but evidently not George, Thomas, Sir George Thomas, Charles Frederick, or Henry) had died before 1 July 1792

when the Society (according to the Minute Books) ordered that his daughter Maria be bound apprentice for seven years to William Fry, trimming maker, of No 9, Riders Street, St James's Street. On 1 September 1799 Mr Fry appeared to express satisfaction with her work, whereupon Maria was given "the usual" award of £5 for her diligence. A similar award was given Catherine Smart on 1 September 1793. On 7 April 1793 Mrs Smart had applied for a "full allowance, in consequence of two of her daughters' having claimed their part of her late husband's estate, leaving her with only £11.12.6 per annum." She was granted £30.7s. 6d. "until further orders."

On 2 March 1800 Mrs Smart informed the Governors that having paid her daughter, by direction of her "late father's will," £100 in stock, her income was reduced to £8 5s. 0d. per annum. She asked and was granted the usual widow's allowance. On the sixth of the following month she reported that Mr [Thomas] Archer, watchmaker, of No 12, Sutton Street, Clerkenwell, was willing to bind her son Joseph James Smart as apprentice.

Joseph James Smart informed the Governor on 6 April 1805 that, because both parents were now dead, he was "in distress for cloaths." On a motion by Dr Callcott he was granted £5. On 7 June 1807, having served out his term "with industry and fidelity," he was given £10. The Minute Books record on 5 October 1806 a request by a Mr Dornford to take over an indenture because "Thomas Archer, master of Henry Smart (apprenticed by this Society) refused to comply with the terms. . . ."

Smart, Mr [*fl.* 1793–1811], *doorkeeper.*

The Covent Garden account books at the Folger Library show a h. use servant named Smart on the roster in 1793–94 but do not specify his function. The British Library Additional Manuscript 29,949 calls him a doorkeeper in 1794–95, at 12s. per week. By 1802–3 he was earning 15s. The last known payment to him—still 15s.—was on 28 December 1811.

Smart, Charles Frederick *b. c.* 1780, *singer, double-bass player.*

The singer and double-bass player Charles Frederick Smart was born in London "c. 1780," according to his minuscule notice in

Grove's Dictionary (fifth edition). He was the son of the musician George Smart (1751–1818) and brother of Henry Smart (1778–1823). Doane's *Musical Directory* (1794) gave his address as No 331, Oxford Street, which was his father's house and the location of the family music publishing business. Doane cited his services as a singer in the Chapel Royal Choir and at the Concerts of Ancient Music. He was probably in the band for the performance of the *Messiah* given for the benefit of the Choral Fund at the Haymarket Theatre on 15 January 1798—"Smart and Sons," said the bill.

Smart, Christopher   *1722–1771, actor, manager, playwright.*

Christopher Smart was born on 11 April 1722 at Sherbourne in Kent, the son of Peter Smart (1697–1733) and his wife Winifred, née Griffiths. Christopher had two sisters, Mary Ann and Margaret, both older. His father was the steward of Christopher Vane, Baron Barnard, after whom the boy was named. Peter Smart bought an estate, Hall Place, at East Barming in 1726, and Christopher was entered at the free grammar school in Maidstone. The elder Smart died when Christopher was 11, and he and his sister Margaret were sent north to relatives in Durham, his mother remaining in Kent. By 1744 she had married William Hunter; a son was born to them in 1745, and in that year Hunter died. (For these and many of the facts in this entry, we are indebted to Arthur Sherbo's admirable biography *Christopher Smart: Scholar of the University* [1967].)

Placed at Durham Grammar School under the Reverend Richard Dongworth, Christopher attracted the patronage of the Duchess of Cleveland, who allowed him £40 a year, a sum continued to him by the Duke after her death.

On 20 October 1739 Smart was admitted to Pembroke College, Cambridge. In 1740 he was awarded a scholarship on the Dr Watts Foundation, which paid him £6 per year. He won the Craven scholarship in 1742, a distinction that brought him an annuity of £25 and the title "Scholar of the University" (which he always took care to cite proudly on his title pages). With his various gifts and stipends he should have fared well. But he began to find Cambridge existence dull and developed a

Pembroke College, Cambridge

CHRISTOPHER SMART

artist unknown

taste for high living in London. His extravagance finally forced him into hiding until his friends could arrange a truce with his creditors. He was seldom to be free of debt for the rest of his life.

Smart was not physically prepossessing. He described himself candidly: "My stature is so very low . . . my eyes, which are extremely small and hollow, may truly be styl'd of the *amorous* kind, for they are always looking at one another." He went about, he said, "on a pair of bandy legs." But his wit and charm attracted companionship all his life. During a period of four years following his rescue from the bailiffs, a time in which he sought to curb his drinking and spending, he improved his friendships with Charles Burney, Thomas Wharton, William Whitehead, and others by correspondence.

Smart turned his attention increasingly to poetry. His Latin translation of Pope's "Ode on St Cecilia's Day" Pope himself praised as "exact." In May 1745, Smart's poem "To Idleness"

1745 1754

For the Benefit of Mifs MIDNIGHT.

AT THE

New Theatre in the *Hay-Market*,

On *Tuefday* next, being the 10th of *September*, will be perform'd

Mrs MIDNIGHT's

Concert of *Vocal* and *Inftrumental Mufick*.

BOXES 5s.   PIT 3s.   GALL. 2s.

N.B. After the Concert, Mrs *Midnight*, for *one Night only*, will give, *Gratis*,

SACK-POSSET.

With a NEW PROLOGUE.

And an EPILOGUE, by particular Defire,

By Mifs MIDNIGHT, riding on an Afs.

Alfo a NEW CONCERTO, fet for the

TAMBOUR DE BASQUE;

ACCOMPANY'D WITH

The Original Jews-Harp, *the* Hurdy-Gurdy, *&c.*

With feveral NEW DANCES, *by*

Sig. Banbaregines, *Sig.* Sambucio, *Sig.* Atterino,

Signora Rerriminonies, *Signora* Remperino, *Signora* Tirenello, *and Others.*

And SINGING, *by Mr* LAUDER.

To which will be added, a Burlefque Entertainment, of *Mufick* and *Dancing*, call'd,

LA PANTOMIME
DU CHARPENTIER.

In which will be introduc'd

A SOLEMN PROCESSION

To the Monuments of the *LUNNS*.

The Doors to be open'd at Six o'Clock, and to begin exactly at Seven.   *Vivat Rex.*

Tickets to be had at Mr *Francis Noble*'s Circulating-Library, *King's-Street*, *Covent Garden*; at *Lawford*'s Coffee-Houfe, in *Marlborough-Street*, *Carnaby-Market*; and at the Theatre: where Places for the Boxes may be taken.

Folger Shakespeare Library

Benefit bill—CHRISTOPHER SMART

National Portrait Gallery

CHRISTOPHER SMART

artist unknown

was the first of his long sequence of contributions to the *Gentleman's Magazine.* In July of that year he was elected a Fellow of Pembroke and in October was made Praelector in Philosophy.

In 1746 Smart gave the first public indication of his interest in the theatre, writing his farce *A Trip to Cambridge; or, The Grateful Fair* and staging it with amateurs in Pembroke College Hall. Thomas Gray wrote to Thomas Wharton, "[H]e acts five parts himself, & is only sorry, he can't do all the rest. . . ." Gray added prophetically, "and for his Vanity & Faculty of Lyeing, they are come to their full Maturity. [A]ll this, you see, must come to a Jayl, or Bedlam, & that without any help, almost without Pity."

By 1749 Smart was living principally in London. Charles Burney introduced him to John Newbery, and Smart became a partner with Newbery in *The Midwife, or Old Woman's Magazine.* Through Newbery, also, he became acquainted with people associated with Vauxhall Gardens, including Jonathan Tyers the proprietor, William Hogarth, who engraved

admission tickets, Francis Hayman, who decorated the boxes, Louis François Roubiliac, sculptor of the statue of Handel which graced the promenade, William Boyce the composer, and the future playwrights Arthur Murphy and John Hawkesworth.

Smart kept some ties to Cambridge. He won the University's first Seatonian poetry prize in 1750, his subject being "On the Eternity of the Supreme Being." He won again in the three years following and again in 1755. The annual prize of £10 was welcome, especially since termination of his College residence in 1750 caused him to forfeit his "Scholar" annuity. His life was now the precarious one of Grub Street poet and pamphleteer. In 1750, under one of his several pseudonyms, "Ebenezer Pentweazle," he published a satire, *The Horatian Canons of Friendship.* From July 1750 he contributed essays and poems to *The Student or Oxford and Cambridge Monthly Miscellany,* and from October 1751 he also undertook sole authorship of *The Midwife,* assuming then his best-known pseudonym, "Mary Midnight."

In 1751 Smart engaged in a paper skirmish with the violent controversialist William Kenrick, published *A Solemn Dirge* on the death of the Prince of Wales, assembled two collections of wit and aphorisms—*The Nutcracker* and *An Index to Mankind*—contributed to Newbery's *Lilliputian Magazine,* and furnished a prologue and an epilogue for a performance of *Othello* by aristocratic amateurs coached by Foote and Macklin at Drury Lane Theatre on 7 March.

On 3 December 1751 Smart took the stage himself as a professional. In the Great Room of the Castle Tavern in Paternoster-Row, *The Old Woman's Oratory, or Henley in Petticoats* (designed at first principally to lampoon the eccentric preacher John "Orator" Henley) was presented, "conducted by Mrs. Mary Midnight, Author of the *Midwife,* and her Family." Mary was Christopher Smart himself, in petticoats. The bill promised "a grand Concert of Vocal & Instrumental Musick by Gentlemen who are eminent performers." The *Oratory* proper consisted of four orations,

after which the 1st of which Signior Antonio Ambrosiano from Naples will perform a Concerto on the Cremona Staccato vulgarly called the Salt Box; after the 2$^{\underline{d}}$ will be presented a Great Creature on a very uncommon instrument; after the 3$^{\underline{d}}$ a Solo on the Viol D'Amore and another piece by the Great Crea-

Harvard Theatre Collection

"Mrs Midnight's Animal Comedians"

artist unknown

ture. Then the Candles will be snuff'd to soft Musick by Signior Claudio Molipitano for his Diversion being the first time of any Gentleman's appearing in that Character. And the whole will conclude with an Oration by Old Time in favour of Matrimony, a Solo on the Violincello by Cupid in Propria Persona; and a Song to the Tune of the Roast Beef of Old England to which all the good Company are desired to join in Chorus.

The bill also announced that "The publication of the next number of Mrs Midnight's Magazine will be deferred till the 16th instant and will contain the Orations delivered at the Oratory."

By 27 December 1751 the *Oratory* had moved to the Haymarket Theatre, where Mrs Midnight spoke her prologue, repeated her Inauguration Address, and presented a various fare, including her speech "In Defence of Her Existence," an "Oration on the Salt-Box by a Rationalist," and the "March in *Judas Maccha-beus*, with the Side-Drum." There were four more performances of the *Oratory* program at the Castle Tavern, and then the regular venue became the Haymarket.

Smart's show was presented under a number of titles—*Mrs Midnight's Grand Concert*, her *New Carnival Concert, The British Roratory, The Old Woman's Concert, Sack Posset,* and so on. Involved in the farrago of satire and nonsense from time to time were various members of Smart's "Band of Originals" under the ridiculous type-names that were his trademark— Signors Ambrosiano, Bombasto, Bombazino, Gapatoono ("first cousin to Farinelli"), Signora Spoonatissima ("dug out of the ruins of Herculaneum"), Twangdilo, Mynheer Puffupandyke, Mynheer von Poop-Poop Broomstickado, and Madame Hophye. There were Bambaregines, Rerriminonies, Piantofugo, Balletino, Don Platto, *et alii,* as well as identifiable performers like Lauder, Noell, Warner, the nine-year-old violinist Benjamin Hallet, and (often) Joseph Woodbridge the kettle-drummer. While "Concertos" on the jews-harp, salt-box, or broomstick were staples of performance, along with hornpipes by performers like "Timbertoe" and ludicrous disquisitions on various subjects, there were also occasional orthodox musical renditions.

Early in the run of performances appeared a "Miss Midnight," like most of the performers never identified. She was later called "Mrs Midnight's Daughter Dorothy," but it is doubtful if she was related to Smart, or even if "she" was female. On 17 March 1752 she performed a "*Solo* of Humour on the French Horn." On 27 March the bill promised that "Miss Midnight will speak a new *Epilogue,* riding on a jack-ass, at the Request of several Persons of Taste." (Betty Rizzo published the epilogue in *Papers of the Bibliographical Society of America,* 73.) Performances from 11 December 1752 until 6 March 1753 usually featured a "Pantomime Entertainment" by the *Animal Comedians* "brought from Italy by one Signor Ballard and including the ape Ballard Mango.

G. W. Stone, in *The London Stage,* tallies 36 performances by Mrs Midnight during the 1751–52 season. In 1752–53 there were 68, by the count of Arthur Sherbo. We count 24 in the spring and early summer of 1754. There was a hiatus in the activities of Mrs Midnight in the seasons of 1754–55, 1755–56, and 1756–57. But in August 1757, both Mother Mary Midnight and Dorothy her daughter were said to be members of Theophilus Cibber's company, which was giving *A Medley Concert and Auction* at the Haymarket. Mary played the kettledrum and Dorothy gave an oration and spoke her equestrienne epilogue. But the fact that Joseph Woodbridge was also in the company gives rise to the suspicion that it was really he who played the drums. Perhaps the opportunistic Cibber had simply taken over the profitable Midnight notoriety, and Smart had ceased to be involved. (There were certainly imitations of the show, and not only in London. Sybil Rosenfeld in *Strolling Players* mentions an *Oratory* in Norwich in 1755, and Betty Rizzo cites one in Canterbury in 1758.)

Horace Walpole viewed Mary Midnight's show with lofty contempt; but Mrs Piozzi defended its "low buffoonery" because "it pretended to nothing better, and was wondrous

droll, and what the wags call funney." Perhaps the enterprise made Smart some money, though. It allowed him briefly to make some generous gestures; he gave benefits for citizens "under Misfortunes" and for "Decay'd and Antient Masons," of which brotherhood Smart himself was a member.

In tandem with his theatrical project, Smart in the 1750s continued his efforts to succeed as both a popular author and a scholarly one. In June 1752 his *Poems on Several Occasions* was published by subscriptions generated by his friends. Subscribers included numbers of his musical and theatrical acquaintances, including Garrick, Foote, Mrs Cibber, Rich, Dr Pepusch, and Thomas Tyers.

Sometime during the summer of 1752, at St Bride's Church, Smart married his publisher John Newbery's stepdaughter Anna Maria Carnan, ten years Smart's junior and a minor. The marriage was without parental sanction, but Newbery forgave the offence and took the couple in at his residence Canonbury House. (On 3 May 1753 was born a daughter, Elizabeth Anne, later Mrs LeNoir, and on 27 October 1754 came a second child, Marianne, later Mrs Thomas Cowslade.) As a result of his marriage Smart lost his Pembroke fellowship and its attendant £10.

Smart made a little money in 1752 doing hack work for his father-in-law by publishing the burlesque *Hilliad* in answer to an attack by "Sir" John Hill in *The Inspector* and by writing the *Drury Lane Journal* (as "Roxana Termagant"). In 1753 (as "Humphrey Humdrum, Esq") he put out *Mother Midnight's Comical Pocket-Book.* In 1754 Newbery published in three volumes *The Midwife,* "Mrs. Midnight's works compleat."

Smart's prose translation of *The Works of Horace* late in 1755 was profitable to the booksellers but brought him nothing. He had signed, with Richard Rolt, a contract to edit *The Universal Visiter, or Monthly Memorialist,* but an increase in the eccentric behavior that had for some time been noted by his intimates obliged some distinguished friends—including Samuel Johnson, Garrick, Percy, Burney, and Murphy—to contribute in his stead.

The onset of Christopher Smart's real madness cannot be surely dated. He had always been a little strange. Neither has a diagnosis been decided. Samuel Johnson's comments on the innocuous nature of his dementia are famous: "My poor friend Smart shewed the disturbance of his mind, by falling upon his knees, and saying his prayers in the street, or in any other unusual place. Now although, rationally speaking, it is a greater madness not to pray at all . . . I am afraid there are so many who do not pray, that their understanding is not called into question." So Johnson "did not think he ought to be shut up. His infirmities were not noxious to society. He insisted on people praying with him; and I'd as lief pray with Kit Smart as any one else. Another charge was, that he did not love clean linen; and I have no passion for it."

Apparently, according to Arthur Sherbo's skillful analysis of the available testimony, Smart was confined, with brief periods of freedom—first in his father-in-law's custody, then in St Luke's Hospital, and finally in the private madhouse of a Mr Potter in Bethnal Green—from early in 1756 until the end of January 1763. He was given a compassionate benefit by Garrick at Drury Lane on 3 February 1759 which netted £285. (Cross the prompter noted, "bft of Mr Chris Smart, an Ingenious young Man in poetry, but now confin'd in a Mad House.") From January 1759 to January 1763, apparently, Smart was engaged in writing the brilliant, fragmentary, and as yet not completely interpreted *Jubilate Agno.* (It was not, as sometimes reported, scrawled on the wainscoting with a key or written with charcoal on a wall.) Evidently Smart was at Potter's house under a light and sympathetic supervision, reading, writing, and playing with his cat Jeoffrey. When Burney asked Johnson's opinion of the prospects for Smart's recovery, Johnson assured him that Smart had plenty of exercise, "for he digs in the garden. Indeed, before his confinement, he used for exercise to walk to the alehouse; but he was *carried* back again."

At his release, Smart took lodgings with a Mrs Barwell in Park Street, where he completed his *magnum opus, A Song to David,* published on 6 April 1763. In July following, his *Poems,* a collection of fables and allegories, appeared, and in November, *Poems on Several Occasions.* On 2 April 1764 his oratorio *Hannah,* with music by John Worgan the Vauxhall organist, failed dismally at the King's Theater. Later in 1764 came another volume of poems

and *A Poetical Translation of the Fables of Phaedrus.* His *Psalms of David* gained 736 subscribers in 1765, thanks to solicitations by his friends Gray, Mason, Burney, and Hawkesworth.

In August 1767 was issued Smart's *Works of Horace, Translated into Verse,* in four volumes. On 8 March 1768 his oratorio *Abimelech,* with music by Samuel Arnold, failed at Covent Garden. At Easter 1768 Smart brought forth 83 *Parables of our Lord and Saviour Jesus Christ,* designed for children. They were charming, but the critics did not like them, and they did not sell. Smart shifted his residence to Chelsea, where he acquired new friends—George Romney the portraitist and George Stubbs the animal painter, John Dixon the mezzotint engraver, and Sir Thomas Robinson, proprietor of Ranelagh.

Smart's unremitting industry and the efforts of friends old and new in his behalf seemed never to keep pace with his obsessive extravagance. Fanny Burney wrote of his desperate application to her father, his staunch friend. Smart "sent a most affecting epistle . . . to entreat him to lend him half-a-guinea!—How great a pity so clever, so ingenious a man should be reduced to such shocking circumstances. He is extremely grave, and has still great wildness in his manner, looks, and voice; but 'tis impossible to *see* him and *think* of his works, without feeling the utmost pity and concern for him. . . ."

In 1768 a cousin, Francis Smart, died. Christopher Smart had, unrealistically, anticipated an inheritance; the fact that he was left nothing was a blow. Several small charities on which he had depended also failed. On 20 April 1770, Smart was arrested for debt, brought before his old friend William Murray, now Lord Chief Justice Mansfield, and sent to King's Bench Prison. Influential friends obtained for him the liberty of the Rules of the prison. Smart wrote to Charles Burney on 26 April 1770: "After being a fortnight at a sponging house, one week at the Marshalsea . . . I am this day safely arrived at the King's Bench.—Seven Years in Madhouses, Eight times arrested in Six years, I beg leave to commend myself to a benevolent friend."

In prison, Smart finished his *Hymns for the Amusement of Children,* which his brother-in-law Thomas Carnan printed. They were dedicated to the five-year-old Prince Frederick, but they did not have the intended effect of procuring Smart's release. He died within the Rules of the King's Bench on 20 May 1771 and was buried in the Church of St Gregory by St Paul's.

Smart was survived by his two daughters and by his wife Anna Maria, a practical businesswoman, who, disgusted by his profligacy, had not lived with him since the beginning of his confinement for madness and had done nothing to assist him, in asylum or in prison. She for many years edited her stepfather's paper the Reading *Mercury* and died in 1809.

Besides the admirable biography by Arthur Sherbo cited above, readers should consult *Christopher Smart: An Annotated Bibliography* by Robert Mahony and Betty Rizzo.

A portrait of Christopher Smart by an unknown artist is at Pembroke College, Cambridge. The book title *Fables* in the background refers to Smart's *A Poetical Translation of the Fables of Phaedrus* (1765). The picture was in the possession of Frederick Cowslade of Reading (the great-great-grandson of the sitter through his eldest daughter Mary Anne, d. 1809). An engraving of it by H. Meyer was published as frontispiece to Smart's *Poems*, 1791. Another portrait generally accepted to be of Smart by an unknown artist is in the National Portrait Gallery (No 3780), bought in 1950 from Irene K. Falkiner, daughter of C. Litton Falkiner, Upper Merrion Street, Dublin, who owned the portrait by 1897. (Smart's sister Mary Anne married in 1750 Richard Falkiner of Mount Falcon, County Tipperary.) A three-panel drawing by an unknown engraver, published in 1753, shows "Mrs Midnight's Animal Comedians" performing a variety of tricks and feats.

Smart, George   *1751–1818, musician, music-publisher.*

The origins and early career of the important London musical figure George Smart are obscure. He was perhaps the Smart who appeared on the Covent Garden Theatre's music list 22 September 1760 to play in the band for 3s. 4d. daily. He is known to have been proficient on violin, double bass, and clarinet. On 30 August and 3 September 1771, a Mr Smart performed a concerto on the violin as part of the entertainment following a play at Finch's Grotto Gardens, George Street, St George's Fields, Southwark.

About that period, or a little after, according to Charles Humphries and William Smith in *Music Publishing in the British Isles,* George Smart was employed at James Bremner's music shop in New Bond Street. He then assisted William Napier, the viola player, who ran a music shop at No 474, the Strand, beginning about 1772. In 1773 or 1774, Smart set up on his own as musical instrument maker, music seller, and publisher, at the corner of Conduit Street, near Savile Row, where he remained until moving, in December 1774, to the corner of Argyll Street, No 331, Oxford Street. There the business remained until 1805, when Smart was succeeded by Walter Turnbull. (Yet, Humphries and Smith list an edition of the *Messiah* "published c. 1810," which was "Printed at Smart and Moreland's Music Warehouse.")

Meanwhile, like some other music sellers, Smart continued to practice his musicianship. He appeared in the Drury Lane account books in 1778–79 as clarinetist and violinist in the band at £2 10s. per week. When the first great Handel Memorial Concerts were given at Westminster Abbey and the Pantheon in May and June of 1784, he played one of the double basses.

The Minute Books of the Royal Society of Musicians state, 3 July 1785, "an error having been discovered in the . . . recommendation of Mr George Smart, signing of the admission book was postponed till the case is laid before a general meeting." The nature of the difficulty was not stated. But Smart reacted to the rejection with indignation. According to Charles Dibdin's *The Musical Tour of Mr Dibdin* (1788) Smart, having read Edward Miller's *Letters in Behalf of Professors of Music, Residing in the Country* (1784), which objected to the exclusion from the Royal Society of Musicians not only of musicians living outside London but of those who practiced a second profession, established the New Musical Fund, on 16 April 1786. (See Michael Kassler on the Fund in the *New Grove*.) Smart was a member of the Court of Assistants and Treasurer of the Fund, according to the membership lists of 1794, 1805, and 1815.

Doane's *Musical Directory* cites Smart's performances with Salomon's Concert, in the band of the the King's Theatre and at the Concerts of Ancient Music. A surviving account of money paid to musicians employed in the 1787–88 season by the Academy of Ancient Music gives G. Smart, "Double Bass," £6 6s. 0d. for the season.

The Dictionary of National Biography says that in 1803 George Smart and his son Henry went into the brewery business, in addition to their musical and other commercial efforts, but that the enterprise quickly failed.

Four collections of popular music selected, edited, printed, and published by George Smart are listed in the *Catalogue of Printed Music in the British Museum: Smart's Annual Collection of Twenty-four Country Dances, for the year 1795, . . . For the Violin and German Flute . . . ;* a collection with similar title for 1798; *Smart's Collection of New & Favorite Country Dances, Waltz's [sic] & Reels. Arranged for the Harp, Piano-forte or Violin . . .* (1800?); and *The Vocal Pocket Companion. Being a Select Collection of . . . Catches, Glees and Duetts for Two & Three Voices . . .* (1800?). Most of the 14 songs and other compositions attributed to his son Henry Smart by the *Catalogue* are far too early and are probably by George Smart.

Smart died at Edinburgh on 4 September 1818, "aged 67 years," according to F. Cansick, in *A Collection of Curious and Interesting Epitaphs* (1869), who reproduced the tablet erected by the subscribers to the New Musical Fund in memory of Smart in St James's Chapel, Hampstead Row, "Lamenting their irreparable loss." A contiguous tablet, "erected by her children" to his wife Anne, buried in the same vault, shows that she survived him for only six weeks, until 19 October 1818.

George Smart was the father of at least three children, all prominent musicians: Charles Frederick, George Thomas, and Henry, with several of whom apparently ("Smart and Sons") he had appeared in the band playing for the *Messiah* under Arnold and Barthélemon at the Haymarket on 15 January 1798.

Smart, George Thomas *1776–1867, organist, violinist, conductor, composer.*

George Thomas Smart was born in London on 10 May 1776, one of at least three sons of

Thomas Coram Foundation for Children

GEORGE THOMAS SMART
by Cawse

the musician and music publisher George Smart (1751–1818). His brothers, Charles Frederick and Henry Smart, were both well-known musicians.

George Thomas sang as a chorister of the Chapel Royal under the tutelage of Dr Edmund Ayrton and studied organ with the eminent executant Thomas Sanders Dupuis. He was taught composition by Dr Samuel Arnold.

In 1791 he was appointed organist of St James's Chapel, Hampstead Road. He was engaged also as a violinist at the subscription concerts conducted by Johann Peter Salomon and began teaching keyboard technique and instructing in voice. Doane's *Musical Directory* (1794) lists among Smart's other accomplishments and activities proficiency on the double bass and attendance at the Concerts of Ancient Music and the Oxford Music Meeting of 1793. In 1794 he lived with his father at No 331, Oxford Street, the address of the family pub-

GEORGE THOMAS SMART
by Hodgson

lishing house. He was a member of the Court of Assistants of the New Musical Fund (which had been founded by his father) in 1805 and in 1815, according to the rosters compiled in those years. In 1811 he went to Dublin, conducted a number of greatly successful concerts, and was knighted by the Lord Lieutenant.

A full account of his nineteenth-century career is furnished in the entry in the *New Grove* by W. H. Husk and Nicholas Temperley. A brief chronology of important events suffices here: in April 1822 he was made organist of the Chapel Royal; in 1825 he went on an extensive tour of Europe to study opera production, during which journey he recorded his important conversations with Beethoven; and he conducted musical festivals at various British cities from 1823 to 1840. His acquaintance among continental musicians was extensive, ranging from Haydn, who once gave him an impromptu lesson in drumming, to Carl Maria von Weber, who died on 3 June 1826 in Smart's house, No 91, Great Portland Street. Because his father had learned Handel's

method of conducting and passed it on to the son, Smart served as a sort of conduit to convey Handelian propriety to singers of the nineteenth century. He married Frances Margaret Hope, daughter of the Rev C. S. Hope of Derby, on 28 February 1832. They had one daughter, Anne Caroline.

Sir George Thomas Smart died in London on 23 February 1867. He left a considerable number of private papers from which H. B. and C. L. E. Cox abstracted *Leaves from the Journals of Sir George Smart* (1907). He also left a few compositions, but they are difficult to discriminate from those of his father and his brother Henry. The *New Grove* account dismisses them as "of little importance." The list given in the *Catalogue of Printed Music in the British Museum* is inaccurate.

Portraits of George Thomas Smart include:

1. By William Bradley, signed and dated 1829. In the National Portrait Gallery (No 1326). For the details of the litigation concerning the bequest of this portrait on the death of Smart's daughter Anne Caroline Smart, see R. Walker, *Regency Portraits in the National Portrait Gallery*. A copy was made of this portrait, with the permission of the Trustees of the National Portrait Gallery, for a branch of the family who were distressed that the original had been given elsewhere. An anonymous engraving was published by Colnaghi & Co.

2. By John Cawse, exhibited at the Royal Academy, 1830 (No 175). In the Foundling Hospital, London, the property of the Thomas Coram Foundation for Children. An engraving by E. Stalker was published by M. Colnaghi.

3. By James Green. Miniature exhibited at the Royal Academy, 1815 (No 740).

4. By Charles Hodgson. Oil, in the possession of the Royal Society of Musicians. Smart at about 80.

5. Engraved lithograph portrait by C. Baugniet. With facsimile autograph. Published by Julien & Co.

6. By F. S. Archer, marble bust exhibited at the Royal Academy, 1839.

7. A photograph of Smart by Ernest Edwards of Baker Street is reproduced in *Men of Eminence* (1864); it shows him full-length, sitting in his library. A half-length cut was printed in the *Illustrated London News* on 16 March 1867 (p 257).

Smart, Henry   *c. 1778–1823, violinist, violist, composer.*

Early musical dictionary accounts, endorsed by the *New Grove,* agree that the instrumentalist Henry Smart, son of the elder George Smart, had a precocious talent. Born about 1778, he began to receive violin lessons very early from the great teacher and executant J. B. Cramer (and not Wilhelm as in the *New Grove*). He is said by the *New Grove* to have been engaged at the King's Theatre in the band of the opera at age 14, but if he was indeed born in 1778, he was nearer 16 at his debut. The New Musical Fund program at the King's Theatre on 6 March 1794 featured a "Concerto by Mr Smart Junior, pupil of J. B. Cramer," his "first appearance in public."

Doane's *Musical Directory* (1794) shows Smart still at his father's address, No 331, Oxford Street. He was said to have been a performer at the concerts of the Academy of Ancient Music and at the Oxford Music Meeting of 1793. He was leader of the band at the Lyceum Theatre when it opened as the English Opera House in 1809 and leader at Drury Lane Theatre from its reopening in 1812 until 1821. The Folger Library's account books from Drury Lane show that his salary was a level £6 per six-day week from 1812–13 through 1817–18 but was reduced to £5 8s. 0d. in the 1818–19 season. Smart was one of four musicians unsuccessfully prosecuted in January 1821 for conspiracy and refusing to play at the theatre, according to James Winston's *Drury Lane Journal,* and on 7 September "Mr Elliston had [an] interview with Smart and he (Smart) quitted the theatre." But though he was often in disagreement with management, his musicians held him in high regard, and they presented him with a silver cup on 12 June 1819.

When his brother George (later Sir George) Smart had assumed the management of the oratorio performances at Drury Lane and Covent Garden Theatres in 1813, Henry Smart had begun to lead the band. He had also been a member and quondam leader of the orchestra of the Philharmonic Society during that period. He was cited as a member of the Court of Assistants of the New Musical Fund on a list of subscribers dated 1815.

In 1821 Henry Smart established a piano factory in London and in 1823 obtained a patent on mechanical improvements in the instrument. He was also a composer. William C. Smith in *The Italian Opera . . . in London 1789–1820* credits him with music for the ballets *Laurette* (King's Theatre, 15 February 1803) and *L'amitié à l'épreuve* (5 May 1803). A considerable number of songs attributed to Henry Smart in the *Catalogue of Printed Music in the British Museum* were published too early to have been his and are probably by his father, George Smart.

Henry Smart went to Dublin to assist in the debut of his pupil Miss Goward. He contracted typhus fever and died there on 27 November 1823. On 16 March 1824 administration of the "goods of Henry Smart late of Berners St p[ari]sh St Marylebone" was granted to his widow. He had married Anne Stanton Bagnold (about 1810, according to the *New Grove*). They had two children, the organist and composer Henry Thomas Smart (1813–1879) and Harriet Anne, who married the painter William Callow.

Smart, J. R.   ₍*fl. 1800*₎, *instrumentalist.*

The *Morning Chronicle* of 4 June 1800 mentions a young instrumentalist operating professionally in London named J. R. Smart.

Smart, Thomas   *1747–1803, singer, instrumentalist.*

Thomas Smart the bass singer was born in 1747. He was listed by Burney as singing in the Handel Memorial Concerts at Westminster Abbey and the Pantheon in May and June 1784. A surviving account of money paid by the Academy of Ancient Music to performers at the Academy's concerts in the 1787–88 season shows that Thomas Smart, "Bass Voice," received £6 6s. 0d. He was organist of St Clement Danes by 1783 and was still there in June 1798.

Thomas Smart was a member of the Royal Society of Musicians by 1 April 1770. On 4 February 1798 the Governors of the Society received a letter from him praying for relief (usually given in cases of illness or infirmity), and he was granted £4 19s. per month. The Society's Minute Books under the date of 7 August 1803 record receipt of his notification that his wife had died, and the Governors granted him £5 for her funeral expenses. By 4 December 1803 he had died, and application was then made for £8 for his funeral, which request was granted.

Thomas Smart's career is obscure and there has been confusion about his life. The statement made by W. H. Husk in the fifth edition of *Grove's Dictionary* that he was "probably" the brother of the elder George Smart was retracted in the *New Grove* by Nicholas Temperley, who finds "no evidence of any relationship." We think, however, that some relationship is probable among the several musical Smarts at the end of the eighteenth century. Husk, citing W. H. Grattan Flood, wrote that our subject Thomas Smart committed suicide on 3 August 1826. But that was obviously some other Thomas Smart.

Smart, Timothy *d. 1781, musician.*

Timothy Smart was bound apprentice to John Ward on 15 September 1752, according to the London Guildhall's list of apprentices of the Worshipfull Company of Musicians. He was made free of the company on 15 April 1761 and was admitted to livery on 18 October 1770, at which time he was living in Fleet Street.

Smart had been admitted on 1 January 1769 to the Royal Society of Musicians, according to the Society's sparse records, which call him a "City Wait" (municipal musician of the City of London). A manuscript now in the Folger Library, endorsed by David Garrick, "List of our Band for the present year 1775," carries the name Timothy Smart. *The Paphian Doves . . . Songs & Music . . . by different Ingenious Masters* [1785?] contains some pieces by "T. Smart." Smart died in 1781.

Smeaton, Mr *[fl.c. 1674–1705], actor.*

Mr Smeaton (or Smeton) performed in Dublin at the Smock Alley Theatre from about 1674 to about 1682, his known part being Doctor in *Macbeth*. He came to London after 1682, but the first role known for him is Rugby in *The Merry Wives of Windsor*, which was performed by the United Company on 31 December 1691. That information comes from a manuscript cast in the Folger Library copy of the play; it would appear that Smeaton was originally intended for the role of Simple, but James Nokes's name was written over Smeaton's.

Smeaton is also known to have played Thummum in *The Marriage-Hater Match'd* in January 1692, Carter to the Lyon and Dulcinea del Toboso in *3 Don Quixote* in November 1695 (with Rich's troupe at Drury Lane), Mr Twang in *The Younger Brother* in February 1696, a Country Tradesman and Fruitful in *Aesop* in December 1696, Father Benedic in *Woman's Wit* in January 1697, a Country Tradesman and Breedwell in *2 Aesop* in March 1697, and Delay in *Imposture Defeated* in September 1697. His name is in the prompt notes in a copy of *Belphegor*, 1690s, and the Gildon version of *Measure for Measure*, dating after 1700. He was not cited in casts again until 22 February 1705, when, at Lincoln's Inn Fields Theatre with Betterton's troupe, he acted Galoon in *The Gamester*.

Smedley, Elizabeth. *See* WILSON, MRS JAMES.

Smedley, Joseph *[fl. 1794–1815], instrumentalist.*

Doane's *Musical Directory* of 1794 listed Joseph Smedley of Trowell, Nottinghamshire, as proficient on the oboe, violoncello, violin, and bass and a participant in the Handel concerts at Westminster Abbey. He was a subscriber to the New Musical Fund and named in the annual benefit program as late as 1815.

Smethergell, William *c. 1751–c. 1836, instrumentalist, composer.*

William Smethergell (or Smetergell), the son of William Smethergell, was christened at St Peter-le-Poer on 6 January 1751 and was presumably born not long before that. His father, a poulterer, apprenticed young William to the organist Thomas Curtis of the Weavers' Company on 1 April 1765. William became a freeman on 4 May 1772. Remarkably, on 22 November 1770 Smethergell had been elected joint organist of Allhallows, Barking, by the Tower (in 1782 or 1783 he became sole organist). The *Public Advertiser* reported a subscription concert at the King's Arms Tavern on 25 January 1775; Smethergell served as steward. He was appointed organist of the united parishes of St Mary at Hill and St Andrew Hubbard on 26 May 1775.

On 4 July 1779 Smethergell was recommended for membership in the Royal Society of Musicians. He was described as an organist, violinist, and violist who played at Vauxhall Gardens, and a teacher. His annual income was £200. He was admitted to the Society on 5 September 1779 but expelled at some later date. In May and June 1784 "Smithergale" played second violin in the Handel Memorial Concerts at Westminster Abbey and the Pantheon. Doane's *Musical Directory* of 1794 gave his address as No 7, Bull's Head Court, Newgate Street. (Doane listed him as organist at "St. Margaret's Hill" [St Margaret, Southwark]—a mistake for St Mary at Hill, for St Margaret's was destroyed in 1676 and a town hall was built on the site ten years later.)

Smethergell published two theoretical works on thorough bass, one in 1794 and the other in 1795. He also composed a number of sonatas, lessons, overtures, and duets.

Smethergell retired from Allhallows in 1823 with a pension of £21 and from St Mary's in 1826 with a pension of £36. He died between Christmas 1835 and 25 March 1836. Smethergell had married Ann Moore on 14 May 1772 and had two daughters, Elizabeth (born in 1773) and Ann (born in 1775). The couple may also have had a son, William.

Smirke, Robert *1753–1845, scene painter, portrait painter, illustrator.*

Robert Smirke was born at Wigton, near Carlisle, on 15 April 1753 "the son," according to *The Dictionary of National Biography,* "of a clever but eccentric travelling artist," who apprenticed him to a London coach-painter named Bromley in 1766. He became a student at the Royal Academy in 1722 and in 1775 joined the Incorporated Society of Artists of Great Britain. With that Society he began to exhibit the same year, with two contemporary portraits, a "classical study" from Ovid and one from Statius, and a conception of Caractacus, according to Redgrave's *Dictionary.*

His address at the time of that exhibition was "at Mr. Bromley's, Little Queen Street, Lincoln's Inn Fields." He had removed to No 29, Newman Street, when, in 1777, inspired by the Ossian fashion, he exhibited "Fingal and the Spirit of Loda." In 1777, also, he was admitted to the Free Society of Artists. He was living at No 2, Portland Row, in 1778 when

ROBERT SMIRKE
engraving by Picart, after Jackson

he exhibited a small, full-length portrait of a gentleman whose identity is not known.

Just when Smirke began to paint scenes for the theatre is not clear. Sybil Rosenfeld and Edward Croft-Murray in 1965 contributed to *Theatre Notebook* a short collected account of all that can now be known about his theatrical activities, taken from the Folger Library's Covent Garden and Drury Lane accounts and the Egerton manuscripts now in the British Library. Smirke (usually spelled "Smirk" in manuscript accounts) worked with John Inigo Richards on scenery for *The Choice of Harlequin,* which played at Covent Garden on 26 December 1781 (*not* 1782, as in *Theatre Notebook*) and following. (One of its scenes, "The Hotel, . . . with the Views of the Temple of Virtue and Pleasure painted by Richards, Dall, and Smirk" was thus advertised as re-used in *Harlequin's Treasure,* 15 March 1796 and following.) Smirke collaborated with Richards, Hodgins, Cotton, and others devising additional machines and painting scenes for *Lord Mayor's Day* on 18 January 1783. *The London Magazine* for January commented that

the idea of the paintings was furnished by Mr Richards and Mr Smirk, and all of them executed by the

National Theatre

Scene from *Love for Love*

by SMIRKE

latter in a style of so much taste and excellence that it is a matter of some wonder to us, where an artist of Mr Smirk's abilities has been so long concealed. . . . The figures are certainly painted with great effect, and yet shew an uncommon delicacy of drawing and colouring, unlike some stage exhibitions on canvass, they will bear the minutest examination, and if they have any fault, it is, that they are more like pictures for a private room, than paintings for scenic exhibition.

Thomas Bellamy's poem *The London Theatres* (1795) asked: "Who, when the garden, and the palace, claim/Their breathing statues, who can paint like thee/Impressive tasteful SMIRKE?"

Smirke was paid £63 on 7 June 1783, £20 on 29 November 1786, at Covent Garden, and £4 at Drury Lane in April 1800, with Bromley. (A Folger manuscript shows a payment to a

Smirke of £130 10s. on 2 November 1813. It may have been to his son Robert.)

Smirke exhibited at the Royal Academy for the first time in 1786 "Narcissus," and, from Milton's *Comus,* "The Lady and Sabrina." In 1791 he was elected an associate of the Royal Academy, exhibiting that year "The Widow." In 1793 he was admitted to full membership in the Academy, painting, as his diploma work, "Don Quixote and Sancho." His revolutionary sentiments are thought to have caused George III to refuse to ratify his election to succeed Joseph Wilton as Keeper of the Royal Academy in 1804. "Infancy" was his last exhibit at the Academy, in 1813. He continued until 1834 to contribute pictures to other exhibitions.

Smirke's pictures were frequently engraved. He designed illustrations for *The Bible, The Picturesque Beauties of Shakespeare,* a translation by his daughter Mary of *Don Quixote,* and many other works. He contributed to Alderman Boydell's great project the *Shakespeare Gallery* a "Katherine and Petruchio," "Juliet and the Nurse," "Prince Henry and Falstaff," and "The Seven Ages of Man." Bryan's *Biographical Dictionary of Painters and Engravers* says that "his last works were the designs for the bas-reliefs in front of the Oxford and Cambridge Club House in Pall Mall, of which his sons were the architects."

Robert Smirke died at No 3, Osnaburgh Terrace, Regent's Park, on 5 January 1845 and was buried in Kensal Green Cemetery. In addition to his daughter Mary, he had four notable sons: Richard (1778–1815), antiquarian and draughtsman; Sir Robert (1781–1867) architect, rebuilder in 1809 of Covent Garden Theatre and, in 1823 and following, of the British Museum; Sir Edward, lawyer and antiquary; and Sydney, architect, who completed the British Museum after his brother Robert's death.

Portraits of Robert Smirke include:

1. By George Dance. Drawing dated 29 March 1793. In the Royal Academy.

2. Attributed to George Dance, 1810. At Sotheby's on 25 May 1955 (lot 49). Possibly a copy by Mary Smirke (Robert Smirke's daughter; see below, Nos 3 & 6).

3. By John Jackson, after Mary Smirke. Watercolor drawing, 9¼" × 8". In the National

Portrait Gallery (No 2672), bought by Meatyard for the NPG from the F. W. Fox sale at Christie's on 22 June 1934 (lot 65). Engraving by C. Picart, "From an original Picture by Miss Smirke Drawn by J. Jackson," published on 2 May 1814 in Cadell's *Contemporary Portraits.* A vignette copy engraved by J. Guillaume was also issued.

4. By William Newton. Several miniatures of Smirke were painted by Newton—"one of rather large dimensions, which his family regard as a most characteristic likeness, is still in our possession" (letter from Sir Edward Smirke, 15 January 1868, in the National Portrait Gallery archive).

5. By H. Singleton. Smirke is one of the many artists shown in Singleton's large canvas, "The Royal Academicians Assembled in their Council Chamber to adjudge the Medals to the successful Students in Painting, Sculpture, Architecture and Drawing in 1793." The picture, now in the Royal Academy, was engraved by C. Bestland and published with a key plate in 1802.

6. By Mary Smirke. Oil painting, about 1810. This portrait was lent by Mary Smirke's brother, Sydney Smirke, to the National Portrait Exhibition in 1868 (No 137). Present location unknown, but see above, No 3.

7. By Robert Smirke, c. 1785. A self-portrait in crayon, reported to be in the family possession in Canada.

8. Attributed to Edward Hodges Baily, c. 1828. Plaster bust, 24" high. In the National Portrait Gallery (No 4525). A marble bust of Smirke, for which the NPG plaster is probably a model, was exhibited by Baily at the Royal Academy in 1828 (No 1169). Smirke's son, Sir Edmund Smirke, described it as a "marble bust made for Sir Thos Lawrence, the best and most important portrait of my father" (letter to Scharf on 15 January 1858, in the NPG archive).

Smith. *See also* SMYTH.

Smith, Mr ₎*fl. 1694*₎, *impresario.*

The *London Gazette* of 12–15 November 1694 said that "A Consort of Musick composed by Mr Grabue, will be performed on Saturday next [17 November], at Mr Smith's in Charles-

National Portrait Gallery

ROBERT SMIRKE

attributed to Bailey

street, Covent-Garden, between the Hours of Seven and Eight." It is probable that Smith's concert room was the one that Johann Wolfgang Franck had developed earlier in the 1690s; Franck had apparently given up his venture by June 1694.

Smith, Mr ₍*fl.* 1703–1708₎, *office keeper.*
Mr Smith worked as office keeper for Thomas Betterton's troupe at the Lincoln's Inn Fields Theatre from as early as 1703. The actor Thomas Doggett wrote to the Lord Chamberlain on 8 November, mentioning Smith as the carrier of a message to him at Bath the previous summer. Among the Coke papers at Harvard is a paylist for the Queen's Theatre dated 8 March 1708; Smith, duty unspecified, is down for 10*s.* daily wages.

Smith, Mr ₍*fl.* 1722?–1727₎, *boxkeeper.*
Mr Smith shared gross benefit receipts of £112 12*s.* 6*d.* with two other house servants at Lincoln's Inn Fields Theatre on 1 June 1722. He was probably the Smith who served as an added boxkeeper at that theatre on 21 January 1727. Perhaps he was related to Thomas Smith, who acted at Lincoln's Inn Fields in the 1720s.

Smith, Mr ₍*fl.* 1745?–1748?₎, *carpenter.*
The Mr Smith who shared a benefit with seven others at the Goodman's Fields Theatre on 1 May 1745 was perhaps the carpenter Smith who was given a solo benefit there on 10 March 1747. He may have been the Smith who was named in the accounts of Covent Garden Theatre as a house servant in 1747–48. That Smith shared a benefit with three others on 6 May 1748.

Smith, Mr ₍*fl.* 1751–1800₎, *house servant.*
Mr Smith, a house servant at Drury Lane Theatre, shared a benefit with five others on 9 May 1751. Later benefit bills identified him as a boxkeeper, but by 9 February 1765 he was listed as a box office keeper at 15*s.* weekly. Between 1766 and 1785 he was not named in the bills, but since the company accounts cited him, it is clear that he was still employed. He probably gave up his benefits in favor of a higher salary. The accounts called him the first gallery office keeper on 5 October 1775 and the pit office keeper on 19 October 1786. Then he was regularly named in benefit bills again through 14 June 1800. The accounts listed numerous Smiths in later years, but the office keeper's last season seems to have been 1799–1800.

Smith, Mr ₍ *fl.* 1760₎. *See* SHAW, CUTHBERT.

Smith, Mr ₍*fl.* 1767–1772₎, *actor. See* SMITH, RICHARD.

Smith, Mr ₍*fl.* 1774₎, *actor, singer. See* SMITH, ADAM.

Smith, Mr ₍*fl.* 1774₎, *dancer. See* SMITH, RICHARD.

Smith, Mr ₍fl. 1781₎, *harpsichordist.*
Among the Richmond Theatre bills at the
Garrick Club is one showing that a Mr Smith
played the harpsichord on 27 August 1781.

Smith, Mr ₍fl. 1784₎, *singer.*
Mr Smith sang countertenor in the Handel
Memorial Concerts at Westminster Abbey and
the Pantheon in May and June 1784.

Smith, Mr ₍fl. 1785–1789₎, *house servant.*
The Mr Smith who was named in the bills
at Astley's Amphitheatre as a ticket-keeper or
place-taker from 28 May 1785 to 22 August
1789 was probably the Smith who was cited
in the Covent Garden Theatre accounts as a pit
office keeper in 1786–87.

Smith, Mr ₍fl. 1787–1799₎, *singer, actor.*
Mr Smith made his first appearance on any
stage on 8 January 1787, when he sang Eustace
in the comic opera *Love in a Village* at the
Haymarket Theatre. That night he was also
Invoice in *The Devil upon Two Sticks*, and on 12
March he acted Stukeley in *The West Indian.*
On 9 April 1788 at the Haymarket Smith
played John in *The Jealous Wife*, and on 13 July
1789 he was named in a bill for the Richmond
Theatre as participating in *The Beggar's Opera*
and *The Author*. (The Smith who acted at the
Haymarket in August and September 1788,
playing the King of the Antipodes in *Chrononhotonthologos*, Jasper in *Miss in Her Teens*, and
Beaufort in *The Citizen*, was possibly our man
but just as possibly William Smith.)
Smith played the Landlord in *She Stoops to
Conquer* at the Haymarket Theatre on 29 September 1790. Perhaps he was the Smith who
acted heroic leads at Bristol in 1790 and
1790–91. Smith played Perez in *The Mourning
Bride* on 26 November 1792 at the Haymarket, and, at Wheatley's Riding School in
Greenwich on 17 May 1799, Sir Felix Friendly
in *The Agreeable Surprise* and Hardcastle in *She
Stoops to Conquer.*

Smith, Mr ₍fl. 1793₎, *dancer.*
Mr Smith danced a Notary in the ballet *The
Governor* at Covent Garden Theatre from 11 to
20 March 1793.

Smith, Mr ₍fl. 1794₎, *singer.*
Mr Smith sang alto for the Choral Fund and
in the oratorios at Drury Lane Theatre, according to Doane's *Musical Directory* of 1794. His
address was No 13, Little Shire Lane.

Smith, Mr ₍fl. 1794₎, *singer.*
Doane's *Musical Directory* of 1794 listed Mr
Smith, a bass, as a singer for the Titchfield
Chapel Society. He lived at No. 4, Whitcomb
Court, Whitcomb Street.

Smith, Mr ₍fl. 1794–1804₎, *dresser,
caller.*
Mr Smith was paid 12s. weekly by Covent
Garden Theatre in 1794–95; he was one of the
men's dressers, and, according to the accounts,
he "Calls ye dancers." He was a dresser at Drury
Lane at 9s. weekly in 1801, and in the summer
of 1804 Smith was a dresser at the Haymarket
Theatre.

Smith, Mr ₍fl. 1797–1801₎, *pyrotechnist.*
Mr Smith was paid £7 19s. by the management of Drury Lane Theatre on 13 April 1798
for presenting fireworks during the 1797–98
season. He worked as a pyrotechnist at Ranelagh Gardens in 1801.

Smith, Mrs ₍fl. 1728–1731₎, *actress.*
Mrs Smith played Abigail in *The Lottery* at
the Haymarket Theatre on 19 November
1728. She returned on 1 May 1730 to act
Cleora in *Tom Thumb*, and on 23 June she was
Cloris in *Rape upon Rape* (later called *The Coffee-
House Politician*). At Southwark Fair on 14 September she played a Peasant in *Harlequin's Contrivance*. At the Haymarket in the fall of 1730
she appeared as Huncamunca in *Tom Thumb* on
23 October and Penelope in *Tunbridge Walks*
and a Peasant in *The Amorous Adventure* on 16
November. Perhaps she was the Mrs Smith
who acted the Maid in Tony Aston's *The Fool's
Opera* in 1731. It was performed, Tony said in
his preface, at the house of a person of quality,
unnamed—but we cannot be certain he was
being serious. A Miss Smith, possibly our subject's daughter, also acted at the Haymarket in
1730. On 30 November she acted Cloris in
The Coffee-House Politician, a role Mrs Smith
had played earlier, unless there was a mistake
in the bill.

Smith, Mrs [*fl. 1761*], *actress.*

Mrs Smith played Emilia in a single performance of *Othello* for Cooke's benefit at Covent Garden Theatre on 23 June 1761.

Smith, Mrs [*fl. 1761–1774*], *singer. See* SMITH, MRS [THOMAS?].

Smith, Mrs [*fl. 1765*], *dresser.*

A paylist for Drury Lane Theatre, dated 9 February 1765, shows Mrs Smith as a dresser at a salary of 9s. weekly.

Smith, Mrs [*fl. 1791–1799*], *actress.*

Mrs Smith played Lady Jane in *Know Your Own Mind* on 19 October 1791 and Lady Sneerwell in *The School for Scandal* on 31 December at Bristol. In 1793 she appeared at Richmond. During the summer of that year, according to the *Thespian Magazine,* she played Widow Warren in *The Road to Ruin* at Manchester (her first appearance there), and in 1794 she performed at the Theatre Royal, Edinburgh, advertised as from Liverpool and Richmond. At Edinburgh some of Mrs Smith's roles were Adeline in *The Battle of Hexham,* Amanda in *A Trip to Scarborough,* Donna Isabella in *The Wonder,* Donna Victoria in *The Castle of Andalusia,* Lady Fairfax in *The Royal Martyr,* Lucinda in *The Conscious Lovers,* Miss Crop in *The Touchstone of Truth,* Miss Neville in *Know Your Own Mind,* and Sophia Dove in *The Brothers.* She repeated Lady Sneerwell at Hammersmith in London on 24 March 1794.

From 4 November to 21 December 1796 Mrs Smith played at Bury, and on 26 December she acted at Stockport. On 1 October 1798 she performed with Mrs Siddons at Lancaster, and on 19 August 1799 she was in *Harlequin Phoenix* in Manchester. She also acted in Birmingham in 1799. Mrs Smith may have been the mother of Sarah Smith.

Smith, Miss [*fl. 1711*], *actress.*

Miss Smith played the young Princess Elizabeth in *Vertue Betray'd* at Drury Lane Theatre on 3 December 1711.

Smith, Miss [*fl. 1716–1721*], *dancer, actress.*

On 2 May 1716 at Lincoln's Inn Fields Theatre Miss Smith, the daughter of the actor Thomas Smith (d. 1766?), made her first appearance on any stage dancing for her father's shared benefit. Bills during the summer cited her as a student of Thurmond. She danced regularly at Lincoln's Inn Fields in 1716–17 and 1717–18. Her dances were seldom titled, but she is known to have performed a *Dutch Skipper* and a *Spanish Dance* with Thurmond Junior, a *Scotch Dance* with Newhouse, and a solo *Peasant* dance. She was in *The Prophetess* on 8 November 1717, played an Hour in *Mars and Venus* on 22 November, and was Scaramouchet in *Amadis* on 24 January 1718.

On 8 October 1718 she and the junior Thurmond danced a comic turn at Drury Lane Theatre, after which she appeared regularly at Drury Lane throughout the 1718–19 season except for two appearances in January and March at Lincoln's Inn Fields as Scaramouchet in *Amadis.* At Drury Lane in the spring of 1719 Miss Smith played a Scaramouch Woman in *The Dumb Farce* and danced a *Pastoral Dance of Myrtillo.*

She remained at Drury Lane through 1720–21, dancing regularly between the acts. A few of her numbers had titles: a *Venetian Peasant* with the younger Thurmond, *Forlanta* with Lally, and *Two Dutch Lasses* with Miss Tenoe. On 7 July 1720 she played Mirtilla in *Love for Money,* her only acting assignment. Her last appearance seems to have been on 25 July 1721.

Smith, Miss [*fl. 1728–1731*], *actress.*

Miss Smith was first noticed on 15 November 1728, when she played Diana in *Perseus and Andromeda* at Drury Lane. She probably acted other roles there, but she was not mentioned in the bills.

At the Haymarket Theatre Miss Smith played an unspecified character in *The Village Opera* on 8 January 1730 and Lusingo in *Hurlothrumbo* on 29 January. On 16 October 1730 Miss Smith made her first appearance on the Goodman's Fields stage, advertised as from Drury Lane, playing Jenny in *The Provok'd Husband.* She went on that season to act Cherry in *The Stratagem,* Mrs Clerimont in *The Tender Husband,* Jenny in *The Fair Quaker of Deal,* Serena in *The Orphan,* Mrs Chat in *The Committee,* Araminta in *The Old Bachelor,* Betty in *Flora,* Leonora in *The Jealous Clown,* Phillida in *Damon and Phillida,* Margery in *The Wedding,* a Spirit in *The Devil of a Wife*, Anne Page in *The Merry Wives of Windsor*, a Maid in *The Cobler of Preston*, Cleone in *The Distrest Mother*, Lais in *The Cynick*, Valeria in *The Rover*, Marinda in *The Merry Throwster*, and Clarissa in *The Temple Beau*. On two nights when she was not busy at Goodman's Fields, she put in appearances at the Haymarket, apparently to help out Fielding: on 18 November 1730 she acted Harriot in *The Author's Farce*, and on 30 November she was Cloris in *The Coffee-House Politician*. Miss Smith played Millwood in *The London Merchant* at Southwark Fair on 8 September 1731 before disappearing from the record.

Smith, Miss [*fl.* 1746–1748], *singer, actress.*

Miss Smith made her first appearance on any stage as Polly in *The Beggar's Opera* at Goodman's Fields Theatre on 4 March 1746. The performance was her shared benefit with Kennedy, and she made tickets available "next door but One to the Old Playhouse in Ayliffe Street." On 4 April 1748 she acted Rose in *The Recruiting Officer* at the New Wells, Clerkenwell.

Smith, Miss [*fl.* 1757–1769], *dancer.*

Miss Smith's benefit tickets were accepted at Drury Lane Theatre on 13 May 1757. She was probably one of the company's minor dancers whose name rarely appeared in the bills. From 23 to 27 November 1762 she was advertised as playing a Bridge Maid in *The Witches,* and from 26 September 1768 to 12 May 1769 she was Miss Harslet in *Harlequin's Invasion.*

Smith, Miss [*fl.* 1771–1778], *actress.*

Miss Smith made her stage debut on 18 September 1771 at the Haymarket Theatre playing an unnamed character in *Madrigal and Truletta*. She returned to the Haymarket on 21 December 1772 to act Charlotte in *The Apprentice.* Miss Smith was in Fox's troupe at Brighton from June to October 1778.

Smith, Miss [*fl.* 1792–1793], *dancer.*

With the Drury Lane troupe at the King's Theatre on 27 December 1792 Miss Smith danced in *Harlequin's Invasion.* Performances continued through 14 January 1793. On some of the same nights another Miss Smith danced

at Covent Garden Theatre; a third Miss Smith was with Astley's troupe in Dublin that winter.

Smith, Miss [*fl.* 1792–1797?], *dancer.*

Miss Smith danced a *Burlesque Pas de Russe* with Byrn at Covent Garden Theatre beginning on 26 December 1792. The turn was repeated through January 1793. In March Miss Smith was Creolian Girl in *The Governor.* On 22 October 1793 she danced Old Kathlane in *Dermot and Kathlane;* a month later she and Byrn danced their *Burlesque Pas de Russe.* In October 1793 she had a role in *Harlequin's Chaplet;* a year later she played Agnes in *The Follies of the Day;* in October 1795 Miss "Smyth" was Susan in *The Shipwreck;* in November 1795 she served as a Maid in *Lord Mayor's Day;* and in April 1796 she danced in *The Lad of the Hills.* In 1794–95 she was earning £1 5s. weekly at Covent Garden. Miss "Smyth" danced Old Kathlane again on 8 April 1796, and the following day she was scheduled to dance in a new Irish ballet by Byrn, *Spinster's Lottery,* but apparently another dance was substituted. On 10 May she danced in *The Humours of a Country Fair.* Perhaps she was the Miss Smyth who performed at the Birmingham Theatre in the summer of 1797.

Smith, Miss [*fl.* 1794], *singer.*

Doane's *Musical Directory* of 1794 listed Miss Smith, of No 12, Upper Charlton Street, as a singer who participated in the oratorios at Drury Lane Theatre.

Smith, A. *See* SMITH, ADAM, and SMITH, WALTER.

Smith, Adam *d. c. 1779, singer, composer, actor, lyricist.*

The Mr Smith named in the bills of the Richmond theatre in August 1765 and in 1766, 1767, and 1769 was evidently the singer and composer Adam Smith, who was advertised as from the Richmond playhouse when he sang at Finch's Grotto Gardens, Southwark, in 1765. The *Catalogue of Printed Music in the British Museum* lists a few songs composed by Smith and sung by him at Richmond and the Grotto Gardens over the years. He was cited regularly as an entertainer at the Gardens through 1771. On 11 March 1771

Smith sang a song of his own composing at the Haymarket Theatre as part of a dance called *The Drunken News-Writer.* One bill for the Gardens, dated 12 September 1771, shows that Smith wrote both the words and music for some songs and sang such pieces as "British Wives," "Russel's triumph," and "The storm or the danger of the seas." He also sang in an entertainment called *The Gamester.* A Mr and Mrs Smith were in Roger Kemble's company at Worcester in November 1772, but we cannot tell if they were Adam and his wife.

The summer of 1774 found Smith as a member of the troupe at Marylebone Gardens. He was Nicholas in the musical work *Don Quixote* on 30 June 1774 and subsequent dates. Perhaps he was the Smith who had a part in *The Duellist* at the Haymarket on 21 September and was with Whitley's troupe at Derby in September 1774. He was surely the singer Smith who sang *The Rejected Lover* at the Grotto Gardens, published about 1775. A[dam] Smith was in Whitley's company at Derby from mid-October 1777 to 9 January 1778. The 1812 edition of the *Biographia Dramatica* called Adam Smith "an actor at the Richmond theatre and a singer at Bermondsey Spa" and "the doer of a piece, called The Noble Foresters. Int. 8vo. 1776." His wife was a singer and actress who had been Miss Spencer and was (after Smith's death) Mrs Woodham. They married about 1765 or 1766. Mr and Mrs Adam Smith's daughter Hannah married John Philip Conway Astley, the amphitheatre manager. Adam Smith seems to have died between 1778 and 1780. The song *Who can describe the Pow'r of Love* by A. Smith was published about 1780.

Smith, Mrs [Adam?], née Spencer, later Mrs Woodham *1743?–1803, actress, singer.*

The career of a Mrs Smith closely parallels that of the actor-musician Adam Smith from 1766 to 1778, so we take it that she was his wife. *The Dictionary of National Biography,* in its entry on Mrs Woodham, states that she had been married to a Mr Smith and had been born Miss Spencer; the dates given for Mrs Woodham are 1743–1803, and she is described as one of London's favorite singers. A close check of the information in the *DNB* entry shows that it has confused Mrs Woodham with the

popular singer-actress Mrs Woodman and the actress Mrs Spencer (who became the second wife of the actor Alexander Pope). The misinformation derives from the *Gentleman's Magazine* and the *Monthly Mirror,* when they reported Mrs Woodham's death; the latter called her Mrs Woodman. But we take the general outline of a Miss Spencer who became Mrs Smith and then Mrs Woodham to be correct.

According to the *DNB* account, Miss Spencer was born in 1743. If we have identified her correctly, that date could be a few years too late. A Miss Spencer was at the Smock Alley Theatre in Dublin in 1755–56 and 1756–57. She was a singer, and on 25 October 1756, according to Esther Sheldon's *Thomas Sheridan of Smock-Alley,* she played Catherine in *Catherine and Petruchio;* the event was advertised as the first time "of her attempting a Character on the Stage." That Miss Spencer, we believe, was the one who had a vocal part in *Harlequin's Invasion* at Drury Lane Theatre in London on 31 December 1759. On 14 April 1760 she was in *Galligantus,* and on 19 May she sang between the acts. About 1760 was published *What tho' the blooming genial Year,* as sung by Miss Spencer at Sadler's Wells. She was still singing at the Wells in September 1765, after which her name dropped from the bills. The *DNB* account states that Miss Spencer went to Dublin after her London stint; we find no evidence of that, but she seems to have been there before coming to London, so the *DNB* is close to correct. She was, the *DNB* reports, "for many years a favourite on the Dublin stage."

Nicely dove-tailing with that career is the appearance of a Mrs Smith in the bills of the Richmond theatre in the summer of 1766; there also was Adam Smith. Mrs Smith played servant roles at Bristol in 1767. She was seen at the New Concert Hall in Edinburgh as Dolly Trull in *The Beggar's Opera* on 23 March 1768 and Mrs Strickland in *The Suspicious Husband* on 13 April. On 28 February 1769 she acted Biddy in *Miss in Her Teens* and Desdemona in *Othello* at the Haymarket Theatre in London, and at Richmond on 1 July 1769 she appeared in *Comus* and *The Recruiting Officer.*

(As *The London Stage* notes, on 17 January 1770 at Covent Garden Theatre Rosetta in *Love in a Village* was played by a young gentlewoman making her first appearance. In his notes in the British Library O. Smith sug-

gested that Miss Spencer played the part, and
the *DNB* account of Mrs Woodham would lead
one to suppose that Miss Spencer was the
woman who later married a Mr Smith; but the
performer in question was almost certainly Mrs
Greville; our entry on her contains details of
the confusion.)

Mrs Smith was at the Haymarket on 14
December 1770, playing Jacinta in *The Mistake*. She appeared as a Housemaid in *Love in a
Village* at the Haymarket on 18 September
1772 and may have been the Mrs Smith who,
with her husband, was in Roger Kemble's
troupe at Worcester in November 1772. Mrs
Smith acted in *The Rival Candidates* at Richmond on 22 July 1775 and was paid £2 10s.
weekly for the summer season at Liverpool in
1776. She had a leading role in *King Henry II*
at Whitley's booth at Stourbridge Fair in Cambridge the same year. She was in Whitley's
company at Derby from mid-October 1777 to
9 January 1778.

At the Haymarket in London Mrs Smith
acted Teresa in *The Spanish Fryar* on 26 February 1778 and was in Fox's company at Brighton in June. From 8 to 25 September she was
again at Derby with Whitley. A Miss Smith
(fl. 1771–1778) was also at Brighton in June
1778. If she was the daughter of Adam Smith,
she was either Hannah Smith, who became
Mrs John Philip Conway Astley, or Hannah's
sister. (The *Hibernian Magazine* in February
1801 stated that Hannah was the granddaugh-
ter of Adam Smith the economist, but there is
no evidence that the actor Adam Smith was
the son of the economist.)

A most curious reference concerning "Mrs
A. Smith" is in the *Catalogue of Printed Music
in the British Museum*. The song *Who can describe
the Pow'r of Love* was published about 1780. It
was composed by A. Smith and sung "at Vauxhall in Birmingham by Mrs. A. Smith, late
Mrs. Woodman." That Mrs Smith may not
have been our subject, but the coincidence of
the name "Woodman" appearing with "Smith"
certainly suggests that she was. We believe
that the statement was confused and should
have read "Mrs Woodham, late Mrs A. Smith."
We have found no references to our Mrs Smith
(except that one) after 1778, nor do references
to Adam Smith continue after 1778, except
for that notice. Our guess is that Adam Smith
died between 1778 and 1780 and that his wife

remarried. The *DNB* says that Miss Spencer
married a man named Smith and had by him
a daughter who married "young" Astley. After
the death of Smith his widow "married a Mr.
Woodham, from whom she was divorced."

Our subject seems not to have performed
much as Mrs Woodham. She lived with her
daughter Hannah in her last years, at Astley's
Amphitheatre. On the morning of 2 September 1803 the Amphitheatre caught fire. Mrs
Woodham had an opportunity to escape, but
she returned—probably to save the house receipts, which were in her charge—and was
burned to death. (The date of the catastrophe
was variously reported: 15 November 1802, 2
February 1803, and 2 and 6 September 1803.)

Smith, Ann [fl. 1763], *singer. See*
LAMPE, MRS CHARLES JOHN FREDERICK.

Smith, Ann [fl. 1776–1827?], *dresser.*
The Miss Smith who worked at Drury Lane
Theatre in 1776–77 as a dresser at a weekly
salary of 9s. was probably Ann Smith. By 16
September 1802 there were two Smiths working in the women's wardrobes: Miss S. and
Miss Ann; Ann was earning 10s. weekly and
Miss S. £1. They were both earning £1 weekly
by 1805–6 and continued at the theatre at
least through 1817. The Miss Smith mentioned by James Winston in his diaries as
wardrobe mistress at Drury Lane in 1827 may
have been Ann.

Smith, Bernard *c. 1630–1708, organist,
organ-builder.*
Bernard Smith (originally Bernhard
Schmidt) was born in Germany about 1630
and came to London in 1660 (the *New Grove*
says 1666) with his nephews Gerard and Christian. The elder Smith was nicknamed "Father"
to distinguish him from his nephew-assistants.
A note in the 8 September 1866 *Notes and
Queries* states that in 1660 Smith built a new
organ for Westminster Abbey for £120. He
built an organ for St Margaret, Westminster,
in 1675, and in 1676 he became organist there
at a salary of £75 annually.

On 30 May 1681 Smith was appointed
organ-maker to the King, replacing James
Farr, and was given apartments in Whitehall.
In 1682, when an organ was needed for the

Faculty of Music, Oxford

BERNARD SMITH

artist unknown

Temple Church, Smith was considered for the task. Benchers of the Inner Temple preferred the organ-builder Renatus Harris, however, and in 1684 organs by both builders were tested. Henry Purcell played Smith's in the competition, and the following year the Middle Temple chose Smith's organ. The benchers of the Inner Temple objected, and Smith had to wait until 1688 before he received his full payment of £1000. *The Calendar of Middle Temple Records* shows that on 26 June 1684 Smith was paid £100. Other payments of £100 were given to him in later years.

Meanwhile Smith was commissioned to build organs for Durham Cathedral in 1683 and St Katherine Kree in London in 1686. Other organs built by Smith were for the Chapel at Hampton Court in 1690 (according to the editor of *The King's Musick*), Westminster Abbey in 1694, St Paul's Cathedral in 1697, the Banqueting Hall at Whitehall in 1699, St James's Chapel in 1699, and, at some point, Windsor Castle. (But see the *New Grove* for a variant list.)

The original agreement between Smith and the Dean and Chapter of Westminster for the organ at Westminster Abbey has survived at the Abbey:

An Agreem[t] made betweene the Deane & Chapter of Westm[r] & Bernard Smyth Organist the 20th of July 1694.

That in consideration of the summe of £200 to be paid by the said Deane & Chapter to the said Bernard Smyth in manner following vizt. £50 in hand £50 more upon the 28th day of November next £50 more upon the 28th day of May then next ensewinge & £50 more residue thereof upon the 28th of Nov. 1695.

The said Bernard Smyth hath undertaken & doth hereby undertake, That by or before the 1st day of November next ensewinge the date hereof he the said Bernard Smyth shall & will make the present organ belongine to the Deane & Chapter of Westm[r] excepting the pipes and case, & add thereto a double sett of Keys & 4 new stops, vizt. one principall of mettle, one stop Diapason of wood, one Nason of wood, & one fifteenth of mettle, wh[ch] are to be added to the present Organ by enlarging the case backwards.

And that such pipes are as defective in the present organ shall be made good by the said Bernard Smyth & he is to compleate and finish the same by or before the 1st day of November next,

That the same shal be veiwed & approved of by Stephen Crespian Clerke Chaunter of the Collegiate of St. Peter in Westm[r] and Henry Purcell gent. organist of the said Church; And what defaults shal be found by them or either of them in the composinge and makinge of the said Organ; shall be altered amended & made good by the said Bernard Smyth.

Ber. Smith

Subscribed by the said
Bernard Smyth in the
presence of STEPH. CRESPION
                HENRY PURCELL
                JOHN NEDHAM

Bernard Smith died in London on 20 February 1708. He had written his will on 4 November 1699, leaving to all of his brothers and sisters and all of their children one shilling each; the rest of his estate he bequeathed to his (second) wife Elizabeth and to Elizabeth Houghton, daughter of Humphry Houghton, deceased. Smith's first wife, Anne, had died in 1689.

A portrait of Bernard Smith by an unknown artist is at the School of Music, Oxford.

Smith, C. J. [*fl. 1794–1806*],   *scene painter, carpenter.*

The Winston catalogue at Harvard cites C. J. Smith as a scene painter. He was evidently the Smith who served as an assistant scene painter at Covent Garden Theatre in August and September 1794 at 7s. 6d. daily (according to Egerton manuscript 2293, reported in *Theatre Notebook* in Autumn 1965). A Sadler's Wells bill for 17 April 1799 named Smith and C. Andrews as having executed the scenery for *The Oracle at Delphi*. Smith was cited as a painter in the Covent Garden accounts in 1801–2 and 1805–6; and Royal Circus bills for June 1802, 1805, and May and June 1806 described Smith as having worked on the scenery as a carpenter.

Smith, Charles   *1701?–1775, actor, singer, dancer.*

The Smith who performed a *Scottish Dance* with Mrs Ogden on 16 August 1726 at Lincoln's Inn Fields Theatre was, we believe, Charles Smith, who was born in 1701 (or 1703). Another Smith, Thomas, had been in the Lincoln's Inn Fields troupe for many years, but our subject seems to have been a younger man who danced, sang, and acted in light entertainments, whereas Thomas Smith was primarily an actor in comedy and tragedy. On 13 February 1727 Charles Smith played an Old Man and a Gardener in *The Rape of Proserpine*, and on 29 January 1728 he was the original Wat Dreary in *The Beggar's Opera*. He was probably the Smith who sang Cleaver in *Penelope* at the Haymarket on 8 May. He danced at Lincoln's Inn Fields in the summer of 1728, one of his turns being a *Swedish Dal Karle* with Mrs Ogden. On 24 August "Young" Smith was Pumpkin in *Bateman* at the Hall-Miller booth at Bartholomew Fair. On 24 September he danced at Bullock's booth at that fair.

Smith repeated his roles in *The Rape of Proserpine* at Lincoln's Inn Fields in January 1729, and he was probably the Smith who was Old Hob in *Dorastus and Faunia* and danced on 25 August at Bullock's booth at Bartholomew Fair.

Charles Smith remained with John Rich's company at Lincoln's Inn Fields Theatre and then at Covent Garden for the rest of his career, making occasional appearances with other troupes, especially at the fairs. He continued dancing, playing roles in pantomimes, and taking some parts that may have required singing. His roles under Rich included a Cyclops in *Perseus and Andromeda*, a Sailor in *Orestes*, a Recruit in *The Recruiting Officer*, a Haymaker in *The Necromancer*, a Citizen in *Julius Caesar*, a Woman in *A City Ramble*, perhaps Day in *The Committee* (at Lincoln's Inn Fields on 31 March 1736, with a mixed group including some from Covent Garden; a Smith also danced that evening), Oldcastle in *The Intriguing Chambermaid*, Davy in *The Mock Doctor*, a Follower in *Cupid and Bacchus*, a Swain and a Villager in *Orpheus and Eurydice*, Trapland in *Love for Love*, a Boor and Ginkes in *The Royal Merchant*, Sly in *The Cheats of Scapin*, Bumpkin in *The Funeral*, Jacques and Charino in *Loves Makes a Man*, a Tradesman in *Aesop*, a Cyclops in *The Lovers of Mars and Venus*, an Outlaw in *The Pilgrim*, a Traveller in *1 Henry IV*, a Hostler in *The Stage Coach*, a Coachman in *The Devil to Pay*, Rugby in *The Merry Wives of Windsor*, and a Keeper in *The Miller of Mansfield*.

In the 1760s Charles Smith performed almost nothing beyond Wat Dreary in *The Beggar's Opera*, Jack Rugby in *The Merry Wives of Windsor*, and the Old Man in *The Rape of Proserpine*. He was distinguished from "Gentleman" Smith, who was also in Rich's troupe in the 1750s and 1760s, by being advertised regularly as C. Smith.

His career did not develop very far at Covent Garden, but an incident in 1736 may have caused John Rich to keep Smith on in smaller parts. The newspapers reported the near-tragedy, which took place on 24 May 1736. One paper reported: "Mr Smith belonging to the Theatre Royal in Covent Garden being disordered in his senses, threw himself out of the window of his Lodgings, up two pair of stairs, near Grays Inn, broke his arm all to shatters and is so much bruised that his life is despaired of." But Smith was sufficiently recovered by the following October to act his parts in *The Rape of Proserpine*.

Charles Smith's utility as a dancer at Covent Garden seems also to have faded with the years. Some of his pantomime parts must have required some dancing, but his entr'acte appearances in the 1730s and later were few: a *Fingalian* with Mrs Ogden on 6 May 1737 and subsequent dates, a part in *The Villagers* on 24 October 1741, and the Clown in a *Drunken Peasant Dance* with Phillips in May 1752. Smith's salary at Covent Garden seems to have remained a pitiful 2s. 6d. daily throughout his tenure.

Charles Smith augmented his small income

under John Rich by appearing elsewhere from time to time, though distinguishing Charles from other Smiths who performed in England during his period is difficult. As has been noted, he made appearances at Bartholomew Fair in the 1720s. He was certainly the Smith from Lincoln's Inn Fields who performed at Richmond in the summer of 1730, playing Sir Francis in *The Busy Body* and Gomez in *The Spanish Fryar*. He also danced with Mrs Ogden. Then he danced at Southwark Fair on 9 September. He danced again at Richmond in July 1731 and played Rugby in *The Merry Wives of Windsor*. At Bullock's booth at Bartholomew Fair on 26 August he danced and, presumably, was the Smith who played Old Hob in *Flora*. He danced at Richmond again in August 1732 and played Sir Humphrey in *The Perjured Prince* at Bullock's Bartholomew Fair booth. He was probably the Smith who appeared as James in *The Miser* and a Masquerader in *Ridotto Al'Fresco* at Bartholomew Fair in August 1733. At that fair in September he danced and played Ragged Wart in *Sir John Falstaff*.

The Smith who danced the *Black Joak* with Miss Mann at the James Street Theatre on 31 May 1734 and danced in *The Force of Inclination* at Bartholomew Fair on 24 August was probably Charles. He may also have been the Smith who acted the Gardener and Puzzlepate in *The Drummer* at Richmond on 26 September 1734, since other players in the troupe were also from Covent Garden. He danced *Two Pierrots* with La Bach at Lincoln's Inn Fields on 31 March 1736. It seems unlikely, in view of his attempted suicide, that he was the Smith who appeared at Bartholomew Fair in August 1736 (and there was another Smith in town that summer, playing at the Haymarket).

After 1736 Charles Smith's appearances away from Covent Garden Theatre decreased for a while, but he seems the most likely candidate for some performances at the summer fairs and minor theatres. We think Charles may have been the Smith who played Falstaff in *The Captive Prince* and Sir Charles in *The Beaux' Stratagem* at May Fair in May and June 1744 and Francisco in *Hamlet* at the Haymarket in June and July 1744. The calendar shows that Smith made no appearances at Covent Garden from the middle of January to October 1744; he may have left the company temporarily and picked up the assignments noted above.

Smith was not mentioned in the bills at Covent Garden from mid-April 1746 to late February 1748 and again sought employment elsewhere. He played Gripe in *Harlequin Captive* at Bartholomew Fair in August 1748. At Southwark Fair in 1748 he was presumably the Smith who danced at the rival Lee-Yeates-Warner booth.

Immediately after that, Smith's activity at Covent Garden picked up dramatically, and, for the first time in years, he played Wat Dreary in *The Beggar's Opera*, from September 1748 to February 1749. A Smith played Tourneclef and Hornpipe in *L'Opera du Gueux* at the Haymarket from 29 April to 29 May 1749—during which period Charles Smith was assigned nothing at Covent Garden. It seems likely that our man was given permission to perform in that Frenchified *Beggar's Opera*.

Smith may have acted Clack in *Modern Madness* at Bartholomew Fair in August 1749, after which we find no record of his activity at the fairs for several years. But if we are correct in guessing that he was in the French *Beggar's Opera* in 1749, then he was the Smith at the Haymarket in February and March 1750 (when he was not advertised at Covent Garden) playing Colin in *L'Officier en Recrue*, Tourneclef in *L'Opéra de Gueux*, and Anselme in *L'Avare*.

Charles Smith was not at Covent Garden in 1763–64, 1764–65, and 1766–67 except for a single performance as Rugby in *The Merry Wives of Windsor* on 17 October 1764 (unless the bill for that date, as transcribed in *The London Stage*, was in error). Dibdin's *Annals of the Edinburgh Stage* place C. Smith in that city in 1766–67. C. Smith was at Covent Garden during the 1767–68 season for only one advertised performance: as a Keeper in *The Miller of Mansfield* on 25 February 1768. He appears then to have gone to Edinburgh again, for a Mr Smith was at the New Concert Hall there in March and April 1768 playing Mat o' the Mint in *The Beggar's Opera*, a Servant in *The Constant Couple*, and Jack Meggot in *The Suspicious Husband*. Sometime during the 1767–68 season he also acted at Norwich.

Smith did not return to London but acted in Carrickfergus, Ireland, in October 1768, advertised as from Edinburgh. With him was Mrs Smith, of whom we know nothing else at all. In March 1769 Smith acted Coxcomb in *The Absent Man* in Edinburgh. He was at Cork, Ireland, on 15 September 1769, after which C. Smith turned up again in the Covent Garden bills in London, beginning on 4 November in *The Rape of Proserpine*. His last appearance was in that work on 28 December 1769, though he was on the payroll at 7*s*. 6*d*. for three days on 28 September 1771.

Charles Smith died, according to the *London Chronicle,* on 13 February 1775 at the age of 74 (the *Morning Chronicle* gave his age as 72). He was buried at St Paul, Covent Garden, on 19 February.

Smith, Charles   *d. 1723?, violinist.*

Charles Smith replaced Charles Powell in the King's Musick on 25 April 1699. He remained attached to the court musical establishment at £40 annually for the rest of his career, but he was one of many who were permitted to play in the opera band at the Queen's Theatre. When he petitioned for a place among the violins he asked for an outrageous £1 nightly, but the Coke papers at Harvard show that he settled for 8*s*. nightly in 1708 and was advanced to 10*s*. about 1713. A second Smith, called Junior, also played in the band; we take him to have been a violist, William; Charles Smith we believe was the one who was several times listed among the second violins and whose annual salary about late December 1707 was £25.

Charles was probably the Smith who played at a concert at York Buildings on 11 December 1703, had a benefit there on 4 January 1705, and performed there again on 4 February 1708. That Smith shared benefit concerts at Stationers' Hall on 11 April 1711 and 14 May 1712. He was still playing in the opera band in 1717. His last known benefit was at York Buildings on 26 March 1718. He was paid £30 about 15 February 1720 for playing violin in the Academy of Music opera orchestra. Charles Smith was replaced in the King's Musick in November 1723, and that probably meant that he had died shortly before.

Smith, Charles   *1786–1856, singer, organist, composer.*

A manuscript biography of Charles Smith, now at the Glasgow University Library, was prepared for Sainsbury's biographical dictionary of musicians in 1823 and contains some details not printed by Sainsbury and consequently not found in *The Dictionary of National Biography* or in Grove. Smith was born in Jermyn Street, London, on 8 September 1786, the son of Felton Smith, who had been a chorister at Christ Church, Oxford. The elder Smith was the son of Edward Smith, page to Princess Amelia. Charles Smith's mother was from Durham County and closely related to the Consitts of Yorkshire. She was largely responsible for encouraging the precocious Charles in his musical career.

At the age of four Charles could play the piano by ear and sing, though sometimes indistinctly, several popular songs by Dibdin. At five he was put under the singing master Thomas Costellow, and at six he composed a song for which his mother wrote the lyrics. When he was eight his parents invited Dr Arnold to hear the boy; Charles played a sonata by Clementi and sang, accompanying himself, "Henry's Cottage Maid" and "In Infancy." Arnold advised the Smiths to place their child in the Chapel Royal under Ayrton. A place for the lad was not available until 1796. In 1798 Charles was withdrawn from the Chapel (because Ayrton, then very old, could not be of much help to the boy) and placed under the tutelage of John Ashley.

In 1799 Charles began singing at private parties, and in 1800 he sang at Ranelagh, in vocal concerts, and in the oratorios. He was regularly at the Prince's Harmonic Club at the Thatched House and sang before the King. He became the darling of many ladies in high society and performed at Edinburgh and Glasgow as well as in and around London. In September 1803 Charles's voice broke and, with Ashley's consent, he retired from singing and devoted himself to playing the organ and teaching. He acted as deputy organist to Knyvett and John Stafford Smith at the Chapel Royal and was appointed Bartleman's successor as organist at Croydon Church.

About 1806 Smith, against his parents' wishes, went to Ireland with a singer and her husband to serve as accompanist. When Smith returned his mind was unsettled due to "some connections he had formed there." Within weeks he left again for Dublin, where he lived for ten months before returning to his family in London. On 2 February 1807, we learn from the Minute Books of the Irish Musical Fund, Charles Smith was proposed for membership; he was admitted on 6 April. That evidently happened during his ten-month stay in Dublin. At some point he was appointed organist of Welbeck Chapel.

Smith had long been writing music, but his songs for *Yes or No,* which opened at the Haymarket Theatre on 31 August 1808, marked the beginning of a considerable career as a theatrical composer. There followed music for *Knapschou* (1809), *The Tourist Friend, Hit or Miss* (Lyceum, 26 February 1810), *Anything New* (1 July 1811), and *How to Die for Love* (1812).

On 7 June 1812 Charles Smith was recommended for membership in the Royal Society of Musicians; he was elected unanimously on 6 September and in the years that followed sometimes performed in the annual St Paul's concerts. In 1815 and 1816 he was a Governor of the Society. Smith also continued his singing career, his voice having settled to a rich bass. In 1813 he sang in the oratorios and after the death of Bartleman was considered England's finest singer of Handel's music. But his voice was not powerful enough for the large theatres, and about 1816 he left the stage.

Charles Smith had married, in 1815, Miss Booth of Norwich, also a musician. He went to Liverpool to sing in 1815 and the following year was given a lucrative position there. He continued composing, some of his ballads being "The Baby Boy," "Far O'er the Sea," and "The Battle of Hohenlinden." Smith retired to Crediton, Devonshire, where he died on 22 November 1856.

Smith, Christopher. *See* SMITH, JOHN CHRISTOPHER *1683–1763.*

Smith, Clara. *See* DIXON, CLARA ANN.

Smith, Clement *1762–1826, harpsichordist, organist, composer.*

Clement Smith was born in 1762, for he was 23 years old when on 6 February 1785 he was recommended for admission to the Royal Society of Musicians. He was then said to be unmarried and a full-time teacher of harpsichord. The vote went against Smith in March

(11 yeas and 14 nays), but he was reconsidered and admitted on 4 September. Smith participated in the Westminster Abbey musical festivals in the late 1780s and by 1794, when Doane's *Musical Directory* was published, had received a bachelor of music degree, was organist at Isleworth Church, and lived in Richmond, Surrey. Smith had a doctorate in music by about 1800, when some of his glees were published. He was also the composer of some piano music. *The Royal Society of Musicians* (1985) states that Clement Smith died on 16 November 1826.

Smith, Mrs E. [*fl.1780–1799*], *dresser, wardrobe keeper.*

The Drury Lane Theatre accounts cite Mrs E. Smith as Mrs Crawford's dresser on 28 October 1780 and regularly through 12 October 1799; her weekly salary was 10s., and by September 1797 she was described as the wardrobe keeper. One entry in the accounts, dated June 1789, described Mrs Smith as a widow.

Smith, Edward [*fl.1794*], *violinist, horn player.*

Doane's *Musical Directory* of 1794 listed Edward Smith, of No 5 or 6, Dean Street, Soho, as a violinist and horn player who performed for the New Musical Fund.

Smith, Edward Woodley *1775–1849, singer, copyist.*

Grove states that Edward Woodley Smith, a chorister at St Paul's Cathedral and lay vicar of St George's Chapel in Windsor, was born on 23 May 1775. Doane's *Musical Directory* of 1794 gave Smith's address as No 3, Sermon Lane, and described him as a tenor and music copyist. Smith sang in the oratorios at Drury Lane Theatre and for the Academy of Ancient Music. His son, George Townshend Smith, was a singer, organist, and composer in the nineteenth century. Edward Woodley Smith died on 17 June 1849.

"Smith, Elephant." *See* UNDERHILL, CAVE.

Smith, Elizabeth, later Mrs Henry Arnold. *See* ARNOLD, MRS HENRY.

Smith, Elizabeth ₍*fl. 1713–1731*₎, *puppeteer, singer, wigmaker.*

"Betty" Smith, one of the puppeteer Powell's assistants, received a benefit at Punch's Theatre on 22 January 1713, when *The Unfortunate Lovers* was performed. She was, we believe, the Elizabeth or Betty Smith active in London musical life in the years that followed.

Elizabeth Smith was, according to Grove's entry on Hickford's Music Room, wigmaker to the King's Theatre about 1715. On 23 March of that year she was given a benefit concert at the Great Room in James Street, Haymarket, and on 18 February 1719 another concert was given for her and Leneker at Hickford's. The *Calendar of State Papers Domestic* cited Elizabeth Smith about 1721 as a ballad singer.

On 31 January 1723 Betty Smith shared a benefit with Mrs Orfeur at the Haymarket Theatre, when *Bonduca* was presented. That night a girl of six sang and danced for her own diversion, but she was not named, and we cannot tell if she was related to Betty Smith or to Mrs Orfeur. At the Haymarket on 22 April 1723 Betty Smith shared a benefit with two others; on 9 March 1724 she shared with three others; and on 2 March 1726 she shared a benefit concert with Bryan, a musician who had in earlier years played at the opera house, where Mrs Smith had worked.

Perhaps our subject was the Mrs E. Smith listed in Humphries and Smith's *Music Publishing in the British Isles* as a pamphlet seller under the New Exchange. That Mrs Smith's name was in the imprint of *The Quaker's Opera,* 1728, a piece that had been performed at Bartholomew Fair. Betty Smith was given benefit concerts on 10 February 1729, 28 February 1730, and 26 March 1731 at Hickford's. In the last bill she was described as "from the Opera House"—that is, the King's Theatre.

Smith, Elizabeth *d. 1774, concessionnaire.*

On 7 November 1775 William Lee published a letter in the *Public Advertiser* concerning himself and Elizabeth Smith. Beginning in 1772, Lee said, he had served refreshments at the King's Theatre in a room that was a passageway to the boxes. Alterations in 1773 enclosed the passage, and Lee was charged £60

annually for the room and had to provide his own fire and light. His concessionnaire was Elizabeth Smith. She died, Lee said, in 1774. Her will was made on 26 May 1774 and proved on 20 August. She was described as of Norris Street in the parish of St James, Westminster, and a spinster. To her godson William Godfrie she left £100; to Peter Crawford of Cold Bath Fields (the King's Theatre treasurer) she left £20; to Elizabeth Stephenson of the Haymarket she gave £10; and to Cisly Wright she gave £10. Her maid, Ann New, was named executrix.

Smith, Felix ₍*fl. 1793?–1815*₎, *violinist, organist, dancing master.*

The Mr Smith who was listed as playing the violin in May 1793 at the annual St Paul's concert sponsored by the Royal Society of Musicians was probably Felix Smith. Felix was described in Doane's *Musical Directory* of 1794 as an organist, violinist, and dancing master from Waterford, Hertfordshire, who performed for the New Musical Fund. He was still a subscriber to the Fund in 1815.

Smith, Frederick ₍*fl. 1739–1758*₎, *kettledrummer, trumpeter.*

On 28 August 1739 Frederick Smith became one of the original subscribers to the Royal Society of Musicians. He replaced Benjamin Gosset as trumpeter in the King's Musick on 7 May 1740. The Lord Chamberlain's accounts listed Smith sometimes as a trumpeter, sometimes as a kettledrummer, and sometimes as both; he was replaced by Walter Rowland on 1 October 1742. Frederick Smith played kettledrums in the performance of the *Messiah* at the Foundling Hospital in May 1754 for 10s. 6d. He participated in the *Messiah* again in May 1758 for the same fee.

Smith, G. ₍*fl. 1776*₎, *actor.*

With other Smiths, G. Smith acted in London at China Hall, Rotherhithe, in the fall of 1776. Smith's only known role was a Coachman in *High Life below Stairs* on 16 October. In the troupe also were J. Smith, who played important roles, and W. Smith, who acted small parts.

GEORGE SMITH, as Robin

engraving by Cooper, after De Wilde

Smith, George *1777–1836?,* *actor,* *singer.*

The Theatrical Inquisitor of October 1812 carried a biographical sketch of George Smith the singer-actor. Smith was born in London in December 1777, the son of a fairly well-off tradesman. When young George displayed a good singing voice, his father took him out of school and placed him under Hudson in St Paul's choir, where George remained until his voice broke at the age of 14. He was then apprenticed to a law stationer named Peacock. Smith did not pursue a career as a stationer after reaching his majority but turned again to singing.

He was probably the G. Smith who played one of several archers in *William Tell* at Sadler's Wells on 12 May 1794, though he would have been only 17 at the time and still serving his apprenticeship. G. Smith also appeared as a Hunter in *Chevy Chase* at Sadler's Wells on 4 August 1795. It certainly seems possible that

George, who evidently did not enjoy his apprenticeship, might have begun frequenting Sadler's Wells in the evenings and playing an occasional bit part. *The Theatrical Inquisitor,* on the other hand, cites as George's initial engagement one at Vauxhall Gardens after he completed his apprenticeship, which would have been in 1798. *The Theatrical Inquisitor* dates his first appearance at Sadler's Wells as Easter 1803, when he was Ralph in *Edward and Susan.*

Smith sang at the Gardens for three seasons, and we take him to have been the Smith who was named in several bills at Sadler's Wells from 1800 to 1808. At the Wells he is known to have been in *Blackenberg* and *Peter Wilkins* in 1800; played Sir John Bull in *British Amazons,* a Rustic in *Barbara Allen,* a Tippling Waterman in *Wizard's Wake,* a Pirate Boatswain in *Philip Quarll,* Perkins in *Red Riding Hood,* a Lambseller "(with a song)" in *Goody Two Shoes,* Giles in *Edward and Susan,* and an Old Woman in *Fire and Spirit* in 1803; and acted a Pedagogue in *The White Witch* and a character in *The Magic Minstrel* in 1808. A contemporary, R. Wheeler, wrote a letter (now in the British Library) saying that George Smith was a natural actor and good singer with a fine voice "but from idleness and sottishness did not get on in his profession and sunk by gradual degrees to a chorus singer." As will be seen, that was not true.

Jones, the proprietor of the Royal Circus, engaged Smith about 1801 for three years. Smith (presumably George) played a Banner Bearer in *Gonsalvo de Cordova* on 16 August 1802; he was a principal character in *The Jubilee of 1802* on 20 September; and he sang a "Negro Duet" with Sleder on 15 November 1803. J. Smith was also at the Royal Circus in 1802; we are guessing that the Smith cited with no initial was George.

For six guineas weekly Smith went with Charles Dibdin's company to Dublin; they performed at the Amphitheatre in Peter Street from 9 November 1805 to 14 February 1806. Smith's success in Dublin was such, according to the *Theatrical Inquisitor,* that he was employed as a bass singer at the Cathedral and sang in the *Dettingen Te Deum* before the Lord Lieutenant to celebrate Nelson's victory at Trafalgar. Jones of the Crow Street Theatre, Dub-

Harvard Theatre Collection

GEORGE SMITH, as Peter
engraving by Cook, after De Wilde

lin, offered Smith an engagement, but Smith did not wish to stay in Dublin.

On 21 February 1806 Smith appeared at Manchester, and *The Thespian Review* reported:

On Friday the 21st of February, the new musical farce, "OUT OF PLACE, or the LAKE of LAUSANNE," was performed here for the first time. . . . Young *Valteline* gave Mr. SMITH an opportunity of displaying his fine voice to much advantage. The ballad of William Tell, and "*Dulce Domum,*" both went to the heart, though part of the effect, in each, was lost from the want of a more clear annunciation of the words, which, instead of injuring the music, would have materially assisted it. Miss STEPHENS in *Laurette,* sung several airs most delightfully, but the duet between her and Mr. Smith, seemed to make the greatest impression. It was a high trait [i.e., treat] to the lovers of

harmony; it rivetted attention, and almost suspended the breathing of the house. . . .

On 19 June 1806 in Liverpool Smith married Miss Stephens.

The following 20 October in London Smith, by permission of the management of Sadler's Wells, was in *Colin Clump* at the Royal Circus. He introduced the song "London Sights; or Colin's Opinion of the Roscius Budget."

Smith's first appearance at Drury Lane, the *Theatrical Inquisitor* noted, was on 10 October 1807 as Hodge. He continued gaining fame with the Drury Lane troupe, being especially successful as Peter in *Up All Night:* "His voice is wonderfully deep and harmonious; in this respect he rises far above Naldi, though not equal in point of science to that celebrated Italian. This defect, however, may be remedied by time and attention, and we look forward with pleasure to the day, when a thorough knowledge in the science will be combined to his extraordinary talents."

Smith began his regular engagement at Drury Lane in September 1808 at a salary of £8 weekly. By 1811–12, when the company was at the Lyceum, his salary had risen to £10 per week, but in 1816–17 he was reduced to £7. He remained at Drury Lane through 1818–19, though Dibdin said Smith was at Sadler's Wells again in 1818. In 1819, from 17 February to 25 September, Smith appeared at the Theatre Royal in Shakespeare Square, Edinburgh, advertised as from Drury Lane. His known parts were Belville in *Rosina,* Macheath in *The Beggar's Opera,* Fiorello in *The Marriage of Figaro,* Henry Bertram in *Guy Mannering,* Masetto in *The Libertine,* Prince Orlando in *The Cabinet,* Young Meadows in *Love in a Village,* and the Traveller in the immensely popular *Rob Roy Macgregor.*

He returned to Drury Lane in 1820 and was mentioned occasionally in James Winston's diaries. Two of Smith's parts there were Father Luke in *The Poor Soldier* and the Gaoler in *Magpie.* On 20 December 1824 "G. Smith [was] arrested for £17 with expenses while coming into [the] theatre this evening."

Such sources as the Harvard and Garrick Club catalogues give George Smith's death as 1836, but we cannot be certain that that is correct. The *Gentleman's Magazine* in January

1836 printed an obituary for a George Smith of Goldicote House who had died on 28 November 1835 at the age of 66, but that George Smith seems not to have been our man.

In his *Memoirs* Charles Dibdin noted that in 1803 at Sadler's Wells Miss Smith, George's sister, was in the troupe. She may not have acted in the eighteenth century in London.

Following are the known likenesses of George Smith:

1. As Bardolph, with William Dowton as Falstaff, in a scene from *1 Henry IV;* oil by George Clint, painted in 1832 and exhibited at the Royal Academy in 1833; now at Harvard University.

2. As Bardolph. Study in oils for painting above; in the Mander and Mitchenson collection; shown at the exhibition "Shakespeare and the Theatre" at the Guildhall Library, London, in 1964.

3. As Peter in *Up All Night.* Pencil and watercolor drawing signed and dated 1810 by Samuel De Wilde; now in the Garrick Club (No 65f). An engraving by H. R. Cook was published as a plate to the *Theatrical Inquisitor* in October, 1812, and another by W. Symms was published by T. and I. Elvey as a plate to *The Drama,* 1823.

4. As Peter. Painting (in oils?) by De Wilde, exhibited at the Royal Academy in 1811; present location unknown.

5. As Robin in *No Song, No Supper;* engraving by R. Cooper, after DeWilde, published as a plate to Terry's *Theatrical Gallery,* 1822.

6. As Schampt in *The Woodman's Hut;* watercolor signed and dated January 1817 by De Wilde; now at the National Theatre, London, from the Maugham Bequest.

7. An engraving with substantial alteration, by J. Thomson, was published as frontispiece to the play in Oxberry's *English Drama,* 1818. Listed incorrectly in the Harvard Theatre Collection catalogue as showing Richard John Smith.

Smith, George ₁*fl. 1786?–1809*₁, *dancer, equestrian, equilibrist.*

The Mr Smith who was in Richards's company at Coopers' Hall in Bristol in 1786 may or may not have been George Smith. The bill for 25 March puffed "The Lilliputian's comic dance by Mr. Smith." He was apparently an equestrian in Handy and Franklin's troupe at the Riding School behind the Full Moon in Stokes Croft, Bristol, on 22 March 1790 and was in *The Taylor Riding to Brentford.*

On 6 March 1792 a Smith rode for Handy and Franklin at the new amphitheatre in Lime-kiln Lane. Smith seems clearly not to have been *the* "Little Devil," for both appeared in the bill for that date, yet Franklin put a notice in the Bristol paper on 4 June that identified Smith:

WHEREAS GEORGE SMITH, (commonly called the *Little Devil*) indentured apprentice to BENJAMIN HANDY, Riding Master, hath absconded from his master's service. This is therefore to caution all persons from employing the said George Smith, as his said master is determined to prosecute any person who shall entertain or employ the said apprentice. The said George Smith may return immediately to his duty by applying to the Printers of the Bristol Mercury; and if he does not return in seven days, a reward will be offered for apprehending him.

If George Smith was Handy's apprentice, he should have been under 21 at the time, so the Mr Smith who was named in the circus bills in Bristol earlier may have been another Smith, perhaps George's father. There seems to have been a mature Smith who acted heroic leads in Bristol in May 1790 and during the 1790–91 season. In any case, the famous equestrian of a few years later was certainly named George Smith, as Dibdin's *Memoirs* prove.

The Smith named in Bristol advertisements of 20 April 1793 and 8 March 1794 as a circus performer with Franklin's company in Lime-kiln Lane may have been George, but we cannot be certain. A Mr Smith, who was puffed as having danced at Sadler's Wells in London, appeared at the Crow Street Theatre in Dublin in 1794–95.

On 17 April 1795, back in London, George Smith performed equestrian exercises at the Royal Circus. After that he was named regularly in the Circus bills as a leading performer. The bill for 20 April 1795 boasted of "SLACK ROPE VAULTING, By Mr. Smith." Later in the evening he and Crossman, assisted by others, performed equestrian exercises, after which Smith took "several surprising Leaps, particularly over Seven Horses with Persons on them." On 11 May he offered "GROUND and LOFTY TUMBLING" and horsemanship, and on 1 October he was given a benefit, hailed as "the First Equestrian Performer in the World" and a pupil of Mr. Hughes. Smith gave the audience full measure:

He will Jump over Three Garters going once round the Ring, and take a surprising Leap through a Balloon, suspended in the air, Ten Feet high, and alight on the Saddle, on a Single horse, which is allowed to be the greatest Feat of Horsemanship ever attempted, and never performed by any other Person.

GRAND TRAMPOLINE TRICKS,
By Mr. Smith

Who will, on the above Evening, take several surprising Leaps: in particular, he will throw a somerset over the Clown standing with a Boy on his head; also over the Clown sitting on Horseback, with a Boy on his Shoulders; likewise over six Horses, with People sitting on them, and through a Balloon of Real Fire.

SLACK ROPE VAULTING,

By Mr. Smith, who will go through several New Feats; in particular, he will stand on the Rope; and turn round like the Fly of a Jack.

Mr. Smith will, for that night only, throw a back somerset, from a . . . horse on full speed, over a Garter Fourteen Feet from the ground.

Tickets for Smith's benefit were available from him at No 2, St George's Crescent.

On 20 August 1796 at the Circus, Smith headed the equestrian troop, called in the bill "that extraordinary Phoenomenon." He displayed "his several excellencies in his much admired Performances with Oranges, Forks, Leaping over the Garter, &c." He was performing on 20 July 1797, but the *Monthly Mirror* that year reported that he was a "sudden deserter" of the Circus, and for a while his name did not appear in the bills.

The *Monthly Mirror* in January 1798 advised readers that "The report of Smith the equestrian, having been killed by a fall during his professional exercise at the Royal Circus, apparently is untrue." The only bill we have seen for the Circus in 1798 named Smith as a performer on the trampoline. On 28 May and 2 June of that year, by permission of the proprietor of the Royal Circus, Smith went through "his wonderful Performances on the Slack Rope" at Covent Garden Theatre.

In 1799 Smith joined William Parker, William David, Robert Handy, John Crossman, and Richard Johannot to form a company of equestrians, according to Charles Dibdin's *Memoirs*. When the troupe went to Bristol,

Dibdin said, Smith's "name and exertions always crammed the house."

On 29 May 1800 Smith returned to the Royal Circus, making his first appearance, the bill said, in two years. He demonstrated his horsemanship, and on 23 June he performed on the trampoline. In September he vaulted on the slack rope. One of his trampoline tricks was a leap over 20 men's heads and through a balloon of fire. He also drew himself up 20 feet by his teeth.

A clipping among James Winston's papers at the Folger Shakespeare Library, dated 3 July 1801, states: "Mr. Smith, of the Circus, was unfortunately drowned on Tuesday night, in stepping out of a boat." The report was false; Smith did not drown. About 1804–5 Smith and three others were admitted to a half share in the new Astley Amphitheatre. Smith retired at the end of the 1809 season. Winston pasted an almost illegible manuscript note near the clipping about Smith's boat accident: "Smith becoming infirm and incapable of his usual exertions & . . . feats quitted Astley, went to Dublin with his family where he had a riding school in Lower Castle Y[ard?] given him by Mr. [?] and broke horses in for the Army & gave private lessons but his infirmities inc^d to that degree that he soon died. . . ." De Castro in his *Memoirs* in 1824 spoke of our subject as "the late celebrated *George Smith*. . . ."

Smith, Mrs [George?]. *See* STEPHENS, MISS.

Smith, Hannah. *See* ASTLEY, MRS JOHN PHILIP CONWAY.

Smith, Henrietta. *See also* SMITH, MRS WALTER.

Smith, [Henrietta?], **later Mrs Edmund John Eyre the second** [*fl. 1792?–1823*], *actress, singer.*

In the fifth volume of this *Dictionary* we supposed that the second Mrs Edmund John Eyre acted only in the nineteenth century, but the late Charles Beecher Hogan believed that she may have been the Miss Smith who made a single London appearance on 15 October 1792 playing Alithea in *The Country Girl* at the Haymarket Theatre. The *Edinburgh Magazine* in February 1823 stated that Mrs Eyre's mother, Mrs Walter Smith, had recently died. Both Mr and Mrs Walter Smith were performers; Mrs Smith was the former Henrietta Scrase. There seems to be no solid evidence that the Miss Smith in London in 1792 was the one who married Eyre, but on the chance that she was, we include her here. It is perhaps worth nothing that Eyre, too, made only a single appearance in London, on 28 May 1791 at Covent Garden Theatre; Miss Smith may have been in London at the time.

A Miss Smith performed in Bury from 4 November to 21 December 1796, after which she appeared in Stockport. She was probably the Miss Smith who acted at Cork in March 1800 and was at Swansea, according to the *Monthly Mirror,* in August 1801. That periodical cited her as a sister to Mrs Hazard. Charles Dibdin in his *Memoirs* said that Miss Smith, the sister of Mr G(eorge) Smith, was engaged for the 1803 season at Sadler's Wells. She was named in the cast of *British Amazons* that year as one of the vocal Amazons; also in the cast were Smith and Mrs Smith (her parents?). That year Miss Smith was also seen as a Slave in *The Old Man of the Mountains.* She was again in the Sadler's Wells troupe in 1804, but no London advertisements have been found for her after 1804.

That fact fits with the report in the *European Magazine* of July 1804 that Miss Smith and Mr Eyre, both of the Bath theatre, had recently been married at Stratford le Bow following an elopement. In the spring of 1805 Edmund John and Henrietta Eyre performed in Edinburgh. She continued acting there until at least 1823, some of her parts being Alithea in *The Country Girl* (the role Miss Smith acted in London in 1792), Calpurnia in *Julius Caesar,* Desdemona in *Othello,* the Duke of York in *Richard III* (which suggests that she was petite), Lady Capulet in *Romeo and Juliet,* Lady Macbeth, Lady Sneerwell in *The School for Scandal,* Millwood in *The London Merchant,* Mrs Page in *The Merry Wives of Windsor,* Patch in *the Busy Body,* the Queen in *Cymbeline,* Gertrude in *Hamlet,* and Yarico in *Inkle and Yarico.* Her husband died in Edinburgh in April 1816; her mother, Mrs Walter Smith, died in Edinburgh in February 1823, at which time Mrs Eyre was still a member of the Edinburgh Theatre Royal.

Smith, Henry *d. 1689, singer.*

Henry Smith, a priest of St Paul's Cathedral, was sworn a Gentleman of the Chapel Royal on 4 October 1666, but he had to wait for a vacancy before he received any pay. When Matthew Penniall died on 12 January 1667, Smith took his place and salary. A tenor, Smith was chosen in the summer of 1671 to attend the King at Windsor at 8s. daily. He was at Windsor again in the late summer of 1678. Smith continued in the Chapel Royal until his death on 23 May 1689. He had made his will on 23 April 1689, describing himself as a clerk and sub-dean of St Paul's and "infirme in body." He left his son Francis 10s. for a mourning ring, noting that Francis had already received his portion of Rev Smith's estate. His daughters Elizabeth (Mrs Peter Lewis), Rebeccka (Mrs Charles Furins), and Mary (Mrs John Clerke) had also received their portions and were given 10s. each for rings. The rest of the estate went to Henry's wife Elizabeth, who proved the will on 27 June 1689.

Smith, Henry [*fl. 1754*], *singer.*

Henry Smith sang at his own benefit at the Haymarket Theatre on 28 November 1754, when an "Aethiopian Concert" was presented.

Smith, Henry [*fl. 1792–1824?*], *singer, actor, dancer.*

The alto singer Henry Smith may have been the Mr Smith who played a Woman Fire-Eater in *The Savages* at Sadler's Wells in 1792. That Smith was also seen that year as a Robber in *La Forêt Noire,* and on 9 April he sang in the musical *Queen Dido* and was in *Maedea's Kettle.* In 1793 at the Wells Smith played Dorcas, another female role, in *Pandora's Box.* The role featured a song in character. That year also saw Smith as a Volunteer and a Sailor in *Sans Culottes* and an unnamed character in *The Witch of the Lakes.* In 1794 the bills named Smith as a dancer in *Irish Courtship,* the Executioner in *William Tell,* and Dorcas (again) in *Pandora's Box.*

Doane's *Musical Directory* of 1794 gave Henry Smith's address as No 75, St Paul's Churchyard, described him as an alto singer late of St Paul's choir, and cited him as singing for the Academy of Ancient Music and in the oratorios at Drury Lane Theatre and Westminster Abbey. A Smith performed at the Theatre Royal, Bath, in late April 1795, but that Smith may have been Walter, William, or Henry Smith. "H. Smith" was a Sailor in *England's Glory* at Sadler's Wells on 31 August and 1 September 1795. Smith (with no initial in the bills) was seen at the Wells on 29 March 1796 as the Genii in *The Talisman* (a singing role) and on 5 April as a comic character in the pantomime ballet *The Strawberry Pickers*.

It seems likely that the singer Smith who appeared at Covent Garden Theatre from 26 December 1798 was Henry. That Smith's first notice was as a vocal character in *Harlequin and Quixotte*. Then he appeared as a Bard in *Oscar and Malvina*, a Soldier and a Sailor in *The Raft*, a singer in *Forecastle Fun*, a Friar and Muleteer in *Raymond and Agnes*, a European in *Ramah Droog*, a Servant in *The Iron Chest*, an Infernal Spirit in *The Volcano*, and a singer in *Joanna*. Smith continued at Covent Garden at least through the 1813–14 season, earning £2 weekly for his chores, which seem to have remained minor.

The will of James Treby, dated 18 January 1824 and proved on the following 10 March named Henry Smith, of Bath, the brother of Treby's wife Frances. A Treby had performed at Covent Garden Theatre from 1810 to 1815, when Mr Smith was active there.

Smith, I. ₁*fl.* 1704₁, *performer?*
Circe and *Acis and Galatea* were performed at Lincoln's Inn Fields Theatre on 14 July 1704 for the benefit of I. Smith. Perhaps he was a performer.

Smith, J. ₁*fl.* 1735?–1737?₁, *actor.*
The Mr Smith who acted Roderigo in *Othello* at York Buildings on 19 March 1735 and appeared at Lincoln's Inn Fields Theatre the following summer was not Charles Smith, we believe; possibly he was J. Smith. At Lincoln's Inn Fields from 16 August through 5 September Smith was seen as Sir Jasper in *The Mock Doctor*, Mrs Nightrail in *Politicks on Both Sides*, the Second Bailiff in *The Tragedy of Tragedies*, a Priest in *Caius Marius*, and a Messenger in *The Carnival*. On 17 September at the Haymarket Theatre he acted Catesby in *Jane Shore*. From 5 March through 30 July 1736 Smith

was at the Haymarket again with Henry Fielding's company, playing Squire Tankard in *Pasquin*, Sir Harry Trueman and Townly in *The Female Rake*, Old Phaeton, a Countryman, Watchman, and Chairman in *Tumble-Down Dick*, and Staytape in *The Temple Rake*. "J. Smith" was the Marquee de Nantal in *The Deposing and Death of Queen Gin* at the Haymarket on 2 August 1736. That is the only instance of Smith's being identified by initial: (T. Smith played Queen Gin). Our man may have been the Smith who acted Sir Nehemiah in *The Modern Pimp* at Bartholomew Fair on 23 August 1736. J. Smith (we believe) returned to the Haymarket on 21 March 1737 to play Banter, Quidam, and a Politician in Fielding's *The Historical Register*. The popular work was performed through 23 May.

Smith, J. ₁*fl.* 1766?–1776₁, *actor.*
A Mr Smith played John Moody in *The Provok'd Husband* at Wrexham, Wales, on 4 July 1766. The play was presented by the Austin-Heatton troupe, which had been appearing in Dublin. We believe that Smith was the J. Smith who acted in October 1768 at Carrickfergus, Ireland, advertised as from Edinburgh. J. Smith may have been the Smith acting with Roger Kemble at Worcester in 1771 and 1772 and with Younger's company at Birmingham in the summer and fall of 1775.

In the summer and fall of 1776 at China Hall, Rotherhithe, Smith, G. Smith, and W. Smith performed. The Smith given no initial in the bills was clearly the best known (or oldest?) of the three (since he needed to be identified merely as Mr Smith) and he played fairly important roles. He seems certainly to have been J. Smith.

He was in *The Rivals* and *The Reprisal* at China Hall, according to a bill at the Guildhall Library hand-dated 3 July 1776. The company was active again from 23 September through 18 October. Smith appeared as Leeson in *The School for Wives*, Lord Foppington in *Miss Hoyden*, Aladin in *Barbarossa*, Lord Lurewell in *The Miller of Mansfield*, Freeman in *A Bold Stroke for a Wife*, Aboan in *Oroonoko*, Soherton in *A Trip to Scotland*, Catesby and the Lieutenant of the Tower in *Richard III*, Lysimachus in *Alexander the Great*, Lovelace in *Marriage à la Mode* (*Three Weeks after Marriage*), Glumdalca in *The*

Life and Death of Tom Thumb the Great, Blunt in *The London Merchant,* Heli in *The Mourning Bride,* a Frenchman in *The Life and Death of Harlequin,* Quildrive in *The Citizen,* Marcus in *Cato,* Sir Harry in *High Life below Stairs,* and Serjeant Kite in *The Recruiting Officer.* He played the last part on 18 October 1776, at a benefit J. Smith shared with two others. Tickets were available from him at the Ship, Seven Houses. A Mrs J. Smith sang in the chorus at Drury Lane that day, but we cannot be certain she was our subject's wife. The Smith in Kemble's troupe at Worcester in 1772 had a wife who acted.

Smith, Mrs J. ₁*fl.*1772?–1778₁, *singer, actress?*

Mrs J. Smith, who was possibly the wife of the J. Smith who acted at China Hall, Rotherhithe, in 1776, was a member of the singing chorus at Drury Lane Theatre from 18 October 1776 through 22 April 1777. She sang in *A Christmas Tale, Romeo and Juliet, Harlequin's Invasion,* and *Macbeth.* She was cited as Mrs J. Smith most of the time, and we take her to have been the Mrs Smith who sang in the chorus of *Romeo and Juliet* on 23 May 1778.

We have guessed that the J. Smith at China Hall in 1776 may have been the Smith in Roger Kemble's company at Worcester in 1772; if so, Mrs Smith also acted in the troupe and may have been our subject.

Smith, J. ₁*fl.*1797–1802₁, *equestrian, actor.*

Mr J. Smith, equestrian, aided Crossman in a performance at the Royal Circus on 20 July 1797. Smith played Medina in *Gonsalvo de Cordova* on 16 August 1802 at the Circus (a Mr Smith, probably George Smith and possibly a relative, was a Banner Bearer). The work was repeated on 20 September 1802.

Smith, James ₁*fl.*1773–1809₁, *violoncellist, violinist.*

James Smith became a member of the Royal Society of Musicians on 1 August 1773. He was certainly the J. Smith who played violoncello in the Handel Memorial Concerts at Westminster Abbey and the Pantheon in May and June 1784 and subsequent years through 1790. Doane's *Musical Directory* of 1794 listed

James Smith as a cellist and violinist, cited him as a member of the Royal Society, and noted that he performed for the Academy of Ancient Music and at the opera house (the King's Theatre). Smith lived in Grange Court. He was still serving on the Court of Assistants of the Royal Society of Musicians in January 1807, a position he had held since March 1785, yet he withdrew from the organization on 31 December 1809.

The violinist and cellist Thomas Smith also lived in Grange Court and may have been related to James.

Smith, James ₁*fl.*1794₁, *singer.*

Doane's *Musical Directory* of 1794 listed James Smith, of No 3, Sermon Lane (where the singer Edward Woodley Smith lived), as a singer, "late" of St Paul's choir. Smith sang for the Academy of Ancient Music and in the oratorios at Drury Lane Theatre and Westminster Abbey. Doane was ambiguous; perhaps Smith was dead by 1794, but Doane also spoke of the singer Henry Smith as having been "late" of St Paul's choir, and Henry Smith was alive after 1794. The relationship between James and Edward Woodley Smith is not known.

Smith, John *c.* 1628–1691, *violist, bass-viol player, violinist.*

John Smith was born about 1628. Perhaps he was the son of the court trumpeter John Smith of pre-Restoration days. That John Smith may have been the John Smith, of Christchurch, London, musician and bachelor, who married Margaret Bonis of St Leonard, Shoreditch, spinster and daughter of Thomas Bonis, deceased, on 6 December 1620.

Our subject replaced the violist John Taylor in the King's Musick on 9 November 1660. His annual salary was £40, his livery allowance £16 2s. 6d. The Lord Chamberlain's accounts frequently cited Smith (sometimes Smyth) over the years. For example, on 4 September 1662 he was to be paid £12 for a new bass viol, and livery warrants almost always named him (and showed that the King was delinquent in his payments to Smith and other royal musicians).

On 16 September 1673 Smith surrendered

his position as violinist in the King's private music to Francis Cruys. Later that month the Lord Chamberlain ordered that Smith was to receive £40 and livery allowances for life, and on 17 November Smith was to be paid £80 12s. 6d. in livery allowances due him from 1664 to 1667 and 1671. On 24 August 1674 John Smith, identified as a former musician in the King's Musick, appointed the court musician Jeoffrey Banister his attorney—that is, gave Banister his power of attorney. In 1676 Smith was just receiving his livery allowances for 1671 and 1672.

It seems probable that our subject was the John Smith who had a book shop in Russell Street, Covent Garden, from as early as 1682. He published *An Heroick Poem to His Royal Highness the Duke of York, on his return from Scotland. With some choice Songs and Medleyes on the Times. By Mat. Taubman, Gent.* (1682). In 1685 Smith published, with John Crouch (the court Violinist and dancing master?), *A New Song, to be sung by a Fop newly come over from France: To an old French tune* and *Three new Songs in Sir Courtly Nice.*

John Singleton, a musician in the King's Musick, had a brother-in-law named John Smith, who may have been our man. Singleton named Smith in his will, which was dated 21 January 1685 and proved on 23 November 1686. No mention was made of a Mrs Smith. John Smith on 8 December had to petition the Lord Chamberlain for his arrears of £252 17s. 6d. He claimed that he had been discharged from the King's Musick because he was Roman Catholic. On 18 October 1688 Smith appointed Thomas Townsend his attorney, so he probably had had no luck getting his money from the crown.

John Smith died on 23 March 1691 at the age of 63. He was buried in the East Cloister of Westminster Abbey (had he converted?) on 26 March. According to the Westminster Abbey registers, Smith drew up his will on 25 February 1691. He was from the parish of St Andrew, Holborn, and had been residing at the house of John Yarling in Baldwin's Gardens. Smith left legacies to several friends but named no relatives. The will was proved on 24 March 1692 by Smith's friend and residuary legatee John Harwood of St Dunstan in the West.

Smith, John [fl. 1784–1794], *violinist, violoncellist.*

The Mr J. Smith who played second violin in the Handel Memorial Concerts at Westminster Abbey and the Pantheon in May and June 1784 was probably the John Smith listed in Doane's *Musical Directory* of 1794. Doane identified Smith as a violinist living in Grange Court (where the violoncellist and violinist James Smith lived) and a participant in performances by the Academy of Ancient Music and at the opera (the King's Theatre). John Smith, according to van der Straeten in his *History of the Violoncello,* made his debut as a cellist in 1784 and performed in the Professional Concerts between 1791 and 1793. He was a teacher of F. W. Crouch.

Smith, John Christopher 1683–1763, *violist, copyist, music seller.*

John Christopher Smith the elder (born Johann Christoph Schmidt on 17 March 1683) was a wool merchant and amateur musician in Anspach, Germany; his wife, according to the *Anecdotes of John Christopher Smith* (the younger), was a lady who brought him a portion of 7000 crowns. Smith's namesake son was born in Anspach in 1712. Smith may have been a friend of Handel at the University of Halle, and in 1716 (?), when Handel was on the Continent visiting his family, he went to Anspach to see Smith. Handel convinced Smith that he should give up his business, devote his life to music, and come to London. Smith followed Handel to England, and in four years Smith's wife and children joined him.

By 1718 the elder Smith was a music copyist (he ultimately turned out masses of copy), and by 1720 he was Handel's treasurer. He also had a music shop in Coventry Street, at the upper end of the Haymarket, not far from the King's Theatre, where Handel served as opera impresario and composer-conductor. Smith advertised in the *Daily Courant* of 2 November 1720 ". . . That Mr. Handel's Harpsichord Lessons neatly Engraven on Copper Plates, will be published on Monday the 14th Instant, and may be had at Christopher Smith's the Sign of the Hand and Musick-Book. . . ." Smith's home as early as 1716 was in Dean Street. He operated his shop in Coventry Street until

1723, when he moved to Meard's Court, Wardour Street, Old Soho, where he had set up residence. There he lived until 1750. He specialized in the sale of Handel's music.

Our subject was perhaps the Mr Smith who was given a benefit concert at Stationers' Hall on 3 April 1723 and another on 10 March 1725. The bills did not indicate any performing on his part, but two warrants in the Lord Chamberlain's accounts, dated 1 April 1724 and 1 March 1726, prove that John Christopher Smith played the tenor (viola). He and other musicians were paid on those dates for performing in the *Te Deum* (Handel's?) at St James's, and they also received office fees, probably as copyists. Smith seems not to have been a regular member of the King's Musick, however.

On 28 August 1739 John Christopher Smith and his son became original subscribers to the Royal Society of Musicians. The elder Smith (called Christopher) gave his parish as St Anne, Westminster. At the Haymarket Theatre on 3 February 1741 a benefit concert was presented for Christopher Smith. The bill stated that he, "at his own Expence, hath provided for, and brought up the Children of the late Mr. Dahuron [the musician], ever since the time of his Death (being near Five Years) and still continues to take Care of the said poor Children, who would otherwise be destitute of all Support."

The elder Smith was still serving as Handel's treasurer and amanuensis in 1750. Otto Deutsch in his *Handel* quotes Smith's receipt for £35—money to be paid to performers who presented the *Messiah* at the Foundling Hospital on 1 May 1750. Both the elder and younger Smith were members of the Court of Assistants of the Royal Society of Musicians beginning in 1751. The elder Smith was again treasurer for Handel when the *Messiah* was given at the Foundling Hospital on 15 April 1752. The Smith who was paid 8s. for playing tenor in the *Messiah* at the Hospital in May 1754 may well have been the elder John Christopher Smith.

Smith joined Handel on at least some of his journeys—to Bath in the summer of 1751 and Tunbridge in 1755, for example. The *Anecdotes* state that it was at Tunbridge (in 1756?) that they had a falling out: "they quarrell'd there and Smith senior left Handel in an abrupt

manner which so enraged him, that he declared he would never see him again." On 1 June 1750 Handel had drawn up his will, bequeathing to his old friend Christopher Smith "my large Harpsichord, my little House Organ, my Musick Books, and five hundred Pounds Sterl:" In the first codicil to his will Handel increased the elder Smith's legacy to £2000; the codicil was made on 6 August 1756, at which point Handel and Smith were clearly on good terms, but between then and 1759 the two had their quarrel. Handel evidently rubbed the elder Smith's name out of his will, and the probate copy of it did not have "senior" after "Mr. Christopher Smith." A receipt for £2470 from the Handel estate to Christopher Smith of Dean Street, Soho, on 2 May 1759 was apparently signed by the younger Smith. Smith junior brought about a reconciliation three weeks before Handel's death.

Smith the elder continued to serve as treasurer for the *Messiah* performances at the Foundling Hospital; he signed the receipt for the presentation that took place on 3 May 1759, just after Handel died. Smith also continued to copy music for his son's performances.

James S. Hall discovered the elder Smith's will and published it in *The Musical Times* in March 1955. The will was dated 16 December 1762 and was proved on 10 January 1763, between which dates Smith died. He bequeathed to his son all the music books and manuscripts ultimately left him by Handel, along with his own books, manuscripts, and musical instruments. The rest of his personal estate he left to the younger Smith in trust. From the trust was to be paid 12 guineas annually to his servant Mary Smith, daughter of Mary Dowling, until such time as she could maintain herself. She was to receive £50 at her marriage. The elder Smith also specified that Mary should be paid £20 if she remained with Smith to his death. Also to be looked after was Mrs Charlotte Ebelin, widow, for whom the elder Smith had cared during his lifetime.

The residue of the estate was to be divided equally between Smith's two daughters, Charlotte Teede (Mrs William) and Judith Rector, widow of John Rector. (William Teede took over Smith's important work as music copyist after Smith's death.) John Christopher Smith the elder was buried on 12 January 1763 and identified as of King's Square Court, where he had lived since 1755.

We are indebted to Barbara Small for her help on this entry.

Smith, John Christopher   *1712–1795, organist, harpsichordist, conductor, composer.*

John Christopher Smith was born in Anspach in 1712, the son of Johann Christoph Schmidt (in England: John Christopher Smith, the elder), a wool merchant and friend of Handel. In 1716 Handel persuaded the elder Smith to come to London and follow his musical interests. Four years later Smith sent for his wife, son, and two daughters. So in 1720 (according to the *New Grove*), by which time the elder Smith was serving as Handel's opera house treasurer, young John Christopher arrived in England, though Otto Deutsch in *Handel* thinks the father and son came together in 1716.

The Dictionary of National Biography states that young John Christopher was enrolled in

JOHN CHRISTOPHER SMITH

engraving by Harding, after Zoffany

Clare's Academy, Soho Square, where he showed his aptitude for music. By 1725 the boy was receiving music lessons from Handel, and he later studied under Pepusch and Thomas Roseingrave.

Andrew McCredie in *Music and Letters* in 1964 identified a number of music manuscripts at the Hamburg State University Library as by Smith, among them "The Mourning Muse of Alexis," a funeral ode composed in 1729, before Smith had come to public attention as a composer. In 1730, when he was 18, Christopher was in poor health from overexertion, and Dr Arbuthnot invited him to stay at his home in Highgate. Smith's consumption was arrested, and his visit with Arbuthnot brought him into contact with some of the literary lights of the time, especially Swift, Pope, and Gay. The Smith who played a lesson on the harpsichord at a concert at Lincoln's Inn Fields Theatre on 2 April 1731 was probably the younger John Christopher Smith. The benefit concert for a Mr Smith held at that theatre on 22 March 1732 may have concerned either the father or the son or yet a third Smith. As William C. Smith noted in *Music and Letters* in 1953, the advertisement stated that Smith would play a lesson of his own on the harpsichord and that tickets could be purchased from him in Vine Street, near Golden Square. Yet the younger J. C. Smith's *Six Suites of Lessons for the Harpsichord,* published in May 1732, were "to be had at the Author's in Meard's Court, Wardour Street, Old Soho"—the elder Smith's address.

The younger John Christopher Smith's first opera, *Teraminta,* was presented at Lincoln's Inn Fields Theatre on 20 November 1732; his second, *Ulysses,* was performed there on 16 April 1733 for his benefit. He gave his address as Meard's Court, Old Soho, and identified himself clearly as Christopher Smith Jr. At the age of 24, according to *Anecdotes of George Frederick Handel and John Christopher Smith* (1799, ascribed to William Coxe),

. . . Mr. Smith married the daughter of Mr. Packenham a gentleman of good fortune, in Ireland. He had reason to suppose that she was entitled to a fortune of £3000, but he never received any portion. They lived together nearly six years, and they had several children; but none survived the age of two years. She died of a decline. Her brother was afterwards created Lord Longford.

Smith and his father were both original subscribers to the Royal Society of Musicians on 28 August 1739. The oratorio (now lost except for one duet in the Hamburg collection), "David's Lamentation over Saul and Jonathan," had been composed in 1738. It was given on 22 February 1740 at Hickford's Music Room. The younger Smith turned out a number of works during the 1740s: *Themesi, Isi, e Proteo, Rosalinda* (performed at Hickford's on 4 January 1740), *The Seasons* (1740), *Issipile* (1743), *Daphne* (1744), *Il Ciro riconosciuto* (1745), *Dario* (1746?), and some arias for *Artaserse* (1748). And in the late 1740s he traveled to the Continent, where he spent about three years. He returned at the request of Handel, whose sight was failing. After Handel became blind, Smith acted as his amanuensis.

Much of Smith's musical activity during the 1750s was with Handel on the one hand and David Garrick on the other. Smith assisted Handel as organist at oratorio performances and in 1754 became first organist at the Foundling Hospital Chapel. In May of that year he played the organ there for the annual performance of the *Messiah* and asked no fee. At some point he composed the opera *The Fairies,* based on *A Midsummer Night's Dream.* The authorship of the libretto was at first attributed to Garrick, but he repudiated it, and it is clear from Garrick's prologue that Smith himself put together the text. The lyrics for the songs came from several sources: Shakespeare, Milton, Waller, Lansdowne, Hammond, and others. Garrick presented the work at Drury Lane Theatre on 3 February 1755, and, according to a letter from Horace Walpole to Richard Bentley on 23 February, it met with great success despite its weaknesses:

Garrick has produced a delectable English opera which is crowded by all true lovers of their country. To mark the opposition to Italian opera, it is sung by some cast singers, two Italians, a French girl and the Chapel boys, and to regale with sense, it is Shakespeare's 'Midsummer Nights Dream', which is forty times more nonsensical than the worst translation of any Italian opera-books.

Smith composed music for *The Tempest,* which Garrick brought out at Drury Lane on 11 February 1756. It, too, was received with much applause. Smith was regularly involved in the Foundling Hospital performances of the

Messiah, conducting in 1755 and 1756 for Handel. The orchestra bill for the performance on 27 April 1758 cites a Smith as having received £5 5s. 6d.; that sum was close to the amounts paid the female soloists and the Smith cited was probably our subject, who would have conducted, probably from the organ. He conducted the *Messiah* again on 3 May 1759, shortly after Handel's death, and he served as conductor regularly through 1768.

Handel and the elder John Christopher Smith had had a falling out in the 1750s, but they were reconciled by the younger Smith before Handel died. Smith senior was bequeathed money, musical instruments, and music books that ultimately became the property of the younger Smith. In 1763, following the death of Dr William Coxe, John Christopher Smith, then a widower, married Coxe's widow.

Smith's oratorio *Paradise Lost* was given its first performance at Covent Garden on 29 February 1760, but it was infrequently revived. *The Enchanter,* Smith's third opera for Garrick, had a libretto by the actor-manager. It was presented successfully at Drury Lane on 13 December 1760. His *Rebecca* received only a single performance, on 4 March 1761 at Covent Garden. Manuscripts for the oratorios *Judith, Medea,* and *The Feast of Darius*—all dating 1760–61 or thereabouts—survive in Hamburg, but no public performances are known. (Thomas Augustine Arne's oratorio *Judith* was given at Drury Lane on 27 March 1761.)

Mortimer's *London Directory* of 1763 listed John "Christian" Smith the younger as a composer and teacher of the harpsichord living in Marylebone Street, Piccadilly. *Nabal,* with music mostly cribbed by Smith from Handel's works, was given at Drury Lane on 16 March 1764. *Jehosaphat* (1764), which survives in manuscript, seems not to have been performed in public. *Gideon* was presented at Covent Garden on 10 February 1769; Smith put it together with music borrowed from Handel's works. It was not successful, the *Theatrical Register* calling it "a very tedious and heavy performance." Smith also composed *Redemption* and several vocal and instrumental pieces. *The Catalogue of Printed Music in the British Museum* lists a number of Smith's compositions.

Sheridan wrote to Linley on 17 November:

"I find Mr. Smith has declined, and is retiring to Bath." Smith lived in a house in Upper Church Street. Handel's bequests to his father, which had passed on to the junior Smith in 1763, Smith gave to George III for the many kindnesses the royal family had shown him, the most important of them the continuance by the King of the pension to Smith which had been originally given him by the King's mother, the Princess Dowager of Wales.

Smith died in London on 3 October 1795. He had drawn up his will on 13 May 1786 at Bath. He provided for the children of his late wife, Martha, by her former husband, Dr Coxe. They were Peter, William, Edward, and Emilia Coxe. A Denner portrait of Handel, which had passed from Handel to Smith's father and then to the younger Smith, was not included in Smith's gift to the King. It was bequeathed to William Coxe. Smith also made a bequest to Sir Peter Rivers, which passed on to Lady Rivers, née Coxe. The will was proved in London on 13 November 1795.

Of the younger John Christopher Smith's personality little is known. Thomas Linley the elder wrote to Richard Brinsley Sheridan on 15 November 1773 commenting negatively about Smith: "I am not satisfied with Smith, who appears to me to be a cunning man." But the *Anecdotes* of 1799 called Smith "scrupulously just" and a religious, caring, and cheerful man.

We are indebted to Barbara Small for a number of the details in this entry.

A portrait of John Christopher Smith the younger by Johann Zoffany shows him seated, with his right elbow leaning on a table covered with manuscript music, holding a quill pen. It was bought at Sotheby's on 30 November 1960 (lot 131) by Gooden and Fox for Gerald Coke and is now in his Handel collection. An engraving by E. Harding was published as a plate to William Coxe's (?) *Anecdotes*, 1799; the engraving was made from a reduced watercolor copy of the portrait made by W. N. Gardiner (contained in an extra-illustrated copy of the *Anecdotes* in the Gerald Coke Handel collection). A watercolor portrait of a "Mr. Smith," musician, was sold in a collection of drawings by George Dance as the property of the artist's grandson, the Rev George Dance, at Christie's on 1 July 1898 (No 132), but that portrait is not now traceable and was not engraved. It

may be of the younger J. C. Smith, or it may be a portrait of the musician John Stafford Smith.

Smith, John Stafford   *1750–1836, organist, singer, composer.*

John Stafford Smith, the son of Martin Smith, organist at Gloucester Cathedral from 1743 to 1782, was born in Gloucester, probably in 1750 (his baptism was 30 March 1750), and received his earliest musical training from his father. He came to London to study under William Boyce and sing in the Chapel Royal under Nares. After leaving the Chapel he concentrated on composition, singing, playing the organ, and collecting music of the twelfth to the eighteenth century. In 1773 he won two prizes given by the Catch Club, for the catch "Here flat" and the canon "O remember not the sins." In the four years that followed he garnered still more prizes for his glees, songs, and catches.

On 7 July 1776 Smith was recommended for membership in the Royal Society of Musicians; at that time he was married but had no children. He was admitted the following 6

JOHN STAFFORD SMITH
engraving by Illman, after Behnes

October. Smith worked closely with Sir John Hawkins in the preparation of Hawkins's *General History* of music, and in 1779 Smith published his own *Collection of English Songs, in score, for three and four voices, composed about the year 1500.* Later years saw a volume of anthems (1793), a collection of songs (1785), and his most important work, *Musica Antiqua* (1812).

Smith appeared regularly at musical performances. He sang tenor in the Handel Memorial Concerts at Westminster Abbey and the Pantheon in May and June 1784, was appointed a Gentleman of the Chapel Royal on the following 16 December, became a lay vicar of Westminster Abbey on 22 February 1785, was made organist of the Gloucester Festival in 1790, became one of the organists of the Chapel Royal in 1802, and succeeded Ayrton as Master of the Children of the Chapel Royal on 14 May 1805, a post he held until 1817. As of 1794, when Doane's *Musical Directory* appeared, Smith was living at No 7, Warwick Street, Charing Cross.

From July 1799 to 1809 he served on the Court of Assistants of the Royal Society of Musicians. Possibly he was the J. Smith who, on 15 July 1815 received £5 16s. 8d. from the management of Drury Lane Theatre for services unspecified. The sum was described as the completion of Smith's salary, but John Stafford Smith is not otherwise known to have had any connection with the London legitimate theatres.

Little is known of John Stafford Smith's personal life. He was surely the father of Julia Stafford Smith, who died on 31 May 1796 at the age of 11 and was buried in the south cloister of Westminster Abbey. Another daughter, Gertrude Stafford Smith, survived him and was his sole heir.

Smith died on 21 September 1836 in London. His will, written on 21 January 1834, identified him as of Paradise Row, Chelsea. He left his entire estate to his daughter Gertrude; she proved the will on 20 October 1836. Some years afterward Gertrude became insane, and her property was ordered invested for her benefit. The contents of Smith's house, including 2191 volumes of printed and manuscript music and other books, were carelessly sold at auction without first bringing the sale to the attention of the music community. Conse-

quently, most of Smith's fabulous collection has now been lost.

A portrait of John Stafford Smith was engraved by T. Illman "from the Original drawing by W. Behnes, in the possession of M.ʳ Rich.ᵈ Clarke," and published by T. Williams as a plate to *Harmonist in Miniature.* A watercolor portrait of "Mr. Smith," musician, was sold in a collection of drawings by George Dance, as the property of the artist's grandson, the Rev George Dance, at Christie's on 1 July 1898 (No 132), but the location of that drawing is not known to us and the portrait was not engraved. It may be a portrait of our subject, or it may be of the younger John Christopher Smith.

Smith, Joseph ₍*fl. 1758–1761*₎, lampman.

Joseph Smith was named for benefit tickets in the bills at Covent Garden Theatre from 12 May 1758 through 15 May 1761 and was cited on a paylist dated 22 September 1760 as a lampman at a daily salary of 1s. 8d.

Smith, Joseph ₍*fl. 1794*₎, singer.

Doane's *Musical Directory* of 1794 listed Joseph Smith as a bass who sang for the Choral Fund. His residence was given as "At the School House" in Stepney Green.

Smith, Katherine. *See* Tofts, Catherine.

Smith, Mariana ₍*fl. 1705–1714*₎, actress, dancer.

On 18 January 1705 Mariana (or Marianna) Smith played Isabella in *Farewell Folly* at Drury Lane Theatre. She and other players signed a petition to the Lord Chamberlain in June or July of that year. On 1 November 1714 she acted Christeta in *Injur'd Virtue* at the King's Arms in Southwark. Ifan Kyrle Fletcher wrote in 1952 to Beecher Hogan, saying that Mariana Smith was also a dancer.

Smith, Martha ₍*fl. 1747*₎, performer?

Mrs Martha Smith was given a solo benefit at Goodman's Fields Theatre on 17 March 1747; the bill did not indicate what, if any, connection she had with the theatre, though she may have been a performer.

Smith, Martin *c. 1715–1786, organist.*

Martin Smith, born about 1715, became one of the original subscribers to the Royal Society of Musicians on 28 August 1739. Smith had served his musical apprenticeship with William Boyce and Maurice Greene. From 1743 to 1782 he was organist of Gloucester Cathedral. According to *The Royal Society of Musicians* (1985) Martin Smith was buried on 13 April 1786. He was the father of the musician John Stafford Smith (1750?–1836).

Smith, Mary *1755?–1779, actress.*

Mary Smith was born in 1755, the daughter of Thomas Smith of Norwich, according to the registers of St Peter Mancroft. At Covent Garden Theatre on 21 October 1778 she made her stage debut as Aurelia in *The Twin Rivals*. The play was repeated on 13 November. Ryan's *Table Talk* quoted a melodramatic letter dated February 1779:

MISS SMITH, a young lady who played the character of *Amelia,* in the comedy of "The Twin Rivals," at Covent Garden Theatre, some years ago, died last week, in this town (Norwich), in the following extraordinary manner. A young gentleman of a good family and great expectancy had long had a *tendre* for her, but did not make her any serious offers, because he feared his friends would object to the match, on account of the young lady's want of fortune, she having given up every shilling of some property which had been bequeathed to her, to rescue her parents from ruin. Her theatrical prospects not appearing very promising, the young gentleman generously told her, that if she would quit the stage, he would make her his wife, in spite of any objections of his friends; as she really loved him, the excess of her joy was such, that she sunk into his arms, and died immediately.

The *Norfolk Chronicle* on 6 February 1779 reported that Mary Smith died on 1 February at the age of 24. The registers of St Peter Mancroft show that she was buried on 4 February; her age was given as 23.

Smith, Mary *[fl. 1800], producer.*

In 1800 Mary Smith and John Dyke were granted a license to put on a play at the Haymarket Theatre. Nothing is known of the production.

Smith, R. *[fl. 1795], actor.*

R. Smith acted Sir Hugh Montgomery in *Chevy Chase* at Sadler's Wells on 4 August 1795.

Smith, Richard *[fl. 1741?–1781?], actor, singer, dancer.*

The advertisement for May Fair on 7 June 1744 listed R. Smith as Bonniface in *The Stratagem*. Though proof is lacking, a number of performances at various minor houses before and after that date may have been by the same Smith, whose Christian name was, we believe, Richard. Our guess is that these appearances were not by Charles Smith (d. 1775), who was active at Covent Garden Theatre during this period.

A Smith played Sir Nehemiah Nestlecock in *The Modern Pimp* on 22 August 1741 at Hallam's Bartholomew Fair booth. On 28 December Smith shared a benefit at the James Street Theatre; no casts were listed for the presentations of *The Earl of Essex* and *The King and the Miller of Mansfield*. On 7 April 1742 at James Street Smith was Nerestan in *Zara*. At Bartholomew Fair on 25 August Smith appeared as Oldcastle in *The Indian Merchant* and the Miser in *The Miser Bit* for Phillips and Yeates. Smith and his wife were at Turbutt and Dove's booth at the Fair on 23 August 1743; they played Tom Thimble and the Landlady in *The Glorious Queen of Hungary*, and Mrs Smith was Gripe in *Harlequin Dissected*.

On 16 March 1744 at James Street the Smiths were playing Modely and Flora in *The Country Lasses;* the performance was a benefit for Smith and an unnamed tradesman. At May Fair on 1 May they were Davy and Angelina in *The Royal Heroe* at Hallam's booth. At that fair on 7 June R. Smith played Bonniface, another Smith (Charles?) played Sir Charles, and Mrs Smith played Dorinda in *The Beaux' Stratagem*.

On 25 August 1746 Smith was Colombine (*sic*) in *Harlequin Incendiary* at the Warner and Fawkes booth at Bartholomew Fair. On 8 September 1746 at Warner's booth at Southwark Fair Smith acted the Father in *The Imprisonment of Harlequin,* and a year later at Chettle's Bartholomew Fair booth Smith played Clodpole in *Frolicksome Lasses*. Smith appeared as the Second Gravedigger in *Hamlet* at Richmond on 13 October 1747. At Phillips's booth at Southwark Fair on 7 September 1748 he acted Stephano in *The Tempest* and Gripe in *Harlequin Imprison'd.* Another Smith (Charles?) was at the Lee-Yeates-Warner booth that day, dancing with Mrs Bullock.

On 23 August 1749 at Phillips's booth at Bartholomew Fair, Smith was Ventoso in *The Tempest;* another Smith (Charles?) at the Cross-Bridges booth, acted Clack in Modern Madness. Smith played Old Muckworm in *The Industrious Lovers* at Phillips's booth at Southwark Fair on 7 September 1749 and subsequent dates. Our Smith (with his wife) was probably the one who arrived in Jamaica with David Douglass in 1751 and acted in Moody's company in Kingston that year. A Smith, perhaps again our man, was back at Southwark Fair in London on 22 September 1752 playing a Servant in *Harlequin Triumphant.*

The R. Smith who acted a Drunken Servant in *The Pilgrim* at Covent Garden Theatre on 11 December 1752 was, we believe, Richard Smith, whose career extended to perhaps as late as 1781. He was referred to in most bills as R. Smith, to distinguish him from William "Gentleman" Smith (cited simply as Smith) until that eminent actor left the company in 1774, after which our subject was listed as Smith. His Christian name is in a cash book at the Folger Shakespeare Library and in Thomas Hull's *The Perplexities,* published in 1767. After appearing in *The Pilgrim* in December 1752 Smith shared a benefit on 5 May 1753 with two others and acted Publius in *Julius Caesar* on 14 May.

Richard Smith served Covent Garden as a utility actor—a "walking gentleman" as the *Morning Chronicle* called him in 1778—until 11 May 1774, playing dozens of secondary roles. Among his many parts were Leander in *The Mock Doctor,* Pindarus in *Julius Caesar,* Jeremy in *The Double Disappointment,* Sir Charles in *The Stratagem,* Sylvius in *As You Like It,* Tom in *The School Boy,* Thomas in *The Virgin Unmask'd,* Sly in *The Cheats of Scapin,* Perez in *The Mourning Bride,* Bernardo, an Officer, and Rosencrantz, in *Hamlet,* James in *The Provok'd Husband,* Balthazar, Gregory, and Paris in *Romeo and Juliet,* Bumpkin in *The Funeral,* Alguazil in *She Wou'd and She Wou'd Not,* Scroop, Bedford, and Westmoreland in *Henry V,* Rugby and Pistol in *The Merry Wives of Windsor,* Peto

and Blunt in *1 Henry IV,* the Lieutenant of the Tower in *Richard III,* Biskey in *The Rover,* Alonzo in *Alzira,* Le Noble in *The Country House,* and Prince Henry in *King John.*

Also, Abel in The *Committee,* Nimming Ned in *The Beggar's Opera,* Martin in *The Jovial Crew,* Seward in *Macbeth,* Colville in *2 Henry IV,* Fantome in *The Drummer,* Sancho in *Love Makes a Man,* Tindal in *The Apprentice,* the Second Spirit in *Comus,* the Corporal in *The What D'Ye Call It,* Sir John Friendly in *The Relapse,* Hephestion and Thessalus in *The Rival Queens,* an Ensign in *The Spanish Lady,* Lord Rake in *The Provok'd Wife,* Belfield in *All in the Right,* Whisper in *The Busy Body,* Theodore in *Venice Preserv'd,* Derby in *Jane Shore,* the Prince of Tannais in *Tamerlane,* Thrassaline in *Philaster,* Freeman in *The Musical Lady,* Traverse and Truman in *The Clandestine Marriage,* the Bailiff in *The Good-Natured Man,* Supple in *The Double Gallant,* Arviragus in *Cymbeline,* the Conjuror in *The Devil to Pay,* Fleece in *Man and Wife,* Friar Peter in *Measure for Measure,* Sir Walter Raleigh in *The Unhappy Favorite,* Robin in *The Author,* Phillip in *The Brothers,* Peregrine in *The Fox,* Simon in *The Suspicious Husband,* Truman in *George Barnwell,* Pedro in *Catherine and Petruchio,* Salarino in *The Merchant of Venice,* Guilford in *Henry VIII,* a Messenger in *The Earl of Warwick,* Verulam in *Henry II,* and Gates in *Lady Jane Grey.* On 13 April 1774 Smith danced in a "Poetical Interlude" called *Henry and Emma.*

Between 1767 and 1772 a Smith appeared with some regularity at the Haymarket Theatre, usually in the summers with Samuel Foote's troupe but occasionally during the winter seasons. Only once, on 23 May 1770, do the bills show the Haymarket Smith and Richard Smith performing on the same day—and the Covent Garden playbill that date could have been in error, since it is a repeat of a cast going back to the previous September. Several roles played by the Haymarket Smith are those in Richard Smith's repertoire, so it seems almost certain that the Haymarket references are to our subject.

Richard's Haymarket activity, if we are correct in our identification, was as follows: Foote opened on 29 May 1767, and Smith was listed on 4 June as playing Gruel in *The Commissary.* The following day he was named in the cast of *The Orators,* and on 22 June he acted Paris in

Romeo and Juliet. Other parts he performed that summer were Theodore in *Venice Preserv'd* on 26 June, Bartholomeau in *The Taylors* on 2 July, Bowman in *Lethe* on 6 July (but the role was omitted on 10 July), Thessalus in *Alexander* on 31 July, Jemmy Twitcher in *The Beggar's Opera* on 5 August, a role in *The Countess of Salisbury* on 21 August, Frank Younger in *The Patron* on 27 August, Beaufort in *The Citizen* on 4 September, Butler in *The Busy Body* on 7 September, Sir James in *The Lyar* on 16 September, and a character in *The Royal Captive* on 18 September.

On 19 December 1768 with some players from Scotland Smith played Gargle in *The Apprentice,* and on 28 February 1769 he was Loveit in *Miss in Her Teens* and Gratiano in *Othello.* On the latter occasion Mrs Smith (related?) played Biddy and Desdemona. In the summer of 1770 Smith played Rosencrantz in *Hamlet,* Frank Younger in *The Patron,* Bedamar in *Venice Preserv'd,* Young Loveit in *The Commissary,* Loader in *The Minor,* Sharper in *The Old Bachelor*—again with Foote's troupe. "Smyth" that summer, surely the same actor, played Albany in *King Lear,* Rossano in *The Fair Penitent,* Sir Charles Freeman in *The Stratagem,* Chatillon in *King John,* and Young Wilding in *The Citizen.* Smith acted Charles in *The Busy Body* on 5 October, and on 14 December he was Sancho in *The Mistake.* On 14 December 1770 he played Don Diego in *The Padlock,* and on 20 April 1771 he was Ernesto in *The Orphan.* Smith acted the title role in *Squire Badger* on 6 March 1771.

Smith acted again with Foote at the Haymarket in the summer of 1772, playing Roger in *The Mayor of Garratt,* Transfer in *The Minor,* a part in *The Devil upon Two Sticks,* a part in *The Nabob,* Helebore in *The Mock Doctor,* one of the Mob in *The Contrivances,* a part in *The Rehearsal,* Ratcliff in *Richard III,* and, on 18 September, a Footman in *Love in a Village.*

From 1774–75 through 1776–77 neither Richard Smith nor "Gentleman" Smith performed at Covent Garden. The Smith who acted at Covent Garden from 18 December 1777 through 19 May 1781 was certainly Richard; he was given some of his earlier roles, and on 17 January 1780 the bill identified him as R. Smith.

During this last portion of Richard Smith's London career he was seen in such characters

as a Stranger in *The Lady's Last Stake,* a Friend in *Isabella,* Theodore in *Venice Preserv'd,* Westmoreland in *Henry V,* Abergavenny in *Henry VIII,* Thessalus in *Alexander the Great* (*The Rival Queens*), Theodore in *Venice Preserv'd,* Whisper in *The Busy Body,* Francisco in *Hamlet,* Sergius in *The Siege of Damascus,* Pedro in *Catherine and Petruchio,* a Gentleman in *The Deaf Lover,* Derby in *Jane Shore,* Simon in *The Suspicious Husband,* Oxford in *Richard III,* and an Officer in *The Earl of Warwick.* On 17 April 1779 Smith joined with others in singing some catches and glees.

Over the years Richard Smith received occasional shared benefits at Covent Garden. A paylist dated 22 September 1760 had him down for a daily salary of 3s. 4d.; the account books at the Folger Shakespeare Library show him at £1 5s. weekly in 1761; and a paylist dated 14 September 1767 in Jesse Foote's *Life of Murphy* lists Richard Smith at 6s. 8d. daily.

Smith, Mrs [**Richard?**] [*fl.* 1741–1757?], *actress, singer, dancer?*

Mrs Smith played a Countrywoman in *Harlequin the Man in the Moon* at Southwark Fair on 14 September 1741. For a number of years thereafter she appeared at the fairs and minor theatres acting, singing, and perhaps dancing, and since she sometimes appeared with the Mr Smith who was, we think, Richard Smith, perhaps she was his wife.

She played the title role in *Zara* at the James Street Theatre on 7 April 1742; the Landlady in *The Glorious Queen of Hungary* and Gripe in *Harlequin Dissected* at Bartholomew Fair on 23 August 1743; Flora in *The Country Lasses* at James Street on 16 March 1744; Angelina in *The Royal Heroe,* Gloriana in *The Captive Prince,* and Dorinda in *The Beaux' Stratagem* at May Fair between 1 May and 7 June 1744; Serina in *The Orphan* at the New Wells, Mayfair, on 6 October 1746; Diana in *The Sacrifice of Iphigenia* and Columbine (a dancing role?) in *Harlequin Mountebank* at the New Wells, Clerkenwell, on 16 April 1750; Aurelia in *The Wife's Relief* at the Haymarket on 26 July 1750; and the Nurse in *Jeptha's Rash Vow* at Southwark Fair on 7 September 1750. She and her husband probably acted in America in 1751.

Arundell in *The Story of Sadler's Wells* claims that Mrs Smith sang "To Song and Dance" from Handel's *Samson* at Sadler's Wells in 1746 and sang there again in 1748. The *New Universal Magazine* in April 1757 contained the song "Spring Returns, the Fawns Advance," as sung by Mrs Smith, but there was no indication when and where she had sung it.

Smith, Richmond [*fl. 1784*], *singer.*

Richmond Smith sang bass in the Handel Memorial Concerts at Westminster Abbey and the Pantheon in May and June 1784.

Smith, Robert *c. 1648–1675, singer, lutanist, composer.*

Robert Smith (or Smyth) was born about 1648 and was one of the Children of the Chapel Royal under Henry Cooke after the Restoration. The boys were taught composition, and Smith, along with his fellow choristers Pelham Humphrey and John Blow, turned out some anthems in 1664. He evidently left the Chapel after his voice broke, but by 20 June 1673 Smith was a musician in ordinary in the King's Musick, and on 3 August 1674 he replaced Pelham Humphrey, deceased. Smith was listed among the lutanists at court.

Playford's collection, *Choice Songs and Ayres* (1673), contains a number of songs composed by Smith for plays produced in 1672–73, and it is evident that Smith was very popular. He contributed songs to *Marriage à la Mode, The Assignation, Amboyna, The Miser, Epsom Wells, The Citizen Turn'd Gentleman, The Morning Ramble, The Fatal Jealousy, The Reformation,* and *The Dutch Lover.* Smith's music also appeared in other collections over the years: Locke's *Melothesia* in 1673, Playford's *Choice Ayres, Songs and Dialogues* of 1676, and Greeting's *The Pleasant Companion* in 1682.

But after a flurry of compositional activity in 1672 and 1673, Robert Smith died, probably in September 1675. On 22 November 1675 he was replaced in the King's Music by Richard Hart.

The playwright and musician Thomas D'Urfey in *The Fool Turn'd Critick* (Drury Lane, 18 November 1676) mentioned Smith; in Act IV Betty is asked by Lady Ancient to sing a song composed by a friend of her kinsman. "The tune was set . . . by a very good friend of his, one Mr. Smith and late composer to the King's playhouse." To which Timothy replies:

Who, Bob! A very excellent fellow, Madam, believe me, and one the town misses very much to my knowledge; for now a dayes what ever is the matter with 'em I know not, but we have such tunes, such lowsy lamentable tunes, that 't would make one forswear all musick. 'Maiden Fair' or 'The Kings Delight', are incomparable to some of these we have now. 'Tis true, the theater musick is something tollerable, because 'tis for their credit; but otherwise—!

Then follows the song, "I found my Caelia one night undressed."

Tom Brown's *Letters from the Dead* in 1703 contained a fictitious letter from Henry Purcell to John Blow. Purcell said that "Robin" Smith was "still as Love mad as ever he was; hangs half a dozen Fiddles at his Girdle . . . and scowers up and down Hell, crying a Reevs, a Reevs as if the Devil were in him."

Smith, Robert [*fl. 1784*], *violinist.*

Robert Smith was one of the second violinists in the Handel Memorial Concerts at Westminster Abbey and the Pantheon in May and June 1784.

Smith, Robert Archibald *1780–1829, violinist, composer.*

Robert Archibald Smith was born in Reading on 16 November 1780, the son of a silkweaver from Paisley, Scotland, according to the *New Grove.* Nothing is known of the musical training of Smith, but *The London Stage* identifies him as the Master Smith who played a concerto (on the violin, presumably) at the King's Theatre in London on 18 June 1793.

The elder Smith, his business declining in Reading, took his family back to Paisley in 1800. In 1807 young Robert was appointed precentor at the Abbey Church in Paisley. Over the years he composed a number of songs, and from 1821 to 1824 he published *The Scottish Minstrel,* a six-volume collection of hundreds of Scottish songs, including many of his own. He was made leader of the psalmody at St George's Church, Edinburgh, in August 1823. Smith continued bringing out collections of songs, secular and religious, until his death from "dyspepsia" on 3 January 1829. He was buried at St Cuthbert's Church.

Smith, Miss S. [*fl. 1776?–1819?*], *dresser.*

Working as dressers in the women's wardrobe at Drury Lane Theatre for a number of years were Miss Ann Smith and Miss S. Smith, relationship unknown. One of them was on the payroll at 9s. weekly as early as the 1776–77 season, and one was still listed as late as 1818–19, at a weekly salary of £1 5s. On 16 September 1802 the two were identified by Christian name and initial respectively, with Miss S. Smith listed as receiving £1 (weekly?). In 1815 one of the women was described as a mantua maker receiving £1 10s. weekly.

Smith, Samuel [fl. 1707], singer.

In the Lord Chamberlain's accounts is a warrant dated 17 February 1707 directing that a clothing allowance be given Samuel Smith, one of the children of the Chapel Royal whose voice had broken.

Smith, Samuel 1758?–1815? singer.

Doane's *Musical Directory* of 1794 listed Samuel Smith, of Plummer's Row, Whitechapel, as an alto who sang for the Handelian Society, the Surrey Chapel Society, and in the oratorios at Westminster Abbey and Covent Garden Theatre. He was probably the S. Smith who sang the role of a Constable in the burletta *George Barnwell* on 3 November 1812 at the Surrey Theatre. Perhaps he was the Samuel Smith, aged 57, of Bow Street, who was buried on 9 February 1815 at St Paul, Covent Garden.

Smith, Sarah d. 1812, actress, singer, dancer.

The Mrs Smith whose benefit tickets for Drury Lane Theatre were accepted on 9 May 1758 was probably Sarah Smith. Not until Mrs Theodore Smith joined the troupe in 1772 was it necessary for the bills to cite Sarah by her initial, so references up to then were simply to Mrs Smith. She performed at Drury Lane as an actress, singer, and dancer—though rarely in major assignments—through 1774–75, though she was not named in the bills in 1762–63 or 1766–67 and may have been absent those seasons.

Her named roles at Drury Lane between 21 May 1759 (when she was an extra in *The Heiress*) through 17 April 1775 (when she played Tib Tatter in *Phebe*) were Cloe in *High Life below Stairs*, Dorcas in *The Mock Doctor*, Myrtilla in *The Provok'd Husband*, Betty in *The Contrivances*, Peggy in *The King and the Miller*, Dolly

in *The Stage Coach*, Betty in *A Bold Stroke for a Wife*, Lettice in *The Plain Dealer*, an Attendant in *Zenobia*, Julia and Delia in *Theodosius*, Milliner in *The Elopement*, Betty in *The Hypocrite*, Betty in *The School for Rakes*, Bianca in *Catherine and Petruchio*, Jenny in *A Word to the Wise*, Lady Capulet in *Romeo and Juliet* (though she usually just sang in the chorus), Clara in *Rule a Wife and Have a Wife*, and a Servant in *The Chances*. The roles in *The Provok'd Husband* and *The Mock Doctor* were performed at Drury Lane on 19 June by members of the company from Richmond, with whom Mrs Smith seems to have performed that summer after Drury Lane's regular season was completed.

Mrs Smith's daily salary at Drury Lane on 9 February 1765 was 2s. 6d., which placed her at the lowest pay scale for actresses (but there were three actors who were paid even less). She was up to 3s. 4d. daily by 24 January 1767, and it may be significant that in 1766 she had begun contributing to the Drury Lane Fund. Mrs Smith's name disappeared from London bills after 1775. She may have moved to Norwich; a Sarah Smith of that city was named in the will of the actress Mary Elmy, signed on 12 October 1780. Mrs Elmy called her "cousin" and left her £1000, a diamond ring, and the residue of her estate.

Sarah Smith was receiving £6 quarterly from the Drury Lane Fund in 1809 and presumably remained an annuitant until her death on 18 May 1812.

Smith, [T.] [fl. 1735?–1736], actor.

At York Buildings on 24 September 1735 with Charlotte Charke's company "Smyth" played Headpiece in *The Art of Management*, and on 1 October he acted Trueman in *George Barnwell*. Perhaps he was the T. Smith (or Smyth) who, at the Haymarket Theatre, played the Beggar in *The Beggar's Opera* and Harry in *The Mock Doctor* on 26 June 1736 and Queen Gin in *The Deposing and Death of Queen Gin* on 2 August.

Smith, Mrs Theodore, Maria, née Harris [fl. 1772–1796], actress, singer.

Maria Smith, the wife of the composer Theodore Smith, was born Maria Harris, according to the manuscript volume "Dramatic Biography" in the Harris collection in the British Library. She had married Smith by the time

Courtesy of the Garrick Club

MARIA SMITH, as Sylvia
by De Wilde

she made her stage debut at Drury Lane on 20 October 1772, as Sylvia in *Cymon,* advertised as "A Young Gentlewoman." In his diary the prompter Hopkins commented, "Mrs Smith made her first Appearance in Sylvia a pretty Innocent looking figure a Sweet Voice & very proper for the Character She had vast Applause & very deservedly." Her second role, Patty in *The Maid of the Mill* on 6 November, she also did "very well and [received] great Applause." She was Polly in *The Beggar's Opera* on 21 November, Miss Serina Violet in *The Rose* on 2 December, and Ophelia in Garrick's alteration of *Hamlet* on 18 December. During the remainder of the season she appeared as Clarissa in *The School for Fathers,* Felicia in *The Wedding Ring,* Helen in *Cymbeline,* Laura in *The Chaplet,* Leonora in *The Padlock,* Miranda in *The Tempest,* and an Attendant in *Zenobia.* A paylist dated 13 February 1773 shows Mrs Smith at £6 6*s.* weekly.

She was at Drury Lane through the 1784–85 season, playing Emma in *Alfred,* Louisa in *The Deserter,* Patty in *The Maid of the Mill,* Camilla in *A Christmas Tale,* a Beggar in *The*

Ladies Frolick, Perdita in *Florizel and Perdita,* Rosetta in *Love in a Village,* Rhodope in *A Peep behind the Curtain,* the title role in *Phebe,* Tragedy in *The Theatrical Candidates,* Narcissa in *The Rival Candidates,* Maria in *The Maid of the Oaks,* Elvira (?) in *The Spanish Lady* (on 9 April 1776; the evening was for Mrs Smith's benefit—she made £28 profit), Betty in *The Way of the World,* Betty in *A Bold Stroke for a Wife,* Ariel in *The Tempest,* a Lady in *The Inconstant,* Judah in *Dissipation,* the Housekeeper in *The West Indian,* Madge in *The Gentle Shepherd,* and unnamed vocal parts in several plays and pantomimes.

Another Mrs Smith (Mrs Tom Smith, we conjecture) was also singing in London while Mrs Theodore Smith was performing at Drury Lane; she was named in bills as early as 1761. But the Mrs Smith who sang Theodore Smith's songs at Vauxhall and Ranelagh about 1775 or 1776 was probably our subject.

Among the theatrical clippings at the British Library is an undated notice on Mrs Smith:

This lady's name was Harris, a scholar of . . . Linley, of Bath. She since married Mr. Smith, a very excellent musician, under whom, Mrs. Smith has so greatly improved her uncommon musical talents. . . .

This Lady has the true Italian method of singing, and never forces her voice beyond its natural strength, and is always perfectly in tune. . . . She is a smart little figure, about twenty-four years old; her face rather sharp, but her features are by no means disagreeable.

William Hawkins in his *Miscellanies in Prose and Verse* in 1775 agreed:

She is a smart little figure, with an admirable sweet musical voice, and sings with the nicest precision. . . . Mrs. Smith, since Mr. Garrick's alteration of Hamlet, has occasionally appeared in that play, in the part of Ophelia, with so much judgement and ease, as for us in reason to hope, we may one day admire her as much [as] an actress, as we now do in her singing. . . .

Lichtenberg also wrote admiringly of Mrs Smith's Ophelia. She had

long flaxen hair hung partly down her back, and partly over her shoulders; in her left hand she held a bunch of loose straw, and her whole demeanour in her madness was as gentle as the passion which caused it. The songs, which she sang charmingly, were fraught with such plaintive and tender mel-

Courtesy of Christie's
MARIA SMITH?
by N. Hone

ancholy that I fancied that I could still hear them far into the night, when I was alone. . . . I wish that Voltaire might have been here and heard Mrs. Smith's interpretation of Shakespeare.

Lichtenberg was writing of the 23 October 1775 performance of *Hamlet* at Drury Lane, with William "Gentleman" Smith in the title role.

The *New Grove Dictionary of Music and Musicians* says that Mrs Theodore Smith retired in the summer of 1774; she ran off with a Mr Bishop (according to Mrs Papendiek in *Court and Private Life in the Time of Queen Charlotte*) and that Theodore Smith fell into a melancholy and took a teaching job at Chiswick girls' school so that he could glimpse his ex-wife when she went there to see her daughter. That may have been a true story, though *The London Stage* has Mrs Smith continuing at Drury Lane through 1784–85, and we find that the Theodore Smiths had a son who was christened on 20 January 1776. Mrs Smith was still alive in January 1796.

A portrait in oils, by Samuel De Wilde, of Maria Smith as Sylvia in *Cymon* is in the Garrick Club (No 459). A portrait by N. Hone of "Miss Smyth, the actress" was in the Exeter sale at Christie's on 25 February 1949 and was bought by Granger. It appeared again at Christie's on 25 November 1955 (lot 91) as the property of the late Francis Howard and was bought by Gooden & Fox. The picture, oval (31½" × 24"), shows the sitter in a blue dress, holding a book. Possibly the sitter is Maria Smith; she was, at any rate, the only actress of that surname in London during Hone's career prominent enough to have been painted by the artist.

Smith, Thomas *d. 1724, violinist.*

The Lord Chamberlain's accounts list Thomas Smith among the instrumentalists at court from as early as 1714, when he received £40 annual wages. He was named from time to time in the years that followed, usually for salary payments. A warrant in 1719 indicated that Smith had been in attendance at Hampton Court from August to October 1718. He was paid £30 in February 1720 for playing violin in the Academy of Music opera orchestra. A warrant dated 4 March 1724 suspended Smith and other court musicians for neglecting their duties, and one in April 1724 shows that Smith, deceased, was replaced by Benjamin Sale on 25 March 1724. It is probable that Smith died very shortly before that date.

Smith, Thomas *[fl. 1754–1755], singer.*

Thomas Smith was, we believe, the son of the Lincoln's Inn Fields and Goodman's Fields actor Thomas Smith. The actor Roger Bridgwater, in his will dated 17 August and proved on 31 August 1754, left £5 to the younger Thomas Smith and noted that the elder resided in Bridgwater's house. Young Thomas made his first appearance on any stage on 5 May 1755 at Drury Lane, singing "All in the Downs." He seems not to have performed in public again.

Smith, Thomas *[fl. 1761–1792], actor, prompter.*

Thomas Smith, cited in the bills as T. Smith, acted Bellmour in *The Upholsterer* on 23 June 1761 at Covent Garden Theatre. He was not mentioned in London bills again until 19 October 1767, when he played a Servant in *The Orphan* at Covent Garden. During the rest of the 1767–68 season Smith acted in *The Roman Father* and played Cornwall's Servant in *King Lear*, a Courtier in *The Miller of Mansfield*, and Thomas in *The Virgin Unmask'd*. In 1768–69 he appeared as James in *The Provok'd Husband* and Cornwall's Servant in *King Lear*. He was surely the Smith named on a paylist dated 14 September 1767 at a salary of 5*s*. daily. Smith's full name was given in the *Theatrical Monitor* on 5 November 1768.

Smith acted in Dublin as early as 1780 and was cited in the *Hibernian Journal* on 18 January 1782 as making his ninth appearance in Ireland at the Crow Street Theatre, Dublin. He was identified as from Covent Garden. Smith was named again in the *Hibernian Journal* on 30 January 1786 as an actor at the Smock Alley playhouse. By 10 January 1792, according to *Faulkner's Daily Journal*, Smith was serving as the prompter at Crow Street.

Smith, Thomas   *d. 1766?, actor, dancer.*

The Mr Smith who acted Peter in *Imposture Defeated* at Drury Lane Theatre in September 1697 was apparently not William Smith, who was in the rival troupe at Lincoln's Inn Fields Theatre, but Thomas Smith, whose Christian name appears in a Lord Chamberlain's warrant dated 23 February 1702. Other parts known for Smith at the beginning of his career are Brisson in *The Unhappy Penitent* on 4 February 1701, Phorbas in *The Virgin Prophetess* on 12 May, Albazer in *The Generous Conqueror* about December, and Phorbas in *Cassandra* (another title for *The Virgin Prophetess?*) in 1702. He was given a benefit on 25 June 1707 at the Queen's Theatre, where players performed for a while during a period of shifting management.

In 1707–8 and 1708–9 he was again at Drury Lane, playing such roles as Duart in *Love Makes a Man*, Ibrahim Bassam in *Irene*, Omar in *Tamerlane*, Stanmore in *Oroonoko*, the High Priest in *The Persian Princess*, Nicusa in *The Sea Voyage*, Rui Gomez in *Don Carlos*, Ferdinand in *The Tempest*, the Keeper in *The Emperor of the Moon*, Alonzo in *Rule a Wife and Have a Wife*, Hephestion in *The Rival Queens*, Brabantio in *Othello*, and C. Numitorius in *Appius and Virginia*. He received a benefit at the Queen's on 25 May 1710, but no roles are

known for him in the 1709–10 season, and after that benefit, his name disappeared from the bills until 1715.

On 7 January 1715, at the new theatre in Lincoln's Inn Fields, Thomas Smith acted Captain Worthy in *The Fair Quaker of Deal*. Thereafter he was seen in such new characters as Southampton in *The Unhappy Favorite*, Aboan in *Oroonoko*, Don Lorenzo in *The Mistake*, Odmar in *The Indian Emperor*, Maximus in *Valentinian*, Torrismond and Bertram in *The Spanish Fryar*, Worthy in *The Recruiting Officer*, Ambrosia in *2 Don Quixote*, Young Worthy in *Love's Last Shift*, Charles in *The Lucky Prodigal*, Woolfort in *The Royal Merchant*, Roderick in *The Perfidious Brother*, Morat in *Aureng-Zebe*, Sir Harry Fillamour in *The Feign'd Curtizans*, the Ghost in *Hamlet*, Haemon in *Oedipus*, Zeydan and Benducar in *Don Sebastian*, Lenox in *Macbeth*, Massinissa in *Sophonisba*, Nuno de Lara in *Mangora*, Douglas in *1 Henry IV*, Altamont in *The Fair Penitent*, Alucius in *Scipio Africanus*, Arviragus in *Cymbeline*, Pisano in *The Traytor*, Sir Julius Caesar in *Sir Walter Raleigh*, Lovewell in *The Gamester*, Villeroy in *Henry IV*, Roderigo in *The Pilgrim*, Trebonius in *Julius Caesar*, and the Duke of Aumerle in *Richard II*. At his shared benefit with Corey in *2 May 1716* (which brought in gross receipts of over £86) his daughter (fl. 1716–1721) made her first stage appearance, dancing between the acts. On 24 August 1719 Smith was at Bartholomew Fair, playing a droll called *The Constant Lovers*. There was a "Benefit for Mr Smith, distress'd by Fire," on 8 May 1721, when *The Spanish Fryar* was presented; the income generated was a bit over £81.

After the 1720–21 season at Lincoln's Inn Fields Smith left for Dublin, where he acted at the Smock Alley playhouse in 1721–22, playing such parts as Bargrave in *The Fatal Extravagance* and Isgello in *The Rival Generals*. He was back at Lincoln's Inn Fields on 6 April 1722 playing Douglas in *1 Henry IV* and may have been acting all season. The S. Smith cited in Fitzgerald's *New History* as a member of the Lincoln's Inn Fields troupe as of 12 April 1722 was, surely, Thomas Smith. Another Smith, a boxkeeper, was also in the company in 1722 and may have been a relative.

Thomas Smith continued to appear at Lincoln's Inn Fields through 1727–28, but his career seems to have gone downhill, for he was not often named in the bills. He is known to have acted Aretious in *Domitian*, Tiresias in *Oedipus* (replacing Ogden), Alcander in *The Fatal Legacy*, Lelius in *Sophonisba*, Vasquez in *The Indian Emperor*, Viceroy in *Massaniello*, a Recruit in *The Recruiting Officer*, Whitebroth in *The Cheats*, Lopez in *The Successful Strangers*, Spitfire in *The Wife's Relief*, and Fumble in *The Fond Husband*. During that period he made a few appearances elsewhere: at Bartholomew Fair in *Darius* in August 1722, at Hampstead Wells on 22 July 1723 as Valentine in *Love for Love*, at Bartholomew Fair in August 1724 as the Father in *The Prodigal Son* (a role not noted in *The London Stage* but listed in a Houghton Library manuscript at Harvard University), and at Bartholomew Fair in August 1727 as Richard the Protector in *Jane Shore*.

The theatre accounts on 1 January 1724 show a payment to Thomas Smith of £2 2s. "to relieve him in prison." He was back on the boards the following summer, but on 29 October 1726 he received 6s. 8d. for his "first appearance since jail," so he was evidently imprisoned again during the fall of 1726. (There were two acting Smiths at Lincoln's Inn Fields at this time, so the incarcerated man may have been Charles, not Thomas; but at this time Thomas's career was clearly failing, and he may well have gone into debt.)

We believe that the Smith playing major roles at the minor Haymarket Theatre in 1728–29 was Thomas. He appeared between 26 October 1728 and 16 July 1729 playing Lorenzo in *The Spanish Fryar*, Polydore in *The Orphan*, the King in *Don Carlos*, Jaffeir in *Venice Preserv'd*, Castalio in *The Orphan*, Plume in *The Recruiting Officer*, Dologodelmo in *Hurlothrumbo*, the title role in *Tamerlane*, Trusty in *The Smugglers*, Alderman Quorum in *The Beggar's Wedding*, and Arcas in *Damon and Phillida* (in *The London Stage*, incorrectly listed as at Drury Lane). In August 1729 Smith had a part in *Hunter* at Bartholomew Fair.

Smith—Thomas, we are guessing—was engaged at the Goodman's Fields Theatre from 1729–30 through 1732–33. There he was first noticed as Worthy in *The Recruiting Officer* on 31 October 1729 and then as Sullen in *The Stratagem* on 3 November, though the bill for 10 November, when he acted Torrismond in *The Spanish Fryar*, stated that Smith was making his first appearance on that stage. He then played some of his earlier roles—Polydore in *The Orphan*, Jaffeir in *Venice Preserv'd*, Duart in *Loves Makes a Man*, the Ghost in *Hamlet*, Aboan in *Oroonoko*, Worthy in *The Fair Quaker of Deal*, and others—and was seen in such new parts as Oroonoko, Essex in *The Unhappy Favorite*, Blunt in *The Committee*, Standard in *The Constant Couple*, Freeman in *A Woman's Revenge*, Alonzo in *The Fatal Villainy*, Whim in *The Fashionable Lady*, Pedro in *The Rover*, Charles in *The Busy Body*, Belmour in *The Old Bachelor*, Rowland in *The Devil of a Wife*, Lucius in *Cato*, Sir Sampson in *Love for Love*, Norfolk in *Richard III*, and Westmoreland in *Henry IV*. He was presumably the Smith who danced *Scaramouch* on 17 May 1731, though that is the only record of his dancing.

Smith appeared on 20 August 1730 at Bartholomew Fair either as Doodle in *The Generous Free Mason* at the Oates-Fielding booth or as Suffolk in *Wat Tyler and Jack Straw* at the Pinkethman-Giffard booth—or both, if the time schedule dovetailed. But two Smiths, Thomas and Charles, may have been involved.

Smith's last appearance at Goodman's Fields was on 11 January 1733; the Smith who acted at Bartholomew Fair in August 1733 was probably Charles, not Thomas.

The *Theatrical Review* in 1763 commented on our subject:

The celebrated Tom Smith, or Tragedy Tom (as he was generally called by his brother actors of Lincolns Inn and Goodmans Fields) used to assert that none but fat men with broad faces were proper figures for Tragedy.—Tom was just such a person himself.—'Betterton (he would often say) had a broad face, Booth too had a broad face, but I—I—have a VERY broad face.'

An obituary in the *Public Advertiser* on 18 December 1766 for Charles Smith must have concerned Thomas (Charles lived until 1775): "Mr. Charles Smith, late of the Old Playhouse in Portugal-Street, near Lincoln's Inn Fields, Upholder and Cabinet-maker deceased." Debtors were advised to leave bills at Smith's house. Smith had presumably died during the year.

It seems likely that the elder of the two Thomas Smiths mentioned in the will of the actor Roger Bridgwater in August 1754 was our man. Bridgwater left £5 to Thomas Smith, son of Bridgwater's friend Thomas Smith, who lived in Bridgwater's house. The younger Thomas we take to have been the Drury Lane singer of 1755.

Smith, Thomas   [*fl. 1769–1778*], *singer, dancer.*

Tom Smith had a benefit at Finch's Grotto Gardens in August 1769. His bill invited the company of his "Brother Masons, Bucks, Antigallicans, &c." At the Haymarket Theatre on 12 August 1771 he danced *The Laughing Bacchanalian.* At that house on 31 March 1778 T. Smith sang "Black Ey'd Susan" and a new "Hunting Song" at a benefit he shared with Follett and another Smith, probably William. Tickets were available from Thomas Smith at the Golden Cross, Charing Cross, and the bill described him as "late of the Bear, Westminster-bridge." Smith had evidently been a publican. He hoped that the benefit would attract his "brother Free Masons, Bucks, &c., Gentlemen of the Welsh, Hereford and Westmoreland Societies. . . ." We believe the Mrs Smith who sang from 1761 to 1774 was his wife.

Smith, Mrs   [Thomas?]   [*fl. 1761–1774*], *singer.*

Mrs Smith sang in a concert at the Haymarket Theatre on 22 August 1761. In August 1765 and again in 1770 she sang at Finch's Grotto Gardens in Southwark, and during the 1768–69 season she appeared at Vauxhall. Mrs Smith sang in the *Messiah* at the Haymarket Theatre on 26 February 1773. On 7 June 1774 at the Haymarket a "Favourite *Cantata* sung at Ranelagh by Mrs Smith" was performed. Her husband may have been Thomas Smith, the singer and dancer who was active from 1769 to 1778.

Smith, Thomas   *b. 1776, instrumentalist.*

Thomas Smith, according to testimony gathered by the Royal Society of Musicians, was born in Wolverhampton, Staffordshire, on 2 November 1776, the son of John Smith, a musical-instrument maker, and his wife Susanna. Thomas was christened at St Peter's in Wolverhampton on 29 January 1777. By the time he was proposed for membership in the Royal Society of Musicians on 5 April 1801, Thomas Smith had practiced music for a livelihood for seven years, been engaged for the

oratorios at Covent Garden Theatre, and was in the band at the Royal Circus. He was proficient on the trumpet, violin, and viola. He was elected on 2 August. Smith played trumpet in the Society's annual St Paul's concert in May 1802 and 1803. He played again in 1804 and 1806, but his instrument was not cited. In 1811 he played violoncello, as he perhaps did in 1812. He was expelled after 1813 for nonpayment of dues. He was probably the Thomas Smith of London Street who was left a mourning ring by the musician John Crosdill; Crosdill's will was dated 30 August 1825 and proved the following 25 October.

Smith, Thomas   [*fl. 1783?–1794?*], *violinist, violoncellist.*

The Lord Chamberlain listed a Mr Smith as a musician at the King's Theatre in 1783. He was probably Thomas Smith, who played first violin in the Handel Memorial Concerts at Westminster Abbey and the Pantheon in May and June 1784. Smith was one of the instrumentalists at a Hanover Square concert on 1 June 1789 and was named as a violoncellist at the Pantheon in 1791. Doane's *Musical Directory* of 1794 listed Smith as a cellist living at No 2, Grainge (probably Grange) Court, Carey Street, who played at Sadler's Wells. Doane did not give his first name. The violinist and violoncellist James Smith also lived in Grange Court.

Smith, Thomas   [*fl. 1794*],   *singer.*

Doane's *Musical Directory* of 1794 listed Thomas Smith as a singer who had been in St Paul's choir and was a performer for the Academy of Ancient Music and in the oratorios at Drury Lane and Westminster Abbey.

Smith, Walter   *1752–1809, actor, treasurer.*

Walter Smith was born in 1752, the son of John and Betty Smith (according to the registers of St Michael le Belfry, York). A Mr Smith performed at York in 1771. We believe he may have been Walter, who acted at the Theatre Royal in Shakespeare Square in Edinburgh from 1773 to 1781. Tate Wilkinson in his *Wandering Patentee* placed Walter Smith at Wakefield in 1774, playing a Masquer in *Old Mother Red-Cap.*

The *Edinburgh Rosciad* in the fall of 1775 called Smith "the genteelest in theatric lore." "He's but beginning" and has a "handsome shape and person." Many of Smith's Edinburgh roles are known through the research of Norma Armstrong: the Abbot in *Henry II*, Aimwell in *The Beaux' Stratagem*, Alonzo in *The Revenge*, Altamont in *The Fair Penitent*, Bardolph in *The Merry Wives of Windsor*, Beaufort in *The Citizen*, Bedamar in *Venice Preserv'd*, Belford in *Isabella*, Bellamy in *The Suspicious Husband*, Belmour in *Jane Shore*, Brother Jolly in *The Ladies' Wish*, Charles in *The Jealous Wife*, Dionysius in *The Grecian Daughter*, Don Louis de Pomposo de Carbino in *The Sailor's Triumph*, Faulkland in *The Rivals*, the First Gentleman in *The Jubilee*, Frederick in *The Wonder*, the Genius of Britain in *The Institution of the Order of the Garter*, the Ghost and an Officer in *Hamlet*, Invoice in *The Devil upon Two Sticks*, Justice in *The Invasion of Harlequin*, the King in *Love and Ambition*, the title role and Worcester in *1 Henry IV*, King Henry in *Richard III*, Lord Raymond in *The Countess of Salisbury*, and Major Oakly in *The Jealous Wife*.

Also Manly in *The Provok'd Husband*, Mendoza in *Braganza*, Narbas in *Merope*, Petruchio in *The Chances*, the Prince in *Much Ado about Nothing*, Pylades in *The Distrest Mother*, Sir John Flowerdale in *Lionel and Clarissa*, Solerino in *The Merchant of Venice*, Stanly in *All the World's a Stage*, Stockwell in *The West Indian*, Tirehack in *The Orators*, Tullus Hostilius in *The Roman Father*, Tycho in *Harlequin Doctor Faustus*, Tyrrel in *The Fashionable Lover*, Worthy in *The Recruiting Officer*, the King in *The Mourning Bride*, and Old Belfield in *The Brothers*.

The *Hibernian Journal* on 30 September 1776 noted the Irish debut at the Crow Street Theatre of a Mr Smith from Edinburgh. He also acted at Cork in 1776, 1777, 1778, and 1779, and in 1779 he also appeared at Waterford. He performed in Dublin again in 1781–82. The dates of his known appearances in Ireland and Scotland dovetail nicely, so there seems to be no question: Walter Smith was the man. *The Authentic Memoirs of the Green Room* identified Smith as having been "accidently wounded by Mr. Reddish on the Dublin stage, while playing Polydore to his Castilio."

In Dublin in 1777 Smith married Miss Henrietta Scrase (or Scrace), an actress from Bath who made her first appearance at the Crow Street Theatre on 28 May 1777. Henrietta was the daughter of Richard and Martha Scrase and the sister of the actress Patty Ann Scrase, who became Mrs James Bates.

Advertised as from the Theatre Royal, Dublin, Walter Smith made his first—and apparently last—appearance in London on 13 September 1777 at the Haymarket Theatre as Hotspur in *1 Henry IV*. A clipping at the Folger Shakespeare Library concerns his performance: "A Mr. Smith, from the Theatre Royal, Dublin, figured away, for the first time, in the character of Hotspur, who, bating his person, seems to have very little requisites for the stage. . . ." The critic said Smith had no feeling and wondered why the management had allowed a "recruit" to play the part when Aickin was available. On 24 September 1777 the *Morning Post* named Smith as playing at Richmond and identified him as from Dublin.

Having made little impression in London, Walter Smith returned to Dublin, and in 1779 he and his wife joined Tate Wilkinson's company at Hull. The Smiths were in the troupe (playing now at Hull, now at York, now at Sheffield) until 1786. Some of Walter's roles in Edinburgh, where he also played, between August 1782 and August 1784, are known: the First Gardener in *The Rival Candidates*, the First Officer in *King Lear*, Francisco in *The Chances*, the Host in *The Merry Wives of Windsor*, Northumberland in *1 Henry IV*, Old Gobbo in *The Merchant of Venice*, Order in *A New Way to Pay Old Debts*, Tyrrel in *Richard III*, and Warwick in *2 Henry IV*. With the York troupe he is known to have played at Hull in *Cymbeline* on 16 December 1783 and *As You Like It* on 8 December 1784. His last benefit with Wilkinson's troupe, shared with his wife, was on 1 April 1786 at York.

The Smiths seem to have been successful enough while they were with Wilkinson's troupe, but Wilkinson found them difficult, especially Mrs. Smith (as her entry indicates). In 1783, for instance, the Smiths had what Wilkinson called "a great house" for their benefit, "but still they were not happy."

In 1788 the Smiths, described as from Dublin, acted at Manchester. She was described as more accomplished than he. Walter acted with the Bath company almost every season from 1789–90 through 1804–5; only 1792–93 is not accounted for. From 1798–99 through

1804–5 he served as the company treasurer. The troupe also performed at Bristol, where "W. Smith" played minor roles in 1799, 1800, 1801, and 1803–4. Walter Smith sustained a dislocated shoulder in a coach accident as he and the company were traveling from Bath to Bristol on 20 April 1801. (Another Smith— probably William Bradford Smith, thinks Kathleen Barker—performed at Bath from 1791 to 1811 and was the uncle of the surgeon and antiquarian Richard Smith the younger.) Perhaps the Smith who acted at Edinburgh in 1801 and 1802 was Walter.

The Smiths had a daughter who made her London debut on 2 October 1805 at Covent Garden as Lady Townly in *The Provok'd Husband*. She became Mrs Knight. Their son, Richard John Smith (1786–1855) acted in the nineteenth century. The *Gentleman's Magazine* in April 1809 reported that Walter Smith, treasurer to the Bath theatre, had died. His wife died in 1822. Among James Winston's notes at the Folger Shakespeare Library is one identifying the son of the Smiths as "A. Smith, Jr.," suggesting incorrectly that the boy's father was A. Smith.

A portrait of Walter Smith was drawn by Joseph Hutchisson and at one time was in the Garrick Club (No 306). The picture is described in the Garrick Club catalogue as pastel on paper (22¾″ × 18¾″), head and shoulders, to right, looking at viewer; dark hair turning gray, brown eyes, white neckcloth, and dark coat. On the back of the paper is written, "James Brownell March 15, 1824 witness^th that this Picture is the Original one of the late Mr Smith of the Theatre of Bath, Joseph Hutchisson No 9 Bath Street Bath." We are informed that this portrait has been sold. The identity of the buyer is not known to us.

Smith, Mrs Walter, Henrietta, née Scrase
1752–1822, actress.

Henrietta Scrase was born in 1752, the daughter of Richard and Martha Scrase and sister of Patty Ann Scrase, later Mrs James Bates, and Edward Scrase. (We were incorrect in Mrs Bates's entry in citing her father as Henry Scrase. The new information above is in the registers of St Michael le Belfry, York.) Henrietta made her Irish stage debut at the Crow Street Theatre, Dublin, on 21 October

1776, according to the *Hibernian Journal*. By 27 May 1777 she had met and married the actor Walter Smith. Mrs Smith performed at Crow Street in 1777, at Cork in 1778 and 1779, and at Belfast in 1779. Advertised as from Dublin, Mrs Smith made her Hull debut on 9 November 1779. Tate Wilkinson wrote in his *Wandering Patentee* that "she acquitted herself well, and promised to be what she afterwards proved, a great favourite." She became his "principal first lady actress" but was a difficult artist to deal with.

In the early months of 1780 and in the summer of 1781 Mrs Smith (with her husband) appeared with Wilkinson's company at the Theatre Royal in Shakespeare Square, Edinburgh. Some of her roles were Angelina in *Love Makes a Man*, Bridget in *The Chapter of Accidents*, Fanny in *The Clandestine Marriage*, Indiana in *The Conscious Lovers*, Jenny in *The Gentle Shepherd*, Juliet, Lady Anne in *Richard III*, Lady Newberry in *Separate Maintenance*, Lady Racket in *Marriage à la Mode*, Lady Teazle in *The School for Scandal*, Marcella in *The Sailor's Triumph*, Miss Dudley and Miss Rusport in *The West Indian*, Miss Tittup in *Bon Ton*, Miss Walsingham in *The School for Wives*, Mrs Racket in *The Belle's Stratagem*, Portia in *The Merchant of Venice*, Rosalind in *As You Like It*, Selima in *Tamerlane*, Tilburnia in *The Critic*, and Volumnia in *Coriolanus*.

Mrs Smith performed in Sheffield in June 1781 and was with Wilkinson at York from 1781–82 through 1785–86; the troupe also played at Hull during those years, as a number of playbills at the London Guildhall show.

Wilkinson was caught in the middle of a rivalry between Mrs Smith and Dorothy Jordan. In the fall of 1782 Mrs Smith was pregnant, but she continued acting rather than yield her parts to Mrs Jordan. Wilkinson described the result:

Mrs SMITH might truly be said to be . . . well in merit, well in friends and prosperity, possessed of situation, &c.; but she certainly was an evil genius to herself. . . .

I am the more particular in mentioning Mrs. Smith's comfortable situation with me, as a jealous eagerness of duty at that juncture in September, was of fatal consequence to her future health and welfare; but I may be, and hope I am mistaken, for she toiled hard in my vineyard and earned her reward. At that time she was in such a situation as women wish to be who love their lords; but fearing her indignant rival Jordan should be prepared at that period in any one of her characters, Mrs. Smith assured me she would wield her pike, and be on duty for three months longer, when it was but a very few days after that assurance, that she was compelled from force irresistible to lay down her arms and be stript of all her accoutrements, and her place was supplied for some time by Mrs. Jordan, who was as happy as the other was unhappy; for she figured away in Emmeline, Lady Racket, Lady Bell, Lady Teazle, Lady Alton, Indiana, &c. the termed property of Mrs. Smith.

. . . Mrs Smith was so eager (though a woman in every respect of delicacy and strict good behaviour) that she would, against all persuasion, though a very remarkable wet September, in a short time after her lying in, walk in a damp garden to get strength for her Sheffield journey of eighteen miles from Doncaster, which was on the 13th of October, and her confinement only took place October 2. She pleased herself in performing her journey it is true, but the consequence was a fixed lameness in her hip, which I was told threatened fatal consequences. I by no means wished her to make her appearance till more recovered, but so eager was she to be on the boards, that act she would, and act she did, and though as lame as Mrs. Amlet, would not suffer Mrs. Jordan to appear in Fanny, but limped and hopped more than myself in Lord Ogleby. It was in vain to remonstrate—I said there is no occasion—do not appear Madam—here comes the *Jordan;* but we will suppose that she replied like Cleopatra,

> *Were she the sister of the thundering Jove,*
> *And bore her brother's light'ning in her eyes,*
> *Thus would I meet my rival.*

and a bad meeting it was for me and herself, for the attempt had so fatal an effect, that from that night, October 28, 1782, till Wednesday December the 18th, she never was able to appear again.

We are not certain which of the Smiths' children was the one born in 1782. But the registers of St Michael le Belfry, York, contain the baptismal notice on 26 February 1786 of Richard John Smith, the sixth child of Walter Smith, comedian, son of John and Betty Smith, and Henrietta, daughter of Richard and Martha Scrase. (Richard John Smith acted in the nineteenth century and died in 1855.)

Mrs Smith's difficult behavior finally led to a break with Wilkinson:

"Fontainbleau, or our Way in France," was got up that season, and I gave its first representation (after being at the expence of Music, Scenery, &c.) for Mrs. Smith's benefit, on Saturday, Feb. 26, 1785: I cast Lady Bull to Mrs Smith; Miss Bull to Mrs. Jordan. Mrs. Smith, though proper for the character, yet disliked so much the playing it, that notwithstanding her having the compliment of it the first representation for her own benefit, yet we quarrelled because I refused a particular requisite when she represented that character; and she was so foolish as to put in practice what she said she would, that was, spoil the character every time she played it; and no compliment to her wisdom or her folly; for she really kept her word most rigidly, and when she was losing her own reputation, gloried in thinking she vexed the manager: We quarrelled so much at Leeds on the subject, that we agreed to part at the expiration of articles, the end of May 1786, and never were friends again in Yorkshire.

Mrs Smith's last benefit with Wilkinson had been on 1 April, when she had played Scrub in *The Stratagem.*

Wilkinson related two other tales, undated, about Mrs Smith. Her jealousy of Mrs Jordan was a constant problem:

Mrs. Smith swelled with indignation, and the constant Green-Room phrase, was, "Pray when, Ma'am, is your benefit? and when is yours, for I see Mrs. Jordan begins with one on Wednesday next?"—And to be sure, if it had not been for my support, she could not have surmounted her difficulties; for by her success, which they attributed to my partiality, not allowing any degree of superior merit to the hated Jordan, she must have sunk under it, for her spirits were never violent, unless when scolding the manager, and with an empty pocket: Her situation, her uncommon labour and study for the Theatre, and so many mouths, whose food were dependent on her bounty, must make the reader feel for her, pity and praise, and rejoice at her good stars and reverse of fortune. . . .

On another occasion Mrs Smith was jealous of Mrs Robinson:

Her making choice of Portia, Mrs. Smith took in great dudgeon; she was tenacious to a folly: In consequence, to prevent the play being acted as I had appointed, Mr. and Mrs. Smith made secret application to Lady M*****, to desire Mrs. Smith might act the part; which her ladyship really did require, and with her own opinion in favour of Mrs. Smith: For though she had not seen Mrs. Robinson on the stage, yet her ladyship conceived a dislike to the seeing her act Portia, as Mrs. Smith had conveyed a notion it interfered with her interest, and would in consequence be an injury to her fame:

But as the bills were printed off the day of the request, it was impossible for me, as manager, with justice or any degree of propriety, to disgrace Mrs. Robinson by such an improper and unprecedented behavior on my part.

In May 1786 Mrs Smith left Wilkinson. On 13 July she made her first appearance in London, playing Phillis in *The Conscious Lovers* at the Haymarket Theatre. The *European Magazine* thought Mrs Smith acquitted herself with spirit and propriety. On 25 July she acted Lady Harriet in *I'll Tell You What*, and on 17 August she was seen as Miss Alscrip in *The Heiress*.

The Mrs Smith who acted at Norwich and Brighton in 1787 was probably our subject. She was certainly the Mrs W. Smith who performed at Bath and Bristol from 1788–89 through 1799–1800, after which she seems to have left the stage. Her husband died in 1809 at Bath. Henrietta Smith died in Edinburgh at the age of 70 on 31 December 1822, according to the *Edinburgh Magazine* in February 1823. She had been a pensioner on the Bath Theatre Fund for some time.

One child of Mr and Mrs Walter Smith was the Miss Smith who became the wife of the actor Edmund John Eyre in 1804; she seems to have been named after her mother. If we have understood our sources correctly, the younger Henrietta Smith was sister to Mrs Hazard, who acted at Swansea in 1801, according to the *Monthly Mirror*, and sister to George Smith, who acted at Sadler's Wells with Henrietta in 1803. In O. Smith's collection at the British Library, Smith noted that he was a son of Henrietta Smith.

Smith, William [*fl. 1680s–1720*], *violist, violinist.*

William Smith apparently became one of the City waits in the 1680s. Harley in *Music in Purcell's London* quotes an anonymous contemporary poem describing the lives of the waits:

The publick waites who Liveryes do own,
And Badges of a City, or some Town,
Who are retain'd in constant Yearly pay,
Do at their Solemn publick Meetings play.
And up and down the Streets, and Town in cold
Dark Nights, when th' Instruments they can scarce
    hold
They play about, and tell what hour it is,
And Weather too, this Course they do not miss,

Most part of Winter, in the Nights; and when
Some Generous Persons come to Town, these Men
As soon as they're Inform'd, do then repair
Unto their Lodgings play them some fine Ayre
Or brisk new tune, such as themselves think fit,
And which they hope, with th' Gallants fancies
    hit,
They cry God Bless you Sirs; again then play,
Expecting Money, e'er they go away . . .

In 1704 William Smith paid £30 5s. for the privilege of being a wait.

Robert Hume has suggested to us that William Smith was the violist Smith who performed in London from 1707 to 1720. About November 1707 Smith was paid 8s. nightly for playing at the Queen's Theatre. In the Coke papers he was sometimes called Smith Junior, to distinguish him from another Smith, who played the violin and was, we believe, Charles Smith. Our subject was named in Coke documents connected with the affairs of the Queen's Theatre through 1711. In the Portland papers at Nottingham Smith was cited as a violist in the Academy of Music opera orchestra in February 1720 at a salary of £30.

Smith, William [*fl. 1685–1690*], *singer.*

William Smith was one of the children of the Chapel Royal and marched in the coronation procession for James II on 23 April 1685. By 25 September 1690 his voice had broken and he had left the Chapel. On that date the Lord Chamberlain ordered maintenance for young Smith.

Smith, William *d. 1695, actor, manager.*

William Smith's will tells us that he was born in Greenwich. According to *The History of the English Stage* (1741) Smith was a barrister of Gray's Inn before he joined Sir William Davenant's Duke's Company at the Lincoln's Inn Fields playhouse, perhaps as early as 1661. Smith's first known role was Antonio in *The Duchess of Malfi* on 30 September 1662 and subsequent dates. During the rest of the 1662–63 season Smith is known to have acted Antonius in *Ignoramus* on 1 November 1662 (at court), Corrigidor in *The Adventures of Five Hours* on 8 January 1663, and Lugo in *The Slighted Maid* on 23 February. Before the closing of the theatres by the plague in 1665 he was seen as Crispus in *The Step Mother*, Buckingham in *Henry VIII*, Colonel Bruce in *The*

Comical Revenge, Burgundy in Boyle's *Henry V* (in which he wore clothes given the company by the Earl of Oxford), Polynices in *The Rivals,* Banquo in *Macbeth,* and Zanger in *Mustapha.*

The Duke's Company resumed performing in October 1666 at court, but we have no information on Smith's activity. On 14 November, however, the actress Mrs Knepp told Samuel Pepys that "Smith, of the Duke's house, hath killed a man upon a quarrel in play; which makes every body sorry, he being a good actor, and, they say, a good man, however this happens. The ladies of the Court do much bemoan him, she says." That statement may have persuaded Montague Summers in *The Playhouse of Pepys* to state positively that Smith was "notably handsome and athletic."

He was notably lucky, certainly, for despite his having killed a man he was back on the boards on 7 March 1667, acting Sir William Stanley in *The English Princess* at Lincoln's Inn Fields. The following 15 August he played Sir John Swallow in *The Feign'd Innocence.* Between then and the opening of the troupe's new playhouse in Dorset Garden William Smith is known to have played Brisac in *The Villain,* Polynices in *The Rivals,* Courtall in *She Wou'd if She Cou'd,* Standford in *The Sullen Lovers,* Cunningham in *The Amorous Widow,* Single in *Sir Salomon,* Philander in *The Forced Marriage,* Foscaris in *The Women's Conquest,* Darius in *Cambyses,* Sharnofsky in *Juliana,* and Tyridates in *Herod and Mariamne.* He was also called upon occasionally to deliver prologues, a responsibility he accepted more and more as his career went on.

Pepys liked Smith's acting, but on 24 October 1667 he could not believe the report that Smith acted Brisac in *The Villain* as effectively as or better than Thomas Betterton, whom he replaced that day. But on 11 February 1668 Pepys saw *Mustapha* and told his Diary, ". . . I never saw such good acting of any creature as Smith's part of Zanger."

Smith's first role at Dorset Garden Theatre was the Prince of Salerne in *Charles VIII,* after which he appeared in such new parts as Ruffle in *The Morning Ramble,* Woodly in *Epsom Wells,* Careless in *The Careless Lovers,* Muly Hamet in *The Empress of Morocco,* Clotair in *Love and Revenge,* Quitazo in *The Conquest of China,* Horatio in *Hamlet,* perhaps Warner in *Sir Martin Marall,* Ibrahim, Sir Fopling Flutter in *The*

Man of Mode, Bruce in *The Virtuoso,* Don Carlos, Philip in *Abdelazer,* Don Diego de Sluniga in *The Wrangling Lovers,* Manley in *Madam Fickle,* Antiochus in *Titus and Berenice,* Mirtillo in *Pastor Fido,* Caesar in Sedley's *Antony and Cleopatra,* Wilmore in both parts of *The Rover,* Ithacus in *Circe,* Rashley in *The Fond Husband,* Perdicas in *The Siege of Babylon,* Alcibiades in Shadwell's *Timon of Athens,* and Lodwick Knowell in *Sir Patient Fancy.*

Also Truman in *Friendship in Fashion,* Peralta in *The Counterfeits,* Henry in *Squire Oldsapp,* Adrastus in *Oedipus,* Ulysses in *The Destruction of Troy,* Sir Harry Fillamour in *The Feign'd Curtizans,* Hector in Dryden's *Troilus and Cressida,* Machiavel in *Caesar Borgia,* perhaps Orsames in *The Young King,* Beauford in *The Virtuous Wife,* Marius Junior (Shakespeare's Romeo Romanized) in *Caius Marius,* Marcello in *The Loving Enemies,* Edward in *The Misery of Civil War,* Chamont in *The Orphan,* Courtine in *The Soldier's Fortune,* Wellman in *The Revenge,* Marcian in *Theodosius,* Lorenzo in *The Spanish Fryar,* Titus in *Lucius Junius Brutus,* Edgar in *King Lear,* The Duke of Suffolk in *1 Henry VI,* Don Carlos in *The False Count,* Ramble in *The London Cuckolds,* Sir Charles Kinglove in *The Royalist,* Pierre in *Venice Preserv'd,* King Harry in *Vertue Betray'd,* and perhaps Loveless in *The Roundheads*—after which, in 1682, the Duke's players absorbed the rival King's Company.

Not only was Smith one of the leading actors in the Duke's troupe in the 1670s, as of 18 July 1674 he held one and a half shares in the acting company, and from 1677–78 through 1681–82 he was co-manager with Thomas Betterton. A survey of the parish of St Bride, Fleet Street, in 1677, now at the Guildhall, shows that Smith had a house on Primrose Hill, not too far from the Dorset Garden Theatre.

On 14 October 1681 Smith, Charles Davenant, and Thomas Betterton signed an underhanded agreement with two actors from the rival troupe, Charles Hart and Edward Kynaston, by which Hart and Kynaston would turn coat and promote a merger of the two companies. That move did not immediately cause the collapse of the King's Company, but in 1682, according to testimony Smith gave later, Charles Killigrew of the King's players approached the Duke's Company about an amalgamation. Smith was one of the signers of the merger agreement on 4 May 1682. In June Drury Lane Theatre (the King's Company house) was leased for £3 daily to Charles Davenant, Thomas Betterton, and William Smith, the leaders of the Duke's players. Smith was also a signer of an agreement to pay the Duke of Bedford £50 ground rent beginning at Michaelmas 1682. On 9 November a new agreement was made leasing Drury Lane to Davenant alone. William Smith seems to have continued as co-manager with Betterton.

Smith's first recorded role with the new United Company was Don Leon in *Rule a Wife and Have a Wife*, which was presented on 15 November 1682 at court. The following day at Drury Lane Smith spoke the epilogue to an unidentified play, and on 28 November he spoke the prologue and played Crillon in *The Duke of Guise*. On 19 January 1683 he delivered the prologue to *City Politicks* at Drury Lane. In July at Dorset Garden he acted Courtine in *The Atheist*. With the United Company at one of their two playhouses or at court through the splitting of the troupe in 1695 Smith is known to have appeared in such new roles as Cassius in *Julius Caesar,* Constantine, Lorenzo in *The Disappointment,* Bruce in *The Virtuoso,* Armusia in *The Island Princess,* Maximus in *Valentinian,* and Norfolk in *Richard III*.

William Smith was clearly one of the more important Restoration actors and was highly respected by his fellows. That did not prevent him from being included in the caustic *Satyr upon the Players* about 1684:

> Then in comes Smith that murders every shape
> The crying Lover & the Squinting Ape,
> So very dull in both, that you may see
> Sorrow turn'd Mirth, & Mirth turn'd Tragedy.
> Passion he Ridicules so whines & cryes
> That you wou'd swear he somewhat more than
>   Dyes,
> Then, by his Antic Postures men of Sence
> Doe say He plays Jack Pudding not a Prince,
> Since so it is, Will, e'en in time be wise
> Stick to ye Bottle; there thy Talent lyes,
> But for ye Stage (Conceited Malapert)
> Thou'rt worse then strowling Coish or strutting
>   Burt.

More is known of Smith's other activities between 1682 and 1695 than of his roles. After April 1684 he left the stage, apparently until 1686–87, when he was next named in theat-rical documents. Hotson in *The Commonwealth and Restoration Stage* states that a cabal of Mohawks forced Smith off the stage in 1685, but perhaps that happened in 1684. In any case, he was certainly back at the theatre by 25–29 November 1686, when a notice in the *London Gazette* cited him: "Whereas Mr Thomas Otway sometime before his Death made Four Acts of a Play, whoever can give Notice in whose Hands the Copy lies, either to Mr Thomas Betterton, or Mr William Smith at the Theatre Royal, shall be well Rewarded for his pains." The missing play was never found.

On 30 August 1687 Charles Davenant signed over to his rascally brother Alexander the residue of the 19-year lease on Drury Lane. On the following 5 November Alexander Davenant deposed Smith and Betterton as managers, replacing them with his unskilled brother Thomas Davenant.

On 19 November 1687 Smith joined the army at his "own expense," he said in his will, made at that time. In his *General History* in 1749 the prompter W. R. Chetwood spoke of Smith's support of James II:

> This gentleman, Mr. *Smith,* was zealously attached to the Interest of King *James* the Second, and serv'd in his Army as a Volunteer, with Two Servants. After the Abdication, Mr. Smith return'd to the Theatre, by the Persuasion of many Friends, and the Desire of the Town who admir'd his Performance. The first Character he chose to appear in was that of *Wilmore* in the *Rover,* his original part in that Comedy; but, being informed that he should be maltreated on account of his Principles, he gave Orders for the Curtain to drop, if any Disturbance should come from the Audience. Accordingly the Play began in the utmost Tranquillity; but when Mr. *Smith* entered in the First Act, the Storm began with the usual Noise upon such Occasions (an Uproar not unknown to all Frequenters of Theatres, and by the Time mightily improved by a particular Set that delight in that agreeable Harmony, that sets all the Village Curs to imitate the Sound), Mr. *Smith* gave the Signal, the Curtain dropp'd, and the Audience [was] dismiss'd.

"Gentleman" Smith (apparently no relation) in his correspondence with Coutts in the early nineteenth century told the story of William Smith's scuffle with a member of the nobility, an incident that seems to have been connected with the *Rover* affair:

Mr Smith one of my great predecessors whose memory Booth in his very excellent classical Epitaph liberally celebrates, struck an Irish Nobleman whose name I . . . forget, for a most insolent outrage offered to an Actress when on the Stage, throwing (as it was said) a [word illegible] at her, wrapp'd up in a Paper, this Smith, who knew 'a Lord opposed against a Man is but a Man' properly resented—& was afterwards hiss'd by a party of Cowards headed by that Lord. . . .

The date of that incident is not known. The first recorded performance of *The Rover* after James II left the throne was at court on 4 November 1690. By April 1691 Smith may again have left the stage, though a manuscript cast of *Richard III* with Smith as Norfolk is listed in *The London Stage* for the 1691–92 season (perhaps it should be redated 1690–91). *The London Stage* keeps Smith on the United Company roster through 1692–93.

The complaints of the older players in the United Company in December 1694 revealed that when Smith retired he was paid £100 and that when he served with Betterton as a co-manager between May 1682 and 1687 he held one share "and half a quarter," the latter being payment for his management duties. He came out of his retirement to play Scandal in the first performance of *Love for Love* on 30 April 1695 at Lincoln's Inn Fields. Chetwood described his return:

No Persuasions could prevail upon him to appear upon the Stage again, till that great Poet, Mr. *Congreve,* had wrote his Comedy of *Love for Love,* which was in the year 1695. . . . This celebrated Author prevailed upon several Persons of the First Rank to move Mr. *Smith* to appear in the Character of Scandal in that excellent Commedy: But he yielded more to the Persuasions of his sincere Friends, Mr. *Betterton* and Mrs. *Barry,* and accepted the Part; and his inimitable Performance added one Grace to the Play. He took his Station in many Plays afterwards, for, I think, three Years.

Smith was a good friend to young players. He had a sister who looked after the youthful actress Mary Porter for some years, and Smith appears also to have concerned himself with Miss Porter's upbringing.

In mid-December 1695 William Smith played Cyaxares in *Cyrus;* Downes said "it was a good Play; but Mr. Smith having a long part in it, fell Sick upon the Fourth Day and

Dy'd. . . ." The *Flying Post* of 26–28 December published a note:

Mr William Smith, a Gentleman, belonging to the Theatre Royal, who had acquired a considerable Estate, and thereupon desisted from Acting, was prevailed upon by the New Play house to remount the Stage; but upon shifting his cloathes in the last New Play, took cold and died thereof this week.

Chetwood's version had it that Smith

died of a Cold, occasion'd by a violent Fit of the Cramp; for when he was first seiz'd, he threw himself out of Bed, and remained so long before the Cramp left him (in that naked Condition) that a Cold fell upon his Lungs, a Fever ensu'd, and Death releas'd him in three Days after.

Fitzgerald in his *New History* claimed that Smith died of apoplexy in 1696 (*recte* late December 1695), and in *Notes and Queries* on 15 February 1879 it was reported that Smith's death was caused by over-exertion in the role of Cyaxares. Smith died in the parish of St Giles, Cripplegate. John Verbruggen withdrew from the Drury Lane troupe and joined Lincoln's Inn Fields to take over some of Smith's roles. Barton Booth the actor wrote a Latin epitaph to go under a portrait of Smith (now lost?) in which he styled Smith a man of much humanity, greatly beloved by his fellow players and his audiences. He was, Booth thought, almost equal to Betterton.

Smith had written his own will on 19 November 1688, just before entering the service, at which time he lived in the parish of St Bride, Fleet Street. He claimed he was "indisposed in body by a fitt of the stone and strangurie which with the dangers and hazards of a Wait now at hand" persuaded him to write his will. The handwriting in the will was certified on 2 January 1696 by Charles Davenant, Thomas Betterton, and others. The will is a lengthy, rambling document that shows Smith a generous and amiable gentleman and supplies some details of his personal life.

To Mrs Chapman, the widow of Smith's uncle Colonel Edmund Chapman, William Smith left an annuity of £8, providing she had less than £100 to her name. Smith provided for Mrs Chapman,

notwithstanding hers and her husbands former unkindness to and neglect of me in his prosperity when he had a paternall Estate of value which he sold without assisting me his next heir at any time or my poor brother tho Orphans with a penny and notwithstanding I can make it appeare I was out six or seaven score pounds in supporting him for seaven or eight years before his death and in his ffunerall expenses and on her since yet in consideration that my deare Brother at my earnest sollicitacon intended him kindness had he liv'd . . .

To Mr Tussingham of the Exchequer office, who married the daughter and only child of "my unfortunate cousin" Henry Smith of Withrock, Leicestershire, Smith left £6 for mourning and a gold ring worth 10*s*.

Smith canceled a bequest of £20 to the widow Allanson, whose son was Smith's friend; the £20 had been owed by Allanson to Smith and had accumulated interest, which Smith decided to cancel. A marginal note by Smith indicates that the debt was settled sometime after the will was made.

To his wife and to her mother Smith left gold rings; to his godson and wife's nephew William Hurkle, son of John Hurkle, town clerk of Leicester, Smith left £20; to his godson Heath (no Christian name given), son of Mr Heath and his wife Grace, he gave £20. Heath had been in the service of Sir John Arundell, master of the horse to the Queen Dowager. The £20 was to go to the parents should the son die. A note for £20 which Grace Heath had given Smith, Smith canceled, along with a seal that he had loaned her. A Cornelian seal also went to Mrs Heath.

Smith left £5 to his brother-in-law John Hurkle of Leicester and canceled a debt of £13. He left the considerable sum of 50 guineas to a youth (perhaps an illegitimate son) named and described in a paper that Smith said he had sealed in a little black trunk.

Smith gave "my Boy's uncle" Thomas Orme of Hanch, Staffordshire, £10 for mourning and a ring. He left ten-shilling rings also to his cousin Arthur Browne, his cousin Baker of Lichfield, Mr Rider of Lichfield, Madam Stanhope of Elvaston and her two sisters, his cousin Richard Brundell of Stonton, Joseph Williams, "old" Mr Coniers alias Connell, Dr (Charles) Davenant, Alexander Davenant, Thomas Davenant, the actor Philip Cademan, his neighbor William Grymes, George Smith of Richmond (a Serjeant at Arms), Captain Wyth, and John Crossby of the pay office of the Navy. Smith also left mourning rings of unspecified value to his "brother" William Orme, cousin C. Agard, and Dr Mollins.

Smith left £20 to his son's nurse Elizabeth Goodchild, widow; to Anne Gutheridge, Smith's maid (if still in his service at his death) Smith gave £10. Thomas Betterton "my friend and oldest acquaintance," received £6 for mourning; Betterton and his wife were given ten-shilling mourning rings. Smith's kinsman Dr William Aglionbey, one of his son's godfathers, was given £6 for mourning and a tenshilling ring. To Mrs Mary Wysley, who had been friendly to his boy, Smith gave £30 and a ring. Twenty-shilling rings were left to Smith's trustees Charles Davenant, Thomas Orme, Dr William Aglionbey, and Thomas Betterton.

All other lands, leases, tenements, goods, and the like Smith left to his only (legitimate?) son and heir Francis Smith. Should he die without issue, the following bequests were to be made: £300 to widow Chapman, £200 to Mary Wysley, £1000 to Thomas Orme, £500 to "my youth," £500 to Tussingham and his wife, £100 to Smith's godson Roger Allanson, £600 to John Hurkle and his children, £100 to Smith's godson Heath, £100 to Smith's cousin Baker, £50 to nurse Goodchild, £500 to Dr Aglionbey, £200 to the two daughters of William Browne of Leicester, evidently £200 to William Browne's brother Henry of Bernard's Inn, £100 to Smith's (?) cousin Arthur Browne, and £100 to his (Arthur's?) two little boys.

Smith also bequeathed £20 to the poor of Greenwich, where Smith was born, £100 to Thomas Betterton, £20 to the poor of the parish of Longdon (where Smith's wife was born), £50 to Dr. Davenant's "pretty prateing eldest daughter," £50 each to Smith's godson Mr Jones's son (of Sheeze Lane), his godson Rider, son of Mr Rider of Lichfield, and Mr Audley and his wife of Fleet Street "where I lodg'd so long." £20 should go to Robin Horknell, his son's servant, £30 to servant Anne Gutheridge, £20 to Thomas Wright, a kinsman "tho a servant" to the Smiths of Wichrock, £20 to the poor of St Bride's, and an unspecified amount (probably £20) to the poor of St Dunstan's parish, where his son "ffranck" was born.

Smith noted that any excess in the estate resulting from the deaths of any legatees before the will was proved should go toward highway repairs and the Seamen's Chest at Chatham. He also noted that if the estate was not large enough and if his son died, the legatees were to reduce the bequests proportionally. Smith's son Francis was to be the executor, but during his minority the trustees named above were to look after the estate and oversee Francis's education. Sir James Butler was to be turned to in case of disagreements among the trustees.

Smith wrote, "And upon recollection and in consideration That I am now goeing into the Kings Army at my own expense which may amount to such a sume as may exhaust most of the ready money I have by me" he wished, in case he should die "in the Expedition" that the trustees should raise money for the legacies by selling his estate. Smith also asked that if he died in the war, mourning rings were to go only to his relatives and relatives of the trustees, "because if I dye as aforesaid I guess I shall have but few of my friends and acquaintance at my Buriall."

He hoped his "Mother" (i.e., -in-law) Orme would pardon him for not making her a legatee, but, Smith observed, she already had a fortune, and what he could provide would "be a small addition." But should she ever need money, Smith wanted his trustees to aid her. She was to have any of Smith's rings she particularly liked (the rings, Smith stated, were in his large trunk). She was to choose one of his diamond rings, though the larger one, which had been Smith's brother's, Smith wished to be saved for his son Francis. Smith had wrapped and marked some rings for certain people to help the trustees in their distribution.

Smith concluded his will saying it was "All of my own handwriting and inditeing" and was to be kept secret until his son came of age. Since there was, apparently, a second probate on 10 August 1705 by Francis Smith and the trustees, we may guess that Francis had just then reached his majority and thus had been born about 1684.

Smith, William [*fl. c.* 1704–1755], *oboist.*
William Smith was an oboist in the royal musical establishment by 1704, if not earlier, and he was one of many court musicians permitted to play in the opera band at the Queen's Theatre, for an annual wage of £25. Smith also worked for a Colonel Harrison in the early years of the eighteenth century, procuring for Harrison a group of oboe players and training them. He was to be paid 25 guineas for gathering the players and 30 guineas for training them over a five-month period. But Smith was not paid for his efforts and had to sue Harrison for the debt. "The Case of William Smith Hautboy" among the Coke papers at Harvard provides us with that information and also reveals that Smith had a large family to support.

Smith played at the Queen's Theatre as late as 1711–12 and at some point was in the service of the Prince of Denmark. He received a pension for the period from 1 October 1714 to 24 June 1716. On 18 July 1726—the last mention of him in the Lord Chamberlain's accounts—he attended the installation of the Duke of Richmond and Sir Robert Walpole at Windsor. On 28 August 1739 William Smith became one of the original subscribers to the Royal Society of Musicians. He remained active until at least 1755.

Smith, William 1730–1819, *actor, manager.*
The actor William Smith was the son of William Smith (b. 1700–d. 19 December 1782), a wholesale grocer and tea importer in the City of London. The younger William Smith was born on 22 February 1730, according to his testimony in a letter in 1818. The author of *The Lives of Eminent & Remarkable Characters . . . in the Counties of Essex, Suffolk, & Norfolk* (1820) declares that Smith's

father having designed him for the clerical profession, sent him in 1737, to Eton, from whence he was removed in 1748, to St. John's College, Cambridge. Young Smith, while at Eton, distinguished himself by his vivacity and spirit, and carrying with him to the university the same levity of disposition, he was soon led into irregularities, which frustrated all the views his father had contemplated in his education. Having one evening drunk too freely with some associates of kindred minds, and being pursued by the proctor he had the imprudence to snap an unloaded pistol at him. For this offense, he was doomed to a punishment to which he would not submit; and in order to avoid expulsion, immediately quitted college.

Tate Gallery

WILLIAM SMITH
by Hoppner

played pretty," but no other criticism, if there was any, survives. Smith himself recalled his debut in two letters to Thomas Coutts 60 years later:

> . . . I can never forget the resplendent Powers of *Barry* & Mrs *Cibber*—I shudder at the thought of so poor a shrub as myself even vegetating under such illustrious excellence. . . .
>
> What a Precipice did I stand on. . . . Every hope at stake! My family affairs almost entirely ruin'd! Father, Mother & Sister looking on me, a very broken reed & deeply weigh'd down by my extravagances, for the slender hope of support. . . .
>
> What a Tryal I surmounted! Rich the Manager had treated me ungenerously & kept me back until I was worn out by attendance on his absurdities & had not Mr [Lacy] Ryan's too advanc'd age render'd him unfit for the part of Theodosius, & his requiring Mr Rich to give me a Tryall in it Heaven knows what would have become of me—Rich said Let the Young Man try it Barry's superiority will ruin him & I shall get rid of Him. . . . What I felt at hearing the sublime and tuneful Notes of Varanes, Where is my Friend, my Theodosius literally froze me—I was petrified & coud have died with shame at my attempt—After the Play Mr B—— & Mrs C—— kindly encouragd me & assurd me of their support & promised to give me a part in each play they reviv'd. . . .

The facts of that account seem substantially correct. Smith himself confirmed the date 1737 for his entry to Eton. Daniel Hipwell, writing to *Notes and Queries* in 1896, confirmed, from the admission register, Smith's matriculation at St John's, as son of a grocer (*aromatarii*) of Middlesex, but corrected "1748" to "23 October 1747."

Smith's father had meanwhile suffered financial reverses, and though some entailed real property seems eventually to have descended to the son, he had no income immediately after his rustication. Smith drifted to the theatre, a recourse probably suggested to him by friends because of the tall figure, striking good looks and bold address that all his critics remarked. On 8 January 1753, as "a Gentleman" said to be making his first appearance on any stage, Smith played the title role in *Theodosius; or, The Force of Love,* supported by the Athenais of the exquisite Susanna Maria Cibber and the Varanes of the polished Spranger Barry. Smith repeated the role on three successive nights. The prompter Cross wrote in his diary: "He

Smith succeeded well enough, however, for John Rich—not the most easily satisfied of managers—to assign him four other substantial roles during the remainder of the spring of 1753: Polydore in *The Orphan,* the original Southampton in Henry Jones's tragedy *The Earl of Essex,* Dolabella in *All for Love,* and Abudah in *The Siege of Damascus.* When he returned to Covent Garden in 1753–54 Smith added 11 new parts to his repertoire: Wat Dreary in *The Beggar's Opera,* Orlando in *As You Like It,* Axalla in *Tamerlane,* Young Mirabel in *The Inconstant,* the original Musidorus in McNamara Morgan's tragedy *Philoclea,* Loveless in *The Relapse,* the original Aurelian in Dr Philip Francis's tragedy *Constantine,* Myrtle in *The Conscious Lovers,* Florizel in *The Sheep Shearing* (when he was allowed to speak the prologue), Carlos in *Love Makes a Man,* and Valentine in *Love for Love.*

Smith was also enlarging his acquaintance among the fashionable, begun as a boy at Eton. The assiduous attention of the *ton,* Smith's education, and his genteel stage manners were already earning him the sobriquet "Gentleman" by which he would always be distinguished from other theatrical Smiths. He was proud of the distinction and recalled in a letter to Charles Payne Crawford in 1813, when Smith was 83, that the dancer Hester Santlow came with the old actress Mrs Horton "behind the Scenes . . . from a Curiosity to see the 'Young Gentleman' as she was pleased to call me (*Gentlemen* not having been often adventurers on the Stage in her Time.)."

Before the end of his first full season on the stage Smith had coolly selected, from among the throng of ladies attracted by his charm, one who could at once help support his growing appetite for French vintages and steeplechasing and extend his acquaintance among the gentry and nobility. On 31 May 1754, he married Elizabeth, second daughter of Edward Richard Montagu, Viscount Hinchinbroke, sister of the notorious "Jemmy Twitcher," John Montagu, Fourth Earl of Sandwich. She was the widow of Kelland Courtenay of Powderham Castle, Devonshire. She must have been a good many years older than Smith, for the eldest of her three children by Courtenay was a captain in the Army when, in 1761, he was killed in Germany.

The *Daily Advertiser* for 7 June 1754 confided: "Mr. Smith, who lately enter'd the Profession of a Player, and with great Reputation appear'd at Covent-Garden Theatre, has, we are inform'd, upon his Marriage declin'd any farther Connection with the Stage." The information was false. All other early accounts agree that, in the words of *Theatrical Biography* (1772):

The marriage was no sooner proclaimed, than the *noble house of Montagu* was all in a flame; comparisons were formed—reflections thrown out—and the words *vagabond* and *nobility* often joined together, to show the separate force of their significations. However, in the midst of this bustle, Smith waited on his noble brother-in-law, and, after telling an *unvarnished tale*, made this proposal—that, if the family he had so much *disgraced*, would allow him for life a sum equal to his theatrical acquisitions, he would cease to dishonour them. . . . Fair as this proposal was, and great as their regards were for the lady, it was rejected. . . .

Smith was to continue on the London stage for another 34 years.

Smith resumed work at Covent Garden—where he was to remain for 20 years—adding nearly 40 roles in his next four seasons: in 1754–55, Heartly in *The Non-Juror*, Hippolitus in *Phaedra and Hippolitus*, Juba in *Cato*, Careless in *The Double Dealer*, Adrastus in *Oedipus, King of Thebes*, Antony in *Julius Caesar*, title roles in *Comus, Henry V,* and *The Earl of Essex*, Hotspur in *Henry IV*, Villeroy in *The Fatal Marriage*, Romeo in *Romeo and Juliet*, Torrismond in *The Spanish Fryar*, the original Icilius in John Moncrieff's tragedy *Appius*, Hastings in *Jane Shore*, and Osmyn in *The Mourning Bride*; in 1755–56, Young Mirabel in *The Inconstant*, Plume in *The Recruiting Officer*, Careless in *The Double Gallant*, Lysimachus in *The Rival Queens*, Edmund in *King Lear*, Telemachus in *Ulysses*, Memnon in *Busiris, King of Egypt*, Colonel Briton in *The Wonder*, and Archer in *The Stratagem*; in 1756–57, Grainger in *The Refusal*, Valentine in *Wit without Money*, the title role in *The Rover*, Glenalvon in the first London performance of *Douglas*, Trueman in *The Twin Rivals*, Lothario in *The Fair Penitent*, and, for his benefit, the title role in *Hamlet*; in 1757–58, Lorenzo in *The Spanish Fryar*, Zamor in *Alzira*, Flaminius in *Marianne*, Maximinian in *The Prophetess*, the title role in *Coriolanus*, and Piercy in *Anna Bullen*.

In the fall of 1758 Spranger Barry deserted London to put into effect his Irish scheme with Woodward, leaving Smith in possession for some years of a near-monopoly of the best roles in tragedy and high comedy at Covent Garden. *The Theatrical Review: for the year 1757 and Beginning of 1758* (1758) took the occasion to try to set Smith on a different course, reproving "the resemblance his manner of acting remarkably bears to that of Mr. Barry. His fond admiration of this actor often betrays him into a likeness, which . . . hurts both, when they are both on the stage together; gestures, deportment, nay even inflections, as far as the inferior pliancy of Mr. Smith's voice will allow it, are the same in both."

In the 1758–59 season Smith studied six new roles: Palador (Guiderius) in William Hawkins's alteration of *Cymbeline*, Sir George in *The Busy Body*, Foppington in *The Careless Husband*, Hastings in *Jane Shore*, Demetrius in *The Humorous Lieutenant*, and Sir Harry Wildair in *The Constant Couple*. (Richard Cross, the prompter at Drury Lane, noted in his diary on 29 May 1759: "We borrow'd Smith from Cov: Garden to do Osmyn [in *The Mourning Bride*]

WILLIAM SMITH, as Iachimo

artist unknown

Mr Mossop's father being dead.") In 1759–60 Smith added Captain Clerimont in *The Tender Husband* and Belmour in *The Old Bachelor,* and in 1760–61, Pierre in *Venice Preserv'd,* the Copper Captain in *Rule a Wife and Have a Wife,* and Riot in *The Wife's Relief.*

On 22 September 1761 young George III was crowned, and by 30 September Garrick had begun to stage a "coronation" at Drury Lane, matched and (Thomas Davies wrote) far surpassed by Rich's elaborate version that opened on 13 November. Covent Garden's coronation was viewed on most evenings through 26 January 1762. Because it was calculated to complement some "royal" play, William Smith found himself acting leading roles in Shakespeare on some 35 nights during the run of *The Coronation:* as Henry v (18 times), as the Bastard Faulconbridge in *King John,* and, for the first time, as Richard III. In addition that season he added the title role in *The Pilgrim,* some part unspecified in the anonymous new comedy *The Love Match,* and Dick in *The City Wives' Confederacy.* He was now deemed worth eight guineas a week.

Smith's noble wife died on 11 December 1762, at her house in Newman Street, in consequence, it was said, of grief over the death of her son in Germany in 1761. Her large estates in Suffolk, Devon, and Cornwall and the London house were of course entailed and thus devolved on her two daughters, the Countess of Corke and the wife of William Poyntz, a wealthy squire of Midgham in Berkshire.

Smith was no longer the master of the Montagus' manor of Leiston Hall, at Saxmundham, Suffolk, near Bury St Edmunds, where he and his wife had summered and spent the Bury race-weeks (though he certainly continued to visit there long after his second marriage). But he had received a sizeable bequest from his wife, he had some property inherited from his father, and he had saved his salary. And soon after his first wife's death he found another heiress, Martha Newsom, daughter of a prominent citizen of Leiston, a coastal village 40 miles from Bury. Smith seems to have married her in 1763.

In 1762–63, Smith added to his repertoire Kitely in *Every Man in His Humour,* Bajazet in *Tamerlane,* Hengist in *The Royal Convert,* and Loveless in *The Relapse.* In 1763–64 he added Edgar in *King Lear,* Leon in *Rule a Wife and Have a Wife,* Belfond in *The Squire of Alsatia,* and the original Belfield in Arthur Murphy's comedy *No Man's Enemy but His Own,* and in 1764–65, Heartfree in *The Provok'd Wife,* Iago in *Othello,* and Ruffle in the *Male Coquette.* Some of those parts he was physically or temperamentally unfitted for (Iago, for instance) but insisted on assuming as experiments.

In 1765–66, Smith added Sir George in *The Drummer,* the original Sir Charles Somerville in Elizabeth Griffith's comedy *The Double Mistake,* Worthy in *The Fair Quaker of Deal,* and Norfolk in *The Albion Queens;* in 1766–67, Mirabell in *The Way of the World,* the original Belford in Arthur Murphy's comedy *The Perplexities,* Alexander in *The Rival Queens,* Juba in *Cato,* Enriquez in *The Double Falsehood,* Cassius in *Julius Caesar,* and Antony in *All for Love;* and in 1767–68, the title role in *Tamerlane,* Publius in *The Roman Father,* Zaphna in *Mahomet,* and Creon in *Medea.*

Smith went on expanding his list at Covent Garden: in 1768–69, Iachimo in *Cymbeline,* Osman in *Zara,* Lovemore in *The Way to Keep Him,* the original Cambyses in John Hoole's tragedy *Cyrus,* the original Lord Clairville in Charlotte Lenox's comedy *The Sister,* and the title role in *Orestes;* and in 1769–70, Townly in *The Provok'd Husband*, the original Belfield Junior in Richard Cumberland's comedy *The Brothers*, Tancred in *Tancred and Sigismunda*, Varanes in *Theodosius*, the title role in *Macbeth*, the original Timanthes in Hoole's tragedy *Timanthes*, the title role in *The Earl of Warwick*, and Biron in *Isabella*. In 1770–71, he added Oakly in *The Jealous Wife* and Leontes in *The Winter's Tale;* in 1771–72, Volpone in *The Fox*, the original Athamond in Joseph Cradock's tragedy *Zobeide*, the original Lord Seaton in Mrs Griffith's comedy *A Wife in the Right*, Don Carlos in *Ximena*, and Phocyas in *The Siege of Damascus;* in 1772–73, the original Athelwold in William Mason's tragedy *Elfrida*, the title role in Murphy's new tragedy *Alzuma*, the Duke of Norfolk in *The Albion Queens*, the title role in *Henry II*, and Dudley in *Lady Jane Grey;* and in 1773–74, the original Captain Boothby in William Kenrick's comedy *The Duellist* and Herod in *Herod and Mariamne.*

Quietly, gradually, with little or no permanent competition at Covent Garden for the roles he wanted to fill, Smith had become a solid favorite of the audiences. His limitations he had learned to compensate for, and criticism had scolded him away from some of the worst of his early affectations. The *Theatrical Review* in 1758 had found him not only an imitator of Barry but "liable to the reproach of distorting his features." Moreover, he had spoken "in a feigned voice." The *Review* critic urged—as critics would always vainly urge—that he confine himself to high comedy and forget tragedy, for "in comedy he is more an original, his performance is more spirited . . . ; his eyes have naturally a rakish leer, which suits very well the modern fine gentleman and the agreeable debauché: would he turn himself that way, few have a chance to equal him. . . ." Still, audiences continued to find him satisfactory and managers to find him useful in tragedy as well as comedy. His salary was £14 a week, and large crowds patronized his benefits.

By 1770 Smith's professional reputation was, like his social one, highly respectable, built upon quiet behavior, good looks, modest talents, a degree of scholarly taste, a wide acquaintance among the fashionable, and—perhaps most—a lucky disposition to stay in one place. He went neither to the provinces nor to the Haymarket to act in the summers. He did not shift from patent house to patent house.

He watched while Barry and Macklin and Foote and other more gifted folk quarreled with managers and invested in imprudent schemes of management, apparently without being tempted to do either. Unlike West Digges, the Dibdins, Theophilus Cibber and dozens of other talented actors, he did not entangle himself in awkward liaisons; and unlike Shuter and the elder Edwin and countless others, he drank like a gentleman.

But as Smith's fortieth year passed a few squalls had begun to agitate the placid surface of his life. Smith had begun to be affected for the first time by symptoms of the managerial itch. He wrote to Colman from Ipswich on 30 June 1769 (*Posthumous Letters*, 1820) to say that he had had a "melancholy" report of the death of William Powell (the actor-patentee then lay ill of pneumonia but did not die until 3 July) and expressed his keen interest in buying Powell's share of the patent. He asked Colman's advice on how to proceed and added jauntily that he had been on "the fortunate side" at the races and that Colman could reply to him at Leiston Hall, where he would be until August.

Later that summer of 1769 Smith seems to have incurred the displeasure of David Garrick because of a reluctance to accept an invitation to participate in Garrick's projected Shakespeare festival at Stratford in early September. In an undated letter (printed by James Boaden) Smith apologized: "Though I am aware that an offer of my services may now seem to come with an ill grace, yet I beg leave to say, if I can be of any use in the Jubilee, you may command, Sir, / Your Sincere servant, / W. Smith." And later, having received an acceptance of that offer, he was all complaisance and cooperation:

Yabley, Aug. 16th, 1769 / Dear Sir, / Your politeness has entirely removed my awkwardness, and I am totally at your disposal. The post and dress you allot for me will be most agreeable to me, and all scruples are removed. If I recollect right, the hat I wear in Richard is very shabby; and the little ornaments I wore in it are locked up in town under a key I have with me. The hat Mr. Powell used in King John is a good one, and I suppose might be had with the ornaments on it; if not, I should be glad of yours. . . .

Smith concluded with a Latin quotation of encouragement, an anxious request for information on where and when to appear at Strat-

Harvard Theatre Collection

WILLIAM SMITH, as the Duke of Norfolk

artist unknown

ford, and the social note: "We set out for York Races tomorrow."

Smith and George Colman were often at odds. The departure of Beard and the advent of a trio of new patentees with competing interests and (in two cases) rival mistresses among the actresses had introduced a turbulence that agitated Covent Garden until the feud was resolved in the lawsuit of 1770 between managerial factions led by Thomas Harris and the elder George Colman. Smith's even-handed testimony in the depositions taken from members of the company was an obvious attempt to palliate, but it only enraged both sides. A letter of 22 May 1771, addressed to Colman from Smith at Beaufort Buildings, sharply demanded, within four days, a resolution to disputed salary arrangements for 1771–72. A reply from Colman the following day reveals that Smith had demanded a rise in pay of nearly £5 a week, much beyond Colman's power to grant. Smith evidently capitulated on the point for the moment. His salary in 1772–73 was still 12 guineas a week. But he had methods of revenge against stubborn managers which he did not scruple to use. Maria Macklin wrote her father (13 March 1773):

Smith has rais'd such a fury in the Town, owing to Colman's having refus'd [to allow] Mrs Yates to

play for [his benefit], that last Saturday [6 March] being the fifth night of *Alzuma,* when the play ought to have begun, the Audience made a most violent noise, called for Colman, insisted that the play should not begin till he was found & the reasons given why Mrs Yates was not suffered to play for Smith. In vain did Bensley endeavor frequently to speak and tell them that Colman was not to be found. They still continued hissing and roaring, and this last [*sic*] till past seven o'clock. Dagge and Harris were behind in a dreadful consternation least the house should be demolished, of which indeed it was in some danger. At last they said something must be said to quiet them, when Smith in the confusion ran on and told them that the managers had consented Mrs Yates should play for him. Then they sent him off to tell them that his day must be settled whenever he thought proper, to give her time to come here. He went off and made them fix it for the 19th of April, went on and told them it was settled. They then insisted that Smith should tell them whether everything was settled to his entire satisfaction. He assured them it was. The play was then ordered to begin. I am told they have given him up his articles for three years, at his desire. Several Gentlemen went round into the Hall and sent for Smith, telling him his private quarrels with the managers were nothing to them. That if Mrs Yates play'd they should be glad to see her, but that as she was not in the company it was not right in him to disturb the play and hinder them from seeing it. He expostulated with them and told his story. The Town rings with this affair. . . .

The squabbling over terms was also renewed that spring and before long spread from Covent Garden to Drury Lane. The dispute's outlines may be followed in the correspondence to and from David Garrick published by James Boaden and by Little, Kahrl, and Wilson. Simply stated, Smith secretly opened negotiations with Garrick while continuing them with Covent Garden. George Garrick, on his brother's behalf, offered him £12 a week, a reduction of 12*s.* from his Covent Garden salary. Smith, who wanted at least £13, "by way of rank," replied with hauteur, speaking of "hard terms" and threatened, since "I have been too ill-treated by Mr. Colman ever to think of an engagement with him without a certainty of better usage than I can expect from so illiberal a mind," to go to "the Yateses"— Richard and Mary Ann Yates were seeking (fruitlessly, it turned out) a license to act with a company at the King's Theatre. Garrick was unmoved. Smith was finally reduced to abject apology and the admission: "I own the golden hopes of a field-marshal's staff misled my judgment." In any event, Garrick did not hire him at that time, simply as a matter of discipline, though Smith was needed.

So, in a letter of 6 August 1773 from Aldeburgh, Suffolk, Smith offered his services, as an "unengaged" actor to another Covent Garden partner, Thomas Harris, saying that he refused to deal with Colman because of their many disagreements. Nevertheless, throughout August and into September, Colman and Smith dickered in a tense correspondence, and Colman stubbornly offered the same sum he had offered for the previous season's engagement.

Smith moved reluctantly back to Covent Garden in the fall of 1773–74 to confront difficulties that would have been more serious to a performer with less depth of personality and fewer financial and social resources. His adversary Colman had engaged the 74-year-old Charles Macklin for the season, and Macklin wanted some of Smith's tragedy roles, notably *Richard III* and *Macbeth*. Macklin finally secured Smith's grudging agreement to an arrangement by which they would alternate performance of the roles in question. But Macklin hadn't reckoned on those resentful Smith partisans in the Covent Garden audiences. When Macklin's carefully prepared and revolutionary production of *Macbeth* was disrupted by them, the old trouper suspected that Smith was one of the instigators and published a letter charging him with complicity. Smith issued an indignant denial and challenged Macklin to a duel. The challenge was accepted. Bloodshed was averted, but the affair finally resulted in a riot that threatened to destroy the theatre. Colman was forced to discharge Macklin. Even if Smith had had a hand in the original attempt to intimidate Macklin, which does not appear from the evidence, it is certain that he did not foresee the difficult old man's discharge, and he regretted it.

That would be Smith's last season with the Covent Garden company, though he did not suspect it. During its course he had begun to be importuned by another emotion besides professional jealousy and the ambition of management. For the first time, gossip began to circulate linking him with one of the actresses at Covent Garden, the alluring Mrs Elizabeth Hartley. When David Garrick had considered hiring her after her Edinburgh debut in 1771, he had asked the comedian John Moody to assess her abilities. Moody had replied to David's brother George, the Drury Lane factotum, on 26 July 1772, that she was "a good figure, with a handsome small face, and very much freckled; her hair red, and her neck and shoulders well-turned." But her voice was harsh and she was "ignorant and stubborn." Besides, she had already been hired for the following season at Covent Garden. A writer in the *Covent Garden Magazine* praised "her beautiful figure and sweet face." When David Garrick himself saw her as Rosamond in Thomas Hull's new tragedy *Henry II* in May 1774, opposite William Smith's King Henry, he wrote in a letter "a finer creature than Mrs Hartly I never saw—her make is prefect." Somewhat before that date she had become the mistress of William Smith.

Mrs Hartley was not, despite her physical charms, the sort of woman to hold Smith long in thrall. Moody had testified: "She has a husband, a precious fool, that she heartily despises. She talks lu[s]ciously, and has a slovenly good-nature about her that renders her prodigiously vulgar." A few days after Garrick witnessed their performance of *Henry II,* Smith and Mrs Hartley eloped to France. On 31 May a letter appeared "in a public journal . . . 'written by a gentleman to his wife previous to his elopement with a beautiful actress,'" according to "The Manager's Notebook" in *The New Monthly Magazine* (1837). The letter, dated from Dover, 27 May 1774, reads:

MY DEAR LOVE,—You and I have long lived happy together, and be assured at this very moment I love you more than any woman in the world. When you hear of the little excursion I am going to make with Mrs. H——, be not alarmed; it is a sudden impulse of passion which I own I have not had the courage to resist. There is something so bewitching and enchanting in beauty, that it baffles our strongest resolutions; but it is an infatuation that will soon be over. You must pardon me this one slip, and believe me when I declare, that though a momentary gust of passion may hurry me into trifling indiscretions, I never can find real felicity and true happiness but in your arms.

I am, my dear Love,
    Your ever affectionate,   ——

Harvard Theatre Collection

WILLIAM SMITH, as Piercy

engraving by Thornthwaite, after Roberts

It is impossible to believe that Smith would have written such a letter, or, if he had, that it could have been purloined from his wife. It was, instead, a personal satire of an original kind. Yet throughout the progress of the Hartley affair, Smith demonstrated a jaunty carelessness about the morality of his actions and their effect on both his marriage and his career which was not far different in tone from that of the published letter. Soon he and Mrs Hartley were in Dublin, whence he began again his courtship of Garrick. On 26 June Smith wrote from "Mr Kisling's, Dorset-street," to describe his and his mistress's successes at the Crow Street Theatre. He protested that he saw nothing very despicable in his conduct. Though the elopement had been much publicized, he said, Mrs Smith had written to him as if she knew nothing of the whole matter. He assured Garrick that he meant to return to her as soon as he arrived in England.

The fact was that Smith had put both his inamorata and himself in a very tight corner professionally. For Dublin had also been chosen by the foppish little comedian James Dodd that summer as his place of assignation with the adulterous Mrs Mary Bulkeley, and the censorious Irish were murmuring against both couples. The Dublin engagements could not be renewed. Covent Garden would not have Mrs Hartley as long as she was allied to Smith, and it would not have Smith at all. His sole hope lay in Garrick, who gave the couple a very bad six weeks before finally relenting and engaging Smith. On 5 August Smith wrote with relief and gratitude and requested that Garrick insert newspaper notices proclaiming the engagement. Mrs Hartley went back to Covent Garden in the fall. On 22 September 1774 Smith stepped onto the Drury Lane stage for the first time, in the title role of *Richard III,* one of Garrick's greatest parts, thus a sign that—for awhile—all was again tranquil between them. But the old, tractable William Smith of his first 20 years in the profession, who got on so well with his fellows and managers, seems for the time being to have vanished.

Smith played at Drury Lane for the following 13 seasons, though often declaring an intention to retire and sometimes requiring again to be disciplined by Garrick. By midseason of 1774–75, Smith, apparently made jealous by rumours of Elizabeth Hartley's flirtatious behavior at Covent Garden, began to intrigue to regain his place there. Garrick was furiously offended and also hurt. On 15 March 1775 he wrote a letter citing some of Smith's pretended injuries and reminding that he had taken Smith in when no one else would. "I had great Satisfaction in being connected with You, & now, I know y^r regard for me I am not Miserable by the seperation." Smith, he concluded, could go back to Covent Garden if he liked. But the canny Garrick was confident Smith could not leave him. He wrote to George Colman, who was no longer manager at Covent Garden, on 10 April:

I must open my heart to you and beg that it be shut up to Everybody else—Smith cannot, with the people the Managers have engag'd, be employ'd at Covent Garden—He has offer'd himself to Me by my Brother in a fit of honour, or Compunction—I still keep aloof, & have written a very spirited & refusing letter to him—this my policy & my Spirit requir'd—but I will not hide a thought

from You—I really think we can't do without
him. . . .

From Garrick's point of view, and for the good
of the Drury Lane company, that was certainly
true. Excepting only Garrick himself and Tom
King, there was no male actor in the company
to rival Smith as a drawing power. The weary
Garrick was planning to retire at the end of
the season, after 33 triumphant years, and he
devoutly wished for a successful and quiet fi-
nale.

But during the 1775–76 season Smith again
had to be reined in, this time over the old
matter of his reluctance to walk in processions,
which he regarded as below the dignity of a
squire with his means and connections. That
attitude was naturally not received patiently
by other leading lights in the Drury Lane company—and poor Garrick, as usual, was caught
in the middle. The great comedian Thomas
King wrote the manager on 22 December
1775, complaining of Smith's refusal to walk
costumed as Benedick in a procession of Shakespeare's characters accompanying the revived
"dramatic entertainment" *The Jubilee,* which
was being prepared for presentation on 26 December. King pointed out that for Garrick to
bend to such arrogance would undermine the
company. Smith wrote again on 24 December
signifying his unwillingness, and Garrick on
26 December penned a reply that survives as a
prime example of Garrick's method of playing
upon his performers' sense of shame, guilt, or
obligation:

Sir/You have prov'd to Me that you have no attach-
ment to me or my affairs—Would your wearing a
domino & Mask, to take turn about with *Me* in
walking down ye Stage, be an injury to your Importance?—I hope not—it would have been of
Consequence to ye Jubilee, which is got up at great
expence to support your & other Performers importance, which without it has suffer'd, & may Suffer
more—but I am now, I must say, fully convinced
that our connection is not rooted in the heart or in
a Mutual desire to Serve each other. . . . I am this
moment come home, and found your Letter upon
the table—I am likewise in a great hurry for *I* am
obliged to make one at ye Jubilee.

But Smith did not do so.

Elizabeth Hartley was soon forgotten.
Smith returned to his wife, to his field sports,

and to the enhanced consequence at Drury
Lane that Garrick's retirement in the spring of
1776 gave him. But the roles (all at Drury
Lane) which he added from 1774–75 until his
retirement in the spring of 1788 were very
few: in 1774–75, Orestes in *The Distress'd
Mother,* the original Edwin in Dr Thomas
Francklin's tragedy *Matilda,* the original Va-
lasquez in Robert Jephson's critically acclaimed tragedy *Braganza,* the Duke in *Measure for Measure,* and Huncamunca in *Tom
Thumb;* in 1775–76, Courtwell in *A Woman Is
a Riddle* and Chamont in *The Orphan;* and in
1776–77, George Hargrave in *The Runaway,*
Publius Horatius in *The Roman Father,* Don
Felix in *The Wonder,* Captain Absolute in *The
Rivals,* Loveless in *A Trip to Scarborough,* and,
on 8 May 1777, the best of all his roles, the
original Charles Surface in R. B. Sheridan's
great comedy *The School for Scandal.*

In 1777–78 Smith added Iachimo in *Cymbeline,* the original Titus in William Shirley's
tragedy *The Roman Sacrifice,* and Mr Ford in
The Merry Wives of Windsor; in 1778–79, the
original Paladore in Jephson's tragedy *The Law
of Lombardy* and Alwin in *The Countess of Salisbury;* in 1780–81, the original Acamas in John
Delap's tragedy *The Royal Suppliants;* and in
1781–82, the title role in *King Arthur* and the
original Mr Morley in Richard Griffith's
comedy *Variety.*

During the last six or seven seasons of
Smith's career there was increasing competition for new roles from John Philip Kemble,
after Kemble's debut on 30 September 1783,
and from other younger actors as well. But
Smith had by 1784 or 1785 built a large repertoire that audiences delighted to see him
return to, led by his Charles Surface and his
Captain Plume, and he tended to stick safely
to those. In 1782–83, Smith added only the
leading male part Biron in *Isabella; or, The
Fatal Marriage* on 10 October 1782, the night
of Mrs Siddons's triumphant return to London
after six years' absence. She played the title
role. In 1784–85, Smith added the original
Saint Valori in Cumberland's tragedy *The Carmelite;* in 1785–86, the original Clifford in
John Burgoyne's comedy *The Heiress;* and after
that, nothing, though he acted two more full
seasons. On 10 March 1788, playing Macbeth,
Smith took his last benefit, clearing the goodly
sum of £291 5*s.* 2*d.* after house charges. In an

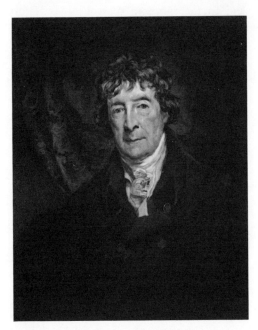

WILLIAM SMITH

engraving by Ward, after Jackson

epilogue of his own composition he announced his intention to retire at season's end:

Full thirty-five campaigns I've urged my way,
Under the ablest generals of the day;
Full oft have stood by Barry's, Garrick's side,—
With them have conquer'd, and with them have died;
I now no more o'er Macbeth's crimes shall lower—
Nor murder my two nephews in the Tower—
Here I no more shall rant "A horse! a horse!"
But mount "White Surrey" for the Beacon *Course.*
No more my hands with tyrants' gore shall stain,
But drag the felon FOX from forth his den!
Then take the circuit of my little fields,
And taste the comfort that contentment *yields;*
And as those sweetest *comforts I review,*
Reflect with gratitude, they come from you.

He retired, with a brief and modest speech of thanks for the "patronage and protection" of his audience, after playing Charles Surface, on 9 June 1788. (He had "created" the youthful role at age 47. He was now 58, but still counterfeited youth tolerably well.) Members of his club, The Phoenix, meeting at the George and Vulture, Cornhill, presented him with a large

silver cup and cover, with the device on top a phoenix rising from the ashes.

Smith returned to Drury Lane just once more, playing Charles Surface to oblige his old friend Tom King, on King's benefit night, 18 May 1798. Smith, at 68, though heavy, still looked remarkably athletic, for he still spent hours on horseback each day. "He was received," said the *Monthly Visitor* for May, "with the most heart-felt gratulations by an audience who did not expect any *apology* for such acting, though he saw fit to deliver one at the conclusion of the play." But the ten years since his final regular appearance in 1788 had almost completed the revolution which had begun in 1776, the year of Garrick's departure and the year the first Kemble reached London. Smith was now a beloved relic to some, a curiosity to others. The critic for the *Monthly Mirror* had "heard so much of this actor, as well in the way of censure as of praise," that he had gone to see him "with many doubts and some fears" for Smith's reputation.

We had been told that Mr. Smith pourtrayed the manners of a *finished gentleman* with more delicacy and characteristic propriety, than any actor of his day: but this does not appear to us to be his particular excellence; he stands too wide to be graceful, and his deportment gains no advantage from a perpetual application of the hand to the lower part of the waist. These habits are far from elegant. His *Charles*, however, is a favourable specimen of that sort of acting which commonly falls under the denomination of the *old school;* light, airy, and natural; which excites applause without any anxious endeavour to produce it; which suffers the points to tell of *themselves,* and does not place them as so many *traps* to ensnare the injudicious parts of the audience.

In fact, as that astonished young critic warmed to his task he found in the aging Smith many of the very virtues—*as a comedian*—that critics had always found: "We had been told too that his *monotony* was disgusting in the extreme; but, on the contrary, we found him possessed of a full, rich, musical voice, somewhat thick in the melody, but by no means ungrateful to the ear, with an articulation sufficiently distinct, and an extent of tone that surprised us."

It was Gentleman Smith's darling delusion that in addition to being excellent in mannered comedy, he was also a great tragedian; and, indeed, he had succeeded with the sober sister often enough, because of his physical attributes and educated taste, to satisfy his public most of the time. But the writing critics, some of them also men of the theatre, had usually sung a different song. Thomas Wilkes, in *A General View of the Stage* (1759), thought "Mr. Smith's figure is very pleasing; and his performance very tolerable: his voice is agreeable, but he wants variety, and [in tragedy] speaks always in the same tone." Charles Churchill's *Rosciad* (1761) dismissed him as "Smith, the genteel, the airy and the smart. . . ." *The Rosciad of C——v——nt G——rd——n* (1762) emphasized his personality and the fact that he had been "Taught and improv'd by learning's sacred lore." The *Macaroni and Savoir Vivre Magazine* (1773) found "a spirit in his comic performance, or, as Dryden terms it, self-breeding: then his figure, which is one of the genteelest on the stage; besides this, there is an agreeableness in his address that suits the characters of gentlemen, &c. In tragedy he wants expression: and . . . his voice, tho' clear and sonorous, wants variation; yet, there are many parts, as, Richard, Alexander, &c. &c. which he supports with judgment, expression, and spirit." The visiting Ernst Brandes, in his *Bemerkungen über das . . . Theater* (Göttingen, 1786), admired Smith's "schönen nervichten Figur" and his manly countenance at age 57.

William Hawkins in his *Miscellanies* (1775) echoed the majority voice in a lengthy critique:

in the parts of the unaffected well-bred gentleman, he irreproachably claims the foremost rank . . . for uniform elegance, ease, and suitable vivacity. . . . What a pity it is, that this actor should so often mistake his abilities, by straying out of that road which nature has so happily placed him in. . . . In tragedy he has too much levity, and wants variation . . . yet he possesses great fervour and manly spirit; particularly in his Richard, his Alexander and the like; his Jachimo, his Phocyas in the Siege of Damascus, &c. are inimitable.

The London Magazine for October 1776, reviewing his Richard III, was sternly judicious.

[Smith] has a good figure, is gentlemanlike, and decent in everything he undertakes. When we allow that, we have said all; he wants both feeling to be affected, and powers to convey his feelings, if he had them. In fine, in spite of all the partiality of his friends, or the ignorant prejudices of those who never judge but at second hand, his performance of

Richard was little more than a strong union of judgement and industry, *unaided* by nature. He should woo genteel Comedy oftener; and not that coy sister of hers, who certainly holds Smith at the point of her lance.

There were critics who remembered Smith's portrayal of Richard principally for its vociferation. The anonymous author of *Thalia to Eliza* (1798) grew ironically nostalgic:

> SMITH *dwells at ease by old Saint Edmund's Cross,*
> *And leaves the echoes to bewail his loss.*
> *Oh, when he led his troops to Bosworth fight,*
> *I pitied the poor pale-fac'd scout his fright;*
> *One at a time, he made five* RICHMOND'*s fall,*
> *Had there been five at once, he'd kill'd them all;*
> *So loud he called to horse, they heard the shout*
> *At Hyde Park Corner, and the grooms led out.*

At about the mid-point of Smith's career Francis Gentleman the actor-critic, who knew him well, delivered a series of more specific judgments on the characters Smith had developed during his first 17 years on stage: as Southampton in *The Earl of Essex*, "Mr Smith gave us much pleasure. . . . [I]t sat easier on him than any other tragic character he ever played." His Bajazet in *Tamerlane* was "lamentable"; his Henry V was "pleasing . . . yet wants consequence and variety"—his effort ranked midway between Spranger Barry and Thomas Sheridan. For Sir George in *The Busy Body,* "Mr. Smith has sufficient vivacity, without diminishing essential elegance; we never desire to see the part better supported. . . ." As Glenalvon in *Douglas* he was totally "out of character" and "simpered like an April fit of sunshine." His Juba in *Cato* was "a tolerable Numidian prince," though not as good as West Digges's. As Lord Townly in *The Provok'd Husband,* "Mr. Smith has freedom and elegance; but a most lamentable sameness of expression hangs heavy on the ears of an audience," a difficulty also troubling his Castalio in *The Orphan*. As the Bastard Faulconbridge he "is pretty and spirited, but wants weight and bluntness." As Hal in the Henry IV plays, "We do not recollect any person better calculated to do the character justice than Mr. Smith."

Gentleman understood but regretted the "terrible necessity which forces Mr. SMITH into an undertaking so opposite to everyone of his requisites, except figure," as Macbeth. In fact "saddling him with the part is an imposi-

Courtesy of the Garrick Club

WILLIAM SMITH as the Bastard, WILLIAM POWELL as King John, and ROBERT BENSLEY as Hubert, in *King John*

by Mortimer

tion upon that good nature and integrity which stimulate him to work through thick and thin, for the support of Covent Garden house." His Archer, in *The Beaux' Stratagem* is "sprightly, agreeable and characteristic." His Captain Plume in *The Recruiting Officer* has "an undoubted superiority for uniform ease, elegance, and suitable vivacity; being the unaffected gentleman in private life, he is necessarily so on the stage." His Richard III was, of course, hardly comparable to Garrick's though it had "considerable spirit." (Smith's Richard, which was later highly regarded, was so to some degree, because it developed between Garrick's departure and Kemble's arrival.)

Gentleman summed up Smith with the usual wish to see him "totally devoted to genteel, sprightly comedy, as his expression and feelings never do justice to the more important passages of passion. . . . [S]carce any performer ever played so much, to affect the heart so little; but an agreeable person, genteel carriage, engaging countenance, and a distinct, smooth, powerful, voice, though monotonous, carry him respectably."

But, of course, neither Gentleman nor any other critic in 1770 had seen the greatest of Smith's portrayals—perhaps his only truly great one—Charles Surface. The character, like all characters in *The School for Scandal* (1777), was deliberately fashioned by Sheridan around the known temperament and personality of the performer who would play the role. Charles Surface *was* Smith, dramatized. There was little for him to do but walk debonairly through the comedy before enchanted audiences. He was young enough at 47 to seem in his twenties, and still able to seem young enough when he was 68 to carry it off. Until his retirement, he had failed to play Charles in only one of the innumerable performances of *The School for Scandal* at Drury Lane.

"Gentleman" Smith lived for more than 30 years after his retirement from the stage, but seldom came to London. His earliest London residence after coming from Cambridge had been in York Buildings, Duke Street. But after his marriage to the Honorable Elizabeth Montagu in 1754, he had lived in a grander style in her house in Newman Street, Marylebone, when in town, and at Leiston Hall during the summers and in race weeks. He was welcome, with his new wife, at Leiston Hall until 1769 at least, as letters dated from there show. But his town address had changed, probably by 1767, certainly by March 1769, to No 7, Beaufort Buildings, the Strand, where he and his second wife lived until his retirement to Bury St Edmunds in 1788. Local records show them living in 1790 and 1800 at what is now No 112, Northgate Street, in Bury. From 1800 to 1809 they lived in the house, No 8, Angel Hill, now occupied by the office of the County Archivist. From 1809 until Smith's death in 1819, they occupied Northgate House, No 8, Northgate Street, along with the second Mrs Smith's spinster sisters Fanny and Mary.

Long before his retirement Smith's attention had been divided between the stage and his fashionable friends in London and the attractions of the country manor of Leiston, which Alfred Suckling's *History and Antiquities of the County of Suffolk* (1848) described as extending four miles along the coast, "in a fine sporting country, and abounding with game." More and more, Smith occupied himself with racing, hunting, and all the pleasures of equitation. It was reported that, during race week, he kept relays of horses on the road down to London to enable him to attend the races and act on the same day. (The assertion is incredible; the distance between Leiston and London is over 90 miles.) He is also said to have required a clause in his contract assuring that he would not be required in London during race week. (That rumor is more credible. We have seen how cavalierly he treated his duty to march in processions, and James Fennell in his *Apology* testified that Smith had boasted to him that he had never blacked his face or gone down a trap.)

Smith was an habitué of the race course and boon companion of the nobility and gentry whom he met there, including the Duke of York. But his acquaintance among the rich and cultivated extended beyond horse fanciers. He kept up with some of his friends of Eton days, like Sir James Mansfield, Lord Chief Justice of the Court of Common Pleas, and Sir George Beaumont, the painter and friend of Wordsworth. But Smith also retained an interest in the theatre and its people. He followed the career of Dorothy Jordan with delight, having first seen her in all her performances at York during race week 1782 and having been (according to Tate Wilkinson's recollection) the "principal agent" of her translation to Drury Lane in 1786. He was flattering to young William Henry West Betty when "the Young Roscius" took London by storm in 1805; Smith gave him a seal ring engraved with Garrick's countenance. But good critical sense asserted itself before long, and Smith registered disappointment in the boy's lack of professional development.

Smith had a deep and abiding dislike for the Kembles which seemed to be caused by something more than what he called John Philip Kemble's "School of strange particularities." Smith lived into the era of Edmund Kean. He watched anxiously the ascent of that meteor, torn between the hope that "Mr Kean is the happy Genius which is to rescue the Drama from Pedantry, Bombast,—false Taste,— [and] restore Nature & excellence to the Stage" and jealousy, as Kean began to be applauded in Smith's best roles.

A delightful and revealing record of Smith's old age at Bury survives in a collection of 77 letters in the Folger Library, written by Smith between 1805 and 1819 to the banker Thomas Coutts (1735–1822), five years younger than Smith and reputedly the richest man in England. (*See* Philip H. Highfill, Jr, "Charles Surface in Regency Retirement," *Studies in Philology*, Extra Series, No 4, January, 1967,

135–166.) Coutts and his mistress, the come-
dienne Harriott Mellon (Coutts's wife after
1815), showered Smith with gifts and flattery,
and Smith repaid them with gossip of the
Court and the turf and recollections of bygone
times.

Smith's latter days were passed with little
illness—his first gout, at 82, was greeted with
Mansfield's advice to increase the intake of
wine "to keep it downwards"—which Smith
did. He gave up the "late Hours & Hot
Rooms" of "Balls & Amusements" when he
passed 85, but he rode to hounds until his
mid-eighties and, at 88, still walked two
hours in his garden each morning. His needs
were well taken care of by a devoted wife and
the cosseting Couttses. Money and property
seemed to gravitate toward him in small bits
and large pieces. He had twice wived it weal-
thily. Lord Chedworth had bequeathed him
£200. Elizabeth Bennett had left to Smith,
King, and Wroughton the library of her lover
William Gibson. Smith's father had left him
some entailed property, saved from the debacle
which sent Smith to the stage in 1753. (In
1818 Smith wrote Coutts "I very *lately* sold an
Estate in *Stepney Rents Bethnal Green,* that had
been many years in my Family. . . .")

Smith declined stylishly into the vale of
years, eating Colchester oysters and riding
blood horses, gossiping with old theatrical
cronies and being entertained by the local gentry. He died on 13 September 1819, at 89,
and was buried (by his direction) in an un-
marked grave in Bury church or churchyard.

William Smith's will left property and investments in stocks valued at about £18,000
for distribution by his executors—his wife and
a relative, Serjeant-at-law William Taddy, Esq.
He left the dwelling house in Bury St Edmunds and the interest for life of £8,000 "in
Navy 5 per cents" to his wife and £4,000 "in
the 8 per cent consols" to "Mrs Elizabeth
White residing at Lymington in Hants." His
wife's sister Fanny Newson was to receive
£1,000 and her sister Mary Newson £500.
Taddy was given £500 and figured, with others, as a residuary legatee.

Portraits of William "Gentleman" Smith include:

1. By John Hoppner, 1788. Canvas, 29" ×
24¼". Exhibited at the Royal Academy, 1789
(No 161), as "Portrait of a Gentleman." The
picture was presented to the National Gallery
in 1837 by Mr Serjeant Taddy; it was deposited
in the National Portrait Gallery in November
1883. It is now in the Tate Gallery.

2. By John Jackson. Painted at Bury St Edmunds when Smith had turned 80. The portrait is now untraced and is known from the
engraving by W. Ward, published by J. Jackson, 1819. A copy engraved by R. Page was
published as a plate to *Essex, Suffolk, and Norfolk Characters,* 1820.

3. Engraved portrait by B. Smith, after H.
Spicer. Published by the engraver, 1789. An-
other impression in sepia was published by
Robert Wilkinson, 1789.

4. By anonymous engraver. With Mrs Hartley. Called "Kitely and Elfrida" and published
as a tête-à-tête in the *Town and Country Magazine,* 8: 233 (1776).

5. As Alexander in *The Rival Queens.* Engraving by Thornthwaite, after J. Roberts.
Published as a plate to *Bell's British Theatre,*
1776. A copy engraved by R. Page was published as a plate to the same work, 1777.

6. As Alexander. By an unknown engraver.
Published by J. Harrison, 1779.

7. As Alonzo, with Mrs Yates as Leonora,
in *The Revenge.* By unknown engraver. Published by R. Sayer, 1773.

8. As Archer in *The Beaux' Stratagem.* By an
unknown engraver, after J. Roberts. Published
as a plate to *Bell's British Theatre,* 1776. A
copy, engraved in reverse by J. Edwards, was
published as a plate to the same work, 1777.

9. As the Bastard, with William Powell as
King John and Robert Bensley as Hubert, in
King John. By J. H. Mortimer, exhibited at
the Society of Artists, 1768, In the Garrick
Club (No 17). Engraving by Valentine Green,
1771.

10. As Biron in *Love's Labour's Lost.* Engraving by N. C. Goodnight.

11. As Charles Surface, with Thomas King
as Sir Peter Teazle, John Palmer as Joseph Surface, and Mrs Abington as Lady Teazle, in *The
School for Scandal.* Canvas. By James Roberts,
1777. In the Garrick Club (15). Reproduced
in this *Dictionary* 9: 33.

12. As the Duke of Norfolk in *The Albion
Queens.* By an unknown engraver. Published by
J. Harrison & Co, 1780.

13. As Hamlet, with Elizabeth Hopkins as
Gertrude, in *Hamlet.* By James Roberts. In the

Thomas Harris sale at Robins on 12 July 1819 (lot 56), now in the Garrick Club (No 439), from the Mathews collection. This picture has been called Spranger Barry and Mrs Elmy in *Hamlet,* by an unknown artist (see our notice of Spranger Barry in Volume 1 of this *Dictionary*), but it is now identified as given here by Geoffrey Ashton in his forthcoming edition of the Garrick Club catalogue.

14. As Hippolytus, with Elizabeth Pope as Phaedra, in *Phaedra and Hippolytus.* Watercolor drawing by J. Roberts. In the British Museum.

15. As Iachimo in *Cymbeline.* Drawing by Lawranson, exhibited at the Society of Artists, 1771. Present location unknown. An engraving by the artist was published by W. Richardson, 1784.

16. As Iachimo. By an unknown engraver. Published by Smith & Sayer, 1773.

17. As King Henry VIII. By an unknown engraver. Published by Harrison & Co, 1781.

18. As Marc Antony in *Julius Caesar.* By an unknown engraver.

19. As Orestes in *Electra.* Engraving by Terry. Published by Harrison & Co, 1780.

20. As Oroonoko in *Oroonoko.* Indian ink drawing by an unknown artist. In the British Museum. An engraving by an anonymous engraver was published by J. Wenman, 1778.

21. As Paladore, with John Henderson as Bireno and Elizabeth Younge as the Princess, in *The Law of Lombardy.* By an unknown engraver, undated, but no doubt 1779, since the engraving is marked "Scene in the New Tragedy of the Law of Lombardy," which opened on 8 February 1779 at Drury Lane. A rare copy of the engraving is in the Huntington Library.

22. As Phocyas in *The Siege of Damascus.* Engraving by B. Reading, after E. Edwards. Published by Lowndes as a plate to *New English Theatre,* 1777.

23. As Phocyas. By an unknown engraver, after J. Roberts. Published as a plate to *Bell's British Theatre,* 1776. A copy, reversed, was published in the same work, 1776.

24. As Phocyas. By an unknown engraver. Published by J. Wenman, 1778.

25. As Phocyas. By an unknown engraver. Published by J. Hand.

26. As Piercy in *Anna Bullen.* Engraving by Thornthwaite, after J. Roberts. Published as a plate to *Bell's British Theatre,* 1777.

27. As Plume in *The Recruiting Officer.* Engraving by Walker, after Taylor. Published by Lowndes as a plate to *New English Theatre,* 1776.

28. As Publius in *The Roman Father.* Engraving by Thornthwaite, after J. Roberts. Published as a plate to *Bell's British Theatre,* 1778.

29. As Richard III in *Richard III.* By an unknown engraver, after J. Roberts. Published as a plate to *Bell's Shakespeare,* 1775.

30. As St Valori, with Aickin as De Courci, Packer as Gyfford, Mrs Siddons as Matilda, and J. P. Kemble as Montgomeri, in *The Carmelite,* Painting by C. R. Ryley, 1785. In the James Winston sale at Puttick & Simpson's on 15 December 1849 (lot 1025); bought for £7 7s. 6d. by Makepeace. Called "The original Picture from which no engraving has been made." Present location unknown.

31. As Lord Townly, with Mary Ann Yates as Lady Townly, in *The Provok'd husband.* Engraving by Thornthwaite, after J. Roberts, published as a plate to *Bell's British Theatre,* 1776.

32. As Lord Townly. Pencil drawing study by J. Roberts of the single figure of Smith for the picture above, No 31. In the Harvard Theatre Collection.

33. As Varanes in *Theodosius.* By an unknown engraver.

34. As Young Mirabel in *The Inconstant.* By an unknown engraver.

35. In a group of 17 Drury Lane performers in various Shakespearean characters (Smith is shown as Hamlet), in the "Immortality of Garrick." Large canvas by G. Carter, 1782. In the Gallery of the Royal Shakespeare Theatre, Stratford-upon-Avon. Engraving by Smith and Caldwell, published with key plate, 1783.

Smith, William, called "Canterbury"

[fl. 1753–1804?],   *actor, manager.*

James Winston in *The Theatric Tourist* spoke of "a man, known by the name of Canterbury Smith" who "bestowed occasional visits" on the Tunbridge Wells theatre sometime before 1753. He was William Smith and probably the Mr Smith who played Sir Philip Modelove in *A Bold Stroke for a Wife* at Widow Yeates's Large Theatrical BARN Facing the Boarding-School in CROYDON On THURSDAY the 2d of OCTOBER, 1775. . . ." We would conjecture also that he was the Smith listed in the

Kentish Post as acting Scrub in *The Beaux'*
Stratagem in Canterbury on 27 July 1756.
Winston stated that Canterbury Smith amused
the people at Maidstone in 1762. "This man,
from an idea that his son resembled the greatest actor in the country, and looking forward
to his becoming another Roscius, had him
christened GARRICK. . . ." Winston identified Smith as a wool-comber from Essex who

conducted the Margate, Canterbury, Dover, Deal,
Maidstone, Feversham, and Rochester Theatres.
The *first* Margate, was a barn, situated in a place
known by the appellation of the *Dean*. This circuit
he continued till the year 1768, when, for particular reasons, though much respected and encouraged, was forced to relinquish the East part of
Kent, exhibiting only in the West.

According to an article in *Notes and Queries*
on 14 March 1931, Smith sold his interest in
the Margate playhouse in 1768 to Thomas
Burton, a former hostler at the Ship Inn, Fav-
ersham, who had worked at the theatre as a
candle-snuffer. The western part of Smith's old
circuit was taken over by William Brown and
John (or James?) Richardson in 1771, when
they also gained control of the Margate theatre.

The Smith who acted in a barn outside
Reading about 1788 may have been our subject, and the editors of Winston's diaries, Nelson and Cross, identify our subject as the
Smith who was Winston's partner at Plymouth
in 1803. A letter dated 27 February 1804 from
W. Smith to Winston gives particulars recollected of the management of the theatres at
Richmond and Bristol. That Smith may have
been William "Gentleman" Smith, but the
provincial nature of his reminiscences suggests
Canterbury Smith.

Smith, William [*fl.* 1776?–1829], ac-
tor.

W. Smith (William, we believe, though he
may have been Walter) acted at China Hall,
Rotherhithe as early as 3 July 1776, when he
was listed in the bills as performing in *The
Rivals* and *The Reprisal*. On 25 September at
China Hall Smith appeared as Mendlegs in
Miss Hoyden and Cromwell in *Henry VIII*. J.
Smith was also in the troupe, playing leading
roles, as was G. Smith.

The Smith who played Raymond in *The
Spanish Fryar* at the Haymarket Theatre on 26
January 1778 was probably William Smith—
not to be confused with either William
"Gentleman" Smith or William "Canterbury"
Smith. Possibly William was the Smith who
acted Hotspur in *1 Henry IV* at the Haymarket
the previous 13 September 1777, but we have
tentatively identified that actor as Walter
Smith. William appeared at the Haymarket
again on 9 February 1778 as Gloster in *Jane
Shore,* on 24 March as Prattle in *The Deuce Is in
Him,* and on 31 March as Colonel Feignwell
in *A Bold Stroke for a Wife* (that night T. Smith
sang between the acts).

On 22 February 1779 Smith returned to the
Haymarket to play Captain O'Cargo in *The
Prejudice of Fashion;* he acted an Officer in *The
Humours of Oxford* on 15 March. The following
19 October he appeared as Mirabel in *The Way
of the World.* From 27 December through 28
March 1780 Smith acted Facias in *The Rival
Milliners,* Slender in *Falstaff's Wedding,* Captain
Starboard in *The Modish Wife,* Martin in *Wit's
Last Stake,* and Lovell in *High Life below Stairs.*
We take him to have been the Smith who
returned to the Haymarket on 21 January
1782 to play Ogle in *The Beaux' Duel.*

On 15 January 1783, stated the *Hibernian
Journal,* a Smith (probably our man) made his
Dublin debut at the Capel Street Theatre; he
was advertised as from Bath. Smith seems to
have stayed on in Dublin through part of the
1783–84 season, but he was back at the Hay-
market in London by 21 January 1784, when
he acted a principal part in *The Talisman.* Be-
tween then and 22 March he appeared as Sir
George Hastings in *A Word to the Wise,* Martin
Sly in *Wit's Last Stake,* a principal character in
The Patriot, Faithful in *The Man's Bewitch'd,*
Lord Falbridge in *The English Merchant,* and
Gayless in *The Lying Valet.* He was Whittle in
The Irish Widow on 13 December.

At the Hammersmith Theatre from 7 June
to 26 July 1786, Smith was seen as Bruin in
The Mayor of Garratt, Lord Randolph in *Doug-
las,* the King in *The King and the Miller of
Mansfield,* Horatio in *Hamlet,* Baptista in *Cath-
erine and Petruchio,* Chicane in *The Agreeable
Surprise,* Priuli in *Venice Preserv'd,* Fairfield in
The Maid of the Mill, Captain Fitzroy in *The
Poor Soldier,* the Earl of Mercia in *Peeping Tom of*

Coventry, Mr Rightly in *The Heiress,* Manly in *The Provok'd Husband,* and Saville in *The Belle's Stratagem. The London Stage* has William Smith at the Haymarket on 27 August 1788, playing the King of the Antipodes in *Chrononhotonthologos.* And we believe he was also the Smith who was there again on 30 September playing Jasper in *Miss in Her Teens* and Beaufort in *The Citizen.*

Genest named William Smith as an annuitant on the Bath Theatre Fund in June 1829; one supposes that Bath was Smith's home theatre and that he came to London to play at the minor theatres in his spare time. Perhaps he was related to Walter Smith, who was in the Bath troupe in the late eighteenth and early nineteenth century.

Smith, William ₁*fl.* 1794₁, *violinist, violoncellist.*

Doane's *Musical Directory* of 1794 listed William Smith, of No 4, Shoemaker Row, Blackfriars, as a violinist and violoncellist who played in the Professional Concerts.

Smithies. *See* SMYTHIES.

Smithson, Mr ₁*fl.* 1749₁, *actor.*

Mr Smithson played a Recruit in *The Recruiting Officer* at Southwark on 9 January 1749.

Smut, Richard. *See* SMYTH, RICHARD.

Smyth. *See also* SMITH.

Smyth, Mr ₁ *fl.* 1770₁. *See* SMITH, RICHARD.

Smyth, Miss ₁*fl.* 1783₁, *actress.*

Miss Smyth played a principal part in *A New Way to Keep a Wife at Home* at the Haymarket Theatre on 17 September 1783.

Smyth, Francis ₁*fl.* 1674–1681₁, *singer.*

Francis Smyth (or Smith) was one of the children of the Chapel Royal who attended the King at Windsor from 18 May to 3 September 1674 at an extra wage of 3*s.* daily. He was under the tutelage of John Blow. The boy singer Smyth who sang in the court masque *Calisto* on 15 February 1675 was probably

Francis, but by 15 April 1678 his voice had broken and he had left the Chapel Royal. Perhaps he went into the service of the royal bellringer Adam Watkins, who, in his will dated 8 August 1678 and proved a month later, left his servant Francis Smyth a suit trimmed with red ribbons. Our subject was still receiving a clothing allowance from the King as late as 23 May 1681. Perhaps he was a descendant of the Francis Smith who played the lute in the King's Musick in pre-Restoration days.

Smyth, George ₁*fl.* 1669₁, *musician.*

On 28 June 1669 the Lord Chamberlain ordered the apprehension of George Smyth and others for "teaching, practicing and executing music in companies or otherwise, without the approbation or lycence of the Marshall and Corporation of musick."

Smyth, Henry *d.* 1670, *violinist.*

Rev Henry Smyth (or Smith) was a member of the Chapel Royal at the time of Charles II's coronation on 23 April 1661. He was a violinist and was named in several Lord Chamberlain's warrants. For example, on 18 April 1662 he was directed to attend the King on a trip to Portsmouth to meet the Queen; on 10 July 1663 he was paid for being in attendance at Windsor; on 14 March 1667 he was one of the twelve violinists at court appointed to an elite group within the regular band of 24; and from 16 May to 4 June 1670 he attended the King at Dover. Joseph Fashion replaced Henry Smyth, deceased, on 25 June 1670. It is probable that Smyth died a few days before that date. On 23 September 1675 his widow, Rebecka, assigned to Fashion all the arrears due her from the King in consideration of £52 paid her by Fashion.

The Lord Chamberlain's accounts, in addition to providing us with Mrs Smyth's maiden name, tell us that the Smyths were from the parish of St Margaret, Westminster. The published registers do not include 1670 burials, but one baptismal entry certainly concerns our subject: on 27 May 1666 Rebecka "Smith," daughter of Henry and Rebecka, was christened. Two other entries may refer to our subject's children: on 11 February 1665 Henry Smith, a child, was buried, and on 11 September 1665 Rebecca Smith, a child, was buried.

Smyth, [John?] [fl. 1675–1699?], dancer.

The Mr Smyth who danced in the court masque *Calisto* on 15 February 1675 may have been John Smith, the dancing master, who was named on 11 November 1699 in the Glasgow Corporation minute books:

The quilk day the Magistrates and Towne Council, upon a supplication given *in re* John Smith, Dancing Master, allow and permit the said John to teach dancing within the burgh, with and under the provisions and conditions under written, viz:— That he shall behave himself soberly, teach at seasonable hours, keep no balls, and that he shall so order his teaching that there shall be noe promiscuous dancing of young men and young women together; but that each sex shall be taught by themselves, and that one sex shall be dismissed and be out of his house before the other enter therein.

Smyth, Richard [fl. 1672–1673], scenekeeper.

The London Stage lists Richard Smut as a scenekeeper in the Duke's Company at the Dorset Garden Theatre in 1672–73; but that is an error for Richard Smyth, who was cited in the Lord Chamberlain's accounts on 23 July 1673.

Smythies, Mr [fl. 1797–1817], actor, costumer.

Mr Smythies was a minor member of the cast of *Sadak and Kalasrade* at Sadler's Wells in 1797 and of *The Oracle at Delphi* on 17 April 1799. He was probably the Smythies (or Smithies) who worked at Sadler's Wells as a costumer from as early as 2 April 1804 to at least 7 April 1817. He was probably related to the two Misses Smithies who danced at Sadler's Wells in 1811–12.

Smythies, Miss [fl. 1725–1726], actress.

Miss (sometimes Mrs) Smythies (or Smithies) shared a benefit with three others at Lincoln's Inn Fields Theatre on 14 May 1725. The gross receipts amounted to over £170. She played Mrs Squeamish in *The Country Wife* on 27 November 1725 and a Peasant Woman in *Apollo and Daphne* on 14 January 1726. With two others she shared a benefit on 13 May 1726, the receipts coming to a little over £100.

Snagg, Thomas. *See* WILKS, THOMAS SNAGGE.

"Sneak, Jerry." *See* RUSSELL, SAMUEL THOMAS.

Snelson, Mr [fl. 1783–1788], house servant.

Mr Snelson was listed in the Lord Chamberlain's accounts as the second gallery money taker at the King's Theatre in 1783. *The London Stage* describes him as the second gallery office keeper in 1786–87 and 1787–88.

Snider, Mr [fl. 1732–1744], singer, actor.

On 13 March 1732 at the Haymarket Theatre Mr Snider made what was apparently his first public appearance, singing Rodulpho in *Amelia*. He shared a benefit on 24 April. "Snyder" sang Liberty in *Britannia* on 16 November and Noodle and the Parson in *The Opera of Operas* on 4 June 1733. On 7 November at Drury Lane he repeated his parts in *The Opera of Operas*, after which he appeared as a Devil in *The Tempest*, Mynheer van Treble in *The Author's Farce*, Apollo in *Cupid and Psyche*, a Shepherd in *Love and Glory*, and a Shepherd in *Britannia*. After a decade "Snyder" returned to the Haymarket on 16 April 1744 to sing Marquis in *The Queen of Spain*.

Snow, Mr [fl. 1737–1741], actor.

Mr Snow played a Bravo in *The Inconstant* at Lincoln's Inn Fields on 20 January 1737 and then, from 1 February to 20 April, a Clerk in *Hymen's Triumph*, On 28 April 1741 he made his first and evidently last appearance on the Goodman's Fields stage as Setter in *The Old Bachelor*.

Snow, Miss [fl. 1765–1781], dancer, singer.

Miss Snow made her stage debut on 10 May 1765 at Covent Garden Theatre dancing a hornpipe in the character of a sailor. On 10 June she offered a new hornpipe at the Haymarket Theatre. She appeared at Finch's Grotto Gardens in 1770, at the Crow Street Theatre in Dublin in 1771 (as a dancer and singer), and at Kilkenny in 1781. Perhaps she was a daughter of the trumpeter Valentine Snow, but we have found no specific evidence of a relationship.

Snow, Charles [fl. 1744–1749], trumpeter.

Charles Snow was listed in the Lord Chamberlain's accounts as a trumpeter in the King's Musick from 1744, when he replaced Charles Marsh, to 1749. He was probably related to the trumpeter Valentine Snow, but in what way we do not know.

Snow, Jonathan b. 1741, harpsichordist, trumpeter, composer?

Master Jonathan Snow was born in 1741, the son of the trumpeter Valentine Snow. At a benefit for the elder Snow at his house in the parish of St Margaret, Westminster, in 1750, master Snow played several pieces on the harpsichord, according to a bill transcribed by Latreille. On 23 April 1751 at the Haymarket Theatre a benefit was held for Jonathan (advertised as ten years old), but the bill did not indicate whether or not he performed. He played the harpsichord and the elder Snow played the trumpet at a concert at the Assembly Room on St Augustine's Back in Bristol on 16 October 1752. On 2 May 1757 Jonathan Snow was given a benefit at the Haymarket. He was a trumpeter in the King's Musick from as early as 1749.

He was the Jonathan Snow of Ealing who married Elizabeth Harrison at St Marylebone on 3 May 1764. Valentine Snow was one of the witnesses. Perhaps Jonathan was the J. Snow listed in the Catalogue of Printed Music in the British Museum; his song Fickle Chloe was published about 1765, and his Variations for the Harpsichord came out about 1760. Jonathan Snow was organist at Marylebone Gardens in 1766.

Snow, Moses 1661–1702, singer, organist, composer.

Moses Snow, son of William and Ellinor Snow, was christened at St Margaret, Westminster, on 7 July 1661. He marched in the coronation procession of James II on 23 April 1685 as a member of the Choir of Westminster. On 30 September 1686 he auditioned for the post of organist at St Katherine Cree and was deemed (by Henry Purcell and John Blow, among other judges) the best of four applicants. Snow had by that time composed a few songs, some of which were published in 1685, 1686, and 1687 by Playford in his Theater of Music: "What cruel pains Corinna takes," "Ah, cruel Beauty!," "When you have broke that tender Loyal Heart," "Proud Strephon!," "Some Wine boys, some Wine," and others.

On 11 July 1689 Snow, a tenor, was appointed to the private and to the vocal music groups at court; on 17 December he was sworn a Gentleman of the Chapel Royal extraordinary (waiting for a salaried post); and on 8 April 1692 following the death of Alphonso Marsh, Snow was admitted to a regular position. In 1692 he was named one of the singers for the St Cecilia's Day celebration, and the following year he sang at the Queen's birthday ball. Snow was made an Epistler in the Chapel Royal on 24 February 1694. His salary at court was £73 annually. He was also active outside the Court, sharing a benefit with Boman on 10 May 1698 at a concert at York Buildings. In 1702 he spent 23 days attending the Queen at Windsor and Hampton Court.

Moses Snow died on 20 December 1702 and was buried four days later in the North Cloister of Westminster Abbey. He had been quite ill and had drawn up his will on 12 December, leaving guinea pieces to Dr John Blow and Rev Dr Ralph Battle (subdean of the Chapel Royal). Everything else he left to his brother George Snow and his sister Sarah Gibbons (Mrs John Gibbons) equally. Sarah was to dispose of her share without her husband's "intermedling or controul." The will was proved on 11 February 1703. Valentine Snow, the eighteenth-century trumpeter, was perhaps the son of Moses Snow.

Snow, Robert. See HARGRAVE, MR.

Snow, Sophia. See BADDELEY, MRS ROBERT.

Snow, Valentine d. 1770, trumpeter.

Valentine Snow was perhaps the son of the court musician Moses Snow, who died in December 1702. Valentine was to become Serjeant Trumpeter to the royal household and the musician for whom Handel composed the trumpet parts in the *Messiah, Samson,* the *Dettingen Te Deum, Judas Maccabaeus,* and other works. Snow's first concert notice came on 30 March 1732, when a benefit was held for him at York Buildings; another benefit, at the Devil Tavern, was presented on 22 March 1734. He was featured as a trumpeter at the Haymarket Theatre on 31 January 1735, had a benefit at the Devil Tavern the following 24 April, and received another benefit on 4 March 1736 at York Buildings. He was by 1735 one of the court trumpeters under John Shore.

Snow played at Hickford's Music Room on 24 March 1737; became one of the original subscribers to the Royal Society of Musicians on 28 August 1739; had a benefit concert at Hickford's on 19 March 1740; and played at Hickford's, the Castle Tavern, and the Haymarket Theatre in the spring of 1741. His address as of 26 February 1741, when he held a benefit at the Haymarket, was at a cabinet maker's in Brewer Street, facing Great Pulteney Street. By the time of his benefit at the Haymarket on 10 March 1743 Snow had a house in Marshall Street, opposite Carnaby Market, near Golden Square. On 9 February 1744 he played at Stationers' Hall, and a year later he shared a benefit with William Douglas at the Haymarket. A benefit for Snow was held at York Buildings in March 1746, and he played at Waltz's benefit at the Haymarket on 9 December 1748. Latreille transcribed a bill for a benefit Valentine Snow held for himself at his house in the parish of St Margaret, Westminster, in 1750. Master Jonathan Snow played several pieces on the harpsichord. At the Assembly Room on St Augustine's Back in Bristol on 18 October 1752, Snow played the trumpet and 11-year-old Master (Jonathan) Snow, his son, played the harpsichord.

The *Public Advertiser* on 2 December 1752 said:

We hear great interest is being made to succeed Mr Serjeant Shore, deceased, as Serjeant Trumpet to his Majesty, which is the gift of his Grace the Duke of Grafton as Lord Chamberlain; and that the contest lies chiefly between that excellent performer Mr Valentine Snow, Trumpet to the First Troop of Horseguards; Mr Du Bourg, the violin; and Mr Beard of the theatre Royal in Drury Lane.

Snow was given the appointment in January 1753 and held it until his death. He presumably inherited Shore's salary of £100 annually. As of 1763, when *Mortimer's London Directory* was published, Valentine Snow was living in Old Palace Yard.

Snow died at Windsor in late December 1770 and was buried at St Margaret, Westminster; his daughter Sophia, who had married the actor Robert Baddeley and become an established actress herself, bore the £40 funeral expenses. The author of *The Memoirs of Sophia Baddeley* claims that at one point Valentine Snow was in such financial straits that he had to pawn his Serjeant Trumpeter's regalia, but Mrs Baddeley's biographer was able to help Sophia bail him out. Administration of Snow's estate was granted to his widow, Mary Snow, on 24 January 1771.

Mary and Valentine Snow had three children: Jonathan, born in 1741; Sophia, born about 1745; and Robert, who died in 1771. Robert, a banker, lived in Red Lyon Square and made an extensive will on 5 November 1766, leaving thousands of pounds to his children, one of whom was Valentina Snow. The will was proved on 14 December 1771.

Dr Burney said Valentine Snow was "justly a favourite [at Vauxhall Gardens], where his silver sounds in the open air, by having room to expand, never arrived at the ears of the audience in a manner too powerful or piercing."

Snowdon. *See* SOWDON.

Snyder. *See* SNIDER.

Soaper, John   *c. 1742–1794, singer, organist.*

Born about 1742, John Soaper sang Damon in a performance of *Acis and Galatea* at the music room in Dean Street, Soho on 1 April 1758. Doane's *Musical Directory* of 1794 listed him as a bass who sang in the choirs of St Paul's Cathedral, the Chapel Royal, and the Madrigal Society. He was vicar choral of St Paul's when he died on 5 June 1794 in his apartment in Sion College, London Wall. Soaper was buried at St Paul's, attended by the choir, on 13 June 1794. The register noted that he was from St Alphage parish and aged 52 years. The *Euro-*

pean *Magazine* spoke of the excellence of his voice and ear and said that after his vocal powers died he turned to composing and playing the organ. His estate went to his sister and only kin Ann Thomas Hayes, widow, on 23 June 1794. He was described in the administration as a bachelor.

Soderigo. *See* SODERINI.

Soderini, Mr ₁*fl.1758–1794*₁, *violinist.*
Mr Soderini played in the band at Marylebone Gardens from 10 June to 19 September 1758 for performances of the popular *La serva padrona*. On 21 August he appeared as a solo violinist. He joined Barthélemon on 5 March 1766 in a Handel concerto for two violins. Soderini played violin in the *Messiah* at the Foundling Hospital in 1769, and in May and June 1784 he performed in the Handel Memorial Concerts at Westminster Abbey and the Pantheon. He was in the opera band at the Pantheon in 1791. Doane's *Musical Directory* of 1794 gave his address as No 5, Carlisle Street, Soho, and listed him as a member of the New Musical Fund (he was on the Court of Assistants) and of the Concert of Ancient Music.

Michael Kelly dined with Soderini in the summer of 1781 in Pisa, where the violinist had gone from England.

He was one of the ugliest men I ever saw. When M. Favar was first ballet-master, Soderini went on the stage, after the rehearsal, and said to him, 'Allow me, my dear Sir, to introduce myself to you;—you are the dearest friend I have on earth,— let me thank you a thousand times for the happiness you have conferred on me by coming amongst us;— command me in any way, for whatever I do for you, I can never sufficiently repay you!'

The ballet-master, who had never seen or heard of Soderini before, was astounded; at last, he said, 'Pray, Sir, to what peculiar piece of good fortune may I attribute the compliments and professions with which you favour me?'

'To your unparalleled ugliness, my dear Sir,' replied Soderini: 'for before *your* arrival, I was considered the ugliest man in Great Britain.'

The ballet-master (strange to say, since he really was so ugly,) took the joke in good part, and they became extremely intimate; but, amiable as they were to each other, they were universally known as the ugly couple! This anecdote Soderini told me himself.

Sodi, Pietro ₁*fl.1741–1775*₁,   *dancer, choreographer.*
The Parfaict brothers' *Dictionnaire* states that Pietro Sodi was a Roman by birth, the younger brother of Carlo Sodi, the composer-choreographer. Pietro was probably a student of Rinaldo Fossano. In 1741–42 he danced in Naples with the San Carlo troupe. Marian Hannah Winter in *The Pre-Romantic Ballet* has Sodi dancing in London in November 1742, though *The London Stage* makes no mention of him until 29 January 1743, when the King's Theatre told balletomanes that Sodi had recovered from his "last disposition" and would dance that night as usual. The inference was that he had been dancing earlier that season, and one supposes that he continued doing so after his January appearance. Sodi then went to France late in 1743 and made his Paris Opéra debut in the spring of 1744.

He returned to London to appear on 6 February 1746 at Covent Garden Theatre. After that he was named regularly in the bills as an entr'acte performer. The dances in which Sodi participated were not often given titles, but a few were: *The Drunken Tyrolese* (a solo), *The Italian Peasants, The Bird Catchers, The Flemish Peasant's Wedding,* and *The Revellers.* He had a solo benefit on 11 April and made his last appearance on 30 April.

Winter places Sodi in Berlin in 1746–47, after which sojourn he returned to the Paris Opéra. He left there in 1752 and, according to Campardon's work on the Paris fairs, Sodi appeared with the Opéra Comique at the St Laurent fair that year, dancing in *Batteurs en grange.* He was ballet master with Dourdet in 1753 in the new Théâtre Français ballet company. The following year Sodi was in Vienna. There in 1756–57 he was the first dancer and associate choreographer at the Vienna Karntnerthor. He was first dancer and ballet master at the Teatro San Samuele in Venice in 1757–58, after which he returned to serve at the Théâtre Italien from 1758 to 1760.

On 9 March 1761 Sodi returned for the first time in ten years to the stage of Covent Garden in London to dance in *The Hungarian Gambols.* He came back for the 1761–62 and 1762–63 seasons at almost £6 weekly, appearing in some pantomimes and other works: *Thomas and Sally, Comus,* as Water and Air in *The Rape of*

Bibliothèque Nationale

Scene from *Prince de Salerne*—ballet by SODI
engraving by Horeolly, after Marvie

Proserpine, The French Country Gentleman, as Apollo in *Apollo and Daphne, The Pleasures of Spring, Romeo and Juliet, The Counterfeit Heiress, Les Sabotiers, The Swedish Gardeners* (his composition), and *Harlequin Sorcerer.* In 1763–64 Sodi moved over to the King's Theatre to become director of dances (Winter mistakenly places him at Covent Garden). He danced Scaramouch in *Le Masquerade* on 31 March 1764 but may not have done much other dancing that season.

Sodi's whereabouts in 1764–65 are not known; he may have continued at the King's, since he was certainly there in 1765–66. A letter quoted in *The London Stage* under 25 January 1766 included a comment on Sodi: "Sg *Sodi* has so often diverted us by his compositions as Ballet master that it were superfluous to bestow any encomiums on him in this place." On 13 March 1766 Sodi danced a minuet and louvre with Miss Capitani (his scholar?). He was again ballet master at the King's in 1766–67.

The next notice we have found of Pietro Sodi comes on 24 April 1773, when he danced at Covent Garden in *The Festival of the Black Prince.* Then he left Europe for America. He arrived in New York, according to Winter, in April 1774 and danced at the Assembly Room on 26 May with his daughter, age nine. Odell in his *Annals of the New York Stage* quotes an announcement in "Rivington's Gazetteer" of 19 May:

At Mr. HULL'S Assembly Room, will be performed a CONCERT, the 26th of this month, for the benefit of
Mr. BIFERI and Mr. SODI
The said Concert will be divided into two acts, each act composed of four pieces. Mr. Biferi, Master of Music from Naples, will perform on the harpsichord a piece of music of his own composition, with the orchestra; in the second act he will perform a solo, accompanied with the violin. There will follow a ball, in which Mr. Sodi will dance the louvre and the minuet, with Miss Sodi, a young lady nine years of age; and Miss Sodi will dance a rigadoon with young Mr. Hulet. It will begin exactly at 7 o'clock.

But Winter quotes a notice from "Remington's Gazeteer" in Philadelphia dated 5 May 1774:

Pietro Sodi—Dancing Master—will teach the minuet and louvre, the Dauphin minuet, the German dance call'd l'Allemand, the cotillion of his

own composition and other figured dances in a short time. He has been dancing master in all the Courts of Europe, and last at London.

Perhaps Sodi worked in both New York and Philadelphia, or there may be some confusion in the sources here. Winter reports that Sodi moved to Charleston, South Carolina, in April 1775 and joined the dancing master John Abercromby.

Among Pietro Sodi's works over the years were a cornemuse (according to Winter) in the opera *Acis et Galatée,* the pantomime *Les Jardiniers* in *Thesée, Les Fous,* in *Le Carnaval et la folie,* a pantomime dance titled *Les Enfans bucherons, Les Mandolines, Les Batteurs en grange, Les Cors de chasse,* and *Les Chasseurs* in *Prince de Salerne.* His specialty was pas de trois pantomimes.

The engraving by Horeolly, after Marvie, shown here, is of Sodi's *Les Chasseurs,* first presented in Paris at the Théâtre Italien on 25 September 1746 and performed at Fontainbleau in November of that year. Sodi's pupil Charles Dubois is seen in a pas de deux with De Hesse's student Camilla Veronese.

Solard. *See* SOULARD.

Solen, N ₁*fl. 1795*₁,   *house servant?*
N. Solen, probably a house servant, was cited in the Drury Lane Theatre accounts on 25 April 1795.

Soler. *See* MARTIN Y SOLER.

Soli. *See* CHAMPVILLE.

Solinus, Andrew ₁*fl. 1739–1767*₁,   *musician.*
On 28 August 1739 Andrew Solinus became one of the original subscribers to the Royal Society of Musicians and was active to at least 1755. He subscribed in 1767 to John Jones's *Lessons for the Harpsichord.*

Solis, E. *b. 1793, singer, composer.*
E. Solis supplied the musical biographer Sainsbury about 1823 with a brief autobiography. Solis described himself as a Professor of Music living in Brixton Hill. He was born in 1793 in Bury Street, St Mary Axe, and studied under Corri. At the age of six he sang "at the

Opera and at most of the public dinners." Solis composed two piano sonatas, an overture, a set of waltzes, and some songs.

Solomon. *See* SALOMON.

"Solon." *See* DOGGETT, THOMAS.

Solway. *See* SALWAY.

Somers. *See also* SUMMERS, ROBERT.

Somers, Maria. *See* WARREN, MARIA.

Somerville, Mrs [*fl. 1782–1792*], *actress.*

Mrs Somerville performed in Derry, Ireland, in 1782. On 26 March 1787 she appeared in London at the Haymarket Theatre as Mandane in *The Orphan of China* and Mrs Brittle in *Barnaby Brittle.* She returned to the Haymarket on 26 November 1792 to appear as Almeria in *The Mourning Bride.*

Sommers. *See* SUMMERS.

Sontlow. *See* BOOTH, MRS BARTON.

Soper, Master [*fl. 1759*], *singer.*

Master Soper sang at Covent Garden Theatre in *Alfred the Great* on 2 February 1759 and in a concert spirituel on 4 May; both were charity benefits. Possibly he should be identified as the singer John Soaper, but Soaper had performed the year before and had not been called Master.

Soper, Guilbert [1674–1683], *actor.*

Guilbert Soper was a minor actor in the King's Company at Drury Lane Theatre in 1674–75, but no roles are known for him. According to an indenture dated 18 April 1678 concerning property owned by the elder Bartholomew Baker (also a King's Company actor, but in the early 1660s), Soper lived on a plot in Drury Lane. The indenture transferred the land to Baker's heirs. Soper was named in the actor Charles Hart's will of 10 July 1683 for a bequest of £10.

A Gilbert Soper, barber surgeon from the parish of St Martin-in-the-Fields, was buried

at St Paul, Covent Garden, on 7 September 1688. He was probably not our subject, but he may well have been related. In his will, dated 29 July 1686 and proved on 8 March 1689, he named several of his kin: his wife Anne, his sister Jane Blakeman, his brother (in law?) John Alford, and his son Gilbert, to whom he left his "study of books." Ann, daughter of Gilbert Soper from St Martin's, was buried at St Paul, Covent Garden, on 26 June 1687.

Sophie, Mlle. *See* LOUILLE, SOPHIE.

Sorace. *See* STORACE.

Sorbelloni, Giovanni. *See* SORBELLONI, PIETRO.

Sorbelloni, Pietro [*fl. 1760–1761*], *singer.*

The London Stage under 25 August 1760 lists Giovanni Sorbelloni as a singer engaged by Signora Mattei as the second man and serious singer in burlettas for the 1760–61 season at the King's Theatre. But during that season the singer named in the bills was Pietro Sorbelloni (variously spelled), and we believe that the citing of Giovanni was an error. Pietro sang Ernesto in *Il mondo della Luna* on 22 November 1760, Tauris in *Arianna e Teseo* on 16 December, Rinaldo in *Il filosofo di campagna* on 6 January 1761, Lucio in *Tito Manlio* on 7 February, and Lindoro in *La pescatrici* on 28 April. Dr Burney said of *Il filosofo* that "The simple and elegant air: *La bella che adora,* sung by Sorbelloni, from the mere tone of his voice, was always applauded. . . ."

Sorin, Joseph *d. c. 1730, dancer, actor, manager.*

The dancer Joseph Sorin's surname was spelled in a variety of ways—Serene, Surrein, Surin, Surene, Sorias—but Sorin is how he signed himself. *The London Stage* lists him as a member of Betterton's company at Lincoln's Inn Fields Theatre in 1695–96, but Sorin's agreement to join the troupe at the end of summer vacation at 30s. weekly was made on 25 July 1696, as the Lord Chamberlain's accounts show. The contract or memorandum reads:

It was then agreed between M.[r] Thomas Betterton, and M.[r] Joseph Sorin, that when y.[e] Vacation is over, y.[e] said M.[r] Joseph Sorin shall be entred among them as one of his Majesties Comedians, and in Consideration of his Acting, Dancing, or performing any other thing proper for him, he shall Receive thirty shillings p.[r] w.[ee]k.[e] after y.[e] manner that all others are paid; and further I promise as y.[e] said M.[r] Joseph Sorin shall please Audiences, and he deserve more his said Sallery shall be from time to time augmented.

The musicians "John Baptist Draghi" and "Balth: Redding" witnessed the agreement. Sorin was cast as Pasquarel in "Natural Magick," a part of a variety entertainment called *The Novelty,* at Lincoln's Inn Fields in June 1697.

Sorin returned to the Continent (whence he had presumably come), for when next mentioned, on 22 August 1702, he was "lately arrived" in England. He and a partner (Richard Baxter) presented a *"Night Scene by a Harlequin and a Scaramouch after the Italian Manner"* at Drury Lane. The pair were referred to as Sieur Allard's "Sons" in *A Comparison Between the Two Stages* that year:

SULL. And the *Sieur* Allard—.

CRI. Ay, the *Sieur* with a pox to him—and the two *Monsieurs* his Sons—Rogues that show at *Paris* for a Groat a piece, and here they were an entertainment for the Court and his late Majesty.

RAMB. Oh—*Harlequin* and *Scaramouch.*

CRI. Ay; What a rout here was with a Night piece of *Harlequin* and *Scaramouch?* with the Guittar and the Bladder! What jumping over Tables and Joint-Stools! What ridiculous Postures and Grimaces! and what an exquisite Trick 'twas to straddle before the Audience, making a thousand damn'd *French* Faces, and seeming in labour with a monstrous Birth, at last my counterfeit Male Lady is deliver'd of her two Puppies *Harlequin* and *Scaramouch.*

SULL. And yet the Town was so fond of this, that these Rascals brought the greatest Houses that ever were known: 'Sdeath I am scandaliz'd at these little things; I am asham'd to own my self of a Country where the Spirit of Poetry is dwindled into vile Farce and Foppery.

John Weaver in his *History of the Mimes and Pantomimes* years later remembered "the Night Scene of the Sieur Allard and his two Sons, performed on the Stage in *Drury-Lane* about seven or eight and twenty Years ago." Indeed,

at the Haymarket Theatre on 20 February 1736 was presented "an Italian night Scene of action which was originally perform'd 25 years ago by Sorrein & Baxter. . . ."

Sorin and Baxter offered their night scene at Drury Lane on 7 October 1703 and 18 August 1704, at Southwark Fair on 18 September 1704, and at Lincoln's Inn Fields Theatre on October 1705. The advertisement for their appearance at the Fair offered ". . . Italian Interludes of Scaramouch and Harlaquin, by these two Great Masters of their kind, Mr. Sorine and Mr. Baxter . . ."

Sorin had performed on the Continent; Campardon in *Les Spectacles de la foire* states that Sorin made his debut at one of the French fairs in mezzetin, "travestis," sultans, and fathers. With him was his long-time partner Baxter; the manager of the company was Nivelon. In 1711 the Nivelon troupe was disbanded and Sorin and Baxter joined Baron's company. The manager (son of the great actor Michel Baron) died, and his widow took over the management, apparently about 1713. To avoid being pursued for her late husband's debts, Mme Baron used Sorin and Baxter's names as the company leaders: "Le Nouvel Opéra Comique de Baxter et de Sorin." The troupe continued until 1716, but in November 1715 the Earl of Stair, minister plenipotentiary to Paris, tried to persuade Sorin and Baxter to take an engagement in London. They were unwilling to come for just a short engagement, and their obligations to Mme Baron prevented them from considering a longer stay.

But in 1716 the Baron troupe disbanded, and Sir Richard Steele was able to engage Sorin and Baxter for Drury Lane, where they appeared in April and May. On 4 April, advertised as lately arrived from Paris, Sorin played Scaramouch in *The Whimsical Death of Harlequin.* The work was repeated on 11 April, and on 20 April and 10 May Sorin and Baxter had benefits.

In 1717–18 Sorin and Baxter performed in the French provinces, and in 1721 they organized an opéra comique troupe to perform at the St Laurent Fair. The venture failed and Baxter retired to the provinces. Campardon says that Sorin left the stage with his parents and died about 1730.

Sorine, Mr ₁*fl. 1713–1716*₁, *guitarist.*
Leonard Ashley in his *Colley Cibber* (1965)
states that manuscript materials pertaining to
Drury Lane Theatre from 1713 to 1716 show
that a Mr Sorine played the guitar in the theatre band.

Sorine, Mr ₁*fl. 1724–1725*₁, *barber.*
The London Stage lists Mr Sorine as a barber
at the Lincoln's Inn Fields Theatre in 1724–
25.

Sorosina, Benedetta ₁*fl. 1722–1732*₁,
singer.
Benedetta Sorosina (or Sorosini) sang in operas in Venice in 1722–23 and in Naples in
1723. She sang in London in the first half of
1725, appearing as Delia in *Dario* on 10 April
and Rosmilda in *Elpidia* on 11 May. The *New
Grove Dictionary of Music and Musicians* states
that she was Nerina in Handel's *Giulio Cesare*
in London, but *The London Stage* does not list

Fondazione Giorgio Cini

BENEDETTA SOROSINA
by Zanetti

her in that role. She sang in Venice in 1727–
28 and in Milan in 1731–32. Caricatures of
her by Zanetti are in the Cini collection in
Venice and at Windsor Castle.

Souchart, Mrs ₁*fl. 1766*₁, *house servant?*
Mrs Souchart shared a benefit with two others at Covent Garden Theatre on 12 May
1766. Perhaps she was one of the house servants.

Soulard, Mons ₁*fl. 1720–1725*₁, *actor,
dancer.*
Monsieur Soulard (or Soulart, Solard) was a
member of the French troupe under De Grim-
bergue playing at the Haymarket Theatre in
1720–21. On 18 April 1721 he replaced
Francisque as the company's harlequin in a
work he had previously acted at foreign courts,
Les Disgraces d'Arlequin. He announced a new
work for 2 May, *Empereur dans la lune,* but *The
London Stage* does not list a performance at the
Haymarket on that day. When Soulard returned in 1724–25 with another company he
was the dottore. He shared a benefit with
Durac on 19 April 1725 at the Haymarket and
played the Eldest Brother in *Les Deux
d'Arlequin* on 7 May.

Soule, Mr ₁*fl. 1708*₁, *bill carrier.*
Mr Soule, according to the Coke papers at
Harvard, was a bill carrier at the Queen's The-
atre as of 8 March 1708.

"South American Dwarfs." *See*
"Monstrous Craws, The."

South, Mr ₁*fl. 1798*₁, *equestrian.*
Mr South was listed as an equestrian in the
Royal Circus bill of 23 April 1798.

Southall, Mr ₁*fl. 1794*₁, *singer.*
Doane's *Musical Directory* of 1794 listed Mr
Southall of Birmingham as an alto singer who
had participated in the Handel performances
at Westminster Abbey in London.

Southall, Mr ₁*fl. 1794*₁, *singer.*
Doane's *Musical Directory* of 1794 listed Mr
Southall of Worcester as an alto singer who had
participated in the Handel performances at
Westminster Abbey in London.

Southby, ₁G.? or J.?₁ ₁fl.1798–1817₁, *actor, clown, acrobat, pyrotechnist. See* SOUTHBY, WILLIAM.

Southby, William ₁fl.1798–1817₁, *actor, clown, pyrotechnist, manager.*

The Pie Powder Court Books at the London Guildhall cite a Southby, possibly William, exhibiting a "pavilion" at Bartholomew Fair in 1791, "Royal Camp" in 1792, a "View of Spithead" in 1793, and puppets in 1794. The "Book" for 1798 lists two Southbys serving as actors at Bartholomew Fair. Sybil Rosenfeld in *The Theatre of the London Fairs* identifies the pair as actors who became celebrated clowns. We take them to be William and either G. or J. Southby, about whom J. E. Varey wrote in *Theatre Notebook*, 8. William Southby managed an English troupe in Madrid in 1816 and 1817. The company made its first appearance on 4 August 1816 and gave five performances through 28 August. In 1817 the group returned to play seven times in January and February and six times in July and August in the Ring outside the Puerta de Alcalá, which belonged to the Royal General Hospital and the Royal Hospital of the Passion, with a portion of the proceeds going to the hospitals.

The performances were a mixture of equestrian exercises; "dangerous leaps upon the spring-board" by J. Southby, G. Southby, and others; tightrope tricks by Mrs Southby (evidently William's wife); and "Brilliant fireworks, directed by Mr. [William] Southby, the foremost pyrotechnician in Europe." J. Southby took over the fireworks displays in the summer of 1817.

In addition to his management and pyrotechnic duties, William Southby performed on the springboard, probably served as ring master, and was apparently a clown. M. Willson Disher in *Clowns and Pantomimes* says that Southby was Laurent's pupil and presented fireworks at Astley's Amphitheatre in 1821 and at Vauxhall Gardens in London in 1822 and 1823. He worked as a clown at Astley's from 1821 to 1824 and as a pyrotechnist at Vauxhall in 1828. In his *Memoirs* Charles Dibdin the younger wrote that at Davis's Amphitheatre in 1822–23 he had "a very good Clown, Mr Southby, the Pyrotechnist, who also furnished me with fireworks, with a 'display' of which, I sometimes in obedience to

Harvard Theatre Collection

WILLIAM SOUTHBY, as Sir Pallinore

artist unknown

public taste, concluded my performances, so that at any rate, some part of the Entertainment, went off well." Perhaps William was a Southby pictured as "Sir Pallinore Knight of the Silver Star," in armor and on horseback, in a print published by Hodgson in March 1835.

Southern, Mr ₁fl.1672₁, *musician.*
The Lord Chamberlain ordered the apprehension of Mr Southern on 15 July 1672 for practicing music without a license.

Sowden, Mr *d. 1740, boxkeeper.*
Latreille, citing an unidentified clipping, says that Mr Sowden, a grocer in Piccadilly and a boxkeeper at the King's Theatre, died on 11 January 1740.

Sowdon, Hester. *See* JACKSON, MRS JOHN.

Sowdon, John *d. 1789?, actor, singer, manager.*
The unnamed gentleman who made his stage debut at Covent Garden Theatre on 4

JOHN SOWDON, as Caled

engraving by Miller, after Lewis

December 1747 playing Pierre in *Venice Preserv'd* was probably John Sowdon, according to Genest's *London Stage.* On 9 January 1748 Sowdon was named in the bills for Othello, and on 29 February he acted Richard III. He moved to Drury Lane for the 1748–49 season, making his first appearance there on 22 September 1748 as Carlos in *Love Makes a Man.* There he remained through 1751–52 playing such characters as Tamerlane, Wellborn in *A New Way to Pay Old Debts,* Banquo in *Macbeth,* Hardy in *the Funeral,* Mustapha in *Mahomet and Irene,* Pyrrhus in *The Distrest Mother,* the Ghost in *Hamlet,* King John in *Edward the Black Prince,* Tullius Hostillius and Publius in *The Roman Father,* Ventidius in *All for Love,* the Elder Brother in *Comus,* Gloster in *Jane Shore,* the Mad Scholar in *The Pilgrim,* Orsino in *Twelfth Night,* Loveless in *Love's Last Shift,* Altamont in *The Fair Penitent,* Don Gabriel in *Gil Blas,* the Danish King in *Alfred,* Villeroy in *The Fatal Marriage,* Edmund in *King Lear,* and Polydore in *The Orphan.*

Tickets for his first benefit, on 5 April 1749, could be had of him at Mr Haymer's in James Street, Covent Garden, and "of Mr. Thomas Sowdon, in Blackman St. Southwark." The relationship between the two Sowdons is not known. John Powel in his "Tit for Tat" manuscript at Harvard noted that "A present was made to [Sowdon] of the charge of the House, because he had acted this season and receiv'd no salary." Receipts for the benefit came to £160. By March 1750 Sowdon was living at the sign of the Sun, a milliner's shop facing Exeter Exchange in the Strand; by April 1752 he had moved next door to the Black Lion on Little Russell Street. Thomas Sowdon continued selling John's benefit tickets in Southwark.

John Sowdon was at the Smock Alley Theatre in Dublin from 1752–53 through 1755–56 and in 1758–59; in 1759–60 he acted at the Crow Street playhouse; and in 1760–61 and 1761–62 he was again at Smock Alley. The *Dublin Journal* of 5–9 June 1753 noted that Sowdon came from a good family and was brother to "Thos Otway of Castle Otway, Esq." Mrs Bellamy said he was originally a horse milliner. The only role known for Sowdon during his Dublin years was his first, Othello, on 18 October 1752 at Smock Alley. West Digges, in his letters to Sarah Ward, mentioned Sowdon as a colleague in 1753.

During the seasons of 1754–55 and 1755–56, when Thomas Sheridan was in England, John Sowdon joined Benjamin Victor in the management of Smock Alley. The anonymous author of *A Letter to Messieurs Victor and Sowdon* in 1755 cautioned the managers not to bow to minority demands for plays with political implications and to quell the savage behavior of the ruffians in the upper gallery, who had evidently made people of distinction stay away from the theatre. But the managers were praised for their "Assiduity and Spirit in engaging the most capital Performers for his Winter's Entertainment. . . ." Wilks in his *General View of the Stage* also commented on Sowdon as a manager, saying that he conducted the theatre "with great regularity." By February 1756, according to a letter written by Victor, Sowdon wanted to drop out of the management and sell his share in the theatre. But, as La Tourette Stockwell shows in *Dublin Theatres and Theatre Customs,* the assignment of Sowdon's property to Spranger Barry was not made until 1 March 1758.

Letters from Dr Thomas Wilson to Samuel

Derrick, now in the Forster collection at the Victoria and Albert Museum, indicate that Sowdon and the actor Mossop had a quarrel in March 1762 in Dublin. It was settled by 14 April, and Wilson commented that "I think Sowdon behaved very well in every Instance. . . ." Still, 1761–62 was Sowdon's last season in Dublin. He performed in Cork in the fall of 1762—a return engagement, for he had been there in July of 1761. After 1762 Sowdon apparently left Ireland. We have found no record of his activity between 1762 and 1767.

Sowdon joined Samuel Foote's troupe at the Haymarket Theatre in London, appearing first on 4 June 1767 as Isaac Fungus in *The Commissary*. The rest of the summer saw him as Sir Jacob Jollup in *The Mayor of Garratt*, Iago in *Othello*, Gloster in *Jane Shore*, Marcian in *Theodosius*, Clytus in *Alexander*, Sealand in *The Conscious Lovers*, Grey in *The Countess of Salisbury*, Polydore in *The Orphan*, and Aboan in *The Royal Captive*. The author of *Momus* in 1767 had nothing good to say about Sowdon:

> See S——w——n, great in capitals appear,
> Disgust the eye and grate the dullest ear;
> For he most surely, of all human kind,
> Was ne'er by nature for the stage design'd:
> Long in Hibernia has he trod the field,
> Where judgment oft to prejudice must yield,
> And with no small indulgence and regard,
> Tho' ev'ry night some noble part he marr'd.

The poet-critic called him "declining, and in age"; "time with years has wrinkled o'er his face." Silas Neville was kinder; he told his diary "Sowdon, Marcian [in *Theodosius*], who tho' ugly, has a pretty good person and is a tolerably good player."

Foote must have been satisfied, for he used Sowdon again in the next three summers in such parts as Lord Crafty in *The Statesman Foil'd*, Leon in *Rule a Wife and Have a Wife*, the Fryar in *The Spanish Fryar*, Friendly in *The Doctor Last in His Chariot*, the Ghost in *Hamlet*, Buckingham in *Richard III*, the title character in *The Old Bachelor*, Cassius in *Julius Caesar*, and Pierre in *Venice Preserv'd*.

Sowdon's winters, at least in 1768, 1770, and 1771, were spent in Edinburgh, first at the New Concert Hall and then, in the last two years, at the Theatre Royal in Shakespeare Square. His characters included Antonio in *The Merchant of Venice*, Banquo in *Macbeth*, Clytus in *The Rival Queens*, Horatio in *The Fair Penitent*, Jaques in *As You Like It*, Leon in *Rule a Wife and Have a Wife*, the Old Bachelor, and Pierre in *Venice Preserv'd*. His appearance in *As You Like It* on 7 January 1771 is the last theatrical record we have found for Sowdon. The *Hibernian Magazine* in April 1789 reported that "Thomas" Sowdon had died recently at L'Orient, France. Since an Irish publication would have been interested in news of John Sowdon, who had spent so many seasons on the Dublin stage, perhaps the obituary notice concerned our subject.

Wilks commented favorably on Sowdon as an actor:

> . . . I believe his performance of Henry the Eighth [of which we have no other record] to be as true a likeness of that monarch as Shakespear or history could draw him. I have seen him also judiciously pleasing in Pyrrhus, Ventidius, Old Bachelor, and Strictland; and he must always be considered as a performer of consequence in the theatrical world.

Charles Dibdin, in the first volume of his *Professional Life*, was not so kind:

> SOWDEN was intended to perform Don Diego, in the *Padlock;* and as I had composed the music, he expected me to teach him, which, by the way, all the world could not have done; for the performance of Peachum, in the *Beggar's Opera*, in which part he sung all the songs out of tune, had been the achme of his musical attempts. As I knew that he was the most penurious skinflint upon earth, I got rid of him by asking him a handsome price for my trouble.

In his *History of the Irish Stage* Robert Hitchcock described Sowdon as "not an actor of the very first merit, yet he supported a variety of business with reputation, and always lived esteemed and respected." Tate Wilkinson in his *Memoirs* wrote:

> He was a sensible shrewd bred man, looked on in general as remarkably insincere; not that I ever met with anything from him in any respect, but the opposite conduct . . . He was very entertaining, and a great epicure: He was possessed of an ample fortune, the consequence of being a good economist, and well knowing how to lend his money to great advantage, yet not without good security: He made himself generally pleasing, as he never contradicted anybody, or disliked any thing at another person's table, but always approved. If a

gentleman had said, "Sowden, that cabbage-leaf those strawberries are on is a fine leaf" he would have sworn a loud oath, that the cabbage leaf not only was a handsome leaf, but by G—d! the handsomest cabbage-leaf that ever grew.

The Thomas Sowdon of Southwark, who sold benefit tickets for John from 1749 to 1752, was possibly the Thomas Sowdon, gentleman, of St George the Martyr, Queen Square, who married Sarah Knight of St Andrew, Holborn, on 24 February 1753. At the Huntington Library is a manuscript of James Winston, whose chief interests were theatrical; he quoted the *Examiner* of 12 August 1811 as reporting that on 2 August 1811 Richard Sowden, a Navy lieutenant, died in Islington. Before the age of 21 he had taken money from his father, which he dissipated in the purlieus of Pall Mall. He seems to have gone on the stage in the early nineteenth century, using the name of Stapleton. He may have been John Sowdon's son.

John Sowdon is pictured as Caled in *The Siege of Damascus* in an engraving by A. Miller, after J. Lewis, published in 1754. A copy, bust only, in reverse, by an unknown engraver, was published by Harding in 1802. In the British Museum and Harvard Theatre Collection catalogues of portraits, he is identified, erroneously, as Thomas Sowdon.

Sowerby, John [*fl. 1781?–1794*], *flutist.*
Doane's *Musical Directory* of 1794 listed John Sowerby, of No 11, Stangate Street, Lambeth, as a flutist who played for the New Musical Fund and the Academy of Ancient Music and in the oratorios at Drury Lane Theatre. The Drury Lane accounts show a payment to a Mr Sowerby of £6 6s. on 5 May 1794; he was probably John the flutist. The oratorio season had run from 12 March to 11 April. Perhaps he was the John Sowerby of St Anne, Westminster, who on 22 December 1781 had married Elizabeth Isabella Litchfield of the same parish at St Paul, Covent Garden.

Soyan. *See* SHOJAN.

Spackman, Mr [*fl. 1741–1742*], *actor.*
At Bartholomew Fair on 22 August 1741 Mr Spackman played the Captain in *The Devil of a Duke.* He appeared at the James Street Theatre on 9 November to speak the prologue and play Barnwell in *George Barnwell* and act Lorenzo in the comic part of *The Spanish Fryar.* Spackman returned to James Street on 7 April 1742 to appear as Chatillion in *Zara.*

Spackman, Mrs [*fl. 1743–1744*], *actress.*
Mrs Spackman played Mrs Motherly in *The Provok'd Husband* at the Lincoln's Inn Fields Theatre on 5 April 1743 and Lady Easy in *The Careless Husband* at the James Street Theatre on 10 December 1744.

"Spagniola, Signora." *See* REDIGÉ, MME PAULO.

Spagnoletti. *See also* SPAGNOLI.

Spagnoletti, Paolo Diana *1768–1834,* *violinist, composer.*
Paolo Diana Spagnoletti was born in Cremona in 1768, according to the *New Grove* (van der Straeten in his *History of the Violin* dates his birth 1761). He exhibited great virtuosity on the violin as a child and made his first English appearance, according to *The London Stage,* on 1 July 1799 at Drury Lane, playing his own *Grand Concerto.* (Grove does not record Spagnoletti coming to London until about 1802.) On 7 April 1802 Spagnoletti was the leader of the band at a benefit for Mrs Franklin at Willis's Rooms on King Street and was that year a second violinist at the King's Theatre. He led the band at the Margravine of Anspach's theatricals on 11 June 1802. Signora Spagnoletti, presumably his wife, was singing at the King's from 1804 to 1806. At some point—perhaps as early as 1804—Spagnoletti became leader of the band at the King's Theatre. He may have been the "Spagniolette" at the Theatre Royal, Edinburgh, in 1807–8; he performed in Dublin with Mme Catalani in 1808; and he led the band at the Pantheon in London in 1812.

In 1813 he became one of the first 28 associates of the Philharmonic Society and played in one of the organization's early concerts on 19 April. From 1815 onward he was the leader of the band at the King's Theatre, and he performed also at the Ancient Concerts, for the Royal Academy of Music, at the Hanover

Royal College of Music

ROBERT LINDLEY, PAOLO SPAGNOLETTI, and WILLIAM LINDLEY
engraving by Sharp, after Wigley

Square Rooms, and at the Argyll Rooms. He led the band at Paganini's concerts in London in 1831. His last appearance may have been on 28 March 1834, when he led the band in the first English performance of Cherubini's *Requiem*.

Spagnoletti had three strokes, the last depriving him of his speech and the use of one side of his body. He died on 23 September 1834. On 9 October administration of his estate was granted to his only child, Ernesto Diana Spagnoletti. The administration described Paolo Spagnoletti as a widower who had been living at No 81, Newman Street, Oxford Street, in the parish of St Anne, Westminster.

A portrait of Spagnoletti with Robert and William Lindley, "Drawn on Stone by Mr Sharp from a Miniature by Mrs Wigley, Salop," was published for the artist by Dickinson in London and Eddowes in Shrewsbury in 1836.

Spagnoli, Clementina [*fl. 1765–1774*], *singer.*
Signora "Spagnolla" sang an unspecified role in *Eumene* at the King's Theatre on 23 November 1765. The *Public Advertiser* on 25 January

Civica Raccolta Stampe A. Bertarelli, Castello Sforzesco, Milan

CLEMENTINA SPAGNOLI

artist unknown

1766 indicated that she had been ill and missed a number of performances:

The Italian opera has suffered considerably, this season, by the inability of Sga Spagnoli to exert her musical talents, owing to a most severe cold; but as she has now recovered her voice, 'tis presumed that she will be a source of as great pleasure, among us, to persons of a musical ear, and who have a true taste for that species of dramas, as she was in her native country, where she was always heard with great applause.

On 19 April she sang in *Sofonisba,* but the papers did not specify her role.

We believe she was the singer Clementina Spagnoli cited in the Milan catalogue of prints and drawings: "Canto nell'opera Armida nel Teatro dell'Accademia Filarmonica, Verona, 1774." She was pictured in an engraving by an unknown artist.

Spagnolla. *See* SPAGNOLI.

Spalden. *See* SPALDING.

Spalding, Mr [*fl. 1694–c. 1700*], *singer.*
Manuscript notes in the music for *Macbeth* in the British Library name Mr Spalding as one of the singers; the work was performed in late 1694 at Drury Lane or Dorset Garden Theatre. About 1700 a duet was published by Eccles from *The Morose Reformer* (possibly the same as *Justice Busy*); Courco and Spalding are named as the singers.

Spalding, Richard [*fl. 1697–1699*], *singer.*
On 28 June 1698 Mrs Sarah Spalding was to be paid £20 and clothing for her son Richard Spalding, a former child of the Chapel Royal whose voice had changed. The payment was for the year 1697. Young Richard was still receiving maintenance in 1699.

Spandau, Herr [*fl. 1773–1780*], *horn player, composer.*
Herr Spandau played French horn in the band of the Stadtholder of the United Provinces and came to London in early 1773 to play at the King's Theatre, beginning on 5 February, and at Covent Garden Theatre, beginning on 26 February. He appeared at both houses

during March and played at the Haymarket Theatre on 19 April. Dr Burney later heard Spandau at the Hague and complimented his expression, taste, and delicacy. Spandau and his son were first and second horn at the Hague opera house in 1780. Spandau composed a few pieces for horn, but they were not published.

"Spangle Jack." *See* KEMBLE, JOHN PHILIP.

"Spaniard, The Famous." *See* "FAMOUS SPANIARD, THE."

"Spaniard, The Little." *See* "LITTLE SPANIARD, THE."

"Spanish Horse." *See* GIBRALTAR.

"Spanish Lady." *See* BALPH, MME, and REDIGÉ, MME PAULO.

"Spanish Little Devil, The," stage name of Felix Balagay [fl. 1784–1790], *acrobat.*

Since the publication of the first volume of this *Dictionary* we have discovered information about Felix Balagay (or Phelix Balaguay), "The Spanish Little Devil." He was with a company for Sadler's Wells, London, performing at Coopers' Hall in Bristol on 11 December 1784 and subsequent dates. His specialty was tumbling, but the bills did not provide any details. When he and his cohorts from Sadler's Wells appeared on 29 October 1787 at Chester, however, the bill declared that "The Spanish LITTLE DEVIL PHELIX BALAGAY, Will perform the Grand SAUT DE TRAMPELIN. With a Variety of SOMERSETS, FLIP-FLAPS, and SAUT DES SINGE, And many other unparalleled PERFORMANCES." Balagay performed again in Bristol on 26 April 1790, this time with Handy's circus.

"Spanish Pig." *See* "REAL GIGANTIC SPANISH PIG, THE."

Sparkes, Mrs [fl. 1776]. *See* SPARKS, MRS G. HUGH.

Sparkling. *See* SPARLING.

Sparks, G. Hugh   1752–1816, *actor, singer, prompter.*

Among the theatrical cuttings at the British Library is a brief biography of the actor Hugh Sparks. He was born in 1752 in Scotland of respectable parents and though intended for the church left college abruptly in 1769 and made his stage debut in Dundee with Fisher's troupe. He remained with that company for "some years."

While attached to it, the company made a voyage to Denmark and Russia. At Copenhagen they performed before the Danish King and Queen; and, at St Petersburg, the Czarina, Catherine II, did not disdain, for a while, to unbend from the cares of government, and witness their representation of several English plays. Mr. Sparks, it is believed, was one of the last survivors of those who formed this expedition. He subsequently belonged to different provincial companies, and was, for a long period, prompter at the Edinburgh theatre, while under the management of Mr. Digges.

Sparks was named in Edinburgh bills as early as 5 April 1777.

Like many prompters, Hugh Sparks amassed a sizable number of roles over the years at Edinburgh, as the research of Norma Armstrong shows. Among his parts were Alderman Gripeall in *The Intriguing Chambermaid*, Alonzo and Gonsalez in *The Mourning Bride*, Antonio in *Love Makes a Man*, Aristander and Cassander in *The Rival Queens*, the banished Duke in *As You Like It*, Banquo, Duncan, and Lennox in *Macbeth*, Belmour in *Jane Shore*, Blunder in *The Honest Yorkshireman*, Bonniface in *The Beaux' Stratagem*, Brabantio, the Duke, and Gratiano in *Othello*, Cacafogo in *Rule a Wife and Have a Wife*, Serjeant Flower, Canton, and Sterling in *The Clandestine Marriage*, Captain Dudley in *The West Indian*, Capulet in *Romeo and Juliet*, Careless, Rowley, and Sir Oliver in *The School for Scandal*, the Chaplain in *The Orphan*, Charon in *Lethe*, Crispin Heeltap in *The Mayor of Garratt*, Cymbeline, Dapper in *The Citizen*, Diggory, the Landlord, and Sir Charles Marlow in *She Stoops to Conquer*, Dr Caius and Page in *The Merry Wives of Windsor*, Dr Hellebore in *The Mock Doctor*, Don Pedro, the Friar, and Leonato in *Much Ado about Nothing*, and Doodle in *Tom Thumb*.

Also the Duke and Tubal in *The Merchant of Venice*, Orsino in *Twelfth Night*, Father Paul in *The Duenna*, Faulkland in *The Rivals*, Gloucester in *King Lear*, Gonzalo in *The Tempest*, the Governor in *Oroonoko*, Hortensio and Baptista in *Catherine and Petruchio*, John Moody in *The Provok'd Husband*, Johnson in *The Rehearsal*, Claudius, the Player King, and Polonius in *Hamlet*, Lord Randolph and Old Norval in *Douglas*, Lord Stanley in *Richard III*, Lockit in *The Beggar's Opera*, Strickland and Tester in *The Suspicious Husband*, Priuli in *Venice Preserv'd*, Sir Archy Macsarcasm in *Love à la Mode*, Sir Jealous Traffic in *The Busy Body*, Sir John Belvil in *The Conscious Lovers*, Sir Sampson Legend in *Love for Love*, Sir William Meadows in *Love in a Village*, Sneer in *The Critic*, a Spirit in *Comus*, and Worcester in *1 Henry IV*. Sparks acted at Edinburgh at least as late as 1794. Perhaps he was the Sparks at the Theatre Royal in Chester in October and November 1787, when he was not listed for any roles in Edinburgh. And he may have been the Sparks at Liverpool on 5 September 1791; only in February and July 1791 was Sparks down for roles in Edinburgh. With Hugh Sparks in Edinburgh was his wife Sarah, née Mills.

On 5 December 1797 Sparks made his London debut, acting Gibby in *The Wonder* at Drury Lane Theatre. The receipts came to a disappointing £88 14s. The *Monthly Mirror* doubted that the house had £30 in it that night but praised Sparks as being "perfectly in character as to the brogue." Mrs Sparks had made her Drury Lane debut the previous October. During the rest of the 1797–98 season Sparks was seen as the Music Master in *Catherine and Petruchio*, the Coachman in *The Wheel of Fortune*, Lord Burleigh in *The Critic*, Ali Beg in *The Mountaineers*, and Paul Peery in *Ways and Means*. Sparks and his wife acted at Birmingham during the summer of 1798.

Hugh Sparks performed at Drury Lane until his death in 1816. His salary in 1798–99 was a modest £1 10s. weekly. By 1804–5 he and his wife earned together £6 weekly, but his value to the company deteriorated over the years, and from 1811–12 until his death he was paid only £1 weekly. Mrs Sparks, on the other hand, climbed to at least £10 weekly.

Over the years Sparks was seen in such parts as Sir Jasper Wilding in *The Citizen*, Seward in *Macbeth*, Oxford in *Richard III*, A Scotchman in *The Apprentice*, Seacoal in *Much Ado about Nothing*, a Muleteer in *The Outlaws*, the First Stockbroker in *A Bold Stroke for a Wife*, Malachi

in *The Young Quaker*, Nimming Ned in *The Beggar's Opera*, Sir Walter Manny in *The Surrender of Calais*, Philip in *High Life below Stairs* (at the Haymarket on 17 December 1798 at a special benefit for the former Drury Lane manager Lacy), the Priest in *Love Makes a Man*, Bonaventure in *Aurelio and Miranda*, Item in *Will and No Will*, a Bravo in *The Inconstant*, Antonio in *The Tempest*, the Second Gravedigger in *Hamlet*, Traverse in *The Clandestine Marriage*, Sawney in *The Embarkation*, a Shoemaker in *A Trip to Scarborough*, Gratiano in *Othello*, a Parish Officer in *Man and Wife*, Pennyman in *John Bull*, the Bailiff in *Honest Thieves*, a Planter in *Inkle and Yarico*, the Jailor in *The Way to Get Married*, Alguazil in *She Wou'd and She Wou'd Not*, and a Witch in *Macbeth*.

On 6 July 1813 he signed himself G. H. Sparks on a receipt for £3 from Drury Lane; on 15 July 1815 he signed himself Hugh Sparks on a similar receipt for £9. We take it that his name was G. Hugh Sparks.

Though Sparks did not earn much at Drury Lane, he was greatly admired. The theatrical cutting at the British Library contains praise for his good judgment of other performers, the esteem in which he was held by his fellows, his good humor, and his benevolent nature. "His tenacious memory was well stored with amusing anecdotes of all the great performers of his day, which, in his convivial hours, he related with great pleasantry."

Hugh Sparks died on 3 March 1816 at the age of 64 at his house on Tavistock Street. He was buried at St James's Chapel, Kentish Town Row, Camden Town. (The *Thespian Magazine* said he was buried at the New Chapel, Tottenham Court Road.) His will, made on 5 June 1815 and proved on 29 April 1816 identified Sparks as of Drury Lane Theatre. He left his entire estate to his wife Sarah.

The relationship between Hugh Sparks and other performers named Sparks is not clear. The *Authentic Memoirs of the Green Room* in 1799 said Sparks was "nearly related to the famous [Isaac] Sparkes, who was renowned in Dublin, by the title of Lord Chief Justice Joker."

Sparks, Mrs G. Hugh, Sarah, née Mills
1754–1837, actress, singer.

Sarah Mills was born in 1754, according to the report of her age at her death. Her parents were Joseph and Mary Mills, and her lineage was most likely theatrical. Earlier in the eighteenth century John Mills (d. 1736) and his wife Margaret had been actors, and their son William (d. 1750) and both his first and second wives were performers. Siblings of Sarah Mills were the Miss Mills who married, first, William Ross and then J. Brown and was the mother of the American actor John Mills Brown; the Eleanor Mills who married the younger James Chalmers; the actor John Mills, who died about 1785; and the Mr Mills who was acting at the Haymarket Theatre in 1786. Yet we have found no evidence of our subject's parents acting or of their relationship to the theatrical Millses of the century.

The only record we have of Sarah Mills acting before her marriage comes from William Dunlap, who has her performing at Berwick (upon Tweed, apparently—near Edinburgh) in the summer of 1773. By April 1776 Sarah was married to the actor G. Hugh Sparks. That month at Edinburgh she had a benefit at which she donned breeches to play Sir Archy Macsarcasm in *Love à la Mode*. She gave her address as the corner of Meuse Lane, New Town. A Mrs "Sparkes" played Lady Ancient in *The Prejudice of Fashion* at the Haymarket Theatre in London on 7 October 1776. She was probably Mrs Hugh Sparks from Edinburgh, since the mainpiece on the bill was the Scottish *Gentle Shepherd*, and *The Prejudice of Fashion* was by an unnamed gentleman from Edinburgh.

Mrs Sparks was named in Edinburgh bills again in 1777 and 1779. Mr and Mrs Sparks were apparently at the Theatre Royal in Chester in October and November 1787, and Mrs Sparks acted at Newcastle in 1788 and 1789. At Edinburgh from 1776 to 1794 Mrs Sparks played a wide variety of characters, as the research of Norma Armstrong has shown. Among her many roles were Ariel in *The Tempest*, Betty, Mrs Heidelberg, and Miss Sterling in *The Clandestine Marriage*, Betty in *Hob in the Well*, Bridget in *The Chapter of Accidents*, Mrs Candour and Lady Sneerwell in *The School for Scandal*, Catherine in *Catherine and Petruchio*, Celia in *As You Like It*, Charlotte in *The West Indian*, Cherry in *The Beaux' Stratagem*, Donna Louisa in *The Duenna*, Elvira and Louisa in *Love Makes a Man*, Emilia in *Othello*, and Flora in *The Wonder*.

Also Goneril in *King Lear*, Jacintha and Lucetta in *The Suspicious Husband*, Jessica and Nerissa in *The Merchant of Venice*, Kitty Pry and Melissa in *The Lying Valet*, Lady Allworth in *A New Way to Pay Old Debts*, Lady Anne in *Richard III*, Lady Macbeth, Lavinia in *The Fair Penitent*, Lucinda and Madge in *Love in a Village*, Lucy and Lydia in *The Rivals*, Lucy, Mrs Slammekin, and Polly in *The Beggar's Opera*, Mademoiselle in *The Provok'd Wife*, Madge in *The Gentle Shepherd*, Margaret in *Much Ado about Nothing*, Miranda in *The Busy Body*, Miss Biddy in *Miss in Her Teens*, Miss Harlow in *The Old Maid*, Miss Hoyden in *A Trip to Scarborough*, Jenny, Myrtilla, and Trusty in *The Provok'd Husband*, Miss Tittup in *Bon Ton*, Mrs Ford and Mrs Page in *The Merry Wives of Windsor*, Mrs Frail and Mrs Foresight in *Love for Love*, Nell in *The Devil to Pay*, Ophelia and Gertrude in *Hamlet*, Phillis in *The Conscious Lovers*, Sysigambis in *The Rival Queens*, and Viletta in *She Wou'd and She Wou'd Not*.

Mr and Mrs Sparks came to London in the fall of 1797 to perform at Drury Lane Theatre. She was first seen on 26 October as Miss Harlow in *The Old Maid*. After that she continued acting more and more important roles, establishing herself as one of the leading Drury Lane comic actresses of the last years of the eighteenth century and the first 20 years of the nineteenth. Among her characters were Lady Restless in *All in the Wrong*, Mrs Sneak in *The Mayor of Garratt*, a Poor Woman in *Knave or Not*, Mrs Goodison in *the Jew*, Olivia in *The Italian Monk*, Mrs Casey in *A Nosegay of Weeds*, Lady Bountiful in *The Beaux' Stratagem*, Dorca in *The Outlaws*, Lady Freelove in *The Jealous Wife* (in a special performance at the Haymarket), Leonella in *Aurelio and Miranda*, Mrs Fardingale in *The Funeral*, Mrs Wisely in *The Miser*, Alice in *The Castle Spectre*, Mrs Gadabout in *The Lying Valet*, Diana Trapes in *The Beggar's Opera*, Dorcas in *Rosina*, Mrs Hardcastle in *She Stoops to Conquer*, Mrs Malaprop in *The Rivals*, the title role in *The Duenna*, Deborah Woodcock in *Love in a Village*, Bianca in *The Cabinet*, Mrs Day in *Honest Thieves*, Mrs Druggett in *Three Weeks after Marriage*, Mrs Quickly in *The Merry Wives of Windsor*, Mrs Amlet in *The Confederacy*, Lady Dunder in *Ways and Means*, the Nurse in *Romeo and Juliet*, the Nurse in *Love for Love*, Isabella in *The Castle of Andalusia*, Lady Oldboy in *Lionel and Cla-*

rissa, Lady Sycamore in *The Maid of the Mill,* Lady Bull in *Fontainebleau,* Dame Ashfield in *Speed the Plough,* and Widow Warren in *The Road to Ruin.*

In 1799 the *Authentic Memoirs of the Green Room* thought that "This lady's theatrical career is almost over—She had her day and many her admirers! Still she is a useful performer, and we hope will retain her engagement at Drury-Lane. . . ." She kept it another 21 years. Her salary increased from £3 to £10 weekly by the 1818–19 season, while her husband's declined. Her fame increased as well. Thomas Dutton in *The Dramatic Censor,* writing of Mrs Sparks as Mrs Heidelberg in *The Clandestine Marriage* in June 1800, claimed that she "only wants to be more generally known, to be more universally approved. She supported the character in a very respectable manner, and evinced herself deserving of greater encouragement than she appears to experience." Gilliland felt that until "the secession of Mrs Walcot" Mrs Sparks's talents were not sufficiently used, but since then she had progressed, to the great satisfaction of the public, specializing in antiquated ladies.

William Hazlitt, writing about *The Hypocrite* at Drury Lane on 17 September 1815, said

Mrs. Sparks's old Lady Lambert, is, we think, one of the finest exhibitions of character on the stage. The attention she pays to Dr. Cantewell, her expression of face and her fixed uplifted hands, were a picture which Hogarth might have copied. The effects of the *spirit* in reviving the withered ardour of youth, and giving a second birth to forgotten raptures, were never better exemplified.

But in the *Examiner* on 4 May 1817 Hazlitt heartily disliked a production of *The Rivals* in which the roles were reversed.

Dowton . . . played *Mrs. Malaprop,* and Mrs. Sparks played *Sir Anthony Absolute.* We cannot say much of these transformations, for the performers themselves remained just the same, breeches and petticoats out of the question; nothing was transformed or ridiculous but their dress. Dowton was as blunt and bluff, and Mrs. Sparks was as keen, querulous, and scolding, as in any of their usual characters. The effect was flat after the first *entrée,* and the whole play was, in other respects, very poorly got up. . . .

Hugh Sparks died in 1816, leaving his entire estate to his widow. She continued per-

forming until 1820, when she retired on a pension from Drury Lane. Harriot Mellon, who became the Duchess of St Albans, settled an annuity on Mrs Sparks which, with the pension, allowed her to live comfortably to the age of 83. She died on 3 or 4 February 1837 at Farnham. The *Observer* of 19 February remembered her as an "excellent woman, who for many years was one of the brightest ornaments of the national stage. . . ."

Sarah Sparks is pictured as Miss Bridget Pumpkin, with other actors, in a scene from *All the World's a Stage,* painted by Samuel De Wilde. Now in the National Theatre, London, the painting is reproduced in this *Dictionary* 5: 284; it is described in detail by Messrs Mander and Mitchenson in *The Artist and the Theatre.*

Sparks, Isaac *1719–1776, actor, singer.*

Isaac Sparks was born on 16 September 1719 in College Street, Dublin, the son of a staymaker, according to the *Hibernian Magazine* of May 1776 and the scrapbooks of W. J. Lawrence. Isaac's older brother was Luke Sparks, and their family was probably related—but in what way is not certain—to the actor Hugh Sparks of later in the century. The *Hibernian Magazine* said that Isaac first appeared as a child playing Peachum in *The Beggar's Opera* to little Peg Woffington's Polly at Signora Violante's booth in George Lane, Dublin.

In 1734–35 and 1735–36 Sparks was acting at the Ransford Street Theatre in Dublin and in about 1736 he played in Sligo. He was at Smock Alley in Dublin in 1738–39 and received a benefit on 5 February 1739, when he made his first appearance as Sir John Brute in *The Provok'd Wife.* In 1739–40 Sparks was again at Smock Alley, three of his parts being the Second Buyer in *The Lottery,* a Servant in *The Hussar,* and the title role in *The Mock Lawyer.* At Smock Alley in 1740–41 he played Hackum in *The Squire of Alsatia.* From 1741–42 through 1743–44 he acted at the Aungier Street playhouse, appearing as Malvolio in *Twelfth Night,* Ben in *Love for Love,* Brazen in *The Recruiting Officer,* Gloster in *Jane Shore,* and Tubal in *The Merchant of Venice.* He was at Smock Alley in 1744–45, one of his new characters being the Miller's Man in *The Necromancer.*

"I. Sparkes" from Dublin played Bonniface

ISAAC SPARKS, as Jobson

artist unknown

Coachman in *The Drummer*, Bardolph in *Henry V*, Major Rakish in *The School Boy*, and the Miller in *The King and the Miller of Mansfield*. As of his shared benefit on 2 May 1748 Isaac Sparks was staying at Mr Pope's at the White Peruke in Russell Street, Covent Garden.

Sparks returned to Dublin to act at Smock Alley from 1748–49 through 1757–58; in 1758–59 and 1759–60 he was at Crow Street, and in 1760–61 and 1761–62 he performed again at Smock Alley. Only two of his parts for that period are known: Jobson in *The Devil to Pay* and Peachum in *The Beggar's Opera*. In the summer of 1761 Sparks played at the Vaults in Belfast with a Dublin company. By then Isaac had grown obese and unwieldly, stated the *Hibernian Magazine*, "but despite his double chin and comic vocation, his person was always majestic and commanding. . . ."

During his career Isaac Sparks acted frequently in the Irish county towns. W. S. Clark traces him to Cork in the summers of 1755, 1757, and 1758, Belfast in the summer of 1761, Cork in the autumns of 1762, 1763, 1765, and 1766, Limerick in October 1768 and September 1771, and Cork in the sum-

in *The Stratagem* at Drury Lane Theatre in London on 19 September 1745. On the twenty-fourth he acted Bluff in *The Old Bachelor;* L. Sparks (his brother Luke) played Heartwell. Isaac remained at Drury Lane through the 1747–48 season, playing such parts as Kite in *The Recruiting Officer*, Glumdalca in *The Tragedy of Tragedies*, Dr Butts in *Henry VIII*, Charles in *As You Like It*, Jolt in *The Stage Coach*, Balderdash in *The Twin Rivals*, a Neighbour in *The Contrivances*, Caliban in *The Tempest*, the Magistrate in *Harlequin Incendiary*, the Constable in *The Lying Lover*, Mixum in *The Vintner Trick'd*, Elbow in *Measure for Measure*, a Carrier in *1 Henry IV*, Old Wilful in *The Double Gallant*, Simon in *The Anatomist*, the Surgeon in *The Sea Voyage*, Serjeant Fileoff in *The Humours of the Army*, Mopsa in *Damon and Phillida*, Quack in *The Country Wife*, Ralph in *Marry or Do Worse*, Moody in *The Provok'd Husband*, the Soothsayer in *Julius Caesar*, Obadiah in *The Committee*, a Traveller in *The Scornful Lady*, a

ISAAC SPARKS—"The Right Comical Chief Joker"

by Delane

mers of 1773 and 1774. At Cork in the 1750s Sparks on his off-nights repaired to the Cork Arms Tavern in Castle Street near the Exchange and the County Court House. In 1753 and later Sparks entertained people by presiding over a weekly mock trial, as he had done at a Nassau Street tavern in Dublin.

Since we have found no Irish activity for Sparks in 1767, he was probably the Sparks in England that year, touring Shrewsbury, Bridgnorth, and Chester. In 1769 he came again to London. On 15 May, hailed as from Dublin and making his first appearance on the Haymarket stage, Sparks played a principal character in *The Devil upon Two Sticks* and Blister in *The Virgin Unmask'd*. He donned a skirt to play Mrs Loveit in *The Commissary* on 24 May and acted Timothy Peascod in *The What D'Ye Call It* on 26 May. During the remainder of the summer Sparks was seen as Foigard in *The Beaux' Stratagem*, Mixum in *The Vintner Trick'd*, Heeltap in *The Mayor of Garratt*, Lockit in *The Beggar's Opera*, the First Gravedigger in *Hamlet*, the Queen of the Giants in *Tom Thumb*, Vamp in *The Author*, the Lord Mayor in *Richard III*, Noll Bluff in *The Old Bachelor*, and a Plebeian in *Julius Caesar*.

On 2 November 1769 "I. Sparks" played John Moody in *The Provok'd Husband* at Drury Lane. He went on that season to appear as Caliban in *The Tempest*, Captain O'Blunder in *The Brave Irishman*, and Sir Sampson in *Love for Love*. In May 1770 Sparks also acted at the Haymarket—playing both there and at Drury Lane on 23 May. In June at the Haymarket he was seen in some new characters: Hob in *Hob in the Well*, Alderman Pentweazle in *Taste*, and Driver in *Oroonoko*. He was at Drury Lane in 1770–71 but seems to have acted only in *The Tempest* and *The Provok'd Husband*. When on 7 May 1771 he acted John Moody in *The Provok'd Husband* his son Richard made his first and last London appearance, playing Lord Townly. (For Richard's suspected piracy of Garrick's *Stratford Jubilee* and Garrick's fury at Isaac and his son, see Richard Sparks's entry.) Father and son were back at the Crow Street Theatre in Dublin in the summer of 1771. After that, Isaac Sparks seems not to have acted again. Perhaps Isaac was the Sparks who, with Waddy and Vandermere, erected the Fishamble Street Theatre in Dublin in the 1770s.

Faulkner's Dublin Journal reported that Isaac Sparks died on 21 April 1776. His wife, the former Ann Holland, had died in May 1756. Chetwood in his *General History* in 1749 had described Sparks in his prime as a tall figure. He had a good vein of humor, Chetwood said, and played Sir Sampson Legend in *Love for Love* to perfection. Yet, according to the *Dublin Evening Post* on 29 May 1779, in his best days Isaac Sparks, "whose merit is universally acknowledged, long laboured for 12s per week. . . ." In *A General View of the Stage* in 1759 Thomas Wilkes wrote:

Mr. J. [i.e., I.] Sparks is not only a useful but a very diverting Comedian: that pleasantry of temper which is habitual to him will not admit him to give a false colouring to any humourous character. In the hearty Old Men of Comedy he has great merit, particularly in Sir Sampson Legend. His Foigard is nearer to nature than any other performer's; but his Teague in the Committee has not the vivacity of Barrington's. In Foigard he is very expressive of that ridiculous gravity which is the result of pedantry and ignorance. He perfectly well supports all the oddity, wildness, and extravagance of Caliban. His Peachum and Serjeant Kite are humourous draughts of nature; and his merit lies in low Comedy.

The *Thespian Magazine* in 1805 wrote of Isaac Sparks as a good comedian and excellent clown in pantomimes. He was "president of a facetious club, and distinguished by the title of Lord Chief Justice Joker. . . . He died upwards of twenty years ago. . . ."

Isaac Sparks is pictured by Solomon Delane as "The Right Comical Chief Joker" in a portrait "Painted from Life" and etched by the artist, published in 1752 by Samuel Price, Dublin. A portrait by an anonymous engraver of Sparks as Foigard in *The Stratagem* was published as a plate to the *Hibernian Magazine*, May 1776; a copy of it, a process print on China paper, is in the Harvard Theatre Collection. An anonymous engraving of Sparks as Jobson in *The Devil to Pay* was published in the *Hibernian Magazine*.

Sparks, James *b. 1753, actor.*

James Sparks was born in 1753, the son of Luke and Grace Sparks. The Richmond parish registers note his baptism on 4 April 1753. When Luke Sparks died in December 1768 he left £1000 to James but directed his executors to decide when the money should be given to the lad. In the fall of 1773 James was one of the rioters at Covent Garden Theatre when Macklin's *Macbeth* caused such a stir. Sparks made his London stage debut at China Hall, Rotherhithe, on 25 September 1776, playing Young Fashion in *Miss Hoyden*. On 14 October he was Young Wilding in *The Citizen*. At the Haymarket Theatre on 11 January 1779 Sparks acted Freeport in *The Students* and then played Whisk in *The Prejudice of Fashion*, Colonel Raymond in *The Foundling*, Saville in *Wit's Last Stake*, and Lord Randolph in *Douglas* by mid-May. He returned to the Haymarket in 1782 to appear as Vermil in *The Temple Beau* on 21 September and Valentine in *Wit without Money* on 25 November.

Sparks, Luke   *1711–1768, actor, manager.*

Luke Sparks, the elder brother of Isaac Sparks, was born in Ireland in 1711. His father was a staymaker, according to the *Hibernian Magazine* of May 1776. The Sparks family was probably related to Hugh Sparks, who acted in the late eighteenth century. W. R. Chetwood in his *General History* in 1749 told a tale (that may be true) of the early acting efforts of Luke Sparks. Signora Violante had a theatrical booth in Dublin which she let

to Mr. *Luke Sparks,* Mr. *John Barrington,* Miss *Mackay* (now Mrs. *Mitchel*), for three Pounds *per* Week: The three mentioned Persons, being all very young, fell desperately in Love with the *Dramatic Poets,* and were resolved to marry them, with their Poetical Fortune, that is, without a Rag to cover their Nakedness, or rather nothing but Rags; for their Scenes had shewed their best Days. However, Cloaths were borrowed, some from Friends, and some to be paid for; and they began with a Comedy of *Farquhar*'s, call'd *The Inconstant,* or, *The Way to win him;* the three chief Parts being performed by the three adventurous Undertakers; *viz.*

Young Mirabel		Mr. Sparks
Duretete	by	Mr. Barrington
Bisarre		Miss Mackay.

Mr. *Sparks* (as having played before, in a Country Company) was the *Manager.* The Play was performed much better than was expected, and their Company soon became more numerous, being join'd by others that look'd more to *Profit* than *Pleasure;* for these three Lovers of the Drama could play Heroes and Heroines, without eating; Love for the Sublime was enough for them: However, other People did not relish this Cameleon Diet, and hun-

ger'd after something more substantial; therefore resolved upon Benefits, and gave the first to Miss *Mackay,* in order to break the Ice. The *Fop's Fortune* was the Play, and she then being a young promising Actress, several Ladies, of the first Rank, espous'd her Cause, and brought upwards of Forty Pounds to her Benefit. They might well say, with the Herald in the *Rehearsal,*
> They had not seen so much the Lord knows when.

The Success of this Benefit alarmed the *Old Smock-alley House,* who applying to the *Lord Mayor,* he sent Orders to forbid their Acting; and it was with much Difficulty they had Leave to play one more, which was, *Woman's a Riddle,* to a good House,
> And that the last.

This was the Spring from whence *Ransford-street* arose, out of the Power of the *Lord Mayor* of *Dublin.*

Luke Sparks began his professional stage career at the Ransford Street playhouse in 1732–33, but his first known role was Ben in *Love for Love* at Smock Alley Theatre on 5 February 1733. He was at Ransford Street from 1733–34 through 1735–36, two of his roles being Florez in *The Royal Merchant* and Iago in *Othello*. At Smock Alley in 1736–37 he played Gloucester in *Richard III* and in 1737–38 acted Belfond junior in *The Squire of Alsatia*, Francesco in *The Sharper*, Volpone, Brazen in *The Recruiting Officer*, and Brisk in *The Double Dealer*. He was at Smock Alley in 1738–39 and 1739–40, acting in the latter season, Maskwell in *The Double Dealer* and Manly in *The Plain Dealer*.

Luke was surely the Sparks who acted Young Wouldbe in *The Twin Rivals* at Covent Garden Theatre in London on 12 April 1739. Sparks shared a benefit on 30 April and repeated Young Wouldbe at Drury Lane Theatre on 18 May. He was identified as from the Theatre Royal, Dublin.

Sparks acted at the Aungier Street Theatre in Dublin from 1741–42 through 1743–44, appearing as the First Spirit in *Comus*, Pyrrhus in *The Distrest Mother*, Myrtle in *The Conscious Lovers*, Pierre in *Venice Preserv'd*, Peachum in *The Beggar's Opera*, Gratiano in *The Merchant of Venice*, Marcian in *Theodosius*, and Ramirez in *Love and Loyalty*. With the United Company at Smock Alley in 1744–45 Sparks played Young Wouldbe in *The Twin Rivals* and Sempronius in *Cato*.

Luke and Isaac Sparks had an engagement at Drury Lane in 1745–46, Luke making his first appearance on 24 September 1745 as

Heartwell in *The Old Bachelor.* He then went on to appear as Dr Wolf in *The Non-Juror,* Syphax in *Cato,* the Bishop of Winchester in *Lady Jane Gray,* Jaques in *As You Like It,* the First Spirit in *Comus,* Hothead in *Sir Courtly Nice,* Don Sebastian in *The Sea Voyage,* Young Wouldbe in *The Twin Rivals,* Frion in *Henry VII,* Wolsey in *Henry VIII,* Buckingham in *Richard III,* Horatio in *The Fair Penitent,* Prospero in *The Tempest,* Iago in *Othello,* Gratiano in *The Merchant of Venice,* and (for his benefit on 9 April 1746) Vizard in *The Vintner Trick'd.* Tickets were available from him at the "Silk Dyer's" near Castle Tavern.

Luke stayed on a Drury Lane for the 1746–47 and 1747–48 seasons, acting such new roles as Lenox in *Macbeth,* Acasto in *The Orphan,* Wilmot in *The Humours of the Army,* the King in *1 Henry IV,* Ventidius in *All for Love,* Renault in *Venice Preserv'd,* Sealand in *The Conscious Lovers,* the Bastard in *King John,* Cassius in *Julius Caesar,* Morochius in *The Merchant of Venice,* Claudius in *Hamlet,* Omar in *Tamerlane,* Albumazar, Antonio in *Twelfth Night,* Phillip in *She Wou'd and She Wou'd Not,* and the Constable of France in *Henry V.* Benefit tickets were available in March 1747 at his lodgings at the corner of Broad Court, Bow Street, Covent Garden; a year later his tickets could be purchased at Courteen's Coffee House in Bow Street.

The Dramatic Censor by Gentleman (1770) had fine things to say of his Claudius: "Sparks was the only person who did not make an insipid figure in it—he was great in the soliloquy . . . peculiarly happy in falling from the throne" when killed. At the New Concert Hall in Edinburgh in the summer of 1748 Luke Sparks played such new characters as Aboan in *Oroonoko,* Clitus in *The Rival Queens,* Gloster in *Jane Shore,* the title role in *The Mock Doctor,* Polydore in *The Orphan,* and Falstaff in *1 Henry IV.*

Sparks began the 1748–49 season at Drury Lane, but after appearing in *Hamlet* on 14 October 1748 he moved to Covent Garden Theatre to act the King in *1 Henry IV* on the seventeenth. There he remained until 1765, playing his standard parts and adding such new ones to his repertoire as Cassander in *The Rival Queens,* Norfolk in *Henry VIII,* Angelo in *Measure for Measure,* Woolfort and Clause in *The Royal Merchant,* Corvino in *Volpone,* Bra-

bantio in *Othello,* Pedro in *The Rover,* Casca and Brutus in *Julius Caesar,* the Governor in *Love Makes a Man,* Doctor Baliardo in *The Emperor of the Moon,* Muley Moluch in *Don Sebastian,* Blunt in *The Committee,* Bajazet in *Tamerlane,* Kite in *The Recruiting Officer,* Kent in *King Lear,* Sciolto in *The Fair Penitent,* the Lord Chief Justice in *2 Henry IV,* the Stranger and Old Norval in *Douglas,* Charinus in *The Prophetess,* Medley in *The Man of Mode,* Duncan in *Macbeth,* Northumberland in *Lady Jane Gray,* Burleigh in *The Unhappy Favorite,* and Canterbury in *Henry V.*

Also Capulet in *Romeo and Juliet,* Antonio in *The Merchant of Venice,* Manly in *The Provok'd Husband,* Banquo in *Macbeth,* Serapion in *All for Love,* Pandulph and the King in *King John,* Lusignan in *Zara,* Roderigo in *The Pilgrim,* Gloucester in *King Lear,* Tamerlane, Leon in *Rule a Wife and Have a Wife,* Pierre in *Venice Preserv'd,* Standard in *The Constant Couple,* Volusius in *Coriolanus,* Balance in *The Recruiting Officer,* Smith in *The Rehearsal,* the King in *The Mourning Bride,* Sullen in *The Strategem,* Oldrents in *The Jovial Crew,* Richard Wealthy in *The Minor,* Strickland in *The Suspicious Husband,* Dominic in *The Spanish Fryar,* Old Knowell in *Every Man in His Humour,* Surly in *Sir Courtly Nice,* and Sir Jealous Traffic in *The Busy Body.*

Sparks was earning £6 weekly at Covent Garden in 1749–50; his salary was over £7 weekly by 1761. At some point he married. His wife Grace had a daughter, Margaret, in 1743; she became Mrs Vernon and, in 1765 Mrs Thomas Death. She seems not to have acted in London. Mrs Death died in 1769. A daughter Elizabeth was born to Luke and Grace Sparks on 1 August 1748 and christened on 3 August, according to the Richmond parish registers. The couple had a son who was christened James at Richmond on 4 April 1753. James appeared briefly on the London stage and is separately entered in this *Dictionary.* Sparks and his wife were living in Crown Court in the spring of 1762.

After the 1764–65 season Luke Sparks retired to Brentford Butts, near Richmond. At the Victoria and Albert Museum is a letter of thanks from Sparks to David Garrick, written in July 1768. In it he said, "I must confess the disposal of my son has laid heavier upon my Mind, than even the cause which forc'd me from the Theatre, he being the youngest and least capable of helping himself. . . ." Young James Sparks had evidently persuaded Garrick to support his quest for a supernumerary civil position; he was turned down, as a letter dated 2 July 1768 from Richard Rigby to Garrick makes clear. What forced Luke Sparks from the stage is not known, but he was ill for about three months in the spring of 1762, and perhaps he retired because of poor health. The *Public Advertiser* reported that Sparks died at Brentford Butts on 29 December 1768. He was buried on 3 January 1769. (The inscription on his tombstone at Brentford states that he died on 28 December 1768 at the age of 57, according to Lysons in his *Environs of London*.)

Sparks's will, undated and unsigned, was proved on 2 June 1769. He asked two of his friends to assist his widow with his estate, checking the worth of his securities and reinvesting if necessary, according to his widow's wishes. Sparks left £1000 to his daughter Sarah and another £1000 to his son James— to be given James when the executors felt he was old enough. Sparks directed that a shilling should be given to his daughter Grace Sparks every 29 February, her birthday. He left nothing to his son Robert or his daughter Mary, having already provided them with large sums. The will and the Richmond registers identify the following Sparks children: Margaret, Elizabeth, James, Sarah, Grace, Robert, and Mary. Elizabeth was not named in the will, so she may have died before the will was drawn up. Margaret, having married, was already provided for. Sparks also left Frances Leigh and her husband £10 each for mourning; Mrs Leigh's daughter Elizabeth Storey was to receive £200.

Luke Sparks, as one can tell from the many important roles he was given, was a popular actor. Samuel Derrick in *The Dramatic Censor* in 1752 thought Sparks was the finest Renault in *Venice Preserv'd* he had seen: "There is not a *line* which he *speaks* in Renault, but he brings us to *listen to* and *observe,* and conveys the true Idea of the part, better than any man among the numbers whom I have *seen*." The author of *The Present State of the Stage* in 1753 wished Sparks had been allowed to take over more of James Quin's roles. "His playing Young Wou'd-be in the *Twin-Rivals,* shews us his

Merits are not entirely confined to the Serious in Comedy; but that he is capable of giving us Pleasure in *funny* parts." The letters of West Digges and Sarah Ward contain praise of Sparks as a teacher. He helped prepare Miss Nossiter for the stage, and Mrs Gregory, later Mrs Fitzhenry, was his pupil.

The prompter Richard Cross noted in his diary on 27 October 1758 that *The Diversions of the Morning* was to be omitted from the Drury Lane bill, "but the audience called for it so violently, that we were obliged to let [Wilkinson] do it.—he took off Foote and Sheridan & wou'd have left out Sparks, but ye audience would not be satisfied without it. . . ."

Sparks had his faults. The *Theatrical Examiner* in 1757 warned him: "when you play Clitus, be less comical: . . . Ventidius is not a droll, Mr. S——s . . . Pierre is also no comical person!—Mr. S——s would have been a good actor, had he been only a useful one, but on becoming great he grew grotesque!" But the critic said Sparks was excellent as Dr Wolf in *The Non-Juror.* Chetwood in 1749 gave a lukewarm assessment:

MR. Sparks was born in this Kingdom, and has, by incessant Attention to the Drama, arrived to be a well-esteemed Person in the Business of the Theatre; and there are many capital Parts in the Compass of his Power; so that he may be accounted a Person in the highest second Class. I have seen him bear up the Burden of a leading Part to please the Audience, without thinking of a better to stand in his Place. He is equally useful in the *Buskin* and *Sock,* and has the Advantage of a good Person and Voice, join'd to diligent Study. He is esteem'd an excellent Oeconomist, which may be accounted a very valuable Disposition in the *theatrical World;* there is something in the very Science of the Stage that urges on to pleasurable Expence. I knew a Gentleman that call'd *London* the Body of Pleasure, and the Theatre the Heart.

A writer in the *Theatrical Review* in 1757– 58 gave a typically mixed report:

Mr. Sparks commenced actor as well as Mr. Dyer in Ireland; his reception there, as well as here, ran into no extream; very good in some parts, he is at least tolerable in any he undertakes. The same understanding and good sense that keep him from mistaking the characters he is put upon, made him discern early those that become best his voice and person; they have both an honest roughness, an emblem, as I hear, of his private character. We might, perhaps, wish in vain for a better Kent in Lear, Clytus in Alexander, Ventidius in All for Love, &c. he has also in his countenance a half laugh, a mischievous leer, which may easily be improved into hypocrisy; and does not look amiss in a Dr. Wollf, a Maskwell, and the Spanish Fryar. The worst of him is his action, which consists of incoherent motions, that are to the body, what a grimace is to the face; but this springs from a laudable source, an eager desire, which he mistakes for the power of affecting strongly his audience; that desire hurries him often out of nature, so as to betray him into uncoothness, when he strives to express more than he can, or should feel; he has great beauties when he personates Mr. Barry's friend; one would imagine there is then something in his looks more than acting, he is so natural.

Thomas Wilkes in *A General View of the Stage* in 1759 was another critic with mixed feelings about Sparks:

Mr. Sparks is an Actor of merit, and shews the strength of his judgment in chusing Acasto, Sciolto, and parts of that cast in Tragedy, which are well adapted to his years and manner. He stands well in Manly, in the Provoked Husband; and in the part of the Old Batchelor. He requires something of agitated passion in Tragedy, and of importance in Comedy to keep him up; but the former he sometimes overdoes; the latter he permits to degenerate into a strut, and an affectation of Quin's voice; otherwise he may be justly allowed preeminent in his walk.

In his *Dramatic Miscellanies* Thomas Davies remembered Sparks as intelligent, though not a scholar. Sparks took possession of the characters he played but sometimes gave too much harshness to his manner, and his coloring was coarse. His step, said Davies, he often "enlarged into a strut." The harshest criticism came in *The Rosciad of C——v——nt G——rd——n* in 1762:

SP——KS (when enough he had admir'd his
  face,
And fix'd upon each action, each grimace;
When he had nicely parted smile from frown,
Each look, each gesture, mark'd distinctly down,)
Put in his claim—And said no Actor e'er
Was half so useful to a Manager;
For who, like him, can shift from part to part,
By nature dull, yet duller made by art?
When he attempts to shew or rage, or fear,
Some frightful grin, or some affected sneer,

*Dwells on his face, his voice no diff'rence knows,
But ever in the same dull channel flows.*

Sparks, Richard I[saac?] d. 1808, actor, prompter.

Richard I. Sparks was the son of the comedian Isaac Sparks. The *Town and Country Magazine* in September 1770 noted that the younger Sparks was "preparing for the Drury-lane stage, under the tuition of Mr. Garrick; and will shortly make his appearance as a disciple of Melpomene." Garrick was later to regret that he ever allowed Richard Sparks to appear on his London stage.

On 7 May 1771 Richard played Lord Townly in *The Provok'd Husband* at Drury Lane, advertised as a "Young Gentleman, first appearance on any stage." His father acted John Moody that night, and Mrs Abington was Lady Townly. The prompter Hopkins noted in his diary that young Sparks had "a fine figure and met with Applause." But that was Richard's first and last appearance in London. He returned to Dublin (where he had probably been born). The expectation of the *Town and Country Magazine* in May 1771 that young Sparks would become "a striking ornament to the stage" was never realized in London.

Richard was accused of being involved in a literary piracy. Sparks had supposedly helped the manager of the Crow Street Theatre in Dublin obtain a copy of a *Stratford Jubilee* closely resembling Garrick's; when Garrick found out, he was livid, as a letter from him to the actor Moody on 6 June 1771 shows:

I shall not let the affair of the Jubilee rest here; I regard so much yᵉ Credit of yᵉ Theatre, & those who belong to it, that I will stir Heav'n & Earth to bring the Thief to Shame, who took yᵉ Advantage of being permitted behind our Scenes, to plunder & betray Us. . . . We took Sparks yᵉ Father into yᵉ house, & paid him a Sallary for Nothing—not one of yᵉ Family shall ever set his or her Foot upon a Stage that belongs to Me, & by yᵉ 12 Lads of yᵉ Net [the Apostles], I will make both Kingdoms Stink wᵗʰ yᵉ Name of yᵉ Traitor—

Richard Cumberland wrote to Garrick on 4 July 1771 assuring him that the Dublin version of the *Jubilee* was not taken from Garrick's but from magazines, song books, and the like. The Sparkses, he wrote, were "entirely innocent of the plagiary: it seemed probable that they had no hand in it." Garrick was apparently not persuaded.

Richard Sparks and his father were back at the Crow Street Theatre in the summer of 1771, and Richard seems to have remained in Ireland for the rest of his career. He married Miss Frances Ashmore in April 1772 (according to some reports; his wife began acting as Mrs Sparks after January 1772). The pair acted in Dublin, sometimes together and sometimes not, at least through 1792–93. Richard also appeared, according to W. S. Clark's *The Irish Stage in the County Towns,* in Limerick in October 1771, Kilkenny in the summer of 1776 and October 1779, Cork in August 1783, and Belfast in February and March 1800. A promptbook of *Pizarro* at the Bodleian, dated November 1799 is signed by Sparks. Richard is said to have been in Edinburgh in 1782, but the Edinburgh records studied by Norma Armstrong show that the actor there was Hugh Sparks. The *Thespian Magazine* of 1805 said that Sparks acted in tragedy and comedy and was "equally indifferent in both."

After his theatrical career Richard Sparks worked at the Custom House, for the *Hibernian Magazine* in June 1808 so declared when it reported his death.

National Library of Ireland

FRANCES SPARKS, as Leonora

artist unknown

Sparks, Mrs Richard I₍saac₎, Frances, née Ashmore *c. 1749–1805, actress.*

The research of the late W. S. Clark shows that Frances Ashmore was born about 1749 and made her stage debut at the Smock Alley Theatre in Dublin on 12 December 1765. She acted as Miss Ashmore in Dublin—at Smock Alley, Crow Street, and Capel Street—until January 1772, when she began appearing as Mrs Richard I. Sparks. In August and September 1769 she performed at Cork, and in the summer of 1770 she was in Belfast. After her marriage to Sparks (which was reported in April 1772) she seems not to have acted much in Dublin, though Clark traced her to Cork in June and September and Limerick in August 1773, Cork in June and August and Limerick in August and September 1774, Kilkenny in the summer of 1776 and October 1779, Derry in October and November 1782, Cork in August and September and Limerick in October 1783, and Carlow in October 1797. Among

her known roles were Desdemona in *Othello,* Lady Townly in *The Provok'd Husband,* and the title role in *The Irish Widow.*

Mrs Sparks acted once in London: on 9 April 1788 she played the Matron in *The Ephesian Mother* at the Haymarket Theatre—unless that Mrs Sparks was Sarah, the wife of Hugh Sparks.

Frances was apparently the Mrs Sparks seen by William Smith in Dublin in July 1774 as Miss Hardcastle in *She Stoops to Conquer.* He reported to Garrick that she was promising, "with a middling person, seemingly inclined to grow fat. She is a favourite here." By 24 July Smith had seen enough of Mrs Sparks to render a final verdict: "She is what may be called handsome, but clumsy, vulgar, and inanimate, and has the brogue very strong." Why Garrick should have been interested in the first place is a wonder, for he had sworn vengeance against all Sparkses three years before.

Tate Wilkinson in *The Wandering Patentee* said he had seen Mrs Sparks in Dublin in May 1772 as Juliet. She was a very handsome woman, he thought

and I expected from her genius and fine eyes, teeth, &c. that she would have proved a beauteous flower ere this time [the 1790s]; but her playing last winter in a country company in Scotland, and not maintaining her popularity at Dublin and Edinburgh, makes me fear she has either not been properly nourished by the public, or that she has neglected herself.

Clark places Mrs Richard Sparks at Drury Lane in 1798, but that is certainly a mistake; Mrs Hugh Sparks was the actress in London then.

Richard and Frances Sparks had twin sons, born on 10 October 1774 at Silvermines, Tipperary, near Limerick, according to the *Monthly Chronicle*. The *Gentleman's Magazine* in September 1805 reported that Frances Sparks had died recently in Dublin.

An anonymous engraving of Frances Sparks as Leonora in *The Padlock* was published in the *Hibernian Magazine*, December 1772.

Sparling, [Joseph?] [d. 1728?], house servant?

Mr Sparling (or Sparkling) shared a benefit with three others at the Haymarket Theatre on 20 February 1724. That playhouse was used that year for occasional benefits for people from other theatres, and it would appear that Sparling was an employee at Lincoln's Inn Fields Theatre, where he had received 8s. 4d. on 23 January 1724. He shared another benefit, this time at Lincoln's Inn Fields, on 22 May 1725. Our guess is that he was one of the house servants, and since his name did not appear in theatre accounts after 1725, possibly he was Joseph Sparling, who was buried at St Paul, Covent Garden, on 1 June 1728. Perhaps the Mrs Sparling who acted Benedict in *The Half Pay Officers* at the Haymarket Theatre on 12 March 1730 was his wife. A Miss Sparling (their daughter?) performed at the Capel Street Theatre in Dublin in 1746–47.

Sparling, Mrs [Joseph] [fl. 1730?], actress. See SPARLING, [JOSEPH?].

Sparrow, Mr [fl. 1776–1783], actor.

Mr Sparrow (or Sparrows) played Cardinal Campeius in *Henry VIII* at China Hall, Rotherhithe, on 25 September 1776. At the Haymarket Theatre he had roles in *The Taylors* on 25 November 1782 and *A New Way to Keep a Wife at Home* on 17 September 1783.

Sparrow, J. [fl. 1794], singer.

Doane's *Musical Directory* of 1794 listed J. and S. Sparrow, both alto singers and both of Tottenham Court Road, as members of the Cecilian Society, participants in the oratorios at Drury Lane Theatre, and entertainers at the Adam and Eve Tea Gardens, St Pancras.

Sparrow, S. [fl. 1794], singer. See SPARROW, J.

Sparroworth, Miss [fl. 1756], actress.

Miss Sparroworth (possibly a pseudonym) played Signor Ferdinando in *Adventures of Half an Hour* at the Swan Inn at Bartholomew Fair on 3 September 1756.

Speare, Mr [fl. 1796–1810?], singer, actor.

Master Speare (or Spear) sang in the chorus of *Harlequin and Oberon* at Covent Garden Theatre on 19 December 1796 and subsequent dates. In 1798–99 he sang in *Ramah Droog* and *Raymond and Agnes,* and in 1799–1800 he sang in the chorus of *The Intriguing Chambermaid.* He was perhaps the singer Spear who performed at a concert in the Assembly Room in New York City on 15 April 1806. He played Sir Charles Cropland in *The Poor Gentleman* in New York at the Park Theatre on 11 September 1807; then he was with Placide's company in Charleston from 1807–8 through 1809–10.

Speechly, Mr [fl. 1793–1795], singer.

At Covent Garden Theatre on 28 November 1793 Mr Speechly played one of the villagers in *Nina.* Doane's *Musical Directory* of 1794 gave his address as Kensington and noted that Speechly was a bass singer in the oratorios at Drury Lane and Covent Garden Theatre. From 31 January through 17 April 1795 at Covent Garden he sang in the chorus of soldiers and sailors in *The Mysteries of the Castle.*

Speer, Mr ₁*fl. 1742*₁, *house servant?*
Mr Speer's benefit tickets were accepted at Drury Lane Theatre on 24 April 1742. Perhaps he was one of the house servants.

Spellman, Mrs ₁*fl. 1733*₁, *actress.*
Mrs Spellman played Phebe in *The Fall of Phaeton* at the Lee and Harper booth at Bartholomew Fair on 23 August 1733.

Speltra, Mr ₁*fl. 1736*₁, *harpsichordist.*
Mr Speltra played a concerto for harpsichord (his instrument) and violoncello with Caporale at a concert held for Speltra's benefit at Hickford's Music Room on 21 January 1736.

Spence, Mr ₁*fl. 1791–1795*₁, *singer.*
The singer Spence made his first public appearance on 11 March 1791 in the oratorios at Drury Lane Theatre. He sang in Handel's *Judas Maccabaeus* on 18 March, *Redemption* on 23 March, *Acis and Galatea* on 1 April, and a selection from *Time and Truth* on 13 April. Mee in *The Oldest Music Room* notes that Spence sang frequently at the Oxford Musical Society concerts and had a benefit in Oxford on 29 April 1795.

Spencer, Mr ₁*fl. 1729*₁, *manager.*
Fog's reported on 19 July 1729: "We hear that Mr Miller having left performing as usual, at Windmill Hill, Mr Spencer intends to Entertain the Town with an antient Catalogue of Plays, which will begin on Monday next [the twenty-first]."

Spencer, Mr ₁*fl. 1740–1741*₁, *actor.*
Mr. Spencer played Phillip in *The Rival Queens* at Covent Garden Theatre on 31 October 1740 and 19 March 1741.

Spencer, Mr ₁*fl. 1749*₁, *music copyist.*
The Covent Garden Theatre accounts show a payment of £6 8*s*. 6*d*. on 30 December 1749 to Mr Spencer for copying out the music for *The Chaplet*.

Spencer, Mrs ₁*fl. 1673–1675*₁, *actress.*
According to the 1673 edition of *Herod and Mariamne*, Mrs Spencer played Mariamne and spoke the epilogue, probably about August

1673, when, according to Robert Hume's revision of the dating in *The London Stage*, the work was performed at the Dorset Garden Theatre by the Duke's Company. On 28 May and 22 June 1675 Mrs Spencer played the breeches part of Vangona in *The Conquest of China* at Dorset Garden.

Spencer, Mrs ₁*fl. 1797–1798*₁? *See* POPE, MRS ALEXANDER THE SECOND, MARIA ANN.

Spencer, Charles *1743–1809, actor.*
At the Crown Inn, Islington, on 15 March 1781 Charles Spencer played Justice Ballance in *The Recruiting Officer*, and on 30 December 1782 at the Haymarket Theatre he was seen as Rossano in *The Fair Penitent*. Documents in the Henderson collection at the Folger Shakespeare Library show that Spencer had first performed on 23 November 1771 at Edinburgh, and the *Gentleman's Magazine* in February 1809 reported Spencer's death at Doncaster at the age of 66.

Spencer, William, stage name of William Barber *1757–1803, actor, dancer, acrobat.*
William Barber was born in 1757 and took the name Spencer for his stage career. He was probably the Spencer who performed in Fox's company at Brighton in 1777. Spencer's first London notice was on 12 May 1780, when he was added to the cast of *Fortunatus* and did an acrobatic turn at Drury Lane Theatre. His solo "vaudeville" was a leap "through" (over) a tub of fire. The evening was a benefit for Spencer and two others and brought in £273 2*s*. before house charges of £105 were deducted. That was Spencer's only appearance of the season. He returned on 19 September to play an unspecified character in *Fortunatus* again, after which he was not named in the bills until 22 May 1781, when he shared a benefit with three others. This time the receipts came to over £251. It seems likely that Spencer was serving the management in some way not evident in the bills.

On 22 and 29 June 1781 he went over to the Haymarket to play "Ditto, Mum!" in *The Genius of Nonsense*. Through the summer of 1784 that pattern continued: occasional notices at Drury Lane in the winters and a few appearances at the Haymarket in the summers. At Drury Lane Spencer was seen in such new parts as a Servant in *The School for Vanity,* Antonio's Servant in *The Merchant of Venice,* a Beggar in *The Ladies' Frolick,* an Officer in *A Duke and No Duke,* and a Clown in *The Elopement.* But most of the time he was simply named as one of the "other" characters in such pieces as *Robinson Crusoe, Harlequin Junior,* or *Lun's Ghost.* He continued sharing benefits.

During the 1782 and 1783 summers at the Haymarket Spencer was advertised as Ditto, Mum! again and as Harlequin in *Harlequin Teague* (on 17 August 1782), Dapper in *The Citizen,* and a Countryman in *The What D'Ye Call It.* After the summer of 1784 he stopped performing at the Haymarket. Except for some work at the Richmond Theatre in the summer of 1788, he remained at Drury Lane until he was discharged in 1791, when the old theatre closed. In the bills from 1784 to 1791 Spencer was named for such new characters as a Spouter in *The Apprentice,* an Officer in the *Earl of Warwick,* Christopherides in *The Taylors,* a Footman in *All in the Wrong,* a Messenger in *Philaster,* Guillamar in *Arthur and Emmeline,* Frank in *The First Floor,* a Lobby Dangler in *The Box-Lobby Loungers,* Kitteau in *The Englishman in Paris,* Rugby in The *Merry Wives of Windsor,* Will in *The Citizen,* and (the role he played at his last appearance on 4 June 1791) a Footman in *The Country Girl.* Despite what appears to have been a very mediocre career, Spencer was remembered by the *Thespian Dictionary* (1805) as a Drury Lane harlequin when he died, and one must suppose that some of the unspecified characters he appeared as, sometimes cited in the bills as "major," were of some importance. He regularly had spring benefits, as in earlier years.

After Drury Lane closed and plans were laid for a new and larger theatre to take its place, William Spencer set up as the master of the Garrick's Head in Bow Street, near by. The *Thespian Dictionary* recalled that Spencer "continually entertained the professors and amateurs of the drama. He died suddenly in 1804, as he was going in a hackney coach, (and in good health when he entered it) to the Gloucester Coffee House, Piccadilly." The date of his death was given in some other publications as 1804, but the *European Magazine* was surely correct in reporting that he died on 23

December 1803. Spencer was buried at St Paul, Covent Garden, on 30 December. The registers there gave his age as 46.

Spencer drew up a most circumstantial will on 15 April 1793:

I William Barber alias Spencer born in Carey Street in the parish of Saint Clement Danes in the Strand, married to Mary Roper of George Street Tottenham Court Road at the New Chapel Kentish Town June 26 in the year of our Lord one thousand seven hundred and eighty-six by whom was born to me on the twenty sixth of April one thousand seven hundred and eighty seven my present Daughter Mary Spencer christened at St. Pauls Covent Garden [on 6 May] in the year of our Lord One thousand seven hundred and eighty seven . . . [To] Elizabeth Spencer my present wife Daughter of Giles Cotterell of Warfield Berks [the *Reading Mercury* reported that Spencer had married Elizabeth Cotterell on 18 October 1788 in Warfield] and my Daughter Mary Spencer above mentioned an Equal Division of all my Goods Chattels Estates . . . allowing my Mother Elizabeth Barber during the term of her Life four shillings per week to be paid her weekly unto my Brother John Barber twenty pounds . . . my Daughter Mary Spencer is to be paid her portion on her coming to the age of twenty one years. . . .

Spencer made his brother John residuary legatee, and after him, Spencer's wife's sister Mary Cotterell of Warfield. He requested the Cotterells to look after his daughter should his wife die before young Mary came of age. To his executors he left mourning rings. The will was proved on 23 January 1804, and administration of the estate was granted not to a Barber, Spencer, or Cotterell, but to Spencer's executors, Richard Atlee and Robert Needham.

Sperati, John [fl. 1787–1794,], violoncellist.

John Sperati played the violoncello in performances of the *Messiah* at Drury Lane on 27 February 1789 and at Covent Garden on 19 February 1790. From 1791 to 1794 he was first cello in the opera band at the King's Theatre and the Pantheon. Haydn listed Sperati in 1792 among the important musical people in London and noted that Sperati made his first appearance in London in 1787—but we do not know where or on what specific date. Doane's *Musical Directory* of 1794 gave Sperati's address as No 26, Castle Street, Oxford Market, and noted that Sperati had played for the Concert of Ancient Music and in the Handel performances at Westminster Abbey. At the same address lived B. Sperati, a pianist but apparently not a public performer. He was a music seller, first with Cianchettini and then, about 1811, alone, at No 34 Bury Street, St James's.

Speres. *See* SPIRES.

Sperin, Benjamin. *See* PERIN, BENJAMIN.

Spicer, Mrs [*fl.* 1723–1724], *actress.*
Mrs Spicer, "who never appear'd on any Stage before," played Portia in *Julius Caesar* at the Lincoln's Inn Fields Theatre on 31 October 1723. She was Gertrude in *The Royal Merchant* on 19 May 1724 and shared a benefit with two others on 25 May. The benefit receipts came to a bit over £80.

Spicer, John [*fl.* 1667–1675], *violinist.*
In his *Descriptive Catalogue of Tokens of the Seventeenth Century,* Burn describes a 1667 token of John Spicer of Crown Court. It is likely that Spicer was operating a music house. On 19 December 1670 he was admitted to the King's Musick as a violinist, but no salary came with his post. He must have gained a salaried position in time, for on 15 February 1675 he played in the court masque *Calisto* as one of the regular band of 24 violins. Perhaps he was the John Spicer of St Margaret, Westminster, who married Margaret Burges on 3 February 1668, but the registers show that there was at least one other John Spicer in the parish. The one who married in 1668 was described as a bachelor about 26 years old.

Spiers, Mr [*fl.* 1774?–1775?], *actor.*
Correspondence in the Forster collection at the Victoria and Albert Museum indicates that a Mr Spiers was a supernumerary actor at Drury Lane Theatre, perhaps in 1774–75.

"Spiletta, La." *See* GIORDANI, NICOLINA.

Spiller, James 1692–1730, *actor, dancer.*
James Spiller was, according to *The Dictionary of National Biography,* born in 1692, the son of "the" Gloucester carrier. He was appren-

Harvard Theatre Collection
JAMES SPILLER
by Bell

ticed to one Ross, a landscape painter, but lost interest and joined a troupe of strolling players. George Akerby's *Life of James Spiller* (1729) reports that during the 1710–11 season (*recte* before 1709–10) Spiller was in the provinces, where he married the actress Elizabeth Thompson. By 6 December 1709, when he made his first recorded appearance at Drury Lane Theatre, playing the Porter in *The Country Wit,* he had gained considerable experience as a low comedian. During the 1709–10 season he appeared in a variety of small and large roles, showing off his special knack for playing old men: Day in *The Committee* on 9 December, Harlequin in *The Emperor of the Moon* on 30 December, Corporal Cuttum in *The Walking Statue* on 9 January 1710, the Fourth Citizen in *Oedipus* on 14 January, Don Francisco in *The Successful Strangers* on 31 January, Don Felix in *The Mistake* on 11 February, and the Boatswain in *Bickerstaff's Burial* on 27 March. On 10 April 1710 he shared a benefit with his wife.

At Pinkethman's theatre at Greenwich from 21 June to 23 September 1710 Spiller played a busy schedule, appearing as Sampson in *The Fatal Marriage,* Polonius in *Hamlet,* Maiden in

Collection of Edward A. Langhans

"For the Benefit of Spiller"

by Hogarth

Tunbridge Walks, Mustacho in *The Tempest*, Jack Locker in *The Fair Quaker*, Kick in *Epsom Wells*, Kite in *The Recruiting Officer*, Hector in *The Gamester*, Pyracmon in *Oedipus*, the title role in *The Busy Body*, Higgen in *The Royal Merchant*, Lopez in *The Mistake*, Ancharius in *Caius Marius*, Coupler in *The Relapse*, Brass in *The Confederacy*, and Bustophia in *The Fair Maid of the Mill*.

He was again at Drury Lane in 1711–12 and remained there through the end of 1713, playing a Citizen in *Philaster*, Anvil in *The Northern Lass*, Ananias in *The Petticoat Plotters*, Smart in *The Female Advocates*, the first Soldier in *The Humours of the Army*, Drawer in *The Wife of Bath*, and Foist in *The Apparition*. He was in competition with Pinkethman at Drury Lane, and that fact, in addition to the bad temper of Robert Wilks, one of the trio of managers at Drury Lane, may have persuaded Spiller to

leave the company and move in 1715 to John Rich's new theatre in Lincoln's Inn Fields.

On 4 January 1715 Spiller acted Setter in *The Old Bachelor* at the new playhouse, after which he was seen during the remainder of the season as a Sailor in *The Fair Quaker*, Lopez in *The Mistake*, Moneytrap in *The Confederacy*, Jeremy in *Love for Love*, Roger in *The Slip*, Crispin in *The Perplexed Couple*, Captain Hackum in *The Squire of Alsatia*, Harlequin in *The Emperor of the Moon*, Don Cholerick in *Love Makes a Man*, Debonair in *Love in a Sack*, and the title character in *The False Count*. At his wife's benefit on 17 May he spoke a prologue on an ass, continuing a comic tradition begun by Joe Haines a generation before, and on 3 August he joined in a *French Peasant* dance with Francis Leigh and Mrs Spiller.

Spiller was seen by Riccoboni, probably in 1715:

When I was in London, a thing happened, which, for its singularity, deserves notice. At the theatre in Lincoln's Inn Fields I saw a comedy taken from "The Crispin Medicine." He who acted the Old Man (Spiller) executed it to the nicest perfection, which one could expect in no player who had not forty years' experience and exercise. As he played the part of an old man, I made no manner of doubt of his being an old comedian, who, instructed by long experience, and at the same time assisted by the weight of years, had performed it so naturally. But how great was my surprise when I learned that he was a young man, about the age of twenty-six! I could not conceive it possible for a young actor, by the help of art, to imitate that debility of nature to such a pitch of exactness; but the wrinkles of his face, his sunk eyes, and his loose and yellow cheeks were incontestible proofs against what they said to me. I knew for certain that the actor, to fit himself for the part of this old man, spent an hour in dressing himself, and disguised his face so nicely, and painted so artificially a part of his eyebrows and eyelids, that, at the distance of six paces, it was impossible not to be deceived. I was desirous to be a witness of this myself, but pride hindered me; so knowing that I must be ashamed, I was satisfied of the confirmation of it from the other actors.

Spiller was a busy player at Lincoln's Inn Fields every season from 1715–16 (his first full one under Rich's management) to his death in 1729. Among the many roles he essayed were Don Lewis in *Love Makes a Man*, Gomez in *The Spanish Fryar*, Costar Pearmain in *The Recruiting Officer*, Snap in *Love's Last Shift*, Sneak in *The Fond Husband*, Toby Guzzle in *The Cobler of Preston*, Bottom in *Pyramus and Thisbe*, Pedro in *The Feign'd Curtizans*, the title role in *The Walking Statue*, Subtleman in *The Twin Rivals*, the (second?) Gravedigger in *Hamlet*, Hob in *The Country Wake*, Ben in *Love for Love*, Hector in *The Gamester*, Setter in *The Old Bachelor*, Old Belfond in *The Squire of Alsatia*, Harlequin in *The Jealous Doctor*, the title role in *Hob*, Clodpole in *Amadis*, Periwinkle in *A Bold Stroke for a Wife*, Jachimo in *Cymbeline*, the Bookseller and Teague in *The Committee*, Francis in *1 Henry IV*, Froth in *The Double Dealer*, the First Boor in *The Royal Merchant*, Moneytrap in *The Confederacy*, and the Murderer in *Macbeth*.

Also, the Mad Englishman in *The Pilgrim*, Daniel and Driver in *Oroonoko*, Higgen in *The Beggar's Bush*, Mustapha in *Don Sebastian*, The Gentleman Usher in *King Lear*, Pistol and Caius in *The Merry Wives of Windsor*, Jobson in *The Devil of a Wife*, Marplot in *The Busy Body*, Pandarus in *Troilus and Cressida*, Razor in *The Provok'd Wife*, the Clown in *Measure for Measure*, Foigard in *The Stratagem*, Dashwell in *The London Cuckolds*, Fourbin in *The Soldier's Fortune*, Butler in *The Drummer*, Gardener in *Don Quixote*, the title part in *Cartouche*, Brush in *Love and a Bottle*, a Citizen in *Oedipus*, Brainworm in *Every Man in His Humour*, the Second Birdcatcher in *Harlequin Sorcerer*, Blunt in *The Rover*, the First Murderer in *Richard III*, Shift in *The Cheats of Scapin*, Quaint in *Aesop*, Rakehell in *She Wou'd If She Cou'd*, a Plebeian in *Julius Caesar*, Antonio in *Venice Preserv'd*, Merryman in *The Amorous Widow*, Sir Politick in *Volpone*, Bilbo in *The Cheats*, and Mat o' the Mint in *The Beggar's Opera*.

Spiller displayed his dancing talent in a number of pantomime roles, but he also appeared as an entr'acte dancer from time to time, as on 12 October 1715, when he performed a *Miller's Dance* with his wife, or on 25 April 1721, when he was a Countryman in a dance titled *Harlequin, Scaramouch, and a Countryman*. He was also popular as a speaker of epilogues, which he sometimes wrote himself. One such was a "New Comi-Tragi-Mechanical Prologue in the gay Stile" which he wrote and delivered on 13 April 1717. His ass-epilogues were performed regularly in the early part of his career but seem to have lost popularity as time went on.

For his benefits at Lincoln's Inn Fields Spiller occasionally worked up something special. On 31 March 1720, for example, he presented three of his staple items, *The Walking Statue*, *Hob*, and *The Cobler of Preston;* he also provided a new epilogue "to Exchange Alley":

For the Entertainment of *Robinson Crusoe*. And whereas I James Spiller of Gloucestershire, having receiv'd an Invitation from Hildebrand Bullock [his fellow actor] of Liquor-Pond-Street, London, to exercise the usual Weapons of the Noble Science of Defence, will not fail to meet this bold Inviter; desiring a full stage, blunt Weapons, and from him much Favour.

There seems to be no report telling us just what kind of a mock combat Spiller and Bullock presented. For his labors at Lincoln's Inn Fields John Rich paid Spiller—in 1724–25— £1 6s. 8d. daily, a very comfortable salary for the time, but not enough to keep the extravagant Spiller out of financial trouble.

Not only did Spiller keep up a busy schedule at Lincoln's Inn Fields during the regular theatrical seasons, but he almost always performed in the summers and was active at the fairs. His earliest appearance may have been on 9 September 1717, when he played Trusty in *Twice Married* at Southwark Fair at a booth run by Pinkethman and Pack. He returned to that Fair in 1718 to play John in *Sir Richard Whittington,* and at Bartholomew Fair in August 1719 he shared the management of a booth with Lee. To attract customers in August 1720 he wrote a facetious letter to the *Weekly Journal* on the thirteenth:

Whereas it was reported in one of your former papers that I James Spiller Comedian was unfortunately slain in Hibernia, these are to certifie all those whom it may concern that the said James Spiller am not dead nor ever was; but on the contrary am fortunately returned [from Ireland?] and do write all my relations friends acquaintances & strangers to see me in Bartholomew fair at the great booth over against the hospital gate Smithfield; in order to put me into a capacity to appear in Change Alley with some other of my brethren. . . .

On 23 September at Bird Cage Alley Spiller played Brazen in *The Recruiting Officer* at Bullock's booth in Southwark.

Though there is no record of his appearing at either of the fairs in 1721, he joined with Lee and Harper to present *Darius,* a droll, at Bartholomew Fair in August 1722. Akerby said that in 1722 (i.e., 1722–23), when Spiller was earning £4 weekly, he was so spendthrift—being a lover of good liquor and good company—that he had to mortgage his salary, borrow at high interest rates, and take shelter in the Mint, a sanctuary in Southwark. He was, according to Akerby, "reduced to having a Play [*The Drummer*] acted for his Benefit in that Place." Indeed, we find that from November 1722 until September 1723 Spiller was not mentioned in any bills. The *St James's Journal* on 5 January 1723 printed an "Epilogue, Written and Spoken by Mr. Spiller, for his own Benefit, in the MINT." Spiller was out to act *Hob* at Pinkethman's booth at Southwark Fair on 25 September 1723. A year later in Southwark he joined with Bullock and Booth to present *Oedipus.*

Spiller was active at both fairs in 1726 after missing them in 1725. With Lee and Harper at Bartholomew Fair in 1726 he produced *The Siege of Troy,* and with Egleton at Southwark Fair he put on *The Unnatural Parents,* in which Spiller played Sir Adam Wealthy. In 1727 at Bartholomew Fair he played the same role, but the booth was run by Lee and Harper. In 1728 at both fairs Spiller and Harper presented *Hero and Leander* and *The Quaker's Opera.* That was Spiller's last activity at the fairs.

Perhaps Spiller wandered as far away from London as Ireland, but his fleeting reference to such a trip (in August 1720) may have been with tongue in cheek. He did perform briefly at Richmond in the summer of 1718 in Pinkethman's company. On 19 July he had unspecified roles in *The Spanish Fryar* and *The Stage Coach.* On 26 July he and Cook danced an *Italian Night Scene between Harlequin and a Countryman.* Then Spiller acted Squib in *Tunbridge Walks,* Ben in *Love for Love,* Hector in *The Gamester,* and the title role in *Hob.* In the summer of 1727 some London players, Spiller among them, were expected to play at York the following season; the arrangements fell through, and Spiller remained in London.

Spiller separated from his wife, according to Akerby, but we do not know when. Akerby said that for some time Spiller lived in intimacy with a very beautiful woman, Mrs Stratford, who lived in Wild Street. Even while he was "on the other side of the Water [in the Mint on the south bank of the Thames? or in Ireland?], [he] allowed her *Fourteen Pence a Week.* . . ."

He was a gregarious fellow and inspired stories—such as stealing a script of Charles Johnson's *The Cobler of Preston* from Pinkethman's pocket during a drinking bout—that may or may not have been true. The tale that he delivered an epilogue on an elephant seems not to be substantiated by any notices in the bills, where one would surely expect it to have been mentioned.

Spiller was popular enough to have a ticket for his *Beggar's Opera* benefit drawn for him by Hogarth. It shows the comedian selling tickets for his benefit—not in 1720, as suggested by Paulson in his study of Hogarth, but in 1728 (the year of *The Beggar's Opera,* in which no normal benefit is recorded for Spiller), as stated in the *Catalogue of Political and Personal Satires in the British Museum.*

Spiller lost the sight in an eye, possibly due to smallpox, and used a squint as part of some characters he played. He died on 7 February 1730 at the age of 37, following an apoplectic seizure while playing Clodpole in *The Rape of Proserpine* at Lincoln's Inn Fields Theatre. He was buried on 10 February at St Clement Danes. Shortly before his death the Bull and Butcher public house in Clare Market, which he had frequented and made popular, was renamed the Spiller's Head, with a sign (showing Spiller) painted by the actor-painter Jack Laguerre.

Akerby quoted an epitaph on Spiller written by a butcher in Clare Market:

He was an inoffensive, merry fellow,
When sober hipp'd, blithe as a bird when mellow.

Spiller's Jests (by Akerby) was published in 1729.

In addition to Hogarth's picture of him on the benefit ticket, Spiller had his portrait engraved by I. Bell, published as a plate to his *Life* by George Akerby, 1729. Copies by T. Gilks and an anonymous engraver were also issued.

Spiller, Mrs James, Elizabeth, née Thompson [*fl.* 1709–1740], *actress, dancer.*

Elizabeth Thompson married James Spiller before 17 December 1709, the first record of her performing in London; on that date Mrs Spiller acted Cloggett in *The Confederacy* at Drury Lane Theatre. Then she was Biancha in *The Successful Strangers* on 31 January 1710, Jenny Private in *The Fair Quaker* on 25 February, and Lucy in *Bickerstaff's Burial* on 27 March; perhaps she had a role in *The Emperor of the Moon* when it was presented on 10 April as a benefit for Mrs Spiller and her husband. Mrs Spiller joined William Pinkethman's troupe at Greenwich in the summer, acting from 15 June through 23 September and appearing as Honoria in *Love Makes a Man*, Julia in *The Fatal Marriage*, Violante in *Sir Courtly Nice*, Ophelia in *Hamlet*, Belinda in *Tunbridge Walks*, Statira in *The Rival Queens*, Flavia in *The Libertine Destroyed*, Jenny in *The Fair Quaker*, Lady Macduff in *Macbeth*, Lucia in *Epsom Wells*, Bellamante in *The Emperor of the Moon*, Sylvia in *The Recruiting Officer*, Angelina in *The Gamester*, Eurydice in *Oedipus*, Patch in

The Busy Body, Maria in *The Fond Husband*, Jaqueline in *The Royal Merchant*, the young Daughter in *The Sea Voyage*, Flippanta in *The Confederacy*, and the title role in *The Maid of the Mill*.

Mrs. Spiller did not appear at Drury Lane again until 7 November 1712, when she acted Lydia in *The Successful Pyrate;* then she was seen in one other role that season: Brush in *The Female Advocates* on 6 January 1713.

With her husband she joined the manager John Rich at Lincoln's Inn Fields Theatre, appearing first on 7 January 1715 as a Sham Quaker in *The Fair Quaker.* During the remainder of the 1714–15 season and into the summer she played Flippanta in *The Confederacy*, Angelica in *Love for Love*, Lucy in *Oroonoko*, Isbel in *The Perplexed Couple*, Lucia in *The Square of Alsatia*, and Angelina in *Love Makes a Man*, and she danced a *French Peasant* with Francis Leigh and her husband.

Mrs Spiller's career paralleled that of her husband up to the end of the 1721–22 season, and though she was given a number of important characters, she was never as popular as her husband. She was, according to Akerby's *Life of James Spiller*, "a good pretty Woman, and one who might have made a tolerable Figure on the stage, was it not for a little too much Affectation. . . ." Some of her parts through 1721–22 were Aurelia in *The Wife's Relief*, Lucy in *The Recruiting Officer*, Hillaria in *Love's Last Shift*, Lydia in *The Northern Heiress*, Laura Lucretia in *The Feign'd Curtizans*, Philadelphia in *Bury Fair*, Melesinda in *Aureng-Zebe*, Clarinda in *Woman Is a Riddle*, Teresia in *The Squire of Alsatia*, Massina in *Sophonisba*, Miranda in *The Busy Body*, Lady Fanciful in *The Provok'd Wife*, Damaris in *The Amorous Widow*, Lavinia in *The Fair Penitent*, Ruth in *The Committee*, Gertrude in *The Royal Merchant*, the Countess of Rutland in *The Unhappy Favorite*, Kate in *1 Henry IV*, Elvira in *The Spanish Fryar*, Constance in *The Twin Rivals*, Gertrude in *Hamlet*, Juletta in *The Pilgrim*, Mrs Termagant in *The Squire of Alsatia*, Lady Piercy in Theobald's alteration of *Richard II*, Portia in *The Merchant of Venice*, Mariana in *Measure for Measure*, Anne in *Richard III*, Gipsy in *The Stratagem*, and Engine in *The London Cuckolds*.

During that period she made only a few appearances away from Lincoln's Inn Fields. On 5 August 1717 she acted Jane Shore in *The*

History of Jane Shore at Tottenham Court Fair, and in September she was Lucia in *Twice Married* at Southwark Fair. At Pinkethman's theatre at Richmond in August 1718 she appeared as Ruth in *The Committee,* Angelica in *Love for Love,* and Angelica in *The Gamester.* In September at Southwark Fair she was Alicia in *Sir Richard Whittington,* and at Angel Court in September she played Sylvia in *The Recruiting Officer.* She was a Bartholomew Fair on 25 August 1722 to appear in a droll called *Darius* at a booth run by her husband, Lee, and Harper. Then she left the stage for almost a year, during which time she was probably in the sanctuary Mint in Southwark with her spendthrift husband.

When she returned to the stage it was as Angelica in *Love for Love* on 22 July 1723 at Hampstead Wells. Then she did not act again, so far as the records show, until 22 August 1724, when she played Lucia in *The Prodigal Son* at Bartholomew Fair. In 1724–25 Mrs Spiller (without her husband) acted at the Smock Alley Theatre in Dublin, playing Damaris in *The Amorous Widow,* Clarinda in *The Double Gallant,* Hillaria in *Tunbridge Walks,* and Octavia in *All for Love.* She did not appear in London again until 22 August 1727, when she was the Fair Maid of the West in *The Unnatural Parents* at Bartholomew Fair. That appearance seems to have been her last on the same stage as her husband.

Mrs Spiller played Judith in *The Siege of Bethulia* at both fairs in August and September 1729, adding, at Southwark Fair, Phebe in *The Beggar's Wedding.* The following 29 November she was Hillaria in *Tunbridge Walks* at the Front Long Room next to the Haymarket; there on 1 December she tried Cherry in *The Stratagem.* In August 1730 at Bartholomew Fair she was again in *The Siege of Bethulia,* and a year later at Tottenham Court she played Selima in *Amurath* and the title role in *Phebe.* In September 1731 she was Britannia in *Whittington* at Southwark Fair. Her sporadic appearances continued, her next one being in August 1733 at Bartholomew Fair, where she acted Lybia in *The Fall of Phaeton.* On 7 September 1734 she was Cassandra in *The Siege of Troy* at Southwark Fair (*The London Stage* carries that performance incorrectly as by Mr Spiller). Her last known role was Tragedy in *Harlequin*

Restor'd at Bartholomew Fair on 23 August 1740.

Spilsbury. *See also* PILSBURY.

Spilsbury, Mr [*fl. 1755–1765*], *doorkeeper.*
Mr Spilsbury was named in the Drury Lane benefit bills from 15 May 1755 through 13 May 1760. The accounts on 9 February 1765 listed Spilsbury as a doorkeeper at 9s. weekly.

Spilsbury, Master [*fl. 1755*], *dancer.*
Master Spilsbury danced in *The Chinese Festival* at Drury Lane on 8 November 1755.

Spilsbury, James [*fl. 1754–1777*], *treasurer.*
The London Stage lists Mr Spilsbury as treasurer of the King's Theatre in 1763. David Garrick wrote to George Colman on 13 July 1766: "Covt Garden Patent &c have been upon Sale—one *Whitworth & Spilsbury* Mrs [Hannah] Pritchard's son in Law are some of ye parties concern'd in ye purchase. . . ." In June 1777 the accounts, apparently for the King's Theatre, named Spilsbury.

The Spilsbury in question was James, about whom little of a theatrical nature is known. On 24 August 1754 he married Judith, the eldest daughter of the actress Hannah Pritchard and her husband William. James Spilsbury was appointed Robe and Habit Maker to Queen Charlotte and was the main operator of Pritchard's Warehouse. He and Whitworth did not purchase the Covent Garden Theatre patent; it was bought by Harris, Rutherford, Colman, and Powell in July 1767.

A number of entries in the parish registers of St Paul, Covent Garden, concern James Spilsbury and his family. On 4 January 1756 William Pritchard Spilsbury, son of James and Judith, was christened; the infant died shortly after his birth and was buried on 15 January. James and Judith had several other children: Hannah Maria, christened on 24 August 1757; Charlote [*sic*] Tamary, christened on 19 November 1758 and buried on 2 February 1759; George, christened on 2 December 1759 and buried on 2 February 1760; Caroline, christened on 31 May 1761 and buried on 29 May 1772; Mary Charlotte, christened on 12 July

1762; Tamary Elizabeth, christened on 25 October 1763; and Jane Caroline, born in 1771. Hannah Pritchard's will was proved on 5 September 1768 and named Judith Spilsbury and her daughter Caroline among her beneficiaries.

Spinacuta, Signor   [fl. 1789–1801], dancer, actor, acrobat, violinist.

Signor Spinacuta was featured as a rope dancer at Astley's Amphitheatre from 20 July to early September 1789. When he appeared at Sollée's French Theatre in Charleston on 10 April 1794 (as Julia Curtis notes in the October 1969 issue of *Educational Theatre Journal*) he had gained appearances in London and at Nicolet's theatre in Paris. In Charleston from April to December 1794 Spinacuta was seen as the Old Man in *Harlequin Doctor,* a Stranger in *The Gamester,* a Servant in *Le Barbier de Seville,* a Thief in *The Old Soldier,* and Pince in *La Forêt Noire.* He also rope-danced, and his wife acted.

The Spinacutas were at the Pantheon in Philadelphia from December 1795 to February 1797, usually performing as a pair: the Clown and Columbine in *Harlequin Statue,* Piero and Columbine in *The Triumph of Virtue, or Harlequin in Philadelphia,* the Clown and Columbine in *Harlequin's Olio,* Piero and Columbine in *Harlequin in the Sun,* and the Clown and Columbine in *Mirth's Medley.* Their daughter made her first appearance on 12 October 1796, playing Columbine to her father's Clown in *The Death and Renovation of Harlequin.* Pollock's *The Philadelphia Theatre* shows Signor and Signora Spinacuta busy at the Pantheon through 14 February 1797, when they shared a benefit.

A Hartford, Connecticut, bill of 25 September 1797 described some of Spinacuta's efforts at the theatre there: "A Dance with Skates. He will throw himself into the Air and perform the Double Serpentaux. He will perform a comic dance [and] . . . a Hornpipe. With the Balance Pole he will perform several Feats with the Hoop—also with a Cane." Spinacuta also played airs on the violin, did some maneuvres with an American flag, and made an ascent and descent on a steep rope. The performance was "the Last Night of his Engagement" in Hartford. No mention was made of his wife and daughter. According to Winter's *Pre-Romantic Ballet,* Spinacuta was serving as a clown to the rope dancer Placide in 1801.

It seems probable that our subject's father was Laurent Spinacuta, who was active in the 1760s.

Spinacuta, Laurent   [fl. 1765–1774], rope dancer, animal trainer.

Campardon in *Les Spectacles de la Foire* speaks of the rope dancer Laurent Spinacuta, who appeared at the Nicolet theatre in Paris in the 1760s and was popular at the French fairs. He was also an animal trainer, two of his most famous pupils being a dog named Caraby and a Monkey called Turco. In 1765 at the Saint Ovide fair Spinacuta exhibited in Hali's menagerie a cassowary, and in 1774 at the Saint Germain fair he showed two tigers, a monkey, an armadillo, a jaguar, and a condor. In addition to training animals and birds, Spinacuta tutored child actors. The Mlles Spinacuta who performed in Paris in 1779–80 were probably his children, and we suppose that the Signor Spinacuta of the 1790's was Laurent's son.

On 27 October 1766 Spinacuta was in Placido's troupe at the Haymarket Theatre in London, vaulting on the slack rope and dancing on the tight rope. In 1767–68 he was popular at Sadler's Wells, where he exhibited his monkey.

An anonymous engraving titled, "Curious & Uncommon Performances of A MONKEY as they will be introduc'd at SADLERS WELLS" shows Spinacuta balancing a monkey on its head in his right hand, surrounded by 18 scenes of monkeys performing.

Spires, Mrs   [fl. 1765–1767], actress.

A Drury Lane Theatre paylist dated 9 February 1765 names Mrs Spires as a minor actress at 2s. 6d. daily. On a paylist dated 24 January 1767 she was called Speres and listed at 3s. 4d. daily. The management loaned her £3 3s. on 4 June 1767.

Spitzer, Mr   [fl. 1794–1801], scene painter.

In August and September 1794 Mr Spitzer was earning 10s. 6d. daily as a scene painter at Covent Garden Theatre. Spitzer painted scenery at Astley's Amphitheatre, according to bills dated 8 September 1794 and 22 August 1795. With others at Sadler's Wells in 1796

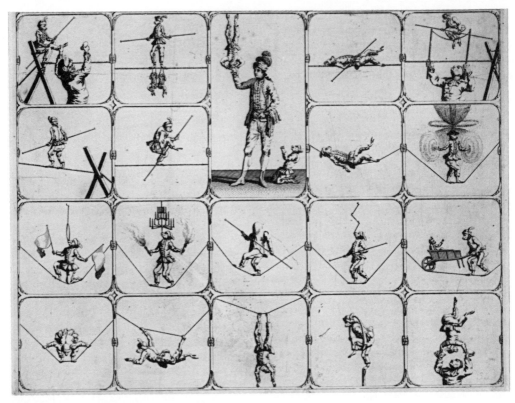

SPINACUTA and his monkeys

artist unknown

he painted the scenes for *Magician of the Rocks*. He was named in the Covent Garden bills and accounts in 1800 and 1801.

Spofforth, Reginald *c. 1768–1827, singer, composer, organist.*

According to Grove, Reginald Spofforth was born in Southwell, Nottinghamshire, between 1768 and 1770. He studied music under his uncle Thomas Spofforth. His first glee may have been "Lightly o'er the village green," composed about 1787 or 1788. In 1789 Spofforth came to London to continue his musical studies under Benjamin Cooke and Daniel Steibelt. On 31 December 1792 at Covent Garden Theatre Spofforth and others sang "God Save the King"; he was omitted from the chorus on 1 January 1793. He was one of the singers in *Harlequin's Chaplet* on 2 October 1793, one of the villagers in *Nina* on 28 No-

vember, and a singer in *Harlequin and Faustus* on 19 December.

Spofforth won two prizes from the Glee Club in 1793, and much of his reputation during the years that followed came from his skill at composing glees. Among his works were "Where are those hours," "Hail, smiling morn," "Fill high the grape's exulting stream," "Hark, the goddess Diana," "Come, bounteous May," and "Mark'd you her eye."

He continued appearing at Covent Garden through the fall of 1796, singing in *Romeo and Juliet, The Mysteries of the Castle, The Battle of Hexham, Merry Sherwood, The Lad of the Hills, A Melocosmiotes, The Witch of the Wood,* and *Harlequin's Treasure*. Doane's *Musical Directory* of 1794 listed Spofforth as an organist, composer, tenor singer, and teacher living in James Street, Westminster. Spofforth sang for the Concert of Ancient Music and in the oratorios at Covent Garden and Westminster Abbey. He was a subscriber to the New Musical Fund as early as 1805 and in 1815 served on the Fund's Committee.

In 1826 Reginald Spofforth inherited a considerable estate from his uncle, but his own health was poor, and he was dead within a year. He died in Brompton on 8 September 1827 and was buried in St Mary Abbots in Kensington.

Spofforth's brother, Samuel (1780–1864), was organist of Peterborough Cathedral and of Lichfield Cathedral.

"Spoonatissima, Signora" [fl. 1752–1760?], *musician.*
One of Christopher Smart's concoctions for his *Old Woman's Oratory,* "Signora Spoonatissima" may have been a man or a woman or perhaps even a trained animal. At the concert on 7 December 1752 at the Haymarket Theatre the performer was called "Signor Spoonatissimo" and played a piece "on an Instrument dug out of the Ruins of Herculaneum, much used by the Ancient Romans, and celebrated by Virgil in his Georgics." On 13 March 1753 Signora Spoonatissima herself was dug out of the ruins of Herculaneum, and on 3 May she shared a benefit with Mynheer Puffupandyke. She was probably the "La Spoonatissiana" who played a concerto of some sort at another Smart concert at the Haymarket on 8 September 1760.

Spooner, Mr [fl. 1776–1777], *box office keeper.*
The London Stage lists Mr Spooner as a box office keeper at China Hall, Rotherhithe, in 1776–77.

"Spotted Indian Youth, The," *and* **"Spotted Negro, The."** *See* "Primrose the Piebald Boy."

Spozzi, Signor [fl. 1786–1787], *dancer.*
From 24 January to 2 May 1786 Signor Spozzi danced at the King's Theatre. He appeared in a new *Divertissement Villageois* and a pas de quatre. A news report from Birmingham on 13 August 1787 said Pozzi was dangerously hurt. "He had in his bills announced a dance by himself in the character of a Daemon, surrounded by fire, and was so impru-

dent as to appear on the stage with five half pound rockets on his head, and one on each arm." When the rockets fired he was thrown over the spikes at the front edge of the stage and into the pit, receiving eleven wounds in different parts of his body in addition to burns.

Spray, John d. *1827, singer.*
John Spray sang at a subscription concert in Bristol on 15 November 1792. *The Dear Village Maid that I Love,* published about 1793 in London, was sung by Spray at the Triennial Meeting at Worcester. Spray was a tenor in some of the Handelian performances at Westminster Abbey in London, according to Doane's *Musical Directory* of 1794. Doane listed Spray as from Lincoln. The singer settled in Dublin about 1797, sang at the Crow Street Theatre from 1798 to 1800, and became vicar-choral of Christ Church and St Patrick's Cathedral. One of the songs he sang, *Bonnie Blue,* was published in Dublin about 1800. By 1800 Spary was a member of the Irish Musical Fund, the minutes of which mention him frequently through 1826. In 1816, according to Ita Hogan's *Anglo-Irish Music,* Spray and his nephew John Smith opened a Logierian Academy in Dublin, and in 1821 Spray was given an honorary doctorate of music by Dublin University. He died in Dublin in 1827.

Spriggs, Mrs James. *See* **Brangin, Rhoda.**

Sprightly, William [fl. 1780], *violinist.*
William Sprightly is identified in the *British Museum Catalogue of Engraved British Portraits* as a violinist who flourished in 1780. A portrait of Sprightly by an unknown engraver shows him with books, violin, and music.

Springer, Mr [fl. 1790–1791], *clarinetist, basset-horn player.*
In the March 1967 issue of the *Galpin Society Journal* Charles Cudworth transcribed lists of Vauxhall musicians who were active in 1790–91. The original lists, in the Minet Library, were probably made by the music copyist John Foulis. A Mr Springer was cited as a clarinetist and basset-horn player.

Squelch. *See* **Quelch.**

WILLIAM SPRIGHTLY

artist unknown

Squibb, George d. 1768, singer.

The "Gentlemen" who made his stage debut singing in *Artaxerxes* at Covent Garden Theatre on 23 November 1764 was George Squibb, who sang La Finesse in *The Guardian Outwitted* on 12 December. For his benefit on 27 April 1765 he appeared as Macheath in *The Beggar's Opera*. He sang in *The Royal Convert* on 16 May. Wroth in *London Pleasure Gardens* notes that Squibb sang at Marylebone Gardens in 1763 and 1764, and the *Jester's Magazine* places him there again in 1765 and 1766.

Squibb continued his engagement at Covent Garden in 1765–66 and 1766–67, adding such new roles as the Chasseur Royal in *The Royal Chace* and singing in the choruses of *Romeo and Juliet*, *The Royal Convert*, and *Comus*. His last appearance at Covent Garden was at his benefit on 29 April 1767, when he made a profit of a bit less than £100. His daily salary was £1. Reed in his "Notitia Dramatica" said that George Squibb died about 27 February 1768.

Squibb, Mrs [George?] [fl. 1768], actress.

At Covent Garden Theatre on 11 May 1768 (not long after the death of the singer George Squibb), a Mrs Squibb played the title character in *Zara* for her shared benefit with Wignell; her profit came to about £85. She seems not to have performed again and should perhaps be treated as an amateur. She may have been the wife of George Squibb.

Squire, James [fl. 1771?-1794], singer, actor?

A Mr Squire was paid £3 15s. by the Covent Garden management on 14 November 1771 for singing in the chorus 15 nights, presumably in *The Institution of the Garter*. He received £3 10s. on 10 January 1772 for 14 nights. Perhaps he was the Mr Squire who acted the Earl of Derby in a performance of *Jane Shore* at the Haymarket Theatre on 20 December 1779. A Mr Squire sang tenor in the Handel Memorial Concerts at Westminster Abbey and the Pantheon in May and June 1784. All of these appearances—or at least the singing ones—were very likely made by James Squire, who was listed in Doane's *Musical Directory* of 1794 as living in Panton Street, St James's. Doane noted that Squire was a member of the Titchfield Chapel Society and had sung in the Handelian performances at Westminster Abbey.

"Squire Ironside." *See* STEELE, RICHARD.

"Squire Sammy." *See* FOOTE, SAMUEL.

St. *See* SAINT.

Stabilini, Girolamo c. 1762–1815, violinist, composer.

Born in Rome about 1762, Girolamo (Hieronymo) Stabilini left Italy in 1783 to take over the leadership of the St Cecilia Hall concerts in Edinburgh. He established himself quickly, and on 14 May 1784, according to David Johnson's *Music and Society in Lowland Scotland*, Stabilini performed his own violin concerto in D at a Musical Society concert. He played solos almost weekly at St Cecilia Hall, and he continued composing works, at least once using

GIROLAMO STABILINI
by Kay

traditional Scots tunes. He became a Mason and a member of the Royal Edinburgh Volunteers.

Doane's *Musical Directory* of 1794 shows that Stabilini came to London at some point to participate in the Handelian concerts at Westminster Abbey. Johnson claims that Stabilini might have moved on to higher accomplishments away from Edinburgh had he not turned to drink. Grove (5th edition) notes that the musician died of dropsy in Edinburgh on 13 July 1815 and was buried in the graveyard of St Cuthbert.

An engraved portrait by John Kay of Stabilini, with three other Edinburgh personalities on the same plate, was published by the engraver in 1786. Captioned "Bucks have at you all or who's afraid," the print shows Dr Eiston, late of the 55th Regiment, Mr Stabilini, an Italian musician, the Laird of Macnab, and Capt M'Kenzie, of Red Castle.

Stables, Mr ₁*fl.1760–1771*₁,   *numberer.*
Mr Stables was mentioned in Egerton and Folger manuscripts as a numberer at Covent Garden Theatre, in 1760, 1761, and 1766. He earned £1 10*s.* weekly, or, as Foote's *Life of Murphy* lists him as of 14 September 1767, 5*s.* daily. He was earning the same salary on 28 September 1771 and was the highest paid house servant named.

Stacey, W. ₁*fl.1795*₁,   *box office keeper.*
Playbills in the Richmond Library for the summer of 1795 show W. Stacey to have been the box office keeper at the Richmond Theatre. Perhaps the Mrs Stacey whose benefit tickets were accepted there on 25 July 1781 was his wife. She presumably worked at the theatre, perhaps as a house servant.

Stacey, Mrs ₁**W.?**₁ ₁*fl.1781*₁,   *house servant? See* STACEY, W.

Stacy, Mr ₁*fl.1776*₁,   *actor.*
Mr Stacy played the Duke of Buckingham in *Henry VIII* at China Hall, Rotherhithe, on 25 September 1776.

"Staffordshire Giant, The" ₁*fl.1759*₁, *actor.*
At the Haymarket Theatre on 1 October 1759 the title role in *Galligantus* was played by "The Staffordshire Giant."

Stagdill. *See* STAGELDOIR.

"Stage King of Grief, The." *See* LEWIS, PHILIP.

Stageldoir, James   *d.1806, dancer, actor, caller, property man.*
A Mr "Steggdoir," a dancer, was in the Smock Alley company in Dublin in 1756, according to a calendar compiled by W. S. Clark. A Miss "Stageldoir," perhaps a younger sister, danced at the theatre as a juvenile on 20 January 1757. (The name Stageldoir was the bane of bill-printers and theatrical treasurers for 50 years and was variously twisted: Stageldiors, Stagledoirs, Stageldour, Staggledior, Staggledore, Stageldoirs, Stegeldoris and Stogadoir.) The Clark manuscript calendar picks up Stageldoir again at Smock Alley in 1758–59 and along with his wife—also a dancer—at the Crow Street Theatre, Dublin, in 1759–60. They were at Cork some part of the autumns of 1760, 1761, and 1762.

For 13 years after 1762 the movements of the Stageldoirs are unknown. James Winston's transcription of the Drury Lane Fund Book in the Folger Library shows that James Stageldoir subscribed his 10*s.* 6*d.* to the theatre's retirement fund in 1775. But his wife's name appears in a paylist of December 1774, so the couple were at the theatre probably during the entire season of 1774–75.

The Folger Library's manuscript treasury accounts of the Liverpool summer theatre in 1778 bear the following notation opposite 12 September: "By Mr & Mrs Stegeldoirs for 7 nights each in the Pantomime 0 14 0." That pittance—a shilling a night for each—cannot have been enough to keep them. Perhaps they relied on the wages of a talented daughter who was being paid sometimes £1 1s. per week, and sometimes £2 for dancing at Liverpool that summer. There were, in fact, three talented dancing and singing daughters—Jane, Martha, and Mary—who from the season of 1775–76 for nearly 20 years were to appear frequently on the Drury Lane boards.

In 1775–76, James Stageldoir was listed as a dancer in the Drury Lane account book and in 1776–77 received £1 per week. But not until 23 May 1783 did his name appear on a bill, and then only in a miscellaneous list of 10 minor house servants and performers who shared a benefit. By that season his daughters were frequently seen as young featured dancers. In 1784, 1785, and 1786, on nearly the same date in May and with nearly the same list of people, Stageldoir shared benefit tickets. He was probably doing chorus dancing during those years.

Stageldoir dropped out of sight in 1786–87 and 1787–88 and until 13 November 1789, when his name (Staggeldior) appeared in the huge cast for the new ballad opera *The Island of St Marguerite*—but his name was not assigned to a part in the bill. John Philip Kemble's notation in British Library Additional Manuscript 31,942 gave Stageldoir a secondary duty at Drury Lane theatre in 1791–92, that of caller. When Colman, taking advantage of the inactivity of the Drury Lane company, ran his Haymarket Theatre through the winter of 1793–94 with Drury Lane performers, Stageldoir was among them and that season achieved his only two identifiable roles: on 10 October 1793, one of two Turnkeys in the pantomime *Royal Clemency* and, on 23 December, one of the Passengers in the pantomime *Harlequin Peasant*. The Folger Fund Book notation has James Stageldoir claiming assistance

from the Fund in "mid-1796" and dying on 1 September 1806.

Stageldoir, Mrs James   d. 1795, dancer, dresser, singer.

Mrs James Stageldoir was the wife of a dancer, actor, and house servant and the mother of three prominent performers—Jane, Martha, and Mary (later Mrs Piele). Mrs Stageldoir's name—spelled correctly—appears first, so far as surviving records show, in the bills for Crow Street Theatre, Dublin, along with her husband's ("Stegadoir") in the 1759–60 season. They were dancers there and at Cork in the summer of 1760 and the autumns of 1761 and 1762.

From 1762 until 24 December 1774, when a notation appeared in the Drury Lane treasury book (now in the Folger Library) showing her salary as £1 per week, nothing is known of her. Very little can be surely known afterward. At some point she abandoned dancing at Drury Lane and began serving as a women's dresser, which function she had assumed by the 1776–77 season, when she was earning only 9s. per week. But she and her husband were evidently dancing at Liverpool in the summer of 1778, when the manuscript account book of that theatre showed them receiving a shilling a night for performing in pantomimes. Both there and in London, however, one or more daughters danced regularly to supplement the family income.

In the 1789–90 season Mrs Stageldoir again received 9s. per week for her work at Drury Lane. In 1790–91 she also sang in the chorus. She died on 25 January 1795, according to the Fund Book.

Stageldoir, Jane   [fl. 1780–1788], dancer, singer, actress.

Jane Stageldoir was the daughter of Mr and Mrs James Stageldoir, dancers and house servants, and the sister—probably the youngest—of the versatile performers Martha and Mary (later Mrs Piele). It is often difficult and sometimes impossible to distinguish among them, but there are enough playbills marked "Miss J. Stageldoir" and other clues to provide Jane with a short but vigorous career.

She was obviously a dancer, like her sisters, from her earliest years, and she remained a dancer always. But by 20 September 1780 she was also acting, if exertions for the slight part of Cupid in *Cymon* can be so described. It was a part she repeated many times, as she continued to do frequent hornpipes and team with her sisters in dancing *The Butterfly*. In 1783 she was still young or short enough to act Prince Edward in *Richard III*. On 5 January 1786 she introduced, with Williamson, Mrs Sutton, and others, "A New Scotch Dance *The Lucky Return*," which she was also to repeat frequently. On 9 March 1786 we first notice "Miss J. Stageldoir" as a singer, one of several delivering an "*Ode* (composed by Dr Cooke)," and from that date she was often present in choruses.

Jane's only other "named" roles of which we are aware, were Colombine in *Harlequin Junior*, which she took over from her sister Martha on 25 January 1788, and Penelope in *The Romp*, on 8 April 1788. On 6 May 1788, she assisted her frequent partner Hamoir and others in a new musical interlude *Le Matin, midi, et le soir.* Their part (Noon) featured the new dance *The Shepherd's Wedding*. The *London Stage* gives several performances in the seasons 1789–90 through 1794–95 to Jane, but we believe they belong to Martha.

Stageldoir, Martha ₍*fl.* 1783–1795?₎, *dancer, singer, actress.*

Martha Stageldoir was a daughter of Mr and Mrs James Stageldoir, dancers and house servants, and the sister of Jane and Mary Stageldoir, for several years well-known at Drury Lane theatre as dancers, singers, and minor actresses. Martha's sister Mary became Mrs John Piele in September 1785. Only in notices after that date is it possible certainly to discriminate Martha and Mary in the bills, since, when first names were regarded at all by the printers, they gave only "Miss *M.* Stageldoir." But many characters in the same "line," and some of the same roles, are given in the bills both to "Miss *M.* Stageldoir" and "Miss Stageldoir" both before and after 1785; we conclude that all such roles belong to Martha rather than to Mary. Before 1785 the dancing must be distributed among the three girls, for sometimes there were "the three Miss Stageldoirs," sometimes only "the Miss Stageldoirs," but most often only one "Miss Stageldoir."

Apparently all three girls danced and sang, and at least two acted.

The following are the named roles known to have been sung, danced, and played in farce and pantomime by "Miss M. Stageldoir" and "Miss Stageldoir," whom we are considering as Martha: in 1783–84, Lucinda in *The Englishman in Paris,* a Bacchant in *Comus,* Colombine in *Fortunatus,* Colombine in *Harlequin Junior,* Miss Prue in *Love for Love,* and a character in *The Camp;* in 1784–85, Patie in *The Gentle Shepherd,* Lucinda in *Love in a Village,* and Cynthia in *The Double Dealer;* in 1785–86, Theodosia in *The Maid of the Mill,* Penelope in *The Romp,* and Colombine in *The Caldron;* in 1788–89, Prissy in *The Lying Valet,* a "principal character" unspecified in *Robinson Crusoe,* and Agnes in *The Follies of the Day;* in 1789–90, a Nun in the new ballad opera by John St. John, *The Island of St Marguerite;* and in 1794–95, a Captive in *Lodoiska,* Marietta in *The Pirates,* and an Amazon in J. H. D'Egville's new afterpiece *Alexander the Great.*

Stageldoir, Mary. *See* PIELE, MRS JOHN.

Stagg, Mr ₍*fl.* 1794₎, *clarinetist, flutist.*

Doane's *Musical Directory* of 1794 listed Mr Stagg, of Virginia Row, Bethnal Green, as a performer on the flute and clarinet at the Royal Circus and in the Guards Third Regiment.

Stagg, Mrs ₍*fl.* 1712₎, *dancer?*

A benefit concert for Mrs Stagg was held on 27 February 1712 at the Dancing Room in Piccadilly. Perhaps she was a dancer. A Mr Stagg was named in 1721 by John Weaver as a dancing master from Bath.

Staggins, Charles ₍*fl.* 1685–1689₎, *violinist, oboist.*

Charles Staggins, one of the sons of the court musician Isaac Staggins and his wife Mary, replaced his father in the King's Musick on 27 January 1685, about two months after his father's death. Charles was hired to play the "tenor hoboy" and violin in the King's private music. Perhaps he was the Charles Staggins who married Mary Brugnie on 3 January 1687 at St Martin-in-the-Fields. He attended the royal family at Windsor in the summer of

1787, receiving 3s. daily above his base salary of £30 annually. He was last mentioned in the Lord Chamberlain's accounts on 25 March 1689, and since he was not named in his mother's will of 1697, perhaps by that time Charles had died.

Staggins, Isaac *d. 1684, violinist, oboist.*

Isaac Staggins was possibly the brother of James Staggins and certainly the father of the more famous Nicholas Staggins. Though Isaac and his wife eventually belonged to St Paul, Covent Garden, the registers of St Andrew, Holborn, show them to have lived in that parish in the 1650s. Alice, the daughter of "Isaacke Staggins musitioner" and his wife Mary, of Cockpit Court in Shoe Lane, was born on 29 November and christened on 2 December 1655. We do not know what happened to Alice; she was not named in her mother's will in 1697 and by that time may have died.

Staggins was possibly a member of the King's Musick as early as 1660, but the Lord Chamberlain's accounts did not mention him until 12 April 1661, when he was one of the violinists receiving livery for the coronation of Charles II. By 25 January 1662 Staggins was a member of the King's "private consort," and in the years that followed he was frequently selected to attend the royal family on trips to Tunbridge, Windsor, Oxford, Hampton Court, Dover, and Newmarket. He was always paid extra for such journeys, his base salary being £46 10s. 10d. annually plus livery. Staggins was also one of several court musicians assigned to play in the band at the Bridges Street Theatre whenever the manager Thomas Killigrew should need his services.

In 1665 Staggins came into a second post at court, one shared with William Young. A warrant concerning it, dated 25 May 1666, cited Staggins as a "tenor hoboy," and the salary for the shared post was 1s. 8d. daily. In addition, Staggins was chosen one of an elite group of 12 violinists within the main band of 24. He played violin in the court production of *Calisto* on 15 February 1675.

In addition to the daughter Alice who was born in 1655, Staggins and his wife had two other daughters (Elizabeth, baptized at St Paul, Covent Garden, on 25 July 1669, and Sarah, buried at that church on 17 December 1667) and three sons (Charles, Nicholas, and

Thomas; the first two have entries in this *Dictionary*). Elizabeth married Summerset Robins and the pair became the executors of Mrs Staggins's will.

Isaac Staggins was buried at St Paul, Covent Garden, on 3 December 1684. Administration of his estate was granted to his wife on 16 December. His wife Mary wrote her will on 15 December 1697; it was proved on 7 April 1701. In the will Mary Staggins described herself as infirm in body in 1697, and she may have spent her last years an invalid. She left her son Nicholas a shilling, noting that he had already received his full portion of Isaac Staggins's estate. Everything else she left to Summerset and Elizabeth Robins.

Staggins, James [*fl. 1660–1661*], *violinist?*

James Staggins may have been a brother of the court musician Isaac Staggins. He seems to have been a member of the King's Musick after the Restoration in 1660, and on 24 January 1661 he was named to receive a New Year's gift as a member of the King's "private consort"—which suggests that he was probably a violinist.

Staggins, Nicholas *d. 1700, violinist, flutist, composer.*

The son of Isaac and Mary Staggins and the brother of Thomas, Charles, Elizabeth, Sarah, and Alice Staggins, Nicholas Staggins was by far the most successful of this family of Restoration court musicians. He was appointed on 21 December 1671 to replace William Young as a violinist in the King's Musick at 20d. daily and 16 2s. 6d. annual livery, but since Young's executors were due arrears in his salary, Staggins received only half pay until the executors were paid off. Moreover, his livery fee was frequently as much as three or more years in arrears. But Staggins had other sources of income: "How unhappy a Lover am I," a song in 2 *Conquest of Granada* (1671), was set by him and published in 1673 in *Choice Songs and Ayres;* so, too, "Whilst Alexis lay prest" from *Marriage à la Mode* (1672). And, perhaps to make up for the fact that his violinist's post brought him only half a salary, a second position was given Staggins in 1673, this one as a flutist. Then, on 15 August 1674, he was promoted to Master of the King's Music and leader of the violins, replacing Lewis Grabu. His new salary was £200 annually.

From time to time Staggins accompanied the royal family on trips to such places as Windsor, Newmarket, Hampton Court, and the Hague. As Master he received as much as 10*s*. daily extra pay for such excursions outside London. The Crown also paid Staggins as a composer or arranger. For example, in July 1675 he was paid for writing out some music for Tiberio Fiorilli, the famous scaramouch, who was visiting London. On 27 January 1676 the Lord Chamberlain ordered that Staggins be paid £92 3*s*. for expenses incurred while writing music for the King; the itemized bill included music paper, ink, chamber rental, fire, and so on. On 9 November 1686 he was to receive £19 11*s*. 6*d*. for writing music for the King's coronation; and on 13 March 1694 he was to be paid over £61 for his services as composer in 1692.

Nicholas Staggins's salary as Master of the King's Musick was continued when James II came to the throne, but William and Mary in 1689 thought £200 excessive, for they cut his salary in half. How long that reduced salary continued is not clear, but by 1697 it was back up to £200. Staggins augmented his income with concerts, two of which were presented at York Buildings in the spring of 1687. The events consisted of "Entertainment of Vocal and Instrumental Musick" composed by Staggins. Modern music historians do not credit Staggins with much talent as a composer, but he seems to have been well enough thought of in his day. John Crowne, who wrote the text for the court masque *Calisto* (February 1675), said in the published edition that "if the judgments of others, and those the most skilful too, be not mistaken, Mr Staggins has not only delighted us with his excellent composition, but with the hopes of seeing in a very short time a master of music in *England* equal to any *France* or Italy have produced."

In 1682 Staggins received his doctorate in music from Cambridge, though, strangely, he did not perform his exercise until two years later. After he did, Cambridge appointed him a professor of music. He may not have spent much time there, however, for his address in 1686 was "Little Chelsey in the parish of Kensington" in London.

Numerous warrants in the Lord Chamberlain's accounts and State Papers cited Nicholas Staggins. Many concerned livery payments due him from previous years (in 1686 he was owed over £193); others directed him to have his band of violins available whenever a play was produced at court; one ordered him to assist the French performers in their preparations for *Rare en Tout* at court in May 1677; one gave him leave to spend a year in Italy and "other foreign parts" in 1676; a few concerned suits brought against Staggins for debts—the quaintest being a 1696 petition by a brewer, Anthony Nurse, for £120 for beer and ale; and others indicated that, like other court musicians waiting for arrears from the King, Staggins sometimes had to assign salary due him to someone who had ready money to lend.

Very few personal notes about Nicholas Staggins have been discovered. Tom Brown in his *Letters from the Dead* in 1703 spoke of Staggins as being bandy-legged. Among the Rochester-Savile letters is one from Savile dated 25 June 1678 in which he said,

From the rising of the sun to the setting thereof, I see noe thing that pleases my eyes, or heare noe thing but what grates my eares; onely I am promised a moments titillation by Mr. Staggins who is come over with great credit and many new aires. Hee may raigne there like Great Turke and cutt whose catts-gutts hee please if the harmony bee not to his liking. With what moderation hee will use this absolute power, I leave it to fate and the immortall gods to determine.

Nicholas Staggins died at Windsor on 13 June 1700 and was succeeded at court by John Eccles. Staggins had written his will on 3 January 1691, leaving to his mother Mary half of his property—his house, courtyards, gardens, and stables in Little Chelsea; after her death the property was to go to his brother Thomas and then to his brother Charles. The other half of the property was to go to Nicholas's sister Elizabeth. His arrears in salary were to be split between his mother and sister. The will was proved on 17 July 1700.

Stainer. *See* STAYNER.

Stamitz, Carl Philipp   *1745–1801, violinist, violist, composer.*

Carl Philipp Stamitz was baptized on 8 May 1745 at Mannheim, a son of the important

Bohemian composer Johann Wenzel Anton Stamitz. Carl studied first with his father, then with Christian Cannabich, Ignaz Holzbauer, and Franz Xavier Richter, according to the account in the *New Grove*. In 1762 Stamitz joined the Mannheim orchestra as a violinist. In 1770 he went to Paris, where he became composer to Duke Louis of Noailles. He performed in the concerts Spirituel, along with his brother Anton, and had other engagements in Paris during the 1770s. In 1772 he lived at Versailles. He travelled widely—composing, performing, and publishing—at Vienna, Frankfurt am Main, Augsburg, and Strasbourg.

The first known mention of Carl Stamitz in London was on the oratorio bill at Covent Garden Theatre on 19 February 1777, when, after Part I of the *Messiah,* there was "a duetto on the tenor [viola] and violin by Stamitz and Lamotte." It may be that after that date Stamitz returned to the Continent; he seems to have been in Paris in 1778. But by March of that year he was serving in the Covent Garden oratorios again. On 18 March, at the end of Part II of *The Ascension,* there was a "*quartetto* for the violin, German flute, tenor and piano forte by Master Weichsel, Florio, Stamitz, and Miss Weichsel." On 25 March following, a "miscellaneous act" after *Acis and Galatea* featured a "*Concerto* on the viole [*sic*] d'amore by Stamitz" and a "*duetto* for the violin and tenor by Master Weichsel and Stamitz."

Stamitz may have been attached to the Italian opera company in London in 1779, for on 25 March that year, when *Enea e Lavinia* was brought out at the King's Theatre, the music for the "second dance" was said to be "entirely new, composed by Charles Stamitz."

About 1779 Stamitz moved to The Hague, and between April 1782 and July 1784 he played 28 concerts, in one of which, that of 23 November 1783, the 12-year-old Beethoven was pianist. Between April 1785, when he arrived in Hamburg, and 1788, when he went to Kassel, Stamitz traveled restlessly in search of a secure living—to Magdeburg, Leipzig, Berlin, Dresden, Prague, and Halle. In 1789 and 1790 he directed the Liebhaber concerts at Kassel.

Before 1790 Stamitz married Maria Josepha Pilz. Several of their children died near birth. By 1795 Stamitz had assumed the post of Ka-

pellmeister at Jena and teacher of music at the University. But the pay was indifferent, and his efforts to supplement it by volunteering compositions for the consideration of princes and publishers were of no avail. The latter part of his life was a series of disappointments, and when he died at Jena on 9 November 1801 (his wife had died on 17 January that year) he was so heavily in debt that his personal effects were sold at auction. Manuscripts of his music, a catalogue of which was published in 1810, have all disappeared.

The *New Grove* has a careful analysis of the published music of Stamitz and a list of his known works.

Stamp, Mr ₍*fl.* 1784₎,   *actor?*
British Library manuscript 29,709 cites a Mr Stamp as ending his engagement (as an actor?) at Drury Lane on 23 October 1784; he received 6s.

Stamper, Francis   *d. 1766, actor, singer, writer, publisher.*
It is probable that the Francis Stamper, silver lace man, whom Leslie Hotson found trading with the King's Company in May 1682, was related (perhaps as father or grandfather) to the actor and literary hack Francis Stamper who was active in the middle of the eighteenth century.

The Francis Stamper of this entry was associated with the miscellaneous writer and public orator William Kenrick as collaborator in or publisher of a number of publications from the middle of 1750 through the middle of 1752. From August 1750 to January 1751, Kenrick and Stamper, as "Whimsey Banter" and "Archimagirus Metaphoricus," wrote and edited the magazine *The Kapélion, or Poetical Ordinary.* In December 1750 they were called by those noms de plume in the mock trial of magazine writers in *The Magazines Blown up; or, They are all in the Suds.*

Other publications either written or published by Stamper or jointly with Kenrick were: *The so much talk'd of and expected Old Woman's Dunciad, A Modern Character, Introduced in the Scenes of Vanbrugh's Aesop. As it was acted at a late private Representation of Henry the Fourth perform'd gratis at the little Opera-House in the Haymarket* (which memorializes some private theatricals in which the authors were engaged); *The Royal Jester, or Cream of the Jest; The Bulfinch, Vol. II, Being a Choice Collection of English Songs;* and *Memoirs of the Life of William Stamper,* all between January and March 1751. Also in the latter month, *A Satirical Dialogue Humbly address'd to the Gentlemen who deformed the play of Othello,* castigating the amateur performance of the brothers Delaval at Drury Lane Theatre on 7 March, was probably by Stamper and Kenrick, despite an emphatic denial inserted by Stamper in the *General Advertiser* on 19 March.

Kenrick's *A Monody to the Memory of his Royal Highness Frederick Prince of Wales* was published by F. Stamper and E. Downham, along with a second edition of *Ben Johnson's Jests* in April 1751. In October following they published *Genuine and Authentic Memoirs of the . . . Robin Hood Society,* probably by Stamper, and Kenrick's *The Grand Question Debated, or an Essay to Prove that the Soul of Man is not, neither can it be, Immortal,* and *A Reply to the Grand Question Debated.* Stamper issued Kenrick's *Fun: A Parodi-tragic-comical Satire* and reissued his two essays on the soul's immortality in 1752.

On 31 August 1750, "Francis Stamper of St. George, Hanover Sq[uare], & Sarah Kirk, of St. Faith under St. Paul's" had been married at St George's Chapel, Hyde Park Corner, according to the register. The Stampers disappeared from the London scene after the spring of 1752. Stamper evidently now was bent on turning his enthusiasm for amateur theatricals to professional account. Walter Baynham in *The Glasgow Stage* (1892) reports evidence that Stamper acted with Digges, Love, and Mrs Ward in a wooden booth in the Castle Yard, Glasgow, in the summer of 1752. He moved on with "Mr. Digge's [*sic*] and Mrs. Ward's company [to] the theatre in the Canongate," Edinburgh, in 1753, according to Arnot's *History of Edinburgh.*

Apparently Stamper remained and acted in Edinburgh through the winter season of 1759–60, his service there broken only by a brief engagement to the Smock Alley Theater in Dublin in October of 1755 and briefer excursions with members of the Edinburgh company into northern England. Evidently he continued to write also. *The Cambridge Bibliography* credits him with *An Essay on the Stage; or, the Art of Acting, A Poem,* published at Edin-

burgh in 1754. But his vocation was now acting.

Norma Armstrong's manuscript calendar of the Edinburgh theatres gives him between 1754 and 1765 a list, which though almost exclusively in comic lines, is greatly varied in the comic talents required: low, suave, broad, sentimental, and melodic: Alderman Smuggler in *The Constant Couple,* Bayes in *The Rehearsal,* Cadwallader in *The Author,* Caliban in *The Tempest,* Charino in *Love Makes a Man,* Corin in *As You Like It,* Cimberton in *The Conscious Lovers,* Dick in *The Apprentice,* Dogberry in *Much Ado about Nothing,* the Drunken Man in *Lethe,* Filch in *The Beggar's Opera,* Fribble in *Miss in Her Teens,* Hypolito in *The Tempest,* an Irish Officer in *The Reprisal,* Jack Meggot in *The Suspicious Husband,* Kent in *King Lear,* Lovegold in *The Miser,* Lusignan in *Zara,* Mercutio in *Romeo and Juliet,* Peachum in *The Beggar's Opera,* Moneytrap in *The City Wives' Confederacy,* Oldcastle in *The Intriguing Chambermaid,* the Old Man in *Lethe,* Old Mirabel in *The Inconstant,* Petruchio in *Catherine and Petruchio,* Polonius in *Hamlet,* Ranger in *The Suspicious Husband,* Razor in *The Provok'd Wife,* Sharp in *The Lying Valet,* Sir Francis Gripe in *The Busy Body,* Sir Francis Wronghead in *The Provok'd Husband,* Squire Somebody in *The Stage Coach,* Trampolin in *A Duke and No Duke,* Will Dowling in *A Hint to the Sailors,* a Witch in *Macbeth,* Witwoud in *The Way of the World,* Cadwallader in *The Author,* Captain Brazen in *The Recruiting Officer,* and unspecified parts in *The Male Coquette* and *The Simpletons.* The *Newcastle Journal* recorded performances of Edinburgh actors at Newcastle and Durham in the fall of 1759 and again in the fall of 1760. Stamper was among them and added to the repertoire listed above Gomez in *The Discovery,* the Gentleman Usher in *The Rehearsal,* and Blunt in *George Barnwell.*

Mrs Stamper also acted and sang at Edinburgh, and though not employed as frequently as her husband, she had roles as various and often more important: Lady Percy in *1 Henry IV,* Phillis in *The Conscious Lovers,* Lucy Lockit in *The Beggar's Opera,* the Nurse in *Romeo and Juliet,* Cephisa in *The Distrest Mother,* Viola in *Twelfth Night,* Harriet in *The Miser,* Isabella in *The Stage Coach,* Fainlove in *The Tender Husband,* and Julia in *The Fatal Marriage,* among others. The *Scots Magazine* for December 1753 thought she played well "for so young an actress." She must have died, however, by October of 1759, for her place had by then been taken by a second Mrs Stamper. "At the particular request of several ladies" that Mrs Stamper's "Concert of Vocal and Instrumental Music" began to be announced in the papers. When that lady gave a concert in the Durham Assembly Room in October 1760 she was identified as "the late Signora Mazzanti." (There is no record of either the first or second Mrs Stamper as a performer in London.)

John Genest, in *Some Account of the English Stage* (1832), wrote that Francis Stamper returned to Dublin to join the Crow Street Theatre for the 1761–62 season. By the spring of 1763 or earlier he had drifted back to London and on 15 April he made his London acting debut at Covent Garden Theatre, as Smuggler in *The Constant Couple*, on the night of Jenny Poitier's benefit. Though not a regular member of the company, Stamper was allowed to share in a benefit with four other performers on 7 May 1763, probably the arrangement to pay him for the service to Miss Poitier and to other performers on 9 and 18 May, when he played, first Oldcastle and then Polonius, for their benefits.

Stamper reappeared at Covent Garden at the beginning of the new season, as Francis the drawer in *1 Henry IV*, on 26 September. But then he went back to Smock Alley for the 1763–64 season. The following season found him again in Edinburgh. Tate Wilkinson in his *Memoirs* recalled Stamper as a favorite there but said that his health had declined after he took to morning drinking. The *Edinburgh Courant* of Monday, 17 March 1766, is quoted by James Dibdin in *The Annals of the Edinburgh Stage:* "Mr Francis Stamper, who performed the tragedy of *Macbeth* last Wednesday night, died about two o'clock on Saturday afternoon, and was interred in the Canongate Churchyard." No reason was given for the seeming extreme haste to bury him.

The comedian George Stayley penned an epitaph:

> *Is Stamper dead? He is!—to all below.*
> *Look in each face—you'll read it in their woe!*
> *He who was wont to raise the general smile,*
> *And for whole nights a world of care beguile:*
> *(Oh sudden change!)—whence comes it, Stamper,*
>   *now,*

> *You fix such gloomy sorrow on the brow?*
> *"Forgive my son'—the comic [G]enius cry'd:*
> *"He never grieved a soul; but when he died!"*

Stamper had developed into a prime favorite with Edinburgh audiences by the time of his death. Mrs Margaret Steuart Calderwood of Polton in one of her letters dated 1756 (published in Alexander Ferguson's edition of her *Letters and Journals* [1886]) described to a friend a rustic character whom she met:

> Peter you have often seen acted by Stamper; he seemed to understand a horse-race or a cock-match much better than the price of corn; he is just the figure of a young squire who would be married to a cast-mistress, if some good-natured person in the drama did not prevent it, for which he would express his thankfulness with many grins and smiles, severall bows and scrapes, shrugs, and rubbing of his hands for gladness.

Though James Boswell and Francis Gentleman, in their *View of the Edinburgh Theatre During the Summer Season, 1759,* disliked Stamper's merry manner of playing Polonius and thought his French pronunciation as Lord Foppington defective, they praised the "ease and gaiety" of his Captain Flash and his conception of Mercutio. Like everyone else, apparently, they reserved their best plaudits for his old men:

> The extraordinary Merit of Mr Stamper, in the old Men in Comedy, has been acknowledged by an elegant Writer of this Country, and confirmed by the general Voice of every Company. The Miser is without dispute his Master-piece. We must say, that we can scarcely form an Idea of the Character's being better performed: He enters so entirely into the Spirit of it, that we absolutely forget the Player, and with Difficulty can bring ourselves to think that it is not a Reality; every Look, every Movement is so particularly just. The Mixture of Astonishment, Grief, and Indignation, at discovering the Loss of his Money, was greatly executed.

Stanard, Mr   [*fl. 1784*],   violinist.

Mr Stanard played second violin in the Handel Memorial Concerts at Westminster Abbey and the Pantheon in May and June 1784.

Standen, Master   *b.c. 1789, actor, singer.*

Master Standen, the son of the strolling player and Covent Garden house servant Charles Standen by his second wife Susanna (née Crump), made his first appearance on the stage in the title role of *Tom Thumb* at Covent Garden on 10 October 1794. When he played that role the second time on 15 October, his young sister appeared as the Duke of York in *Richard III*. On 6 May 1795 he again played Tom Thumb, and was described as a child only six years of age. On 28 May he appeared as Little Bob in the premiere of Bernard's *The Poor Sailor*.

In the summer of 1795 Master Standen performed at Birmingham, where his father probably was working. At Covent Garden on 2 October 1795 he played Little Bob again and was the Drummer Boy in the premiere of O'Keeffe's *The Doldrum* on 23 April 1796, Tom Thumb again on 18 May, and Little Bob once more on 4 June 1796. The following season, 1796–97, he was seen as Tom Thumb, the Drummer Boy, Little Bob, and a Young Devil in *Duke and No Duke*. On 8 June 1797 he sang "The Little Farthing Rushlight" (from *Tom Thumb*) as a specialty number. On 2 October 1797 he was the Duke of York in *Richard III* and on 13 October the Page in *The Orphan*. He sang in the chorus of *The Genoese Pirate*, Cross's ballet pantomime that premiered on 15 October 1798, played Kenrick in the premiere of Cobb's comic opera *Ramah Droog* on 12 November 1798, and sang in the premiere of Cumberland's *Joanna* on 16 January 1800.

Master Standen continued to perform at Covent Garden at least through 1802–3. He also played at the Royal Circus in 1802, appearing as a Little Old Bachelor in *The Golden Farmer; or, Harlequin Ploughboy,* which opened on 28 June.

Standen, Miss [*fl.* 1790–1799], *actress, dancer.*

Miss Standen, the daughter of the actor and house servant Charles Standen by his second wife Susanna (née Crump), first appeared at Covent Garden Theatre, as a child, on 18 October 1790 playing the Duke of York in *Richard III*. On 11 February 1791 she played the Child in *Isabella*. At the Haymarket Theatre in the summer of 1791 she acted Goliah in *The Young Quaker* on 23 June and subsequently appeared as the Negro Boy in *The Son-in-Law*, the Duke of York again, and the Maid in *The Double Amour*. After playing the Page in *The Orphan* at Covent Garden on 28 October 1791,

she acted the Duke of York for the Drury Lane company at the King's Theatre on 14 November 1791, then returned to Covent Garden to appear as the Child in *Medea* on 26 March 1792. Again at the Haymarket she played Goliah in *The Young Quaker* on 15 June 1792 and danced in *The Enchanted Wood* on 25 July.

Miss Standen played similar roles at Covent Garden through 1798–99. She acted an unassigned role in the premiere of T. J. Dibdin's *The Magic Oak* on 29 January 1799, and was in a total of 32 performances that season.

Her brother Master Standen acted at Covent Garden in the 1790s. Her sister Sophia Standen, born in 1791, was performing at Covent Garden in 1809, when she signed a salary receipt. Sophia was probably the Miss Standen at the theatre in 1813–14.

Standen, Charles 1731–1800, *actor, house servant.*

Charles Standen, born in 1731, probably was the Mr Standen who with his wife acted in *Love and Duty,* a new tragedy by John Slade, at the Haymarket Theatre on 12 August 1756. In 1762 and 1765 Standen was acting at Edinburgh, in the New Concert Hall Theatre, where surviving bills record him for the Prince in *Romeo and Juliet* and Swad in *Phoebe* on 13 April 1762 and Mr Melinder in *Zara* on 10 August 1765. According to Edward Cape Everard, Charles Standen was a strolling player in Essex in the late 1770s. In 1777 he managed a company at Hastings. He and Everard were with a group of actors that played at China Hall, Rotherhithe, South London, in June 1778, though Standen's name appeared in none of the surviving notices.

Between 1787 and May 1791 a Mr Standen shared in benefit tickets at Drury Lane Theatre with a group of house servants, and from June 1791 to 11 June 1800 a Mr Standen shared tickets with servants at Covent Garden Theatre. We have assumed that the same person was involved and that as a minor house servant or perhaps a supernumerary, he moved from one theatre to the other in 1791. We have also assumed that the house servant was the former stroller, for on 31 July 1800 one Charles Standen was buried at St Paul, Covent Garden, "aged 69 years." Despite his age at death, he was probably the Charles Standen whose daughter Sophia by his wife Susanna had been baptized at St Paul, Covent Garden, on 14 April 1791. The *Oracle* on 23 February 1791 had reported that Charles Standen had testified at proceedings to establish his son's legitimacy, stating that he had separated from his first wife because they had been illegally married (only two banns had been read) and that later he had married Miss Crump.

The circumstances and their sequence are not quite clear, but we believe them to have been as follows. Standen's first wife, with whom he had appeared at Drury Lane in August 1756, was Anne Standen (who may have been born Lewis), whom he had married on 4 August 1755. She acted as Mrs Standen at Edinburgh in 1761–62, but when she made her debut at Covent Garden Theatre on 27 September 1762 as the Queen in *Hamlet,* she was billed as Mrs Lewis. The *Theatrical Review* (January 1763) described Mrs Lewis as "from Edinburgh, where she played by the name of Standen." In his *London Journal 1762–63* Boswell calls her "Louisa," an actress in the provinces whose marriage had dissolved, and "just twenty-four."

Sometime after his separation from Anne Standen, Charles married Susanna Crump, who was probably the daughter of the Worcester manager William Crump (d. 1791) and his wife, the provincial actress Elizabeth Crump. Standen's second marriage had occurred by 18 September 1778, when the new Mrs Standen acted Lady Wronghead in *The Provok'd Husband* at the Haymarket Theatre, in a specially licensed performance for the benefit of Mrs Jewell.

It was the second Mrs Standen who was the mother of Standen's three known children: the aforesaid Sophia, who was baptized in 1791 and became an actress in the early part of the nineteenth century; another Miss Standen, who danced at the Haymarket and Drury Lane in the 1790s; and Master Standen, who at about the age of six made his debut as Tom Thumb at Covent Garden on 10 October 1794.

Standen, Mrs Charles the first, Anne ("Louisa"), née Lewis?, later Mrs Vaughan *b.c. 1739, actress.*

According to information provided in *The Oracle* on 23 February 1791, the actor Charles Standen had married his first wife, Anne, on

4 August 1755. At that time Ann Standen was only about 16 years old, if the statement by James Boswell that she was "just twenty-four" in early 1763 is correct. Perhaps she had some provincial acting experience by the time she and her husband came to London to play principal characters in a special performance of *Love and Duty* to Drury Lane Theatre on 12 August 1756, for the benefit of the play's author, John Slade.

With her husband Mrs Standen acted in the New Concert Hall at Edinburgh in February 1761. The *Norwich Mercury* of 26 December 1761 reported that she was performing with the Norwich company at Yarmouth that month.

When she made her debut at Covent Garden Theatre as the Queen in *Hamlet* on 27 September 1762, she was announced as Mrs Lewis, "from Edinburgh where she played under the name of Standen." The *Theatrical Review* in January 1763 described her figure as "most happily adapted" for the Queen, and stated she "might have been more agreeably received, had she not expressed less sensibility in her speaking, than affectation in her address." Why she assumed the name of Lewis is unclear. By that time she was separated from Standen, who had decided that their marriage was not valid because only two banns had been read. Perhaps she had reverted to her maiden name, which may have been Lewis. It seems unlikely that she had remarried by then, for when Boswell met her late in 1762 he described her as a former provincial actress whose marriage had been dissolved.

Acting as Mrs Lewis, her other roles at Covent Garden that season were Mrs Ford in *The Merry Wives of Windsor* on 20 October 1762, Lady Darling in *The Constant Couple* on 15 April 1763, and the Queen in *Hamlet* again on 18 May. On 7 May 1763 she shared benefit tickets with several minor performers, though she seems not to have appeared that night.

In his *London Journal 1762–1763,* James Boswell gave an entertaining account of his affair with a handsome Covent Garden actress "whom I shall distinguish in this my journal by name of LOUISA." Frederick Pottle, on the basis of evidence in the Boswell memoranda, identifies "Louisa" as Mrs Lewis. During the course of their relationship between mid-December 1762 and mid-February 1763, she had told Boswell that, when a girl, she had been taken by two aunts to France and consequently "could once speak French as fluently as English." She also had a brother who was present during several of Boswell's visits to her London lodgings. By the end of January 1763 Boswell was cursing "Louisa" in his journal for giving him gonorrhea. Though she confessed to having been infected "about three years ago," she claimed that for the past 15 months she had been "quite well." Boswell concluded that she was "in all probability a most consummate dissembling whore."

Sometime after leaving London at the end of that season, she became Mrs Vaughan. She seems not to have returned to act in London under any one of her three names, nor was she related by marriage to Henry and William Vaughan, Drury Lane actors, and their sister, the famous Hannah Pritchard. Perhaps she was the Mrs Vaughan who with her husband was a member of Roger Kemble's strolling company between January 1767 and May 1768. She played the Queen in *Charles I* at Worcester on 12 February 1767. Mr and Mrs Vaughan were acting at Derby between 29 November 1771 and February 1772.

After his separation from Anne, Charles Standen married Susanna Crump, who was probably the daughter of the provincial players William Crump (d. 1791) and his wife Elizabeth. As Mrs Standen, his second wife acted at the Haymarket on 18 September 1778. She was also the mother of his three known children.

Standen, Mrs Charles the second, Susanna, née Crump [*fl.* 1778–1815?], *actress.*

The second wife of the actor Charles Standen made a single appearance on the London stage in the eighteenth century, when on 18 September 1778 she acted Lady Wronghead in *The Provok'd Husband* at the Haymarket Theatre, for the benefit of Mrs Jewell. She was Susanna Crump, probably the daughter of the provincial performers William Crump (d. 1791) and Elizabeth Crump.

Perhaps she was the Mrs Standen who worked at Covent Garden from 1810–11 through 1814–15 at £1 10*s.* per week, though possibly that person was her daughter, Miss Sophia Standen. Information about the second

Mrs Standen's children is given in the notice of Charles Standen.

Stanley, Mrs. *See* TWISLETON, MRS THOMAS JAMES.

Stanley, [C.?] [*fl.* 1782?–1810?], *actor.*

On 21 April 1782 a Mr Stanley played an unspecified "Principal Character" in *Love at a Venture* when a group of "performers engaged from the different theatres" performed at the Haymarket by special permission of the Lord Chamberlain. It may be that he was the Stanley who was in the Richmond, Surrey, company in the summer of 1788. Conceivably he was the Stanley whom the *Thespian Magazine* placed in Duckworth's company in the new theatre on Parson's Green, Fulham, early in 1792; and it seems likely that the Fulham Stanley was the one who joined a pickup company at the Haymarket Theatre on 26 November following to give a benefit performance for the actor Silvester. Stanley at that time acted Wingate in *The Apprentice,* and the *Public Advertiser* furnished his first name's initial: C.

There were several provincial Stanleys, one of whom could have been our man, like the one touring Ireland in 1796 and after. He was at Kilkenny in January 1796, and George Frederick Cooke met him at Cork on 21 September 1798. He had "for some weeks been on a visit on board the Ramilies Man of War . . . now at the cove of Cork," according to Cooke's manuscript diary in the Harvard Theatre Collection.

Stanley, Charles [*fl.* 1785?–1794], *singer.*

A bass singer named Charles Stanley was recorded in Doane's *Musical Directory* (1794). He resided in Durham, sang in the Durham Choir, subscribed to the New Musical Fund, and had sung in one or more of the Handelian memorial performances in Westminster Abbey.

Stanley, John 1712–1786, *organist, conductor, composer.*

John Stanley was born on 17 January 1711 / 12 and christened at St Swithin, London Stone, on 1 February, according to that

By permission of the Trustees of the British Museum

JOHN STANLEY

engraving by Scott, after Gainsborough

church's registers. Remarkably, *The Royal Society of Musicians* (1985) gives his year of birth as 1713. Glyn Williams and H. Diack Johnstone in the October 1976 *Musical Times* discuss in detail the confusion over the year. Stanley's parents were John Stanley (d. 18 August 1735) and Elizabeth Davy Stanley (d. August 1730). The couple had six children, only three of whom survived infancy. Young John was blinded at the age of two in a domestic accident described in the *European Magazine and London Review* in September 1784: "he fell down with a china bason in his hand; the bason breaking, a pointed fragment cut through one of his eyes, which occasioned the loss of the other" (sympathetic ophthalmia, probably).

John studied music with John Reading and then with Maurice Greene. Dr Burney reported that Stanley studied "with great diligence, and a success that was astonishing." He had a phenomenal memory for music, and at the age of 11 he was made organist of All Hallows, Bread Street. On 16 August 1726 Stanley became organist of St Andrew, Holborn, and resigned the All Hallows post. On

13 May 1734 he added the position of organist of the Middle Temple. In July 1729 he received his bachelor of music degree at Oxford; he was the youngest music graduate on record, Williams and Johnstone point out. He became one of the original governors of the Royal Society of Musicians in 1738 and remained active to at least 1755. After Handel's death in 1759, according to Malcolm Boyd in the October 1976 *Musical Times*, Stanley was invited to share with John Christopher Smith and Thomas Linley the direction of the Lenten oratorio seasons. He was able to perform a composition after only two hearings. Stanley composed a number of organ voluntaries and other works. Williams and Johnstone provide a list.

Boyd researched Stanley's clandestine marriage. At Lambeth Palace Library is a register entry dated 22 July 1738:

On which day appeared personally John Stanley of the Parish of St. Stephens Walbrook London aged upwards of Twenty five years and a Batchelor, and alledge he intends to marry with Sarah Arlond of the Parish of Low Layton in the County of Essex aged upwards of twenty one years and a spinster. . . .
This deponent . . . made Oath and prayed Licence to solemnize the said Marriage in the Parish Church of St. Bridgets otherwise St. Brides London.

The entry was signed by Robert Chapman, surrogate of the Archbishop of Canterbury, and William Legard, notary public. The young couple did not marry at St Bride's but at Fleet Prison, where many clandestine marriages were performed. The reason for the secrecy was the difference in social standing. Sarah was worth £7000; her father was a wealthy merchant. Further, Sarah's father was Catholic.

John and Sarah Stanley lived in Walbrook after their marriage. In 1751 they moved to Hatton Garden, close to St Andrew, Holborn. Sarah's sister Ann lived with them. Sarah Stanley died in 1780; John Stanley died on 19 May 1786, leaving Ann Arlond his personal effects, the freehold of two houses in Hatton Garden, an insurance policy, and the proceeds from the sale of his books, music, and instruments at Christies.

Thomas Hearne in his *Remarks and Collections* (1907) said that in 1725 Stanley was "look'd upon as the best Organist in Europe,

JOHN STANLEY

engraving by McArdell, after Williams

it may be, in the World." Dr Burney in his *General History of Music* wrote:

Few professors have spent a more active life in every branch of his art, than this extraordinary musician; having been not only a most neat, pleasing, and accurate performer, but a natural and agreeable composer, and an intelligent instructor. He was the conductor and soul of the Swan and Castle concerts in the city, as long as they subsisted. . . . This ingenious and worthy professor, whose blindness excited the pity, and performance the admiration, of the public, for so many years, will be long lamented by his surviving friends; for they have lost in him, exclusive of his musical talents, a most intelligent and agreeable companion, who contributed to the the pleasures of society as much by his conversation in private, as by his professional merit in public.

John Stanley's portrait was painted by Thomas Gainsborough, about 1763. The painting was last recorded in 1807, and it is known by M. A. Scott's engraving published in 1781. Prints were also issued from the same plate, with the engraver's name altered from

Scott to Rigg after she became Mrs Rigg. A portrait of Stanley engraved by J. McArdell, after J. Williams, was published by E. Fisher and Ryland & Bryer. An anonymous engraver pictured Stanley when he was a young man; and another anonymous engraver showed him playing the organ in a plate to the *European Magazine,* October 1784.

Stanmore, Miss [*fl.* 1769], *singer.*

Miss Stanmore, advertised as "A Young Gentlewoman," played Polly in *The Beggar's Opera* at Covent Garden Theatre on 11 November 1769. When she appeared as Polly on 26 December, her name was given in the bill, but that evidently ended her professional career.

Stannard, Mr [*fl.* 1780–1796], *actor, singer.*

A Mr Stannard made infrequent appearances in London between 1780 and 1796. His first noticed performance was as Rushlight in the premiere of the anonymous *The Detection* on 13 November 1780 at the Haymarket Theatre. His other performances at that theatre included Fairman in *A Wife to Be Lett* and a character in *The Sharper's Last Shift* on 22 January 1781, Sandman in the premiere of Charles Stuart's interlude *Damnation* on 29 August 1781, Lord Stanley in *Richard III* on 15 December 1783, a character in *The Talisman* on 21 January 1784 (benefit of the Masons), Sir Geoffrey Constant in *The Man's Bewitch'd* (in which Stannard Junior acted Slouch) on 8 March 1784, and a Recruit in the premiere of Wewitzer's *The Gnome* on 5 August 1788.

At Drury Lane Theatre Stannard sang in the chorus of Guards for *The Mountaineers* on 31 October 1794 and 11 January 1796, though he seems not to have been a regular member of that company.

This Stannard may well have been related to Abraham Stannard, a musician who was at Norwich, it seems, as early as 1751–52. He was a violinist at Birmingham in the summer of 1775, and in 1779 he was employed for £1 1*s*. per week at the Liverpool Theatre Royal from June through 19 October. His son was also on the payroll at 10*s*. per week. On 28 May 1779 the Committee of the Norwich Theatre Royal "order'd that Mr Stannard & Son be engaged at two pound p week, for performing in the Orchestra, teaching, & writing music

& &." On 19 December 1783, the Norwich Committee replaced Stannard and his son with Mr Sharp, from London. A Joseph Stannard, Junior, in 1810 and 1811 attended meetings of the Norwich Theatre Committee as a proprietor.

Stannard, Mr [*fl. 1784*], *actor. See* STANNARD, MR [*fl. 1780–1796*].

Stanton, Charlotte. *See* GOODALL, MRS THOMAS.

Stanton, Elizabeth. *See* NUNNS, MRS JOHN.

Staples, Master [*fl. 1777–1778*], *dancer.*
Master Staples danced a hornpipe at Drury Lane on 15 May 1777, advertised as a scholar of Blurton. He danced his hornpipe again when he made his second and last appearance, on 8 May 1778.

Staples, John [*fl. 1673*], *musician.*
The Lord Chamberlain on 17 July 1673 ordered the apprehension of John and William Staples for playing music without a permit.

Staples, William [*fl. 1673*], *musician. See* STAPLES, JOHN.

Starkey, Mrs [*fl. 1742*], *actress, dancer.*
At the New Wells, London Spa, Clerkenwell, on 27 December 1742 Mrs Starkey played Colombine in *Harlequin Englishman* and danced between the acts.

Starkey, Joseph *d. 1791, singer, oboist.*
The Starkey from Oxford who sang countertenor in the Handel Memorial Concerts at Westminster Abbey and the Pantheon in May and June 1784 was evidently Joseph Starkey. *Jackson's Oxford Journal* on 9 April 1791 reported his death:

Last Monday [4 April] died, after a lingering Illness, Mr. Joseph Starkey, First Oboe in the Oxford Band; which Appointment he had held for many Years. His ready Wit and remarkable Vivacity had introduced him into Company, who regret his Loss, as one of those cheerful, thoughtless Companions who are said to be 'no one's Enemy but their own.'

Staunton, Richard Collet [*fl. 1780–1788*], *actor.*
Richard Staunton made his London debut at the Haymarket Theatre on 7 July 1780 playing Douglas in *Percy,* billed only as "A Gentleman." He was identified as Mr Staunton by the *Westminster Magazine,* which stated that he was from the Crow Street Theatre, Dublin. A writer for the *London Chronicle,* also identifying him and calling him for some years a stock hero of the Dublin theatres, essayed a criticism:

This gentleman's stage requisites are somewhat negative. His figure is rather manly than majestic; his features are regular, but not very expressive, and his voice, though extremely powerful, wants variety of tone. He nevertheless played the character in such a manner as served to convince us that with proper instruction, and due care, he might be rendered, if not a capital actor (which no person can be *made,* but must be *born,* as it depends solely upon genius, the gift of nature!) at least as good a performer as any now to be found in our Theatres.

The critic, having given, then proceeded to take away, advising Staunton sternly to modulate his delivery, acquire elegance of carriage, and rid himself of violence of deportment, hardness of manner, perpetual motion of the body, and provincial style of enunciation. To what effect he used those suggestions is not known. But he seems to have acquired other defects by 1785 when Henry James Leigh wrote in *The New Rosciad:*

The well-fed STAUNTON next, with awkward
    gait,
And hollow voice appear'd—but not in state;
He's pleasant faith! Some humour he displays,
And might act better, if he'd not wear stays.

And "Anthony Pasquin" (John Williams) in *The Pin-basket to the Children of Thespis* (1797) looked back and sneered:

What animal's this! like the daw in his plumes?
Is it STAUNTON who thus on your presence
    presumes?
Who the deuce was it thrust such a man in
    ORSINO?
He's as far from the truth as Pall Mall from
    Urbino.
See, his essays have made poor propriety puke,
And the best we can say is—he makes a rum Duke.

Staunton returned to the Haymarket in the summers of 1781 and 1782 after acting in the winters at Portsmouth. He first appeared at Drury Lane on 6 March 1783 and acted there frequently for the rest of that season. He remained on the Drury Lane roster for the winter seasons through 1787–88. He came only once more to the Haymarket, to play Carlos in *Isabella* for Mrs Wells's benefit on 5 August 1784.

Staunton's other London roles, in order, were: at the Haymarket in 1781, an Officer in *The Genius of Nonsense*, Young Cape in *The Author*, Captain Harcourt in *The Chapter of Accidents*, a Serjeant in *The Baron Kinkvervankotsdorsprakingatchdern*, Bever in *The Patron*, The Ghost in *The School of Shakespeare*, Townly in *A Preludio*, Dick in *The Confederacy*, and Drama in *Damnation*; in 1782, Danford in *The East Indian*, Captain Allspice in *The Candidate*, Beverly in *The Female Dramatist*, Altamont in *The Fair Penitent*, Serjeant Drill in *The Camp*, Steady in *The Quaker*, a Bacchanal in *Comus*, the title role in *Belphegor*, Hatchway in *The Fair Quaker*, and Russet in *The Deserter*.

At Drury Lane, in 1783–84 he added Jenkins in *A School for Fathers*, Vincent in *The Ladies' Frolick*, Salisbury in *King John*, a Magician in *Harlequin Junior*, Ranger in *The Suspicious Husband* (for his benefit), Don Diego in *The Padlock*, Merlin in *Cymon*, and Lavinio in *A Duke and No Duke*. He sang "Hearts of Oak" and "Stand to Your Guns" at Drury Lane on 20 May 1784, and in May and June that year participated as a singer in the Handel Memorial Concerts at Westminster Abbey and the Pantheon.

In 1784–85 Staunton added to his repertoire Horatio in *Hamlet*, Lord Lovel in *A New Way to Pay Old Debts*, a character in *The Caldron*, Osmond in *Arthur and Emmeline*, the original Lord Lofty in Charles Dibdin's comic opera *Liberty Hall*, Rakish in *The Intriguing Chambermaid*, Batholomeus in *The Taylors*, Wilding in *The Citizen*, the title role in *Comus*, Duke Senior in *As You Like It*, and Colonel Blunt in *The Committee*; in 1785–86, Orsino in *Twelfth Night*, Edric in *Percy*, Sir William Worthy in *The Gentle Shepherd*, and Bundle in *The Waterman*; in 1786–87, Regnalto in *The Strangers at Home*, Arcas in *The Grecian Daughter*, Sir John Buck in *The Englishman in Paris*, the title role in *Cymbeline*, Sir William Belmont in *All in the Wrong*, and Alonzo in *The Tempest*; and in 1787–88, Lord Stanley in *Richard III*, Verulam in *Henry II*, Cornwall in *King Lear*, Corex

in *The Fate of Sparta*, and the Lord Mayor in *Richard III*.

Richard Staunton had put down his 10s. 6d. to join the Drury Lane Fund in 1783, and he "claimed" in 1788, according to James Winston's transcriptions in the Folger Library. A notation in the Drury Lane accounts, dated 21 February 1789, reads "Mr. Staunton off List lower'd 13s/4d per diem." (His salary, then, had been £4 per six-day week.) Staunton had changed his residence while in London from No 9, St Martin's Street, in May 1785 to No 54, Drury Lane, in May 1786 and then to lodgings in Gloucester Street, Queen Square, in May 1788.

Richard Collet Staunton had married Miss Sarah Carr of Portsmouth at St Peter's, Bristol, on 17 September 1785, according to the transcript of the parish register now in the City Archivist's office.

Staunton is liable to confusion with the numerous members of the Stanton family of performers because of the careless orthography of the printers of playbills, but there is no obvious connection.

Stayner, Daniel   [fl. 1761–1784], violinist, music copyist?

Daniel Stayner became a member of the Royal Society of Musicians on 4 October 1761. He played violin in the *Messiah* at the Foundling Hospital in 1769. Parke's *Musical Memoirs* of 1830 named Stayner as leader of the band at Drury Lane Theatre in 1775. The playhouse accounts sometimes spelled his name Stainer. On 23 October 1775 he was paid £6 18s. for music books—suggesting that he may have served also as a copyist. Stayner was cited in the accounts as late as June 1778. He played second violin in the Handel Memorial Concerts at Westminster Abbey and the Pantheon in May and June 1784. According to *The Royal Society of Musicians* (1985) Stayner was expelled from the organization for non-attendance at a St Paul's concert.

Stead. *See also* STEDE.

Stead, Mr   [fl. 1785], performer?

A benefit was held at Hammersmith for a Mr Stead on 2 July 1785. Tickets were available from him at the Angel.

Stede, Mrs ₁*fl. 1742*₁. *See* STEDE, JOHN.

Stede, John 1687–1768, *prompter.*

John Stede (or Steed) was born in 1687. He may have been the Mr. Steed who was paid £1 3*s*. 6*d*. about 13 January 1708 for opera materials for the Queen's Theatre. His hand can be seen in the manuscript promptbook of *The Force of Friendship* (1710) at the Folger Shakespeare Library; the work was performed at the Queen's in April and May 1710, and Stede was probably serving as underprompter to Thomas Newman. Our subject may have been the John Steed cited in the parish registers of St Giles in the Fields in the first quarter of the eighteenth century: on 17 August 1712 Samuel, the son of John and Jane Steed was baptized, and on 13 December 1719 their daughter Elizabeth was christened.

Stede shared a benefit with the numberer Cross at Lincoln's Inn Fields Theatre on 17 May 1717. For many years thereafter Stede was cited for benefits at that house and, beginning in 1733, Covent Garden Theatre—the playhouses managed for years by John Rich. Stede's benefits were sometimes shared, sometimes solo, and usually did well. In 1721, for example, he and the house servant Gwinn shared gross receipts of over £120; in 1724 he split over £100 with Mrs Parker; and in 1725 he shared over £133 with Hall. Stede's daily salary, the account books reveal, was 11*s*. in the 1720s (5*s*. 6*d*. nightly plus money for copying out parts); in 1746–47 he was earning 15*s*. weekly, but that was probably only a portion of his income; he was paid 10*s*. daily as one of three prompters at Covent Garden on 22 September 1760. (*The London Stage* lists a benefit for a Mrs Stede on 21 May 1742, but that is clearly an error for John, since 1742 was the only year in the decade when Stede was not named for a benefit.)

His duties would have involved not only the copying out of parts and the routine prompting during performances but the preparation of promptbooks, several of which, such as those for *The Perfidious Brother* and *Money the Mistress,* have survived (at the Bodleian Library). Stede would also have been responsible for the company's library of scripts. By 19 December 1762, according to Boswell, Stede was "late Prompter and now in the Cabinet Council of Covent Garden Theatre." He was

still on the company's paylist, at 3*s*. 4*d*. daily, on 14 September 1767—but that was probably a pension, for Stede was then 80 years old. Before he died he told Charles Dibdin about the many actors and actresses he had observed over the years, but in his memoirs Dibdin did not identify Stede's reminiscences.

John Stede died in September 1768 at the age of 81. The exact date was reported by Reed in his "Notitia Dramatica" as the second of September, but another British Library manuscript (11826) gives the thirtieth.

British Library Additional Charter 9308, dated 12 April 1722, lists "Mr Steed" as a Drury Lane Theatre employee; curiously, *The London Stage* for 1721–22 lists the regular Drury Lane prompter, Chetwood, as working that season at Lincoln's Inn Fields, and no prompter is named for Drury Lane. Perhaps Stede and Chetwood traded places that season. Under 9 June 1733 *The London Stage* cites "Steede" as the Drury Lane prompter; that is surely an error, for Stede had been given his usual benefit at Covent Garden on 2 May.

Stede, Mrs ₁ John?₁, ₁ Jane?₁ ₁*fl. 1708?–1729*₁, *dresser?*

A Mrs Steed was listed in Vice Chamberlain Coke's papers at Harvard as a dresser at the Queen's Theatre on 8 March 1708 at a daily wage of 5*s*. Perhaps she was Mrs John Stede, wife of the prompter who worked for many years at Lincoln's Inn Fields and Covent Garden. A John and Jane Steed are named in the registers of St Giles in the Fields in 1712 and 1719. On 26 April 1729 at Lincoln's Inn Fields a benefit was held for "a Gentlewoman and her Daughter"; *The London Stage* identifies the woman as Mrs Stede. The gross receipts came to over £125.

Stede, Mary ₁*fl. 1768–1776*₁, *dancer, actress.*

Mary Stede was employed occasionally as a dancer at Covent Garden Theatre from the spring of 1768 until that of 1774. In no single season does her name appear in the bills more than a few times, in some seasons only once. That she was sometimes useful in other capacities than as a dancer is suggested by the first mention of her services in the Covent Garden account book, on 23 February 1768: "Paid Miss Stede for walking 2 nights in *The Roman*

Father [on 13 and 22 February] 10*s*." On 23 April following, the entry was "Paid Miss Stede extra dancer for 6 nights £1."

Her first known notice in a playbill was on 12 May 1768: "A Hornpipe by Miss Stede, 1st Time (Scholar to [James] Fishar)," on the occasion of a benefit for the actor Bennet and the old prompter John Stede, to whom, obviously, she was in some way related. She is not likely to have been his daughter, inasmuch as he was then 81 years old and she was still a "scholar" and thus probably a juvenile.

Despite the absence of her name from the bills, she may have been employed with some frequency in the corps de ballet in 1768–69, for she shared a benefit with four others on 19 May 1769. On 18 May 1770 she was among 20 minor folk permitted benefit tickets. She appeared at Kniveton's benefit on 8 May 1771, dancing her hornpipe. She, "Pilfold, and others" divided a benefit on 25 May 1771, when there was "A Minuet by Fishar and Miss Stede (his scholar)."

The first organized and titled ballet in which Mary Stede participated was on 1 May 1772, "A New Grand Pantomimical Dance call'd *The Recruits.*" There were named characters, but she was only one of the "wives and country girls." On 23 May she again shared a benefit, with Mrs Heard, Mrs Williams, Abbot, and Furkins. On 24 April 1773, for her master Fishar's benefit, she appeared as one of numerous "dancers and attendants" in Fishar's ballet *The Festival of the Black Prince* and on 22 May again shared a benefit with Hollingsworth and Master Jones. On 7 May 1774 she shared a benefit with Thomas Ansell and on 12 May did a *Sixfold Hornpipe.* The last mention of her in a London playbill was when she danced a minuet with Blurton on 16 May 1774.

She never, so far as is known, did anything more strenuous in the dramatic line in London than the two nights of "walking." But she had at least one night of dramatic prominence, in Roger Johnston's company at Brighton. That was in a special performance, after the regular season was over, 19 December 1774, when she played both Irene in *Barbarossa* and Leonora in *The Padlock* and presented an entr'acte dance. She returned to Johnston's company to dance (and perhaps act) in the summer and fall of 1776. After that, the trail grows cold.

Mary Stede's first name is furnished in a letter to George Colman signed by Covent Garden performers and published in the *Theatrical Monitor* for 5 November 1768.

Stedman, Francis [*fl.* 1794–1805], *violinist.*

Francis Stedman, of No 52, Red Lion Street, Clerkenwell, was listed in Doane's *Musical Directory* of 1794 as a violinist who played in concerts presented by the New Musical Fund. He was still a member of that organization in 1805.

Steed. *See* STEDE.

Steel, Mrs [*fl.* 1734–1742], *actress, singer.*

Mrs Steel (or Steele) played Jezebel in *Don Quixote in England* at the Lincoln's Inn Fields playhouse on 1 October 1734. At York Buildings on 21 March 1735 she was Louisa in *Love Makes a Man* and Kissinda in *The Covent Garden Tragedy.* She acted at Norwich later that year. After an absence from London of a few years, Mrs Steel returned to play the 1740–41 and 1741–42 seasons at the Goodman's Fields Theatre. She first appeared as Selima in *Tamerlane* on 4 November 1740 and then acted such important roles as Oriana in *The Inconstant,* Lavinia in *The Fair Penitent,* the Duchess of Suffolk in *Lady Jane Gray,* Hermione in *The Distrest Mother,* Lady Graveairs in *The Careless Husband,* Melinda in *The Recruiting Officer,* Queen Elizabeth in *The Unhappy Favorite,* Gertrude in *Hamlet,* Narcissa in *Love's Last Shift,* Lady Macbeth, Bullfinch in *Love and a Bottle,* Paulina in *The Winter's Tale,* Leonora in *The Spanish Fryar,* Mrs Peachum in *The Beggar's Opera,* Agnes in *The Fatal Curiosity,* the Countess in *All's Well that Ends Well,* Melissa in *Timon of Athens,* Millwood in *George Barnwell,* Widow Lackit in *Oroonoko,* Zara in *The Mourning Bride,* Lucy in *The Lover's Opera,* Alicia in *Jane Shore,* Mrs Trippit in *The Lying Valet,* and Wishwell in *The Double Gallant.*

In the middle of her stay at Goodman's Fields Mrs Steel went to Bartholomew Fair to play Queen Eleanor in *Fair Rosamond* on 22 August 1741.

Steel, Miss F. W. [*fl.* 1789], *performer?*

One of the subscribers in 1789 to *George Parker, Life's Painter* was Miss F. W. Steel of

"T. R. London"—that is, one of the theatres royal. *The London Stage* makes no mention of her, but she could have been a minor performer never named in any playbill.

Steele. *See also* STEIL.

Steele, Mr. [*fl. 1744–1747*], *house servant.*

Mr Steele was listed in benefit bills at Drury Lane Theatre on 21 May 1744, 8 May 1745, and 8 May 1747. Others named with him were house servants, as doubtless Steele was.

Steele, Mr [*fl. 1773–1784*], *singer.*

Mr Steele sang as an Arval Brother in *Ambarvalia* at Marylebone Gardens on 3, 6, and 9 September 1773. He was in the singing chorus at Drury Lane Theatre in 1774–75 and was hired as an extra tenor at 5*s.* per performance in 1776–77. "Steel" sang in *Macbeth* at the Haymarket Theatre on 7 and 9 September 1778 and returned in the summer of 1783 to serve as an Anchor Smith in *Harlequin Teague.* In May and June 1784 Steele sang in the Handel Memorial Concerts at Westminster Abbey and the Pantheon.

Steele, Nicholas *d. 1785, organist.*

The musician Nicholas Steele of the parish of St Marylebone married Margaret Judith Claridge of Bushy, Hertfordshire, on 17 March 1770. That information was collected by the Royal Society of Musicians when Steele was recommended for membership in January 1780. He was then described as having practiced music for seven years. He was organist of St Bartholomew the Great, member of St Peter's, Westminster (Westminster Abbey), and vicar choral of St George's Chapel in Windsor and of Eton College. Steele was admitted to the Society on 6 February 1780. He died childless in 1785. His widow was recommended for financial aid from the Society on 1 October 1785 and was granted two guineas per month.

Steele, Richard *1672–1729, manager, playwright, essayist.*

Richard Steele was born in Dublin, the son of Richard and Elinor (née Sheyles) Steele. He was christened at St Bride's on 12 March 1672.

National Gallery of Ireland

RICHARD STEELE
by Kneller

The elder Steele was a well-to-do attorney with an estate at Monkstown; his wife, who married him in 1670, was the widow of Thomas Sims. A daughter, Katherine, was born in March 1671. The elder Steele died about 1677, and apparently Mrs Steele died soon afterward. Young Katherine and Richard were cared for by their uncle, Henry Gascoigne, secretary to James Butler, first Duke of Ormonde. Through the influence of Ormonde, Richard was nominated to the Charterhouse in London in November 1684. In 1686 young Joseph Addison was admitted to the same school, and a long friendship began.

In November 1689 Steele was elected to Oxford, where Addison had already begun his studies; he matriculated on 13 March 1690 at Christ Church College and became postmaster of Merton College on 27 August 1691. Though Steele was a good scholar, he did not complete his degree, preferring in 1694 to join the second troop of life guards under the second Duke of Ormonde. By 1696 Steele was employed by John, Lord Cutts, colonel of the

Coldstream regiment of foot guards, and by 1702 was a Captain. He had developed friendships with such men of letters as Congreve, Sedley, and Vanbrugh, and in 1701 he published his first major work, *The Christian Hero,* a moralistic treatise. Later the same year he wrote his second comedy, *The Funeral; or, Grief a-la-Mode* (the first, written in college, he had burned). It was presented at Drury Lane Theatre in December with what the actor Colley Cibber called "more than expected Success." In the cast with Cibber were some of the theatre's best players: Robert Wilks, William Pinkethman, Susanna Verbruggen, and Anne Oldfield. For the following 20 years Steele was to be intimately associated with Drury Lane and her players.

Still in the army, Steele began his next comedy, *The Election of Goatham,* which he took to Drury Lane in January 1703; it was never produced and may never have been completed. *The Lying Lover,* however, was performed at Drury Lane on 2 December 1703. It was a pious work and did not have wide appeal. *The Tender Husband* came out at Drury Lane on 23 April 1705, and though it was well-written and later became popular, it was not an immediate success. When the play was published, it was dedicated to Addison, who had written the prologue. Steele then turned to other creative efforts and did not bring out another play until 1722.

Soon after March 1705 Steele married, perhaps for her money, Margaret Stretch, née Ford, who had inherited estates in Barbados worth, it was said, £850 annually. But the property was encumbered by a debt of £3000 and may never have yielded much to the spendthrift Steele. Mrs Steele, who was evidently a good bit older than her husband, died in December 1706, and the estate came into Steele's hands. His other sources of income at the time were Prince George of Denmark, to whom he was a gentleman waiter at £100 annually, and Queen Anne, who paid Steele £300 yearly (before taxes) to serve as gazetteer.

At his wife's funeral Steele met Mary Scurlock, daughter and heiress of Jonathan Scurlock of Llangunnor, Carmarthen. They were married, in secret apparently, on 9 September 1707, and set up housekeeping in Bury Street, not too far from Steele's office in the Cockpit, Whitehall. The erratic Steele, genial, impulsive, and extravagant, was constantly in debt and on the lookout for advancement. But he often failed to gain posts he tried for, and with the death of Prince George in 1708 he lost the position of gentleman waiter he had held (though he received a pension). Yet he kept a chariot and pair of horses and a place at Hampton Wick. He was evidently behind in his rent on the house in Bury Street, but he and his wife started a family. Their daughter Elizabeth was born in March 1709.

On 12 April Steele began his career as an essayist by publishing the first issue of the *Tatler,* which, with Steele writing under the pseudonym Isaac Bickerstaff, ran for 271 issues, to 2 January 1711. Though Addison contributed to many numbers, Steele was responsible for about 188.

In January 1710 Steele was appointed commissioner of stamps, a post which brought him £300 annually, but he lost his gazetteership in October 1710 when Harley, whom he had satirized in the *Tatler,* became head of the government. On 1 March 1711 the *Spectator* began publication; the periodical was wonderfully successful, sometimes selling 10,000 copies per week. Though the writers claimed that they would remain neutral between the Whigs and Tories, Steele's contributions became more political as time went on. In March 1713, after the *Spectator* had ceased publication, Steele began issuing the *Guardian,* espousing the Whig philosophy. He carried on a running battle with the Tory *Examiner* (to which Swift contributed).

Steele gave up his position as commissioner of stamps on 4 June 1713, ran for parliament for Stockbridge, Hampshire, and was elected in August. The *Guardian* ceased publication in September, and Steele brought out its successor, the *Englishman,* on 6 October 1713. He was accused of seditious libels and, on 18 March 1714, was expelled from the House of Commons. Steele returned to his writing; the *Englishman* had ceased publication in February 1714, to be followed by the *Lover,* then the *Reader,* both of which ceased publication in May. Steele then turned to pamphleteering.

On 1 August 1714 Queen Anne died, and on 18 September George I arrived in England. Steele's support of the Hanoverian succession was amply rewarded, but not in the way he had hoped—a ministerial post, perhaps. Instead, he was made a justice of the peace, deputy-lieutenant for Middlesex, surveyor of the royal stables at Hampton Court, and co-manager of Drury Lane Theatre.

Though Steele had set aside playwriting after *The Tender Husband* in 1705, he had kept up his contacts with the players and frequently puffed their benefits in his periodicals. Indeed, we are greatly indebted to Steele for his comments on the performers of his time and his whimsical discussions of performances. He was the person to whom the players at Drury Lane turned when, upon the death of Queen Anne, they needed to procure a new license.

Steele had championed a more moral drama, putting into practice a philosophy that owed much to Jeremy Collier's attacks on the immorality of the stage at the turn of the century. The players, for their part, needed a man with Steele's court connections and concern for the good of the theatre, especially since John Rich was about to open the new Lincoln's Inn Fields playhouse and provide Drury Lane with some serious competition. Steele was evidently first asked to take over Drury Lane in 1713, but at that time the offer from the government was a political one, and Steele turned it down. The second offer came at a time when the political climate had changed, and Steele was able to accept. Indeed, given his constant money problems, he could hardly have turned down what was clearly a lucrative opportunity.

This time it was the group of actor-managers at Drury Lane—Colley Cibber, Robert Wilks, Barton Booth, and Thomas Doggett—who invited Steele to join them in the management of the theatre. They had been paying William Collier, a Tory attorney, £700 annually as their representative at court; Steele, a Whig, a playwright, and a friend of the players, was a more logical choice. Though in later years the players claimed that one of Steele's duties as a co-manager was the training of the younger actors, surely he was not expected to be an acting coach; he had no performing experience, and it seems certain that his responsibilities were chiefly administrative.

Steele was able to obtain a license for his co-managers with no difficulty. It was passed on 18 October 1714. Before the 1714–15 season was over, Steele changed his annual fee for a share of the profits—a shrewd move that sea-

son, for the company made £1700 in the first three months. But Drury Lane had to operate under a license, not a patent, and that meant that the players performed at the pleasure of the Lord Chamberlain and were subject to the licensing fee for new plays collected by the Master of the Revels. The old patents, issued by Charles II to Thomas Killigrew and Sir William Davenant, had been inherited by John Rich and his brother, and under them Lincoln's Inn Fields Theatre was operated.

Steele petitioned the King for a patent in December 1714 or January 1715; his request is among the *State Papers Domestic:*

> To the King's most Excellent Majesty,
> The humble Petition of Richard Steele,
> Sheweth

That the use of the Theatre has for many years last past been much perverted to the great Scandal of Religion and Good Government.

That it will require much time to remedy so inveterate an evil, and will expose the Undertaker to much Envy and Opposition.

That an affair of this Nature cant be accomplished without a lasting Authority.

That your Maj^{ty} has given to your Pet^r in conjunction with others a Licence to form and establish a Company of Commedians for the Service of your Maj^{tie}.

That your Pet^r did not desire this Favour in so ample a manner as your Maj^{tie} was graciously disposed to bestow it upon him, till he had taken a View of the State of the Theatre, under your Maj^{ties} Licence, and after mature deliberation thereupon promised himself he should be able to act therein in some degree to your Maj^{ties} Satisfaction.

That your Pet^r has observed great inconveniences to have arisen from a grant of this kind, to Men and their Heirs.

Your Pet^r therefore most humbly prays that your Ma^{ty} would graciously please to grant your Petitioner your Letters Patents for forming a company of Commedians for the Service of your Majesty during your Pet^{rs} natural Life and for three Years after his Death, &c

The patent was issued on 19 January 1715. It seems likely that Steele's success in getting it was due to his emphasis on reforming the theatre. His pious approach was evident in his petition and was spelled out in the patent itself:

George, by the grace of God, etc. We having informed Ourselves, since Our accession to Our crown, of the state of Our theatre, and finding, to Our sorrow, that through the neglect and ill management thereof, the true and only end of its institution is greatly perverted; and instead of exhibiting such representations of human life as may tend to the encouragement and honour of religion and virtue and discountenancing vice, the English stage hath been the complaint of the sober, intelligent, and religious part of Our people, and by indecent and immodest expressions, by profane allusions to Holy Scriptures, by abusive and scurrilous representations of the clergy, and by the success and applause bestowed on libertine characters, it hath given great and insufferable scandal to religion and good manners. And in the representations of civil government care has not been taken to create in the minds of Our good subjects just and dutiful ideas of the power and authority of magistrates, as well as to preserve a due sense of the rights of Our people; and, through many other abuses, that which under a wise discretion and due regulation would be useful and honourable has proved, and if not repressed will continue, a reproach to Government and a dishonour to religion. And it being Our pious resolution, which with the blessing of God We will steadily pursue through the whole course of Our reign, not only by Our own example but by all other means possible, to promote the honour of religion and virtue, and on every occasion to encourage good literature and to endeavor the establishment of good manners and discipline among all Our loving subjects in all stations and ranks of men whatsoever; these being, in Our opinion, the proper means to render Our kingdoms happy and flourishing: We, having seriously resolved on the premises, and being well satisfied of the ability and good disposition of Our trusty and well-beloved Richard Steele, Esq., for the promoting these Our royal purposes, not only from his public services to religion and virtue, but his steady adherence to the interest of his country; know ye that We, of Our special grace, certain knowledge, and meer motion, and in consideration of the good and faithful services which the said Sir Richard Steele hath done Us, and doth intend to do for the future, have given and granted, and by these presents for Us, and for Our heirs and successors, do give and grant unto him, the said Richard Steele, his exors, etc., for and during the term of his natural life, and for and during in full end and term of three years to be computed next and immediately after the decease of him, the said Richard Steele, full power, licence, and authority to gather together, form, entertain, govern, privilege, and keep a company of comedians for Our service, to exercise and act tragedies, plays, operas, and other performance of the stage, within the house in Drury Lane, wherein the same are now exercised by virtue of a licence granted by Us to him, the said Richard Steele, Robert Wilks, Colley Cibber, Thomas Dogget, and Barton Booth, or within any other house built, or to be built, wherever they can best be fitted for the purpose, within Our cities of London and Westminster, or the suburbs thereof. Such house or houses so to be built (if occasion shall require) to be assigned, allotted out by the surveyour of Our works for a theatre or playhouse, with necessary tiring and retiring rooms, and other places convenient, of such extent and dimensions as the said Richard Steele, his executors, administrators, or assigns shall think fitting, wherein tragedies, comedies, plays, operas, musick, scenes, and all other entertainments of the stage whatsoever may be showed and presented. Which said company shall be Our servants, and styled the Royal Company of Comedians, and shall consist of such members as the said Sir Richard Steele, his exors., etc., shall from time to time think meet. And We do hereby, for Us, Our heirs, and successors, grant unto the s^d Sir Richard Steele, his exors., etc., full power, licence and authority to permit such persons, at and during the pleasure of the s^d Sir Richard Steele, his exors., etc., from time to time to act plays and entertainments of the stage of all sorts peaceably and quietly, without the impeachment or interruption of any person or persons whatsoever, for the honest recreation of such as shall desire to see the same: nevertheless, under the regulations hereinafter mentioned, and such other as the s^d Sir R. Steele from time to time in his direction shall find reasonable and necessary for Our service. And We do for Ourselves, Our heirs and successors, further grant to him, the said R. Steele, his exors., etc., as aforesaid, that it shall be lawful to and for the s^d R. Steele, his exors., etc., to take and receive of such Our subjects as shall resort to see or hear any such plays, scenes, and entertainments whatsoever, such sum or sums of money as either have accustomably been given and taken in the like kind, or as shall be thought reasonable by him or them in regard of the great expenses of scenes, musick, and such new decorations as have not formerly been used. And further for Us, Our heirs and successors, We do hereby give and grant unto the s^d R. Steele, his executors, etc., full power to make such allowances out of that which he shall so receive by the acting of plays and entertainments of the stage, as aforesaid, to the actors and other persons employed in acting, representing, or in any quality whatsoever about the s^d theatre, as he or they shall think fit. And that the said company shall be under the sole gov^t and authority of the said R. Steele, his executors, etc., and all scandalous and mutinous persons shall from time to time by him and them be ejected and disabled from playing in the s^d theatre. And for the better attainment of Our Royal purposes in this

National Portrait Gallery

RICHARD STEELE
by Kneller

behalf, We have thought fit hereby to declare that henceforth no representations be admitted on the stage by virtue, or under colour, of these Our Letters Patent, whereby the Christian religion in general or the Church of England may in any manner suffer reproach, strictly inhibiting every degree of abuse or misrepresentations of sacred characters, tending to expose religion itself, and bring it into contempt; and that no such character be otherwise introduced, or placed in other light, than such as may enhance the just esteem of those who truly answer the end of their sacred function. We further enjoin the strictest regard to such representations as any way concern Civil Policy, or the Constitution of Our Government, that these may contribute to the support of Our sacred authority, and the preservation of order and good Government. And it being Our Royal desire that, for the future, Our theatre may be instrumental to the promotion of virtue and instructive to humane life, We do hereby command and enjoin that no new play, or any old or revived play, be acted under the authority hereby granted containing any passages or expressions offensive to piety and good manners, until the same be corrected and purged by the s^d governor from all such offensive and scandalous passages and expres-

sions. And these Our Letters Patents, etc., shall be good and effectual, anything in these presents contained, or any Law, Statute, Act, Proclamation, etc., or anything whatsoever to the contrary, in any wise notwithstanding.

> Witness Our self at Westminster, Jan. 19th, 1st year of Our reign. By Writ of Privy Seal.

As soon as he received the patent, Steele, as he had agreed, assigned equal shares to the actor-managers (now Cibber, Wilks, and Booth). Armed with the patent, the players were able to defy the authority of the Lord Chamberlain, for the patent, said Cibber, "made us sole Judges of what Plays might be proper for the Stage, without submitting them to the Approbation of License of any other particular Person." For almost five years the players were able to keep that authority.

Though Steele did not (or could not) carry out all the theatrical reforms he planned, his statement in *Town Talk* No 6 in the winter of 1715–16 clarified his good intentions:

This PATENT . . . is the LAW of the THEATRE; and by the rule of it, we are to expect that nothing new shall hereafter come upon the Stage, that may in the least offend decency or good-manners. The indulgence at present given to what is represented there, is a sufferance which it is to be hoped will be made up to the audience in future plays. If every thing that shall be represented is not virtuous, let it at least be innocent. This will bring a new audience to the house; and it is from the hope of entertaining those who at present are terrified at the Theatre, that the sharers must hope for their success hereafter. This will naturally have the desired effect, and Folly will be ridiculous without being at the same time so mixed with Vice, as to make it also terrible. The daughter may be agreeable and blooming, though the mother is at the same time discreet, careful, and anxious for her conduct. No necessary imperfections, such as old age, and misfortune, shall be the objects of derision and buffoonery. The fine gentleman is not absolutely obliged to wrong his friend in the most unpardonable instance, that of his bed; nor is the fine lady of course to like him best, who lavishes his youth among the abandoned of her sex.

One reason for Steele's failure to reform Drury Lane was his overriding interest in making money, and the managers recognized that theatrical clap-trap such as pantomimes and spicy plays such as revived Restoration comedies were more likely to make money than pious didactic works such as Steele himself wrote.

An anonymous author in *The State of the Case . . . Restated* castigated Steele for his ineffectual government of Drury Lane. Steele, he said,

has not at any time, during his administration, made one step towards those glorious ends proposed by his Majesty, for the service of religion and virtue, nor reformed the least abuse of either. The same lewd Plays being acted and revived without any material alteration, which gave occasion for that universal complaint against the English Stage, of lewdness and debauchery, from all the sober and religious part of the nation; the whole business of Comedy continuing all his time to be the criminal intrigues of fornication and adultery, ridiculing of marriage, virtue, and integrity, the giving a favourable turn to vicious characters, and instructing loose people who to carry on their lewd designs with plausibility and success; thus, among other Plays, they have revived "The Country Wife;" "Sir Fopling Flutter;" "The Rover;" "The Libertine destroyed;" and several others. . . .

Or Steele may have been lax in carrying out his intended reforms because of his other interests.

As early as 1711 Steele had become interested in English music and had used the pages of the *Spectator* to promote it over Italian opera, which was gaining great popularity. It was a losing cause, but Steele supported the efforts of the composer Thomas Clayton. Clayton had written two English operas "in the Italian manner," *Arsinoe* in 1705 and *Rosamond* in 1707. In 1711 Clayton and others ran a series of concerts at York Buildings featuring English poetry with musical settings. The series was puffed in the *Spectator* in the summer of 1711, as were Clayton's subscription concerts in the winter of 1711–12. Steele finally took over the concert room in York Buildings and turned it into his own "Censorium."

The Censorium was a kind of private theatre in which Steele invested his time and money from about 1712 to perhaps as late as 1723. At the Censorium Steele proposed to present entertainments of all sorts. "All Works of Invention, All the Sciences, as well as mechanick Arts will have their turn," he wrote in a manuscript now at Blenheim Palace. He appealed to Alexander Pope for support and contribu-

tions in the way of poems to be set to music, but Pope was not enthusiastic.

Steele's Censorium venture was still in the planning stage in the spring of 1713. On 7 March George Berkeley wrote:

He [Steele] is likewise proposing a noble entertainment for persons of a refined taste. It is chiefly to consist of the finest pieces of eloquence translated from the Greek and Latin authors. They will be accompanied with the best music suited to raise those passions that are proper to the occasion. Pieces of Poetry will be there recited. These informations I have from Mr. Steele himself. I have seen the place designed for these performances: it is in York Buildings, and he has been at no small expence to embellish [it] with all imaginable decorations. It is by much the finest chamber I have seen, and will contain seats for a select company of 200 persons of the best quality and taste, who are to be subscribers.

But Steele's involvement in political affairs prevented him from opening the Censorium until 1715.

On 28 May 1715 Steele presented his first entertainment, in celebration of the King's birthday and (probably) Steele's recent (April) knighthood. For the occasion Steele had the walls of the room decorated with paintings, and a speaker's rostrum was installed. Miss Younger of Drury Lane delivered a prologue, after which came an ode to the royal family spoken by a performer representing Liberty, an ode of Horace set to music, and other songs and instrumental music. Finally, an epilogue about Steele's career as a reformer and pamphleteer was spoken by Robert Wilks. Steele did not offer another entertainment for some time, but in manuscripts now at Blenheim he made clear that he intended his Censorium to augment his reforming work at Drury Lane: "This Project will be to the Stage, what an Under-plot is to a play." But it was a costly venture.

A letter at Blenheim, written by Steele perhaps in March 1716 and perhaps to Spencer Compton, describes Steele's financial woes:

I tooke the liberty at my Lord Treasurers to desire you'd please to speake for me to His Lordship that two hundred and fifty pounds due to me as pension from the Queen might be payd. I have at my own private Charge and Expence prepared a Roome in York Buildings for select Audiences, where there will, I doubt not, be performances in Eloquence and Musick transcending, if I may believe men of good Judgement, what has ever appeared before in any Age or any Nation. This matter has already cost me a thousand pounds, and made me very bare of money. The Generall purpose of my Studies and actions is the promotion of Elegant delights and Stirring Generous Principles. And when I consider what admirable things by my procurement or sollicitation have been produced to the learned world within this four years last past, I cannot but think any pertinaciousnesse in private opinion ought to be over-looked, and I, if not received in particular favour, ought at least [to be] distinguished from the Crowd of those who partake the Queen's Bounty by a prompt payment of it. If my Lord would be pleased to order me this money it would quicken affairs . . . and your mediation in my behalfe would extremely oblige, S[r]

> Y[r] Most Obedient & Most
> Humbe Servant

Steele apparently hoped to present didactic dramatizations of ancient historical events at the Censorium, and an academy with directors was to conduct the operation. On 16 March 1716 a lecture was presented at Steele's Room; Mr Whiston spoke on "the surprizing Appearances in the Air" of 10 days before. Whiston had evidently rented the Censorium for his lecture. His talk seems not to have been a part of Steele's plan, though it was the sort of thing Steele had said he would sponsor.

The Censorium may have succeeded for a while, but information is lacking on just how many presentations were given. It was not often mentioned in the newspapers. In June 1717 there were concerts in the "Great Room" at York Buildings, but Steele may have done no more than rent out his hall for them. When his wife died in December 1718 Steele moved into apartments in York Buildings and activity at his Room increased. On 17 November 1719 the *Daily Post* carried an advertisement for a series of scientific lectures at "Sir *Richard Steele's* great Room in Villars' street, York Buildings" beginning on 1 December.

John Loftis, who wrote a detailed study of the Censorium in the *Huntington Library Quarterly* in November 1950, quotes an amusing satirical attack on Steele in *The Original Weekly Journal* in April 1720. It made fun of

an Oration, or Speech, spoken at the Opening of a sort of Meeting, or Assembly, call'd the Capricioso, set up by the Chevalier of the brazen Countenance

[Steele], an eminent Member of the Family of the Wrong Heads, and a great Projector, of whom I shall have Occasion to speak more hereafter. In the Capricioso there are Orations spoken pro and con on several Subjects, from a Certain Desk, or Rosteram, not very unlike our Pulpits, and in the intervals of these Speeches, the Company are entertain'd with Musick, Vocal and Instrumental. The first Speech that was made was to prove the Excellence of human Nature, by a young Bonzi, or Philosopher; the next that mounted was a middle aged Man, and one of the Cacafuogos, which is the Name of the establish'd Teachers of that Country. . . .

Other references to Steele's activities in York Buildings came in the newspapers in 1721 and 1722, and he may have presented entertainments of lectures and music until he left London in 1724. On 17 August 1724 he advertised that his Room was for rent; after that the place was still referred to as "Sir Richard Steele's Great Musick Room," though he was no longer the proprietor. Aaron Hill in *The Prompter* in 1735 still identified the room as Steele's.

Meanwhile, Steele's responsibilities at Drury Lane were either not heavy or were neglected, and in time the actor-managers turned against him. His duties were (as the actor-managers stated on 23 June 1726) "to write plays and other performances and to sollicite persons of Quality and other persons of distinction to resort to the . . . Theatre and to use his best endeavours to support the interest thereof. . . ." Steele also aided Drury Lane through his periodicals, especially *Town Talk*, which came out in the winter of 1715–16 and through which he again urged the reformation of the stage.

Steele apparently served also as an agent for the troupe on occasion. In December 1715, for example, he corresponded with the Earl of Stair in Paris, trying to arrange for a visit to London by the *commedia* actors Baxter and Sorin; they came to Drury Lane for a short engagement in the spring of 1716. But at the end of the 1716–17 season Steele wrote a letter to his wife that suggests that Wilks, not Steele, was representing Drury Lane at court:

I write this from Richmond, where I have been since yesterday morning at a Lodging near Wilks, who I believe, will bring matters to bear so that there will be no Play-House but Ours, allowing Rich, who is almost broke, a Sallary while there is but one House. I am in hopes one way or other let the Courtiers do as unthankfully as they please, I shall pick up a Comfortable fortune.

As things turned out, Rich put Keene and Bullock in charge of Lincoln's Inn Fields, and London continued having two playhouses and an opera house.

It was Steele, on the other hand, who served as intermediary between Drury Lane and the critic-playwright John Dennis in 1718 and the years that followed. (He seems to have acted frequently as the theatre's literary adviser.) He arranged for Cibber and Booth to attend a reading of Dennis's *The Invader of His Country* in February 1718. The players promised to produce the play, and at that point Steele evidently thought his share in the negotiations was concluded. When the production was delayed, however, Dennis felt that Steele was at least partly to blame for not being his champion. The play failed in performance, and Dennis fumed at the actor-managers. When in 1720 Steele (using the pseudonym Sir John Edgar) defended Cibber and the actors in the theatre, Dennis felt insulted and castigated Cibber (and Steele) in *The Characters and Conduct of Sir John Edgar*. In the second part of that work Dennis attempted to discredit Steele. Dennis's hostility did not fade until the beginning of 1723, by which time Steele's theatrical activity had ended.

Though he did not manage to hang on to his income from Drury Lane, Steele was well paid for his services. He began with a stipend of £700 annually when he joined the management, but he quickly realized that his chances of profit would be greater if he were a sharer. Cibber estimated that the co-managers averaged £1000 per year each, though that figure is judged by Loftis as exaggerated. Some years, when the theatre prospered, Steele certainly realized that much, but the figures we have suggest that the average may have been closer to £700. After 1715–16 most of Steele's playhouse income, whatever it may have been, went to his creditors.

Steele's association with Drury Lane began to deteriorate when the Duke of Newcastle was made Lord Chamberlain on 13 April 1717. Even before Newcastle's appointment his predecessor, the Duke of Bolton, had raised the question of government control of Drury Lane. In a letter written in March 1717, now at the Public Record Office, Bolton directed his secretary to write the following letter; it was almost certainly addressed to the Attorney General or his assistant, the Solicitor General, who would have been charged with giving legal opinions to the Crown on constitutional questions. The Solicitor General in 1717 was Sir William Thomson.

My Ld Chamberln has directed me by his maties command to send yu the inclosed copy of Sr Richard Steels patent for erecting a Company of Comedians, in order to yr giving yr opinions upon ye following Querys for his Maties information.
Q Whether his Matie may not by his Ld Chamberln give orders from time to time for ye better regulation & govermt of ye Playhouse as formerly notwithstanding ye present grant to Sr Richard Steel ye Patentee & of ye players under him
Q In case of refusal to obey or comply with such orders of ye Ld Chamberln what may be done to compell ym.

Newcastle, anxious to regain the control over theatrical affairs that the Lord Chamberlain had once had, called in Steele and his fellow managers. Steele later (in the *Theatre* on 25 January 1720) published the letter he wrote to Newcastle.

When your Grace came to be Chamberlain, from a generous design of making every office and authority the better for your wearing, your Grace was induced to send for me and the other Sharers, and in an absolute manner offered us a Licence, and demanded a resignation of the Patent, which I presumed as absolutely to refuse. This refusal I made in writing, and petitioned the King for his protection in the grant which he had given me.

In October 1718 Newcastle took a new tack, asking the Attorney General:

Whether Sr. Richd. Steele has power to Sell, Alienat or dispose of his Interest in the Said patent, or any part or Share of the profitts thereof and whether he may Appoint and impower any person to be Managers and Governes. of the Said Company, and assigne over and vest in them the Authority and power granted to him by the Said patent, and in Case he has no Such power, how far his patent may be Affected by it.

In 1718 he also asked Thomas Pengelly, serjeant-at-law,

1. Whether a patent granted for erecting and forming a company of comedians or stage players to act

National Portrait Gallery

RICHARD STEELE

by Richardson

in any part of the kingdom be not against law? 2. Whether the patent to Sir R. Steele be not against law? 3. Whether the King may not by the Lord Chamberlain make orders for the government of the players under Steele, notwithstanding the patent? 4. In case of disobedience, whether the Lord Chamberlain may not silence the company?

Newcastle found an occasion to take strong action in the winter of 1719–20. Cibber offended Newcastle in his dedication (to Steele) of *Ximene* in September 1719, and when Newcastle wanted a certain actor to play a role usually assigned to one of the actor-managers, Cibber refused. Newcastle, on 19 December 1719, ordered Steele, Wilks, and Booth to dismiss Cibber; the suspension lasted until 28 January 1720. Steele understood that the suspension of Cibber was a veiled attack on himself, and on 22 January 1720 he wrote to the King, begging protection. The following day Steele's old licence (not the patent) was revoked, and on 25 January Drury Lane was silenced. Wilks, Cibber, and Booth made their

submission to the Lord Chamberlain, received a licence on 27 January, and reopened the theatre the following day.

On 28 January 1720 Steele wrote to Cibber, Wilks, and Booth, reminding them that the patent was in his name, and authority for performances at Drury Lane lay with him. Then he said,

Whereas I am informed you intend to act this Night in the said Theatre without having consulted me I do hereby order you to desist from acting yourself in any Play or Performance whatsoever in the said Theatre or in causing any Play or Performance to be this Evening or any other Evening Acted till you receive further orders from, Gentlemen,
Y^r Affectionate Governour
Richard Steele

The players, fearful that Steele might still have authority over them, asked Pengelly for a legal opinion. He wrote to Newcastle on 1 February:

There is nothing further to be said, but that the managers stand upon their Defense and take care to secure the Lease or quit rent of the House, thereby to preserve the Possession of it; and also that they promise Sir Richard's part of the Cloathes and Scenery to be at their own Disposal, which I believe may be obtained upon moderate Terms from Mr. Gry [Gery] the mortgager, and this will deprive Sir Richard of the power & opportunity of giving them any inconvenient Disturbance. I am apt to think that Sir Richard's process, his artillery upon which he chiefly depended, has been discharged, not only without Direction, but without Terrors, and I Do not apprehend anything more terrible even from the Thunderer Himselfe, as he is pleased to call his Director. It will not be proper to ask any new order or Direction from His Majesty to defend the Players, until Sir Richard has Commenced some Prosecution, that it may be known in what method he intends to proceed against them; His Tuesday and Saturday's Process did not attack the managers in Drury Lane—I intend to pay my Duty to yr Grace tomorrow morning at 11 if it may be convenient. . . .

Pengelly was correct; the Lord Chamberlain's case against Steele was solid.

Steele's position was described by Sir John Vanbrugh in a letter to Jacob Tonson dated 18 February 1720:

But Sir R. Steel is grown such a Malecontent, That he now takes the Ministry directly for his Mark; and treats them (in the House) for some days past in so very frank a manner that they grow quite angry; and 'tis talked as if it would not be impossible, to see him very soon expel'd the House. I don't know whether you have heard, he has a month ago work'd a Quarrel So high with my Lord Chamberlain, That a New Licence has been granted to Wilks, Cibber & Booth which they accepting of, and acting under; have Left him with his Patent, but not one Player, and so the Lord Chamberlain's Authority over the Playhouse is restor'd, and the patent ends in a joke. I take hold of this Turn, to call upon those three Gentlemen about the Stock they had of mine, and think they will be willing to come to some tollerable Composition.

On 4 March the Drury Lane actors were sworn, but under the license, not a patent, and thus they were made subservient to the Lord Chamberlain.

In March 1720 Steele published *The State of the Case,* setting forth his legal position as patentee, but he was not in favor with the Lord Chamberlain nor was he in the good graces of the Whig ministry after his opposition to the peerage bill and the South Sea bill. Consequently, at the beginning of 1720 Steele had no standing at Drury Lane, no powers as governor, and no salary. To make matters worse, his health was declining. But on 9 April 1721 Steele wrote of his hopes for recovery of his theatrical position:

I have this morning resolved to pursue very Warmly my being restor'd in my Government of the Theatre Royall which is my right, under the Title of the Governor of the Royall Company of Comedians & from which I have been violently dispossessed by the Duke of Newcastle Lord Chamberlain of his Majesty's Household, upon a frivolous pretence of Jurisdiction in His office which He has been persuaded to assert against the Force of the King's Patent to me. This Violation of Property I take to have been instigated by the late Secretaryes Stanhope and Craggs for my opposition to the Peerage Bill by Speeches in the House and Printed Pamphlets.

Help was at hand, from Sir Robert Walpole.

When Walpole became Chancellor of the Exchequer in the spring of 1721, Steele was restored as head of Drury Lane. Newcastle wrote to the players on 2 May 1721:

Whereas Application has been made to me in behalf of Sr. Richd. Steele on Occasion of the Regulation under which his Mat.'s Company of Comedians has been lately placed Exclusive of the said Sr. Richd. Steele and his pretentions. I do hereby Order and Direct You to Account with the said Sr. Richd. Steele for all the past and future Share arising from the Profits of the Theatre as he would have been Entitled to by an Agreement between You and him, if the said Regulation had never been made, and to Pay him hereafter from time to time his said Share till further Orders from me, or Determination of that point be made by due course of Law. For wch. this shall be your Sufficient Warrant. . . .

For the time being Steele and his co-managers were at peace. His last play, upon which he had been working for years, came out at Drury Lane on 7 November 1722. It was *The Conscious Lovers,* and all three actor-managers were in the cast. The *Daily Journal* on 8 November claimed that "a greater Concourse of People was never known to be assembled." Indeed, the play received an initial run of 18 performances, brought Steele over £300 in benefit receipts, and remained immensely popular during the rest of the century. Steele dedicated the play to the King when it was published in 1723, and the King bestowed a gift of £500 upon him. Steele began but did not complete two other plays, *The School of Action* and *The Gentleman.*

By 1723 relations among the Drury Lane managers had deteriorated again. Steele was absenting himself from the theatre and had been mortgaging his profits. The actor-managers on 28 January 1720 had begun deducting £5 every acting day from Steele's salary to pay themselves for doing his work. But he probably received more than he deserved, his services to the theatre having been negligible since 1720. The players explained the situation in a Chancery deposition:

. . . And Yr. Oratrs. Cibber, Wilks, and Booth shew that ever since the sd. day of Janry 1719 / 20 aforesd being the time the sd. Sr. Richd. Steele began to absent him self from the business of the sd. Theatre Your Orators have had reced and taken to their own Use respectively 1.13.4 apiece for every day there has been a play Acted at the sd. Theatre in Consideration of such their attendance and Actings as aforesd. and the same has been always Entred in the daily Charge of the Accots. of the sd. Theatre . . . and he the sd Sr Richd Steel was so conscious to himself that Your Oratrs. Deserved a much greater sume . . . that he the sd. Sr. Richd. Steele allowed the Accots. of the sd Theatre wherein the sd 1.13.4 p Diem was Charged and never made any Objection thereto and in particular the sd. Sr. Richd. Steele upon the 18th of June 1723 passed and setled ye Accots. of the sd. Theatre

& reced his proportion of the profits thereof and gave a receipt. . . .

On 3 June 1724 a four-part indenture was drawn up to protect the interest of the managers and Steele's creditors, and about that time Steele, paralytic but still genial, retired permanently to Wales.

In September 1725 Steele and his trustee, David Scurlock, brought suit against the Drury Lane leaders for holding back Steele's share in the theatre income. Cibber, Wilks, and Booth countered with a suit on 11 January 1726, claiming that Steele had neglected his duties since January 1720 and had mortgaged his share without their consent. The litigation did not come to an end until 10 July 1728. The actor-managers were upheld in the taking of extra fees, but Steele was paid his back profits. Steele himself, of course, never appeared; he was represented by his trustee.

Dame Mary Steele had died on 26 December 1718 at the age of 40 and had been buried on 30 December at Westminster Abbey. She left a son Eugene and daughters Elizabeth and Mary; another son, Richard, had died in 1716. On 1 September 1729 Sir Richard Steele died in Carmarthen. He was privately buried in the church there. His patent passed to Anne Oldfield and continued in force until 1 September 1732, when the actor-managers were issued a new one, good for 21 years.

Steele's two daughters survived him, though the younger died within months of her father's death. The surviving daughter inherited Steele's share of the Drury Lane properties; the actor-managers paid her £1200 for Steele's share. According to John Nichols in *The Epistolary Correspondence of Sir Richard Steele,*

Steele's interest in Drury Lane Theatre became, after his death, the joint property of his two daughters, and on the death of the younger of them, devolved to Elizabeth, the elder, who sold it for no inconsiderable sum. But as if a fatality attended the business, the attorney who received the money for her ran away with the whole, and she never received a penny.

Steele at Drury Lane by John Loftis has been of great help in the preparation of this entry. See also Calhoun Winton's *Captain Steele* and *Sir Richard Steele, M.P.* and Richard H. Dammers's *Richard Steele.*

Portraits of Richard Steele include:

1. By J. B. Closterman. Portrait of a Gentleman, said to be Richard Steele. Small bust-length; in blue coat, contemporary giltwood frame. Sold at Christie's on 13 February 1981 for £1200.

2. By Godfrey Kneller, 1711. One of the Kit-Cat portraits commissioned by Jacob Tonson and for many years in the possession of Tonson's descendants at Bayfordbury, Hertfordshire. In the National Portrait Gallery (No 3227), presented in June 1945 with the Kit-Cat collection by the National Art Collections Fund. A variant of the Kneller, in oval, 24" × 28½", with a portrait of a woman in similar oval, called "Sir Richard Steele and Wife" were sold at C. G. Sloane and Co., Washington, D.C., on 12–13 October 1962 (illustrated in the sale catalogue). Engravings by J. Simon 1712–13 (reversed); by G. Vertue (reversed) as frontispiece to Steele's *Dramatic Workers,* 1723; by J. Faber Jr, 1733; by J. Houbraken, for Birch's *Heads,* 1748; and later by many others. A drawing, after Kneller, is in the Byng albums in the British Museum.

3. By Godfrey Kneller. In the National Gallery of Ireland (No 296), purchased at Christie's in 1889. This portrait and No 2 above were sold by Mr Slade at Christie's on 13 November 1801 and were bought by Williamson.

4. By Edward Lutterell. Head and shoulders, wearing brown coat. Pastel on metal, 9¾" × 7¾, signed and dated 1700. Sold at Sotheby's on 20 November 1963 (lot 24); bought for £90 by Fine Art Society.

5. By Jonathan Richardson, 1712. Once in the collection of Sir Richard Phillips, and then with Colnaghi, it was bought by the National Portrait Gallery (No 160) in March 1863. Engravings by J. Smith (reversed); by F. Bartolozzi, 1803; by S. Freeman; by R. M. Meadows as a plate to *The Cabinet,* 1808; and by an unknown engraver, "Sold in May's Buildings."

6. By Jonathan Richardson. Three-quarter-length, wearing a gray coat and a white cravat, left hand resting on the hilt of his sword, 49" × 39½". Sold at Christie's on 21 March 1975.

7. By Christian Richter, c. 1720. One of four miniatures attributed to Richter of Steele and his three children, in the National Portrait Gallery (No 1506a).

8. By James Thornhill, c. 1712. Depicts Steele in cap and tassel, wigless, with plain

undercoat undone. The turban on his head is pushed back to reveal a bit of cropped hair above his forehead. Highlights on his shiny face and nose. This portrait would seem to be the painting attributed to Kneller and reproduced as frontispiece to Willard Connely's *Sir Richard Steele* (1934). It was given to the Stationers' Company in 1798 by John Nichols, the early editor of Steele's correspondence. Steele writing in *The Theatre* called it an "*indolent*" pose. A three-quarter-length portrait (either the original or a copy) was in the Darnley collection at Cobham Hall, and was sold at Sotheby's on 23 July 1957 (lot 353) as "Portrait of a Gentleman;" it was bought for Her Majesty's Ministry of Works. The Cobham Hall version was engraved by Vertue in 1713. A copy by an anonymous engraver was published with the title "Isaac Bickerstaff, Esq.," and an engraving of it by "J. F." (and drawn by L. F. Dubourg) was published in a small oval plate, "Les Free Masons," in Picart's *Religious Ceremonies*, 1738.

9. By unknown artist. Miniature. Oil on copper. In the Victoria and Albert Museum, the Dyce Bequest. Reproduced in Rae Blanchard's *Correspondence of Richard Steele*.

10. By unknown artist. With Joseph Addison, shaking hands, about 1712. Painting in Chetham's Hospital and Library, Manchester. Reproduced in Willard Connely's *Sir Richard Steele*, 1934.

11. By unknown artist. A portrait of Steele was owned by the singer John Braham and is found in an inventory of his property at South Lodge, No 69, Baker Street, about 1838. It was also listed in the inventory of the property of Braham's heirs at No 21, Green Street, Leicester Square, on 9 November 1870. These manuscript inventories are now in the Strachie collection, Somerset Record Office, Taunton.

12. Engraved portrait by J. Sturt, after B. Lens. Sold by Sturt, 1710. A fanciful picture of Steele seated at a bureau, writing; with title: "Isaac Bickerstaff."

Steer, Mr ₁*fl.1795*₁,   *house servant?*

Benefit tickets sold by Mr Steer, probably a house servant, were accepted for 13 June 1795 at Covent Garden Theatre.

Steers, Mrs. *See* SALMON, MRS.

Steevens. *See* STEPHENS and STEVENS.

Steevenson. *See* STEPHENSON and STEVENSON.

Steffkins, Christian   *d. 1714, violist.*

Christian (sometimes Christopher) Steffkins was the son of the court musician Theodore Steffkins (or Stiffkins, Stofkins, Stephkin). He was appointed a violist in the King's private music on 19 July 1689, at an annual salary of £40, and thereafter he was frequently mentioned in the Lord Chamberlain's accounts in connection with livery payments. From 1 January to 13 April 1691 he was with William III at the Hague. Steffkins was buried at St Clement Danes on 2 December 1714. At Stationers' Hall on 5 May 1715 a benefit concert was presented for Steffkins's widow and children.

Steffkins, Dietrich   *d. c. 1675?, bass viol player.*

Dietrich (or Diedrich) Steffkins was sworn a musician in ordinary in the King's Musick on 2 January 1636, replacing Maurice Webster. In 1637 he was paid £5 for strings for the bass viols—of which he was apparently the leader. In 1660 he was again in the King's Musick, at £46 10*s.* 10*d.* per year. The last mention of him in the Lord Chamberlain's accounts was in 1668. Westrup, in his article in *Musical Quarterly* (1941) on foreign musicians in London, states that the Steffkins family was originally from Germany, that Dietrich returned to Hamburg during the Commonwealth, and that he was probably the Steffkins who died late in 1674 or early 1675.

Steffkins, Frederick   ₁*fl.1689–1705*₁, *violist?*

On 19 July 1689, according to the Lord Chamberlain's accounts, Frederick Steffkins was appointed to the private music of William III. He was, we believe, the son of Frederick William Steffkins, who was a violist in the 1660s and 1670s, and Frederick was probably also a violist. (Grove, however, states that Frederick was the son of Theodore Steffkins.) The accounts mentioned Steffkins several times, usually in connection with livery payments. He was on an annual salary of £40. Steffkins accompanied William III to the Hague in January 1691, but most of his service appears to have been in London. He was probably the Frederick Steffkins who married Eve Guidet at St Marylebone on 3 June 1696. He advertised on 20 December 1703 that he would "undertake to set the frets of viols brought to his house at the lower end of Basinghall Street in perfect proportions and to give necessary directions for correct performances." On 29 November 1705 George Hill was sworn a musician in ordinary in the King's Musick on the surrender of Frederick Steffkins. That would suggest that Steffkins had retired but was still alive.

The Frederick Steffkins who was bequeathed a violin in the will of John Hingeston in 1683 must have been our subject.

Steffkins, Frederick William d. 1675?, violist.

Frederick William (or Wilhelm) Steffkins and his father Theodore Steffkins were sworn into the King's Musick on 29 November 1662 as musicians in ordinary on the viola at 1s. 8d. daily each plus livery allowances of £16 2s. 6d. annually each, retroactive to 24 June 1660. On 3 June 1675 Sarah Steffkins, executrix for Frederick (William?) Steffkins, "a former musician," was ordered by the Lord Chamberlain's accounts to pay Thomas Ward £11 4s. 4d.— evidently a sum owed him by the deceased Steffkins. One must suppose that Frederick William Steffkins died shortly before that date, and that the Frederick Steffkins mentioned in the Lord Chamberlain's accounts in the 1680s was his son.

Steffkins, Theodore [fl. 1660–1675?], violist, composer.

Grove (fifth edition) notes that Theodore Steffkins came to England (presumably from Germany) at the Restoration. He was the brother of Dietrich and father of Frederick William and Christian Steffkins. (The New Grove treats Theodore and Dietrich as the same person.) The Lord Chamberlain's accounts show that on 16 July 1661 Theodore Steffkins was paid £10 to buy a bass viol, though his ordinary instrument appears to have been the viola. On 29 November 1662 he and Frederick William Steffkins were admitted to the King's Musick as musicians in ordinary for the viola, with wages of 1s. 8d. daily and livery allowances of £16 2s. 6d. annually, retroactive to John the Baptist 1660.

On 14 May 1663 Theodore Steffkins was to be paid £12 for a lyra viol. By about 1667 Steffkins was admired by his musical friends John Jenkins and Roger North and seems to have been the most talented of the Steffkins family of royal musicians. A Steffkins, presumably Theodore, played bass viol in the court masque Calisto on 15 February 1675. One of his works has survived: a suite written in 1664 for unaccompanied bass viol.

Steggeldolt and Stegeldoirs. See STAGELDOIR.

Steibelt, Daniel 1765–1823, pianist, composer.

The New Grove states that Daniel Steibelt was born in Berlin on 22 October 1765, the son of a harpsichord player and builder of pianofortes. Steibelt was patronized by Frederick William II, and the King placed him with Kirnberger to study harpsichord and composition. After a brief period in the military service, Steibelt left Berlin about 1784, settling in the late 1780s in Paris, where his abilities as a pianist and composer blossomed. His opera Romeo et Juliette was given at the Théâtre Feydeau on 10 September 1793.

Steibelt came to London by way of Holland about the end of 1796, performing first, perhaps, on 1 May 1797 at Salomon's benefit concert. His third piano concerto was probably performed at Salomon's concert on 19 March 1798. He and Attwood composed and selected the music for Albert and Adelaide, which opened at Covent Garden Theatre on 11 December 1798. While in England Steibelt established himself as a music teacher and married a young Englishwoman who was an accomplished piano player.

He journeyed to Hamburg late in 1799 and gave performances in Dresden, Prague, Berlin, and Vienna in 1800. In Vienna he contested with Beethoven, lost, and found his own recitals poorly attended. By August 1800 he was again in Paris, performing his alteration of Haydn's Creation on Christmas eve at the Opéra. On 3 March 1802 his ballet La Vellée de Tempé was given at the Opéra, and on 22 March Steibelt returned to London.

Steibelt divided his time between London and Paris in the early years of the nineteenth century. On 24 May 1804 his ballet Le Jugement du berger Paris was given at the King's Theatre, and La Belle Laitrère was produced there on 26 January 1805. At the Paris Opéra on 4 February 1806 La Fête de Mars was presented. An opera, La Princesse de Babylone, was in rehearsal at the Opéra in 1808, but an accumulation of debts forced Steibelt to flee Paris. During these years he also busied himself with composing piano music.

Tsar Alexander invited Steibelt to St Petersburg late in 1808, and by the end of 1810 Steibelt was director of the French opera there and maître de chapelle. His ballet La Fête de l'empereur was produced in 1809 and Der blöde Ritter by 1812. Steibelt also composed two operas in Russia, Cendrillon and Sargines, and he revised his Roméo et Juliette and worked on but did not complete Le Jugement de Midas. He died in St Petersburg on 20 September 1823, leaving behind a vast number of works for piano, voice, and chamber ensembles. The Catalogue of Printed Music in the British Museum lists a number of his works that were published in London, Edinburgh, and Paris.

An engraving by Landseer, published in 1801 and designed by De Loutherbourg from miniature cameos by H. de Janvry, shows Daniel Steibelt with 25 other leading musicians of the period.

Steiner, Mr ₁fl. 1783₁, musician.
According to the Lord Chamberlain's accounts, Mr. Steiner was a musician at the King's Theatre in 1783.

Stenson, Mr ₁fl. 1794₁, singer.
Doane's Musical Directory of 1794 listed Mr Stenson, of Derby, as a tenor who sang in the Handelian performances at Westminster Abbey.

"Stentor." See FARLEY, CHARLES.

Stephanoff, N. Fileter ₁fl. 1777–1791₁, scene painter.
The painter N. Fileter Stephanoff, born in Russia, resided in England for some years during the last quarter of the eighteenth century. The date of his arrival in London is unknown, but on 6 May 1777 Drury Lane Theatre paid £25 to "Stepanoff painter on acct.," and he was paid £47 9s. the following 19 June, for services

unspecified. He exhibited several paintings at the Royal Academy in 1778 and 1781, and, in 1782 at the Free Society of Artists, several drawings and watercolors of landscapes. His commissions, according to Edwards's Anecdotes of Painters, included ceiling decorations.

Stephanoff painted scenery for the Royal Circus in 1790. During the 1791 season at the Pantheon he assisted William Hodges with scene painting.

Sometime in the early 1790s Stephanoff committed suicide. His wife Gertrude Stephanoff was a still-life painter; two of her pictures were exhibited at the Royal Academy in 1782.

Stephens. See also STEVENS.

Stephens, Mr ₁fl. 1773₁, constable.
The Morning Chronicle of 23 April 1773 cited Mr Stephens as the constable at Covent Garden Theatre.

Stephens, Mr ₁fl. 1775–1776₁. See STEVENS, WILLIAM.

Stephens, Mrs ₁fl. 1700–1701₁, actress.
As a member of Christopher Rich's troupe at Drury Lane Theatre Mrs Stephens played Cloe in The Reform'd Wife in March 1700 and Dearnwell in The Bath on 31 May 1701.

Stephens, Mrs ₁fl. 1755–1770₁, actress, singer.
Mrs Stephens played Mrs Vixen in The Beggar's Opera at Covent Garden Theatre on 17 October 1755. She was Isabel in Henry V on 3 December, Mrs Sealand in The Conscious Lovers on 5 December, Goneril in King Lear on 26 February 1756, and Isabella in A Duke and No Duke on 29 April. Mrs Stephens remained at Covent Garden through the 1767–68 season, appearing in such new parts as Lucetta in The Rover, Honoria in Love Makes a Man, Cephania in Alzira, Cassana in The Prophetess, Jenny Diver and Mrs Peachum in The Beggar's Opera, Lady Percy in 1 Henry IV, Alicia in Jane Shore, a Beggar Woman in The Jovial Crew, Bianca in Catherine and Petruchio, Doll Tearsheet in 2 Henry IV, the Widow of Florence in All's Well that Ends Well, Lamorce in The Inconstant, Margery in Love in a Village, Melinda in The Recruiting Officer, Teresa in The Spanish Fryar, Pro-

serpine in *Harlequin Sorcerer,* Charmion in *All for Love,* Lady Anne in *Richard III,* Juno in *Midas,* Lucy in *Oroonoko,* Cleone in *The Distrest Mother,* Megra in *Philaster,* and Lady Scrape in *The Musical Lady.* She also sang in the *Macbeth* chorus. Her daily salary at Covent Garden, as of 22 September 1760, was 5*s.*

In the summer of 1765 Mrs Stephens was engaged by Love to act at the new playhouse in Richmond. The *Universal Museum* in August reported that "Mrs. *Stephens,* of Covent-Garden house, who, when in town, seldom rises to a part of fifty lines, has played the Lady in *Comus* with a more merited share of success perhaps, than it has received for the last twenty years at either of the theatres [i.e., the patent houses, Covent Garden and Drury Lane]. . . ." She was again at Richmond in the summers of 1766 and 1767.

Mrs Stephens transferred to Drury Lane in the fall of 1768, and there she acted through the spring of 1770. Her first part was Lady Brute in *The Provok'd Wife* on 8 September 1768, after which she appeared as Mila in *Zingis,* Lavinia in *The Fair Penitent,* Isabella in *The Wonder,* Lady Freelove in *The Jealous Wife,* Lady Anne in *Richard III,* Mrs Strickland in *The Suspicious Husband,* Maria in *The London Merchant,* Goneril in *King Lear,* Lady Percy in *1 Henry IV,* Laura in *Tancred and Sigismunda,* Lady Grace in *The Provok'd Husband,* Lady Constant in *The Way to Keep Him,* Araminta in *The Confederacy,* Mrs Page in *The Merry Wives of Windsor,* Emilia in *Othello,* and Margaretta in *Rule a Wife and Have a Wife.*

Stephens, Mrs ₍*fl.* 1782₎, *impresario.*

The Lord Chamberlain's papers show that a Mrs Stephens was granted a license to present an entertainment at the Haymarket Theatre on 18 September 1782. *The London Stage* lists *The Beggar's Opera* and *Harlequin Teague* there on that date, a benefit for Massey. Mrs Stephens was not mentioned and may have been only the promoter of the event.

Stephens, Miss, later Mrs ₍George?₎ Smith *d. 1828?, singer, actress.*

On 29 November 1798 at Drury Lane Theatre Miss Stephens made her stage debut singing Polly in *The Beggar's Opera.* The *Monthly Mirror* in December stated flatly that

this lady's voice is unequalled, except by Mrs. Bland's, on the English stage; her tones are firm, clear, full, and exquisitely harmonious; and, we think, peculiarly calculated for ballads, and the old English melodies; nature, and not art, has made her a singer, and if she means to continue in the profession, we are not aware of any obstacle that can possibly impede her advancement to the first situation in the theatre. She possesses, also, no inconsiderable abilities as an actress, and seems to feel that degree of confidence, which is so necessary to give energy and effect to exertion. Miss Stevens has performed this character four times with distinguished applause, and we know no instance where it has been so justly and so universally bestowed.

The *Authentic History of the Green Room* in 1801 and the *Authentic Memoirs of the Green Room* in 1806 provided some background on the talented Miss Stephens. Her father was a respectable tradesman in Park Street, Grosvenor Square, and her singing teachers were De Lanza (who also taught her younger sister, Catherine) and Benelli. The *Authentic History* felt that Miss Stephens wanted "sprightliness, vivacity, and animation" as an actress, but, since she was very young, she would doubtless improve. In private life she was "highly respected among the first circles, her company being courted by persons of the first distinction. . . ." Mrs Sheridan was her patroness and protector. Miss Stephens's sister Catherine had a considerable career as a singer in the early nineteenth century, and in 1838 she married the fifth Earl of Essex. Another sister, who became Mrs Carter, acted at Drury Lane in the 1800–1801 season.

After her success in *The Beggar's Opera* Miss Stephens sang in *Pizarro* and added to her repertoire Margaretta in *No Song No Supper,* Patty in *The Maid of the Mill,* Sophia in *Of Age Tomorrow,* the title part in *Rosina,* and a Nun in *De Montfort.* At her benefit on 7 June 1800 she entertained between the acts with "The Soldier tir'd of War's alarms" and a new ballad. The receipts came to almost £327 before house charges of £212 were subtracted; that was a very respectable showing for a beginner. In September 1799 her salary for five days came to £3 6*s.* 8*d.*

At Drury Lane after the turn of the century Miss Stephens was seen in such new characters as Rosetta in *Love in a Village* and Violetta in

The Egyptian Festival. By 1802 she was earning £5 16s. 8d. weekly. She may not have stayed at Drury Lane after 1803.

Early in 1806 Miss Stephens was performing at Manchester. The *Thespian Review* reported her appearance on 21 February, when *Out of Place*, a new musical farce, was presented. "Miss STEPHENS [as] *Laurette,* sung several airs most delightfully, but the duet between her and Mr. Smith, seemed to make the greatest impression. It was a high trait [i.e., treat] to the lovers of harmony; it rivetted attention, and almost suspended the breathing of the house. . . ." The Smith in question was almost certainly the popular singer George Smith. The *Gentleman's Magazine* in June 1806 announced that Miss Stephens and Smith were married in Liverpool on 19 June. A Mrs Smith, according to a British Library manuscript, died in April 1828, but we cannot be certain she was our subject.

Stephens, Mary, née Capon   *b. 1751, dancer.*

Born in 1751, Mary Capon made her first stage appearance at the age of 16 dancing at Covent Garden Theatre on 27 April 1767. The bill stated that she was an apprentice to the ballet master James Fishar. The performance was for his benefit. Miss Capon was given a regular engagement at Covent Garden in 1767–68 at 6s. 8d. daily, a handsome salary for a youngster. She repeated the serious dance in which she had made her stage debut the previous spring and during the season was also seen in a comic dance.

Miss Capon continued at Covent Garden through 1774–75, offering entr'acte dances— usually untitled—and appearing in such dances, plays, and pantomimes as *Henry VIII, The Sylphs, The Fair, The Druids, The Florist, Harlequin's Jubilee, The Corsican Sailor's Punch House, The Italian Gardener, Daphne and Amintor, The Festival of the Black Prince, The Recruits, The Frolick, Rural Merriment, The Generous Pirate,* and *The Indiaman Return'd.* She also played Ceres in *The Rape of Proserpine,* her first character part, on 28 December 1770.

Though Mary Capon was not given leading assignments, she was evidently popular, and a poem in the *Gentleman's Magazine* in January 1772 included a fleeting reference to her: "C

was a Capon, who dances with ease." She was still advertised as a scholar of Fishar's in the spring of 1772, but her apprenticeship must have ended that year. In 1773 she began appearing at Sadler's Wells and at Covent Garden. The Covent Garden bill for 10 May 1774 indicated that she had become Mrs Stephens. The *Morning Chronicle* noted the following September that she had married "some time since." After 1774–75 she left Covent Garden and confined her dancing to Sadler's Wells. The bill there for 28 September 1775 said benefit tickets could be had of Mrs Stephens at Mr Selth's the peruke maker under the great piazza in Covent Garden. She was still performing at the Wells in 1776.

A Mary Capon was in Birmingham in 1770, and Timothy Plain (Moncrieff Threepland), in *Letters Respecting the Performances at the Theatre Royal, Edinburgh,* placed a Miss Capon there in 1782. Both of those references may have been to our subject; if our Mary Capon reverted to her maiden name by 1782, her marriage to Mr Stephens may have failed or Stephens may have died. There is no evidence to relate Mary Capon to the scene designer William Capon, though since she was born in 1751 and he in 1757 they may have been siblings or cousins.

Stephens, Samuel   *d. 1764, actor, manager.*

The tale of Samuel Stephens the buttonmaker who became an actor was told in several eighteenth-century sources; Kirkman's *Memoirs of Macklin* contains a fairly complete version:

In the history of the Stage, there is scarcely any thing more singular than the circumstances which have attended the performance of this character [Othello] by a person of the name of Stephens, a button-maker, who resided in Paternoster Row. Mr. Samuel Stephens had been for many years a constant attendant at the Theatre, and especially at that period when Mr. [Barton] Booth acted the principal characters in Tragedy. Among his acquaintances he had frequently repeated speeches, or favourite portions of Plays, especially from *Othello.* He was told by his friends, that his voice resembled that of Mr. Booth, both in strength and melody, and his imitation of that great actor's manner was just, as well as pleasing. He was, at length, tempted to make an offer of his services to Mr.

Rich, who had just lost his great Tragedian, Mr. Quin, who had left his old master, and was engaged at Drury Lane. In consequence of some temporary agreement with Mr. Rich, Stephens ventured in 1734, to perform his favourite character of Othello.

His figure was not unsuitable to the part, and he had, by close attention, acquired some of Mr. Booth's happy tones. The audience were equally surprised and delighted at the performance; and, during that passionate scene between the Moor and Iago, in the 3d act, the pit cried out, "Bravo! bravo! better than Quin! better than Quin!" For six or seven nights successively, this man drew after him very large audiences. During this time Mr. Quin avoided going to the Coffee House that he usually frequented, lest he should be affronted by the loud praises bestowed upon the button-maker. However, the charm was not wound up so powerfully as to last long; Rich, either through mistake or design, persuaded the new Actor to choose Polydore, in the Orphan, for his second character, than which nothing could have been more ill-advised. Stephens was in form, bulky; in the management of his voice, aukward, and advanced beyond his fortieth year. This act of indiscretion was equally hurtful to the Actor and Manager. The ladies, more especially, were displeased with such a misrepresentation of a young, gay libertine, dressed in a large full-bottomed wig, and red stockings, though they had been laid aside by all the fashionable people for some time. . . .

The London Stage shows that the debut of button-maker Stephens took place at Covent Garden Theatre on 19 October 1734. The bill said that the impersonator of Othello would be Stephens, "a citizen of London, who never appeared on any stage before." In Aaron Hill's *Works* is a letter dated 23 October 1734. He told Stephens that "The pleasure you gave me, in *Othello*, was so new and suprizing" Hill could not forbear acknowledging it. But he advised Stephens to "assume, from your very first step upon the stage, all that warlike boldness of air" Othello should have. Hill cautioned Stephens not to lose lines of dialogue through improper articulation or turning his face away from the audience, and he advised him to take his breath in well-chosen places and use pointed pauses. A voice "of such compass as yours, may, in the highest torrent of passion, rise still stronger and clearer. . . ." Hill especially liked Stephens' "impressive attention" in listening to others on stage.

After performing five times as Othello, Stephens acted the Ghost in *Hamlet* (another role

Booth had played) on 31 October. On 4 November he tried Tamerlane, and on 4 January 1735 he appeared as Polydore in *The Orphan*. Despite his failure in *The Orphan* Stephens continued to the end of the season, acting such important new roles as Herod in *Mariamne*, Hannibal in *Sophonisba*, King Lear, the King in 1 *Henry IV*, and Aboan in *Oroonoko*.

Samuel Stephens went on to become a regular member of the Covent Garden company, playing some leading parts and a number of lesser ones through 1743–44. Among the new characters Stephens (often Stevens) tried were Marcian in *Theodosius*, Acasto in *The Orphan*, Aegeon and the Ghost of Laius in *Oedipus*, Pyrrhus and Pylades in *The Distrest Mother*, Hastings in *Jane Shore*, Lennox in *Macbeth*, Casca in *Julius Caesar*, Sciolto in *The Fair Penitent*, Mahomet in *Abra Mule*, Marcus and Cato in *Cato*, Clytus in *The Rival Queens*, Bellarius in *Cymbeline*, Salisbury in *King John*, Falstaff in 1 *Henry IV*, Raymond in *The Spanish Fryar*, York in *Richard II*, Shallow and the King in 2 *Henry IV*, Exeter in *Henry V*, the King and Heli in *The Mourning Bride*, Sir Thomas in *The Gamester*, Tradelove in *A Bold Stroke for a Wife*, Pericles in *Marina*, Pelopidas in *Mithridates*, Falstaff in *The Merry Wives of Windsor*, Trusty in *The Funeral*, Norfolk in *Richard III*, Duke Senior in *As You Like It*, a General in *The Rehearsal*, Bajazet in *Tamerlane*, Leontes in *The Winter's Tale*, and Sealand in *The Conscious Lovers*. Stephens's last appearance at Covent Garden was in *As You Like It* on 23 May 1744.

Rich paid Stephens £200 per season and granted him annual benefits. Tickets were available at Stephens's house in Paternoster Row until April 1744, when he was at the Jar, opposite Red Lion Street, Holborn. A Stephens (or Stevens) appeared at Bartholomew Fair in August 1741, but we take him to have been a different person.

Since reports of Stephens's career stated that he left London and became an itinerant actor, perhaps he was the "Stevens" who acted King Henry in *Richard III* at the New Concert Hall in Edinburgh on 17 February 1750. Samuel Stephens is known to have associated himself with the Bath theatre in 1751, so we believe the Stephens who was at the related Jacob's Wells theatre in Bristol from 12 June to 4 September 1745 was Samuel. By 1748 he was serving as the Bristol company treasurer at 5s.

nightly. The records of the Orchard Street Theatre, Bath, show Samuel Stephens active there from 1751–52 through 1760–61. He was named as one of the playhouse managers in the *Bath Journal* of 2 December 1751. Stephens was given a special benefit at Bath in March 1759, according to Penley's *The Bath Stage;* he had been the principal sufferer in a fire in May 1758 in which £2000 in clothing and scenes were burned in a wagon crossing Salisbury plain. Samuel Stephens died at Bath in 1764.

Stephenson. *See also* STEVENSON.

Stephenson, Mr ₁*fl. 1767–1784*₁, *constable.*

Mr Stephenson is listed in *The London Stage* as a constable earning 2s. daily at Covent Garden Theatre as of 14 September 1767. He was named in benefit bills through 29 May 1784.

Stephenson, John ₁*fl. 1674–1715*₁, *scene designer.*

The London Stage lists a Mr Stephenson as a member of the Duke's Company at the Dorset Garden Theatre in 1674–75. He was probably the painter John Stephenson (or Steevenson) who worked on pageants for the Lord Mayor's show in 1677 and was mentioned in the Painter-Stainer's book in 1715, according to Croft-Murray's *Decorative Painting in England.*

Stephenson, Thomas ₁*fl. 1669–1679*₁, *scene designer.*

Thomas Stephenson (or Stevenson) studied under the scene painter Robert Aggas and was, according to Buckeridge (*A Note Towards an English School* [1706]), "a good painter, not only in landskip, but also in figures and architecture in distemper. . . ." He was in his day considered eminent in scene painting. In 1669 he was living in Nightingale Lane. Stephenson designed the scenery for Shadwell's *Psyche* in 1675 and worked with John Fordham on the Lord Mayor's Show from 1674 to 1676. Croft-Murray in *Decorative Painting in England* thinks our subject was probably the Thomas Stephenson who painted a portrait of a lady, now at King's College, Newcastle. His son was John Stephenson, also a scene painter.

The scenery for *Psyche* caused considerable stir. The prompter John Downes wrote that it

cost over £800. In 1678–79 Stephenson acted as Rentee Warden to the Painter-Stainer's Company.

"Stephen Stuffbags." *See* KEMBLE, STEPHEN.

Stergess, Mr. ₁*fl. 1760*₁, *attendant.*

The accounts at Covent Garden Theatre on 26 May 1760 show a payment of £14 14s. 6d. to Mr Stergess and his son for attending Mr Saunders on the wire for 48 nights.

Stergess, Master ₁*fl. 1760*₁, *attendant. See* STERGESS, MR.

Sterling, Mrs. *See* DIXON, CLARA ANN.

Sterling, Miss ₁*fl. 1768–1772*₁, *actress.*

A Miss Sterling played Jenny in *Patie and Roger* at the Haymarket Theatre on 21 September 1772 with a group, most of whom were from Scotland. She was surely one of the two Misses Sterling who were at the Norwich Theatre Royal in 1768, one of whom was called Miss Sterling and the other Miss Fanny Sterling.

Sterling, Mrs James, née Lyddal *d.c. 1733, actress, singer, author.*

Mrs James Sterling, wife of the poet-playwright, made her first London appearance on 2 October 1723 at the Lincoln's Inn Fields Theatre, playing Desdemona to James Quin's *Othello.* She has hailed as "lately arrived from the Theatre in Dublin." Her maiden name, according to La Tourette Stockwell, was Lyddal (or Lyddall), and she was the sister of the Lyddal girl who married Henry Giffard. So far as we can determine, Giffard married, first, Mary (Molly) Lyddal, who died about 1729; then he married Anna Marcella (Nancy) Lyddal, Mary's sister. The Christian name of the Lyddal girl who married James Sterling we do not know. Her parents were actors at the Smock Alley Theatre in Dublin.

Mrs Sterling (or Stirling) played Marcella in *Don Quixote* at Lincoln's Inn Fields on 4 October 1723 and, in character, sang the popular "I burn, I burn." During the rest of the 1723–24 season she appeared as Miranda in *The Busy Body*, Selima in *Tamerlane*, Ophelia in *Hamlet,*

Silvia in *The Soldier's Fortune,* Cressida in *Troilus and Cressida,* Lavinia in *Titus Andronicus,* Belinda in *The Old Bachelor,* Belinda in *The Provok'd Wife,* Morayma in *Don Sebastian* (for her benefit on 29 April 1724, shared with Mrs Brett; gross income came to only about £78), Angelina in *Love Makes a Man,* and Melinda in *The Recruiting Officer.* Her daily salary during the season was 13s. 4d. On 2 September 1724 Mrs Sterling played Artesia in *Merlin* at Southwark Fair.

She returned to Smock Alley in Dublin, where she probably had acted before coming to London. There she remained to the end of her career in 1732. Her parts at Smock Alley are not fully known, but W. S. Clark's notes show that she acted Philadelphia in *The Amorous Widow,* Flora in *She Wou'd and She Wou'd Not,* Sylvia in *The Double Gallant,* Belinda in *Tunbridge Walks,* Quisara in *The Island Princess,* Mrs Constance in *The Northern Lass,* Lady Diana Talbot in *Vertue Betray'd,* Arethusa in *Philaster,* Estifania in *Rule a Wife and Have a Wife,* Mrs Sullen in *The Beaux' Stratagem,* Phebe in *The Beggar's Wedding,* Ruth in *The Committee,* the title role in *Flora,* Leonora in *The Revenge,* Lady Anne in *Richard III* (on 22 March 1731, when she also spoke and sang a humorous opera epilogue in the character of Lady Anne's ghost!), Statira in *The Rival Queens,* Ophelia, Rachel in *The Jovial Crew,* Maria in *The London Merchant,* and Leiza in *Love and Ambition.*

On 22 May 1732 at Smock Alley *The Beggar's Opera* was presented for Mrs Sterling's benefit, "being the last time of her performance on the stage." Perhaps she sang a role; the bill said only that she spoke an epilogue, presumably one she had written herself. Among W. J. Lawrence's notes is one saying that Mrs Sterling was "in the habit of writing and singing epilogues" and presenting epilogues written for her by her husband. Since James Sterling remarried in 1734, our guess is that Mrs Sterling died about 1733.

According to notes left by W. J. Lawrence in the National Library of Ireland, a print showing Mrs Sterling as Polly and Lewis Layfield as Macheath in *The Beggar's Opera* had been published by Thomas Benson in Dublin on 7 December 1728. We have been unable to locate a copy.

Sterne, Everard, stage name of John Knight ₁*fl.* 1777–1787₁, *actor, manager.*

The *Morning Chronicle* on 27 February 1777 reported that Booth of Drury Lane Theatre (probably John Booth) testified at a trial in Bow Street that he had seen Everard Sterne, then a prisoner, on the Edinburgh stage. The *Morning Post* on the same day identified Sterne as John Knight, who used Everard Sterne as an alias. With Mrs Sterne, our subject appeared in *Barbarossa* at the Red Lion Inn, Stoke Newington, on 28 March 1787, he playing Selim and she Irene; she acted Sally in the afterpiece, *Thomas and Sally.* The bill contained the following statement:

Mr Sterne presents his respectful Compliments to the Ladies and Gentlemen of Newington and its Vicinity, and now begs leave to inform them that he has been at considerable Expence in procuring several Performers, in order that every Performance may give Satisfaction to those Ladies and Gentlemen who have so generously exerted their Interest for him and his Company; and as their Stay will be but *very* short, he hopes that this Care by obtaining so many *fresh Members* may meet with the Encouragement of a candid Public. N.B. Any Lady or Gentlemen who will honor the company by bespeaking a Play, their Commands will be thankfully received and attended to by applying to Mr Sterne.

Sterne, Mrs Everard ₁*fl.* 1787₁, *actress.* See STERNE, EVERARD.

Stevenart, Mr ₁*fl. c.* 1797₁, *singer, composer.*

The *Catalogue of Printed Music in the British Museum* lists *'Twas Paddy O'Flanaghan sett out one Morning,* a song composed by Mr Stevenart and sung by him at the Royal Circus. It was published about 1797.

Stevens. *See also* STEPHENS.

Stevens, Mr ₁*fl.* 1728–1733₁, *actor.*

A Mr Stevens shared a benefit with two others at the Haymarket Theatre on 3 April 1728. He may have been a member of the Violante troupe, which had been appearing at the Haymarket during the season. On 31 January 1729 at the same house Stevens shared a benefit with Patrick. That Stevens was prob-

265 STEVENS

ably the "Stephens" who had a role in *The Amorous Lady* on 26 July 1733 at the Haymarket and then went over to Covent Garden Theatre to act the First Player in *The Stage Mutineers* on 27 July and Honestus in *The Fancy'd Queen* on 14 August.

Stevens, Mr ₁*fl. 1737–1742*₁, *actor.*

In the late 1730s and early 1740s, when the button-maker Samuel Stephens was pursuing his acting career at Covent Garden Theatre, there was a player named Stevens also in the Covent Garden troupe. They often appeared in the same plays, and usually the bills distinguished them by the different spellings of their names. But it is clear that Stephens was sometimes spelled Stevens in the bills, so we cannot be certain of the accuracy of some of the following assignments.

Stevens first came to notice at the Lincoln's Inn Fields Theatre on 26 July 1737, when he acted Wildman in *The Woman Captain*. He then appeared as a Player in *The Beggar's Opera* on 2 August and a Player in *Three Hours after Marriage* on 5 August. In the cast of *The Woman Captain* was Mrs Stevens, presumably his wife.

Stevens joined the Covent Garden company, his first part being Cassio in *Othello* (at Lincoln's Inn Fields) on 7 September 1737, with Samuel Stephens playing Othello. During the rest of the season Stevens was seen as Supple in *The Double Gallant*, Fitzwalter and Salisbury in *Richard II*, Mortimer and Young Talbot in *1 Henry IV*, Moreton in *2 Henry IV*, Grey in *Henry V*, Pyracmon in *Oedipus*, Slango in *The Honest Yorkshireman*, Freeman in *A Bold Stroke for a Wife*, Loveworth in *Tunbridge Walks*, Leonine in *Marina*, and Lovewell in *Love and a Bottle*. Other roles he added to his repertoire in the seasons that followed were Sancho in *Rule a Wife and Have a Wife*, Hotman in *Oroonoko*, Spinosa in *Venice Preserv'd*, Mirvan in *Tamerlane*, Fetch in *The Stage Coach*, Buckram in *Love for Love*, Termagant in *The Squire of Alsatia*, Young Rakish in *The School Boy*, and Diego in *Don Quixote*.

Stevens left Covent Garden after the 1738–39 season. In the fall of 1740 he acted at Drury Lane Theatre, appearing first as Dowglass in *1 Henry IV* on 13 October. Between then and the end of the year he was seen as Freehold in *Robin Goodfellow*, Pistol in *The Merry Wives of Windsor*,

Ben in *The Beggar's Opera*, and Pyracmon in *Oedipus*. Our man was most likely the "Stephens" and the "Stevens" who acted at the Lee and Woodward booth at Bartholomew Fair on 22 August 1741, playing Anglicanus in *Darius* and Mars in *The Wrangling Deities*.

He returned to Covent Garden on 25 September 1741 to act Leander in *The Mock Doctor* and then such new parts as Jaques in *Love Makes a Man*, Jack Stanmore in *Oroonoko*, the Lieutenant of the Tower in *Richard III*, Jaques in *As You Like It*, Guildenstern in *Hamlet*, the Lieutenant General in *The Rehearsal*, Axalla in *Tamerlane*, Dion in *The Winter's Tale*, Jaques in *The Pilgrim*, Matchlock in *The Funeral*, Catesby in *Jane Shore*, Perez in *The Mourning Bride*, and Young Bernard in *The Country House*. His last notice seems to have been on 20 May 1742.

Stevens, Mr ₁*fl. 1739–1744*₁, *house servant.*

Mr Stevens shared benefits at Drury Lane Theatre from 31 May 1739 through 22 May 1744; once, on 3 June 1743, the benefit had to be held at Lincoln's Inn Fields Theatre. Stevens was described in 1742 as a doorkeeper and in 1744 as the gallery boxkeeper.

Stevens, Mr ₁*fl. 1745–1752?*₁, *actor.*

At Drury Lane Theatre on 12 October 1745 a young actor, not named in the playbill, attempted *Hamlet*. Charles Beecher Hogan in *Shakespeare in the Theatre* identified him as Mr Stevens. He seems not to have been the Stevens who acted at Covent Garden Theatre and Drury Lane a few years earlier, nor the Stevens who performed in London in the 1750s. Young Stevens remained at Drury Lane for the 1745–46 season, appearing as Axalla in *Tamerlane*, Cromwell in *Henry VIII*, the Younger Brother in *Comus*, and the King of Scotland in *Henry VII*. Mrs Cibber wrote to David Garrick in January 1746, after Macklin's *Henry VII* had opened (and closed), telling him what a bad play it was. But, she wrote, ". . . I must ask Mr Stevens's pardon, to whom I have done injustice, for I think he may dispute the pass downstairs with Perkin [Warbeck, played by Goodfellow], and as his head seems to be the heaviest of the two, I think he has the best right to it."

Perhaps our subject was the "Stephens" who was given a benefit at the New Wells, Shepherd's Market, on 20 August 1750 and the Stephens who had benefit tickets out at Covent Garden on 10 April 1752.

Stevens, Mr [fl. 1761], singer.

The Covent Garden Theatre accounts show a payment of 5s. on 11 November 1761 to a Mr Stevens for serving as a supernumerary in *Comus;* on 13 November he received another 5s. for singing in the chorus in *The Coronation.*

Stevens, Mr [fl. 1768–1782], house servant?

A Mr Stevens had benefit tickets out at Drury Lane Theatre on 24 May 1768, 1 June 1772, 16 May 1774, 19 May 1775, 18 May 1779, and 4 May 1782. All of those citations may have concerned one man—probably a house servant—or those before 1773 may have concerned Stevens the Drury Lane tailor. A Stevens, perhaps our man, was down for 18s. weekly in 1776 and 1777.

Stevens, Mr d. 1773, tailor.

The *Morning Chronicle* reported on 12 June 1773 that Mr Stevens, the master tailor at Drury Lane Theatre, had died on the ninth. A Stevens had shared benefit tickets at Drury Lane in 1768 and 1772, but we cannot tell if he was our subject or a second Stevens, who shared in tickets from 1774 to 1782. We have tentatively assigned the early dates to the other Stevens. But Stevens the tailor may well have been the Stevens who rented space from Drury Lane at £10 per year from as early as 23 March 1767. A note in the accounts dated 4 May 1772 is a receipt for Stevens's payment of the previous year's rent. After that the accounts are silent on Stevens the renter.

Stevens, Mr [fl. 1783–1785], dresser.

The Lord Chamberlain's accounts show a Mr Stevens working as a dresser at the King's Theatre from 1783 to 1785.

Stevens, Mr [fl. 1792–1800], watchman.

A Mr Stevens had benefit tickets out at Drury Lane Theatre from 15 June 1792 (when the company was at the King's Theatre), through 13 June 1800. He was probably Stevens the watchman, who was cited in the company's account books on 23 September 1797 at a weekly salary of 12s.

Stevens, Mr [fl. 1792–1803], house servant?

A Mr Stevens, probably a house servant, was named in the Drury Lane Theatre accounts from 1792 to 1803. His weekly salary in 1800 was 5s.

Stevens, Mr [fl. 1795–1796], dancer.

The dancer Stevens played a Giant in *Merry Sherwood* at Covent Garden Theatre from 21 December 1795 through 8 February 1796.

Stevens, Mr [fl. 1798–1801], performer?

The Drury Lane Theatre accounts list a Mr Stevens on 29 December 1798 at a salary of 13s. 4d. daily; in 1801 he was cited again at £1 16s. d. weekly. At that salary he was probably a minor performer.

Stevens, Mrs, stage name of Priscilla Wilford, later Mrs John Rich the third c. 1713–1783, actress, dancer?

The *London Evening Post* reported that on 25 November 1744 Mrs Priscilla Stevens became the third wife of the Covent Garden Theatre manager John Rich; she was said to have been 21 years younger than Rich, which would suggest a birth date about 1713. She was born Wilford; her brother Edward worked at Covent Garden Theatre as a pit doorkeeper and in the Exchequer Office. Their cousin Charles Wilford's daughter Mary had an extensive acting career as Mrs George Bulkley. (In our second volume we incorrectly said that Mary was Edward's daughter. Michael Bulkley, a descendant, kindly gave us the correction.) According to George Anne Bellamy, Priscilla Stevens was employed as a barmaid at Bret's Coffee House before trying the stage. When she first appeared on the theatrical scene she called herself Mrs Stevens.

On 20 August and 9 September 1730 at the Oates-Fielding booths at Bartholomew and Southwark fairs she acted Jenny in *The Generous Free-Mason,* after which she joined John Rich's company at Lincoln's Inn Fields Theatre. She played Betty in *Flora* there on 30 October and then Cloris in *The Coffee-House Politician* on 4 and 5 December. Though no other roles were listed for Mrs Stevens that season, she received a solo benefit on 17 March 1731.

Mrs Stevens was named for a number of parts in 1731–32: Trusty in *The Provok'd Husband*, a Woman Peasant in *Apollo and Daphne* (perhaps she was a dancer), Flora in *She Wou'd and She Wou'd Not*, Honoria in *Love Makes a Man*, Prudence in *The Amorous Widow*, Betty in *The Fond Husband*, Pinwell in *The Married Philosopher*, Juletta in *The Pilgrim*, Lucy in *The London Merchant*, and a Country Lass in *The Rape of Proserpine*. She was granted a benefit at the Haymarket Theatre on 12 May 1732. In the fall of 1732 at Lincoln's Inn Fields she added to her repertoire Emilia in *Othello*, Charlotte in *Oroonoko*, and Lucy in *Tunbridge Walks*. *The London Stage* lists her as "Miss" Stevens on 28 October 1732, but that is clearly a misprint in the bill.

At the opening of John Rich's new theatre in Covent Garden on 7 December 1732 Mrs Stevens acted Foible in *The Way of the World*, after which at Covent Garden and sometimes at Lincoln's Inn Fields for the remainder of the 1732–33 season she was seen in such new characters as Valeria in *The Rover*, Lucy in *The Recruiting Officer*, Flametta in *A Duke and No Duke*, Altea in *Rule a Wife and Have a Wife*, Caelia in *Volpone* (for her benefit with Hall on 19 April 1733), Lesbia in *Achilles*, Chloe in *Timon of Athens*, and Mrs Squeamish in *The Stage Mutineers*.

Mrs Stevens continued acting in Rich's company through October 1744, appearing in such new roles as Lucy in *The Old Bachelor*, Florella in *The Orphan*, Moretta in *The Rover*, Engine in *The London Cuckolds*, Jacinta in *The False Friend*, Sentry in *She Wou'd If She Cou'd*, Edging and later Lady Easy in *The Careless Husband*, a Haymaker in *The Necromancer*, Patch in *The Busy Body*, Leonora in *The Mourning Bride*, Victoria in *The Fatal Marriage*, Inis in *The Wonder*, Clarinda in *The Double Gallant*, Massina in *Sophonisba*, Favourite in *The Gamester*, Lettice in *The Double Deceit*, Tattleaid in *The Funeral*, Lucilla and later Lavinia in *The Fair Penitent*, the Widow in *The Scornful Lady*, the Doctor's Wife in *The Royal Chace*, Lady Macduff in *Macbeth*, Desdemona in *Othello* (on 21 April 1737 for her shared benefit with Mrs

Wright), Mercury in *Momus Turn'd Fabulist*, Hillaria in *Love's Last Shift*, Lucia in *Cato*, the title role in *The Woman Captain*, Ursula in *Much Ado about Nothing*, Blanche in *King John*, Lady Grace in *The Provok'd Husband*, the First Constantia in *The Chances*, Mrs Fainall in *The Way of the World*, Fainlove in *The Tender Husband*, Salome in *Mariamne*, Mrs Frail in *Love for Love*, Amanda in *The Relapse*, Isabinda in *The Busy Body*, Belinda in *The Man of Mode*, Elvira in *Love Makes a Man*, Lady Lurewell in *The Constant Couple*, Alithea in *The Country Wife*, Melinda in *The Recruiting Officer*, Margaritta in *Rule a Wife and Have a Wife*, and Anne Bullen in *Henry VIII*.

The Covent Garden account books show that Mrs Stevens was earning 6s. 8d. daily in 1740–41, and two notes in the books call her "Kitty Stevens," one on 29 November 1740, when Mrs S. White was to lay out clothes for her, and another on 16 February 1741, when she was advanced £2 2s. The playbills only referred to her as Mrs Stevens, so it would appear that "Kitty" was an occasional personal nickname. A Mrs Stephens—possibly our actress—was paid 4s. per performance at the Jacob's Wells Theatre in Bristol from 8 June to 2 September 1741.

After playing Anne Bullen on 20 October 1744 Mrs Stevens left the stage to marry her manager. The ceremony took place at St Paul, Covent Garden, on 25 November, she giving her name as Priscilla Wilford. (The Mrs Stevens listed in *The London Stage* as active at Covent Garden in 1746–47 seems not to have been Priscilla; the Mrs Stevens who played Emilia in *Othello* at Drury Lane on 7 March 1751 was yet another woman—an amateur actress, the wife of Captain Stevens.)

George Anne Bellamy wrote of Priscilla Rich in her *Apology*: "That lady's regards were only shewn to those who Bask in sunshine; and not to poor beings enveloped in a cloud of distress." Mrs Rich was a Methodist convert and "thought of nothing but praying and accumulating wealth for herself and her spouse." In *Roderick Random* Smollett said of Rich that "the poor man's head, which was not naturally very clear, had been disordered with superstition, and he laboured under the tyranny of a wife and the terror of hell-fire at the same time." Priscilla had been, according to Mrs Bellamy, Rich's housekeeper for several years before they were married; under her prodding, Rich reformed his libertine ways within three years after their marriage.

Though Mrs Rich gave up her stage career when she married, she may have remained active in some way at the theatre. The Covent Garden accounts show payments to her on 13 October 1759 of £26 5*s.* for five nights and on 20 October of £31 10*s.* for six nights; on 22 October 1760 "Mrs. P. R." was on the paylist at 10*s.* daily.

When John Rich died in November 1761, Mrs Rich and the singer John Beard (who had married Rich's daughter Charlotte) assumed the management of Covent Garden Theatre, as Rich had requested in his will. Though Rich had specified that they should act jointly, Beard appears to have done most of the work, with Mrs Rich remaining—apparently of her own volition—a silent partner. Rich's will had divided the profits from his patent equally among Priscilla and Rich's four daughters: Henrietta Bencraft, Charlotte Beard, Mary Morris, and Sarah Voelcker. Priscilla was to receive Rich's house, gardens, and income from bonds and other investments. Rich specified that Priscilla had the right to sell the Covent Garden patent as long as she did not remarry. She did not, and in 1767 the patent was sold for £60,000.

Priscilla Rich died, following a long illness, at her brother's house in Chelsea on 28 February 1783, according to Reed in his "Notitia Dramatica." She had made a lengthy will on 9 November 1778. To her brother Edward Wilford of the King's Receipt of Exchequer, Esquire, she left her two-fifths share in a property on the west side of Bow Street and south side of Playhouse Passage, Covent Garden, and her two-fifths share of a property on the west side of Bow Street and south side of Hart Street, Covent Garden. She named three trustees: Charles Ellys, a Captain in the Royal Navy; Thomas Tibbs of St Andrew, Holborn; and Theodosius Forrest of St Martin-in-the-Fields. Her annuities in the Bank of England, totalling £4,000, were to be transferred to their account, and the interest was to be paid as follows: an unspecified amount to Edward Wilford, a £100 annuity to her friend Susanna White, who was in 1778 residing with Mrs Rich, and, after Edward Wilford's death, £400

toward the maintenance and education of William Fisher Bulkley (or Bulkeley), age about seven, the second son of the musician George Bulkley and his wife Mary. Should Susanna White die in Edward Wilford's lifetime, the residue of the £4,000 was to go to young Bulkley. To her nephew Richard Rich Wilford (Edward's son) Mrs Rich gave £1,000 toward his advancement in the Queen's Royal Regiment of Foot, in which he was then a Captain.

To Henrietta Bencraft of Hillingdon, James Bencraft's widow and John Rich's daughter, Mrs Rich left £100, and she provided in like manner for Charlotte Beard, John Beard's wife and John Rich's daughter, and for Mary Horsley, wife of John Horsley of Burton, widow of James Morris and daughter of John Rich. To Mary Horsley's son James Morris of the East India Company in Asia Mrs Rich left £400 in annuities; to Mary's daughter Mary Morris, £400 in annuities; and to Mary's daughter Elizabeth Morris when she should reach 21 and marry with the consent of her mother, £400 in annuities.

Mrs Rich bequeathed ten guineas each for mourning rings to Sarah Melosina and Sophia Henrietta, the daughters of Sarah Voelcker, deceased; Sarah had been the wife of George Voelcker, also deceased, and another daughter of John Rich. To Mary Dorothy Potts, daughter of Christopher Mosyer Rich and now wife of Cuthbert Potts of Pall Mall, Mrs Rich gave ten guineas for a ring, as she did to Elizabeth Rich, widow of John Bewley Rich, son of Christopher Mosyer Rich. Also named for rings were John Horsley, Martha Gumley, and Hannah Norsa of Brumpton Road. To Elizabeth Carne, widow of John Carne and now residing at Covent Garden Theatre (as a housekeeper) Mrs Rich left £5, and to Mrs Rich's servant Martha, widow of Thomas Lloyd she left £10.

To Harriet Bencraft, the eldest daughter of Henrietta Rich Bencraft, at age 21 and if she should marry with her mother's consent, Priscilla Rich bequeathed £400, as she did to Henrietta's second daughter, Mary Bencraft. Mrs Rich left £100 of her three percent consolidated annuities to the Covent Garden Theatre relief fund.

To Catherine Colville, late Catherine Benson, spinster, now the wife of Lieutenant William Colville of the Royal Liverpool Regiment of Foot, Mrs Rich left an annuity of £15. Catherine was John Rich's illegitimate daughter. To her cousin Ann Nicholls of Drury Lane, Mrs Rich bequeathed an annuity of £16; to her cousin Catherine Goodman, wife of James Goodman of Featherstone Street, Bunhill Row, she gave an annuity of £15; to Elizabeth Doane of Snow Hill, St Sepulchre, widow, she left an annuity of £10; and to Ann Boulby of Islington she bequeathed an annuity of £5. Mrs Rich apologized for not leaving the Voelcker girls as much as her other step-grandchildren, but she noted that they were provided for by the wills of both their grandfather and father. Apologies were hardly needed; Mrs Rich was remarkably generous to a sizable number of people who were related to her only by marriage. She certainly made up for any covetousness she may have displayed in earlier years. The will was proved on 12 March 1783.

Edward Wilford's will was proved on 31 July 1789; in it he arranged for payment of the annuities left in trust by his sister Priscilla Rich.

A portrait of Priscilla Rich by Johann Zoffany was offered at Christie's on 21 March 1975 (lot 65). The present location is unknown to us. In the sale catalogue the picture was described as half-length, 29½" × 24½", with Mrs Rich wearing a blue dress, seated at a tea table.

Stevens, Mrs [fl. 1785–1789], dancer.

Mrs Stevens was named in the bills for Astley's Amphitheatre from 1785 through 1789. She danced in *Love from the Heart* on 4 September 1786 and was a Rower in *The Royal Navy Review* on 4 September 1789.

Stevens, Mrs [fl. 1799], pit money taker.

The bills in the Richmond Reference Library for the Richmond Theatre in 1799 show Mrs Stevens as the pit money taker.

Stevens, Master [fl. 1733], actor.

"Young" Stevens acted Filch in *The Beggar's Opera* on 14 February 1733 at the Haymarket Theatre. He was possibly the son of the Mr Stevens who acted at the Haymarket and at Covent Garden Theatre in 1733.

Stevens, Miss [fl. 1746–1753?], actress, singer.

On 24 February 1746 Miss Stevens played Drab in *Phebe* at Covent Garden Theatre. On 23 April she was Friskit in *A Plot and No Plot*. The accounts cited her in 1746–47 for a salary of 5s. daily. On 14 April 1748 she appeared as Dolly Trull in *The Beggar's Opera*, and on 29 April her benefit tickets were accepted. She was most likely the Miss Stevens who sang Babeau Catin in *L'Opéra du gueux*—a French version of *The Beggar's Opera*—at the Haymarket Theatre on 29 April 1749. Her benefit tickets were accepted there on 26 May. Perhaps she was the "Mrs Stevens" named in the Covent Garden accounts on 29 September 1749 for £1 for two days' work. The Miss or Mrs Stevens who performed at the Smock Alley Theatre in Dublin in 1752–53 may have been our subject.

Stevens, Miss [fl. 1786], actress.

Miss Stevens played the Maid in *She Stoops to Conquer* and Mrs Trippit in *The Lying Valet* at the Hammersmith Theatre on 5 June 1786.

Stevens, C. *See* STEVENS, WILLIAM.

Stevens, George Alexander 1710–1784, actor, lecturer, author, manager, puppeteer.

The eccentric George Alexander Stevens was born in the parish of St Andrew, Holborn, in 1710, the son of a tradesman. George was apprenticed to a trade, according to the *European Magazine* and *The Dictionary of National Biography*, but fled London to join a touring company. Poems by George Alexander Stevens were published in the *Norwich Mercury* in 1743, and a Stevens, presumably George, was acting with the Norwich company that year. He seems to have joined the troupe in 1741. Gerald Kahan in his invaluable *George Alexander Stevens and The Lecture on Heads* (1984) tracked down the parts Stevens played at Norwich in 1744 and 1745 (and supplied much other useful information used in this entry): Sir John Brute in *The Provok'd Wife*, Hengist in *The Royal Convert*, the title role in *Don Quixote in England*, Petruchio in *Sauny the Scot*, the Bridegroom in *The Bridegroom Bilked*, the title

Harvard Theatre Collection

GEORGE ALEXANDER STEVENS

engraving by Cook, after Dodd

role in *Macbeth*, Scandal in *Love for Love*, Gloster in *Jane Shore*, Squire Gawkey in the *Birth and Adventures of Harlequin*, Loveless in *Love's Last Shift*, Worthy in *The Relapse*, Gratiano in *The Universal Passion*, Mirabell in *The Inconstant*, the Uncle in *The London Merchant*, Foigard in *The Beaux' Stratagem*, Riot in *The Wife's Relief*, Campley in *The Funeral*, Young Rakish in *The School Boy*, Claudius in *Hamlet*, Carlos in *The Fatal Marriage*, Richard III, Dioclesian in *The Roman Maid*, Edgar in *King Lear*, Hannibal in *Sophonisba*, the Mad Scholar in *The Pilgrim*, the Colonel in *The Non-Juror*, Pounce in *The Tender Husband*, Colonel Cuttum in *The Walking Statue*, and Varanes in *Theodosius*. His recorded performances stretch from 16 January 1744 through 6 May 1745.

Stevens was acting in Lincoln by 1750 and married Elizabeth, the daughter of the Lincoln manager Dennis Herbert, probably about that time. (Kahan and *The London Stage* place G. A. Stevens in London in 1745–46, acting at Drury Lane, but that Stevens was probably another, younger man. If our Stevens played Claudius in the provinces, it is unlikely he

would play Hamlet in London. On the other hand, the Stevens who wrote a "Dialogue" that was sung at the James Street Theatre in London on 26 December 1748 may well have been our subject.)

From 1751 to 1753 Stevens (or Stephens) acted at the Smock Alley Theatre in Dublin, his first appearance being on 27 September 1751 as Richmore in *The Twin Rivals*. Kahan retrieved his other roles: Obadiah in *The Committee*, Orasmin in *Zara*, the Shoemaker in *The Man of Mode*, Harlequin in *The Necromancer*, Trinculo in *The Tempest*, Hothead in *Sir Courtly Nice*, Lory in *The Relapse*, Vizard in *The Vintner Trick'd*, Setter in *The Old Bachelor*, Razor in *The Provok'd Wife*, Squire Richard in *The Provok'd Husband*, Waitwell in *The Way of the World*, Ben in *Love for Love*, Face in *The Alchemist*, Harlequin in *The Constant Captives*, Gibbet in *The Stratagem*, Don Pedro in *The Rover*, Henry VIII, Ben Budge in *The Beggar's Opera*, the Host in *The Merry Wives of Windsor*, the Duke in *Rule a Wife and Have a Wife*, and other roles, chiefly in comedies.

While in Dublin, Stevens and Isaac Sparks founded the Nassau Court, a club that held mock trials on winter Sunday evenings. Perhaps the Stevens who shared a benefit concert at the Assembly Rooms on St Augustine's Back in Bristol on 28 April 1753 was George, but *Felix Farley's Bristol Journal*, which reported the event, did not supply clarifying details.

On 12 November 1753 Stevens acted Corvino in *Volpone* at Covent Garden Theatre in London. He remained there through the 1754–55 season, playing Lory in *The Relapse*, Marcellus in *Constantine*, the Clown in *The Sheep Shearing*, Slango in *The Honest Yorkshireman*, Charles in *As You Like It*, Stratocles in *Tamerlane*, Decius in *Cato*, Brutus in *Coriolanus*, Metellus in *Julius Caesar*, Alonzo in *The Mourning Bride*, and Bluff in *The Old Bachelor* (at his shared benefit on 12 May 1755).

The *Public Advertiser* announced that on 24 December 1754:

AT the LECTURE ROOM, formerly the Theatre in James-street, near the Tennis-Court, Haymarket, This evening will be read, A Comic Lecture on the Pilgrim's Progress, A Disquisition on the Inquisition, and Orators Oratorised By GEORGE ALEX. STEVENS. The Question, in which Specimens of true and false Eloquence will be given by the ROSTRATOR, is How far the Parabola of a Comet affects the Vegetation of a Cucumber. Ladies will be admitted—not to speak.

He altered the entertainment and took it to the Haymarket on 8 January 1755, calling it *A Course of Comic Lectures*. The bill explained that

an Orator's head will be dissected *secundum artem*. The Orators will be shewn lying in state with Heiroglyphicks and Monumental Inscriptions. The Question will be whether they will be allow'd Christian burial? If 't'is granted, a funeral Oration will be pronounced by Martinus Scriblerus. Places for the Boxes to be taken at the theatre.

> "Thus orator to orator succeeds
> Another and another after him
> and the last."

On 28 January, when Stevens was advertised as playing Metellus in *Julius Caesar* at Covent Garden, he delivered "A Praemium and peroration" at the Haymarket as part of *The Female Inquisition*, during which Miss Wilkinson performed on the wire. That entertainment was in a short time changed to *A Short Comic Oratorio*. The lectures turned out to be far more successful for Stevens than his appearances as an actor. Stevens was welcomed to such clubs as The Choice Spirits, near Covent Garden, for which group he wrote (probably the lyrics only) several songs.

By then George Alexander Stevens had published a number of odds and ends: *Religion, or The Libertine Repentant* in 1751; *Distress upon Distress* (a "Heroi-Comi-Parodi-Tragedi-Farcical Burlesque in two acts," not intended for the stage, by Sir Henry Humm, with notes by Paulus Purgantius Pedasculus) in 1752; *The Choice Spirits' Feast* (a comic ode) in 1754; and *The Birthday of Folly* (a poem) in 1755. He also wrote songs and speeches for the actor Ned Shuter and others. In 1760 was published *The History of Tom Fool*, an autobiographical piece. *The English Sailors in America* (also called *The French Flogged* and *The True-Born Irishman*) by Stevens was presented by Shuter at his benefit at Covent Garden on 20 March 1760. That piece seems to have evolved into *The English Tars in America; or The Good Woman Without a Head*, which Shuter offered at Covent Garden on 30 March 1761.

In his study of Hogarth, Ireland reprinted a letter written by G. A. Stevens on 27 May 1761 from "Yarmouth Gaol." Kahan quotes an almost identical letter dated 27 March 1761 from Nottingham Gaol, so we will give the Yarmouth version. The letter was evidently addressed to one of his fellow players from the Lincoln circuit—perhaps his father-in-law Dennis Herbert.

When I parted from you at Lincoln, I thought, long before now, to have met with some oddities worth acquainting you with. It is grown a fashion of late to write lives; I now, and for a long time, have had leisure sufficient to undertake mine, but want materials for the latter part of it: for my existence *now* cannot properly be called living, but what the painters term still life, having ever since March 13th been confined in this town gaol for a London debt. As the hunted deer is always shunned by the happier herd, so am I deserted by the company; my share taken off, and no support left me, except what my wife can spare out of hers:

> Deserted, in my utmost need,
> By those my former bounties fed.

With an economy, which till now I was ever a stranger to, I have made a shift hitherto to victual my little garrison; but then it has been by the assistance of some good friends: and alas! my cloaths furnish me this week with my last resort. . . . A wig has kept me two days; the trimmings of a waistcoat as long; a ruffled shirt has paid my washer-woman; a pair of velvet-breeches discharged my lodgings; my coat I swallow by degrees, the sleeves I breakfasted upon for three days, the body, skirts, &c. served me as long; and two pair of pumps enabled me to smoke several pipes. . . . I here think myself *poor* enough to *want* a favour, and *humble* enough to *ask* it. Then, Sir, I could draw an encomium on your good sense, humanity, &c. but I will not pay so bad a compliment to your understanding, as to endeavour by a parade of phrases to win it over to my interest. If at the concert you could make a gathering for me, it would be a sense of obtaining my liberty.

Did he have a form letter for begging assistance?

Stevens' chief recorded activity in the early 1760s was authorial, though he was the Stevens who acted at Drury Lane from 1761–62 through 1763–64. His roles included the Doctor in *Macbeth*, Cornelius in *Cymbeline*, Falstaff in *The Merry Wives of Windsor*, Glendower in *1 Henry IV*, Mowbray in *2 Henry IV*, Panthino in *The Two Gentlemen of Verona*, Hartwell in *The Old Maid*, Spinner in *The Male Coquette*, and the Sheriff in *1 Henry IV*. He turned out a

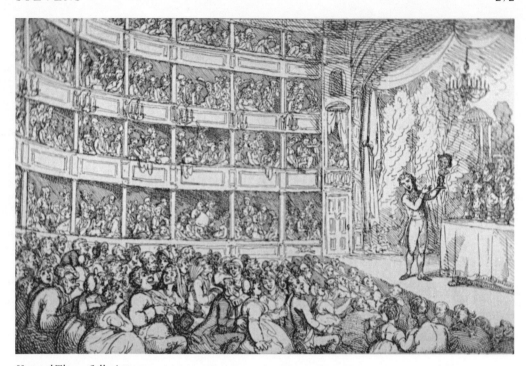

Harvard Theatre Collection

GEORGE ALEXANDER STEVENS delivering his Lecture upon Heads
engraving by Rowlandson, after Woodward

periodical called *The Beauties of All the Magazines Selected* between 1762 and 1764. Kahan, following Baker in his *Biographia Dramatica* and *The London Stage,* credits Stevens with the song and dance piece *Hearts of Oak,* which was presented at Drury Lane on 15 January 1762, but *The Dictionary of National Biography* questions that attribution. In 1763 came *The Dramatic History of Master Edward, Miss Anne, and others the extraordinaries of these times,* a libel on Shuter and Nancy Dawson, which contained the germ of what came to be Stevens's famous *Lecture upon Heads* of 1764.

In 1762 *The Battle of the Players* attacked the Drury Lane and Covent Garden managers (David Garrick and John Rich) and Stevens:

Two *Richerian* Officers endeavour to stop the Fury of his Arms, and oppose his further Progress. The first was named Stevinus:* A Man, who having been Link-boy to the Muses, thought himself beloved by them; and who, mistaking Scurrility for Satire, and the grossest Dulness for the purest Wit,

had been permitted by Cloacina, with Permission to deposite the excrementitious Works of his hard-bound Brain, in her sacred Temple; and, elated with a real Confidence, and an imaginary Valour, was grown so military mad in the Cause of Obscenity, that he swore he would wage eternal War with Delicacy and Virtue. . . .

*Author of a thousand bawdy Songs and obscene Treatises; a constant Attendant at the Bucks nocturnal Meetings, and a great Pretender to Wit and Humour.

(An editorial note mentions—correctly—that Stevens was not then at Covent Garden but at Drury Lane.)

The London Stage strangely omits George Alexander Stevens's very successful series of 12 presentations at the Haymarket Theatre of his *Lecture,* which opened on 30 April 1764. Kahan helped fill that gap in a paper presented in 1975 in Washington and then with his book in 1984. On 26 April 1764 Stevens puffed his event:

. . . A LECTURE upon HEADS; and NO HEADS. Being a CAPUT-all Exhibition, with proper Apparatus, of Antique and Modern Sculptures, Bronzes, Pictures, &c. &c. With Observations on the LEXONICAL and PHYZICAL CONSEQUENCE of WIGS; wherein a Full-bottom Oration, and SECUNDUM ARTEM dissertation, will by CARICATURED, HORNS will be accounted for AB ORIGINE: And the Genealogical Table of NOBODY, properly explained. To conclude with a Dissection of THREE HEADS viz. 1st, a STOCKJOBBER's; 2d, An AUTHOR's; 3d, A CRITIC's. Attempted by G. STEVENS N. B. NO HEAD FOR POLITICS. Gallery 2s. Pit 3s. Boxes 4s.

The presentation was scheduled for 12:30 P.M.

What the audience got was a one-man hodge-podge of satire, wit, and silliness that in its various published forms does not come off well but must have been saved by Stevens's presentation. There is no certainty that the following excerpt is authentic Stevens, but perhaps it comes close:

Ladies and Gentlemen,

By all the laws of laughing, every man has an undoubted right to play the fool with himself; under that licence this Exhibition is attempted.— Good wine needs no bush;—the bad deserves none:—If what I have to offer meets with your approbation, you will applaud it; if otherwise, it will meet with the contempt it deserves.—Some of these heads are manufactured in wood, and others in pasteboard, to denote, that there are not only Blockheads, but Paper Sculls.

This is one of those extraordinary personages called Conquerors. He was called Alexander the Great, from the great number of people his ambition had cut to pieces, he was a most dexterous slaughterman, and thought mankind only made for him to cut away with; he was a great hero, warrior, and mankiller.—Formerly. And—This is the head of a Cherokee Chief, called Sachem-Swampum-Scalpo-Tomahauk;—He was a great hero, warrior, and man-killer—Lately. And

This is the head of a Quack-Doctor:—a greater man-killer than either of the other two. This head of the quack-doctor is exhibited to shew the weakness of Wisdom, and the strength of folly; for if wisdom was not so weak, would such fellows as Carmen, Coblers and Potters be permitted to vend their unwholsome mixtures, under letters patent;—and if folly was not too strong, wou'd any body swallow their compositions!—The madness of this head [Alexander's], made him a conqueror.—The folly of the town dubb'd this a doctor.—The exploits of Alexander are celebrated by half the great writers of the age; and yet this Alexander was nothing more than a murderer and a

madman; who ran from one end of the world to the other, seeking whom he might cut to pieces;—and this copper-complexioned hero [Cherokee Chief] wants nothing to make him as great as Alexander, but the rust of antiquity to varnish over his crimes, and the pens of writers to illustrate his actions.— The Quack-doctor is his own historian; and publishes, in the Daily Advertiser and Gazeteer, accounts of cures never performed, and copies of affidavits never sworn to.

Stevens went on like that for hours, ridiculing human foibles through such characters as Sir Full Fed Domine Double Chin and Sir Languish Lisping. Mrs Montagu saw Stevens's *Lecture* during its initial year and wrote, "In short an hour of the best theatrical entertainment I have seen. He is infinitely beyond Mr. Foote, whose excellence is mere personal mimicry."

Stevens then toured his lecture to Dublin, Manchester, Bath, and Bristol. His advertisement in the *Bristol Journal* of 15 December 1764 shows how he worked variations on his basic format:

At the COOPERS-HALL in *King-Street*,
On MONDAY, TUESDAY, THURSDAY, and
FRIDAY EVENINGS
next,
The Lecture upon HEADS
will be exhibited,
By *George Alexander Stevens,*
Divided into THREE PARTS.
The first Part, Contains an Exhibition of Men's Heads, with the History of Nobody's Family, and a No-Head.
The second Part, An Exhibition of Ladies Head-Dresses, with the History of Flattery and its Family.
The third Part, Is a Physical Dissertation upon Sneezing and Snuff-taking, with a Dissection of Heads, viz. a Virtuoso's, a Stock-jobber's, a Critic's, a Politician's, a Wit's, and the Section of a Methodist's, with a Methodistical Preachment. To conclude with a Mock Italian Cantata.

He brought his *Lecture* back to the Haymarket in March 1765 and then to the Long Room, opposite Sadler's Wells, in July. The latter performances were puffed in the *Public Advertiser* of 24 July. Topics included, in addition to Alexander, the Cherokee Chief, and the Quack Doctor, "Daniel against the Dishclout," jockies, "Everybody's coats of arms," architecture, painting, poetry, astronomy, music, Venus's girdle, Cleopatra, an old maid, a young married lady, a Quaker, a Spitalfields

Harvard Theatre Collection

GEORGE ALEXANDER STEVENS, as a Quack Doctor

artist unknown

weaver, a woman of the town, a tea table critic, a gambler's three faces, and a gambler's funeral. The paper reported on 25 July that some noblemen who had attended the performance "testified their great satisfaction at the performance by the most unbounded marks of applause." In August Stevens gave his *Lecture* at the old Richmond theatre, tickets being available at his lodgings on Richmond Hill, opposite the Star and Garter.

The *European Magazine* stated that Stevens toured his one-man show to Scotland, Ireland, and North America as well as to the English provinces. An American tour must be questioned, as Kahan points out, though once the *Lecture upon Heads* was published in 1765 (and there were other editions after that, some unauthorized), performers anywhere could capitalize on Stevens's successful idea. Ned Shuter gave Stevens's lecture at Covent Garden on 18

March 1765, and someone presented it at Bartholomew Fair, apparently in September of that year. In America David Douglass is known to have delivered a *Lecture on Heads* in Charleston, South Carolina, in April 1766. Douglass was the first of many to acquaint the colonists with Stevens's show. Kahan found no evidence of Stevens's ever having gone to America. A new lecture, called *The Supplement,* was brought out by Stevens at the Haymarket on 25 February 1766.

Late in 1767 Stevens was in Stratford-upon-Avon and helped persuade David Garrick to provide a statue of Shakespeare for the new town hall, as Christian Deelman in *The Great Shakespeare Jubilee* shows.

In December 1768 Stevens returned to Bristol to present his *Lecture.* In his notice in *Felix Farley's Bristol Journal* on 17 December he felt obliged to complain about illegal publication and use of his *Lecture:*

N. B. Some Time after the Author had been favoured with the Approbation of the Public, a most wretched Compilation appeared in the Magazines, and was sold as a Pamphlet, call'd *George Alexander Stevens's Lecture upon Heads;* and Head Lecturers immediately spread over England; some of them taking his Name, some gave out he had taught them for a Sum of Money, some published in their Bills he was a Partner with them in the Profits, and others advertised they had bought his Apparatus, and were his Successors, as he had left off Lecturing upon receiving from them a large Premium.

Thus he has been most iniquitously Pilfer'd, not only of his Property, but even of his Reputation, as a man of either common Sense, or common Education (as far as the *Lecture upon Heads,* as Printed, may be supposed to be his Writing). In Justification of himself, he has ever since exerted his utmost Abilities towards enriching the Lecture with *new Characters,* and by making such other Alterations, as appeared requisite for keeping Pace with the *Foibles* as well as the *Fashions* of the *Times.*

Stevens's Bristol appearances were at Coopers' Hall.

He returned to London to give his entertainment at the Haymarket on 28 March 1769 and subsequent dates. At Covent Garden on 5 January 1770 *The Court of Alexander* was presented; the text was by G. A. Stevens and the music by John Abraham Fisher. The piece was a burlesque of Lee's *The Rival Queens* and had a fair run. Stevens returned to acting on 5 April 1771 at Covent Garden, when he played

Touchstone in *As You Like It* for Mrs Bulkley's benefit. According to the *Cambridge Bibliography of English Literature*, two works by Stevens were published in 1771: *The Fair Orphan*, a comic opera, and *The Choice Spirits' Chaplet* (edited by Stevens but published at Whitehaven without his permission). Perhaps *The Fair Orphan* was the play reported in the *Biographia Dramatica* of 1814 as having been performed "at Lynn, by G. A. Stevens's company of comedians." The play presented there was published in 1771, but the *Biographia Dramatica* did not indicate that Stevens was the author.

In the fall of 1771 Thomas Snagg (according to his *Recollections*) came from Norwich to London:

This might be ranked as one of the most unfortunate of my travels, for here I had formed a kind of wild goose scheme with Mr G. A. Stevens to establish a Burletta Company, which was to be our joint property and to be conducted under my direction on a small scale with few performers and at little expense.

It was to comprise musical and comic dramas in which Mr Stevens was to assist, with writing new and whimsical pieces. To accomplish this, cash was necessary for our apparatus, as scenes, clothes, music and the numberless etceteras that would be properly wanting to embark in this mad business. . . . The scenes were painting, the dresses making, the performers engaging and myself labouring and calculating without ceasing, to hatch this egg of improbability. Mr Stevens was likewise not idle, for his ideas on success were as blooming as my own. We purposed to take the field not very distant from the Capital of Norfolk, because of the expense and as our few performers were nearly all upon the spot. . . .

Thus everything went before the wind and we invested [Yarmouth] in form, pasted up a large posting bill and announced for our first representation the Burletta of *The Mad Captain*. (To be sure the title might have been construed into some little affinity to our undertaking.) This was an altered piece from an old and obsolete farce with songs and local jokes written and appropriated by Mr G. A. Stevens and music compiled and set by Mr Wat Clagget and an introductory prelude which I, the Manager, delivered.

The venture did not succeed in Yarmouth, even when Stevens did his *Lecture*. The company tried a small town near Harleston, and though they met with some success, "We then weighed seriously our situation and the improbability of profit or reputation ensuing and resolved to disband our troop and lay down our Managerial dignities."

An Essay on Satirical Entertainments, published in 1772 as part of an edition of his *Lecture*, included Stevens's new *Lecture* and indicated that it was then being delivered by Stevens at the Haymarket. He performed at the Haymarket, according to Kahan, from 26 March to 11 May 1772 (a run not shown in *The London Stage*). Stevens poked fun at himself in that version of his piece, saying "Before I presume to meddle with the heads of other people, it may seem necessary to say something by way of apology on my own. . . ."

That year Stevens again had a troupe of strolling players, according to Sybil Rosenfeld in *Studies in English Theatre History*. The *Cambridge Chronicle* of 12 September 1772 reported that Stevens had a booth at Cheese Fair and presented *The Clandestine Marriage, Midas, Douglas, The Mayor of Garratt, The West Indian*, and *The Padlock*. Stevens presumably acted, and in his company was Master Thomas Blanchard, who sang. The *London Chronicle* on 12 January 1773 announced that "Mr. Foote and Mr. George Alexander Stevens are going to amuse the town with a new species of entertainment, or rather an old one revived, called 'A Puppet-shew, where will be laughing Tragedies, weeping Comedies, and squeaking Operas, by Figures as large as some living Theatrical heroes.'" The *Westminster Magazine* the same month said, "G. A. Stevens entered into partnership with the Son of Fun, and began to compose a new species of creatures, with features so similar to the originals, that you will not know the man of paste-board from the man of nature. . . . Such are the imitative perfections of Stevens, who surpasses all statuaries we have seen!" The show opened at the Haymarket on 15 February.

Stevens acted Stephano in *The Tempest* at Drury Lane on 12 May 1773 for Ackman's benefit. On 11 August at the Haymarket was presented *The Trip to Portsmouth;* that afterpiece was written by Stevens, with music by Arne (according to Grove) and songs by Dibdin.

David Garrick wrote on 24 September 1773 to his brother Peter in Lichfield, where Stevens was to present his *Lecture*. Garrick called Stevens

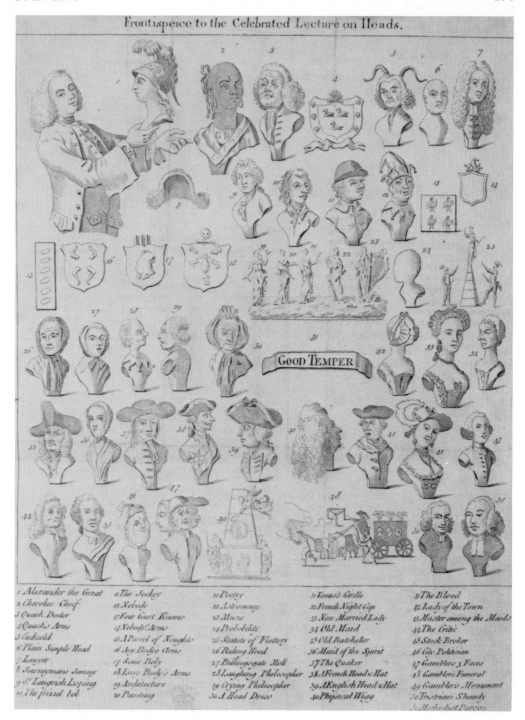

"Frontispiece to the Celebrated Lecture on Heads"

by O. Neale

a Person deservedly applauded, for his Peculiarity of Genius, & Universal Love of Mirth & Letters— He has great Merit, & more than all he is a very honest, liberal-minded Man, & deserves Every Encouragement that has been given to him—As he is travelling Your Way with his heads, I must beg leave to introduce him to You, & y^r friends, not my dear Peter, that I think You & Y^r friends want the least Amendment of Y^r Own, but that You may laugh with my Friend Stevens at ye heads of other People—In short, I have so great a desire that he Should be well receiv'd, & approv'd at my own Native Place, (as I always call it, tho dropt at Hereford) that I beg You will let ye Whole Town know that I beg it, as a particular favour, that they will attend his Lectures—If any should be discontented with his Performance, I beg that I may treat them, & that You will pay for all the Malcontents, & draw upon Me for the Sum total—I need not desire You, to let him taste y^r Lichfield Mutton & best Ale, Your Own Heart always prevents [i.e., anticipates] my Wishes in these Matters. always in a hurry—

Dear Peter

If the Ladies expect a Maccaroni Player [i.e., a fop] in Master George, they will be dreadfully disappointed—

We do not know how successful Stevens was in Lichfield, but with that kind of help he could hardly have failed.

In November 1774 Stevens was again in Bristol, presenting the 1774 version of his *Lecture* at Coopers' Hall. He stated in his advertisements that this was the last time he would be presenting his lecture in Bristol. In August 1775 he appeared at the Mill Street Theatre in Belfast, and that year he also performed in Dublin. On 11 March 1777 Stevens lectured at the Haymarket, saying that it would be his final exhibition in London of his *Lecture*. His run lasted until 5 May. *The Dictionary of National Biography* has it that Stevens sold his *Lecture* to the actor Charles Lee Lewes in 1774, but that date is too early in view of Stevens's presentations in 1777.

Creswick delivered a parody on Shakespeare's "Seven Ages of Man" at the Haymarket on 23 March 1778; *The London Stage* attributes the piece to Stevens. At Lincoln's Inn Fields Theatre on 28 October 1779 Creswick gave Stevens's remarks on the origin of lectures, and Lee Lewes, without much success, presented Stevens's *Lecture* at Covent Garden on 26 June 1780. That version of the lecture—the official one, with additions by Pilon—was published

in 1785. Stevens had not yet retired, however; he gave his *Lecture* in Manchester in the summer of 1779, in Chester in November and December, and on 8 and 10 December in Wrexham, Wales—his last appearances.

After selling his entertainment, Stevens turned his talents to a new piece called *The Cabinet of Fancy,* which was first given at the Haymarket in London on 30 October 1780. The puff said the work would consist of a

variety of Paintings, serious and comic; Satirical, Portrait and Caricature Designs; Emblematical, Pantomimical, Farcical and Puppet-showical Representations, mostly Transparency. Instead of delivering a Catalogue, the Designs will be explained by at present an unknown Artist [Wilks, the stage name of Thomas Snagg, Stevens's old partner]. As the Time of viewing the Exhibition is limited, and as it is the wish to render it as amusing as possible, an excellent band of Music will be provided for the entertainment of the Spectators. In the course of the explanation of the Pictures several Songs will be introduced.

The songs, written by Stevens, were sold at the theatre. That statement in the bill and the attribution to Stevens of the song *Drink and let's be jolly* (published about 1780) in the *Catalogue of Printed Music in the British Museum,* imply that Stevens was a composer, though it is more likely that he merely wrote the lyrics. *The Dictionary of National Biography* notes that one of his songs, "Cease, rude Boreas, blustering railer," was adapted to the tune of "Old Hewson the cobbler." It seems probable that other songs by Stevens were also lyrics by him set to existing tunes.

By 1780 Stevens had retired to Hampstead, already declining mentally. He "died in a state of imbecility" at Baldock in Hertfordshire on 6 September 1784, according to the *DNB.* Reed in his "Notitia Dramatica" transcribed a somewhat different notice: "Died at Baldock Herts. Geo. Alexander Stevens. The papers say that on the 24th last he ment^d to his wife & others that he sho'd die within a fortnight & desired them to take notice of the day & a few days after reminded them he sho'^{d} keep his time. He was then as well as he had usually been." The *Gentlemen's Magazine* claimed that Stevens died at nearby Biggleswade, Bedfordshire. The notice of his death cited him as famous for his *Lecture upon Heads* and mentioned the £10,000 he was said to have earned from that entertainment. About George Alexander Stevens's other accomplishments they were silent.

According to Mark Moore's *Memoirs* (1795) Stevens had a sister Katharine, who became Mrs Craven and performed in Rugby. Thomas Snagg was said to have been the offspring of Stevens in a note in the *Morning Post* of 31 October 1781, but no other source we have found states that. Despite Garrick's admiration for Stevens's character, the *Biographia Dramatica* of 1812 spoke of his behavior as "despicable for its meanness and irregularity."

In his book on Stevens, Kahan supplies a very complete bibliography of Stevens's works, a text of the *Lecture,* and a detailed production history (including American performances).

Portraits of George Alexander Stevens include:

1. In the character of a Poet, speaking the epilogue to *The Disquisition.* Engraving by T. Cook, after D. Dodd, published by Fielding & Walker, 1780. A vignette copy was engraved by "AB."

2. Delivering his *Lecture upon Heads,* standing on the stage of a theatre. Engraving by Rowlandson, after Woodward. Published by T. Tegg, 1808.

3. Standing behind a table, delivering his lecture to a group. Engraving by T. Trotter, after C. Fox. Published by G. Kearsley as a plate to Stevens's *Lecture upon Heads,* 1785.

4. As the Quack Doctor. Standing behind a table, wearing wig, hands in a large muff. By an unknown engraver. Published by S. W. Fores, 1793.

5. Satirical print, "Frontispiece to the Celebrated Lecture on Heads," 1765. Designed by "Mr O. Neale." The design shows six rows of heads, busts, monuments, and shields, with a reference key below. In the first row is a half-figure of the lecturer. *Catalogue of Political and Personal Satires in the British Museum,* No 4113.

Stevens, Mrs George Alexander, Elizabeth, née Herbert *1729–1813, actress.*

Miss Elizabeth Herbert, the daughter of the Lincoln manager Dennis Herbert (1695–1770), married George Alexander Stevens, probably about 1750, when Stevens is known to have performed in Lincoln. When Stevens appeared at the Smock Alley Theatre in Dublin in 1752–53, Mrs Stevens was also there,

presumably acting. She certainly acted with Stevens in Yarmouth or Nottingham in 1761. The Mrs "Steevens" who made her first Drury Lane appearance on 13 April 1763 as Melissa in *The Lying Valet* was probably our subject, for George Alexander Stevens was performing there at the time and had benefit tickets out that night.

On 10 March 1766 Stevens petitioned the Lord Chamberlain: "May I beg his Grace's Permission for Mrs. Stevens to repeat part of my Lecture with me." In February 1766 Stevens had begun presenting a new version of his *Lecture upon Heads,* called *The Supplement,* at the Haymarket Theatre. Mrs. Stevens may have been allowed to join him in some of the performances.

Mrs Stevens was named in her father's will in 1770, from which source we learn her Christian name. She presumably joined Stevens in his retirement at Hampstead about 1780 and was with him when he died in 1784 (for details, see his entry). The *European Magazine* reported that Mrs Stevens died at the age of 84 on 2 September 1813 in Setch, Norfolk. She had a brother, Nathaniel Herbert, who died in 1787.

Stevens, Giles *b. 1650?, violinist.*

Foster in his compilation of London marriages records the wedding of Giles Stevens of Richmond, Surrey, a bachelor about 21 years of age, marrying, with his father's consent, Sarah Wilkins of Richmond, a spinster about 20 years old, marrying with the consent of her mother Mary, a widow, on 18 March 1671. The registers of St Margaret, Westminster, which contain many entries for court musicians, show the baptism of Alice Stephens, daughter of Giles and Sarah, on 26 October 1676. On the previous 12 August Giles Stevens, violinist, replaced Henry Dove in the King's Musick, and as of 13 December 1679, he was earning £46 12s. 3d. annually. Giles accompanied the King to Windsor in 1681 or 1682, for which journey he was paid £11 13s. on 17 May 1682. On 8 May 1690 Stevens assigned £100 due him from the Crown to Richard Robinson.

Stevens, J. ₁*fl.* 1748₁, *actor.*

On 14 June 1748 a Mr Stevens, a bookseller, made his stage debut at the James Street Theatre playing "(by Desire)" Barnwell in *The London Merchant* for his benefit. The *Daily Advertiser* on 5 September 1748 published a note signed J. Stevens telling of his appearance that night as Nicanor in *Busiris* at the Haymarket Theatre for his benefit. He identified himself as "late a Bookseller in Cornhill."

Stevens, John   [*fl. 1691*]. *See* STEVENSON, JOHN.

Stevens, Katharine, later Mrs Craven
[*fl. 1760–1789*],   *actress.*
The provincial actress Mrs Katharine Craven, whom Mark Moore in his *Memoirs and Adventures* in 1795 called the sister of the actor-monologist George Alexander Stevens, evidently did not perform in London, as we implied under Craven by cross-indexing her to Stevens. We have traced her only to Rugby, to Durravan's company in Derby in the spring of 1760, and to a theatre in Abington in January 1789.

Stevens, Richard John Samuel   *1757–1837, singer, organist, composer.*
Richard John Samuel Stevens, son of John Stevens, was born in London on 27 March 1757, according to the inscription on his tombstone. He became a choir boy at St Paul's Cathedral, receiving his musical instruction from William Savage, whose biography he later wrote. After his voice broke, young Stevens studied organ and, evidently, composition. On 9 July 1776, having served his seven-year apprenticeship, he was recommended for membership in the Royal Society of Musicians. He was then single. The Society admitted him on 1 September. In 1781 he was elected organist of St Michael, Cornhill, at £40 per year. We take him to have been the Stevens who sang tenor in the Handel Memorial Concerts at Westminster Abbey and the Pantheon in May and June 1784.
  Stevens was appointed organist of Temple Church in 1786, succeeding John Stanley. By that time he had begun his career as a composer, especially of glees, winning Catch Club prizes in 1782 and 1786. In 1786, too, he published three harpsichord sonatas. A number of his glees over the years were settings for lines from Shakespeare, and they were very

RICHARD JOHN SAMUEL STEVENS
artist unknown

popular at the London theatres. Many of them are in manuscript at the Fitzwilliam Museum in Cambridge, but, as the *Catalogue of Printed Music in the British Museum* shows, Stevens published a large number of his songs. Grove states that Stevens also wrote music for *The Widow of Malabar,* which was performed at Covent Garden Theatre on 5 May 1790.
  Doane's *Musical Directory* of 1794 gave Stevens's address as Lambeth Walk. He was made organist of the Charterhouse in 1796, and on 17 March 1801, through the influence of his friend Samuel Birch, he was appointed Gresham professor of music. The following year Stevens brought out the last of three volumes of sacred music, selected from Italian and English composers, and, as Charles Cudworth noted in *Music and Letters* in 1964, he wrote his memoirs, now in manuscript at Cambridge. In 1808 he became music master at Christ's Hospital. In view of Stevens's interests and musical training, we suppose he was not

the Mr Stevens who played in the band at the Haymarket Theatre in the summers from 1804 to 1810 nor the Stevens who was a Choral Sprite in *The Hall of Mischief* at the Surrey Theatre in April 1814.

Stevens was a member of the Court of Assistants of the Royal Society of Musicians for a number of years, but he resigned in 1835. He died at Peckham at the age of 81 on 23 September 1837. He was buried in the cloister of Charterhouse Chapel. His will had been written on 8 August 1833, with a codicil dated 8 July 1835. To Mary Liffen, daughter of Henry Liffen of Glasshouse Street, Vauxhall, he left £500. He bequeathed £100 each to his executors; to Elizabeth, Richard, and John Peake, the children of his sister Sophia (Mrs Thomas Peake); and to Richard and Lucy Warr, the children of his sister Henrietta Maria (the widow of Thomas Warr). Stevens left gifts of 10 guineas each to Kitty King, Elizabeth King, William Clarke, and a Mrs Holmes. The rest of his estate he bequeathed to his wife Anna Maria Stevens (née Jeffery). A son, Richard George (b. 1810), was not mentioned. Stevens asked his executors to take over the executorship of the estate of Ann Haylock, for whom Stevens had served as executor. The will was proved on 30 October 1837. Mrs Stevens, who had been born on 24 May 1768, died at Peckham on 19 December 1847 and was buried beside her husband in the cloisters of the Charterhouse Chapel.

A miniature portrait by an unknown artist of Richard Stevens as a young man was owned by Mrs E. B. Dykes when it was reproduced in *Musical Times*, November-December 1962 and July 1967.

Stevens, Stephen *d. 1802?, house servant.*

Stephen Stevens was cited in the Lord Chamberlain's accounts as a messenger at the King's Theatre from 1783 to 1785. He may well have been the S. Stevens, of No 6, New Street, Brighton, who was the box bookkeeper at the Brighton theatre in 1789. A Mr Stevens, certainly Stephen, was named in the Drury Lane accounts as early as June 1800 as a boxkeeper. A note in the 1801 accounts shows him at a weekly salary of 15s.; one dated 11 April 1801 cites him as a bookkeeper. The management paid £6 4s. for Stephen Stevens's

funeral toward the end of March 1802. He was then identified as a boxkeeper.

Stevens, William, stage name of William Castevens *d. 1790, actor, manager.*

On 24 May 1775 at the Haymarket Theatre Mr Castevens played Robin in *Cross Purposes.* On 7 July he was Harry in *The Mock Doctor,* on 31 July an unspecified character in *The Rehearsal,* on 4 September a character in *A Trip to Portsmouth,* and on 16 September Bagshot in *The Beaux' Stratagem.* William Castevens, the *European Magazine* of May 1790 explained, was the real name of the actor William Stevens. We believe he began using the name Stevens (sometimes Stephens) after his 1775 summer stint, that the Stevens who played Eustace in *Love in a Village* at the Haymarket on 30 October 1775 was our subject, and that the Stephens (or Stephens) acting at Covent Garden Theatre in 1775–76 was also he. "Stephens" acted a principal but unspecified character in *Prometheus* from 26 December 1775 through 23 January 1776 and from 15 February through 3 May was an Officer in *A Duke and No Duke.* When his benefit tickets were admitted on 11 May the bill called him Castevens.

On 20 May 1776 "Stephens" joined Foote's troupe at the Haymarket to play Harry in *The Mock Doctor.* During the rest of the summer he appeared in *The Devil upon Two Sticks, The Bankrupt, The Cozeners, The Maid of Bath,* and *The Orators* and was Dick in *The Minor,* Roger in *The Mayor of Garratt,* John in *The Patron,* Timotheus in *The Tailors,* Gadshill in *1 Henry IV,* and Pedro in *Catherine and Petruchio.* As will be seen, several of those assignments for "Stephens" were in later seasons given to William Stevens.

Stevens performed at Covent Garden during the winter seasons through 1788–89 and at the Haymarket in the summers through 1785, occasionally rising to parts of some size but often playing minor roles. At Covent Garden in 1776–77 he was a Servant in *Harlequin's Frolicks* on 27 December 1776, after which he played a Servant in *Sir Thomas Overbury* and the Counsel in *Cross Purposes.* For Colman at the Haymarket from 28 May to 18 September 1777 he appeared as Timotheus in *The Tailors,* Rosencrantz in *Hamlet,* Quildrive in *The Citizen,* Dick in *The Minor,* a Servant in *Rule a Wife and Have a Wife*, a Gentleman in *The Sheep Shearing*, Roger in *The Mayor of Garratt*, John in *The Maid of Bath*, Oxford in *Richard III*, a Mutineer in *Cato*, Mignon in *Bon Ton*, a Notary in *The Spanish Barber*, Pistol in *The Merry Wives of Windsor*, the Tailor in *The Provok'd Wife*, and an unspecified character in *The Nabob*.

At Covent Garden over the years Stevens added to his repertoire such roles as a Witch in *Macbeth*, Sancho and Monsieur in *Love Makes a Man*, the Apothecary and Peter in *Romeo and Juliet*, Buckingham in *The Earl of Warwick*, Scrub in *The Stratagem*, the Cook in *Chrononhotonthologos*, Ned in *The Flitch of Bacon*, William in *The Deaf Lover*, the Clown in *The Norwood Gypsies*, Tester in *The Suspicious Husband*, Finder and Supple in *The Double Gallant*, Bristle in *The Humours of an Election*, Mirvan in *Tamerlane*, Amble and Marall in *A New Way to Pay Old Debts*, Simon in *The Apprentice*, a Clown in *The Choice of Harlequin*, a Watchman in *The London Cuckolds*, Isaac and Lopez in *The Duenna*, Jeffrey in *Barnaby Brittle*, Vasquez in *The Castle of Andalusia*, the Printer's Devil in *The Author*, Camphire in *The Devil upon Two Sticks*, Whalebone in *Lord Mayor's Day*, Peto in *1 Henry IV*, Pedro in *A Bold Stroke for a Husband*, Pierrot in *The Royal Chace*, a Jailer in *The Beggar's Opera*, Fabian in *Twelfth Night*, Slender and Rugby in *The Merry Wives of Windsor*, Corrigidore and Alguazile in *She Wou'd and She Wou'd Not*, the Doctor's Servant in *More Ways than One*, Peter in *The Chances*, Thomas in *The Agreeable Surprize*, John in *The Son-in-Law*, a Clown in *Harlequin Rambler*, an Outlaw in *The Two Gentlemen of Verona*, Dick in *Hob in the Well*, the Music Master in *Catherine and Petruchio*, Bounce in *The Follies of a Day*, Whisper in *The Busy Body*, Jubilee Dicky in *The Constant Couple*, a Smuggler in *Barataria*, Lucianus in *Hamlet*, Smith in *The Rehearsal*, a Servant in *She Stoops to Conquer*, a Clown in *Omai*, Aminadab in *A Bold Stroke for a Wife*, Wolfe in *The School for Wives*, Feeble in *The Provok'd Wife*, Dapper in *The Citizen*, Satin in *The Miser*, and the Undertaker in *Aladin*. His last appearance at Covent Garden was as a Servant in *She Stoops to Conquer* on 5 June 1789.

William Stevens's roles at the Haymarket during the summers, from 1778 through 1785, included some of his regular parts at Covent Garden—Dick in *The Minor*, Ned in *The Flitch of Bacon*, and John in *The Son-in-Law*

are examples. But many of his summer characters were different, and among the new ones he attempted were Jasper in *Miss in Her Teens*, Sir Thomas Lovell in *Henry VIII*, a Waiter in *The Suicide*, a Soldier in *Bonduca*, Fleece in *Man and Wife*, Simon in *The Apprentice*, Forceps in *The Devil upon Two Sticks*, the Constable in *The Provok'd Wife*, Tom in *The Jealous Wife*, an Officer in *Douglas*, Flint in *The Deserter*, Launcet in *The Wedding Night*, Tubal in *The Merchant of Venice*, an Attendant and Pantaloon in *The Genius of Nonsense*, the Devil in *The Author*, Sheers in *The Dead Alive*, Pedro in *The Spanish Fryar*, Sir Roger in *The Patron*, Mrs Coaxer in *The Beggar's Opera*, a Lord in *Cymbeline*, Harlequin in *The Life and Death of Common Sense*, Flint in *The Deserter*, and many unspecified parts in other works.

Stevens made occasional appearances at the Haymarket during the winter months when he was not needed at Covent Garden: on 24 March 1778 he acted Oxford in *Richard III*, a role he had played there the previous summer; he was probably the "Stephens" who played Fountain in *Wit without Money* and a role in *The Tailors* on 25 November 1782; and on 15 March 1785 he acted a Hostler in *All the World's a Stage*—unless that was another Stevens.

A newspaper took notice of William Stevens on 30 December 1780; the previous night he had been in *Harlequin Freemason*. No one, the reviewer said,

tried more successfully to keep the piece alive than Mr. Stevens. This young man has not afforded any great promise to become a capital comedian, though he is considerably improved of late, but in pantomime he seems determined to stand conspicuously forward, and to show that he knows, what few comedians are master of, the art of expressing a good deal when he does not utter a syllable.

As of his shared benefit with Miss Besford on 17 May 1786 William Stevens was living at No 54, Drury Lane. That year he became interested in the Richmond theatre, having given up performing at the Haymarket after the summer of 1785. The Lord Chamberlain granted him a license to present entertainments at Richmond up to 30 September 1786, and, as a Richmond bill of 11 September shows, he had left his lodgings in Drury Lane for a house on Richmond Green adjoining the theatre. On that date—his benefit—he played

Euston in *I'll Tell You What!* Stevens managed the Richmond playhouse each summer through 10 October 1788. His last benefit there was on 9 October 1788, a night when he was not required at Covent Garden.

Stevens may also have been the C. Stevens (Castevens?) mentioned by James Winston in *The Theatric Tourist* as buying Waldron's interest in the Windsor Theatre, perhaps in 1789, after his retirement from Covent Garden, for Winston said C. Stevens was "formerly of Covent Garden." If William Stevens did obtain an interest in the Windsor playhouse, he did not live to enjoy it. The *European Magazine* reported that William Stevens died on 19 May 1790 at his house on Richmond Green.

Stevenson. *See also* STEPHENSON.

Stevenson,   Mr   [*fl. 1784–1794?*],
singer.

Mr Stevenson of Huntingdon was a countertenor who sang in the Handel Memorial Concerts at Westminster Abbey and the Pantheon in May and June 1784. Doane's *Musical Directory* of 1794 named Stevenson but did not indicate whether or not he was still performing.

Stevenson, Mr [*fl. 1785*], *actor.*

Mr Stevenson performed at Hammersmith from 17 June through 27 July 1785, playing Vasquez in *The Wonder,* Trippit in *The Lying Valet,* a Countryman in *The Quaker,* the Watchman in *The Apprentice,* Porter in *Jane Shore,* Traverse in *The Clandestine Marriage,* and a small part in *Robinson Crusoe.*

Stevenson, Mr [*fl. 1795–1817*], *boxkeeper, office keeper.*

Mr Stevenson was listed as a boxkeeper at Drury Lane Theatre in the benefit bill of 30 May 1795. The bills continued naming him in the years that followed, and the accounts show him to have been paid 12s. weekly during most of his career, though he was up to 18s. weekly in 1812–13 and 1813–14. He was at 12s. weekly in 1816–17, the last season the accounts mentioned him. We take him to have been the Stevenson, office keeper, cited in the accounts in 1797. He was probably related to the other Stevensons working at Drury Lane

near the end of the eighteenth century and may have been the son of Thomas Stevenson.

Stevenson, Mr [*fl. 1799*], *caller.*

The Drury Lane Theatre accounts on 29 May 1799 cited Mr Stevenson as a caller at a salary of 4s. (daily, presumably).

Stevenson, Mr [*fl. 1799*], *watchman.*

The Drury Lane Theatre accounts on 24 September 1799 cited Mr Stevenson as a watchman at a salary of £1 1s. weekly.

Stevenson, Miss [*fl.c. 1740–c. 1760*],
singer.

The *Catalogue of Printed Music in the British Museum* contains numerous references to the singer Miss Stevenson (or Stephenson), who appeared at Vauxhall Gardens from about 1740 to about 1760. Among the songs she sang were *Forgive ye Fair, nor take it wrong, Ye Swains that are courting a Maid, Did you see e'er a shepherd, I'll sing to my lover all night and all day, Young Jockey who teaz'd me, Love and Folly were at Play, You tell me I'm handsome, By a pratt'ling Stream, Tell me, Lasses have ye seen, Since we went out a Maying, Sure a Lass in her bloom, More bright the Sun began to dawn, The other Day to grief betray'd, Attend ye nymphs, As I went o'er the Meadows, Where's my Swain so blithe and clever?, Hence, fly hence* (with Miss Burchell and Mr Lowe), *Sweet William, Daphne and Chloe, Long, long I despair'd,* and *Haste, haste, Phillis, haste.* Alick Williams has supplied us with a list of performers at Norwich; a Miss Stevenson was there in 1759 and may have been our subject.

Stevenson,   Miss [*fl. 1785–c. 1790*],
singer.

In *The London Pleasure Gardens* Wroth states that Miss Stevenson sang from 1785 to 1788 at Bermondsey Spa Gardens. She may have been the Miss Stevenson who appeared at Brighton in 1785, apparently in the summer. Miss Stevenson had a vocal part in *The Roman Father* at Covent Garden Theatre on 21 October 1786. The *Catalogue of Printed Music in the British Museum* cites the song *When Phoebus wakes the rosy hours* as sung by Miss Stevenson at the Royalty Theatre; the piece was published about 1790.

Stevenson, John [*fl.1684–1714*], *trumpeter.*

John Stevenson, trumpeter, was admitted to the King's Musick on 13 February 1684 as a replacement for Milbert Meares, deceased. He was reappointed under James II and William III and accompanied the latter on a trip to Holland in the winter of 1690–91. Stevenson was, we believe, the John Stevens, trumpeter, mentioned in the Lord Chamberlain's accounts on 30 December 1791 as receiving a new silver trumpet. Other warrants show Stevenson at an annual salary of £91 5s. annually and assigned to travel in 1697 with the King's ambassadors for the "Treaty of Peace," for which he received extra pay. Stevenson was still listed as a trumpeter in the King's Musick in 1714.

Stevenson, Thomas *d. 1802, music porter.*

A Mr Stevenson was cited in the Drury Lane Theatre accounts frequently from 1793 through 1795 as a music porter. His daily salary seems to have been 2s. We take the music porter to have been Thomas Stevenson, who died in 1802; the Drury Lane books show a payment on 10 April 1802 for "Thos. Stevenson, by his Son on Acct. to Bury him 6/6/-." Perhaps the son in question was Stevenson the Drury Lane boxkeeper.

Steventon, Mrs [*fl.1791*], *actress.*

Mrs Steventon played Miss Noel in *The Double Amour* at the Haymarket Theatre on 26 September 1791.

Steward, Mr [*fl.1740–1754*], *equilibrist, instrumentalist.*

At Hallam's booth at Bartholomew Fair on 23 August 1740 Mr Steward and others presented a tumbling act. On 18 and 19 September 1752 at the Great Tiled Booth on the Bowling Green in Southwark *The Rake Reformed* was presented:

The whole to conclude with several curious performances by the famous Steward on the Slack Wire. Scarcely perceptible [!] he plays on a violin, sounds a trumpet, beats the drum and balances a coach wheel on the wire; likewise puts a straw on his left foot, tosses it thence to his face, from thence to his right foot, from thence to his face again, and shoulders and keeps it in balance the whole time;

he also stands on his head and quits it with his hands, the wire in full swing.

He was probably the acrobat and slack wire performer "Stewart" who performed at the Edinburgh theatre on 5, 7, and 14 December 1752. And we take him to have been "Stuart" the equilibrist who began performing at the Smock Alley Theatre in Dublin on 30 November 1753. He appeared several times through 29 January 1754, one of his specialties being the balancing of "a Pyramid of Fireworks, which will be discharged while he is in full Swing."

Stewart. *See also* STUART *and* STURT.

Stewart, Mrs [*fl.1736*], *actress.*

At the Haymarket Theatre on 16 February 1736 Mrs Stewart played Lady Graveairs in *The Careless Husband.*

Stewart, Mrs, later Mrs Bellair [*fl.1791–1796*], *actress, singer.*

Mrs Stewart (often Stuart) was in Stephen Kemble's troupe in Edinburgh in the spring of 1791 and during the 1791–92 season, her earliest known appearance being as Donna Clara in *The Duenna* at the Theatre Royal in Shakespeare Square on 28 May 1791. After that she was seen as Angelina in *Robin Hood*, Antonio in *Richard Coeur de Lion*, Eliza in *The Flitch of Bacon*, Euphrosyne in *Comus*, Fatima in *Selima and Azor*, Ismene in *The Sultan*, Madelon in *The Surrender of Calais*, Margaretta in *No Song No Supper*, Rosetta in *Love in a Village*, Urganda in *Cymon*, Venus in *Arthur and Emmeline*, and Wilhelmina in *The Waterman*.

The *Hibernian Journal* on 20 June 1792 reported Mrs Stewart's Irish debut at the Crow Street Theatre in Dublin the previous day. She was advertised as from Edinburgh, where she had "played Clara, Leonora, &c. with considerable applause." She toured to Cork and Derry later in 1792 and to Derry and Belfast in early 1793 before coming to London for her Haymarket debut on 5 November 1793 as Leonora in *The Padlock*. She was advertised as "A Gentlewoman" from the Crow Street Theatre in Dublin. The *European Magazine,* which identified her as Mrs "Stuart," thought her figure pretty and engaging, though small, her voice melodious but not powerful, and her manner of singing cultivated and agreeable. The *Thespian Magazine* in 1793, however, called her voice "powerful as well as harmonious." She sang Amphitrite in the masque *Neptune and Amphitrite* in the last act of *The Tempest* on 19 November, Susan in *The Mariners* on 30 November, Eliza in *The Flitch of Bacon* on 14 December, and The Genius of Gratitude in *Harlequin Peasant* on 23 December and subsequent dates through 2 February 1794. On 8 July 1796 Mrs Stewart performed at Brighton, advertised as late of the Haymarket Theatre in London. In time, according to information provided us by Charles Beecher Hogan, she became Mrs Bellair.

Stewart, James ₁*fl.1772–1782*₁, *singer, actor, playwright.*

James Stewart, evidently a performer from Scotland, made some isolated appearances at the Haymarket Theatre in London: as Roger in *Patie and Roger* on 21 September 1772 and 20 February 1775, Bauldy in the same play (now called *The Gentle Shepherd*) on 13 October 1777, Roger again on 11 January 1779, Bauldy again on 17 January 1780, Roger (with the song "There's my Thumb, I'll ne'er beguile ye") on 25 September 1780, and Roger on 18 March 1782. Stewart was also a playwright, his farce *The Students* being presented at the Haymarket, for his shared benefit with Walker, on 13 October 1777. Stewart spoke the prologue and played an unspecified role in the play. When it was repeated on 11 January 1779, Stewart was down for the part of Macdowell, the Exciseman. Stewart apparently made an adaptation of *The Students,* calling it *The Exciseman Trick'd;* it was first presented on 18 March 1782 at the Haymarket for Stewart's benefit. Tickets were available at Stewart's china shop, No 201, Ratcliff Highway.

The *Hibernian Magazine* in March 1804 reported that James Stewart, ex-comedian, had died recently "in an advanced age." Possibly that reference was to our subject, but we think it more likely the death was that of the Irish performer James Beattie Stewart.

Stewart, Mrs James R., née Griffiths, *b. 1783, singer, actress.*

Miss Griffiths was born in 1783. According to the singer Michael Kelly in his *Reminiscences,* She was the daughter of the stage-door keeper of the Edinburgh theatre, and was employed about the house to sweep the stage, &c. when Mrs. Crouch and myself acted at Edinburgh. She was so delighted with Mrs. Crouch's performance, that some time after we had quitted the theatre, without intimating her intention to her father, or any person belonging to her, she travelled *on foot* all the way from Edinburgh to London, and found out Mrs. Crouch in Lisle Street, who took her under her tuition and patronage, and bestowed the greatest pains in instructing her. She had a sweet voice, a fine ear, and a great share of intellect.

Miss Griffiths did not arrive in London without some theatrical experience. By 7 April 1794 she was acting Princess Elizabeth in *The Royal Martyr* at the Theatre Royal in Shakespeare Square, Edinburgh. On 29 April 1795 she appeared as Little Pickle in *The Spoiled Child.* Yet she was advertised as making her first appearance on any stage when, on 13 June 1798, she appeared as Polly in *The Beggar's Opera* at the Haymarket Theatre in London. The *Monthly Mirror* gave her an extensive review:

Miss Griffith, a pupil of [Michael] Kelly, made her appearance in Polly. This lady is extremely young—scarcely fifteen, as we are informed—her voice is sweet and flexible, but not powerful: it is what is called a soprano. Some of the tones are shrill and offensive; but it is probable they may not yet have found their true compass and modulation, and as the lady has taste, feeling, and expression, we have every thing to expect from her future exhibitions, under the able and scientific tuition of such a man as Kelly. In addition to her musical talent, she speaks, acts, and deports herself with the confidence of a veteran. Siddons could not be more perfect in her bye-play, and her self-possession commenced with the moment of her appearance on the stage. Her figure is low and slight. Her features are not pretty, but they bear the character of intelligence. On the whole we never witnessed a debût so well regulated, at such an age. We have no high opinion of premature merit, for it has seldom answered its promise; but there are exceptions to every thing, and this may be one.

On 21 June 1798 Miss Griffiths played Florella in *My Grandmother,* and on 5 July she attempted Clarissa in *Lionel and Clarissa.* A critic protested "against the extravagant comments of the diurnal prints. There is no warranty for such excessive praise: it *may* do her a momentary service, but it *must* lead to eventual injury." He thought that her Clarissa, as well as her Polly, discovers taste, spirits and sensibility; and some, not *all* of her songs, are very well executed. In Florella she is not equally happy, for the part requires depth of tone . . . of which she is not yet mistress; for the same reason she should have avoided Margaretta [in *No Song No Supper,* which was performed on 13 July], as unsuitable to her powers.

During the remainder of the 1798 summer season at the Haymarket Miss Griffiths was seen as Caroline in *The Dead Alive,* Louisa in *The Farmer,* Lauretta in *False and True,* Norah in *The Poor Soldier,* Angelica Goto in *The Ship- wreck,* the title character in *Rosina,* and Miss Goodwill in *Bannian Day.* The *Authentic Mem- oirs of the Green Room* in 1799 thought Miss Griffiths's acting "far beyond Kelly's" and her "recitation and deportment were that of a vet- eran's: in short, we never knew a performer so young, to be so wonderfully great the first night. She afterwards performed Clarissa, in Lionel and Clarissa, Margaretta, in No Song, No Supper, &c. with encreased reputation."

In the summer of 1799 Miss Griffiths re- turned to the Haymarket to play some of her earlier roles and appear as the title character in *Rosina,* Rosina in *The Castle of Sorrento,* and a singing part in *The Red-Cross Knights.* She also ventured to Drury Lane, on 4 July 1799, to play Margaretta in *No Song No Supper* ("By permission of the Proprietor [Colman] of the Theatre Royal, Hay-Market").

Miss Griffiths then left London for Man- chester. Hodgkinson and Pogson note that the new season there opened on 16 December 1799 with Miss Griffiths performing the title role in *Rosina.* She was in *Pizarro* in February 1800 and on 24 March played Cecilia in *The Son-in-Law.* A Shrewsbury bill of 6 October 1800 has Miss Griffiths as Peggy ("with a song") in *The King and the Miller of Mansfield.* The *Monthly Mirror* reported that in the 1800– 1801 season Miss Griffiths was greatly im- proved in person, manner, and voice and had established herself as a favorite with Manches- ter audiences. A critic called "Fidelis" observed that Miss Griffiths was also singing in concert rooms and sang in the *Redemption* at St John's Church. At her benefit in 1801 she made £110, the second highest income in the troupe. The *Monthly Mirror* on 11 April 1801 said, "It is with pleasure I view this young

lady rising in public estimation, both as a performer and singer."

By 8 May 1802 Miss Griffiths was in Dub- lin, singing in *The Tempest.* We assume that our subject was the Miss Griffith who sang in the Irish Musical Fund's spring concert in Dublin in 1803. The *Hibernian Magazine* in December 1803 reported that Miss Griffiths had recently married the Irish actor James R. Stewart and was then performing at the Crow Street Theatre Royal in Dublin. On 15 April 1805 Mrs Stewart, hailed as from Dublin, made her first appearance at the Royal Circus in London, singing Rosabella in *Abellino.* She was Lucy in *The Knights of the Garter* on 29 April. Mrs Stewart evidently applied to the managers of the Manchester theatre to sing there in 1805, for *The Townsman* chided the managers for not hiring her and her husband. She was named in Crow Street, Dublin, bills in 1807 and 1810 and in the minutes of the Irish Musical Fund in March 1810.

James R. Stewart performed in Ireland from as early as 1790, according to W. S. Clark's *The Irish Stage in the County Towns,* became a popular favorite in Dublin, and died there on 16 November 1806, at the age of 35.

Stewart, Thomas [*fl.* 1780–1798], *ac- tor, playwright.*

The London Stage notes that the author of the unpublished afterpiece, *The Double Amour,* which was given at the Haymarket Theatre on 25 September 1780, was Thomas Stewart. That night, in the cast of *The Gentle Shepherd,* was James Stewart, and it may be that the two were related, though the *Index to The London Stage* lists them, confusingly, as the same per- son. On 23 February 1784 at the Haymarket a prologue by Thomas Stewart was spoken, and on 24 January 1785 Stewart wrote and spoke a prologue there. He was, according to *The London Stage,* the Stewart who played Lord Randolph in *Douglas* at the Haymarket on 23 April 1798 for Lady Perrot's benefit.

Stewartson, Mr [*fl.* 1791], *watchman.*

The Drury Lane accounts on 8 October 1791 list Mr Stewartson as a watchman at 12*s.* weekly.

Stich. *See* PUNTO, GIOVANNI.

Stichbury. *See* TOUCHBURY.

Stichel, Mrs _[fl.1792]_, *actress.*
Mrs Stichel played Mause in *The Gentle Shepherd* at the Haymarket Theatre on 22 October 1792.

Stiffkin. *See* STEFFKINS.

Stiles. *See* STYLES.

Stint, Mr _[fl.1738]_, *candlesnuffer.*
Testimony given at the trial of Theophilus Cibber in 1738 names Mr Stint, a candlesnuffer at Drury Lane Theatre, as the guard Cibber placed over his estranged wife Susanna in his house in Wild Court, Great Wild Street.

Stitchbury. *See* TOUCHBURY.

Stivaux, Mme _[fl.1757–1758]_, *dancer.*
Madame Stivaux danced Harliquinette in *Le Carneval de Venice* at the Haymarket Theatre on 26 December 1757 and 6 January 1758.

Stock, Mr _[fl.1786]_, *actor.*
Mr Stock played Porter in *Jane Shore* at Covent Garden Theatre on 6 October 1786. He was Buckram in *Love for Love* on 15 November.

Stock, [?] Mr _[fl.1799]_, *performer.*
A Mr Stock (or Stoch?) was one of several performers at the King's Theatre who petitioned the Lord Chamberlain on 12 November 1799 to refuse a license to the manager William Taylor until he paid their salaries.

Stockdale, Mr _[fl.1715]_, *musician.*
A Mr Stockdale, with Banister and the two Bastons, performed some new music at the Lincoln's Inn Fields Theatre on 9 May 1715.

Stockdale, Mrs _[fl.1715]_, *actress.*
Mrs Stockdale played the Fourth Whore in *The City Ramble* at Lincoln's Inn Fields Theatre on 2 June 1715. She was presumably the wife of the musician Stockdale.

Stockdale, George _[fl.1709–1710]_, *housekeeper.*
The *Daily Courant* of 30 May 1709 named George Stockdale as the housekeeper at Drury Lane Theatre. Among Vice Chamberlain Coke's papers is a letter from Aaron Hill to William Collier concerning the actors' riot at Drury Lane on 5 June 1710. Hill said he had sent an order to Stockdale not to open the theatre's doors until Hill could send a guard of constables.

Stockdon. *See* STOCKTON.

Stockley, Mr _[fl.1735–1736]_, *house servant.*
The accounts for Covent Garden Theatre in 1735–36 list a Stockley (presumably a male) as a house servant at 18*d.* daily or £13 8*s.* 6*d.* for 179 days.

Stockley, Mrs _[fl.1735]_, *house servant?*
Mrs Stockley's benefit tickets were accepted at Covent Garden Theatre on 26 May 1735. She was probably a house servant and the wife of the house servant Stockley.

Stockton, Thomas *d. 1783?, instrumentalist.*
Thomas Stockton was paid 10*s.* for playing violin in the *Messiah* at the Foundling Hospital in May 1754. For the performance on 27 April 1758 he played the viola for 8*s.* He was a violist in the *Messiah* again in 1759, 1760, and 1763. Thomas was most likely the "Stockdon" who was on the music list at Covent Garden Theatre on 20 September 1760 at a wage of 3*s.* 4*d.* daily. *Mortimer's London Directory* of 1763 named Thomas Stockton as a violist and oboist living in Leicester Street, Leicester Fields. Perhaps he was the Thomas "Stockden" who was buried at St Paul, Covent Garden, on 3 March 1783, though Leicester Fields is not in that parish.

Stoded[?]le, Ann _[fl.1727]_, *house servant?*
The accounts for the Lincoln's Inn Fields Theatre at Harvard contain an entry on 23 May 1727 that reads "M.r Chr. Rich 2. by Ann Stoded[?]le" (unreadable in the manuscript). Presumably that means that two tickets for Christopher Mosyer Rich, who had a share of the theatre's patent, were arranged for by Ann Stoded[?]le, who was probably a house servant.

Stoeskin and **Stofkins.** *See* STEFFKINS.

Stogadoir. *See* STAGELDOIR.

Stokes, Mr [*fl. 1772–1778?*], *actor.*

On 17 September 1772 a young gentleman played Richard III at the Haymarket Theatre; the *Morning Chronicle* identified him as Stokes, a "young grocer (for the attempter of King Richard was a dealer in figs). . . ." When Stokes "came to the combat scene with Richmond, he was encored in his fall and death, and wondrous as it may seem, he that night lived to die three several times before the curtain dropt." On 18 September Stokes gave the audience a "Variety of Imitations."

In the summer of 1776 he turned up at China Hall, Rotherhithe, playing in *The Rivals* on 3 July. Then he appeared as Cardinal Wolsey in *Henry VIII,* Selim in *Barbarossa,* and Juba in *Cato.* The *Morning Post* on 26 August, which identified Stokes as from Deptford, stated that he was "wretched" and called him the "celebrated Gentleman who perform'd Richard." On 25 June 1777 at China Hall he acted Hastings in *Jane Shore,* and perhaps he was the Stokes who played at York in March 1778. In 1778 at China Hall he tried the title role in *Douglas* on 27 May and, on 26 July, just before the theatre burned to the ground, he again appeared as Richard III. At the Haymarket on 25 September 1780 Stokes had a role in *The Double Amour;* on 15 March 1781 at the Crown Inn, Islington, he played Captain Plume in *The Recruiting Officer* and Harlow in *The Old Maid.*

Stokes, Mr [*fl. 1792–1801*], *actor.*

The *Thespian Magazine* in May 1792 reported that a Mr Stokes played Shylock in *The Merchant of Venice* at Richmond (Yorkshire?) "with great animation & judgment." He was identified in August as Steward to the Duke of Clarence. On 2 July 1800 at the Haymarket Theatre in London, Stokes acted an Officer of the Government in *The Jew and the Doctor.* Stokes was again at the Haymarket in the summer of 1801.

Stokes, Mrs [*fl. 1731*], *actress.*

Mrs Stokes played Betty in *The Letter Writers* on 24 March 1731 at the Haymarket Theatre.

Stokes, James *d. c. 1818, prompter.*

There were possibly two men named Stokes at Drury Lane Theatre in the 1790s and the early years of the nineteenth century: James, who served as an underprompter (Wrighten and then Powell were the prompters), and John G., who was a copyist. The sources—account books, benefit bills, promptbooks—are not very specific, and it could be that there was only one Stokes (James G.?). The citations seldom say more than "Stokes." Was it James who was cited in the Drury Lane benefit bill of 31 May 1793? As of 1 May 1794 Stokes was earning £1 1*s.* weekly. Remarkably, a prompt copy of Sheridan's *The Critic* at the Folger Shakespeare Library, dating about 1794, contains a Stokes signature, but the writing is so florid that the initials cannot be deciphered accurately. By 17 September 1807 Stokes was being paid £3 10*s.* weekly as "Dep.^y Prom.^r" A note dated 1 January 1796 ordered "Stokes to ascertain the half Price at Covent Garden Theatre on the first Night of a New Pantomime by Order of Mr. Kemble." For that piece of spying Stokes received 3*s.* He was probably the Stokes named in benefit bills from 1793 through 1799.

The Lord Chamberlain granted James Stokes a license to present a play and entertainment at the Haymarket Theatre on 27 January 1812; Stokes was probably acting for someone else, perhaps for the younger George Colman. A Drury Lane salary receipt dated 10 July 1813 was signed by a Stokes, but the Christian name was omitted. From at least 1804 to 1808 or 1810 Stokes served as prompter at the Haymarket Theatre during the summers.

The baptismal registers of St Giles in the Fields name James Stokes and his wife Elizabeth, of No 137, Tottenham Court Road, St Pancras, identifying James as a prompter at Drury Lane Theatre. He died before 7 June 1818 at Ebsworth.

Stokes, John G. [*fl. 1793–1817*], *copyist.*

The second (?) Stokes working at Drury Lane Theatre in the late eighteenth century was evidently named John G. He was cited in several documents as a copyist. A Rylands manuscript of Colman's *The Mountaineer,* which played at the Haymarket Theatre on 3 August 1793, has a notation reading, "This copy made by STOKES, the copyist of the Theatre DL for G. Colman, who has corrected some errors in it." Stokes had evidently prepared the copy for the printer. As early as April 1795 Stokes was also serving Drury Lane as a secretary, sending notes to playwrights about rehearsals of their works. The Drury Lane accounts name John Stokes or J. G. Stokes as a copyist through 1817. His salary was £3 10s. in 1805, but it appears to have dropped to £2 10s. by 1812. From 1815 to 1817 the copyist worked for £2 weekly at the Haymarket, presumably during the summers.

Stokes, Thomas ₍fl. 1761–1768₎, *singer, instrumentalist.*

According to the accounts for Covent Garden Theatre, a Mr Stokes was paid 5s. for serving as a chorus singer in *The Coronation* on 13 November 1761. He was, we believe, Thomas Stokes, who became a member of the Royal Society of Musicians on 3 June 1764 and in 1768 was a member of the King's band.

Stone, Mr ₍fl. 1735₎, *actor.*

In 1735 Mr Stone acted Fantome in *The Drummer* at Tottenham Court on 28 May and, for his shared benefit with Freeman, Foppington in *The Relapse* at York Buildings on 17 July.

Stone, Anne *d. 1724?, actress.*

On 13 November 1719 Miss Anne Stone played Prue in *Love for Love* at the Lincoln's Inn Fields Theatre. During the rest of the 1719–20 season she was seen as Rose in *The Recruiting Officer*, Lucia in *The Squire of Alsatia*, Lady Jane in *The Pretenders*, Angelina in *Love Makes a Man*, Charlotte in *The Half Pay Officers*, Lucia in *Hob's Wedding*, Dorcas in *The Fair Quaker*, Ophelia in *Hamlet*, Jessica in *The Merchant of Venice*, the epilogue speaker for *The Imperial Captives*, Corinna in *The Confederacy*, Morayma in *Don Sebastian*, Cydaria in *The Indian Emperor*, and Jaqueline in *The Royal Merchant*. She shared a benefit with Harper on 3 May 1720.

In 1720–21 and 1721–22 Miss Stone appeared in such new roles as Anne Page in *The Merry Wives of Windsor*, Juliet in *Measure for Measure*, Arabella in *The Committee*, Prince Edward in *Richard III*, Malapert in *The Quaker's Wedding*, Ciss in *The Cheats*, Serina in *The Orphan*, Lucy in *Oroonoko*, Charmilla in *Injured Love*, and Sylvia in *The Old Bachelor*. She was

cited (by her full name) in a list of Lincoln's Inn Fields performers on 12 April 1712.

In his *Dramatic Miscellanies* in 1784 Thomas Davies said that Miss Stone also played Cordelia to Anthony Boheme's *King Lear*, though *The London Stage* contains no record of such casting. Davies said Miss Stone had a pleasing voice and agreeable face and in a variety of roles pleased the public. She won the attentions of a young gentleman of wealth, a "Mr. C——," who married her. The young man's father found the match indiscreet and unworthy, commanded his son home to the country estate, not far from London, and thus the couple was separated. The father set about trying to make a permanent separation, one of his schemes being to intimidate Lincoln's Inn Fields manager John Rich into driving the young actress from the stage. That accomplished, father and son conspired with a young man of fashion to compromise Anne; she, now near poverty, fell prey to him. He then forsook her, and she died soon after, "in great affliction and distress."

Anne may have reverted to her maiden name after her separation from her husband; if so, perhaps she was the Anne Stone, from St Martin-in-the-Fields, who was buried at St Paul, Covent Garden, on 30 March 1724.

Stone, Thomas ₍fl. 1671₎, *musician.*

On 31 March and again on 4 August 1671 Thomas Stone was ordered apprehended for "exercising musique without lycense" from the Corporation of Music.

Stone, William ₍fl. 1748₎, *recruiter.*

On 15 December 1780 in the *British Mercury and Evening News* appeared a series of letters purported to have been exchanges between David Garrick and one "Wm. Stone" in 1748. Richard Ryan picked up the letters in his *Dramatic Table Talk* in 1825, saying that at Drury Lane "it was Garrick's department to engage all performers, etc. and he had a humorous fellow in his pay, whose office it was to procure persons competent to act subordinate characters, and for whom he received a certain sum per head." In 1748 Stone wrote that he had "a few cupids you may have cheap, as they belong to a poor journeyman Shoemaker, who I drink with now and then." Garrick replied,

You are the best fellow in the world—bring the

Cupids to the Theatre to-morrow. If they are under six, and well made, you shall have a guinea apiece for them. . . .

If you can get me two good murderers, I will pay you handsomely, particularly the spouting fellow who keeps the apple-stand on Tower-hill; the cut in his face is quite the thing. Pick me up an Alderman or two, for Richard if you can, and I have no objection to treat with you for a comely Mayor. The Barber will not do for Brutus, although I think he will succeed in Mat.

And so on. This all reads like a fabrication.

Stonecastle, Mr [fl. 1734–1735], actor.

Mr Stonecastle played Ramilie in *The Miser* at the James Street Theatre on 29 May 1734 and Clodio in *Love Makes a Man* at York Buildings on 21 March 1735.

Stooskin. *See* STEFFKINS.

Stopeler and Stoplear. *See* STOPPELAER.

Stoppelaer, Charles d. 1772, actor, singer, painter.

Charles Stoppelaer was cited by Edward Edwards in his *Anecdotes of Painting:* "STOPPELAER, A portrait painter, and one of those who might be considered an itinerant artist. He was an exhibitor in the years 1761 and 1762, about which time he visited Norfolk. He had a brother who was well known upon the stage of Drury-lane. . . ." That brother was Michael, who did indeed have a long acting career, but most of it was spent at Covent Garden Theatre, not Drury Lane. He, too, was a painter, as was yet another brother (or Charles's son?), Herbert, who also acted, but evidently not in London. Edwards went on to say, "Of the comparative merits of the two brothers [Charles and Michael] in their different professions, no correct estimate can be made, for the abilities of the player [Michael] are forgotten, and the works of the artist [Charles] do not possess any superiority that can distinguish them from the multitude of . . . common-place portraits. . . ." Edwards noted that Stoppelaer the artist (he did not know his Christian name) exhibited paintings in 1772, "which period he did not long survive."

About 1738 Charles Stoppelaer painted a portrait of the comedian Jo Miller as Teague in *The Committee*. It was engraved by A. Miller,

W. Greatbach, N. G., H. Burgh, and an anonymous engraver. The A. Miller copy is reproduced in this *Dictionary* with Jo Miller's entry. Another portrait by Charles, of an unknown gentleman, signed and dated 1745, is in the National Gallery of Ireland. Art dictionaries cite Charles Stoppelaer (or Stopler, Stopplear, Stoppeler, etc.) as working as an artist in London and Dublin from 1703 to 1738.

Theatrical records cite a Stoppelaer in London as early as 1729: "Stoplar" had a role in *The Beggar's Wedding* and played Clodden in *Southwark Fair* at Reynolds's booth at Southwark Fair on 8 September. At Blackheath Fair on 30 September "Stoplar" acted Hunter in *The Beggar's Wedding* and then moved to the Haymarket Theatre for the 1729–30 season. That performer, through the roles assigned him, can be traced (accurately, we hope, but the dangers of mistaking him for a second Stoppelaer in London are great) through the spring of 1740, acting in many pantomimes and comedies and singing roles in popular musical pieces and even in Handel operas.

Stoppelaer (Charles, we are supposing) appeared throughout the 1729–30 season at the Haymarket Theatre, beginning on 12 November 1729 as Mulligrub in *Love and Revenge*. He went on to play Hunter in *The Beggar's Wedding*, Damon in *Damon and Phillida*, Theorby in *Hurlothrumbo*, a role in *The Village Opera*, Alonzo in *Fatal Love*, Sir Charles in *The Stratagem*, a role in *The Cheshire Comicks*, Polly in *The Metamorphosis of the Beggar's Opera*, Sparkish and Signor Opera in *The Author's Farce*, Constant in *Rape upon Rape*, Ludovico in *Othello*, and Forester in *The Amorous Adventure*. After the Haymarket season ended, Stoppelaer went to Tottenham Court to play an unspecified role in *The Rum Duke and the Queer Duke* and Opera in *Punch's Oratory* on 1 August 1730. On 22 August at Bartholomew Fair he was seen as Lelius in *Scipio's Triumph* and Forester in *Harlequin's Contrivance*.

Stoppelaer repeated some of his earlier parts at the Haymarket in September, October, and November 1730 and sang between the acts. On 16 December he turned up at Goodman's Fields Theatre, where he completed the season. His first part was Lovewell in *The Jealous Clown*, after which he offered entr'acte singing and appeared as Damon in *Damon and Phillida*, Peartree in *The Wedding*, Friendly in *Flora*,

Worthy in *The Merry Throwster,* Cleara in *Tom Thumb,* Melton in *The Cobler's Opera,* and Drivewell in *The Sailor's Wedding.* He was granted a solo benefit on 29 April 1731. On 6 July he made his first appearance on the stage of Drury Lane, playing Hunter in *Phebe.* On 20 July he acted Vincent in *The Jovial Crew,* and then he appeared as Cantato in *Bayes's Opera,* Sir John Loverule in *The Devil to Pay,* Filbert in *The What D'Ye Call It,* and Damon in *The Triumphs of Love.* On 20 August he sang a pastoral dialogue with Miss Oates and on 26 August returned to Bartholomew Fair to play the Uncle in *The London Merchant* and Friendly in *Flora.*

Stoppelaer was again at Drury Lane in 1731–32, adding such new roles as Cephalus in *Cephalus and Procris,* Nightingale in *Bartholomew Fair,* a Servant of Pierrot in *Perseus and Andromeda,* Lovemore in *The Lottery,* Edgar in *The Lover's Opera,* Rovewell in *The Contrivances,* Octavio in *The Comical Revenge,* Leander in *The Mock Doctor,* Macheath in *The Beggar's Opera,* and Bruneto in *The Devil of a Duke.* In August 1732 he acted again at Bartholomew Fair, in *The Envious Statesman.* At Drury Lane in 1732–33 his new parts included Thomas in *The What D'Ye Call It,* a Farmer in *The Country Revels,* Jerry in *Betty,* Warble in *The Boarding School,* Mercury in *The Judgment of Paris,* Mercury, Beau Mordecai, and Mezzetin in *The Harlot's Progress,* Lelius in *The Imaginary Cuckolds,* Hymen in *Damon and Daphne,* and Damon in *Venus, Cupid, and Hymen.* He was at Bartholomew Fair in August and September 1733, playing Clerimont in *The Miser,* a Masquerader and a Doctor in *Ridotto Al' Fresco,* and Silence in *Sir John Falstaff.* Stoppelaer remained at Drury Lane in 1733–34, choosing not to join Theophilus Cibber and his rebel Drury Lane players at the Haymarket. He played some of his earlier parts—Cephalus, Sir John, Leander, Macheath, Beau Mordecai, Opera, and others—and added some new ones: a Spaniard and Jupiter in *Cupid and Psyche,* Oronces in *Aesop,* Pedro in *The Spanish Fryar,* Ramilie in *The Miser,* King Arthur in *The Opera of Operas,* Neptune in *The Tempest,* the Second Musician and a Shepherd in *The Cornish Squire,* Tom in *The Livery Rake,* Valentine in *The Intriguing Chambermaid,* Marplay senior in *The Author's Farce,* Dick in *The Confederacy,* and a Follower of Mars in *Love and Glory.* At the Goodman's

Fields Theatre that season, as in 1732–33 and 1734–35, was another Stoppelaer—Michael, it would seem—playing a similar line of characters.

On 15 April 1734 Charles Stoppelaer appears to have performed at Drury Lane and at Lincoln's Inn Fields at the same time, but the Drury Lane bill in *The London Stage* has conflicting information on casts, the newspapers differing in at least three instances. We believe that Jupiter in *Cupid and Psyche* was probably not played by Charles that night and that at Lincoln's Inn Fields, for his Drury Lane benefit, he acted his usual roles in *The Miser* and *The Contrivances.* On 24 August at the Fielding-Oates booth at Bartholomew Fair, both Stoppelaers were in *The Constant Lovers:* Stoppelaer senior (Charles) acted Springtime and Stoppelaer junior (Michael) played Mactrot. On 2 September Charles played his old role of Friendly in *Flora* at Covent Garden Theatre at a charity benefit.

By 1734–35, if not earlier, Charles Stoppelaer's singing had attracted the attention of Handel. Stoppelaer joined Handel in the opera at Covent Garden, acting also with the regular company either there or at their second theatre in Lincoln's Inn Fields. His first appearance of the season seems to have been on 20 September, when he played Lovemore in *The Lottery.* Three days later he was Sir John in *The Devil to Pay.* During the season he appeared in other old roles and tried some new ones: a Spirit and Genius in *The Necromancer,* Jupiter in *The Rape of Proserpine,* Perseus in *Perseus and Andromeda,* Macheath in *Macheath in the Shades,* Octavio in *The Mock Countess,* and Valentine in *The Mock Lawyer.* For Handel, beginning on 8 January 1735, Charles Stoppelaer lent his tenor to the part of Odoardo in *Ariodante.* Dean in *Handel's Dramatic Oratorios and Masques* says Stoppelaer also sang in *Alcina* in 1735. One assumes he sang in Italian. During the season he also entertained with entr'acte songs, one being "The Original Words of the Play," which he sang with Richard Leveridge. On 26 September 1735 Charles or Michael went over to the Haymarket to play Archer in a drastically revised version of *The Stratagem* and Damon in *Damon and Phillida.* Both had played Damon previously.

Both Stoppelaers were at Covent Garden in 1735–36. On 1 October 1735 the bill listed

Mat in *The Beggar's Opera* as being played by (Michael?) Stoppelaer. Thereafter the bills distinguished the brothers by identifying Michael by his initial or an abbreviation of his Christian name; Charles, having established himself in London and having spent a season at Covent Garden, was cited as just Stoppelaer. New roles for Charles in 1735–36 included Apollo in *Momus Turned Fabulist,* Bacchus in *Apollo and Daphne,* Fabian in *The Fatal Marriage,* Sir Charles in *The Stratagem,* Mercury in *The Royal Chace,* and Polydore in *The Orphan* (at his benefit on 30 April 1736). Dean believes he also may have sung in *Acis and Galatea.* Stoppelaer was living at the Star and Anchor in Tavistock Street, Covent Garden, at the time of his benefit. During 1735–36 Charles's salary at Covent Garden was 13s. 4d. daily for 172 days. Michael, a newcomer, was paid 2s. 6d. daily.

In 1736–37 one Stoppelaer was at Drury Lane and the other at Covent Garden. The Drury Lane Stoppelaer was the one we have been following since 1729, as one can tell from certain assignments: Sir John in *The Devil to Pay,* Leander in *The Mock Doctor,* Lovemore in *The Lottery,* Macheath in *The Beggar's Opera,* Valentine in *The Intriguing Chambermaid,* and singing appearances. He began the season as the Spaniard in *Columbine Courtezan* on 4 September 1736, after which, in addition to several old assignments, Stoppelaer was seen in such new characters as Shamwell in *Damon and Phillida,* Longbib and a Ballad Singer in *Harlequin Restored,* Quaver in *The Virgin Unmask'd,* a Priest of Aurora and Mercury in *The Fall of Phaeton,* the Ghost of Darius in *The Rival Queens* (a singing role), and Joe in *The King and the Miller of Mansfield.*

Stoppelaer seems then to have left London, but he returned to sing an Amalekite in Handel's *Saul* at the King's Theatre on 16 January 1739 and make a few appearances in the spring of 1740 at Drury Lane, performing as Sir John in *The Devil to Pay,* Lovemore in *The Lottery,* and Valentine in *The Intriguing Chambermaid.* He received a solo benefit on 13 May, at which he sang in *Macbeth* and played Sir John in *The Devil to Pay* for the Ancient and Honourable Order of Gregorians.

Charles was surely the Stoppelaer at the Smock Alley Theatre in Dublin in the summer of 1740, singing Macheath in *The Beggar's Opera* and playing Sir John in *The Devil to Pay* and

Beau Mordecai in *The Harlot's Progress.* He was probably the Stoppelaer who was in the company at the Jacob's Wells Theatre in Bristol, which was managed by the actor John Hippisley. Stoppelaer was a witness to Hippisley's will of 1748.

Notes in the Burney papers at the British Library and in the manuscripts at the Folger Shakespeare Library claim that a Stoppelaer died in 1751; a note in British Library manuscript 18,586 puts Stoppelaer's death in 1754. Those citations cannot have referred to either Charles or Michael Stoppelaer, so perhaps one of them concerned Herbert. Charles died in 1772, perhaps at Manchester, for administration of the estate of Charles Stoppelaer was granted there that year to Michael Stoppelaer, natural and lawful brother and next of kin.

Stoppelaer, Michael   c. 1710–1777, actor, singer, dancer, painter.

Michael Stoppelaer (or Stopler, Stopplear, Stoppeler, etc.) was born in Ireland about 1710, according to the *New Grove.* He acted for many years in London, but another Stoppelaer, Charles, seems to have preceded him and was identified in the 1735–36 season as Stoppelaer senior. We have evidence that he was the brother of Michael (not his father, as is suggested by Merchant in *The Artist and the Theatre*). Yet a third Stoppelaer, Herbert, is identified in the Redgrave and Bryan dictionaries of artists as a painter and an actor. Michael and Charles, too, were artists and performers. Merchant says that Herbert Stoppelaer came to London from Dublin about 1730 with the artist and engraver Thomas Frye. "He appeared at Covent Garden Theatre for Rich in a pantomime *Harlequin Skeleton,* after which he seems to have given up the stage and devoted his time to art." But the earliest record in *The London Stage* of a Stoppelaer in *Harlequin Skeleton* dates from 1754 and clearly concerns Michael. Herbert seems not to have acted in London. The assignments of parts below should be treated with some caution, for it is obvious that the careers of the three Stoppelaers have been much confused.

On 26 October 1732, when Charles Stoppelaer was with the Drury Lane troupe, at Goodman's Fields a "Mimick Song" was sung "by Mr. Stoppelaer, from the Theatre Royal in Dublin, in the character of a ballad singer."

MICHAEL STOPPELAER(?) as Tubal and CHARLES MACKLIN as Shylock

by H. Stoppelaer

The wording certainly suggests a newcomer and a different person from the Stoppelaer who had been appearing in London since 1729. We take it, then, that the singer was Michael, Charles's brother. The roles assigned to him during his first season at Goodman's Fields were sometimes identical with those played by the Drury Lane Stoppelaer, but Michael tried a number of parts his brother seems not to have acted. Michael's first role at Goodman's Fields was Ben in *Love for Love* on 3 November 1732. During the rest of the 1732–33 season he appeared as a Citizen in *Julius Caesar*, an Attendant in *The Amorous Sportsman*, Moody in *The Lovers' Opera*, Damon in *Damon and Phillida*, Mr Xenodocky in *The Decoy*, Leander in *The Mock Doctor*, Master Johnny in *The Mad Captain*, and Hob in *Flora* (for his shared benefit with Collet on 27 April 1733).

In 1733–34 at Goodman's Fields, Stoppe-

laer's new parts included Diana in *The Beggar's Opera* (he tried other skirts parts later), Hottman in *Oroonoko*, and a Waterman and a Citizen in *Britannia*. He also sang in the chorus of *Macbeth*. At his solo benefit on 27 April 1734 Stoppelaer sang his "Mimick Song" and acted in *The Mad Captain*. On 24 August he and his brother played at the Fielding-Oates booth at Bartholomew Fair, Charles acting Springame and Michael Mactrot in *The Constant Couple*. Michael was cited as Stoppelaer junior. In 1734–35 at Goodman's Fields Michael attempted such new characters as a Witch in *Macbeth*, Teague in *The Committee*, and a Witch in *Jupiter and Io*.

In 1735–36 both Stoppelaers were engaged by Rich at Covent Garden, and the bills usually distinguished them by citing Michael by his initial or an abbreviation of his name. For 2s. 6d. daily for 167 days he appeared as Mat in *The Beggar's Opera* (on 1 October 1735, probably his first Covent Garden appearance), Vulcan (a Blacksmith) in *Momus Turned Fabulist*, Strut in *The Double Gallant*, Kate Matchlock in *The Funeral*, Gaffer Gabble in *Sylvia*, a Constable in *The City Ramble*, a Bravo in *The Inconstant*, and Cymon in *Damon and Phillida*. He was not granted a benefit at Covent Garden, so he shared one with two others at Lincoln's Inn Fields on 16 June 1736, playing Sullen in *The Stratagem*.

Michael Stoppelaer remained at Covent Garden for the rest of his career, leaving only during two summers, 1746 and 1753, to perform at Richmond. At Covent Garden he continued in some of his old parts—Cymon in *Damon and Phillida*, Strut in *The Double Gallant*, Teague in *The Committee*, Mat in *The Beggar's Opera*, Kate Matchlock in *The Funeral*, a Bravo in *The Inconstant*, and others—and added a large number of new roles to his repertoire.

Among them were Mouldy, Silence, and Bardolph in *2 Henry IV*, Nym in *Henry V*, a Citizen in *Oedipus*, Dorcas Guzzle in *The Cobler of Preston*, Sapscull in *The Honest Yorkshireman*, Dorante in *The Gamester*, Mrs Mandrake and the Captain in *The Twin Rivals*, Mrs Hackem in *The Squire of Alsatia*, Ferret in *The Royal Merchant*, the Orange Woman in *The Man of Mode*, Stave in *The What D'Ye Call It*, the Landlord in *The Stage Coach*, Cacafogo in *Rule a Wife and Have a Wife*, Tyrrel in *Richard III*, Monsieur and Antonio in *Love Makes a Man*, the Constable in *The Recruiting Officer*, Caius in *The Merry Wives of Windsor*, the Second Gravedigger in *Hamlet*, a Murderer in *Macbeth*, Serjeant Ploden in *The Plain Dealer*, Joe in *The King and the Miller of Mansfield*, Barnardine in *Measure for Measure*, Dr Butts in *Henry VIII*, Tubal in *The Merchant of Venice*, Wormwood in *The Virgin Unmask'd*, Mump in *Phebe*, Bull in *The Relapse*, Poundage in *The Provok'd Husband*, the Mad Welshman in *The Pilgrim*, Peto in *1 Henry IV*, the Dragon in *The Dragon of Wantley*, Helebore in *The Mock Doctor*, the Anatomist in *Harlequin Skeleton*, Dick in *The Lying Valet*, one of the Kings of Brentford in *The Rehearsal*, the Cook in *The Devil to Pay*, Timon in *The Humorous Lieutenant*, Benedict in *The School Boy*, a Suitor in *The Prophetess*, a Plebeian in *Coriolanus*, and the Duke in *Othello*.

Like his brother, Michael Stoppelaer was a singer, though evidently not as talented. He sang in the chorus of *Macbeth* regularly, and on 12 May 1741 he sang "Arra my Judy" at his shared benefit (with three others). A year later, on 26 April 1742, Stoppelaer sang a "Gregorean Song" and the following month he offered "Arra my Judy" again. On 3 May 1745 at his solo benefit he sang some Masonic songs for his brethren. He danced in *The Villagers* and *The Metamorphosis of Harlequin* in October and November 1741. But as the years went on Stoppelaer seems to have been used less and less as an entr'acte entertainer at Covent Garden. His salary is a clear indication of his lowly status in the company. In 1740–41 he was earning 3s. 4d. daily. He remained at that rate at least through 1767. He was at a scale next to the bottom for actors.

With the Richmond-Twickenham troupe in the summer of 1746 Stoppelaer played Tom Errand in *The Constant Couple* on 19 June, Mump in *Phebe* on 9 August, a Recruit in *The Recruiting Officer* and Peter in *The Resolute Husband* on 13 September, and Captain Hackum in *The Squire of Alsatia* on 15 September. On 28 July 1753 at Richmond he acted Duncan in *Macbeth*.

The *County Magazine* in January 1789 said that "Stoppelaer died about twenty years ago—his most remarkable performance was the *Doctor* in *Harlequin Skeleton*." (Michael Stoppelaer played the Anatomist in *Harlequin Skeleton* as early as 5 November 1754 at Covent Garden.) But the only Stoppelaer who is known to have died near 1769 was Charles. In 1772 administration of Charles Stoppelaer's estate was granted to his brother and next of kin, Michael. Michael's last notice was on 15 May 1777, when he and five others had benefit tickets out at Covent Garden. The *New Grove* (which gives Charles's Handel roles to Michael) says Michael's will was proved on 4 July 1777.

Davies in his *Dramatic Miscellanies* spoke in 1784 of Michael Stoppelaer, "of blundering memory"—a reference explained in Ryan's *Dramatic Table Talk*:

This votary of the mimic art was a native of the Sister Isle, and had been educated at Trinity College, Dublin; but imbibing a love for acting, he quitted those academic bowers for the stage, in which pursuit he attained but little eminence. He was more celebrated for his blunders than for his acting, and for a singular faculty he possessed of uttering absurd speeches, and disagreeable truths, without any design to offend the party to whom they were addressed: one sample of his ability in that way will give the reader a more perfect idea of his character.

Rich [the Covent Garden manager and harlequin] was talking to some of his performers, when Stoppelaer was present, concerning the very disproportioned agreement he had just entered into with one of his tragedians, named Halland [probably Holland], when Stoppelaer stepped up to him and said, "Upon my soul, sir, he got *the blind side* of you there." Rich was somewhat nettled at this remark, and being apprehensive of hearing something from the same quarter still more offensive, he left the company. As soon as the manager was out of hearing, one of the party observed to Stoppelaer, that his speech was exceedingly improper, and greatly affronting, as every body knew that Mr. Rich had a great blemish in one of his eyes. "Upon my word (replied the unconscious Stoppelaer) I never heard of it before: I'll set the thing to rights, for I'll go immediately, and ask his pardon."

Davies said Stoppelaer had played the Abbot of Westminster in *Richard II* but was by no means equal to that part. He was remarkable, Davies said, for his singing of Irish and Scottish songs. Davies evidently did not know that there had been a second Stoppelaer acting in London in the 1730s; he may have supposed that all references to a performer of that name concerned Michael.

Michael Stoppelaer was a caricaturist, according to Merchant, and his work was published by Carrington Bowles. In his *Anecdotes* Edward Edwards noted that Michael was also a portrait painter. A Stoppelaer, presumably Michael, painted scenery for the Patagonian Theatre from Dublin, which performed puppet plays in the Great Room over the Exeter 'Change from October 1776.

Edwards, in his listing of (Charles) Stoppelaer, had this to say about his brother (Michael):

He had a brother who was well known upon the stage of Drury-lane [*recte* Covent Garden] where he for several years supported the inferior but useful characters of the drama, such as the Grave-digger in Hamlet, and Ben Budge [*recte* Mat?] in the Beggar's Opera, which last occasioned the following whimsical event: He was accustomed to pass part of his summer vacations at Windsor, to which place as he was once travelling in the stage, a man well mounted, rode up to the coach-door, and surveying the passengers, repeated the following quotations:

"Pry' thee Mat, what is become of thy brother Tom? I have not seen him since my return from transportation;" and then, without further question, turned his horse's head and rode off, to the great joy of the travellers. Of the comparative merits of the two brothers in their different professions, no correct estimate can be made, for the abilities of the player are forgotten, and the works of the artiste do not possess any superiority that can distinguish them from the multitude of . . . common-place portraits.

The actor was living in 1770, and the artist exhibited again in 1771, which period he did not long survive.

The author [Edwards] has lately been informed by Mr. Richards, of the Royal Academy, that the actor had also practised portrait painting.

A painting attributed to Herbert Stoppelaer of a scene from *The Merchant of Venice* shows Charles Macklin as Shylock and perhaps Michael Stoppelaer as Tubal. The picture was once owned by Lord Aberdare, then Sir Hubert Hughes-Stanton, and in 1960 by Lewis Kirstein, who gave it to the American Shakespeare Theatre at Stratford, Connecticut. In 1975 it was acquired by the Yale Center for British Art. The pose of Shylock in this picture is based on Zoffany's small full-length of Macklin (but with the arms altered) at the National Theatre, London, and is similar to the larger painting of the trial scene by Zoffany which is at the Tate Gallery. See Geoffrey Ashton, *Shakespeare and British Art* (Yale Center for British Art, 1981), for details.

Stoppelaer, Mrs [**Michael?**] [*fl.* 1760– 1778], *actress.*

At Michael Stoppelaer's benefit at Covent Garden Theatre on 9 May 1760 Mrs Stoppelaer, presumably his wife, made her stage debut playing Phyllis in *The Conscious Lovers*. A year later, on 28 April 1761, again at Stoppelaer's benefit, she made her second appearance, as Cherry in *The Stratagem*. After Michael's death, Mrs Stoppelaer was named in a codicil to the will of the actor William Havard. In the codicil, dated 25 February 1778, Havard left "to the Widow Stoppelaer wife of my old ffriend Mich! Stoppelaer twenty pounds."

Storace, Ann Selina, later Mrs John Abraham Fisher the second 1765– 1817, *singer, actress.*

Ann Selina Storace, who was known profes-

Courtesy of the Garrick Club

ANN STORACE, as Catherine

by Sharp

sionally as Anna and was commonly called Nancy, was born in London on 27 October 1765. Until recently her year of birth has been given as 1766, because, as Roger Fiske tells us in the *New Grove,* her father falsified her age and that of her brother in order to further their careers as child prodigies. Her father Stephen (anglicized from Stefano) Storace had immigrated from Naples by 1747, played double bass in Dublin and London, and was band director at Marylebone Gardens from about 1758 to 1772. Her mother, Elizabeth Trusler, a daughter of John Trusler, proprietor of Marylebone Gardens, had married Storace in 1761.

Nancy's career and that of her elder brother Stephen John Seymour Storace (1762–1796), who became a successful composer and conductor of theatre music, were guided in their earlier years by the ambitions of their father. After instruction by the elder Storace, Nancy took singing lessons from Sacchini and Rauzzini. Perhaps her first appearance in public occurred in the summer of 1773 at Southampton, when as "a Child not eight Years old," she was advertised in the *Hampshire Chronicle* of 23

August to sing at a public breakfast to take place at Mr Martin's Long Rooms. Sharing the program with her was the violinist Signor Ximinez. The success of that entertainment encouraged Storace, who had taken lodgings at No 13, Bugle Street, to advertise a benefit for his daughter at Martin's Rooms for 17 September, with Signor Ximinez offering a violin solo and with Nancy singing "a Set of new Songs." Obliged to appear at the Three Choirs Festival in Worcester, Storace left his daughter, no doubt with her mother, at Southampton to enjoy her sudden popularity. In an advertisement in the local press he thanked the public for the notice they had taken of her and expressed his hope that "by his Absence . . . his Child will find protection from the Nobility and Gentry to whom she will respectfully pay her Devoirs at their several Habitations."

The following month Nancy and her 11-year-old brother were engaged with their father at the Salisbury annual musical festival, held that year in the Assembly Rooms (the Cathedral being closed) on 6 to 8 October 1773. The *Salisbury Journal* announced that "Signiora Storace, a child of eight years old will oblige the company with several Italian songs." The principal singer at the festival was Cecilia Grassi in *Samson;* she soon would marry Johann Christian Bach, who delighted the audience with "an elegant performance on the harpsichord." The Salisbury press reported that Miss Storace sang several songs "with great spirit and judgment and shewed uncommon signs of an early genius to music."

According to *The Dictionary of National Biography,* Nancy sang at the Haymarket Theatre on 15 April 1774, in a concert given by the harper Evans, a performance not recorded in *The London Stage.* It was about that time that she became Rauzzini's pupil. In 1777 she appeared in the Covent Garden oratorios, first on 14 February in *Judas Maccabaeus* with the estimable singers Tenducci and Reinhold. On 13 March of that year she sang Cupido in Rauzzini's *L'ali d'amore* at the King's Theatre, for her master's benefit. That opera was repeated on 20 March. The next night she sang again in the Covent Garden oratorio. She returned to the King's Theatre on 5 July to appear again in *L'ali d'amore,* and before the last ballet she and Rauzzini sang an *Address of Thanks,* composed by him. She traveled with Rauzzini to

Brighton, where they sang on 30 August 1777 in a special concert at the theatre under Joseph Fox's first year of management. She was so successful that a second concert was demanded on 3 September. That year she also appeared at the Hereford Three Choirs Festival.

A benefit concert for Nancy at the Tottenham Street Room (later the Prince of Wales Theatre) on 27 April 1778 provided funds for her parents to take her that December to Naples, where her brother was studying at the San Onofrio Conservatorio. It is said that she sang in the Lenten oratorios at the San Carlo Theatre in that city. With plans for launching young Nancy's operatic career, the family traveled north in 1779. Michael Kelly in his *Reminiscences* provides a colorful account of the young Storaces abroad, though his narrative (filtered through an amanuensis) is devoid of dates and is cavalier about accuracy of details.

In 1780 she made her debut, at the age of 15, in *Achilles in Sciro* at the Pergola Theatre in Florence. Kelly relates a good story of the circumstances that presumably brought Nancy into renown with Florentine auditors. The eminent tenor Marchesi had displayed such exquisite power and strength in singing Bianchi's celebrated *cavatina* "Sembianza amabile de mio bel sole," especially in a particular passage in which "he ran up a violetta of semitone octaves," that it was called "La bomba di Marchesi!" At the Pergola one night, Nancy had to sing her solo immediately after Marchesi's virtuoso song, and she was determined

to show the audience that she could bring a bomba into the field also. She attempted it, and executed it, to the admiration and astonishment of the audience, but to the dismay of poor Marchesi. Campigli, the manager, requested her to discontinue it, but she peremptorily refused, saying, that she had as good a right to shew the power of her bomba as anybody else.

Whereupon Marchesi threatened to leave the theatre if 15-year-old Nancy remained, so the manager was obliged to dismiss her.

The Storaces went thence to Lucca and Leghorn. At Leghorn, Kelly first met the children. Nancy sang in Parma in 1781, and, at the age of 17, at La Scala in Milan in 1782. About 1783 the elder Stephen Storace died in Italy, but Nancy's mother continued to guide her career.

By the spring of 1783 they were in Vienna, where Nancy was to be the *prima donna* in *opera buffa* at the imperial court theatre for four years, at the high salary of 3247 florins per year. The Italian opera company began performing in April 1783, and Nancy experienced success after success. The Hungarian poet Kazinczy reported that "Storace, the beautiful songstress, bewitches eye, ear, and soul," and a critic in *Allgemeine Musikalische Zeitung* wrote, "She united in her person, like none other alive, and only a few singers of the past, all the gifts of nature, education, and technique which one may desire for performance in Italian comic opera."

Nancy's mother seems to have failed in her duties as chaperone, for in the autumn of 1783, Nancy, now turned 18, married at the chapel of the Dutch ambassador the vain English musician John Abraham Fisher, then resident in Vienna. In a manuscript notation to Mozart's unfinished *La sposo deluso,* which he abandoned in December 1783, the composer indicated that the role of Emilia in that comic opera was intended for "Signora Fischer." Nancy was Vienna's first Rosina in Paisiello's *Il barbiere di Siviglia* (to Kelly and Mandini alternating as Almaviva). In Mozart's setting of Beaumarchais's sequel, *Le Nozze di Figaro,* which had its premier performance on 1 May 1786, instead of playing the mature and more dignified Rosina she was assigned to Susanna, the maid. Vienna heard her brother's first opera, *Gli sposi malcontenti,* at the Burgtheater on 1 June 1785, when in the middle of the first act, Sga Storace, before the Emperor, completely lost her voice, and she had to be replaced by Celestini Coltellini. (Legend has it that the Duke of York was among the dignitaries in the audience, but his visit to Vienna occurred 12 months earlier.) She did not sing for three months. Her return in September was celebrated by a cantata, *Per la ricuperata salute di Ophelia,* written in collaboration by Mozart, Salieri, and Cornetti (the last name perhaps being a pseudonym for Stephen Storace).

Nancy's marriage to John Abraham Fisher, tempestuous from the outset, was destined to be short-lived. He was 21 years her elder and had previously been married to Elizabeth Powell, the widow of the fine actor William Powell (d. 1769). After Elizabeth Fisher's death in May 1780, Fisher had embarked on a concert tour of the Continent, which brought him to Vienna in 1783 and his marriage to Nancy Storace. By the end of 1784, Emperor Joseph II, who seems also to have had some special interest in Nancy, heard of Fisher's cruel treatment of his new wife and expelled him from Austria. Later, in her will drawn in 1797 while Fisher was still alive, Nancy did not mention her marriage to the musician. According to documentation in Otto Michtner's *Das Alte Burgtheater als Opernbühne* (*Theatergeschichte Österreichs,* 1970), in July 1785 Nancy had a daughter, presumably by Fisher, but the child soon died because Nancy's stinginess caused her to dismiss the wetnurse, and the child starved. Nancy never remarried. There is no evidence that her relationship with Mozart was ever deeper than a feeling of strong friendship, though Mozart was evidently smitten by her and dedicated his concert aria "Ch'io mi scordi di te" to her. The emperor, it was said, wanted her for his mistress, but there is no evidence to support an actual liaison.

Nancy sang Sofronia in her brother's second opera, *Gli equivoci,* composed to an excellent libretto by Lorenzo da Ponte, based on *The Comedy of Errors,* and produced at the Burgtheater on 27 December 1786. In performances of that opera Nancy substituted for one of her brother's arias a song called "The Yellow-haired Laddie," in an arrangement by J. C. Bach. Stephen Storace, who was part of the boisterous English colony in Vienna, wrote to J. Serres in London on 21 February 1787 that he had lived in "one continual scene of riot" for six weeks and had been jailed several days for brawling at a ridotto. Late that month Nancy, Stephen, and their mother left Vienna, in the company of Michael Kelly and Thomas Attwood.

Kelly went to work at Drury Lane Theatre, where he made his London debut on 20 April 1787. Nancy and her brother were engaged at the King's Theatre, where the opera was under the new management of John Gallini, with Joseph Mazzinghi as the musical director. Billed as Sga Storace, she made her season's debut (and her first appearance in London since, at the age of 12, she had left the city) as Gelinda in *Gli schiavi per amore* on 24 April 1787. Bisiello's comic opera was under the direction of her brother, who had begun to supervise opera productions. Her success con-

tributed greatly to that opera's run of 19 performances before the end of the season. In that piece she took her benefit on 24 May 1787, when tickets were available from her at No 23, Howland Street, Rathbone Place. Her welcome at the King's Theatre, however, had not been the warm one that she and her brother had expected. These young intruders with reputations from Vienna perhaps were resented by Cherubini, the incumbent King's Theatre composer, and Madame Mara, the leading singer. On 3 July Stephen wrote to the British ambassador at Vienna: "My sister's success in London upon the whole has been as much as we could expect, though she had great opposition from the Italians, who consider it an infringement on their rights that any person should be able to sing that was not born in Italy. . . ."

In September 1787 she sang in the oratorios given in St Thomas's Church during the Salisbury Musical Festival. The *Salisbury Journal* reported "Signiora Storace's vocal powers and good taste prove her to have few superiors in the serious style; and in the comic she confessedly stands unrivalled." A month later at Salisbury she again sang, for the benefit of Joseph Corfe, and was once again "admired for her comic powers."

Nancy remained at the King's Theatre for two more seasons. She sang Lisetta in Paisiello's *Il re Teodoro in Venezia* on 8 December 1787. When she sang the role again on 12 January 1788 the orchestra played badly, but Sga Storace, reported the *Public Advertiser* on 17 January, "baffled the efforts of the musicians to make her sing out of tune, quick or slow. As they fiddled, she modulated." On 15 January 1788 she was Brillante in Cimarosa's *La locandiera,* and played Gelinda in *Gli schiavi per amore* on 5 February. On 5 March 1788 she appeared as Violetta in the premiere of her brother's *La cameriera astuta.* She took her benefit in that comic opera on 6 March 1788, when her address was still in Howland Street. And on 15 May 1788 she played an unspecified role in Paisiello's *La frascatana.* While singing in a performance of the oratorio *Israel in Egypt* at the Tottenham Street Concert Room on 22 February 1788, she went hoarse, and, evidently ill, "she sunk on her seat in a fit during the first act," reported the *Morning Chronicle* on 25 February, and "was so overcome with fatigue" that Madame Mara was sent for to sing a few numbers, she having finished her work that night in the Drury Lane oratorio. Sga Storace recovered sufficiently by the second act, however, to sing with Harrison the fine duet "The Lord is my strength." The following season she sang in the Covent Garden oratorios in February and March 1789. At the King's Theatre her roles were Agatina in *La vendemmia* and Rosina in the London premiere of Paisiello's setting of *Il barbiere di Siviglia*. The latter was premiered on 11 June 1789, when Sga Storace, still living in Howland Street, took her benefit. That season she also sang with Harrison and others in the concerts of ancient music in Tottenham Street. On 15 May 1789 she sang in the *Messiah* at the Freemasons' Hall and on 27 May she contributed to a program of Handelian music at St Margaret, Westminster, followed on 1 June by a concert for Marchesi at the Hanover Square Rooms. On 24, 25, and 26 of that month she went to sing for the Musical Society at the Oxford Music Room, where she returned many times during the rest of her career.

After the King's Theatre burned in 1789, Nancy and her brother went over to Drury Lane. She made her debut there as Adela in the premiere of James Cobb's *The Haunted Tower*, with music by Stephen Storace, on 24 November 1789. The critic in *The Country Magazine* for January 1790 reported that she spoke the dialogue "very articulately," and though her first song "shewed embarrassment," the acting in it was good, and her second song "was charmingly sung." That comic opera firmly established her reputation. It was a professional triumph for both Storaces and achieved 56 performances that season. *The Haunted Tower,* according to Roger Fiske, was "the most successful full-length opera that Drury Lane staged in the entire century." Stephen received £105 on 5 June 1790 "for 25th Night of Haunted Tower," but Nancy was paid more handsomely. The account books reveal that she received £10 each night she appeared in the piece. She received the first payment of £150 for 15 nights on 19 December 1789, other payments being made throughout the season.

Her only other role at Drury Lane in 1789–90 was Margaretta in Prince Hoare's *No Song No Supper,* again with Storace's music. She also

appeared as Mandina in *La villanella rapita* at the Haymarket Theatre on 27 February 1790 and eight other times. She was a featured singer in the oratorios at Drury Lane that season. She returned to the Haymarket to play Rosina in *Il barbiere di Siviglia* on 3 and 10 June; on the latter night she and Borselli sang "Orchietta Furbetti" from *La villanella rapita.* That summer she was also engaged to sing with Harrison and Meredith in the Norwich music festival led by Michael Sharp.

Still commanding £10 per night in 1790–91, Nancy played Adela and Margaretta and on 1 January 1791 appeared as Lilla in the premiere of James Cobb's *The Siege of Belgrade,* with music by Storace. The excellent cast, including Kelly as the Seraskier and Mrs Crouch as Catherine, contributed to the great success of that comic opera, which brought a nightly average of £250 during the 47 nights it ran. Nancy took her benefit as Lilla on 5 February 1791, when the net receipts were £239 (£357 less house charge of £118). Her only other role that season was Daphne in Prince Hoare and Storace's unsuccessful comic opera, *The Cave of Trophonius,* which had a single performance on 3 May 1791. The following season it played only twice.

For the next several seasons, while the new Drury Lane playhouse was being erected, the company played first at the new King's Theatre and then at the Haymarket. At the King's in 1791–92, she appeared infrequently, despite her salary of £60 for the season. Over fewer than 20 nights, most of them toward the beginning of the season, she played Adela, Margaretta, Daphne, and Lilla. After playing Lilla in *The Siege of Belgrade* on 24 October 1791, she was absent from the company for over six months, evidently recuperating from an operation. She reappeared on 21 May 1792 as Margaretta in *No Song No Supper.* She took her benefit in *The Siege of Belgrade* on 30 May 1792. Receipts were £525 less £159 house charges, and she still resided in Howland Street, Rathbone Place, now, however, at No 36.

In 1792–93 her salary was raised to £10 10s. per night. On 21 November 1792 she was the original Fabulina in Cobb and Storace's *The Pirates,* which had 30 performances that season. She sang in *Il barbiere di Siviglia* on 26 January and in the oratorio on 26 February 1793. She took her benefit on 11 March as

Harvard Theatre Collection

ANN STORACE, as Euphrosyne

engraving by Condé, after De Wilde

Fabulina, and in the afterpiece was the original Caroline in Hoare and Storace's *The Prize.* One reviewer described her as "clumsey" in person, with a face "coarse and ordinary," but she possessed "so much enchanting vivacity . . . that she always delights whenever she appears." In the summer of 1793, with Kelly, Morelli, and Rovedino she sang selections from *Le nozze di Dorina* and *I zingari in fiera* at the King's Theatre on 25 and 29 June. Advertised as making her only appearance of the season at the little Haymarket Theatre, she played Caroline in *The Prize* on 30 August 1793, for Bannister's benefit.

In the early part of 1793–94 the Drury Lane company disbanded temporarily, to await the opening of their new playhouse. With other performers from that company, Sga Storace joined the younger Colman, who took advantage of the situation by running his Haymarket Theatre, usually open only in summers, during the regular season. She played there as Caroline in *The Prize* on 30 September 1793 and as Margaretta in *No Song No Supper* on 23

October. Concerning the latter performance, the *Thespian Magazine* judged, "two or three songs were charmingly sung by Storace, but of her acting the less is said the better; she cannot look like a fine lady, let her disguise herself how she will." On 23 November she created the role of Fantast in the anonymous comic opera *Wives in Plenty!; Or, the More the Merrier,* which concluded with a musical medley by her and the younger Bannister. On 16 December 1793, for her benefit, she acted her usual role of Adela in *The Haunted House* and in the afterpiece was the original Florella in the premiere of Prince Hoare and Storace's *My Grandmother.* Her brother's songs, reported the *Public Advertiser* of 18 December, were very lively and well calculated "to afford her a complete opportunity of displaying that mixture of laughable levity, friskiness and merriment which on the stage give her so much attraction."

In February 1794 Sga Storace drew some criticism for failing to respond to a command for a performance at Buckingham Palace. The press reported that she "thought it a Fatigue" to play before their majesties in three different pieces on the same night, and that she was relieved from the command and was "condemn'd to the Mortification of not playing at all." In *More Money! Or, Odes of Instruction to Mister Pitt* (1794), "Peter Pindar" (John Wolcot) called her the "perverse Storace" and claimed that she had not obliged because she was expected to sing at "the old price"—"My compliments to your Master and Mistress," she is said to have told their Majesties' envoy, the violinist Nicolai, "and tell them I am better engaged."

On 6 March 1794 she offered a song in a concert program at the King's Theatre to benefit the New Musical Fund, to which she was listed as an honorary subscriber. The next month, on 14 April, she participated in a concert of sacred music with Incledon and Master Phelps at St Michael's Church in Bristol.

Sga Storace sang in the series of concerts of Handel's music that began on 12 March 1794 to celebrate the opening of the new Drury Lane Theatre. The first theatre piece she was seen in at the new theatre was *No Song No Supper* on 26 April 1794. She played Lilla in *The Siege of Belgrade* on 3 May, Florella in *My Grandmother* on 12 May, Caroline in *The Prize* the next night, and Fabulina in a revival of *The Pirates* on 16 May. On 2 July 1794 Sheridan presented the first night of his two-act entertainment *The Glorious First of June,* for the benefit of the widows and orphans of the men who had fallen in that recent naval action under Lord Howe; Sga Storace played Margaretta in five performances of that concoction, which was described by the *European Magazine* that month as "a sort of continuation of *No Song No Supper* . . . hastily put together for the occasion." The prompter recorded that on the first night it brought in better than 1300 guineas for the cause, free of house charges, and Sheridan generously paid the usual salaries of the performers, including Sga Storace's, which in her case came to £10 10*s.* per night.

In 1794–95 Sga Storace's salary at Drury Lane remained at £10 10*s.* per night, but she delayed her appearance that season until 20 October 1794, when she played Adela in *The Haunted Tower.* (She was to have played in *The Siege of Belgrade* on 13 October, but she informed Kemble that she would not play and "said Mr. Sheridan knew she was not to play; so did Stephan Storace.") After offering several roles in her regular repertoire, she was the original Eleanor in Cobb and Storace's *The Cherokee,* which was introduced on 20 December 1794 and ran 16 nights. Her next new character was Emma in the younger James Hook's comic opera, *Jack of Newbury* (with music by his father), on 6 May 1795. For her benefit on 18 May 1795, at which the receipts totaled £443 12*s.* free of charges, she made her first appearance as Clara in Sheridan's *The Duenna* and also sang a specialty lullaby. Her address was given as No 26, Howland Street, Fitzroy Square.

In the season of 1795–96 at Drury Lane, Sga Storace played intermittantly about 25 nights at £11 per night. She appeared as Rosina in the elder Colman's *The Spanish Barber* on 16 November 1795 and on 20 February 1796 created Letitia in Cobb's musical farce *The Shepherdess of Cheapside.* She was the original Barbara in the younger Colman's *The Iron Chest* on 12 March 1796, which Stephen Storace's music helped make a modest success despite Kemble's catatonic performance of the leading role of Sir Edward Mortimer. But soon after, on 19 March, the 33-year-old composer died from a violent "gout and fever." Sga Storace refused to play in the piece at its second performance, on the night her brother died, and was replaced by Miss Leak.

Stephen Storace had been preparing a production of a new music drama, *Mahmoud; or, The Prince of Persia,* in collaboration with Prince Hoare. Nancy and Kelly vamped up the music (which included adaptations from Paisiello, Haydn, and Sarti) and presented the opera at Drury Lane on 30 April 1796, with Nancy as Zelica, Kelly as Mossafer, and Kemble as the nonsinging Mahmoud. John Braham, whom Storace had heard sing at Bath and had hired for Drury Lane, was introduced in the role of Noureddin. Braham was encored three times and was an immediate success; the *Morning Herald* of 2 May 1796 pronounced him to be "the first public singer of the present day." On 9 May Sga Storace took her benefit, singing in *Mahmoud* and *My Grandmother* (in which Braham played opposite her as Woodly). According to *The London Stage* the receipts were £402, less £261 house charges. Nancy's address was then given as No 36, Howland Street. The accounts in the Folger Library record that the benefit was free of house charges. In addition to 15 performances in *Mahmoud* that season, Sga Storace appeared with many of London's principal singers and dancers on 25 May 1796 in a commemoration of Stephen Storace called *A Dramatic Cento,* presented at Drury Lane for the benefit of the composer's widow and son. On 8 June Nancy and Braham sang some favorite songs from *Mahmoud* and *The Haunted Tower,* for the benefit of the widow and children of the actor Robert Benson, who had recently committed suicide.

Nancy quickly fell in love with John Braham, who was 12 years her junior, and they formed an enduring relationship. When Braham joined the King's Theatre in 1796–97, Nancy, distressed by her brother's death and disillusioned with Drury Lane, also returned to the opera. John Williams (writing as Anthony Pasquin) in *A Pin Basket to the Children of Thespis* (1796) suggested that she had left Drury Lane because she was not being sufficiently paid (£11 per night), and he mentioned her reputation for being mercenary and stingy.

Before joining the company Sga Storace went to sing at Bath and Bristol, where she enjoyed great notice and received a benefit gift of £50 from the Duchess of York, who attended all her performances. The Royal Family attended a performance at Bath on 3 January 1797, and Mrs Powys recorded in her diary that when Sga Storace sang *"God save the King, I do believe half the audience shed Tears, as her manner, voice & action was beyond anything one could imagine."* On 14 March 1797 she reappeared at the King's Theatre as Gelinda in *Gli schiavi per amore.* On 18 April she sang Amore to Braham's Silvio in the first London performance of *L'albero di Diana,* a comic opera by Martini that had been popular all over Europe. The *Monthly Mirror* commented that Nancy had sung well but, "as this lady's figure is not of the most requisite form, we submit to her better judgment, the propriety of not again coming forward in *Breeches.*" She went over to Covent Garden on 26 April 1797 (her first appearance at that theatre) to sing Margaretta in *No Song No Supper* (and her lullaby) for Miss Wallis's benefit. She returned to Drury Lane to sing in *The Haunted Tower* for the benefit of her old friend Kelly, and on 21 June was once again at Covent Garden to sing with Braham in *The Duenna,* for the benefit of the General Lying-In Hospital. Announced as from the Opera House, Sga Storace and Braham played six nights, beginning on 21 July 1797, at the Birmingham Theatre.

In the autumn of 1797 Nancy and Braham left England for a concert tour of the Continent. They arrived first in Paris where they remained for eight months, both giving concerts under the patronage of Josephine Beauharnais. According to Oxberry, whose *Dramatic Biography* must be approached cautiously, the Paris public thronged to hear them, paying a louis per ticket although general admission to concerts was usually only six francs; and Braham and Storace, had they chosen, could have remained in Paris at an annual salary of 1400 louis. The *Monthly Mirror* in October 1797 printed a dispatch from Paris about their debut at the Theatre de la Rue Federace: "these singers, besides two solo pieces, performed a duet, in which they displayed that unison, harmony, and happy execution which belongs, we repeat, only to Italians." The *Mirror* took umbrage at the failure of its French correspondent to discern that both singers had been born in London. Arriving in Italy in 1798, they performed in Florence, Milan, Venice, Leghorn, Trieste, and Genoa. They moved on to Vienna, where offers from the London managers reached them, and they soon made their way home through Hamburg, arriving in London early in the winter of 1801.

With Braham she made her reappearance at Covent Garden Theatre on 9 December 1801 in *The Chains of the Heart,* a comic opera by Hoare and Mazzinghi, in which Sga Storace played Zulima. On 15 March 1802 she was Lilla to Braham's Seraskier in *The Siege of Belgrade.* Soon after, their son William Spencer Harris Braham was born at their lodgings in Leicester Square on 3 May 1802.

Nancy continued with Braham at Covent Garden through 1804–5, playing such roles as Katherine in T. Dibdin's *The English Fleet in 1342* on 13 December 1803, Eliza (to Braham's Herbert) in Prince Hoare's *The Paragraph* on 3 March 1804, Rosanna in T. Dibdin's *Thirty Thousand* on 10 December 1804, and Lauretta in Reynolds's *Out of Place* on 28 February 1805. In the summer of 1805 they sang for six nights at Brighton. Subsequently they engaged at Drury Lane, where her first appearance was as Lilla in *The Siege of Belgrade* on 2 November 1805. Then she performed Floretta in *The Cabinet* on 12 November 1805, the Marchioness Merida in *The Travellers* on 22 June 1806, the original Susan in Kenney's *False Alarms* on 12 January 1807, Wowski in *Inkle and Yarico* for her benefit on 13 April 1807, the original Rozella in Brandon's *Kais; or, Love in the Deserts* on 11 February 1808 (with music by Braham), and the first Mammora in Cumberland's *The Jew of Mogadore* on 3 May 1808. By that time her salary was no longer at its former high mark of £11 per night, but was set, according to an account book now in the British Library (Add. 29710) at £15 per week. On 6 June 1807 she was paid £5000 "on Account of Salary," and her benefit on 13 April 1807 brought in £430 1s. 6d.

She took her farewell benefit at Drury Lane on 30 May 1808, playing Floretta in *The Cabinet* (not Margaretta in *No Song No Supper,* as Kelly incorrectly recalled) and delivering an address written for her by the younger Colman. The receipts were £251 5s. 6d. She then retired to her Herne Hill Cottage, in Dulwich, where her mother also lived. (In the Garrick Club is a letter from Nancy to carpet installers about measurements of a carpet that was in her drawing room in Great Russell Street but was to be placed in the drawing room at Herne Hill.)

Nancy's liaison with John Braham lasted some 20 years. Byron designated the *amour* as the "Only thing of this kind known to last." But Braham in 1816 deserted the soprano who had lived with him so long as his wife. He ran off to France with a Mrs Wright, whose husband promptly sued Braham for criminal conversation. The great vocalist was hissed for his actions by the audience at the Drury Lane oratorio on 16 March 1816. Damages of £1000 were awarded to Wright that year. But then Braham married Miss Frances Elizabeth Bolton of Ardwick, near Manchester. Numerous letters between Nancy Storace and Braham now in the Sir John Soane Museum, as Roger Fiske has pointed out, reveal their personalities. They "reflect no credit" on John Braham, especially, though perhaps it was understandable that he should have wanted a legitimate family. Miss Bolton gave him two daughters and four sons.

Braham's desertion and marriage, it was said, hastened Nancy Storace's death. She died of a brain hemorrhage about a year and a half after his departure, at Dulwich on 24 August 1817, and was buried at St Mary's Church in Lambeth, where her mother placed a memorial tablet.

In her will drawn on 10 August 1797 (20 years prior to her death), she called herself Anna Selina Storace, of Howland Street, parish of Saint Pancras. Her executors Joseph Burchell and Prince Hoare were directed to pay interest from her £5000 in East India stocks to her mother Elizabeth Storace so long as she should live, and thereafter it was to be applied to the education of her nephew Brinsley John Storace, son of Stephen Storace, until the age of 21, whereupon he was to receive the principle. If he should die before 21 then the whole should go to the children of her cousin Emily Toosy, of Duke Street, Bloomsbury. The same sequence of descent, beginning with her mother, was to apply to the leasehold on her house in Howland Street, and the plate, linen, and furnishings. (As it turned out, the nephew Brinsley John Storace died in February 1807 at the age of 19.) Nancy left £500 to her aunt Miss Catherine Trusler and £200 to her aunt Miss Sarah Trusler. To Mary Storace, her brother's widow, she gave £500 and all her clothes.

(In the autumn of 1801, Mary Storace married the Rev. J. Kennedy, curate of Kimcotte.) Her harp and all her music Nancy bequeathed to her old singing teacher, the eminent Bath musician Venanzio Rauzzini. (But he had died in 1810, and Nancy and Braham had erected a monumental plaque to him in Bath Abbey.) Other bequests included £500 to Arthur Corfe, a musician of Salisbury, £100 to Joseph Burchell, and £50 to Prince Hoare. She generously contributed £1000 to the Old Musical Fund (the Royal Society of Musicians) and the same amount to the New Musical Fund.

The will is also distinguished by a bequest of £2000 to John Braham, of Air Street, Piccadilly. The will was made about a year after she first met him, and there is no evidence that it was altered or that any codicils were added, so Braham probably received the money when the will was proved on 11 October 1817. Nancy made no mention of her husband John Abraham Fisher, who did not die until 1806, at which time she would have been free to marry Braham.

Bequests in her will totaled £11,200, not including real estate and personal property. The estate was sworn at probate at under £50,000.

Not mentioned in her will of 1797, of course, was her son William Spencer Harris Braham, born in 1802. After Nancy's death he was cared for by his grandmother Elizabeth Storace, who sent him to Winchester College and, by her will, dated 12 September 1817, left him her estate in trust, provided that at the age of 23 he would take the surname of Storace instead of or in addition to Braham. Elizabeth Storace died in May 1821, at 82. Her funeral of the twenty-first of that month was attended by John Braham.

In the spring of 1824 William Spencer Harris Braham had considered suing for the whole of his mother's estate, which had passed to his recently deceased grandmother Elizabeth Storace. A long letter from him to his father John Braham, written shortly before mid-April 1824 (and now in the Strachie collection, Somerset Record Office, Taunton), is worth quoting at length:

My mother, Anna Selina Storace, was married to a M⸰ Fisher, at the age of eighteen or nineteen, in Vienna, about 1780, and I believe in the English

Harvard Theatre Collection

ANN STORACE, as Clara

engraving by Ryder, after Craven

also I gained thus much of the above statement). . . . I hear she allowed Mr Fisher a sum of money not to molest her, but that he would retire, and live quite away from her. There exists a Will made by my Mother, the original of which is in her own handwriting, and dated the 10th of August 1797, five years previous to my birth, by which she has distributed her property among certain of her relatives and when it was the only will found at her death in Sept^{tr} 1817, and which has since been acted upon. Mr Joseph Burchell principal Executor, under idea of a more recent document appearing threw it unto Chancery, and has reserved for himself a power of *Indemnity*. The question of importance then is this: had Madame Storace a legal right, being at the time a married woman, to make a Will at all? and to sign that will in her maiden name Storace, instead of Fisher, her name by right of Marriage: it is quite certain Fisher was living at the time of her making this will, and that he did not die till the year 1800 according to the opinion of some, though I am inclined to believe it was not till 1804 or 1805 [*evidently 1806*]: if the latter, which I have since ascertained to be the case, my claim is still stronger, as the law would consider me as the child of M^r & Mrs Fisher being born in wedlock, unless *non access* be proved, which I hear is extremely difficult: and in that case supposing this Will to be invalid, I should claim the property as her heir at law, she having died as *intestate:* supposing Fisher has died previous to the year of my birth (1802) that claim would be done away with but then Mrs Storace my Grandmother was the legal heiress of my mother and I residuary legatee of Mrs Storace thus, I should have a double claim. Fisher at the time of his death was a Doctor of music, I suppose: but he was a natural Son of Lord Tyrawley's and consequently could have no heirs in wedlock, as I hear died *intestate*. Therefore I have no fear of any one else starting up with a claim from that quarter. Mr Fisher taught music in the family of Sir O. Wynn of Hazelwood near Sligo, in Ireland, and who now is present M. P. for Sligo, and died in his house dependent upon him. . . .

His father replied on 15 April 1824, urging Spencer—as he called his son—not to press the suit as it could prove to be very costly in financial and personal terms. Spencer seems to have heeded the advice. And on 21 May 1824 administration of his grandmother's will was granted to him. He had matriculated at Lincoln College, Oxford, in 1822, and received his B. A. in 1826 and his M. A. in 1829. Eventually he took orders in the Anglican Church, changed his name to Meadows, and served out his days as a Minor Canon

Protestant Church. How long they lived together as Man and Wife I am unable to say, but I understand not for any considerable time. They separated by mutual consent, and the Emperor . . . granted her a *Release* or *Immunity* from all obligations to her husband, but which did not amount to a legal divorce; and the question is whether even such an agreement made in that country could be valid here? and this will induce me to believe there was no divorce; the circumstances of her having transferred the whole of her property to the hand of three individuals to act as trustees, namely Mr Joseph Burchell Senr the late Dr Parsons of Doctor's Commons and Mr Prince Hoare travelling associate of the Royal Academy in London, who was present at Vienna during the years 1780–82 (and from whom at Canterbury Cathedral and as a rector of Coldon.

(The possibility that Nancy actually had a total of three children by Braham should be noted, though no mention of more than one has survived. In a satirical print published at the time of Braham's elopement with Mrs Wright in 1816, Sga Storace is pictured as the deserted woman in England, reclining on the ground in a theatrical pose, singing a lament. Standing behind her are three children, of equal height, singing vigorously.)

When Nancy Storace had returned to London to make her adult debut as a singer, Dr Burney judged her "a lively and intelligent actress, and an excellent performer in comic operas," but, as he wrote in his *History of Music,* "her voice, in spite of all her care, does not favour her ambition to appear as a *serious* singer. There is a certain crack and toughness." But Nancy seems to have had no ambition for *"serious"* singing, and confined herself to lighter fare. She did, of course, appear regularly in the spring oratorios, and was especially magnificent in the Handelian memorial concerts at Westminster Abbey, "for in that space," wrote Lord Mount-Edgecumbe, "the harsh part of her voice was lost, while its power and clearness filled the whole of it." Fiske in *English Theatre Music in the Eighteenth Century* (where a detailed discussion of the musical pieces in which she appeared can be found) credits her with setting "new standards in comic opera by her vivacity and infectious good humour." Nancy possessed a short and clumsy figure, a lusty dark complexion, and a certain vulgarity of manner. John Williams (as Anthony Pasquin) in *A Pin Basket to the Children of Thespis* wrote, however:

> With her jigs and her jerks and her tartness of manner,
> She has form'd a new corps, and uprais'd her own banner.
> She's a pye-bald exotic our ballad lays chanting,
> But her naivete's triumphant where beauty is wanting;
> She has fire unfelt by the commonknit throng,
> And happily mingles her mind with her song. . . .

Unfortunately she persisted well beyond her prime in playing characters no longer suited to her growing girth, so that her retirement was not universally regretted. But she had been a fine comic actress and an admirably finished singer, who perhaps enjoyed more acclaim abroad than at home. It has been suggested that her obituaries and posthumous accounts of her talents were downplayed in deference to Braham.

In his *Dramatic Biography* (1825), Oxberry repeated stories about her reputed stinginess to her brother and her husband Fisher. Supposedly after Fisher was driven from Vienna and was suffering consumption in Ireland he applied to her for £10 to relieve his distresses and she refused him. It was also said that she insisted on being paid her usual nightly salary of £10 when she was asked to appear for the benefit of the Drury Lane Theatrical Fund, but she returned the fee when the story got into the papers. It should be noted, however, that she bequeathed large sums of money to professional organizations.

A number of songs which were published as sung by her in the various comic operas are listed throughout the *Catalogue of Printed Music in the British Museum.*

Portraits of Sga Storace include:

1. By Louis d'Ami Artaud. Exhibited at the Royal Academy, 1796. Present location unknown.

2. By Thomas Beach. Half-length, 29″ × 24¼″, wearing a white dress with a black hat, holding sheets of music. At one time in the possession of the Hoskens family, Ellenglaze Manor, Newquay, Cornwall. Sold at Sotheby's on 18 November 1987 (lot 53) for £3080; illustrated in the sale catalogue.

3. By John Downman. Blue chalk and wash drawing. In the collection of J. P. Hesletine in 1920; offered in the Leverhulme sale at Anderson's, New York, 2–4 March 1926. Present location unknown; a photograph of it is in the Witt Library, Courtauld Institute of Art.

4. By William Grimaldi (8th Marquis of Grimaldi). Miniature signed and dated 1795. Once in the possession of the Earl of Wharncliffe. Owned by Daphne Foskett and reproduced in her *British Portrait Miniaturists* (1963), plate 117.

5. By unknown artist. Miniature in the Sir John Soane Museum.

6. Engraved portrait by P. Bettelini. Published by Molteno, Colnaghi & Co, 1788.

7. Engraved portrait by J. Condé. Published as a plate to the *Thespian Dictionary,* 1793.

8. Engraved portrait by J. Godefroy. Published by Molinari, 1797.

9. Engraved portrait, in silhouette, by Loeschenkohl, Vienna. In the collection of the Hoftheater, Vienna.

10. As Adela in *The Haunted Tower*. Pencil, grey wash and watercolor by John Nixon, 1790. In the Garrick Club.

11. As Catherine in *The English Fleet in 1342*. By Michael W. Sharp, exhibited at the Royal Academy, 1804. In the Thomas Harris sale on 12 July 1819 (lot 26); then in the Charles Mathews collection. Now in the Garrick Club (No 416).

12. As Clara in *The Duenna*. Engraving by T. Ryder, after Miss Craven. Published by S. Watts, 1790.

13. As Euphrosyne in *Comus*. By Samuel De Wilde. Present location unknown. An engraving by Condé—"from the original Picture which was painted from life by De Wilde"—was published by Bell, 1791; a copy was engraved by Thornthwaite and published as a plate to *Bell's British Theatre*, 1791; another copy, engraved by Thomas, was also issued.

14. As Euphrosyne. Engraving by Thornthwaite, after Corbould. Published by J. Bell, 1791.

15. As Euphrosyne. By unknown engraver. Similar to above, No 13. Printed by C. Cooke, 1809.

16. As Euphrosyne. Caricature, standing, full-face, feathers in hair and flowers in right hand. By unknown engraver. Published as a plate to the *Attic Miscellany*, 1 July 1792.

17. As Lilla, with John Bannister as Leopold, in *The Siege of Belgrade*. Engraving by Barlow, after Cruikshank. Published by J. Roach, 1790.

Storace, Stephen   *d. c. 1783, double-bass player, composer, band director, fireworks designer.*

Stephen Storace, a native of Torre Annunziata near Naples, had immigrated to England by 1747. He anglicized his first name from Stefano, but, as Roger Fiske points out in *English Theatre Music in the Eighteenth Century*, there is no evidence to support Michael Kelly's story that he also changed his surname from Sorace because of its vulgar connotation if pronounced in the French manner. It does seem that Storace continued to sound his surname

according to the Italian pronunciation, and in the first notice we have of him, in fact, his name was spelled Storachi. It appeared in an advertisement of a concert for Castiglione's benefit at Cooper's Hall in Bristol on 11 September 1747; he was announced as one of the musicians, without an instrument specified.

By 1749–50 Storace was in Dublin, serving as director of the band at the New Gardens. In the spring of 1751 he was involved in a dispute with Thomas Sheridan concerning permission for the Crow Street Theatre musicians to play at the New Gardens. In 1751 Storace and four others (John Baxted Murell, Joseph de Boeck, Daniel Sullivan, and Samuel Lee) leased the Crow Street Music Hall from Peter Bardin for six years at an annual rent of £113 15s. The hall was located on the north side of Cecilia Street, near Crow Street. The lease granted Bardin two free tickets to the premises "to view any play, opera, or music meeting exhibited or performed there." Storace's grasp of English was demonstrated in a letter to the *Gentleman's Magazine* in September 1753 describing how the deadly effect of the bite of the tarantula could be averted by the victim dancing a wild tarantella.

By the late 1750s Storace was in London. According to the *Thespian Dictionary* (1805), he was performing with "considerable celebrity" on the double bass and was engaged for that instrument in the band of the King's Theatre; but no record survives to that effect.

In his *Dramatic Biography* (1825), Oxberry stated that at one time Storace kept Marylebone Gardens, where he was assisted by his wife and sisters in making fancy pastries. But Oxberry confused Storace with John Trusler, who was the proprietor there from about 1751 to 1763. Storace, however, was very much involved in the entertainments at Marylebone Gardens in 1758. With the younger John Trusler (his future brother-in-law), Storace adapted and translated the first burletta to be given at Marylebone Gardens, Pergolesi's *La serva padrona*, which opened on 8 June 1758 and proved to be exceedingly popular, playing almost every night that summer. The following year *La serva padrona*, announced to be under the direction of Signor Storace and Mr Oswald, was scheduled for production at the Haymarket Theatre on 12 January 1759, but the performance was canceled by "a particular order of the Lord Chamberlain." The *Public Advertiser* that day affirmed that "as a great many of the Nobility and Quality are very desirous to see this Entertainment, it will be soon presented at another theatre." On 21 February 1759 a license was granted to Stephen Storace and James Oswald, "the Managers of the Burletta, exhibited last year at Marylebone to perform the said Burletta at the Little Theatre in the Haymarket for 3 Nights only & those not to be Opera Nights." *La serva padrona* finally made its way to the Haymarket stage on 29 March 1759 and was repeated on 2 and 5 April. That year Oswald published the "Favourite Songs," with Storace's translation. During the following decade the burletta was revived regularly at Marylebone Gardens.

The Coquette, translated from Goldoni's *La Cicisbea alla moda,* by Storace, who also adapted Galuppi's original music, was played at Marylebone Gardens in 1759, as was Storace's adaptation of *La strattaggemma,* ascribed variously to Pergolesi and to Hasse. In the summer of 1760 Storace and the Truslers disputed the ownership of the rights to the "Books" (libretti) of the burlettas performed at the Gardens. The Truslers contended that the only "genuine Books" were "to be had of Mrs. Trusler at the Bar of the Gardens" and warned that others were counterfeit. Storace published a counter-claim in the *Public Advertiser* (quoted by Mollie Sands in *The Eighteenth-Century Pleasure Gardens of Marylebone*) assuring "that the Books of the several Burlettas sold at the Door are the same Books that have been performed there, and those sold at the Bar are Copies pirated from me. . . ."

In September and October 1760 Signor Storace was working at the Theatre Royal in Norwich. On 16 June 1761 at St James, Piccadilly, he married Elizabeth Trusler (1739–1821), one of the daughters of the Marylebone proprietor. He continued to be involved at the Gardens until at least 1772. In the summer of 1769 he designed an intricate firework display for the pyrotechnist Clanfield's execution, on the occasion of his benefit. In 1770 *La serva padrona* was performed several times, and Storace had a benefit on 7 August, when the bills announced, "The Whole adapted to the original Music of Pergolesi by Storace." His adaptation of *The Coquette* was revived in August 1771 and was published that year. His benefit

at Marylebone Gardens that summer was on 20 August 1771. The following summer, when *The Coquette* was again played, he enjoyed two benefits, on 31 August and 2 September 1772.

From 1759, Storace also had played double bass at the annual Three Choirs Festival, and he was the arranger of the appearances made by Elizabeth Linley (later Mrs R. B. Sheridan) at those meetings. In 1773 Storace was living at No 72, Marylebone High Street, where the Sheridans came to visit after their honeymoon. With his wife and daughter, Storace went to Naples at Christmas 1778 to visit his son. Fiske suggests that the elder Storace died in Italy about 1783. In 1784 the *European Magazine* referred to him as the "late Stephen Storace so well known for his performance on the double Bass for many years in this kingdom."

The death of Storace's widow occurred at Brompton on 13 May 1821, at the age of 82, and she was buried on 21 May. Some information about Mrs Storace's parents and sisters is given in our notice of John Trusler. Stephen and Elizabeth Storace's children, Stephen Storace (1762–1796), a prominent composer and music director, and Ann Selina Storace (1765–1817), a famous singer, are noticed separately in these pages.

Storace, Stephen John Seymour   *1762–1796, composer, conductor, instrumentalist, manager.*

An affidavit in the files of the Royal Society of Musicians establishes that Stephen John Seymour Storace was born on 4 April 1762 and baptized at St James, Westminster, on 6 May 1762. That document corrects the date of 4 January 1763 given for his birth in previous biographies. He was the son of Stephen Storace (d. c. 1783), a Neapolitan immigrant who played double bass in Dublin and London and was band director at Marylebone Gardens from about 1758 to 1772. The younger Stephen's mother was Elizabeth Trusler, a daughter of John Trusler, proprietor of Marylebone Gardens.

Tutored by his father, by the age of ten Storace was a violin virtuoso. By 1776 he was placed in the San Onofrio Conservatorio at Naples for the study of composition, harpsichord, and violin. While at Naples he lived with an uncle who was a bishop. In 1779

By permission of the British Library Board

STEPHEN JOHN SEYMOUR STORACE

artist unknown

Storace joined his sister, the singer Anna Selina Storace, in her concert tour of the Continent. Colorful accounts of the young Storaces abroad are provided by their companion Michael Kelly in his *Reminiscences*. According to Roger Fiske, *English Theatre Music in the Eighteenth Century*, Storace returned to England several times during the period that his sister stayed in Europe. About 1782 he published a set of canzonets, one set to verses from Gray's *Elegy*. He also published two quintets and a sextet, and *Three Sonatas for the Harpsichord or Pianoforte* (1785?).

While in Vienna Storace became acquainted with Mozart, who influenced his style, but there is no evidence that he was tutored by that genius, as is sometimes claimed. Vienna heard Storace's first opera, *Gli sposi malcontenti,* at the Burgtheater on 1 June 1785 when in the middle of the first act, Sga Storace, before the Emperor, completely lost her voice. The opera, to a libretto by Brunati, was never performed in London, though it played subsequently in several German cities and in Paris. It was never published, but a full manuscript score survives in the Dresden Sächisches Landeshauptarchiv Museum. Storace's second opera, *Gli equivoci,* with an excellent libretto by Da Ponte based on *The Comedy of Errors,* was produced at the Burgtheater on 27 December 1786. Manuscript full scores of this opera, described as "Eines italienisches Singspiel," are at Dresden and Vienna. In the Harvard Theatre Collection is a letter by Storace written on 21 February 1787 from Vienna to J. Serres at London, in which he explains that owing to a ridiculous circumstance which happened the previous night he was composing the letter from a prison cell. From Storace's account it is evident that the English colony at Vienna was prone to cutting up in boisterous fashion, and that he had the last six weeks lived in "one continual scene of riot." He had been jailed for starting a row at a ridotto, after some unmannerly gentleman kept bumping into his sister Anna and her escort Lord Barnard and addressing them in vulgar language. Expecting to be "liberated" soon, Storace informed Serres he planned to leave Vienna the next Saturday, visit the Bavarian cities, then move on to Paris.

In March 1787 Storace returned to England with his sister, mother, and Kelly. At Drury Lane Theatre, on 20 April 1787, the occasion of Kelly's first appearance on the London stage, Kelly sang a duet composed by himself and Storace. By that time, Storace was supervising opera production at the King's Theatre, where on 24 April 1787 Sga Storace returned after an absence of 10 years to sing in *Gli schiavi per amore,* Paisiello's comic opera, under the direction of her brother.

Quarrels and petty jealousies at the King's, it is said, soon drove Storace to Bath, where he taught drawing for a while and considered giving up music. He was, however, again working in the London theatres in 1787–88. Some of his music, selected by Shield, was used in the premiere of O'Keeffe's *The Farmer* at Covent Garden Theatre on 31 October 1787. At the King's Theatre on 8 December 1787 a mixture of airs by Storace, Mazzinghi, and Corri were used in the premiere of Paisiello's burletta *Il re Teodoro;* his song *Care donne che bramate,* sung in the opera by Sga Storace, was published that year. That season Storace was again directing operas at the King's, where on 4 March 1788 his own comic opera *La cameriera astuta* was premiered, with his sister as Violetta. On 6 March the critic in the *Public Advertiser* observed:

. . . Signor Storace does not appear to have studied that art [of music] much in Italy; for he has entirely deviated from the usual plan of Italian authors. . . . The overture announces entirely a French author, and the finales are in the German style of Gluck, loaded with harsh, terrifying music of trumpeting and drumming.

Scores for the overture, a favorite quartet, and several airs from *La cameriera astuta* were published in 1788.

On 3 August 1788 Samuel Arnold recommended Storace for membership in the Royal Society of Musicians, at which time he was described as a teacher of harpsichord and singing, and a composer and publisher of music, age 26, and single. A note was added to the file on 7 September 1788 revealing that since the original date of recommendation Storace had married. His new wife, whom he had married on 23 August 1788, was Mary Hall, the third daughter of the London engraver John Hall (1739–1797), who is noticed in *The Dictionary of National Biography,* and his wife Mary de Gilles. (Her brother, George William Hall [1770–1843], became master of Pembroke College, Oxford.) Storace was admitted to the Society on 7 December 1788 and served as a governor in 1793. He played violin in the Society's annual May benefit concerts at St Paul's from 1789 to 1792.

Storace advanced his reputation as a composer by providing additional music and arranging Dittersdorf's score of the opera *The Doctor and the Apothecary,* which was presented at Drury Lane on 25 October 1788 in an adaptation by James Cobb. The score was also published that year. Some of Storace's music was added to Gazzaniga's score of *La vendemmia* at the King's on 9 May 1789. Great success came to Storace's three-act opera *The Haunted Tower,* with text by Cobb, which opened at Drury Lane on 24 November 1789 and played

a total of 56 times that season. The score was published that year, and several songs from the opera were issued separately. On 5 June 1790 Cobb and Storace were paid £105 "for 25th Night of Haunted Tower." Also introduced that season on 16 April 1790 was Prince Hoare's *No Song No Supper,* with music composed chiefly by Storace, who also selected pieces from Pleyel, Harrington, Gluck, and others.

The rest of Storace's career was devoted mainly to Drury Lane, where his operas were supported by his sister and Kelly in the leading roles. He provided most of the music for Cobb's comic opera *The Siege of Belgrade* on 1 January 1791, Hoare's *The Cave of Trophonius* on 3 May 1791, Cobb's *Poor Old Drury* on 23 September 1791, a musical adaptation of Garrick's *Cymon* on 31 December 1791, and *Dido Queen of Carthage* (with the *Masque of Neptune's Prophesy*) on 23 May 1792.

Among his greater successes was the score for Cobb's comic opera *The Pirates,* which was premiered by the Drury Lane company at the King's Theatre on 21 November 1792 and ran 30 performances that season. It is said that Greenwood's scenery for that opera, which is set on the coast south of Naples, was based on sketches Storace had made when visiting that area earlier in his life. Greenwood's scene of the Bay of Naples and the eruption of Mount Vesuvius was published as the title-page to the vocal score of *The Pirates* in 1792; the view is reproduced with Storace's entry in the *New Grove* and in volume 7 of the *New Oxford History of Music* (1973). Storace wrote additional music for a tournament introduced into *Cymon* on 23 January 1793 and provided the score to Hoare's *The Prize* on 11 March 1793, in which Sga Storace played. She took a benefit that evening.

In 1792–93 Storace also was employed as composer to the theatre and harpsichordist for the operas at the King's Theatre, where under his direction were produced Paisiellos' *Il barbiere di Siviglia* on 26 January 1793, *La nozze di Dorina,* with music by Storace, Sarti, and Martini on 26 February (it contained Noverre's ballet *Venus and Adonis,* with Storace's music), and the London premiere of Paisiello's *I zingari in fiera* on 14 May. In the oratorio at Covent Garden on 20 February 1793 Mrs Crouch sang

Storace's ballad "Captivity," supposed to have been sung by Marie Antoinette during her confinement in the Tower of the Temple.

Some of Storace's music was used in *Wives in Plenty,* an anonymous comic opera produced on 23 November 1793 at the Haymarket. There also, on 16 December 1793, was first performed Hoare's *My Grandmother,* composed by Storace, the night his sister took a benefit. The *Public Advertiser* of 18 December reported that the very lively and agreeable tunes afforded Sga Storace "a complete opportunity of displaying that mixture of laughable levity, friskiness, and merriment which on the stage give her so much attraction." That year Storace was involved in some legal action: the Minute Books of the Royal Society of Musicians record on 1 December 1793 that "Mr Charles Manners having paid the Storaces £100 to avoid indictment, they presented it to the society."

With the elder Thomas Linley, Storace directed the series of oratorios with which the new Drury Lane Theatre was inaugurated in March 1794. On 9 January 1794 Kemble's *Lodoiska* was presented there with some music composed by Storace and other pieces adapted by him from Cherubini, Kreutzer, and Androzzi. He also composed the music for Sheridan and Cobb's entertainment *The Glorious First of June* on 2 July 1794. It was a busy year for Storace, for he also served as co-acting manager with Kelly of the operas at the King's Theatre.

Storace and Cobb's successful comic opera *The Cherokee* was introduced at Drury Lane on 20 December 1794, and his and Hoare's musical farce *The Three and the Deuce* was produced by the younger Colman at the Haymarket on 2 September 1795.

Sometime in 1795 Storace was invited by Sheridan to join him in the proprietorship of Drury Lane. The composer declined the partnership, writing to Sheridan (in an undated letter) of "the absurdity of my entering into any engagement with you *singly.*" He did offer a counterproposal to buy some 29 or 37 shares that Sheridan intended to put forward. When the theatre opened for the 1795–96 season, Sheridan's new partners were John Grubb and Joseph Richardson.

At Drury Lane on 12 March 1796 Colman's *The Iron Chest* was performed for the first time,

with Storace's music making it a modest success, though later it became a repertory standby. The anxieties and problems of bringing the music drama to production, however, took a heavy toll on Storace, already considerably weakened by severe attacks of gout. He caught cold and developed a dangerous fever. "Poor Storace is so ill with gout and fever," reported the *True Briton,* "that it is hardly supposed he will recover. He is principally attacked in the head, and it is said that on Saturday (the first night of *The Iron Chest*) his disorder was so violent as to deprive him wholly of his sight." He died on 19 March 1796 at his home, No 27, Percy Street, Rathbone Place, about a month short of his thirty-fourth birthday. He was buried in a small church at the top of Marylebone High Street. When it was torn down in 1949, Storace's memorial was removed to the parish church nearby; the inscription incorrectly gives 16 March 1796 as his date of death.

Before he died Storace had been preparing the production of a new music drama, *Mahmoud; or, The Prince of Persia,* again in collaboration with Hoare. Kelly and Sga Storace completed Storace's part of the music (Paisiello, Haydn, and Sarti were also represented), and *Mahmoud* was presented at Drury Lane on 30 April 1796, with John Braham and Sga Storace as leading singers and Kemble in the title role. The piece was deemed long and tedious, but Braham's singing kept it running for 15 performances, one of which, on 25 May 1796, was given for the benefit of Storace's "Widow and Orphan." The performance, at which selections from others of Storace's operas were also played, was intended as a "Commemoration" to him and brought his widow £657, less £244 house charges. Prince Hoare also gave over his proceeds as author to the widow.

Administration of Storace's estate, valued under £5000, was granted on 3 May 1796 to his widow Mary Storace, formerly of Percy Street, but late of Hayes, where he had left her a house. (It was subsequently used as council offices until it was demolished about 1960.) Their only child, Brinsley John Storace, who became a pupil of John Soane, died in February 1807; if at the time of his death he was 19, as claimed by the *Gentlemen's Magazine,* then he would have been born prior to the marriage of his parents in August 1788.

In 1797 Mrs Storace printed *The Favourite Operas of Mahmoud & the Iron Chest . . . adapted for the Piano Forte or Harpsichord by J. Maz-zinghi*, at the high price of 25s. The list of some 400 subscribers, headed by the Princess of Wales and the Duchess of York, included many stage people. Mary Storace continued to receive periodic payments from Drury Lane Theatre—for example £50 on 12 March 1799 and £100 on 4 January 1800—evidently in payment of salary and other fees still owed her husband by a notoriously debt-ridden Sheridan. The *Monthly Mirror* in November 1801 announced that the widow of the late eminent musician Stephen Storace had been recently married to the Rev J. Kennedy, curate of Kim-cotte.

His friend and colleague Michael Kelly called Storace "the most gifted creature I ever met with! an enthusiast and a genius. But in music and painting he was positively occult! I have often heard Mr. Sheridan say, that if he had been bred to the law, he thought he would have been Lord Chancellor."

A list of Storace's published works, which includes some 15 operas, various songs, overtures, and instrumental music, is provided in the *Catalogue of Printed Music in the British Museum*. Many of his songs were also published in America. Fiske in the *New Grove* states that except for *No Song No Supper* the full scores and orchestral parts of his operas were lost in the several fires that plagued London theatres early in the nineteenth century. Storace's operas were rendered popular in their time by his gift for melody. Mozart's influence can be heard in his instrumentation, and he frequently borrowed from the Italians. His more elaborate arias in the Italian style, it is said, were devised to show off his sister and Kelly in that technique. But Storace also had an original talent for English songwriting. As Fiske points out, Storace "was trying to write opera of a kind new to the playhouse." Instead of standing in a straight line facing the audience, his singers continued to act in the scenes as they sang. A fine account and analysis of Storace's music is provided by Fiske in *English Theatre Music in the Eighteenth Century.*

The portrait of Stephen Storace on the title page of the 1797 edition of *The Favourite Operas*

of Mahmoud & The Iron Chest evidently was drawn from memory by an unknown artist after the composer's death.

Storer, Charles *d. c. 1765, actor, singer.*

Charles Storer was born "in the Town of Lancaster," according to W. R. Chetwood in *A General History of the Stage* (1749). He played in country companies for some years before he entered into any established theatre. Storer's wife Elizabeth (née Clark) was playing in the Smock Alley troupe in Dublin as early as 1742–43, but there is no trace of her husband in surviving records until 1746–47, when both husband and wife turned up on the Smock Alley roster. They, with the rest of the company, signed a petition to the Lord Lieutenant, submitted at the end of February 1747, beseeching him to reopen the theatre, closed by the Lords Justices after the Kelly riots against Thomas Sheridan.

Both the Storers played in the company which was at Richmond and Twickenham from August through mid-October 1747. The scattered bills yield only the roles of Fribble in *Miss in Her Teens,* Billy Fluter in *Diversions of the Morning,* and Laertes in *Hamlet* for Charles. Her entr'acte singing, already acclaimed in Dublin, may have secured the offers of the contracts at Covent Garden which both Elizabeth and Charles signed for the next season. Certainly she was to outshine her husband wherever they went. Charles made his debut at Covent Garden on 23 November in the minor farcical role of Pallas in *The Rehearsal.* During the balance of the season he added several minor supporting parts in his comic line—Guildenstern in *Hamlet,* Vulture in *The Country Lasses,* and Lieutenant (Brakenbury) in *Richard III,* Jack Stanmore in *Oroonoko,* the Second Merchant in *The Royal Merchant,* Cabinet in *The Funeral,* Bellamoure in *Wit without Money,* Easy in *The Fair Quaker of Deal,* Lissardo in *The Wonder,* Westmoreland in *1 Henry IV,* Beau in *Drums Demolish'd,* Dr Bolus in *The Double Gallant,* and Coupée in *The Virgin Un-mask'd.* During the season Storer and his wife lodged at the corner of New Broad Court, Bow Street. Charles Storer found employment at the Bartholomew Fair booth of Bridges, Cross, Burton, and Vaughan in the George Inn Yard on 24 August 1748 playing Slim in *The Volunteers.* The Storers also played again in the

Richmond-Twickenham summer company and returned to Dublin in time for the opening of the Smock Alley season of 1748–49.

In 1749 Chetwood gave Charles Storer his only surviving criticism:

His good Understanding keeps him within the Bounds of his own Power, which is the ready Road never to meet with Displeasure. I think his Talent leads him to old Men in Comedy, and the artificial Wrinkles in his Face seem to content him best, which is something singular with young Persons in a Theatre. . . . I have seen him give great Satisfaction in *Gomez* in the *Spanish Fryar,* Foresight in *Love for Love,* with other Parts of the same Cast.

In the season of 1749–50 Mrs Storer again acted and sang at Smock Alley. Charles was not on the company list but shared a benefit with his wife on 2 April 1750. She signed a contract with Thomas Davies and Henry Thomson to sing and act, along with Isabella Lampe, in the New Concert Hall in Edinburgh from 29 October 1750 through 29 April 1751, but the Storers were delayed at sea or on the road, the *Caledonian Mercury* reporting on 6 November: "Last night Mrs Storer, the celebrated singer, arrived here from Dublin, and is to perform to-morrow night at the New Concert Hall." She represented a long list of characters. So did Charles. In fact, the manuscript calendar of Edinburgh performances compiled by Mrs Norma Armstrong gives us the first extensive review of his roles: Brazen in *The Recruiting Officer,* Cassio in *Othello,* Castalio in *The Orphan,* the Constable in *Merlin,* the Duke of Gloucester in *Jane Shore,* Fribble in *Miss in Her Teens,* Hubert in *King John,* King Henry in *Richard III,* Laertes in *Hamlet,* Peachum in *The Beggar's Opera,* Petit Maître in *The Hussar,* Shylock in *The Merchant of Venice,* Tom in *The Conscious Lovers,* Capulet in *Romeo and Juliet,* the Ghost in *Hamlet,* Mark Antony in *Julius Caesar,* and Sable in *The Funeral.*

The Storers made another try at London in the summer of 1751. Both played at Richmond (he as Sir Francis Gripe in *The Busy Body* on 24 July) and she sang at Ranelagh. They were perhaps in the English provinces during the winter, for one London performance is recorded for her in April 1752. They were not to be found in playbills anywhere in 1752–53. They were back at Smock Alley in 1753–54, and then the record again fails, this time for over three years.

W. S. Clark in *The Irish Stage in the County Towns* located Charles in a Cork performance on 5 August 1757, and he was certainly again at Smock Alley in 1757–58, as was his wife. On 25 April 1758 mention of some of the couple's children occurs in the bill for *The Oracle:* "All the Characters to be performed by Mrs Storer's Children. With the Epilogue to be spoke by Miss Storer in the Character of Cynthia." The performance was for the "Benefit of Mrs. Storer's Children." There was no mention of Mr Storer. Other bills in 1757–58 and in 1758–59 mention the Misses Fanny (Frances), Jenny (Jane), Nancy (Ann) and M. (Maria).

In 1758–59 again the Storers played at Smock Alley, but in 1759–60 she only was at Crow Street. On 23 June 1761 Storer was both Iago in *Othello* and Quidnunc in *The Upholsterer* at Covent Garden for Cooke's benefit. When the new season, 1761–62, opened both he and his wife were on the rolls at Covent Garden. He played Shylock, Westmoreland in *2 Henry IV* (a dozen times) Orasmin in *Zara,* and Dervise in *Tamerlane* that season, being paid £2 per week, according to the account books at the Folger Library.

Nothing further is known about the activities of either Charles or Elizabeth Storer until they departed with their seven daughters— Ann (Nancy), Elizabeth, Frances (Fanny), Hannah, Jane (Jenny, baptized at Richmond, Surrey, on 1 August 1747), Maria, and Sarah—for Jamaica in 1762. No record remains of their activities there. The murderous fevers of the island soon claimed the lives of Charles and two of the daughters, Elizabeth and Hannah, according to the *Public Advertiser* of 3 December 1767.

Mrs Charles Storer, her daughters Sarah and Jane, and two of her grandchildren, died in a conflagration aboard the brig *Dolphin* on a voyage from Jamaica to New York in August 1767.

Storer, Mrs Charles, Elizabeth, née Clark *d. 1767, actress, singer.*

The Miss Clark who walked on as the Page in *The Contrivances* at Covent Garden Theatre on 6 April 1736 is now probably identifiable as Elizabeth Clark, who would in time become Mrs Charles Storer. (*See* Clark, Miss [fl. 1736–1747?] in Volume 3 of this *Dictionary.*) On 29

June and 7 July she essayed Manly in *The Provok'd Husband* as a member of a company of Lilliputians while "Miss Clark Junior," her sister, was Myrtilla. On 7 July the sisters also sang a dialogue song. Elizabeth was in Charlotte Charke's peripatetic troupe at the Old Playhouse at the Bottom of Mermaid Court during the time of Southwark Fair, in September, acting Peggy in *The Innocent Wife* from 10 A.M. to 9 P.M. After one more London performance, at Covent Garden and in her debut role, on 26 April 1737, Miss Clark disappeared from the bills. The 1742 and 1743 performances previously attributed to her must be given now to her sister or to some other Miss Clark.

By 22 November 1742 Elizabeth had married the actor Charles Storer and was performing (as "from Covent Garden") at Smock Alley Theatre, Dublin. On that date she was Belinda in *The Old Bachelor* and Arethusa in *The Contrivances*. Through 22 December 1742 she performed Polly in *The Beggar's Opera* (three times), both Dorinda and Amphitrite in the musical version of *The Tempest*, Lucy in *The Virgin Unmask'd*, and Farinelli (burlesquing Italian opera) in *The Queen of Spain*. When the short Dublin season ended, Mrs Storer had established herself as a favorite singer of the town.

So she continued with the Smock Alley and then the united companies through the 1746–47 season, entertaining in entr'actes, singing in concerts and oratorios, and adding such roles as Chloe in *The Lottery,* Margery in *The Double Dealer,* Phillida in *Damon and Phillida,* Jacqueline in *The Royal Merchant,* Arabella in *The Honest Yorkshireman,* Nell in *The Devil to Pay,* Master Johnny in *The School-Boy,* Dorcas in *The Mock Doctor,* and Leander in *The Necromancer.*

Faulkner's Dublin Journal of 24 March 1747 announced "Mrs. Storer left Ireland today." The London *General Advertiser* of 4 April reported that the "celebrated" Mrs Storer had arrived "a few days since" and would perform the following week in "Handel's Oratorios" (a promise that was perhaps fulfilled: the cast for *Judas Maccabaeus* on 13 April was not listed). At Drury Lane on 29 April, a benefit night for Kitty Clive's brother James Raftor and two minor house servants, she was hired to sing between the acts and perform Arethusa in *The Contrivances.* But she did not join the permanent company. In the summer she acted and sang at Richmond and Twickenham where she was joined by her husband. In the fall both signed articles at Covent Garden. Her parts were more important and the reputation that had preceded her was obviously larger. She would receive £2 per week.

Mrs Storer opened her Covent Garden season singing her winning Polly on 31 October 1747 opposite the great tenor John Beard as Captain Macheath. She repeated that part and Belinda, Phillida, Nell, and Jenny and added to her repertoire Venus in *Apollo and Daphne,* Aura in *The Country Lasses,* Modesty in *The Muses' Looking Glass,* and Hoyden in *The Relapse.* In the summer she and Charles acted once more with the Richmond-Twickenham troupe. They had lodged that year at the corner of New Broad Court, Bow Street.

During the next two seasons Mrs Storer was at Smock Alley, continuing to charm her Dublin audiences with her lilting soprano voice. W. R. Chetwood, writing in his *A General History of the Stage* (1749) at this point in her career, gave her enthusiastic praise:

[She] recommends herself by her amiable Person, Good-nature, and her excellent sweet harmonious Manner in Singing; therefore she is too much desired to shew her Excellence that Way, to perform many Speaking Parts, but where her exalted Talent is required: and then, whatever she says, or sings, thus properly introduced, she doubly charms in. I shall end with four Lines of a Poem on *Ranelagh* Gardens, written last Summer in *London.*

Then Storer—with her sweet inchanting Strains,
Steals to our Hearts, and o'er our Senses reigns;
With ravish'd Ears we hear the pleasing Sounds,
And heav'nly Joys the vaulted Roof resounds.

Evidently Mrs Storer acted and sang at both Smock Alley and Aungier Street in 1749–50. Charles Storer was not in the Smock Alley company list, but husband and wife shared a benefit there on 2 April 1750. On 13 June 1750 Elizabeth was singing in a concert at the Assembly Room in Belfast. Managerial interests had been dickering for Mrs Storer's services for some time. She was advertised to sing in *The Beggar's Opera* at the Concert Hall in the Canongate in Edinburgh on 30 July, but the performance was not given. On 22 August her husband and the musician John Frederick

Lampe signed the following document (now in the Library of the University of Edinburgh):

Memorandum—/ It is this day agreed upon between Henry Thomson and Thomas Davies managers and sole Proprietors of the New Concert Hall in Edinburgh on the one Part and Charles and Elizabeth Storer his Wife and John Frederick Lampe and Isabella Lampe his Wife on the other Part. That for and in Consideration of the Sum of Three Hundred Pounds to be paid in Weekly Payments . . . they . . . shall Act and Sing in the said Concert Hall for the space of Six Calendar Months, viz: From the Twenty-Ninth April following in all such Parts as shall be allotted them by the said Davies and Thomson. NB The weekly payments are to consist of twelve pounds twelve shillings to be equally divided between the said Elizabeth Storer and Isabella Lampe at six pounds & six shillings each.

(Isabella Lampe was one of the most talented of the celebrated Young sisters.)

Mrs Storer was somehow delayed and did not arrive until 5 November, according to the *Caledonian Mercury,* which promised that she would perform on the seventh at the Concert Hall. Mrs Norma Armstrong's manuscript calendar, gleaned from surviving bills, shows her extensive collection of parts, most of which Mrs Storer had done before. Apparent additions to her repertoire were Queen Dollalolla in *Tom Thumb the Great,* Portia in *The Merchant of Venice,* and Ophelia in *Hamlet.*

With the coming of spring the Storers made their way back to London, both of them playing at Richmond and she singing occasionally at Ranelagh. Their activities from the summer of 1751 until she acted Arethusa in the afterpiece *The Contrivances* at Covent Garden on 6 February 1752 (when she was said to be making her first appearance there in three years) are not known. She played in London only once more that season, again at Covent Garden, for her benefit on 13 April, a night when she and Mrs Lampe descended to Mauxalinda and Margery, respectively, in Harry Carey's old burlesque opera *The Dragon of Wantley.* Charles Storer seems to have found no employment at all.

The Storers seem, indeed, to have fallen upon hard times. The record fails in 1752–53. Were they in Dublin? They were certainly at Smock Alley in 1753–54, but after that there is another blank period, this time three years

long. She (alone?) came back to Smock Alley in 1756–57, according to the company lists, and one bill acknowledges her three-year absence. But no roles are known.

In 1757–58, when both Storers were at Smock Alley, audiences were introduced to at least four of the seven daughters they are known to have had: Ann (Nancy), Elizabeth, Frances (Fanny), Hannah, Jane (Jenny, baptized at Richmond, Surrey, on 1 August 1747), Maria, and Sarah. The debutantes, if we may judge from the scattered bills, were Fanny, Jenny, Nancy and Maria ("M."). On 25 April "All the Characters [in *The Oracle* were] to be performed by Mrs Storer's Children," for their benefit.

The Storers remained at Smock Alley through 1758–59; she acted at the Crow Street Theatre in 1759–60; they seem not to have been engaged anywhere in 1760–61; and by January 1761 they were attempting London again. She sang at the Great Room in Dean Street, Soho, for Ferdinando Tenducci's benefit and began to act at Covent Garden again with Arethusa in *The Contrivances* on 25 March. In the 1761–62 season the Storer family sailed for Jamaica. By about 1765 Charles Storer and two of his daughters had sickened and died in that climate, fatal to so many adventurers from Britain. Mrs Storer determined to move on to the American continent, to act with the American Company, with the family, which now included the young actor John Henry, who had married Jane Storer, and the couple's two infant children. For Mrs Storer, the second voyage was even more disastrous than the first. It ended four miles from Newport, Rhode Island, in the fiery destruction of the brig *Dolphin,* when Jane, her children, Sarah, and Mrs Storer herself perished. The disaster was reported in the *Newport Mercury* for 24–31 August 1767 (quoted by Richardson Wright in *Revels in Jamaica*):

The following is a particular and authentic Account of the melancholy Accident which happened on board of the Brig Dolphin, commanded by Capt. John Malbone, of this town, viz. Last Wednesday night she arrived off Point Judith, from Jamaica and when within five Miles from Land, at half after ten o'clock the same Night, a Negro Boy went down between the Decks, amongst the Rum where there stood several Puncheons of Water, and (as he says) with an Intention to draw some Water, but mistook, and broached a Cask of Rum; at the same Time the Door of the Lantern, in which he carried the Candle, being open, and the Candle falling into the Rum, set it on Fire; This so affrighted the Boy, that he neglected to stop the Running of the Rum, and in less than half a Minute the Head of the Cask flew out, and the Flames were immediately communicated to fifteen Casks more, all between Decks, so that all possible Means to extinguish it proved ineffectual; the Vessel was all in Flames in a very few Minutes, and consequently reduced twenty-six Persons, being the Number of People, including Passengers, on board, to a Distress and Horror that must be left to the Reader's imagination;—among many of them subsisted the tender and endearing Connections of Husband and Wife, Parent and Child, Brother and Sister, etc., between whom the merciless Flames were now effecting a cruel and inevitable Separation; and it was with the utmost Difficulty that a Soul on board saved his Life.—There were eleven Passengers, viz.—Mr. John Henry, Mr. William Brooks Simson, Mr. Nathaniel Green, Mrs. Storer, Mrs. Henry, Miss Ann Storer, and Mr. Henry's two children, one sixteen months and the other four months old; five of whom perished in the following Manner, viz. Mrs. Storer, Miss Sarah Storer, and Mr. Henry's two Children being in the Cabbin, were suffocated with the Smoke before the two small Boats could be got out, they being thrown over with the utmost Difficulty, not having any Thing ready to hoist them; Mrs. Henry was upon the Deck, with her Sisters, and might have been saved with them, but overcome with maternal Love and Affection on having her Mother cry out, *The Children,* oh the Children, she ran and threw herself headlong down the Companion, into the Flames, and was there instantly consumed. The Remainder of the People, to the number of twenty-one, got ashore with Difficulty, in the two small Boats, not without being wet in landing; some of them, the same Night, with Trouble and Fatigue, got up to the House of Mr. Silas Niles, who received them with great Humanity, and afforded them all the Assistance in his power. The vessel burned till eight o'clock the next Day, when she sunk.

The survivors picked up their lives and continued to perform. John Henry and Ann Storer began housekeeping together almost immediately and by 1768 she had assumed his name in theatrical bills. But by 1775 she had gone to Dublin to act, and Henry to Jamaica again. (Years later, apparently in 1794, she married the American actor John Hogg, acted as Mrs Hogg, and bore him several children.) Charles and Elizabeth Storer's daughter Maria, who had (like Jane and Frances) acted as a child in Dublin, in Jamaica, and on the mainland of America, returned to perform in London and on the Bath-Bristol circuit and came back to America where by 1788 she had assumed, probably legitimately, the name and status of the third Mrs John Henry. (See her entry under that name in Volume 7 of this *Dictionary.*) The remaining daughter Frances has no record of a London performance. She survived the holocaust of the *Dolphin* to become for some years a dependable actress in the Old American Company of Henry and Douglass, performing in New York and Philadelphia, and on trips along the Atlantic seaboard from Albany to Charleston. She was the Miss Storer at the theatre in Montego Bay, Jamaica, in 1784. She later married a Mr Mechtler and settled in England.

Storer, Maria. *See* HENRY, MRS JOHN THE THIRD.

Storey, Mrs ₁*fl. 1730*₁, *actress.*
Mrs Storey played Gipsey in *The Stratagem* at the Haymarket Theatre on 18 September 1730. The Mrs "Story" listed in *The London Stage* as dancing at Drury Lane on 2 October 1744 was surely Miss Story and not our subject.

Story, Mr ₁*fl. 1799–1819?*₁, *actor, singer.*
A young gentleman made his stage debut on 28 June 1799 at the Haymarket Theatre playing Belville in *Rosina;* he was identified as Mr Story. The *Monthly Mirror* reported: "He is a pupil, it is said, of [Michael] Kelly; and certainly does his master no discredit." On 16 July Story made his third appearance (his second is not on record), playing Niccolo in *False and True.* Between then and 16 September Story sang in *The Red-Cross,* sang "Rule Britannia" with a group, and sang (solo) Purcell's "Mad Tom." He was probably the Mr Story who was acting and singing at the Federal Street Theatre in Boston in March 1801. And he may have been the Story who was a Slave in *Aladdin* at the Theatre Royal in Shakespeare Square, Edinburgh, from 25 March through 28 April 1819.

Story, Miss [*fl. 1740–1745*], *dancer, actress.*

Miss Story played a Gipsy in *The Fortune Tellers* at Drury Lane Theatre on 15 January 1740. On 29 April she was a Maid in the same piece, and on 22 May she acted Margaret in *The Squire of Alsatia.* She remained at Drury Lane through the 1741–42 season, appearing as a Peasant in *Robin Goodfellow,* a Peasant in *The Rural Sports,* a Peasant and a Haymaker in *Harlequin Shipwrecked,* Jenny in *The Harlot's Progress,* Scentwell in *The Busy Body,* and a Lady of Honour in *Chrononhotonthologos.* She also had a part in *The Rehearsal.* As an entr'acte dancer she was seen in a minuet with Leviez, and Miss Story danced in *Comus, Le Genereux Corsaire, A Voyage to the Island of Cytherea, Les Satires puny,* an untitled ballet, and *The Peasants.*

On 3 December 1742 she appeared at the Lincoln's Inn Fields Theatre in a comic ballet. During the rest of the 1742–43 season she played a Peasant in *The Imprisonment of Harlequin* and Hoyden in *The Relapse* and danced between the acts. In 1744–45 she was back at Drury Lane. She was certainly the "Mrs" Story who was in a *Grand Turkish Dance* on 2 October 1744. Then Miss Story was a Shepherdess in *The Amorous Goddess,* danced in *Comus,* and appeared in a minuet with Baudouin. Her benefit tickets were accepted on 8 May 1745.

Stott, Mrs John. *See* LESSINGHAM, JANE.

Stracchini, Antonio [*fl. 1791*], *prompter.*

The London Stage lists Antonio Stracchini as the prompter at the Pantheon in 1791 for the spring opera season.

Strada Del Pò, Signora Aurelio, Anna Maria [*fl. 1720–1740*], *singer.*

According to the *New Grove Dictionary of Music and Musicians,* the Italian soprano Anna Maria Strada del Pò was a native of Bergamo and in 1720–21 served the governor of Milan, Count Colloredo. She also sang that season in Venice, and from 1724 to 1726 she performed at the San Bartolomeo theatre in Naples. During her stay in Naples she married that theatre's manager, Aurelio del Pò. He is said to have married her because he owed her 2000 ducats and had no other way to pay her.

Gerald Coke Handel Collection
(Photograph courtesy of Sotheby's)

ANNA MARIA STRADA DEL PÒ

by Verelst

At the King's Theatre in London on 2 December 1729 she sang Adelaide in Handel's *Lotario.* Handel had recruited her for his opera company for £600 per season. Jean Jaques Zambino had written to Count Manteuffel the previous July saying that Signora "Trada" "Has an excellent voice of great beauty and is a person of outstanding merit" (quoted in Deutsch's *Handel*). The *Daily Journal* on 2 July had also reported that she "hath a very fine Treble Voice" and was "a Person of singular Merit." The librettist Paolo Rolli wrote to his friend Riva after seeing *Lotario:*

Strada pleases mightily, and *Alto* [Handel] says that she sings better than the two who have left us [Signoras Cuzzoni and Faustina], because one of them never pleased him at all and he would like to forget the other. The truth is that she has a penetrating thread of a soprano voice which delights the ear, but oh how far removed from Cuzzona! Bononcini, who was with me at the opera, agrees with me as to this. (Deutsch translation.)

During the rest of the 1729–30 season Signora Strada sang the title role in *Partenope,*

A. R. Gellman Collection

ANNA MARIA STRADA DEL PÒ

artist unknown (Ricci?)

Artenice in *Ormisda,* and Seleuce in *Tolomeo.* She received a solo benefit on 21 March 1730. In 1730–31 she sang Berenice in *Scipio,* Cleofide in *Poro,* Almirena in *Rinaldo,* and the title role in *Rodelinda.*

The composer Bononcini in 1732 proposed a performance of one of his works at the King's, but a letter to the *Daily Post* on 9 June 1732 from Signora Strada's husband shows that he was denied:

Whereas Signor Bononcini intends after the Serenata composed by Mr. Handel has been performed, to have one of his own at the Opera-house, and has desired Signora Strada to sing in that Entertainment.

Aurelio del Po, Husband of the said Signora Strada, thinks it incumbent on him to acquaint the Nobility and Gentry, that he shall ever think himself happy in every opportunity wherein he can have the Honour to contribute to their Satisfaction; but with respect to this particular Request of Signor Bononcini, he hopes he shall be permitted to decline complying with it, for Reasons best known to the said Aurelio del Po and his Wife; and therefore the said Aurelio del Po flatters himself that the Nobility and Gentry will esteem this a sufficient

Cause for his Noncompliance with Signor Bononcini's Desire; and likewise judge it to be a proper Answer to whatever the Enemies of the said Aurelio del Po may object against him or his Wife upon this Occasion.

The refusal probably concerned the charge of plagiarism against Bononcini and the rivalry between him and Handel.

Signora Strada appears to have been faithful to Handel, even to allowing arrears in salary to accumulate during Handel's financially troubled period in the late 1730s. Indeed, most of Handel's singers deserted him in 1733 to join the rival Opera of the Nobility under Porpora, but Signora Strada remained with Handel. She was compassionate, too, to a fellow countryman, "Anthony l'Anglodge" alias "l'Anglois," according to *The Bee* on October 1734. "Porta Anthony" was condemned to die for stealing 15 guineas from the desk of Joseph Teddy. Signora Strada petitioned the King for a pardon. It was granted, but apparently too late; the Italian died in Newgate.

She sang regularly for Handel at the King's through 1733–34 and then at Covent Garden through 1736–37. Her new roles at the King's included Antinona in *Admeto,* Fulvia in *Ezio,* Elmira in *Sosarme,* Volumnia in *Coriolano,* Emilia in *Flavio,* the title role in *Esther,* Papira in *Lucio Papira,* Galatea in *Aci, e Galatea,* Rossane in *Alessandro,* Angelica in *Orlando,* the title role in *Deborah,* Marzia in *Cato,* Theophane in *Ottone,* Sextia in *Cajo Fabricio,* the title role in *Arianne,* Clio in *Il Parnasso in festa,* Amarilli in *Il pastor fido,* and, at Covent Garden, Erato in *Terpsicore,* Ginevra in *Ariodante,* Josabeth in *Athalia,* the title role in *Alcina,* Tusnelda in *Arminio,* Arianna in *Giustino,* Bellezza in *Il trionfo del tempo e della verita,* and the title role in *Berenice.* She also sang in *Alexander's Feast* and at concerts and was in Handel's oratorios at Oxford.

Dr Burney said that Signora Strada had a "fine and brilliant shake" but "so little of Venus in her appearance, that she was usually called the *Pig.*" But Handel helped her "from a coarse singer with a fine voice" to the "equal at least to the first performer in Europe." On 21 June 1738 the *Daily Post* carried the following story:

On Saturday last, set out for Breda, Signora Strada del Pò, to which place she goes in obedience to the commands of her royal highness the princess of Orange, from whence she intends to go to Italy, but before her departure desires the English nobility and gentry, from whom she has received so many signal marks of favour, might be acquainted that it is no way owing to her, that the present scheme for performing operas next winter, in the Hay-market [i.e., the King's Theatre], under the direction of Mr. Heidegger, has miscarried, as has been maliciously reported; she having agreed with Mr. Heidegger above a month ago, as the said gentleman can testify.

She had apparently been offered 1000 guineas.

Signora Strada sang with Senesino in Naples in 1739–40, after which she retired to Bergamo, according to the *New Grove*.

A portrait, three-quarter-length 48½" × 39", by John Verelst said to be of Anna Maria Strada del Pò was offered at Christie's on 19 November 1986 (lot 38), and was bought by Gerald Coke for his superb Handel collection. It was sold at that time by the person who had bought it at Sotheby's on 17 June 1983 (lot 182), when it was called a portrait of an unknown sitter. A drawing by Amigoni in the possession of the Princeton University Art Museum is a copy of or a sketch for the Verelst portrait. A caricature sketch attributed to Ricci of Strada wearing a plumed headdress with pendant veil and an embroidered hooped skirt is in the Royal Library, Windsor Castle; a copy in pen and brown ink over pencil is in the Albert R. Gellman collection.

Stradiotti, Signora [*fl. 1714*], *singer, harpsichordist.*

At Hickford's Music Room on 29 April 1714 Signora Stradiotti sang and played a solo on the harpsichord. At the King's Theatre she sang Cecina in *Arminio* on 23 October and Edelberto in *Ernelinda* on 16 November 1714. In his "Opera Register" Colman called her "a very bad singer."

Strahan, Mr [*fl. 1788–1817*], *doorkeeper.*

The doorkeeper Strahan was named in Covent Garden Theatre playbills and accounts from as early as 24 May 1788, when he had benefit tickets out, until 5 June 1817, when he was cited as a doorkeeper in the accounts. His weekly salary was 15*s.*

Strang, Mr [*fl. 1783–1785*], *constable.*

The Lord Chamberlain's accounts list Mr Strang as the constable at the King's Theatre from 1783 to 1785.

Strange, Mr [*fl. 1762?–1771?*], *actor.*

A Mr Strange was named on the Birmingham Theatre bill of 14 June 1762. He may have been the Strange who had an unspecified role in *Philaster* at Drury Lane Theatre in London on 8 October 1763 and subsequent dates. During the rest of the 1763–64 season Strange was seen as a member of the Mob in *The Mayor of Garratt*, a character in *The Dupe*, Rosencrantz and Bernardo in *Hamlet*, and a Slave in *The Rival Queens*.

Strange was at Drury Lane through 1768–69, playing minor roles for 3*s.* 4*d.* daily or £1 weekly—near the bottom of the actors' salary scale—as of February 1765; by 1767 he was up to 4*s.* 5*d.* daily. Many of his assignments were supernumerary, but some had names: Blunt in *1 Henry IV*, Clermont in *Philaster*, Elliot and Spinoza in *Venice Preserv'd*, Gower in *2 Henry IV*, Ratcliff in *Richard III*, Brush in *All in the Wrong*, Sideboard in *The Way to Keep Him*, Melidor in *Zara*, Hali in *Tamerlane*, Ali in *Mahomet*, Thomas in *The Virgin Unmask'd*, Selim in *The Mourning Bride*, Fenton in *The Merry Wives of Windsor*, Catesby and Belmour in *Jane Shore*, Eumenes in *The Rival Queens*, Butler in *The Busy Body*, Silvius in *As You Like It*, Laroches in *The Countess of Salisbury*, Item in *Wit's Last Stake*, Conrade in *Much Ado about Nothing*, Sir James Elliot in *The Lyar*, Tipstaff in *The Hypocrite*, Nadir in *Zingis*, Mervin in *A Peek behind the Curtin*, Buckle in *The Suspicious Husband*, Calmar in *The Fatal Discovery*, Stanmore in *The Royal Slave*, Antonio in *The Tempest*, William in *The Jealous Wife*, Beaufort in *The Citizen*, and Harwood in *The Register Office*.

In the summers of 1768 and 1769 Strange joined Samuel Foote's company at the Haymarket Theatre, making his first appearance there on 13 July 1768 as Harpy in *The Commissary*. He was also seen as a Player in *The Beggar's Opera* and Jasper in *Miss in Her Teens* that summer; in 1769 he was a Soldier in *The What D'Ye Call It*, Loveit in *Miss in Her Teens*, Rosencrantz in *Hamlet*, Catesby in *Richard III*, and Elliot in *Venice Preserv'd*. At the Haymarket on 29 October 1770 Strange was with a pick-up company, playing Elliot again.

Since his name disappeared from London playbills after that, perhaps he was the Mr Strange in Dublin spoken of by George Garrick in a letter to his brother David on 25 June 1771. Strange had reported seeing a letter from Richard Sparks in May saying that Sparks had obtained a copy of *The Jubilee* for the Dublin manager Dawson.

Strange, Mrs ₍*fl.* 1733₎, *actress.*

At the Haymarket Theatre Mrs Strange played Dorcas in *The Mock Doctor* on 20 March and 23 April 1733, Isabella in *The Old Debauchees* on 27 March, and Lucy in *The Recruiting Officer* on 18 April.

Stratford, Mr ₍*fl.* 1784₎, *actor.*

Mr Stratford played Richmond in *Richard III* at the Haymarket Theatre on 17 September 1784.

Streater. *See* STREETER.

Street. *See also* STUART.

Street, Mr ₍*fl.* 1783–1788₎, *callboy?*

The Drury Lane Theatre accounts on 15 March 1783 show a payment of 8*s.* to one Street "for calling." One supposes Street was a callboy. He was named in the benefit bill of 4 June 1787 and cited in the accounts again on 18 October 1788 for £40 on account.

Street, Miss ₍*fl.* 1761–1770₎, *dancer.*

Miss Street, a student of Gherardi, was one of the dancers in *The Gardeners* at the Haymarket Theatre on 23 June 1761. The dance was repeated on 27 June and 30 July, and on 3 August she and other youngsters danced *The Reapers.* Except for 1762 and 1767, Miss Street was advertised as dancing at the Haymarket in the summers through 1770, appearing in such pieces as *The Venetian Gardeners* with Master Rogier, *The Provincial Dance* with Master Clayton, a comic dance with Master Clinton, a solo serious dance, *The Carpenter and the Fruit Dealer, The Dutchman and Provincials, The Shepherdess and the Faux Aveugle, La Chasseur, La Berge, The English Sailor at Marseille,* a double hornpipe with Vandemere, and *The Sailor's Re-turn* with Tassoni. On 27 August 1766 she went down the street to the King's Theatre to appear in an untitled dance with Arnauld.

Miss Street had made her first Drury Lane appearance on 14 October 1763 in a comic turn with Master Clinton called *"Provansale."* The prompter Hopkins noted that the children were "greatly applauded." During the rest of the season Miss Street was in a *Fairy Dance* in *A Midsummer Night's Dream,* a similar dance (or perhaps the same one) in *The Fairy Tale* (a farce taken from *A Midsummer Night's Dream*), *Shepherdesses, The Hunters,* and *The Gypsies.*

Street, Ann. *See* BARRY, MRS SPRANGER.

Street, James ₍*fl.* 1791–1812₎, *singer, actor.*

James Street was first noticed in the bills on 20 October 1791, when he had an unspecified part in *Oscar and Malvina* at Covent Garden Theatre. His only other advertised assignment that season was participation in *Orpheus and Eurydice.* He had benefit tickets out on 25 May 1792. Street sang in choruses and acted small parts through 1811–12, never earning more than £2 weekly. Among his roles were a Shipwright in *Harlequin's Museum,* a Mariner in *The Midnight Wanderers,* a Mate in *Inkle and Yarico,* a Servant in *The Travellers in Switzerland,* a Robber in *The Battle of Hexham,* Wat Dreary in *The Beggar's Opera,* an Undertaker in *The Way to Get Married,* a Gipsy in *Harlequin and Oberon,* Bardolph in *The Merry Wives of Windsor,* a Coachman in *The Devil to Pay,* a Huntsman in *The Round Tower,* a Bowman in *Robin Hood,* an Upholsterer in *The Miser,* Thomas in *The Spoiled Child,* a Recruit in *The Magic Oak,* a Chandler in *The Turnpike Gate,* Peto in *Henry IV,* and a Daemon in *The Volcano.* He also sang in the chorus in *Hamlet, Romeo and Juliet,* and other plays.

The critics had nothing favorable to say of Street. In 1793 the *Theatrical Journal* wished that Helm would sing instead of Street, and in 1799 the complete entry for Street in the *Authentic Memoirs of the Green Room* read, "Mr. Street may be very great in the country, but in town, he serves only to join with Linton, Abbot, Usher, &c." Yet he was listed in Doane's *Musical Directory* of 1794, where it was observed that he was a tenor who belonged to the New Musical Fund and the Academy of An-

cient Music and sang at Covent Garden Theatre, in the oratorios, at the 1793 Oxford
Meeting, and in the Handelian performances
at Westminster Abbey. His address was No
27, Princes Street, Soho.

Street, Simon ₁*fl.*1739₁, *musician.*
Simon Street was one of the original subscribers to the Royal Society of Musicians when
it was founded on 28 August 1739.

Streeter, Robert   *1624–1679, scene designer.*
Bainbrigg Buckeridge in *An Essay towards
an English School of Painting* (1706), placed
Robert Streeter's birth in 1624. Vertue said
Streeter was the son of a painter who lived in
Covent Garden, but when Streeter was first
cited in the Minutes of the Painter-Stainers he
was described as "a forrin"—which suggests
that he had been born on the Continent. He is
said to have received his training from one Du
Moulin, presumably a Frenchman but otherwise unknown. In any case, Streeter apparently
went to the Continent during the Commonwealth and did not return to England until
about 1658.
By the Restoration, Streeter had already
done some decorative art work, including
plates to Stapleton's *Mores Hominum* in 1660.
In 1661 he was called the King's Serjeant
Painter and paid for painting and gilding
coaches and other royal vehicles, but his official
appointment did not come until 28 February
1663. By that time he had received permission
to build a house and workshop in Longacre. In
Decorative Painting in England, Croft-Murray
has assembled the known facts about Streeter's
work, most of which has long-since vanished.
The prime example of his skill is the ceiling of
Wren's Sheldonian Theatre at Oxford, which
work indicates that Streeter at least partly deserved his reptutation as "the greatest and most
universal painter that England ever bred" but
was hardly worthy of Robert Whitehall's pre-
diction in *Urania* in 1669:

> *That Future ages must confess they owe
> To* STREETER *more than* Michael Angelo.

Evelyn saw a perspective by Streeter at Mr
Povey's house in Lincoln's Inn Fields and found
it "indeede excellent, with the Vasas in Imita-

Henry E. Huntington Library and Art Gallery

ROBERT STREETER
by Vertue?

tion of Porphyrie," and Pepys was impressed
when, on 1 February 1669, Povey

> carried me to Mr. Streeter's, the famous history-
> painter over the way, whom I have often heard of,
> but did never see him before; and there I found
> him, and Dr. Wren, and several Virtuosos, looking
> upon the paintings which he is making for the new
> Theatre at Oxford: and, indeed, they look as if they
> would be very fine, and the rest think better than
> those of Rubens in the Banqueting-house at White
> Hall, but I do not so fully think so. But they will
> certainly be very noble; and I am mightily pleased
> to have the fortune to see this man and his work,
> which is very famous; and he is a very civil little
> man, and lame, but lives very handsomely.

Streeter spent some of his time painting for
the court and public theatres. The Lord Chamberlain's accounts tell us of payments to him
for building and painting wings and shutters
for the Hall Theatre at Whitehall in January
1671; the items included four pairs of "wings
of boscage" and a pair of shutters. The following month he was paid again for a pair of
shutters depicting a garden, a scene of a mill,
and clouds (borders, evidently). These may
have been the scenes for the production of
Dryden's *The Conquest of Granada,* which was

By gracious permission of Her Majesty Queen Elizabeth II

View of Whiteladies Priory, Boscabel House

by STREETER

presented at court by the King's Company. On 9 February Evelyn saw a performance and said "there were indeede very glorious scenes & perspectives, the work of Mr. *Streeter,* who well understands it. . . ."

Streeter did the decorative painting showing "the Gyants War" in the cedar dining room at Sir Robert Clayton's new house; Evelyn saw the work and told his diary on 26 September 1672 that the painting was handsome but "the figures are too neere the Eye. . . ." Streeter's grand style was probably well suited to scene painting, and he continued working on items for the theatre at Whitehall: in March 1673 a backcloth showing rustic stonework and a border showing a matching arch and crosspiece; in May "two rock peices and ye long peices of sky," a backcloth showing the sea, and two "long bourds of sea" (probably low sliding pieces that could simulate ocean waves); and in early 1675 a boscage scene on shutters and a "paire of side Relieses [relieves]," repairs to the frontispiece (proscenium arch), a peacock,

an eagle, a flowery bank, seats in the clouds, and the like. Streeter painted the scenes for the court masque *Calisto,* which was performed on 15 February 1675.

From Streeter's will we learn that his wife's name was Ruth and that they lived in the parish of St Martin-in-the-Fields. The following entries in the registers of St Martin's, therefore, surely concern the painter. On 17 May 1652 Charles Streeter, the son of Robert and Ruth, was christened; on 1 July 1653 their son Paul was christened; on 27 July 1655 their son Benjamin was born, and on 5 August he was christened. We have not found baptismal records for the Streeters' other sons, Robert the younger and Thomas.

By early 1675 Streeter was suffering from the stone. On 20 January Evelyn visited him "to comfort, & encourage him to be cut from the stone, with which that honest man was exceedingly afflicted." Charles II brought over a surgeon from France to perform the operation, but it was to no avail. Robert Streeter was buried at St Martin's on 23 April 1679. His will, dated 28 March 1679 and proved the following 12 May, specified that the rents and profits from his property in Longacre and £20 should go to his wife Ruth; his son Thomas was to receive £80 and Charles £50; to young Robert was to go the lease on the property in Longacre and "all my Prints Drawings and Plaister-peeces belonging to my Trade which shall be and remaine in my own Closet above staires" plus £100 and some property near the Stone-Bridge held on lease from Sir William Poultney. Streeter made small bequests to his goddaughter Isabella Fillebay and her mother and to a kinswoman, Elizabeth Hatler. The rest of the estate was to go to Ruth Streeter.

Robert Streeter is said to have done a self-portrait that is untraced but is known by A. Bannerman's engraving, published as a plate to Walpole's *Anecdotes, 1762*. But a wash drawing portrait of Streeter in the Huntington Library, credited to Vertue, seems to be the original (or a copy of it) upon which the Bannerman engraving is based.

Streeter, Robert *d. 1711, scene designer.*

The younger Robert Streeter, the son of Robert and Ruth, followed in his father's footsteps and became a scene designer, but none of his work has survived, and the references to him are scarce. His father left him his collection of art works when he died in 1679. "Rebecka" Streeter, a child, was buried at St Martin-in-the-Fields on 15 April 1683, and it seems likely that she was the younger Robert Streeter's daughter. In July 1687 Streeter was paid for "mending ye cloth of ye clouds" and painting them at the Hall theatre at Whitehall, and in October 1697 he was paid £2 for repairing some scenery at the court theatre. In *Decorative Painting in England,* Croft-Murray notes that the elder Streeter's pictures were sold at the death of his son Robert in 1711. We find in the registers of St Martin's that Mr Robert Streeter, "man," was buried on 25 August 1711.

Strensham, Mr [fl. 1736], *actor.*

As a member of Henry Fielding's troupe at the Haymarket Theatre Mr Strensham played Ignorance in *Pasquin* on 5 March 1736. He

may have remained in the cast through the work's long run, which ended in July.

Strollger, [James?] [fl. 1730–1740?], *musician?*

A Mr Strollger received a solo benefit at the Goodman's Fields Theatre on 6 July 1730. Perhaps he was James Strollger, who is listed in the *Catalogue of Printed Music in the British Museum* as having published three songs: *When modest Cloe's downcast Eyes* (with words by the actor John Boman; 1735?), *Imagination* (1740?), and *Lucinda by a secret art* (1740?). Master Strologer may have been related to him.

Strologer, Master [fl. 1744], *organist.*

Wroth in *The London Pleasure Gardens* states that the landlord of Lord Cobham's Head tavern, Robert Leeming, announced that for one of his concerts in 1744 a concerto on the organ would be played by Master Strologer.

Strong, Edward *d. 1663, instrumentalist.*

Edward Strong (or Stronge) was admitted to the King's Musick on 9 November 1660 at an annual salary of £46 12s. 8d., replacing the violinist John Hopper. The same warrant that gave him that position also listed Strong as replacing Francis Smith, oboist, at £66 2s. 6d. annually. Since there is no evidence to suggest two Edward Strongs, it would appear that our subject had a double position—a not uncommon practice in the King's Musick. A warrant in the Lord Chamberlain's accounts dated 3 September 1662 indicates that Edward, John, and Robert Strong (brothers) all played bass violins, that is, violoncellos. On 30 August 1662 a warrant directed Edward and Robert Strong to attend at Whitehall with their double curtalls (bassoons), and another warrant of the same date ordered that Edward be paid 5s. daily for having attended the King at Hampton Court in the summer of 1662. He attended at Windsor in 1663.

Edward Strong died sometime before 9 November 1663, when his will of 19 February 1661 was proved. If he attended the King at Windsor in the summer of 1663, his death probably occurred in the late summer or fall. In his will he identified himself as of the parish of St Sepulchre and said he was "sick and weake of body." He left his mother Ellen a mourning ring worth 20s., his sister Elizabeth Steward £5, his brother John "my best hatt and a mourning Ring," his brother Stephen "my two duble Sagbutts and a mourning Ring," his sister (-in-law) Mary (Stephen's wife) a mourning ring, his cousin Lightfoote (William, the pageant painter?) and his wife mourning rings, and his niece Mary Strong (John's daughter) a mourning ring.

To his brother Robert he left his houses in the parish of St Giles without Cripplegate, provided that Robert give Edward's widow Elizabeth £30 annually and Elizabeth not pester Robert. The legacy was to cease if she bothered him. Robert was named residuary legatee and executor. Edward Strong was replaced in the King's Musick on 24 December 1663 (the violin position) and 25 October 1664 (the wind instrument position).

Strong, John   *d. 1675, instrumentalist.*

John Strong was sworn wind instrumentalist in the King's Musick on 5 November 1634. His salary, as of 10 December 1641, was 1s. 8d. daily and a livery allowance of £16 2s. 6d. annually. He was reappointed at the Restoration and listed in 1660 as a violinist; his salary was exactly what it had been years before. Since on 9 March 1661 Strong was paid £30 for two double sackbuts, he was probably proficient on that instrument. For the coronation of Charles II, however, Strong played the violin. In the summer of 1661 he attended the King at Windsor for 5s. daily, and in 1662 he journeyed with the King to Portsmouth to meet the Queen. On 3 September 1662 he and his brothers Edward and Robert were listed in the Lord Chamberlain's accounts as bass violinists (violoncellists). It would appear from the records that John, like his brother Edward, held a double position in the court musical establishment.

In 1663 and 1664 John attended the King at Windsor, and on 20 December 1664 he and other court musicians were ordered to attend Thomas Killigrew at the Bridges Street Theatre whenever he should need them. In 1667 Strong was a member of John Banister's elite group of 12 violinists within the regular band of 24. As of June 1672 he was a member of the Corporation of Music. Strong's last official notice in the court records was in February 1675, when he played violin in the court masque *Calisto*. He died between 9 and 21 August 1675, the composition and probate dates on his will.

Out of the arrears owed to him by the King, John left £100 each to his godchildren, Ann Taylor and John Taylor, to be paid them when they reached 21 or set up their trades. Should they die before then, the money was to go to John's daughter Mary. To his brother Robert he left his "Books Musick Instruments" and £20 for a mourning ring. To his son-in-law Thomas Payne, Strong left £20 for a ring. From his arrears in salary he bequeathed £10 each to his cousin Lightfoote and his daughter Mary. Strong left his clothes to John Taylor. Everything else was bequeathed to Robert Strong in trust for John Strong's daughter Mary. Mary was evidently married, but her husband's name is not clear in the will; it appears to have been Kent.

Strong, Robert   *d. 1694, instrumentalist.*

Robert Strong was sworn a wind instrument player in the King's Musick on 20 June 1638, to serve temporarily on the double sackbut and the violin in place of Robert Parker, who was then absent because of age and infirmity. When Parker died in 1640, Strong was given a permanent position among the wind instrumentalists at 1s. 8d. daily and £16 2s. 6d. annually for livery.

During the Commonwealth Strong turned to teaching, one of his students being Henry Hazard, who was apprenticed to Strong in October 1657 for eight years. Strong was presumably able to continue being a music master after he was reappointed to the King's Musick on 18 June 1660. At court his annual wage was £46 12s. 8d., and he was now listed among the violinists as well as among the wind players. Warrants dated 30 August and 3 September 1662 cited Robert Strong as a bass violinist (violoncellist) and a performer on the double curtall (bassoon).

From time to time Strong journeyed with the King away from London: in 1662 to Portsmouth, in 1663 to Windsor, in 1670 to Dover. For such trips he received additional pay. Strong may also have increased his income when he was selected on 14 March 1667 to serve in the elite group of 12 violinists within the regular band of 24. Strong was evidently a good friend of the court musician John Gamble. On 18 August 1683 Gamble gave Strong his power of attorney for a half year, and Gamble's will, dated 30 June 1680 and proved 3 December 1687, shows that Gamble's grandson John was a servant to Robert Strong.

Robert Strong died between 2 and 18 June 1694. He had made his will on 9 February 1694, when he described himself as sick and weak. He added a codicil on 2 June. The will left everything to his wife Mary and daughter Mary equally. The codicil specified that his wife should have certain items, such as three silver tankards, six lockets, rings, a silver spoon, two silver trenchers, and the like. Mrs Strong proved the will on 18 June 1694.

Robert Strong was the last of the musical Strongs of the Restoration. His brothers Edward, John, and Stephen, all court musicians, died before him.

Strong, Stephen   *d. 1665?, sackbut player.*

Stephen Strong was appointed to the King's Musick as a double sackbut player, effective 13 November 1661. He received the usual livery allowance, £16 2s. 6d., and an annual salary unspecified. Strong attended the King at Windsor in 1663, but the Lord Chamberlain's accounts made very little mention of him except for notices that his livery payments were in arrears. Strong probably died shortly before 6 April 1665, when he was replaced by Theophilus Fitz. Such appointments were usually, but not always, made within days of a court musician's death. We have found no will for Stephen Strong. He was the brother of the court musicians Edward, John, and Robert Strong.

Strong, William   *ₗfl. 1671–1672ₗ, scenekeeper.*

The London Stage lists William Strong as a scenekeeper in the King's Company in 1671–72. He was named in a Lord Chamberlain's warrant dated 23 November 1671.

Strong Man. *See also* Ducrow, Peter, and Joy, William.

"Strong Man From Islington, The"   *b. c. 1704, strong man.*

At the Haymarket Theatre on 2 March 1734 "the strong Man from Islington (not in Defiance to Mynheer Cajanus) as was Yesterday improperly advertis'd, but out of good Will to the Author [Henry Carey, whose benefit it was], and to oblige the Audience, for that Night only, will perform several surprizing proofs of Manly Strength, unequall'd yet by any." The Earl of Egmont was in the audience and described the Strong Man's performance:

After dinner I went to the Haymarket playhouse, where among other representations I saw the strong man show one of his feats. Two chairs were placed on the stage at such a distance as that laying himself along, his head and a small part of his shoulders rested on one, and his feet on the other, so that his body and legs were suspended in the air. Then six grown men (two of whom I observed to be remarkably tall [got] up, and stood perpendicular upon his body, two on his chest, two on his body, and two on his legs. He bore them all a quarter of a minute, and bending his body downward till it almost touched the ground between the chairs, with a surprising spring and force raised his body with all that weight upon it, not only level as he lay at first, but higher in the air. The mob in the gallery not satisfied with this, hissed, whereupon he refused to show any other of his tricks.

From the gallery had they been able to see some trickery?

Egmont noted that the Strong Man was then about 30 years of age; his father had been 70 and his mother 52 when he was born. "He is very fond of music and goes a note lower than Montagnana, the deep voiced Italian now here, wherefore he is now learning to sing."

Strong Woman. *See* Alchorne, Mrs.

Stroud, Mr   *ₗfl. 1747ₗ,   French horn player.*

Mr Stroud and Mr Baker played French horns between the acts at the Goodman's Fields Theatre on 24 March 1747.

Stroud, Charles   *c. 1705–1726, organist, composer.*

Charles Stroud, according to Grove, was born about 1705 in London and received his musical education from William Croft as a

choruster in the Chapel Royal. He was made
deputy organist to Croft upon leaving the
choir and was appointed organist of Whitehall
Chapel. Stroud composed the anthem "Hear
my prayer, O God." He died on 26 April 1726
and was buried in the west cloister of Westminster Abbey. Perhaps the musician Stroud
of 1747 was related to him.

Struke, Mrs ₍fl. 1713–1716₎, *cook.*
Leonard Ashley in his dissertation on the
management of Drury Lane Theatre from 1713
to 1716 notes that on the theatre's payroll was
Mrs Struke, a cook.

Strutton, Mr ₍fl. 1766₎, *actor.*
At the Haymarket Theatre under Samuel
Foote's management, Mr Strutton played a
Constable in *The Minor* on 18 June 1766. He
repeated his part at the King's Theatre on 20
August.

Strutts, Mr ₍fl. 1698–1699₎, *exhibitor.*
Advertisements in the *Flying Post* from 10
December 1698 to 3 January 1699 called at-
tention to a freak being shown by Mr Strutts:

There is arrived from *Germany,* a Man born without
Arms: He Fences with his Foot, Flings a Dart or
Sword through a Board; lays one Foot behind his
Neck and Hops on the other; stands on a Stool and
reaches a Glass from under it with his Mouth, holds
a Cane so fast with his Foot, that the strongest Man
cannot pull it from him; writes with his Feet and
Mouth Five several Languages, cuts the Pen himself; lays one Foot on his Neck and with his other
brings a Glass into that Foot, &c. He is to be seen
at Mr. *Strutts* at the *Civet Cat* over against *Exeter
Change* in the *Strand.* Was never in *England* before
and will stay but a short time.

Stuart. *See also* Stewart.

Stuart, Mr ₍fl. 1785₎, *actor.*
Mr Stuart played the Cryer in *The Follies of
a Day* at the Hammersmith Theatre on 25 July
1785. The company performed there from 17
June through 27 July, but Stuart was not
named in any other bill.

Stuart, Mr ₍fl. 1792–1810₎, *actor.*
Mr Stuart acted at Cork in May 1792 and
appeared at the Crow Street Theatre in Dublin
during the 1792–93 season. He was in a com-

pany playing at Bolton, Lancashire, on 14
March 1798; *The Road to Ruin* was presented,
but Stuart's role was not given in the bill. In
June and July 1799 at Darlington, Durham,
Stuart was seen in *Secrets Worth Knowing, The
Maid of the Oaks, Lovers' Vows,* and *The Poor
Soldier.* He may have been the Stuart in Well-
man's troupe in Albrighton on 22 July 1799.
A Stuart was at the Theatre Royal in Shake-
speare Square, Edinburgh, from January to
April 1800 playing Twig in *The Young Quaker,*
a Sailor in *The Brothers,* and Muley in *The
Sultan.* He was probably the Stuart who had a
company at the Star and Garter, Kew Bridge,
London, on 18 July 1800. A Shrewsbury bill
for 6 October 1800 has Stuart down as Fripo-
neau in *The East Indian,* Monsieur Chateau in
Roast Beef and Soup Maigre, and a Keeper in *The
King and the Miller of Mansfield.* He was in
Manchester in April and May 1801 and on the
Drury Lane paylist in London in 1801–2 at £2
weekly. A Stuart was with the Butler troupe
from Richmond, Yorkshire, performing in
Whitby in 1803–4. The last notice of Stuart
(assuming that we have been following the
correct person) has him in Stanton's company
at Burton on 2 January 1810.

Stuart, Mr ₍fl. 1794₎, *house servant?*
On 16 June 1794 benefit tickets for Covent
Garden Theatre were delivered by a Mr
Stuart—unless that was a misprint in the bill
for the minor actor Street, who was in the
Covent Garden company at the time.

Stuart, Mrs ₍fl. 1776₎, *proprietor.*
On 25 June 1776 Marylebone Gardens were
rented by a Mrs Stuart for a *Festivale di Campagna,* according to Mollie Sands in her history
of the Gardens. A Temple of Apollo, with
transparencies by Biaggio Rebecca, was
erected on the grounds to serve as a ballroom.
Advertisements for the evening proposed concerts of instrumental and vocal music, masked
dancing, a cold collation, and a representation
of the Almeida of Cadiz. Tickets were a guinea
(or a guinea and a half for two persons) and
could be obtained from Mrs Stuart at 40 Portland Street.

Complaint was made in the *Public Advertiser*
that neither the entertainment nor the decorations came up to expectations; and Mrs
Stuart herself complained that the manage-

ment of the Gardens gave her no part in the profits for that night. Nevertheless, the Festivale was repeated several times, and on 11 July Mrs Stuart received a benefit.

Stuart, Mrs ₁*fl. 1788–1794*₁, *singer, actress.*

A Mrs Stuart (or Stewart) sang James Hooks's songs at Vauxhall in 1788, according to the *Catalogue of Printed Music in the British Museum*. She was probably the singer who was a soloist at the Pantheon in June 1789. At Covent Garden on 7 March 1794 Mrs Stuart sang in the oratorio selections. Certain identification of Mrs Stuart is difficult, for a second Mrs Stuart, Ann, also a singer and actress, was in London in the 1793–94 season.

Stuart, Miss ₁*fl. 1735*₁, *actress.*

Miss Stuart played Desdemona in *Othello* at York Buildings on 19 March 1735.

Stuart, Miss ₁*fl. 1795–1802?*₁, *actress.*

On 12 February 1795 Miss Stuart played an Amazon in *Alexander the Great* at Drury Lane Theatre, her first notice in the bills. Between then and 20 May she appeared also as Diana in *Jack of Newbury.* In 1795–96 she sang in the choruses of *The Cherokee, The Pirates, The Surrender of Calais, Harlequin Captive, The Iron Chest,* and *Mahmoud* and played Kitty Willis in *The Belle's Stratagem* (on 13 May 1796— unless that was Ann Stuart from Covent Garden) and Isabella in *Don Juan.* Perhaps she was the Miss "Stewart" who acted at Ennis, Ireland, in June 1796. Her name did not appear in London bills again until 28 April 1797, when she had an unspecified role in *The Queen of Carthage* at Drury Lane. She was earning £1 10s. weekly. In May she played in *The Wandering Jew* and *Linco's Travels.*

Miss Stuart went over to the Haymarket Theatre on 9 September 1797 to play Harriet in *The Guardian,* and the *Monthly Mirror* said her "performance proved that she is worthy a better situation than the one she held last winter at Drury Lane." Drury Lane took notice and raised Miss Stuart to £4 weekly in 1797–98 and gave her such new assignments as a Chambermaid in *The Clandestine Marriage,* Stella in *Cheap Living!,* and Charlotte in *The Stranger.* In August 1798 she returned to the Haymarket to act in *The Guardian* again.

Miss Stuart continued at Drury Lane through 1800–1801, earning £4 weekly and adding to her repertoire such new characters as Lady Anne in *Richard III,* Harriet in *The Jealous Wife,* and Lady Clara Modish in *The East Indian.*

Possibly our subject was the Miss "Stewart" of the Theatre Royal, Margate, who married her fellow actor Mr Lancaster in April 1802 at Minster, according to the *Monthly Mirror.*

Stuart, Ann *d. 1809, actress, singer.*

The Covent Garden Theatre performer Miss Stuart of the 1780s and 1790s was, we take it, the Miss Stewart (and, at least once in London bills, Mrs Stuart) who was active from perhaps as early as 1772 through 1795 and who was a different performer from the Miss Stuart who appeared from 1795 through 1800 at Drury Lane and the Haymarket Theatre. Her Christian name, Ann, we learn from an extra-

Harvard Theatre Collection

ANN STUART, as Joan

engraving by Newnham, after Ramberg

illustrated set of Genest's *English Stage* at the Huntington Library.

Perhaps she was the Miss Stuart who acted Peggy in *Patie and Roger* at the Haymarket on 21 September 1772. Also in the cast was James Stewart, who may have been related to her. On 18 September 1776 at the Haymarket a Miss "Stewart" played June in *Midas*, and on the twentieth she acted Mrs Vixen in *The Beggar's Opera*. On 30 November Miss Stewart played Chloe in *High Life below Stairs*.

Our actress seems not to have been mentioned in London bills again until 20 March 1779, when Miss "Stewart" was a Passenger in a Stage in *A New Prelude and Prologue* at Covent Garden Theatre. On 8 November 1779 she sang in the solemn dirge in *Romeo and Juliet* at Covent Garden. Then she was active at Covent Garden regularly throughout the rest of the 1779–80 season, playing parts in *The Bondman* and *The Islanders*, the Nurse in *The Chances*, Sally in *The Invasion*, a Lady in *The Deaf Lover*, a principal but unspecified character in *The Belle's Stratagem*, Amie in *The Jovial Crew*, Parisatis in *The Rival Queens*, and a part in *The Female Orators*. In 1780–81 the Covent Garden bills cited her sometimes as Miss Stewart but more often as Miss Stuart—which we take to be the proper spelling of her name. She was named for some of her old parts as well as for Gipsey in *The Beaux' Stratagem*, Galatea in *Philaster*, the Milliner in *The Suspicious Husband*, a chorus member in *Macbeth*, a Maid in *Sir Courtly Nice*, Arante in *King Lear*, and a Woman of the Town in *Thelypthora*. Her salary was £1 10s. weekly. Miss Stuart donned breeches to play Carlos in *The Duenna* at the Haymarket Theatre on 15 August 1781.

Ann Stuart remained at Covent Garden Theatre through the 1795–96 season, playing such new parts as Ben Budge in a female *Beggar's Opera* called *The Lady's Opera*, Juliet in *Measure for Measure*, Trusty and Myrtilla in *The Provok'd Husband*, Phoebe in *As You Like It*, a Lady in *Which Is the Man?*, Kitty Willis in *The Belle's Stratagem*, Molly Brazen in *The Beggar's Opera*, Cicily in *The Quaker*, Marmalet in *All in the Wrong*, the Fool in *The Pilgrim*, a Girl in Brobdignag in *Friar Bacon*, Columbine in *Harlequin Rambler*, Lady Bab Lardoon in *The Maid of the Oaks*, a Shepherdess in *Cymon*, the Player Queen in *Hamlet*, Iris in *All for Love*, Mavis in *Epicoene*, Lucinda in *Love in a Village*, Betty in

The Hypocrite, Corinna in *The Citizen*, Trippet in *The Lying Valet*, Charlotte in *The Mock Doctor*, Mignionet in *The Way to Keep Him*, a Bacchante in *Comus*, the Duchess in *Barataria*, Lucy in *The West Indian*, Miss Audley in *Appearance Is against Them*, Jenny in *The Commissary*, Florella in *The Orphan*, Grace in *Poor Vulcan*, Sittup in *The Double Gallant*, Scentwell and Patch in *The Busy Body*, Cleone in *The Distrest Mother*, Laura in *Werter*, Lettice in *The Plain Dealer*, Flametta in *A Duke and No Duke*, Katherina in *The Bird in a Cage*, Tawdry in *The Country Mad Cap*, Phryne in *Timon of Athens*, Penelope in *The Romp*, Clara in *The Cheats of Scapin*, Betty in *He Wou'd Be a Soldier*, Helen in *Cymbeline*, Dorcas in *The Winter's Tale*, and Wheedle in *The Miser*.

She also played Lucy Waters in *The Brothers*, Charlotte in *The Apprentice*, Toilet in *The Jealous Wife*, Isabella in *The Revenge*, Susan in *Love and War*, Damaris in *Barnaby Brittle*, Altea in *Rule a Wife and Have a Wife*, Muslin in *The Way to Keep Him*, Fib in *The Toy*, Jenny Diver in *The Beggar's Opera*, Catalina in *The Castle of Andalusia*, Tattleaid in *The Funeral*, Mrs Casey in *Fontainebleau*, Betty in *Hob in the Well*, Annette in *Robin Hood*, Parley in *The Constant Couple*, Lucilla in *The Fair Penitent*, Foible in *The Way of the World*, Mrs Dimity in *The Wives Revenged*, Leonora in *Two Strings to Your Bow*, Kitty Maple in *The Woodman*, a Prisoner in *The Crusade*, Lady Dash in *Blue-Beard*, Penelope in *The Romp*, Lucy in *The Rivals*, Mary in *The Prisoner at Large*, Lucy in *The Recruiting Officer*, a Bar Maid in *Hartford Bridge*, Flounce in *Modern Antiques*, Alice in *The Speechless Wife*, Mrs Bullrush in *The Town before You*, a Country Girl in *The Mysteries of the Castle*, a Maid at the Inn in *Crotchet Lodge*, Jenny in *The Road to Ruin*, Miss Clare in *Life's Vagaries*, and Lucy in *The Devil to Pay*. By the end of May 1796 Miss Stuart's name seems to have dropped from the Covent Garden bills.

During her career Ann Stuart worked her way up to £3 weekly only to drop to £2 weekly by 1795–96, and her line—mostly maids and other minor characters—received little notice. The *Biographical and Imperial Magazine* in January 1790 called her Mignionet in *The Way to Keep Him* "execrable."

The *Druriad* in 1798 (when Miss Stuart may have been performing still, but in very minor roles) said,

Let black-ey'd Heard, and Stuart tattling fast
Of vixen chambermaids divide the cast.

A British Library manuscript reveals that Miss Stuart lived in King Street, St James's Square in 1802. Wewitzer and the *Gentleman's Magazine* reported that she died on 5 July 1809 and was buried in the Savoy.

Ann Stuart is pictured as Jeanne la Pucelle in *1 Henry VI* in an engraving by Newnham, after J. H. Ramberg, published as a plate to *Bell's Shakespeare,* 1786. She never played that role in London; the play was not produced there during the second half of the eighteenth century.

Stuart, Thomas [*fl. 1794*], *violinist.*
Doane's *Musical Directory* of 1794 listed Thomas Stuart as a violinist who had played in the oratorios at Covent Garden Theatre and Westminster Abbey and at Vauxhall Gardens. By 1794 he had gone to America and was living in Philadelphia.

"Student, Kellom's." *See* FRANCIS, MISS [*fl. 1719–1723*], and TOPHAM, JOHN.

Sturgeon, Mr [*fl. 1791–1814*], *scene painter.*
Mr Sturgeon was first mentioned in Covent Garden benefit bills on 14 June 1791. The accounts show him at 15s. weekly through 1813–14 and identify him as a scene painter.

Sturges, Master [*fl. 1754–1769*], *tumbler.*
Master Sturges, surely the son of the tumbler Charles Sturges, performed at Sadler's Wells from as early as 1754 to as late as 1769, according to bills in the Percival collection at the British Library. He shared a benefit with the senior Sturges (or Sturgess) on 22 September 1769; the bill did not describe their performance but gave their address as in Rosoman's Row.

Sturges, Charles [*fl. 1760–1769*], *tumbler, rope dancer, actor.*
Charles Sturges presented a tumbling act at Sadler's Wells as early as 1760, according to advertisements in the Percival collection at the British Library. Bills from 1764 cited Sturges (or Sturgess) as a rope dancer as well. He was

described in the bill of 22 September 1764 as flying over 12 men with three boys on their shoulders and then through a hogshead with fire in the middle. On 29 September 1766 he was Harlequin in *The Custom of the Manor.* He played the title role in *Harlequin Restored* on 26 September 1767.

The newspapers on 8 December 1768 reported that "Among the persons wounded by the Mob at Brentford is Mr. Charles Sturges, the Tumbler at Sadler's Wells, who . . . was knocked off his Horse, and cut and slashed about the Head in a most dreadful Manner. . . ." Charles was living in Rosoman's Row at the time of his benefit at Sadler's Wells on 22 September 1769, which he shared with Sturges junior, presumably his son. Perhaps Charles was related to J. Sturgess.

Sturges, William Henry [*fl. 1794*], *violoncellist.*
Doane's *Musical Directory* of 1794 listed William Henry Sturges, of No 18, Little Trinity Lane, Queen Hithe, as a violoncellist who played for the Cecilian Society.

Sturgess, J. *d. 1754?,* *actor, singer, rope dancer.*
A Mr Sturges played Pluto in *Orpheus and the Death of Eurydice* on 23 August 1740 at Bartholomew Fair. He was probably the Sturgess (or Sturges) who was again active at the fair booths and minor theatres in London in 1748–49. On 24 August 1748 at Bartholomew Fair he played the Third Witch in *The Universal Parents,* a work that was repeated at Southwark Fair on 7 September and at Blackheath on 1 October as *The Fair Maid of the West.* On 31 October Sturgess acted Thorogood in *The London Merchant* at the James Street Theatre and had his benefit tickets accepted at Southwark. He was Tradelove in *A Bold Stroke for a Wife* at the New Wells, Clerkenwell, on 26 December. At Southwark on 2 January 1749 Sturgess sang Peachum in *The Beggar's Opera,* and on 9 January he appeared there as Bullock in *The Recruiting Officer.*

We believe he was the slack-rope dancer Sturgess who performed in May and June 1754 at Gordon's Long Room in Charleston, South Carolina, advertised as recently arrived from London. J. Sturgess, "Comedian," was buried at St Philip's Church in Charleston on 4 January 1755. We assume he died a few days earlier, perhaps before the end of 1754.

Sturmer, Mr ₍*fl.* 1794₎, *performer, puppeteer.*

Mr Sturmer, his wife (the former Ann Flockton, niece of the puppeteer John Flockton), and two of their children performed in the musical drama *The Purse* at Bartholomew Fair in 1794, according to Sybil Rosenfeld in *The Theatre of the London Fairs.* Sturmer was listed as a puppeteer in the Pie Powder Court Book that year. Ann Sturmer's uncle died on 12 April 1794, leaving her his two houses in Old Street, one a freehold and the other a leasehold.

Sturmer, Ann, née Flockton ₍*fl.* 1794₎, *performer. See* STURMER, MR.

Sturpesi, Mr ₍*fl.* 1766–1767₎, *tumbler.*

Mr Sturpesi was a tumbler in a troupe performing at the Haymarket Theatre from 27 October 1766 through 14 January 1767.

Sturt, Mr ₍*fl.* 1751–1762?₎, *actor.*

Mr Sturt was named in the Drury Lane benefit bill on 13 May 1751. He was a minor actor in the company and is known to have played the Fine Gentleman in *Lethe* at his shared benefit (with three others) on 11 May 1753 and a character in *The Chinese Festival* on 8 November 1755 and subsequent dates. He was named in benefit bills at Drury Lane through 9 May 1757. During the summers he acted at Richmond and Twickenham, his first notice being at Richmond on 17 August 1751, when he played John in *Two Nights from Land's End.* He then went on there to play Ratcliff in *Jane Shore,* Snival in *Diversions of the Morning,* Sir Walter Blunt in *Henry IV,* and a Bravo in *The Inconstant.* At Twickenham he played Percy in *The Mourning Bride* and Paris in *Romeo and Juliet.* He returned to Richmond in the summer of 1753 to act the Second Murderer in *Macbeth* on 28 July and then Coupée in *The Virgin Unmask'd,* a Bravo in *The Inconstant,* Vale in *The Suspicious Husband,* Palemon in *The Chaplet,* Sir Charles Freeman in *The Beaux' Stratagem* (at his solo benefit on 24 July), Whisper in *The Busy Body,* and Harlequin in *Harlequin Skeleton.*

Perhaps our subject was the Mr Sturt who was in David Douglass's company in America in 1761–62, performing in Newport and New York. Seilhamer lists Sturt's known roles in America as Guildenstern in *Hamlet,* the Lieutenant in *Richard III,* Montague in *Romeo and Juliet,* Lucius in *Theodosius,* a Magician in *Harlequin Collector,* Sapscull in *The Honest Yorkshireman,* Mercury in *Lethe,* and Leander in *The Mock Doctor.*

Style, Miss ₍*fl.* 1789₎, *actress.*

Advertised as "A Young Gentlewoman," Miss Style made her first and last stage appearance on 1 August 1789 at the Haymarket Theatre as the title character in *Polly Honeycomb.* The *European Magazine* identified her and noted that she had

rendered herself conspicuous at some late Masquerades for her representation of a few dramatic characters. . . . [She] made her first theatrical attempt at the Haymarket in the character of Polly Honeycombe. Her figure is rather short than elegant. She possesses a pleasing voice and is mistress of an easy deportment. Her talents however seem entirely without cultivation and she has much both to learn and unlearn.

Styles, Mr ₍*fl.* 1677₎, *actor.*

Mr Styles, an actor trained at the "Nursery," played Abraham in *The Country Innocence* in March 1677 and Sir Jasper Sympleton in *Wits Led by the Nose* the following mid-June at Drury Lane Theatre.

Subbeys, Mr ₍*fl.* 1795₎, *showman.*

The Pie Powder Court Book shows that Mr Subbeys had a medley at Bartholomew Fair in 1795.

Subligny, Marie-Thérèse Perdou de 1666–*c.* 1735, *dancer.*

Marie-Thérèse Perdou de Subligny, according to Campardon in his *Académie Royale de Musique,* was born in 1666 and from 1688 was attached to the Paris Opéra. She danced many small roles between 1689 and 1707, including three parts in *Atys* in 1689 and 1699, a Peasant in *Cadmus et Hermione* in 1690, a Peasant in the *Ballet de Villeneuve-Saint-Georges* in 1692, two parts in *Didon* in 1693 and 1704, two parts in *L'Europe galante* in 1697 and 1706, three parts in *Issé* in 1698, a Peasant in *Amadis*

Harvard Theatre Collection

MARIE-THÉRÈSE PERDOU DE SUBLIGNY

artist unknown

de Grèce in 1699, three parts in *Marthésie* in 1699, a Ghost in *Proserpine* in 1699, three parts in *Canente* in 1700, two parts in *Les Saisons* in 1700, a Nymphe of Diane in *Aréthuse* in 1701, two parts in *Acis et Galatée* in 1702 and 1704, a Follower of Thomiris in *Médus* in 1702, a Peasant in *Les Muses* in 1703, two parts in a revival of *Psiché* in 1703, three parts in *Le Carnaval et la Folie* in 1704, a Nymphe in *Iphegénie en Tauride* in 1704, Flore in *Alcide* in 1705, two parts in *Télémaque* in 1705, and two parts in *Tancrède* in 1707.

Thomas Betterton tried to boost theatre attendance at the Lincoln's Inn Fields Theatre in London by bringing over Mme Subligny between December 1701 and February 1702. According to the *Memoires* of the Abbé Trublet, she came armed with a letter of introduction to the philosopher John Locke, who had noted the value of dancing in his *Education* in 1693. Though Trublet said Locke became her "l'homme d'affaires," by 1702 Locke may not

have aided her much. In any case Mme Subligny made enough of a mark in London that later dancers—the Devonshire Girl, among them—imitated her, and the *Diverting Post* on 16 December 1704 compared Mme De La Valle to her.

On 3 August 1704, as Genest in *Les Divertissements de Sceaux* (1712) reported, Mme Subligny appeared at a fête at Chastenay, but in 1705 she retired from the stage, having impressed critics with her "noble and graceful dancing" (as Castil-Blaze put it in *La Danse et les ballets* in 1832). She died, according to the *Histoire de l'Opéra,* before 1736. Compardon cites documents dating from May 1735 concerning "demoiselle Marie-Thérèse de Subligny et Madeline Bailleul, filles majeures" of the Rue St Honoré, who were involved in a lawsuit, but that Subligny could hardly have been our subject. She may have been a daughter.

A portrait of Mme Subligny, by an unknown engraver, shows her standing with her arms extended.

"Succianoccioli."   *See*   MANZUOLI, GIOVANNI.

Suck, Charles J. [*fl. 1781–1784*], *oboist, flutist, composer.*

The *New Grove Dictionary of Music and Musicians* says that Charles J. Suck performed in London in 1781. He was a pupil of J. C. Fischer and played oboe in the Handel Memorial Concerts at Westminster Abbey and the Pantheon in May and June 1784. The *European Magazine* described him as proficient on the oboe and the German flute. Grove (fifth edition) notes that six trios by Suck have survived. The musician lived at No 15, Great Russell Street, Bloomsbury.

Sudlow, William *1772–1848, violoncellist, organist, composer.*

In his *History of the Violoncello* van der Straeten gives William Sudlow's dates as 1772–1848. Sudlow was from Manchester, where he was an organist, violoncellist, and composer of vocal music. His brother Edward was a violist. William was listed in Doane's *Musical Directory* in 1794 as having played cello in the Handelian performances at Westminster Abbey and at the Manchester Meeting.

"Sue." *See* VERBRUGGEN, MRS JOHN.

Suett, Richard   *c. 1758?–1805, actor, singer, composer.*

Richard Suett was born in Chelsea about 1758. At the time of his death in July 1805 the *Morning Herald* reported his age as 50, but the *Gentleman's Magazine* stated he had died in his forty-seventh year. When acting at York, he was called Master Suett through 1772, but in 1773 was designated Mr Suett. Had that change occurred at his majority then he would have been born in 1752. He was the son of John Suett, a butcher, who at the time of his death on 20 October 1783 was reported in the *Gentleman's Magazine* to be "one of the servants" at St Paul's Cathedral. Evidently he was a verger. Nothing is known of Suett's mother, though she may have been referred to in the will of Thomas Ludford dated 12 January 1776. Ludford made bequests of property to his daughter Elizabeth, the wife of the singer

Courtesy of the Garrick Club

RICHARD SUETT
by De Wilde

Richard Bellamy, and her children, with the proviso that they were to forfeit the inheritances in case they ever had anything to do with a person whom he designated as "that infernal hussey Suett." Richard Bellamy had associations in the 1770s with the royal musical establishment, and in 1777 became a vicar choral of St Paul's. His son Thomas Ludford Bellamy was educated in the late 1770s in the choir of the Westminster Abbey under Benjamin Cooke, where young Richard Suett, according to *The Dictionary of National Biography,* was entered at the age of ten. In his *Reminiscences,* however, Thomas J. Dibdin wrote that Suett had been in the choir of St Paul's under Robert Hudson.

Perhaps Suett did stints in both choirs. But it should be noted that from about 1760 to 1775 Hudson was organist at the Grotto Gardens, where Master Suett was performing by 1771 and perhaps as early as the year 1769 claimed by the *DNB.* (Supposedly, he also made appearances in that earlier year at Ranelagh Gardens and at Marylebone Gardens. The *DNB* notes that he acted in some unnoted juvenile parts at the Haymarket Theatre in the summer of 1770.)

The first performance by Suett for which a notice has been found occurred on 22 June 1771, when he sang at the Grotto Gardens in a musical entertainment by Bates called *The Gamester.* The advertisements, which called him "Master Suett," promised repetitions on Tuesdays, Thursdays, and Saturdays. On 8 August, one of the nights *The Gamester* was performed, he sang "a Favourite Song." That summer, according to Wroth in *The London Pleasure Gardens,* he also was at Ranelagh Gardens. Advertised as Master "Sewett," he appeared as Cupid in the premiere of Hook's comic opera *Dido* at Foote's Haymarket on 24 July 1771 and then on several other nights that summer.

In the autumn of 1771, upon the recommendation of Charles Bannister, Suett was engaged for the York circuit by Tate Wilkinson, who in his *Wandering Patentee* described Suett at that time as "about the age of seventeen" and possessed of "a most unpromising pair of legs." Suett made his first appearance at Hull on 20 November 1771, singing "Chloe's my Myrtle and Jenny's my Rose." York first heard Master Suett on 22 January 1772 when he sang

"Soldier Tir'd of War's Alarms." On 22 February he appeared with other young people in *Lilliput,* and on the twenty-ninth he sang a duet with Miss Hitchcock. During the ten years that Suett remained under Wilkinson's tutelage he steadily improved and became, as the manager put it, "of real importance" to the company. In 1773–74 his name began to appear as *Mr* Suett. When Garrick offered him a position at Drury Lane in 1780, Wilkinson generously released him from his articles and assisted him in obtaining a three-year contract in London. Suett took a benefit at York on 28 May 1780, as Scrub in *The Stratagem,* at which performance it was announced that his departure was imminent.

On 7 October 1780 Suett made his first appearance at Drury Lane, as Ralph in *The Maid of the Mill.* He next played Squire Richard in *The Provok'd Husband* on 26 October and subsequently was seen as Mungo in *The Padlock,* Simon in *The Apprentice,* Metaphor in *Dissipation,* and Tipple in *A Flitch of Bacon.* He was the original Moll Flagon in the premiere of Burgoyne's *The Lord of the Manor* on 27 December 1789, and on 25 April 1781 he sang "Poor Thomas Day" with Bannister and Gaudry in an entertainment called *A Fête.*

In the summer of 1781 Suett returned to Wilkinson to play at Leeds and Sheffield in June, and in July and August he performed at the Theatre Royal, Shakespeare Square, Edinburgh, where his roles included Tipple, Westmoreland in *2 Henry IV,* Doodle in *Tom Thumb the Great,* and Deputy Dimity in *The Wives Revenged.*

Before beginning his second season at Drury Lane, on 8 September 1781 Suett married at St Michael le Belfrey in York the dancer Louisa Margaretta West, whom he had met when they were both young performers in Wilkinson's company in the 1770s. She was the daughter of the sometime London performers Mr and Mrs D. West and the sister of William West, who danced in London and the provinces for over 55 years, and of Miss D. West, who had a modest career in the provinces and danced once in London, at the Royalty Theatre on 3 July 1787. When Suett had first joined the York company in 1772 he had lodged at Mr Mountain's in Stangate, where the West family were also boarders.

Suett reappeared at Drury Lane on 20 Sep-

tember 1781, in an unspecified role in *Robinson Crusoe.* His original roles that season were Tom in Jackman's *The Divorce* on 10 November 1781, Piano in Tickell's opera *The Carnival of Venice* on 10 December, an unspecified part in the anonymous pantomime *Lun's Ghost* on 3 January 1782, and Carbine in *The Fair American* on 18 May. The role of Carbine he took over from Dodd "at a few minute's notice," according to the *Morning Herald* on 21 May, and "went through the reading as though he had studied the character." His other roles included Daniel in *Oroonoko,* Glaud in numerous performances of *The Gentle Shepherd,* Lubin in *The Quaker,* Bundle in *The Waterman,* Diego in *She Wou'd and She Wou'd Not,* Squire Richard in *The Provok'd Husband,* Filch in *The Beggar's Opera,* Dick in *The Lying Valet,* a Recruit in *The Recruiting Serjeant,* Linco in *Cymon,* Hobbinol in *The Capricious Lovers,* Kecksey in *The Irish Widow,* Waitwell in *The Way of the World,* and Diggery in *All the World's a Stage.* On 7 March 1782 he replaced Parsons as Sir Timothy Valerian in the seventh performance of Griffith's

Harvard Theatre Collection

RICHARD SUETT, as Colonel Oldboy
engraving by Woodman, after De Wilde

Variety. For his benefit on 3 May 1782 (when he acted Jarvis in *The Runaway*) tickets were available at his house, No 20, Gloucester Street, Queen's Square, Bloomsbury, and he shared net benefit receipts of about £117 with Wright.

In 1782–83 he continued in many of the above roles and added Supple in *The Double Gallant,* Davy in *Bon Ton,* Inkhorn in the premiere of M. P. Andrews's *The Best Bidder* on 11 December 1782, an unspecified role in the premiere of King's *The Triumph of Mirth* on 26 December, Launcelot in *The Merchant of Mirth,* and a Strolling Player in *Imitation.* For his benefit on 26 April 1783 he played Booze in *Belphegor,* and his address was given as No 24, King Street, Holborn.

Suett remained engaged at Drury Lane throughout his career. He made occasional appearances at the Haymarket, and beginning in 1793 he had regular summer engagements there until 1803. Indeed the story of his life is told mainly by listing the numerous parts he played in his 24 years on the London stage, mostly in the line of low comedy characters and Shakespearean clowns. Because of his good musical skills and training, he also played many roles in comic operas. A selection of roles at Drury Lane before the turn of the century includes Cimberton in *The Conscious Lovers,* Marall in *A New Way to Pay Old Debts,* Lord Plausible in *The Plain Dealer,* Binnacle in *The Fair Quaker,* the Clown in *The Winter's Tale,* the Clown in *Twelfth Night,* Touchstone in *As You Like It,* Pistol in *Henry V,* Cob in *Every Man in His Humour,* a Citizen in *Coriolanus,* Gibbet in *The Beaux' Stratagem,* Hardcastle in *She Stoops to Conquer,* Lint in *The Mayor of Garratt,* Colonel Oldboy in *The School for Fathers,* Thurio in *Two Gentlemen of Verona,* a Witch in *Macbeth,* a Gravedigger in *Hamlet,* and the Old Woman in *Rule a Wife and Have a Wife.*

His original roles were extensive. In addition to those already cited, they included: Sir Ephraim Rupee in C. Dibdin's *Liberty Hall* on 8 February 1785, Dr Bilioso in Cobb's *The Doctor and the Apothecary* on 25 October 1788, Oliver in Cumberland's *The Imposters* on 26 January 1789, Lewis in Cobb's *The Haunted Tower* on 24 November 1789, Old Pickle in Bickerstaff's *The Spoil'd Child* on 22 March 1790, Endless in Hoare's *No Song No Supper* on 16 April 1790, Yuseph in Cobb's *The Siege of*

Ashmolean Museum, Oxford

RICHARD SUETT, as Dicky Gossip
by De Wilde

Belgrade on 1 January 1791, Aldobrand in Cobb's *The Algerine Slave* on 17 March 1792, and Don Gasparo in Cobb's *The Pirates* on 21 November 1792. With the Drury Lane company at the Haymarket Theatre he created the original Label in Hoare's *The Prize* on 11 March 1793, Apathy in Morton's *The Children of the Wood* on 1 October 1793, Dicky Gossip in Hoare's *My Grandmother* on 16 December 1793, Justice Rackrent in Waldron's *Heigho for a Husband* on 14 January 1794, and Squire Robert in Cumberland's *The Box-Lobby Challenge* on 22 February 1794.

After the company moved into the new Drury Lane Theatre in 1794, his original roles were Jabal in Cumberland's *The Jew* on 8 May 1794, Varbel in Kemble's *Lodoiska* on 9 June 1794, Jeremy in Cobb's *The Cherokee* on 20 December 1794, Weazel in Cumberland's *The Wheel of Fortune* on 28 February 1795, Consol in Holcroft's *The Man of Ten Thousand* on 23 January 1796, Samson in Colman's *The Iron Chest* on 12 March 1796, Barakka in Hoare's

Mahmoud on 30 April 1796, Stave in Arnold's *The Shipwreck* on 10 December 1796, Realize in Reynold's *The Will* on 19 April 1797, the Governor in Porter's *The Chimney Corner* on 7 October 1797, Old Woodland in Reynolds's *Cheap Living* on 21 October 1797, Ibrahim in Colman's *Blue-Beard* on 16 January 1798, Peter in Thompson's *The Stranger* on 24 March 1798, Nicholas in Colman's *Feudal Times* on 19 January 1799, Old Lizard in Morris's *The Secret* on 2 March 1799, Diego in Sheridan's *Pizarro* on 24 May 1799, Ramrod in Franklin's *The Embarkation* on 3 October 1799, and Baron Piffleberg in T. J. Dibdin's *Of Age Tomorrow* on 1 February 1800.

On 16 September 1785, at the Haymarket Theatre, where he had appeared 15 years earlier as a child, Suett replaced Edwin in a vocal part in *The Sons of Anacreon*. In the summer of 1793 he was engaged by the younger Colman at the Haymarket where he reappeared on 11 June as Cranky in *The Son-in-Law* and Tallboy in *The Spanish Barber,* and also that summer played such roles as Governor Harcourt in *The Chapter of Accidents,* Roundfree in *Ways and Means,* Old Philpot in *The Citizen,* and Sir Felix Friendly in *The Agreeable Surprise.* On 29 June 1793 he was the original Whimsey in O'Keeffe's *The London Hermit.* He returned to the Haymarket each summer thereafter through 1803, playing his line of low comedy and clown characters and appearing in numerous musical roles. Among the original roles he acted at the Haymarket were Robin Gray in Arnold's *Auld Robin Gray* on 29 July 1794, Fustian in Colman's *New Hay at the Old Market* on 9 June 1795, Amalekite in Morton's *Zorinski* on 20 June 1795, Bobby Notice in Brewer's *Bannian Day* on 11 June 1796, Daniel Dowlas, alias Baron Duberly, in Colman's *The Heir at Law* on 15 July 1797, Germain in Heartwell and Colman's *The Castle of Sorrento* on 13 July 1799, Von Snarl in Hoare's *Sighs* on 30 July 1799, Steinberg in C. Kemble's *The Point of Humour* on 15 July 1800, Don Miguelde Lara in Holman's *What a Blunder!* on 14 August 1800, and Mr Deputy Bull in Colman's *The Review* on 1 September 1800. Among many other roles played by Suett at the Haymarket were the Carpenter in *The Surrender of Calais,* Snarl in *The Village Lawyer,* Dowdle in *The Prisoner at Large,* Perriwinkle in *A Bold Stroke for a Wife,* Rorey in *Gretna Green,* Sir Francis Gripe in *The Busy Body,* and Antonio in *The Follies of the Day.*

Suett's only appearance at Covent Garden Theatre was on 23 April 1799, when by special permission of the proprietors of Drury Lane he acted Samson in *The Iron Chest,* evidently in place of his son Theophilus Suett, who had been cast in the role.

In the early years of the nineteenth century his roles at Drury Lane included the original Dominique in Holcroft's *Deaf and Dumb* on 24 February 1801. His salary by his last season, 1804–5, was £12 per week, having risen steadily from £6 in 1789–90. Benefit notices gave his address as No 230, High Holborn in 1784; No 14, Broad Street, Bloomsbury, in 1785; No 21, King Street, Bloomsbury Square, from 1790 to 1793; No 19, Martlett Court, Covent Garden, in 1796; No 10, Hart Square, Covent Garden, in 1797; No 18, Clement's Inn in 1798; No 1, Martlett Court in 1799; and back at No 21, King Street, Bloomsbury Square, in 1800.

Suett's last appearance was at Drury Lane on 10 June 1805, when he acted Lampedo in *The Honeymoon.* He died on 6 July 1805, at a small public house in Denzell Street, Clare Market, according to the *DNB,* or, according to other sources, at his lodgings in Paradise Row. He was buried in St Paul's Cathedral churchyard, on the north side, on 15 July.

In his will, made on 16 June 1805, Suett described himself as a comedian of Denzell Street, Clare Market, and declared that he was drawing the will "to prevent controversies" after his decease. That precaution seems to have been pointed at his estranged wife Louisa, "who I verily believe at this time and for a long time lives in a state of adultery with Mr Grindal a distiller in St Giles." He left her "one shilling and no more." After directing that his funeral expense should not exceed £20, he bequeathed £150 to Lucy Wood of Denzell Street, Clare Market; she was to receive also all sums due him in arrears from Drury Lane, and all his household goods, including his china, plate, apparel, musical instruments, and books. No doubt she was living with Suett. Lucy Wood, the named executrix, proved the will on 8 July 1805.

No mention was made in Suett's will of his two sons by Louisa Margaretta Suett, who after her marriage to him in 1781 retired from the stage. One son, Theophilus Suett, sang as Master Suett at the Haymarket in 1799 and 1800 and acted at Drury Lane in 1800. He died on naval service in the Mediterranean on 28 April 1817. The other son, John Suett, born in 1785, died on 11 October 1848 and was buried at Doncaster Parish Church, where his mother, who died on 13 May 1832, was also buried. She is noticed in this *Dictionary* as Louisa Margaretta West.

"Dicky" Suett, as he was called, was a sociable man, who enjoyed the fellowship of his colleagues. He was a member of "The Strangers at Work," a singing society formed about 1791 by 21 performers, including Bannister, Johnstone, Quick, Holman, Blanchard, and Munden. He had close ties in Birmingham, where he played during the summers. He was a member of the famous Birmingham Anacreontic Society, instituted on 24 October 1793, which met at Joseph Warden's tavern, the Eagle and Ball, in Colmore Street. The society consisted of illustrious citizens of Birmingham and London visitors; these included John Emery, John Braham, Admiral Lord Duncan, Admiral Nelson, and General Lord Hutchinson. The press in that city reported on 13 August 1792 the loss by Suett of his "Curious Collection of Wigs, Which were unfortunately burned . . . in the Fire at Birmingham Theatre." He was well known for his wigs. Indeed, John Williams in *A Pin Basket to the Children of Thespis* (1797) claimed that "Half Suett's comedy lies in—his wig." Williams also mentioned that a brown suit worn by Suett as Foresight in *Love for Love* had been made for the late Mrs Woffington to wear as Sir Harry Wildair.

Suett was extremely fond of low company and was a frequenter of public houses in Chelsea and Clare Market. Genest reported that Suett had ruined himself by drinking, and related a story of someone's calling on the actor one morning at breakfast and finding him at the table with a bottle of rum and a bottle of brandy. It was said that Suett frequently used spirits to get himself ready for a night's work on the stage.

Indeed drunken characters were one of his specialties, and no part more suited him than the drunken Porter in *Feudal Times*. The playwright O'Keeffe called him "the most natural

Courtesy of the Garrick Club

RICHARD SUETT, as Endless
by De Wilde

actor of any," whose "tall, thin, ungainly figure, was very comic." He was adept at make-up, upon which he heavily relied. He was prone to mugging and ad-libbing. Hazlitt called him "the delightful old croaker, the everlasting Dicky Gossip of the stage." In the *Dramatic Censor* (1800), Thomas Dutton praised his Label in *The Prize,* his old character Varbel in *Lodoiska,* and his Baron Piffleberg in *Of Age Tomorrow,* and commented on his "natural disposition for drollery" and his "irresistible comic force." Of his Clown in *Twelfth Night,* Williams in his *Children of Thespis* (1786) wrote:

> *Go, ask why that Folly should thus be his debtor,*
> *The argument's us'd, that they can't find a better.*

High praise was accorded his portrayal of one of the gravediggers in *Hamlet*—but he was "deficient," according to the *Theatrical Review* (1783), in "that high style of colouring which characterizes the *vis-comica* of Parsons."

Suett was often compared to Parsons, whose death in 1795 left a gap in the Drury Lane company. Suett took on many of his characters, and was generally successful, but he was not Parsons' equal. Waldron wrote in his *Candid and Impartial Strictures on the Performers* (1795):

. . . Mr. Suett's comedy is deficient of that strength and richness of humour so luxuriously possessed by Parsons. His figure is too thin for its height. His turned-in tottering knees and lathy body, when performing old men, give us more an idea of an aged Spaniard than any other character. He is too fond of distorting his features into grimace, and saying more than is set down for him. His method of delivering dialogue is however entirely his own, and not in the least borrowed from any other actor.

Suett's reputation rests perhaps on the praise given him by Charles Lamb in *Essays of Elia:*

I think he was not altogether of that timber out of which cathedral seats and sounding-boards are hewed. But if a glad heart—kind, and therefore glad—be any part of sanctity, then might the robe of Motley, with which he invested himself with so much humility after his deprivation, and which he wore so long with so much blameless satisfaction to himself and to the public, he accepted for a surplice,—his white stole and *albe.* . . .

He was the Robin Goodfellow of the stage. . . . Thousands of hearts yet respond to the chuckling *O La!* of Dicky Suett, brought back to their remembrance by the faithful transcript of his friend Mathew's mimicry. The "force of nature could no further go." He drolled upon the stock of these two syllables richer than the cuckoo. . . .

Shakspeare foresaw him, when he framed his fools and jesters. They have all the true Suett stamp, a loose and shambling gait, a slippery tongue, this last the ready midwife to a without-pain-delivered jest; in words, light as air, venting truths deep as the centre; with idlest rhymes tagging conceit when busiest, singing with Lear in the tempest, or Sir Toby at the buttery-hatch.

Jack Bannister and he had the fortune to be more of personal favorites with the town than any actors before or after. The difference, I take it, was this:— Jack was more *beloved* for his sweet, good-natured, moral pretensions. Dicky was more *liked* for his sweet, good-natured, no pretensions at all. Your whole conscience stirred with Bannister's performance of Walter in the Children in the Wood,—but Dicky seemed like a thing, as Shakspeare says of

Love, too young to know what conscience is. He put us into Vesta's days. Evil fled before him,—not as from Jack, as from an antagonist,—but because it could not touch him, any more than a cannon-ball a fly. He was delivered from the burden of that death; and, when death came himself, not in metaphor, to fetch Dicky, it is recorded of him by Robert Palmer, who kindly watched his exit, that he received the last stroke, neither varying his accustomed tranquillity, nor tune, with the simple exclamation, worthy to have been recorded in his epitaph—*O La! O La! Bobby!*

Suett was also a good musician. He set the music for the songs of Fernside's *The Female Duellist,* an afterpiece acted by the Drury Lane company at the King's Theatre on 22 May 1793. In that farce Suett acted Don Alvarez. Compositions by Suett listed in the *Catalogue of Printed Music in the British Museum* include *Six Canzonets with an Accompaniment for a Harp or Piano-Forte* (1794); *Six Glees . . . Composed for . . . Members of the Ad Libitum Society* (1794); *The Kiss—an Enigma* (1800?); *Of Cruel Absence. A Favorite Ballad* (1800?); *The celebrated Pastoral of Corin and Joan* (1800?); *The Signs of Faithfull Love* (1800?); *Soft Music, let my humble lay,* sung by Miss Farren in *False Colours* (1793); *Three Sonatas for the Piano Forte or Harpsichord* (1785?); *Sometimes when Absent. A Favorite Canzonet* (1795?); *Sylvia again is true and Kind. A Favorite Canzonet* (1790?); *The Tranquil Thatch. A favorite Ballad,* sung by Mr Incledon (1795?).

Portraits of Richard Suett include:

1. By Samuel De Wilde. Oil painting in the Garrick Club (No 196). Engraving by W. Ridley, published in the *Monthly Mirror,* August 1803; a copy by an unknown engraver was published by De Wilde and Cawthorn, 1811.

2. As Bayes in *The Rehearsal.* Painting by John Graham. Sold at Leigh & Sotheby's on 25 May 1805. In the Victoria and Albert Museum. Engraving by W. Skelton published as a plate to *Bell's British Library,* 1796.

3. As Bayes. Engraving by J. Rogers, after W. Smith. Published as a plate to Oxberry's *Dramatic Biography,* 1825.

4. As Colonel Oldboy in *The School for Fathers.* Painting by Samuel De Wilde, c. 1790. In the National Theatre. Engraving by R. Woodman published as a plate to *The Cabinet,* 1808. For details see R. Mander and J. Mitch-

Courtesy of the Garrick Club

JOHN BANNISTER as Sylvester Daggerwood and RICHARD SUETT as Fustian
by De Wilde

enson, *The Artist and the Theatre* (1955), 76–81.

5. As Dicky Gossip in *My Grandmother.* Painting by Samuel De Wilde, 1797. In the Ashmolean Museum, Oxford, presented by A. Buttery in 1924.

6. As Diggery Duckling, with eight other actors, in a scene in *All the World's a Stage,* as revived at Drury Lane Theatre on 12 March 1803. Painting by Samuel De Wilde. In the National Theatre. Details and provenance are given by Messrs Mander and Mitchenson, *The Artist and the Theatre* (1955), pp. 122–127. The painting is reproduced in this *Dictionary,* 6:284.

7. As Endless in *No Song No Supper.* Painting by Samuel De Wilde. In the Garrick Club (No 479).

8. As Endless. Pencil and watercolor drawing by Samuel De Wilde, inscribed June 17, 1794. In the Garrick Club (No 552). Similar to No 7 above.

9. As the First Gravedigger in *Hamlet.* By unknown artist. Sold in the sale of the property of the American Shakespeare Theater at Sotheby Parke Bernet, New York, 15 January 1976.

10. With John Bannister, as the Gravediggers in *Hamlet.* By Johann Zoffany, canvas, 20½" × 17½". Sold at Sotheby's on 7 January 1970 and bought for £25 by Farlow.

11. As Fustian, with John Bannister as Sylvester Daggerwood, in *Sylvester Daggerwood.* Painting by Samuel De Wilde, 1797. In the Garrick Club. Another version by De Wilde, dated 1798, once belonged to Henry Irving. It was part of the Maugham bequest to the National Theatre, where it now hangs.

12. As the Ghost in *Hamlet.* Slight caricature, after T. H. Tuthill, published as a plate to *The Green-Room Remembrancer,* 1828.

13. As Ibrahim in *Blue-Beard.* Engraving by R. Page, after T. Wageman. Published as a plate to Oxberry's *New English Drama,* 1823.

14. As Louis in *The Haunted Tower.* Watercolor drawing by W. Loftis. In the Folger Shakespeare Library.

15. As Pistol in *Henry V.* Watercolor drawing by W. Loftis. In the Folger Shakespeare Library.

16. As Ralph in *The Maid of the Mill.* Engraving by T. Cole after De Wilde. Published

by C. Cook, 1797. A copy was published by Cooke as a plate to *British Drama,* 1809.

17. As the Turnkey in *The Island of St. Marguerite.* Watercolor drawing by W. Loftis. In the Folger Shakespeare Library.

Suett, Mrs Richard. *See* WEST, LOUISA MARGARETTA.

Suett, Theophilus   *d. 1817, singer, actor.*

Theophilus Suett, one of the two sons of the actor Richard Suett by his wife, the dancer Louisa Margaretta (née West), made his first appearance in public at the Haymarket Theater on 13 August 1799. Announced as Master Suett, after the mainpiece he sang Haydn's "My mother bids me bind my hair." That night his father acted Amalekite in *Zorinski* and Antonio in *The Follies of a Day.* At his father's benefit on 22 August 1799 Master Suett acted David Rawbold in *The Iron Chest* and Dick in *The Shipwreck.* He played David Rawbold again on 5 and 16 August.

The following season, at Drury Lane Theatre on 23 May 1800, Master Suett sang an unspecified song in Act II of *The Sultan.* At the end of *The Clandestine Marriage* on 5 June he sang "Strike the Harp," with Master Heather, and on 10 June Master Suett sang "Soft Musick let my humble lay," a song composed by his father.

On 23 September 1800 at Drury Lane a Master Suett acted the Prince of Wales in *Richard III.* Since he was announced as making his first appearance on any stage, that youngster may have been John Suett (1785–1848).

Master Suett, obviously the singing Theophilus, sang at Sadler's Wells in the summer of 1801.

Theophilus Suett died on naval service in the Mediterranean on 28 April 1817.

Sulivan. *See* SULLIVAN.

Sullivan, Daniel   *d. 1764, singer, actor, composer.*

Though the Irish countertenor Daniel Sullivan did not make his official acting debut until 1743, he may have been singing in public before that. The *Catalogue of Printed Music in the British Museum* cites him as singing

Lampe's *The Shepherd's Invitation,* a song published about 1730. The *New Grove* notes that he may have begun as a boy singer in Dublin in 1737. He was the Sullivan listed as the composer of *Gentle Parthenissa* (1740?), and he sang Lampe's *The Wish* (1740?). At Chester in 1741, according to Sands, Sullivan sang with Mr and Mrs Lampe, and in 1743 he sang at Ranelagh.

At Drury Lane Theatre on 2 February 1743 Sullivan made his "1st appearance any stage" playing Moore of Moore Hall in *The Dragon of Wantley.* On 24 March at the Haymarket Theatre he sang Casimir in *Amelia* for Mrs Lampe's benefit. At Drury Lane he sang "Gentle Parthenissa" on 15 April, and on 23 May "The Noontide Air." In the fall of 1743 at Drury Lane, Sullivan was a regular entr'acte singer, but on 19 January 1744 he went over to the Haymarket to sing Farinelli in Lampe's *The Queen of Spain; or, Farinelli at Madrid.* On 10 February he was at Covent Garden Theatre, singing Athamas in Handel's *Semele,* and on 24 February he sang Micah in *Samson.* Sullivan was Joseph in *Joseph and His Brethren* on 2 March. Mrs Delaney had written to Mrs Dewes on 25 February that "Handel is mightily out of humour about it, for Sullivan, who is to sing Joseph, is a *block* with a very fine voice. . . ." At the Haymarket on 16 April Sullivan was Lysander in *The Kiss Accepted and Returned,* another work by Lampe. The performance was for Sullivan's benefit and also included a repetition of *The Queen of Spain.*

On 14 February 1745 at the Haymarket Sullivan had another benefit, singing the lead in *The Queen of Spain* again, and on 1 April he sang in a concert there. In 1745 Sullivan also sang at Bath. About that year Lampe's *To Sylvia* was published, as sung by Sullivan at Drury Lane. A benefit concert was held for Sullivan on 16 December 1745 at the Exchange Tavern in Bristol; then the singer headed for Ireland. David Garrick wrote from Dublin to Draper on 2 January 1746 that "Mr. Sullivan is just arrived; but what he intends, or where, is not yet fixed: he looks as gay and sensible as usual. . . ." Sullivan sang at the Music Hall in Fishamble Street on 3 March and at Smock Alley Theatre on 5 March. On 13 March at Smock Alley he was Moore in *The Dragon of Wantley.*

At Drury Lane on 7 November 1746 Sulli-van sang in *Macbeth* and on 15 December in *Theodosius.* In the spring of 1747 he was Gubbins in *The Dragon of Wantley* and appeared in *King John* and in entr'acte entertainments. He was again at Drury Lane in 1747–48, and he returned to Smock Alley in 1748–49 and 1749–50. With four others he rented the Crow Street Music Hall in Dublin in 1751 for a period of six years, though he performed in 1752–53 and 1753–54 at Smock Alley. Sullivan sang at Coopers' Hall in Bristol on 7 May 1755 and then appeared at the Orchard Street Theatre in Bath in 1756–57, 1757–58, 1759–60, and 1762–63. Many of his performances at Bath were in Handel oratorios. He sang in Bristol in September 1757 and apparently in January 1763. Daniel Sullivan died in Dublin on 13 October 1764, according to *Faulkner's Dublin Journal.*

Sully, Matthew   *d. 1815?, dancer, singer, acrobat, actor.*

Little is known of the early life of Matthew Sully, whose real name was O'Sullivan. His family had roots for generations in the village of Long Crendon (east of Oxford). His brother John O'Sullivan served as aide-de-camp to Prince Charles in Scotland. Accounts of Matthew Sully relate that soon after his entry into a theological seminary he met young Sarah Chester, married her against his father's wishes, and was disowned; in desperation, Matthew and his wife turned to the provincial stage. Such a story must be met with skepticism, for Sully's sister, Margaretta Sully, was already an actress, performing in the provinces before 1776, the year she came to London with her husband, the actor Thomas Wade West. She made her first known appearance in the metropolis in William Bailey's company at China Hall, Rotherhithe, on 7 August 1776. (It is also possible that Matthew Sully's parents had been country actors. We find a Miss Shepherd who was announced at Limerick in 1767 as Mrs Sully, having recently been married, according to *Faulkner's Dublin Journal* of 13 October 1767.)

We first notice Matthew Sully, as a dancer, on a Sadler's Wells bill for 11 May 1778. He was tumbling and singing at the Wells in 1781 and 1782. On 1 April 1782 he sang there with Lowe and Mrs Saunders and tumbled with Huntly, Placide and the Little Devil (Paulo

Redigé). Earlier that year he had been at Portsmouth, where from 11 to 16 January 1782 after the play were "exhibited many surprizing Feats of ACTIVITY, By Mr. SULLY, alias the English LITTLE DEVIL, and Mr. HUNTLY, the favorite and principal performers from SADLER'S WELLS." Sully returned to Portsmouth for a "few nights" in February and March 1782. Evidently Sully had called himself the English Little Devil to capitalize on the popularity of Redigé, recently arrived from France, who was billed as the Little Devil. (In the 1780s the equestrians George Smith and Giles Sutton also took on the title.)

According to Iola Willis's *The Charleston Stage,* Sully lived in Horncastle, Lincolnshire, for nine years before he went to America in 1792, and his son the artist Thomas Sully was born in Horncastle in 1783. In his *History of the Rise and Progress of the Arts and Design in the United States,* William Dunlap, who must have known Sully, stated that before coming to America the Sullys settled in Edinburgh, playing with the company managed by Jones and Parker.

Early in 1790 Sully's sister Margaretta and her husband Thomas Wade West went to America, arriving in Philadelphia in September of that year; and soon they established a theatre in Richmond, Virginia. The company expanded, and the Wests persuaded the Sully family to join them. After building a theatre in Norfolk, Virginia, West and his partner John Bignall opened a new theatre in Charleston on 11 February 1793. On 19 February Sully appeared as Sir Benjamin Backbite in *The School for Scandal.* In the same cast were his son Matthew, Jr, as Crabtree, and his daughters, Elizabeth as Maria and Julia as the Maid. The bills that season featured Mr M. Sully—"who was justly the admiration of Britain"—in surprising feats of manly activity. Among roles that he played at Charleston in 1794 were the Lieutenant of the Tower in *The Earl of Essex* and Filch in *The Beggar's Opera,* in 1795 the Gentleman Usher in *King Lear,* and in 1796 the Duke of Venice in *Venice Preserv'd.* His son Matthew appeared in such roles as Roundy in *The Farmer* and Suffredi in *Tancred and Sigismunda.* Probably it was the elder Matthew who acted at Philadelphia occasionally between 1795 and 1798.

W. Stanley Hoole in *The Ante-Bellum*

Charleston Theatre lists Matthew, Sr, as appearing in that city from 1803–4 into 1810–11, but he seems to have confused the elder with the younger Matthew. According to Dunlap both the senior Mr and Mrs Sully were dead by 1799. But in *The Life and Works of Thomas Sully,* Edward Biddle and Mantle Fielding list a portrait of the elder Sully by his son Thomas, which according to the artist's "Register," was painted at Richmond in the summer of 1803, begun on 8 July and finished on 18 August. Biddle and Fielding give the elder Matthew's year of death as 1815, without documentation.

Matthew Sully had a numerous family, four sons and six daughters, most of whom acted in America for a while. His eldest son, Lawrence Sully (1769–1803), became a miniature-and-device-painter in America; he lived for a time in Richmond, Virginia, with his wife, the former Sarah Annis of Annapolis. He moved to Norfolk about 1801, where he helped to train his brother Thomas. Lawrence died at Richmond in 1803.

The younger Matthew Sully was a great favorite on the Charleston and Richmond stages. He died in Augusta, Georgia, on 7 April 1812. By his wife, Elizabeth Robertson of Virginia, he had a son, Robert Matthew Sully, born in Petersburg, Virginia, on 17 July 1803, who became an artist.

The elder Matthew Sully's third son, Chester Sully, was probably the Master Sully who acted in Charleston in 1794, appearing in such roles as the Waiter in *The Farmer* on 22 January; he also acted with the family at Richmond.

The fourth son, Thomas Sully (1783–1872), no doubt also acted as a child, but it is difficult to distinguish his roles from those of Chester Sully. One of them played Isabella's Child in *Isabella* at Richmond in 1792. (Every member of the family seems to have acted there on 6 October 1792 when the comic opera *The Woodman* was performed.) Thomas married his late brother Lawrence's widow in 1805, supported her three daughters by Lawrence and sired six daughters and three sons. Thomas Sully became a prominent American artist who is noticed in the *Dictionary of American Biography* and is the subject of the aforesaid study by Biddle and Fielding, which unfortunately, tells us little about his father and mother.

Matthew Sully's daughter Sarah (probably the eldest) danced at Hull from 3 to 25 November 1788. She was married in Edinburgh on 23 April 1791 to the equestrian Joseph Jenkinson (1770–1797). She performed in the provinces and with her husband at the Haymarket in 1795, the only one of the Sully children, so far as we can determine, to have acted in London. Jenkinson died on 16 October 1797, leaving her with three children.

Charlotte Sully acted as a child with the family and married the former London actor A. A. Chambers at Charleston on 30 May 1793. As Mrs Chambers she acted for several years with her husband in the American Company, at Hartford in 1795 and at Philadelphia in 1796 and 1797.

Another daughter, Harriet Sully (1788–c. 1866), acted in Charleston in 1793 when five years old. About 1805 she married Joseph Du Prá Porcher (b. 1784), a physician and a member of the prominent South Carolina family, details about whom are given in the *Transactions of the Huguenot Society of South Carolina* for 1976 (No 81). A copy of Harriet Porcher's will, made on 6 August 1866, is in the Charleston County Court House (box 181, No 15). Her daughter Mary Porcher married Josiah P. Hughes. The will also mentions her "unfortunate Son William" and an unmarried daughter Eliza.

Matthew Sully's daughter Elizabeth acted in Charleston in 1793 in such roles as Iris in *Widow's Vow,* Miss Audley in *The Adventures of a Shawl,* Penelope in *The Romp,* Miss Neville in *She Stoops to Conquer,* and Maria in *The School for Scandal.* She eventually married Henry Middleton Smith of Charleston, son of Peter Smith and Mary Middleton. She died in 1860 without issue.

A daughter Julia made her debut in Charleston on 24 January 1794, as Lucy in *The West Indian.* On 26 November of that year she married Jean Zolbins, an eccentric French miniature painter who had been driven to America by the French Revolution. Upon returning from their honeymoon they adopted the stage name Belzons. He painted scenery in Charleston until 1812.

Matthew Sully's sixth daughter, Jane, is noted by Biddle and Fielding as having married one J. B. LeRoy.

Thomas Sully's register of sitters notes five portraits of his father Matthew. One at least seems to have been painted from life, a portrait (10″ × 12″), begun on 8 July and finished on 18 August 1803. A miniature in red coat, head to right, oval on ivory, was owned by Mrs E. O. Bolling of Brooklyn, Virginia. A portrait copy of the miniature was begun on 14 May and finished on 12 June 1815. Another portrait (15″ × 18″), nearly full-face, with gray hair, fur collar on coat, was inscribed on the back of the canvas, "Painted from sketches, TS, 1826." It was owned by Miss Sarah Sully Rawlins of Philadelphia. A portrait (20″ × 17″), copied from a portrait painted for the artist's sister Elizabeth, was begun on 27 March 1829 and finished that April. It was owned by Edward W. Hughes of Charleston. A miniature of Matthew Sully, signed by T. Sully in 1801 but not listed in his register, was for a time owned by Dr Francis Peyre Porcher of Charleston. Later it was located at "Woodside," the home of the Wickham family near Richmond, Virginia. The miniature is now owned by Mr and Mrs Charles W. Porter III.

Sully, Sarah. *See* JENKINSON, MRS JOSEPH.

Sumbel, Mrs Joseph. *See* WELLS, MRS EZRA.

Summers, George   1757–1787, *dancer, actor.*

George Summers, son of the performers Mr and Mrs Robert Summers, was probably "the child 4 years old" who spoke "Mr Foote's *Epilogue to the Minor*" in the "Entertainment" after a benefit performance of *Richard III* at Drury Lane Theatre on 29 June 1761.

Master Summers accompanied his parents to the Norwich company in 1764. He was still billed as a juvenile at Bath in 1772–73, 1774–75, and 1775–76 and at Bristol in 1774. He played as an adult harlequin and took comic parts at Bristol every season from 1778–79 through 1786–87.

George Summers died on 1 March 1787 of an illness that also killed his mother on 15 March.

Summers, Robert   *d. 1791, actor, dancer.*

The Summers who danced a hornpipe at Marylebone Gardens after the comic opera *La strattagemma* on 9 August 1759 was probably Robert Summers. We believe him also to have been the "Somers" who was at Smock Alley Theatre in Dublin in the 1760–61 season and who (sometimes as "Sommers") was among several actors whom Samuel Foote hired for 24 presentations of his *Oratorical Lectures* at the Haymarket Theatre from 1 May through 16 September 1762.

Summers returned to the Haymarket on 18 July 1763 (as "Sommers") to play Quildrive in *The Citizen*. He was "Somers" when on 5 August he played a Servant in *An Enligshman Returned from Paris*. But he was "Summers" on 5 September when he played Hounslow in *The Beaux' Stratagem* and also two days later when he played Monsieur in *Love Makes a Man*.

Summers was at Norwich in the 1764–65 seasons, according to a company check-list furnished us by Alick Williams. We do not know where he was during the four years following, but he was almost certainly in Ireland in 1768. The Haymarket manager Samuel Foote was in Dublin with Mossop during that winter and brought back some players with him; and Summers was again in Foote's summer company, among some actors indubitably from Dublin, in 1769. On 15, 22, and 26 May and 7 June he took a principal character unspecified in *The Devil upon Two Sticks*. On 24 May he played Dr Catgut in *The Commissary* (Francis Gentleman commented, in *The Dramatic Censor* [1770]: "as to the sick, monkey-face, Mr SUMMERS looked it inimitably"). On 25 May he was Justice Statute in *The What D'Ye Call It*, on 29 May one of the Mob in *The Mayor of Garratt*, on 2 June some character in *The Orators*, and on 7 August Lucianus in *Hamlet* and Doodle in *Tom Thumb*.

Robert Summers then joined the company at the Orchard Street Theatre, Bath, with which troupe he and his wife seem to have been associated every season from 1769–70 through 1789–90. Summers was also at Bristol, as a harlequin, according to Kathleen Barker's manuscript calendar, in 1774 and in most seasons from 1779–80 through 1789–90. He was also, perhaps, the Summers who played at Richmond, Surrey, on 27 June 1778 (though

that actor could have been his son George). That Mr Summers acted the Constable in *The Provok'd Husband* in a benefit performance for Mrs Jewell by a company of casuals at the Haymarket on 18 September 1778.

Robert Summers seems to have been the father of the Bath-Bristol actors George and Elizabeth Summers. (Genest, in *Some Account of the English Stage*, establishes the latter relationship, declaring that Miss Summers [1751–1826] had been, at her retirement in 1820, "on the Bath stage for 56 years, without being absent for a single season." Miss Summers, "when young, was reckoned a very good Columbine—her brother was a good Harlequin.")

Some illness of dire effect swept through the Summers family in 1787. Miss Summers's benefit bill of 1 March referred to the illness of mother, father, and brother. The brother, George, died on 1 March, according to the *Bath Chronicle* of the eighth. Robert Summers's wife died on 15 March. Robert Summers himself survived that disease but succumbed to some other on 27 December 1791, reported the *Bristol Mirror*.

Sumner, Mr   [*fl. 1742*], *doorkeeper?*

The Drury lane bill for 15 May 1742 read "Benefit Doorkeepers &c., Buckley, Fen, Fuller, Fulwood, Sumner." Perhaps Sumner was a doorkeeper, but one cannot be certain.

Sumner, Mrs   [*fl. 1737*], *singer.*

A bill transcribed by Latreille has Mrs Sumner, who "never appeared on any stage," singing Venus in *Momus Turned Fabulist* on 28 April 1737 at Covent Garden Theatre.

Sumney, Signor   [*fl. 1777*], *acrobat.*

Signor Sumney was part of an exhibition of Egyptian pyramids at Astley's Amphitheatre on 23 September 1777.

Sunderland, Mr   [*fl. 1740*], *actor.*

At Bartholomew Fair on 23 August 1740 Mr Sunderland played Comedy in *Harlequin Restored*. On 9 September at Southwark Fair he was a Fury in *Harlequin Doctor Faustus*. Perhaps he was related to the Mrs Sunderland who performed at Norwich from 1746 to 1757 but who seems not to have appeared in London.

Sureis. *See* DE SURLIS.

Surel. *See also* SURRELL.

Surel, Mr [*fl.* 1728–1733], *dancer, choreographer.*

Mr Surel played Harlequin in *Perseus and Andromeda* at Drury Lane Theatre on 6 December 1728. On 8 May 1729 for his shared benefit he danced Harlequin in his own composition, *The Cheats of Harlequin.* He was Harlequin in *Harlequin Doctor Faustus* on 26 December 1729, and for his benefit on 15 May 1730 he was Harlequin in his own *Fairy Queen.* In October 1730 he was again in *Harlequin Doctor Faustus* and played a Wind in *Cephalus and Procris.* On 10 October 1733 he danced a Statue in *Harlequin Doctor Faustus.*

"Surintendant des plaisirs d'Angelterre." *See* HEIDEGGER.

Surmont, Mr [*fl.* 1798–1807], *actor, singer.*

Mr Surmont's first Drury Lane appearance was on 25 September 1798, when he played Tressel in *Richard III.* He was then seen as Marcellus in *Hamlet,* Conrade in *Much Ado about Nothing,* a Gentleman in *Measure for Measure,* a Greek Herald in *The Grecian Daughter,* an Officer in *The Surrender of Calais,* John in *The Jealous Wife* and Freeman in *High Life below Stairs* (at the Haymarket Theatre, with other Drury Lane players), Orlando in *Feudal Times,* Alonzo in *Rule a Wife and Have a Wife,* Valentine in *Twelfth Night,* Le Beau in *As You Like It,* an Officer in *Douglas,* Lenox in *Macbeth,* Charles in *The Village Lawyer,* Alonzo in *The Mourning Bride,* Gomez in *Pizarro,* and Theodore in *The Purse*—all in the 1798–99 season. He spent the summer of 1799 performing at the Birmingham theatre.

Surmont continued at Drury Lane as late as 1802, apparently never earning more than £2 weekly. He continued playing many of the small parts he acted in his first season and such new ones as Mushroom in *The Embarkation,* Simon in *The First Floor,* Leander in *The Mock Doctor,* Robert in *The Will,* Blunt in *The London Merchant,* an Irishman in *The Apprentice,* Gustavus in *Lodoiska,* Canteen in *The Deaf Lover,* Fag in *The Rivals,* Selwyn in *The Shipwreck,* La

Varole in *A Trip to Scarborough,* Davilla in *Pizarro,* Lord Alford in *The Children in the Wood,* Quaver in *The Virgin Unmask'd,* Kedah in *The Egyptian Festival,* Don Carlos in *The Pannel,* Simon Pure in *A Bold Stroke for a Wife,* Rakeland in *The Wedding Day,* Percy in *The Castle Spectre,* Don Lewis in *She Wou'd and She Wou'd Not,* and Ganem in *The Mountaineers.*

The Haymarket Theatre accounts show Surmont to have joined the company there in the summer of 1807. Mrs Surmont, presumably his wife, was in the chorus at the Haymarket about 1810 but seems not to have stayed there long.

"Surprising Heifer, The" [*fl.* 1791], *freak animal.*

In April and June 1791 Gilbert Pidcock exhibited his "Surprising HEIFER, with Two Heads, Four Horns, Four Eyes, Four Ears, Four Nostrils, &c." at the Lyceum in the Strand.

Surrein. *See* SORIN.

Surrell. *See also* SUREL.

Surrell, Mr [*fl.* 1728–1731], *boxkeeper.*

The account books for Lincoln's Inn Fields Theatre show that Mr Surrell was hired as an extra boxkeeper for the night of 22 April 1728. He evidently became a regular employee, for he shared a benefit with two others on 10 May 1731. Receipts came to over £111.

Sutherland, John [*fl.* 1766–1767], *piper.*

The Covent Garden Theatre accounts show a payment of 15*s.* to John Sutherland for playing the bagpipes in *Midas* for three nights, beginning on 14 October 1766. On 22 November he received £1 for playing four nights in *Harlequin Doctor Faustus,* and he continued receiving 5*s.* nightly for performing throughout the season. On 12 October 1767 he again began taking payments for playing in *Faustus.* The last payment came on 6 November.

Sutton, Mr [*fl.* 1742], *actor.*

Mr Sutton played the Upholsterer in *The Miser* at Goodman's Fields Theatre on 18 May 1742. He had benefit tickets out that night.

Sutton, Mr [*fl. 1761–1780*], *actor.*

Mr Sutton made his first stage appearance as Paris in *Romeo and Juliet* on 13 January 1761 at Covent Garden Theatre. The accounts on 24 January note that Sutton was paid 3*s*. 4*d* (daily, presumably) from 17 January, but no other roles are known for him. He left London at some point after that, and when he returned on 13 November 1780 to the Haymarket Theatre, he was advertised as from the Theatre Royal, Edinburgh. He acted Timothy Remnant in *The City Association* and delivered Shuter's comic monologue, *Post Haste Observations on His Journey to Paris*.

Sutton, Mr [*fl. 1772–1785?*], *performer.*
See SUTTON, GILES.

Sutton, Mrs, neé Froment *1756–1797,* *dancer, singer, actress.*

Miss Froment, the daughter (?) and student of John Baptiste Froment, was born in 1756 and made her stage debut at the age of six on 12 May 1762 at Drury Lane Theatre dancing a serious piece called *Les Caractères de la danse.* She danced another solo, *The Lilliputian Fisherman,* and played a Lilliputian in *The Witches* on 20 and 23 November, respectively. Froment seems to have withdrawn her from the stage after that, for the next notices of her in the bills are on 7 and 8 July 1767, when she did a comic dance at the Haymarket Theatre as a member of Samuel Foote's troupe. She appeared regularly in untitled dances during the following two weeks. On 22 July she danced a hornpipe, and when Silas Neville saw her on 27 July he told his diary that "The little girl who dances is more applauded than anyone who appears on that stage." During the remainder of the summer Miss Froment appeared regularly in such dances as *The Italian Peasant, The Gallant Peasant,* and numerous untitled turns. Then her name again disappeared from London bills.

Miss Froment returned to the Haymarket on 2 May 1771 to perform for her benefit. She played Polly in *The Beggar's Opera* and danced a louvre and minuet with Froment. The bill noted that she was the principal dancer in the late Harmonical Meeting in Soho. In the summer of 1771 she sang and danced at Sadler's Wells, and she returned there on 29 September 1772 to sing, dance in *The Plough Boy* and *The Sailor's Return,* and play Colombine in *Trick upon Trick.* About that time she must have married, for the previous day's bill had called her Mrs Sutton, late Miss Froment. Sometime in September (the thirteenth? suggest Little and Kahrl in their edition of Garrick's letters, but we would guess later), David Garrick wrote to his brother George:

> Should you not take care that *Sutton* does not make some fine story for the papers, that the managers would not pay if she was with-child, or some such stuff with which they are always fill'd—He should be told that we cannot engage her unless she is able to do the part on some general term that may include our thoughts and opinions, and indeed our wants.

The identity of Sutton is not clear. He seems not to have been a minor performer and may have been related in some way to the performing Suttons later in the century. Giles Sutton, sometimes called "The Little Devil," was perhaps the son of our subject.

Mrs Sutton was given an engagement at Drury Lane that lasted until the spring of 1778. Her weekly salary at the beginning was £5. Her first appearance was on 23 October 1772 in a dance called *The Irish Fair.* The prompter Hopkins noted that she "displayed great spirit and activity." On 30 October she was Colombine in *The Witches,* following which she was seen as the colombine in *The Elopement* and *The Pigmy Revels;* she also danced in a quadrille and did a solo hornpipe. On 24 April 1773 she was given a benefit, her profits coming to nearly £75. Monsieur Froment choreographed a special *Turkish Dance* for her in which she was a Sultana. The two danced a louvre, a minuet, and a turn titled *Dauphin Minuet.* In the summer of 1775 Mrs Sutton performed at Richmond, dancing in *The Highland Reel* and playing Colombine in *Harlequin Gipsey.*

In the Drury Lane seasons that followed her first one Mrs Sutton was a colombine in *The Genii* and *Harlequin's Jacket* and danced in such other works as *A Christmas Tale, Florizel and Perdita, Cymbeline, The Suspicious Husband, A Trip to Scotland,* and *The Fair Quaker.* She also continued her appearances as an entr'acte dancer. In 1777–78 she did not make her first appearance until 8 May 1778, after which performance she left Drury Lane. Exactly a year later she turned up at Covent Garden to dance with Harris.

Mrs Sutton's address in April 1776 was near the end of Tottenham Court Road; a year later she was at No 8, Great Wild Street, Lincoln's Inn Fields. On 27 May 1777 she danced at Sadler's Wells, and the following August and September she and Froment danced at Richmond. She had a house on Barnes Common that summer. A year later she was again at Sadler's Wells and had moved to No 70, Gray's Inn Lane. She continued performing at Sadler's Wells in 1779, moving again, this time to No 209, near the Turnstile, Holborn. By 1782, when she was still dancing at the Wells, she lived at No 48, Jermyn Street, St James's, but by September of that year she again gave her address as No 70, Gray's Inn Lane. Perhaps she was dodging creditors after losing her position at Drury Lane. The theatre's Fund Book shows that, though she had begun contributing to the Fund in 1775, she was delinquent in 1779.

The 1783–84 season found Mrs Sutton serving as a colombine in Bristol; in the summers of 1785 and 1786 she appeared at Sadler's Wells. She returned to Drury Lane for the 1785–86 season, dancing with Hamoir on 17 October 1785 for her first appearance. Then she danced in *The Caldron, The Market, Hurly Burly, The Lucky Return, Highland Reel, Daphne and Amintor,* and other pieces. She was earning 16s. 8d. nightly at Drury Lane. After the summer of 1786 Mrs Sutton's name dropped from the London bills.

The *Hibernian Journal* of 17 January 1798 reported that Mrs Sutton was a member of Astley's company and that in December 1797 she and others drowned crossing St George's Channel on their way to perform in Ireland.

Sutton, George ₁*fl. 1691*₁, *oboist.*
George Sutton was one of several "Hooboys" from the King's Musick who accompanied William III to the Hague on a trip that lasted from 1 January to 13 April 1691.

Sutton, Giles, sometimes called "The Little Devil" ₁*fl. 1785–1802?*₁, *equestrian, acrobat, dancer.*
Giles Sutton was a youthful equestrian performer at Hughes's Royal Circus in St George's Fields by 1785. It is likely that he was the son

of the dancer and singer Miss Froment (1756–1797) who in the autumn of 1772, at the age of 16, married some obscure performer named Sutton. Mrs Sutton was no doubt the daughter of the choreographer Jean Baptiste Froment, who flourished at London between 1739 and 1777. She drowned with members of Astley's troupe while crossing St George's Channel in December 1797.

Though our subject was usually advertised until 1793 as "Master Sutton," the first notice we have of him, dating from 21 October 1785, calls him Giles Sutton. On that day at the Royal Circus, dressed in yellow, he rode "Chiliby" in a jockey race. It is possible that there were two equestrians of that name, father and son, but, having no firm evidence of the elder Sutton's performing, we have assumed that all notices of an equestrian called Sutton pertain to our subject.

Press clippings at the British Library reveal that Master Sutton, along with Masters King and Ricketts, exhibited feats of horsemanship at Jones's Equestrian Amphitheatre in Union Street, Whitechapel, on 25 April 1786. At the Royal Circus he performed on the trampoline in April 1787. Again with Masters King and Ricketts he rode for Jones in Union Street on 8 April 1788. Dancing on the tightrope that day was "the Little Devil from Sadler's Wells;" we take that "Little Devil" to have been Paulo Redigé, who had adopted that name in France and had used it at the Wells since 1781. At Stourbridge Fair at Cambridge in 1788 Giles Sutton was riding with Hughes's troupe and, advertised as Hughes's apprentice, he challenged Handy, who headed up a rival troupe also working the Fair.

Called Master Sutton, he rode at Astley's Amphitheatre, Westminster Bridge, in August and September 1791. When he was advertised there again in August and November 1793 he was called "Mr Giles Sutton, the original Little Devil," who would "ride with his head upon the saddle, full speed, likewise will leap over a garter placed in four different parts of the riding school."

In April and May 1795 Sutton performed in equestrian exercises at the Royal Circus. Also at the Circus at that time was George Smith (fl. 1786–1809), an equestrian who at Bristol in 1792 had sometimes been called the Little Devil. It was a title that Matthew Sully the elder also had used in England before he emigrated to America in 1792.

Probably Giles Sutton was the Mr Sutton who was identified as playing Laf in a cast list of *Alfred the Great,* an historical entertainment presented at Sadler's Wells and published in 1797. He was again riding at the Royal Circus in 1798. A performer named Sutton was a dancer at Covent Garden in 1800–1801. Probably our subject was the Sutton who played Conrad in *Puss in Boots* at the Royalty Theatre on 5 October 1801 and during the season there also performed some acrobatics. He was in the dancing chorus of *British Amazons* and danced Health in *Fire and Spirit,* pantomimes given at Sadler's Wells in 1803. Sutton's name appeared fairly regularly in advertisements for performances at the Royal Circus, in pantomimes and on horseback, between June 1806 and April 1808. In the later year he also performed at Sadler's Wells, particularly in *The White Witch.* A Sutton's name was in the bills for the Wells in 1812, 1814, and 1820; Master Sutton, probably his son, was at the Wells in 1806, 1809, and 1814.

Sutton, James [*fl. 1783*], *house servant?*
On 17 July 1783, according to *The Case of the Opera-House Disputes Fairly Stated,* the proprietor Taylor, being in debtors' prison, executed a deed of trust to James Sutton and five others to act in his stead. Sutton was apparently a house servant at the King's Theatre, probably an employee connected with the administration of the opera house.

Sutton, John [*fl. 1668–1673*], *scenekeeper.*
John Sutton was a scenekeeper in the King's Company at the Bridges Street Theatre from as early as 1668–69. He was named in the Lord Chamberlain's accounts at least three times, twice for debt. On 28 April 1670 Walter Pryor sued him, and on 1 January 1673 Valentine Heward sued him.

Sutton, Thomas [*fl. 1794*], *singer.*
Doane's *Musical Directory* of 1794 listed Thomas Sutton, of the Black Dog, Oxford Market, as a bass who sang in the oratorios at Drury Lane Theatre.

Svoglio. *See* AVOGLIO.

Swaine, Mr [*fl. 1770*], *actor.*
Mr Swaine played the title role in *The Miller of Mansfield* and spoke an "Ode in Honor of Shakespeare" at the Haymarket Theatre on 21 November 1770.

Swaine, Benjamin [*fl. 1784–1794*], *singer.*
Benjamin Swaine sang countertenor in the Handel Memorial Concerts at Westminster Abbey and the Pantheon in May and June 1784. Doane's *Musical Directory* of 1794 noted that Swaine had also participated in the Concert of Ancient Music and oratorios at Covent Garden Theatre. He lived at Mr Steel's in Cranbourn Alley.

Swan, Daniel [*fl. 1784–1794*], *singer.*
A Mr Swan was listed among the countertenors at the Handel Memorial concerts at Westminster Abbey and the Pantheon in May and June of 1784. Doane's *Musical Directory* (1794) furnished his first name and stated that he sang in oratorios at Drury Lane Theatre. His residence was at No 111, High Holborn.

Swan, John [*fl. 1784–1794*], *singer.*
John Swan is listed as a bass among the vocal performers at the Handel Memorial Concerts at Westminster Abbey and the Pantheon in May and June of 1784. Doane's *Musical Directory* (1794) added the statements that he had performed in oratorios at Drury Lane Theatre (not confirmed in any extant bill) and resided in Rose Street, Longacre.

Swan, Joseph [*fl. 1784–1794*], *singer.*
Joseph Swan is listed as a bass among the vocal performers at the Handel Memorial Concerts at Westminster Abbey and the Pantheon in May and June of 1784. Doane's *Musical Directory* (1794) asserted that he had also performed in oratorios at Drury Lane Theatre, but his name is not to be found in any bill.

Swartz, Herr [*fl. 1717*], *animal trainer.*
According to Fitzgerald's *New History of the English Stage,* a German animal trainer named Swartz brought two dancing dogs to London. He was engaged by Rich at Lincoln's Inn Fields Theatre at £10 nightly and brought 20 full houses. But the bills in *The London Stage* make no mention of the animals or their trainer.

Swartz, Mr [fl. 1733], *singer*.

Mr Swartz (or Swartzs) sang a part in *Deborah* at the King's Theatre on 17 March 1733.

"Swedish Giant, The." *See* CAJANUS, DANIEL.

Sweedes, Mr [fl. 1755–1756], *proprietor*.

A Mr Sweedes was a partner with John Trusler in the management of Marylebone Gardens in 1755 and 1756, according to Mollie Sands in her study of the Gardens.

Sweeney, Owen. *See* SWINEY, OWEN MAC.

Sweeny, Esther. *See* HAMILTON, MRS JOHN.

Sweet, James [fl. 1660?], *singer*.

James Sweet had been one of the children of the Chapel Royal, but a warrant in the Lord Chamberlain's accounts dated 14 December— apparently 1660—indicated that his voice had changed. He was granted an allowance for livery. Forty years later, on 14 December 1700, another James Sweet, presumably the son of the earlier Sweet, left the Chapel Royal when his voice changed. On 27 January 1707 the younger Sweet shared a benefit concert with Isham at York Buildings.

Sweet, James [fl. 1700–1707], *singer*. *See* SWEET, JAMES [fl. 1660?].

"Sweet Cowslip." *See* WELLS, MRS EZRA.

"Sweetlips, Miss" [fl. 1756], *actress*.

An actress masquerading under the name of "Miss Sweetlips" played Don Jacomo in *Adventures of Half an Hour* with Hallam's troupe at the Swan Inn at Bartholomew Fair on 3 September 1756.

Swendale. *See* SWENDALL.

Swendall, James [fl. 1777–1810], *actor, manager*.

Among the scattered bills of the theatre at Richmond, Surrey, is one for 4 September 1777 with the name of a Mr "Swindall,"

doubtless James Swendall. He appeared as Charles in *The Jealous Wife* in a specially licensed benefit performance at the Haymarket Theatre on 23 March 1778, and played Freeman in *A Bold Stroke for a Wife* on 31 March, Polydore in *The Orphan* on 9 May, and Heartwell in *The Country Lasses* on 29 May, in other benefits.

It would be nearly a decade before Swendall would return to London, and then only briefly. His extensive and respectable career was to be spent almost entirely in the provinces of England, Ireland, and Scotland. His peripatetic progress can be partially traced in country playbills, criticisms, and company rosters. He was in the Bristol company in 1778–79. In 1780–81 he was in the Crow Street company at Dublin (though apparently he acted first in Dublin at Smock Alley in the spring of 1780). He was at Smock Alley from the season of 1783–84 through 1786–87, but acted also at Kilkenny in January 1783 and January 1784, at Cork in September 1784, and at Waterford and Cork in July and August 1786. Sybil Rosenfeld found that he also joined William Palmer's pickup company that went to Stourbridge Fair near Cambridge in 1786 to oppose the Norwich company's monopoly.

Swendall was briefly in John Palmer's employ at the ill-fated Royalty Theatre in Wellclose Square, London, at some time during 1787. His roles are not known. When Joseph Fox opened his new theatre in Duke Street, Brighton, on 18 July 1788, Swendall was of his company, and so was Jane Bannister, to whom Swendall was very soon married. The couple appeared on the bills as man and wife at Dublin's Crow Street Theatre in the 1789– 90 season, but apparently left in February to join Stephen Kemble's troupe at Coventry, in which troupe they remained until June.

When Fox opened Duke Street Theatre in Brighton on 13 July 1790 the Swendalls settled in for the summer. They dwelt then at No 34, Middle Street, Brighton. Swindall was reported by the *Thespian Magazine* to be at Margate in May, 1791—"a performer of much merit from Dublin," he had "performed here with great applause. . . ." When the Court of Session interdicted Stephen Kemble's performance of plays at his new theatre in Edinburgh he opened his 1792–93 season, according to J. C. Dibdin "with an Entertainment called

Esperance, being a concert of vocal and instrumental music, including imitations by Mr Swindall." But by 21 January at latest Swindall was beginning to perform dramatic roles; on that date he played Sir Lucius O'Trigger in *The Rivals*. His other parts that season were: a role unknown in *The Murdered Baron*, Admiral Cleveland in *The Fugitive*, Barton in *The Battle of Hexham*, Colonel Hubbub in *Notoriety*, the Earl of Moray in *Owen of Carron*, the Governor in *The Surrender of Calais*, Malcolm Canmore in *Birnam Wood*, Sir Charles Cullender in *Cross Partners*, Sir Oliver Surface in *The School for Scandal*, and Sir William Douglas in *The English Merchant*. His wife, meanwhile, was given half a dozen substantial parts in comedy.

The Swendalls' progress can be followed only sporadically for a while after that: Richmond again in the summer of 1795 and Manchester, in Ward's company, in January 1796. Swendall was brought there 27 May 1797, for one performance only, to substitute in Tom King's accustomed part, Moody, in *The Country Girl*, for the benefit of Swendall's father-in-law Bannister. Swendall was advertised as "from the Theatre Royal, Dublin" and as making his "first appearance this stage." A press clipping in the Enthoven collection commended "Mr Swendall, a gentleman well known in the provincial theatres" who "acquitted himself with credit." The Swendalls were again at Richmond in the summer of 1797 where he, at least, succeeded well, according to a contemporary press clipping in the Richmond Library in which he was called "a very chaste, sensible, and gentlemanly actor." Both Swendalls went again to the Birmingham Theatre in the summer of 1798.

On 15, 17, 18, and 19 June 1799 James Swendall made what were apparently his last appearances in London when he played Harrington in *Family Distress* at the Haymarket. The winter-spring season of 1800 saw him in Edinburgh, where he performed the following roles: Ava Theanoe in *The Wise Men of the East*, Bonniface in *The Beaux' Stratagem*, Captain Ironsides in *The Brothers*, Charino in *Love Makes a Man*, Farmer Ashfield in *Speed the Plough*, Las Casas in *Pizarro*, and Old Chronicle in *The Young Quaker*.

On 12 August 1800, Blogg and Alexander Archer, co-lessees, opened the Brighton Theatre with a company which included Mrs Wil-

liam Powell (the prompter's widow), Mrs Miles, Leah Sumbell (Becky Wells), Ralph Wewitzer and others. Apparently at some time late in that season the lessees had a falling-out and Swendall was hired as manager for the rest of the summer. He was at Manchester in April and May 1801 and returned to manage Brighton in the summer.

Scattered bills show Swendall to have been at Manchester again in 1802. But he apparently resigned because of a disagreement over salary early in 1803. The *Townsman*, a critical periodical of Manchester, lamented his absence from that theatre's company and agitated for his restoration in the fall: "Mr. Swendell [*sic*] is at this time, or was a few days since, wholly disengaged, and expressed himself, in a letter lately written to a friend in this town [the critic?], extremely desirous to visit Manchester again, provided he could obtain such a salary as could allow him to exist." On 4 January the Townsman wrote: "I begin my paper for this week by congratulating the managers on their valuable addition of Mr. Swendall to the company, who made his first appearance this season, on Thursday [29 December 1803], in the character of Humphrey Dobbins" in *The Poor Gentleman*. Later in the month of January, "A more chaste and finished piece of acting was scarcely ever witnessed than Mr. Swendall's Adam" in *As You Like It*. "The faithful old steward" had an "elegantly smooth placidity"—a rather strange interpretation of the character.

The *Townsman* thought him "correct and natural" as Polonius, and "very good" as Farmer Ashfield in *Speed the Plough*, though in "the scene where his daughter's letter is found in the box, he overacted, almost to buffoonery." His Sir Tunbelly Clumsy in *A Trip to Scarbro'* was "a great piece of acting," but "Mr. S——ll's good sense must tell him the impropriety of repeating some words so very often; it is not pleasant to the audience, nor is it justice to the author." The *Thespian Dictionary*, finding him "chaste and energetic" in performance, wondered "that his abilities did not recommend him to Drury Lane on the death of Mr. [James] Aicken, or to the Haymarket, on the change of the company, in 1803."

Swendall remained in the Manchester company through 1805–6, and we have found several other of his roles: Sir Charles Raymond in *The Foundling,* Old Norval in *Douglas,* Sciolto in *The Fair Penitent,* Old Dornton in *The Road to Ruin,* Balthazar in *The Honeymoon,* and Governor Heartall in Andrew Cherry's new comedy *The Soldier's Daughter.* The *Townsman* cheered his efforts: "I have seldom seen Mr. Swendall to more advantage. . . . Had Mr. Cherry . . . taken compleat measure of Mr. Swendall's abilities, he could not have more successfully hit off a Character, better suited to his talents." As for Old Dornton, when he repeated it "he played it with that feeling and pathos with which his performances are frequently distinguished." His benefit in 1805 yielded £102.

James Swendall was with is wife at Brighton in the summers of 1809 and 1810. After that, his trail disappears.

Swendall, Mrs James, Jane, née Bannister ₍*fl. 1783–1829*₎, *actress.*

Jane Bannister was the daughter of the popular singer and actor Charles Bannister (1741–1804) and his wife Sarah. Jane was the sister—apparently younger—of the even more popular performer John Bannister (1760–1836). She made her "first appearance on any stage" at the Haymarket Theatre on 27 August 1783 for her brother's benefit, as Amelia in *The English Merchant.* Her second appearance, also for John Bannister's benefit, was at Drury Lane Theatre on 28 April 1784 when she essayed Marcia in *Cato.* Her father and brother both being of the Drury Lane company, she was in the spring of 1785 again pressed into service for their benefit nights—as Miranda in *The Tempest* on 28 March and as Perdita in *The Winter's Tale* on 18 April. Those were probably her last appearances in London.

Jane Bannister's career is inscrutable until the summer of 1788, when she turned up in the Brighton company. In addition to her regular professional endeavors she was pressed into service at least once by the Earl of Barrymore's troupe of amateurs at Wargrave, playing Ursula in the farce *The Minor* on 11 September, with his lordship acting Smirk. That summer James Swendall was also acting in the Brighton company. They were both in the company again in the summer of 1790 and residing together at No 34, Middle Street; by that time they had married.

Mrs Swendall followed her husband's for-

tunes thereafter, frequently acting with him and apparently almost always engaged in the same companies: successively at Crow Street, Dublin, then at Coventry, Brighton again for several summers, Richmond, Surrey, in another summer, the Manchester-Chester circuit from 1803 through 1806, and Edinburgh in both 1793 and 1800. Only her Edinburgh roles survive: In January and February 1793, Honoria in *Notoriety,* Lady Eleanor Conmore in *Birnam Wood,* Louisa in *Cross Partners,* Maria in *The School for Scandal,* and Miss Godfrey in The *Lyar* and in April and May 1800, Agatha in *Lovers' Vows,* Elmira in *The Sultan,* Isabella in *The Wonder!,* Louisa in *The Irishman in London,* Mrs Doggerel in *The Register Office,* and Violette in *The Brothers.*

Jane Swendall was named in John Bannister's will; so she was still alive in 1829.

Swindall. *See* SWENDALL.

Swiney, Owen Mac 1680–1754, *manager, playwright.*

Owen Mac Swiney (or Swiny, Swinny, MacSwinny, Macawinnen) was born near Enniscorthy, Ireland, in 1680 (according to early editions of Grove), and by the spring of 1703 had associated himself with Christopher Rich at the Drury Lane Theatre in London. Swiney shared benefits with Hall on 23 April, 15 October, 6 April 1704, and 21 June. The pattern is similar to that followed by John Rich and his brother at Lincoln's Inn Fields a decade later and suggests that Swiney received benefits at Drury Lane in lieu of a salary. His function is not known, but he was probably helping Christopher Rich with the management of the company.

Colley Cibber in his *Apology,* wrote of the Irishman's early connection with Christopher Rich:

At this time [c. 1705–6] the Master of *Drury-Lane* happen'd to have a sort of premier [*sic*] Agent in his Stage-Affairs, that seem'd in Appearance as much to govern the Master as the Master himself did to govern his Actors: But this Person was under no Stipulation or Sallary for the service he render'd, but had gradually wrought himself into the Master's extraordinary Confidence and Trust, from an habitual Intimacy, a cheerful Humour, and an indefatigable Zeal for his Interest. . . . [T]his Person was Mr. *Owen Swiney,* and . . . it was to him Sir

By permission of the Trustees of the British Museum

OWEN MAC SWINEY
by Van Bleeck

John Vanbrugh, in his Exigence of his Theatrical Affairs [the Queen's Theatre project foundering], made an Offer of his Actors, under such Agreements of Sallary as might be made with them; and of his House, Cloaths, and Scenes, with the Queen's License to employ them, upon Payment of only the casual Rent of five Pounds upon every acting Day, and not to exceed 700 *l.* in the Year.

At that time Swiney was £200 in debt to Rich, but his venture at the Queen's so prospered that he was soon able to pay it off.

Swiney tried his hand at play translation and adaptation. *The Quacks,* which, after some censorship, was performed at Drury lane on 29 March 1705, was based on Molière's *L'Amour Médecin.* The work had been scheduled for 22 March, but the Lord Chamberlain, at the urging of Sir John Vanbrugh, delayed the opening, partly because Swiney's work contained an attack on Jacob Tonson and the Kit-Cat Club and partly because the rival players at The Lincoln's Inn Fields Theatre complained that they were preparing a play based on the same source. No play based on Molière's work seems to have been brought out by the rival troupe that season. Swiney also translated the

libretto of *Camilla* from the Italian Stampiglio; the opera was presented at Drury Lane on 30 March 1706 with considerable success. Swiney's translation of the libretto of *Pirro e Demetrio* came out at the Queen's on 14 December 1708.

In August 1706 Vanbrugh leased the Queen's Theatre (which he had built) to Swiney. Congreve wrote to his friend Keally on 10 September (the letter is in the Summers edition of Congreve's *Works*):

The playhouses have undergone another revolution; and Swinny, with Wilks, Mrs. Oldfield, Pinkethman, Bullock, and Dicky ["Jubilee Dicky" Norris], are come over to the Hay-Market [i.e., the Queen's]. Vanbrugh resigns his authority to Swinny, which occasioned the revolt. Mr. Rich complains and rails like Volpone when counterplotted by Mosca. My Lord Chamberlain approves and ratifies the desertion; and the design is, to have plays only at the Hay-Market, and operas only at Covent Garden [i.e., Drury Lane Theatre]. I think the design right to restore acting; but the houses are misapplied, which time may change.

Swiney wrote to Colley Cibber on 5 October 1706 (the letter is now in the Osborn collection at Yale; transcription courtesy of Robert Hume):

Dear Colley
I undertook the management of the playhouse in the Haymarket by and w.th the advice of some who were M.r Rich's best friends but incensed against him because he trifled w.th 'em about Vanbrugh's businesse, he never really intending any thing (but the gaining of time) by the treaty, his old play. Well What's that to me yol say—why I'll tell thee puppy. Know then that Rich was to make a union of the houses and I was to manage under him My Angel at 100 Guineas p annū Salary & I was to have a place at court and the Devil and all you know upon this I quitted my post in the Army. in about a fortnights time after this, I found that M.r Rich intended nothing but the going on his old way of paying Singers and dancers & not paying the Actors, I did not think it was my Interest to be Concerned on the wrong side, since I had no obligation to stay w.th M.r Rich, he discharging me of my promise the minute he broke of w.th Vanbrugh. further my Angel I thought if I had reason to complain now I was not in his power I thought it wou'd be too late to seek redresse when ever I shou'd be so unluckly as to fall into his hands for you must know My Dear that Rich is as tyrannycall as Lewis Le Grand, and I have as many grievances to com-

plain off as Prince Rogotzki, I thought the best way of doing my selfe right was to take up Arms and declare for the liberty of the Actors who were oppressed by Singers and dancers (Jesuits of a playhouse) And I think I shall be as successfull as my Brother Princes who turn out another upon the pretence of Mal administration and secure themselves a greater power. but to be serious I will Exhibit a few Articles against my Late Soveraign viz.

1 He sent for me from my Quarters in the North, I was at a great charge in coming to town and you know it cost me a great deal of mony last winter, I served him night and day, nay all night and all day, for Nine Months. he sent me forty pound by Jack Hall as a return for my services, I bid him carry back the mony to his Master w.th a bill of Jobs or porterage to whites Chocolate house, Ld Whatons, Mr Manwarings, & Mr Boyles, wch at 2.^{s} a jobb came to above 50.^{li} 13.^{s} and 4.^{d}

2 It was impossible for him to have had the Opera of Camilla without me, he told me if I coud get a Subscription he woud give me 100.^{li} 50. to be disposed off to a gentleman that was concern'd in the writing it, the other for the Industrious Mr Swiny. I applyd to Ld Wharton and his Grace of Richmond, the Subscription was gott and Rich told me in the Winter he would let me have a part of a benefit from the performance of it one day, he not being in a Condition to keep his word W.th me Tho' he received 1400. Guineas for it besides the Gallerys that time that the subscription was got by my Ld Wharton was for the Scotch Nobility. Item for a great parcell of Ill language at several times and places, but that I think he never got the better of me at Except when Collonel Brett was by. Successe will determine who is in the right.

I did design to have communicated this matter to you as soon as you came from Windsor and was w.th Mr Wilks at ye house the Thursday friday Saturday Sunday & Monday before the businesse was discovered, It was to have been kept Secret a fortnight longer till I had gott the people I had pitchd upon among whom was Mr Cibber among the Betterton's Wilks's Barry's &c the paper delivered to My Ld Chamberlain will be my Voucher, his Lordship was big of the plot and was afraid if any body shou'd let it be known at Court before him, he shou'd be Robbed of the glory of Establishing the Stage upon a foot of going on, he told it at the Dutchesse of Malbro's the same day Wilks & Oldfield signed and if I had not been pretty brisk the whole matter might have miscarried, for on Monday Mills Bullock Keen Newman & Norris Signed,

so that you may see I had no such mean design of lowering the Actors or starving 'em into a compliance w.th me, I am satisfied that it can't be worse w.th the Actors any where than where they were as to their Salary, And to show you that I have a very great regard for Mr Cibber he shall be welcome to me when he sees which side is strongest tho' it shou'd be ours. Estcourt must be had tho' he has addrest Mr Rich: I think y.^{r} first question is answered. As to y.^{r} Second Mr Rich might have had the house for 3.^{li} or 3.^{li} 10.^{s} a day. I have taken a lease for 7: yeares at 5.^{li} p day. I think y.^{r} second is reasonably well answered. I have given every Actor greater Salarys than Rich did and most of 'em benefit's playing [sic] 40.^{li} charge now I've here y.^{u} answered, if you have any difficulties upon y.^{r} mind if I can ease you by answering I will. I shall begin on Tuesday 7: night and play the Earle of Essex or the spanish Fryar. The Bellman has frightened me out of some other things wch you shall have when I hear from you, My Duty to my Co.^{li} and most humble respects in the most obliging manner you can to M.^{der} Brett Mr Brent &c

Unbeliver thine
Owen Swiny

Swiney's company opened the 1706–7 season with *The Spanish Fryar*. Rich stumbled along in October and November 1706 with a weakened troupe, playing at the old Dorset Garden Theatre instead of Drury Lane. By agreement, Swiney did not present any entr'acte turns, leaving those "Exotick Entertainments" to Rich's troupe. By mid-season Swiney's venture was succeeding, even against opera productions at Drury Lane.

On 15 August 1707 Swiney was accosted by Lord Tunbridge. Thomas Dean, a bystander, testified in support of Swiney:

Thomas Dean of ye Parish of St James's Westminster Victualler came this daye before me one of her Majesties Justices of ye Peace for ye said County & liberty and made oath that he this Deponent upon Friday ye 15th of that instant August did see Mr Owen Swiny going into ye Play house in ye Hay markett in ye said Parish of St James's Westminster and he this Deponent did see two Gentlemen meet the said Owen Swiny who ask'd him what he woud have, Mr Swiny answerd I would have nothing upon which one of them drew his Sword and ye other laid his hand upon his Sword, but did not draw it and they both pursued Mr Swiny within the Gates of ye Play house but ye said Mr Owen Swiny did not draw his Sword or offer so to do or say anything to provoke them and further this Deponent sayeth not.

A second bystander gave similar testimony, yet Swiney was forced by the Lord Chamberlain to apologize to Tunbridge.

The competition between Swiney and Rich continued until the end of 1707, when the Lord Chamberlain ordered that the Queen's be used only for operas (for which it was accoustically better suited anyway) and Drury Lane for drama. A union of the Rich and Swiney forces was effected on 13 January 1708, with Swiney (working for Vanbrugh) in charge of the Queen's. Swiney engaged such singers as Cassani, Leveridge, Valentini, "The Baroness," Signora de l'Épine, Mrs Tofts, and a number of dancers.

As of 24 February 1708, according to a letter from Vanbrugh to the Earl of Manchester, Vanbrugh and Peregrine Bertie were "now the sole adventurers and undertakers of the opera, for I have bought Mr. Swiney quite out: only pay him as manager. . . ." But on 11 May Vanbrugh wrote to Manchester, thanking him for his interest in improving the opera troupe and indicating that Swiney was now in full charge:

Henry E. Huntington Library and Art Gallery

OWEN MAC SWINEY

engraving by Faber, after Van Loo

What your Lordship says of having one or two of the top voices is most certainly right; as to myself, I have parted with my whole concern to Mr Swiny, only reserving my rent; so that he is entire possessor of the Opera, and, most people think, will manage it better than anybody. He has a good deal of money in his pocket, that he got before by the acting company, and is willing to venture it upon the singers. I have been several times with him lately in consultations with the Vice-Chamberlain Coke (who being a great lover of music and promoter of operas, my Lord Chamberlain leaves that matter almost entirely to him). I have acquainted him with what your Lordship writes, and Mr. Swiny has engaged before him to allow a thousand pounds for Nicolini, to stay here two winters. . . . As for Santini, Mr. Swiny offers the same conditions to her, if your Lordship can prevail with her to come; or if she won't, and you think Regiana would do as well, he leaves it to your judgement, and will allow her the same. If neither of these women will come, he would venture at half his allowance—viz. 600 Pistoles . . . for the two winters, if a young, improving woman could be found that had a good person and action. . . . If your Lordship can get any of these people over, on the terms here mentioned, Mr Swiny desires me to assure you of punctual performance of his part; nor is there any reason to doubt him, for he has behaved himself so as to

get credit in his dealings with the actors, and I know the Vice-Chamberlain does not the least question his making good all he offers on this occasion. Besides, he has power sufficient to oblige him to it, the license being only during the Queen's pleasure. . . .

Did Vanbrugh protest too much in favor of Swiney? It seems evident that Swiney himself did not have the necessary connections with the nobility to approach Manchester directly, and Vanbrugh's multiple assurances that Swiney could be trusted makes one wonder if in earlier years Swiney had been unreliable. Later events show that Swiney was quite willing to run out on his debts.

Swiney was able to engage Nicolini, the eminent *castrato,* but he did not get Signora Santini or any other new female. The proposal for Nicolini is among the Coke papers at the Westminster Public Library. Vanbrugh, having lost money on the opera venture, had less and less to do with it, though he seemed certain that opera would in time thrive in London. After the 1707–8 season Swiney was without Vanbrugh's influence with the aristocracy.

Christopher Rich was silenced on 6 June 1709, and during the following season plays were offered at both theatres with rival companies, the Queen's troupe being managed by Swiney. Swiney had the stronger group and was able to open the 1709–10 season two months before the players at Drury Lane. The Queen's Theatre was altered to improve the acoustics, and the company offered both plays and operas. Still, the expenses ran high, and the troupe did not prosper.

According to the Coke papers at Harvard and transcriptions by James Winston of other Coke papers at the British Library, Swiney moved in the spring and summer of 1709 to consolidate his monopoly, but, as will be seen, his power did not last long.

Among the Coke papers at Harvard is a letter dated 18 May 1710 from the singer Nicolini to Vice Chamberlain Coke, complaining about Swiney and the new "directors" of the Queen's Theatre, Cibber, Wilks, and Doggett; he said that he had suffered disgrace and mortification and found the new directors full of malice and insolence. His venom appears to have been directed less at Swiney than at the actor-managers. (His complaints are quoted in his entry.)

According to Mollie Sands in *Theatre Notebook*, 20, Swiney went to Venice (to recruit singers?) about 1710 or 1711. William Collier held the Drury Lane patent, and with his influence at court he obtained a reversion to the earlier arrangement whereby Swiney and the actors performed at Drury Lane while Collier and the singers presented operas at the Queen's.

On 6 November 1710 Swiney, Cibber, Wilks, and Doggett received a license to perform at Drury Lane. The new agreement put the actor-managers in firm control, and they set about establishing the company administration that was to make Drury Lane a stable troupe for two decades. Among other reforms, they reduced Swiney's salary to a fourth of the company's net receipts, refused his plea to pay off debts from the 1709–10 season, and told the treasurer not to make any payments without the permission of at least three of the managers. That effectively prevented Swiney

from interfering, and, when he saw his partners drawing sizable amounts of money from the treasury, he complained to the Lord Chamberlain

Mr Swiny took a Lease of the Theatre in ye Haymarket with ye Clothes Scenes and Utensills thereunto belonging for 14 years from Mr Vanbrugh with an Assignment of his License from her Majesty for Acting Plays Operas &ca for a Yearly Consideration payable to ye said Mr. Vanbrugh. Some time after Mr Swiny took Mr Wilks Mr Dogget and Mr Cibber into partner ship with himselfe for the remainder of the said terme subject to the following Conditions as may be seen more at large by the Indented Articles of Agreement Sign'd by them.

ffirst it is Agreed that they shall with Mr Swiny be Copartners not only in the profits and loss that may happen in ye Theatre in the Haymarket, but in any other play house they shall think fit to remove to, without engaging in any other Society of Players whatever.

2 dly that Mr Wilks Mr Dogget and Mr Cibber shall do their utmost by managing Acting &ca to support ye Company.

3 dly That Mr Swiny shall Employ his constant care & pains in governing &ca and has not nor shall make over any part of his Interest in the Lease or License, but with ye consent of his partners.

4 thly That Mr Wilks shall Attend and take care of all Rehearsalls.

5 ly that a plain and true Account shall be kept of all Receipts and disbursements, that Mr Swiny shall out of those Receipts in the first place, and preferrably to all other deductions or payments discharge ye Rent to Mr Vanbrugh due to his Lease and Conditions with him. That he shall next discharge and satisfye all Agreements with performers and servants Expences in Cloths Scenes &ca which shall be Allow'd to him in passing his Accounts. That after all charges thus paid and clear'd Mr Swiny shall Receive £300 a Year out of the profits in consideration of his pains and care in the governent &ca. That Mr Wilks Mr Dogget and Mr Cibber shall for their care in managing and for their Acting on ye Stage receive each £200 a year. And Mr Wilks £50 more for Attending and taking care of Rehearsals. And after these payments made, the clear profits shall be divided into two equall parts, one of which to be detain'd by Mr Swiny and the other to be Equally divided between Mr Wilks Mr Doggett and Mr Cibber. The Losses if any to be allow'd for after the same proportion.

6 ly That Mr Wilks Mr Dogget and Mr Cibber shall have every year each of them a play Acted for their Benefit without any deduction for ye charges of ye House.

Henry E. Huntington Library and Art Gallery

OWEN MAC SWINEY

by Grisoni

7 ly That if Mr Swiny dyes before the Expiration of the Lease His salary of £300 a year shall cease and his Executors be Entituled only to one 4th part of the clear profits, And lyable only to the same proportion of Loss. That if any of the other three dye their salary and share both shall cease but their widow or children shall have a Benefit play paying £40 for the Charges of the House. That within six months after such decease an other Actor shall be chosen by the surviving partners to supply the vacancy.

8 ly That the government and Management shall be in ye Majority, Mr Swiny to have but one voice and in Case of equality of voices to be determin'd by Lott. All Law suits to be at the Common Expence, ffarther writings to be signd if Necessary for the strengthning these Articles, & a penalty of £2000 for non performance.

But the Queen having since thought fit to divide ye Operas from the Comedys. And in Order to it, to grant distinct Licenses, Mr Swiny's partners complaining they had not that power in Managing which they conceiv'd themselves entituled to by their Agreement with him pray'd that their names might be inserted with his in the new License, which being done Accordingly they now pretend they are by that means freed from all the former Contracts, That Mr Swiny is Entituled to Nothing more than one fourth part of the profits and that they are no longer subject with him to make good the Engagements of Rent to Mr Vanbrugh Tho' they at this very time have no other stock of Cloathes Scenes &ca but those Mr Swiny has furnish'd them with and is possest of by Vertue of his Lease from Mr Vanbrugh And which are all to Revert to Mr Vanbrugh at ye termination of the said Lease with whatever is Added in the mean time.

Mr Swiny therefore most humbly prays that my Lord Chamberlain will please by his Authority to Compell the said Mr Wilks Mr Dogget and Mr Cibber to proceed According to ye true tenure and meaning of the above Receited Contract, And that it may be enter'd in the Books of his Grace's Office That by inserting their names in the License, there was nothing intended to Annull or Invalidate their former Agreements but only to give them an Equall power in the Management.

On 12 January 1711 Swiney sued the trio in Chancery; a settlement was reached out of court by 19 May. Swiney's income was fixed at £600 annually; the articles of 1709 were canceled. Swiney, frustrated, decided to deal with William Collier. In April 1712 an exchange took place and the "troublesome" Swiney (as Doggett described him) received a license for the opera and Collier, Cibber, Wilks, and Doggett were given a license for plays.

When Swiney returned to the opera house for the 1711–12 season, he found the financial situation precarious, but the troupe struggled through and continued into the following season. On 10 January 1713 Handel's *Teseo* was presented; Colman in his "Opera Register" noted the occasion:

Mr O. Swiny ye Manager of ye Theatre was now setting out a New Opera, Heroick, all ye Habits new & richer than ye former with 4 New Scenes, & other Decorations & Machines. Ye Tragick Opera was called Theseus. Ye Musick composed by Mr Handel. . . . ye Opera being thus prepared Mr Swiny would have got a Subscription for Six times, but could not.—he then did give out Tickets at half a Guinea each [i.e., little more than the usual price for boxes], for two Nights ye Boxes lay'd open to ye Pit, ye House was very full these two Nights. . . . After these two Nights [10 and 14 January] Mr Swiny Brakes & runs away & leaves ye Singers unpaid ye Scene & Habits also unpaid for.

The Singers were in Some confusion but at last concluded to go on with ye operas on their own accounts, & divide ye Gain amongst them.

Swiney's abrupt departure evidently caused not only confusion among the singers but a bad performance on the thirteenth, for on 24 January they advertised their apology for not giving "the Nobility and Gentry all the Satisfaction they could have wished . . . having been hindered by some unforeseen Accidents at that time insurmountable." Later, on 1 January 1715, Vanbrugh wrote himself a note describing the situation:

I have accepted of Mr Swinys Resignation of his Lease of the Playhouse as on the 10th of May last, to which time having settled the Account between us (with Mr. Sexton his Agent, he himself being in France) I paid him part of the Ballance, and Sign'd a note to him payable to Michaelmass next, of £125. for the remainder, which is in full, of All Accounts between him and me. The Surrender of his Lease is only by a Writing sent from France; the lease it self being lock'd up with things of his at Leyden as likewise a Mortgage he had upon the Playhouse for £1000. But I have his Receipts for the Whole Sum Written upon the Counterpart or annex'd to it.

(That memorandum is quoted in Downes's *Vanbrugh.*)

Swiney went first to France and later to Italy. In Venice he met Consul Joseph Smith, who about 1716 or 1717 married the English singer Catherine Tofts. Swiney lived at the Smiths' Palazzo Balbi from 1720. Between 1720 and 1730 Swiney commissioned (as an agent, evidently) a number of portraits by a variety of artists for *Monuments to the Remembrance of a Set of British Worthies*. The paintings are listed in Edward Croft-Murray's *Decorative Painting in England*.

Cibber in 1740 wrote warmly of Swiney:

. . . I should farther say, that this Person has been well known in almost every Metropolis in *Europe;* that few private Men have, with so little Reproach, run through more various Turns of Fortune; that, on the wrong side of Three-score, he has yet the open Spirit of a hale young Fellow of five and twenty; that though he still chuses to speak what he thinks to his best Friends with an undisguis'd Freedom, his is, notwithstanding, acceptable to many Persons of the first Rank and Condition; that any one of them (provided he likes them) may now

send him, for their Service, to *Constantinople* at half a Day's Warning; that Time has not been able to make a visible Change in any Part of him but the Colour of his Hair, from a fierce coal-black to that of a milder milk-white.

During his years in exile Swiney may at first have lost contact with England, but Elizabeth Gibson in *Musical Times* in 1984 reported that letters in the Goodwood Estate archives show Swiney to have been involved in London opera affairs by the spring of 1724. Letters to the Duke of Richmond show Swiney recommending continental singers to the Royal Academy of Music and serving as the Academy's agent in negotiating contracts. Swiney also reported on opera librettos and successful Continental (especially Italian) opera productions. He was paid for his services, but the letters do not reveal his salary.

Swiney recruited opera singers for Handel in 1730 and returned to London by 26 February 1735, when he was given a benefit at Drury Lane. Cibber came out of retirement that season and played Fondlewife in *The Old Bachelor* for Swiney. On 1 April 1736 John Rich gave Swiney a benefit at Covent Garden Theatre, and the accounts for Covent Garden show that on 14 April 1741 £30 was given "Mr. Swinny for a Note of hand." About that time Horace Walpole wrote of going to a party at Sir Thomas Robinson's, where there were "none but people of the first fashion except Mr Kent, Mr Cibber, Mr Swiney, and the Parsons family, and you know all these have an alloy."

About 1749 Swiney traveled to Paris for John Rich to arrange for the visit of a French troupe headed by Jean Monnet in 1749–50. The visit was a disaster, with English audiences picqued at the French.

At some point Swiney was appointed examiner of the office securities in the custom house and storekeeper at the King's mews. His posts evidently provided him with sufficient income to enjoy himself with Cibber at the spas and indulge in a flirtation with Peg Woffington. Both Cibber and Swiney were attracted to Mrs Woffington, Swiney went off to France with her for a spell and was so enamoured that he left most of his estate to her in his will. Davies tells a story of the elderly Swiney championing Peg in a scuffle in the

Green Room at Drury Lane in 1754 after she appeared as Lady Percy in *1 Henry IV.*

Owen Swiney died on 2 October 1754 and was buried on the fifth at St Martin-in-the-Fields. He had made his will on 1 August 1752, leaving his estate in trust to the Duke of Dorset (Lord Lieutenant of Ireland) and Francis Andrews, a lawyer and fellow of Trinity College, Dublin, for Margaret Woffington. Swiney left £20 each to his housekeeper Elizabeth London and her daughter Elizabeth. His household furniture, books, pictures (of which he had a considerable collection), and other moveables he asked to be sold for Mrs Woffington's benefit. The will was proved on 7 October 1754.

Portraits of Swiney include:

1. In a picture by Robert Crone called "The Ship Cabin," Swiney is shown in the cabin of Lord Boyne's yacht, sailing to the Levant; also depicted are Lord Boyne, Robert Wood, and others. The picture was painted in Italy for Lord Boyne and then belonged to the Rt Hon Nathaniel Clements. Present location unknown.

2. By Grisoni, in Padua, August 1716. Drawing in the Huntington Library.

3. By Laroon. According to Vertue, Swiney sat for Laroon, but no portrait has been found.

4. By Peter Van Bleeck, 1747. The original painting seems lost, but the National Portrait Gallery has a copy, after Van Bleeck (No 1417), oil on canvas, 30½" × 25⅛". An engraving of the original was made by Van Bleeck, 1749. In the painting the sitter's hand rests on a book; in the engraving it rests on a cane.

5. By Jean-Baptiste Van Loo. Painted shortly after the artist's arrival in London in December 1737. For some time the portrait was untraced and was known by the engraving done by J. Faber, Jr, 1752. The painting appeared at Christie's on 7 March 1927 (lot 113), when it was bought by an anonymous buyer. It, or another version, oil on canvas, 44¼" × 33¼", was at Sotheby's, New York, on 27 March 1987. An oval version sketched by Scharf, October 1859, was offered that year to the National Portrait Gallery by J. Mara, Caledonian Road, London, but was not accepted.

Swiny, Mrs. *See* HAMILTON, MRS JOHN.

"Swiss, The." *See* HEIDEGGER, JOHN JAMES.

"Swiss, The Little." *See* "LITTLE SWISS, THE."

Swords, William [*fl. 1778–1795*], *actor, singer.*

William Swords made his first stage appearance on 28 December 1778, playing an unspecified role in *The Macaroni Adventurer* at the Haymarket Theatre. That evening he also acted Mother Punchbowl in *The Covent Garden Tragedy.* On 11 January 1779 he played Graspall in *The Students* and before the end of May appeared as Caveat in *Wit's Last Stake,* Conundrum in *The Humours of Oxford,* Lopes in *The Wrangling Lovers,* and an Officer in *Douglas.*

In 1779 Swords acted at Brighton in Joseph Fox's company, and he was presumably the Swords named as the singer of *The Farmer's Dog leapt o'er the Stile* at the Haymarket, a song published about 1780. He was again at the Haymarket on 13 November 1780, playing

Folger Shakespeare Library

WILLIAM SWORDS
by Harding

Dr M'Drugg and Powell in *The Detection* and Gregory Last in *The City Association*. Swords then went to the Smock Alley Theatre in Dublin, making his first appearance in Ireland on 2 January 1781. On 12 November 1781 he played again at the Haymarket, this time in *The Spendthrift*. He remained at the Haymarket through September 1782, trying such new parts as Young Clincher in *The Constant Couple*, Addlepot in *An Adventure in St James's Park*, Careful in *The Beaux' Duel*, Mrs Slammekin in *The Beggar's Opera* (women played the male roles), Vane in *The Chapter of Accidents*, Wrinkle in *The Candidate*, Sneer in *The Life and Death of Common Sense*, Sir Jasper in *The Citizen*, and Sir Harry in *The Temple Beau*.

In the summer of 1783 at the Haymarket, Swords acted, among other new characters, Creon in *Medea and Jason*, Ostler in *Man and Wife*, and Crack in *Gretna Green;* and in the spring and summer of 1784 he essayed Trusty in *The Man's Bewitch'd*, Jerry Sneak in *The Mayor of Garratt*, Gomez in *The Spanish Fryar*, Juggins in *The Suicide*, a Brother in *Comus*, Jarvis in *The Good Natur'd Man*, and Peter Nettle and the Serjeant in *The What D'Ye Call It*. In 1785 he tried Muskato in *'Tis Well It's No Worse*, Lady Pentweazel in *The Diversions of the Morning*, John in *The Agreeable Surprise*, Marcellus in *Hamlet*, Alguazile in *The Spanish Barber*, Major Benbow in *The Flitch of Bacon*, Dr Caterpillar in *Harlequin Teague*, and Chronicle in *The Young Quaker*.

In the fall of 1785 Swords began an engagement at Covent Garden Theatre that lasted through 1786–87. His first appearance came on 21 September 1785, when he played the Irishman in *Rosina*. He was then seen in such parts as a Gardener in *Barataria*, Wat Dreary in *The Beggar's Opera*, Order in *A New Way to Pay Old Debts*, Pedro in *Catherine and Petruchio*, the Apothecary in *Romeo and Juliet*, Simon in *The Commissary*, a Constable in *Omai*, a Drummer in *Love in a Camp*, Carlo in *The Bird in a Cage*, Old Gobbo in *The Merchant of Venice*, Bardolph in *1 Henry IV* and *The Merry Wives of Windsor*, Slap in *The Intriguing Chambermaid*, and Sour Crout in *The Maid of Bath*. Between seasons, in the summer of 1786, Swords returned to the Haymarket to act several of his old roles and such new ones as Varnish in *The Separate Maintenance*, Crab in *Summer Amuse-*

ment, John in *The Son-in-Law*, Omar in *A Mogul Tale*, and an Italian Merchant in *Harlequin Teague*. In the summer of 1787 at the Haymarket some of his new characters were Thomas in *The Virgin Unmask'd*, Elliot in *Venice Preserv'd*, Solarino in *The Merchant of Venice*, Bounce in *The Follies of a Day*, and Derby in *Jane Shore*. He then went off to Dublin to spend the 1787–88 season at Smock Alley.

On 5 August 1788 William Swords was back at the Haymarket playing a Covent Garden Doctor (and perhaps also a Blacksmith) in *The Gnome*. After that appearance Swords may have left London again, for he was not mentioned in any bills until 26 September 1791, when he played Sir Oliver Oafby in *The Double Amour*, advertised as making his first Haymarket appearance in three years. Then he acted Linger in *Wit's Last Stake* on 22 October 1792 and dropped from sight once more. At some point he performed in Canterbury. The last date we have found for him is July 1795, when he published a poem in the *Universal Magazine*. Swords had a wife who was an actress, but her career was brief.

A drawing of Swords (in oval, 4 ⅝" × 3 ¾") by Harding is in the Folger Library.

Swords, Mrs William ₁*fl. 1784–1786*₁, *actress, singer*

Mrs William Swords played Charlotte in *The Apprentice* at the Haymarket Theatre on 17 September 1784. On 19 October 1785 at Covent Garden Theatre she acted Furnish in *The Way to Keep Him*, and on 21 November she sang in *Romeo and Juliet*. On 24 April 1786 she played Mardona in *The Bird in a Cage*.

Sworms, John Adam *d. c. 1778?, double-bass player.*

John Adam Sworms (or Schworm), according to *The Royal Society of Musicians* (1985) was "upwards of seventy Years of Age" in 1776 and thus born near the turn of the century. On 1 March 1752 he was admitted to the Royal Society, and at the chapel of the Foundling Hospital on 27 April 1758 he played double bass in a performance of the *Messiah*. He performed in the *Messiah* again in 1759, 1760, 1763, and 1767. Sworms died before 24 June 1778.

"Sybilla, Mrs," stage name of Sybilla Gronaman, later Mrs Thomas Pinto the first [*fl.* 1742–1748], *singer, actress.*

Sybilla Gronaman, a German soprano, seems to have gone to Ireland late in 1742. She was first noticed, as "Mrs Sybilla," at the Aungier Street Theatre, Dublin, on 10 January 1743, when she played the second Nymph in *Comus.* She was in the title role of the opera *Rosamond* and sang Princess Huncamunca in *The Tragedy of Tragedies* on 7 May 1743.

On 17 January 1745 Mrs Sybilla (her constant stage name) sang at Drury Lane Theatre in the first performance of Arne's musical afterpiece *The Temple of Dulness,* taking the role of the Goddess of Dulness. It was advertised as "the first time of her performing in England," and to at least one admirer her singing was a success. "S. G." published a poem in the *Gentleman's Magazine* for February 1745 entitled *To Mrs Sybilla, on her Acting the Goddess of Dullness and persuading her to attempt Melantha in Dryden's Marriage Alamode.* There is no evidence that she ever took the advice.

When on 31 January 1745 the opera *Rosamond* was staged at Drury Lane, she dropped down to the secondary part of Grideline, behind Miss Young's Rosamond. On 20 March, when James Thomson and David Mallet's masque *Alfred, King of England,* with music by Arne, was brought to Drury Lane from the theatre at the Prince of Wales's residence at Clivedon, she was in the cast, but her role is not known. She was the original Lady Abbess in *King Pepin's Campaign,* William Shirley's new afterpiece, with music by Arne, on 15 April.

Mrs (often Signora) Sybilla returned to Drury Lane in 1745–46 and in 1746–47, adding Ceres ("Mrs Sibella") in the "Grand Masque" attached to *The Tempest* and a "vocal part" in the chorus to Macbeth and singing between the acts. On 14 November 1747 she appeared for the first time in England in Italian-style opera, as Flavius in Handel's *Lucio Vero,* repeated eight times. She probably had a role in Galuppi's *Enrico,* on 23 January and subsequently in Handel's *Rossane,* 20 February 1748 and following. She was certainly Aspasia in Handel's dramatic oratorio *Alexander Balus* on 23 March at Covent Garden. On 9 December 1748 Signora Sybilla headed a list of eminent names performing a *Concert of Vocal and Instrumental Music* at the Haymarket for the benefit of the singer Gustavus Waltz. She sang Handel's "Come ever smiling Liberty." Her last recorded appearances at a patent theatre were at Covent Garden on 10, 15, and 17 February as an Attendant in Handel's oratorio *Susanna,* though she may have been also in the opera company at the King's Theatre that season; the bills there furnished no casts. On 23 May 1748 Cuper's Gardens opened with her as a featured singer.

Miss Gronaman had married the violinist Thomas Pinto in 1745, but had never performed under her married name. The date of her death is not known, but Pinto remarried in November 1766. At least two of Pinto's children (discussed in his entry) were Sybilla's.

Sydney. *See also* SIDNEY.

Sydney, Grace. *See* WALCUP, GRACE.

Sydow. *See* SEEDO.

Sykes, Mr [*fl.* 1769], *violinist.*
Mr Sikes played violin in a benefit performance of the *Messiah* at the Foundling Hospital sometime in 1769.

Sylvester. *See also* SILVESTER.

Sylvester, Mr [*fl.* 1776–1777], *boxkeeper.*
The Drury Lane Theatre accounts reveal that Mr Sylvester was a boxkeeper at 12s. weekly in 1776–77.

Sylvester, Mr [*fl.* 1786–1789], *waxworks exhibitor.*
At the Lyceum exhibition room about 1786, according to Altick's *The Shows of London,* Mr and Mrs Sylvester (or Silvester) exhibited "A Cabinet of Royal Figures, most curiously moulded in wax, as large as Nature." Represented were the French and British royal families, a sleeping Venus, Warren Hastings, Benjamin Franklin, and Voltaire. In 1788 the Sylvesters took their show to Ansell's Large Room in Spring Gardens; a feature was a representation of a seraglio. The visitors could have their portraits taken in wax or miniature,

and Sylvester announced that he would charge nothing "should the portraits not be thought the most striking and correct likenesses."

On 4 April 1789 at Merchant Taylors' Hall in Bristol, Sylvester, advertised as having just arrived from the Lyceum in London, showed his wax figures. "The Crowned heads are all in their Court dress, and the Admirals in their Uniforms." Sylvester described himself as "late pupil of the Royal Academy at Paris." Mrs Sylvester exhibited waxworks in Bristol in 1795 and 1796; perhaps by that time her husband had died.

Sylvester, Mrs ₍*fl. 1786–1796*₎, *waxworks exhibitor. See* SYLVESTER, MR ₍*fl. 1786–1789*₎.

Sylvester, Mr ₍*fl. 1791–1801?*₎, *tumbler, actor?*
At Astley's Amphitheatre in July 1791 one of the tumblers was Mr Sylvester. Perhaps he was the Sylvester mentioned by the *Thespian Magazine* as being at the theatre in Chesterfield in December 1792, or the actor in the Drury Lane company in London in 1800–1801.

Sylvester, Mr ₍*fl. 1800–1801*₎, *machinist.*
The Haymarket Theatre bill for 2 July 1800 named Sylvester and Ronaldson as responsible for the machinery for the new production of *Obi.* Sylvester was one of the machinists for *Corsair* when it was presented at the same theatre on 29 July 1801.

Sylvester, Harriett. *See* LITCHFIELD, MRS JOHN, HARRIETT.

Symcoll, Richard ₍*fl. 1670*₎, *singer.*
On 20 July 1670 Richard Symcoll was given a suit of clothes upon his leaving the Chapel Royal; he had been one of the boy singers, and presumably his voice had broken.

Symmons, Mr ₍*fl. 1722–1744*₎, *actor.*
Mr Symmons (or Symonds) was a member of the Drury Lane troupe as of 12 April 1722, when an inventory of players was drawn up. He played Demetrius in *Timon of Athens* at his shared benefit with May on 29 May 1722, and on 3 June 1723 he had a solo benefit. At the

Haymarket Theatre on 15 October 1728 Symmons acted Trickwell in *The Metamorphosis* and Trap in *The Craftsman* and spoke the epilogue. At Southwark Fair on 8 September 1731 he played Old Barnwell in *The London Merchant*. On 1 May 1744 at May Fair he was the Lieutenant in *The Royal Heroe*.

Symms, Edward ₍*fl. 1673*₎, *wardrobe keeper.*
A warrant in the Lord Chamberlain's accounts dated 19 March 1673 admitted Edward Symms as wardrobe keeper for the Duke's Company at the Dorset Garden Theatre.

Symonds. *See also* SIMMONS, SIMONDS, SIMONS.

Symonds, John *d. 1739, organist, harpsichordist, composer, impresario.*
The Political State of Great Britain recorded the death of the musician John Symonds on 6 January 1739 at his house in Princes Street, Bedford Row. He was described as a music master, organist of West Ham Church, Essex, and of St John's Chapel in St John's Square. *A Dictionary of Musicians* (1824) described Symonds as a member of the King's band and organist, not at West Ham but at St Martin, Ludgate, and at St John's. The *Dictionary* said Symonds had published six sets of lessons for the harpsichord, but that source was surely in error in calling Symonds Henry and saying he died about 1730. A clipping in the Burney papers at the British Library advertises a benefit concert for Kenny "At Mr. Symonds's Great Room at the King's Head in Engfield" on 15 August 1726. The concert was to be followed by a ball. That Symonds was very likely our subject, and he may have held a number of other musical events about which no information has been found.

Symonds, William *d. 1777, hall keeper.*
William Symonds served Covent Garden Theatre as a hall keeper from at least as early as 3 June 1768, on which date he shared a benefit. On 17 June the patentee Thomas Harris and others broke into the theatre, collared Symonds (who had lodgings there), and threatened him. That was part of the violent squabble between Colman and Harris; Harris had been locked out of the playhouse.

Symonds (sometimes Symmonds) was named in benefit bills in the 1770s. The *Morning Chronicle* reported that the hall keeper died on 16 September 1777.

Symone, Mons ₁*fl.*1792₁, *dancer.*
Monsieur Symone danced a pas seul at the Haymarket Theatre on 26 November 1792.

Symons. *See* SIMMONDS.

Sympson. *See* SIMPSON.

"Syphace" or "Syphax." *See* "SIFACE."

Syrmen. *See* SIRMEN.

Tacet, Joseph [*fl. 1751–1780*], *flutist, composer.*

The Burney papers at McGill University reveal that Joseph Tacet played in the Concerts Spirituels in Paris in 1751. His first notice in London was on 13 February 1755, when he played a solo on the German flute at the Haymarket Theatre. For the following 20 years he was a regular soloist at concerts and oratorios at the London theatres and music rooms. Usually he performed for the benefit of others, at the annual King's Theatre charity benefits for indigent musicians, or at a "Concerto Spirituale" at Drury Lane or Covent Garden. In January 1761, for example, he played at Tenducci's benefit at the music room in Dean Street, Soho; in February 1769 he supplied music on the German flute at *An Attic Evening's Entertainment* (readings) at the Haymarket; in June 1770 he played between sections of *La Passione* at the King's; and in March 1774 he did the same at a performance of the *Messiah* at the Haymarket. The final year that events are listed for Tacet, 1775, he played at the King's Theatre several times in March and April, when *Samson*, the *Messiah*, *Alexander's Feast*, and *Judas Maccabaeus* were performed.

Tacet was also a composer and a collector of music, mostly works for the flute. His musical publications date from about 1770 to about 1775. He was named in the *ABC Dario Musico*, which was published at Bath in 1780.

Taddy. *See* TADY.

Tadwell. *See* TIDSWELL.

Tady, Mr [*fl.c. 1671–1672*], *actor.*

Mr Tady (or Taddy) was associated with the actor John Coysh and is named in the promptbook of *The Comedy of Errors* at the University of Edinburgh for the parts of a Merchant and Pinch. The notes may have been for a performance about 1671–72, most likely at the Barbican "Nursery" training theatre for young players or on tour. Tady is also down for the role of Sir Harry in the promptbook of *The Wise Woman of Hogsdon* at the Folger Shakespeare Library; that work also dates about 1671–72 at the Nursery or on tour.

Tagg, Mr [*fl. 1794*], *flutist.*

Doane's *Musical Directory* of 1794 listed Mr Tagg, of No 75, Wood Street, Cheapside, as a flutist who played for the Cecilian Society.

Tagnoni, Madelena [*fl. 1764*], *singer.*

At the King's Theatre on 21 February 1764 Signora Madelena Tagnoni sang Fenicia in *Senocrita*. The bill for 27 March noted that she had been unwell but would perform again that night.

Taimes, William [*fl. 1673–1674*], *scenekeeper, machinist.*

William Taimes was a member of the King's Company in 1673–74, the season during which they moved from their temporary home at the Lincoln's Inn Fields Theatre to their new playhouse in Drury Lane. A Lord Chamberlain's warrant dated 14 November 1673 cited Taimes as a scenekeeper and machinist.

Tajana, Giovanni [*fl. 1791*], *singer.*

Giovanni Tajana sang at a musical entertainment at the King's Theatre on 26 March 1791; the event was repeated a month later and again in May and June. His last notice was on 2 June.

Talbot, Mrs [*fl. 1730–1740*], *actress.*

Mrs Talbot acted Dorinda in *The Stratagem* in Lee and Harper's booth at Southwark Fair on 24 September 1730, when the *Daily Journal* identified her as "a Gentlewoman" playing "for *her* Diversion." Probably this lady was the "Miss" Talbot who was seen as Harriot in *The*

Author's Farce at the Haymarket Theatre on 21 October 1730. On 27 April 1732 Mrs Talbot acted Sylvia in *The Recruiting Officer* at the Haymarket, and that summer she was in the employ of Fielding and Hippisley during Bartholomew Fair, where she appeared in an unspecified role in *The Envious Statesman* on 22 August 1732 at the George Inn.

On 21 February 1733 Mrs Talbot, acting Sylvia, shared a benefit with Mrs Martin at the Haymarket. At that theatre on 19 March she was Cherry in *The Beaux' Stratagem*. At Bartholomew Fair again in the summer of 1733, she acted Widow Widely in *The Miser* and Mrs Cribcole in *The Comical Humours of Sir John Falstaff*. During the summer of 1734 Mrs Talbot played a number of roles at the Haymarket, including Mrs Cribcole, Cherry, Lucy in *George Barnwell*, Mrs Vixen in *The Beggar's Opera, Tragediz'd*, Tippet in *The Beggar's Wedding*, Lady Wronghead in *The Provok'd Husband*, Mrs Soaker in *The Humorous Election*, and Mariana in *The Miser*. She also appeared with the company hired by Fielding and Oates for Bartholomew Fair in 1734, one of her roles being Henrietta in *Don Carlos, Prince of Spain*, on 24 August.

Over the next six years, Mrs Talbot, who never had an engagement with a winter patent house, reappeared in the various summer houses and booths. At Lincoln's Inn Fields Theatre in the summer of 1735, she played Mrs Squeamish in *The Stage Mutineers*, Lady Charlot in *Squire Basinghall*, Constantia in *Politicks on Both Sides*, Mustacha in *The Tragedy of Tragedies*, the Nurse in *Caius Marius*, Valentine in *Bartholomew Fair*, and Mrs Peachum in *The Beggar's Opera*. As a member of Mrs Charke's Company Mrs Talbot acted Lucy in *George Barnwell* at York Buildings on 1 October 1735. That season she appeared at the Haymarket as Sylvia in *The Recruiting Officer* on 13 December 1735 and Pleadwell in *The Rival Milliners; or, The Humours of Covent Garden* on 19 January 1736; at Lincoln's Inn Fields as Flippanta in *The Confederacy* and Pleadwell on 24 March (also in the latter role on 3 March), Phillis in *The Female Rake* on 26 April, and Sylvia in *The Soldiers' Fortune* on 29 April; and at the Haymarket again as Lucy in *The Beggar's Opera* on 26 June and Pleadwell on 30 July 1736. During this period she operated a coffee house in the passage to Drury Lane Theatre.

When she acted Hypolita in *She Wou'd and She Wou'd Not* for her benefit at the Haymarket on 2 March 1737, tickets were available at Mrs Talbot's Coffee House.

Mrs Talbot also performed at Bartholomew Fair in 1736, 1739, and 1740; her last appearance of record was as Loveit in *Harlequin Scapin* at Hippisley and Chapman's booth on 23 August 1740.

Talbot, Miss [*fl.* 1744–1748], *actress, singer.*

A Miss Talbot acted Mariana in *The Miser* at the Haymarket Theatre on 20 April 1744. That night, which was for her benefit, Miss Talbot also sang "Tell me, Gentle Shepherd Where," from *Solomon*. No doubt she was one of the pupils of Charles Macklin who that season presented several performances by his students; also in that group was Samuel Foote. On 16 May Miss Talbot again appeared as Mariana.

Probably she was the same Miss Talbot who sang at the Smock Alley Theatre in Dublin on 22 April 1748, when the advertisements announced that "at the Request of several Persons of Quality Miss Talbot will sing . . . celebrated Songs, being the first Time of her appearing in this Kingdom."

Talbot, Miss [*fl.* 1750], *actress.*

A Miss Talbot, on an occasion announced as "Being the first time of her appearing on the Stage," played Melinde in *L'Officier en recrue*, a French version of *The Recruiting Officer*, which was performed at the Haymarket Theatre on 9 February 1750. On 16 February the company played a French version of *The Beggar's Opera*, called *L'Opéra du gueux*, in which Miss Talbot acted Mlle Lucie. On 13 March she played Mme du Melange in *Arlequin Fourbe Anglois*, and on 9 April 1750 she appeared as Melinda in the English version of *The Recruiting Officer*.

Talbot, Montague 1774–1831, *actor, manager, author.*

Montague Talbot was born about 1774 in Boston, Massachusetts, where his mother had joined his father Captain John Talbot, of the Irish line of Talbot, who was on military service. Montague's paternal grandfather had been killed in the battle of the Boyne, and other Talbots had died in his Majesty's service

MONTAGUE TALBOT, as Colonel Cohenberg

artist unknown

in America or India. On the voyage home in 1782 Captain Talbot went down with the *Grosvenor* East Indiaman off the coast of Kaffraria.

Young Talbot was educated at Exeter and then entered the Temple to study law. But after participating in some private theatricals he determined to head for the stage, thus causing his uncle, Dr Geech, to revoke his will in which Talbot was intended as joint heir with his cousin, the Rev Dr Crossman, to a fortune of £60,000. Advertised as a young gentleman making his first appearance on any stage, Talbot acted Douglas in *Douglas* at Covent Garden Theatre on 13 January 1794. His name was given by the *European Magazine* of that month and his attempt was recorded as a failure. The critic admonished him for not waiting a few

years until his person, voice, and judgment had matured and he had studied parts within the reach of his powers. Not until the end of the season did he appear again, when on 28 May 1794 he acted Cassander in *Alexander the Great*, billed as the gentleman who has been "so very favourably received in Douglas."

In 1794–95 he acted under the name Montague at the Crow Street Theatre, Dublin. In the summer of 1795 he played at Cork. In September 1795 he left Ireland for London with Charles Mathews, a fellow member of the Crow Street company, stopping at Swansea, where, it was reported by the December 1795 *Monthly Mirror*, that Mr Montague acted Othello, Penruddock in *The Wheel of Fortune*, Jaffeir in *Venice Preserv'd*, and other roles. The purpose of his trip to London, according to *The Dictionary of National Biography*, was to see the production of *Vortigern*, Ireland's Shakespearean hoax, which Talbot himself helped to perpetrate. But the performance of *Vortigern* at Drury Lane occurred on 2 April 1796, and by the previous 8 January Talbot had returned to Crow Street, the theatre which served as his base in 1796–97 and 1797–98.

Talbot had met William Henry Ireland, son of the engraver Samuel Ireland, at law school. Talbot claimed to have surprised young Ireland in the act of forgery, and having been sworn to secrecy, to have been drawn into the fraud. Talbot connived at allowing Ireland to attribute the discovery of the manuscripts to him: in a letter dated 10 November 1795 young Ireland wrote to his father, "I was at chambers, when Talbot called, and shewed me a deed signed Shakespeare." Indeed, Talbot elaborated with enthusiasm, claiming in a letter to the elder Ireland, "The gentleman in whose possession these things were found was *a friend of mine*, and *by me* your son Samuel was *introduced to his acquaintance*." Talbot had an agreement with Samuel Ireland to share any profits from the deception. In a letter to Samuel Ireland, apparently written from Dublin on 15 April 1796 (thereby making it unlikely that Talbot was in London when *Vortigern* was produced), the lawyer-turned-actor offered to make an affidavit admitting his complicity.

In August 1798 Talbot left Dublin for Liverpool, where, still using the name of Montague, he acted with Charles Mayne Young and was highly regarded. He returned to London the following spring to make his debut at Drury Lane Theatre on 27 April 1799 as Young Mirable in *The Inconstant,* on which occasion he was advertised as Mr Talbot. *The Monthly Mirror* for May 1799 noted that he had formerly acted at Covent Garden some years back, had improved his talents under the name of Montague in Dublin, and had been seriously implicated in the Shakespeare forgery. In this debut, for which he had assumed his real name, the actor revealed "considerable ease, vivacity and fashionable address; a genteel figure, a correct judgment, and a tolerable acquaintance with mechanism of the stage; but we think his voice wants harmony and flexibility for the proper delivery of comic dialogue." Talbot repeated the role on 18 May 1799. He was probably the Talbot who performed with the adventuress Mary Ann Talbot (no apparent relation) in a private theatre in Tottenham Court Road about November 1799; he acted Octavian to her Floranthe in *The Mountaineer.*

On 14 December 1799 Talbot was paid £6 for a week's salary at Drury Lane, but his name did not appear in that season's bills until he acted Charles Surface in *The School for Scandal* on 12 February 1800. (The performance, originally scheduled for 2 January, had been postponed several times because of "the indisposition of a principal performer," probably Charles or John Kemble.) In his *Dramatic Censor* Thomas Dutton reported Talbot's figure "not unpleasing," nor his voice "absolutely inharmonious," though he did not understand how to manage the latter. That season Talbot also acted Young Mirable, Roderigo in *Othello,* Rezenvelt in the premiere of Baillie's *De Montfort* on 29 April, and Algernon in the premiere of Hoare's *Indiscretion* on 10 May 1800. The role of Rezenvelt had originally been intended for Charles Kemble, who became ill. Talbot acquitted himself well, according to Dutton, "and would succeed still better, if he did not, by an affectation of ease, degenerate into slovenliness. His pronunciation is distinct, but rather too flippant." On 3 March 1800 he was paid £11 for 11 days.

Almost all of the remainder of Talbot's career was spent in Ireland, with excursions to Scotland, Wales, and the English provinces. The *Morning Post* of 24 October 1800 announced that he had "lately" at Derry married the pro-

vincial actress Emily Coote Binden, who had made her stage debut at Crow Street on 2 March 1799 as Miss Hoyden in *A Trip to Scarborough.* Talbot acted six nights at Belfast in December 1800, when he lived at Captain Scott's, No 26, Waring Street.

In June and July 1801 at Edinburgh he acted Bassanio in *The Merchant of Venice,* Charles Surface in *The School for Scandal,* Horatio in *Hamlet,* Orlando in *As You Like It,* Ranger in *The Suspicious Husband,* Sydenham in *The Wheel of Fortune,* Young Philpot in *The Citizen,* and Young Wilding in *The Lyar.* In August he was at Swansea and that year also played at Liverpool, Bath, and Bristol. He became a favorite in the Dublin company, playing such serious roles as Aufidius in *Coriolanus,* Lysimachus in *The Rival Queens,* Lothario in *The Fair Penitent,* and Romeo. His forte was comedy, and he received warm praise for Ranger in *The Suspicious Husband,* Rolando in *The Honeymoon,* Monsieur Morbleu in *Monsieur Tonson,* and Lord Ogleby in *The Clandestine Marriage.* J. W. Croker in his *Familiar Epistles* on the Irish stage wrote of Talbot's "trifling air" and "baby face," attributes that prevented him from competing with leading tragedians like J. P. Kemble, despite his taste and superior feeling; but in comedy Talbot reigned "supreme" in Dublin, and there was no actor in London, claimed Croker, who

Can paint the rakish Charles so well,
Give so much life to Mirabel,
Or show for light and airy sport
So exquisite a Doricourt.

Talbot returned to London to make his first appearance at the Haymarket on 5 July 1812, as Ranger in *The Suspicious Husband;* that summer he was also seen as Duke Aranga in *The Honeymoon* and in other roles.

In the summer of 1808 Talbot bought Bellamy's interests in the theatres at Belfast, Newry, and Derry. His plans for opening in Belfast before Christmas were announced in the Dublin *Evening Post* in early October; later in the month it was reported in the Belfast *Newsletter* that Talbot had gone to Scotland and his acting manager Gordon had gone to England to recruit actors. The Belfast theatre opened a month later than expected, on 23 January 1809, with Talbot acting Young Mirable in *The Inconstant.* Talbot ended his first

Harvard Theatre Collection

MONTAGUE TALBOT, as Monsieur Morbleau

engraving by Maguire

season by inducing John Philip Kemble to come over for six nights.

In late 1810 Talbot thoroughly renovated the Belfast theatre and reopened it on 14 January 1811. That season he experienced difficulty in forming his company because so many performers were being enticed to America, but on 16 January 1811 he introduced Miss O'Neill as Mrs Haller in *The Stranger,* with himself in the title role.

Struggling against the constant tribulations of acquiring and holding good actors, Talbot managed and acted at Belfast and Newry—and also played irregularly at Dublin—until in the fall of 1820 he leased out his theatrical holdings to Mason, the Glasgow manager. Talbot continued to act a few nights each year at Belfast, but from 1821 to the end of his career he was a member of the Crow Street company. At Dublin he was such a favorite that audiences refused to allow anyone else to appear in

his roles, as Charles Mathews discovered to his embitterment when cries of "Talbot" drove the intruder from his engagement at Crow Street.

Talbot died at Belfast on 26 April 1831, after a lingering illness, at the age of 58, and was buried in Friars Bush cemetery. His wife, who had retired from the stage after her marriage, died at Belfast on 29 January 1832, at 53. They had five children; two sons settled in South America. Talbot had been a freemason; two of his benefits at Newry were attended by local brothers in regalia.

Though he lacked sufficient merit to retain a London engagement, Talbot was generally well regarded as an actor in Ireland. The author of *A Few Reflections occasioned by the Perusal of a Work entitled "Familiar Epistles to Frederick J———, Esq"* thought Talbot played with ease and judgment; his manner was gentlemanly, his action cheerful and sprightly, and his elocution distinct. These attributes were sometimes diminished by his ranting and waving his arms about. The reviewer in *Walker's Hibernian Magazine* for March 1805 described Talbot at about the age of 30:

[H]is figure is tall, slender, and flexible; his face (which, with a dark complexion, large dark eyes, and well-formed eyebrows, give him much the appearance of a foreigner) is small, but very expressive; his voice possesses naturally very agreeable tones, but is sometimes, by the warmth of his feelings, extended to a pitch beyond its strength, and is then discordant. In Tragedy characters, a prudent reservation of its force, for the impassioned scenes, would produce a greater variety. . . .

Talbot was especially praised by the same critic for his Aufidius, Pierre, the Count of Narbonne, Lothario, Hamlet, and Edgar (in *King Lear*), the last being "a beautiful picture of feigned madness and real feeling." He was spirited and elegant as Ranger and "lively, pointed, and diverting" as Mirable, and yet commendable in older characters like Lusignan and Cardinal Wolsey.

Talbot translated Boissy's *Le Babillard* and produced it at Belfast on 11 March 1817 as *Myself in the Plural Singular,* in which as Captain Allelack, surrounded by mute characters, he had all the lines. That piece was acted at Crow Street in December 1817. For his Dublin benefit on 18 May 1822 he wrote and produced a sequel to *Monsieur Tonson* called *Morbleu Restored.*

Portraits of Montague Talbot include:

1. As Colonel Cohenberg in *The Siege of Belgrade*. By an unknown engraver. In the National Library of Ireland.

2. As Young Mirable in *The Inconstant*. By an unknown engraver. Published as a plate to the *Hibernian Magazine,* March 1805. A copy was published as a plate to the *Dublin Theatrical Observer,* 1821.

3. As Monsieur Morbleu in *Monsieur Tonson*. Watercolor drawing by Samuel Lover, in the possession of W. J. Lawrence when Talbot's notice was published in *The Dictionary of National Biography.* Present location unknown.

4. As Monsieur Morbleu. Engraving by C. Maguire. Published by Del Vecchio.

5. As Monsieur Morbleu. By an unknown engraver. Published in Dublin by McCleary.

6. As Monsieur Morbleu. By an unknown engraver. Published as a plate to the *Dublin Theatrical Observer,* 1821.

"Tall Man from Finland, The" ₁*fl.1741*₁, *giant.*

At Covent Garden Theatre on 26 November 1741 and subsequent dates through the end of the year, a "Tall Man from Finland" played the part of the Giant in *Perseus and Andromeda*.

"Tall Man from Germany, The." *See* CAJANUS, DANIEL.

"Tall Woman from Leicestershire, The." *See* WEBB, MRS ₁*fl.1734*₁.

"Tambourina, Signora" ₁*fl.1760*₁, *performer.*

On 14 February 1760 Christopher Smart held one of his one-night stands at the Haymarket Theatre, presenting "Mrs Midnight's Concert and Oratory." Among the performers operating under one of the pseudonyms devised by Smart was a "Signora Tambourina."

Tame, Mrs. *See* TURNER, MRS ₁*fl.1728–1743*₁.

Tamplin, Henry ₁*fl.1794–1838*₁, *trumpeter.*

Doane's *Musical Directory* of 1794 listed a trumpeter named Tamplin who played in the Guards Second Regiment and at Astley's Am-

phitheatre. His address was in King Street, Westminster. He was surely Henry Tamplin, a subscriber to the New Musical fund in 1794 and subsequent years. By 1801 Tamplin was playing in the band at Drury Lane Theatre for £1 15*s.* weekly. He continued there until at least 1816–17. The accounts named him several times, once as "Tamplin, Bugle Horn" and once, on 4 December 1802, as "Mr. Tamplin for 7 Nights Tambourine." At some point he became a member of the Royal Society of Musicians, for on 1 January 1837 he was given a donation of £1 10*s;* his letter of thanks was dated 4 February 1838. A Mrs Tamplin, presumably his wife, had sent thanks to the Society for a benefaction in January 1822.

Tanner, Mr ₁*fl.1792*₁, *actor, singer.*

At a single performance of *The Merchant of Venice* at the Haymarket Theatre on 20 February 1792 a Mr Tanner played Lorenzo "(with *songs)*" and sang a song at the end of the play.

Tanner, Edmund *d. 1671, violinist.*

Edmund Tanner was appointed to the King's Musick as a violinist without fee on 20 February 1663. He seems not to have been given a salaried position until July 1665, following the death of Walter Youckney. Tanner was to receive wages of 1*s.* 8*d.* daily plus livery. His yearly salary as of 1668 was £45 10*s.* 10*d.* His service seems to have been routine except for a trip with the King to Dover in May and June 1670. The Lord Chamberlain's accounts show that by 6 November 1671 Tanner had died; John Twist replaced him, and such appointments usually came within a few days of the death of a court musician. That leads us to believe that the following will concerned our subject.

On 12 September 1671 an Edmund Tanner of St Margaret, Westminster (a parish in which many court musicians lived), drew up his will, noting that he was "very weake and infirme in body." He left his son Michael £10 to purchase glass and tools necessary for his trade—but Tanner did not say what the trade was. To his son Culpepper he left 5*s.*, having already given him "what I could spare." His daughter Elizabeth was to receive £50 when she reached 21. The rest of the estate was to go to Tanner's wife Jane.

Tanner's son Culpepper became a servant to

the Earl of Exeter. Culpepper wrote his will on 9 January 1695; it was proved by his daughter Susanna Butcher on 14 February 1701. When the will was written his brother Michael was still alive. Culpepper left bequests to his wife Susan, his sons Edward and Culpepper, and his daughters Sarah Belling and Susanna Butcher.

Tanner, Robert *d. 1696, singer.*

On 23 April 1685 Robert Tanner marched in the coronation procession of James II as a member of the Choir of Westminster. That is all we know of his professional life as a singer. He was buried on 14 November 1696 in the west cloister of Westminster Abbey. His wife Ann, née Shorter, was buried there on 3 August 1727. The Tanners had at least two sons: Robert died in infancy and was buried in the cloisters on 26 October 1684; Shorter was baptized on 9 July 1690 at the Abbey. The Tanner's daughter Sarah was baptized there on 23 June 1687.

Tanner, Thomas [*fl. 1661–1664*], actor.

No roles are known for Thomas Tanner. On 17 December 1661 a canceled warrant in the Lord Chamberlain's accounts named Tanner. A list of the household of Charles II in the fall of 1663, in the State Papers, includes Tanner among the actors, but "dead" was noted after his name at some later date. *The London Stage* includes Tanner in the roster of the King's Company for 1663–64. Just when he died is not clear, but his name was in the Lord Chamberlain's accounts as late as 12 November 1664.

Tannett, B. [*fl. 1772–1794*], actor, manager.

Master Tannett was in *Cupid's Revenge* at the Haymarket Theatre on 27 August 1772, probably playing Cupid (as he certainly did in June 1773). At Marylebone Gardens on 3 September 1773 he was an Arval Brother in *Ambarvalia*. By 9 October 1777, when he was in *The Coquette* at the Haymarket, he was called Mr Tannett, so we suppose he had come of age. Later sources identified him as B. Tannett.

From June through 19 October 1778 Tannett performed at the Theatre Royal in Liverpool for £1 1s. weekly, and from 1782 to 1784 he acted at the Theatre Royal in Shakespeare

Square, Edinburgh. A number of his Edinburgh roles have been recovered by Norma Armstrong, among them Alonzo in *Rule a Wife and Have a Wife*, Amiens in *As You Like It*, Balthazar in *Much Ado about Nothing*, Belvinne in *Rosina*, Captain Greville in *The Flitch of Bacon*, Catesby in *Richard III*, Cymon, Dawson in *The Gamester*, Don Carlos in *The Duenna*, Eustace and Young Meadows in *Love in a Village*, Fag in *The Rivals*, Freeman in *The Clandestine Marriage*, the Gentleman Usher in *King Lear*, Hippolito in *The Tempest*, Leander in *The Padlock*, Lionel in *Lionel and Clarissa*, Lorenzo in *The Merchant of Venice*, Marcellus in *Hamlet*, Paris in *Romeo and Juliet*, Peter Simple in *The Merry Wives of Windsor*, Planter in *Oroonoko*, Ratcliffe in *Jane Shore*, Roger in *She Stoops to Conquer*, Sir Charles in *The Beaux' Stratagem*, Sir John Loverule in *The Devil to Pay*, Stukely in *The West Indian*, Trip in *The School for Scandal*, Westmoreland in *1 Henry IV*, and William in *The Deaf Lover*.

By December 1792, according to the *Thespian Magazine*, Tannett was playing at the theatre in Gainsborough, and Tate Wilkinson reported that Tannett (Wilkinson called him Taunton) was the manager of the theatre at Malton. Tannett's wife performed with him at Edinburgh and Gainsborough; she was a columbine and took small parts in comedies.

Tantini, Anna [*fl. 1779–1783*], dancer.

Signora Anna Tantini made her first appearance in England dancing in a *Pastoral Ballet* at the King's Theatre on 27 November 1779. She was listed in the company as one of the first dancers, "Demi-Caractere." She remained at the King's for two seasons, appearing in such dances as a *Masquerade Dance*, *La Bergère Coquete*, a *Chaconne of Jomelli's*, *Le Fête Pastorale*, *Il Filosofo*, a *Grand Chaconne*, *The Fortunate Escape*, *The Country Gallant*, *The Pert Country Maid*, *The Rural Sports*, *The Country Diversions*, *Les Caprices de Galatée*, and *Medée et Jason*. On 12 March 1781 she and another King's Theatre dancer, Traffieri, appeared at Drury Lane Theatre in *The Dutch Quaker*. Anna Tantini's full name was given in the libretto of *Mendonte*, published in Naples in 1783.

Tanton Samuel [*fl. 1671*], actor.

On 25 February 1671 the Lord Chamberlain ordered Samuel Tanton and Robert Parker apprehended for illegally staging plays, presumably in London.

Tape, Mr ₁*fl. 1720*₁, *dancer.*

Mr Tape, a scholar of the elder Topham, made his stage debut at Lincoln's Inn Fields Theatre on 29 April 1720 dancing with Rice. The bills did not mention him again so far as we know.

Taplin, Mr ₁*fl. 1795*₁, *equestrian.*

Mr Taplin was one of the equestrians in Handy's New Circus at the Lyceum in the Strand in 1795.

Tapp, Mr ₁*fl. 1794*₁, *singer?*

Doane's *Musical Directory* of 1794 listed one Tapp, from Woolwich, Kent, as a bass (singer?) who performed in the Handel concerts at Westminster Abbey.

"Tar, The Jolly." *See* "JOLLY TAR, THE."

Tarchi, Angelo *c. 1760–1814, composer, music director.*

Angelo (or Angiolo) Tarchi was born in Naples about 1760 and studied at the Pietà dei Turchini conservatory there beginning in 1771. His teachers included Fago and Sala, and by 1778 Tarchi had turned out his first opera. He was in Rome from 1781 to 1785 before going to Florence and then, in 1787, Milan. In 1787–88 and in the spring of 1789 Tarchi was music director and composer at the King's Theatre in London, his *opera seria Il Disertore* and *La generosità d'Alessandro* being well received. The *World* on 3 June 1789 reported that the audience the previous night had shouted "'Bravo Tarchi,' 'Bravo Maestro.'" His works were also performed in Paris.

Tarchi was ill in Naples in 1793 and his prodigious output of operas (four to six annually in the 1780s) dropped. After 1797 he worked in Paris, concluding his career as a singing teacher. Tarchi died there on 19 August 1814. The *New Grove* contains a list of his works.

Taretti, Mr ₁*fl. 1774*₁, *singer.*

Between the acts of the opera at the King's Theatre on 17 March 1774 "A favourite Song" was sung by Taretti. He seems not to have been mentioned in the bills again.

Tariot, Mr ₁*fl. 1759–1761*₁, *dancer.*

Mr and Mrs Tariot (or Tarriot, Terrier) were entered on the books at Covent Garden Theatre on 13 October 1759 (retroactive to the eighth) at 5s. each per night. Mr Tariot had evidently danced at Sadler's Wells before that. At Covent Garden during the 1759–60 season the Tariots danced in *The Fair,* beginning on 10 December 1759, and *Comus,* beginning on 18 January 1760. Miss Tariot, their daughter, also danced in *Comus* and was paid £21 for her season's work. On 2 June at the Haymarket Theatre, for the benefit of J. Philips and Master Tariot (their son, one assumes), Mr and Mrs Tariot and Master Tariot offered several new dances. The boy was described in the bill as being from the opera, that is, the King's Theatre. On 5 June Master Tariot danced in a new *Terzetta* at the Haymarket.

In September and October 1760 Master "Taryot" danced at the Theatre Royal, Norwich. Perhaps the rest of the family was there, too, but we have found no mention of them. Mr Tariot danced at the King's Theatre in London in 1760–61, appearing first on 22 November 1760. In *The Case of Anthony Minelli* (Dublin, 1761) we learn that Minelli promised Mossop to provide dancers for Dublin and "engaged for that Purpose, in *London,* Mr. and Mrs. *Tarrot,* and gave them seventeen Guineas, in order to defray their Expences to Chester, sent with them several Trunks, with Cloaths, and Dresses for Dancers, which they run away with. . . ."

Tariot, Mrs ₁*fl. 1759–1761*₁, *dancer. See* TARIOT, MR.

Tariot, Master ₁*fl. 1760*₁, *dancer. See* TARIOT, MR.

Tariot, Miss ₁*fl. 1760*₁, *dancer. See* TARIOT, MR.

Tarr, Mrs ₁*fl. 1730*₁, *singer.*

Mrs Tarr sang between the acts at the Goodman's Fields Theatre on 31 October 1730 and may have continued appearing throughout the season.

"Tartar, The Irish." *See* JOHNSON, THOMAS.

"Tarteraro, Signora" [*fl. 1753*], *performer.*

At Bartholomew Fair on 3 September 1753 "Mrs Midnight" (Christopher Smart) presented a variety program that included "a new Concerto on the Salt-Box, by Signora Tarteraro, accompanied by Mrs. Midnight's Band of Originals." *The London Stage* contains only a brief portion of the bill and transcribes the performer's name as "Tatteraro." Our transcription is from the bill in the Huntington Library.

Tasca, Luigi [*fl. 1784–1786*], *singer.*

The basso Luigi Tasca made his first appearance in England singing Titta in *I rivali delusi* at the King's Theatre on 6 January 1784. He sang at the King's through the spring season of 1786, appearing in such characters as Asdrubale in *La schiava*, Cacchino in *Le gelosie villane*, Don Tiburzio in *Le gemelle*, Il Marchese Calandrano Curioso in *Il curioso indescreto*, Il Barone Cricca in *Il pittor parigino*, Don Gastone in *I viaggiatori felici*, Iarba in *Didone abbandonata*, Blasio in *La scuola de gelosi*, and Don Pasticcio in *L'Inglese in Italia*. When he shared a benefit with Signora Dorta on 28 April 1785 he gave his address as No 5, Great Pultney Street, Golden Square. His season salary in 1784–85 was £350.

Tasca also sang in the Handel Memorial Concerts in Westminster Abbey and the Pantheon in May and June 1784, at the Tottenham Court Music Room on 13 March 1786, and at a Hanover Square Concert on 12 May 1786 (when he gave his address as No 81, Haymarket).

Dr Burney said that Tasca

had a powerful voice, and seemed to be a good musician. . . . He had been here three years, during which time he was not only a useful performer at the opera, but in the oratorios and performances in Westminster Abbey. His voice, however, wanted mellowness and flexibility; for, like an oaken plant, though *strong*, it was *stiff*.

Tasca also taught singing, one of his students being Thomas Ludford Bellamy. He returned to Italy after the 1785–86 season.

Tasca. *See also* "LA SANTINA."

Tasher, James *d. 1662?, fifer.*

James Tasher (or Tasker) was sworn a "phife" extraordinary—without salary—in the King's Musick in February 1637. He had still not come into a salaried position in 1641 and perhaps did not before the civil war. On 23 June 1662 Richard Vaux was appointed to succeed the deceased Tasher. Such appointments were usually made within days of a musician's death.

Tasnett, Master [*fl. 1773*], *actor.*

Master Tasnett played Cupid in *Cupid's Revenger* at the Haymarket Theatre on 4, 14, and 21 June 1773.

Tassa. *See* TASCA.

Tasset. *See* TACET.

Tassey, Mr [*fl. 1794–1795*], *dresser.*

Mr Tassey worked at Covent Garden Theatre in 1794–95 as a men's dresser at 7s. 6d. weekly.

Tassie, Mrs [*fl. 1785*], *actress.*

Mrs Tassie made her first and apparently only appearance on the London stage on 24 January 1785, when she acted Jenny in *The Gentle Shepherd* at the Haymarket Theatre.

Tassoni, Signor [*fl. 1762–1774*], *dancer.*

Signor Tassoni danced with Signora Radicati at the King's Theatre on 20 March 1762. In 1762–63 he was in the Covent Garden troupe, dancing first in *Comus* on 8 October 1762 and then appearing in *The Jealous Woodcutter, Harlequin Sorcerer, The Rape of Proserpine,* and *Catalonian Marriage.* He moved to Drury Lane Theatre in 1763–64, remaining there through the 1769–70 season. His first appearance was as a Cherokee in *The Witches* on 28 October 1763. Other works in which Tassoni danced over the years included *The Rites of Hecate, Cymbeline, Daphne and Amintor, The Hermit, The Jealous Peasant, Catalonian Peasants, The National Prejudice,* and *The Medley.*

During his engagement at Covent Garden Tassoni was paid £1 10s. weekly (as of February 1765), and by January 1767 he had risen to £2. He augmented his income by performing occasionally at Sadler's Wells in 1766 and 1767, and he appeared at the Haymarket Theatre in the summer of 1769, dancing between the acts. After 1770 Signor Tassoni seems to have confined himself to teaching. On 6 and 13 May 1772 one of his pupils, seven years of age, danced a hornpipe at Drury Lane; the following January another (or possibly the same) student danced there. His pupils were seen at Drury Lane in April and May 1773 as well, and on 29 January 1774 (the last reference to him) one of his students danced at the King's Theatre.

Taswell, James   *d. 1759, actor, manager.*

According to Samuel Foote, James Taswell was educated at Oxford and was originally designed for a clerical life, but he neglected everything for the stage. Davies, in his biography of David Garrick, on the other hand, said Taswell was bred at Cambridge and was brought upon the stage by Charles Macklin. Manuscript notes in William Taswell's copy of Davies' *Life of David Garrick* explain the confusion:

He was educated at Westminster School, of which he was Captain, & was upon the Point of succeeding to a Fellowship at Trinity College in Cambridge, or a studentship at Ch: Church Coll: Oxford: But an unlucky riot in which with more Fire & spirit (the attendants commonly of fine Parts) than Prudence, He acted a principal Part & an unwillingness to submit to a Discipline from a Birchen scepter'd Tyrant, which, He thought, disgrac'd a young man of seventeen, oblig'd him (to adopt the Court Language) to resign, that is He was turn'd out of the school. He was sent from thence to university Coll: Oxford, where his Parts and his eccentricities soon distinguish'd him.

The William Taswell who owned the copy of Garrick's biography may have made the manuscript notes and was probably related to James Taswell, but in what way we do not know. The copy is now owned by Anthony Vaughan, who kindly informed us of the notes.

Perhaps James Taswell was the Taswell who was in the troupe of players performing in the theatre on St Augustine's Back in Bristol in 1728. He was named in the cast of *The Beggar's Opera* and received a shared benefit with Warren on 2 September 1728, when *The Beaux' Stratagem* was presented. That Taswell played

Darony in *Hurlothrumbo* at the Haymarket Theatre in London on 29 March and 13 May 1729. James Taswell seems to have made his first Drury Lane appearance on 16 January 1739, when he played Obadiah Prim in *A Bold Stroke for a Wife.* Then he was seen as Goodwill in *The Virgin Unmask'd*, Northumberland in *1 Henry IV*, Petulant in *The Plain Dealer*, a Bravo in *The Inconstant*, Diascordium in *The Mother-in-Law*, the Orange Woman in *The Man of Mode*, Lopez in *The Pilgrim*, and the Player King in *Hamlet.*

Except for an occasional excursion elsewhere, Taswell remained at Drury Lane to November 1758, two months before his death, playing mostly secondary and tertiary characters. Among them were Dr Tackem in *Robin Goodfellow*, the Lord Mayor in *Richard III* (Davies said George II greatly admired Taswell in that part), Francisco in *The Chances*, the Statue in *Don Juan*, Isidore in *Timon of Athens*, Cimberton in *The Conscious Lovers*, Polonius in *Hamlet*, Princess Huncamunca in *The Tragedy of Tragedies*, Moneytrap in *The Confederacy*, Foigard in *The Stratagem*, Ireton in *An Historical Play*, Scrapeall and Hackum in *The Squire of Alsatia*, Sir Francis in *The Busy Body*, the Surgeon, Sir Tunbelly, and Coupler in *The Relapse*, Ligarius in *Julius Caesar*, Tribulation in *The Alchemist*, Caius and Shallow in *The Merry Wives of Windsor*, Tipkin in *The Tender Husband*, the Constable in *The Twin Rivals*, a Citizen in *Oedipus*, a Murderer in *Macbeth*, Sycorax in *The Tempest*, the Bailiff in *The Committee*, Charino in *Love Makes a Man*, the Duke in *Venice Preserv'd*, Plausible in *The Plain Dealer*, Corin in *As You Like It*, Tubal in *The Merchant of Venice*, Gripus in *Amphitryon*, the Duke in *Othello*, a Justice in *The Harlot's Progress*, a Messenger in *The Comedy of Errors*, Dr Bolus and Sir Solomon in *The Double Gallant*, the Surveyor and Gardiner in *Henry VIII*, Bullock and the Collier in *The Recruiting Officer*, Ernesto in *The Orphan*, Davy and Sir Jasper in *The Mock Doctor*, Old Mutable in *The Wedding Day*, Foresight in *Love for Love*, Guttle in *The Lying Valet*, Decius in *Cato*, Driver in *Oroonoko*, Father Benedict in *The School Boy*, Smuggler in *The Constant Couple*, and Heli in *The Mourning Bride.*

He also appeared as Learchus in *Aesop*, the Old Man in *King Lear*, Aristander in *The Rival Queens*, Old Gerald in *The Anatomist*, Sir

Thomas and Dotanti in *The Gamester,* the Doctor in *Macbeth,* Cambridge in *2 Henry IV,* Attilus Regulus in *Regulus,* Justice Clack in *The Jovial Crew,* Testimony in *Sir Courtly Nice,* Sir William in *Love's Last Shift,* Father Martin in *The Debauchees,* Corydon in *Damon and Phillida,* Morecraft in *The Scornful Lady,* LeCaster in *The Wild Goose Chase,* Old Bellair in *The Man of Mode,* Nym in *Henry V,* Doodle in *The London Cuckolds,* Dogberry in *Much Ado about Nothing,* Gregory in *Romeo and Juliet,* Elbow in *Measure for Measure,* the Miser in *Lethe,* Sir Simon in *Miss in Her Teens,* Justice Clement in *Every Man in His Humour,* Alderman Pentweazel in *Taste,* Guzzle in *Don Quixote in England,* a Servant in *Coriolanus,* Codicil in *The Upholsterer,* and Bluff in *The Old Bachelor.*

Away from Drury Lane Taswell acted Antipater in *Darius* at Bartholomew Fair on 22 August and Goodwill in *The Virgin Unmask'd* at Goodman's Fields on 8 September 1741, before he was needed at Drury Lane; at Southwark on 30 March 1743 he appeared as Bullock in *The Recruiting Officer,* and on 3 April he was Sir Francis in *The Busy Body* at Lincoln's Inn Fields; at Goodman's Fields on 1 February 1745 he acted Ernesto in *The Orphan;* at Bartholomew Fair in August 1748 he appeared as Bransby Bustle in *The Consequences of Industry and Idleness;* and he was Sir Tristram in *The Wife's Relief* at the Haymarket on 26 July 1750.

The critics blew hot and cold about James Taswell. Thomas Davies called him a man of humor and a scholar both in acting and private conversation.

He was a confined actor but what he did was generally distinguished by marks of genius; his Polonius was good, and his Cimberton still better—in Dogberry his dryness of humour, and laughable cast of features will never be excelled—he buffooned Gardiner in Henry 8th sadly.

In his *Dramatic Biography* Oxberry quoted a communication from Edgar Darlington: "Taswell's Gardiner degenerated into absolute trick and buffoonery; and, when he followed Cranmer off, he held his crutch over his head, that the ignorant might laugh. For this he sometimes paid dearly, by a well-merited hiss from the judicious portion of the audience."

Not much else is known about Taswell. He was a co-patentee of the Birmingham Theatre

from 1755, and one might guess that he spent some of his summers there. He published *Deviliad,* a "heroic" poem, in 1744. Taswell's wife was a dresser and property woman at Covent Garden Theatre.

The Drury Lane prompter Richard Cross wrote in his diary on 8 January 1759: "Mr Taswell dy'd—an excellent Actor, the best in that way since [Benjamin] Johnson." Taswell had suffered a lingering illness. He had drawn up his will on 7 February 1754 and may even then have been unwell. He named his wife Elizabeth his sole heir. His estate consisted of an annuity granted on a house and land known as Broadstone in Sussex, then in the possession of the Duke of Dorset; an interest in the Birmingham theatre, "held upon Lease by Mr. Richard Yates of London;" and personal belongings and household goods. The will was proved on 10 January 1759.

Taswell, Mrs James, Elizabeth ₁*fl.1754–1759*₁, *house servant.*
Elizabeth Taswell, the wife of the Drury Lane actor James Taswell, was apparently a dresser and property woman at Covent Garden Theatre, but when she worked there is not known. Taswell named Elizabeth his sole heir in his will, dated 7 February 1754 and proved on 10 January 1759.

Tatam, Mr ₁*fl.1795*₁, *actor.*
Mr Tatam played the Keeper of the Wild Beasts in *Harlequin Invincible* at Astley's Amphitheatre on 22 August 1795.

Taterell. *See* TATTNEL.

Tatley, Miss. *See* CATLEY, ANN, and TETLEY, ELIZABETH.

Tatnall. *See* TATTNAL.

"Tatteraro, Signora." *See* "TARTERARO, SIGNORA."

Tattnal, Mr ₁*fl.1704*₁, *actor.*
Mr Tattnal (or Tattnel) acted Macahone in *The Stage Coach* at Lincoln's Inn Fields Theatre on 2 February 1704.

Tattnall, John [fl. 1764–1766], *musician.*

The records of the Worshipfull Company of Musicians show that John Tattnall, of Exeter 'Change, became a freeman on 17 November 1764. On the twenty-ninth he took on what may have been his first apprentice, Mark Samuel Tattnall, surely a relative. On 7 May 1766 John Tattnall, then of St Mary le Strand, took John Dickson as an apprentice. John Tattnall's son Edward was bound apprentice to Mark Tattnall on 6 July 1778.

Tattnall, Mark Samuel [fl. 1764–1778], *musician.*

According to the records of the Worshipfull Company of Musicians, Mark Samuel Tattnall was bound apprentice to John Tattnall on 29 November 1764. Mark became a freeman on 23 October 1772, at which time his address was Windsor Court, Exeter Street, near the Strand. Edward Tattnall, son of John, was apprenticed to Mark Tattnall on 6 July 1778.

Tattnall, Samuel *d. 1825, violinist, clarinetist, music copyist.*

On 5 June 1783 Samuel Tattnall (or Tatnell, Tatterell) was paid £10 10s. for attending "Practices" at Drury Lane during the 1782–83 season. Those practices were doubtless dance or music rehearsals, for Tattnall was, among other things, a violinist. He was surely related to the musical Tattnalls of the previous decade; indeed, there is a possibility that he was Mark Samuel Tattnall, though we have treated them as different persons.

The Drury Lane accounts make frequent references to Samuel Tattnall over the years, often in connection with his work as a music copyist. But he was paid for tuning a harp, for attending music rehearsals, and for playing in the band. For his work in the band he earned £2 weekly in the early years of the nineteenth century. He worked at Drury Lane at least through 1807.

Samuel Tattnall was also a member of the Royal Society of Musicians (membership date 2 July 1775), for whom he played violin at the St Paul's concerts in May 1785, 1789, 1790, and 1794. He also had apprentices, one of whom, Thomas Ebworth, was bound to him on 20 August 1789, at which time Tattnall's

address was given as New Tunbridge Wells—perhaps a summer address. Doane's *Musical Directory* of 1794 placed Tattnall at No 5, Windmill Street, Rathbone Place, London, and called him a violinist and clarinetist. Tattnall, in addition to playing at Drury Lane, participated in the Handel concerts at Westminster Abbey.

By 1796 Tattnall had been made a Governor of the Royal Society of Musicians, a post he held at least through the following year. On 7 November 1813 he petitioned the Society for financial aid, and he was granted, the Minute Books said, the "usual" allowance. On 2 October 1814 he informed the Society that the allowance would no longer be needed, since he had obtained a position at Worthing, but the following February found him requesting aid again. In March 1825 the Society provided money for medical aid to Tattnall; on the sixth his niece was granted £12 for his funeral expenses.

Tattnel. *See* TATTNAL.

"Tattoo, Mr" [fl. 1759–1761], *musician.*

In *The Fair,* which ran at Covent Garden Theatre from 10 December 1759 through 26 May 1760, the part of Drummer was played by a musician called "Mr Tattoo"—presumably a pseudonym. He played in *The Fair* again when it was revived on 13 October 1761.

Taunton. *See* TANNETT.

"Tawny Tuscan, The." *See* DE L'ÉPINE.

Tayler. *See* TAYLOR.

Taylor, Mr [fl. 1720–1729], *boxkeeper.*

Mr Taylor shared a benefit with his fellow boxkeeper Lovelace at Lincoln's Inn Fields Theatre on 10 May 1720. When the pair shared again on 22 May 1721, the receipts came to a healthy £135 18s. And so it went for Taylor through 22 May 1729, when he shared over £126 with Mr Lawrence. Taylor may have been a relative of the house servant Taylor who was at Drury Lane from 1728 to 1743.

Taylor, Mr [*fl. 1728–1743*], *gallery keeper, boxkeeper.*

At Drury Lane Theatre on 22 May 1728 the first gallery keeper Taylor shared a benefit with Jones. (A week later at the rival Lincoln's Inn Fields house another Taylor, a boxkeeper, shared a benefit; the two Taylors were possibly related.) When Taylor and Jones shared a benefit on 9 May 1729, Taylor was called a box-keeper, and he retained the post until 1743. At first he shared benefits, but by the spring of 1735 he was getting them alone. A bill in the Enthoven Collection, dated 23 May 1739, stated that tickets for Taylor's benefit could be had at "Mr. Taylor's Grocer, in Greek-street, Soho." Like many theatre personnel, Taylor had another source of income. The bill for his 18 May 1743 benefit stated that "As Mr. Tay-lor's long and violent illness has prevented his personal application, he humbly hopes those Gentlemen and Ladies who us'd to honour him with their Company, will continue their fa-vour, and send for tickets to his house in Greek Street, Soho." Taylor was not mentioned in benefit bills after that and must have retired or died.

Taylor, Mr [*fl. 1729–1744?*], *actor, dancer, dancing master.*

Mr Taylor played Verdict in *The Smugglers* at the Haymarket Theatre on 7 May 1729. He was at Tottenham Court on 9 August 1731, playing the Crying Brother in *Damon and Phil-lida* and at the Lee and Harper booth at South-wark Fair the following 8 September, acting Ranger in *The Devil to Pay.* He turned up next on 27 May 1732 at the Great Booth on Wind-mill Hill playing "Simon" (i.e., Cymon) in *Damon and Phillida,* a part he repeated at Yeates's booth in Upper Moorfields on 19 June. At Windmill Hill Taylor also danced three pieces: *Harlequin and Country Man, Harlequin Turn'd into a Dog,* and *Drunken Man.* He was apparently the Taylor who acted Lorenzo in *The Spanish Fryar* for his benefit at York Build-ings on 24 April 1734. Other parts were taken "by a sett of Gentlemen his Friends." Taylor's address was in Fountain Court, Cheapside. On 7 September 1734 Taylor danced a hornpipe at Southwark Fair.

In 1734–35 Taylor had an engagement at the Goodman's Fields Theatre, his first ap-pearance being on 28 October 1734 as a De-mon in *The Necromancer.* He spent the rest of the season in that part and as a Waterman in *Britannia.* In the summer of 1735, according to *The London Stage,* Taylor danced at the Hay-market Theatre, but his name seems not to have appeared in any bills. On 23 August, however, he was at Bartholomew Fair, dancing *Two Pierrots* with Rosoman and a solo horn-pipe. On 2 and 5 September Taylor was at the Lincoln's Inn Fields playhouse dancing his hornpipe.

Taylor joined the Drury Lane company for the 1735–36 season, playing for his first ap-pearance a Chinese Guard in *Harlequin Grand Volgi.* He then appeared as a Lover and Squire Flash in *Harlequin Restor'd,* Pearmain in *The Recruiting Officer,* Scaramouch in *The Harlot's Progress,* and Scaramouch in *Columbine Courte-zan.* In 1736–37 he was advertised only as Flash in *Harlequin Restor'd.* On 8 November 1737 Taylor received a solo benefit at Covent Garden Theatre and was cited as a dancing master. The date of the benefit would suggest that he was not a regular member of the troupe, and the bills for the 1737–38 season do not mention him again. He danced a horn-pipe at Covent Garden on 8 December 1738, however, but "by desire," so perhaps he was again not a regular company member. Simi-larly, he danced his hornpipe there on 8 De-cember 1739. Goodman's Fields gave him a benefit on 4 May 1741, styling him as dancing master.

On 22 August 1741 Taylor played Solyman in *Thamas Kouli Kan* at *Bartholomew Fair.* He danced his hornpipe at Covent Garden on 9 and 11 December 1741, and on 3 January 1743 at Lincoln's Inn Fields he danced a *Sailor's Dance.* On the seventh he offered *The English Sailor.* Perhaps he was the Taylor whose benefit tickets were available at Covent Garden on 21 April 1744.

Taylor, Mr [*fl. 1748*], *scene painter.*

A promptbook for Ravenscroft's *The London Cuckolds* at the Folger Shakespeare Library, probably used at Drury Lane Theatre on 29 October 1748, contains a note reading "Tay-lors C 2 G"—a chamber setting in the second grooves. Taylor is otherwise unknown.

Taylor, Mr [*fl. 1764-c. 1770?*], *actor.*

Mr Taylor was a member of Samuel Foote's

summer company at the Haymarket Theatre in 1764. On 26 June he was in the cast of *The Orators,* after which he was seen as the First King of Brentford in *The Rehearsal* on 20 August and a Servant in *Every Man in His Humour* on 1 September. Perhaps he was the Taylor who managed a theatre in the Borough about 1770.

Taylor, Mr ₁*fl. 1783–1785*₁, *box and lobby keeper.*
The Lord Chamberlain's accounts name Mr Taylor as a box and lobby keeper at the King's Theatre from 1783 to 1785.

Taylor, Mr ₁*fl. 1784*₁, *singer.*
Mr Taylor, a bass, sang in the Handel Memorial Concerts at Westminster Abbey and the Pantheon in May and June 1784.

Taylor, Mr ₁*fl. 1784*₁, *singer.*
Mr Taylor, a countertenor, sang in the Handel Memorial Concerts at Westminster Abbey and the Pantheon in May and June 1784.

Taylor, Mr ₁*fl. 1784*₁, *singer.*
Mr Taylor, a tenor, sang in the Handel Memorial Concerts at Westminster Abbey and the Pantheon in May and June 1784.

Taylor, Mr ₁*fl. 1791*₁, *dancer.*
William C. Smith in *The Italian Opera* says that a Mr Taylor danced with the opera company at the Pantheon in the spring of 1791, though *The London Stage* does not reveal his name in any bills.

Taylor, Mrs ₁*fl. 1723–1741*₁, *actress.*
Mrs Taylor played Belinda in *The Recruiting Officer* at the Haymarket Theatre on 15 April 1723. On 22 April she was Beatrice in *The Anatomist.* She was evidently playing minor parts at the Lincoln's Inn Fields Theatre in 1723–24, for on 28 May 1724 she and two others shared a benefit that brought in over £100. She played Lucy in *The Old Bachelor.* At the Haymarket on 15 October 1728, Mrs Taylor was Carolina in *The Metamorphosis.* At the Lee-Harper booth at Bartholomew Fair on 24 August 1731, she played Jilt in *Guy, Earl of Warwick* and at Southwark Fair on 8 September Mrs Fitzwarren in *Whittington.* She returned to

Bartholomew Fair on 22 August 1741 to appear as the First Widow in *The Devil of a Duke.*

Taylor, Mrs. ₁*fl. 1735–1736*₁, *dresser.*
The Covent Garden Theatre accounts by R. J. Smith, studied by Judith Milhous, list a Mrs Taylor working as a dresser in 1735–36.

Taylor, Mrs ₁*fl. 1789*₁, *actress.*
A Mrs Taylor played Patty in *Inkle and Yarico* and Venus in *Chrononhotonthologos* at the White Horse Inn, Fulham, on 9 November 1789. She was probably not Mary Taylor, who was acting at the Theatre Royal in Edinburgh in 1789–90; but Mary acted on the fourth and not again until December, and so might have come to London.

Taylor, Mrs ₁*fl. 1791–1792*₁, *actress.*
At the Haymarket Theatre on 12 December 1791 a Mrs Taylor acted Anna in *Douglas* (a role taken in 1770 by a Miss Taylor—a relative?). On 26 December Mrs Taylor was seen as Ethelinda in *Henry II,* and on 6 February 1792 she played Tagg in *Miss in Her Teens.* The last two roles were in the repertoire of Mary Taylor, but she was performing with Tate Wilkinson's company on the York Circuit in 1791–92.

Taylor, Master ₁*fl. 1793–1796*₁, *equestrian, actor.*
On 21 August 1793 Master Taylor was one of the young equestrians at Astley's Amphitheatre. On 22 August 1795 he played a Cupid in *Harlequin Invincible* and on 16 Mary 1796 Fame in *The Magician of the Rocks.* He was probably the son of Mr and Mrs John Taylor, also equestrians.

Taylor, Miss ₁*fl. 1744*₁, *actress.*
At the Haymarket Theatre in the summer of 1744 Miss Taylor played Dorinda in *The Stratagem* on 16 May and the Player Queen in *Hamlet* from 29 June to 7 July.

Taylor, Miss ₁*fl. 1765–1773*₁, *dancer, actress.*
On 22 May 1765 Miss Taylor danced a hornpipe at Drury Lane Theatre. She was to have danced a double hornpipe with Master Cape there on 13 May 1768, but the performance

was canceled, and they offered their turn on 23 May instead. Advertised as from Drury Lane, Miss Taylor performed at the Theatre Royal in Norwich in 1768 and 1769. *The London Stage* lists a Miss Taylor acting at the Haymarket in the 1769–70 season; she played Anna in *Douglas* on 19 March 1770. *The Index to the London Stage* calls her Elizabeth Taylor but provides no evidence for the Christian name. The *Index* also conflates her with the singer Mrs. Taylor.

Miss Taylor was discharged from the Norwich troupe on 24 August 1772, according to the Committee Books of the theatre there. In 1773 she played in *The Chaplet* with Bailley's company at Stourbridge Fair, Cambridge.

Taylor, Miss [fl. 1776–1778], actress.

In the summer and fall of 1776 Miss Taylor acted at China Hall, Rotherhithe, London. A bill at the Guildhall, hand-dated 3 July, has her in the casts of *The Rivals* and *The Reprisal;* on 23 September she was Miss Leeson in *The School for Wives* and Daphne in *Midas.* Between then and 18 October she was seen as Kate in *The King and the Miller of Mansfield,* Betty in *A Bold Stroke for a Wife,* Lucy Weldon in *Oroonoko,* Miss Flack in *A Trip to Scotland,* Lady Ann in *Richard III,* Parisatis in *Alexander the Great,* Nancy in *Marriage à la Mode (Three Weeks after Marriage),* Lucy in *The Minor,* Mustacha in *The Life and Death of Tom Thumb the Great,* Lucy in *The London Merchant,* Marcia in *Cato,* Lady Charlotte in *High Life below Stairs,* and Lucy in *The Recruiting Officer.* Her solo benefit was on 23 September; she made tickets available at Sergeant's in Paradise Street. Miss Taylor returned to China Hall on 30 July 1778 to play Portia in *The Merchant of Venice.*

Taylor, Charles [fl. 1685], singer.

In the coronation procession of James II, in 1685, Charles Taylor marched as a member of the Choir of Westminster.

Taylor, Elizabeth, later Mrs William Bayzand [fl. 1787–1796], dancer, singer.

The London Stage identifies the Miss Taylor who danced a minuet and cotillion with Master Warburton and others at Drury Lane on 4 June 1787 as Elizabeth Taylor, who married William Bayzand in 1792. On 11 June 1787 she was paid £1 16s. for a week's work. Perhaps she was the Miss Taylor who was in *The Magic Grot* at Sadler's Wells on 3 October 1791. Miss Taylor on 22 December 1791 at Covent Garden Theatre danced an Aerial Spirit in *Blue-Beard,* and on 12 April 1792 she sang in *Alexander the Great.* In our first volume we did not identify that Miss Taylor was Mrs Bayzand, but *The London Stage* is certainly correct.

She married Bayzand at St Martin-in-the-Fields on 14 June 1792. She continued singing in small parts to the end of the 1795–96 season. (Our entry under Mrs Bayzand omitted some of this information.)

Taylor, George Thomas 1769–c. 1804, bassoonist, horn player.

According to information collected by the Royal Society of Musicians in 1794, George Thomas Taylor was born on 30 April 1769 and baptized the following 25 May. His parents were William and Elizabeth Taylor of the parish of St George, Hanover Square. George Thomas subscribed to the New Musical Fund in 1794, and that year Doane's *Musical Directory* listed Taylor as a bassoonist and horn player who had played in the Handelian concerts at Westminster Abbey. Taylor was living in Castle Lane, Westminster.

On 6 April 1794 Taylor was proposed for membership in the Royal Society of Musicians; he was elected unanimously two months later. The Minute Books reveal that in 1794 he was engaged at Ranelagh Gardens and played in the oratorios at Covent Garden Theatre. He was married and had a daughter, Ann, then a year old. Taylor played bassoon in the annual St Paul's concerts from 1794 to 1803, and he participated in the yearly oratorios at Covent Garden Theatre to the end of the century.

George Thomas Taylor died sometime before 1 April 1804, when the Royal Society of Musicians was asked for financial aid for his three children. On 6 May the Society granted Taylor's executor an allowance of three guineas, probably monthly.

Taylor, Gideon [fl. 1673], musician.

On 17 July 1673 the Lord Chamberlain ordered the apprehension of Gideon Taylor and six others for playing music without a permit.

Taylor, Guy [*fl. 1796–1807*], *instrumentalist.*

The Drury Lane accounts cited Guy Taylor as a musician as early as 1 October 1796 and as late as 16 September 1807. He played the flageolet and pipes for £1 15s. weekly.

Taylor, [**J.?**] [*fl. 1784?–1822?*], *singer, actor?*

As early as 1794 Mr Taylor (initial possibly J.) was singing during the summers at Vauxhall Gardens. Perhaps our subject was the Master Taylor who had sung "treeble" in the Handel Memorial Concerts at Westminster Abbey and the Pantheon in May and June 1784. The *Catalogue of Printed Music in the British Museum* lists a number of songs published about 1794 and 1795 that were sung at Vauxhall by Taylor: *The British Fair with Three Times Three, The True Honest Heart, Tell the Maid I Love Her, No Waist at All,* and *The Pleasures of Hunting.*

A Mr Taylor was in the cast of *The Magician of the Rocks* at Astley's Amphitheatre on 16 May 1796. On 20 April 1798 at Covent Garden Theatre, Taylor made what was called his first appearance on any stage playing Tug in *The Waterman* and singing "Old England's Tree of Liberty." The *Monthly Mirror* in April said that "A Mr. Taylor, from Vauxhall, gave his assistance in Tug in the Waterman. He has a good, plain English voice; clear, firm, and full; but there was no striking display of taste."

Perhaps he was the tenor singer listed in 1799 as a member of the Bath Harmonic Society and the Taylor who played Pierrotton in *Puss in Boots* at the Royalty Theatre on 5 October 1801. Taylor was again at Vauxhall in 1812, earning £290 for the season, and by 1822 he (or possibly Charles Taylor, the Covent Garden singer) was director at Vauxhall, earning £200 for the season.

Another singer named Taylor—Charles (1777–c. 1848)—performed for a number of years at Bath and Bristol, came to London in 1803 to sing at the Haymarket, and performed at Covent Garden from 1804 to at least 1815. The two Taylors are often confused in the records.

Taylor, John *1754–1768, singer.*

The Westminster Abbey registers record the death of John Taylor on 10 August 1768 at the age of 14 years and nine months. He had been one of the Abbey choristers. *The Chronicle* on 11 August reported that "Last night as Master Taylor, one of the Singing Boys belonging to the Choir of Westminster, was washing, off the wooden bridge at Westminster, in the Thames, he was drowned."

Taylor, John [*fl. 1767?–1805*], *actor, prompter.*

The provincial actor John Taylor was probably the Mr Taylor who acted in Roger Kemble's troupe at Worcester in the early months of 1767 and had a benefit there on 4 May. He may have been the Taylor at Birmingham in the summers of 1775 and 1776. Perhaps John was the Taylor who acted at China Hall, Rotherhithe, in the fall of 1776 with Miss Taylor (his daughter?); on 14 October "Taylor of Deptford" played Old Wilding in *The Citizen.* John Taylor also served as a prompter. His name is on a promptbook of *Every Man in His Humour* at the Folger Shakespeare Library; the notes appear to date from the 1770s or 1780s on the York circuit. A copy of *The Belle's Stratagem* at Harvard also contains Taylor's name; the notes belong to Edinburgh and date from the late eighteenth century.

In the summer of 1777 Taylor was an extra at Liverpool at 1s. nightly. He appeared at the Haymarket Theatre in London on 17 September 1778 as Albany in *King Lear,* and the following day he acted Basset in *The Provok'd Husband.* In 1778 and 1779 he was in Edinburgh, playing Westmoreland in *1 Henry IV* at the Theatre Royal in Shakespeare Square on 13 March 1779. Advertised as from the Theatre Royal in Edinburgh, Taylor played Count Almaviva in *The Spanish Barber* on 5 June 1782 at Portsmouth. A Taylor was a member of the company at Brighton in the summer of 1787. Taylor's first name was given when his wife acted at Drury Lane in London on 28 October 1800. In July 1801 Taylor performed at Margate.

The *Thespian Dictionary* in 1805, speaking of John Taylor as still alive and performing, said that he had acted several seasons at Margate and was "a very articulate sententious speaker, but rather of the old school. In private life he is a worthy character, and much esteemed. His wife appeared in London *once.*"

Taylor, John *d. 1797, equestrian, dancer, actor, swordsman, acrobat.*

John Taylor was a nephew of Philip Astley, according to James De Castro in his *Memoirs,* or the brother-in-law of Astley, according to the *Bristol Mercury* of 26 March 1792. Our earliest notice of Taylor (presumably John) is a Birmingham bill for December 1776 for performances by Astley's company. Taylor and others presented *A Roman Battle; or Un Combat de Batons.* Taylor shared a benefit with Birt at Astley's Amphitheatre at the south end of Westminster Bridge in London on 19 September 1777. The Astley bills show Taylor and his wife performing in 1781, he taking a benefit on 19 September. Presumably the Master Taylor who appeared at Astley's in the 1790s was their son, but we cannot be certain; also at Astley's during the 1780s, when John Taylor performed, was T. Taylor. We have supposed that references to a Taylor with no initial were to John, since he appears to have been the more important performer.

John Taylor performed at Astley's Amphitheatre on 21 March 1782, offering tumbling and horsemanship. The few surviving bills suggest that he may then have left Astley's until 1785, when he appeared again as an equestrian. In the summer of 1786 he danced in *The Ethiopian Festival,* did equestrian exercises, and played a dancing attendant in *Love from the Heart.* He went with the Astley troupe to Paris, but Philip Astley wrote back to Mr Pownall in London on 4 December 1786 that John Taylor was "a little crack'd," for the company had not been in Paris a week when Taylor packed up to return to London; when prevented from leaving Paris, Taylor had holed up in his room like someone just out of Bedlam.

In 1787 at Astley's Amphitheatre Taylor played a Servant in *The Siege of Quebec,* and in 1788 he impersonated a Savage Chief in an entertainment with young Astley involving a broadsword. He rode for Astley again in 1790, was with the Handy-Franklin circus in Bristol in March 1792, and in 1793 was in *Maternal Affection* and equestrian exhibitions at the Amphitheatre in London. On 13 July 1795 in *The Tythe Sheaf* Taylor did a peasant dance, a hornpipe, and a flag dance on a single horse, and on 22 August he played the title role in *Harlequin Invincible.* The *Hibernian Journal* of 17 January 1798 reported that Taylor and

his wife, with others from the Astley company, had drowned in December 1797 when the packet *Viceroy* went down in St George's Channel.

Taylor, Mrs John *d. 1797, equestrian.*

Mrs John Taylor, the wife of the Astley performer, was one of eight performers added to the Astley troupe on 11 October 1780. She did equestrian exercises at Astley's Amphitheatre on 27 February 1781. Mrs Taylor presented "a variety of unparalleled feats" on horseback at her husband's benefit on 19 September and rode again on 10 December. Some bills called her "a young lady from Vienna." She seems not to have continued her equestrian career. Mrs Taylor drowned with her husband in December 1797 crossing St George's Channel.

Taylor, Mrs. John. *See also* DUILL, MRS JOHN LEWIS.

Taylor, Littleton *c. 1665–1701, singer.*

Nothing is know of Littleton Taylor's career beyond the note in the Westminster Abbey registers that he was a member of the Abbey choir. Littleton and Mary Taylor were married at the Abbey on 24 November 1692. Mary was the daughter of John Tynchare and his wife Elizabeth; the Tynchares were a musical family, and church records always identify the Tynchares as "alias Littleton." It seems probable, then, that Littleton Taylor and Mary Tynchare (alias Littleton) were cousins. In any case, the pair had a son William, who was baptized at the Abbey on 16 January 1696, and a son Littleton, who was baptized on 20 May 1698 and buried in the north cloister nine days later. Their daughter Anne-Barbara was baptized at the Abbey on 7 September 1693. Littleton Taylor died in 1701 at the age of 36 and was buried on 10 November in the north cloister. His wife Mary was buried on 2 November 1705.

Taylor, [R.?] [*fl. 1757?–1790*], *singer, composer?, organist?*

R. Taylor of Marylebone Gardens is credited with a number of songs and some instrumental music dating from 1764 to 1790 in the *Catalogue of Printed Music in the British Museum.* One

Marylebone bill in 1764 said he was "late of His Majesty's Chapel Royal." It seems likely that he was the singer Taylor who was active in London during much of the same period, and perhaps he was Taylor the bookseller, who had a shop in the Haymarket opposite the King's Theatre and had published songs from the opera *Antigono* in 1757. An R. Taylor, according to the *European Magazine*, played organ at Marylebone Gardens, probably in the early 1760s. The earliest notice we have found of a Taylor singing is the publication about 1760 of *Away to the Field, see the Morning looks grey*, as sung by Taylor at Marylebone Gardens.

Taylor sang in *Solomon* on 6 August 1765 at the Gardens, and on 26 September 1766 under Thomas Lowe, Taylor sang in *Acis and Galatea*. Sometime during 1766 Taylor and others sang Boyce's "A New Musical Address to the Town" there. He was there again on 7 August 1767, singing songs, glees, and catches with other singers. In 1768 his salary at the Gardens was three guineas for six nights. At the New Concert Hall in Edinburgh in July and August 1769 Taylor and his wife sang Artaxerxes and Mandane in *Artaxerxes*. *Pleasure, Goddess all divine*, published about 1770, named Taylor as the singer at Marylebone Gardens.

He was not cited as a singer after that, so far as we can determine, though songs by him continued to be published up to 1790. Among his works were *The British Soldier, The Flowing Bowl*, and *Summer*. He also adapted for harpsichord a number of songs and an overture and composed a *Symphony to the new Interlude of 'The Gates of Calais', . . . now performing . . . at Sadler's Wells, Composed and Adapted for the Harpsichord, G. Flute, or Violin* (1786). In 1790 was published *Jack the Guinea Pig*, a song from *The Guardian Frigate*, performed at Sadler's Wells.

R. Taylor may have been related to the musician Raynor Taylor.

Taylor, Mrs [R.?] [fl. 1756–1776?], singer, actress.

Mrs. (R?) Taylor was singing at Finch's Grotto Gardens in George Street, St George's Fields, Southwark, as early as August 1756. According to Wroth's *London Pleasure Gardens* Mrs Taylor was singing at the Grotto Gardens again or perhaps still in August 1765 and that year sang with Thomas Lowe at Marylebone

Gardens, as did her husband. Mrs Taylor sang Mandane in *Artaxerxes* in July and August 1769 at the New Concert Hall in Edinburgh. In 1770 *A New Rosciad* was published in Edinburgh. It included the lines:

And though in speech and gesture wrong,
T——Y——R is still admir'd in song.

She was perhaps the Mrs Taylor singing with the Austin and Heatton troupe at Whitehaven in October 1770, by which time her husband seems to have given up performing.

She was again at the Grotto Gardens on 22 June 1771, playing a part in *The Gamester*. Perhaps she was the Mrs Taylor at the Theatre Royal, Norwich, in 1772 and the Mrs Taylor at the Orchard Street Theatre in Bath in 1772–73. A Mrs Taylor sang at Bristol in 1774, and perhaps the same Mrs Taylor played Lucy in *The Gamester* and Mignionet in *The Way to Keep Him* at the King Street Theatre in Birmingham on 20 July 1774, with Younger's company. Our subject was probably the Mrs Taylor who was performing at the Theatre Royal in Liverpool in the summer of 1776. She was paid at the rate of £1 6s. 3d. for a five-day week.

Taylor, Raynor 1747–1825, singer, organist, composer.

The *European Magazine* reported that Raynor Taylor, born in 1747, spent his formative years as a chorister in the King's Chapel under Gates and Nares. He was an organist and music teacher at Chelmsford, Essex, after which he became composer and director of music at Sadler's Wells, according to Sonneck's *Bibliography*. (The *European Magazine* has it that, before going to Chelmsford, Taylor sang and played the organ at Marylebone Gardens, which may be true, though the R. Taylor at Marylebone was probably a different person of an earlier generation, possibly Raynor's relative.) Raynor Taylor composed *Fye! nay prithee John*, a catch published about 1775, some variations on a minuet by Martini (San Martini?) (1775?), and some music for the burletta *Buxom Joan* (1778).

In October 1792 Taylor, having given up England, set up in Baltimore, Maryland, as a "music professor, organist and teacher of music in general, lately arrived from London." That year he became organist of St Anne's in Annapolis, but for financial reasons he moved to Philadelphia within a few months. In Philadelphia he served as organist of St Peter's and, in 1820, founded the Musical Fund Society. Sonneck provides an extensive list of Taylor's songs, some of them sung in the theatres. In Boston on 6 April 1796 his music for the pantomime ballet *The Shipwrecked Mariners Preserved* was heard. Raynor Taylor died in Philadelphia on 17 August 1825.

Taylor, T. ₍*fl. 1786–1809?*₎, *equestrian, aerialist, acrobat, dancer, tumbler.*

On 24 July 1786 at Astley's Amphitheatre, equestrian exhibitions were presented by T. Taylor, J. (John) Taylor, and others. The two Taylors were probably related, and when a Taylor was named in the bills with no initial, we have assumed it was John, though we cannot be certain. On 4 September T. Taylor was a Dancing Shepherd in *Love from the Heart*, and on 9 October he displayed his expertise on two horses. James Winston recorded a Royalty Theatre bill of 1801 which cited Taylor as an equestrian, aerialist, acrobat, and tumbler. Our subject was probably the Taylor who danced a hornpipe in fetters on 10 and 17 July 1809 at the Royal Circus.

Taylor, Mrs Thomas?, Mary, née Valentine *1753–1834, actress, singer.*

Mary Valentine was born in 1753, perhaps in Leicester, where, according to *The Secret History of the Green Room*, her mother kept a music shop in 1792. "She obtained a tolerable reputation in the Provincial Theatres, not only as a Singer, but as an Actress, when she came to London on a visit to a friend, and was introduced to Mr. TIGHE, a Gentleman of distinction in Ireland, who interested himself so much in her behalf, as to obtain her an engagement at the Haymarket, 1789." Mary had evidently acted in the provinces as Miss Valentine but had married a Mr Taylor by the time she came to London. Her husband, said the *Thespian Dictionary* of 1805, had been bred an attorney but had become a provincial actor.

Mary Taylor's first London appearance was at the Haymarket Theatre on 25 May 1789, when, cited in the bill only as a young lady, she acted Sukey in *Half an Hour after Supper*. The *Biographical and Imperial Magazine* that month said she "played with vivacity." On 5 June she sang Madge in *Love in a Village*, and on 22 June she was Lisette in *The Swop*. From

then through 15 September she appeared as Daphne in *Midas*, Emily in *The Comet*, Sophia Bountiful in *Thimble's Flight from the Shopboard*, Gillian in *The Quaker*, Fanny in *A Mogul Tale*, and, on 15 September, Adeline in *The Battle of Hexham*, which she read in the absence of Mrs Goodall "much to the satisfaction of the public," according to *The Secret History.*

The *Thespian Dictionary* placed Mary Taylor in Edinburgh in 1789, where "she was much admired." Norma Armstrong provided us with a number of roles played by Mrs Taylor at the Theatre Royal in Shakespeare Square in Edinburgh in 1789–90: Adeline in *The Battle of Hexham*, Amelia in *The English Merchant*, Anna in *The Doctor and the Apothecary*, Ariel and Sylvia in *The Tempest*, Eliza in *The Flitch of Bacon*, Emma in *Peeping Tom of Coventry*, a Prisoner in *Such Things Are*, Flippant in *The Confederacy*, Flora in *The Country Lasses*, Harriet in *The Jealous Wife*, Isabella in *The Wonder*, Ismena in *The Sultan*, Jenny in *The Highland Reel*, Jessica in *The Merchant of Venice*, Kate in *The King and the Miller of Mansfield*, Kathleen in *The Poor Soldier*, Lady Frances Touchwood in *The Belle's Stratagem*, Lady Harriet Trifle in *The Divorce*, Lady Minikin in *Bon Ton* (a role played in January 1781 by a Mrs Taylor, possibly Mary), Lady Trueman in *The Drummer*, Leonora in *The Padlock*, Louisa in *The Farmer*, Louisa Dudley in *The West Indian*, Miss Alton in *The Heiress*, Miss Grantham in *The Lyar*, Phillida in *A Laugh and a Cry*, Polly in *The Beggar's Opera*, the title role in *Rosina*, a singing Witch in *Macbeth*, Sylvia in *Cymon*, and Yarico in *Inkle and Yarico*. Ms Armstrong tentatively identifies Mary as Mrs Thomas Taylor and does not mention her Christian name; clearly, however, several roles above were played by Mary Taylor before and after her Edinburgh engagement. Acting with Mary in Edinburgh was her husband, who had performed there in the late 1770s and early 1780s but seems not to have acted in London.

At the Haymarket in 1790 Mrs Taylor appeared from 14 June to mid-September as Sukey in *Half an Hour after Supper*, a Villager in *The Battle of Hexham*, Jessica (with a song) in *The Merchant of Venice*, Irene in *A Mogul Tale*, Lauretta in *Try Again*, Sophia in *Thimble's Flight*, Bell in *The Deuce Is in Him*, and Letty in *Tit for Tat*. In the summers of 1791 and 1792 she added such new characters as Beatrice in *The Kentish Barons,* an Attendant and Madelon in *The Surrender of Calais,* Joan in *The Northern Inn,* Anna in *Douglas,* Lady Minikin in *Bon Ton,* Ethelinda in *Henry II,* Kitty in *Young Men, and Old Women,* Tagg in *Miss in Her Teens,* Kitty in *Seeing is Believing,* Mrs Evans in *Next Door Neighbours,* Aetheria in *The Enchanted Wood,* and Patty in *Inkle and Yarico.* She also had a part in *The Rights of Women.*

Between those two summers, in the fall of 1791, Mary Taylor was with Tate Wilkinson's troupe on the York circuit. She joined the company at Wakefield. In *The Wandering Patentee* Wilkinson said of her:

Mrs. Taylor is not so well known in London as she ought to be, for she not only possesses a powerful voice, and a pleasing person, but adds a talent of singing to that of acting far beyond the mediocrity of more leading singers.

Mrs. Taylor was well received the Monday following the race-week in the character of Polly [presumably in *The Beggar's Opera*].

The company moved next to Doncaster and then opened at Hull on 1 November 1791 with Mrs Taylor playing Miss Hardcastle in *She Stoops to Conquer* and Eliza in *The Flitch of Bacon.* She was "not only well received, but in the course of the season by assiduity and a portion of merit, grew into a deserved degree of more than being a common favourite." On 7 February 1792, four days after closing at Hull, the troupe opened at York. On 11 February Mrs Taylor played Lucy in *The Beggar's Opera.*

From 1793 to 1801 Mary Taylor was a member of the company at the Theatre Royal in Norwich. In *Theatre Notebook,* 9, A. Stuart Brown collected information on Mrs Taylor's roles at Norwich. At her benefit on 26 April 1797 she played in *The Pilgrim* and sang a "Hunting Song." On 21 April 1800 at her benefit *The Wheel of Fortune* was presented and Mrs Taylor sang "Crazy Jane." Her last Norwich performance was on 21 May 1801, when she acted in *The Gamester* and *Of Age Tomorrow* and delivered a farewell address.

Lord Chedworth died in Ipswich in October 1804, leaving sizeable bequests to various Norwich performers. To Mary Taylor, widow, formerly of the Theatre Royal in Norwich and a resident (Chedworth believed) at No 4, Millman Street, Bedford Row, he left £13,000 pro-

vided she cancelled an annuity bond of £100; until she was paid the £13,000 she was to receive £300 annually. Mary's daughter Harriet Taylor was given £4,000, and Mary's sister Fanny Valentine received £3,000. The will was signed on 18 July 1804 and proved in London the following 13 November.

The *Dramatic Register* reported that Mary Taylor died in Liverpool on 13 July 1834 at the age of 81.

Taylor, Thomas   *b. 1787, singer, composer, pianist, organist.*

Thomas Taylor, according to information supplied to the biographer Sainsbury by his son Richard Taylor, was born on 2 May 1787 in Chester. He was the eldest son of the elder Richard Taylor. Young Thomas played piano in the subscription concerts at the Royal Hotel in Chester featuring Mme Catalani and the violinist Felix Janiewicz, probably in the 1790s. Doane's *Musical Directory* of 1794 cited Thomas Taylor as an alto singer who sang for the Portland Chapel Society and in the oratorios at Drury Lane Theatre and Westminster Abbey. He was a member of the Court of Assistants of the New Musical Fund and was living at No 31, Clerkenwell Close, in London. When his son Richard supplied Sainsbury with information about his father, he spoke of him as an organist and music master and listed some sacred music, songs, and Welsh airs Thomas Taylor had composed.

Taylor,   [Thomas?]   [*fl. 1791-c. 1804?*], actor, manager?

A Mr Taylor, whose Christian name may have been Thomas, was active near London and in the provinces in the 1790s.

At Bristol on 19 October 1791 a Taylor played Captain Bygrove in *Know Your Own Mind,* and in the summer of 1792 at the Theatre Royal in Richmond, Surrey, Taylor is listed in the bills for Sir George Touchwood in *The Belle's Stratagem,* Oliver in *As You Like It,* Milford in *The Road to Ruin,* Orloff in *A Day in Turkey,* Captain Dash in *The Highland Reel,* and unspecified roles in *Wild Oats* and *Rosina.* The *Thespian Magazine* called Taylor an actor from the Theatre Royal, York, when in the 1790s it cited him at Windsor, Richmond, Manchester, Nottingham, and Lancashire. In Manchester on 31 March 1794 he appeared for

Mrs Taylor's benefit, and on 2 June 1794 he acted Woodville in *The Chapter of Accidents* at the Haymarket Theatre in London, advertised as from Edinburgh. The Derby bills show him there in the spring of 1799, and on 17 January 1800 Taylor acted Ataliba in *Pizarro* in Chesterfield. He may have been the Taylor who shared the management of the Sheffield theatre until 1804 and was a manager at Nottingham and Derby in the early 1800s.

Taylor, William *c. 1753–1825, manager, proprietor, house servant?*

According to the *Survey of London*, 29, William Taylor was born about 1753. Perhaps as a lad he was the William Taylor who served as an assistant to the housekeeper of Covent Garden Theatre in 1768. In 1781 Taylor purchased for £12,333 Richard Brinsley Sheridan's interest in the King's Theatre, but he was not alone in the transaction. A manuscript in the Widener collection at Harvard, dating from early 1781, notes that Richard Stone, William Brummell, Albany Wallis, and Robert Burton were trustees for securing a payment of £20,000 to Giovanni Andrea Gallini, to whom Sheridan and Harris had mortgaged the property in 1778. Stone and the others were acting in behalf of S. and William Taylor, who were named as proprietors of the King's Theatre. The identity of S. Taylor is not clear, but one supposes he was William's relative. According to *The Case of the Opera-House Disputes, Fairly Stated* (1784), Taylor, a native of Scotland, had been a clerk for the bankers Messrs Mayne and Graham and was completely unqualified for theatre affairs. In *Opera House. A Review of this Theatre* by "Veritas," Taylor was said never to have known "a note of music or a word of any tongue but English."

William Taylor's first season as proprietor of the King's Theatre, 1781–82, was a successful one. The opera *I viaggiatori felici* was extremely popular, being presented 28 times, and Jean Georges Noverre returned to London to stage some of his ballets. Lord Chamberlain's warrants show that Taylor was granted permission to hold masquerades at the King's on 9 April 1782, an unspecified date in May and on 10 June. Taylor then had the scene designer and architect Michael Novosielski carry out an extensive renovation of the opera house (at the same time that changes were being made at

Drury Lane, the Haymarket, and Covent Garden—those at the latter being a fairly complete reconstruction.)

The cost of making revisions to the King's Theatre was high; Taylor increased the number of boxes and the cost of a season subscription in order to double the income (to £10,000). The 1782–83 season, which might have helped pay the expenses of the renovation, was not nearly as successful as Taylor's first season had been. Bills could not be paid, and performers' salaries were in arrears. By the middle of May 1783 no operas could be presented, and in June his investment was attached and the property put in trust for six years.

Sylas Neville told his *Diary* on 27 May 1783

The unfair & rascally management of Mr Taylor having at last produced a Bankruptcy in the Opera leaving the performers, particularly the inferior ones, in a very disagreeable situation, the proprietors of the Pantheon with a truly liberal spirit gave them the use of their magnificent room for a concert with dancing to be performed this evening.

A new subscription was also raised to help the performers.

Taylor ignored such things as rent, taxes, mortgages, and salaries, and as the season proceeded went deeper and deeper in debt. He owed £25,000, according to some reports, but *The Case of the Opera-House Disputes* indicated that £15,000 of that was "supposititious." On 17 July 1783 Taylor executed the deed of trust to a group of six men, one of them Novosielski, and arrangements were made to pay the interest due on the mortgage, which Gallini held, to pay interest at 5 percent to Taylor's creditors, and to pay all bills and salaries. Taylor languished in jail, but his lawyers found a flaw in the sale, and Taylor, through the trustees, still controlled the theatre. The Lord Chamberlain put an end to that by refusing to grant the trustees a license and awarding it instead to Gallini, who took over as proprietor. But in June 1789 the King's Theatre burned.

Gallini, Taylor, and Gallini's attorney Robert Bray O'Reilly all had an interest in building a new opera house. Taylor had held the old patent, but with the building gone, the patent was gone as well. Gallini was persuaded to withdraw from any concern in the opera house by subscribers who had raised some funds, and he and O'Reilly began planning a new theatre in Leicester Square. Taylor, though he had no patent, found sufficient subscribers to begin building a new King's Theatre on the old site. Gallini and O'Reilly managed to get a new patent for their proposed theatre, but the King and the Lord Chamberlain, not wanting another theatre in London, forced them to give up their plans. On 30 June 1790 O'Reilly obtained a patent to perform operas at the Pantheon, so Taylor had a theatre under construction but no patent or license, while his rivals had a patent and no theatre.

Taylor, in a petition to the Privy Council in 1810, reviewed the situation:

That your petitioner became possessed twenty-nine years ago of the property of the said opera house, which was unfortunately consumed by fire in the month of June, 1789. That your petitioner rebuilt the present theatre in the following year (1790), and having provided the usual company of singers and dancers, he made the customary application to the Lord Chamberlain for the usual license to carry on operas, which, however, was refused, upon the pretext that a license for the same purpose had been previously granted to a Mr. O'Reilly, who had then recently fitted up the Pantheon, in Oxford Street, as a theatre; in consequence of which refusal, and being unable to open the present opera house for Italian operas, your petitioner lost above 9700 *l.* in the winter of the year 1791.

That the said Mr. O'Reilly having, within the same year, contracted debts at the Pantheon Theatre to the amount of 30,000 *l.*, and having, in consequence thereof, left the kingdom, a negotiation was set on foot with those principally concerned with Mr. O'Reilly in that enterprise, who were His Grace the late Duke of Bedford, and the then Lord Chamberlain (the Marquis of Salisbury), for the restoration not only of the former licence, but even for a patent and permanent exclusive right to carry on Italian operas at the said [King's] theatre in the Haymarket, which was brought to a conclusion in the autumn of 1791, under the auspicious mediation of His Royal Highness the Prince of Wales, the said late Duke of Bedford, and the said Lord Chamberlain, who respectively sanctioned the same with the signature of their names thereto, and which was called, "An Outline for a General Opera Arrangement," in which also the interests of the said two theatres in Covent Garden and Drury Lane were comprehended.

That by the said arrangement it was (among other things) stipulated and agreed, that your petitioner should take upon himself, and secure upon the said Haymarket Theatre [i.e. the King's Theatre], by yearly payments, for the term of fifteen years, the said sum of 30,000 *l.* of debts so contracted at the said Pantheon Theatre, and which sum your petitioner fully paid and satisfied in the year 1796, without waiting for the stipulated instalments; and it was likewise by the said arrangement, which was considered as a recognition of the said three theatres, and the monopoly thereto belonging, that in order to extinguish the risk of the establishment of a third English playhouse, that the proprietors of Drury Lane Theatre and your petitioner should give the proprietors of Covent Garden Theatre a compensation, to put at rest what was called the dormant or third patent; and it was accordingly agreed that the proprietors of Drury Lane Theatre should pay in respect of such compensation the sum of 11,500 *l.* (and which they did actually pay), and that your petitioner should pay 5000 *l.*, other part thereof, to be charged upon the said theatre in the Haymarket, which was agreed to.

What Taylor received in 1790–91 from the Lord Chamberlain was a license that allowed him to operate the King's Theatre as a concert hall, presenting ballets, songs, instrumental music, but no operas—since O'Reilly at the Pantheon held that right. According to the singer Michael Kelly in his *Reminiscences,* Richard Brinsley Sheridan sided with Taylor when the King's was being rebuilt, writing to the Duke of Bedford that "the carrying on Italian operas at the Pantheon was most unjust and unfair towards the claimants on the Opera House in the Haymarket, as well as to Mr. Taylor, the chief proprietor, who was making every effort to rebuild it. . . ."

Taylor opened the King's Theatre unofficially, before his license was granted, on 23 February 1791, by holding a semiprivate rehearsal of the opera *Pirro.* Another rehearsal was held on 10 March. The *Oracle* the following day reported that "Last night the Proprietors of this undertaking saw company to the number we imagine of Four Thousand Persons. . . . Davide, in the Opera of Pirro, engrossed the whole of the applause that so matchless a singer may well merit." The rehearsal evasion was tried again on 22 March.

The King's officially opened on 26 March with *Entertainments of Music and Dancing.* The evening consisted of two parts, with dancing following the first part (serious music and songs) and the ballet *Orpheus and Eurydice* following part II (comic music and songs). Taylor advised the public:

As the Proprietors would not presume, even to save themselves from utter ruin, to offend either the Authority of the King, or of the Laws, they forbear all idea of performing Operas until the hardship and injustice of their case shall produce the proper influence upon his Majesty's benevolent mind; and, under the circumstances in which they stand, with a Company of the most celebrated singers and dancers in the world, in their respective departments, engaged at an expense of £18,000, they confide in the liberality of the Public that they will countenance and support such an Entertainment as they are legally warranted to give, until they shall recover their just right of performing Operas under his Majesty's license.

Clearly, the authorities had disliked the rehearsal ruse, but Taylor did not give up.

Walpole wrote on 31 March, "There is no peace between the opera theatres; the Haymarket [King's] rather triumphs. They have opened twice, taking money in an evasive manner, pretending themselves concerts; the singers are in their own clothes, the dancers dressed, and no recitative—a sort of opera déshabillé." The King's continued with the concert format, aided by the presence of Haydn, who presided at the harpsichord when his music was played. The season ended in July, a success, but Taylor could clearly not operate the second largest theatre in Europe (only La Scala in Milan was larger) without being able to perform operas. In 1791–92, the Drury Lane company moved into the unoccupied King's while their new theatre was being built.

When the Pantheon burned in 1792 and O'Reilly fled to Paris, Taylor's chances revived. A *General Opera Trust Deed* (called *The Final Arrangement*) was signed on 24 August 1792, transferring the Pantheon patent to the King's Theatre. The company opened on 26 January 1793 with *Il barbiere di Siviglia* (music mostly by Paisiello) and for the rest of the season shared the theatre with the Drury Lane troupe; from 1793–94 on, Taylor and his opera company had the splendid new King's Theatre to themselves.

Taylor had been nominally imprisoned since 1783 under the rules of the King's Bench, but he rather liked running theatrical affairs while technically not free, as John Ebers in *Seven Years of the King's Theatre* (1828) explained:

"How can you conduct the management of the King's Theatre," I said to him one day, "perpetually in durance as you are?"

"My dear fellow," he replied, "how could I possibly conduct it if I were at liberty? I should be eaten up, Sir, devoured. Here comes a dancer— 'Mr Taylor, I want such a dress'; another, 'I want such and such ornaments.' One singer demands to sing in a part not allotted to him; another to have an addition to his appointments. No,—let *me* be shut up, and they go to Masterson (Taylor's secretary): he, they are aware, cannot go beyond his line, but if they get at *me*—pshaw! no man at large can manage that theatre; and in faith," added he, "no man that undertakes it ought to go at large."

William Taylor remained the King's Theatre proprietor until 1813, with Michael Kelly serving as what we would probably call production manager. In the Public Record Office are numerous annual licenses granted to Taylor for masquerades, oratorios, concerts, and Italian opera presentations. Complaints against him were many. In his *London Notebook* Haydn commented on Taylor and the financial arrangements of the King's Theatre in 1794–95:

The *Entrepreneur* of the Haymarket Theatre, of which the Duke of Pedfort is the principal figure, pays that miserable cur Taylor £21,000 Sterling every year for the expenses of the opera house; which sum is never sufficient, so that a group of various Lords, bankers, merchants, & c. (but in all more than 200 of them) helps out. Moreover the house brings in not less than £500. The present contract was established in 1791 and lasts for 17 years. Each backer gets 15 percent annually, but he loses the capital entirely after the 17 years are up.

Taylor had a knack for not being available when he was needed. Haydn told of an incident at the King's on 28 April 1795, when the audience began demanding Mme Hilligsberg's new ballet instead of the scheduled one; "at last a dancer came forward and said, very submissively: 'Ladies and Gantleman: since . . . Mr Taylor cannot be found, the whole Ballet Company promises to perform the desired ballet next week, for which, however, the Impresario must pay Madam Hilligsberg £300."

In 1795–96 Taylor was involved in disputes with his subscribers. On 6 February 1796 the spectators rioted. Michael Kelly managed to appease the audience, but Taylor put notices in the papers saying he was perfectly within his rights in evicting disorderly subscribers or in cancelling their subscriptions. A public resolution against him was passed, and he saved his position only by recanting and apologizing.

The *Monthly Mirror* in May 1797 complained:

There is a confusion pervades the management of the Opera, which, while it exists, will deprive the town of the variety of new operas and ballets to which it is entitled. Why these continual broils between Mr. Gallet [the ballet master] and Mr. Taylor, Mr. Didelot and Madame Hilligsberg [principal dancers]? Surely, as we visit those places for our entertainment, we ought not to be pestered in the public prints with a ridiculous correspondence between a *ballet-master* and a *dancing master;* nor is it to the credit of some person or other, high in office in the department of the Opera, to permit the arrest of the first female singer in the country (for a small debt) to meet the public eye.

The following month in the same periodical was another complaint against Taylor:

The whole concerns of this magnificent theatre, for want of system and regularity, are rapidly going to destruction. The subordinate performers expostulate with the treasurer Jewell, than whom there is not a more able or worthy man, but he is debarred the means;—the cash is laid hold of by higher powers, and that which should satisfy the cravings of nature, and the wants of the necessitous, is, perhaps, appropriated to *bribery* and *corruption,* for the purpose of obtaining a seat in parliament, and that end being at length accomplished, *bills, bonds,* and *ejectments* become waste paper!

In July the *Monthly Mirror* called for Jewell to be made sole manager. (Taylor did, indeed, become a Member of Parliament: for Leominster from 1797 to 1802 and for Barnstaple from 1806 to 1812. He was thus given immunity from his creditors, but not after his loss in 1802, when he fled to France.) Yet in 1796–97, despite heavy running expenses, Taylor managed to pay off £30,000 indebtedness that he had inherited in 1792 when the Pantheon burned, and he managed to get the opera license he needed.

Typically, he was in trouble before the end of the season, and some wealthy patrons had to help. By the fall of 1799 the performers could suffer no more, and they petitioned the

Lord Chamberlain to suspend the King's Theatre license until Taylor paid their salaries. George III supported the performers, and the opera season did not open on 21 December as planned. By 11 January 1800 Taylor must have paid the salaries, for the season finally began. (Kevin Pry in *Theatre Notebook* [1985] examines in detail the petition and its aftermath.)

In January 1803 Taylor sold a third share in the theatre property to Francis Goold for £13,335; in 1804 Goold paid Taylor £14,165, and by the end of the year Taylor mortgaged his remaining interest to Goold for £5,700 and dropped into the background until Goold's death on 17 January 1807, after which, as the surviving partner, Taylor had nominal control. Edmund Waters, Goold's executor, complained that Taylor had mismanaged the theatre's affairs and disregarded the 1803 agreement made with Goold, according to William C. Smith's *Italian Opera*. Waters fought more and more during the 1806–7 season, and in the fall of 1807 the situation became absurd. Taylor and Waters each had renovation plans for the King's Theatre, and each engaged workmen. Taylor managed to get the annual license for performing and advertised the opening of the theatre season. Waters protested to the Lord Chamberlain, and in January 1808 differences were settled by arbitration in Waters's favor. That did not deter Taylor, who continued to act independently. The situation was so unsettled that Mme Catalani refused to sing under a contract for the season and demanded payment after each performance.

Attacks on Taylor's management increased with the years. The *Examiner* on 30 December 1810 contained a scathing letter from "H.R.":

The Opera-House has opened for the season, with all its usual symptoms of bad management, exemplified by its internal appearance, disfigured by rags and dirt, and by the wretchedness of its scenery, dresses, and decorations, which would produce murmurs from the audience of a puppet-show. But nothing better can be expected while the public continue so indifferent to the insults they receive, and while the theatre is in the hands of a manager so destitute of taste and liberality as Mr. TAYLOR. The talents most esteemed by him are those which can be procured for the least money, and consequently the authors and composers that he employs are the very refuse of their professions.

The same writer blasted Taylor again on 19 May 1811: "his mind appears devoid of all relish for the elegant arts;—poets are to him far less interesting personages than bailiffs, and the only music that can affect him is the discordant clamour of his duns."

In 1812 a group of disgruntled opera lovers tried to establish an opera at the new Pantheon, but the venture failed. That was small comfort for Taylor, however, for he was in such financial difficulties by early 1813 that the sheriff took some of his property to meet a liability of some £1,300. Taylor did not help matters by neglecting his managerial duties. "H." wrote to *The Theatrical Inquisitor* in April 1813:

It was our first intention to remark, at considerable length, on the mismanagement of Mr. Dunne [Taylor], and on the imperfection of the scenery, the deficiensy of the *corps de ballette,* and the irregularities that occur at every performance. But we have turned from the task in disgust and disappointment; nor shall we readily resume our criticism of this dirty, degraded temple of the Italian muses, till the property be consigned to the management of other hands, or till we shall be enabled to distinguish the voices of the performers, without being distracted by perpetual clamors of "Tramezzani! Tramezzani!" [the singer] and shouts of *"No Squallini!"* "Let Mr. Taylor come forward." "No Tayloring Dunnes!" and "Explanation! Explanation!" . . .

But what can be expected beneath the management of an individual who, without the power to superintend the theatre in person, has neither the discrimination to select an active and able substitute, nor the prudence to conciliate those who might render the various plans that have been adopted for his benefit, effectual? Eternal litigation, and perpetual quarrels are the favourite objects of Mr. Taylor's pursuits, and even when some small portion of civility would command the services of useful friends, or obtain the forbearance of dangerous enemies; he is obliged to pay enormous sums for the reluctant services of those who would come forward to gratify the public, under any other management, at one half of their present salaries; and the efforts of his new partner [Waters], his composers, and his performers, are debarred and counteracted by the confusion, the bustle, the inconvenience of arrangement, and the petty observances of economy, that accompany the presentation of a new, or the revival of a favourite opera. . . . When Catalani and her rivals subject themselves to the capricious insults of Mr. Taylor, they *will* be paid for it; and the public is ultimately condemned to *feel* the rudeness and indiscretion of the manager. We do not blame him for making the best terms he could, but for not abiding by the engagements that he actually forms, and nothing can be clearer than that, in this instance, Signior Tramezanni has a full claim to exemption from performing in comic operas. [He had been engaged to sing serious, not comic opera and had protested in the papers.]

The Lord Chamberlain finally had enough. In December 1813 he ordered that the whole of Goold's share in the theatre was to be sold, and Taylor was specifically forbidden to interfere in the management. Waters purchased Goold's share for £35,000 and became co-proprietor with Taylor and mortgagee of Taylor's share. Waters opened the opera season on 12 March 1814.

Taylor continued to meddle. Ebers wrote that "Taylor, now entirely out of the concern, found great amusement in practicing on the fears of Mr Chambers [the holder of Waters's mortgage] by means of anonymous letters, and otherwise prophesying the inevitable ruin of Waters, and the consequent loss to ensue to Mr. Chambers." In 1817 the French actor Talma was to give recitations in the concert room at the King's Theatre. The *British Stage and Literary Cabinet* in July reported:

Mr Taylor, in his infinite wisdom, has applied to the Court of Chancery to issue an injunction restraining Mr Waters from letting the theatre for these performances, upon the pretense that it is solely insured as a place for the performance of Italian Operas, and that consequently should any accident occur, the Insurance Offices would not hold themselves liable to make good the loss . . . for if English and French plays are allowed to be acted, the Opera House, instead of being open two nights in the week, would be open every night, consequently there would be the risk of four additional nights of performance.

(As Nalbach in *The King's Theatre* points out, Taylor himself had rented the opera house to the Covent Garden company in 1808–9.) The Lord Chamberlain did not grant the injunction.

According to *Notes and Queries* on 19 September 1916 William Taylor died on 1 May 1825, but that cannot be true, for a codicil to his will was dated 4 June 1825. He died between then and the eighth, when the will was proved. The will is a fascinating and informative document and is worth quoting at length:

This is my last Will and Testament written with my own hand this fifteenth day of ffebruay 1823 I hereby will and bequeath all the monies that may arise from the sale of the Operahouse in the Haymarket for the purpose of paying all my just debts and the surplus to be divided among the children of my Brother Captain George Taylor of the City of Dublin. I also will and bequeath all my interest in the property boxes in the said Operahouse marked or numbered vizt. the Coutts box in the Pit Tier N°. 20 and the Ground Tier e LVIII on the first tier upstairs the Opera Season of 1824 the late Duke of Queensbury's box marked R No 5 Coutts Box and L in the Pit tier for 1825 and for the same year or season of Operas the boxes N°. 2–5–7–8–15–23–24 & 36 upon the ground Tier and for the same year or season of Operas the boxes N°. 38–41–48–54–55–56–57–LVIII–69–70–71 & 72 upon the first tier upstairs to Ann Dunn who has lived with me mostly as my reputed Wife since 1807 a period of 16 years during which time she has constantly acted the part of a true and sincere ffriend in doing which she has gone through a world of anxiety trouble and fatigue in return for which it is my most earnest desire wish and will to leave her the means of ease and comfort for the remainder of her life for which purpose it is my will and request that the Executors . . . shall let all the aforementioned boxes for the year or opera seasons at the best rents that can be obtained for the same and of the rent of such boxes to set apart for the use and benefit of said Ann Dunn the sum of six thousand pounds (£6,000) of which it is my wish that a moiety may be laid out in the purchase of an annuity and the remaining £3,000 to be invested in the Public funds or the whole £6,000 laid out in the purchase of houses at annual rents not exceeding £60.

He wanted matters arranged to provide Ann Dunn with an annual income of at least £400. She was not to have the power to dispose of the £6,000 during her lifetime (was she a spendthrift?) but she could bequeath £3,000 of it freely. The residuary legatees were Captain George Taylor's children.

William Taylor had a house in Southampton Row he called Bordeau House. He bequeathed the furniture in it to Ann Dunn but did not indicate in his will the disposition of the house itself or its other furnishings. Taylor left £250 to an attorney named Birkett. The 4 June 1825 codicil specified an alternative to the renting of the boxes if some of them were already assigned. Taylor must not have had full control of the boxes. One of Taylor's executors was the dancer James Harvey D'Egville. The will was proved on 8 June 1825.

William Taylor appears in a caricature engraving by Dent entitled "High Committee, or Operatical Contest," along with other figures representing the nobility and opera personnel who were involved in the rivalry between the two opera companies in 1791; that engraving is reproduced in this *Dictionary*, 11:117.

Taylor, William Perkins   *1769–1800, actor, manager.*

The Mr Taylor who acted several times in London and environs between 1792 and 1794 was, we believe, the provincial performer and manager William Perkins Taylor (though possibly the Margate manager John Taylor). In June 1792 a Taylor was in the company at Richmond, Surrey; he was announced as from Edinburgh, where William P. Taylor and his wife had often appeared. In September 1793 that Taylor was at Windsor, announced as from York, for, when he acted Woodville in *The Chapter of Accidents* in a specially licensed production at the Haymarket Theatre on 2 June 1794, he was again reported to be from Edinburgh.

William P. Taylor managed the Nottingham circuit in the 1780s and 1790s. In February 1790 he bought the Cheltenham license from Watson. He also acted at Derby in the 1790s and at Bath from 1788 to 1792.

At Edinburgh sometime in the earlier half of 1786 Taylor had married the actress Mrs Hannah Henrietta Robinson, whose husband had died in January 1786. She was the daughter of the provincial manager David Pritchard and sister to the younger David Pritchard and Miss Pritchard (later Mrs Henry F. Thornton). The *Gentleman's Magazine* of July 1787 stated that Taylor and Mrs Robinson had been married "lately." They played at Edinburgh that season, and that autumn the new Mrs Taylor went south for a season's engagement at Drury Lane Theatre. When they were together at Bath and Bristol in 1791–92, Taylor complained in the press that his wife was being unfairly hissed.

The *Gentleman's Magazine* of May 1800 reported Taylor's death at Derby on 18 May 1800, at the age of 31. He was described as from "Wymondham."

In his will dated 6 August 1794 and proved on 5 September 1800, Taylor left his estate to his wife, who was some years his senior. She managed the Nottingham theatre until at least 1805. In 1793 the license for Chelmsford evidently had been turned over by Taylor to Henry F. Thornton, the brother-in-law of Hannah Taylor. About 1805 Mrs Taylor married the actor Benjamin Wrench (1778–1843). The date of her death is unknown, though she was still alive in 1827. No issue of her marriage to Taylor is known, though she evidently had two daughters by her first marriage to Robinson.

Taylor, Mrs William Perkins, Hannah Henrietta, née Pritchard, earlier Mrs ₍Joseph?₎ Robinson, later Mrs Benjamin Wrench ₍fl. 1777–1827₎, *actress, manager.*

Hannah Henrietta Pritchard, not related to the great actress Hannah Pritchard, was the daughter of the country manager David Pritchard. Her brother David Pritchard, the younger, had an active provincial career but seems not to have acted in London in the eighteenth century; his wife, née Caulfield, probably was the Mrs Pritchard who acted Barbara in *Love and Money* at Covent Garden Theatre on 31 May 1796. Hannah's sister married the actor Henry F. Thornton and as Mrs Thornton acted in the provinces in the 1790s; her husband acted in London and is noticed separately in this *Dictionary.*

Brought up in a theatrical family, Hannah Henrietta when a child may have appeared on some country stage. She may have been already married when, advertised as "A Young Lady," she made her debut at Bath on 3 April 1777 as Jane Shore. A manuscript notation on a copy of the Bath playbill in the Harvard Theatre Collection identifies her as Mrs Robinson. On 19 April 1777, now advertised as the "Gentlewoman that perform'd Jane Shore," she acted Lady Townly in *The Provok'd Husband.* Her name did appear on the bill of her third appearance on 22 May 1777, when she played Calista in *The Fair Penitent.*

Announced as from the Theatre Royal,

Bath, Mrs Robinson played the Queen in a specially licensed performance of *The Spanish Fryar,* "at the Desire of the Jerusalem Lodge," for a benefit she shared with "Brother" Herricks at the Haymarket Theatre on 26 January 1778. She returned to the Haymarket that season to act Queen Elizabeth in *Richard III* on 24 March 1778 and Miss Sterling in *The Clandestine Marriage* on 30 May 1778. Other appearances at the Haymarket included Rosetta in *The Foundling* on 22 February 1779 and Clarinda in *The Humours of Oxford* and Lady Charlotte in *High Life below Stairs* on 28 March 1780.

She was an itinerant for several years, acting in Gosli's company at Derby in January and February 1782. That year she also acted at Portsmouth.

Advertised as "A Lady" making her first appearance on that stage, Mrs Robinson acted Rosamond in *King Henry the Second* at Covent Garden Theatre on 31 December 1782. A notation in Reed's "Notitia Dramatica" in the British Library identifies her and states that she came from the Portsmouth company. When she acted Alicia in *Jane Shore* on 27 January 1783 she was named in the bills. On 24 February she played Cordelia in *King Lear* and on 25 February Victoria in the premiere of Mrs Cowley's *A Bold Stroke for a Husband.* She appeared as Oriana in *The Knight of Malta* on 23 April, and on 7 May at very short notice she took over Miss Younge's role of Viola in *Twelfth Night.* On 9 May 1783, Mrs Robinson played Alinda in *The Pilgrim.* Her salary for the season had been £3 per week.

Not reengaged by Covent Garden, Mrs Robinson returned to the provinces. When Tate Wilkinson employed her in May 1785 for his York circuit she had been engaged the previous winter season at Manchester and Liverpool and had been principal actress at Birmingham the previous summer. She made her first appearance for Wilkinson at Leeds as Elwina in *Percy,* which, according to his *Wandering Patentee,* "she played with credit, but not equal to her forms of fancy." She was much superior in the title role of the comic afterpiece, *The Irish Widow.* "Her figure in the small clothes was neat to a degree of perfection," thought Wilkinson, "and her deportment, spirit, and conception of that part was . . . the best I had then, or have since seen." Next at Leeds she acted Isabella in *The Fatal Marriage* and on 1 June 1785 finished the stay there as Rosalind in *As You Like It.* During Race Week at Wakefield she acted Portia in *The Merchant of Venice* and the Irish Widow. She completed her engagement with Wilkinson at York on 16 June 1786, when she acted Horatia in *The Roman Father* and the Irish Widow for her benefit. The house was sparse, and, to make matters worse, Mrs Jordan, an arch-rival, came behind the scenes and tried to steal the attention of the audience by coming to the very edge of the wings while Mrs Robinson was doing the last act of the farce.

Wilkinson described Mrs Robinson as "a person well made, and is as neat as if she had a dozen virgins at her toilet to decorate her person." She had good powers but her voice, not musical, sometimes ran sharp. She was prone "to let affectation peep where the characters should only take place" and thus often projected her pretty self rather than the character. Wilkinson thought she was wrong in perpetually acting tragedies when her features were "much better calculated for the line of genteel comedy."

In January 1786 Mrs Robinson's husband died at Hull. "His dissolution had been weekly expected from a rapid decay, which baffled all art," wrote Wilkinson. No contemporary memoirs note Robinson's first name or mention whether or not he was a member of the profession. C. B. Hogan identified him as Joseph Robinson, the York actor.

After leaving Wilkinson, Mrs Robinson went to act in Ireland, appearing at the Smock Alley Theatre in Dublin and playing at Waterford in July 1786 and at Cork in August and October. Also acting at Cork in October 1786 were Miss Robinson and Miss M. Robinson, no doubt her daughters.

Sometime in 1786 Mrs Robinson married William Perkins Taylor, manager of the Nottingham circuit. In his *Annals of the Edinburgh Stage,* J. C. Dibdin wrote that Mrs Robinson, from Dublin, was at Edinburgh, with her husband, in February 1787, but Dibdin mistook her for Mary Robinson. The *Gentleman's Magazine* on July 1787 states that she had been married "lately" at Edinburgh.

Announced as Mrs Taylor and as making her

first appearance on that stage, she began an engagement at Drury Lane Theatre on 29 September 1787 as Elwina in *Percy.* The *World* on 1 October reported "there was nothing to recommend her." The critic in the *European Magazine* found her "certainly improved" since her former appearance in London when Mrs Robinson, but she was still not good enough to serve as an occasional substitute for Mrs Siddons. On her debut night she played Widow Brady in the afterpiece *The Irish Widow.* On 26 October she acted Alinda in *The Pilgrim.* Her other roles that season were Imogen in *Cymbeline* on 5 November, Lady Touchwood in *The Double Dealer* on 29 November, Charlotte Rusport in *The West Indian* on 8 December, the Queen in *Richard III* on 10 December, Rosamond in *Henry the Second* on 26 December, Alicia in *Jane Shore,* on 19 January, Lady Lurewell in *The Constant Couple* on 31 March 1788, and Miranda in *The Invisible Mistress* on 21 April. For her benefit on 28 April 1788 she acted Miss Walsingham in *The School for Wives.* That night total receipts were £173 (less £109 11s. 11d. house charges) and tickets were available from her at No 10, Charles Street, Covent Garden; her ticket money came to £97 16s., so she suffered a deficit of £34 7s. 11d.

Once again her engagement in a London theatre lasted but one season, and in 1788–89 Mrs Taylor was in the Manchester company. She engaged at York in 1789 but quarreled with Wilkinson over her choice of roles and within a few days broke her engagement and left York. She was at Manchester when the new Theatre Royal opened there in 1790; that summer she also acted at Birmingham. In April 1791 she was again at Manchester and in August 1791 at Derby. Over the next decade and more her peregrinations took her throughout England and Scotland, including the Orchard Street Theatre, Bath, and the Bristol Theatre Royal in 1791–92. In February 1792 her husband complained to the press that Mrs Taylor was being unjustifiably hissed. She was at Chelmsford in September 1792, after a summer engagement in Manchester. The *Thespian Magazine* that year also placed her at Edinburgh and Glasgow. She returned in the summer of 1793 to Chelmsford, where the proprietor of the recently-built theatre was Henry F. Thornton, her brother-in-law, who also ran theatres at Reading and Guildford. In 1794 she spent much of the year at Manchester and also acted at Chester. In the spring of 1799 she was at Derby, and that summer she returned to Nottingham.

When her husband, who was somewhat younger than she, died on 18 May 1800 at the age of 31, Mrs Taylor became the Nottingham manager, which position she held until 1805, when she sold her share to Adcock. Advertised as manager of the Nottingham company, she performed six nights at Liverpool in the summer of 1801 and that year was again at Bath and Bristol. She even returned to York, for one night only, when on 5 May 1801 she acted Euphrasia in *The Grecian Daughter.*

In 1805 the *Thespian Dictionary,* calling her Mrs Robinson Taylor, described her as a lady "of very considerable abilities" and sister to Mrs Thornton and David Pritchard; she was, the editor reported, married now "to a *third* husband, a Mr. Wrench; of whose figure and abilities we have no doubt, being the selected choice of so judicious and experienced a matron, who preferred him for a *husband,* rather than a *son-in-law.*" That statement was an allusion to the fact that at one point Mrs Taylor and her daughter Miss Robinson were engaged, respectively, to Thomas H. W. Manly and Benjamin Wrench, but they ultimately changed partners, with the daughter marrying Manly and the mother marrying Wrench.

Benjamin Wrench (1778–1843) had been a member of the Nottingham company and had been coached and prepared for the stage with great care by Mrs Taylor. The date of their marriage is not known, but when she appeared at Liverpool on 27 May 1805 it was as Mrs Wrench. She also acted as Mrs Wrench at Edinburgh that year.

The date of Hannah Wrench's death is unknown, but in 1827 she still was receiving an annuity of £54 12s. from Manly and the Nottingham Theatre. Her third husband, Benjamin Wrench, died in 1843. He did not act in London in the eighteenth century, but his long career in the capital, after he made his debut with the Drury Lane company at the Lyceum Theatre on 7 October 1809 as Belcour in *The West Indian* and Tristam Fickle in *The Weathercock,* is noticed in *The Dictionary of National Biography.* On 12 December 1843 administration of his estate (about £3,000) was granted

to Jonathan Fountain Wrench and Esther Rebecca Wrench, spinster, his brother and sister and only next of kin. In the administration he was described as a widower.

By her earlier marriage to Robinson, Hannah had two daughters, the younger of whom married the provincial manager Thomas H. Wilson Manly (d. 1840). By Manly that daughter had a large family, including two sons, Charles and Tom (1807–1834), who became actors on the Nottingham circuit. Some additional information on Manly and his children is given by Sybil Rosenfeld in *Theatre Notebook,* October–December 1952.

Teano. *See* TENOE.

Teasdell, Roger [*fl. 1686*], *singer. See* PARKER, MRS [*fl.c. 1686*].

Tebbett. *See* TIBET.

Tedeli. *See* FIDELI.

Tedeschi, Signora [*fl. 1741–1742*], *singer.*
Signora Tedeschi was the "third woman" in the opera company at the King's Theatre in 1741–42. She had a role in *Alessandro in Persia* on 31 November 1741 and then was heard as Alethes in *Polidoro* on 19 January 1742 and Druso in *Scipione in Cartagine* on 2 March.

Tedeschini, Christiano [*fl. 1760–1761*], *singer.*
Christiano Tedeschini sang Cecco in *Il mondo della luna* at the King's Theatre on 22 November 1760, Capocchio in *Il filosofo di campagna* on 6 January 1761, Il Barone Macacco Tartaglia in *I tre gobbi rivali* on 9 March, and Mastricco in *La pescatrice* on 28 April. At the Great Room in Dean Street, Soho, on 21 January 1761 he sang in the oratorio *Issac.*

Tedway. *See* TUDWAY.

Teede, Jacob [*fl. 1767?–1794*], *oboist.*
Doane's *Musical Directory* of 1794 listed Jacob Teede as an oboist living at No 3, Warren Place, Hampstead Road. He was a member of the Court of Assistants of the New Musical Fund. Teede was presumably the son of Wil-

liam Teede and was the "Teed Junr." listed as playing oboe in the *Messiah* at the Foundling Hospital in 1767.

Teede, William [*fl.1739–1784*], *oboist, flutist, copyist.*

On 28 August 1739 William Teede (or Teed, Teide) became one of the original subscribers to the Royal Society of Musicians. He played oboe in the *Messiah* at the Foundling Hospital in May 1754 for 10*s.* and in May 1758 for 10*s.* 6*d.* He performed in the *Messiah* again in 1759, 1760, 1763, and 1767. *Mortimer's London Directory* of 1763 gave Teede's address as King's Square Court, Soho, and noted that he also played the German flute. In May and June 1784 Teede played second oboe in the Handel Memorial Concerts at Westminster Abbey and the Pantheon.

He was married to Charlotte, the daughter of the elder John Christopher Smith. Teede took over Smith's music copying work after Smith's death, in 1762–63. Charlotte and William Teede had a son, presumably the Jacob Teede cited in Doane's *Musical Directory* in 1794.

"Telegraphic Actor, The." *See* ELLISTON, ROBERT WILLIAM.

Tellier, Mons [*fl.1718–1719*], *actor.*

Monsieur Tellier was a member of Francisque Moylin's troupe of French players who performed at Lincoln's Inn Fields from 7 November 1718 and then at the King's Theatre from 11 February to 19 March 1719. Tellier's one known role was Orgon in *Tartuffe,* which he acted on 13 January 1719.

"Tell-Truth, Paul." *See* CAREY, GEORGE SAVILLE.

Temple, Mr [*fl.1730–1737*], *boxkeeper.*

Mr Temple shared benefits at Goodman's Fields Theatre from 25 June 1730 through 22 May 1733; he was one of the boxkeepers. His benefit tickets were accepted at Lincoln's Inn Fields Theatre on 10 May 1737.

Temple, Diana 1675–1705, *actress, dancer, singer.*

Diana Temple was born in 1675, according to Musgrave's *Obituary.* She danced in *The Rape*

of *Europa* with the United Company at Dorset Garden Theatre in the winter of 1693–94. When the troupe split in 1694–95 she chose to remain with Christopher Rich's group at Drury Lane and Dorset Garden and during 1695–96 played the Princess in *Agnes de Castro* in December 1695, Teresia in *The Younger Brother* in February 1696, Ariena in *Neglected Virtue* in mid-February, and Clarinda in *The Cornish Comedy* in June. Before the end of the century she spoke the epilogue to *Brutus of Alba* and acted Calista in *The Female Wits,* Euphronia in both parts of *Aesop,* Marcella in *Imposture Defeated,* Cleonista in *The Fatal Discovery,* Julia in *Caligula,* and Cassiope in *Phaeton.*

Other roles Diana Temple played before her death in 1705 included Phylante in *The Grove,* Sylvia in *The Reform'd Wife,* Timandra in *Courtship à la Mode,* Angelina in *Love Makes a Man,* Lucia in *Vice Reclaimed,* Lucinda in *The Quacks,* Honora in *The Loyal Subject,* and Jessina in *The Fashionable Lover.* She was one of the Drury Lane players who petitioned the Lord Chamberlain in June or July 1705, signing her full name. Musgrave reported that she died in 1705 at the age of 30. She was still remembered in *Wit and Mirth* in 1719, where she was named as the singer of "I seek no more."

Templer, Mrs [*fl.1728–1739*], *actress.*

Mrs Templer's first recorded appearance was on 7 December 1728, when she acted Euryone in *The Virgin Queen* at the Lincoln's Inn Fields Theatre, though she may have played small parts there at other times during the 1728–29 season. On 26 August 1729 she had the title role in *Maudlin* at the Hall and Oates booth at Bartholomew Fair. She continued acting for the manager John Rich at Lincoln's Inn Fields and, from December 1732, at Covent Garden Theatre through the 1738–39 season.

Among her parts were Regan in *King Lear,* Florella in *Sir Walter Raleigh,* Parisatis in *The Rival Queens,* Florinda in *The Wife of Bath,* Althea in *The Country Wife,* Marcella in 2 *Don Quixote,* Lady Townly and Myrtilla in *The Provok'd Husband,* the Countess of Rutland in *The Unhappy Favorite,* Isabella in *The Coffee House Politician,* Clarinda in *Periander,* Timoclea in *Merope,* the Ghost of Clytemnestra in *Orestes,* Sukey in *The Beggar's Opera,* Isabella in *The Mistake,* Maria in *The London Merchant,* Rosara in *She Wou'd and She Wou'd Not*, Isabella in *The Conscious Lovers*, Belinda in *The Fair Quaker of Deal* (her first appearance at Covent Garden, on 14 December 1732), Prudentia in *A Duke and No Duke*, Lucinda and Lavinia in *The Fair Penitent*, Eugenia in *The London Cuckolds*, Mariana in *Measure for Measure*, Monimia and Serina in *The Orphan*, Florinda in *The Rover*, Araminta in *The Old Bachelor*, Dorinda in *The Stratagem*, Hillaria in *Love's Last Shift*, Mrs Fainall in *The Way of the World*, Belinda in *Turnbridge Walks*, Zaida in *Abra Mule*, Cleopatra in *Macheath in the Shades*, Salome in *Mariamne*, Jenny in *The Double Deceit*, Cephisa in *The Distrest Mother*, Marina in *Theodosius*, Eugenia in *Cymbeline*, Kate in *1 Henry IV*, and Hero in *Much Ado about Nothing*. Her last role was Marcella in *Don Quixote* on 17 May 1739.

Mrs Templer made a number of appearances elsewhere, her first being on 27 June 1730, when she played the Queen in *The Spanish Fryar* at Richmond. During July at Richmond she acted Lady Lurewell in *The Constant Couple*, Mrs Ford in *The Merry Wives of Windsor*, Amanda in *Love's Last Shift*, and Indiana in *The Conscious Lovers*. She returned to Richmond on 8 June 1731 to play Mrs Ford again, and there on 17 August 1732 she repeated Amanda. In June 1734 she was Kate in *1 Henry IV*, and the following September, when she was not scheduled to perform at Covent Garden, she went out to Richmond to play Lady Trueman in *The Drummer*.

She also made two appearances at Bartholomew Fair after 1729: as Fidelia in *The Emperor of China, Grand Volgi* on 24 August 1731 and in *The Envious Statesman* on 22 August 1732. After Covent Garden opened, Mrs Templer put in occasional appearances at Lincoln's Inn Fields. On 12 October 1734 she acted Melinda in *The Recruiting Officer* at a widow's benefit; with the Covent Garden troupe she was Philadelphia in *The Amorous Widow* on 23 April and Dorinda in *The Stratagem* on 30 April 1735—both benefits; on 31 March 1736 she was Ruth in *The Committee* at another benefit; and with Covent Garden players on 18 October 1736 she played Althea in *The Country Wife*.

Little else is known about Mrs Templer except that in 1735–36 at Covent Garden she was paid £43 for 172 acting days.

Templeton, Mr ₁*fl. 1773–1777*₁,   *actor.*
A Mr Templeton was employed at the Smock Alley Theatre in Dublin in 1773–74, according to the research of W. J. Lawrence. He was, perhaps, the actor Templeton who worked for £1 weekly at Drury Lane Theatre in London in 1776–77 (as the theatre accounts show; he is not listed in *The London Stage*). (He seems not to have been the Templeton who performed on the slack wire in Philadelphia in 1780 or the Templeton who acted at Cork, Ireland, in 1796.)

Templeton, Mrs ₁*fl. 1780–1785*₁,   *actress, singer.*
Mrs Templeton was named as a beneficiary at Covent Garden Theatre on 23 May 1780. She was presumably the Mrs Templeton who played the Abbess in *Harlequin Rambler* on 29 January 1784 and Molly Brazen in *The Beggar's Opera* on 30 September 1785, earning £1 weekly for her chores.

Templin. *See* TAMPLIN.

Tench, Miss ₁*fl. 1747*₁,   *singer.*
Miss Tench and others sang between the acts at Goodman's Fields Theatre on 5 January 1747.

Tench, Fisher, alias Fisher Tench Charke ₁*fl. 1729–1755?*₁,   *dancer, actor.*
When he was first mentioned in playbills, Fisher Tench was called Fisher Tench Charke; he played Harry Paddington and a Player in *The Beggar's Opera* on 1 January 1729 with a Lilliputian troupe at the Lincoln's Inn Fields Theatre. But when he danced there on 9 May he was styled Fisher Tench; the evening was his shared benefit (as "Young Tench") with two others, the receipts for which, before house charges, came to over £123. He must have been related in some way to the musician Richard Charke, who was at the Haymarket Theatre in May and June 1729. On 26 May at the Haymarket Tench played a Shepherd and a Sylvan in *The Humours of Harlequin*. At Bartholomew Fair on 23 August at Fielding's booth Richard Charke played Hunter in *Hunter; or, the Beggar's Wedding*, and "Fisher-Tench" Charke danced *Dusty Miller* and *French Peasant*.

Both were members of the Drury Lane company in 1729–30. Master Tench made his first appearance on 28 April 1730, at Richard Charke's benefit, dancing between the acts. (*The London Stage* transcribes the bill as saying Tench was making his first appearance on the stage, but Latreille reported it as the first time on "this" stage—that is, Drury Lane.) "Young Master Tench" was a Follower in *The Fairy Queen* on 15 May. He seems to have dropped Charke from his name before joining the Drury Lane troupe. One wonders if that could have had anything to do with the fact that in February 1730, before young Tench danced at Drury Lane, Richard Charke married the eccentric Charlotte Cibber.

Fisher Tench remained at Drury Lane through the 1732–33 season. Also at Drury Lane, dancing and acting, was Henry Tench, surely Fisher's relative and apparently older than Fisher. The bills distinguished between the two when both were in the same cast, but often the bills simply said "Tench." We are supposing that those references are to Fisher, who clearly had the more extensive career. In 1730–31 Fisher Tench danced a Gardener and a Wind in *Cephalus and Procris*, an Infernal Spirit in *The Tempest*, Nadir in *The Devil to Pay*, and, with Miss Brett, a turn called *Bartholomew Fair*. The young pair danced at both Bartholomew and Southwark fairs in August and September.

During the rest of his stay at Drury Lane, Fisher Tench added to his pantomime parts a Triton, Mandarin Gorgon, and Peasant in *Cephalus and Procris*, a Gorgon, a Brideman, and a Follower in *Perseus and Andromeda*, a Peasant in *The Country Revels*, a Huntsman or a Countryman in *Betty*, a Frenchman in *Harlequin Restor'd*, a Shepherd in *The Judgment of Paris*, and Pierrot, a Shepherd, and a Companion of Paris in *The Harlot's Progress*. He also appeared regularly as a specialty dancer between the acts. Some of his titled pieces were *Le Chasseur royal*, *The Masques* (he was a Punch), *The Masqueraders*, *Les Bergeries*, a *Grand Dance of Moors*, a *Spanish Entry*, and *The Country Revels* (he was a Peasant). Tench returned to Bartholomew Fair on 23 August 1733 to dance with Mlle Delorme. He was at the Fielding-Hippisley booth; at the Cibber-Griffin-Bullock-Hallam booths at both fairs that fall was Henry Tench.

The London Stage notes that at Goodman's Fields Theatre on 5 May 1733 benefit tickets for Tench were taken. No person named Tench is known to have been in the troupe at that theatre; on that date Fisher Tench was advertised as dancing at Drury Lane, and two days earlier Henry Tench had performed there. Perhaps Fisher or Henry had benefit tickets out at a rival theatre, or perhaps there was a mistake in the Goodman's Fields bill.

When Theophilus Cibber rebelled against the Drury Lane management in the fall of 1733 and took a group of Drury Lane discontents to the Haymarket Theatre, Fisher Tench went along, making his first appearance on that stage in an entr'acte turn on 26 September. Henry was also in the troupe, acting small roles in plays and pantomimes. The bills at the Haymarket usually identified Fisher by his initial and called Henry simply Tench. Through January 1734 at the Haymarket, Fisher danced in such entr'acte turns as *Punches*, *The Whim*, *Les Bergeries*, *Les Amantes constants*, a *Mock Minuet*, *Les Polichinelles*, and *Les Ombres des amants fideles*. He also played Doodle in *The Opera of Operas* and was a College Youth in *An Impromptu Revel Masque*, a Swain in *The Festival* (a revision of the *Impromptu Revel Masque*), and a Peasant in *The Burgomaster Trick'd*.

The rebel players returned to Drury Lane in mid-March. Fisher was a Sailor and perhaps a Satyr in *Cupid and Psyche* and possibly a Mandarin Gormogon in *Cephalus and Procris*. He danced *Pierrots* with Davenport between the acts. The Drury Lane season ended early, and Fisher Tench danced at the Haymarket on 27 May 1734 and at Lincoln's Inn Fields two days later. He was at Bartholomew Fair at the Hippisley-Bullock-Hallam booth in August to conclude a very busy season.

Henry Tench left the London stage after the 1733–34 season—possibly because of illness, as his benefit bill of 10 July suggests—but Fisher continued until 1737–38. In 1734–35 Fisher had an engagement at Goodman's Fields Theatre, where he made his first appearance on 11 September 1734, dancing with Mrs Woodward in *La Follette c'est ravisez*. That season he was assigned such pantomime roles as a Fury and a Demon in *The Necromancer* and a Follower in *Jupiter and Io*. He was used mostly as an entr'acte dancer, two of the pieces in which he appeared being a *Scot's Dance* and a *Moors' Dance*. His pas de deux with Mrs Woodward was especially popular and was danced throughout the season.

Fisher Tench danced at Covent Garden Theatre from 1735–36 through 1737–38. He began (and perhaps ended) at 6s. 8d. daily. Among his pantomime roles were a Pierrot Man in *The Necromancer*, a Polonese Man and a Spaniard in *Apollo and Daphne*, Fire and a Demon in *The Rape of Prosperine*, Mars and a Zephyr in *The Royal Chace*, and an Infernal in *Perseus and Andromeda*. Entr'acte turns in which he appeared included *The Faithful Shepherd*, a *Scot's Dance*, Peasant, a *Dance of Sailors*, French Peasants, *Je ne scai quoi*, and a number of untitled ballets. In July and August 1737 Tench danced a few times at Lincoln's Inn Fields.

After the 1737–38 season Fisher Tench was not named in London playbills. Doubtless he was the Fisher Tench, dancing master, whose son Richard was christened on 18 April 1755 at Holy Trinity, Chester.

Tench, Henry [*fl.* 1729–1734], dancer, actor.

Henry Tench (once, in error, Fench) played a Shepherd and a Sylvan in *The Humours of Harlequin* on 25 February 1729 at the Haymarket Theatre. He was certainly related to Fisher Tench, who was also a performer in pantomimes, often performing at the same theatre; the bills did not always distinguish the two carefully. Henry appears to have been the elder Tench and the one who acted small parts in straight plays as well as dancing roles.

On 6 August 1731 at Drury Lane, Henry played Abishog in *The Devil to Pay*. Then, at Drury Lane for the 1731–32 season, he appeared as Pan in *Perseus and Andromeda* on 25 November 1731 and subsequent dates. In 1732–33 at Drury Lane, Henry Tench played the Parson in *The Tragedy of Tragedies* and then joined the Cibber-Griffith-Bullock-Hallam troupe at Bartholomew Fair in August and September to play a Masquerader and then Mezzetin in *Ridotto Al'Fresco* and Mirvan in *Tamerlane*.

At the Haymarket Theatre with Theophilus Cibber's company in the first half of the 1733–34 season, Henry Tench played Jaques in *Love Makes a Man*, a College Youth in *The Festival*

(a role that Fisher Tench also played), a Peasant in *The Burgomaster Trick'd*, Joseph in *The Mother-in-Law*, the Cook in *Chrononhotonthologos*, and a series of other small roles: Pearmain in *The Recruiting Officer*, the Poet in *The Scornful Lady*, a Neighbor in *The Alchemist*, the Bailiff in *The Opera of Operas*, and a Servant in *The Burgomaster Trick'd*. Henry then returned with Cibber's players to Drury Lane to complete the 1733–34 season, playing Punch in *The Harlot's Progress* and perhaps a Satyr in *Cupid and Psyche*, a Soldier in *The Country House*, and Richard in *The Provok'd Husband*. He was most likely the Tench who acted Feeble in *The Humours of Sir John Falstaff* at the Haymarket on 3 June 1734 and Hellebore in *The Mock Doctor* on 5 June. The advertisements said that "Mr Tench having labour'd under a violent Fit of Illness, and not being quite recover'd, humbly hopes his Friends will excuse his not waiting on them as he could wish, and favour him with their Company." He then appears to have left the stage.

Tenducci, Giusto Ferdinando *c.* 1735–1790, *singer, composer.*

Giusto Ferdinando Tenducci was born in Siena. He was therefore sometimes called "Senesino," leading to occasional confusion with the earlier and greater Sienese singer Francesco Bernardi (c. 1680–c. 1759), who went always under that designation. Tenducci's year of birth was variously reported but appears to have been in or about 1735. He underwent the operation of castration at about nine years and entered the Conservatorio at Naples shortly thereafter. Charles Baroe, an Italian grocer in Dublin, recalled in a deposition of 1775 having seen and heard Tenducci in the spring of 1750 singing in an opera at Cagliari on Sardinia, "upon the occasion of the nuptials of the son of the King of Sardinia." The singer had continued at Cagliari "about eight months" and then returned to Naples.

Tenducci sang first in Venice in Bertoni's *Ginevra* in 1753. In 1756 he sang at Naples in *Farnace*. A newspaper clipping dated 12 October 1758, in the Burney collection at the British Library, states: "Yesterday arrived [in London] from Italy two new singers, Signor Tenduci [*sic*] and Signor Quilice, with the rest of the performers engaged for the ensuing season of Operas, at the King's Theatre in the Haymarket." On 11 November the King's

The Barber Institute of Fine Arts, University of Birming-ham

GIUSTO FERDINANDO TENDUCCI
by Gainsborough

Theatre opened its season with Galuppi's *Attalo* with Gaetano Quilici in the title role and "Ferdinano [*sic*] Tenducci detto il Senesino" singing the second-man role of Idaspe. On 16 December the *pasticcio Demetrio* was first presented at the King's. No casts were given, but the bill assured patrons that "All the Songs are new of Tenducci and Quilici."

Tenducci's performance as Cambises in Cocchi's *Il Ciro riconosciuto,* which opened on 16 January 1759 and was given frequent performances for the rest of the season, brought him critical and popular acclaim. His role in the production of *Il trionfo della gloria,* 29 January and following, is not known.

Tenducci sang at the Theatre Royal, Norwich, in September 1759 and it is likely that he appeared in other provincial towns that summer and fall. On 13 November the King's company opened the season with *Vologeso,* a *pasticcio,* with Tenducci in the secondary role of Amiceto. During the season he added Annio in *La clemenza di Tito,* Sigismundo in *Arminio,* Learcho in *Antigona,* and probably a part in

Farnace, which was performed for his benefit on 3 March 1760. In addition, he sang with others in a *Charlottenburg Festegiante,* at Hickford's Great Room in Soho on 14 February; in performances (his part unknown) of *L'isola disabitata* at the Haymarket on 27 March and at Hickford's on 13 March and 29 May; and probably in the performances of the *Messiah* at the King's on 15 and 24 April 1760. On 5 June he sang for the benefit of Polly Capitani in a concert at the Haymarket.

But when Signora Mattei announced in September 1760 her roster for the new season of operas at the King's, where she was assuming the direction, Tenducci's name was absent. His name did not appear in public notices again until 28 January 1761, when Signora Calori, Mrs Storer, and various prominent instrumentalists appeared with Tenducci himself in a compassionate benefit performance arranged for him and directed by Abel. The bill stated that he had been arrested for debt and had been eight months in the King's Bench prison. Perhaps he had been released from confinement for the evening—an arrangement not unknown. In the next notice we have, that of 23 February in the *Public Advertiser* concerning Arne's oratorio *Judith,* to be sung at Drury Lane on 27 February, "we are assured . . . that Sg Tenducci has obtained permission from his Plaintiff, to sing the part which Sga Eberhardi was so obliged as to understudy for him, in case he could not obtain such indulgence." Evidently, then, he had run himself heavily into debt and had been in debtor's prison ever since July 1760. A display of fireworks and a masque at Ranelagh on 12 June 1761 were also given for Tenducci's benefit.

Tenducci did not sign on with Signora Mattei for the 1761–62 season but was said to have appeared briefly in Scotland late in 1761. He was Arbaces in Thomas Augustine Arne's new opera *Artaxerxes* at Covent Garden on 2 February and was in a performance of Handel's setting of Dryden's *Alexander's Feast* at Drury Lane on 3 March 1762. He sang two nights later at the same theatre in Arne's oratorio *The Sacrifice; or, the Death of Abel* and on 16 March was given a benefit concert at the Haymarket at which he also sang. On 3 April 1762 he sang between the acts of *The Merry Wives of Windsor* at a special benefit for Luke Sparks at Covent Garden. He sang on 18 May at Lock

Hospital Chapel, Hyde Park Corner, in a performance of sacred music for the hospital's benefit; on 22 May in an entertainment of music at Aynscombe's benefit at the Haymarket; and on 16 June in still another of his own benefits, at Ranelagh Gardens.

In the fall of 1762 Tenducci went to Covent Garden to join a rather distinguished chorus that included Beard, Polly Young, Mrs Lampe, Peretti, Mattocks, Dibdin, and other good voices. His principal contributions during the 1762–63 season were his repeated performances of Artabanes in *Artaxerxes*. On 27 April he went over to Drury Lane to sustain a vocal part in *The Cure of Saul*.

In the summer of 1762 Tenducci had begun fairly regular performances at Ranelagh, which he resumed in 1763, when he published *Six New English Songs Composed by Ferdinando Tenducci and to be Sung by him at Ranelagh Price 5s. Printed for the Author, and to be had of him at his Lodgings in the Great Piazza, Covent Garden, the Corner of James Street. . . .* It was at Ranelagh that Liddy Melford in Smollett's *Humphrey Clinker* saw and heard "a thing from Italy. It looks for all the world like a man, though they say it is not. The voice, to be sure, is neither man's nor woman's; but it is more melodious than either; and it warbled so divinely that, while I listened, I really thought myself in Paradise." But Tenducci was in financial straits again, and on 2 January 1763, he was "Excluded [from the Royal Society of Musicians] for non-payment," according to the Society's records.

At Covent Garden in 1763–64 Tenducci was again employed in choruses and again often performed Artabanes. On 29 February 1764 he once more contributed to the charity benefit at Lock Hospital by singing a part in the oratorio *Judith*. He was featured in some part in the oratorio *Pellegrini* at Spilsbury's benefit at the King's on 6 April. He figured in one more performance of *Artaxerxes* in November 1764 and then went back to the King's to assume Valentiniano in *Ezio,* a new opera, on 24 November. On 26 January 1765 he sang the title role in the first performance of Johann Christian Bach's *Adriano in Syria*. On 15 February he had a part in the oratorio *Judith* and on 28 March, for his benefit, sang Alessandro in *Antigono*. The Mozarts had come to London in April 1764, and Tenducci became intimate with them, especially with the eight-year-old prodigy, who wrote for him a special aria.

In the summer of 1765 Tenducci adventured to Ireland, where he was to have some of his greatest successes and most bizarre and devastating experiences. His first appearance in Dublin was at Mossop's Smock Alley Theatre in July. His roles during 1765–66 are unknown. But on 3 July 1766 his singing of the aria "Water parted from the sea" in *Artaxerxes* was acclaimed. He was lionized by Dublin society.

A few weeks after Tenducci's triumph he was invited by Thomas Maunsell, Esq., a well-known counsellor-at-law, to his house in Molesworth Street to give singing lessons to his 16-year-old daughter Dorothea. She immediately became infatuated with the handsome stranger. On 19 August 1766 they were secretly married by the Rev Patrick Egan, a Roman Catholic priest. Shortly thereafter, while Dorothea was visiting her sister in Tipperary, Tenducci contrived one night to carry her off. (He had chosen to break his 1765–66 engagement with Rich at Covent Garden rather than leave Dorothea.) In May 1766 Tenducci had contracted with Spranger Barry to sing at Cork in the summer of 1766 and at Crow Street Theatre Dublin in the winter of 1766–67. On 11 July 1767 Tenducci announced in the *Public Advertiser* that he had "renounced the Errors of Popery." Both at Cork and at Dublin Maunsell used his influence to persecute Tenducci, according to a pamphlet, *A True and Genuine Narrative of Mr. and Mrs. Tenducci in a Letter to a Friend at Bath.* It was signed "D[orothea] Tenducci From the place of our Retreat, August the 26th, 1767." The pamphlet is of uncertain authorship, despite the subscription. It alleges complicity between Maunsell, other relatives, and the magistrates in attempts to force the couple apart. Their bedchamber was invaded at midnight, her chairmen were assaulted and wounded, and belongings and papers were rifled. Dorothea was threatened with confinement for life in a mad house. Tenducci was twice imprisoned and released only after a physician swore he was near death. Maunsell repeatedly tried to interrupt public performances.

In mid-July 1767, after somehow obtaining a license from the Consistory Court of the Bishop of Waterford and Lismore, the couple

GIUSTO FERDINANDO TENDUCCI
engraving by Bastin, after Bruscett

was married again, according to the rites of the Church of Ireland, by the Rev William Hobbs at the parish church of Shanrahan, Tipperary. In October they returned to Dublin, taking lodgings in November first at Porto Bello and then removing (probably because of harassment) after a few days to a house in Dame Street, Dublin. During the 1767–68 season Tenducci sang in concert and gave music lessons at his house. Evidently public sentiment had swung in his favor, for his benefit recital of 2 March 1768 at Fishamble Street Music Hall was reportedly a great success.

By 27 May 1768, perhaps earlier, the Tenduccis had gone to Scotland, according to records of the Edinburgh Musical Society concerts now in the library of the University of Edinburgh. From that date until 11 November 1769 Tenducci sang in concert at least 45 times. Norma Armstrong's manuscript calendar credits him, in addition, with five opera performances at the New Concert Hall: three as Amintas in *The Royal Shepherd* and two as Arbaces in *Artaxerxes*.

Dorothea evidently began her own brief professional career at Edinburgh. On 9 September and 11 November she sang duets with her husband. And when Tenducci departed for London to take up singing engagements, she

remained in Edinburgh, singing in at least 10 additional vocal performances through 26 January 1770.

Tenducci's activities for some time after he left Edinburgh are dimly known. He evidently was relegated principally to the chorus at Covent Garden. When he sang the title role in *Amintas* there on 15 December 1769, he was erroneously billed as making his first appearance at that theatre. And when, on 2 February, Guadagni declined to sing in the benefit performance for the Royal Society of Musicians at the King's, Tenducci was "so obliging" as "to favour the Society." When he sang Arbaces to Mrs Mattocks's Mandane in *Artaxerxes* on 7 April 1770, he was said to be singing the part for the first time in four years. He had a part unknown in *Gioas re di Guida* at the King's, appeared in a concert of catches and glees, and traveled to York to appear in the oratorios, all in March 1770. When he assumed Amintas again at the Haymarket on 3 May, Thamitis was sung by a "young lady, scholar of Tenducci, her first appearance." She was certainly Dorothea Maunsell Tenducci, and that seems to have been her sole recorded performance in London.

From there, the Tenduccis' odd odyssey can be followed with fair accuracy by means of depositions taken in the action of annulment, though the recollections of the deponents stretched back a quarter of a century. We know from the opera bills of the King's and Haymarket theatres that Tenducci sang in London at least through mid-March 1771, and Thomas Maunsell's deposition recalled that his daughter and Tenducci left London "in or about the month of March, 1771." (Tenducci's contributions to the season of 1770–71 at the King's are not known in detail. But Burney wrote that "in the few serious operas that were performed TENDUCCI was the immediate successor of [Gaetano] Guadagni. This performer, who came here first . . . only as a singer of the second or third class, was now so much improved, during his residence in Scotland and Ireland, as not only to be well received as the first man on our stage, but, afterwards, in all the great theatres of Italy.") So Charles Baroe's positive recollections of the Tenducci's movements in Europe must be adjusted by one year. Baroe remembered that he had seen the pair in August 1770 (i.e., 1771), "the said Tenducci, being then engaged there as a singer at the Opera House, and the said Miss Maunsell being then resident with . . . Tenducci's mother and sister" at their house in Florence. The following December Tenducci left his wife in his relatives' care while he went to Rome to sing during *carnevale*. In March (1772) Tenducci returned to Florence and about April or May left for Venice to sing for the Festival of Ascension, returning in June.

Tenducci, the account continues, sang a summer season in Siena (in 1772) and then returned to Florence, where he "Sang for the English gentlemen in the autumn." But when the singer went again to Rome in November, leaving his wife behind, she "went in a post-chaise, with a woman-servant, and escorted by a servant-man of Mr. Kingsman's, from Florence to Naples." Baroe affirmed that Tenducci had never during their Italian sojourn acknowledged Dorothea as his wife, because of the severe Italian statutes against a eunuch's marrying, but "passed the said Miss Maunsell as an English young lady, put under his tuition as a scholar. . . ." Thomas Maunsell's deposition stated that he had received a letter from Dorothea posted from Naples about February 1773, repenting of her flight with Tenducci, asking forgiveness, and desiring to return to Ireland. Maunsell sent her £200, and she came home.

Evidently Dorothea had met William Long Kingsman during one of her husband's absences and it was to his protection at Naples that she fled. He was one of the parties in the suit for an annulment, which was granted in July 1775. In the official transcript she is called "Dorothea Kingsman, wife of William Long Kingsman, Esq. of the parish of St. James, Westminster." Tenducci was located in "the parish of St. Martin in the Fields."

Casanova later told a story (as incredible as many another among the great lover's collection) that at Covent Garden

the castrato Tenducci surprised me greatly by presenting me to his legitimate wife, by whom he had two children. He laughed at those who argued that, as he was a castrato, he could not reproduce his kind. Nature had made him a monster to keep him a man: he was a *Triorchis*, and as in the operation only two of his seminal glands had been removed, that which remained was sufficient to prove his vitality.

But the annulment was granted "by reason of impotency," after testimony by divers friends of Tenducci which included physical details precisely clinical, and there was no mention of children. Further, Casanova was in London in 1763–64, not afterward, and Tenducci did not meet Dorothea Maunsell until 1766.

An unidentified newsclipping dated 5 February 1776 also included a curious admiring-condemnatory review:

Signor TENDUCCI, who was formerly so great a favourite with the Town as a singer, was last night, after an absense of several years, introduced to his old friends by the Managers of Drury-Lane Theatre in The Maid of the Oaks. The new Opera of Orpheus not being ready for exhibition, and Mr. Tenducci being engaged at Covent-Garden for the Oratorios, the Managers of Drury House wisely determined that their engagement with him should not be damped by his first singing in the other Theatre, they therefore introduced him in a drama which, like the wire that runs across the stage at a puppet-show, seems peculiarly calculated to hold new figures as time and occasion may require. The audience, for the most part, received Mr. Tenducci with their wonted kindness and generosity, some John Bulls aloft disliked his singing so much *more Italiano,* and therefore hissed heartily. We honestly confess we felt a little like *Jack Roast Beef* upon the occasion; the Managers certainly deserve thanks for engaging Tenducci, because they evidently have incurred a large additional expence, in hopes of additionally pleasing the town; Mr. Tenducci, as a singer, and a singer of uncommon merit, is also undoubtedly entitled to candour and applause; but we do not not admire the idea of making Drury-lane Theatre similar, we might add superior, to the Opera House, even on its own plan. We hope next season to find the flare of tinsel dresses, the legions of foreign dancers, and the auxiliary force of foreign singers, banished from Bridges-street to the Hay Market. The latter is the proper field for empty sound and ridiculous pageantry. Let our Theatres be more nobly employed in instructing the mind, and at once pleasing and amending the heart, with the sterling sense of Shakespear, Johnson, Row, Otway, Savage and other manly dramatists.

Tenducci was hired by Sheridan at Drury Lane in 1776–77 and 1777–78 at a salary of £500 plus a benefit. He sang in chorus and solo and was a notable Second Spirit in 16 performances of *Comus* there in 1777–78. He also sang at least twice in *Judas Maccabaeus* at Covent Garden and twice presented miscella-

GIUSTO FERDINANDO TENDUCCI

engraving by Dickinson, after Beach

neous concerts at that theatre. During the concert season, January to May 1778, Tenducci was also a leading singer in the series presented by Johann Christina Bach and Carl Friedrich Abel at the Hanover Square Rooms.

In August 1778 Mozart wrote to his father from St Germain, speaking of the arrival in Paris of Bach and Tenducci and explaining that he wrote in haste because he had to compose, in three days, a *scena* for Tenducci to be performed by the orchestra of the Maréchal de Noailles at his palace in St Germain.

News of Tenducci after about 1779 is sketchy indeed, though we know that he was soloist at the Oxford Music Room in 1781. He was on the roster at Smock Alley, Dublin, in 1782–83 and 1783–84. He returned to London to direct the Handel festivals in Westminster Abbey and the Pantheon in May and June 1784. He continued to teach. The anonymous author of the *Memoirs of Mrs Billington* heard him sing Arbaces in Dublin in 1784. He made his last appearances in May and June 1785 at the King's Theatre, singing the title role in a

revival of Gluck's *Orfeo*. Lord Mount Edgcumbe found it the "performance of an old man, who had never been very capital."

When he was given a benefit at the King's Theatre on 19 May 1785 he was living at No 63, Dean Street, Soho. He sang at a concert conducted by Cramer and Raimondi at the Tottenham Street Music Room on 23 February 1786.

Tenducci composed *Six New English Songs . . . to be Sung by Him at Ranelagh*, 1763; *A Collection of New French Songs, with a Thorough Bass for the Harpsicord* (1770?); *Instruction by Mr Tenducci to his Scholars* (1785?); and several separate songs. Many songs by other composers, "as sung by" Tenducci at Bath, at the Pantheon, at Ranelagh, and in operas, were published. He selected music for the opera *The Revenge of Attridates*, produced at Smock Alley, Dublin, in 1765. Tenducci altered Richard Rolt's *The Royal Shepherd* to the opera *Amintas*, which was produced at Covent Garden in 1769. He composed music for Henry Lucas's comic opera *The Triumph of Vanity*, produced at Crow Street Theatre, Dublin, in 1772, and for Jephson's comic opera *The Campaign* (1784).

The *Scots Magazine* for March 1790 reported that "Tenducci, the celebrated singer," had died "lately at Genoa. . . . In paying the debt to nature, he has discharged other demands to a large amount," meaning perhaps that he died in debt.

Portraits of Tenducci include:

1. By Thomas Beach, 1782, exhibited at the Society of Artists, 1783, as "A Gentleman." The *Connoisseur* of July 1913 reported it to be in the collection of Lord Hylton, Radstock, Somerset. An engraving by W. Dickinson was published in 1782. Another version, attributed to Gainsborough Dupont, is in the Garrick Club (No 411) and shows the sitter's wig and dress altered and the hat removed. The latter picture was in the Harris sale at Robins on 12 July 1819 (lot 2), as by Gainsborough, and came to the Garrick Club in the Mathews collection; an anonymous engraving, in reverse, was published by Longman & Broderip.

2. By J. Bruscett. Seated behind a table, his left hand holding a copy of the music of "Water parted from the sea." Location unknown. An engraving by J. Finlayson, titled "Mr. Tenducci." was published by T. Bowen, 1770; two

other impressions of the same plate were issued, one with title altered to "Justus Ferdinand Tenducci," and the other reworked, with wig altered and star added on breast. An engraving by T. Bastin is also in the British Museum.

3. By Thomas Gainsborough. Oil on canvas, 30¼" × 25¼". Previously in the collections of Samuel Archbutt and John Neeld; in the Sir Audley Neeld sale at Christie's on 9 June 1944 (lot 7), bought by the Barber Institute of Fine Arts, University of Birmingham.

4. By Thomas Gainsborough. Oil on canvas, 26½" × 24½". Owned by the great tenor, John Braham, and sold from his collection of paintings at Grange Villa, Brompton, on 8 June 1842, George Lewis auctioneer. At Christie's: in the Hogarth sale on 24 May 1867 (lot 110), bought in; in the John Heugh sale on 24 April 1874 (lot 163), bought by Agnew; in the A. Levy sale on 6 April 1876 (lot 291), bought by Gray Hill. Present location unknown.

5. By John Nixon. Drawing, in the Gerald Coke Handel Collection, Bentley, Hants.

6. By unknown engraver. Oval, facing front, in chair, holding music. Titled "Instruction of Mr. Tenducci, to his Scholars." Published by Longman & Broderip (n.d.). In the Huntington Library, extra-illustrated copy of *The Tavern Hunter,* volume 3, plate 89.

7. An engraving after a design by A. Fedi, published between 1801 and 1807, shows Tenducci in a large group of singers.

Tenducci, Signora Giusto Ferdinando, Dorothea, née Maunsell, later Mrs William Long Kingsman *b. c.1750, singer, actress.* See TENDUCCI, GIUSTO FERDINANDO.

Tenell, Mr [*fl.1799–1802*], *house servant.*

A Mr Tenell was cited three times in the Drury Lane accounts between 12 October 1799, when he was paid £1 13s. 4d., through 1801–2, when his weekly salary was given as 11s. 1d. The salary indicates that Tenell was probably a house servant. Mrs Tenell, though she seems not to have been active before the end of the eighteenth century, was paid £3 10s. by the Drury Lane management on 17 June 1801 for 21 days' work.

Tennant, Miss, later Mrs Thomas Vaughan [*fl.1797?–1822*], *singer.*

Miss Tennant may have sung in the oratorios in 1797, as some notices of her husband state, but her name first appeared in the advertisements for oratorios at Covent Garden Theatre on 28 February 1800, when she sang Handel's "Awful pleasing being" from *Joshua.* On 5 March she joined others in singing "Like a bright cherub." In the remaining oratorios that month she and Master Elliot offered "My faith and truth" from *Samson* on the fourteenth, and she sang "Tune your Harps" from *Esther* on the nineteenth, and, again with Master Elliot, "My faith and truth" on the twenty-first.

In his *Dramatic Censor* (1800), Thomas Dutton reported that Miss Tennant had promised Thomas Busby, the composer, to sing a major part in his *Britannia,* a new "Commemorative Oratorio" that was performed at Covent Garden on 16 June 1800 for the benefit of the Humane Society, but she was prevented by "the sordid mercenary disposition of a certain person (whose name, from a regard to the family, we forbear to mention)." Consequently Miss Holland sang in her place. Dutton had written the concluding stanzas for Part I of the oratorio. His forbearance results in a kept secret, but the person who prohibited her appearance was no doubt her singing master. She was, then, probably still young enough to be a musical apprentice.

Also in 1800 Miss Tennant was engaged at the Concert of Ancient Music, and on 21 June of that year she sang in a "Choral Evening" at the Oxford Musical Society. Soon she became popular in concert circles and in provincial festivals. On 25 February 1805 Miss Tennant sang in the Concert Room of the King's Theatre.

In 1806 she married the vocalist Thomas Vaughan (1782–1843) and thereafter became well known as Mrs Vaughan, singing at the Oxford Music Room and the Festivals of the Three Choirs. They separated after about 12 years. In a manuscript journal (now in the Folger Shakespeare Library) kept by Edmund Simpson, stage manager at the Park Street Theatre in New York, during his visit to London to recruit talent, is a notation in June 1818 that Mrs Vaughan had run away after a concert with "a young Roscius" and had left six children behind her. She then began to call herself

Mrs Tennant. Her name was on the Drury Lane company paylist in 1821–22 for £6 per week.

Her husband Thomas Vaughan, a tenor, was a chorister at Norwich Cathedral and in June 1799 was elected lay-clerk of St George's Chapel, Windsor. Subsequently he became a Gentleman of the Chapel Royal and was appointed vicar-choral of St Paul's and lay-vicar of Westminster Abbey. He succeeded Samuel Harrison as principal tenor in the Concert of Ancient Music, a position he held for more than 25 years. He died on 9 January 1843 and was buried in the West Cloister of Westminster Abbey.

When Thomas Vaughan made his will on 16 July 1828, he did not mention his estranged wife. He left his estate to six minor children, no doubt by the former Miss Tennant, all born between 1807 and about 1817: Elizabeth Sarah, Anne, Thomas Charles, Edward William, John Stephen, and James. The will was proved in London on 23 February 1843, by William Knyvett, one of the executors.

Teno, Mr ₍fl. 1743₎, *house servant.*

A players' petition in the Lord Chamberlain's accounts (LC5/204) dated September 1743 lists a house servant at Drury Lane Theatre named Teno or Jeno. His daily salary was 1s. 6d. The management owed him £8.

Tenoe, Mr ₍fl. 1729–1734₎, *singer, actor, dancer?*

On 24 June 1729 at Drury Lane Mr Tenoe and Rainton sang "A Dialogue between a Rake and a Widow" with Tenoe apparently taking the skirts part. We believe that this Tenoe was not the singer of earlier years, though he was probably related, perhaps a son. Our subject appeared next on 28 October 1730 at Drury Lane, as a Forester and a Triton in *Cephalus and Procris. The London Stage* lists him as a dancer that season because of his characters in pantomimes, though Tenoe may have taken only singing parts. During the rest of the 1730–31 season he was an Infernal Spirit in *The Tempest* and continued appearing in *Cephalus and Procris.* At Bartholomew and Southwark fairs in August and September he was the King and Plausey in *The Banish'd General.* He was not noticed in the Drury Lane bills in 1731–32

but may have played bit parts; in August 1732 he was Northumberland in *Henry VIII.*

Tenoe was supposed to be one of the Priests in *Venus, Cupid and Hymen* at Drury Lane in May 1733, and at Bartholomew Fair that year he acted Forgewell in *Jane Shore.* He joined Theophilus Cibber's rebel players at the Haymarket Theatre for the first part of the 1733–34 season, playing Bull in *The Relapse* and a Neighbor in *The Alchemist.* He seems not to have returned to Drury Lane. On 4 November 1734 at the Great Room at the Ship Tavern, Tenoe played Dervise in *Tamerlane* and then disappeared from London playbills.

Tenoe, Miss ₍fl. 1740₎, *performer?*

On 28 May 1740 the benefit tickets of a Miss Tenoe were accepted at Drury Lane Theatre. She may have been a minor performer.

Tenoe, ₍**Stephen?**₎ ₍fl. 1706?–1739?₎, *singer, composer?*

Perhaps the Mr Tenoe who sang in London in the early eighteenth century was the father of Mary "Tinoy," a "Musician's Child," who was buried at St Clement Danes on 23 January 1706. The earliest notice of Tenoe the singer came on 12 November 1707, when he held a concert at Stationers' Hall. He shared a benefit concert with Beeston on 26 July 1708 at the Bowling Green, Epsom, according to the notes of Emmett L. Avery, and he sang in 1709 at concerts at Hampstead Wells, Stationers' Hall, and York Buildings. The girl of nine, his pupil, who sang at the Great Room at Hampstead Wells on 22 July 1710, may have been Theodosia Tenoe, his daughter. Theodosia performed regularly from 1717 onward and married the actor William Mills.

In 1711 Tenoe had a benefit concert at Stationers' Hall in March, sang at Richmond Wells in July, and was at Pinkethman's theatre in Greenwich in September. After a period during which he received no notices, Tenoe had a benefit concert at Stationers' Hall on 6 April 1715. From May through August he sang at Drury Lane Theatre. He held another benefit at Stationers' Hall in March 1716 and was advertised as singing at Drury Lane on 14 May 1719. It seems very likely that he was the "S. Teno" who set two songs, the lyrics of which were published in *Wit and Mirth* in 1719, "Three Glorious Things" and "Cupid no

Physician." Perhaps he was Stephen Tenoe, who became one of the original subscribers to the Royal Society of Musicians in August 1739.

Tent. *See* KENT *and* TYNTE.

Teresia, Maria, called "The Corsican Fairy" *1743–c. 1790, dwarf.*

Morley in his *Memoirs of Bartholomew Fair* quotes a typical puff for Madame Teresia, probably dating about 1770:

There is to be seen in a commodious Apartment, at the corner of Cow-Lane, facing the Sheep-Pens, West Smithfield, During the short time of Bartholomew Fair,

MARIA TERESIA

the Amazing CORSICAN FAIRY, who has had the Honour of being shown three Times before their Majesties.

☞She was exhibited in Cockspur-Street, Haymarket, at two-shillings and sixpence each person; but that Persons of every Degree may have a Sight

of so extraordinary a Curiosity, she will be shown to the Gentry at sixpence each, and to Working People, Servants, and Children, at Three-pence, during this Fair.

This most astonishing Part of the Human Species was born in the Island of Corsica, on the Mountain of Stata Ota, in the year 1743. She is only thirty-four Inches high, weighs but twenty-six Pounds, and a child of two Years of Age has larger Hands and Feet. Her surprising Littleness makes a strong Impression at first Sight on the Spectator's Mind. Nothing disagreeable, either in Person or Conversation, is to be found in her; although most of Nature's productions, in Miniature, are generally so in both. Her Form affords a pleasing Surprise, her Limbs are exceedingly well proportioned, her admirable Symmetry engages the attention; and, upon the whole, is acknowledged a perfect Beauty. She is possessed of a great deal of Vivacity of Spirit; can speak Italian and French, and gives the inquisitive Mind an agreeable Entertainment. In short, she is the most extraordinary Curiosity ever known, or ever heard of in History; and the Curious, in all countries where she has been shown, pronounce her to be the finest Display of Human Nature, in Miniature, they ever saw.

⁑She is to be seen, by any Number of Persons, from Ten in the Morning till Nine at Night.

The exhibitor Zucker showed her in Exeter Exchange in the Strand in 1770. He boasted that she danced a minuet and other turns "with the utmost Ease and Elegance," and stated that she was available for private meetings in the homes of the nobility and gentry.

She was exhibited at the Fourteen Stars, near the Cross in Temple Street, Bristol, in March 1773 and rode Philip Astley's horse and danced a Corsican jig in Dublin on 8 April 1774. In 1775–76 she played Columbine in *Harlequin from the Moon* at the Theatre Royal in Shakespeare Square, Edinburgh.

According to Le Fanu's *Royal College of Surgeons,* Maria Teresia died in Norwich about 1790, in labor. There is an account of her by Philip Martineau of Norwich among the Hunterian manuscripts at the Royal College of Surgeons.

A portrait of Maria Teresia by William Hincks, singed "Hincks Dublin 1774," is in the Hunterian Museum, Royal College of Surgeons. An engraved portrait of her by R. Cooper shows her standing full-length, with a fan in her hand, and a woman of ordinary height standing in back of her. That engraving was published by J. Robins & Co, 1821.

Reproduced by kind permission of the President and Council of the Royal College of Surgeons of England

MARIA TERESIA

by Hincks

MARIA TERESIA
by T. Worlidge

Thomas Worlidge's engraving of her, standing in a large hoop and holding a fan, with the sketch of a woman of ordinary height behind her, was published in 1769.

Térodat, Mons [fl. 1740–1752], *actor.*
Monsieur Térodat, whose name also appeared as Cadoret, Kérodack, Kérodat, Térodack, Térodak, Théroday, and Thérodax, made his debut at the Comédie Italienne in Paris on 3 September 1740, according to Fuch's *Lexique.* He performed in Strasbourg in 1745 and came to London in Monnet's troupe in 1749, appearing at the Haymarket Theatre on 14 November in *Les Amans réunis.* The company met with much anti-Gallic sentiment, and Drury Lane Theatre on 22 May 1750 gave the manager a benefit to help recoup his losses. Térodat had contracted for a salary of £52 10s.

but had been paid only £39 2s. Térodat performed in Strasbourg again in 1752 and in Vienna after 1752.

Terravese. *See* FERRARESE.

Terrier or **Terriot.** *See* TARIOT.

Terry, George [fl. 1749–1763], *violoncellist.*
The Lord Chamberlain's accounts in the Public Record Office name George Terry as a member of the King's Musick as early as 1749 at an annual salary of £40 and livery. He lived in Denmark Street, Soho, and about 1760 published and sold *Six Trios for two German Flutes or two Violins with a Thorough Bass for the Harpsichord,* composed by Androux. *Mortimer's London Directory* of 1763 named Terry as a violoncellist in the royal musical establishment.

Tersi, Alexander [fl. 1770–1780], *musician, street entertainer.*
Alexander Tersi was the father of Maria Theresa Catherine Tersi, later Mrs George Bland. Tersi was a strolling musician from Rome; his wife Catherine Zeli was a Jew from the parish of St Paul's, Florence. According to Winston's notes at the Folger Shakespeare Library, on 10 April 1773 Maria Theresa and her father were in England, appearing at Bristow. Tersi may have been responsible for the fantoccini performance in Piccadilly on 24 May 1780, which was held for his daughter's benefit.

Tersi, Maria Theresa. *See* BLAND, MRS GEORGE.

Terwin, Mr [fl. 1734–1740], *puppeteer.*
The puppeteer Terwin was active at Southwark Fair in 1734, according to Speaight's *History of the English Puppet Theatre.* On 23 August 1740 at Bartholomew Fair, Terwin, Fawkes, and Pinchbeck offered *Britons Strike Home,* "by Punch's Celebrated Company of Comedians, formerly Mrs Charke's."

Tessarini, Carlo *c. 1690–c. 1767, violinist, composer.*
The *New Grove Dictionary of Music and Musicians* states that Carlo Tessarini was born in Rimini about 1690 and by 15 December 1720

Civica Raccolta Stampe A. Bertarelli, Castello Sfor-zesco, Milan

CARLO TESSARINI

artist unknown

was a violinist at St Mark's in Venice. He later was a violinist at SS Giovanni e Paolo in the same city. From about 1733 he probably worked at Urbino Cathedral. He eventually went into the service of Cardinal Wolfgang Habbibal at Brno, in what is now Czechoslo-vakia. In 1739 he went on concert tours, and in 1740 and 1742 he visited Rome. In 1743 he called himself "*direttore perpetuo*" of the Ac-cademia degli Anarconti of Fano, near Urbino. Tessarini may have lived in Paris, and he cer-tainly gave concerts in the Netherlands in 1747.

Grove does not record Tessarini as perform-ing in London, but a clipping at the Garrick Club, apparently belonging to 22 April 1748, advertises a concert at Hickford's Music Room at which Tessarini played first violin.

He was in Urbino Cathedral again from 1750 to 1757, though he was frequently away on concert tours. In 1761 he was in Arnheim,

and it is likely that he lived in Holland the rest of his life. Gerber says that in 1762, when Tessarini performed in Amsterdam, he was still vigorous. His final appearance was in Arnheim on 15 December 1766. He died about 1767. The *Catalogue of Printed Music in the British Museum* lists a number of Tessarini's composi-tions, several of which were published in Lon-don.

The catalogue of the Civiche Raccolta D'Arte Applicata ed Incisione states that Tes-sarini died in Amsterdam about 1765. A por-trait of him by an unknown engraver is in that collection. The catalogue's date for Tessarini's death is clearly incorrect; he must have died sometime after his last appearance on 15 De-cember 1766.

Tessier. *See* LE TEXIER.

Tetherington, Mrs. *See* COLLET, CATHERINE.

Tetley, Master [*fl. 1761*], *dancer.*
At the Haymarket Theatre on 23 June 1761 Master Tetley danced, along with his sister Elizabeth, Miss Twist, Master Rogier, Miss Buckinger and Miss Street, in three exercises: *Les Chasseures et les bergères, The German Coopers,* and *The Gardeners.* They repeated the dances on 31 July and 3 August. Though Miss Tetley went on dancing for some years, Master Tetley was not seen again in London.

Tetley, Elizabeth, later Mrs George Gar-rick the second *d. 1822, dancer.*
Elizabeth Tetley first appeared profession-ally at the Haymarket Theatre on 23 June 1761, along with her brother Master Tetley, Master "Rogers" (Rogier), Miss Buckingham, Miss Twist, and Miss Street. All were juvenile dancers and were executing dances devised by Jean-Baptiste Gherardi: *Les Chasseurs et les ber-gères, The German Coopers,* and *The Gardeners.* Elizabeth danced again on 27 June, 30 July, and 3 August.

She was first seen (Miss "Tatley") at Drury Lane Theatre as one of several Bride's Maids in *The Witches; or Harlequin Cherokee* on 23 No-vember 1762, which was repeated many times that season. By the spring of 1764 she had transferred her services to the King's Theatre, where on 10 March she danced a "new *Terzetto*" with Duvall and Berardi. That trio presented evolutions called *The Turkish Coffee House* on 20 March. On 31 March both Miss Tetley and Duvall were harlequins in *Le Masquerade,* and on 5 May Miss Tetley was in "a new dance" along with Fischar, Berardi, and Miss Auretti.

Elizabeth Tetley was again at Drury Lane in the late spring of 1765, on 16 April dancing (for "the first time") a hornpipe. On 23 April she essayed a "Double Hornpipe" with Walker and repeated it half a dozen times thereafter. She was paid £1 per week that season. Again, she appeared a few times only so far as the bills show, at Drury Lane in 1765–66, 1766–67 (when she was paid £1 10s. per week) and 1767–68. But dances were not always listed. She was noticed only a few times in the next few seasons, and after 1769–70 not at all.

The date on which she became the second wife of George Garrick, Drury Lane factotum and brother of the great actor-manager, is not known. The first Mrs Garrick had died in 1758. But the *Morning Post* of 5 February 1779 assured its readers that George Garrick and Miss Tetley had been "privately married" and, by then, had two children. Apparently only one child, George, born in June 1775, survived. The wording of the elder George Garrick's will of 30 January 1779, just four days before his death, is strangely inexplicit: "Whereas my children by my first marriage are all amply provided for now in order to make provision for my present wife Elizabeth and my issue by her" £10,000 in trust was provided. Little and Kahrl, in *The Letters of David Garrick,* give 1822 as the year of the death of Elizabeth Tetley Garrick.

Tetlow, John [fl. 1717–1739], violinist.

John Tetlow was a valet-violinist at Cannons in the employ of the Duke of Chandos about 1717–1720. In 1736, according to the Bakers' biography of Chandos, the Duke recommended Tetlow for a place in the King's Musick, saying that there were few "who are not profest masters who perform better than he doth on the violin." The Lord Chamberlain's accounts, however, give no indication that Tetlow was given a position as a court musician. The Cannons accounts at the Huntington Library show a payment to Tetlow of £11 9s. 8d. on 1 October 1739.

Tett, Mr [fl. 1784], singer.

A Mr Tett sang tenor in the Handel Memorial Concerts at Westminster Abbey and the Pantheon in May and June 1784. Perhaps he was Benjamin Tett, but Doane's *Musical Directory* of 1794 described Benjamin as a bass.

Tett, Benjamin d. 1807, singer.

Benjamin Tett was possibly the brother of Joseph Tett, also a singer. Both were said by Doane in his *Musical Directory* of 1794 to be basses, though Dr Burney in his list of performers in the Handel Memorial Concerts in May and June 1784 listed J. Tett as a tenor and a Mr Tett (yet another relative?) also as a tenor. *The London Stage* treats all calendar references to a singer named Tett as being to Benjamin, but Doane makes it clear that the singer who worked at Covent Garden Theatre was Joseph and the one at Drury Lane was Benjamin. Indeed, each was often performing at his respective theatre on the same nights.

The earliest mention of Benjamin Tett in the Drury Lane bills was on 23 May 1792, when he sang in the chorus of *Dido Queen of Carthage* at the King's Theatre—the company's temporary home. He was not mentioned in 1792–93 and rarely in 1793–94, but he sang in *The Pirates* in May 1794. His assignments were invariably minor throughout his career; he sang in the choruses of *The Cherokee, Richard Coeur de Lion, The Honeymoon, The Prisoner, Blue-Beard, The Captive of Spilburg, Feudal Times, Lodoiska, The Surrender of Calais, The Iron Chest, Theodosius, Aurelio and Miranda, Pizarro, The Tempest,* and *De Montfort.* Tett was still singing at Drury Lane in 1800.

Doane noted that Benjamin Tett was also active in the Portland Chapel Society, the Oxford Meeting in 1793, and oratorio performances. He was living in 1794 at No 2, Portsmouth Street, Clare Market. The *Gentleman's Magazine* reported his death as 4 February 1807.

Tett, Joseph [fl. 1784?–1815], singer.

The J. Tett who sang in the Handel Memorial concerts at Westminster Abbey and the Pantheon in May and June 1784 was presumably Joseph Tett, but while Burney identified J. Tett as a tenor, in 1794 Doane in his *Musical Directory* described Joseph as a bass. *The London*

Stage conflates the performing careers of Joseph and Benjamin Tett and creates further confusion. Doane specified that Benjamin worked at Drury Lane Theatre while Joseph was employed at Covent Garden. Joseph, in addition, subscribed to the New Musical Fund and sang in the Covent Garden oratorios. He lived at No 29, Princes Street, Soho.

His earliest notice in the Covent Garden bills was on 20 October 1791, when he sang in the chorus of *Oscar and Malvina*. Like Benjamin, who was perhaps his brother, he confined his activities at the theatre to choruses and over the years sang in *Harlequin's Chaplet, The Ward of the Castle, He Wou'd Be a Soldier, Romeo and Juliet, Macbeth, Harlequin and Oberon, The Village Fête, Alexander the Great, Joanna, Orpheus and Eurydice, The Midnight Wanderers, Nina, Merry Sherwood, Bantry Bay, The Genoese Pirate, Ramah Droog, The Magic Oak, The Old Cloathsman,* and *The Volcano.* As of 1801–2 Tett was being paid £1 10s. weekly for his services; by 1811–12 he was down to £1 5s. He was last mentioned in the theatre accounts in the 1814–15 season and, coincidentally, he was last named in a New Musical Fund program in 1815.

There were other musical Tetts in addition to Benjamin and Joseph. One, whose Christian name is not known, worked at Covent Garden from 1811 to 1815; another, C. Tett, worked there in 1813–14 and 1814–15. Samuel Tett was named in the New Musical Fund program of 1815.

Teuve, Stephen ₍*fl.* 1739₎, *musician.*
On 28 August 1739 Stephen Teuve became one of the original subscribers to the Royal Society of Musicians.

Texier. *See* LE TEXIER.

Teyfer. *See* TYFER.

Thackeray, Mr ₍*fl.* 1783–1816₎, *barber.*
Mr Thackeray (or Thackray, Thackery) was a hairdresser at the King's Theatre from as early as 1783. He worked as a hairdresser at the Haymarket Theatre in 1793 and probably for a number of years thereafter, for he was named in the accounts as a barber in the summer of 1804 and again in 1815. His salary on the latter date was £1 10s., presumably per

week. He was last named in the Haymarket accounts in 1816.

Thackeray, Thomas ₍*fl.* 1770–1793₎, *violinist, violoncellist, guitarist, composer.*
Thomas Thackeray (or Tackray, Thackray) played violoncello in the band at the York Theatre in 1770. He performed at Marylebone Gardens in London in 1776. By 1779 Thackeray had become a musician in ordinary to the King in London and may have been in debt, for in the Lord Chamberlain's accounts is a power of attorney he gave to Thomas Gibbon of Downing Street, giving him permission to draw his salary. In May and June 1784 Thackeray played first violin in the Handel Memorial Concerts at Westminster Abbey and the Pantheon. The last record we have of him dates from 1793, when he was still listed in the Lord Chamberlain's accounts as a member of the King's Musick. Thackeray published a number of works for guitar, his first volume dating about 1770.

"Thalia." *See* ABINGTON, MRS JAMES.

Thatcher, John ₍*fl.* 1678–1683₎, *singer.*
John Thatcher was one of the children of the Chapel Royal who journeyed with the King to Windsor from 14 August to 26 September 1678. By 1682 his voice had broken and he had left the royal service. The last mention of him in the Lord Chamberlain's accounts is a note dated 26 October 1683 granting money for clothing for him.

Thebbett, Mr ₍*fl.* 1793–1800₎, *violinist.*
A member of the Royal Society of Musicians, Mr Thebbett was named in 1793 and 1794 to play violin in the annual benefit concert at St Paul's Cathedral. On 5 January 1800 he declined the office of governor in the Society, was fined, and was replaced by Joseph Woodham.

Théodore, Mlle. *See* D'AUBERVAL, MME JEAN.

Theresa, Maria ₍*fl.* 1790–1791₎, *performer.*
The bills for Astley's Amphitheatre name Mlle Maria Theresa of St Orre from 22 October

1790 to 9 July 1791, the bill in June 1791 noting that she "is supposed to possess the finest Head of Hair ever seen." What she did besides exhibit her coiffure is not known.

Thérodats or **Thérodax**. *See* TÉRODAT.

Thicknesse, Mrs Philip. *See* FORD, ANN.

Thistleton, Mr [*fl. 1783–1785*], *scene painter*.
The Lord Chamberlain's accounts show that Mr Thistleton was an assistant to the scene painter Novosielski at the King's Theatre in 1783, 1784, and 1785. Mrs Thistleton was employed there as a dresser during those years.

Thistleton,   Mrs [*fl. 1783–1785*], *dresser. See* THISTLETON, MR.

Thobald, Mr [*fl. 1790*], *actor*.
A Bartholomew Fair bill of 1790 collected by Lysons shows that *The Spaniard Well Drub'd* was performed at the old Yates-Shuter theatre with Mr Thobald as Alonzo.

Thomas. *See also* TOMS.

Thomas, Mr [*fl. 1708*], *pit keeper*.
A paylist for the Queen's Theatre, now in the Coke papers at Harvard, names Mr Thomas as one of the pit keepers at a daily wage of 2s. 8d. in 1708.

Thomas, Mr [*fl. 1723–1735*], *actor*.
Mr Thomas was an amateur making his first stage attempt with other neophytes when at the Haymarket Theatre on 12 December 1723 he played Sir Obstinate Lecture in *The Female Fop.* But he acted again on 5 February 1724, playing Hothead in *Sir Courtly Nice,* and on 27 February he shared a benefit with Hawker and probably had a part in *Love and a Bottle.* He was perhaps the Thomas who came back to the Haymarket on 26 October 1728 to appear as Raymond in *The Spanish Fryar.* On 19 June 1732, at Yeates's booth in Upper Moorfields, Thomas acted Arcas in *Damon and Phillida;* on 28 September 1733 at Mile End Green he was Waggoner in *The Harlot's Progress;* and at York Buildings on 29 September 1735 he played Ratcliff in *Jane Shore.* We have supposed that

one Mr Thomas gave all those performances, but we cannot be certain.

Thomas, Mr [*fl. 1765*], *singer*.
According to Wroth's *London Pleasure Gardens,* a Mr Thomas sang at Finch's Grotto Gardens in George Street, St George's Field, Southwark, in August 1765.

Thomas, Mr [*fl. 1776–1797*], *actor*.
At China Hall, Rotherhithe, from 4 through 18 October 1776 Mr Thomas played Oxford in *Richard III,* Aristander in *Alexander the Great,* and a Follower in *The Life and Death of Tom Thumb the Great.* On 13 November 1780 at the Haymarket Theatre he was Samuel Slender in *The City Association,* and on 25 November 1782 at the same house he acted an unspecified role in *The Taylors.* He was probably the Thomas who was Jack Top-Gallant in *The Spaniard Well Drub'd* at Bartholomew Fair in 1790. At the Haymarket on 4 December 1797 Thomas played Marcus in *Cato* and Dapper in *The Citizen.*

Thomas, Mr [*fl. 1796–1805?*], *singer*.
Mr Thomas sang in *The Mountaineers* at Covent Garden Theatre on 6 October 1796, after which, to the end of the century, he was regularly in small parts and choruses of musical pieces. His assignments included an Irish Peasant in *Bantry Bay,* a Recruit in *The Magic Oak,* a Bard in *Oscar and Malvina,* a Robber in *The Iron Chest,* a Gipsy in *The Norwood Gipsies,* a Bacchanal in *Comus,* a Soldier in *Ramah Droog,* an Infernal Spirit in *The Volcano,* and a Shepherd in *A Peep behind the Curtain.* On 18 and 19 July at the Haymarket Theatre Thomas sang in the chorus of Negroes in *Obi.* Thomas also sang in the choruses of *Macbeth, Romeo and Juliet, Joanna, The Italian Villagers,* and *Raymond and Agnes.*

Perhaps he was the Thomas who performed at the Birmingham Theatre in the summer of 1799. He was very likely the singer Thomas who was in choruses at the Haymarket in the summers of 1801 and 1802. He was one of two Thomases active at Covent Garden in the early years of the nineteenth century, both of whom earned £1 10s. weekly. We are guessing that our subject was the one whose name dropped from the accounts after 7 December 1805.

Thomas, Mr [*fl.* 1797–1808?], *scene painter.*

Mr Thomas was one of the scene painters at Covent Garden Theatre from as early as 30 December 1797, when he was paid £3 12*s.* for an unspecified purpose. The accounts named him for similar amounts from time to time during the rest of the 1790s. His salary, apart from his occasional special payments (perhaps for supplies), was £1 10*s.* weekly. He was probably the Thomas whose benefit tickets were accepted on 8 June 1799, and we are supposing that he was the Thomas who was last named in the accounts on 30 April 1808. However, there was a singer named Thomas performing at Covent Garden during some of the years the scene painter was active.

Thomas, Mrs. *See also* SIMPSON, MRS GEORGE.

Thomas, Mrs [*fl.* 1723–1731], *actress, dancer, singer.*

Mrs Thomas appeared as an amateur at the Haymarket Theatre on 12 December 1723 playing Eudemia in *The Female Fop.* Also performing was Mr Thomas, presumably her husband, who seems to have acted sporadically in London after that until 1735. Mrs Thomas, too, appears to have gone on after her initial appearance and found regular theatrical employment, through September 1731.

On 31 January 1729 Mrs Thomas began an engagement at the Haymarket that lasted through 26 July. She was seen as Sylvia in *The Recruiting Officer,* Venus, a Grace, and a Nymph in *The Humours of Harlequin,* Sermentory in *Hurlothrumbo,* Mrs Vulcan in *The Smugglers,* Mrs Chaunter in *The Beggar's Wedding,* and Betty in *Flora.* She repeated her role in *The Beggar's Wedding* at Reynold's booths at Bartholomew and Southwark fairs in August and September. On 23 September at Southwark she played in *The Recruiting Officer* again.

She attracted the attention of Henry Giffard, the manager of the Goodman's Fields Theatre, for she spent the 1729–30 and 1730–31 seasons there. She began her tenure on 31 October 1729 as Sylvia in *The Recruiting Officer* and then went on in 1729–30 to play Lady Bountiful in *The Stratagem,* Serina in *The Orphan,* Lucy in *Tunbridge Walks,* the Countess of Nottingham in *The Unhappy Favorite,* Mrs Prim in *A Bold*

Stroke for a Wife, Lucy in *The Old Bachelor,* Mrs Security and Angelica in *The Gamester,* Lamorce in *The Inconstant,* Parly in *The Constant Couple,* Mrs Mixem in *A Woman's Revenge,* Honoria in *Love Makes a Man,* Isabella in *The Conscious Lovers,* Myrtilla in *The Provok'd Husband,* Lady Graveairs in *The Careless Husband,* Jenny and Arabella in *The Fair Quaker of Deal,* Smooth in *The Fashionable Lady,* Moretta in *The Rover,* Clara in *Rule a Wife and Have a Wife,* a Peasant Woman in *Harlequin Turn'd Dancing Master,* Flareit in *Love's Last Shift,* Lucy in *The Man's Bewitch'd,* Isabinda in *The Busy Body,* Regan and Goneril in *King Lear,* Friendly in *Flora,* Parly in *Constant Couple,* Hunter in *Phebe,* Charlotte in *Oroonoko,* and Lady Wronghead in *The Provok'd Wife.* During the season she also appeared as an entr'acte dancer, and on 29 June 1739 she donned man's clothes to sing "The White Joke." After that impressive display she went to Tottenham Court on 1 August to play Lady Numscul in *Mad Tom of Bedlam,* and on 31 August she was seen at Bartholomew Fair as Suky Tyler in *Wat Tyler and Jack Straw.*

In 1730–31 at Goodman's Fields Mrs Thomas added to her repertoire such roles as Dorinda and Gypsy in *The Stratagem,* a Spirit and Lady Lovemore in *The Devil of a Wife,* Jenny and Lucy in *The Beggar's Opera,* Haly in *Tamerlane,* Fainlove in *The Tender Husband,* Friendly in *The Jealous Clown,* Cephisa in *The Distrest Mother,* the title role in *Flora,* Betty Wheadle in *The Merry Throwster,* Noodle in *Tom Thumb,* Situp in *The Double Gallant,* Jenny Pyfleet in *The Cobler's Opera,* Maria in *The Man's Bewitch'd,* Massina in *Sophonisba,* and Hippolito in *The Tempest.* She also put on "a Gentleman's Habit" again to deliver a prologue. At Tottenham Court in August she was Zara in *Amurath* and Tippet in *Phebe,* and on 28 September 1731 at Southwark she made her last recorded appearance, as Mrs Prim in *A Bold Stroke for a Wife.*

Thomas, Mrs [*fl.* 1754], *See* THOMAS, MISS [*fl.* 1752?–1776]?

Thomas, Mrs [*fl.* 1771], *See* THOMAS, MISS [*fl.* 1752?–1776].

Thomas, Master [*fl.* 1799], *actor.*
Master Thomas played Jack Slang in *She*

Stoops to Conquer at Wheatley's Riding School in Greenwich on 17 May 1799.

Thomas, Miss [*fl.* 1752?–1776], *singer, actress.*

In his will, written on 9 July 1752, the musician John Christopher Pepusch left a Miss Thomas five guineas. She may well have been the Miss Thomas who made her first stage appearance on 1 March 1753 singing Laura in *The Chaplet* at Drury Lane Theatre, and Pepusch may have been her teacher. The prompter Cross said she did "very well" at her debut. During the remainder of the season Miss Thomas was seen as Miranda in *Bayes in Petticoats* on 22 March and Phillis in *The Shepherd's Lottery* on 27 April. In her first full season, 1753–54, she repeated Laura, sang in *Macbeth* (advertised in error as Mrs Thomas) and *Henry VIII*, was Miranda in *The Rehearsal*, and took a part in *The London Prentice*. She was also heard in entr'acte songs, one of them being Arne's "A Pastoral Dialogue," which she sang with Beard, and another "Damon and Chloe," a duet with Master Reinhold.

Miss Thomas was again at Drury Lane in 1754–55, playing Humdrumeda in *The London Prentice*, Nancy in *Britannia*, and some of her earlier parts. She also sang between the acts, but she was not used nearly as often as she had been in the previous season. Still, she shared a benefit with Scrase on 26 April 1755, making her tickets available at the Ring and Pearl in Duke's Court, Bow Street. In 1755–56 she made at least two appearances: at her shared benefit with the younger Cross at the Haymarket on 15 December 1755, when *Acis and Galatea* was performed, and at the Great Room in Soho on 16 March 1756, when she took part in *Alexander's Feast*. In 1756 was published one of the songs she sang at Drury Lane: *Confin'd to the House till the Age of Fifteen*, also called *The Novice*.

In 1757 the song *At the foot of a hill in a neat lonely cott*, as sung by Miss Thomas, was published. No mention was made about where she sang it. *Felix Farley's Bristol Journal* reported that the subscription concerts for the winter of 1759–60 would include the singer Miss Thomas from London and Mr Richards, a violinist. The first concert was scheduled for 17 September 1759. Possibly in the summer of either 1759 or 1760 Miss Thomas sang *At the foot of a hill* at Marylebone Gardens in London; the song was reprinted about 1760. *The Judicious Fair*, as sung by her, was also published about 1760. In 1761, *I told my nymph, I told her true*, as sung by Miss Thomas at Ranelagh Gardens, was published.

On 2 February 1762 Miss Thomas sang Semira in *Artaxerxes* at Covent Garden Theatre. She then went over to Drury Lane to sing in *Alexander's Feast*, in Arne's *The Sacrifice*, and Virtue in *Beauty and Virtue*, under Arne's direction. At Ranelagh on 11 June 1762 she joined others to sing songs from *Artaxerxes*. From February to mid-May 1763 she was again at Covent Garden singing Semira in *Artaxerxes*. In 1764–65 Miss Thomas sang at the Smock Alley Theatre in Dublin, hailed as from Covent Garden in London; in August 1765, according to Wroth's *London Pleasure Gardens*, she sang at Finch's Grotto Gardens, one of her songs being *O lead me to some safe retreat*, published that year. In 1769 Thomas Gray wrote in a letter that Miss Thomas was one of the singers, "well-versed in Judas Maccabeus," who sang at the Gloucester Music Festival. Miss Thomas was an entr'acte singer at Marylebone Gardens in June, July, and August 1771 (sometimes called in the bills Mrs Thomas); she sang in *The Magnet* and *A Cure for Dotage*. About 1771 was published one of the songs sung by her at the Gardens, *I search'd the Fields of Ev'ry Kind*. She appeared there again in 1776.

Rendle called her "A singer of great promise and expectation, who had been brought forward by W. Kitchener, Esq. father of the later Dr. [William] Kitchener. She appeared in public only as a concert performer, and died very young in consequence of mental derangement." The date of her death is not known.

Thomas, Miss [*fl.* 1782], *actress.*
On 4 March 1782 Miss Thomas played Prince Edward in *Richard III* at the Haymarket Theatre.

Thomas, Andrew [*fl.* 1728?–1755], *trumpeter.*
The Lord Chamberlain's accounts list Andrew Thomas as a trumpeter in the King's Musick from perhaps as early as 1728 to 1749. On 28 August 1739 he became one of the original subscribers to the Royal Society of

Musicians. Thomas was replaced in the King's Musick by Daniel Wardle, evidently in 1749, but he remained active in the Royal Society of Musicians to at least 1755.

Thomas, Benjamin ₁*fl.*1784₁, *singer.*
Benjamin Thomas sang bass in the Handel Memorial Concerts at Westminster Abbey and the Pantheon in May and June 1784.

Thomas, Elizabeth ₁*fl.*1794–1795₁, *actress.*
Miss Elizabeth Thomas was granted a license to present a play at the Haymarket Theatre on 22 May 1794; she chose to act Sigismunda in *Tancred and Sigismunda* and Lady Racket in *Three Weeks after Marriage*. Bills in the Richmond Library show that Miss Thomas was a member of the company at Richmond in the summer of 1795.

Thomas, James ₁*fl.*1794₁, *singer.*
Doane's *Musical Directory* of 1794 listed James Thomas, of St Mary's Chapel, Park Lane, as a bass who subscribed to the New Musical Fund, was the clerk of the Park Lane Chapel, and sang in the Handelian performances in Westminster Abbey.

Thomas, Jo ₁*fl.*1733–1734₁, *violinist?*
Benefits were given for "Jo. Thomas" at Stationers' Hall on 19 March 1733 and 28 March 1734. Perhaps he was the Thomas who played violin at the Earl of Egmont's concert on 22 March 1734.

Thomas, John ₁*fl.*1784₁, *singer.*
John Thomas sang bass in the Handel Memorial concerts at Westminster Abbey and the Pantheon in May and June 1784.

Thomas, Joseph ₁*fl.*1700₁, *swordsman?*
The *Protestant Mercury* of 24–26 April 1700 carried the following notice:

On Wednesday in the afternoon [24 April] a tryal of skill was performed between Joseph Thomas, Master of the noble science of defence, and one Mʳ. Jones, a gentleman, that came out of North-Wales on purpose to fight him, at the Theater in Dorset Gardens, where were abundance of the nobility and gentry; and between each bout was a very fine

consort of musick; but in the conclusion Mʳ. Jones gained the day, with great applause.

The wording does not make clear whether the fighters were pugilists or swordsmen.

Thomas, Tobias ₁*fl.*1696–1704₁, *actor.*
Tobias Thomas's earliest known role was Lord Whiffle in *The Female Wits*, which was presented at Drury Lane in September 1796. After that he appeared as Geraldo in *Sauny the Scot*, the Duke of Venice in *Imposture Defeated*, Conall in *The Fatal Discovery*, Cassius Cheraea in *Caligula*, Kinglove in *The Campaigners*, Piniero in *The Island Princess*, Catesby in *Richard III*, Nicias in *The Grove*, the Mad Scholar in *The Pilgrim*, Alonzo in *The Perjured Husband*, Lord Brumpton in *The Funeral*, Graville in *The Unhappy Penitent*, Rodorick in *The Generous Conqueror*, and, about May 1704, Oliman in *The Faithful Bride*.

He may have been the Tobias Thomas whose stillborn child was buried at St Martin-in-the-Fields on 13 August 1697. Thomas was possibly the author of *The Life of the Late Famous Comedian Jo. Haynes* (1701).

Thomlinson. *See* TOMLINSON.

Thompson. *See also* THOMSON *and* TOMSON.

Thompson, Mr ₁*fl.*1728–1741₁, *boxkeeper.*
The Lincoln's Inn Fields Theatre accounts at Harvard show a Mr Thompson turning in after-money on 3 May 1728; he was named again on 2 January 1729, this time as a boxkeeper. Latreille listed him as a boxkeeper at Covent Garden Theatre in 1735–36 at 2s. 6d. nightly. Our subject was probably the "Thomson" whose benefit tickets were accepted at Covent Garden on 13 May 1740, and he was certainly Thomson the boxkeeper who shared a benefit with two others on 11 May 1741, when receipts came to £100. In 1740–41 he was earning 3s. 4d. nightly. Other references in the bills to a Thompson or Thomson may be to the boxkeeper, but there were two other Thompsons in the company during the same period.

The *Index to The London Stage* is clearly confused in its listing for a Thomson, boxkeeper: the 16 May 1734 citation probably concerns Edward Thompson, and the 28 March 1745 listing clearly refers to the playwright James Thomson.

Thompson, Mr ₍*fl. 1735–1736*₎, *lampman.*
Latreille cites a Mr Thompson as a lampman at Covent Garden Theatre in 1735–36 at 1*s.* nightly. Another British Library list has Thompson down for 179 days at 20*d.*

Thompson, Mr ₍*fl. 1767*₎. *See* BARDIN, PETER.

Thompson, Mr ₍*fl. 1776–1785*₎, *actor, singer.*
Mr Thompson made his Hull debut on 6 November 1776. We take him to have been the Thompson who appeared occasionally at the Haymarket Theatre in London during the winter months from 1778 to 1785. Also in London was the Covent Garden actor James Thompson, who sometimes performed at his theatre the same night as our Thompson acted at the Haymarket. On 9 February 1778 our Thompson acted Derby in *Jane Shore,* and on 23 March, when James Thompson was acting in *Iphigenia* at Covent Garden, our subject was playing Paris in *The Jealous Wife* at the Haymarket. The following night Mr Thompson was seen as the Duke of Buckingham in *Richard III,* and on 31 March he played Simon Pure in *A Bold Stroke for a Wife* at the Haymarket, while James Thompson was acting in *The Citizen* at Covent Garden. On 29 April Thompson had a role in *All the World's a Stage* and acted Doublejugg in *The Country Lasses.*

Thompson was at the Crown Inn, Islington, from 27 March to 5 April 1781, playing Altamont in *The Fair Penitent,* Oxford in *Richard III,* Derby in *Jane Shore,* and Joe in *The King and the Miller of Mansfield.* On 4 March 1782 he was again at the Haymarket, acting Fairlove in *Don Quixote in England.* Thompson returned to the Haymarket on 15 December 1783 to play Buckingham in *Richard III* again and act the Nephew in *The Irish Widow.* On 21 January 1784 "Thomson" performed in *The Talisman* at the Haymarket. In January 1785 he acted

Glaud in *The Gentle Shepherd,* Bradshaw in *King Charles I,* and Peachum in *The Beggar's Opera.*

Perhaps he was the Thompson who had played old men at Bristol in the summer of 1778 and acted in Fox's troupe at Brighton in 1779.

Thompson, Mr ₍*fl. 1783–1784*₎, *house servant.*
Places for boxes at the Royal Circus on 3 and 21 November 1783 and 3 February 1784 could be obtained from Mr Thompson (or Thomson) "at the Academy." The bill for 26 May 1784 said that tickets were available from Thompson at the Circus.

Thompson, Mr. ₍*fl. 1783–1785*₎, *boxkeeper, lobby keeper.*
The Lord Chamberlain's accounts name Mr Thompson as a boxkeeper and lobby keeper at the King's Theatre from 1783 to 1785.

Thompson, Mr ₍*fl. 1786–1811?*₎, *actor.*
We have found a number of references to a Thompson (or Thompsons) in provincial playbills; we cannot be certain all concern the same person, but perhaps they did. At one point Thompson turned up at Bartholomew Fair and Richmond, Surrey, within the London area.

At Liverpool a Mr Thompson shared a benefit with "Maddocks" (George Mattocks?) on 18 August 1786. A Cheltenham bill for July 1788 listed Thompson as Statuary in *Harlequin's Whim.* At Bartholomew Fair in London in 1788 Thompson played Dr Hellebore in *The Mock Doctor.* On 11 August 1790 at Richmond Thompson was Sir Richard in *The Minor,* and that year at Bartholomew Fair he acted Captain Driv'em in *The Spaniard Well Drub'd.* A Thompson was at Derby on 14 March 1793, and the Tunbridge Wells bills listed Thompson in 1794. The Birmingham bills for the summers of 1795, 1796, and 1797 named a Thompson. Rosenfeld in *The Georgian Theatre of Richmond, Yorkshire* places Thompson at Harrogate with the Richmond troupe in 1797. He acted there in *Which Is the Man?* and was in it again at Tunbridge Wells in 1800. The Bath-Bristol company had a Thompson playing minor roles in farces in 1803–4 and 1804–5, and the Bristol bills named him through 1806–7. Thompson was at Harrogate in 1806, advertised as from Edinburgh, and a Thompson acted at Norwich in 1806 and at Edinburgh from 1809 to 1811, playing such roles as Charles Dudley in *The West Indian,* Joseph Surface in *The School for Scandal,* Lovewell in *The Clandestine Marriage,* and Young Malfort in *The Soldier's Daughter.*

Thompson, Mrs [*fl. 1726–1736*], dresser.

The accounts for Lincoln's Inn Fields Theatre list Mrs Thompson as a dresser at 9*s.* weekly as early as 14 January 1726. She was last named in 1735–36 as working 172 days for £12 18*s.*

Thompson, Mrs [*fl. 1736*], actress.

Mrs Thompson played Lady Betty in *The Careless Husband* at the Haymarket Theatre on 16 February 1736.

Thompson, Mrs [*fl. 1738–1747*], dancer.

There were apparently two female dancers named Thompson (or Thomson) at Drury Lane from 1738 to 1747, Miss and Mrs, perhaps daughter and mother. (If Miss Thompson spent part of the 1739–40 season in Dublin, her initial was E.) Mrs Thompson was first mentioned on 19 January 1738, when she appeared in a new ballet. On 28 January she participated in a *Grand Polish Dance,* and beginning on 4 March she danced in *Comus.* During the rest of the season she was seen in such entr'acte pieces as *La Folie amoureuse, La Pieraite, French Peasant,* and some untitled dances. She continued at Drury Lane through 24 January 1747, though her activity slackened noticeably after 1744.

Mrs Thompson danced regularly in *Comus* and was also seen in dances in *The Fall of Phaeton, Robin Goodfellow,* and *The Harlot's Progress.* She was the Second Wife in *Don John,* a Nymph and Pallas in *The Rural Sports,* Mrs Coaxer and Molly in *The Beggar's Opera,* and a Fantastic Spright and Shepherdess in *The Amorous Goddess.* She danced also in such entr'acte turns as *Les Amant volages,* a *Peasant Dance, Shepherds and Shepherdesses, A Voyage to the Island*

of *Cytherea* (she was a Pilgrim), *Le Jardiniers Suedois, Les Masons & les sabotiers, Les Satires puny* (she was a Shepherdess), a *Tyrolean Dance,* and *The Italian Masquerade.*

Thompson, Mrs [*fl. 1752*]. See THOMPSON, MISS [*fl. 1752*].

Thompson, Mrs [*fl. 1767–1774*]. See POITIER, JANE.

Thompson, Mrs [*fl.1784–1794?*], actress.

Mrs Thompson played Lucy in *The Man's Bewitch'd* and Mrs Bruin in *The Mayor of Garratt* at the Haymarket Theatre on 8 March 1784. The following 16 November at that house Mrs "Thomson" acted Lady Rachel Mildew in *The School for Wives.* A Mrs Thompson, possibly our subject, was at the Haymarket on 22 May 1794 playing Mrs Drugget in *Three Weeks after Marriage.*

Thompson, Miss [*fl.1752*], singer.

The *General Advertiser* on 27 January 1752 carried a notice of a concert at the King's Arms Tavern in Cornhill that day, a benefit for Miss Thompson, who was to sing Galatea in *Acis and Galatea.* "Mrs" Thompson (most likely an error for Miss) also sang two other songs by Handel.

Thompson, Miss [*fl.1769*], actress.

Miss Thompson played Emilia in *Othello* at the Haymarket Theatre on 28 February 1769.

Thompson, Miss [*fl. 1773*]. See POITIER JANE.

Thompson, Miss [*fl.1791–1804?*], singer, actress.

Miss Thompson sang "Hark, hark, to the Woodlands" at the Haymarket Theatre on 12 December 1791. (The Miss Thompson in *The Merchant of Venice* at the Haymarket in February 1792 was evidently Mary Anne Thompson, a different person.) Our subject acted Dorcas in *The Jew* at the Haymarket on 26 March 1798. In the summer of 1804 a female Thompson, possibly our Miss Thompson, sang in the chorus at the Haymarket.

Thompson, Albion *d. 1683?, trumpeter.*

On 11 June 1660 the Lord Chamberlain issued a warrant naming Melker Goldt as a trumpeter in ordinary; after his name was a note: "at pension and Thompson in his place." It is not certain that the note was written in 1660, since other mentions of the trumpeter Albion Thompson in the accounts date from the 1670s; indeed, one dated 6 May 1674 contains the same information about Thompson replacing Goldt.

On 18 November 1672 Thompson was appointed to attend the Duke of Monmouth, evidently outside England, for a warrant dated September 1673 provided liveries to Thompson and Simon Pierson "at sea." They were in the Troop of Guards under Monmouth's command. On 15 February 1675 Thompson played trumpet in the court masque *Calisto* in London, but a year later he was off again, this time with Lawrence Hyde in Poland. That assignment lasted until February 1677.

Thompson and his wife Margaret had a son, Albion, who was christened at St Margaret, Westminster, on 26 July 1674. Their daughter Elizabeth was christened on 8 November 1681. Albion Thompson was recorded in the Lord Chamberlain's accounts as deceased and replaced on 16 February 1683; ordinarily such action was taken within days of a court musician's death.

Thompson, B. *[fl. 1790–1801?], box office keeper.*

The Drury Lane accounts cite B. Thompson as a member of the box office staff on 4 June 1791. He was one of at least five male Thompsons working at the theatre in the 1790s, the other four being John the box office keeper and supernumerary player, a younger John (son of B.?) the gallery doorkeeper, Joseph the property man, and William the dancer. Consequently, the accounts are very confusing, and our distinguishing of the Thompsons should be considered tentative. Since we are certain of the salary of the elder John (£2 weekly, and he held an important position), references to an office worker at a lower salary probably concern B. Thompson. A box office keeper Thompson was earning £1 10*s.* weekly in 1801, and we would guess him to have been our subject. We guess, too, that the Thompson (function not given) getting £1 6*s.* 8*d.* on 5 May 1792 was probably our man. And the Thompson cited with many others in benefit bills on 29 May 1790, 31 May 1791 (identified as "of box office"), and 15 June 1792 was also probably B. Thompson.

Thompson, Mrs *[B?] [fl. 1792], house servant?*

The Mrs Thompson cited in the Drury Lane accounts on 5 May 1792 may have been the wife of B. Thompson. She was listed at a weekly salary of 16*s.* 8*d.*, as was a Thompson junior—their son, probably, and, we think, named John. Mrs Thompson was probably a house servant; the junior Thompson was a gallery doorkeeper.

Thompson, Miss *[E?] [fl. 1738–1747], dancer, actress.*

From 1738 to 1747 two female Thompsons danced at Drury Lane Theatre—Miss and Mrs Thompson, probably daughter and mother. Since they did the same kind of chores, the bills may on occasion have confused the one with the other. Miss Thompson was first noticed on 11 January 1738, when she was in an untitled dance with two others. Two days later the same trio was in a *Grand Ballet* added to *The Fall of Phaeton,* and on 20 January Miss Thompson was named again as an entr'acte dancer. During the rest of the season she appeared in various untitled dances and in *La Pieraite* (a dance Mrs Thompson also did on occasion) and a *Scots Dance.*

Throughout the 1738–39 season Miss Thompson played Mrs Taffata in *Robin Goodfellow* and appeared as a Haymaker in *Harlequin Shipwrecked* and as a Grace and Thetis in *Mars and Venus.* She also danced between the acts, one of her turns being a *Dutch Dance* with Baudouin. In 1739–40 our Miss Thompson was not very active at Drury Lane. The bills show her in *Harlequin Shipwrecked* from September 1739 to January 1740, so it is quite possible that she was the Miss E. Thompson who appeared at the Smock Alley Theatre in Dublin during the season—perhaps during the spring and summer, when our subject is not known to have been dancing in London. Also at Smock Alley was another Miss Thomson, also a dancer and actress.

In 1740–41 Miss Thompson was again at Drury Lane, dancing a Peasant in *Robin Goodfellow* in October and November 1740 and appearing in a *Peasant Dance* and as a Pierot Woman in *The Enchanted Garden* in October and December. *The London Stage* notes that in 1741–42 either a Miss or Mrs Thompson danced at Drury Lane; the bills make it clear that the woman was Mrs Thompson and that Miss Thompson was not named again until 1744–45: on 2 October 1744 she was in a *Grand Turkish Dance* at Drury Lane, and unless that was an error for Mrs Thompson, our subject had only that assignment during the season. She was not named in 1745–46 and 1746–47, but she was mentioned in 1747: on 2 November she was in a *Polish Dance,* on 13 November she danced in *Comus,* and on 16 November she was in *The Gardener's Revels.*

Thompson, Edward   *d. 1748, actor, singer, dancer.*

Edward Thompson was probably the "Y." or "Young" Thompson cited in the accounts for the Lincoln's Inn Fields Theatre as early as 15 February 1724, when he was paid £3 5s. for singing "last year." He was named frequently in the accounts through 1728–29, sometimes cited as Ned Thompson, but his name did not appear in the bills. One citation, on 1 November 1727, concerned "Ed. Thompson's Father," who was given complimentary tickets.

Thompson was named in the bills beginning with the 1729–30 season. On 3 October 1729 he sang in the *Macbeth* chorus; on 2 January 1730 he was an Ethiopian in *Perseus and Andromeda;* and on 14 May he again sang in *Macbeth.* His chores were very similar in 1730–31, and either he or the house servant Thompson shared a benefit on 28 May 1731; receipts came to over £116. Thompson (occasionally Thomson) performed at Lincoln's Inn Fields and then at Covent Garden through the 1747–48 season, never rising above small parts in pantomimes and chorus singing. He was named over and over as an Ethiopian in *Perseus and Andromeda,* and beginning on 18 November 1731 he was advanced to the First Ethiopian. He was also Evil, a Pierot Man, and a Fury in *The Necromancer,* a Savoyard in *The Rape of Proserpine,* Stheno and an Infernal in *Perseus and Andromeda,* a Follower in *Cupid and Bacchus,* Goody Gurton and a Villager in *Orpheus and*

Eurydice, and an Attendant in *Comus.* He sang in the choruses of *Macbeth* and *Henry VIII.*

Thompson also served as an entr'acte entertainer, but infrequently. He was a Villager in the dance *The Italian Peasants* on 24 October 1741, and he sang in "The English Hero's Welcome Home" on 8 January 1746. Edward Thompson was paid for 172 nights in the 1735–36 season at 20d. nightly; in 1746–47 he was paid 10s. weekly.

Thompson made occasional appearances elsewhere. On 5 June 1734 he went over to the Haymarket Theatre to play a Drawer in *The Humours of Sir John Falstaff.* On 23 August 1737 he danced at Bartholomew Fair, and on 7 September he danced at Southwark Fair. At Bartholomew Fair in August 1739 Thompson was a Triton in *The Sailor's Wedding.* On 19 February 1746 a Thompson, very likely Edward, made his first appearance at the Smock Alley Theatre in Dublin.

The Drury Lane prompter Richard Cross wrote in his diary on 21 March 1748 that Ned Thompson had died on 19 March. Possibly our subject was the Edward Thompson from St George, Bloomsbury, whose daughter Jane was christened on 13 December 1747.

Thompson, Elizabeth. *See* Spiller, Mrs James.

Thompson, J.   [*fl.* 1739], *dancer.*
J. Thompson danced a hornpipe at Covent Garden Theatre on 11, 28, and 29 May 1739.

Thompson, James   [*fl.* 1770–1812?], *actor, singer, dancer, manager?*
James Thompson was on the Covent Garden boards for many years, rarely playing parts of much consequence. He was apparently not the Thompson who appeared at the Haymarket Theatre in the summer of 1767; that person seems to have been Peter Bardin, using a pseudonym. On 24 April 1770 at Covent Garden a Thompson played Octavian in *The Cheats of Scapin.* That Thompson shared a benefit on 19 May but had to settle for half value and received only £2 15s. 6d. On 23 October he was an Officer in *Venice Preserv'd,* and on 29 December he was added to the cast of *Mother Shipton.* On 6 February 1771 he acted Francis in *The Brothers,* on 29 April Lopez in *The Merry Counterfeit,* on 1 May Dr Catgut in *The Commissary,*

and on 15 May a Gambler in *Harlequin Doctor Faustus*. On 22 May he shared a benefit with four others. Since some of those parts were associated with James Thompson in later years, we take the above notices to have concerned him.

Those assignments are fairly typical of the whole career of James Thompson. Season after season to the end of the eighteenth century and beyond he played bit parts with no names—officers, servants, bailiffs, sportsmen, villagers, sailors, planters, citizens, coachmen, cooks, robbers, soldiers, and the like. In 1798 the *Authentic Memoirs of the Green Room* said that Thompson "seldom soars higher than an officer or attendant; and if a lord or king, says very little." Yet he was clearly a useful actor, one of those utility drudges without whom theatres cannot operate. By 1780–81 at Covent Garden Thompson was earning £2 weekly. He went up to £2 10s. in 1786–87.

Among his many parts (with names) over the years were Traverse in *The Clandestine Marriage*, Guildenstern and the Player King in *Hamlet*, Gruel in *The Commissary*, Stanmore, Captain Driver, and Hotman in *Oroonoko*, Ratcliff and Stanley in *Richard III*, Hali, the Prince of Tanais, Stratocles, and Dervise in *Tamerlane*, Cash in *Every Man in His Humour*, Jaques and Don Antonio in *Love Makes a Man*, Seyton in *Macbeth*, Derby in *Jane Shore*, Quildrive in *The Citizen*, the Duke, Tubal, and Salarino in *The Merchant of Venice*, Polyperchon in *All's Well That Ends Well*, Alexas and Serapion in *All for Love*, a Brother in *Comus*, Paris, Montague, and Friar John in *Romeo and Juliet*, Humphrey in *The Conscious Lovers*, Martin and Oldrents in *The Jovial Crew*, Antonio in *Much Ado about Nothing*, Burgundy and Cornwall in *King Lear*, Corin and Duke Frederick in *As You Like It*, Atticus in *Theodosius*, Sullen in *The Strategem*, Westmoreland and Bardolph in *1 Henry IV*, Blunt in *George Barnwell*, Woodley in *Three Weeks after Marriage*, the Bishop of Ely in *Henry V*, Moody in *The Provok'd Husband*, Sir Jealous Traffic in *The Busy Body*, Kilderkin in *The Flitch of Bacon*, Sir Harry Atall in *The Double Gallant*, Sancho in *The Pilgrim*, Sir William Meadows in *Love in a Village*, Friar Peter in *Measure for Measure*, and Tapwell in *A New Way to Pay Old Debts*.

He was also Strickland and Buckle in *The Suspicious Husband*, Fulmer in *The West Indian*, Fabian in *The Count of Narbonne*, Perez in *The Mourning Bride*, Loveday in *The London Cuckolds*, Father Paul in *The Duenna*, Lockit and Mat o'the Mint in *The Beggar's Opera*, Spinosa in *Venice Preserv'd*, Pistol and the Host in *The Merry Wives of Windsor*, Hugh Clump and Puzzle in *The Funeral*, Montano in *Othello*, Ambrose in *The Midnight Hour*, Ernesto in *The Orphan*, Decoy in *The Miser*, Tradelove in *A Bold Stroke for a Wife*, and dozens of other small parts in more obscure works. Thompson was cast in pantomime parts that probably required some dancing ability, and he occasionally had to do some singing.

James Thompson rarely strayed from Covent Garden, and occasional references to a Thompson at other houses—at the Haymarket during the winter seasons in the 1780s and 1790s—are usually to another person. But perhaps James was the Thompson who played an Officer in *Edward and Eleonora* at Drury Lane on 18 March 1775, a night when he was not busy at Covent Garden. Similarly, he may have been the Servant in *The Busy Body* at the Haymarket on 19 September 1775, just before the Covent Garden season began. On 2 June 1783 he played his old part of Sir William Meadows in *Love in a Village* at the Haymarket. When he went over to Drury Lane on 12 November 1783 to act Stockwell in *The West Indian* he was identified as Thompson from Covent Garden. On 28 May and in June, July, and August 1784 Thompson was Chicane in *The Agreeable Surprise* at the Haymarket—a part he played regularly at Covent Garden. He was again identified as from Covent Garden when he played Russet in *The Jealous Wife* at Drury Lane on 26 May 1786. He was probably the Thompson who acted Montano in *Othello* at the Haymarket on 6 February 1792, since that was a part in his repertoire. The Thompson at Drury Lane in 1796–97 was another person, probably William Thompson. But our man may well have been the Thompson who played Pillage in *The Romance of an Hour* at the Haymarket on 10 May 1797, when he was not active at Covent Garden.

The London bills rarely account for James Thompson's summer activity. He may have been the Thompson who spent the summers of 1776 and 1777 at the Theatre Royal in Liverpool at £2 a week, though that seems too high a salary, since at Covent Garden Thompson earned only £1 10s. weekly at that time in his career. He may, however, have played larger roles if he went to the provinces. Perhaps he was the Thompson who joined with Benson and Macready in the management of the Richmond theatre in 1791, a venture that lasted only a year. In July 1792 James was certainly at the Liverpool Theatre Royal, advertised as from Covent Garden; he acted Mr Silky in *The Road to Ruin*. After that he seems to have given up activity outside London. He was certainly the Thompson earning £2 10s. weekly at Covent Garden as late as 1802–3, and he was probably the Thompson earning £3 in 1811–12.

The Secret History of the Green Room in 1792 spoke of the humble capacity of Thompson at Covent Garden:

[We] must confess that in Old Men he sometimes delivers a tender passage with great feeling; but he is made so much the pack-horse of every evening, and that in such obscure parts, that whatever judgment he has, it must be smothered by his load of business. He is too old to think of attaining any greater eminence in his profession. . . .

We learn his first name from his membership in 1794 in the Theatrical Fund and from the report of the *Morning Chronicle* on 17 November 1775 that James Thompson of Covent Garden Theatre had married a Miss Thompson. She seems not to have been of the theatre.

Thompson, Jane. *See* POITIER, JANE.

Thompson, John [fl. 1777–1813], *box office keeper.*
Of the several Thompsons working at Drury Lane Theatre in the late eighteenth century and early nineteenth century, John the box office keeper seems clearly to have been the most important. John was cited in the confusing accounts as early as 4 October 1777, and during the 1780s he received sums from time to time that were marked for the supernumeraries, over whom he appears to have had some kind of jurisdiction. He was certainly responsible for paying them and may have had a hand in selecting them. By 1789–90 he was being called a box office keeper, and his duties still included paying the supers. His weekly salary as of 1791–92 was £2, but he seems to have been the Thompson who was important

enough to receive benefits shared with only two or three others. His earliest such notice was on 7 May 1779, when his address was given as No 7, Great Marlborough Street. A Thompson, perhaps John, joined the Haymarket troupe in the summer of 1808. John Thompson, the gallery doorkeeper, was probably the son of a second box office keeper, B. Thompson. Since the accounts show that yet another Thompson, William the dancer, was a brother of our John Thompson, it is likely that all the Thompsons at Drury Lane were related.

Thompson, John [fl. 1789–1821], *gallery doorkeeper.*
The younger John Thompson was probably the Thompson cited in the Drury Lane accounts in 1789–90 at a weekly salary of 15s. "Thompson, Jr." was down for 16s. 8d. weekly on 5 May 1792; he was grouped with (B.?) Thompson and Mrs Thompson, so our guess is that he was their son. John was called the gallery doorkeeper on 27 January 1796. James Winston in his *Diary* mentioned John as the check-taker at the gallery door on 2 May 1821.

Thompson, Joseph [fl. 1790–1813], *property man.*
Joseph Thompson served Drury Lane Theatre as a property man (perhaps the head property man, for he earned a respectable £2 weekly) from as early as 1790–91. John Philip Kemble in his notes at the British Library indicated in 1791–92 that Thompson had the same job at the Haymarket Theatre during the summers. The Covent Garden accounts on 17 September 1807 cited Thompson by his full name. He worked through the 1812–13 season. Perhaps Joseph was the Thompson, "scene man," who was employed at the Haymarket Theatre in the summer of 1804.

Thompson, Joshua d. 1761, *musician.*
Joshua Thompson (or Thomson) was a member of the King's Musick at £40 annually as early as 1746, according to the Establishment accounts among the Lord Chamberlain's papers. In addition to his salary Thompson was paid £16 2s. 6d. for livery. On 5 August 1750 he became a member of the Royal Society of Musicians, and on 30 April 1753 "Josh Thompson" and the musician Maurice Greene

deposited over £94 at Drummond's Bank—probably in connection with a concert. *The Royal Society of Musicians* (1985) gives Thompson's death date tentatively as 1786; Musgrave's *Obituary* notes the death of Thompson, of the King's Musick, on 10 June 1761.

Thompson, Mary Anne, later Mrs Joseph Clarke *1776–1852, actress.*

On 20 February 1792 at the Haymarket Theatre "A Young Lady" played Portia in *The Merchant of Venice* and Miranda in *The Busy Body. The London Stage* identifies her as probably Mary Anne Clarke, on the basis of Elizabeth Taylor's statement in the *Authentic Memoirs of Mrs. Mary Anne Clarke* (neé Thompson) that Mary Anne at some unspecified date played Portia at the Haymarket. We provide this entry only to indicate that the conjecture has been made; the evidence seems to us to be flimsy at best, and if the young lady was, in fact, Mary Anne Thompson, that was the beginning and end of her stage career and suggests an amateur rather than professional performance. *The Dictionary of National Biography* contains an account of Mary Anne's extravagant life.

Thompson, Peter *d. 1757?, violinist, oboist.*

Peter Thompson was one of a long line of musical-instrument makers, music sellers, and music publishers who had premises at the west end of St Paul's churchyard. Humphries and Smith's *Music Publishing in the British Isles* lists the various Thompsons and provides most of the following information. Nathaniel Thompson may have been one of the earliest members of the line. He was a bookseller in Dublin and London from 1666 to 1688 and printed some music. The first of the Thompsons to operate out of a shop in St Paul's churchyard may have been our subject, Peter Thompson. He was proficient on the violin and oboe, and for a while during the period 1746–1757 he hung the sign of the Violin and Hautboy over his shop. At the sign of the Dolphin in St Paul's Churchyard in 1750, a Mr Thompson, surely related to Peter, sold a hymn from the fifth book of *Paradise Lost*. Peter Thompson played violin and oboe at St Paul's Cathedral, according to van der Straeten's *History of the Violin.*

Peter Thompson's business was taken over by his widow and son, who operated at the Violin and Hautboy from about 1757 to 1761.

Mrs Thompson was joined in the business by a second son from 1761 to 1763, after which she perhaps retired or died. *Mortimer's London Directory* lists the Thompsons as eminent for making violins. From about 1763 to 1776 Charles and Samuel Thompson, surely the sons of Peter, operated as music sellers and publishers at No 75, St Paul's Church Yard. Samuel Thompson alone ran the establishment about 1776–77; then Samuel and Ann Thompson (probably son and mother) continued the business as musical instrument makers and music publishers and sellers from 1777 to 1779. Samuel, Ann, and Peter Thompson ran the shop from 1779 to 1793; they were joined by Henry Thompson in 1794, when Peter dropped out of the business. One supposes that Peter and Henry were also sons of the elder Peter Thompson and his wife Ann.

Doane's *Musical Directory* of 1794 listed Samuel and Peter Thompson as instrument makers and music sellers. The business became Ann and Henry Thompson in August 1795, when Samuel died. They continued it until 1798, when Ann either died or retired, and the enterprise was called, until 1805, simply Henry Thompson. After 1805 Purday and Button ran the shop.

The elder Peter Thompson was one of two (or more) Thompsons from this clan who was also a professional performer. Robert Thompson (d. 1786), probably related but in what way is not clear, also had a shop in St Paul's Church Yard and was a performer.

Thompson, Robert *d. 1786, double-bass player.*

Humphries and Smith's *Music Publishing in the British Isles* lists Robert Thompson as a musical instrument maker and music publisher at the sign of the Bass Violin (that is, the bass viol) at No 1, Paul's Alley, St Paul's Church Yard, from 1748 to December 1769. He played double bass in the *Messiah* at the Foundling Hospital in May 1754 at a fee of 10s. 6d. and in the Three Choirs Festival in 1756. Robert Thompson became a member of the Royal Society of Musicians on 7 August 1757. In 1760 he again performed in the *Messiah* at the Hospital. *Mortimer's London Directory* of 1763 listed Thompson as a double-bass player, confirming the evidence of 1754 and 1760 and showing that van der Straeten's assumption in his *History of the Violoncello* that Thompson's sign meant a cello is incorrect.

Thompson moved from Paul's Alley to No 8, Lombard Street, in January 1770 and kept those premises until 1785. He played double bass in the Handel Memorial Concerts at Westminster Abbey and the Pantheon in May and June 1784. He died, according to *The Royal Society of Musicians* (1985), in 1786. Robert Thompson was surely related to the Thompson family of musical instrument makers and publishers who operated out of St Paul's Church Yard. Information on the family may be found in Peter Thompson's entry.

Thompson, Robert *d. 1823, trumpeter, oboist, clarinetist, music copyist.*

Robert Thompson, a trumpeter in the Second Troop of Life Guards, was admitted to the Royal Society of Musicians on 6 February 1780. He was single at the time, had practiced music as a livelihood for seven years, played trumpet, and was proficient as well on the oboe and clarinet. We take him to have been the Thompson who was frequently named in the accounts of Drury Lane Theatre as a trumpeter. His earliest notice in the accounts was on 22 October 1787, when he was paid £4 for music paper—which fact suggests he may have been a music copyist. On 11 June 1790 the accounts show a payment of £3 to Hogg and Thompson, "Extra Trumpets." For another year Thompson was paid for music paper, but after October 1791 the accounts mentioned him only as a trumpeter. Such citations continued through 1803–4.

As a member of the Royal Society of Musicians Thompson played trumpet in the annual St Paul's concerts in 1792, 1796, 1797, and 1798. He was listed in Doane's *Musical Directory* of 1794 as also having participated in the Handelian concerts at Westminster Abbey. Thompson's address was No 18, Pitt Street, Tottenham Court Road. On 3 June 1804 the Society granted Robert Thompson's petition for financial aid and awarded him four guineas per month. That would indicate that Thompson was probably retired, and it is significant that his name disappeared from the Drury Lane

accounts about the same time. He died on 31 March 1823.

Thompson, T. ₁*fl. 1768*₁, *performer.*

The *Theatrical Monitor* on 5 November 1768 published a letter to George Colman signed by a group of Covent Garden Theatre performers; among them was T. Thompson, who is otherwise unknown. The *Index to the London Stage* lists a T. Thompson but gives him performance dates earlier in the century belonging mostly to Edward Thompson.

Thompson, William ₁*fl. 1671–1678*₁, *doorkeeper, gallery keeper.*

William Thompson was a doorkeeper and then gallery keeper for the King's Company from 1671–72 through 1677–78. *The Theatrical Inquisitor* of July 1816, a late source and one to be treated with caution, contained income figures for performances of *All for Love* and *The Rival Queens* in December 1677. Thompson was named as a keeper, evidently of the upper gallery.

Thompson, ₁**William**₁ ₁*fl. 1796–1801*₁, *dancer.*

Mr and Mrs Thompson danced at Drury Lane Theatre in 1796–97, but Mrs Thompson died on 12 November 1796, before the season was very old. Thompson's first notice came on 1 October 1796, when he danced a Shepherd in *The Triumph of Love*, a piece attached to *The Country Girl*. He was in the chorus of Peasants in *Richard Coeur de Lion* on 19 October. On 29 October he danced in a specialty number called *The Scotch Ghost*. Thompson was a Countryman in *Harlequin Captive* on 9 November. His wife died three days later, and Thompson was given some time off. He returned on 26 December to dance in *Robinson Crusoe,* and on 10 January 1797 he was a Spirit in *Comus.* His benefit tickets were accepted on 10 June.

Though Thompson was not named in bills during the rest of the 1790s, he might have been dancing in the chorus at Drury Lane. A William Thompson, who was probably our dancer, was named in the accounts on 20 December 1800 at a weekly salary of £2 2s. William was the brother of John Thompson, the Drury Lane box office keeper. The bills name our Thompson in Drury Lane crowds and dancing choruses in 1800–1801. He was in a new Scotch ballet, *Our Dancing Days,* on 11 February 1801.

Thompson, Mrs [William] *d. 1796, dancer.*

Mrs (William) Thompson danced a Nymph in *The Triumph of Love* at Drury Lane on 1 October 1796. She and Mr Thompson were Villagers in *The Scotch Ghost* on 29 October, but she was omitted from the dance when it was repeated on 1 November. She was doubtless ill, for the account books record her death on 12 November. Her salary had been 4s. 2d. nightly.

Thomson. *See also* THOMPSON *and* TOMSON.

Thomson, Mr [fl. 1748–1757?], *actor, manager?*

The Mr "Thompson" who acted a Gardener in *The Unnatural Parents* at the Lee and Yeates booth at Bartholomew Fair on 24 August 1748 could not have been Edward Thompson, since Edward had died the previous March, but he may have been the "Thomson" who that same day played Count Piper in *The Northern Heroes* at the Bridges-Cross-Burton-Vaughan booth—if the schedules meshed. Those two works (with *The Unnatural Parents* called *The Fair Maid of the West*) were repeated at Southwark Fair on 7 September; again, one man may have played at both booths. *The Fair Maid of the West* was given again by Lee and Yeates at Blackheath Fair on 1 October. Perhaps the man we have been following was the Thomson who was at the Edinburgh theatre from 1748 to 1752 and lived in the area of the concert hall. Dibdin in his *Annals of the Edinburgh Stage* noted that on 16 March 1757 there was a benefit for Thomson, "late manager of the [Canongate] theatre." Tickets were available at his house at the Abbey. Dibdin thought that Thomson was bankrupt and in jail at the time, but the bill said only that since "Mr Thomson's state of health will not permit him personally to wait on his friends, he humbly hopes that will plead his excuse, and that they will favour him with their company that night."

Thomson, Mr [fl. 1798], *singer.*

The singer Thomson was a Slave in *Blue-Beard* at Drury Lane Theatre from 16 January through 12 June 1798.

Thomson, Master [fl. 1771–1772], *singer.*

According to the Drury Lane Theatre accounts on 31 October 1771, Master Thomson was paid £3 5s. for singing in the chorus for 13 nights. He was paid periodically at the same rate through 25 May 1772. It would appear that he sang in *Harlequin's Invasion* and *The Witches.*

Thomson, Miss [fl. 1739–1769], *dancer, actress.*

A Miss Thomson acted in *The Careless Husband* at Edinburgh on 9 January 1739. With her there was a male Thomson, who may have been her brother or father. Miss Thomson danced at the Aungier Street Theatre in Dublin on 4 December 1740, and on 21 October 1741 she danced in *Le Genereux Corsaire* at Drury Lane Theatre in London. Miss Thomson danced in *Comus* from 11 February through 14 April 1743, and at the Haymarket Theatre on 17 December 1744 she played a Page in *Romeo and Juliet.* She was in the company at Taylors' Hall, Cowgate, Edinburgh, in 1745 and probably earlier; and at the New Concert Hall in Edinburgh from 1746 to 1748 she is known to have acted Douglas in *The Albion Queens,* the Grand Turk's Daughter in *The Amours of Harlequin and Columbine,* Harlequinet in *Love Triumphant,* and Tagg in *Miss in Her Teens.* At the Haymarket in London on 28 February 1769 a Miss Thomson played Tagg and acted Emilia in *Othello.*

There is a distinct possibility that we have confused Mrs Thompson, Miss E. Thompson, and Miss Thomson, for the bills were not always careful to distinguish them, and they had similar lines.

Thomson, Michael *d. 1797, organist.*

Dr Michael Thomson, organist of Hillsborough Cathedral, Ireland, published six anthems in 1786. Among the Lord Chamberlain's papers at the Public Record Office is a list of musicians in the royal band in London in 1793, and Dr Michael "Thompson" is named. Ita Hogan in *Anglo-Irish Music* gives Thomson's death date as 1797.

Thomson, William [fl.c. 1775–1789], singer, organist, composer.

W. Thomson sang tenor for the Academy of Ancient Music in 1787–88 for a fee of £4 10s. W. "Thompson" sang in the chorus of *Romeo and Juliet* on 14 September 1789 at Covent Garden Theatre. From Humphries and Smith's *Music Publishing in the British Isles* we learn that he was William Thomson, a book and music seller in Exeter 'Change from about 1775 to 1780 or later. He composed *Six Easy Lessons for the Harpsichord,* published about 1775; the *Catalogue of Printed Music in the British Museum* identifies him as from Leominster. Thomson was at one point librarian to the Academy of Ancient Music and organist of St Michael, Cornhill.

Thomuth. *See* THUMOTH.

Thoral, Mr [fl.1735], actor.

Mr Thoral played Sir Thomas in *Flora* at the Great Booth on the Bowling Green, Southwark, on 7 April 1735.

Thorndell, Gregory d. 1671, singer.

Gregory Thorndell shared with Dubartus Hunt the role of Villerius in the historic production of *The Siege of Rhodes* at Rutland House about September 1656. On 9 November 1660 Thorndell was appointed to the King's Musick as a Gentleman of the Chapel Royal at an annual salary of £40, plus livery of £16 2s. 6d.—which was seldom paid on time. He was apparently a member of the Corporation of Music shortly before his death on 17 January 1671. Thorndell left no will, but a memorandum dating about 28 December 1670, identifying him as one of the Gentlemen of the Chapel Royal, left all of his estate to John Thornton. The probate date was 7 May 1672. The court musician Henry Cooke mentioned in his will of 6 July 1672 that he was executor for Thorndell and was still owed £96 10s. in back livery payments.

Thorne, Mr [fl.1785–1786], actor.

At the Haymarket Theatre on 25 April 1785 Mr Thorne played Don Ferdinand in *'Tis Well It's No Worse,* and at the Hammersmith Theatre on 25 July (advertised as making his second appearance on that stage) he acted Count Almaviva in *The Follies of a Day* and Dermot in *The Poor Soldier.* He also appeared that summer at the Richmond Theatre, and the bills for the Royal Circus show him to have performed in *Who's Who,* a burletta, in the spring (probably) of 1786. He had a role in a new pantomime at the Royal Circus on 26 and 28 October 1786. The *Index to The London Stage* conflates his career with that of the scene designer Thorne of later years.

Thorne, Mr [fl.1794–1822], scene painter.

Mr Thorne worked as a scene painter at Covent Garden Theatre from as early as 2 August 1794 at 8s. daily. Between then and 1808 he helped paint scenery for such productions as *Mago and Dago, Merry Sherwood, Harlequin and Oberon, Raymond and Agnes, The Magic Oak, Harlequin Quicksilver, Harlequin's Magnet, The Ogre and Little Tom, The Blind Boy,* and *Harlequin and His Element,* according to the census of scene painters in *Theatre Notebook* in 1965. He designed scenery at Ipswich in 1815 and may have been the Thorne who was discharged from Drury Lane Theatre in London on 4 April 1820 (though Nelson and Cross, the editors of Winston's *Drury Lane Journal,* call that Thorne a performer). The painter Thorne worked at Vauxhall Gardens in 1822.

Thorne, Thomas d. 1764, carpenter.

The earliest notice we have found of Thomas Thorne, the Covent Garden Theatre master carpenter, is a note in the account books dated 28 June 1760; he and Thomas Hall were paid £1 13s. for a week's work in the women's wardrobe—making repairs or alterations one supposes. The following year Thorne was twice cited in the accounts for payments of over £12 "for the Scenemen," over whom he evidently had authority. The *Public Advertiser* reported that Thomas Thorne died on 29 June (May?) 1764. He had written his will on 27 May, describing himself as of the parish of St Giles in the Fields, carpenter. He left his estate to Mary Thorne, his daughter, and Mary Chitty, widow, "who had resided & cohabited with me for 16 years or thereabout as my wife." Thomas

Emery, also a Covent Garden employee, proved Thorne's will on 12 June 1764.

Thornhill, Dr _[fl. 1720]_, _singer, actor?_

For his own benefit at the Great Booth in the Queen's Arms Tavern, Southwark, on 3 October 1720 Dr Thornhill presented _Love for Love_ (and perhaps played a role in it) and sang "A Comical Dialogue between Dr Thornhill and his Old Merry Andrew." The performers were supposedly drawn from both Drury Lane and Lincoln's Inn Fields, but Thornhill may have been an amateur.

Thornhill, Mrs _[fl. 1720]_, _actress._

Mrs Thornhill played Araminta in _The Confederacy_ at Lincoln's Inn Fields Theatre on 28 March 1720. According to British Library Additional Charter 9306, she was still in the company on 1 November 1720.

Thornhill, James _1675–1734, scene painter._

James Thornhill was born on 25 July 1675 or 1676 at Woolland, Melcombe Regis, Dorsetshire, the son of Walter and Mary Thornhill. His mother had been Mary Sydenham, the daughter of William Sydenham of Winford Eagle; his father was the eighth son of George Thornhill (or Thornhull). A Parliamentarian, Walter Thornhill's fortunes deteriorated at the Restoration and he became a grocer in Dorchester. Young James was sent to London, and with the help of his uncle, Dr Thomas Sydenham, he was apprenticed on 9 May 1689 to Thomas Highmore, later the King's Serjeant Painter. James was made free of the Painter-Stainers Company on 1 March 1704. He may have worked under Verrio or Laguerre or both, and _The Dictionary of National Biography_ states that he traveled on the Continent, studying the works of Carracci, Nicholas Poussin, and others. His sketchbook, now at the British Museum, also shows the influence of Pellegrini and Sebastiano Ricci.

Thornhill's first known theatrical commission was the scenery for Thomas Clayton's opera _Arsinoe_, which opened on 16 January 1705 at Drury Lane Theatre. Sketches for the scenery are now at the Victoria and Albert Museum, along with many other Thornhill drawings. A sketch labeled "The 1st Great flat Scene" is at the Art Institute in Chicago and may also relate to Drury Lane and the production of _Arsinoe_. Thornhill also designed scenery for productions by the Drury Lane troupe at Hampton Court Palace in 1718.

Most of his career, however, was devoted to baroque decorative painting. Among his works were the interior of the dome of St Paul's Cathedral (against Wren's wishes), the Great Hall at Blenheim, the saloon and hall of the mansion at Moor Park, apartments at Hampton Court, the hall and staircase at Baston Neston, the Chapel at Wimpole, the Great Hall at Greenwich Hospital (the greatest history painting commission in England, a task which occupied him for 20 years), and paintings at Chatsworth, Bastwell, Stoke Edith, and Oxford. He toured the Low Countries in 1711, keeping an illustrated diary, one of two now at the Victoria and Albert Museum. His second diary dates from 1716–17, when he visited France. Thornhill was also a portrait painter whose sitters included Sir Isaac Newton, Sir Richard Steele, and himself.

National Portrait Gallery

JAMES THORNHILL
by Richardson

National Portrait Gallery

JAMES THORNHILL

self-portrait

Thornhill tried to establish a national school of art. He was made one of the directors of Kneller's academy in Great Queen Street in 1711 and became the Governor in 1716, but he and Kneller were often at odds. Then he began his own academy in James Street, Covent Garden, behind his own house at No 12, the Piazza (he had previously lived at No 75, Dean Street, Soho). William Hogarth attended Thornhill's academy and noted that it was not successful and soon closed.

Dudley Ryder recorded in his *Diary* an encounter on 28 August 1716 with Thornhill when the artist was painting the dome of St Paul's:

[T]he man that keeps the keys for the whispering gallery told me that nobody ever went up there. Mr. Thornhill would not admit it. However, I desired him to show me the door into it, which he did, and told me if I would ring the bell and ask for Mr. Thornhill they would admit me up and I must then make my excuse to Mr. Thornhill. This shocked me a little at first. However, I thought it could be no such great crime to beg the favour of seeing his painting and design. Accordingly I ventured and was admitted up by his servant. When I came I made my bow to Mr. Thornhill and told him I had a great curiosity to see so extraordinary

a piece of painting as that of the Dome of St. Paul's and begged the favour of being allowed the liberty to view what was done of it. He told me this was a liberty which he did not usually allow to anybody, because if it was people would come in so great crowds that they would interrupt him in his study and painting. However, since I was come, I might go about it and view any part of it. I thanked him for the liberty and began to look about me, and then told him we should now be able to vie at last with Paris for history painting which we have been so deficient in before. He told me he had been about this a year already and expected to finish it in a year more.

After Ryder had observed a while

Mr. Thornhill came up to me again and talked with me about painting and told me he supposed I was a virtuoso. I told him I took pleasure in seeing fine painting. He asked me if I did not paint myself. I told him no. He took me, I believe, for one that understood it pretty well, but I was afraid of talking to him lest I should discover my ignorance. He at length seemed mighty complaisant and glad that anybody that was a judge would come to take notice of his performance. He said there were but few that took a pleasure in viewing these things, and would give themselves the trouble to come and see him, and therefore he was not much troubled upon that account with many people. I went up to the top of the scaffolds where the very top of the Dome is painted chiefly with roses gilded within squares. It will be exceeding rich. There are two or three more persons who are under-workers that are working at these figures but Mr. Thornhill himself comes and overlooks them and directs them.

The anecdote reveals nicely the sometimes arrogant, sometimes whining personality of Thornhill. Vain, fawning, sensitive, domineering, some of his commissions and honors he gained as much by having good connections at court as by his artistic talent. His patron, Lord Sunderland, was persuaded by Thornhill's friend John Huggins to urge the King to knight the painter.

He was made Serjeant painter to the King in March 1720, succeeding his master, Highmore, and the following May he was knighted, the first native painter so honored. Other posts held by Thornhill were History Painter in Ordinary to the King and Master of the Painter-Stainers Company. He was elected M.P. for Weymouth in 1722 and a Fellow of the Royal Society in May 1723. Thornhill's son John (1700–1757) succeeded him as Serjeant

Art Institute of Chicago, Leonora Hall Gurley Memorial Collection

Great flat Scene

by THORNHILL

Painter in 1732. James Thornhill died on 13 (or 4?) May 1734 at Thornhill Park in Dorsetshire. He was buried in the churchyard at Stalbridge. Administration of his estate was granted to his widow Judith (1673–1757) on 20 May 1734. The Thornhills had a daughter, Jane, who was clandestinely married to the artist William Hogarth on 23 March 1729.

In 1967 the Victoria and Albert Museum published *Sketches by Thornhill,* with a biography and catalogue of plates by Edgard de N. Mayhew. Also valuable is the sixth chapter of Ronald Paulson's *Hogarth,* Colvin's *Biographical Dictionary of British Architects,* and "Thornhill at Wimpole," by Brian Allen, in the September 1985 issue of *Apollo.*

Victoria and Albert Museum

Scene for *Arsinoe, Queen of Cyprus*

by THORNHILL

Not all portraits called "Sir James Thornhill" can be authenticated. The following list includes both those portraits that have been authenticated and those sometimes said to be of him. Because it is not always possible to follow the various items through the sales rooms with certainty, some duplications may occur in the list:

1. By Charles Boit, oval enamel. Sold at Christie's on 8 May 1878 (lot 131). Present location unknown.

2. By Michael Dahl. Three-quarter length. Listed in Cock's sale catalogue of the collection of Edward, Earl of Oxford, March 1741 (lot 34); bought by Maddison. Present location unknown.

3. By Michael Dahl. Head only, according to Vertue's "Notes" in the British Library (Add MSS 23076, fol 12d). Present location unknown.

4. By Gawen Hamilton. Called Sir James Thornhill showing his friends the famous Poussin he had bought. In the Beaverbrook Art Gallery, Frederickburg, New Brunswick; the gift of Sir Alec Martin.

5. By Gawen Hamilton. "An Elegant Company Playing Cards." Oil on canvas, 23¼" × 21". Possibly the picture in the collection of the Rev Charles Onley, Stisted Hall, Essex, by 1794; by descent to Onley Savill-Onley, on whose death it was sold at Christie's on 16 June 1894 (lot 56), as by Hogarth, and bought by Colnaghi. By 1929 it was with O. Bondy, Vienna, as "by Hogarth: A Card Table with Peg Woffington." Offered at Sotheby's on 15 November 1989 (lot 31, illustrated in the sale catalogue), but withdrawn or not sold. Two other versions exist: one at the Tate Gallery, unfinished; and the other, a contemporary copy, at the Walker Art Gallery, Liverpool. The painting is now considered to be by Gawen Hamilton. The couple on the right of the painting are probably Sir James and Lady Thornhill.

6. By Joseph Highmore, 1723. Untraced, but a profile etching signed "*J. Highmore/pinx & fecit/1723*" was exhibited at Colnaghi's in 1972 (No 32). A corresponding profile in oil, 21½" × 16", facing the opposite direction, was with Christie's in September 1974, from

the collection of Lady Angela Oswald; provenance unknown, but perhaps the original? The latter is bust length, with sitter in green coat; it was bought by Stewart for 180 guineas.

7. By Joseph Highmore. Thornhill at age 57. The picture is untraced but it is known through various engravings:

a. By J. Baker. Oval frame on pedestal.

b. By Barrett. Published as a plate to *Biographical Magazine*, 1795.

c. By J. Faber Jr. Sold by J. Faber at the Green Door in Craven Buildings. Another impression has Faber's address changed to "ye Golden Head."

d. By unknown engravers: four versions, including one published as a plate d'Argenville's *Vies des plus fameux peintres*, 1762.

8. By William Hogarth. Head and shoulders. Painted in 1734. The portrait survives only in S. Ireland's engraving, published by W. Dickinson in 1786 and reduced for Ireland's *Graphic Illustrations*, 1794. Probably it was the portrait of Thornhill by Hogarth that was in the Ireland sale at Sotheby's on 12 May 1801, and was bought by Vernon for 14*s*. (see No 8), and again sold, by Thomas Winstanley at Christie's on 15 March 1805 (lot 72). A portrait engraved by J. Whessell, after Hogarth, and published in Ireland's *Graphic Illustrations* with the erroneous title "Mr. Jas. Thornhill," is actually Hogarth's portrait of John Thornhill, Sir James's son.

9. By William Hogarth. Sir James and Lady Thornhill, "kit-kat" size. Sold by Samuel Ireland at Sotheby's on 12 May 1801; bought by Vernon for 14*s*.

10. By William Hogarth. Called Sir James Thornhill, but identification doubtful. Oil, 34½" × 28½". The photograph in the Witt Library places it in the Drury-Lowe collection, No 185.

11. By William Hogarth. Said to be Sir James Thornhill. Oil on paper, 5½" × 4½", head and shoulders. Sold at Sotheby's on 16 February 1972; buyer unknown to us.

12. By William Hogarth. Said to be Thornhill painting a picture of his daughter Jane (Hogarth's wife). The property of Charles B. Braham (the singer John Braham's son) when sold at Messrs Foster, No 54, Pall Mall, on 21 June 1871. Probably the picture described as Thornhill painting a portrait of his daughter,

10" × 7", that was sold at Sotheby's on 13 October 1971.

13. Attributed to William Hogarth and called James Thornhill. Perhaps a copy of the portrait by Hogarth that was engraved by Ireland. Given by Carlo Loeser in 1909 to the Ufizzi Gallery, Florence. Photograph in the Witt Library.

14. By William Hogarth. In Hogarth's painting of Jane Thornhill, c. 1738, she is shown holding an oval portrait of her father on her lap. Owned by the Earl of Rosebery.

15. By William Hogarth? In the Huntington Library art file is a notation of a portrait of Thornhill by Hogarth in the "Bell Collection." The portrait and the collection are otherwise unknown.

16. By William Hogarth. Thornhill is said to be one of the figures in Hogarth's group picture of "The Fleet Prison Committee, 1729." The oil sketch on paper is in the Fitzwilliam Museum and the finished canvas is in the National Portrait Gallery. Both are reproduced in Ronald Paulson's *Hogarth: His Life, Art, and Times* (1971), 1, plates 65a and 65b.

17. By William Hogarth. In a group portrait of a family said to be the Thornhill, but that is doubtful. When it was exhibited at York in 1866 it was called "Sir James Thornhill exhibiting a picture to his uncle and patron, Dr. Sydenham," but the latter died eight years before Hogarth was born. The picture was with A. Tooth in London, 1946; it was sold at Christie's on 18 June 1971, bought by Mostyn for £900. Its provenance was given as from the collections of J. Andrews and Dr Donovan when it was offered at Christie's on 22 November 1974 (illustrated in the sales catalogue), and bought by Fitzwilliam Howard for 3000 guineas.

18. By William Hogarth. A painting, 25" × 26½", called "The Broken Fan" possibly represents members of the Thornhill family. Once in the collection of J. Holme, then W. Cuningham; bought in 1849 by Thomas Baring, from whom it was passed by descent to the present owner, Lord Northbrook.

19. Attributed to Hogarth. Called James Thornhill, 28½" × 23½", in brown cloak and white cravat. Sold at Christie's on 5 March 1954 (lot 97); bought for five guineas by Bell.

20. By William Hogarth and James Thornhill, 1730. The two artists collaborated on a

Royal Naval College, Greenwich

"George I and his Family"—with JAMES THORNHILL standing in lower right corner
by THORNHILL

painting of the sitting of the House of Commons during the administration of Sir Robert Walpole. Hogarth painted Thornhill into the bottom row. With the National Trust, the Earl of Onslow collection, Clandon Park. Another version, in the possession of the Earl of Hardwicke in 1888, was in the Colville sale at Christie's on 24 February 1939, and was bought by Nicholls. An engraving by R. Page (and A. Fogg) was published by E. Harding, 1863.

21. By Thomas Hudson. Sold as the property of Nathaniel Smith at Wells's on 8 October 1803.

22. By Jonathan Richardson, c. 1730–34. In the National Portrait Gallery (No 3962). Related to a drawing by Richardson dated July 1733 which is now in the British Museum. In his National Portrait Gallery catalogue David Piper suggested that Richardson may have painted more than one version, and that the NPG's is a repetition.

23. By Jonathan Richardson. Drawing inscribed with Thornhill's name in Richardson's hand and dated by Richardson August 1733. In the British Museum. A copy drawn by James Alexander and dated 20 October 1813 is in the Huntington Library.

24. By J. P. Richter, 1718. Miniature in the collection of Mrs Blofeld in 1963.

25. Self-portrait. Thornhill's sketch of his family, c. 1730. Pen and violet wash, shows him standing, center, pointing to one of the Raphael cartoons on his easel, with family members and Hogarth gathered around. In the collection of the Marquess of Exeter; reproduced in Ronald Paulson's *Hogarth: His Life, Art, and Times* (1971), 1: 211.

26. Self-portrait. A pen and wash drawing, called "The Connoisseurs and Sir James Thornhill," c. 1719, contains figures by Thornhill, including a self-portrait, seated at table with papers, head resting on left hand. Other figures are M. Dahl, John Wooton, James Gibb, Matthew Prior, and Humphrey Wanley. A sketch evidently intended for a painting at Wimpole Hall, country seat of Edward Harley, second Earl of Oxford, in 1721. Reproduced in *Apollo* 122 (September 1985). In the Art Institute of Chicago, Leonora Hall Gurley Memorial collection.

27. Self-portrait. Half-length in oval, with wig. In the National Portrait Gallery (No

4688), given in 1969 by Douglas H. Gordon of Baltimore. This picture presumably is a sketch for his figure in the upper west wall of the Painted Hall, Royal Naval Hospital, Greenwich.

28. Self-portrait. Half-length, holding a pencil, in a painted oval, 29½" × 24". Offered at Sotheby's on 17 June 1981 (illustrated in the catalogue); buyer unknown to us.

29. Self-portrait. Owned about 1838 by the singer John Braham at South Lodge, his home at No 69, Baker Street. It is also listed in an inventory for No 21, Green Street, Leicester Square, dated 9 November 1870, the property of Braham's descendants (manuscript in Strachie collection, Somerset Records Office, Taunton). Present location unknown. Perhaps one of the self-portraits on this list.

30. Self-portrait. Hanging in the Chapter House, St Paul's Cathedral.

31. Self-portrait. Sold by Philip James Tassaert at Christie's on 28 November 1803 (lot 101); bought for 5s. by Woodin.

32. Self-portrait. Thornhill painted himself, full-length, standing, into the lower right of his large mural of "George I and his Family," on the wall of the Upper Hall, Royal Naval Hospital, Greenwich.

33. By Thomas Worlidge. Pencil study, 5¼" × 4½". Sold by Elizabeth Richardson Simmons at Christie's on 12 November 1968, and bought for 120 guineas by Sanders. Illustrated in the sales catalogue. With it was sold an unfinished state of Worlidge's etching of Thornhill at his easel, for which this drawing is a study.

34. By Thomas Worlidge. Thornhill standing before easel, holding brush and palette. Engraving; an unfinished state was sold at Christie's on 12 November 1968 with Worlidge's study drawing (see above, No 32). The only engraved state listed in the *Catalogue of Engraved British Portraits in the British Museum* is by H. Robinson, after Worlidge, which was published as a plate to Walpole's *Anecdotes*, 1828.

35. By unknown artist (called "school of Zincke"). Miniature enamel, oval 1⅓", three-quarter-length, looking at viewer, wearing powdered wig, green and gold embroidered vest, and brown coat. Offered at Sotheby's on 1 November 1965 (lot 5).

36. By unknown artist. In the entry to the

Painted Hall, Royal Naval Hospital, Greenwich, from the National Maritime Museum, Greenwich Hospital collection.

37. By unknown artist. In the National Portrait Gallery (No 118). Inscribed on the stretcher in a nineteenth-century hand: "Portrait of Sir James Thornhill Painted by Himself Late the Property [of] Mr Hamlet." Now called "Unknown Youth," by unknown artist, c. 1702–1705.

38. Plaster bust attributed to Charles Stanley. Both attributions of sitter and sculptor are doubtful. Owned by Lord Faringdon at Barnsley Park, Bibury.

Thornhill, John *1700–1757, scene painter.*

John Thornhill was christened at St Giles in the Fields on 5 May 1700. He was the son of James (later Sir James) Thornhill and his wife Judith. John succeeded to his father's post as serjeant painter in July 1732. In 1735 John became one of the original 24 members of the

By permission of the Trustees of the British Museum

JOHN THORNHILL (mistitled)
engraving by J. Whessell, after Hogarth

Sublime Society of Beefsteaks and may by then have been working for the founder, John Rich, manager of Covent Garden Theatre. Thornhill was made free (by patrimony) of the Painter-Stainers Company in 1739. He was certainly employed as a scene painter at Covent Garden in 1746–47, when he received payments of £21 and £34 10s. He served as Master of the Painter-Stainers Company in 1748–49.

John Thornhill died in September 1757. As Paulson notes in his *Hogarth,* Thornhill had resigned the post of serjeant painter in favor of his brother-in-law William Hogarth in July 1757. On 12 August Thornhill made his will, naming, among others, Ebenezer Forrest and George Lambert the painter, both fellow members of the Beefsteaks. To each member of that Society Thornhill left mourning rings.

Thornhill's portrait was engraved by J. Whessell, after Hogarth, published as a plate to Ireland's *Graphic Works* in 1799 and incorrectly titled "Mr. Jas. Thornhill."

Thornowets, Miss [*fl.* 1729–1736], *singer, actress.*

Miss Thornowets made her first Goodman's Fields appearance on 9 December 1729 as a singer. She presumably had had previous stage experience, though we have found no earlier mention of her in playbills. She sang frequently throughout the 1729–30 season and was cast as the Visiting Lady in *Harlequin Turn'd Dancing Master* on 16 April 1730. At her shared benefit (with only one other person) on 16 June Miss Thornowets sang in Italian and English. *The London Stage* mistakenly lists her as a dancer in 1729–30.

A Miss Thornowets played Cupid in *King Arthur* at Goodman's Fields on 17 December 1736, and though she was advertised as making her first appearance on any stage, she seems to have been our subject. She was a Shepherdess in *Harlequin Shipwrecked* on 20 February. *The London Stage* again lists her as a dancer in 1736–37 at Lincoln's Inn Fields, but the bills show her to have been a singer. She sang in the chorus of *King Arthur* on 30 September 1736 and was then Mrs Lovepuppy in *The Worm Doctor,* a Follower in *Harlequin Shipwrecked,* and Mrs Slammekin in *The Beggar's Pantomime.* Her name disappeared from the bills after 31 December 1736.

Thornton, Mr ₍*fl. 1776–1777*₎, *dresser.*
During the 1776–1777 season a Mr Thornton was employed at Drury Lane Theatre as a men's dresser, earning nine shillings a week.

Thornton, Henry F., real name Ford?
b. 1748, actor, manager.

Henry F. Thornton, whose real name was said by the author of the *Thespian Dictionary* (1805) to have been Ford, was a native of Claire, Sussex. He was born about 1748. John Bernard said that Thornton was 25 in 1773. He is both an ubiquitous and an elusive figure in the history of the English provincial theatre. James Winston, in describing one of his ventures in *The Theatric Tourist* (1805), remarked, "As Mr. THORNTON maintains so many theatres; or, rather, as so many theatres contribute to the maintenance of Mr. THORNTON, we shall have frequent occasion to note his eccentricities, which are almost as many and as ludicrous as the celebrated [James Augustus] WHITLEY's." But aside from a tame anecdote having to do with bribing a bailiff, one about absent-mindedness, and some testimony about his devotion to ad-libbing, Winston tells us little about Thornton's personality.

Certainly he was energetic and versatile. He was acting and prompting in Wheeler's company at Plymouth and Portsmouth in the 1770s. He was on some playbills at King's Lynn in 1779. He was acting in low comedy at Bristol in 1778 and 1779 and again at Plymouth in 1780 (a bill of 19 July 1780 shows him playing the Lay Brother in *The Duenna* and Mr Woodley in *Three Weeks after Marriage*).

Just when the managerial fever struck Thornton is uncertain. Winston says towns were "adopted by him, when deserted by all other theatrical campaigners" and that he was "particularly careful never to lose by any of his adventures, as his schemes are conducted on so confined a principle, that a nightly average of a few pounds will amply repay him; and but for his constant rage for building, must have realized a handsome independence."

About 1787, wrote Winston, Thornton "ventured to rent a large thatched barn, on lease for ten years, at ten pounds per year, situate in the yard of the Angel Inn [at Andover], after agreeing with the proprietor (a carpenter by trade), to enlarge and make it fit,

at a considerable expense: the decorations were better than could have been reasonably expected. . . ." But when the lease expired the barn was sold by the owner. Thornton had to contract with a printer named Rawlins who agreed to erect the shell of a theatre and give Thornton a long lease. That house also was fitted up at Thornton's expense. He opened there on Easter Monday 1803.

Thornton, meanwhile, in 1788, had erected a theatre in Friar Street, Reading, holding "upwards of forty pounds"; and he built another at Guildford the same year. By 1792 he had added Newbury, Croydon, Gosport, and Chelmsford to his occasional circuit, according to the *Thespian Dictionary* of September 1792; and the *Theatrical Journal* in 1793 added Windsor to the list. He had finished building the Newbury Theatre in November 1802. Winston described the interior: "It is a small House, but neatly fitted up—the Boxes are lined with crimson damask: the centre Box is private, and is decorated for the reception of the Margravine of Anspach, who occasionally distinguishes it with her presence. . . ." A letter from J. Foley to Winston, now in the Birmingham Public Library, speaks of the terms under which the Croydon house was obtained. It was "let to Thornton from Year to Year for the season only which commences the 2d of October of Croydon Fair-day and continues the space of Six weeks or two Months." Another Winston transcription in that collection states that Thornton held forth at Reading "during Race Week and two months afterwards."

A. H. W. Fynmore in *Notes and Queries* (1931) cites a February 1809 notation in the diary of John Cole Tomkins in *Sussex Archaelogical Collections*: "Last Year Mr. Thornton built the Theatre at Arundel adjoining my Mothers house, Cost £1,300, on leasehold Ground for 60 years." (The site in 1931 was No 18, Maltravers Street). The Lord Chamberlain's records show licenses granted to Thornton in 1795 and 1796, and each year, 1809 through 1813, for theatrical performances "at Windsor during Eton vac., Whilst HM is resident." The *Authentic Memoirs of the Green Room* (c. 1814) found Thornton still active, at Gosport and Arundel. His acting specialty was elderly eccentrics.

Henry Thornton is rather typical of a number of actor-managers operating busily on circuits all over England and not much concerned with what went on in the capital. He enters this *Dictionary* by reason of one performance. When Edward Cape Everard, himself for many years a provincial actor, organized his own benefit at the Haymarket Theatre in London on 22 April 1795, he invited Henry Thornton to play Lord Ogleby in *The Clandestine Marriage,* advertised "for that night only." So far as we know, he had never acted in London before and never acted there again.

Thornton, Margaret. *See* MARTYR, MARGARET.

Thornton, Martha. *See* NORTON, MARTHA.

Thorp, Mr ₁*fl. 1726–1736*₁, *billsticker, watchman.*

The accounts for John Rich's Lincoln's Inn Fields Theatre in 1726 show a payment of 2*s.* 6*d.* to Mr Thorp, "watchman in the front," for his Christmas box. Rich's accounts for Covent Garden Theatre in 1735–36, in R. J. Smith's transcription at the British Library, list "Thorpe" as a billsticker (or billsetter).

Thrustans, Thomas ₁*fl. 1784?–1794*₁, *violinist, pianist.*

Farmer in his *History of Music in Scotland* notes that at some point between 1785 and 1788 the leader of the band at the Aberdeen Musical Society Concerts, Robert Mackintosh, was moved down to second violin and replaced by Mr Thrustans from London. The Londoner was Thomas Thrustans, identified in Doane's *Musical Directory* of 1794 as a violinist and pianist living in London at No 8, opposite the Orange Coffee House, in Chelsea. It seems likely that Thrustans was the Mr "Thurstan" who had played first violin in the Handel Memorial Concerts at Westminster Abbey and the Pantheon in May and June 1784.

Thumoth, Burk, stage name of Burke of Thumond *1717–1747, instrumentalist, composer.*

Burke of Thumond, who took Burk Thumoth (or Thumont) as his professional name, was born in 1717, presumably in Ireland. At

Goodman's Fields Theatre on 13 May 1730 a lesson on the harpsichord was played by Burk, who was advertised as 13 years of age. On 22 May he played a harpsichord lesson by Handel and a trumpet piece, and on 2 June, accompanied by the Goodman's Fields band on stage, Burk played a "Trumpet Farce, call'd *See-larce.*" On 9 April 1731 he was advertised as 14 when he had a benefit concert at Hickford's Music Room, and on 23 April he played harpsichord and trumpet pieces at the Devil Tavern at Temple Bar. On 10 May he was featured at the Haymarket Theatre, and on 9 August he played at the Great Room in St Alban's Street. Latreille transcribed a bill that differs from that in *The London Stage* for the Haymarket Theatre on 10 May 1731; Latreille's bill reads: "A Concerto on the Trumpet by Burk Thumoth, a youth of 14 years of age, belonging to Sir Charles Wills [Major General Sir Charles Wills?]." The concert was a benefit for a family in distress.

Burk was similarly active in the spring of 1732, performing at Hickford's, Goodman's Fields, the Haymarket, and the Fielding-Hippisley booth at Bartholomew Fair. He repeated that pattern in the spring of 1733, and on 22 October 1733 he played a solo on the German horn (according to *The London Stage;* the German flute, according to Latreille) at Drury Lane Theatre. He made fairly regular solo appearances in London through 1737–38, though he was sometimes advertised only once or twice a year. He returned to Drury Lane to play a concerto on the German flute on 16 September 1742. He had probably spent the interim in Dublin, for the *New Grove* (unaware of Thumoth's London activity and his age) notes that references to Thumoth appeared in Dublin newspapers in 1739 and 1740. About 1745 or shortly afterward Thumoth edited two books of traditional Irish, Scottish, and English airs. Since Thumoth died in 1747, the publication probably came out before that year. About 1746 in London *Six Solos for a German Flute* were published, the first three being Thumoth's compositions.

He performed regularly as a flutist at Drury Lane in 1742–43, taking time off on 9 February 1743 to appear at Stationers' Hall and on 30 March to play at Southwark. In 1743–44 he made isolated appearances at Covent Garden Theatre and the Haymarket, and in the fall of 1745 he played occasionally at the Haymarket. On 12 December 1744 a benefit was held for Thumoth at the Swan Tavern in Cornhill, the last discovered mention of him in London papers.

On 27 August 1745 in Bristol, stated the Bristol *Oracle,* "For the BENEFIT of Mr. THUMOTH, Belonging to his Majesty's First Regiment of Foot Guards," a concert was held at Castiglione's Long Room. Thumoth played the German flute and offered, after the concert, "several favourite Scots and Irish Airs. . . ." Thumoth seems to have spent the rest of his career at Bristol. *The London Stage* cites a newspaper report on 9 February 1747 reporting the death of Burk Thumoth, at Bristol, "A few days since." He was "well known for his excellent manner of performing on the German Flute."

Thunderwood, Mr [*fl.* 1794–1795], *carpenter.*

Mr Thunderwood was being paid £1 weekly in 1794–95 as a carpenter at Covent Garden Theatre.

Thurmond, John *d. 1727, actor, dancer.*

The earliest discovered date for the elder John Thurmond is mid-December 1695, when he played Artabasus in *Cyrus* with Betterton's troupe at Lincoln's Inn Fields Theatre. During the rest of the 1695–96 season Thurmond was seen as Frederick in *The She-Gallants* and Friendly in *The City Bride,* a play for which he spoke the prologue. Before the turn of the century he also acted Don Juan in *Rule a Wife and Have a Wife,* Antony in *Julius Caesar,* Rodrigo in *The Italian Husband,* Lord Courtipoll in *The Pretenders,* Bellgard in *Fatal Friendship,* Thyrrold in *Queen Catharine,* Ubaldo in *Rinaldo and Armida,* Cleontes in *Xerxes,* Spinola in *The Princess of Parma,* Lorenzo in *The False Friend,* and Belvoir in *The Beau Defeated.*

According to W. S. Clark in *The Early Irish Stage,* Thurmond joined the company at the Smock Alley Theatre in Dublin in the fall of 1699, though *The London Stage* suggests that Thurmond was still in London in mid-March 1700, acting in *The Beau Defeated.* The only known Dublin role for Thurmond is Colonel Peregrine in *The Spanish Wives* in 1707–8. By that time he had become one of the sharers in the Smock Alley troupe. His wife Winifred, who had become Mrs Thurmond as early as 1697–98, and their young son John were also in the company.

The prompter W. R. Chetwood in his *General History of the Stage* (1749) wrote that Thurmond

was an Actor of Repute in this Kingdom [Ireland] about Thirty Years past, and stood in many capital Parts, being then a Sharer in old *Smock-Alley* Theatre with Mr. *Thomas Elrington,* &c.

To let you see how formerly even Tragedy Heroes were now-and-then put to their Shifts, I'll tell you a short Story that befel Mr. *Thurmond.*

It was a Custom, at that Time, for Persons of the First Rank and Distinction to give their Birth-Day Suits to the most favoured Actors. I Think Mr. *Thurmond* was honour'd by General *Ingoldby* with his. But his Finances being at the last Tide of Ebb, the rich Suit was put in Buckle (a Cant Word for Forty in the Hundred Interest): One Night, Notice was given that the General would be present with the *Government* at the Play, and all the Performers on the Stage were preparing to dress out in the Suits presented. The Spouse of *Johnny* (as he was commonly called) try'd all her Arts to persuade Mr. *Holdfast* the Pawnbroker (*as it fell out, his real Name*) to let go the Cloaths for that Evening, to be returned when the Play was over: But all Arguments were fruitless; nothing but the *Ready,* or Pledge of full equal Value. . . . At last *Winny* the Wife (that is *Winifrede*) put on a compos'd Countenance (but, alas! with a troubled Heart); stepp'd to a neighbouring Tavern, and bespoke a very hot *Negus,* to comfort *Johnny* in the great Part he was to perform that Night, begging to have the Silver Tankard with the Lid, because, as she said, *A Covering, and the Vehicle Silver, would retain Heat longer than any other Metal.* The Request was comply'd with, the *Negus* carry'd to the Play-house piping hot— popp'd into a vile earthen Mug—the Tankard *L'argent* travelled *Incog.* under her Apron (like the *Persian* Ladies veil'd), popp'd into the Pawnbroker's Hands, in exchange for the Suit—put on, and play'd its Part, with the rest of the Wardrobe; when its Duty was over, carried back to remain in its old Depository—the Tankard return'd the right Road; and, when the Tide flow'd with its Lunar Influence, the stranded Suit was wafted into safe Harbour again, after paying a little for *dry Docking,* which was all the Damage receiv'd.

By 13 January 1708, Fitzgerald tells us in his *New History,* John Thurmond was in the new united company of players at the Drury Lane Theatre in London, though he and Powell did not act at first due to infirmities. On 4 June 1708 Thurmond is recorded as playing

Jaffeir in *Venice Preserv'd,* and on 10 July he acted Muly Labas in *The Empress of Morocco.* At Drury Lane in 1708–9 he was seen in such characters as Plume in *The Recruiting Officer,* Hamlet (his first attempt at the role in England, which implies that he had acted it earlier in Dublin), Macduff in *Macbeth,* Villeroy in *The Fatal Marriage,* Southampton in *The Unhappy Favourite,* Alexander in *The Rival Queens,* Antonio in *The Libertine Destroyed,* Cortez in *The Indian Emperor,* Torrismond in *The Spanish Fryar,* Othello (for his benefit on 9 October 1708, not a normal benefit month), Haemon in *Oedipus,* Hamond in *Rollo,* Horatius in *Appius and Virginia,* Antony in *All for Love* (for his second benefit, on 2 May 1709), and Ulysses in *Troilus and Cressida.* Acting with him that season was the younger John Thurmond.

Thurmond was at the Queen's Theatre in 1709–10, playing the Duke in *The Chances,* the Governor in *Love Makes a Man,* Carlos in *The Fatal Marriage,* Pedro in *The Rover,* the Mad Scholar in *The Pilgrim,* and Brisac in *The Villain.* Then he joined Pinkethman's troupe at Greenwich in the summer of 1710 to play Carlos in *Love Makes a Man,* Othello, Villeroy in *The Fatal Marriage,* Jaffeir in *Venice Preserv'd,* Surly in *Sir Courtly Nice,* Laertes in *Hamlet,* Loveworth in *Tunbridge Walks,* Don Antonio in *The Libertine Destroyed,* Worthy in *The Fair Quaker,* Macduff in *Macbeth,* Haemon in *Oedipus,* Lavinio in *A Duke and No Duke,* and Worthy in *The Relapse.*

Company management shifted again, and in 1710–11 the elder Thurmond began the season at the Queen's Theatre and finished it at Drury Lane, adding to his repertoire such new parts as Lenox in *Macbeth,* the Governor in *Oroonoko,* Diphilus in *The Maid's Tragedy,* and Oldrents in *The Jovial Crew.* He remained at Drury Lane at least through 28 November 1712, his known new parts being Don Antonio in *Don John* and Alonzo in *Ximena.* On 9 June 1712 he made his first public appearance as a dancer, in *Two Skippers,* with Wade; it was Thurmond's benefit.

He was in Dublin in 1715 (and probably earlier), according to the notes of the late Emmett Avery, one of his parts being Phaeax in *Timon of Athens.* On 24 May 1715 he played the title role in *Valentinian* at Lincoln's Inn Fields Theatre in London, advertised as acting

for the first time since his arrival from Ireland. His son John had been dancing earlier that month at Drury Lane and Lincoln's Inn Fields, also hailed as lately arrived from Ireland. The bills after that usually identified the elder Thurmond as Thurmond senior, since his son was now appearing regularly in London (usually as a dancer), but we cannot always be certain we have separated the references to the two Thurmonds correctly.

In 1715–16 we believe the elder Thurmond acted, at Lincoln's Inn Fields, Ranger in *The Fond Husband,* Vernish in *The Plain Dealer,* Hubert in *The Royal Merchant,* and the King in *1 Henry IV.* In 1716–17 he was at Drury Lane, acting such new characters as Honorius in *Lucius,* the Lieutenant in *The Old Troop,* and Saturnius in *Titus Andronicus.* In 1717–18 the elder Thurmond seems to have acted at Drury Lane, while the younger Thurmond and his wife were at Lincoln's Inn Fields. Our subject played the King in *Henry IV,* the Duke in *The Chances,* Champernell in *The Little French Lawyer,* Brumpton in *The Funeral,* Kent in *King Lear,* Lucius in *Cato,* Pounce in *The Tender Husband,* Pylades in *The Distrest Mother,* Balance in *The Recruiting Officer,* a role in *The Tempest,* Don Philip in *Love in a Vail,* Blunt in *The Committee,* and Antonio in *Don John.*

The elder John Thurmond remained at Drury Lane until his death in 1727, acting such new parts as Bonario and Voltore in *Volpone,* Worthy in *Greenwich Park,* Serapion in *All for Love,* Claudius in *Hamlet,* Bertran in *The Spanish Fryar,* Syphoces in *Busiris,* the King in *The Humorous Lieutenant,* Casca in *Julius Caesar,* Heartwell in *The Old Bachelor,* Archidamus in *The Bondman,* Bernard in *The Earl of Warwick,* Cominius in *The Invader of His Country,* Lysander in *The Spartan Dame,* Gloucester in *King Lear,* Abudah in *The Siege of Damascus,* Sullen in *The Stratagem,* Sir Edward in *The Squire of Alsatia,* the Archbishop of York in *2 Henry IV,* Pelopidas in *Mithridates,* Don Alvarez in *The Revenge,* Caesar in *Julius Caesar,* Sosybius in *Cleomenes,* Leontine in *Theodosius,* Omar in *Tamerlane,* Arimant in *Aureng-Zebe,* Portius in *Cato,* Mitza in *The Ambitious Stepmother,* Didius in *The Briton,* Gonsalez in *The Mourning Bride,* Oliver in *Love in a Forest,* the Earl of Salisbury in *Humphrey, Duke of Gloucester,* the King of France in *Henry V,* Northumberland in *Vertue Betray'd,* Maherbal in *So-*

phonisba, Brabantio in *Othello,* Ulysses in *Heroick Love,* Fairbank in *The Twin Rivals,* Acasto in *The Orphan,* and Sylla in *Caius Marius.*

The bills make it clear that the elder John Thurmond also danced, but though he evidently appeared as a dancer on occasion, we take most of the references to a Thurmond dancing at Drury Lane during those years to be to his son John, who served as dancing master and composed a number of pantomimes.

The elder Thurmond died on 7 September 1727 of an apoplectic fit, according to the *St James's Evening Post;* he had been scheduled to act in *Othello* that night. He was buried at St Paul, Covent Garden, on 9 September. Chetwood called him "a merry good-natured Companion to the last."

Mrs John Thurmond, Winifred, evidently did not perform in London, though her daughter-in-law, Sarah Lewis Thurmond, had a considerable acting career. Winifred Thurmond was buried at St Paul, Covent Garden, on 5 October 1736.

Thurmond, John   *d. 1754, dancer, choreographer, actor.*

The younger John Thurmond, according to W. S. Clark in *The Early Irish Stage,* was in the Smock Alley Theatre troupe in Dublin as early as 1707–8, though no specific roles are known for him. He was the son of John and Winifred Thurmond, who had married as early as 1697–98; since young John was acting adult roles by 1708, the Thurmonds may have married earlier, or John may have been born out of wedlock. *The London Stage* lists Thurmond junior as acting Edgeworth in *Bartholomew Fair* at Drury Lane Theatre in London on 31 August 1708 and then Osric in *Hamlet* on 9 September and (for his father's benefit on 2 May 1709) Alexas in *All for Love.* The Lord Chamberlain's accounts show John and his father to have been at the Queen's Theatre in 1709–10, and Thurmond the younger was named in the bill as dancing with Mrs Bicknell on 16 March 1710.

In June and July 1710 at Pinkethman's playhouse in Greenwich the younger Thurmond (regularly distinguished in the bills from his father) acted Clodio in *Love Makes a Man,* Frederick in *The Fatal Marriage,* Guildenstern in *Hamlet,* and Lysimachus in *The Rival Queens.*

On 3 July 1710 *Italian Scaramouch* was danced at Greenwich by young Thurmond and others, "it being the first time of his Performance in Dancing from the Operas." He also danced at the Queen's Theatre on 16 August.

Thurmond's dancing was clearly successful, for the bills from 1711 onward show him devoting his energies to dancing and choreography rather than dramatic parts, and one supposes that when the bills show a Thurmond acting, he was very likely the elder Thurmond. The younger man was the Thurmond who danced at the Queen's Theatre on 2 May 1711, and he was the one who danced a *Spanish Entry* on 13 September in Greenwich; the bill said he had performed it "in the Opera at the Hay-Market [i.e., the Queen's Theatre] last Winter with great Applause." He danced at a concert at Coachmakers' Hall in December 1711 and was the Thurmond who danced at Drury Lane in May 1712. He performed in Ireland after that, returning to London to dance a *Spanish Entry* and *Scaramouch* at Lincoln's Inn Fields Theatre on 16 May 1715. He was advertised as "lately arriv'd from Ireland."

Three Thurmonds were at Lincoln's Inn Fields in 1715–16, the third being the younger John's wife, Sarah, née Lewis. The younger John danced between the acts and the elder acted; one of the dances in which John junior appeared was *Dutch Skipper* with Mrs Cross. On 10 August 1716 Thurmond junior acted Tattle in *Love for Love* and was described as one "who never acted on the Stage before." That does not jibe with the acting *The London Stage* attributes to the younger Thurmond in 1708, 1709, and 1710. In 1716–17 he danced frequently in specialty turns and appeared as Scaramouch in *The Cheats* and Plotwell (Scaramouch) in *The Jealous Doctor.* That season he also choreographed at least two dances, a *Grand Comic Dance* and a *Spanish Dance.* He shared a benefit with his fellow dancer Shaw on 21 May 1717, but the receipts were only £51 5s. Thurmond and his wife remained at Lincoln's Inn Fields in 1717–18, though the elder Thurmond moved to Drury Lane. Our man continued his entr'acte appearances, repeated his earlier roles in pantomime-like pieces, composed at least two new dances, and played Scaramouch in *Harlequin Executed,* the King in *The Humorous Lieutenant,* and a Fury in *Amadis.*

Scene from THURMOND'S *Harlequin Doctor Faustus*

artist unknown

In 1718–19 Thurmond junior joined his father at Drury Lane, and there, except for two seasons at Goodman's Fields in the early 1730s, he continued his career through 1736–37. One might speculate that Thurmond left Lincoln's Inn Fields because the manager there, John Rich, was a harlequin and made prospects for Thurmond's advancement dim. At Drury Lane Thurmond became dancing master and chief contriver of pantomimes. His first appearance there seems to have been on 8 October 1718, when he danced with Miss Smith. He appeared regularly as an entr'acte dancer throughout the season and in the seasons that followed. On 12 February 1719 his *Dumb Farce,* "A new Dramatick Entertainment of Dancing," was presented, with Thurmond as Scaramouch, and his pantomime-like *A Duke and No Duke* came out on 4 December 1719 with Thurmond in the title role. By his benefit night on 27 April 1722 he was designated the theatre's dancing master.

The younger John Thurmond is best known for contriving *Harlequin Doctor Faustus,* which had its premiere on 26 November 1723 at Drury Lane, with Thurmond dancing Mars. He called it "A new Grotesque Entertainment. . . . in the Character of Harlequin, Mephostophilus, Scaramouch, Pierrot, Punch, and the Spirit of Helen: The whole concluding with a grand Masque of the Heathen Deities, (viz.), Apollo, Mars, Bacchus, Mercury,

Diana, Ceres, Flora, and Iris." Though pantomime-like pieces had been presented earlier in the century, *Harlequin Doctor Faustus* is often cited as the first English pantomime; it set a pattern for pantomimes in later years.

The *Universal Journal* on 11 December described the show in detail:

At the drawing of the curtain, Dr. Faustus's study is discovered; the Doctor enters, pricks his finger, and with the blood signs a contract: it thunders; and a Devil, riding on a fiery dragon, flies swiftly cross the stage: the Devil alights, receives the contract, and embraces Dr. Faustus, delivers him a wand, and vanishes. Two countrymen and women enter to be told their fortunes; the Doctor waves his wand, and four pictures turn out of the scenes opposite to these country people, representing a Judge, a Soldier, a dressed Lady, and a Lady in a riding habit: Dr. Faustus, by his action, shews them they are to be what is represented in those pictures. The scene changes, and discovers the outside of a handsome house; the two men and women enter, as returning home; as they are going off the Doctor seizes the two women; the countrymen return to rescue their wives; the Doctor waves his wand, four Devils enter, the men are frighted, run up the steps of the house, clap their back against the door, the front of the house immediately turns, and the husbands are thrown out of the stage; the wives remain with the Doctor; and at the same instant the machine turns, a supper ready dressed, rises swiftly up, and a Devil is transformed into an agreeable shape, who dances whilst they are regaling, and then vanishes. The husbands appear at the window, threatening the Doctor, who by art magic have large horns fixed to their heads, that they can neither get out nor in. Dr. Faustus and the women go out; he beckons the table, and it follows him off. The scene changes to the street. Punch, Scaramouch, and Pierro enter in scholars gowns and caps; they are invited into the Doctor's house by a Devil: they enter, and the scene changes to the inside of the house: the Doctor receives them kindly, and invites them to sit down to a bottle of wine; as they are drinking, the table rises, upon which they start back affrighted: then the spirit of Helen rises in a chair of state, with a canopy over her; she entertains them with a dance, goes to her seat again, and sinks. While the scholars are drinking, the Doctor waves his wand, and large asses ears appear, at once, upon each of their heads: they join in a dance, each pointing and laughing at the others; the Doctor follows them out, pointing and laughing at them all. The scene being changed to the street, a Usurer crosses the stage with a bag of money, goes into the Doctor's house; the scene opens, and discovers the Doctor at a table; the Usurer enters, lends the Doctor the money, but refuses his bond, and demands a limb of him; the Doctor suffers him to cut off his leg, and carry it away. Several legs appear upon the scene, and the Doctor strikes a woman's leg with his wand, which immediately flies from the rest, and fixes to the Doctor's stump, which dances with it ridiculously. A bawd next enters with a courtezan; she presents her to the Doctor, for whom he gives the bawd the bag of money; they all join in a dance, and the Doctor is going off; the bawd stops him, to demand more money; he hangs his hat against the scene, and points to that, and goes out with his mistress. The bawd holds her apron under the hat, from whence a considerable quantity of silver drops; she advances to the front of the stage with a great deal of pleasure, but going to review her money, finds she has none, and runs off. The scene changes to the street, four watchmen enter, and join in a dance adapted to their character. The scene opens, and discovers the Doctor's study, he enters affrighted, the clock strikes one, the figures of Time and Death appear, and in a short piece of recitative declare his latest minute is come. Several Devils enter, tear him in pieces, some fly up, others sink, each bearing a limb of him away; flashes of fire arise, and thunder is heard.

The last, which is the grand scene, whether proper or not I shall not pretend to determine, is the most magnificent that ever appeared upon the English Stage. The Gods and Goddesses discovered there are, Apollo, Mars, Mercury, Bacchus, Ceres, Iris, Flora, and Pales. Apollo advances and sings, inviting the Gods to revel, the power of Faustus being at an end. The rest of the deities (Pales excepted) advance, and dance agreeable to their several characters, in the greatest order and exactness. Apollo again advances, and invites Diana to appear; upon which a machine flies up and discovers Diana in her chariot, the crescent in an azure sky hanging over her head; she descends, beckons two nymphs who take her bow and quiver; which done, she dances. They then all join in a chorus of singing and dancing; which concludes the entertainment.

The London *Journal* reported that the theatre received £260 in entrance money, which indicates the success of Thurmond's work.

His "New Night Scene" *Harlequin Shepard* came out on 18 November 1724, capitalizing on the escapades and hanging of the notorious Jack Sheppard. The *Weekly Journal or Saturday's Post* said it "was dismiss'd with a universal hiss.—And, indeed, if Shepherd had been as wretched, and as silly a Rogue in the World, as the ingenious and witty Managers have made him upon the Stage, the lower Gentry, who attended him to Tyburn, wou'd never have pittied him when he was hang'd." Nathaniel Mist in his *Journal* attacked the Drury Lane's co-manager and actor-author Colley Cibber and Thurmond on 2 January 1725. Cibber had brought out his *Caesar in Aegypt* shortly after Thurmond's *Harlequin Shepard* appeared:

As for Cleopatra, [Cibber] has made her a perfect Moll Frisky and I suspect that while he was writing this character he designed it for the farce *Harlequin Sheppard* in order to help out his brother wit Mr Thurmond. These two gentlemen may have parts but it seems to me as if they had misapplied them: to make myself better understood, I would have Cibber *dance* and Thurmond *write*, which may tend much towards improving our public diversions.

Thurmond's *Apollo and Daphne; or, Harlequin's Metamorphoses* (different from the anonymous *Apollo and Daphne; or, Harlequin Mercury* of 1725) came out at Drury Lane on 11 February 1726 with Thurmond as Apollo (he had danced Apollo in the earlier work as well). *The Miser; or, Wagner and Abericock,* another Thurmond pantomime and a sequel to *Harlequin Doctor Faustus,* appeared on 30 December 1726 with the author dancing a Statue. *Harlequin's Triumph* was first presented on 27 February 1727 with Thurmond again as a Statue. (The *Index to The London Stage* mistakenly assigns John's pantomimes to his father, but Chetwood makes it clear who composed them.)

The younger Thurmond continued at Drury Lane through September 1732, but he seems not to have contrived any more pantomimes. He was active as an entr'acte dancer, however, and he performed such pantomime parts as Harlequin and Mars in *Harlequin Doctor Faustus,* Scaramouch (a Magician), Medusa, and a Triton in *Perseus and Andromeda,* and a Sea God and a Gormogon in *Cephalus and Procris.* His annual salary at Drury Lane was £166.

On 20 December 1732 Thurmond made his first appearance on the stage of the Goodman's Fields Theatre, dancing the leading part in *The Amorous Sportsman.* Though he composed no new pantomimes while at Goodman's Fields, he did create occasional entr'acte

dances, such as a *Masquerade Dance,* which was first performed on 27 December 1732. And he was seen as Scaramouch in *The Tavern Bilkers,* Clodio in *Love Makes a Man* (his first time in that character since 1710, evidently), Scaramouch in *The Cheats,* and a Swain in *Britannia.*

Thurmond returned to Drury Lane in the fall of 1734 and remained there for the rest of his career. He made his first appearance on 5 October, as Pan in *Cupid and Psyche,* after which he was seen in such parts as a Wind in *The Tempest,* a Countryman and Innkeeper in *Harlequin Orpheus,* a Hussar and a Dutchman in *Colombine Courtezan,* a Turk in *The Fall of Phaeton,* and a Mandarin Gormogon in *Harlequin Grand Volgi.* He and his wife lived next door to the Bedford Arms Tavern in Covent Garden. At the end of the 1736–37 season Thurmond seems to have left the stage.

The younger John Thurmond was buried at St Paul, Covent Garden, on 31 January 1754. He had written his will on 30 December 1749. In it he left his wife Sarah all of his household goods and clothes; the rest of his estate was to be divided into four parts, Sarah to receive two and his daughters Mary and Catherine one each. The two parts left to Mrs Thurmond were to go to the girls after her death. The will was proved on 18 February 1754. The *Biographia Dramatica* in 1812 remembered the younger Thurmond as a dancing master who "in that walk acquired considerable reputation. He was the composer of several pantomimes; and Chetwood intimates that he was living in the year 1749, having quitted the practice of his profession before he was disabled by age or infirmities." Chetwood said Thurmond "is a Person of a clean Head and a clear Heart, and inherits the Mirth and Humour of his late Father."

In the British Museum is a sketch in pencil and sepia ink by an unknown artist of a scene from *Harlequin Doctor Faustus* at Drury Lane in 1724. The scene shows Pantaloon and Scaramouch, but not Mars (Thurmond's character).

Thurmond, Mrs John, Sarah, née Lewis
d. 1762, actress, singer.

Sarah Lewis, according to *The Dictionary of National Biography,* was born in Epsom, Surrey, and is listed by Sybil Rosenfeld in *Strolling Players* as acting in Pinkethman's troupe at

Greenwich in 1711. Also in the company was the younger John Thurmond, who went with her to act in Dublin from 1712 to 1715 and who became her husband in 1713. Three of Mrs Thurmond's known Dublin roles were Evandra in *Timon of Athens*, Arpasia in *Tamerlane*, and Ruth in *The Committee*—all in 1715—unless those parts belonged to Winifred Thurmond, the wife of the elder John Thurmond, who had acted in Dublin in 1707–8.

On 23 June 1715 in London Sarah Thurmond played Cosmelia in *The Doting Lovers* and spoke the epilogue at Lincoln's Inn Fields Theatre, her first appearance there. Her husband had performed in dances there earlier in the month. On 8 July she played Portia in *The Jew of Venice;* on 3 August she and Hall sang "'Tis Sultry Weather, Pretty Maid"; and on 11 August she acted Julia in *The False Count*. She remained at Lincoln's Inn Fields through the 1717–18 season playing a number of important roles, among them Arabella in *The Wife's Relief*, Belinda in *The Provok'd Wife*, Alinda in *The Pilgrim*, the title part in *The Woman Captain*, Belinda in *The Artful Husband*, Ophelia in *Hamlet*, the Countess of Nottingham in *The Unhappy Favorite*, Laetitia in *The Old Bachelor*, Arabella in *The Fair Quaker of Deal*, Lady Plotwell in the main play and Paulina in the masque *Decius and Paulina* in *The Lady's Triumph*, Eugenia in *Cymbeline*, and Marcella in *2 Don Quixote*.

Mrs Thurmond made her first appearance at Drury Lane Theatre on 8 November 1718 acting Aspasia in *The Maid's Tragedy*. She was then seen during the rest of the 1718–19 season as Almeria and Zara in *The Mourning Bride*, Lady Frances Ombre in *The Masquerade*, Moderna in *Chit Chat*, Myris in *Busiris*, Hypolita in *She Wou'd and She Wou'd Not*, Alcmena in *Amphitryon*, the Countess of Rutland in *The Unhappy Favorite*, Cleora in *The Bondman*, and Eliza in *The Earl of Warwick*.

She stayed at Drury Lane through the 1731–32 season, acting such new characters as Angelica in *Love for Love*, Desdemona in *Othello*, Clarinda in *The Double Gallant*, Lady Macduff in *Macbeth*, Maria in *Don John*, Imoinda in *Oroonoko*, Leonora in *Sir Courtly Nice*, the Queen in *The Spanish Fryar*, Gertrude in *Hamlet*, Narcissa in *Love's Last Shift*, Portia in *Julius*

Caesar, Cassandra in *Cleomenes*, Epicoene in *The Silent Woman*, Isabella in *The Conscious Lovers*, Mrs Termagent in *The Squire of Alsatia*, Bisarre in *The Inconstant*, Cordelia in *King Lear*, Sylvia in *The Recruiting Officer*, Lady Wronghead in *The Provok'd Husband*, Lucy in *The Lover's Opera*, Creusa in *Medea*, the title role in *Jane Shore*, Berinthia in *The Relapse*, and Mrs Marwood in *The Way of the World*. She was also popular as an entr'acte singer and speaker of prologues and epilogues. Davies in his *Dramatic Miscellanies* claimed that Barton Booth was partly responsible for Mrs Thurmond's training in tragedy.

Some evidence suggests that Mrs Thurmond may have been a heavy drinker. *The Way of the World* was deferred on 10 February 1729 due to the "sudden illness of Mrs Thurmond," and *The Village Opera* was deferred the following night for the same reason. Then, when the latter work was presented on 27 February it was met with "a Serenade of cat Calls, Penny-Trumpets, Clubs, Canes, Hoarse Voices, whistling in Keys, Heels, Fists; and Vollies of whole Oranges. . . . When Mrs T—— appeared, they call'd out for a Quartern of Gin, to chear up her Spirits." So reported the *Flying Post*.

On 18 October 1732 Mrs Thurmond played for the first time at Goodman's Fields Theatre, appearing as Almeria in *The Mourning Bride*. She brought some of her earlier parts with her—Angelica, Arpasia, Ruth, Lady Wronghead, Laetitia, Clarinda, Portia, Jane Shore, and others—but she was also given some new assignments, most notably Anne Bullen in *Vertue Betray'd*, Lady Easy in *The Careless Husband*, and Polly in *The Beggar's Opera*. She was granted two benefits, one on 12 February 1733 and another on 30 March; tickets were available at Thurmond's house in Haydon Square. In 1733–34 at Goodman's Fields Mrs Thurmond's new parts included Elizabeth in *The Unhappy Favorite*, Lady Sharlot in *The Funeral*, Roxana in *The Rival Queens*, and Prince Germanicus in *Britannia*. She and her husband went back to Drury Lane after the season ended.

For her return on 7 September 1734 Mrs Thurmond chose Angelica in *Love for Love*. She continued at Drury Lane thorugh 1736–37, adding to her repertoire such new characters as Marcia in *Cato,* Queen Katherine in *Henry VIII,* Belvidera in *Venice Preserv'd,* Queen Elizabeth in *Richard III,* Hellena in *The Christian Hero,* Lady Graveairs in *The Careless Husband,* Dorinda in *The Man of Taste,* Lady Pliant in *The Double Dealer,* Mrs Ford in *The Merry Wives of Windsor,* and Lady Brute in *The Provok'd Wife.* Her last appearance was on 5 May 1737, as Lady Wronghead in *The Provok'd Husband.* By then she and her husband had returned to lodgings next door to the Bedford Arms Tavern in Covent Garden.

Aaron Hill in the 27 December 1734 issue of *The Prompter* commented on Mrs Thurmond's artificial vocal style:

I Take this public Opportunity to beg Pardon of a celebrated *Actress,* who begins the Tragedy of the *Mourning Bride,* with this extraordinary Encomium on the Power of *Musick.*

Mu-u-sick has Cha-a-arms, to so-o-oth a savage Breast,
To so-o-often Rocks, or be-e-end the Knotted Oak.

I must confess, I was under the Mistake of supposing this Lady *affected* when I herad her *whining* out good Verses, in a *Drawl* so unpleasingly extended: Little dreamt I, all the while, that she was *topping* her *Character,* and deriving her Ideas of *Musick,* from the fashionable Present State of the Art, as it *flourishes* under Royal Encouragement.

The prompter W. R. Chetwood in his *General History* in 1749 noted that Mrs Thurmond had "an amiable Person and good Voice: She wisely left the Bustle and Business of the Stage, in her full and ripe Performance; and, at that time, left behind her but few that excell'd her."

Mrs Thurmond lost her husband in 1754 and lived a widow for eight years. She was buried at St Paul, Covent Garden, on 18 May 1762. She had drawn up her will on 13 July 1761, describing herself as of the parish of St Martin-in-the-Fields. Her estate was left to her daughter Catherine Thurmond; she asked Catherine to be "kind as lays in her power to my Dear Daughter Mary Jackson and her children." Catherine proved the will on 14 May (*recte* June?) 1762. Soon after that, Catherine married John Addy, and before 6 June 1764 she died; administration of Sarah Thurmond's estate passed to Mr Addy.

Thurmond, Mary, later Mrs John Jackson *b. 1727, actress.*

Mary Thurmond, the daughter of the performers Sarah and John (the younger) Thurmond, was christened at St Paul, Covent Garden, on 22 January 1727. She played Lady Harriot in *The Funeral* at Drury Lane Theatre on 13 January 1749, advertised as making her first appearance on any stage. Mary acted the part again on 14 January and 25 February, after which her name dropped from the bills. Mary Thurmond of St Paul, Covent Garden, married John Jackson of St Mary Aldermary, widower, on 4 February 1755. She was still alive in 1761, when her mother wrote her will, naming Catherine Thurmond (Sarah's daughter) executor and legatee but asking Catherine to "be kind as lays in her power to my Dear Daughter Mary Jackson and her children."

Thurstan. *See* THRUSTANS.

Thurston, Mr [*fl. 1751–1752*], *doorkeeper.*

In 1751–52 Mr Thurston was the stage doorkeeper at Drury Lane Theatre, and from him places for the boxes could be purchased.

Thwaites, Mr [*fl. 1798*], *actor.*

Sybil Rosenfeld in her *Theatre of the London Fairs* notes that in 1798 at Bartholomew Fair Mr Thwaites played "the first line of business" in Richardson's company.

Thynne, Miss [*fl. 1736–1742*], *actress, singer, dancer.*

At Drury Lane Theatre on 31 December 1736 Miss Thynne played Molly in *The Beggar's Opera.* She was not mentioned in the bills again until 21 October 1737, when she acted Margaret in *The Squire of Alsatia;* she played in *The Beggar's Opera* on 25 October. Her name was dropped again from the bills, reappearing on 23 September 1738, when she was Jenny in *The Harlot's Progress.* During the rest of 1738–39 season she was mentioned as Mrs Muslin in *Robin Goodfellow,* a Lady of Pleasure in *The Harlot's Progress,* Lisetta in *The Man of Taste,* and Molly in *The Beggar's Opera.* On 3 May 1739 she sang in Italian between the acts.

She was again at Drury Lane in 1739–40, appearing in such new parts as Jenny in *The*

Beggar's Opera, Kitty in *The Harlot's Progress,* Flora in *Don John,* Charlotte in *The Mock Doctor,* Mrs Squeamish in *The Country Wife,* and the Duke of York in *An Historical Play (King Charles I).* She was also used briefly as a dancer in *The Harlot's Progress.* Unaccountably, after having shown considerable progress, Miss Thynne seems to have left Drury Lane. She turned up at Bartholomew Fair on 25 August 1742 to play Lucia in *Scaramouch Scapin* for Hippisley and Chapman and then dropped from sight.

Previously Published